C++

HOW TO PROGRAM

THIRD EDITION

Deitel & Deitel
Books, Cyber Classrooms and Complete Training Courses
published by
Prentice Hall

How to Program Series **[Books]**
e-Business and e-Commerce How to Program
Internet and World Wide Web How to Program
Java™ How to Program, 3/e
C How to Program, 3/e
C++ How to Program, 3/e
Visual Basic® 6 How to Program

Multimedia Cyber Classroom Series
[These are interactive multimedia CD versions of *How to Program Series* books.]
e-Business and e-Commerce Programming Multimedia Cyber Classroom
Internet and World Wide Web Programming Multimedia Cyber Classroom
Java™ Multimedia Cyber Classroom, 3/e
C++ Multimedia Cyber Classroom, 3/e
Visual Basic® 6 Multimedia Cyber Classroom

The Complete Training Course Series
[These contain a *How to Program Series* book and the corresponding *Cyber Classroom* CD.]
The Complete e-Business and e-Commerce Programming Training Course
The Complete Internet and World Wide Web Programming Training Course
The Complete Java™ Training Course, 3/e
The Complete C++ Training Course, 3/e
The Complete Visual Basic® 6 Training Course

Visual Studio® Series
Getting Started with Microsoft® Visual C++™ 6 with an Introduction to MFC
Visual Basic® 6 How to Program
Getting Started with Microsoft® Visual J++® 1.1

Fall 2000 Publications
[A separate *Cyber Classroom* and a *Complete Training Course* will be published for each of these.]
Perl How to Program
XML How to Program
Internet and World Wide Web How to Program: Microsoft® Technologies Edition
Internet and World Wide Web How to Program: Open Source Edition
Advanced Java™ How to Program

For continuing updates on Prentice Hall and Deitel & Associates, Inc. publications visit the Prentice Hall web site

    `http//www.prenhall.com/deitel`

To communicate with the authors, send email to:

    `deitel@deitel.com`

For information on corporate on-site seminars and public seminars offered by Deitel & Associates, Inc. worldwide, visit:

    `http://www.deitel.com`

C++
HOW TO PROGRAM
THIRD EDITION

H. M. Deitel
Deitel & Associates, Inc.

P. J. Deitel
Deitel & Associates, Inc.

PRENTICE HALL, Upper Saddle River, New Jersey 07458

Library of Congress Cataloging-in-Publication Data
on File

Vice President and Editorial Director: *Marcia Horton*
Acquisitions Editor: *Petra J. Recter*
Assistant Editor: *Sarah Burrows*
Project Manager: *Crissy Statuto*
Editorial Assistant: *Karen Schultz*
Production Editor: *Camille Trentacoste*
Managing Editor: *David A. George*
Executive Managing Editor: *Vince O'Brien*
Chapter Opener and Cover Designer: *Tamara Newnam Cavallo*
Art Director: *Heather Scott*
Marketing Manager: *Jennie Burger*
Manufacturing Buyer: *Pat Brown*
Manufacturing Manager: *Trudy Pisciotti*
Assistant Vice President of Production and Manufacturing: *David W. Riccardi*

© 2001, 1998, 1994 by Prentice-Hall, Inc.
Upper Saddle River, New Jersey 07458

The authors and publisher of this book have used their best efforts in preparing this book. These efforts include the development, research, and testing of the theories and programs to determine their effectiveness. The authors and publisher make no warranty of any kind, expressed or implied, with regard to these programs or to the documentation contained in this book. The authors and publisher shall not be liable in any event for incidental or consequential damages in connection with, or arising out of, the furnishing, performance, or use of these programs.

Many of the designations used by manufacturers and sellers to distinguish their products are claimed as trademarks and registered trademarks. Where those designations appear in this book, and Prentice Hall and the authors were aware of a trademark claim, the designations have been printed in initial caps or all caps. All product names mentioned remain trademarks or registered trademarks of their respective owners.

Printed in the United States of America

10 9 8 7 6 5 4 3 2

ISBN 0-13-089571-7

Prentice-Hall International (UK) Limited, *London*
Prentice-Hall of Australia Pty. Limited, *Sydney*
Prentice-Hall Canada Inc., *Toronto*
Prentice-Hall Hispanoamericana, S.A., *Mexico*
Prentice-Hall of India Private Limited, *New Delhi*
Prentice-Hall of Japan, Inc., *Tokyo*
Pearson Education Asia Pte. Ltd., *Singapore*
Editora Prentice-Hall do Brasil, Ltda., *Rio de Janeiro*

TO

Don Kostuch:

For your steadfast commitment to excellence in teaching and writing about C++ and object technology.

Thank you for being our mentor, our colleague and our friend.

Thank you for a decade of being our most critical, yet most constructive reviewer.

Thank you for the sacrifices of your personal time that you have made unselfishly to help us meet our publishing deadlines.

It is a privilege for us to be your students.

We look forward to co-authoring *Advanced C++ How to Program* with you.

Harvey and Paul Deitel

Contents

Illustrations

6 Classes and Data Abstraction   389

7 Classes: Part II   452

16   Bits, Characters, Strings and Structures   849

21   Standard C++ Language Additions   1067

A   Operator Precedence Chart   1102

B   ASCII Character Set   1104

C   Number Systems   1105

Preface

Welcome to ANSI/ISO Standard C++! This book is by an old guy and a young guy. The old guy (HMD; Massachusetts Institute of Technology 1967) has been programming and/or teaching programming for 39 years. The young guy (PJD; MIT 1991) has been programming for 18 years and has caught the teaching and writing "bug." The old guy programs and teaches from experience; the young guy does so from an inexhaustible reserve of energy. The old guy wants clarity; the young guy wants performance. The old guy appreciates elegance and beauty; the young guy wants results. We got together to produce a book we hope you will find informative, interesting and entertaining.

These are exciting times in the C++ community with the approval of the ANSI/ISO C++ Standard. ANSI (the American National Standards Institute) and ISO (the International Standards Organization), have cooperated to develop what has become one of the most important worldwide standards for the computing community.

When we wrote the second edition of *C++ How to Program*, we aimed the book at college-level courses which at the time were primarily being taught in Pascal or C, emphasizing the procedural programming paradigm. Writing a C++ textbook for the Computer Science I and II audiences presented a difficult challenge to us. We would need to describe two programming paradigms, both procedural programming (because C++ still includes C) and object-oriented programming. This practically doubled the amount of material that would need to be presented at the introductory level. We chose a strategy of presenting the C-like material on primitive data types, control structures, functions, arrays, pointers, strings and structures in the first five chapters of the book. We then presented object-oriented programming in Chapters 6 through 15.

C++ How to Program became the most widely used college-level C++ textbook in the world. We delayed writing the new edition for two reasons:

1. C++ was under active development over this time period, with new drafts of the standards document appearing on a regular basis, but with no clear signs from the standards committee that the draft standard was going to be accepted "as is" within a short period of time.

2. We were waiting for a key sign that it was time for a new edition of *C++ How to Program*. That came in July 1997 with the publication of Bjarne Stroustrup's third edition of his book *The C++ Programming Language: Third Edition*. Stroustrup created C++ and his books are the definitive works on the language. At this point, we felt that the "new definition" of C++ was sufficiently stable for us to publish *C++ How to Program: Second Edition*.

We diverted our attention for a time to produce five Java publications. But the excitement of the impending acceptance of the ANSI/ISO C++ Draft Standard drew our attention back to C++.

C++ How to Program: Third Edition

We performed an extensive review process on this *Third Edition* that led to thousands of polishing changes. We also completely updated the programs in the text to conform to the C++ standard's use of namespaces.

The major new feature of this *Third Edition* is a complete, fully-implemented case study on object-oriented design using the Unified Modeling Language™ (UML). We felt that a commitment to larger-scale object-oriented design projects is something that has been lacking in introductory programming textbooks. This optional case study is highly recommend because it will considerably enhance the students' experience in a first-year university programming sequence. This case study provides students with an opportunity to immerse themselves in a 1000+ line C++ program that was carefully scrutinized by a team of distinguished industry and academic reviewers.

In the previous editions of this book, we included special "Thinking About Objects" sections at the ends of Chapters 1 through 7. These sections walked the student through the steps needed to design the software simulator for an elevator system. We asked the student to complete these steps and to implement their design in C++. For *C++ How to Program: Third Edition*, we have completely remodeled this case study. At the ends of Chapters 1 through 7 and the end of Chapter 9, we use the "Thinking About Objects" sections to present a carefully paced introduction to object-oriented design using the UML. The UML is now the most widely used graphical representation scheme for modeling object-oriented systems. The UML is a complex, feature-rich graphical language. In our "Thinking About Objects" sections, we present a concise, simplified subset of these features. We then use this subset to guide the reader through a first design experience with the UML intended for the novice object-oriented designer/programmer. We present this case study in a fully solved format. This is not an exercise; rather, it is an end-to-end learning experience that concludes with a detailed walkthrough of the C++ code.

In each of the first five chapters we concentrate on the "conventional" methodology of structured programming, because the objects we will build will be composed, in part, of structured-program pieces. We then end each chapter with a "Thinking About Objects" section in which we present an introduction to object orientation using the Unified Modeling Language (UML). Our goal in these "Thinking About Objects" sections is to help students develop an object-oriented way of thinking, so they can immediately put to use the object-oriented programming concepts that they begin learning in Chapter 6. In the first of these sections at the end of Chapter 1, we introduce basic concepts (i.e., "object think") and terminology (i.e., "object speak"). In the optional "Thinking About Objects" sections at the ends of Chapters 2 through 5 we consider more substantial issues as we attack a challenging problem with the techniques of object-oriented design (OOD). We analyze a typical problem statement that requires a system to be built, determine the objects needed to implement that system, determine the attributes the objects will need to have, determine the behaviors these objects will need to exhibit and specify how the objects will need to interact with one another to meet the system requirements. We do all this even before we discuss how to write object-oriented C++ programs. In the "Thinking About Objects" sections at the ends of Chapters 6, 7 and 9, we discuss a C++ implementation of the object-oriented system we designed in the earlier chapters.

This case study is significantly larger than any other project attempted in the book. We feel that the student gains significant experience by following this complete design and implementation process. This project forced us to incorporate topics that we do not discuss in any other section of the book, including object interaction, an in-depth discussion of handles, the philosophy of using references vs. pointers and the use of forward declarations to avoid the circular include problem. This case study will help prepare students for the kinds of substantial projects encountered in industry.

"Thinking About Objects" Sections

In Chapter 2, we begin the first phase of an object-oriented design (OOD) for the elevator simulator—identifying the classes needed to implement the simulator. We also introduce the UML use case, class and object diagrams and the concepts of associations, multiplicity, composition, roles and links.

In Chapter 3, we determine many of the class attributes needed to implement the elevator simulator. We also introduce the UML statechart and activity diagrams and the concepts of events and actions as they relate to these diagrams.

In Chapter 4, we determine many of the operations (behaviors) of the classes in the elevator simulation. We also introduce the UML sequence diagram and the concept of messages sent between objects.

In Chapter 5, we determine many of the collaborations (interactions between objects in the system) needed to implement the elevator system and represent these collaborations using the UML collaboration diagram. We also include a bibliography and a list of Internet and World Wide Web resources that contain the UML 1.3 specifications and other reference materials, general resources, tutorials, FAQs, articles, whitepapers and software.

In Chapter 6, we use the UML class diagram developed in previous sections to outline the C++ header files that define our classes. We also introduce the concept of handles to objects in the system and we begin to study how to implement handles in C++.

In Chapter 7, we present a complete elevator simulator C++ program (approximately 1000 lines of code) and a detailed code walkthrough. The code follows directly from the UML-based design created in previous sections and employs our good programming practices, including the use of **static** and **const** data members and functions. We also discuss dynamic-memory allocation, composition and object interaction via handles and how to use forward declarations to avoid the circular include problem.

In Chapter 9, we update the elevator simulation design and implementation to incorporate inheritance. We also suggest further modifications so that the student may then design and implement, using the tools presented in the previous sections.

We sincerely hope that this newly updated elevator simulation case study provides a challenging and meaningful experience for both students and instructors. We employ a carefully developed, incremental object-oriented process to produce a UML-based design for our elevator simulator. From this design, we produce a substantial working C++ implementation using key programming notions, including classes, objects, encapsulation, visibility, composition and inheritance. We would be most grateful if you would take a moment to send your comments, criticisms and suggestions for improving this case study to us at **deitel@deitel.com**.

C++ How to Program: Third Edition Ancillary Package

We have worked hard to produce a textbook and ancillaries that we hope you and your students will find valuable. The following ancillary resources are available:

- *C++ How to Program: Third Edition's 268 program examples* are included on the CD-ROM in the back of the textbook. This helps instructors prepare lectures faster and helps students master C++. The examples are also available for download at **www.deitel.com**. When extracting the source code from the ZIP file, you must use a ZIP-file reader such as WinZip (**http://www.winzip.com/**) or PKZIP (**http://www.pkware.com/**) that understands directories. The file should be extracted into a separate directory (e.g., **cpphtp3e_examples**).

- *Microsoft Visual C++ 6 Introductory Edition software* is provided on the textbook's CD-ROM. This software allows students to edit, compile and debug C++ programs. We have provided at no charge a short Visual C++ 6 tutorial (in Adobe PDF format) on our Web site (**www.deitel.com**).

- This *C++ How to Program: Third Edition Instructor's Manual* on CD contains answers to most of the exercises in the textbook. The programs are separated into directories by chapter and exercise number.

- The optional *C++ Multimedia Cyber Classroom: Third Edition* is an interactive multimedia CD version of the book for Windows. Its features include audio walk-throughs of programs, section review questions (which are available only on the *C++ Multimedia Cyber Classroom: Third Edition*), a text-search engine, the ability to execute example programs and more. The *Cyber Classroom* helps students get more out of their courses. The *Cyber Classroom* is also useful for students who miss a lecture and have to catch up quickly. The *Cyber Classroom* is available as a stand-alone product (see the last few pages of the textbook for the ISBN number) or bundled with the textbook (at a discount) in a product called *The Complete C++ Training Course: Third Edition* (ISBN# 0-13-089563-6). We discuss the *Cyber Classroom* in further detail later in the Preface.

- *Companion Web site* (**www.prenhall.com/deitel**) provides instructor and student resources. Instructor resources include textbook appendices (e.g., Appendix D, "C++ Internet and Web Resources") and a syllabus manager for lesson planning. Student resources include chapter objectives, true/false questions, chapter highlights, reference materials and a message board.

- Customizable *PowerPoint*® *Instructor Lecture Notes*, with many complete features including source code and key discussion points for each program and major illustration. These lecture notes are available for instructors and students at no charge at our Web site **www.deitel.com**.

- *Lab Manual* (available Spring 2001)—a for-sale item containing closed-lab sessions.

A Revolution in Software Development

For years, hardware has been improving dramatically, but software, for some reason, seemed to resist almost every attempt to build it faster and to build it better. Today we are in the middle of a revolution in the way software is being designed and written. That revolution is based on the common-sense, hardware notion of standardized, interchangeable parts, exactly as used by Henry Ford in the days of the Model T Ford. These software components are called "objects"—more properly, "classes," which are the "cookie cutters" out of which objects are produced.

The most mature of the well-known object-oriented languages is Smalltalk, developed in the early 1970s at Xerox's Palo Alto Research Center. But the most widely used object-oriented language—by a factor of 10 over Smalltalk—is C++ developed by Bjarne Stroustrup and others in the early 1980s at AT&T. In the time between the publication of the first and second editions of this book, another contender appeared on the scene—the Java object-oriented programming language, developed in the early 1990s by James Gosling and others at Sun Microsystems.

Why a major new object-oriented programming language every 10 years? Smalltalk was truly ahead of its time as a research experiment. C++ was right for its time and for today's high-performance systems programming and applications development needs. Java™ offered developers the ability to create highly portable multimedia-intensive and networking-intensive Internet/World Wide Web-based applications.

Procedural Programming, Object-Based Programming, Object-Oriented Programming and Generic Programming

In this book, you will master the five key components of C++ as well as four contemporary programming paradigms:

1. C *procedural programming*—Chapters 1–5 and 16–18; key topics include data types, control structures, functions, arrays, pointers, strings, structures, bit manipulation, character manipulation, preprocessing and others.

2. C++ *procedural programming enhancements to C*—Sections 3.15–3.21; key topics include **inline** functions, references, default arguments, function overloading and function templates.

3. C++ *object-based programming*—Chapters 6–8; key topics include abstract data types, classes, objects, encapsulation, information hiding, member access control, constructors, destructors, software reusability, constant objects and member functions, composition, friendship, dynamic memory allocation, **static** members, **this** pointer and others.

4. C++ *object-oriented programming*—Chapters 9–15, 19 and 21; key topics include base classes, single inheritance, derived classes, multiple inheritance, **virtual** functions, dynamic binding, polymorphism, pure **virtual** functions, abstract classes, concrete classes, stream input/output, class templates, exception handling, file processing, data structures, strings as full-fledged objects, data type **bool**, cast operators, namespaces, run-time type information (RTTI), **explicit** constructors and **mutable** members.

5. C++ *generic programming*—Chapter 20—the largest chapter in the book; key topics include the Standard Template Library (STL), templatized containers, sequence containers, associative containers, container adaptors, iterators that traverse templatized containers and algorithms that process the elements of templatized containers.

Evolving from Pascal and C to C++ and Java™

C++ has replaced C as the systems implementation language of choice in industry. But C programming will continue to be an important and valuable skill because of the enormous amount of C legacy code that must be maintained. Dr. Harvey M. Deitel has been teaching introductory programming courses in college environments for two decades with an emphasis on developing clearly written, well-structured programs. Much of what is taught in these courses is the basic principles of programming with an emphasis on the effective use of control structures and functionalization. We have presented this material exactly the way HMD has done in his college courses. There are some pitfalls, but where these occur, we point them out and explain procedures for dealing with them effectively. Our experience has been that students handle the course in about the same manner as they handle introductory Pascal or C courses. There is one noticeable difference though: Students are highly motivated by the fact that they are learning a leading-edge language (C++) and a leading-edge programming paradigm (object-oriented programming) that will be immediately useful to them as they leave the college environment. This increases their enthusiasm for the material—a big help when you consider that C++ is more difficult to learn than Pascal or C.

Our goal was clear: Produce a C++ programming textbook for introductory college-level courses in computer programming for students with little or no programming experience, yet offer the depth and the rigorous treatment of theory and practice demanded by traditional, upper-level C++ courses. To meet these goals, we produced a book larger than other C++ texts—this because our text also patiently teaches the principles of procedural programming, object-based programming, object-oriented programming and generic programming. Hundreds of thousands of people have studied this material in academic courses and professional seminars worldwide.

Until the early 1990s, computer science courses were focused on procedural programming in Pascal and C. Since then, these courses have largely switched to object-oriented programming in C++ and Java. At Deitel & Associates, Inc., we are focussed on producing quality educational materials for today's leading-edge programming languages. As *C++ How to Program: Third Edition* goes to the presses, we are working on *Java How to Program: Fourth Edition*, *Advanced C++ How to Program* and *Advanced Java How to Program*.

Introducing Object Orientation from Chapter 1!

We faced a difficult challenge in designing this book. Should the book present a pure object-oriented approach? Or should it present a hybrid approach balancing procedural programming with object-oriented programming?

Many instructors who will teach from this text have been teaching procedural programming (probably in C or Pascal). C++ itself is not a purely object-oriented language. Rather it is a hybrid language that enables both procedural programming and object-oriented programming.

So we chose the following approach. The first five chapters of the book introduce procedural programming in C++. They present computer concepts, control structures, functions, arrays, pointers and strings. These chapters cover the C portion of C++ and the C++ "procedural enhancements" to C.

We have done something to make these first five chapters really unique. At the end of each of these chapters, we have included a special section entitled, "Thinking About Objects." These sections introduce the concepts and terminology of object orientation to help students begin familiarizing themselves with what objects are and how they behave.

The Chapter 1 "Thinking About Objects" section introduces the concepts and terminology of object orientation. The sections in Chapters 2 through 5 present a requirements specification for a substantial object-oriented system project, namely building an elevator simulator and carefully guide the student through the typical phases of the object-oriented design process. These sections discuss how to identify the objects in a problem, how to specify the objects' attributes and behaviors, and how to specify the interactions among objects. By the time the student has finished Chapter 5, he or she has completed a careful object-oriented design of the elevator simulator and is ready—if not eager—to begin programming the elevator in C++. Chapters 6 and 7 cover data abstraction and classes. These chapters also contain "Thinking About Objects" sections that ease students through the various stages of programming their elevator simulators in C++. Chapter 9's "Thinking About Objects" section applies C++ inheritance concepts to the elevator simulator.

About this Book

C++ How to Program contains a rich collection of examples, exercises and projects drawn from many fields to provide the student with a chance to solve interesting real-world problems. The book concentrates on the principles of good software engineering and stresses program clarity. We avoid arcane terminology and syntax specifications in favor of teaching by example.

This book is written by educators who spend most of their time teaching and writing about edge-of-the-practice programming languages.

The text places a strong emphasis on pedagogy. For example, virtually every new concept of either C++ or object-oriented programming is presented in the context of a complete, working C++ program immediately followed by a window showing the program's output. Reading these programs is much like entering and running them on a computer. We call this our "live-code approach."

Among the other pedagogical devices in the text are a set of *Objectives* and an *Outline* at the beginning of every chapter; *Common Programming Errors*, *Good Programming Practices*, *Performance Tips*, *Portability Tips*, *Software Engineering Observations* and

Testing and Debugging Tips enumerated in, and summarized at, the end of each chapter; comprehensive bullet-list-style *Summary* and alphabetized *Terminology* sections in each chapter; *Self-Review Exercises and Answers* in each chapter; and the richest collection of *Exercises* in any C++ book.

The exercises range from simple recall questions to lengthy programming problems to major projects. Instructors requiring substantial term projects will find many appropriate problems listed in the exercises for Chapters 3 through 21. We have put a great deal of effort into the exercises to enhance the value of this course for the student.

In writing this book, we have used a variety of C++ compilers. For the most part, the programs in the text will work on all ANSI/ISO compilers.

This text is based on the C++ programming language as developed by Accredited Standards Committee X3, Information Technology and its Technical Committee X3J16, Programming Language C++, respectively. This language was approved by the International Standards Organization (ISO). For further details, contact:

> X3 Secretariat
> 1250 Eye Street NW
> Washington DC 20005

The serious programmer should read these documents carefully and reference them regularly. These documents are not tutorials. Rather they define C++ and C with the extraordinary level of precision that compiler implementors and "heavy-duty" developers demand.

We have carefully audited our presentation against these documents. Our book is intended to be used at the introductory and intermediate levels. We have not attempted to cover every feature discussed in these comprehensive documents.

Objectives

Each chapter begins with a statement of objectives. This tells the student what to expect and gives the student an opportunity, after reading the chapter, to determine if he or she has met these objectives. It is a confidence builder and a source of positive reinforcement.

Quotations

The learning objectives are followed by a series of quotations. Some are humorous, some are philosophical and some offer interesting insights. Our students enjoy relating the quotations to the chapter material. You may appreciate some of the quotations more *after* reading the chapters.

Outline

The chapter outline helps the student approach the material in top-down fashion. This, too, helps students anticipate what is to come and set a comfortable and effective learning pace.

Sections

Each chapter is organized into small sections that address key C++ topics.

13,741 Lines of Syntax-Colored Code in 268 Example Programs (with Program Outputs)

We present C++ features in the context of complete, working C++ programs; each program is immediately followed by a window containing the outputs produced when the program is run—we call this our "live-code approach." This enables the student to confirm that the programs run as expected. Relating outputs back to the program statements that produce those outputs is an excellent way to learn and to reinforce concepts. Our programs exercise the diverse features of C++. Reading the book carefully is much like entering and running these programs on a computer. The code is "syntax colored" with C++ keywords, comments and other program text each appearing in different colors. This makes it much easier to read the code—students will especially appreciate the syntax coloring when they read the many more substantial programs we present.

469 Illustrations/Figures

An abundance of colorized charts and line drawings is included. The discussion of control structures in Chapter 2 features carefully drawn flowcharts. (Note: We do not teach the use of flowcharting as a program development tool, but we do use a brief flowchart-oriented presentation to specify the precise operation of C++'s control structures.) Chapter 15, "Data Structures," uses colorized line drawings to illustrate the creation and maintenance of linked lists, queues, stacks and binary trees. The remainder of the book is abundantly illustrated.

625 Programming Tips

We have included six design elements to help students focus on important aspects of program development, testing and debugging, performance and portability. We highlight hundreds of these tips in the form of *Good Programming Practices*, *Common Programming Errors*, *Performance Tips*, *Portability Tips*, *Software Engineering Observations* and *Testing and Debugging Tips*. These tips and practices represent the best we have been able to glean from almost six decades (combined) of programming and teaching experience. One of our students—a mathematics major—told us recently that she feels this approach is somewhat like the highlighting of axioms, theorems and corollaries in mathematics books; it provides a basis on which to build good software.

112 Good Programming Practices

Good Programming Practices are highlighted in the text. They call the student's attention to techniques that help produce better programs. When we teach introductory courses to nonprogrammers, we state that the "buzzword" of each course is "clarity," and we tell the students that we will highlight (in these *Good Programming Practices*) techniques for writing programs that are clearer, more understandable and more maintainable.

216 Common Programming Errors

Students learning a language—especially in their first programming course—tend to make certain kinds of errors frequently. Focusing on these *Common Programming Errors* helps students avoid making the same errors. It also helps reduce long lines outside instructors' offices during office hours!

87 Performance Tips

In our experience, teaching students to write clear and understandable programs is by far the most important goal for a first programming course. But students want to write the programs that run the fastest, use the least memory, require the smallest number of keystrokes, or dazzle in other nifty ways. Students really care about performance. They want to know what they can do to "turbo charge" their programs. So we have include *Performance Tips* to highlight opportunities for improving program performance.

37 Portability Tips

Software development is a complex and expensive activity. Organizations that develop software must often produce versions customized to a variety of computers and operating systems. So there is a strong emphasis today on portability, i.e., on producing software that will run on a variety of computer systems with few, if any, changes. Many people tout C++ as an appropriate language for developing portable software, especially because of C++'s close relationship to ANSI/ISO C and the fact that ANSI/ISO C++ is the global C++ standard. Some people assume that if they implement an application in C++, the application will automatically be portable. This is simply not the case. Achieving portability requires careful and cautious design. There are many pitfalls. We include numerous *Portability Tips* to help students write portable code.

146 Software Engineering Observations

The object-oriented programming paradigm requires a complete rethinking about the way we build software systems. C++ is an effective language for performing good software engineering. The *Software Engineering Observations* highlight techniques, architectural issues and design issues, etc. that affect the architecture and construction of software systems, especially large-scale systems. Much of what the student learns here will be useful in upper-level courses and in industry as the student begins to work with large, complex real-world systems.

27 Testing and Debugging Tips

This "tip type" may be misnamed. When we decided to incorporate *Testing and Debugging Tips* into this new edition, we thought these tips would be suggestions for testing programs to expose bugs and suggestions for removing those bugs. In fact, most of these tips tend to be observations about capabilities and features of C++ that prevent bugs from getting into programs in the first place.

Summary

Each chapter ends with additional pedagogical devices. We present an extensive, bullet-list-style *Summary* in every chapter. This helps the student review and reinforce key concepts. There is an average of 37 summary bullets per chapter.

Terminology

We include a *Terminology* section with an alphabetized list of the important terms defined in the chapter—again, further reinforcement. There is an average of 72 terms per chapter.

Summary of Tips, Practices and Errors

We collect and list from the chapter the *Good Programming Practices, Common Programming Errors, Performance Tips, Portability Tips, Software Engineering Observations* and *Testing and Debugging Tips*.

554 Self-Review Exercises and Answers (Count Includes Separate Parts)
Extensive *Self-Review Exercises* and *Answers to Self-Review Exercises* are included for self study. This gives the student a chance to build confidence with the material and prepare to attempt the regular exercises.

877 Exercises (Count Includes Separate Parts; 1431 Total Exercises)
Each chapter concludes with a substantial set of exercises including simple recall of important terminology and concepts; writing individual C++ statements; writing small portions of C++ functions and classes; writing complete C++ functions, classes and programs; and writing major term projects. The large number of exercises enables instructors to tailor their courses to the unique needs of their audiences and to vary course assignments each semester. Instructors can use these exercises to form homework assignments, short quizzes and major examinations.

550-page Instructor's Manual with Solutions to the Exercises
The solutions for the exercises are included on the *Instructor's CD* and on the disks *available only to instructors* through their Prentice Hall representatives. [**NOTE: Please do not write to us requesting the instructor's CD. Distribution of this CD is limited strictly to college professors teaching from the book. Instructors may obtain the solutions manual only from their Prentice Hall representatives.**] Solutions to approximately half of the exercises are included on the *C++ Multimedia Cyber Classroom: Third Edition* CD (available September 2000; please see the last few pages of this book for ordering instructions).

4523 Index Entries (Total of 7653 Counting Multiple References)
We have included an extensive *Index* at the back of the book. This helps the student find any term or concept by keyword. The *Index* is useful to people reading the book for the first time and is especially useful to practicing programmers who use the book as a reference. Most of the terms in the *Terminology* sections appear in the *Index* (along with many more index items from each chapter). Thus, the student can use the *Index* in conjunction with the *Terminology* sections to be sure he or she has covered the key material of each chapter.

A Tour of the Book

The book is divided into several major parts. The first part, Chapters 1 through 5, presents a thorough treatment of procedural programming in C++ including data types, input/output, control structures, functions, arrays, pointers and strings. The "Thinking About Objects" section at the ends of Chapters 1–5 introduce object technology, present an interesting and challenging optional case study in designing and implementing a substantial object-oriented system.

The second part, Chapters 6 through 8, presents a substantial treatment of data abstraction with classes, objects and operator overloading. This section might effectively be called, "Programming with Objects." The "Thinking About Objects" sections at the ends of Chapters 6 and 7 develop and present a 1000-line C++ program that implements the design presented in Chapters 2–5.

The third part, Chapters 9 and 10, presents inheritance, virtual functions and polymorphism—the root technologies of true object-oriented programming.

The "Thinking About Objects" section at the end of Chapter 9 incorporates inheritance into the design and implementation of the elevator simulator.

The fourth part, chapters 11 and 14, presents C++-style stream-oriented input/output including using stream I/O with the keyboard, the screen, files and character arrays; both sequential file processing and direct-access (i.e., random access) file processing are discussed.

The fifth part, Chapters 12 and 13, discusses two of the more recent additions to C++, namely templates and exception handling. Templates, also called parameterized types, encourage software reusability. Exceptions help programmers develop more robust, fault-tolerant, business-critical and mission-critical systems.

The sixth part, Chapter 15, presents a thorough treatment of dynamic data structures such as linked lists, queues, stacks and trees. This chapter, when supplemented with the treatment of the Standard Template Library (STL) in Chapter 20, creates a rich treatment of data structures that makes a nice C++ supplement to traditional computer science data structures and algorithms courses.

The seventh part, Chapters 16 through 18 discuss a variety of topics including bit, character and string manipulation; the preprocessor and miscellaneous "Other Topics."

The last part of the main text, Chapters 19 through 21, is devoted to the latest enhancements to C++ and to the C++ Standard Library which have been included in the ANSI/ISO C++ Standard. These include discussions of class **string**, string stream processing, the Standard Template Library and a potpourri of other recent additions to C++.

The end matter of the book consists of reference materials that support the main text including Appendices on operator precedence, the ASCII character set, number systems (binary, decimal, octal and hexadecimal) and C++ Internet/World Wide Web resources. A bibliography is included to encourage further reading. The text concludes with a detailed index that helps the reader locate any terms in the text by keyword. Now let us look at each of the chapters in detail.

Chapter 1—Introduction to Computers and C++ Programming—discusses what computers are, how they work and how they are programmed. It introduces the notion of structured programming and explains why this set of techniques has fostered a revolution in the way programs are written. The chapter gives a brief history of the development of programming languages from machine languages, to assembly languages, to high-level languages. The origin of the C++ programming language is discussed. The chapter includes an introduction to a typical C++ programming environment and gives a concise introduction to writing C++ programs. A detailed treatment of decision making and arithmetic operations in C++ is presented. We have introduced a new, more open, easier to read "look and feel" for our C++ source programs, most notably using syntax coloring to highlight keyword comments and regular program text; and to make programs more readable. After studying this chapter, the student will understand how to write simple, but complete, C++ programs. We discuss the explosion in interest in the Internet that has occurred with the advent of the World Wide Web and the Java programming language. We discuss **namespaces** and the **using** statement for the benefit of readers with access to standard-compliant compilers. We use the new-style header files. It will take a few years to "clear out" the older compilers that are still widely used. Readers plunge right in with object-orientation in the "Thinking About Objects" section which introduces the basic terminology of object technology.

Chapter 2—Control Structures—introduces the notion of algorithms (procedures) for solving problems. It explains the importance of using control structures effectively in producing programs that are understandable, debuggable, maintainable and more likely to work properly on the first try. It introduces the sequence structure, selection structures (**if**, **if/else** and **switch**) and repetition structures (**while, do/while** and **for**). It examines repetition in detail and compares counter-controlled loops and sentinel-controlled loops. It explains the technique of top-down, stepwise refinement that is critical to the production of properly structured programs and presents the popular program design aid, pseudocode. The methods and approaches used in Chapter 2 are applicable to effective use of control structures in any programming language, not just C++. This chapter helps the student develop good programming habits in preparation for dealing with the more substantial programming tasks in the remainder of the text. The chapter concludes with a discussion of logical operators—**&&** (and), **||** (or) and **!** (not). The keyword table was enhanced with the new C++ keywords introduced in the ANSI/ISO C++ Standard. We introduce the new-style **static_cast** operator. This is safer than using the old-style casting C++ inherited from C. We added the "Peter Minuit" exercise so students can see the wonders of compound interest—with the computer doing most of the work! We discuss the new scoping rules for loop counters in **for**-loops. In the "Thinking About Objects" section, we begin the first phase of an object-oriented design (OOD) for the elevator simulator—identifying the classes needed to implement the simulator. We also introduce the UML use case, class and object diagrams and the concepts of associations, multiplicity, composition, roles and links.

Chapter 3—Functions—discusses the design and construction of program modules. C++'s function-related capabilities include standard-library functions, programmer-defined functions, recursion, call-by-value and call-by-reference capabilities. The techniques presented in Chapter 3 are essential to the production of properly structured programs, especially the kinds of larger programs and software that system programmers and application programmers are likely to develop in real-world applications. The "divide and conquer" strategy is presented as an effective means for solving complex problems by dividing them into simpler interacting components. Students enjoy the treatment of random numbers and simulation, and they appreciate the discussion of the dice game of craps which makes elegant use of control structures. The chapter offers a solid introduction to recursion and includes a table summarizing the dozens of recursion examples and exercises distributed throughout the remainder of the book. Some texts leave recursion for a chapter late in the book; we feel this topic is best covered gradually throughout the text. The extensive collection of 60 exercises at the end of the chapter includes several classical recursion problems such as the Towers of Hanoi. The chapter discusses the so-called "C++ enhancements to C," including **inline** functions, reference parameters, default arguments, the unary scope resolution operator, function overloading and function templates. The header files table has been modified to include many of the new header files that the reader will use throughout the book. Please do Exercise 3.54 on adding a wagering capability to the craps program. In "Thinking About Objects" section, we determine many of the class attributes needed to implement the elevator simulator. We also introduce the UML statechart and activity diagrams and the concepts of events and actions as they relate to these diagrams.

Chapter 4—Arrays—discusses the structuring of data into arrays, or groups, of related data items of the same type. The chapter presents numerous examples of both single-subscripted arrays and double-subscripted arrays. It is widely recognized that structuring data properly is just as important as using control structures effectively in the development of properly structured programs. Examples in the chapter investigate various common array manipulations, printing histograms, sorting data, passing arrays to functions and an introduction to the field of survey data analysis (with simple statistics). A feature of this chapter is the discussion of elementary sorting and searching techniques and the presentation of binary searching as a dramatic improvement over linear searching. The 94 end-of-chapter exercises include a variety of interesting and challenging problems such as improved sorting techniques, the design of an airline reservations system, an introduction to the concept of turtle graphics (made famous in the LOGO language) and the Knight's Tour and Eight Queens problems that introduce the notion of heuristic programming so widely employed in the field of artificial intelligence. The exercises conclude with many recursion problems including the selection sort, palindromes, linear search, binary search, the Eight Queens, printing an array, printing a string backwards and finding the minimum value in an array. This chapter still uses C-style arrays which, as you will see in Chapter 5, are really pointers to the array contents in memory. We are certainly committed to arrays as full-fledged objects. In Chapter 8, we use the techniques of operator overloading to craft a valuable **Array** class out of which we create **Array** objects that are much more robust and pleasant to program with than the arrays of Chapter 4. In Chapter 20, "Standard Template Library (STL)," we introduce STL's class **vector** which, when used with the iterators and algorithms discussed in Chapter 20, creates a solid treatment of arrays as full-fledged objects. In the "Thinking About Objects" section, we determine many of the operations (behaviors) of the classes in the elevator simulation. We also introduce the UML sequence diagram and the concept of messages sent between objects.

   Chapter 5—Pointers and Strings—presents one of the most powerful and difficult-to-master features of the C++ language, namely pointers. The chapter provides detailed explanations of pointer operators, call by reference, pointer expressions, pointer arithmetic, the relationship between pointers and arrays, arrays of pointers and pointers to functions. There is an intimate relationship between pointers, arrays and strings in C++, so we introduce basic string-manipulation concepts and include a discussion of some of the most popular string-handling functions, namely **getline** (input a line of text), **strcpy** and **strncpy** (copy a string), **strcat** and **strncat**, (concatenate two strings) **strcmp** and **strncmp** (compare two strings), **strtok** ("tokenize" a string into its pieces) and **strlen** (compute the length of a string). The 49 chapter exercises include a simulation of the classic race between the tortoise and the hare, card shuffling and dealing algorithms, recursive quicksort and recursive maze traversals. A special section entitled "Building Your Own Computer" is also included. This section explains machine-language programming and proceeds with a project involving the design and implementation of a computer simulator that allows the reader to write and run machine language programs. This unique feature of the text will be especially useful to the reader who wants to understand how computers really work. Our students enjoy this project and often implement substantial enhancements, many of which are suggested in the exercises. In Chapter 15, another special section guides the reader through building a compiler; the machine language produced by the compiler is then executed on the machine language simulator produced in Chapter 7. Information is communicated from the compiler to the simulator in sequential files which we discuss in Chapter 14. A second special section includes challenging string-manipulation exercises related to text analysis, word processing, printing dates in various formats, check protection, writing the word equivalent of a check amount, Morse Code and metric-to-English conversions. The reader will want to revisit these string-manipulation exercises after studying class **string** in Chapter 19. Many people find that the topic of pointers is, by far, the most difficult part of an introductory programming course. In C and "raw C++" arrays and strings are really pointers to array and string contents in memory. Even function names are pointers. Studying this chapter carefully should reward you with a deep understanding of the complex topic of pointers. Again, we cover arrays and strings as full-fledged objects later in the book. In Chapter 8, we use operator overloading to craft customized **Array** and **String** classes. In Chapter 19, we discuss Standard Library class **string** and show how to manipulate **string** objects. In Chapter 20 we discuss class **vector** for implementing array objects. Chapter 5 is loaded with challenging exercises. Please be sure to try the *Special Section: Building Your Own Computer.* In the "Thinking About Objects" section, we determine many of the collaborations (interactions between objects in the system) needed to implement the elevator system and represent these collaborations using the UML collaboration diagram. We also include a bibliography and a list of Internet and World Wide Web resources that contain the UML 1.3 specifications and other reference materials, general resources, tutorials, FAQs, articles, whitepapers and software.

Chapter 6—Classes and Data Abstraction—begins our discussion of object-based programming. The chapter represents a wonderful opportunity for teaching data abstraction the "right way"—through a language (C++) expressly devoted to implementing abstract data types (ADTs). In recent years, data abstraction has become a major topic in introductory computing courses. Chapters 6 through 8 include a solid treatment of data abstraction. Chapter 6 discusses implementing ADTs as **struct**s, implementing ADTs as C++-style **class**es and why this approach is superior to using **struct**s, accessing **class** members, separating interface from implementation, using access functions and utility functions, initializing objects with constructors, destroying objects with destructors, assignment by default memberwise copy and software reusability. The chapter exercises challenge the student to develop classes for complex numbers, rational numbers, times, dates, rectangles, huge integers and for playing tic-tac-toe. Students generally enjoy game-playing programs. The "Thinking About Objects" section asks you to write a class header file for each of the classes in your elevator simulator. The more mathematically inclined reader will enjoy the exercises on creating class **Complex** (for complex numbers), class **Rational** (for rational numbers) and class **HugeInteger** (for arbitrarily large integers). In the "Thinking About Objects" section, we use the UML class diagram developed in previous sections to outline the C++ header files that define our classes. We also introduce the concept of handles to objects in the system and we begin to study how to implement handles in C++.

Chapter 7—Classes Part II—continues the study of classes and data abstraction. The chapter discusses declaring and using constant objects, constant member functions, composition—the process of building classes that have objects of other classes as members, **friend** functions and **friend** classes that have special access rights to the **private** and **protected** members of classes, the **this** pointer that enables an object to know its own address, dynamic memory allocation, **static** class members for containing and manipulating class-wide data, examples of popular abstract data types (arrays, strings and queues), container classes and iterators. The chapter exercises ask the student to develop a savings account class and a class for holding sets of integers. In our discussion of **const** objects, we briefly mention keyword **mutable** which, as we will see in Chapter 21, is used in a subtle manner to enable modification of "non-visible" implementation in **const** objects. We discuss dynamic memory allocation with **new** and **delete**. When **new** fails, it returns a 0 pointer in pre-standard C++. We use this pre-standard style in Chapters 7-12. We defer to Chapter 13 the discussion of the new style of **new** failure in which **new** now "throws an exception." We motivate the discussion of **static** class members with a video-game-based example. We emphasize throughout the book and in our professional seminars how important it is to hide implementation details from clients of a class; then, we show **private** data on our class headers, which certainly reveals implementation. We discuss proxy classes, a nice means of hiding even **private** data from clients of a class. The "Thinking About Objects" section asks you to incorporate dynamic memory management and composition into your elevator simulator. Students will enjoy the exercise creating class **Integerset**. This serves as excellent motivation for the treatment of operator overloading in Chapter 8. In the "Thinking About Objects" section, we present a complete elevator simulator C++ program (approximately 1000 lines of code) and a detailed code walkthrough. The code follows directly from the UML-based design created in previous sections and employs our good programming practices, including the use of **static** and **const** data members and functions. We also discuss dynamic-memory allocation, composition and object interaction via handles and how to use forward declarations to avoid the circular include problem.

Chapter 8—Operator Overloading—as one of the most popular topics in our C++ courses. Students really enjoy this material. They find it a perfect match with the discussion of abstract data types in Chapters 6 and 7. Operator overloading enables the programmer to tell the compiler how to use existing operators with objects of new types. C++ already knows how to use these operators with objects of built-in types such as integers, floats and characters. But suppose we create a new string class—what would the plus sign mean when used between string objects? Many programmers use plus with strings to mean concatenation. In Chapter 8, the programmer will learn how to "overload" the plus sign so that when it is written between two string objects in an expression, the compiler will generate a function call to an "operator function" that will concatenate the two strings. The chapter discusses the fundamentals of operator overloading, restrictions in operator overloading, overloading with class member functions vs. with nonmember functions, overloading unary and binary operators and converting between types. A feature of the chapter is the collection of substantial case studies including an array class, a string class, a date class, a huge integer class and a complex numbers class (the last two appear with full source code in the exercises). The more mathematically inclined student will enjoy creating the polynomial class in the exercises. This material is different from what you do in most programming languages and courses. Operator overloading is a complex topic, but an enriching one. Using operator overloading wisely helps you add that extra "polish" to your classes. The discussions of class **Array** and class **String** are particularly valuable to students who will go on to use the Standard Library classes **string** and **vector**. With the techniques of Chapters 6, 7 and 8, it is possible to craft a **Date** class that, if we had been using it for the last two decades, could easily have eliminated a major portion of the so-called "Year 2000 (or Y2K) Problem." The exercises encourage the student to add operator overloading to classes **Complex**, **Rational** and **HugeInteger** to enable convenient manipulation of objects of these classes with operator symbols—as in mathematics—rather than with function calls as the student did in the Chapter 7 exercises.

Chapter 9—Inheritance—deals with one of the most fundamental capabilities of object-oriented programming languages. Inheritance is a form of software reusability in which new classes are developed quickly and easily by absorbing the capabilities of existing classes and adding appropriate new capabilities. The chapter discusses the notions of base classes and derived classes, **protected** members, **public** inheritance, **protected** inheritance, **private** inheritance, direct base classes, indirect base classes, constructors and destructors in base classes and derived classes and software engineering with inheritance. The chapter compares inheritance ("is a" relationships) with composition ("has a" relationships) and introduces "uses a" and "knows a" relationships. A feature of the chapter is its several substantial case studies. In particular, a lengthy case study implements a point, circle, cylinder class hierarchy. The chapter concludes with a case study on multiple inheritance—an advanced feature of C++ that enables a derived class to be formed by inheriting attributes and behaviors from several base classes. The exercises ask the student to compare the creation of new classes by inheritance vs. composition; to extend the various inheritance hierarchies discussed in the chapter; to write an inheritance hierarchy for quadrilaterals, trapezoids, parallelograms, rectangles and squares; and to create a more general shape hierarchy with two-dimensional shapes and three-dimensional shapes. We modify our inheritance hierarchy for university community members to show a nice example of multiple inheritance. In Chapter 21 we continue our discussion of multiple inheritance by exposing the problems caused by so-called "diamond inheritance" and showing how to solve these problems with **virtual** base classes. In the "Thinking About Objects" section, we update the elevator simulation design and implementation to incorporate inheritance. We also suggest further modifications so that the student may then design and implement, using the tools presented in the previous sections.

Chapter 10—Virtual Functions and Polymorphism—deals with another of the fundamental capabilities of object-oriented programming, namely polymorphic behavior. When many classes are related through inheritance to a common base class, each derived-class object may be treated as a base-class object. This enables programs to be written in a general manner independent of the specific types of the derived-class objects. New kinds of objects can be handled by the same program, thus making systems more extensible. Polymorphism enables programs to eliminate complex **switch** logic in favor of simpler "straight-line" logic. A screen manager of a video game, for example, can simply send a draw message to every object in a linked list of objects to be drawn. Each object knows how to draw itself. A new object can be added to the program without modifying that program as long as that new object also knows how to draw itself. This style of programming is typically used to implement today's popular graphical user interfaces (GUIs). The chapter discusses the mechanics of achieving polymorphic behavior through the use of **virtual** functions. It distinguishes between abstract classes (from which objects cannot be instantiated) and concrete classes (from which objects can be instantiated). Abstract classes are useful for providing an inheritable interface to classes throughout the hierarchy. A feature of the chapter is its two major polymorphism case studies—a payroll system and another version of the point, circle, cylinder shape hierarchy discussed in Chapter 9. The chapter exercises ask the student to discuss a number of conceptual issues and approaches, add abstract classes to the shape hierarchy, develop a basic graphics package, modify the chapter's employee class—and pursue all these projects with **virtual** functions and polymorphic programming. The chapter's two polymorphism case studies show a contrast in inheritance styles. The first example (of a payroll system) is a clear, "sensible" use of inheritance. The second, which builds on the point, circle, cylinder hierarchy developed in Chapter 9, is an example of what some professionals call "structural inheritance"—not as natural and sensible as the first, but "mechanically correct" nevertheless. We use this second example because of the section entitled "Polymorphism, **virtual** Functions and Dynamic Binding "Under the Hood." We deliver C++ professional seminars to senior software engineers. These people appreciated the two polymorphism examples in the first edition, but they felt something was missing from our presentations. Yes, they said, we showed them how to program with polymorphism in C++. But they wanted more. They told us they were concerned about the operating overhead of programming polymorphically. It is a nice feature, they said, but it clearly has costs. So our professional audiences insisted that we provide a deeper explanation that showed precisely how polymorphism is implemented in C++, and hence, precisely what execution time and memory "costs" one must pay when programming with this powerful capability. We responded by developing an illustration that shows the *vtables* (**virtual** function tables) that the C++ compiler automatically builds to support the polymorphic programming style. We drew these tables in our classes in which we discussed the point, circle, cylinder shape hierarchy. Our audiences indicated that this indeed gave them the information to decide whether polymorphism was an appropriate programming style for each new project they would tackle. We have included this presentation in Section 10.10 and the *vtable* illustration in Fig. 10.2. Please study this presentation carefully. It will give you a much deeper understanding of what is really occurring in the computer when you program with inheritance and polymorphism.

Chapter 11—C++ Stream Input/Output—contains a comprehensive treatment of C++ object-oriented input/output. The chapter discusses the various I/O capabilities of C++ including output with the stream insertion operator, input with the stream extraction operator, type-safe I/O (a nice improvement over C), formatted I/O, unformatted I/O (for performance), stream manipulators for controlling the stream base (decimal, octal, or hexadecimal), floating-point numbers, controlling field widths, user-defined manipulators, stream format states, stream error states, I/O of objects of user-defined types and tying output streams to input streams (to ensure that prompts actually appear before the user is expected to enter responses). The extensive exercise set asks the student to write various programs that test most of the I/O capabilities discussed in the text.

Chapter 12—Templates—discusses one of the more recent additions to C++. Function templates were introduced in Chapter 3. Chapter 12 presents an additional function template example. Class templates enable the programmer to capture the essence of an abstract data type (such as a stack, an array, or a queue) and then create—with minimal additional code—versions of that ADT for particular types (such as a queue of **int**, a queue of **float**, a queue of strings, etc.). For this reason, template classes are often called parameterized types. The chapter discusses using type parameters and nontype parameters and considers the interaction among templates and other C++ concepts, such as inheritance, **friends** and **static** members. The exercises challenge the student to write a variety of function templates and class templates, and to employ these in complete programs. We greatly enhance the treatment of templates with the discussion of the Standard Template Library (STL) containers, iterators and algorithms in Chapter 20.

Chapter 13—Exception Handling—discusses one of the more recent enhancements to the C++ language. Exception handling enables the programmer to write programs that are more robust, more fault tolerant and more appropriate for business-critical and mission-critical environments. The chapter discusses when exception handling is appropriate; introduces the basics of exception handling with `try` blocks, `throw` statements and `catch` blocks; indicates how and when to rethrow an exception; explains how to write an exception specification and process unexpected exceptions; and discusses the important ties between exceptions and constructors, destructors and inheritance. A feature of the chapter is its 43 exercises that walk the student through implementing programs that illustrate the diversity and power of C++'s exception handling capabilities. We discuss rethrowing an exception and we illustrate both ways `new` can fail when memory is exhausted. Prior to the C++ draft standard `new` failed by returning 0, much as `malloc` fails in C by returning a `NULL` pointer value.We show the new style of `new` failing by throwing a `bad_alloc` (bad allocation) exception. We illustrate how to use `set_new_handler` to specify a custom function to be called to deal with memory exhaustion situations. We discuss the `auto_ptr` class template to guarantee that dynamically allocated memory will be properly `delete`d to avoid memory leaks. We present the new Standard Library exception hierarchy.

Chapter 14—File Processing—discusses the techniques used to process text files with sequential access and random access. The chapter begins with an introduction to the data hierarchy from bits, to bytes, to fields, to records, to files. Next, C++'s simple view of files and streams is presented. Sequential-access files are discussed using programs that show how to open and close files, how to store data sequentially in a file and how to read data sequentially from a file. Random-access files are discussed using programs that show how to sequentially create a file for random access, how to read and write data to a file with random access and how to read data sequentially from a randomly accessed file. The fourth random-access program combines many of the techniques of accessing files both sequentially and randomly into a complete transaction-processing program. Students in our industry seminars have told us that after studying the material on file processing, they were able to produce substantial file-processing programs that were immediately useful in their organizations. The exercises ask the student to implement a variety of programs that build and process both sequential-access files and random-access files. The closely related material on string stream processing has been positioned at the end of Chapter 19.

Chapter 15—Data Structures—discusses the techniques used to create and manipulate dynamic data structures. The chapter begins with discussions of self-referential classes and dynamic memory allocation and proceeds with a discussion of how to create and maintain various dynamic data structures including linked lists, queues (or waiting lines), stacks and trees. For each type of data structure, we present complete, working programs and show sample outputs. The chapter really helps the student master pointers. The chapter includes abundant examples using indirection and double indirection—a particularly difficult concept. One problem when working with pointers is that students have trouble visualizing the data structures and how their nodes are linked together. So we have included illustrations that show the links and the sequence in which they are created. The binary tree example is a superb capstone for the study of pointers and dynamic data structures. This example creates a binary tree; enforces duplicate elimination; and introduces recursive pre-order, inorder and postorder tree traversals. Students have a genuine sense of accomplishment when they study and implement this example. They particularly appreciate seeing that the inorder traversal prints the node values in sorted order. The chapter includes a substantial collection of exercises. A highlight of the exercises is the special section "Building Your Own Compiler." The exercises walk the student through the development of an infix-to-postfix-conversion program and a postfix-expression-evaluation program. We then modify the postfix evaluation algorithm to generate machine-language code. The compiler places this code in a file (using the techniques of Chapter 14). Students then run the machine language produced by their compilers on the software simulators they built in the exercises of Chapter 5! The 67 exercises include a supermarket simulation using queueing, recursively searching a list, recursively printing a list backwards, binary-tree node deletion, level-order traversal of a binary tree, printing trees, writing a portion of an optimizing compiler, writing an interpreter, inserting/deleting anywhere in a linked list, implementing lists and queues without tail pointers, analyzing the performance of binary tree searching and sorting and implementing an indexed list class. After studying Chapter 15, the reader is prepared for the treatment of STL containers, iterators and algorithms in Chapter 20. The STL containers are pre-packaged, templatized data structures that most programs will find sufficient for the vast majority of applications they will need to implement. STL is a giant leap forward in achieving the vision of reuse, reuse and reuse.

Chapter 16—Bits, Characters, Strings and Structures—presents a variety of important features. C++'s powerful bit-manipulation capabilities enable programmers to write programs that exercise lower-level hardware capabilities. This helps programs process bit strings, set individual bits on or off and store information more compactly. Such capabilities, often found only in low-level assembly languages, are valued by programmers writing system software such as operating systems and networking software. As you recall, we introduced C-style `char *` string manipulation in Chapter 5 and presented the most popular string-manipulation functions. In Chapter 16, we continue our presentation of characters and C-style `char *` strings. We present the various character-manipulation capabilities of the `<cctype>` library—these include the ability to test a character to see if it is a digit, an alphabetic character, an alphanumeric character, a hexadecimal digit, a lowercase letter, an uppercase letter, etc. We present the remaining string-manipulation functions of the various string-related libraries; as always, every function is presented in the context of a complete, working C++ program. Structures are like records in Pascal and other languages—they aggregate data items of various types. Structures are used in Chapter 14 to form files consisting of records of information. Structures are used in conjunction with pointers and dynamic memory allocation in Chapter 15 to form dynamic data structures such as linked lists, queues, stacks and trees. A feature of the chapter is its high-performance card shuffling and dealing simulation. This is an excellent opportunity for the instructor to emphasize the quality of algorithms. The 38 exercises encourage the student to try out most of the capabilities discussed in the chapter. The feature exercise leads the student through the development of a spell checker program. Chapters 1–5 and 16–18 are mostly the "C legacy" portion of C++. In particular, this chapter presents a deeper treatment of C-like, `char *` strings for the benefit of C++ programmers who are likely to work with C legacy code. Again, Chapter 19 discusses class `string` and discusses manipulating strings as full-fledged objects.

Chapter 17—The Preprocessor—provides detailed discussions of the preprocessor directives. The chapter includes more complete information on the `#include` directive that causes a copy of a specified file to be included in place of the directive before the file is compiled and the `#define` directive that creates symbolic constants and macros. The chapter explains conditional compilation for enabling the programmer to control the execution of preprocessor directives and the compilation of program code. The `#` operator that converts its operand to a string and the `##` operator that concatenates two tokens are discussed. The various predefined preprocessor symbolic constants (`__LINE__`, `__FILE__`, `__DATE__` and `__TIME__`) are presented. Finally, macro `assert` of the header file `<cassert>` is discussed; `assert` is valuable in program testing, debugging, verification and validation. We have used `assert` in many examples, but the reader is urged to begin using exception handling instead, as we discussed in Chapter 13.

Chapter 18—C Legacy Code Topics—presents additional topics including several advanced topics not ordinarily covered in introductory courses. We show how to redirect program input to come from a file, redirect program output to be placed in a file, redirect the output of one program to be the input of another program (piping), append the output of a program to an existing file, develop functions that use variable-length argument lists, pass command-line arguments to function `main` and use them in a program, compile programs whose components are spread across multiple files, register functions with `atexit` to be executed at program termination, terminate program execution with function `exit`, use the `const` and `volatile` type qualifiers, specify the type of a numeric constant using the integer and floating-point suffixes, use the signal-handling library to trap unexpected events, create and use dynamic arrays with `calloc` and `realloc`, use `union`s as a space-saving technique and use linkage specifications when C++ programs are to be linked with legacy C code. As the title suggests, this chapter is intended primarily for C++ programmers who will be working with C legacy code.

Chapter 19—Class `string` and String Stream Processing—The chapter also discusses C++'s capabilities for inputting data from strings in memory and outputting data to strings in memory; these capabilities are often referred to as in-core formatting or string-stream processing. Class `string` is a required component of the Standard Library. Although we placed this material in a chapter near the end of the book, many instructors will want to incorporate the discussion of "strings as full-fledged objects" early in their courses. We preserved the treatment of C-like strings in Chapter 5 and later for several reasons. First, we feel it strengthens the reader's understanding of pointers. Second, we feel that for the next decade, or so, C++ programmers will need to be able to read and modify the enormous amounts of C legacy code that have accumulated over the last quarter of a century and this code processes strings as pointers, as does a large portion of even the C++ code that has been written in industry over the last many years. In Chapter 19 we discuss `string` assignment, concatenation and comparison. We show how to determine various `string` characteristics such as a `string`'s size, capacity and whether or not it is empty. We discuss how to resize a `string`. We consider the various *find* functions that enable us to find a substring in a `string` (searching the `string` either forwards or backwards), and we show how to find either the first occurrence or last occurrence of a character selected from a `string` of characters, and how to find the first occurrence or last occurrence of a character that is not included in a `string`. We show how to replace, erase and insert characters in a `string`. We show how to convert a `string` object to a C-style `char *` string.

Chapter 20—Standard Template Library (STL)—We emphasize here again that this is not an STL book, nor is there any discussion of actual STL features in the first 18 chapters. Chapter 19 does make brief mention of iterators, but states that the real discussion of iterators is in Chapter 20. With the inclusion of Chapter 20, *C++ How to Program: Third Edition* now discusses four programming paradigms: procedural programming, object-based programming, object-oriented programming and generic programming (with the STL). The challenges of teaching object-oriented programming will increase as class libraries and class template libraries grow. We believe that there will be exponential growth in reusable componentry over the next few decades. The early computer science curriculum will need to present the root language, indicate how to craft valuable classes, overview key existing class libraries and show how to reuse these components. Upper-level computer science courses, and, in fact, courses in most any topic for which computers are used (i.e., today that means most any topic, period) will cover their bodies of knowledge and these will include discussion and use of the class libraries that apply to that subject area. Many efforts are underway to support reuse across platforms, so it will not matter what language your classes are written in; you will be able to reuse them from many different languages.

Chapter 21—ANSI/ISO C++ Standard Language Additions—This chapter is a collection of miscellaneous additions to the language. We discuss data type **bool** with data values **false** and **true**—a more natural representation than using non-zero and zero values (although these may still be used). We discuss the four new cast operators: **static_cast**, **const_cast**, **reinterpret_cast** and **dynamic_cast**. These provide a much more robust mechanism for dealing with casts than the style of casts C++ inherited from C. We discuss **namespace**s, a feature particularly crucial for software developers building substantial systems, especially when using a variety of class libraries. Namespaces prevent the kinds of naming collisions that previously hindered such large software efforts. We consider run-time type information (RTTI) which allows existing programs to check the type of an object, something they could not do previously unless the programmer explicitly included a type code (an undesirable programming practice). We discuss the use of operators **typeid** and **dynamic_cast**. We discuss the new operator keywords; these are useful for programmers who do not like cryptic operators, but their primary use is in international markets where certain characters are not normally available on local keyboards. We consider the use of keyword **explicit** that prevents the compiler from invoking conversion constructors when it would be undesirable to do so; **explicit** conversion constructors can only be invoked through constructor syntax, not through implicit conversions. We discuss keyword **mutable**, which allows a member of a **const** object to be changed. Previously this was accomplished by "casting away **const**-ness," a dangerous practice. We also discuss a few features that are not new, but which we chose not to include in the main portion of the book, because they are relatively obscure, namely pointer-to-member operators **.*** and **->*** and using **virtual** base classes with multiple inheritance.

Appendix A—Operator Precedence Chart—We have reformatted the table to be more useful. Each operator is now on a line by itself with the operator symbol, its name and its associativity.

Appendix B—ASCII Character Set—We resisted the temptation to expand this substantially to include the relatively new international Unicode character set. By the next edition, we expect to discuss Unicode in detail.

Appendix C—Number Systems—discusses the binary, octal, decimal and hexadecimal number systems. It considers how to convert numbers between bases and explains the one's complement and two's complement binary representations.

Appendix D—C++ Internet and Web Resources—contains a huge listing of valuable C++ resources such as demos, information about popular compilers (including freebies), books, articles, conferences, job banks, journals, magazines, help, tutorials, FAQs (frequently asked questions), newsgroups, copies of the ANSI/ISO C++ Standard document, Web-based courses, product news and C++ development tools.

Bibliography—lists 125 books and articles—some of historical interest and most quite recent—to encourage the student to do further reading on C++ and OOP.

Index—The book contains a comprehensive index to enable the reader to locate by keyword any term or concept throughout the text.

The C++ Multimedia Cyber Classroom: Third Edition

We have implemented an interactive, CD-ROM-based, software version of *C++ How to Program: Third Edition* called the *C++ Multimedia Cyber Classroom: Third Edition*. It is loaded with features for learning and reference. The *Cyber Classroom* is wrapped with the textbook in a publication called *The Complete C++ Training Course: Third Edition*. If you have already purchased the textbook, you can get a copy of the *C++ Multimedia Cyber Classroom* CD directly from Prentice Hall. Please see the ordering instructions on the last few pages of this book.

There is an introductory presentation in which the authors overview the Cyber Classroom's features. The 268 live-code example C++ programs in the textbook truly "come alive" in the *C++ Multimedia Cyber Classroom*. We have placed executables for all these examples "under the hood" of the *C++ Multimedia Cyber Classroom*, so if you are viewing a program and want to execute it, you simply click the lightning bolt icon and the program runs. You will immediately see—and hear (for the audio-based multimedia programs)—the program's outputs. If you want to modify a program and see the effects of your changes, simply click the floppy-disk icon that causes the source code to be "lifted off" the CD and "dropped into" one of your own directories so you can edit the text, recompile the program and try out your new version. Click the audio icon and Paul Deitel will talk about the program and "walk you through" the code. (You will not hear Harvey Deitel's voice in these audios—our friends at Prentice Hall like Paul's voice better!)

C++ How to Program: Third Edition contains thousands of exercises that are divided into groups and have varying levels of difficulty. Approximately half of the solutions are provided on the *C++ Multimedia Cyber Classroom* (the remaining exercise solutions are reserved for instructors who wish to assign these exercises as homework). For the *Cyber Classroom*, we carefully selected at least one exercise solution from each group. This allows a student looking at the solution for one exercise in a group to apply the techniques shown in that solution to other exercises.

The *C++ Multimedia Cyber Classroom* provides various navigational aids including extensive hyperlinking. The *C++ Multimedia Cyber Classroom* remembers in a "history list" recent sections you have visited and allows you to move forward or backward in that history list. The thousands of index entries are hyperlinked to their text occurrences. You can key in a term and the *C++ Multimedia Cyber Classroom* will locate its occurrences throughout the text. The *Table of Contents* entries are "hot," so clicking a chapter or section name immediately takes you to that chapter or section. You can insert "bookmarks" at places to which you may want to return.

This third edition Cyber Classroom has been completely redesigned using a Web-browser-based interface. The Cyber Classroom comes in two forms—a CD-ROM version for Microsoft® Windows® platforms and a Web-based version. The Web-based version is ideal for students who prefer the convenience of Internet delivery or who want to run the Cyber Classroom on non-Windows platforms.

Students and professional users of our *Cyber Classrooms* tell us they like the interactivity and that the *Cyber Classroom* is an effective reference because of the extensive hyperlinking and other navigational features. We received an email from a person who said that he lives "in the boonies" and cannot take a live course at a college, so the *Cyber Classroom* was a nice solution to his educational needs.

Professors have sent us emails indicating their students enjoy using the *Cyber Classroom*, spend more time on the course and master more of the material than in textbook-only courses. Also, the *Cyber Classroom* helps shrink lines outside professors' offices during office hours. Prentice Hall is now publishing Cyber Classrooms for most of our books—we will soon publish our books in Web-based training (WBT) format.

Acknowledgments

One of the great pleasures of writing a textbook is acknowledging the efforts of many people whose names may not appear on the cover, but whose hard work, cooperation, friendship and understanding were crucial to the production of the book.

Many other people at Deitel & Associates, Inc. devoted long hours to this project.

- Tem Nieto, a graduate of the Massachusetts Institute of Technology, is one of our full-time colleagues at Deitel & Associates, Inc. and was recently promoted to Director of Product Development. Tem teaches C++, C and Java seminars and works with us on textbook writing, course development and multimedia authoring efforts. Tem co-authored Chapter 19, Chapter 21 and the Special Section entitled "Building Your Own Compiler" in Chapter 15. He also contributed to the Instructor's Manual and the *C++ Multimedia Cyber Classroom: Third Edition.*

- Barbara Deitel managed the preparation of the manuscript and coordinated with Prentice Hall all the efforts related to production of the book. Barbara's efforts are by far the most painstaking of what we do to develop books. She has infinite patience. She handled the endless details involved in publishing a 1200-page, four-color book; a 550-page instructor's manual and the 650 megabyte CD *C++ Multimedia Cyber Classroom.* She spent long hours researching the quotations at the beginning of each chapter. She did all this in parallel with handling her extensive financial and administrative responsibilities at Deitel & Associates, Inc.

- Abbey Deitel, a graduate of Carnegie Mellon University's industrial management program, and now President and Director of Worldwide Marketing at Deitel & Associates, Inc., wrote Appendix D and suggested the title for the book. We asked Abbey to surf the World Wide Web and track down the best C++ sites. She used every major Web search engine and collected this information for you in Appendix D. For each resource and demo, Abbey has provided a brief explanation. She rejected hundreds of sites and has listed for you the best she could find. Abbey will be keeping this resources and demos listing on our Web site `www.deitel.com`. Please send URLs for your favorite sites to her by email at `deitel@deitel.com` and she will post links to these on our site.

Deitel & Associates, Inc. student interns who worked on this book include:

- Ben Wiedermann—a computer science major at Boston University—was the lead developer, programmer and writer working with Dr. Harvey M. Deitel on the UML case study. We wish to acknowledge Ben's extraordinary commitment and contributions to this project.

- Sean Santry—a computer science and philosophy graduate of Boston College—worked on the coding and code walkthroughs of the UML Case Study. Sean has joined Deitel & Associates, Inc. full time and is working as a lead developer with Paul Deitel on our forthcoming book, *Advanced Java How to Program*.

- Blake Perdue—a computer science major at Vanderbilt University—helped develop the UML Case Study.

- Kalid Azad—a computer science major at Princeton University—worked extensively on the book's ancillaries including the PowerPoint® Instructor Lecture Notes and the test bank.

- Aftab Bukhari—a computer science major at Boston University—performed extensive program testing and verification and worked on the book's ancillaries including the PowerPoint Instructor Lecture Notes and the Instructor's Manual.

- Jason Rosenfeld—a computer science major at Northwestern University—worked on the book's ancillaries including the Instructor's Manual.

- Melissa Jordan—a graphic design major at Boston University—colorized the art for the entire book and created several original illustrations.

- Rudolf Faust—a freshman at Stanford University—helped create the test bank.

We are fortunate to have been able to work on this project with a talented and dedicated team of publishing professionals at Prentice Hall. This book happened because of the encouragement, enthusiasm and persistence of our computer science editor, Petra Recter, and her boss—the best friend we have had in 25 years of publishing—Marcia Horton, Editor-in-Chief of Prentice-Hall's Engineering and Computer Science Division. Camille Trentacoste did a marvelous job as production manager. Sarah Burrows did a marvelous job with her work on both the review process and the book supplements.

The *C++ Multimedia Cyber Classroom: Third Edition* was developed in parallel with *C++ How to Program: Third Edition*. We sincerely appreciate the "new media" insight, savvy and technical expertise of our editor Mark Taub and his colleague Karen McLean. Mark and Karen did a remarkable job bringing the *C++ Multimedia Cyber Classroom: Third Edition,* to publication under a tight schedule. They are surely among the world's leaders in new-media publishing.

We owe special thanks to the creativity of Tamara Newnam Cavallo (**smart-art@earthlink.net**) who did the art work for our programming tips icons and the cover. She created the delightful creature who shares with you the book's programming tips. Please help us name this endearing little bug. Some early suggestions: D. Bug,

InterGnat, Ms. Kito, DeetleBug (an unfortunate moniker that was attached to the old guy in high school) and Feature ("It's not a bug, it's a feature").

We wish to acknowledge the efforts of our *Third Edition* reviewers and to give a special note of thanks to Crissy Statuto of Prentice Hall who managed this extraordinary review effort.

Reviewers of C++ Material

- Tamer Nassif (Motorola)
- Christophe Dinechin (Hewlett Packard)
- Thomas Kiesler (Montgomery College)
- Mary Astone (Troy State University)
- Simon North (Synopsis)
- Harold Howe (Inprise)
- William Hasserman (University of Wisconsin)
- Phillip Wasserman (Chabot College)
- Richard Albright (University of Delaware)
- Mahe Velauthapilla (Georgetown University)
- Chris Uzdavinis (Automated Trading Desk)
- Stephen Clamage (Chairman of ANSI C++ Standards Committee)
- Ram Choppa (Akili Systems; University of Houston)
- Wolfgang Pelz (University of Akron)

Reviewers of the UML Case Study

- Spencer Roberts (Titus Corporation)
- Don Kostuch (You Can C Clearly Now)
- Kendall Scott (Independent consultant; UML author)
- Grant Larsen (Blueprint Technologies)
- Brian Cook (Technical Resource Connection; OMG)
- Michael Chonoles (Chief of Methodology, Lockheed Martin Adv. Concepts; OMG)
- Stephen Tockey (Construx Software; OMG)
- Cameron Skinner (Advanced Software Technologies; OMG)
- Rick Cassidy (Advanced Concepts Center)
- Mark Contois (NetBeans)
- David Papurt (Independent consultant; C++ lecturer and author)
- Chris Norton (AD2IT; Independent consultant)

We wish to acknowledge again the efforts of our previous edition reviewers (some first edition, some second edition and some both):

- Richard Albright (University of Delaware)
- Ken Arnold (Sun Microsystems)
- Ian Baker (Microsoft)
- Pete Becker (Member of ANSI/ISO C++ Committee; Dinkumware, LTD.)
- Timothy D. Born (Delta C-Fax)

- John Carson (George Washington University)
- Steve Clamage (Chairman of ANSI/ISO C++ Standards Committee; Sunsoft)
- Marian Corcoran (Member ANSI/ISO C++ Standards Committee)
- Edgar Crisostomo (Siemens/Rolm)
- David Finkel (Worcester Polytechnic Institute)
- Rex Jaeschke (Chairman, ANSI/ISO C Committee)
- Frank Kelbe (Naval Postgraduate School)
- Chris Kelsey (Kelsey Associates)
- Don Kostuch (You Can C Clearly Now)
- Meng Lee (Co-creator of STL; Hewlett-Packard)
- Barbara Moo (AT&T Bell Labs)
- David Papurt (Consultant)
- Wolfgang Pelz (University of Akron)
- Jandelyn Plane (University of Maryland College Park)
- Paul Power (Borland)
- Kenneth Reek (Rochester Institute of Technology)
- Larry Rosler (Hewlett-Packard)
- Robin Rowe (Halycon/Naval Postgraduate School)
- Brett Schuchert (ObjectSpace; Co-Authored *STL Primer*)
- Alexander Stepanov (Co-creator of STL; Silicon Graphics)
- William Tepfenhart (AT&T; Author *UML and C++: A Practical Guide to Object-Oriented Development*)
- David Vandevoorde (Member of the ANSI/ISO C++ Committee; Hewlett-Packard)
- Terry Wagner (University of Texas)

Under tight deadlines, they scrutinized every aspect of the text and made countless suggestions for improving the accuracy and completeness of the presentation.

We would sincerely appreciate your comments, criticisms, corrections and suggestions for improving the text. Please address all correspondence to:

deitel@deitel.com

We will respond immediately. Well, that is it for now. Welcome to the exciting world of C++, object-oriented programming, the UML and generic programming with the STL. We hope you enjoy this look at contemporary computer programming. Good luck!

Dr. Harvey M. Deitel
Paul J. Deitel

About the Authors

Dr. Harvey M. Deitel, CEO of Deitel & Associates, Inc., has 39 years experience in the computing field including extensive industry and academic experience. He is one of the world's leading computer science instructors and seminar presenters. Dr. Deitel earned

B.S. and M.S. degrees from the Massachusetts Institute of Technology and a Ph.D. from Boston University. He worked on the pioneering virtual memory operating systems projects at IBM and MIT that developed techniques widely implemented today in systems like UNIX®, Windows NT,™ OS/2 and Linux. He has 20 years of college teaching experience including earning tenure and serving as the Chairman of the Computer Science Department at Boston College before founding Deitel & Associates, Inc. with Paul J. Deitel. He is author or co-author of several dozen books and multimedia packages and is currently writing five more. With translations published in Japanese, Russian, Spanish, Elementary Chinese, Advanced Chinese, Korean, French, Portuguese, Polish and Italian the Deitels' texts have earned international recognition.

Paul J. Deitel, Executive Vice President of Deitel & Associates, Inc., is a graduate of the Massachusetts Institute of Technology's Sloan School of Management where he studied Information Technology. Through Deitel & Associates, Inc. he has delivered Java, C, C++, Internet and World Wide Web courses for industry clients including Compaq, Sun Microsystems, White Sands Missile Range, Rogue Wave Software, Computervision, Stratus, Fidelity, Cambridge Technology Partners, Open Environment Corporation, One Wave, Hyperion Software, Lucent Technologies, Adra Systems, Entergy, CableData Systems, NASA at the Kennedy Space Center, the National Severe Storm Center, IBM and many other organizations. He has lectured on C++ and Java for the Boston Chapter of the Association for Computing Machinery, and has taught satellite-based Java courses through a cooperative venture of Deitel & Associates, Inc., Prentice Hall and the Technology Education Network.

The Deitels are co-authors of the best-selling introductory college computer-science programming language textbooks, *C How to Program: Third Edition, Java How to Program: Third Edition, Visual Basic 6 How to Program (co-authored with Tem R. Nieto)* and *Internet and World Wide Web How to Program (co-authored with Tem R. Nieto).* The Deitels are also co-authors of the *C++ Multimedia Cyber Classroom: Third Edition* (the first edition of this was Prentice Hall's first multimedia-based textbook), the *Java 2 Multimedia Cyber Classroom: Third Edition,* the *Visual Basic 6 Multimedia Cyber Classroom* and the *Internet and World Wide Web Programming Multimedia Cyber Classroom.* The Deitels are also co-authors of *The Complete C++ Training Course: Third Edition,* The *Complete Visual Basic 6 Training Course, The Complete Java 2 Training Course: Third Edition and The Complete Internet and World Wide Web Programming Training Course*—these products each contain the corresponding *How to Program Series* textbook and the corresponding *Multimedia Cyber Classroom.*

About Deitel & Associates, Inc.

Deitel & Associates, Inc. is a rapidly growing, internationally recognized corporate training and publishing organization specializing in programming languages, Internet, World Wide Web and object technology education. The company provides courses on C++, Java, C, Visual Basic, Internet and World Wide Web programming and object-technology. The principals of Deitel & Associates, Inc. are Dr. Harvey M. Deitel and Paul J. Deitel. The company's clients include some of the world's largest computer companies, government agencies and business organizations. Through its publishing partnership with Prentice Hall, Deitel & Associates, Inc. publishes leading-edge programming textbooks and professional books, interactive CD-ROM-based multimedia *Cyber Classrooms* and Web-based training courses. Deitel & Associates, Inc. and the authors can be reached via email at

deitel@deitel.com

To learn more about Deitel & Associates, Inc., its publications and its on-site course curriculum, visit:

www.deitel.com

To learn more about Deitel/Prentice Hall publications, visit:

www.prenhall.com/deitel

For a current list of Deitel/Prentice Hall publications including textbooks and *Cyber Classrooms*, *Complete Training Courses* and Web-Based Training products, and for complete worldwide ordering information, please see the last few pages of this book.

1

Introduction to Computers and C++ Programming

Objectives

- To understand basic computer science concepts.
- To become familiar with different types of programming languages.
- To understand a typical C++ program development environment.
- To be able to write simple computer programs in C++.
- To be able to use simple input and output statements.
- To become familiar with fundamental data types.
- To be able to use arithmetic operators.
- To understand the precedence of arithmetic operators.
- To be able to write simple decision-making statements.

High thoughts must have high language.
Aristophanes

Our life is frittered away by detail ... Simplify, simplify.
Henry Thoreau

My object all sublime
I shall achieve in time.
W. S. Gilbert

Outline

1.1 Introduction

Welcome to C++! We have worked hard to create what we hope will be an informative, entertaining and challenging learning experience for you. C++ is a difficult language that is normally taught only to experienced programmers, so this book is unique among C++ textbooks:

- It is appropriate for technically oriented people with little or no programming experience.

- It is appropriate for experienced programmers who want a deeper treatment of the language.

How can one book appeal to both groups? The answer is that the common core of the book emphasizes achieving program *clarity* through the proven techniques of *structured programming* and *object-oriented programming*. Non-programmers learn programming the right way from the beginning. We have attempted to write in a clear and straightforward manner. The book is abundantly illustrated. Perhaps most importantly, the book presents hundreds of complete working C++ programs and shows the outputs produced when those programs are run on a computer. We call this the "live-code approach." All of these example programs are provided on the CD-ROM that accompanies this book. You may also download all these examples from our Web site **www.deitel.com**. The examples are also available on our interactive CD-ROM product, the *C++ Multimedia Cyber Classroom: Third Edition*. The Cyber Classroom also contains extensive hyperlinking, audio walkthroughs of the program examples in the book and answers to approximately half the exercises in this book (including short answers, small programs and many full projects). The Cyber Classroom's features and ordering information appear at the back of this book.

The first five chapters introduce the fundamentals of computers, computer programming and the C++ computer programming language. Novices who have taken our courses tell us that the material in Chapters 1 through 5 presents a solid foundation for the deeper treatment of C++ in the remaining chapters. Experienced programmers typically read the first five chapters quickly then find the treatment of C++ in the remainder of the book both rigorous and challenging.

Many experienced programmers have told us that they appreciate our treatment of structured programming. Often they have been programming in structured languages like C or Pascal, but because they were never formally introduced to structured programming, they are not writing the best possible code in these languages. As they review structured programming in the early chapters of this book, they are able to improve their C and Pascal programming styles as well. So whether you are a novice or an experienced programmer, there is much here to inform, entertain and challenge you.

Most people are at least somewhat familiar with the exciting things computers do. Using this textbook, you will learn how to command computers to do those things. It is *software* (i.e., the instructions you write to command the computer to perform *actions* and make *decisions*) that controls computers (often referred to as *hardware*). C++ is one of today's most popular software development languages. This text provides an introduction to programming in the version of C++ standardized in the United States through the *American National Standards Institute (ANSI)* and worldwide through the efforts of the *International Standards Organization (ISO)*.

The use of computers is increasing in almost every field of endeavor. In an era of steadily rising costs, computing costs have been decreasing dramatically because of the rapid developments in both hardware and software technology. Computers that filled large rooms and cost millions of dollars 25 to 30 years ago are now inscribed on the surfaces of silicon chips smaller than a fingernail and that cost perhaps a few dollars each. Ironically, silicon is one of the most abundant materials on the earth—it is an ingredient in common sand. Silicon-chip technology has made computing so economical that hundreds of millions of general-purpose computers are in use worldwide helping people in business, industry, government and their personal lives. That number could easily double in a few years.

This book will challenge you for several reasons. Your peers over the last few years probably learned C or Pascal as their first programming language. You will actually learn both C and C++! Why? Simply because C++ includes C and adds much more.

Your peers probably learned the programming methodology called *structured programming*. You will learn both structured programming and the exciting newer methodology, *object-oriented programming*. Why do we teach both? Object-orientation is certain to be the key programming methodology for the next decade. You will create and work with many *objects* in this course. But you will discover that the internal structure of those objects is often best built using structured programming techniques. Also, the logic of manipulating objects is occasionally best expressed with structured programming.

Another reason we present both methodologies is that there currently is a massive migration occurring from C-based systems to C++-based systems. There is a huge amount of so-called "legacy C code" in place. C has been in wide use for about a quarter of a century and its use in recent years has been increasing dramatically. Once people learn C++, they find it more powerful than C and often choose to move to C++. They begin converting their legacy systems to C++. They begin using the various C++ features generally called "C++ enhancements to C" to improve their style of writing C-like programs. Finally, they begin employing the object-oriented programming capabilities of C++ to realize the full benefits of the language.

An interesting phenomenon in programming languages is that most of the vendors simply market a combined C/C++ product rather than offering separate products. This gives users the ability to continue programming in C if they wish then gradually migrate to C++ when appropriate.

C++ has become the implementation language of choice for building high-performance computing systems. But can it be taught in a first programming course, the intended audience for this book? We think so. Nine years ago we took on a similar challenge when Pascal was the entrenched language in first computer science courses. We wrote *C How to Program*. Hundreds of universities worldwide now use the third edition of *C How to Program*. Courses based on that book have proven to be equally effective to their Pascal-based predecessors. No significant differences have been observed, except that students are better motivated because they know they are more likely to use C rather than Pascal in their upper-level courses and in their careers. Students learning C also know that they will be better prepared to learn C++ and the new Internet-ready, C++-based language called *Java*.

In the first five chapters of the book you will learn structured programming in C++, the "C portion" of C++ and the "C++ enhancements to C." In the balance of the book you will learn object-oriented programming in C++. We do not want you to wait until Chapter 6, however, to begin appreciating object-orientation. Therefore, each of the first five chapters concludes with a section entitled "Thinking About Objects." These sections introduce basic concepts and terminology about object-oriented programming. When we reach Chapter 6, Classes and Data Abstraction, you will be prepared to start using C++ to create objects and write object-oriented programs.

This first chapter has three parts. The first part introduces the basics of computers and computer programming. The second part gets you started immediately writing some simple C++ programs. The third part helps you start "thinking about objects."

So there you have it! You are about to start on a challenging and rewarding path. As you proceed, if you would like to communicate with us, please send us email at

deitel@deitel.com

or browse our World Wide Web site at

http://www.deitel.com/

We will respond immediately. We hope you enjoy learning with *C++ How to Program*. You may want to consider using the interactive CD-ROM version of the book called the *C++ Multimedia Cyber Classroom: Third Edition*. Please see the ordering instructions at the back of this book.

1.2 What is a Computer?

A *computer* is a device capable of performing computations and making logical decisions at speeds millions and even billions of times faster than human beings can. For example, many of today's personal computers can perform hundreds of millions of additions per second. A person operating a desk calculator might require decades to complete the same number of calculations a powerful personal computer can perform in one second. (Points to ponder: How would you know whether the person added the numbers correctly? How would you know whether the computer added the numbers correctly?) Today's fastest *supercomputers* can perform hundreds of billions of additions per second—about as many calculations as hundreds of thousands of people could perform in one year! And trillion-instruction-per-second computers are already functioning in research laboratories!

Computers process *data* under the control of sets of instructions called *computer programs*. These computer programs guide the computer through orderly sets of actions specified by people called *computer programmers.*

A computer is comprised of various devices (such as the keyboard, screen, "mouse," disks, memory, CD-ROM and processing units) that are referred to as *hardware*. The computer programs that run on a computer are referred to as *software*. Hardware costs have been declining dramatically in recent years, to the point that personal computers have become a commodity. Unfortunately, software development costs have been rising steadily as programmers develop ever more powerful and complex applications, without significantly improved technology for software development. In this book you will learn proven software development methods that can reduce software development costs—structured programming, top-down stepwise refinement, functionalization, object-based programming, object-oriented programming, object-oriented design and generic programming.

1.3 Computer Organization

Regardless of differences in physical appearance, virtually every computer may be envisioned as being divided into six *logical units* or sections. These are:

1. *Input unit.* This is the "receiving" section of the computer. It obtains information (data and computer programs) from various *input devices* and places this information at the disposal of the other units so that the information may be processed. Most information is entered into computers today through keyboards and mouse

devices. Information can also be entered by speaking to your computer and by scanning images.

2. *Output unit.* This is the "shipping" section of the computer. It takes information that has been processed by the computer and places it on various *output devices* to make the information available for use outside the computer. Most information output from computers today is displayed on screens, printed on paper, or used to control other devices.

3. *Memory unit.* This is the rapid access, relatively low-capacity "warehouse" section of the computer. It retains information that has been entered through the input unit so that the information may be made immediately available for processing when it is needed. The memory unit also retains processed information until that information can be placed on output devices by the output unit. The memory unit is often called either *memory* or *primary memory.*

4. *Arithmetic and logic unit (ALU).* This is the "manufacturing" section of the computer. It is responsible for performing calculations such as addition, subtraction, multiplication and division. It contains the decision mechanisms that allow the computer, for example, to compare two items from the memory unit to determine whether or not they are equal.

5. *Central processing unit (CPU).* This is the "administrative" section of the computer. It is the computer's coordinator and is responsible for supervising the operation of the other sections. The CPU tells the input unit when information should be read into the memory unit, tells the ALU when information from the memory unit should be used in calculations and tells the output unit when to send information from the memory unit to certain output devices.

6. *Secondary storage unit.* This is the long-term, high-capacity "warehousing" section of the computer. Programs or data not actively being used by the other units are normally placed on secondary storage devices (such as disks) until they are again needed, possibly hours, days, months, or even years later. Information in secondary storage takes much longer to access than information in primary memory. The cost per unit of secondary storage is much less than the cost per unit of primary memory.

1.4 Evolution of Operating Systems

Early computers were capable of performing only one *job* or *task* at a time. This form of computer operation is often called single-user *batch processing.* The computer runs a single program at a time while processing data in groups or *batches.* In these early systems, users generally submitted their jobs to a computer center on decks of punched cards. Users often had to wait hours or even days before printouts were returned to their desks.

Software systems called *operating systems* were developed to help make it more convenient to use computers. Early operating systems managed the smooth transition between jobs. This minimized the time it took for computer operators to switch between jobs and hence increased the amount of work, or *throughput,* computers could process.

As computers became more powerful, it became evident that single-user batch processing rarely utilized the computer's resources efficiently because most of the time was spent waiting for slow input/output devices to complete their tasks. Instead, it was thought that many jobs or tasks could be made to *share* the resources of the computer to achieve better utilization. This is called *multiprogramming*. Multiprogramming involves the "simultaneous" operation of many jobs on the computer—the computer shares its resources among the jobs competing for its attention. With early multiprogramming operating systems, users still submitted jobs on decks of punched cards and waited hours or days for results.

In the 1960s, several groups in industry and the universities pioneered *timesharing* operating systems. Timesharing is a special case of multiprogramming in which users access the computer through *terminals*, typically devices with keyboards and screens. In a typical timesharing computer system, there may be dozens or even hundreds of users sharing the computer at once. The computer does not actually run all the users simultaneously. Rather, it runs a small portion of one user's job then moves on to service the next user. The computer does this so quickly that it may provide service to each user several times per second. Thus the users' programs *appear* to be running simultaneously. An advantage of timesharing is that the user receives almost immediate responses to requests rather than having to wait long periods for results as with previous modes of computing.

1.5 Personal Computing, Distributed Computing and Client/Server Computing

In 1977, Apple Computer popularized the phenomenon of *personal computing*. Initially, it was a hobbyist's dream. Computers became economical enough for people to buy them for their own personal or business use. In 1981, IBM, the world's largest computer vendor, introduced the IBM Personal Computer. Literally overnight, personal computing became legitimate in business, industry and government organizations.

But these computers were "standalone" units—people did their work on their own machines then transported disks back and forth to share information (this is often called "sneakernet"). Although early personal computers were not powerful enough to timeshare several users, these machines could be linked together in computer networks, sometimes over telephone lines and sometimes in *local area networks (LANs)* within an organization. This led to the phenomenon of *distributed computing* in which an organization's computing, instead of being performed strictly at some central computer installation, is distributed over networks to the sites at which the work of the organization is performed. Personal computers were powerful enough to handle the computing requirements of individual users, and to handle the basic communications tasks of passing information back and forth electronically.

Today's most powerful personal computers are as powerful as the million dollar machines of just a decade ago. The most powerful desktop machines—called *workstations*—provide individual users with enormous capabilities. Information is easily shared across computer networks where some computers called *file servers* offer a common store of programs and data that may be used by *client* computers distributed throughout the network, hence the term *client/server computing*. C and C++ have become the programming languages of choice for writing software for operating systems, for computer networking and for distributed client/server applications. Today's popular operating systems such as UNIX, Linux and Microsoft's Windows-based systems provide the kinds of capabilities discussed in this section.

1.6 Machine Languages, Assembly Languages, and High-level Languages

Programmers write instructions in various programming languages, some directly under-standable by the computer and others that require intermediate *translation* steps. Hundreds of computer languages are in use today. These may be divided into three general types:

1. Machine languages,

2. Assembly languages,

3. High-level languages.

Any computer can directly understand only its own *machine language*. Machine lan-guage is the "natural language" of a particular computer. It is defined by the hardware design of that computer. Machine languages generally consist of strings of numbers (ulti-mately reduced to 1s and 0s) that instruct computers to perform their most elementary oper-ations one at a time. Machine languages are *machine-dependent,* i.e., a particular machine language can be used on only one type of computer. Machine languages are cumbersome for humans, as can be seen by the following section of a machine language program that adds overtime pay to base pay and stores the result in gross pay.

```
+1300042774
+1400593419
+1200274027
```

As computers became more popular, it became apparent that machine language pro-gramming was too slow, tedious and error prone. Instead of using the strings of numbers that computers could directly understand, programmers began using English-like abbreviations to represent the elementary operations of the computer. These English-like abbreviations formed the basis of *assembly languages. Translator programs* called *assemblers* were devel-oped to convert assembly language programs to machine language at computer speeds. The following section of an assembly language program also adds overtime pay to base pay and stores the result in gross pay, but more clearly than its machine language equivalent:

```
LOAD    BASEPAY
ADD     OVERPAY
STORE   GROSSPAY
```

Although such code is clearer to humans, it is incomprehensible to computers until trans-lated to machine language.

Computer usage increased rapidly with the advent of assembly languages, but these still required many instructions to accomplish even the simplest tasks. To speed the programming process, *high-level languages* were developed in which single statements accomplish sub-stantial tasks. Translator programs called *compilers* convert high-level language programs into machine language. High-level languages allow programmers to write instructions that look almost like everyday English and contain commonly used mathematical notations. A payroll program written in a high-level language might contain a statement such as:

```
grossPay = basePay + overTimePay
```

Obviously, high-level languages are much more desirable from the programmer's stand-point than either machine languages or assembly languages. C and C++ are among the most powerful and most widely used high-level languages.

The process of compiling a high-level language program into machine language can take a considerable amount of computer time. *Interpreter* programs were developed that can directly execute high-level language programs without the need for compiling those programs into machine language. Although compiled programs execute faster than interpreted programs, interpreters are popular in program development environments in which programs are changed frequently as new features are added and errors are corrected. Once a program is developed, a compiled version can be produced to run most efficiently.

1.7 History of C and C++

C++ evolved from C, which evolved from two previous programming languages, BCPL and B. BCPL was developed in 1967 by Martin Richards as a language for writing operating systems software and compilers. Ken Thompson modeled many features in his language B after their counterparts in BCPL and used B to create early versions of the UNIX operating system at Bell Laboratories in 1970 on a DEC PDP-7 computer. Both BCPL and B were "typeless" languages—every data item occupied one "word" in memory and the burden of treating a data item as a whole number or a real number, for example, was the responsibility of the programmer.

The C language was evolved from B by Dennis Ritchie at Bell Laboratories and was originally implemented on a DEC PDP-11 computer in 1972. C uses many important concepts of BCPL and B while adding data typing and other features. C initially became widely known as the development language of the UNIX operating system. Today, most operating systems are written in C and/or C++. C is now available for most computers. C is hardware independent. With careful design, it is possible to write C programs that are *portable* to most computers.

By the late 1970s, C had evolved into what is now referred to as "traditional C," "classic C," or "Kernighan and Ritchie C." The publication by Prentice-Hall in 1978 of Kernighan and Ritchie's book, *The C Programming Language*, brought wide attention to the language.

The widespread use of C with various types of computers (sometimes called *hardware platforms*) unfortunately led to many variations. These were similar, but often incompatible. This was a serious problem for program developers who needed to write portable programs that would run on several platforms. It became clear that a standard version of C was needed. In 1983, the X3J11 technical committee was created under the American National Standards Committee on Computers and Information Processing (X3) to "provide an unambiguous and machine-independent definition of the language." In 1989, the standard was approved. ANSI cooperated with the International Standards Organization (ISO) to standardize C worldwide; the joint standard document was published in 1990 and is referred to as *ANSI/ISO 9899: 1990*. Copies of this document may be ordered from ANSI. The second edition of Kernighan and Ritchie, published in 1988, reflects this version called ANSI C, a version of the language now used worldwide.

Portability Tip 1.1

Because C is a standardized, hardware-independent, widely available language, applications written in C can often be run with little or no modifications on a wide range of different computer systems.

C++, an extension of C, was developed by Bjarne Stroustrup in the early 1980s at Bell Laboratories. C++ provides a number of features that "spruce up" the C language, but more importantly, it provides capabilities for *object-oriented programming*.

There is a revolution brewing in the software community. Building software quickly, correctly and economically remains an elusive goal, and this at a time when the demand for new and more powerful software is soaring. *Objects* are essentially reusable software *components* that model items in the real world. Software developers are discovering that using a modular, object-oriented design and implementation approach can make software development groups much more productive than is possible with previous popular programming techniques such as structured programming. Object-oriented programs are easier to understand, correct and modify.

Many other object-oriented languages have been developed, including Smalltalk, developed at Xerox's Palo Alto Research Center (PARC). Smalltalk is a pure object-oriented language—literally everything is an object. C++ is a hybrid language—it is possible to program in C++ in either a C-like style, an object-oriented style, or both. In Section 1.9 we discuss the exciting new C and C++-based language, Java.

1.8 C++ Standard Library

C++ programs consist of pieces called *classes* and *functions*. You can program each piece you may need to form a C++ program. But most C++ programmers take advantage of the rich collections of existing classes and functions in the C++ standard library. Thus, there are really two parts to learning the C++ "world." The first is learning the C++ language itself and the second is learning how to use the classes and functions in the C++ standard library. Throughout the book, we discuss many of these classes and functions. The book by Plauger is must reading for programmers who need a deep understanding of the ANSI C library functions that are included in C++, how to implement them and how to use them to write portable code. The standard class libraries are generally provided by compiler vendors. Many special-purpose class libraries are supplied by independent software vendors.

Software Engineering Observation 1.1

Use a "building block approach" to creating programs. Avoid reinventing the wheel. Use existing pieces where possible—this is called "software reuse" and it is central to object-oriented programming.

Software Engineering Observation 1.2

When programming in C++ you will typically use the following building blocks: classes and functions from the C++ standard library, classes and functions you create yourself, and classes and functions from various popular third-party libraries.

The advantage of creating your own functions and classes is that you will know exactly how they work. You will be able to examine the C++ code. The disadvantage is the time-consuming and complex effort that goes into designing, developing and maintaining new functions and classes that are correct and that operate efficiently.

Performance Tip 1.1

Using standard library functions and classes instead of writing your own comparable versions can improve program performance because this software is carefully written to perform efficiently and correctly.

Portability Tip 1.2

Using standard library functions and classes instead of writing your own comparable versions can improve program portability because this software is included in virtually all C++ implementations.

1.9 Java and *Java How to Program*

Many people believe that the next major area in which microprocessors will have a profound impact is in intelligent consumer electronic devices. Recognizing this, Sun Microsystems funded an internal corporate research project code-named Green in 1991. The project resulted in the development of a C and C++ based language which its creator, James Gosling, called Oak after an oak tree outside his window at Sun. It was later discovered that there already was a computer language called Oak. When a group of Sun people visited a local coffee place, the name *Java* was suggested and it stuck.

But the Green project ran into some difficulties. The marketplace for intelligent consumer electronic devices was not developing as quickly as Sun had anticipated. Worse yet, a major contract for which Sun competed was awarded to another company. So the project was in danger of being canceled. By sheer good fortune, the World Wide Web exploded in popularity in 1993 and Sun people saw the immediate potential of using Java to create Web pages with so-called *dynamic content*.

Sun formally announced Java at a trade show in May 1995. Ordinarily, an event like this would not have generated much attention. However, Java generated immediate interest in the business community because of the phenomenal interest in the World Wide Web. Java is now used to create Web pages with dynamic and interactive content, to develop large-scale enterprise applications, to enhance the functionality of Web servers (the computers that provide the content we see in our Web browsers), to provide applications for consumer devices (such as cell phones, pagers and personal digital assistants), and more.

In 1995, we were carefully following the development of Java by Sun Microsystems. In November 1995 we attended an Internet conference in Boston. A representative from Sun Microsystems gave a rousing presentation on Java. As the talk proceeded, it became clear to us that Java would play a significant part in the development of interactive, multimedia Web pages. But we immediately saw a much greater potential for the language.

We saw Java as a nice language for teaching first-year programming language students the essentials of graphics, images, animation, audio, video, database, networking, multithreading and collaborative computing. We went to work on the first edition of *Java How to Program* which was published in time for fall 1996 classes. *Java How to Program: Third Edition* was published in 1999.

In addition to its prominence in developing Internet- and intranet-based applications, Java is certain to become the language of choice for implementing software for devices that communicate over a network (such as cellular phones, pagers and personal digital assistants). Do not be surprised when your new stereo and other devices in your home will be networked together using Java technology!

1.10 Other High-level Languages

Hundreds of high-level languages have been developed, but only a few have achieved broad acceptance. *FORTRAN* (FORmula TRANslator) was developed by IBM Corporation between 1954 and 1957 to be used for scientific and engineering applications that require complex mathematical computations. FORTRAN is still widely used, especially in engineering applications.

COBOL (COmmon Business Oriented Language) was developed in 1959 by computer manufacturers, government and industrial computer users. COBOL is used primarily for commercial applications that require precise and efficient manipulation of large amounts of data. Today, more than half of all business software is still programmed in COBOL.

Pascal was designed at about the same time as C by Professor Niklaus Wirth and was intended for academic use. We will say more about Pascal in the next section.

1.11 Structured Programming

During the 1960s, many large software development efforts encountered severe difficulties. Software schedules were typically late, costs greatly exceeded budgets and the finished products were unreliable. People began to realize that software development was a far more complex activity than they had imagined. Research activity in the 1960s resulted in the evolution of *structured programming*—a disciplined approach to writing programs that are clearer than unstructured programs, easier to test and debug and easier to modify. Chapter 2 discusses the principles of structured programming. Chapters 3 through 5 develop many structured programs.

One of the more tangible results of this research was the development of the Pascal programming language by Niklaus Wirth in 1971. Pascal, named after the seventeenth-century mathematician and philosopher Blaise Pascal, was designed for teaching structured programming in academic environments and rapidly became the preferred programming language in most universities. Unfortunately, the language lacks many features needed to make it useful in commercial, industrial and government applications, so it has not been widely accepted outside the universities.

The Ada programming language was developed under the sponsorship of the United States Department of Defense (DOD) during the 1970s and early 1980s. Hundreds of separate languages were being used to produce DOD's massive command-and-control software systems. DOD wanted a single language that would fulfill most of its needs. Pascal was chosen as a base, but the final Ada language is quite different from Pascal. The language was named after Lady Ada Lovelace, daughter of the poet Lord Byron. Lady Lovelace is generally credited with writing the world's first computer program in the early 1800s (for the Analytical Engine mechanical computing device designed by Charles Babbage). One important capability of Ada is called *multitasking;* this allows programmers to specify that many activities are to occur in parallel. The other widely used high-level languages we have discussed—including C and C++—generally allow the programmer to write programs that perform only one activity at a time.

1.12 The Key Software Trend: Object Technology

One of the authors, HMD, remembers the great frustration that was felt in the 1960s by software development organizations, especially those developing large-scale projects. During his undergraduate years, HMD had the privilege of working summers at a leading computer vendor on the teams developing time-sharing, virtual memory operating systems. This was a great experience for a college student. But in the summer of 1967 reality set in when the company "decommitted" from producing as a commercial product the particular system that hundreds of people had been working on for many years. It was difficult to get this software right. Software is "complex stuff."

Hardware costs have been declining dramatically in recent years, to the point that personal computers have become a commodity. Unfortunately, software development costs have been rising steadily as programmers develop ever more powerful and complex applications, without being able to improve significantly the underlying technologies of software development. In this book you will learn many software development methods that can reduce software development costs.

There is a revolution brewing in the software community. Building software quickly, correctly and economically remains an elusive goal, and this at a time when demands for new and more powerful software are soaring. *Objects* are essentially reusable software *components* that model items in the real world. Software developers are discovering that using a modular, object-oriented design and implementation approach can make software development groups much more productive than is possible with previous popular programming techniques such as structured programming. Object-oriented programs are often easier to understand, correct and modify.

Improvements to software technology did start to appear with the benefits of so-called *structured programming* (and the related disciplines of *structured systems analysis and design)* being realized in the 1970s. But it was not until the technology of object-oriented programming became widely used in the 1980s, and especially widely used in the 1990s, that software developers finally felt they had the tools they needed to make major strides in the software development process.

Actually, object technology dates back at least to the mid 1960s. The C++ programming language developed at AT&T by Bjarne Stroustrup in the early 1980s, is based on two languages—C, which was initially developed at AT&T to implement the UNIX operating system in the early 1970s, and Simula 67, a simulation programming language developed in Europe and released in 1967. C++ absorbed the capabilities of C and added Simula's capabilities for creating and manipulating objects. Neither C nor C++ was intended for wide use beyond the AT&T research laboratories. But grass-roots support rapidly developed for each.

What are objects and why are they special. Actually, object technology is a packaging scheme that helps us create meaningful software units. These are large and highly focussed on particular applications areas. There are date objects, time objects, paycheck objects, invoice objects, audio objects, video objects, file objects, record objects and so on. In fact, any noun can be represented as an object.

We live in a world of objects. Just look around you. There are cars, planes, people, animals, buildings, traffic lights, elevators, and so on. Before object-oriented languages appeared, programming languages (such as FORTRAN, Pascal, Basic and C) were focussed on actions (verbs) rather than things or objects (nouns). Programmers living in a world of objects would get to the computer and have to program primarily with verbs. This paradigm shift made it a bit awkward to write programs. Now, with the availability of popular object-oriented languages such as Java and C++ and many others, programmers continue to live in an object-oriented world and when they get to the computer they can program in an object-oriented manner. This means they program in a manner similar to the way in which they perceive the world. This is a more natural process than procedural programming and has resulted in significant productivity enhancements.

One of the key problems with procedural programming is that the program units programmers created do not easily mirror real-world entities effectively. So they are not particularly reusable. It is not unusual for programmers to "start fresh" on each new project and wind up writing very similar software "from scratch." This wastes precious time and money resources as people repeatedly "reinvent the wheel." With object technology, the software entities created (called *objects*), if properly designed, tend to be much more reusable on future projects. Using libraries of reusable componentry such as *MFC (Microsoft Foundation Classes)* and those produced by Rogue Wave and many other software development organizations can greatly reduce the amount of effort it takes to implement certain kinds of systems (compared to the effort that would be required to reinvent these capabilities on new projects).

Some organizations report that software reuse is not, in fact, the key benefit they get from object-oriented programming. Rather, they indicate that object-oriented programming tends to produce software that is more understandable, better organized and easier to maintain, modify and debug. This can be significant because it has been estimated that as much as 80% of software costs are not associated with the original efforts to develop the software, but are associated with the continued evolution and maintenance of that software throughout its lifetime.

Whatever the perceived benefits of object-orientation are, it is clear that object-oriented programming will be the key programming methodology for the next several decades.

[*Note*: We will include many of these *Software Engineering Observations* throughout the text to explain concepts that affect and improve the overall architecture and quality of a software system, and particularly, of large software systems. We will also highlight *Good Programming Practices* (practices that can help you write programs that are clearer, more understandable, more maintainable, and easier to test and debug), *Common Programming Errors* (problems to watch out for so you do not make these same errors in your programs), *Performance Tips* (techniques that will help you write programs that run faster and use less memory), *Portability Tips* (techniques that will help you write programs that can run, with little or no modification, on a variety of computers) and *Testing and Debugging Tips* (techniques that will help you remove bugs from your programs, and more important, techniques that will help you write bug-free programs in the first place). Many of these techniques and practices are only guidelines; you will, no doubt, develop your own preferred programming style.]

The advantage of creating your own code is that you will know exactly how it works. You will be able to examine the code. The disadvantage is the time-consuming and complex effort that goes into designing and developing new code.

Performance Tip 1.2

Reusing proven code components instead of writing your own versions can improve program performance because these components are normally written to perform efficiently.

Software Engineering Observation 1.3

Extensive class libraries of reusable software components are available over the Internet and the World Wide Web. Many of these libraries are available at no charge.

1.13 Basics of a Typical C++ Environment

C++ systems generally consist of several parts: a program development environment, the language and the C++ Standard Library. The following discussion explains a typical C++ program development environment shown in Fig. 1.1.

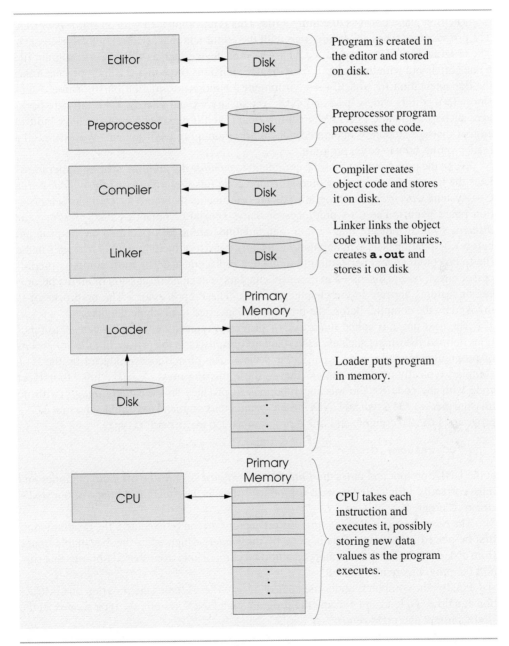

Fig. 1.1   A typical C++ environment.

C++ programs typically go through six phases to be executed (Fig. 1.1). These are: *edit, preprocess, compile, link, load and execute.* We concentrate on a typical UNIX-based C++ system here (Note: the programs in this book will run with little or no modification on most current C++ systems, including Microsoft Windows-based systems). If you are not using a UNIX system, refer to the manuals for your system, or ask your instructor how to accomplish these tasks in your environment.

The first phase consists of editing a file. This is accomplished with an *editor program.* The programmer types a C++ program with the editor and makes corrections if necessary. The program is then stored on a secondary storage device such as a disk. C++ program file names often end with the **.cpp**, **.cxx** or **.C** extensions (note that **C** is in uppercase). See the documentation for your C++ environment for more information on file-name extensions. Two editors widely used on UNIX systems are **vi** and **emacs**. C++ software packages such as Borland C++ and Microsoft Visual C++ for personal computers have built-in editors that are smoothly integrated into the programming environment. We assume the reader knows how to edit a program.

Next, the programmer gives the command to *compile* the program. The compiler translates the C++ program into machine language code (also referred to as *object code*). In a C++ system, a *preprocessor* program executes automatically before the compiler's translation phase begins. The C++ preprocessor obeys special commands called *preprocessor directives* which indicate that certain manipulations are to be performed on the program before compilation. These manipulations usually consist of including other text files in the file to be compiled and performing various text replacements. The most common preprocessor directives are discussed in the early chapters; a detailed discussion of all the preprocessor features appears in the chapter entitled, "The Preprocessor." The preprocessor is invoked by the compiler before the program is converted to machine language.

The next phase is called *linking.* C++ programs typically contain references to functions defined elsewhere, such as in the standard libraries or in the private libraries of groups of programmers working on a particular project. The object code produced by the C++ compiler typically contains "holes" due to these missing parts. A *linker* links the object code with the code for the missing functions to produce an *executable image* (with no missing pieces). On a typical UNIX-based system, the command to compile and link a C++ program is *CC*. To compile and link a program named **welcome.C** type

```
CC welcome.C
```

at the UNIX prompt and press the *Enter* key (or *Return* key). If the program compiles and links correctly, a file called **a.out** is produced. This is the executable image of our **welcome.C** program.

The next phase is called *loading.* Before a program can be executed, the program must first be placed in memory. This is done by the *loader,* which takes the executable image from disk and transfers it to memory. Additional components from shared libraries that support the program are also loaded.

Finally, the computer, under the control of its CPU, executes the program one instruction at a time. To load and execute the program on a UNIX system, we type **a.out** at the UNIX prompt and press *return*.

Programs do not always work on the first try. Each of the preceding phases can fail because of various errors that we will discuss. For example, an executing program might attempt to divide by zero (an illegal operation on computers just as it is in arithmetic). This would cause the computer to print an error message. The programmer would then return to the edit phase, make the necessary corrections and proceed through the remaining phases again to determine that the corrections work properly.

Common Programming Error 1.1

Errors like division-by-zero errors occur as a program runs, so these errors are called run-time errors or execution-time errors. Divide-by-zero is generally a fatal error, i.e., an error that causes the program to terminate immediately without having successfully performed its job. Non-fatal errors allow programs to run to completion, often producing incorrect results. (Note: On some systems, divide-by-zero is not a fatal error. Please see your system documentation.)

Most programs in C++ input and/or output data. Certain C++ functions take their input from **cin** (the *standard input stream*; pronounced "see-in") which is normally the keyboard, but **cin** can be connected to another device. Data is often output to **cout** (the *standard output stream*; pronounced "see-out") which is normally the computer screen, but **cout** can be connected to another device. When we say that a program prints a result, we normally mean that the result is displayed on a screen. Data may be output to other devices such as disks and hardcopy printers. There is also a *standard error stream* referred to as **cerr**. The **cerr** stream (normally connected to the screen) is used for displaying error messages. It is common for users to route regular output data, i.e., **cout**, to a device other than the screen while keeping **cerr** assigned to the screen so the user can be immediately informed of errors.

1.14 Hardware Trends

The programming community thrives on the continuing stream of dramatic improvements in hardware, software and communications technologies. Every year, people generally expect to pay at least a little more for most products and services. The opposite has been the case in the computer and communications fields, especially with regard to the hardware costs of supporting these technologies. For many decades, and with no change in the foreseeable future, hardware costs have fallen rapidly, if not precipitously. This is a phenomenon of technology, another driving force powering the current economic boom. Every year or two, the capacities of computers, especially the amount of memory they have in which to execute programs, the amount of secondary storage (such as disk storage) they have to hold programs and data over the longer term, and their processor speeds—the speed at which computers execute their programs (i.e., do their work)—each tend to approximately double. The same has been true in the communications field with costs plummeting, especially in recent years with the enormous demand for communications bandwidth attracting tremendous competition. We know of no other fields in which technology moves so quickly and costs fall so rapidly.

When computer use exploded in the sixties and seventies, there was talk of huge improvements in human productivity that computing and communications would bring about. But these improvements did not materialize. Organizations were spending vast sums on computers and certainly employing them effectively, but without realizing the productivity gains that had been expected. It was the invention of microprocessor chip technology and its wide deployment in the late 1970s and 1980s that laid the groundwork for the productivity improvements of the 1990s that have been so crucial to economic prosperity.

1.15 History of the Internet

In the late 1960s, one of the authors (HMD) was a graduate student at MIT. His research at MIT's Project Mac (now the Laboratory for Computer Science—the home of the World Wide Web Consortium) was funded by ARPA—the Advanced Research Projects Agency of the Department of Defense. ARPA sponsored a conference at which several dozen ARPA-funded graduate students were brought together at the University of Illinois at Urbana-Champaign to meet and share ideas. During this conference, ARPA rolled out the blueprints for networking the main computer systems of about a dozen ARPA-funded universities and research institutions. They were to be connected with communications lines operating at a then-stunning 56KB (i.e., 56,000 bits per second), this at a time when most people (of the few who could be) were connecting over telephone lines to computers at a rate of 110 bits per second. HMD vividly recalls the excitement at that conference. Researchers at Harvard talked about communication with the Univac 1108 "supercomputer" across the country at the University of Utah to handle calculations related to their computer graphics research. Many other intriguing possibilities were raised. Academic research was about to take a giant leap forward. Shortly after this conference, ARPA proceeded to implement what quickly became called the *ARPAnet*, the grandparent of today's *Internet*.

Things worked out differently from what was originally planned. Rather than the primary benefit being that researchers could share each other's computers, it rapidly became clear that simply enabling the researchers to communicate quickly and easily among themselves via what became known as *electronic mail* (*e-mail*, for short) was to be the key benefit of the ARPAnet. This is true even today on the Internet with e-mail facilitating communications of all kinds among millions of people worldwide.

One of ARPA's primary goals for the network was to allow multiple users to send and receive information at the same time over the same communications paths (such as phone lines). The network operated with a technique called *packet switching* in which digital data was sent in small packages called *packets*. The packets contained data, address information, error-control information and sequencing information. The address information was used to route the packets of data to their destination. The sequencing information was used to help reassemble the packets (which—because of complex routing mechanisms—could actually arrive out of order) into their original order for presentation to the recipient. Packets of many people were intermixed on the same lines. This packet-switching technique greatly reduced transmission costs compared to the cost of dedicated communications lines.

The network was designed to operate without centralized control. This meant that if a portion of the network should fail, the remaining working portions would still be able to route packets from senders to receivers over alternate paths.

The protocols for communicating over the ARPAnet became known as *TCP—the Transmission Control Protocol*. TCP ensured that messages were properly routed from sender to receiver and that those messages arrived intact.

In parallel with the early evolution of the Internet, organizations worldwide were implementing their own networks for both intra-organization (i.e., within the organization) and inter-organization (i.e., between organizations) communication. A huge variety of networking hardware and software appeared. One challenge was to get these to intercommunicate. ARPA accomplished this with the development of *IP—the Internetworking Protocol*), truly creating a "network of networks," the current architecture of the Internet. The combined set of protocols is now commonly called *TCP/IP*.

Initially, use of the Internet was limited to universities and research institutions; then the military became a big user. Eventually, the government decided to allow access to the Internet for commercial purposes. Initially there was resentment among the research and military communities—it was felt that response times would become poor as "the net" became saturated with so many users.

In fact, the exact opposite has occurred. Businesses rapidly realized that by making effective use of the Internet they could tune their operations and offer new and better services to their clients, so they started spending vasts amounts of money to develop and enhance the Internet. This generated fierce competition among the communications carriers and hardware and software suppliers to meet this demand. The result is that *bandwidth* (i.e., the information carrying capacity of communications lines) on the Internet has increased tremendously and costs have plummeted. It is widely believed that the Internet has played a significant role in the economic prosperity that the United States and many other industrialized nations have enjoyed over the last decade and are likely to continue enjoying for many years.

1.16 History of the World Wide Web

The *World Wide Web* allows computer users to locate and view multimedia-based documents (i.e., documents with text, graphics, animations, audios and/or videos) on almost any subject. Even though the Internet was developed more than three decades ago, the introduction of the *World Wide Web* was a relatively recent event. In 1990, *Tim Berners-Lee* of CERN (the European Laboratory for Particle Physics) developed the World Wide Web and several communication protocols that form its backbone.

The Internet and the World Wide Web will surely be listed among the most important and profound creations of humankind. In the past, most computer applications ran on "stand-alone" computers, i.e., computers that were not connected to one another. Today's applications can be written to communicate among the world's hundreds of millions of computers. The Internet mixes computing and communications technologies. It makes our work easier. It makes information instantly and conveniently accessible worldwide. It makes it possible for individuals and small businesses to get worldwide exposure. It is changing the nature of the way business is done. People can search for the best prices on virtually any product or service. Special-interest communities can stay in touch with one another. Researchers can be made instantly aware of the latest breakthroughs worldwide.

1.17 General Notes About C++ and This Book

C++ is a complex language. Experienced C++ programmers sometimes take pride in being able to create some weird, contorted, convoluted usage of the language. This is a poor programming practice. It makes programs more difficult to read, more likely to behave strangely, more difficult to test and debug and more difficult to adapt to changing requirements. This book is geared for novice programmers, so we stress program *clarity*. The following is our first "good programming practice."

Good Programming Practice 1.1

Write your C++ programs in a simple and straightforward manner. This is sometimes referred to as KIS ("keep it simple"). Do not "stretch" the language by trying bizarre usages.

You have heard that C and C++ are portable languages, and that programs written in C and C++ can run on many different computers. *Portability is an elusive goal.* The ANSI C standard document contains a lengthy list of portability issues and complete books have been written that discuss portability.

Portability Tip 1.3

Although it is possible to write portable programs, there are many problems among different C and C++ compilers and different computers that can make portability difficult to achieve. Simply writing programs in C and C++ does not guarantee portability. The programmer will often need to deal directly with compiler and computer variations.

We have done a careful walkthrough of the ANSI/ISO C++ standard document and audited our presentation against it for completeness and accuracy. However, C++ is a rich language, and there are some subtleties in the language and some advanced subjects we have not covered. If you need additional technical details on C++, we suggest that you read the C++ standard document. You can order the C++ standard document from the ANSI web site

```
http://www.ansi.org/
```

The title of the document is "Information Technology – Programming Languages – C++" and its document number is ISO/IEC 14882-1998. If you prefer not to purchase the document, the older draft version of the standard can be viewed at the World Wide Web site

```
http://www.cygnus.com/misc/wp/
```

We have included an extensive bibliography of books and papers on C++ and object-oriented programming. We also have included a C++ Resources appendix containing many Internet and World Wide Web sites relating to C++ and object-oriented programming.

Many features of the current versions of C++ are not compatible with older C++ implementations, so you may find that some of the programs in this text do not work on older C++ compilers.

Good Programming Practice 1.2

Read the manuals for the version of C++ you are using. Refer to these manuals frequently to be sure you are aware of the rich collection of C++ features and that you are using these features correctly.

Good Programming Practice 1.3

Your computer and compiler are good teachers. If after carefully reading your C++ language manual you are not sure how a feature of C++ works, experiment using a small "test program" and see what happens. Set your compiler options for "maximum warnings." Study each message you get when you compile your programs and correct the programs to eliminate the messages.

1.18 Introduction to C++ Programming

The C++ language facilitates a structured and disciplined approach to computer program design. We now introduce C++ programming and present several examples that illustrate many important features of C++. Each example is analyzed one statement at a time. In Chapter 2 we present a detailed treatment of *structured programming* in C++. We then use the structured approach through Chapter 5. Beginning with Chapter 6, we study object-oriented programming in C++. Again, because of the central importance of object-oriented programming in this book, each of the first five chapters concludes with a section entitled "Thinking About Objects." These special sections introduce the concepts of object orientation and present a case study that challenges the reader to design and implement a substantial object-oriented C++ program.

1.19 A Simple Program: Printing a Line of Text

C++ uses notations that may appear strange to non-programmers. We begin by considering a simple program that prints a line of text. The program and its screen output are shown in Fig. 1.2.

This program illustrates several important features of the C++ language. We consider each line of the program in detail. Lines 1 and 2

```
// Fig. 1.2: fig01_02.cpp
// A first program in C++
```

each begin with **//** indicating that the remainder of each line is a *comment*. Programmers insert comments to *document* programs and improve program readability. Comments also help other people read and understand your program. Comments do not cause the computer to perform any action when the program is run. Comments are ignored by the C++ compiler and do not cause any machine language object code to be generated. The comment **A first program in C++** simply describes the purpose of the program. A comment that begins with **//** is called a *single-line comment* because the comment terminates at the end of the current line. [Note: C++ programmers may also use C's comment style in which a comment—possibly containing many lines—begins with **/*** and ends with ***/**.]

Good Programming Practice 1.4

Every program should begin with a comment describing the purpose of the program.

Line 3

```
#include <iostream>
```

```
1   // Fig. 1.2: fig01_02.cpp
2   // A first program in C++
3   #include <iostream>
4
5   int main()
6   {
7       std::cout << "Welcome to C++!\n";
8
9       return 0;          // indicate that program ended successfully
10  }
```

```
Welcome to C++!
```

Fig. 1.2　Text printing program.

is a *preprocessor directive,* i.e., a message to the C++ preprocessor. Lines beginning with **#** are processed by the preprocessor before the program is compiled. This specific line tells the preprocessor to include in the program the contents of the *input/output stream header file* **<iostream>**. This file must be included for any program that outputs data to the screen or inputs data from the keyboard using C++-style stream input/output. Figure 1.2 outputs data to the screen, as we will soon see. The contents of **iostream** will be explained in more detail later.

Common Programming Error 1.2

Forgetting to include the **iostream** *file in a program that inputs data from the keyboard or outputs data to the screen causes the compiler to issue an error message.*

Line 5

```
int main()
```

is a part of every C++ program. The parentheses after **main** indicate that **main** is a program building block called a *function.* C++ programs contain one or more functions, exactly one of which must be **main**. Figure 1.2 contains only one function. C++ programs begin executing at function **main**, even if **main** is not the first function in the program. The keyword **int** to the left of **main** indicates that **main** "returns" an integer (whole number) value. We will explain what it means for a function to "return a value" when we study functions in depth in Chapter 3. For now, simply include the keyword **int** to the left of **main** in each of your programs.

The *left brace,* **{**, (line 6) must begin the *body* of every function. A corresponding *right brace,* **}**, (line 10) must end the body of each function. Line 7

```
std::cout << "Welcome to C++!\n";
```

instructs the computer to print on the screen the *string* of characters contained between the quotation marks. The entire line, including **std::cout**, the **<<** *operator,* the *string* **"Welcome to C++!\n"** and the *semicolon* (**;**), is called a *statement.* Every statement must end with a semicolon (also known as the *statement terminator*). Output and input in C++ is accomplished with *streams* of characters. Thus, when the preceding statement is executed, it sends the stream of characters **Welcome to C++!** to the *standard output stream object*—**std::cout**—which is normally "connected" to the screen. We discuss **std::cout**'s many features in detail in Chapter 11, *Stream Input/Output.*

Notice that we placed **std::** before **cout**. This is required when we use the preprocessor directive **#include <iostream>**. The notation **std::cout** specifies that we are using a name, in this case **cout**, that belongs to "namespace" **std**. Namespaces are an advanced C++ feature. We discuss namespaces in depth in Chapter 21. For now, you should simply remember to include **std::** before each mention of **cout, cin** and **cerr** in a program. This can be cumbersome—in Fig. 1.14, we introduce the **using** statement, which will enable us to avoid having to place **std::** before each use of a namespace **std** name.

The operator **<<** is referred to as the *stream insertion operator.* When this program executes, the value to the right of the operator, the right *operand,* is inserted in the output stream. The characters of the right operand normally print exactly as they appear between the double quotes. Notice, however, that the characters **\n** are not printed on the screen. The backslash (****) is called an *escape character.* It indicates that a "special" character is to be output. When a backslash is encountered in a string of characters, the next character is combined with the backslash to form an *escape sequence*. The escape sequence **\n** means *newline*. It causes the *cursor* (i.e., the current screen position indicator) to move to the beginning of the next line on the screen. Some other common escape sequences are listed in Fig. 1.3.

Common Programming Error 1.3

Omitting the semicolon at the end of a statement is a syntax error. A syntax error is caused when the compiler cannot recognize a statement. The compiler normally issues an error message to help the programmer locate and fix the incorrect statement. Syntax errors are violations of the language. Syntax errors are also called compile errors, compile-time errors, or compilation errors because they appear during the compilation phase.

Line 9

```
return 0;   // indicate that program ended successfully
```

is included at the end of every **main** function. C++ keyword **return** is one of several means we will use to *exit a function*. When the **return** statement is used at the end of **main** as shown here, the value **0** indicates that the program has terminated successfully. In Chapter 3, we discuss functions in detail and the reasons for including this statement will become clear. For now, simply include this statement in each program, or the compiler may produce a warning on some systems.

The right brace, **}**, (line 10) indicates the end of **main**.

Good Programming Practice 1.5

*Many programmers make the last character printed by a function a newline (**\n**). This ensures that the function will leave the screen cursor positioned at the beginning of a new line. Conventions of this nature encourage software reusability—a key goal in software development environments.*

Good Programming Practice 1.6

Indent the entire body of each function one level of indentation within the braces that define the body of the function. This makes the functional structure of a program stand out and helps make programs easier to read.

Escape Sequence	Description
\n	Newline. Position the screen cursor to the beginning of the next line.
\t	Horizontal tab. Move the screen cursor to the next tab stop.
\r	Carriage return. Position the screen cursor to the beginning of the current line; do not advance to the next line.
\a	Alert. Sound the system bell.
\\	Backslash. Used to print a backslash character.
\"	Double quote. Used to print a double quote character.

Fig. 1.3   Some common escape sequences.

Good Programming Practice 1.7

Set a convention for the size of indent you prefer then uniformly apply that convention. The tab key may be used to create indents, but tab stops may vary. We recommend using either 1/4-inch tab stops or (preferably) three spaces to form a level of indent.

Welcome to C++! can be printed several ways. For example, Fig. 1.4 uses multiple stream insertion statements (lines 7 and 8), yet produces identical output to the program of Fig. 1.2. This works because each stream insertion statement resumes printing where the previous statement stopped printing. The first stream insertion prints **Welcome** followed by a space and the second stream insertion begins printing on the same line immediately following the space. In general, C++ allows the programmer to express statements in a variety of ways.

A single statement can print multiple lines by using newline characters as in Fig. 1.5. Each time the **\n** (newline) escape sequence is encountered in the output stream, the screen cursor is positioned to the beginning of the next line. To get a blank line in your output, simply place two newline characters back to back as in Fig. 1.5.

```
1   // Fig. 1.4: fig01_04.cpp
2   // Printing a line with multiple statements
3   #include <iostream>
4
5   int main()
6   {
7       std::cout << "Welcome ";
8       std::cout << "to C++!\n";
9
10      return 0;   // indicate that program ended successfully
11  }
```

```
Welcome to C++!
```

Fig. 1.4   Printing on one line with separate statements using **cout**.

```
1   // Fig. 1.5: fig01_05.cpp
2   // Printing multiple lines with a single statement
3   #include <iostream>
4
5   int main()
6   {
7       std::cout << "Welcome\nto\n\nC++!\n";
8
9       return 0;   // indicate that program ended successfully
10  }
```

```
Welcome
to

C++!
```

Fig. 1.5   Printing on multiple lines with a single statement using **cout**.

```
int integer2;
```

could have been placed immediately before the line

```
std::cin >> integer2;
```

and the declaration

```
int sum;
```

could have been placed immediately before the line

```
sum = integer1 + integer2;
```

Good Programming Practice 1.12

Always place a blank line between a declaration abd adjacent executable statements. This makes the declarations stand out in the program and contributes to program clarity.

Good Programming Practice 1.13

If you prefer to place declarations at the beginning of a function, separate those declarations from the executable statements in that function with one blank line to highlight where the declarations end and the executable statements begin.

Line 9

```
std::cout << "Enter first integer\n";   // prompt
```

prints the string **Enter first integer** (also known as a *string literal* or a *literal*) on the screen and positions to the beginning of the next line. This message is called a *prompt* because it tells the user to take a specific action. We like to pronounce the preceding statement as "**cout** *gets* the character string **"Enter first integer\n"**."

Line 10

```
std::cin >> integer1;                    // read an integer
```

uses the *input stream object* **cin** (of namespace **std**) and the *stream extraction operator,* **>>**, to obtain a value from the keyboard. Using the stream extraction operator with **std::cin** takes character input from the standard input stream which is usually the keyboard. We like to pronounce the preceding statement as, "**std::cin** *gives* a value to **integer1**" or simply "**std::cin** *gives* **integer1**."

When the computer executes the preceding statement, it waits for the user to enter a value for variable **integer1**. The user responds by typing an integer (as characters) then pressing the *Enter* key (sometimes called the *Return* key) to send the number to the computer. The computer then converts the character representation of the number to an integer and assigns this number (or *value*) to the variable **integer1**. Any subsequent references to **integer1** in the program will use this same value.

The **std::cout** and **std::cin** stream objects facilitate interaction between the user and the computer. Because this interaction resembles a dialogue, it is often called *conversational computing* or *interactive computing*.

Line 11

```
std::cout << "Enter second integer\n"; // prompt
```

prints the words **Enter second integer** on the screen, then positions to the beginning of the next line. This statement prompts the user to take action. Line 12

```
std::cin >> integer2;                    // read an integer
```

obtains a value for variable **integer2** from the user.

The assignment statement in line 13

```
sum = integer1 + integer2;        // assignment of sum
```

calculates the sum of the variables **integer1** and **integer2** and assigns the result to variable **sum** using the *assignment operator* **=**. The statement is read as, "**sum** *gets* the value of **integer1 + integer2**." Most calculations are performed in assignment statements. The **=** operator and the **+** operator are called *binary operators* because they each have two *operands*. In the case of the **+** operator, the two operands are **integer1** and **integer2**. In the case of the preceding **=** operator, the two operands are **sum** and the value of the expression **integer1 + integer2**.

 Good Programming Practice 1.14

Place spaces on either side of a binary operator. This makes the operator stand out and makes the program more readable.

Line 14

```
std::cout << "Sum is " << sum << std::endl; // print sum
```

displays the character string **Sum is** followed by the numerical value of variable **sum** followed by **std::endl** (**endl** is an abbreviation for "end line;" **endl**, also, is a name in namespace **std**)—a so-called *stream manipulator*. The **std::endl** manipulator outputs a newline then "flushes the output buffer." This simply means that on some systems where outputs accumulate in the machine until there are enough to "make it worthwhile to display on the screen," **std::endl** forces any accumulated outputs to be displayed at that moment.

Note that the preceding statement outputs multiple values of different types. The stream insertion operator "knows" how to output each piece of data. Using multiple stream insertion operators (**<<**) in a single statement is referred to as *concatenating, chaining* or *cascading stream insertion operations*. Thus, it is unnecessary to have multiple output statements to output multiple pieces of data.

Calculations can also be performed in output statements. We could have combined the statements at lines 13 and 14 into the statement

```
std::cout << "Sum is " << integer1 + integer2 << std::endl;
```

thus eliminating the need for the variable **sum**.

The right brace, **}**, informs the computer that the end of function **main** has been reached.

A powerful feature of C++ is that users can create their own data types (we will explore this capability in Chapter 6). Users can then "teach" C++ how to input and output values of these new data types using the **>>** and **<<** operators (this is called *operator overloading*—a topic we will explore in Chapter 8).

1.21 Memory Concepts

Variable names such as **integer1**, **integer2** and **sum** actually correspond to *locations* in the computer's memory. Every variable has a *name*, a *type*, a *size* and a *value*.

In the addition program of Fig. 1.6, when the statement

```
std::cin >> integer1;
```

is executed, the characters typed by the user are converted to an integer that is placed into a memory location to which the name **integer1** has been assigned by the C++ compiler. Suppose the user enters the number **45** as the value for **integer1**. The computer will place **45** into location **integer1** as shown in Fig. 1.7.

Whenever a value is placed in a memory location, the value replaces the previous value in that location. The previous value is lost.

Returning to our addition program, when the statement

```
std::cin >> integer2;
```

is executed, suppose the user enters the value **72**. This value is placed into location **integer2** and memory appears as in Fig. 1.8. Note that these locations are not necessarily adjacent locations in memory.

Once the program has obtained values for **integer1** and **integer2**, it adds these values and places the sum into variable **sum**. The statement

```
sum = integer1 + integer2;
```

that performs the addition also replaces whatever value was stored in **sum**. This occurs when the calculated sum of **integer1** and **integer2** is placed into location **sum** (without regard to what value may already be in **sum**; that value is lost). After **sum** is calculated, memory appears as in Fig. 1.9. Note that the values of **integer1** and **integer2** appear exactly as they did before they were used in the calculation of **sum**. These values were used, but not destroyed, as the computer performed the calculation. Thus, when a value is read out of a memory location, the process is nondestructive.

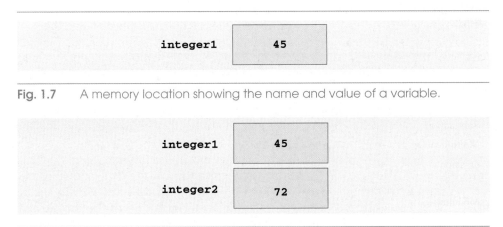

Fig. 1.7   A memory location showing the name and value of a variable.

Fig. 1.8   Memory locations after values for two variables have been input.

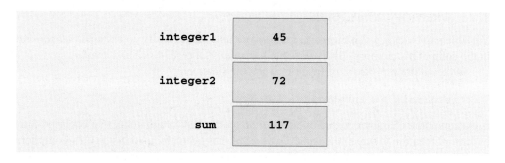

Fig. 1.9   Memory locations after a calculation.

1.22 Arithmetic

Most programs perform arithmetic calculations. The *arithmetic operators* are summarized in Fig. 1.10. Note the use of various special symbols not used in algebra. The *asterisk (*)* indicates multiplication and the *percent sign (%)* is the *modulus* operator that will be discussed shortly. The arithmetic operators in Fig. 1.10 are all binary operators, i.e., operators that take two operands. For example, the expression **integer1 + integer2** contains the binary operator **+** and the two operands **integer1** and **integer2**.

Integer division (i.e., both the numerator and the denominator are integers) yields an integer result; for example, the expression **7 / 4** evaluates to **1** and the expression **17 / 5** evaluates to **3**. Note that any fractional part in integer division is simply discarded (i.e., *truncated*)—no rounding occurs.

C++ provides the *modulus operator*, **%**, that yields the remainder after integer division. The modulus operator can be used only with integer operands. The expression **x % y** yields the remainder after **x** is divided by **y**. Thus, **7 % 4** yields **3** and **17 % 5** yields **2**. In later chapters, we will discuss many interesting applications of the modulus operator such as determining if one number is a multiple of another (a special case of this is determining if a number is odd or even).

 Common Programming Error 1.4

Attempting to use the modulus operator, %, with non-integer operands is a syntax error.

C++ operation	Arithmetic operator	Algebraic expression	C++ expression
Addition	+	$f + 7$	**f + 7**
Subtraction	–	$p - c$	**p - c**
Multiplication	*	bm	**b * m**
Division	/	x / y or $\frac{x}{y}$ or $x \div y$	**x / y**
Modulus	%	$r \bmod s$	**r % s**

Fig. 1.10   Arithmetic operators.

Arithmetic expressions in C++ must be entered into the computer in *straight-line form*. Thus, expressions such as "**a** divided by **b**" must be written as **a / b** so that all constants, variables and operators appear in a straight line. The algebraic notation

$$\frac{a}{b}$$

is generally not acceptable to compilers, although some special-purpose software packages do exist that support more natural notation for complex mathematical expressions.

Parentheses are used in C++ expressions in much the same manner as in algebraic expressions. For example, to multiply **a** times the quantity **b + c** we write:

```
a * (b + c)
```

C++ applies the operators in arithmetic expressions in a precise sequence determined by the following *rules of operator precedence,* which are generally the same as those followed in algebra:

1. Operators in expressions contained within pairs of parentheses are evaluated first. Thus, *parentheses may be used to force the order of evaluation to occur in any sequence desired by the programmer.* Parentheses are said to be at the "highest level of precedence." In cases of *nested,* or *embedded,* parentheses, the operators in the innermost pair of parentheses are applied first.

2. Multiplication, division and modulus operations are applied next. If an expression contains several multiplication, division and modulus operations, operators are applied from left to right. Multiplication, division and modulus are said to be on the same level of precedence.

3. Addition and subtraction operations are applied last. If an expression contains several addition and subtraction operations, operators are applied from left to right. Addition and subtraction also have the same level of precedence.

The rules of operator precedence enable C++ to apply operators in the correct order. When we say that certain operators are applied from left to right, we are referring to the *associativity* of the operators. For example, in the expression

```
a + b + c
```

the addition operators (**+**) associate from left to right. We will see that some operators associate from right to left. Fig. 1.11 summarizes these rules of operator precedence. This table will be expanded as additional C++ operators are introduced. A complete precedence chart is included in the appendices.

Now let us consider several expressions in light of the rules of operator precedence. Each example lists an algebraic expression and its C++ equivalent.

The following is an example of an arithmetic mean (average) of five terms:

Algebra: $m = \dfrac{a + b + c + d + e}{5}$

C++: **m = (a + b + c + d + e) / 5;**

Operator(s)	Operation(s)	Order of evaluation (precedence)
( )	Parentheses	Evaluated first. If the parentheses are nested, the expression in the innermost pair is evaluated first. If there are several pairs of parentheses "on the same level" (i.e., not nested), they are evaluated left to right.
*, /, or %	Multiplication Division Modulus	Evaluated second. If there are several, they are evaluated left to right.
+ or −	Addition Subtraction	Evaluated last. If there are several, they are evaluated left to right.

Fig. 1.11 Precedence of arithmetic operators.

The parentheses are required because division has higher precedence than addition. The entire quantity **(a + b + c + d + e)** is to be divided by **5**. If the parentheses are erroneously omitted, we obtain **a + b + c + d + e / 5** which evaluates incorrectly as

$$a + b + c + d + \frac{e}{5}$$

The following is an example of the equation of a straight line:

Algebra: $y = mx + b$

C++: **y = m * x + b;**

No parentheses are required. The multiplication is applied first because multiplication has a higher precedence than addition.

The following example contains modulus (**%**), multiplication, division, addition and subtraction operations:

Algebra: $z = pr\%q + w/x - y$

C++: **z = p * r % q + w / x − y;**
       ⑥ ① ② ④ ③ ⑤

The circled numbers under the statement indicate the order in which C++ applies the operators. The multiplication, modulus and division are evaluated first in left-to-right order (i.e., they associate from left to right) since they have higher precedence than addition and subtraction. The addition and subtraction are applied next. These are also applied left to right.

Not all expressions with several pairs of parentheses contain nested parentheses. For example, the expression

    a * (b + c) + c * (d + e)

does not contain nested parentheses. Rather, the parentheses are said to be "on the same level."

To develop a better understanding of the rules of operator precedence, consider how a second-degree polynomial is evaluated.

The circled numbers under the statement indicate the order in which C++ applies the operators. There is no arithmetic operator for exponentiation in C++, so we have represented x^2 as **x * x**. We will soon discuss the standard library function **pow** ("power") that performs exponentiation. Because of some subtle issues related to the data types required by **pow**, we defer a detailed explanation of **pow** until Chapter 3.

Suppose variables **a**, **b**, **c** and **x** are initialized as follows: **a = 2, b = 3, c = 7** and **x = 5**. Figure 1.12 illustrates the order in which the operators are applied in the preceding second degree polynomial.

The preceding assignment statement can be parenthesized with unnecessary parentheses for clarity as

```
y = ( a * x * x ) + ( b * x ) + c;
```

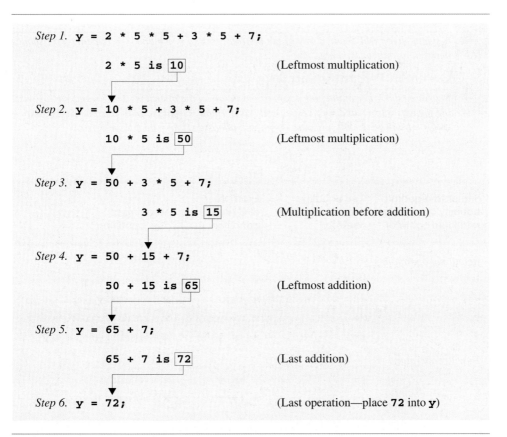

Fig. 1.12   Order in which a second-degree polynomial is evaluated.

Good Programming Practice 1.15

As in algebra, it is acceptable to place unnecessary parentheses in an expression to make the expression clearer. These parentheses are called redundant parentheses. Redundant parentheses are commonly used to group subexpressions in a large expression to make that expression clearer. Breaking a large statement into a sequence of shorter, simpler statements also promotes clarity.

1.23 Decision Making: Equality and Relational Operators

This section introduces a simple version of C++'s **if** *structure* that allows a program to make a decision based on the truth or falsity of some *condition*. If the condition is met, i.e., the condition is **true**, the statement in the body of the **if** structure is executed. If the condition is not met, i.e., the condition is **false**, the body statement is not executed. We will see an example shortly.

Conditions in **if** structures can be formed by using the *equality operators* and *relational operators* summarized in Fig. 1.13. The relational operators all have the same level of precedence and associate left to right. The equality operators both have the same level of precedence, which is lower than the precedence of the relational operators. The equality operators also associate left to right.

Common Programming Error 1.5

A syntax error will occur if any of the operators **==**, **!=**, **>=** *and* **<=** *appears with spaces between its pair of symbols.*

Common Programming Error 1.6

Reversing the order of the pair of operators in any of the operators **!=**, **>=** *and* **<=** *(by writing them as* **=!**, **=>** *and* **=<**, *respectively) is normally a syntax error. In some cases, writing* **!=** *as* **=!** *will not be a syntax error, but will almost certainly be a logic error.*

Standard algebraic equality operator or relational operator	C++ equality or relational operator	Example of C++ condition	Meaning of C++ condition
Relational operators			
>	>	**x > y**	**x** is greater than **y**
<	<	**x < y**	**x** is less than **y**
≥	>=	**x >= y**	**x** is greater than or equal to **y**
≤	<=	**x <= y**	**x** is less than or equal to **y**
Equality operators			
=	==	**x == y**	**x** is equal to **y**
≠	!=	**x != y**	**x** is not equal to **y**

Fig. 1.13   Equality and relational operators.

Common Programming Error 1.7

Confusing the equality operator **==** *with the assignment operator* **=**. *The equality operator should be read "is equal to" and the assignment operator should be read "gets" or "gets the value of" or "is assigned the value of." Some people prefer to read the equality operator as "double equals." As we will soon see, confusing these operators may not necessarily cause an easy-to-recognize syntax error, but may cause extremely subtle logic errors.*

The following example uses six **if** statements to compare two numbers input by the user. If the condition in any of these **if** statements is satisfied, the output statement associated with that **if** is executed. The program and the input/output dialogs of three sample executions are shown in Fig. 1.14.

```cpp
1   // Fig. 1.14: fig01_14.cpp
2   // Using if statements, relational
3   // operators, and equality operators
4   #include <iostream>
5
6   using std::cout;   // program uses cout
7   using std::cin;    // program uses cin
8   using std::endl;   // program uses endl
9
10  int main()
11  {
12      int num1, num2;
13
14      cout << "Enter two integers, and I will tell you\n"
15           << "the relationships they satisfy: ";
16      cin >> num1 >> num2;   // read two integers
17
18      if ( num1 == num2 )
19         cout << num1 << " is equal to " << num2 << endl;
20
21      if ( num1 != num2 )
22         cout << num1 << " is not equal to " << num2 << endl;
23
24      if ( num1 < num2 )
25         cout << num1 << " is less than " << num2 << endl;
26
27      if ( num1 > num2 )
28         cout << num1 << " is greater than " << num2 << endl;
29
30      if ( num1 <= num2 )
31         cout << num1 << " is less than or equal to "
32              << num2 << endl;
33
34      if ( num1 >= num2 )
35         cout << num1 << " is greater than or equal to "
36              << num2 << endl;
37
38      return 0;   // indicate that program ended successfully
39  }
```

Fig. 1.14   Using equality and relational operators (part 1 of 2).

```
Enter two integers, and I will tell you
the relationships they satisfy: 3 7
3 is not equal to 7
3 is less than 7
3 is less than or equal to 7
```

```
Enter two integers, and I will tell you
the relationships they satisfy: 22 12
22 is not equal to 12
22 is greater than 12
22 is greater than or equal to 12
```

```
Enter two integers, and I will tell you
the relationships they satisfy: 7 7
7 is equal to 7
7 is less than or equal to 7
7 is greater than or equal to 7
```

Fig. 1.14   Using equality and relational operators (part 2 of 2).

Lines 6 through 8

```
using std::cout;    // program uses cout
using std::cin;     // program uses cin
using std::endl;    // program uses endl
```

are **using** *statements* that help us eliminate the need to repeat the **std::** prefix. Once we include these **using** statements, we can write **cout** instead of **std::cout**, **cin** instead of **std::cin** and **endl** instead of **std::endl**, respectively, in the remainder of the program. [*Note:* From this point forward in the book, each example contains one or more **using** statements.]

Line 12

```
int num1, num2;
```

declares the variables used in the program. Remember that variables may be declared in one declaration or in multiple declarations. If more than one name is declared in a declaration (as in this example), the names are separated by commas (**,**). This is referred to as a *comma-separated list*.

The program uses cascaded stream extraction operations (line 16) to input two integers. Remember, that we are allowed to write **cin** (instead of **std::cin**) because of line 7. First a value is read into variable **num1**, then a value is read into variable **num2**.

The **if** structure at lines 18 and 19

```
if ( num1 == num2 )
    cout << num1 << " is equal to " << num2 << endl;
```

compares the values of variables **num1** and **num2** to test for equality. If the values are equal, the statement at line 19 displays a line of text indicating that the numbers are equal. If the conditions are **true** in one or more of the **if** structures starting at lines 21, 24, 27, 30 and 34, the corresponding **cout** statement displays a line of text.

Notice that each **if** structure in Fig. 1.14 has a single statement in its body and that each body is indented. Indenting the body of an **if** structure enhances program readability. In Chapter 2 we show how to specify **if** structures with multiple-statement bodies (by enclosing the body statements in a pair of braces, **{ }**).

Good Programming Practice 1.16

*Indent the statement in the body of an **if** structure to make the body of the structure stand out and to enhance program readability.*

Good Programming Practice 1.17

There should be no more than one statement per line in a program.

Common Programming Error 1.8

*Placing a semicolon immediately after the right parenthesis after the condition in an **if** structure is often a logic error (although not a syntax error). The semicolon would cause the body of the **if** structure to be empty, so the **if** structure itself would perform no action regardless of whether or not its condition is **true**. Worse yet, the original body statement of the **if** structure would now become a statement in sequence with the **if** structure and would always be executed, often causing the program to produce incorrect results.*

Notice the use of spacing in Fig. 1.14. In C++ statements, *white space* characters such as tabs, newlines and spaces are normally ignored by the compiler. So, statements may be split over several lines and may be spaced according to the programmer's preferences. It is incorrect to split identifiers, strings (such as **"hello"**) and constants (such as the number **1000**) over several lines.

Common Programming Error 1.9

*It is a syntax error to split an identifier by inserting white space characters (e.g., writing **main** as **ma in**).*

Good Programming Practice 1.18

A lengthy statement may be spread over several lines. If a single statement must be split across lines, choose breaking points that make sense such as after a comma in a comma-separated list, or after an operator in a lengthy expression. If a statement is split across two or more lines, indent all subsequent lines.

Figure 1.15 shows the precedence of the operators introduced in this chapter. The operators are shown top to bottom in decreasing order of precedence. Notice that all these operators, with the exception of the assignment operator **=**, associate from left to right. Addition is left associative, so an expression like **x + y + z** is evaluated as if it had been written **(x + y) + z**. The assignment operator **=** associates from right to left, so an expression like **x = y = 0** is evaluated as if it had been written **x = (y = 0)** which, as we will soon see, first assigns **0** to **y** then assigns the result of that assignment—**0**—to **x**.

Operators	Associativity	Type
( )	left to right	parentheses
* / %	left to right	multiplicative
+ -	left to right	additive
<< >>	left to right	stream insertion/extraction
< <= > >=	left to right	relational
== !=	left to right	equality
=	right to left	assignment

Fig. 1.15   Precedence and associativity of the operators discussed so far.

 Good Programming Practice 1.19

Refer to the operator precedence chart when writing expressions containing many operators. Confirm that the operators in the expression are performed in the order you expect. If you are uncertain about the order of evaluation in a complex expression, break the expression into smaller statements or use parentheses to force the order, exactly as you would do in an algebraic expression. Be sure to observe that some operators such as assignment (=) associate right to left rather than left to right.

We have introduced many important features of C++ including printing data on the screen, inputting data from the keyboard, performing calculations and making decisions. In Chapter 2, we build on these techniques as we introduce *structured programming*. You will become more familiar with indentation techniques. We will study how to specify and vary the order in which statements are executed—this order is called *flow of control*.

1.24 Thinking About Objects: Introduction to Object Technology and the Unified Modeling Language™

Now we begin our early introduction to object orientation. We will see that object orientation is a natural way of thinking about the world and of writing computer programs.

In each of the first five chapters we concentrate on the "conventional" methodology of structured programming, because the objects we will build will be composed in part of structured-program pieces. We then end each chapter with a "Thinking About Objects" section in which we present a carefully paced introduction to object orientation. Our goal in these "Thinking About Objects" sections is to help you develop an object-oriented way of thinking, so that you can immediately put to use the knowledge of object-oriented programming that you begin to receive in Chapter 6. We will also introduce you to the *Unified Modeling Language (UML)*. The UML is a graphical language that allows people who build systems (e.g., software architects, systems engineers, programmers, etc.) to represent their object-oriented designs using a common notation.

In this required section (1.24), we introduce basic concepts (i.e., "object think") and terminology (i.e., "object speak"). In the optional "Thinking About Objects" sections at the ends of Chapters 2 through 5 we consider more substantial issues as we attack a challenging problem with the techniques of *object-oriented design (OOD)*. We will analyze a typical problem statement that requires a system to be built, determine the objects needed to implement the system, determine the attributes the objects will need to have, determine the behaviors these objects will need to exhibit and specify how the objects will need to interact with one another to meet the system requirements. We will do all this even before we have learned how to write object-oriented C++ programs. In the optional "Thinking About Objects" sections at the ends of Chapters 6, 7 and 9, we discuss a C++ implementation of the object-oriented system we will design in the earlier chapters.

This case study will help prepare you for the kinds of substantial projects encountered in industry. If you are a student, and your instructor does not plan on including this case study in your course, please consider covering the case study on your own time. We believe it will be well worth your while to walk through this large and challenging project. You will experience a solid introduction to object-oriented design with the UML, and you will sharpen your code-reading skills by touring a carefully written and well-documented 1000-line C++ program that solves the problem presented in the case study.

We begin our introduction to object orientation with some of the key terminology of object orientation. Look around you in the real world. Everywhere you look you see them— *objects*! People, animals, plants, cars, planes, buildings, computers, etc. Humans think in terms of objects. We have the marvelous ability of *abstraction* that enables us to view screen images as objects such as people, planes, trees and mountains, rather than as individual dots of color. We can, if we wish, think in terms of beaches rather than grains of sand, forests rather than trees and houses rather than bricks.

We might be inclined to divide objects into two categories—animate objects and inanimate objects. Animate objects are "alive" in some sense. They move around and do things. Inanimate objects, like towels, seem not to do much at all. They just kind of "sit around." All these objects, however, do have some things in common. They all have *attributes* like size, shape, color, weight, etc. And they all exhibit *behaviors* (e.g., a ball rolls, bounces, inflates and deflates; a baby cries, sleeps, crawls, walks and blinks; a car accelerates, brakes and turns; a towel absorbs water; etc.)

Humans learn about objects by studying their attributes and observing their behaviors. Different objects can have similar attributes and can exhibit similar behaviors. Comparisons can be made, for example, between babies and adults and between humans and chimpanzees. Cars, trucks, little red wagons and roller skates have much in common.

Object-oriented programming (OOP) models real-world objects with software counterparts. It takes advantage of *class* relationships where objects of a certain class—such as a class of vehicles—have the same characteristics. It takes advantage of *inheritance* relationships, and even *multiple inheritance* relationships where newly created classes of objects are derived by absorbing characteristics of existing classes and adding unique characteristics of their own. An object of class "convertible" certainly has the characteristics of the more general class "automobile," but a convertible's roof goes up and down.

Object-oriented programming gives us a more natural and intuitive way to view the programming process, namely, by *modeling* real-world objects, their attributes and their behaviors. OOP also models communication between objects. Just as people send *messages* to one another (e.g., a sergeant commanding a soldier to stand at attention), objects also communicate via messages.

OOP *encapsulates* data (attributes) and functions (behavior) into packages called *objects;* the data and functions of an object are intimately tied together. Objects have the property of *information hiding.* This means that although objects may know how to communicate with one another across well-defined *interfaces,* objects normally are not allowed to know how other objects are implemented—implementation details are hidden within the objects themselves. Surely it is possible to drive a car effectively without knowing the details of how engines, transmissions and exhaust systems work internally. We will see why information hiding is so crucial to good software engineering.

In C and other *procedural programming languages,* programming tends to be *action-oriented,* whereas in C++ programming tends to be *object-oriented.* In C, the unit of programming is the *function.* In C++, the unit of programming is the *class* from which objects are eventually *instantiated* (a fancy term for "created"). C++ classes contain functions (that implement class behaviors) and data (that implement class attributes).

C programmers concentrate on writing functions. Groups of actions that perform some common task are formed into functions, and functions are grouped to form programs. Data is certainly important in C, but the view is that data exists primarily in support of the actions that functions perform. The *verbs* in a system specification help the C programmer determine the set of functions that work together to implement the system.

C++ programmers concentrate on creating their own *user-defined types* called *classes* and *components.* Each class contains data as well as the set of functions that manipulate that data. The data components of a class are called *data members.* The function components of a class are called *member functions* (typically called *methods* in other object-oriented programming languages like Java). Just as an instance of a built-in type such as **int** is called a *variable,* an instance of a user-defined type (i.e., a class) is called an *object.* The programmer uses built-in types as the "building blocks" for constructing user-defined types. The focus of attention in C++ is on classes (out of which we make objects) rather than on functions. The *nouns* in a system specification help the C++ programmer determine the set of classes from which objects will be created that will work together to implement the system.

Classes are to objects as blueprints are to houses. We can build many houses from one blueprint, and we can instantiate many objects from one class. Classes can also have relationships with other classes. For example, in an object-oriented design of a bank, the **BankTeller** class needs to relate to the **Customer** class. These relationships are called *associations.*

We will see that when software is packaged as classes, these classes can be *reused* in future software systems. Groups of related classes are often packaged as reusable *components.* Just as real-estate brokers tell their clients that the three most important factors affecting the price of real estate are "location, location and location," we believe the three most important factors affecting the future of software development are "reuse, reuse and reuse."

Indeed, with object technology, we will build most future software by combining "standardized, interchangeable parts" called classes. This book will teach you how to "craft valuable classes" for reuse, reuse and reuse. Each new class you create will have the potential to become a valuable software asset that you and other programmers can use to speed and enhance the quality of future software development efforts. This is an exciting possibility.

Introduction to Object-Oriented Analysis and Design (OOAD)

By now, you have probably written a few small programs in C++. How did you create the code for your programs? If you are like many beginning programmers, you may have turned on your computer and simply started typing. This approach may work for small projects, but what would you do if you were asked to create a software system to control the automated teller machines for a major bank? Such a project is too large and complex to sit down and simply start typing.

For creating the best solutions, you should follow a detailed process for obtaining an *analysis* of your project's *requirements* and developing a *design* for satisfying those requirements. You would go through this process and have its results reviewed and approved by your superiors before writing any code for your project. If this process involves analyzing and designing your system from an object-oriented point of view, we call it an *object-oriented analysis and design (OOAD) process.* Experienced programmers know that no matter how simple a problem appears, time spent on analysis and design can save innumerable hours that might be lost from abandoning an ill-planned system development approach part of the way through its implementation.

OOAD is the generic term for the ideas behind the process we employ to analyze a problem and develop an approach for solving it. Small problems like the ones in these first few chapters do not require an exhaustive process. It may be sufficient to write *pseudocode* before we begin writing code. (Pseudocode is an informal means of expressing program code. It is not actually a programming language, but we can use it as a kind of "outline" to guide us as we write our code. We introduce pseudocode in Chapter 2.)

Pseudocode may suffice for small problems, but as problems and the groups of people solving these problems increase in size, the methods of OOAD become more involved. Ideally, a group should agree on a strictly defined process for solving the problem and on a uniform way of communicating the results of that process with one another. Many different OOAD processes exist; however, a graphical language for communicating the results of any OOAD process has become widely used. This language is known as the *Unified Modeling Language (UML).* The UML was developed in the mid-1990s, under the initial direction of a trio of software methodologists: Grady Booch, James Rumbaugh and Ivar Jacobson.

History of the UML

In the 1980s, increasing numbers of organizations began using OOP to program their applications, and a need developed for an established process with which to approach OOAD. Many methodologists—including Booch, Rumbaugh and Jacobson—individually produced and promoted separate processes to satisfy this need. Each of these processes had their own notation, or "language" (in the form of graphical diagrams), to convey the results of analysis and design.

By the early 1990s, different companies, and even different divisions within the same company, were using different processes and notations. Additionally, these companies wanted to use software tools that would support their particular processes. With so many processes, software vendors found it difficult to provide such tools. Clearly, standard processes and notation were needed.

In 1994, James Rumbaugh joined Grady Booch at Rational Software Corporation, and the two began working to unify their popular processes. They were soon joined by Ivar Jacobson. In 1996, the group released early versions of the UML to the software engineering community and requested feedback. Around the same time, an organization known as the *Object Management Group™ (OMG™)* invited submissions for a common modeling language. The OMG is a not-for-profit organization that promotes the use of object-oriented technology by issuing guidelines and specifications for object-oriented technologies. Several corporations—among them HP, IBM, Microsoft, Oracle and Rational Software—had already recognized the need for a common modeling language. These companies formed the *UML Partners* in response to the OMG's request for proposals. This consortium developed and submitted the UML version 1.1 to the OMG. The OMG accepted the proposal and, in 1997, assumed responsibility for the continuing maintenance and revision of the UML. In 1999, the OMG released the UML version 1.3 (the current version at the time this book was published).

What is the UML?

The Unified Modeling Language is now the most widely used graphical representation scheme for modeling object-oriented systems. It has indeed unified the various notational schemes that existed in the late 1980s. Those who design systems use the language (in the form of graphical diagrams) to model their systems.

One of the most attractive features of the UML is its flexibility. The UML is extendable and is independent of the many OOAD processes. UML modelers are free to develop systems using various processes, but all developers can now express those systems with one standard set of notations.

The UML is a complex, feature-rich graphical language. In our "Thinking About Objects" sections, we present a concise, simplified subset of these features. We then use this subset to guide the reader through a first design experience with the UML intended for the novice object-oriented designer/programmer. For a more complete discussion of the UML, refer to the Object Management Group's Web site (**www.omg.org**) and to the official UML 1.3 specifications document (**www.omg.org/uml/**). Many UML books have been published. *UML Distilled: Second Edition*, by Martin Fowler (with Kendall Scott) provides a detailed introduction to the UML version 1.3, with many examples. *The Unified Modeling Language User Guide*, written by Booch, Rumbaugh and Jacobson, is the definitive tutorial to the UML.

Object-oriented technology is ubiquitous in the software industry, and the UML is rapidly becoming so. Our goal in these "Thinking About Objects" sections is to encourage you to think in an object-oriented manner as early, and as often, as possible. Beginning in the "Thinking About Objects" section at the end of Chapter 2, you will apply object technology to implement a solution to a substantial problem. We hope that you will find this optional project to be an enjoyable and challenging introduction to object-oriented design with the UML and to object-oriented programming.

SUMMARY

- A computer is a device capable of performing computations and making logical decisions at speeds millions and even billions of times faster than human beings can.
- Computers process data under the control of computer programs.
- The various devices (such as the keyboard, screen, disks, memory and processing units) that comprise a computer system are referred to as hardware.
- The computer programs that run on a computer are referred to as software.
- The input unit is the "receiving" section of the computer. Most information is entered into computers today through typewriter-like keyboards.

- The output unit is the "shipping" section of the computer. Most information is output from computers today by displaying it on screens or by printing it on paper.
- The memory unit is the "warehouse" section of the computer and is often called either memory or primary memory.
- The arithmetic and logic unit (ALU) performs calculations and makes decisions.
- Programs or data not actively being used by the other units are normally placed on secondary storage devices (such as disks) until they are again needed.
- In single-user batch processing, the computer runs a single program at a time while processing data in groups or batches.
- Operating systems are software systems that make it more convenient to use computers and to get the best performance from computers.
- Multiprogramming operating systems enable the "simultaneous" operation of many jobs on the computer—the computer shares its resources among the jobs.
- Timesharing is a special case of multiprogramming in which users access the computer through terminals. The users' programs appear to be running simultaneously.
- With distributed computing, an organization's computing is distributed via networking to the sites where the work of the organization is performed.
- Servers store programs and data that may be shared by client computers distributed throughout a network, hence the term client/server computing.
- Any computer can directly understand only its own machine language. Machine languages generally consist of strings of numbers (ultimately reduced to 1s and 0s) that instruct computers to perform their most elementary operations one at a time. Machine languages are machine-dependent.
- English-like abbreviations form the basis of assembly languages. Assemblers translate assembly language programs into machine language.
- Compilers translate high-level language programs into machine language. High-level languages contain English words and conventional mathematical notations.
- Interpreter programs directly execute high-level language programs without the need for compiling those programs into machine language.
- Although compiled programs execute faster than interpreted programs, interpreters are popular in program development environments in which programs are recompiled frequently as new features are added and errors are corrected. Once a program is developed, a compiled version can then be produced to run more efficiently.
- It is possible to write programs in C and C++ that are portable to most computers.
- FORTRAN (FORmula TRANslator) is used for mathematical applications. COBOL (COmmon Business Oriented Language) is used primarily for commercial applications that require precise and efficient manipulation of large amounts of data.
- Structured programming is a disciplined approach to writing programs that are clearer than unstructured programs, easier to test and debug and easier to modify.
- Pascal was designed for teaching structured programming in academic environments.
- Ada was developed under the sponsorship of the United States Department of Defense (DOD) using Pascal as a base.
- Multitasking allows programmers to specify parallel activities.
- All C++ systems consist of three parts: the environment, the language and the standard libraries. Library functions are not part of the C++ language itself; these functions perform operations such as popular mathematical calculations.

- C++ programs typically go through six phases to be executed: edit, preprocess, compile, link, load and execute.

- The programmer types a program with an editor and makes corrections if necessary. C++ file names on a typical UNIX-based system end with the **.C** extension.

- A compiler translates a C++ program into machine language code (or object code).

- The preprocessor obeys preprocessor directives which typically indicate files to be included in the file being compiled and special symbols to be replaced with program text.

- A linker links the object code with the code for missing functions to produce an executable image (with no missing pieces). On a typical UNIX-based system, the command to compile and link a C++ program is **CC**. If the program compiles and links correctly, a file called **a.out** is produced. This is the executable image of the program.

- A loader takes an executable image from disk and transfers it to memory.

- A computer, under the control of its CPU, executes a program one instruction at a time.

- Errors like division-by-zero errors occur as a program runs, so these errors are called run-time errors or execution-time errors.

- Divide-by-zero is generally a fatal error, i.e., an error that causes the program to terminate immediately without having successfully performed its job. Non-fatal errors allow programs to run to completion, often producing incorrect results.

- Certain C++ functions take their input from **cin** (the standard input stream) which is normally the keyboard, but **cin** can be connected to another device. Data is output to **cout** (the standard output stream) which is normally the computer screen, but **cout** can be connected to another device.

- The standard error stream is referred to as **cerr**. The **cerr** stream (normally connected to the screen) is used for displaying error messages.

- There are many variations between different C++ implementations and different computers that make portability an elusive goal.

- C++ provides capabilities to do object-oriented programming.

- Objects are essentially reusable software components that model items in the real world. Objects are made from "blueprints" called classes.

- Single-line comments begin with **//**. Programmers insert comments to document programs and improve their readability. Comments do not cause the computer to perform any action when the program is run.

- The line **#include <iostream>** tells the C++ preprocessor to include the contents of the input/output stream header file in the program. This file contains information necessary to compile programs that use **std::cin** and **std::cout** and operators **<<** and **>>**.

- C++ programs begin executing at the function **main**.

- The output stream object **std::cout**—normally connected to the screen—is used to output data. Multiple data items can be output by concatenating stream insertion (**<<**) operators.

- The input stream object **std::cin**—normally connected to the keyboard—is used to input data. Multiple data items can be input by concatenating stream extraction (**>>**) operators.

- All variables in a C++ program must be declared before they can be used.

- A variable name in C++ is any valid identifier. An identifier is a series of characters consisting of letters, digits and underscores (_). Identifiers cannot start with a digit. C++ identifiers can be any length; however, some systems and/or C++ implementations may impose some restrictions on the length of identifiers.

- C++ is case sensitive.

- Most calculations are performed in assignment statements.
- Every variable stored in the computer's memory has a name, a value, a type and a size.
- Whenever a new value is placed in a memory location, it replaces the previous value in that location. The previous value is destroyed.
- When a value is read from memory, the process is nondestructive, i.e., a copy of the value is read leaving the original value undisturbed in the memory location.
- C++ evaluates arithmetic expressions in a precise sequence determined by the rules of operator precedence and associativity.
- The **if** statement allows a program to make a decision when a certain condition is met. The format for an **if** statement is

> **if (** *condition* **)**
>   *statement***;**

If the condition is **true**, the statement in the body of the **if** is executed. If the condition is not met, i.e., the condition is **false**, the body statement is skipped.
- Conditions in **if** statements are commonly formed by using equality operators and relational operators. The result of using these operators is always simply the observation of **true** or **false**.
- The statements

```
using std::cout;
using std::cin;
using std::endl;
```

are *using statements* that help us eliminate the need to repeat the **std::** prefix. Once we include these **using** statements, we can write **cout** instead of **std::cout**, **cin** instead of **std::cin** and **endl** instead of **std::endl**, respectively, in the remainder of a program.
- Object-orientation is a natural way of thinking about the world and of writing computer programs.
- Objects have attributes (like size, shape, color, weight and the like) and they exhibit behaviors.
- Humans learn about objects by studying their attributes and observing their behaviors.
- Different objects can have many of the same attributes and exhibit similar behaviors.
- Object-oriented programming (OOP) models real-world objects with software counterparts. It takes advantage of class relationships where objects of a certain class have the same characteristics. It takes advantage of inheritance relationships and even multiple inheritance relationships where newly created classes are derived by inheriting characteristics of existing classes, yet contain unique characteristics of their own.
- Object-oriented programming provides an intuitive way to view the programming process, namely by modeling real-world objects, their attributes and their behaviors.
- OOP also models communication between objects via messages.
- OOP encapsulates data (attributes) and functions (behavior) into objects.
- Objects have the property of information hiding. Although objects may know how to communicate with one another across well-defined interfaces, objects normally are not allowed to know implementation details of other objects.
- Information hiding is crucial to good software engineering.
- In C and other procedural programming languages, programming tends to be action-oriented. Data is certainly important in C, but the view is that data exists primarily in support of the actions that functions perform.

- C++ programmers concentrate on creating their own user-defined types called classes. Each class contains data as well as the set of functions that manipulate the data. The data components of a class are called data members. The function components of a class are called member functions or methods.

TERMINOLOGY

abstraction
action
action-oriented
analysis
ANSI/ISO standard C
ANSI/ISO standard C++
arithmetic and logic unit (ALU)
arithmetic operators
assembly language
assignment operator (=)
association
associativity of operators
attribute
attributes of an object
behavior
behaviors of an object
binary operator
body of a function
Booch, Grady
C
C++
C++ standard library
case sensitive
central processing unit (CPU)
cerr object
cin object
clarity
class
client/server computing
comma-separated list
comment (//)
compile error
compile-time error
compiler
component
computer
computer program
condition
cout object
CPU
"crafting valuable classes"
data
data member
decision

declaration
design
distributed computing
editor
encapsulation
equality operators
   == "is equal to"
   != "is not equal to"
escape character (****)
escape sequence
execution-time error
fatal error
file server
flow of control
function
hardware
high-level language
identifier
if structure
information hiding
inheritance
input device
input/output (I/O)
instantiate
int
integer (**int**)
integer division
interface
interpreter
iostream
Jacobson, Ivar
left-to-right associativity
linking
loading
logic error
machine dependent
machine independent
machine language
main
member function
memory
memory location
message
method

modeling
multiple inheritance
modulus operator (**%**)
multiple inheritance
multiplication operator (*****)
multiprocessor
multiprogramming
multitasking
nested parentheses
newline character (**\n**)
non-fatal error
nouns in a system specification
object
Object Management Group (OMG)
object-oriented analysis and design (OOAD)
object-oriented design (OOD)
object-oriented programming (OOP)
operand
operator
operator associativity
output device
parentheses (**)**
precedence
preprocessor
primary memory
procedural programming
procedural programming language
programming language
prompt
pseudocode
Rational Software Corporation
relational operators
     < "is less than"
     <= "is less than or equal to"
     > "is greater than"
     >= "is greater than or equal to"

requirements
reserved words
"reuse, reuse and reuse"
right-to-left associativity
rules of operator precedence
Rumbaugh, James
run-time error
semicolon (**;**) statement terminator
software
software asset
software reusability
standard error object (**cerr**)
standard input object (**cin**)
standard output object (**cout**)
statement
statement terminator (**;**)
std::cerr
std::cin
std::cout
std::endl
string
structured programming
syntax error
translator program
Unified Modeling Language (UML)
user-defined type
using
using std::cerr;
using std::cin;
using std::cout;
using std::endl;
variable
variable name
variable value
verbs in a system specification
white-space characters

COMMON PROGRAMMING ERRORS

1.1   Errors like division-by-zero errors occur as a program runs, so these errors are called run-time errors or execution-time errors. Divide-by-zero is generally a fatal error, i.e., an error that causes the program to terminate immediately without having successfully performed its job. Non-fatal errors allow programs to run to completion, often producing incorrect results. (Note: On some systems, divide-by-zero is not a fatal error. Please see your system documentation.)

1.2   Forgetting to include the **iostream** file in a program that inputs data from the keyboard or outputs data to the screen causes the compiler to issue an error message.

1.3   Omitting the semicolon at the end of a statement is a syntax error. A syntax error is caused when the compiler can not recognize a statement. The compiler normally issues an error message to help the programmer locate and fix the incorrect statement. Syntax errors are violations of the language. Syntax errors are also called compile errors, compile-time errors, or compilation errors because they appear during the compilation phase.

1.4   Attempting to use the modulus operator, **%**, with non-integer operands is a syntax error.

1.5   A syntax error will occur if any of the operators **==**, **!=**, **>=** and **<=** appears with spaces between its pair of symbols.

1.6   Reversing the order of the pair of operators in any of the operators **!=**, **>=** and **<=** (by writing them as **=!**, **=>** and **=<**, respectively) is normally a syntax error. In some cases, writing **!=** as **=!** will not be a syntax error, but will almost certainly be a logic error.

1.7   Confusing the equality operator **==** with the assignment operator **=**. The equality operator should be read "is equal to" and the assignment operator should be read "gets" or "gets the value of" or "is assigned the value of." Some people prefer to read the equality operator as "double equals." As we will soon see, confusing these operators may not necessarily cause an easy-to-recognize syntax error, but may cause extremely subtle logic errors.

1.8   Placing a semicolon immediately after the right parenthesis after the condition in an **if** structure is often a logic error (although not a syntax error). The semicolon would cause the body of the **if** structure to be empty, so the **if** structure itself would perform no action regardless of whether or not its condition is **true**. Worse yet, the original body statement of the **if** structure would now become a statement in sequence with the **if** structure and would always be executed, often causing the program to produce incorrect results.

1.9   It is a syntax error to split an identifier by inserting white space characters (e.g., writing **main** as **ma in**).

GOOD PROGRAMMING PRACTICES

1.1   Write your C++ programs in a simple and straightforward manner. This is sometimes referred to as KIS ("keep it simple"). Do not "stretch" the language by trying bizarre usages.

1.2   Read the manuals for the version of C++ you are using. Refer to these manuals frequently to be sure you are aware of the rich collection of C++ features and that you are using these features correctly.

1.3   Your computer and compiler are good teachers. If after carefully reading your C++ language manual you are not sure how a feature of C++ works, experiment using a small "test program" and see what happens. Set your compiler options for "maximum warnings." Study each message you get when you compile your programs and correct the programs to eliminate the messages.

1.4   Every program should begin with a comment describing the purpose of the program.

1.5   Many programmers make the last character printed by a function a newline (**\n**). This ensures that the function will leave the screen cursor positioned at the beginning of a new line. Conventions of this nature encourage software reusability—a key goal in software development environments.

1.6   Indent the entire body of each function one level of indentation within the braces that define the body of the function. This makes the functional structure of a program stand out and helps make programs easier to read.

1.7   Set a convention for the size of indent you prefer then uniformly apply that convention. The tab key may be used to create indents, but tab stops may vary. We recommend using either 1/4-inch tab stops or (preferably) three spaces to form a level of indent.

1.8   Some programmers prefer to declare each variable on a separate line. This format allows for easy insertion of a descriptive comment next to each declaration.

1.9   Place a space after each comma (**,**) to make programs more readable.

1.10   Choosing meaningful variable names helps a program to be "self-documenting," i.e., it becomes easier to understand the program simply by reading it rather than having to read manuals or use excessive comments.

1.11   Avoid identifiers that begin with underscores and double underscores because C++ compilers may use names like that for their own purposes internally. This will prevent names you choose from being confused with names the compilers choose.

1.12   Always place a blank line between a declaration and adjacent executable statements. This makes the declarations stand out in the program and contributes to program clarity.

1.13   If you prefer to place declarations at the beginning of a function, separate those declarations from the executable statements in that function with one blank line to highlight where the declarations end and the executable statements begin.

1.14   Place spaces on either side of a binary operator. This makes the operator stand out and makes the program more readable.

1.15   As in algebra, it is acceptable to place unnecessary parentheses in an expression to make the expression clearer. These parentheses are called redundant parentheses. Redundant parentheses are commonly used to group subexpressions in a large expression to make that expression clearer. Breaking a large statement into a sequence of shorter, simpler statements also promotes clarity.

1.16   Indent the statement in the body of an **if** structure to make the body of the structure stand out and to enhance program readability.

1.17   There should be no more than one statement per line in a program.

1.18   A lengthy statement may be spread over several lines. If a single statement must be split across lines, choose breaking points that make sense such as after a comma in a comma-separated list, or after an operator in a lengthy expression. If a statement is split across two or more lines, indent all subsequent lines.

1.19   Refer to the operator precedence chart when writing expressions containing many operators. Confirm that the operators in the expression are performed in the order you expect. If you are uncertain about the order of evaluation in a complex expression, break the expression into smaller statements or use parentheses to force the order, exactly as you would do in an algebraic expression. Be sure to observe that some operators such as assignment (**=**) associate right to left rather than left to right.

PERFORMANCE TIP

1.1   Using standard library functions and classes instead of writing your own comparable versions can improve program performance because this software is carefully written to perform efficiently and correctly.

1.2   Reusing proven code components instead of writing your versions can improve program performance because these components are normally written to perform efficiently.

PORTABILITY TIPS

1.1   Because C is a standardized, hardware-independent, widely available language, applications written in C can often be run with little or no modifications on a wide range of different computer systems.

1.2   Using standard library functions and classes instead of writing your own comparable versions can improve program portability because this software is included in virtually all C++ implementations.

1.3   Although it is possible to write portable programs, there are many problems among different C and C++ compilers and different computers that can make portability difficult to achieve. Simply writing programs in C and C++ does not guarantee portability. The programmer will often need to deal directly with compiler and computer variations.

1.4   C++ allows identifiers of any length, but your system and/or C++ implementation may impose some restrictions on the length of identifiers. Use identifiers of 31 characters or fewer to ensure portability.

SOFTWARE ENGINEERING OBSERVATIONS

1.1   Use a "building block approach" to creating programs. Avoid reinventing the wheel. Use existing pieces where possible—this is called "software reuse" and it is central to object-oriented programming.

1.2   When programming in C++ you will typically use the following building blocks: classes and functions from the C++ standard library, classes and functions you create yourself, and classes and functions from various popular libraries provided by third-party vendors.

1.3   Extensive class libraries of reusable software components are available over the Internet and the World Wide Web. Many of these libraries are available at no charge.

SELF-REVIEW EXERCISES

1.1   Fill in the blanks in each of the following:
   a) The company that popularized personal computing was _____.
   b) The computer that made personal computing legitimate in business and industry was the _____.
   c) Computers process data under the control of sets of instructions called computer _____.
   d) The six key logical units of the computer are the _____, _____, _____, _____, _____ and the _____.
   e) The three classes of languages discussed in the chapter are _____, _____ and _____.
   f) The programs that translate high-level language programs into machine language are called _____.
   g) C is widely known as the development language of the _____ operating system.
   h) The _____ language was developed by Wirth for teaching structured programming in universities.
   i) The Department of Defense developed the Ada language with a capability called _____ which allows programmers to specify that many activities can proceed in parallel.

1.2   Fill in the blanks in each of the following sentences about the C++ environment.
   a) C++ programs are normally typed into a computer using an _____ program.
   b) In a C++ system, a _____ program executes before the compiler's translation phase begins.
   c) The _____ program combines the output of the compiler with various library functions to produce an executable image.
   d) The _____ program transfers the executable image of a C++ program from disk to memory.

1.3   Fill in the blanks in each of the following.
   a) Every C++ program begins execution at the function _____.
   b) The _____ begins the body of every function and the _____ ends the body of every function.
   c) Every statement ends with a _____.

    d) The escape sequence **\n** represents the _____ character which causes the cursor to position to the beginning of the next line on the screen.

    e) The _____ statement is used to make decisions.

1.4   State whether each of the following is *true* or *false*. If *false*, explain why. Assume the statement **using std::cout;** is used.

    a) Comments cause the computer to print the text after the **//** on the screen when the program is executed.

    b) The escape sequence **\n** when output with **cout** causes the cursor to position to the beginning of the next line on the screen.

    c) All variables must be declared before they are used.

    d) All variables must be given a type when they are declared.

    e) C++ considers the variables **number** and **NuMbEr** to be identical.

    f) Declarations can appear almost anywhere in the body of a C++ function.

    g) The modulus operator (**%**) can be used only with integer operands.

    h) The arithmetic operators *****, **/**, **%**, **+** and **–** all have the same level of precedence.

    i) A C++ program that prints three lines of output must contain three output statements using **cout**.

1.5   Write a single C++ statement to accomplish each of the following: (Assume that **using** statements have not been used)

    a) Declare the variables **c, thisIsAVariable, q76354** and **number** to be of type **int**.

    b) Prompt the user to enter an integer. End your prompting message with a colon (**:**) followed by a space and leave the cursor positioned after the space.

    c) Read an integer from the user at the keyboard and store the value entered in integer variable **age**.

    d) If the variable **number** is not equal to **7**, print **"The variable number is not equal to 7"**.

    e) Print the message **"This is a C++ program"** on one line.

    f) Print the message **"This is a C++ program"** on two lines where the first line ends with **C++**.

    g) Print the message **"This is a C++ program"** with each word of the message on a separate line.

    h) Print the message **"This is a C++ program"** with each word separated from the next by a tab.

1.6   Write a statement (or comment) to accomplish each of the following: (Assume that **using** statements have been used)

    a) State that a program will calculate the product of three integers.

    b) Declare the variables **x, y, z** and **result** to be of type **int**.

    c) Prompt the user to enter three integers.

    d) Read three integers from the keyboard and store them in the variables **x, y** and **z**.

    e) Compute the product of the three integers contained in variables **x, y** and **z**, and assign the result to the variable **result**.

    f) Print **"The product is "** followed by the value of the variable **result**.

    g) Return a value from **main** indicating that the program terminated successfully.

1.7   Using the statements you wrote in Exercise 1.6, write a complete program that calculates and displays the product of three integers. Note: you will need to write the necessary **using** statements.

1.8   Identify and correct the errors in each of the following statements (assume that the statement **using std::cout;** is used):

a) `if ( c < 7 );`
   `cout << "c is less than 7\n";`
b) `if ( c => 7 )`
   `cout << "c is equal to or greater than 7\n";`

1.9   Fill the correct "object speak" term into the blanks in each of the following:
a) Humans can look at a TV screen and see dots of color, or they can step back and see three people sitting at a conference table; this is an example of a capability called _____.
b) If we view a car as an object, the fact that the car is a convertible is a(n) attribute/behavior (pick one) _____ of the car.
c) The fact that a car can accelerate or decelerate, turn left or turn right, or go forward or backward are all examples of _____ of a car object.
d) When a new class inherits characteristics from several different existing classes, this is called _____ inheritance .
e) Objects communicate by sending each other _____.
f) Objects communicate with one another across well-defined _____.
g) Each object is ordinarily not allowed to know how other objects are implemented; this property is called _____.
h) The _____ in a system specification help the C++ programmer determine the classes that will be needed to implement the system.
i) The data components of a class are called _____ and the function components of a class are called _____.
j) An instance of a user-defined type is called a(n) _____.

ANSWERS TO SELF-REVIEW EXERCISES

1.1   a) Apple. b) IBM Personal Computer. c) programs. d) input unit, output unit, memory unit, arithmetic and logic unit, central processing unit, secondary storage unit. e) machine languages, assembly languages, high-level languages. f) compilers. g) UNIX. h) Pascal. i) multitasking.

1.2   a) editor. b) preprocessor. c) linker. d) loader.

1.3   a) **main**. b) Left brace (`{`), right brace (`}`). c) Semicolon. d) newline. e) **if**.

1.4   a) False. Comments do not cause any action to be performed when the program is executed. They are used to document programs and improve their readability.
b) True.
c) True.
d) True.
e) False. C++ is case sensitive, so these variables are unique.
f) True.
g) True.
h) False. The operators `*`, `/` and `%` have the same precedence, and the operators `+` and `-` have a lower precedence.
i) False. A single output statement using cout containing multiple `\n` escape sequences can print several lines.

1.5
a) `int c, thisIsAVariable, q76354, number;`
b) `std::cout << "Enter an integer: ";`
c) `std::cin >> age;`
d) `if ( number != 7 )`
   `std::cout << "The variable number is not equal to 7\n";`
e) `std::cout << "This is a C++ program\n";`

```
f) std::cout << "This is a C++\nprogram\n";
g) std::cout << "This\nis\na\nC++\nprogram\n";
h) std::cout << "This\tis\ta\tC++\tprogram\n";
```

1.6   a) // Calculate the product of three integers
      b) int x, y, z, result;
      c) cout << "Enter three integers: ";
      d) cin >> x >> y >> z;
      e) result = x * y * z;
      f) cout << "The product is " << result << endl;
      g) return 0;

1.7   // Calculate the product of three integers

```
// Calculate the product of three integers
#include <iostream>

using std::cout;
using std::cin;
using std::endl;

int main()
{
    int x, y, z, result;

    cout << "Enter three integers: ";
    cin >> x >> y >> z;
    result = x * y * z;
    cout << "The product is " << result << endl;

    return 0;
}
```

1.8   a) Error: Semicolon after the right parenthesis of the condition in the if statement. Correction: Remove the semicolon after the right parenthesis. Note: The result of this error is that the output statement will be executed whether or not the condition in the if statement is true. The semicolon after the right parenthesis is considered an empty statement—a statement that does nothing. We will learn more about the empty statement in the next chapter.
      b) Error: The relational operator =>. Correction: Change => to >=.

1.9   a) abstraction. b) attribute. c) behaviors. d) multiple. e) messages. f) interfaces. g) information hiding. h) nouns. i) data members; member functions or methods. j) object.

EXERCISES

1.10   Categorize each of the following items as either hardware or software:
      a) CPU
      b) C++ compiler
      c) ALU
      d) C++ preprocessor
      e) input unit
      f) an editor program

1.11   Why might you want to write a program in a machine-independent language instead of a machine-dependent language? Why might a machine-dependent language be more appropriate for writing certain types of programs?

1.12   Fill in the blanks in each of the following statements:

a)   Which logical unit of the computer receives information from outside the computer for use by the computer? _____.

b)   The process of instructing the computer to solve specific problems is called _____.

c)   What type of computer language uses English-like abbreviations for machine language instructions? _____.

d)   Which logical unit of the computer sends information that has already been processed by the computer to various devices so that the information may be used outside the computer? _____.

e)   Which logical unit of the computer retains information? _____.

f)   Which logical unit of the computer performs calculations? _____.

g)   Which logical unit of the computer makes logical decisions? _____.

h)   The level of computer language most convenient to the programmer for writing programs quickly and easily is _____.

i)   The only language a computer directly understands is called that computer's _____.

j)   Which logical unit of the computer coordinates the activities of all the other logical units? _____.

1.13   Discuss the meaning of each of the following objects:

a)   **std::cin**

b)   **std::cout**

c)   **std::cerr**

1.14   Why is so much attention today focused on object-oriented programming in general and C++ in particular?

1.15   Fill in the blanks in each of the following:

a)   _____ are used to document a program and improve its readability.

b)   The object used to print information on the screen is _____.

c)   A C++ statement that makes a decision is _____.

d)   Calculations are normally performed by _____ statements.

e)   The _____ object inputs values from the keyboard.

1.16   Write a single C++ statement or line that accomplishes each of the following:

a)   Print the message **"Enter two numbers"**.

b)   Assign the product of variables **b** and **c** to variable **a**.

c)   State that a program performs a sample payroll calculation (i.e., use text that helps to document a program).

d)   Input three integer values from the keyboard and into integer variables **a**, **b** and **c**.

1.17   State which of the following are *true* and which are *false*. If *false*, explain your answers.

a)   C++ operators are evaluated from left to right.

b)   The following are all valid variable names: **_under_bar_**, **m928134**, **t5**, **j7**, **her_sales**, **his_account_total**, **a**, **b**, **c**, **z**, **z2**.

c)   The statement **cout << "a = 5;";** is a typical example of an assignment statement.

d)   A valid C++ arithmetic expression with no parentheses is evaluated from left to right.

e)   The following are all invalid variable names: **3g**, **87**, **67h2**, **h22**, **2h**.

1.18   Fill in the blanks in each of the following:

a)   What arithmetic operations are on the same level of precedence as multiplication? _____.

b)   When parentheses are nested, which set of parentheses is evaluated first in an arithmetic expression? _____.

c)   A location in the computer's memory that may contain different values at various times throughout the execution of a program is called a _____.

1.19   What, if anything, prints when each of the following C++ statements is performed? If nothing prints, then answer "nothing." Assume **x = 2** and **y = 3**.

    a) `cout << x;`
    b) `cout << x + x;`
    c) `cout << "x=";`
    d) `cout << "x = " << x;`
    e) `cout << x + y << " = " << y + x;`
    f) `z = x + y;`
    g) `cin >> x >> y;`
    h) `// cout << "x + y = " << x + y;`
    i) `cout << "\n";`

1.20   Which of the following C++ statements contain variables whose values are replaced?

    a) `cin >> b >> c >> d >> e >> f;`
    b) `p = i + j + k + 7;`
    c) `cout << "variables whose values are destroyed";`
    d) `cout << "a = 5";`

1.21   Given the algebraic equation $y = ax^3 + 7$, which of the following, if any, are correct C++ statements for this equation?

    a) `y = a * x * x * x + 7;`
    b) `y = a * x * x * ( x + 7 );`
    c) `y = ( a * x ) * x * ( x + 7 );`
    d) `y = (a * x) * x * x + 7;`
    e) `y = a * ( x * x * x ) + 7;`
    f) `y = a * x * ( x * x + 7 );`

1.22   State the order of evaluation of the operators in each of the following C++ statements and show the value of **x** after each statement is performed.

    a) `x = 7 + 3 * 6 / 2 - 1;`
    b) `x = 2 % 2 + 2 * 2 - 2 / 2;`
    c) `x = ( 3 * 9 * ( 3 + ( 9 * 3 / ( 3 ) ) ) );`

1.23   Write a program that asks the user to enter two numbers, obtains the two numbers from the user and prints the sum, product, difference, and quotient of the two numbers.

1.24   Write a program that prints the numbers 1 to 4 on the same line with each pair of adjacent numbers separated by one space. Write the program using the following methods:

    a) Using one output statement with one stream insertion operator.
    b) Using one output statement with four stream insertion operators.
    c) Using four output statements.

1.25   Write a program that asks the user to enter two integers, obtains the numbers from the user, then prints the larger number followed by the words **"is larger."** If the numbers are equal, print the message "**These numbers are equal**."

1.26   Write a program that inputs three integers from the keyboard and prints the sum, average, product, smallest and largest of these numbers. The screen dialogue should appear as follows:

```
Input three different integers: 13 27 14
Sum is 54
Average is 18
Product is 4914
Smallest is 13
Largest is 27
```

1.27   Write a program that reads in the radius of a circle and prints the circle's diameter, circumference and area. Use the constant value 3.14159 for π. Do these calculations in output statements. (Note: In this chapter, we have discussed only integer constants and variables. In Chapter 3 we will discuss floating-point numbers, i.e., values that can have decimal points.)

1.28   Write a program that prints a box, an oval, an arrow and a diamond as follows:

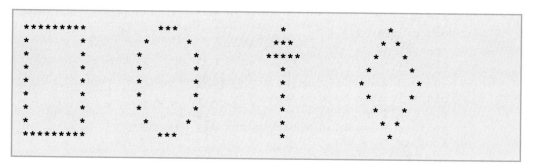

1.29   What does the following code print?

```
cout << "*\n**\n***\n****\n*****\n";
```

1.30   Write a program that reads in five integers and determines and prints the largest and the smallest integers in the group. Use only the programming techniques you learned in this chapter.

1.31   Write a program that reads an integer and determines and prints whether it is odd or even. (Hint: Use the modulus operator. An even number is a multiple of two. Any multiple of two leaves a remainder of zero when divided by 2.)

1.32   Write a program that reads in two integers and determines and prints if the first is a multiple of the second. (Hint: Use the modulus operator.)

1.33   Display a checkerboard pattern with eight output statements, then display the same pattern with as few output statements as possible.

1.34   Distinguish between the terms fatal error and non-fatal error. Why might you prefer to experience a fatal error rather than a non-fatal error?

1.35   Here is a peek ahead. In this chapter you learned about integers and the type **int**. C++ can also represent uppercase letters, lowercase letters and a considerable variety of special symbols. C++ uses small integers internally to represent each different character. The set of characters a computer uses and the corresponding integer representations for those characters is called that computer's *character set*. You can print a character by simply enclosing that character in single quotes as with

```
cout << 'A';
```

You can print the integer equivalent of a character using **static_cast** as follows:

```
cout << static_cast< int >( 'A' );
```

This is called a *cast* operation (we formally introduce casts in Chapter 2). When the preceding statement executes, it prints the value 65 (on systems that use the *ASCII character set*). Write a program that prints the integer equivalents of some uppercase letters, lowercase letters, digits and special symbols. At a minimum, determine the integer equivalents of the following: **A B C a b c 0 1 2 $ * + /** and the blank character.

1.36   Write a program that inputs a five-digit number, separates the number into its individual digits and prints the digits separated from one another by three spaces each. (Hint: Use the integer division and modulus operators.) For example, if the user types in **42339** the program should print:

```
4    2    3    3    9
```

1.37   Using only the techniques you learned in this chapter, write a program that calculates the squares and cubes of the numbers from 0 to 10 and uses tabs to print the following table of values:

```
number  square  cube
0       0       0
1       1       1
2       4       8
3       9       27
4       16      64
5       25      125
6       36      216
7       49      343
8       64      512
9       81      729
10      100     1000
```

1.38   Give a brief answer to each of the following "object think" questions:
   a) Why does this text choose to discuss structured programming in detail before proceeding with an in-depth treatment of object-oriented programming?
   b) What are the typical steps (mentioned in the text) of an object-oriented design process?
   c) How is multiple inheritance exhibited by human beings?
   d) What kinds of messages do people send to one another?
   e) Objects send messages to one another across well-defined interfaces. What interfaces does a car radio (object) present to its user (a person object)?

1.39   You are probably wearing on your wrist one of the world's most common types of objects—a watch. Discuss how each of the following terms and concepts applies to the notion of a watch: object, attributes, behaviors, class, inheritance (consider, for example, an alarm clock), abstraction, modeling, messages, encapsulation, interface, information hiding, data members and member functions.

2

Control
Structures

Objectives

- To understand basic problem solving techniques.
- To be able to develop algorithms through the process of top-down, stepwise refinement.
- To be able to use the **if**, **if/else** and **switch** selection structures to choose among alternative actions.
- To be able to use the **while**, **do/while** and **for** repetition structures to execute statements in a program repeatedly.
- To understand counter-controlled repetition and sentinel-controlled repetition.
- To be able to use the increment, decrement, assignment and logical operators.
- To be able to use the **break** and **continue** program control statements.

Let's all move one place on.
Lewis Carroll

The wheel is come full circle.
William Shakespeare, King Lear

Who can control his fate?
William Shakespeare, Othello

The used key is always bright.
Benjamin Franklin

Outline

2.1 Introduction

Before writing a program to solve a particular problem, it is essential to have a thorough understanding of the problem and a carefully planned approach to solving the problem. When writing a program, it is equally essential to understand the types of building blocks that are available and to employ proven program-construction principles. In this chapter, we discuss all of these issues in our presentation of the theory and principles of structured programming. The techniques that you will learn here are applicable to most high-level languages, including C++. When we begin our treatment of object-oriented programming in C++ in Chapter 6, we will see that the control structures we study here in Chapter 2 are helpful in building and manipulating objects.

2.2 Algorithms

Any computing problem can be solved by executing a series of actions in a specific order. A *procedure* for solving a problem in terms of

1. the *actions* to be executed and

2. the *order* in which these actions are to be executed

is called an *algorithm*. The following example demonstrates that correctly specifying the order in which the actions are to be executed is important.

Consider the "rise-and-shine algorithm" followed by one junior executive for getting out of bed and going to work: (1) Get out of bed, (2) take off pajamas, (3) take a shower, (4) get dressed, (5) eat breakfast, (6) carpool to work.

This routine gets the executive to work well prepared to make critical decisions. Suppose that the same steps are performed in a slightly different order: (1) Get out of bed, (2) take off pajamas, (3) get dressed, (4) take a shower, (5) eat breakfast, (6) carpool to work.

In this case, our junior executive shows up for work soaking wet. Specifying the order in which statements are to be executed in a computer program is called *program control*. In this chapter, we investigate the program-control capabilities of C++.

2.3 Pseudocode

Pseudocode is an artificial and informal language that helps programmers develop algorithms. The pseudocode we present here is useful for developing algorithms that will be converted to structured C++ programs. Pseudocode is similar to everyday English; it is convenient and user-friendly although it is not an actual computer programming language.

Pseudocode programs are not actually executed on computers. Rather, they help the programmer "think out" a program before attempting to write it in a programming language such as C++. In this chapter, we give several examples of how pseudocode can be used effectively in developing structured C++ programs.

The style of pseudocode we present consists purely of characters, so programmers can conveniently type pseudocode programs using an editor program. The computer can display a fresh copy of a pseudocode program on demand. A carefully prepared pseudocode program can be converted easily to a corresponding C++ program. This is done in many cases simply by replacing pseudocode statements with their C++ equivalents.

Pseudocode consists only of executable statements—those that are executed when the program has been converted from pseudocode to C++ and is run. Declarations are not executable statements. For example, the declaration

```
int i;
```

simply tells the compiler the type of variable **i** and instructs the compiler to reserve space in memory for the variable, but this declaration does not cause any action—such as input, output, or a calculation—to occur when the program is executed. Some programmers choose to list variables and briefly mention the purpose of each at the beginning of a pseudocode program.

2.4 Control Structures

Normally, statements in a program are executed one after the other in the order in which they are written. This is called *sequential execution*. Various C++ statements we will soon discuss enable the programmer to specify that the next statement to be executed may be other than the next one in sequence. This is called *transfer of control*.

During the 1960s, it became clear that the indiscriminate use of transfers of control was the root of much difficulty experienced by software-development groups. The finger of blame was pointed at the **goto** *statement* that allows the programmer to specify a transfer of control to one of a very wide range of possible destinations in a program. The notion of so-called *structured programming* became almost synonymous with "*goto elimination*."

The research of Bohm and Jacopini[1] had demonstrated that programs could be written without any **goto** statements. The challenge of the era became for programmers to shift their styles to "**goto**-less programming." It was not until the 1970s that programmers started taking structured programming seriously. The results have been impressive as software development groups have reported reduced development times, more frequent on-time delivery of systems and more frequent within-budget completion of software projects. The key to these successes is that structured programs are clearer, easier to debug and modify and more likely to be bug-free in the first place.

Bohm and Jacopini's work demonstrated that all programs could be written in terms of only three *control structures*, namely the *sequence structure*, the *selection structure* and the *repetition structure*. The sequence structure is built into C++. Unless directed otherwise, the computer executes C++ statements one after the other in the order in which they are written. The *flowchart* segment of Fig. 2.1 illustrates a typical sequence structure in which two calculations are performed in order.

A flowchart is a graphical representation of an algorithm or of a portion of an algorithm. Flowcharts are drawn using certain special-purpose symbols, such as rectangles, diamonds, ovals and small circles; these symbols are connected by arrows called *flowlines*.

Like pseudocode, flowcharts are useful for developing and representing algorithms, although pseudocode is strongly preferred by most programmers. Flowcharts clearly show how control structures operate; that is all we use them for in this text.

Consider the flowchart segment for the sequence structure in Fig. 2.1. We use the *rectangle symbol*, also called the *action symbol,* to indicate any type of action, including a calculation or an input/output operation. The flowlines in the figure indicate the order in which the actions are to be performed—first, **grade** is to be added to **total**, then **1** is to be added to **counter**. C++ allows us to have as many actions as we want in a sequence structure. As we will soon see, anywhere a single action may be placed, we can place several actions in sequence.

When drawing a flowchart that represents a *complete* algorithm, an *oval symbol* containing the word "Begin" is the first symbol used in the flowchart; an oval symbol containing the word "End" is the last symbol used. When drawing only a portion of an algorithm, as in Fig. 2.1, the oval symbols are omitted in favor of using *small circle symbols* also called *connector symbols*.

---

1. Bohm, C. and G. Jacopini, "Flow Diagrams, Turing Machines, and Languages with Only Two Formation Rules," *Communications of the ACM*, Vol. 9, No. 5, May 1966, pp. 336–371.

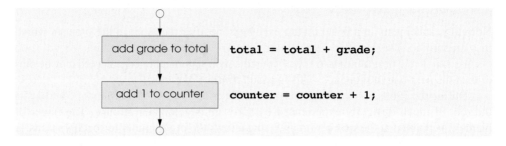

Fig. 2.1   Flowcharting C++'s sequence structure.

Perhaps the most important flowcharting symbol is the *diamond symbol*, also called the *decision symbol,* that indicates a decision is to be made. We will discuss the diamond symbol in the next section.

C++ provides three types of selection structures. The **if** selection structure either performs (selects) an action if a condition (predicate) is **true** or skips the action if the condition is **false**. The **if/else** selection structure performs an action if a condition is **true** and performs a different action if the condition is **false**. The **switch** selection structure performs one of many different actions depending on the value of an integer expression.

The **if** selection structure is a *single-selection structure*—it selects or ignores a single action. The **if/else** selection structure is a *double-selection structure*—it selects between two different actions. The **switch** selection structure is a *multiple-selection structure*—it selects the action to perform from many different actions.

C++ provides three types of repetition structures, namely **while**, **do/while** and **for**. Each of the words **if**, **else**, **switch**, **while**, **do** and **for** is a C++ *keyword*. These words are reserved by the language to implement various features such as C++'s control structures. Keywords must not be used as identifiers, such as for variable names. A complete list of C++ keywords is shown in Fig. 2.2.

Common Programming Error 2.1

Using a keyword as an identifier is a syntax error.

Well, that is all there is. C++ has only seven control structures: sequence, three types of selection and three types of repetition. Each C++ program is formed by combining as many of each type of control structure as is appropriate for the algorithm the program implements. As with the sequence structure of Fig. 2.1, we will see that each control structure is flowcharted with two small circle symbols, one at the entry point to the control structure and one at the exit point. These *single-entry/single-exit control structures* make it easy to build programs—the control structures are attached to one another by connecting the exit point of one control structure to the entry point of the next. This is similar to the way a child stacks building blocks, so we call this *control-structure stacking*. We will learn that there is only one other way to connect control structures—called *control-structure nesting*.

Software Engineering Observation 2.1

Any C++ program we will ever build can be constructed from only seven different types of control structures (sequence, **if**, **if/else**, **switch**, **while**, **do/while** *and* **for***) combined in only two ways (control-structure stacking and control-structure nesting).*

C++ Keywords

Keywords common to the C and C++ programming languages

auto	break	case	char	const
continue	default	do	double	else
enum	extern	float	for	goto
if	int	long	register	return
short	signed	sizeof	static	struct
switch	typedef	union	unsigned	void
volatile	while			

C++ only keywords

asm	bool	catch	class	const_cast
delete	dynamic_cast	explicit	false	friend
inline	mutable	namespace	new	operator
private	protected	public	reinterpret_cast	
static_cast	template	this	throw	true
try	typeid	typename	using	virtual
wchar_t				

Fig. 2.2   C++ keywords.

2.5 The `if` Selection Structure

A selection structure is used to choose among alternative courses of action. For example, suppose the passing grade on an exam is 60. The pseudocode statement

> *If student's grade is greater than or equal to 60*
> *Print "Passed"*

determines if the condition "student's grade is greater than or equal to 60" is **true** or **false**. If the condition is **true**, then "Passed" is printed and the next pseudocode statement in order is "performed" (remember that pseudocode is not a real programming language). If the condition is **false**, the print statement is ignored and the next pseudocode statement in order is performed. Note that the second line of this selection structure is indented. Such indentation is optional, but it is highly recommended because it emphasizes the inherent structure of structured programs. When you convert your pseudocode into C++ code, the C++ compiler ignores *whitespace characters* like blanks, tabs and newlines used for indentation and vertical spacing.

Good Programming Practice 2.1

Consistently applying reasonable indentation conventions throughout your programs greatly improves program readability. We suggest a fixed-size tab of about 1/4 inch or three blanks per indent.

The preceding pseudocode *If* statement can be written in C++ as

```
if ( grade >= 60 )
    cout << "Passed";
```

Notice that the C++ code corresponds closely to the pseudocode. This is one of the properties of pseudocode that makes it such a useful program development tool.

Good Programming Practice 2.2

Pseudocode is often used to "think out" a program during the program-design process. Then the pseudocode program is converted to C++.

The flowchart of Fig. 2.3 illustrates the single-selection **if** structure. This flowchart contains what is perhaps the most important flowcharting symbol—the *diamond symbol*, also called the *decision symbol*, which indicates that a decision is to be made. The decision symbol contains an expression, such as a condition, that can be either **true** or **false**. The decision symbol has two flowlines emerging from it. One indicates the direction to be taken when the expression in the symbol is **true**; the other indicates the direction to be taken when the expression is **false**. We learned in Chapter 1 that decisions can be based on conditions containing relational or equality operators. Actually, a decision can be based on any expression—if the expression evaluates to zero, it is treated as **false** and if the expression evaluates to nonzero, it is treated as **true**. The C++ standard provides the data type **bool** to represent **true** and **false**. The keywords **true** and **false** are used to represent values of type **bool**.

Note that the **if** structure, too, is a single-entry/single-exit structure. We will soon learn that the flowcharts for the remaining control structures also contain (besides small circle symbols and flowlines) only rectangle symbols to indicate the actions to be performed and diamond symbols to indicate decisions to be made. This is the *action/decision model of programming* we have been emphasizing.

We can envision seven bins, each containing only control structures of one of the seven types. These control structures are empty. Nothing is written in the rectangles or in the diamonds. The programmer's task, then, is assembling a program from as many of each type of control structure as the algorithm demands, combining those control structures in only two possible ways (stacking or nesting), then filling in the actions and decisions in a manner appropriate for the algorithm. We will discuss the variety of ways in which actions and decisions may be written.

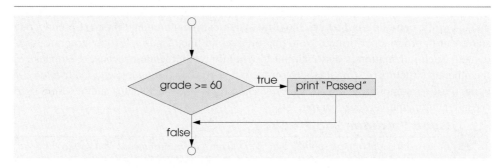

Fig. 2.3   Flowcharting the single-selection **if** structure.

2.6 The `if/else` Selection Structure

The **if** selection structure performs an indicated action only when the condition is **true**; otherwise the action is skipped. The **if/else** selection structure allows the programmer to specify that a different action is to be performed when the condition is **true** than when the condition is **false**. For example, the pseudocode statement

> *If student's grade is greater than or equal to 60*
> *Print "Passed"*
> *else*
> *Print "Failed"*

prints *Passed* if the student's grade is greater than or equal to 60 and prints *Failed* if the student's grade is less than 60. In either case, after printing occurs, the next pseudocode statement in sequence is "performed." Note that the body of the *else* is also indented.

Good Programming Practice 2.3

Indent both body statements of an **if/else** *structure.*

Whatever indentation convention you choose should be applied carefully throughout your programs. It is difficult to read programs that do not obey uniform spacing conventions.

Good Programming Practice 2.4

If there are several levels of indentation, each level should be indented the same additional amount of space.

The preceding pseudocode *If/else* structure can be written in C++ as

```
if ( grade >= 60 )
    cout << "Passed";
else
    cout << "Failed";
```

The flowchart of Fig. 2.4 nicely illustrates the flow of control in the **if/else** structure. Once again, note that (besides small circles and arrows) the only symbols in the flowchart are rectangles (for actions) and a diamond (for a decision). We continue to emphasize this action/decision model of computing. Imagine again a deep bin containing as many empty double-selection structures as might be needed to build any C++ program. The programmer's job is to assemble these selection structures (by stacking and nesting) with any other control structures required by the algorithm, and to fill in the empty rectangles and empty diamonds with actions and decisions appropriate to the algorithm being implemented.

C++ provides the *conditional operator (?:)* that is closely related to the **if/else** structure. The conditional operator is C++'s only *ternary operator*—it takes three operands. The operands, together with the conditional operator, form a *conditional expression*. The first operand is a condition, the second operand is the value for the entire conditional expression if the condition is **true** and the third operand is the value for the entire conditional expression if the condition is **false**. For example, the output statement

```
cout << ( grade >= 60 ? "Passed" : "Failed" );
```

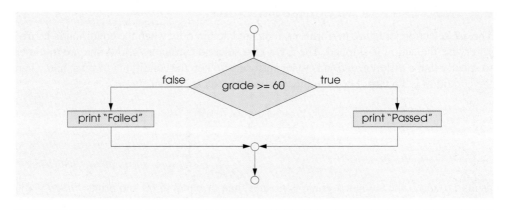

Fig. 2.4   Flowcharting the double-selection **if/else** structure.

contains a conditional expression that evaluates to the string **"Passed"** if the condition **grade >= 60** is **true** and evaluates to the string **"Failed"** if the condition is **false**. Thus, the statement with the conditional operator performs essentially the same as the preceding **if/else** statement. As we will see, the precedence of the conditional operator is low, so the parentheses in the preceding expression are required.

The values in a conditional expression can also be actions to execute. For example, the conditional expression

```
grade >= 60 ? cout << "Passed" : cout << "Failed";
```

is read, "If **grade** is greater than or equal to **60**, then **cout << "Passed"**; otherwise **cout << "Failed"**." This, too, is comparable to the preceding **if/else** structure. We will see that conditional operators can be used in some situations where **if/else** statements cannot.

Nested **if/else** *structures* test for multiple cases by placing **if/else** selection structures inside **if/else** selection structures. For example, the following pseudocode statement will print **A** for exam grades greater than or equal to 90, **B** for grades in the range 80 to 89, **C** for grades in the range 70 to 79, **D** for grades in the range 60 to 69 and **F** for all other grades.

> *If student's grade is greater than or equal to 90*
>> *Print "A"*
> *else*
>> *If student's grade is greater than or equal to 80*
>>> *Print "B"*
>> *else*
>>> *If student's grade is greater than or equal to 70*
>>>> *Print "C"*
>>> *else*
>>>> *If student's grade is greater than or equal to 60*
>>>>> *Print "D"*
>>>> *else*
>>>>> *Print "F"*

This pseudocode can be written in C++ as

```
if ( grade >= 90 )
   cout << "A";
else
   if ( grade >= 80 )
      cout << "B";
   else
      if ( grade >= 70 )
         cout << "C";
      else
         if ( grade >= 60 )
            cout << "D";
         else
            cout << "F";
```

If **grade** is greater than or equal to 90, the first four conditions will be **true**, but only the **cout** statement after the first test will be executed. After that **cout** is executed, the **else**-part of the "outer" **if/else** statement is skipped. Many C++ programmers prefer to write the preceding **if** structure as

```
if ( grade >= 90 )
   cout << "A";
else if ( grade >= 80 )
   cout << "B";
else if ( grade >= 70 )
   cout << "C";
else if ( grade >= 60 )
   cout << "D";
else
   cout << "F";
```

The two forms are equivalent. The latter form is popular because it avoids the deep indentation of the code to the right. Such indentation often leaves little room on a line, forcing lines to be split and decreasing program readability.

Performance Tip 2.1

*A nested **if/else** structure can be much faster than a series of single selection **if** structures because of the possibility of early exit after one of the conditions is satisfied.*

Performance Tip 2.2

*In a nested **if/else** structure, test the conditions that are more likely to be **true** at the beginning of the nested **if/else** structure. This will enable the nested **if/else** structure to run faster and exit earlier than will testing infrequently occurring cases first.*

The **if** selection structure expects only one statement in its body. To include several statements in the body of an **if**, enclose the statements in braces (**{** and **}**). A set of statements contained within a pair of braces is called a *compound statement*.

Software Engineering Observation 2.2

A compound statement can be placed anywhere in a program that a single statement can be placed.

The following example includes a compound statement in the **else** part of an **if/else** structure.

```
if ( grade >= 60 )
   cout << "Passed.\n";
else {
   cout << "Failed.\n";
   cout << "You must take this course again.\n";
}
```

In this case, if **grade** is less than 60, the program executes both statements in the body of the **else** and prints

```
Failed.
You must take this course again.
```

Notice the braces surrounding the two statements in the **else** clause. These braces are important. Without the braces, the statement

```
cout << "You must take this course again.\n";
```

would be outside the body of the **else**-part of the **if** and would execute regardless of whether the grade is less than 60.

Common Programming Error 2.2

Forgetting one or both of the braces that delimit a compound statement can lead to syntax errors or logic errors in a program.

Good Programming Practice 2.5

*Always putting the braces in an **if/else** structure (or any control structure) helps prevent their accidental omission, especially when adding statements to an **if** or **else** clause at a later time.*

A syntax error is caught by the compiler. A *logic error* has its effect at execution time. A *fatal logic error* causes a program to fail and terminate prematurely. A *nonfatal logic error* allows a program to continue executing, but might produce incorrect results.

Software Engineering Observation 2.3

*Just as a compound statement can be placed anywhere a single statement can be placed, it is also possible to have no statement at all, i.e., the empty statement. The empty statement is represented by placing a semicolon (**;**) where a statement would normally be.*

Common Programming Error 2.3

*Placing a semicolon after the condition in an **if** structure leads to a logic error in single-selection **if** structures and a syntax error in double-selection **if** structures (if the **if**-part contains an actual body statement).*

Good Programming Practice 2.6

Some programmers prefer to type the beginning and ending braces of compound statements before typing the individual statements within the braces. This helps avoid omitting one or both of the braces.

In this section, we introduced the notion of a compound statement. A compound statement can contain declarations (as does the body of **main**, for example). If so, the compound statement is called a *block*. The declarations in a block are commonly placed first in the block before any action statements, but declarations can be intermixed with action statements. We will discuss the use of blocks in Chapter 3. The reader should avoid using blocks (other than as the body of **main**, of course) until that time.

2.7 The `while` Repetition Structure

A *repetition structure* allows the programmer to specify that an action is to be repeated while some condition remains true. The pseudocode statement

> *While there are more items on my shopping list*
> *Purchase next item and cross it off my list*

describes the repetition that occurs during a shopping trip. The condition, "there are more items on my shopping list" is either true or false. If it is true, then the action, "Purchase next item and cross it off my list" is performed. This action will be performed repeatedly while the condition remains **true**. The statement(s) contained in the *while* repetition structure constitute the body of the *while*. The *while* structure body can be a single statement or a compound statement. Eventually, the condition will become **false** (when the last item on the shopping list has been purchased and crossed off the list). At this point, the repetition terminates and the first pseudocode statement after the repetition structure is executed.

Common Programming Error 2.4

*Not providing, in the body of a **while** structure, an action that eventually causes the condition in the **while** to become **false** normally results in an error called an "infinite loop" in which the repetition structure never terminates.*

Common Programming Error 2.5

*Spelling the keyword **while** with an uppercase **W**, as in **While** (remember that C++ is a case-sensitive language), is a syntax error. All of C++'s reserved keywords such as **while**, **if** and **else** contain only lowercase letters.*

As an example of an actual **while**, consider a program segment designed to find the first power of 2 larger than 1000. Suppose the integer variable **product** has been initialized to 2. When the following **while** repetition structure finishes executing, **product** will contain the desired answer:

```
int product = 2;

while ( product <= 1000 )
   product = 2 * product;
```

The flowchart of Fig. 2.5 illustrates the flow of control in the **while** structure that corresponds to the preceding **while** structure. Once again, note that (besides small circles and arrows) the flowchart contains only a rectangle symbol and a diamond symbol. Imagine a deep bin of empty **while** structures that can be stacked and nested with other control structures to form a structured implementation of an algorithm's flow of control. The empty rectangles and diamonds are then filled in with appropriate actions and decisions. The flowchart clearly shows the repetition. The flowline emerging from the rectangle wraps back to the decision that is tested each time through the loop until the decision becomes **false**. Then, the **while** structure exits and control passes to the next statement in the program.

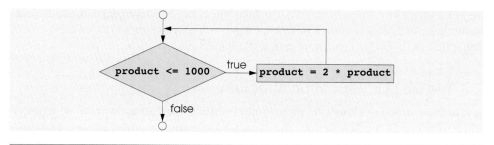

Fig. 2.5   Flowcharting the **while** repetition structure.

When the **while** structure is entered, the value of **product** is 2. The variable **product** is repeatedly multiplied by 2, taking on the values 4, 8, 16, 32, 64, 128, 256, 512 and 1024 successively. When **product** becomes 1024, the **while** structure condition, **product <= 1000**, becomes **false**. This terminates the repetition—the final value of **product** is 1024. Program execution continues with the next statement after the **while**.

2.8 Formulating Algorithms: Case Study 1 (Counter-Controlled Repetition)

To illustrate how algorithms are developed, we solve several variations of a class-averaging problem. Consider the following problem statement:

> *A class of ten students took a quiz. The grades (integers in the range 0 to 100) for this quiz are available to you. Determine the class average on the quiz.*

The class average is equal to the sum of the grades divided by the number of students. The algorithm for solving this problem on a computer must input each of the grades, perform the averaging calculation and print the result.

Let us use pseudocode to list the actions to be executed and specify the order in which these actions should be executed. We use *counter-controlled repetition* to input the grades one at a time. This technique uses a variable called a *counter* to control the number of times a set of statements will execute. In this example, repetition terminates when the counter exceeds 10. In this section, we present a pseudocode algorithm (Fig. 2.6) and the corresponding program (Fig. 2.7). In the next section, we show how pseudocode algorithms are developed. Counter-controlled repetition is often called *definite repetition* because the number of repetitions is known before the loop begins executing.

Note the references in the algorithm to a total and a counter. A *total* is a variable used to accumulate the sum of a series of values. A counter is a variable used to count—in this case, to count the number of grades entered. Variables used to store totals should normally be initialized to zero before being used in a program; otherwise, the sum would include the previous value stored in the total's memory location.

Lines 11 through 14

```
int total,        // sum of grades
    gradeCounter, // number of grades entered
    grade,        // one grade
    average;      // average of grades
```

declare variables **total**, **gradeCounter**, **grade** and **average** to be of type **int**. Variable **grade** will store the value the user inputs into the program.

Set total to zero
Set grade counter to one

While grade counter is less than or equal to ten
    Input the next grade
    Add the grade into the total
    Add one to the grade counter

Set the class average to the total divided by ten
Print the class average

Fig. 2.6   Pseudocode algorithm that uses counter-controlled repetition to solve
            the class average problem.

```
1   // Fig. 2.7: fig02_07.cpp
2   // Class average program with counter-controlled repetition
3   #include <iostream>
4
5   using std::cout;
6   using std::cin;
7   using std::endl;
8
9   int main()
10  {
11     int total,          // sum of grades
12         gradeCounter,   // number of grades entered
13         grade,          // one grade
14         average;        // average of grades
15
16     // initialization phase
17     total = 0;                        // clear total
18     gradeCounter = 1;                 // prepare to loop
19
20     // processing phase
21     while ( gradeCounter <= 10 ) {    // loop 10 times
22        cout << "Enter grade: ";       // prompt for input
23        cin >> grade;                  // input grade
24        total = total + grade;         // add grade to total
25        gradeCounter = gradeCounter + 1;  // increment counter
26     }
27
28     // termination phase
29     average = total / 10;             // integer division
30     cout << "Class average is " << average << endl;
31
32     return 0;     // indicate program ended successfully
33  }
```

Fig. 2.7   C++ program and sample execution for the class average problem with
            counter-controlled repetition (part 1 of 2).

```
Enter grade: 98
Enter grade: 76
Enter grade: 71
Enter grade: 87
Enter grade: 83
Enter grade: 90
Enter grade: 57
Enter grade: 79
Enter grade: 82
Enter grade: 94
Class average is 81
```

Fig. 2.7   C++ program and sample execution for the class average problem with counter-controlled repetition (part 2 of 2).

Notice that the preceding declarations appear in the body of function **main**. Remember that variables declared in a function definition's body are *local variables* and can be used only from the line of their declaration in the function to the closing right brace (**}**) of the function definition. The declaration of a local variable in a function must appear before the variable is used in that function.

Lines 17 and 18

```
total = 0;                    // clear total
gradeCounter = 1;             // prepare to loop
```

are assignment statements that initialize **total** to **0** and **gradeCounter** to **1**.

Note that variables **total** and **gradeCounter** are initialized before they are used in a calculation. Counter variables are normally initialized to zero or one, depending on their use (we will present examples showing each of these uses). An uninitialized variable contains a *"garbage" value* (also called an *undefined value*)—the value last stored in the memory location reserved for that variable.

Common Programming Error 2.6

If a counter or total is not initialized, the results of your program will probably be incorrect. This is an example of a logic error.

Good Programming Practice 2.7

Initialize counters and totals.

Good Programming Practice 2.8

Declare each variable on a separate line.

Line 21

```
while ( gradeCounter <= 10 ) {        // loop 10 times
```

indicates that the **while** structure should continue as long as **gradeCounter**'s value is less than or equal to 10.

Lines 22 and 23

```
cout << "Enter grade: ";        // prompt for input
cin >> grade;                   // input grade
```

correspond to the pseudocode statement *"Input the next grade."* The first statement displays the prompt "**Enter grade:**" on the screen. The second statement inputs the grade value from the user.

Next, the program updates **total** with the new **grade** entered by the user. Line 24

```
total = total + grade;          // add grade to total
```

adds **grade** to the previous value of **total** and assigns the result to **total**.

The program is now ready to increment the variable **gradeCounter** to indicate that a grade has been processed, then read the next grade from the user. Line 25

```
gradeCounter = gradeCounter + 1;  // increment counter
```

adds **1** to **gradeCounter**, so the condition in the **while** structure will eventually become **false** and terminate the loop.

Line 29

```
average = total / 10;           // integer division
```

assigns the results of the average calculation to variable **average**. Line 30

```
cout << "Class average is " << average << endl;
```

displays the string "**Class average is** " followed by the value of variable **average**.

Note that the averaging calculation in the program produced an integer result. Actually, the sum of the grades in this example is 817, which, when divided by 10, should yield 81.7, i.e., a number with a decimal point. We will see how to deal with such numbers (called floating-point numbers) in the next section.

 Common Programming Error 2.7

In a counter-controlled loop, because the loop counter (when counting up by one each time through the loop) is one higher than its last legitimate value (i.e., 11 in the case of counting from 1 to 10), using the counter value in a calculation after the loop is often an off-by-one-error.

In Fig. 2.7, if line 29 used **gradeCounter** rather than 10 for the calculation, the output for this program would display an incorrect value of 74.

2.9 Formulating Algorithms with Top-Down, Stepwise Refinement: Case Study 2 (Sentinel-Controlled Repetition)

Let us generalize the class-average problem. Consider the following problem:

> *Develop a class-averaging program that will process an arbitrary number of grades each time the program is run.*

In the first class-average example, the number of grades (10) was known in advance. In this example, no indication is given of how many grades are to be entered. The program must process an arbitrary number of grades. How can the program determine when to stop the input of grades? How will it know when to calculate and print the class average?

One way to solve this problem is to use a special value called a *sentinel value* (also called a *signal value*, a *dummy value* or a *flag value*) to indicate "end of data entry." The user types grades in until all legitimate grades have been entered. The user then types the sentinel value to indicate that the last grade has been entered. Sentinel-controlled repetition is often called *indefinite repetition* because the number of repetitions is not known before the loop begins executing.

Clearly, the sentinel value must be chosen so that it cannot be confused with an acceptable input value. Because grades on a quiz are normally nonnegative integers, –1 is an acceptable sentinel value for this problem. Thus, a run of the class-average program might process a stream of inputs such as 95, 96, 75, 74, 89 and –1. The program would then compute and print the class average for the grades 95, 96, 75, 74 and 89 (–1 is the sentinel value, so it should not enter into the averaging calculation).

Common Programming Error 2.8

Choosing a sentinel value that is also a legitimate data value is a logic error.

We approach the class average program with a technique called *top-down, stepwise refinement*, a technique that is essential to the development of well-structured programs. We begin with a pseudocode representation of the *top:*

> *Determine the class average for the quiz*

The top is a single statement that conveys the overall function of the program. As such, the top is, in effect, a complete representation of a program. Unfortunately, the top (as in this case) rarely conveys a sufficient amount of detail from which to write the C++ program. So we now begin the refinement process. We divide the top into a series of smaller tasks and list these in the order in which they need to be performed. This results in the following *first refinement*.

> *Initialize variables*
> *Input, sum and count the quiz grades*
> *Calculate and print the class average*

Here, only the sequence structure has been used—the steps listed are to be executed in order, one after the other.

Software Engineering Observation 2.4

Each refinement, as well as the top itself, is a complete specification of the algorithm; only the level of detail varies.

Software Engineering Observation 2.5

Many programs can be divided logically into three phases: an initialization phase that initializes the program variables; a processing phase that inputs data values and adjusts program variables accordingly; and a termination phase that calculates and prints the final results.

The preceding Software Engineering Observation is often all you need for the first refinement in the top-down process. To proceed to the next level of refinement, i.e., the *second refinement*, we commit to specific variables. We need a running total of the numbers, a count of how many numbers have been processed, a variable to receive the value of each grade as it is input and a variable to hold the calculated average. The pseudocode statement

Initialize variables

can be refined as follows:

Initialize total to zero
Initialize counter to zero

Notice that only the variables *total* and *counter* need to be initialized before they are used; the variables *average* and *grade* (for the calculated average and the user input, respectively) need not be initialized, because their values will be written over as they are calculated or input.

The pseudocode statement

Input, sum and count the quiz grades

requires a repetition structure (i.e., a loop) that successively inputs each grade. Because we do not know in advance how many grades are to be processed, we will use sentinel-controlled repetition. The user will type legitimate grades in one at a time. After the last legitimate grade is typed, the user will type the sentinel value. The program will test for the sentinel value after each grade is input and will terminate the loop when the sentinel value is entered by the user. The second refinement of the preceding pseudocode statement is then

Input the first grade (possibly the sentinel)
While the user has not as yet entered the sentinel
    Add this grade into the running total
    Add one to the grade counter
    Input the next grade (possibly the sentinel)

Notice that, in pseudocode, we do not use braces around the set of statements that form the body of the *while* structure. We simply indent the statements under the *while* to show that they belong to the *while*. Again, pseudocode is only an informal program-development aid.

The pseudocode statement

Calculate and print the class average

can be refined as follows:

If the counter is not equal to zero
    Set the average to the total divided by the counter
    Print the average
else
    Print "No grades were entered"

Notice that we are being careful here to test for the possibility of division by zero—a *fatal logic error* that, if undetected, would cause the program to fail (often called *"bombing"* or *"crashing"*). The complete second refinement of the pseudocode for the class average problem is shown in Fig. 2.8.

Common Programming Error 2.9

An attempt to divide by zero causes a fatal error.

Initialize total to zero
Initialize counter to zero

Input the first grade (possibly the sentinel)
While the user has not as yet entered the sentinel
    Add this grade into the running total
    Add one to the grade counter
    Input the next grade (possibly the sentinel)

If the counter is not equal to zero
    Set the average to the total divided by the counter
    Print the average
else
    Print "No grades were entered"

Fig. 2.8   Pseudocode algorithm that uses sentinel-controlled repetition to solve the class-average problem.

Good Programming Practice 2.9

When performing division by an expression whose value could be zero, explicitly test for this case and handle it appropriately in your program (such as by printing an error message) rather than allowing the fatal error to occur.

In Fig. 2.6 and Fig. 2.8, we include some completely blank lines in the pseudocode to make the pseudocode more readable. The blank lines separate these programs into their various phases.

The pseudocode algorithm in Fig. 2.8 solves the more general class-averaging problem. This algorithm was developed after only two levels of refinement. Sometimes more levels are necessary.

Software Engineering Observation 2.6

The programmer terminates the top-down, stepwise refinement process when the pseudocode algorithm is specified in sufficient detail for the programmer to be able to convert the pseudocode to C++. Implementing the C++ program is then normally straightforward.

The C++ program and a sample execution are shown in Fig. 2.9. Although only integer grades are entered, the averaging calculation is likely to produce a number with a decimal point, i.e., a real number. The type **int** cannot represent real numbers. The program introduces the data type **double** to handle numbers with decimal points (also called *floating-point numbers*) and introduces a special operator called a *cast operator* to force the averaging calculation to produce a floating-point numeric result. These features are explained in detail after the program is presented.

In this example, we see that control structures can be stacked on top of one another (in sequence) just as a child stacks building blocks. The **while** structure (lines 30 through 35) is immediately followed by an **if/else** structure (lines 38 through 45) in sequence. Much of the code in this program is identical to the code in Fig. 2.7, so we concentrate in this example on the new features and issues.

Line 20 declares **double** variable **average**. This change allows us to store the class-average calculation's result as a floating-point number. Line 24 initializes the variable **gradeCounter** to **0**, because no grades have been entered yet. Remember that this program uses sentinel-controlled repetition. To keep an accurate record of the number of grades entered, variable **gradeCounter** is incremented only when a valid grade value is entered.

Notice that both input statements (lines 28 and 34)

```
cin >> grade;
```

are preceded by an output statement that prompts the user for input.

```
1   // Fig. 2.9: fig02_09.cpp
2   // Class average program with sentinel-controlled repetition.
3   #include <iostream>
4
5   using std::cout;
6   using std::cin;
7   using std::endl;
8   using std::ios;
9
10  #include <iomanip>
11
12  using std::setprecision;
13  using std::setiosflags;
14
15  int main()
16  {
17     int total,          // sum of grades
18         gradeCounter,   // number of grades entered
19         grade;          // one grade
20     double average;     // number with decimal point for average
21
22     // initialization phase
23     total = 0;
24     gradeCounter = 0;
25
26     // processing phase
27     cout << "Enter grade, -1 to end: ";
28     cin >> grade;
29
30     while ( grade != -1 ) {
31        total = total + grade;
32        gradeCounter = gradeCounter + 1;
33        cout << "Enter grade, -1 to end: ";
34        cin >> grade;
35     }
36
```

Fig. 2.9 C++ program and sample execution for the class-average problem with sentinel-controlled repetition (part 1 of 2).

```
37        // termination phase
38        if ( gradeCounter != 0 ) {
39            average = static_cast< double >( total ) / gradeCounter;
40            cout << "Class average is " << setprecision( 2 )
41                 << setiosflags( ios::fixed | ios::showpoint )
42                 << average << endl;
43        }
44        else
45            cout << "No grades were entered" << endl;
46
47        return 0;    // indicate program ended successfully
48    }
```

```
Enter grade, -1 to end: 75
Enter grade, -1 to end: 94
Enter grade, -1 to end: 97
Enter grade, -1 to end: 88
Enter grade, -1 to end: 70
Enter grade, -1 to end: 64
Enter grade, -1 to end: 83
Enter grade, -1 to end: 89
Enter grade, -1 to end: -1
Class average is 82.50
```

Fig. 2.9   C++ program and sample execution for the class-average problem with sentinel-controlled repetition (part 2 of 2).

Good Programming Practice 2.10

Prompt the user for each keyboard input. The prompt should indicate the form of the input and any special input values (such as the sentinel value the user should enter to terminate a loop).

Good Programming Practice 2.11

In a sentinel-controlled loop, the prompts requesting data entry should explicitly remind the user what the sentinel value is.

Study the difference between the program logic for sentinel-controlled repetition compared with that for the counter-controlled repetition in Fig. 2.7. In counter-controlled repetition, we read a value from the user during each pass of the **while** structure for the specified number of passes. In sentinel-controlled repetition, we read one value (line 28) before the program reaches the **while** structure. This value is used to determine if the program's flow of control should enter the body of the **while** structure. If the **while** structure condition is **false** (i.e., the user has already typed the sentinel), the body of the **while** structure does not execute (no grades were entered). If, on the other hand, the condition is **true**, the body begins execution and the value entered by the user is processed (added to the **total** in this example). After the value is processed, the next value is input from the user before the end of the **while** structure's body. As the closing right brace (**}**) of the body is reached at line 35, execution continues with the next test of the **while** structure condition, using the new value just entered by the user to determine if the **while** structure's body should execute again. Notice that the next value is always input from the user immediately before the **while** structure condition is evaluated. This allows us to determine if the value just entered by the user is the sentinel value *before* that value is processed (i.e., added to the **total**). If the value entered is the sentinel value, the **while** structure terminates and the value is not added to the **total**

Notice the compound statement in the **while** loop in Fig 2.9. Without the braces, the last three statements in the body of the loop would fall outside the loop, causing the computer to interpret this code incorrectly, as follows:

```
while ( grade != -1 )
    total = total + grade;
gradeCounter = gradeCounter + 1;
cout << "Enter grade, -1 to end: ";
cin >> grade;
```

This would cause an infinite loop if the user does not input –1 for the first grade.

Averages do not always evaluate to integer values. Often, an average is a value that contains a fractional part, such as 7.2 or –93.5. These values are referred to as floating-point numbers and are represented in C++ by the data types **float** and **double**. A variable of type **double** can store a value of much greater magnitude or with greater precision than **float**. For this reason, we tend to use type **double** rather than type **float** to represent floating-point values in our programs. Constants (like **1000.0** and **.05**) are treated as type **double** by C++.

The variable **average** is declared to be of type **double** to capture the fractional result of our calculation. However, the result of the calculation **total / counter** is an integer, because **total** and **counter** are both integer variables. Dividing two integers results in *integer division*, in which any fractional part of the calculation is lost (i.e., *truncated*). Because the calculation is performed first, the fractional part is lost before the result is assigned to **average**. To produce a floating-point calculation with integer values, we must create temporary values that are floating-point numbers for the calculation. C++ provides the *unary cast operator* to accomplish this task. The statement

```
average = static_cast< double >( total ) / gradeCounter;
```

includes the cast operator **static_cast< double >( )**, which creates a temporary floating-point copy of its operand in parentheses—**total**. Using a cast operator in this manner is called *explicit conversion*. The value stored in **total** is still an integer. The calculation now consists of a floating-point value (the temporary **double** version of **total**) divided by the integer **counter**.

The C++ compiler knows how to evaluate only expressions in which the data types of the operands are identical. To ensure that the operands are of the same type, the compiler performs an operation called *promotion* (also called *implicit conversion*) on selected operands. For example, in an expression containing the data types **int** and **double**, **int** operands are *promoted* to **double**. In our example, after **counter** is promoted to **double**, the calculation is performed and the result of the floating-point division is assigned to **average**. Later in this chapter, we discuss all the standard data types and their order of promotion.

Cast operators are available for any data type. The **static_cast** operator is formed by following keyword **static_cast** with angle brackets (**<** and **>**) around a data type name. The cast operator is a *unary operator*, i.e., an operator that takes only one operand. In Chapter 1, we studied the binary arithmetic operators. C++ also supports unary versions of the plus (**+**) and minus (**-**) operators, so that the programmer can write expressions like **-7** or **+5**. Cast operators have higher precedence than other unary operators such as unary **+** and unary **-**. This precedence is higher than that of the *multiplicative operators* *****, **/** and **%**, and lower than that of parentheses. We indicate the cast operator with the notation **static_cast<** *type***>()** in our precedence charts.

The formatting capabilities in Fig. 2.9 are explained in depth in Chapter 11 and discussed here briefly. The call **setprecision(2)** in the output statement

```
cout << "Class average is " << setprecision( 2 )
     << setiosflags( ios::fixed | ios::showpoint )
     << average << endl;
```

indicates that **double** variable **average** is to be printed with two digits of *precision* to the right of the decimal point (e.g., 92.37). This call is referred to as a *parameterized stream manipulator*. Programs that use these calls must contain the preprocessor directive

```
#include <iomanip>
```

Lines 11 and 12 specify the names from the **<iomanip>** header file that are used in this program. Note that **endl** is a *nonparameterized stream manipulator* and does not require the **<iomanip>** header file. If the precision is not specified, floating-point values are normally output with six digits of precision (i.e., the *default precision*), although we will see an exception to this in a moment.

The stream manipulator **setiosflags(ios::fixed | ios::showpoint)** in the preceding statement sets two output formatting options, namely **ios::fixed** and **ios::showpoint**. The vertical bar character (**|**) separates multiple options in a **setiosflags** call (we will explain the **|** notation in depth in Chapter 16). [*Note:* Although commas (,) are often used to separate a list of items, they can not be used with the stream manipulator **setiosflags**; otherwise, only the last option in the list will be set.] The option **ios::fixed** causes a floating-point value to be output in so-called *fixed-point format* (as opposed to *scientific notation*, which we will discuss in Chapter 11). The **ios::showpoint** option forces the decimal point and trailing zeros to print even if the value is a whole number amount such as 88.00. Without the **ios::showpoint** option, such a value prints in C++ as 88 without the trailing zeros and without the decimal point. When the preceding formatting is used in a program, the printed value is *rounded* to the indicated number of decimal positions, although the value in memory remains unaltered. For example, the values 87.945 and 67.543 are output as 87.95 and 67.54, respectively.

Common Programming Error 2.10

Using floating-point numbers in a manner that assumes they are represented precisely can lead to incorrect results. Floating-point numbers are represented only approximately by most computers.

Good Programming Practice 2.12

Do not compare floating-point values for equality or inequality. Rather, test that the absolute value of the difference is less than a specified small value.

Despite the fact that floating-point numbers are not always "100% precise," they have numerous applications. For example, when we speak of a "normal" body temperature of 98.6 we do not need to be precise to a large number of digits. When we view the temperature on a thermometer and read it as 98.6, it may actually be 98.5999473210643. The point here is that calling this number simply 98.6 is fine for most applications.

Another way floating-point numbers develop is through division. When we divide 10 by 3, the result is 3.3333333… with the sequence of 3s repeating infinitely. The computer allocates a fixed amount of space to hold such a value, so clearly the stored floating-point value can only be an approximation.

2.10 Formulating Algorithms with Top-Down, Stepwise Refinement: Case Study 3 (Nested Control Structures)

Let us work another complete problem. We will once again formulate the algorithm by using pseudocode and top-down, stepwise refinement and write a corresponding C++ program. We have seen that control structures can be stacked on top of one another (in sequence) just as a child stacks building blocks. In this case study, we will see the only other structured way control structures can be connected in C++, namely through *nesting* of one control structure within another.

Consider the following problem statement:

> *A college offers a course that prepares students for the state licensing exam for real estate brokers. Last year, several of the students who completed this course took the licensing examination. Naturally, the college wants to know how well its students did on the exam. You have been asked to write a program to summarize the results. You have been given a list of these 10 students. Next to each name is written a 1 if the student passed the exam and a 2 if the student failed.*
>
> *Your program should analyze the results of the exam as follows:*
>
> 1. *Input each test result (i.e., a 1 or a 2). Display the message "Enter result" on the screen each time the program requests another test result.*
> 2. *Count the number of test results of each type.*
> 3. *Display a summary of the test results indicating the number of students who passed and the number of students who failed.*
> 4. *If more than 8 students passed the exam, print the message "Raise tuition."*

After reading the problem statement carefully, we make the following observations:

1. The program must process 10 test results. A counter-controlled loop will be used.
2. Each test result is a number—either a 1 or a 2. Each time the program reads a test result, the program must determine if the number is a 1 or a 2. We test for a 1 in our algorithm. If the number is not a 1, we assume that it is a 2. (An exercise at the end of the chapter considers the consequences of this assumption.)
3. Two counters are used—one to count the number of students who passed the exam and one to count the number of students who failed the exam.
4. After the program has processed all the results, it must decide if more than 8 students passed the exam.

Let us proceed with top-down, stepwise refinement. We begin with a pseudocode representation of the top:

Analyze exam results and decide if tuition should be raised

Once again, it is important to emphasize that the top is a complete representation of the program, but several refinements are likely to be needed before the pseudocode can be naturally evolved into a C++ program. Our first refinement is

Initialize variables
Input the ten quiz grades and count passes and failures
Print a summary of the exam results and decide if tuition should be raised

Here, too, even though we have a complete representation of the entire program, further refinement is necessary. We now commit to specific variables. Counters are needed to record the passes and failures, a counter will be used to control the looping process and a variable is needed to store the user input. The pseudocode statement

Initialize variables

can be refined as follows:

Initialize passes to zero
Initialize failures to zero
Initialize student counter to one

Notice that only the counters and totals are initialized. The pseudocode statement

Input the ten quiz grades and count passes and failures

requires a loop that successively inputs the result of each exam. Here it is known in advance that there are precisely ten exam results, so counter-controlled looping is appropriate. Inside the loop (i.e., *nested* within the loop), a double-selection structure will determine whether each exam result is a pass or a failure and will increment the appropriate counter accordingly. The refinement of the preceding pseudocode statement is then

While student counter is less than or equal to ten
Input the next exam result

If the student passed
Add one to passes
else
Add one to failures

Add one to student counter

Notice the use of blank lines to set off the *If/else* control structure to improve program readability. The pseudocode statement

Print a summary of the exam results and decide if tuition should be raised

can be refined as follows:

Print the number of passes
Print the number of failures

If more than eight students passed
Print "Raise tuition"

The complete second refinement appears in Fig. 2.10. Notice that blank lines are also used to set off the *while* structure for program readability.

Initialize passes to zero
Initialize failures to zero
Initialize student counter to one

While student counter is less than or equal to ten
    Input the next exam result

    If the student passed
        Add one to passes
    else
        Add one to failures

    Add one to student counter

Print the number of passes
Print the number of failures

If more than eight students passed
    Print "Raise tuition"

Fig. 2.10   Pseudocode for examination-results problem.

This pseudocode is now sufficiently refined for conversion to C++. The C++ program and two sample executions are shown in Fig. 2.11.

```
1   // Fig. 2.11: fig02_11.cpp
2   // Analysis of examination results
3   #include <iostream>
4
5   using std::cout;
6   using std::cin;
7   using std::endl;
8
9   int main()
10  {
11     // initialize variables in declarations
12     int passes = 0,           // number of passes
13         failures = 0,         // number of failures
14         studentCounter = 1,   // student counter
15         result;               // one exam result
16
17     // process 10 students; counter-controlled loop
18     while ( studentCounter <= 10 ) {
19        cout << "Enter result (1=pass,2=fail): ";
20        cin >> result;
21
22        if ( result == 1 )          // if/else nested in while
23           passes = passes + 1;
```

Fig. 2.11   C++ program and sample executions for examination-results problem (part 1 of 2).

```
24          else
25              failures = failures + 1;
26
27          studentCounter = studentCounter + 1;
28      }
29
30      // termination phase
31      cout << "Passed " << passes << endl;
32      cout << "Failed " << failures << endl;
33
34      if ( passes > 8 )
35          cout << "Raise tuition " << endl;
36
37      return 0;    // successful termination
38  }
```

```
Enter result (1=pass,2=fail): 1
Enter result (1=pass,2=fail): 1
Enter result (1=pass,2=fail): 1
Enter result (1=pass,2=fail): 1
Enter result (1=pass,2=fail): 2
Enter result (1=pass,2=fail): 1
Enter result (1=pass,2=fail): 1
Enter result (1=pass,2=fail): 1
Enter result (1=pass,2=fail): 1
Enter result (1=pass,2=fail): 1
Passed 9
Failed 1
Raise tuition
```

```
Enter result (1=pass,2=fail): 1
Enter result (1=pass,2=fail): 2
Enter result (1=pass,2=fail): 2
Enter result (1=pass,2=fail): 1
Enter result (1=pass,2=fail): 1
Enter result (1=pass,2=fail): 1
Enter result (1=pass,2=fail): 2
Enter result (1=pass,2=fail): 1
Enter result (1=pass,2=fail): 1
Enter result (1=pass,2=fail): 2
Passed 6
Failed 4
```

Fig. 2.11   C++ program and sample executions for examination-results problem (part 2 of 2).

Lines 12 through 15

```
int passes = 0,          // number of passes
    failures = 0,        // number of failures
    studentCounter = 1,  // student counter
    result;              // one exam result
```

declare the variables used in **main** to process the examination results. Note that we have taken advantage of a feature of C++ that allows variable initialization to be incorporated into declarations (**passes** is assigned **0**, **failures** is assigned **0** and **student-Counter** is assigned **1**). Looping programs may require initialization at the beginning of each repetition; such initialization would normally occur in assignment statements.

Good Programming Practice 2.13

Initializing variables when they are declared helps the programmer avoid the problems of uninitialized data.

Software Engineering Observation 2.7

Experience has shown that the most difficult part of solving a problem on a computer is developing the algorithm for the solution. Once a correct algorithm has been specified, the process of producing a working C++ program from the algorithm is normally straightforward.

Software Engineering Observation 2.8

Many experienced programmers write programs without ever using program development tools like pseudocode. These programmers feel that their ultimate goal is to solve the problem on a computer and that writing pseudocode merely delays the production of final outputs. Although this may work for simple and familiar problems, it can lead to serious errors and delays on large, complex projects.

2.11 Assignment Operators

C++ provides several assignment operators for abbreviating assignment expressions. For example, the statement

        c = c + 3;

can be abbreviated with the *addition assignment operator* **+=** as

        c += 3;

The **+=** operator adds the value of the expression on the right of the operator to the value of the variable on the left of the operator and stores the result in the variable on the left of the operator. Any statement of the form

   variable **=** *variable operator expression***;**

where *operator* is one of the binary operators **+**, **−**, *****, **/**, or **%** (or others we will discuss later in the text), can be written in the form

   *variable operator***=** *expression***;**

Thus the assignment **c += 3** adds **3** to **c**. Figure 2.12 shows the arithmetic assignment operators, sample expressions using these operators and explanations.

Performance Tip 2.3

Programmers can write programs a bit faster and compilers can compile programs a bit faster when the "abbreviated" assignment operators are used. Some compilers generate code that runs faster when "abbreviated" assignment operators are used.

Assignment operator	Sample expression	Explanation	Assigns
Assume: `int c = 3, d = 5, e = 4, f = 6, g = 12;`			
`+=`	`c += 7`	`c = c + 7`	10 to `c`
`-=`	`d -= 4`	`d = d - 4`	1 to `d`
`*=`	`e *= 5`	`e = e * 5`	20 to `e`
`/=`	`f /= 3`	`f = f / 3`	2 to `f`
`%=`	`g %= 9`	`g = g % 9`	3 to `g`

Fig. 2.12   Arithmetic assignment operators .

Performance Tip 2.4

Many of the performance tips we mention in this text result in nominal improvements, so the reader might be tempted to ignore them. Significant performance improvement is often realized when a supposedly nominal improvement is placed in a loop that repeats many times.

2.12 Increment and Decrement Operators

C++ also provides the **++** unary *increment operator* and the **--** unary *decrement operator*, which are summarized in Fig. 2.13. If a variable **c** is incremented by 1, the increment operator **++** can be used rather than the expressions **c = c + 1** or **c += 1**. If an increment or decrement operator is placed before a variable, it is referred to as the *preincrement* or *predecrement operator,* respectively. If an increment or decrement operator is placed after a variable, it is referred to as the *postincrement* or *postdecrement operator,* respectively. Preincrementing (predecrementing) a variable causes the variable to be incremented (decremented) by 1, then the new value of the variable is used in the expression in which it appears. Postincrementing (postdecrementing) a variable causes the current value of the variable to be used in the expression in which it appears, then the variable value is incremented (decremented) by 1.

Operator	Called	Sample expression	Explanation
`++`	preincrement	`++a`	Increment **a** by 1, then use the new value of **a** in the expression in which **a** resides.
`++`	postincrement	`a++`	Use the current value of **a** in the expression in which **a** resides, then increment **a** by 1.
`--`	predecrement	`--b`	Decrement **b** by 1, then use the new value of **b** in the expression in which **b** resides.
`--`	postdecrement	`b--`	Use the current value of **b** in the expression in which **b** resides, then decrement **b** by 1.

Fig. 2.13   The increment and decrement operators.

The program of Fig. 2.14 demonstrates the difference between the preincrementing version and the postincrementing version of the **++** operator. Postincrementing the variable **c** causes it to be incremented after it is used in the output statement. Preincrementing the variable **c** causes it to be incremented before it is used in the output statement.

The program displays the value of **c** before and after the **++** operator is used. The decrement operator (**--**) works similarly.

Good Programming Practice 2.14

Unary operators should be placed next to their operands with no intervening spaces.

The three assignment statements in Fig 2.11

```
passes = passes + 1;
failures = failures + 1;
studentCounter = studentCounter + 1;
```

```cpp
1   // Fig. 2.14: fig02_14.cpp
2   // Preincrementing and postincrementing
3   #include <iostream>
4
5   using std::cout;
6   using std::endl;
7
8   int main()
9   {
10      int c;
11
12      c = 5;
13      cout << c << endl;              // print 5
14      cout << c++ << endl;            // print 5 then postincrement
15      cout << c << endl << endl;      // print 6
16
17      c = 5;
18      cout << c << endl;              // print 5
19      cout << ++c << endl;            // preincrement then print 6
20      cout << c << endl;              // print 6
21
22      return 0;                       // successful termination
23  }
```

```
5
5
6

5
6
6
```

Fig. 2.14   The difference between preincrementing and postincrementing.

can be written more concisely with assignment operators as

```
passes += 1;
failures += 1;
studentCounter += 1;
```

with preincrement operators as

```
++passes;
++failures;
++studentCounter;
```

or with postincrement operators as

```
passes++;
failures++;
studentCounter++;
```

Note that, when incrementing or decrementing a variable in a statement by itself, the preincrement and postincrement forms have the same effect, and the predecrement and postdecrement forms have the same effect. It is only when a variable appears in the context of a larger expression that preincrementing the variable and postincrementing the variable have different effects (and similarly for predecrementing and postdecrementing). Also, preincrement and predecrement operate slightly faster than postincrement and postdecrement.

For now, only a simple variable name may be used as the operand of an increment or decrement operator. (We will see that these operators can be used on so-called *lvalues*.)

Common Programming Error 2.11

Attempting to use the increment or decrement operator on an expression other than a simple variable name, e.g., writing ++(x + 1), *is a syntax error.*

Figure 2.15 shows the precedence and associativity of the operators introduced up to this point. The operators are shown top-to-bottom in decreasing order of precedence. The second column describes the associativity of the operators at each level of precedence. Notice that the conditional operator (**? :**), the unary operators increment (**++**), decrement (**--**), plus (**+**), minus (**-**) and casts, and the assignment operators **=, +=, -=, *=, /=** and **%=** associate from right to left. All other operators in the operator precedence chart of Fig. 2.15 associate from left to right. The third column names the various groups of operators.

2.13 Essentials of Counter-Controlled Repetition

Counter-controlled repetition requires the following:

1. the *name* of a control variable (or loop counter);
2. the *initial value* of the control variable;
3. the condition that tests for the *final value* of the control variable (i.e., whether looping should continue);
4. the *increment* (or *decrement*) by which the control variable is modified each time through the loop.

Operators						Associativity	Type
()						left to right	parentheses
++	--	static_cast<*type*>()				left to right	unary (postfix)
++	--	+	-			right to left	unary (prefix)
*	/	%				left to right	multiplicative
+	-					left to right	additive
<<	>>					left to right	insertion/extraction
<	<=	>	>=			left to right	relational
==	!=					left to right	equality
?:						right to left	conditional
=	+=	-=	*=	/=	%=	right to left	assignment
,						left to right	comma

Fig. 2.15   Precedence of the operators encountered so far in the text.

Consider the simple program shown in Fig. 2.16, which prints the numbers from 1 to 10. The declaration at line 10

```
int counter = 1;
```

names the control variable (**counter**), declares it to be an integer, reserves space for it in memory and sets it to an *initial value* of **1**. Declarations that require initialization are, in effect, executable statements. In C++, it is more precise to call a declaration that also reserves memory—as the preceding declaration does—a *definition*.

```cpp
1   // Fig. 2.16: fig02_16.cpp
2   // Counter-controlled repetition
3   #include <iostream>
4
5   using std::cout;
6   using std::endl;
7
8   int main()
9   {
10      int counter = 1;              // initialization
11
12      while ( counter <= 10 ) {     // repetition condition
13         cout << counter << endl;
14         ++counter;                 // increment
15      }
16
17      return 0;
18  }
```

Fig. 2.16   Counter-controlled repetition.

```
1
2
3
4
5
6
7
8
9
10
```

Fig. 2.16   Counter-controlled repetition.

The declaration and initialization of **counter** could also have been accomplished with the statements

```
int counter;
counter = 1;
```

We use both methods of initializing variables.

The statement

```
++counter;
```

increments the loop counter by 1 each time the loop is performed. The loop-continuation condition in the **while** structure tests if the value of the control variable is less than or equal to **10** (the last value for which the condition is **true**). Note that the body of this **while** is performed even when the control variable is **10**. The loop terminates when the control variable is greater than **10** (i.e., **counter** becomes **11**).

The program in Fig. 2.16 can be made more concise by initializing **counter** to **0** and by replacing the **while** structure with

```
while ( ++counter <= 10 )
   cout << counter << endl;
```

This code saves a statement because the incrementing is done directly in the **while** condition before the condition is tested. Also, this code eliminates the braces around the body of the **while**, because the **while** now contains only one statement. Coding in such a condensed fashion takes some practice and can lead to programs that are more difficult to debug, modify and maintain.

Common Programming Error 2.12

Because floating-point values are approximate, controlling counting loops with floating-point variables can result in imprecise counter values and inaccurate tests for termination.

Good Programming Practice 2.15

Control counting loops with integer values.

Good Programming Practice 2.16

Indent the statements in the body of each control structure.

Good Programming Practice 2.17

Put a blank line before and after each control structure to make it stand out in the program.

Good Programming Practice 2.18

Too many levels of nesting can make a program difficult to understand. As a general rule, try to avoid using more than three levels of indentation.

Good Programming Practice 2.19

Vertical spacing above and below control structures, and indentation of the bodies of control structures within the control-structure headers, give programs a two-dimensional appearance that greatly improves readability.

2.14 The `for` Repetition Structure

The **for** repetition structure handles all the details of counter-controlled repetition. To illustrate the power of **for**, let us rewrite the program of Fig. 2.16. The result is shown in Fig. 2.17. The program operates as follows.

When the **for** structure begins executing, the control variable **counter** is declared and initialized to 1. Then, the loop-continuation condition **counter <= 10** is checked. Because the initial value of **counter** is 1, the condition is satisfied, so the body statement prints the value of **counter**, namely 1. The control variable **counter** is then incremented in the expression **counter++** and the loop begins again with the loop-continuation test. Because the control variable is now equal to 2, the final value is not exceeded, so the program performs the body statement again. This process continues until the control variable **counter** is incremented to 11—this causes the loop-continuation test to fail and repetition terminates. The program continues by performing the first statement after the **for** structure (in this case, the **return** statement at the end of the program).

```
1   // Fig. 2.17: fig02_17.cpp
2   // Counter-controlled repetition with the for structure
3   #include <iostream>
4
5   using std::cout;
6   using std::endl;
7
8   int main()
9   {
10      // Initialization, repetition condition, and incrementing
11      // are all included in the for structure header.
12
13      for ( int counter = 1; counter <= 10; counter++ )
14         cout << counter << endl;
15
16      return 0;
17   }
```

Fig. 2.17   Counter-controlled repetition with the **for** structure.

Figure 2.18 takes a closer look at the **for** structure of Fig. 2.17. Notice that the **for** structure "does it all"—it specifies each of the items needed for counter-controlled repetition with a control variable. If there is more than one statement in the body of the **for**, braces are required to enclose the body of the loop.

Notice that Fig. 2.17 uses the loop-continuation condition **counter <= 10**. If the programmer incorrectly wrote **counter < 10**, then the loop would be executed only 9 times. This is a common logic error called an *off-by-one error*.

Common Programming Error 2.13

Using an incorrect relational operator or using an incorrect final value of a loop counter in the condition of a **while** *or* **for** *structure can cause off-by-one errors.*

Good Programming Practice 2.20

Using the final value in the condition of a **while** *or* **for** *structure and using the* **<=** *relational operator will help avoid off-by-one errors. For a loop used to print the values 1 to 10, for example, the loop-continuation condition should be* **counter <= 10** *rather than* **counter < 10** *(which is an off-by-one error) or* **counter < 11** *(which is nevertheless correct). Many programmers nevertheless prefer so-called zero-based counting, in which, to count 10 times through the loop,* **counter** *would be initialized to zero and the loop-continuation test would be* **counter < 10**.

The general format of the **for** structure is

> **for** (*initialization*; *loopContinuationTest*; *increment*)
>   *statement*

where the *initialization* expression initializes the loop's control variable, *loopContinuationTest* is the loop-continuation condition (containing the final value of the control variable for which the condition is true) and *increment* increments the control variable. In most cases, the **for** structure can be represented by an equivalent **while** structure, as follows:

> *initialization*;
>
> **while** (*loopContinuationTest*) {
>   *statement*
>   *increment*;
> }

There is an exception to this rule, which we will discuss in Section 2.18.

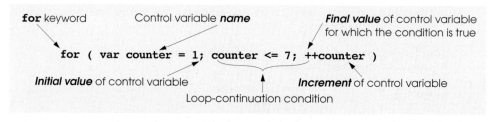

Fig. 2.18   Components of a typical **for** header.

If the *initialization* expression in the **for** structure header defines the control variable (i.e., the control variable's type is specified before the variable name), the control variable can be used only in the body of the **for** structure, i.e., the value of the control variable will be unknown outside the **for** structure. This restricted use of the control variable name is known as the variable's *scope*. The scope of a variable specifies where it can be used in a program. Scope is discussed in detail in Chapter 3, "Functions."

Common Programming Error 2.14

*When the control variable of a **for** structure is initially defined in the initialization section of the **for** structure header, using the control variable after the body of the structure is a syntax error.*

Portability Tip 2.1

*In the C++ standard, the scope of the control variable declared in the initialization section of a **for** structure is different from the scope in older C++ compilers. C++ code created with old C++ compilers can break when compiled on compilers that are compatible with the C++ standard. These are two defensive programming strategies that can be used to prevent this problem: Either define control variables with different names in every **for** structure, or, if you prefer to use the same name for the control variable in several **for** structures, define the control variable outside and before the first **for** loop.*

Sometimes, the *initialization* and *increment* expressions are comma-separated lists of expressions. The commas, as used here, are *comma operators* that guarantee that lists of expressions evaluate from left to right. The comma operator has the lowest precedence of all C++ operators. The value and type of a comma-separated list of expressions is the value and type of the rightmost expression in the list. The comma operator is most often used in **for** structures. Its primary application is to enable the programmer to use multiple initialization expressions and/or multiple increment expressions. For example, there may be several control variables in a single **for** structure that must be initialized and incremented.

Good Programming Practice 2.21

*Place only expressions involving the control variables in the initialization and increment sections of a **for** structure. Manipulations of other variables should appear either before the loop (if they execute only once, like initialization statements) or in the loop body (if they execute once per repetition, like incrementing or decrementing statements).*

The three expressions in the **for** structure are optional. If the *loopContinuationTest* is omitted, C++ assumes that the loop-continuation condition is true, thus creating an infinite loop. One might omit the *initialization* expression if the control variable is initialized elsewhere in the program. One might omit the *increment* expression if the increment is calculated by statements in the body of the **for** or if no increment is needed. The increment expression in the **for** structure acts like a stand-alone statement at the end of the body of the **for**. Therefore, the expressions

```
counter = counter + 1
counter += 1
++counter
counter++
```

are all equivalent in the incrementing portion of the **for** structure. Many programmers prefer the form **counter++** because the incrementing occurs after the loop body is executed.

The postincrementing form therefore seems more natural. Because the variable being in-cremented here does not appear in an expression, both preincrementing and postincrement-ing have the same effect. The two semicolons in the **for** structure are required.

Common Programming Error 2.15

*Using commas instead of the two required semicolons in a **for** header is a syntax error.*

Common Programming Error 2.16

*Placing a semicolon immediately to the right of the right parenthesis of a **for** header makes the body of that **for** structure an empty statement. This is normally a logic error.*

Software Engineering Observation 2.9

*Placing a semicolon immediately after a **for** header is sometimes used to create a so-called delay loop. Such a **for** loop with an empty body still loops the indicated number of times doing nothing other than the counting. For example, you might use a delay loop to slow down a program that is producing outputs on the screen too quickly for you to read them.*

The initialization, loop-continuation condition and increment portions of a **for** struc-ture can contain arithmetic expressions. For example, assume that **x = 2** and **y = 10**. If **x** and **y** are not modified in the loop body, the statement

```
for ( int j = x; j <= 4 * x * y; j += y / x )
```

is equivalent to the statement

```
for ( int j = 2; j <= 80; j += 5 )
```

The "increment" of a **for** structure can be negative (in which case it is really a decre-ment and the loop actually counts downwards).

If the loop-continuation condition is initially false, the body of the **for** structure is not performed. Instead, execution proceeds with the statement following the **for**.

The control variable is frequently printed or used in calculations in the body of a **for** structure, but it does not have to be. It is common to use the control variable for controlling repetition while never mentioning it in the body of the **for** structure.

Good Programming Practice 2.22

*Although the value of the control variable can be changed in the body of a **for** loop, avoid doing so, because this practice can lead to subtle logic errors.*

The **for** structure is flowcharted much like the **while** structure. Figure 2.19 shows the flowchart of the **for** statement

```
for ( int counter = 1; counter <= 10; counter++ )
    cout << counter << endl;
```

The flowchart makes it clear that the initialization occurs once and that incrementing occurs each time *after* the body statement executes. Note that (besides small circles and arrows) the flowchart contains only rectangle symbols and a diamond symbol. Imagine, again, that the programmer has a bin of empty **for** structures—as many as needed to stack and nest with other control structures to form a structured implementation of an algorithm. The rect-angles and diamonds are filled with actions and decisions appropriate to the algorithm.

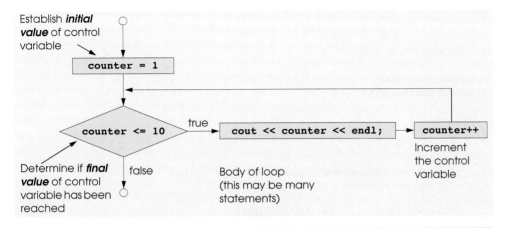

Fig. 2.19   Flowcharting a typical **for** repetition structure.

2.15 Examples Using the **for** Structure

The following examples show methods of varying the control variable in a **for** structure. In each case, we write the appropriate **for** header. Note the change in the relational operator for loops that decrement the control variable.

a) Vary the control variable from **1** to **100** in increments of **1**.

```
for ( int i = 1; i <= 100; i++ )
```

b) Vary the control variable from **100** to **1** in increments of **−1** (decrements of **1**).

```
for ( int i = 100; i >= 1; i-- )
```

Common Programming Error 2.17

Not using the proper relational operator in the loop-continuation condition of a loop that counts downwards (such as incorrectly using **i <= 1** *in a loop counting down to 1) is usually a logic error that will yield incorrect results when the program runs.*

c) Vary the control variable from **7** to **77** in steps of **7**.

```
for ( int i = 7; i <= 77; i += 7 )
```

d) Vary the control variable from **20** to **2** in steps of **−2**.

```
for ( int i = 20; i >= 2; i -= 2 )
```

e) Vary the control variable over the following sequence of values: **2, 5, 8, 11, 14, 17, 20**.

```
for ( int j = 2; j <= 20; j += 3 )
```

f) Vary the control variable over the following sequence of values: **99, 88, 77, 66, 55, 44, 33, 22, 11, 0**.

```
for ( int j = 99; j >= 0; j -= 11 )
```

The next two examples provide simple applications of the **for** structure. The program of Fig. 2.20 uses the **for** structure to sum all the even integers from **2** to **100**.

```cpp
1   // Fig. 2.20: fig02_20.cpp
2   // Summation with for
3   #include <iostream>
4
5   using std::cout;
6   using std::endl;
7
8   int main()
9   {
10     int sum = 0;
11
12     for ( int number = 2; number <= 100; number += 2 )
13        sum += number;
14
15     cout << "Sum is " << sum << endl;
16
17     return 0;
18  }
```

```
Sum is 2550
```

Fig. 2.20   Summation with **for**.

Note that the body of the **for** structure in Fig. 2.20 could actually be merged into the rightmost portion of the **for** header, by using the comma operator as follows:

```cpp
for ( int number = 2;                  // initialization
      number <= 100;                   // continuation condition
      sum += number, number += 2) // total and increment
    ;
```

The assignment **sum = 0** could also be merged into the initialization section of the **for**.

Good Programming Practice 2.23

*Although statements preceding a **for** and statements in the body of a **for** can often be merged into the **for** header, avoid doing so, because it can make the program more difficult to read.*

Good Programming Practice 2.24

Limit the size of control structure headers to a single line, if possible.

The next example computes compound interest using the **for** structure. Consider the following problem statement:

> *A person invests $1000.00 in a savings account yielding 5 percent interest. Assuming that all interest is left on deposit in the account, calculate and print the amount of money in the account at the end of each year for 10 years. Use the following formula for determining these amounts:*
>
> $a = p (1 + r)^n$

where

    p is the original amount invested (i.e., the principal),

    r is the annual interest rate,

    n is the number of years and

    a is the amount on deposit at the end of the nth year.

This problem involves a loop that performs the indicated calculation for each of the 10 years the money remains on deposit. The solution is shown in Fig. 2.21.

The **for** structure executes the body of the loop 10 times, varying a control variable from 1 to 10 in increments of 1. C++ does not include an exponentiation operator, so we use the *standard library function* **pow** for this purpose. The function **pow(x, y)** calculates the value of **x** raised to the **y**th power. In this example, the algebraic expression $(1 + r)^n$ is written as **pow(1 + rate, year)** where variable **rate** represents *r* and variable **year** represents *n*. Function **pow** takes two arguments of type **double** and returns a **double** value.

This program would not compile without the inclusion of **<cmath>**. Function **pow** requires two **double** arguments. Note that **year** is an integer. The **<cmath>** file includes information that tells the compiler to convert the value of **year** to a temporary **double** representation before calling the function. This information is contained in **pow**'s *function prototype*. Function prototypes are explained in Chapter 3. We provide a summary of the **pow** function and other math library functions in Chapter 3.

Common Programming Error 2.18

Forgetting to include the **<cmath>** *file in a program that uses math library functions is a syntax error.*

Notice that we declared the variables **amount**, **principal** and **rate** to be of type **double**. We have done this for simplicity because we are dealing with fractional parts of dollars and we need a type that allows decimal points in its values. Unfortunately, this can cause trouble. Here is a simple explanation of what can go wrong when using **float** or **double** to represent dollar amounts (assuming **setprecision(2)** is used to specify two digits of precision when printing): Two dollar amounts stored in the machine could be 14.234 (which prints as 14.23) and 18.673 (which prints as 18.67). When these amounts are added, they produce the internal sum 32.907 which prints as 32.91. Thus your printout could appear as

```
    14.23
+ 18.67
  -------
    32.91
```

but a person adding the individual numbers as printed would expect the sum 32.90! You have been warned!

Good Programming Practice 2.25

Do not use variables of type **float** *or* **double** *to perform monetary calculations. The imprecision of floating-point numbers can cause errors that will result in incorrect monetary values. In the exercises, we explore the use of integers to perform monetary calculations. Note: C++ class libraries from third-party vendors are available for properly performing monetary calculations.*

```
1   // Fig. 2.21: fig02_21.cpp
2   // Calculating compound interest
3   #include <iostream>
4
5   using std::cout;
6   using std::endl;
7   using std::ios;
8
9   #include <iomanip>
10
11  using std::setw;
12  using std::setiosflags;
13  using std::setprecision;
14
15  #include <cmath>
16
17  int main()
18  {
19     double amount,            // amount on deposit
20            principal = 1000.0,  // starting principal
21            rate = .05;          // interest rate
22
23     cout << "Year" << setw( 21 )
24         << "Amount on deposit" << endl;
25
26     // set the floating-point number format
27     cout << setiosflags( ios::fixed | ios::showpoint )
28         << setprecision( 2 );
29
30     for ( int year = 1; year <= 10; year++ ) {
31        amount = principal * pow( 1.0 + rate, year );
32        cout << setw( 4 ) << year << setw( 21 ) << amount << endl;
33     }
34
35     return 0;
36  }
```

```
Year    Amount on deposit
   1             1050.00
   2             1102.50
   3             1157.62
   4             1215.51
   5             1276.28
   6             1340.10
   7             1407.10
   8             1477.46
   9             1551.33
  10             1628.89
```

Fig. 2.21   Calculating compound interest with **for**.

The output statement

```
cout << setiosflags( ios::fixed | ios::showpoint )
    << setprecision( 2 );
```

before the **for** loop and the output statement

```
cout << setw( 4 ) << year << setw( 21 ) << amount << endl;
```

in the **for** loop combine to print the values of the variables **year** and **amount** with the formatting specified by the parameterized stream manipulators **setw**, **setiosflags** and **setprecision**. The call **setw(4)** specifies that the next value output is printed in a *field width* of 4, i.e., the value is printed with at least 4 character positions. If the value to be output is less than 4 character positions wide, the value is *right justified* in the field by default. If the value to be output is more than 4 character positions wide, the field width is extended to accommodate the entire value. The call **setiosflags(ios::left)** can be used to specify that values should be output *left justified*.

The other formatting in the preceding output statements indicates that variable **amount** is printed as a fixed-point value with a decimal point (specified with the stream manipulator **setiosflags(ios::fixed | ios::showpoint)**) right-justified in a field of 21 character positions (specified with **setw(21)**) and two digits of precision to the right of the decimal point (specified with **setprecision(2)**). We will discuss the powerful input/output formatting capabilities of C++ in detail in Chapter 11. We placed the **setiosflags** and **setprecision** stream manipulators in a **cout** before the for loop because these settings remain in effect until they are changed. Thus, they do not need to be applied during each iteration of the loop.

Note that the calculation **1.0 + rate**, which appears as an argument to the **pow** function, is contained in the body of the **for** statement. In fact, this calculation produces the same result each time through the loop, so repeating the calculation is wasteful.

Performance Tip 2.5

Avoid placing expressions whose values do not change inside loops—but, even if you do, many of today's sophisticated optimizing compilers will automatically place such expressions outside loops in the generated machine language code.

Performance Tip 2.6

Many compilers contain optimization features that improve the code you write, but it is still better to write good code from the start.

For fun, be sure to try our Peter Minuit problem in the chapter exercises. This problem demonstrates the wonders of compound interest.

2.16 The `switch` Multiple-Selection Structure

We have discussed the **if** single-selection structure and the **if/else** double-selection structure. Occasionally, an algorithm will contain a series of decisions in which a variable or expression is tested separately for each of the constant integral values it can assume and different actions are taken. C++ provides the **switch** multiple-selection structure to handle such decision making.

The **switch** structure consists of a series of **case** labels and an optional **default** case. The program in Fig. 2.22 uses **switch** to count the number of each different letter grade that students earned on an exam.

```
1   // Fig. 2.22: fig02_22.cpp
2   // Counting letter grades
3   #include <iostream>
4
5   using std::cout;
6   using std::cin;
7   using std::endl;
8
9   int main()
10  {
11     int grade,          // one grade
12         aCount = 0,     // number of A's
13         bCount = 0,     // number of B's
14         cCount = 0,     // number of C's
15         dCount = 0,     // number of D's
16         fCount = 0;     // number of F's
17
18     cout << "Enter the letter grades." << endl
19          << "Enter the EOF character to end input." << endl;
20
21     while ( ( grade = cin.get() ) != EOF ) {
22
23        switch ( grade ) {        // switch nested in while
24
25           case 'A':  // grade was uppercase A
26           case 'a':  // or lowercase a
27              ++aCount;
28              break;   // necessary to exit switch
29
30           case 'B':  // grade was uppercase B
31           case 'b':  // or lowercase b
32              ++bCount;
33              break;
34
35           case 'C':  // grade was uppercase C
36           case 'c':  // or lowercase c
37              ++cCount;
38              break;
39
40           case 'D':  // grade was uppercase D
41           case 'd':  // or lowercase d
42              ++dCount;
43              break;
44
45           case 'F':  // grade was uppercase F
46           case 'f':  // or lowercase f
47              ++fCount;
48              break;
49
50           case '\n': // ignore newlines,
51           case '\t': // tabs,
52           case ' ':  // and spaces in input
53              break;
```

Fig. 2.22   An example using **switch** (part 1 of 2).

```
54
55              default:    // catch all other characters
56                  cout << "Incorrect letter grade entered."
57                      << " Enter a new grade." << endl;
58                  break;   // optional
59          }
60      }
61
62      cout << "\n\nTotals for each letter grade are:"
63          << "\nA: " << aCount
64          << "\nB: " << bCount
65          << "\nC: " << cCount
66          << "\nD: " << dCount
67          << "\nF: " << fCount << endl;
68
69      return 0;
70  }
```

```
Enter the letter grades.
Enter the EOF character to end input.
a
B
c
C
A
d
f
C
E
Incorrect letter grade entered. Enter a new grade.
D
A
b

Totals for each letter grade are:
A: 3
B: 2
C: 3
D: 2
F: 1
```

Fig. 2.22   An example using **switch** (part 2 of 2).

In the program, the user enters letter grades for a class. Inside the **while** header,

```
while ( ( grade = cin.get() ) != EOF )
```

the parenthesized assignment **(grade = cin.get())** is executed first. The **cin.get()** function reads one character from the keyboard and stores that character in integer variable **grade**. The dot notation used in **cin.get()** will be explained in Chapter 6, "Classes." Characters normally are stored in variables of type **char**; however, an important feature of C++ is that characters can be stored in any integer data type because they are represented as 1-byte integers in the computer. Thus, we can treat a character as either an integer or a character depending on its use. For example, the statement

```
cout << "The character (" << 'a' << ") has the value "
    << static_cast< int > ( 'a' ) << endl;
```

prints the character **a** and its integer value as follows:

```
The character (a) has the value 97
```

The integer 97 is the character's numerical representation in the computer. Many computers today use the *ASCII (American Standard Code for Information Interchange) character set*, in which 97 represents the lowercase letter **'a'**. A list of the ASCII characters and their decimal values is presented in the appendices.

Assignment statements as a whole have the value that is assigned to the variable on the left side of the **=**. Thus, the value of the assignment **grade = cin.get()** is the same as the value returned by **cin.get()** and assigned to the variable **grade**.

The fact that assignment statements have values can be useful for initializing several variables to the same value. For example,

```
a = b = c = 0;
```

first evaluates the assignment **c = 0** (because the **=** operator associates from right to left). The variable **b** is then assigned the value of the assignment **c = 0** (which is 0). Then, the variable **a** is assigned the value of the assignment **b = (c = 0)** (which is also 0). In the program, the value of the assignment **grade = cin.get()** is compared with the value of **EOF** (a symbol whose acronym stands for "end-of-file"). We use **EOF** (which normally has the value –1) as the sentinel value. *However, you do not type the value –1 nor do you type the letters EOF as the sentinel value.* Rather, you type a system-dependent keystroke combination to mean "end-of-file," i.e., "I have no more data to enter." **EOF** is a symbolic integer constant defined in the **<iostream>** header file. If the value assigned to **grade** is equal to **EOF**, the program terminates. We have chosen to represent characters in this program as **int**s because **EOF** has an integer value (again, normally –1).

Portability Tip 2.2

The keystroke combinations for entering end-of-file are system dependent.

Portability Tip 2.3

*Testing for the symbolic constant **EOF** rather than –1 makes programs more portable. The ANSI standard states that **EOF** is a negative integral value (but not necessarily –1). Thus, **EOF** could have different values on different systems.*

On UNIX systems and many others, end-of-file is entered by typing the sequence

<*ctrl-d*>

on a line by itself. This notation means to simultaneously press both the **ctrl** key and the **d** key. On other systems such as Digital Equipment Corporation's VAX VMS or Microsoft Corporation's MS-DOS, end-of-file can be entered by typing

<*ctrl-z*>

Note: In some cases, you may have to press *Enter* after the preceding key sequence.

The user enters grades at the keyboard. When the *Enter* (or *Return*) key is pressed, the characters are read by the **cin.get()** function, one character at a time. If the character entered is not end-of-file, the **switch** structure is entered. The keyword **switch** is followed by the variable name **grade** in parentheses. This is called the *controlling expression*. The value of this expression is compared with each of the **case** *labels*. Assume the user has entered the letter **C** as a grade. **C** is automatically compared to each **case** in the **switch**. If a match occurs (**case 'C':**), the statements for that **case** are executed. For the letter **C**, **cCount** is incremented by **1** and the **switch** structure is exited immediately with the **break** statement. Note that, unlike other control structures, it is not necessary to enclose a multistatement **case** in braces.

The **break** statement causes program control to proceed with the first statement after the **switch** structure. The **break** statement is used because the **case**s in a **switch** statement would otherwise run together. If **break** is not used anywhere in a **switch** structure, then, each time a match occurs in the structure, the statements for all the remaining **case**s will be executed. (This feature is sometimes useful when performing the same actions for several **case**s, as in the program of Fig. 2.22.) If no match occurs, the **default** case is executed and an error message is printed.

Each **case** can have one or more actions. The **switch** structure is different from all other structures in that braces are not required around multiple actions in a **case** of a **switch**. The general **switch** multiple-selection structure (using a **break** in each **case**) is flowcharted in Fig. 2.23.

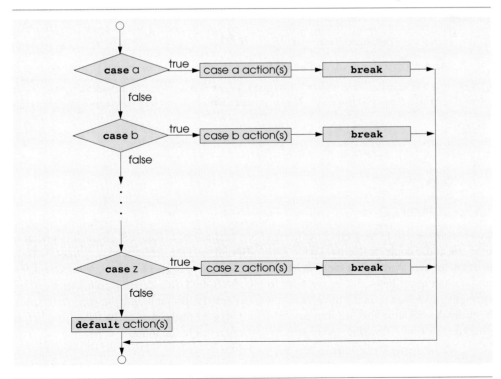

Fig. 2.23   The **switch** multiple-selection structure with **break**s.

The flowchart makes it clear that each **break** statement at the end of a **case** causes control to immediately exit the **switch** structure. Again, note that (besides small circles and arrows) the flowchart contains only rectangle symbols and diamond symbols. Imagine, again, that the programmer has access to a deep bin of empty **switch** structures—as many as the programmer might need to stack and nest with other control structures to form a structured implementation of an algorithm's flow of control. And again, the rectangles and diamonds are then filled with actions and decisions appropriate to the algorithm. Nested control structures are common, but it is rare to find nested **switch** structures in a program.

Common Programming Error 2.19

*Forgetting a **break** statement when one is needed in a **switch** structure is a logic error.*

Common Programming Error 2.20

*Omitting the space between the word **case** and the integral value being tested in a **switch** structure can cause a logic error. For example, writing **case3:** instead of writing **case 3:** simply creates an unused label. (We will say more about this in Chapter 18.) The problem is that the **switch** structure will not perform the appropriate actions when the **switch**'s controlling expression has a value of 3.*

Good Programming Practice 2.26

*Provide a **default** case in **switch** statements. Cases not explicitly tested in a **switch** statement without a **default** case are ignored. Including a **default** case focuses the programmer on the need to process exceptional conditions. There are situations in which no **default** processing is needed. Although the **case** clauses and the **default** case clause in a **switch** structure can occur in any order, it is considered a good programming practice to place the **default** clause last.*

Good Programming Practice 2.27

*In a **switch** structure when the **default** clause is listed last, the **break** statement is not required. Some programmers include this **break** for clarity and symmetry with other cases.*

In the **switch** structure of Fig. 2.22, lines 50 through 53

```
case '\n':
case '\t':
case ' ':
   break;
```

cause the program to skip newline, tab and blank characters. Reading characters one at a time can cause some problems. To have the program read the characters, they must be sent to the computer by pressing the *Enter key* on the keyboard. This places a newline character in the input after the character we wish to process. Often, this newline character must be specially processed to make the program work correctly. By including the preceding cases in our **switch** structure, we prevent the error message in the **default** case from being printed each time a newline, tab or space is encountered in the input.

Common Programming Error 2.21

Not processing newline and other whitespace characters in the input when reading characters one at a time can cause logic errors.

Note that several case labels listed together (such as **case 'D': case 'd':** in Fig. 2.22) simply means that the same set of actions is to occur for each of the cases.

When using the **switch** structure, remember that it can only be used for testing a *constant integral expression,* i.e., any combination of character constants and integer constants that evaluates to a constant integer value. A character constant is represented as the specific character in single quotes such as **'A'**. An integer constant is simply an integer value.

When we get to the part of the book on object-oriented programming, we will present a more elegant way to implement **switch** logic. We will use a technique called polymorphism to create programs that are often clearer, more concise, easier to maintain and easier to extend than programs using **switch** logic.

Portable languages like C++ must have flexible data type sizes. Different applications might need integers of different sizes. C++ provides several data types to represent integers. The range of integer values for each type depends on the particular computer's hardware. In addition to the types **int** and **char**, C++ provides the types **short** (an abbreviation of **short int**) and **long** (an abbreviation of **long int**). The minimum range of values for **short** integers is -32,768 to 32,767. For the vast majority of integer calculations, **long** integers are sufficient. The minimum range of values for **long** integers is –2,147,483,648 to 2,147,483,647. On most computers, **int**s are equivalent either to **short** or to **long**. The range of values for an **int** is at least the same as the range for **short** integers and no larger than the range for **long** integers. The data type **char** can be used to represent any of the characters in the computer's character set. The data type **char** can also be used to represent small integers.

Portability Tip 2.4

*Because **int**s vary in size between systems, use **long** integers if you expect to process integers outside the range –32,768 to 32,767 and you would like to be able to run the program on several different computer systems.*

Performance Tip 2.7

In performance-oriented situations where memory is at a premium or execution speed is crucial, it might be desirable to use smaller integer sizes.

Performance Tip 2.8

Using smaller integer sizes can result in a slower program if the machine's instructions for manipulating them are not as efficient as for the natural-size integers (e.g., sign extension must be done on them).

Common Programming Error 2.22

*Providing identical case labels in a **switch** structure is a syntax error.*

2.17 The do/while Repetition Structure

The **do/while** repetition structure is similar to the **while** structure. In the **while** structure, the loop-continuation condition is tested at the beginning of the loop before the body of the loop is performed. The **do/while** structure tests the loop-continuation condition *after* the loop body is performed; therefore, the loop body will be executed at least once. When a **do/while** terminates, execution continues with the statement after the **while** clause. Note that it is not necessary to use braces in the **do/while** structure if there is only one statement in the body; however, the braces are usually included to avoid confusion between the **while** and **do/while** structures. For example,

    while (*condition*)

is normally regarded as the header to a **while** structure. A **do/while** with no braces around the single statement body appears as

    do
        statement
    while (*condition*);

which can be confusing. The last line—**while**(*condition*);—might be misinterpreted by the reader as a **while** structure containing an empty statement. Thus, the **do/while** with one statement is often written as follows to avoid confusion:

    do {
        statement
    } **while** (condition);

Good Programming Practice 2.28

*Some programmers always include braces in a **do/while** structure, even if the braces are not necessary. This helps eliminate ambiguity between the **while** structure and the **do/while** structure containing one statement.*

Common Programming Error 2.23

*Infinite loops are caused when the loop-continuation condition in a **while**, **for** or **do/while** structure never becomes **false**. To prevent this, make sure the value of the condition does change somewhere in the header or body of the loop so the condition can eventually become **false**.*

The program in Fig. 2.24 uses a **do/while** repetition structure to print the numbers from 1 to 10. Note that the control variable **counter** is preincremented in the loop-continuation test. Note also the use of the braces to enclose the single-statement body of the **do/while** structure.

```
1   // Fig. 2.24: fig02_24.cpp
2   // Using the do/while repetition structure
3   #include <iostream>
4
5   using std::cout;
6   using std::endl;
7
8   int main()
9   {
10     int counter = 1;
11
12     do {
13        cout << counter << "  ";
14     } while ( ++counter <= 10 );
```

Fig. 2.24   Using the **do/while** structure (part 1 of 2).

```
15
16        cout << endl;
17
18        return 0;
19   }
```

```
1   2   3   4   5   6   7   8   9   10
```

Fig. 2.24   Using the **do/while** structure (part 2 of 2).

The **do/while** structure is flowcharted in Fig. 2.25. This flowchart makes it clear that the loop-continuation condition is not executed until after the action is performed at least once. Again, note that (besides small circles and arrows) the flowchart contains only a rectangle symbol and a diamond symbol. Imagine, again, that the programmer has access to a deep bin of empty **do/while** structures—as many as the programmer might need to stack and nest with other control structures to form a structured implementation of an algorithm's flow of control. And again, the rectangles and diamonds are then filled with actions and decisions appropriate to the algorithm.

2.18 The **break** and **continue** Statements

The **break** and **continue** statements alter the flow of control. The **break** statement, when executed in a **while**, **for**, **do/while** or **switch** structure, causes immediate exit from that structure. Program execution continues with the first statement after the structure. Common uses of the **break** statement are to escape early from a loop or to skip the remainder of a **switch** structure (as in Fig. 2.22). Figure 2.26 demonstrates the **break** statement in a **for** repetition structure. When the **if** structure detects that **x** has become **5**, **break** is executed. This terminates the **for** statement and the program continues with the **cout** after the **for**. The loop executes fully only four times.

Note that the control variable **x** in this program is defined outside the **for** structure header. This is because we intend to use the control variable both in the body of the loop and after the loop completes its execution.

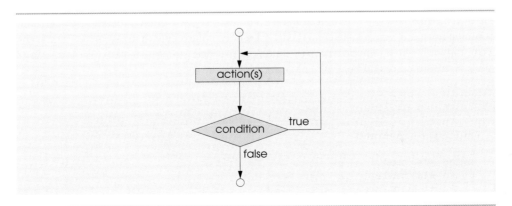

Fig. 2.25   Flowcharting the **do/while** repetition structure.

```
1   // Fig. 2.26: fig02_26.cpp
2   // Using the break statement in a for structure
3   #include <iostream>
4
5   using std::cout;
6   using std::endl;
7
8   int main()
9   {
10     // x declared here so it can be used after the loop
11     int x;
12
13     for ( x = 1; x <= 10; x++ ) {
14
15        if ( x == 5 )
16           break;      // break loop only if x is 5
17
18        cout << x << " ";
19     }
20
21     cout << "\nBroke out of loop at x of " << x << endl;
22     return 0;
23  }
```

```
1 2 3 4
Broke out of loop at x of 5
```

Fig. 2.26   Using the **break** statement in a **for** structure .

The **continue** statement, when executed in a **while**, **for** or **do/while** structure, skips the remaining statements in the body of that structure and proceeds with the next iteration of the loop. In **while** and **do/while** structures, the loop-continuation test is evaluated immediately after the **continue** statement is executed. In the **for** structure, the increment expression is executed, then the loop-continuation test is evaluated. Earlier, we stated that the **while** structure could be used in most cases to represent the **for** structure. The one exception occurs when the increment expression in the **while** structure follows the **continue** statement. In this case, the increment is not executed before the repetition-continuation condition is tested and the **while** does not execute in the same manner as the **for**. Figure 2.27 uses the **continue** statement in a **for** structure to skip the output statement in the structure and begin the next iteration of the loop.

```
1   // Fig. 2.27: fig02_07.cpp
2   // Using the continue statement in a for structure
3   #include <iostream>
4
5   using std::cout;
6   using std::endl;
7
```

Fig. 2.27   Using the **continue** statement in a **for** structure (part 1 of 2).

```
8   int main()
9   {
10      for ( int x = 1; x <= 10; x++ ) {
11
12          if ( x == 5 )
13              continue;   // skip remaining code in loop
14                          // only if x is 5
15
16          cout << x << " ";
17      }
18
19      cout << "\nUsed continue to skip printing the value 5"
20          << endl;
21      return 0;
22  }
```

```
1 2 3 4 6 7 8 9 10
Used continue to skip printing the value 5
```

Fig. 2.27   Using the **continue** statement in a **for** structure (part 2 of 2).

Good Programming Practice 2.29

Some programmers feel that **break** *and* **continue** *violate structured programming. Because the effects of these statements can be achieved by structured programming techniques we will soon learn, these programmers do not use* **break** *and* **continue**.

Performance Tip 2.9

The **break** *and* **continue** *statements, when used properly, perform faster than the corresponding structured techniques we will soon learn.*

Software Engineering Observation 2.10

There is a tension between achieving quality software engineering and achieving the best-performing software. Often, one of these goals is achieved at the expense of the other.

2.19 Logical Operators

So far we have studied only *simple conditions*, such as **counter <= 10**, **total > 1000** and **number != sentinelValue**. We have expressed these conditions in terms of the relational operators **>**, **<**, **>=** and **<=**, and the equality operators **==** and **!=**. Each decision tested precisely one condition. To test multiple conditions while making a decision, we performed these tests in separate statements or in nested **if** or **if/else** structures.

C++ provides *logical operators* that are used to form more complex conditions by combining simple conditions. The logical operators are **&&** *(logical AND)*, **||** *(logical OR)* and **!** *(logical NOT, also called logical negation)*. We consider examples of each of these.

Suppose we wish to ensure that two conditions are *both* **true** before we choose a certain path of execution. In this case we can use the logical **&&** operator as follows:

```
if ( gender == 1 && age >= 65 )
    ++seniorFemales;
```

This **if** statement contains two simple conditions. The condition **gender == 1** might be evaluated, for example, to determine if a person is a female. The condition **age >= 65** is evaluated to determine if a person is a senior citizen. The simple condition to the left of the **&&** operator is evaluated first because the precedence of **==** is higher than the precedence of **&&**. If necessary, the simple condition to the right of the **&&** operator is evaluated next because the precedence of **>=** is higher than the precedence of **&&** (as we will discuss shortly, the right side of a logical AND expression is evaluated only if the left side is **true**). The **if** statement then considers the combined condition

```
gender == 1 && age >= 65
```

This condition is **true** if and only if both of the simple conditions are **true**. Finally, if this combined condition is indeed **true**, then the count of **seniorFemales** is incremented by **1**. If either or both of the simple conditions are **false**, then the program skips the incrementing and proceeds to the statement following the **if**. The preceding combined condition can be made more readable by adding redundant parentheses

```
( gender == 1 ) && ( age >= 65 )
```

Common Programming Error 2.24

Although **3 < x < 7** *is a mathematically correct condition, it does not evaluate correctly in C++. Use* **(3 < x && x < 7)** *to get the proper evaluation in C++.*

The table of Fig. 2.28 summarizes the **&&** operator. The table shows all four possible combinations of **false** and **true** values for expression1 and expression2. Such tables are often called *truth tables*. C++ evaluates to **false** or **true** all expressions that include relational operators, equality operators and/or logical operators.

Portability Tip 2.5

For compatibility with earlier versions of the C++ standard, the **bool** *value* **true** *can also be represented by any nonzero value and the* **bool** *value* **false** *can also be represented as the value* **0**.

Now let us consider the **||** (logical OR) operator. Suppose we wish to ensure at some point in a program that either *or* both of two conditions are **true** before we choose a certain path of execution. In this case we use the **||** operator as in the following program segment:

```
if ( semesterAverage >= 90 || finalExam >= 90 )
   cout << "Student grade is A" << endl;
```

expression1	expression2	expression1 && expression2
false	false	false
false	true	false
true	false	false
true	true	true

Fig. 2.28   Truth table for the **&&** (logical AND) operator.

This preceding condition also contains two simple conditions. The simple condition **semesterAverage >= 90** is evaluated to determine if the student deserves an "A" in the course because of a solid performance throughout the semester. The simple condition **finalExam >= 90** is evaluated to determine if the student deserves an "A" in the course because of an outstanding performance on the final exam. The **if** statement then considers the combined condition

```
semesterAverage >= 90 || finalExam >= 90
```

and awards the student an "A" if either or both of the simple conditions are **true**. Note that the message "**Student grade is A**" is not printed only when both of the simple conditions are **false**. Figure 2.29 is a truth table for the logical OR operator (**||**).

The **&&** operator has a higher precedence than the **||** operator. Both operators associate from left to right. An expression containing **&&** or **||** operators is evaluated only until truth or falsehood is known. Thus, evaluation of the expression

```
gender == 1 && age >= 65
```

will stop immediately if **gender** is not equal to **1** (i.e., the entire expression is **false**) and continue if **gender** is equal to **1** (i.e., the entire expression could still be **true** if the condition **age >= 65** is **true**).

Common Programming Error 2.25

In expressions using operator **&&**, *it is possible that a condition—we will call this the dependent condition—might require another condition to be* **true** *for it to be meaningful to evaluate the dependent condition. In this case, the dependent condition should be placed after the other condition, or an error might occur.*

Performance Tip 2.10

In expressions using operator **&&**, *if the separate conditions are independent of one another make the condition that is most likely to be* **false** *the leftmost condition. In expressions using operator* **||**, *make the condition that is most likely to be* **true** *the leftmost condition. This can reduce a program's execution time.*

C++ provides the **!** (logical negation) operator to enable a programmer to "reverse" the meaning of a condition. Unlike the **&&** and **||** operators, which combine two conditions (binary operators), the logical negation operator has only a single condition as an operand (unary operator). The logical negation operator is placed before a condition when we are interested in choosing a path of execution if the original condition (without the logical negation operator) is **false**, such as in the following program segment:

```
if ( !( grade == sentinelValue ) )
    cout << "The next grade is " << grade << endl;
```

The parentheses around the condition **grade == sentinelValue** are needed because the logical negation operator has a higher precedence than the equality operator. Figure 2.30 is a truth table for the logical negation operator.

In most cases, the programmer can avoid using logical negation by expressing the condition differently with an appropriate relational or equality operator. For example, the preceding statement can also be written as follows:

```
if ( grade != sentinelValue )
    cout << "The next grade is " << grade << endl;
```

This flexibility can often help a programmer express a condition in a more "natural" or convenient manner.

Figure 2.31 shows the precedence and associativity of the C++ operators introduced to this point. The operators are shown from top to bottom, in decreasing order of precedence.

expression1	expression2	expression1 || expression2
false	false	false
false	true	true
true	false	true
true	true	true

Fig. 2.29   Truth table for the || (logical OR) operator.

expression	!expression
false	true
true	false

Fig. 2.30   Truth table for operator ! (logical negation).

Operators	Associativity	Type
( )	left to right	parentheses
++ -- static_cast<*type*>()	left to right	unary (postfix)
++ -- + -	right to left	unary (prefix)
* / %	left to right	multiplicative
+ -	left to right	additive
<< >>	left to right	insertion/extraction
< <= > >=	left to right	relational
== !=	left to right	equality
&&	left to right	logical AND
||	left to right	logical OR
?:	right to left	conditional

Fig. 2.31   Operator precedence and associativity (part 1 of 2).

Operators						Associativity	Type
=	+=	-=	*=	/=	%=	right to left	assignment
,						left to right	comma

Fig. 2.31   Operator precedence and associativity (part 2 of 2).

2.20 Confusing Equality (==) and Assignment (=) Operators

There is one type of error that C++ programmers, no matter how experienced, tend to make so frequently that we felt it was worth a separate section. That error is accidentally swapping the operators **==** (equality) and **=** (assignment). What makes these swaps so damaging is the fact that they do not ordinarily cause syntax errors. Rather, statements with these errors ordinarily compile correctly and the programs run to completion, probably generating incorrect results through run-time logic errors.

There are two aspects of C++ that cause these problems. One is that any expression that produces a value can be used in the decision portion of any control structure. If the value is 0, it is treated as **false**, and if the value is nonzero, it is treated as **true**. The second is that C++ assignments produce a value, namely the value that is assigned to the variable on the left side of the assignment operator. For example, suppose we intend to write

```
if ( payCode == 4 )
    cout << "You get a bonus!" << endl;
```

but we accidentally write

```
if ( payCode = 4 )
    cout << "You get a bonus!" << endl;
```

The first **if** statement properly awards a bonus to the person whose **paycode** is equal to 4. The second **if** statement—the one with the error—evaluates the assignment expression in the **if** condition to the constant 4. Because any nonzero value is interpreted as **true**, the condition in this **if** statement is always **true** and the person always receives a bonus regardless of what the actual paycode is! Even worse, the paycode has been modified when it was only supposed to be examined!

Common Programming Error 2.26

Using operator == for assignment and using operator = for equality are logic errors.

Testing and Debugging Tip 2.1

Programmers normally write conditions such as **x == 7** *with the variable name on the left and the constant on the right. By reversing these so that the constant is on the left and the variable name is on the right as in* **7 == x**, *the programmer who accidentally replaces the == operator with = will be protected by the compiler. The compiler will treat this as a syntax error because only a variable name can be placed on the left-hand side of an assignment statement. At least this will prevent the potential devastation of a run-time logic error.*

Variable names are said to be *lvalues* (for "left values") because they can be used on the left side of an assignment operator. Constants are said to be *rvalues* (for "right values") because they can be used on only the right side of an assignment operator. Note that *lvalues* can also be used as *rvalues*, but not vice versa.

The other side of the coin can be equally unpleasant. Suppose the programmer wants to assign a value to a variable with a simple statement like

```
x = 1;
```

but instead writes

```
x == 1;
```

Here, too, this is not a syntax error. Rather the compiler simply evaluates the conditional expression. If **x** is equal to **1**, the condition is **true** and the expression returns the value **true**. If **x** is not equal to **1**, the condition is **false** and the expression returns the value **false**. Regardless of what value is returned, there is no assignment operator, so the value is simply lost and the value of **x** remains unaltered, probably causing an execution-time logic error. Unfortunately, we do not have a handy trick available to help you with this problem!

Testing and Debugging Tip 2.2

*Use your text editor to search for all occurrences of **=** in your program and check that you have the correct operator in each place.*

2.21 Structured-Programming Summary

Just as architects design buildings by employing the collective wisdom of their profession, so should programmers design programs. Our field is younger than architecture is and our collective wisdom is considerably sparser. We have learned that structured programming produces programs that are easier than unstructured programs to understand and hence are easier to test, debug, modify, and even prove correct in a mathematical sense.

Figure 2.32 summarizes C++'s control structures. Small circles are used in the figure to indicate the single entry point and the single exit point of each structure. Connecting individual flowchart symbols arbitrarily can lead to unstructured programs. Therefore, the programming profession has chosen to combine flowchart symbols to form a limited set of control structures and to build structured programs by properly combining control structures in two simple ways.

For simplicity, only single-entry/single-exit control structures are used—there is only one way to enter and only one way to exit each control structure. Connecting control structures in sequence to form structured programs is simple—the exit point of one control structure is connected to the entry point of the next control structure, i.e., the control structures are simply placed one after another in a program; we have called this "control structure stacking." The rules for forming structured programs also allow for control structures to be nested.

Figure 2.33 shows the rules for forming properly structured programs. The rules assume that the rectangle flowchart symbol may be used to indicate any action, including input/output. The rules also assume that we begin with the simplest flowchart (Fig. 2.34).

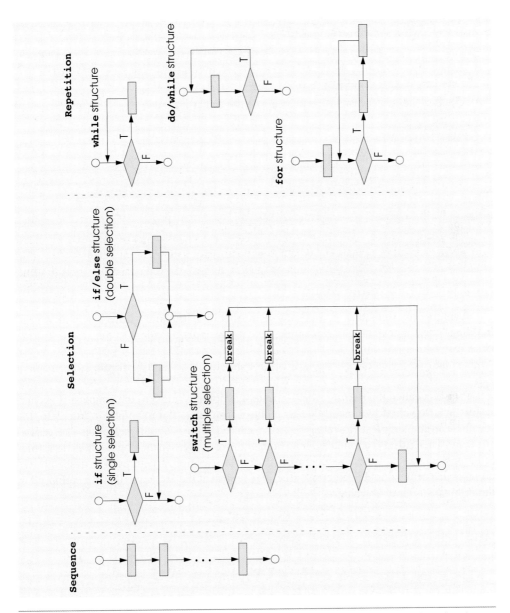

Fig. 2.32   C++'s single-entry/single-exit sequence, selection and repetition structures.

Rules for Forming Structured Programs

1)   Begin with the "simplest flowchart" (Fig. 2.34).
2)   Any rectangle (action) can be replaced by two rectangles (actions) in sequence.

Fig. 2.33   Rules for forming structured programs (part 1 of 2).

Rules for Forming Structured Programs

3)   Any rectangle (action) can be replaced by any control structure (sequence, **if**, **if/else**, **switch**, **while**, **do/while** or **for**).

4)   Rules 2 and 3 can be applied as often as you like and in any order.

Fig. 2.33   Rules for forming structured programs (part 2 of 2).

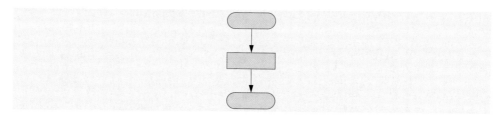

Fig. 2.34   The simplest flowchart.

Applying the rules of Fig. 2.33 always results in a structured flowchart with a neat, building-block appearance. For example, repeatedly applying rule 2 to the simplest flowchart results in a structured flowchart containing many rectangles in sequence (Fig. 2.35). Notice that rule 2 generates a stack of control structures, so let us call rule 2 the *stacking rule*.

Rule 3 is called the *nesting rule*. Repeatedly applying rule 3 to the simplest flowchart results in a flowchart with neatly nested control structures. For example, in Fig. 2.36, the rectangle in the simplest flowchart is first replaced with a double-selection (**if/else**) structure. Then rule 3 is applied again to both of the rectangles in the double-selection structure, replacing each of these rectangles with double-selection structures. The dashed boxes around each of the double-selection structures represent the rectangle that was replaced in the original simplest flowchart.

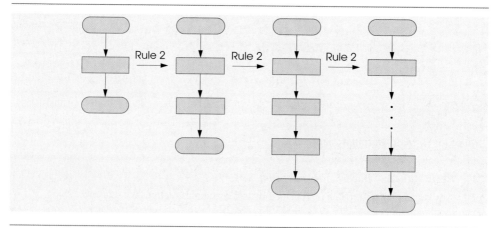

Fig. 2.35   Repeatedly applying rule 2 of Fig. 2.33 to the simplest flowchart.

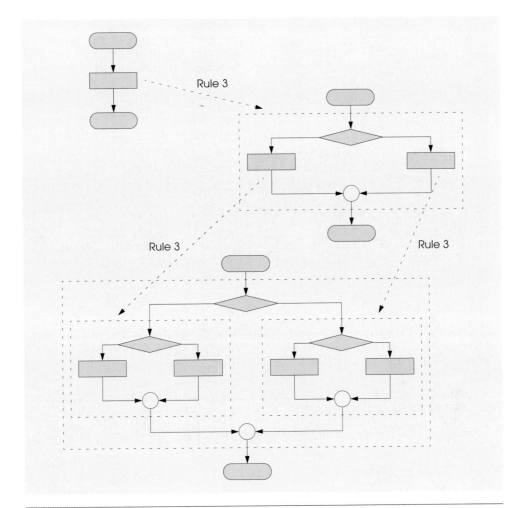

Fig. 2.36   Applying rule 3 of Fig. 2.33 to the simplest flowchart.

Rule 4 generates larger, more involved and more deeply nested structures. The flowcharts that emerge from applying the rules in Fig. 2.33 constitute the set of all possible
structured flowcharts and hence the set of all possible structured programs.

The beauty of the structured approach is that we use only seven simple single-entry/
single-exit pieces and we assemble them in only two simple ways. Figure 2.37 shows the
kinds of stacked building blocks that emerge from applying rule 2 and the kinds of nested
building blocks that emerge from applying rule 3. The figure also shows the kind of overlapped building blocks that cannot appear in structured flowcharts (because of the elimination of the **goto** statement).

If the rules in Fig. 2.33 are followed, an unstructured flowchart (such as that in Fig.
2.38) cannot be created. If you are uncertain if a particular flowchart is structured, apply
the rules of Fig. 2.33 in reverse to try to reduce the flowchart to the simplest flowchart. If
the flowchart is reducible to the simplest flowchart, the original flowchart is structured; otherwise, it is not.

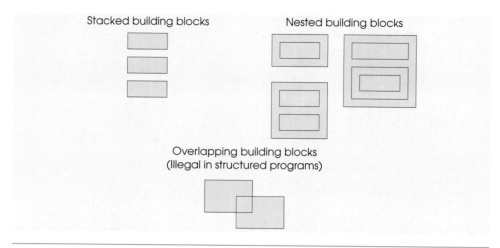

Fig. 2.37   Stacked, nested and overlapped building blocks.

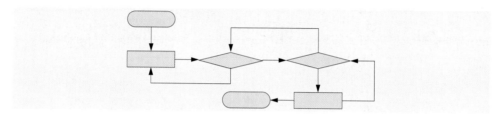

Fig. 2.38   An unstructured flowchart.

Structured programming promotes simplicity. Bohm and Jacopini have given us the result that only three forms of control are needed:

- Sequence
- Selection
- Repetition

Sequence is trivial. Selection is implemented in one of three ways:

- **if** structure (single selection)
- **if/else** structure (double selection)
- **switch** structure (multiple selection)

In fact, it is straightforward to prove that the simple **if** structure is sufficient to provide any form of selection—everything that can be done with the **if/else** structure and the **switch** structure can be implemented by combining **if** structures (although perhaps not as clearly and efficiently).

Repetition is implemented in one of three ways:

- **while** structure
- **do/while** structure
- **for** structure

It is straightforward to prove that the **while** structure is sufficient to provide any form of repetition. Everything that can be done with the **do/while** structure and the **for** structure can be done with the **while** structure (although perhaps not as smoothly).

Combining these results illustrates that any form of control ever needed in a C++ program can be expressed in terms of the following:

- sequence
- **if** structure (selection)
- **while** structure (repetition)

and that these control structures can be combined in only two ways—stacking and nesting. Indeed, structured programming promotes simplicity.

In this chapter, we discussed how to compose programs from control structures containing actions and decisions. In Chapter 3, we will introduce another program-structuring unit called the *function*. We will learn to compose large programs by combining functions that, in turn, are composed of control structures. We will also discuss how functions promote software reusability. In Chapter 6, we will introduce C++'s other program-structuring unit called the *class*. We will then create objects from classes and proceed with our treatment of object-oriented programming. Now, we continue our introduction to objects by introducing a problem that the reader will attack with the techniques of object-oriented design.

2.22 (Optional Case Study) Thinking About Objects: Identifying the Classes in a Problem

Now we begin our optional, object-oriented design/implementation case study. These "Thinking About Objects" sections at the ends of this and the next several chapters will ease you into object orientation by examining an elevator simulation case study. This case study will provide you with a substantial, carefully paced, complete design and implementation experience. In Chapters 2 through 5 we will perform the various steps of an object-oriented design (OOD) using the UML. In Chapters 6, 7 and 9, we will implement the elevator simulator using the techniques of object-oriented programming (OOP) in C++. We present this case study in a fully solved format. This is not an exercise; rather it is an end-to-end learning experience that concludes with a detailed walkthrough of the C++ code. We have provided this case study so you can become accustomed to the kinds of substantial problems that are attacked in industry. We hope you enjoy this experience.

Problem Statement
A company intends to build a two-floor office building and equip it with an elevator. The company wants you to develop an object-oriented *software simulator* in C++ that models the operation of the elevator to determine whether or not it will meet their needs.

Your simulator should include a clock that begins with its time, in seconds, set to zero. The clock ticks (increments the time by one) every second; it does not keep track of hours and minutes. Your simulator should also include a scheduler that begins the day by randomly scheduling two times: the time when a person will step onto floor 1 and press the button on the floor to summon the elevator, and the time when a person will step onto floor

2 and press the button on the floor to summon the elevator. Each of these times is a random integer in the range of 5 to 20, inclusive (i.e., 5, 6, 7, ..., 20). [Note: You will learn how to schedule random times in Chapter 3.] When the clock time equals the earlier of these two times, the scheduler creates a person, who then walks onto the appropriate floor and presses the floor button. [Note: It is possible that these two randomly scheduled times will be identical, in which case people will step onto both floors and press both floor buttons at the same time.] The floor button illuminates, indicating that it has been pressed. [Note: The illumination of the floor button occurs automatically when the button is pressed and needs no programming; the light built into the button turns off automatically when the button is reset.] The elevator starts the day waiting with its door closed on floor 1. To conserve energy, the elevator moves only when necessary. The elevator alternates directions between moving up and moving down.

For simplicity, the elevator and each of the floors have a capacity of one person. The scheduler first verifies that a floor is unoccupied before creating a person to walk onto that floor. If the floor is occupied, the scheduler delays creating the person by one second (thus giving the elevator an opportunity to pick up the person and clear the floor). After a person walks onto a floor, the scheduler creates the next random time (between 5 and 20 seconds into the future) for a person to walk onto that floor and press the floor button.

When the elevator arrives at a floor, it resets the elevator button and sounds the elevator bell (which is inside the elevator). The elevator then signals its arrival to the floor. The floor, in response, resets the floor button and turns on the floor's elevator arrival light. The elevator then opens its door. [Note: The door on the floor opens automatically with the elevator door and needs no programming.] The elevator's passenger, if there is one, exits the elevator, and a person, if there is one waiting on that floor, enters the elevator. Although each floor has a capacity of one person, assume there is enough room on each floor for a person to wait on that floor while the elevator's passenger, if there is one, exits.

A person entering the elevator presses the elevator button, which illuminates (automatically, without programming) when pressed and turns off when the elevator arrives on the floor and resets the elevator button. [Note: Because there are only two floors, only one elevator button is necessary; this button simply tells the elevator to move to the other floor.] Next, the elevator closes its door and begins moving to the other floor. When the elevator arrives at a floor, if a person does not enter the elevator and the floor button on the other floor has not been pressed, the elevator closes its door and remains on that floor until a button on a floor is pressed.

For simplicity, assume that all the activities that happen once the elevator reaches a floor, and until the elevator closes its door, take zero time. [Note: Although these activities take zero time, they still occur sequentially, e.g., the elevator door must open before the passenger exits the elevator.] The elevator takes five seconds to move from either floor to the other. Once per second, the simulator provides the time to the scheduler and to the elevator. The scheduler and elevator use the time to determine what actions each needs to take at that particular time, e.g., the scheduler may determine that it is time to create a person; and the elevator, if moving, may determine that it is time to arrive at its destination floor.

The simulator should display messages on the screen describing the activities that occur in the system. These include a person pressing a floor button, the elevator arriving on a floor, the clock ticking, a person entering the elevator, etc. The output should resemble the following:

```
Enter run time: 30
(scheduler schedules next person for floor 1 at time 5)
(scheduler schedules next person for floor 2 at time 17)


*** ELEVATOR SIMULATION BEGINS ***

TIME: 1
elevator at rest on floor 1

TIME: 2
elevator at rest on floor 1

TIME: 3
elevator at rest on floor 1

TIME: 4
elevator at rest on floor 1

TIME: 5
scheduler creates person 1
person 1 steps onto floor 1
person 1 presses floor button on floor 1
floor 1 button summons elevator
(scheduler schedules next person for floor 1 at time 20)
elevator resets its button
elevator rings its bell
floor 1 resets its button
floor 1 turns on its light
elevator opens its door on floor 1
person 1 enters elevator from floor 1
person 1 presses elevator button
elevator button tells elevator to prepare to leave
floor 1 turns off its light
elevator closes its door on floor 1
elevator begins moving up to floor 2 (arrives at time 10)

TIME: 6
elevator moving up

TIME: 7
elevator moving up

TIME: 8
elevator moving up

TIME: 9
elevator moving up

TIME: 10
elevator arrives on floor 2
elevator resets its button
elevator rings its bell
floor 2 resets its button
floor 2 turns on its light
```

```
elevator opens its door on floor 2
person 1 exits elevator on floor 2
floor 2 turns off its light
elevator closes its door on floor 2
elevator at rest on floor 2

TIME: 11
elevator at rest on floor 2

TIME: 12
elevator at rest on floor 2

TIME: 13
elevator at rest on floor 2

TIME: 14
elevator at rest on floor 2

TIME: 15
elevator at rest on floor 2

TIME: 16
elevator at rest on floor 2

TIME: 17
scheduler creates person 2
person 2 steps onto floor 2
person 2 presses floor button on floor 2
floor 2 button summons elevator
(scheduler schedules next person for floor 2 at time 34)
elevator resets its button
elevator rings its bell
floor 2 resets its button
floor 2 turns on its light
elevator opens its door on floor 2
person 2 enters elevator from floor 2
person 2 presses elevator button
elevator button tells elevator to prepare to leave
floor 2 turns off its light
elevator closes its door on floor 2
elevator begins moving down to floor 1 (arrives at time 22)

TIME: 18
elevator moving down

TIME: 19
elevator moving down

TIME: 20
scheduler creates person 3
person 3 steps onto floor 1
person 3 presses floor button on floor 1
floor 1 button summons elevator
(scheduler schedules next person for floor 1 at time 26)
```

```
elevator moving down

TIME: 21
elevator moving down

TIME: 22
elevator arrives on floor 1
elevator resets its button
elevator rings its bell
floor 1 resets its button
floor 1 turns on its light
elevator opens its door on floor 1
person 2 exits elevator on floor 1
person 3 enters elevator from floor 1
person 3 presses elevator button
elevator button tells elevator to prepare to leave
floor 1 turns off its light
elevator closes its door on floor 1
elevator begins moving up to floor 2 (arrives at time 27)

TIME: 23
elevator moving up

TIME: 24
elevator moving up

TIME: 25
elevator moving up

TIME: 26
scheduler creates person 4
person 4 steps onto floor 1
person 4 presses floor button on floor 1
floor 1 button summons elevator
(scheduler schedules next person for floor 1 at time 35)
elevator moving up

TIME: 27
elevator arrives on floor 2
elevator resets its button
elevator rings its bell
floor 2 resets its button
floor 2 turns on its light
elevator opens its door on floor 2
person 3 exits elevator on floor 2
floor 2 turns off its light
elevator closes its door on floor 2
elevator begins moving down to floor 1 (arrives at time 32)

TIME: 28
elevator moving down

TIME: 29
elevator moving down
```

```
TIME: 30
elevator moving down

*** ELEVATOR SIMULATION ENDS ***
```

Our goal (over these "Thinking About Objects" sections in Chapters 2 through 7 and Chapter 9) is to implement a working software simulator that models the operation of the elevator for the number of seconds entered by simulator user.

Analyzing and Designing the System

In this and the next several "Thinking About Objects" sections, we perform the steps of an object-oriented design process for the elevator system. The UML is designed for use with any OOAD process—many such processes exist. One popular method is the *Rational Unified Process*™ developed by Rational Software Corporation. For this case study, we present our own simplified design process for your first OOD/UML experience.

Before we begin, we must examine the nature of simulations. A simulation consists of two portions. One contains all the elements that belong to the world we want to simulate. These elements include the elevator, the floors, the buttons, the lights, etc. Let us call this the *world portion*. The other portion contains all the elements needed to simulate this world. These elements include the clock and the scheduler. We call this the *controller portion*. We will keep these two portions in mind as we design our system.

Use Case Diagrams

When developers begin a project, they rarely start with a detailed problem statement, such as the one we have provided at the beginning of this section (Section 2.22). This document and others are usually the result of the *object-oriented analysis* (OOA) phase. In this phase you interview the people who want you to build the system and the people who will eventually use the system. You use the information gained in these interviews to compile a list of *system requirements*. These requirements guide you and your fellow developers as you design the system. In our case study, the problem statement contains the system requirements for the elevator system. The output of the analysis phase is intended to specify clearly *what* the system is supposed to do. The output of the design phase is intended to clearly specify *how* the system should be constructed to do what is needed.

The UML provides the *use case diagram* to facilitate the process of requirements gathering. The use case diagram models the interactions between the system's external clients and the *use cases* of the system. Each use case represents a different capability that the system provides the client. For example, an automated teller machine has several use cases, including "Deposit," "Withdraw" and "Transfer Funds."

Figure 2.39 shows the use case diagram for the elevator system. The stick figure represents an *actor*. Actors are any external entities such as people, robots, other systems, etc., that use the system. The only actors in our system are the people who want to ride the elevator. We therefore model one actor called "Person." The actor's "name" appears underneath the stick figure.

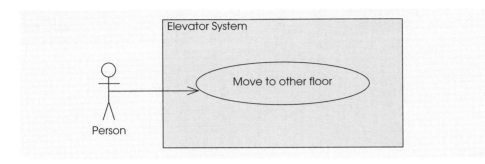

Fig. 2.39   Use case diagram for elevator system.

The *system box* (i.e., the enclosing rectangle in the figure) contains the use cases for the system. Notice that the box is labeled "Elevator System." This title shows that *this use case model focuses on the behaviors of the system we want to simulate* (i.e., elevator transporting people), *as opposed to the behaviors of the simulation* (i.e., creating people and scheduling arrivals).

The UML models each use case as an oval. In our simple system, actors use the elevator for only one purpose: to move to another floor. The system provides only one capability to its users; therefore, "Move to other floor" is the only use case in our elevator system.

As you build your system, you rely on the use case diagram to ensure that all the clients' needs are met. Our case study contains only one use case. In larger systems, use case diagrams are indispensable tools that help systems designers remain focused on satisfying the users' needs. The goal of the use case diagram is to show the kinds of interactions users have with a system without providing the details of those interactions.

Identifying the Classes in a System
The next step of our OOD process is to *identify the classes* in our problem. We will eventually describe these classes in a formal way and implement them in C++ (we begin implementing the elevator simulator in C++ in Chapter 6). First we review the problem statement and locate all the *nouns*; with high likelihood, these represent most of the classes (or instances of classes) necessary to implement the elevator simulator. Figure 2.40 is a list of these nouns.

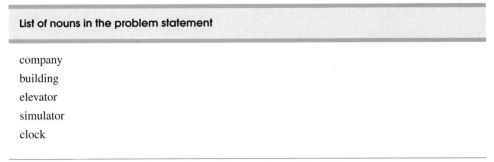

List of nouns in the problem statement

company
building
elevator
simulator
clock

Fig. 2.40   List of nouns in problem statement (part 1 of 2).

List of nouns in the problem statement

---

time

scheduler

person

floor 1

floor button

floor 2

elevator door

energy

capacity

elevator button

elevator bell

floor's elevator arrival light

person waiting on a floor

elevator's passenger

Fig. 2.40   List of nouns in problem statement (part 2 of 2).

We choose only the nouns that perform important duties in our system. For this reason we omit the following:

- company
- simulator
- time
- energy
- capacity

We do not need to model "company" as a class, because the company is not part of the simulation; the company simply wants us to model the elevator. The "simulator" is our entire C++ program, not an individual class. The "time" is a property of the clock, not an entity itself. We do not model "energy" in our simulation (although electric, gas or oil companies might certainly be interested in doing so in their simulation programs) and, finally, "capacity" is a property of the elevator and of the floor—not a separate entity itself.

We determine the classes for our system by filtering the remaining nouns into categories. Each remaining noun from Fig. 2.40 refers to one or more of the following categories:

- building
- elevator
- clock
- scheduler
- person (person waiting on a floor, elevator's passenger)

- floor (floor 1, floor 2)

- floor button

- elevator button

- bell

- light

- door

These categories are likely to be the classes we will need to implement for our system. Notice that we create one category for the buttons on the floors and one category for the button on the elevator. The two types of buttons perform different duties in our simulation—the buttons on the floors summon the elevator, and the button in the elevator tells the elevator to begin moving to the other floor.

We can now model the classes in our system based on the categories we derived. By convention, we will capitalize class names. If the name of a class contains more than one word, we run the words together and capitalize each word (e.g., **MultipleWordName**). Using this convention, we create classes **Elevator**, **Clock**, **Scheduler**, **Person**, **Floor**, **Door**, **Building**, **FloorButton**, **ElevatorButton**, **Bell** and **Light**. We construct our system using all of these classes as building blocks. Before we begin building the system, however, we must gain a better understanding of how the classes relate to one another.

Class Diagrams

The UML enables us to model the classes in the elevator system and their relationships via the *class diagram*. Figure 2.41 shows how to represent a class using the UML. Here, we model class **Elevator**. In a class diagram, each class is modeled as a rectangle. This rectangle can then be divided into three parts. The top part contains the name of the class.

The middle part contains the class's *attributes*. We discuss attributes in the "Thinking About Objects" section at the end of Chapter 3. The bottom contains the class's *operations*. We discuss operations in the "Thinking About Objects" section at the end of Chapter 4.

Classes relate to one another via *associations*. Figure 2.42 shows how our classes **Building**, **Elevator** and **Floor** relate to one another. Notice that the rectangles in this diagram are not subdivided into three sections. The UML allows the truncation of class symbols in this manner in order to create more readable diagrams.

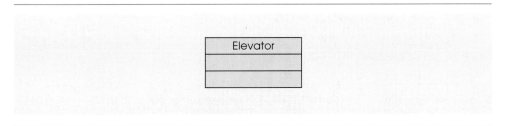

Fig. 2.41   Representing a class in the UML.

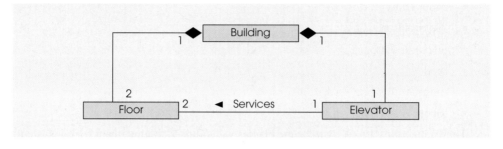

Fig. 2.42   Associations between classes in a class diagram.

In this class diagram, a solid line that connects classes represents an association. An association is a relationship between classes. The numbers near the lines express *multiplicity* values. Multiplicity values indicate *how many* objects of a class participate in the association. From the diagram, we see that two objects of class **Floor** participate in the association with one object of class **Building**. Therefore, class **Building** has a *one-to-two* relationship with class **Floor**; we can also say that class **Floor** has a *two-to-one relationship* with class **Building**. From the diagram, you can see that class **Building** has a *one-to-one* relationship with class **Elevator** and vice versa. Using the UML, we can model many types of multiplicity. Figure 2.43 shows the multiplicity types and how to represent them.

An association can be named. For example, the word "Services" above the line connecting classes **Floor** and **Elevator** indicates the name of that association—the arrow shows the direction of the association. This part of the diagram reads: "one object of class **Elevator** services two objects of class **Floor**."

The solid diamond attached to the association lines of class **Building** indicates that class **Building** has a *composition* relationship with classes **Floor** and **Elevator**. Composition implies a whole/part relationship. The class that has the composition symbol (the solid diamond) on its end of the association line is the whole (in this case, **Building**), and the class on the other end of the association line is the part (i.e., **Floor** and **Elevator**). [2]

Symbol	Meaning
0	None.
1	One.
m	An integer value.

Fig. 2.43   Multiplicity table (part 1 of 2).

---

2. According to the UML 1.3 specifications, classes in a composition relationship observe the following three properties: 1) only one class in the relationship may represent the whole (i.e., the diamond can only be placed on one end of the association line); 2) composition implies coincident lifetimes of the parts with the whole, and the whole is responsible for the creation and destruction of its parts; 3) a part may only belong to one whole at a time, although the part may be removed and attached to another whole, which then assumes responsibility for the part.

Symbol	Meaning
0..1	Zero or one.
$m..n$	At least m, but not more than n.
*	Any non-negative integer.
0..*	Zero or more
1..*	One or more

Fig. 2.43　Multiplicity table (part 2 of 2).

Figure 2.44 shows the full class diagram for the elevator system. All the classes we created are modeled, as well as the associations between these classes. [Note: In Chapter 9, we expand our class diagram by using the object-oriented concept of *inheritance*.]

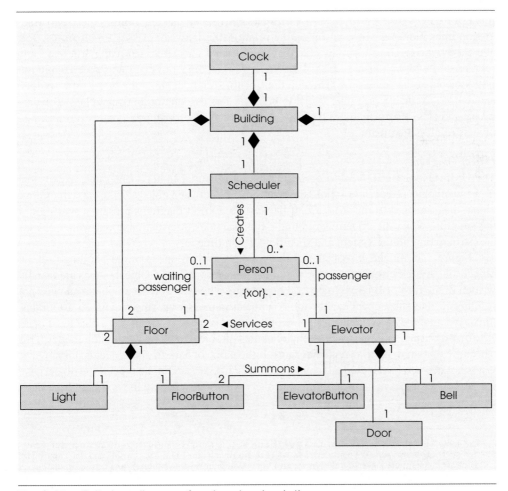

Fig. 2.44　Full class diagram for elevator simulation.

Class **Building** is represented near the top of the diagram and is composed of four classes, including **Clock** and **Scheduler**. These two classes make up the controller portion of the simulation.[3] Class **Building** is also composed of class **Elevator** and class **Floor** (notice the one-to-two relationship between class **Building** and class **Floor**).

Classes **Floor** and **Elevator** are modeled near the bottom of the diagram. Class **Floor** is composed of one object each of classes **Light** and **FloorButton**. Class **Elevator** is composed of one object each of classes **ElevatorButton**, class **Door** and class **Bell**.

The classes involved in an association can also have *roles*. Roles help clarify the relationship between two classes. For example, class **Person** plays the "waiting passenger" role in its association with class **Floor** (because the person is waiting for the elevator.) Class **Person** plays the passenger role in its association with class **Elevator**. In a class diagram, the name of a class's role is placed on either side of the association line, near the class's rectangle. Each class in an association can play a different role.

The association between class **Floor** and class **Person** indicates that an object of class **Floor** can relate to zero or one objects of class **Person**. Class **Elevator** also relates to zero or one objects of class **Person**. The dashed line that bridges these two association lines indicates a *constraint* on the relationship between classes **Person**, **Floor** and **Elevator**. The constraint says that an object of class **Person** can participate in a relationship with an object of class **Floor** or with an object of class **Elevator**, but not both objects at the same time. The notation for this relationship is the word "xor" (which stands for "exclusive or") placed inside braces.[4] The association between class **Scheduler** and class **Person** states that one object of class **Scheduler** creates zero or more objects of class **Person**.

Object Diagrams

The UML also defines *object diagrams*, which are similar to class diagrams, except that they model objects and *links*—links are relationships between objects. Like class diagrams, object diagrams model the structure of the system. Object diagrams present a snapshot of the structure while the system is running—this provides information about which objects are participating in the system at a specific point in time.

Figure 2.45 models a snapshot of the system when no one is in the building (i.e., no objects of class **Person** exist in the system at this point in time). Object names are usually written in the form: **objectName : ClassName**. The first word in an object name is not capitalized, but subsequent words are. All object names in an object diagram are underlined. We omit the object name for some of the objects in the diagram (e.g., objects of class **FloorButton**). In large systems, many names of objects will be used in the model. This can cause cluttered, hard-to-read diagrams. If the name of a particular object is unknown or if it is not necessary to include the name (i.e., we only care about the type of the object), we can leave the object name out. In this instance, we simply display the colon and the class name.

---

3. The composite relationship between class **Building** and classes **Clock** and **Scheduler** represents a design decision on our part. We consider class **Building** to be part of both the "world" and the "controller" portions of our simulation. In our design we give the building the responsibility of running the simulation.
4. Constraints in UML diagrams can be written with what is known as the **Object Constraint Language** (**OCL**). The OCL was created so that modelers could express constraints on a system in an clearly defined way. To learn more, visit *www-4.ibm.com/software/ad/standards/ocl.html*.

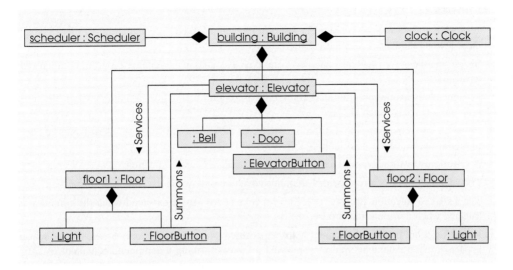

Fig. 2.45   Object diagram of empty building.

Now we have identified the classes for this system (although we may discover others in later phases of the design process). We have also examined the system's use case. In the "Thinking About Objects" section at the end of Chapter 3, we use this knowledge to examine how the system changes over time. As we expand our knowledge, we will also discover new information that will enable us to describe our classes in greater depth.

Notes

1. You will learn how to implement randomness in the next chapter (Chapter 3), where we study random number generation. Random number generation helps you simulate random processes like coin tossing and dice rolling. It will also help you simulate people arriving at random to use the elevator.

2. Because the real world is so object-oriented, it will be quite natural for you to pursue this project, even though you have not yet formally studied object orientation.

Questions

1. How might you decide whether the elevator is able to handle the anticipated traffic volume?

2. Why might it be more complicated to implement a three-story (or taller) building?

3. It is common for large buildings to have many elevators. We will see in Chapter 6 that once we have created one elevator object, it is easy to create as many as we want. What problems or opportunities do you foresee in having several elevators, each of which may pick up and discharge passengers at every floor in a large building?

4. For simplicity, we have given our elevator and each floor a capacity of one passenger. What problems or opportunities do you foresee in being able to increase these capacities?

SUMMARY

- A procedure for solving a problem in terms of the actions to be executed and the order in which these actions should be executed is called an algorithm.

- Specifying the order in which statements are to be executed in a computer program is called program control.

- Pseudocode helps the programmer "think out" a program before attempting to write it in a programming language such as C++.

- Declarations are messages to the compiler telling it the names and attributes of variables and telling it to reserve space for variables.

- A selection structure is used to choose among alternative courses of action.

- The **if** selection structure executes an indicated action only when the condition is true.

- The **if/else** selection structure specifies separate actions to be executed when the condition is true and when the condition is false.

- Whenever more than one statement is to be executed where normally only a single statement is expected, these statements must be enclosed in braces forming a compound statement. A compound statement can be placed anywhere a single statement can be placed.

- An empty statement indicating that no action is to be taken is indicated by placing a semicolon (**;**) where a statement would normally be.

- A repetition structure specifies that an action is to be repeated while some condition remains true.

- The format for the **while** repetition structure is

    while (*condition* **)**
        statement

- A value that contains a fractional part is referred to as a floating-point number and is represented by the data types **float** or **double**.

- The unary cast operator **static_cast< double >( )** creates a temporary floating-point copy of its operand.

- C++ provides the arithmetic assignment operators **+=**, **-=**, ***=**, **/=** and **%=** that help abbreviate certain common types of expressions.

- C++ provides the increment (**++**) and decrement (**--**) operators to increment or decrement a variable by 1. If the operator is prefixed to the variable, the variable is incremented or decremented by 1 first, then used in its expression. If the operator is postfixed to the variable, the variable is used in its expression, then incremented or decremented by 1.

- A loop is a group of instructions the computer executes repeatedly until some terminating condition is satisfied. Two forms of repetition are counter-controlled repetition and sentinel-controlled repetition.

- A loop counter is used to count repetitions for a group of instructions. It is incremented (or decremented), usually by 1, each time the group of instructions is performed.

- Sentinel values are generally used to control repetition when the precise number of repetitions is not known in advance and the loop includes statements that obtain data each time the loop is performed. A sentinel value is entered after all valid data items have been supplied to the program. Sentinels should be different from valid data items.

- The **for** repetition structure handles all the details of counter-controlled repetition. The general format of the **for** structure is

    for (*initialization***;** *loopContinuationTest***;** *increment* **)**
        statement

where *initialization* initializes the loop's control variable, *loopContinuationTest* is the loop-continuation condition and *increment* increments the control variable.

- The **do/while** repetition structure tests the loop-continuation condition at the end of the loop, so the body of the loop will be executed at least once. The format for the **do/while** structure is

```
do
     statement
while ( condition );
```

- The **break** statement, when executed in one of the repetition structures (**for**, **while** and **do/while**), causes immediate exit from the structure.

- The **continue** statement, when executed in one of the repetition structures (**for**, **while** and **do/while**), skips any remaining statements in the body of the structure and proceeds with the next iteration of the loop.

- The **switch** statement handles a series of decisions in which a particular variable or expression is tested for values it can assume and different actions are taken. In most programs, it is necessary to include a **break** statement after the statements for each **case**. Several **case**s can execute the same statements by listing the **case** labels together before the statements. The **switch** structure can only test constant integral expressions. It is not necessary to enclose a multistatement **case** in braces.

- On UNIX systems and many others, end-of-file is entered by typing the sequence

    <ctrl-d>

on a line by itself. On VMS and DOS, end-of-file is entered by typing

    <ctrl-z>

possibly followed by pressing the *Enter* key.

- Logical operators can be used to form complex conditions by combining conditions. The logical operators are **&&**, **||** and **!**, meaning logical AND, logical OR and logical NOT (negation), respectively.

- Any nonzero value implicitly converts to **true**; 0 (zero) implicitly converts to **false**.

TERMINOLOGY

! operator
&& operator
|| operator
++ operator
-- operator
?: operator
action/decision model
algorithm
arithmetic assignment operators:
    +=, **-=**, ***=**, **/=** and **%=**
ASCII character set
block
body of a loop
bool
break

case label
cast operator
char
cin.get() function
compound statement
conditional operator (**?:**)
continue
control structure
counter-controlled repetition
decrement operator (**--**)
default case in **switch**
definite repetition
definition
delay loop
do/while repetition structure

double
double-selection structure
empty statement (**;**)
EOF
false
fatal error
field width
fixed-point format
float
for repetition structure
garbage value
if selection structure
if/else selection structure
increment operator (**++**)
indefinite repetition
infinite loop
initialization
integer division
ios::fixed
ios::left
ios::showpoint
keyword
logic error
logical AND (**&&**)
logical negation (**!**)
logical operators
logical OR (**||**)
long
loop counter
loop-continuation condition
looping
lvalue ("left value")
multiple-selection structure
nested control structures
nonfatal error

off-by-one error
parameterized stream manipulator
postdecrement operator
postincrement operator
pow function
predecrement operator
preincrement operator
pseudocode
repetition
repetition structures
rvalue ("right value")
selection
sentinel value
sequential execution
setiosflags stream manipulator
setprecision stream manipulator
setw stream manipulator
short
single-entry/single-exit control structures
single-selection structure
stacked control structures
static_cast< *type* **>()**
structured programming
switch selection structure
syntax error
ternary operator
top-down, stepwise refinement
transfer of control
true
unary operator
undefined value
while repetition structure
whitespace characters
|| operator

"Thinking About Objects" Terminology

actor
association
association name
class diagram
composition
constraint
controller portion of a simulation
identify the classes in a system
link
multiplicity
Object Constraint Language (OCL)
object diagram
object-oriented analysis (OOA)
object-oriented analysis and design (OOAD)

object-oriented design (OOD)
one-to-one relationship
one-to-two relationship
Rational Unified Process
rectangle symbol in UML class diagram
role
software simulator
solid diamond symbol in UML class and
    object diagram
solid line symbol in UML class and
    object diagram
static structure of a system
system box
system requirements

two-to-one relationship
use case
use case diagram

"what vs. how"
world portion of a simulation
xor

COMMON PROGRAMMING ERRORS

2.1   Using a keyword as an identifier is a syntax error.

2.2   Forgetting one or both of the braces that delimit a compound statement can lead to syntax errors or logic errors in a program.

2.3   Placing a semicolon after the condition in an **if** structure leads to a logic error in single-selection **if** structures and a syntax error in double-selection **if** structures (if the **if**-part contains an actual body statement).

2.4   Not providing, in the body of a **while** structure, an action that eventually causes the condition in the **while** to become **false** normally results in an error called an "infinite loop" in which the repetition structure never terminates.

2.5   Spelling the keyword **while** with an uppercase **W**, as in **While** (remember that C++ is a case-sensitive language), is a syntax error. All of C++'s reserved keywords such as **while**, **if** and **else** contain only lowercase letters.

2.6   If a counter or total is not initialized, the results of your program will probably be incorrect. This is an example of a logic error.

2.7   In a counter-controlled loop, because the loop counter (when counting up by one each time through the loop) is one higher than its last legitimate value (i.e., 11 in the case of counting from 1 to 10), using the counter value in a calculation after the loop is often an off-by-one-error.

2.8   Choosing a sentinel value that is also a legitimate data value is a logic error.

2.9   An attempt to divide by zero causes a fatal error.

2.10   Using floating-point numbers in a manner that assumes they are represented precisely can lead to incorrect results. Floating-point numbers are represented only approximately by most computers.

2.11   Attempting to use the increment or decrement operator on an expression other than a simple variable name, e.g., writing **++(x + 1)**, is a syntax error.

2.12   Because floating-point values are approximate, controlling counting loops with floating-point variables can result in imprecise counter values and inaccurate tests for termination.

2.13   Using an incorrect relational operator or using an incorrect final value of a loop counter in the condition of a **while** or **for** structure can cause off-by-one errors.

2.14   When the control variable of a **for** structure is initially defined in the initialization section of the **for** structure header, using the control variable after the body of the structure is a syntax error.

2.15   Using commas instead of the two required semicolons in a **for** header is a syntax error.

2.16   Placing a semicolon immediately to the right of the right parenthesis of a **for** header makes the body of that **for** structure an empty statement. This is normally a logic error.

2.17   Not using the proper relational operator in the loop-continuation condition of a loop that counts downwards (such as incorrectly using **i <= 1** in a loop counting down to 1) is usually a logic error that will yield incorrect results when the program runs.

2.18   Forgetting to include the **<cmath>** file in a program that uses math library functions is a syntax error.

2.19   Forgetting a **break** statement when one is needed in a **switch** structure is a logic error.

2.20   Omitting the space between the word **case** and the integral value being tested in a **switch** structure can cause a logic error. For example, writing **case3:** instead of writing **case 3:** simply creates an unused label. (We will say more about this in Chapter 18.) The problem is that the **switch** structure will not perform the appropriate actions when the **switch**'s controlling expression has a value of 3.

2.21   Not processing newline and other whitespace characters in the input when reading characters one at a time can cause logic errors.

2.22   Providing identical **case** labels in a **switch** structure is a syntax error

2.23   Infinite loops are caused when the loop-continuation condition in a **while**, **for** or **do/while** structure never becomes **false**. To prevent this, make sure the value of the condition does change somewhere in the header or body of the loop so the condition can eventually become **false**.

2.24   Although **3 < x < 7** is a mathematically correct condition, it does not evaluate correctly in C++. Use **(3 < x && x < 7)** to get the proper evaluation in C++.

2.25   In expressions using operator **&&**, it is possible that a condition—we will call this the dependent condition—might require another condition to be **true** for it to be meaningful to evaluate the dependent condition. In this case, the dependent condition should be placed after the other condition, or an error might occur.

2.26   Using operator **==** for assignment and using operator **=** for equality are logic errors.

GOOD PROGRAMMING PRACTICES

2.1   Consistently applying reasonable indentation conventions throughout your programs greatly improves program readability. We suggest a fixed-size tab of about 1/4 inch or three blanks per indent.

2.2   Pseudocode is often used to "think out" a program during the program-design process. Then the pseudocode program is converted to C++.

2.3   Indent both body statements of an **if/else** structure.

2.4   If there are several levels of indentation, each level should be indented the same additional amount of space.

2.5   Always putting the braces in an **if/else** structure (or any control structure) helps prevent their accidental omission, especially when adding statements to an **if** or **else** clause at a later time.

2.6   Some programmers prefer to type the beginning and ending braces of compound statements before typing the individual statements within the braces. This helps avoid omitting one or both of the braces.

2.7   Initialize counters and totals.

2.8   Declare each variable on a separate line.

2.9   When performing division by an expression whose value could be zero, explicitly test for this case and handle it appropriately in your program (such as by printing an error message) rather than allowing the fatal error to occur.

2.10   Prompt the user for each keyboard input. The prompt should indicate the form of the input and any special input values (like the sentinel value the user should enter to terminate a loop).

2.11   In a sentinel-controlled loop, the prompts requesting data entry should explicitly remind the user what the sentinel value is.

2.12   Do not compare floating-point values for equality or inequality. Rather, test that the absolute value of the difference is less than a specified small value.

2.13   Initializing variables when they are declared helps the programmer avoid the problems of un-initialized data.

2.14   Unary operators should be placed next to their operands with no intervening spaces.

2.15   Control counting loops with integer values.

2.16   Indent the statements in the body of each control structure.

2.17   Put a blank line before and after each control structure to make it stand out in the program.

2.18   Too many levels of nesting can make a program difficult to understand. As a general rule, try to avoid using more than three levels of indentation.

2.19   Vertical spacing above and below control structures, and indentation of the bodies of control structures within the control-structure headers give programs a two-dimensional appearance that greatly improves readability.

2.20   Using the final value in the condition of a **while** or **for** structure and using the **<=** relational operator will help avoid off-by-one errors. For a loop used to print the values 1 to 10, for example, the loop-continuation condition should be **counter <= 10** rather than **counter < 10** (which is an off-by-one error) or **counter < 11** (which is nevertheless correct). Many programmers nevertheless prefer so-called zero-based counting, in which, to count 10 times through the loop, **counter** would be initialized to zero and the loop-continuation test would be **counter < 10**.

2.21   Place only expressions involving the control variables in the initialization and increment sections of a **for** structure. Manipulations of other variables should appear either before the loop (if they execute only once, like initialization statements) or in the loop body (if they execute once per repetition, like incrementing or decrementing statements).

2.22   Although the value of the control variable can be changed in the body of a **for** loop, avoid doing so because this practice can lead to subtle logic errors.

2.23   Although statements preceding a **for** and statements in the body of a **for** can often be merged into the **for** header, avoid doing so because it can make the program more difficult to read.

2.24   Limit the size of control structure headers to a single line, if possible.

2.25   Do not use variables of type **float** or **double** to perform monetary calculations. The imprecision of floating-point numbers can cause errors that will result in incorrect monetary values. In the exercises, we explore the use of integers to perform monetary calculations. Note: C++ class libraries from third-party vendors are available for properly performing monetary calculations.

2.26   Provide a **default** case in **switch** statements. Cases not explicitly tested in a **switch** statement without a **default** case are ignored. Including a **default** case focuses the programmer on the need to process exceptional conditions. There are situations in which no **default** processing is needed. Although the **case** clauses and the **default** case clause in a **switch** structure can occur in any order, it is considered a good programming practice to place the **default** clause last.

2.27   In a **switch** structure when the **default** clause is listed last, the **break** statement is not required. Some programmers include this **break** for clarity and symmetry with other cases.

2.28   Some programmers always include braces in a **do/while** structure, even if the braces are not necessary. This helps eliminate ambiguity between the **while** structure and the **do/while** structure containing one statement.

2.29   Some programmers feel that **break** and **continue** violate structured programming. Because the effects of these statements can be achieved by structured programming techniques we will soon learn, these programmers do not use **break** and **continue**.

PERFORMANCE TIPS

2.1 A nested **if/else** structure can be much faster than a series of single-selection **if** structures because of the possibility of early exit after one of the conditions is satisfied.

2.2 In a nested **if/else** structure, test the conditions that are more likely to be **true** at the beginning of the nested **if/else** structure. This will enable the nested **if/else** structure to run faster and exit earlier than will testing infrequently occurring cases first.

2.3 Programmers can write programs a bit faster and compilers can compile programs a bit faster when the "abbreviated" assignment operators are used. Some compilers generate code that runs faster when "abbreviated" assignment operators are used.

2.4 Many of the performance tips we mention in this text result in nominal improvements, so the reader might be tempted to ignore them. Significant performance improvement is often realized when a supposedly nominal improvement is placed in a loop that repeats many times.

2.5 Avoid placing expressions whose values do not change inside loops—but, even if you do, many of today's sophisticated optimizing compilers will automatically place such expressions outside loops in the generated machine language code.

2.6 Many compilers contain optimization features that improve the code you write, but it is still better to write good code from the start.

2.7 In performance-oriented situations where memory is at a premium or execution speed is crucial, it might be desirable to use smaller integer sizes.

2.8 Using smaller integer sizes can result in a slower program if the machine's instructions for manipulating them are not as efficient as for the natural-size integers (e.g., sign extension must be done on them).

2.9 The **break** and **continue** statements, when used properly, perform faster than the corresponding structured techniques we will soon learn.

2.10 In expressions using operator **&&**, if the separate conditions are independent of one another make the condition that is most likely to be **false** the leftmost condition. In expressions using operator **||**, make the condition that is most likely to be **true** the leftmost condition. This can reduce a program's execution time.

PORTABILITY TIPS

2.1 In the C++ standard, the scope of the control variable declared in the initialization section of a **for** structure is different from the scope in older C++ compilers. C++ code created with old C++ compilers can break when compiled on compilers that are compatible with the C++ standard. These are two defensive programming strategies that can be used to prevent this problem: Either define control variables with different names in every **for** structure, or, if you prefer to use the same name for the control variable in several **for** structures, define control variable outside and before the first **for** loop.

2.2 The keystroke combinations for entering end-of-file are system dependent.

2.3 Testing for the symbolic constant **EOF** rather than –1 makes programs more portable. The ANSI standard states that **EOF** is a negative integral value (but not necessarily –1). Thus, **EOF** could have different values on different systems.

2.4 Because **int**s vary in size between systems, use **long** integers if you expect to process integers outside the range –32,768 to 32,767 and you would like to be able to run the program on several different computer systems.

2.5 For compatibility with earlier versions of the C++ standard, the **bool** value **true** can also be represented by any nonzero value and the **bool** value **false** can also be represented as the value **0**.

SOFTWARE ENGINEERING OBSERVATIONS

2.1   Any C++ program we will ever build can be constructed from only seven different types of control structures (sequence, **if**, **if/else**, **switch**, **while**, **do/while** and **for**) combined in only two ways (control-structure stacking and control-structure nesting).

2.2   A compound statement can be placed anywhere in a program that a single statement can be placed.

2.3   Just as a compound statement can be placed anywhere a single statement can be placed, it is also possible to have no statement at all, i.e., the empty statement. The empty statement is represented by placing a semicolon (**;**) where a statement would normally be.

2.4   Each refinement, as well as the top itself, is a complete specification of the algorithm; only the level of detail varies.

2.5   Many programs can be divided logically into three phases: an initialization phase that initializes the program variables; a processing phase that inputs data values and adjusts program variables accordingly; and a termination phase that calculates and prints the final results.

2.6   The programmer terminates the top-down, stepwise refinement process when the pseudocode algorithm is specified in sufficient detail for the programmer to be able to convert the pseudocode to C++. Implementing the C++ program is then normally straightforward.

2.7   Experience has shown that the most difficult part of solving a problem on a computer is developing the algorithm for the solution. Once a correct algorithm has been specified, the process of producing a working C++ program from the algorithm is normally straightforward.

2.8   Many experienced programmers write programs without ever using program development tools like pseudocode. These programmers feel that their ultimate goal is to solve the problem on a computer and that writing pseudocode merely delays the production of final outputs. Although this may work for simple and familiar problems, it can lead to serious errors and delays on large, complex projects.

2.9   Placing a semicolon immediately after a **for** header is sometimes used to create a so-called delay loop. Such a **for** loop with an empty body still loops the indicated number of times doing nothing other than the counting. You might use a delay loop, for example, to slow down a program that is producing outputs on the screen too quickly for you to read them.

2.10   There is a tension between achieving quality software engineering and achieving the best-performing software. Often, one of these goals is achieved at the expense of the other.

TESTING AND DEBUGGING TIPS

2.1   Programmers normally write conditions such as **x == 7** with the variable name on the left and the constant on the right. By reversing these so that the constant is on the left and the variable name is on the right as in **7 == x**, the programmer who accidentally replaces the **==** operator with **=** will be protected by the compiler. The compiler will treat this as a syntax error because only a variable name can be placed on the left-hand side of an assignment statement. At least this will prevent the potential devastation of a run-time logic error.

2.2   Use your text editor to search for all occurrences of **=** in your program and check that you have the correct operator in each place.

SELF-REVIEW EXERCISES

Exercises 2.1 through 2.10 correspond to Sections 2.1 through 2.12.
Exercises 2.11 through 2.13 correspond to Sections 2.13 through 2.21.

2.1   Answer each of the following questions.
  a) All programs can be written in terms of three types of control structures: _____, _____ and _____.
  b) The _____selection structure is used to execute one action when a condition is **true** and another action when that condition is **false**.
  c) Repeating a set of instructions a specific number of times is called _____ repetition.
  d) When it is not known in advance how many times a set of statements will be repeated, a _____value can be used to terminate the repetition.

2.2   Write four different C++ statements that each add 1 to integer variable **x**.

2.3   Write C++ statements to accomplish each of the following:
  a) Assign the sum of **x** and **y** to **z** and increment the value of **x** by 1 after the calculation.
  b) Test if the value of the variable **count** is greater than 10. If it is, print "**Count is greater than 10.**"
  c) Decrement the variable **x** by 1 then subtract it from the variable **total**.
  d) Calculate the remainder after **q** is divided by **divisor** and assign the result to **q**. Write this statement two different ways.

2.4   Write a C++ statement to accomplish each of the following tasks.
  a) Declare variables **sum** and **x** to be of type **int**.
  b) Initialize variable **x** to **1**.
  c) Initialize variable **sum** to **0**.
  d) Add variable **x** to variable **sum** and assign the result to variable **sum**.
  e) Print **"The sum is: "** followed by the value of variable **sum**.

2.5   Combine the statements that you wrote in Exercise 2.4 into a program that calculates and prints the sum of the integers from 1 to 10. Use the **while** structure to loop through the calculation and increment statements. The loop should terminate when the value of **x** becomes 11.

2.6   Determine the values of each variable after the calculation is performed. Assume that, when each statement begins executing, all variables have the integer value 5.
  a) **product *= x++;**
  b) **quotient /= ++x;**

2.7   Write single C++ statements that do the following:
  a) Input integer variable **x** with **cin** and **>>**.
  b) Input integer variable **y** with **cin** and **>>**.
  c) Initialize integer variable **i** to **1**.
  d) Initialize integer variable **power** to **1**.
  e) Multiply variable **power** by **x** and assign the result to **power**.
  f) Increment variable **y** by **1**.
  g) Test **y** to see if it is less than or equal to **x**.
  h) Output integer variable **power** with **cout** and **<<**.

2.8   Write a C++ program that uses the statements in Exercise 2.7 to calculate **x** raised to the **y** power. The program should have a **while** repetition control structure.

2.9   Identify and correct the errors in each of the following:
  a) ```while (c <= 5) {
       product *= c;
       ++c;```

b) `cin << value;`

c) ```
if (gender == 1)
    cout << "Woman" << endl;
else;
    cout << "Man" << endl;
```

2.10    What is wrong with the following **while** repetition structure?

```
while ( z >= 0 )
    sum += z;
```

2.11   State whether the following are true or false. If the answer is false, explain why.

a) The **default** case is required in the **switch** selection structure.

b) The **break** statement is required in the default case of a **switch** selection structure to exit the structure properly.

c) The expression (x > y && a < b) is **true** if either the expression x > y is **true** or the expression a < b is **true**.

d) An expression containing the || operator is **true** if either or both of its operands are **true**.

2.12   Write a C++ statement or a set of C++ statements to accomplish each of the following:

a) Sum the odd integers between 1 and 99 using a **for** structure. Assume the integer variables **sum** and **count** have been declared.

b) Print the value **333.546372** in a field width of **15** characters with precisions of **1, 2** and **3**. Print each number on the same line. Left-justify each number in its field. What three values print?

c) Calculate the value of **2.5** raised to the power **3** using the **pow** function. Print the result with a precision of **2** in a field width of **10** positions. What prints?

d) Print the integers from 1 to 20 using a **while** loop and the counter variable **x**. Assume that the variable **x** has been declared, but not initialized. Print only 5 integers per line. Hint: Use the calculation x % 5. When the value of this is 0, print a newline character, otherwise print a tab character.

e) Repeat Exercise 2.12 (d) using a **for** structure.

2.13   Find the error(s) in each of the following code segments and explain how to correct it (them).

a) ```
x = 1;
while (x <= 10);
    x++;
}
```

b) ```
for (y = .1; y != 1.0; y += .1)
    cout << y << endl;
```

c) ```
switch ( n ) {
    case 1:
        cout << "The number is 1" << endl;
    case 2:
        cout << "The number is 2" << endl;
        break;
    default:
        cout << "The number is not 1 or 2" << endl;
        break;
}
```

d) **The following code should print the values 1 to 10.**
```
n = 1;
while ( n < 10 )
    cout << n++ << endl;
```

ANSWERS TO SELF-REVIEW EXERCISES

2.1   a) Sequence, selection and repetition. b) **if/else**. c) Counter-controlled or definite. d) Sentinel, signal, flag or dummy.

2.2   ```
x = x + 1;
x += 1;
++x;
x++;
```

2.3    a) `z = x++ + y;`
b) ```
if ( count > 10 )
    cout << "Count is greater than 10" << endl;
```
c) `total -= --x;`
d) ```
q %= divisor;
q = q % divisor;
```

2.4    a) `int sum, x;`
b) `x = 1;`
c) `sum = 0;`
d) `sum += x;` or `sum = sum + x;`
e) `cout << "The sum is: " << sum << endl;`

2.5    See below.

```
1   // Calculate the sum of the integers from 1 to 10
2   #include <iostream>
3
4   using std::cout;
5   using std::endl;
6
7   int main()
8   {
9      int sum, x;
10     x = 1;
11     sum = 0;
12     while ( x <= 10 ) {
13        sum += x;
14        ++x;
15     }
16     cout << "The sum is: " << sum << endl;
17     return 0;
18  }
```

2.6   a) **product = 25, x = 6;**
b) **quotient = 0, x = 6;**

2.7   a) `cin >> x;`
b) `cin >> y;`
c) `i = 1;`
```

d) **power = 1;**

e) **power *= x; or power = power * x;**

f) **i++;**

g) **if (i <= y)**

h) **cout << power << endl;**

2.8   See below.

```
1   // raise x to the y power
2   #include <iostream>
3
4   using std::cout;
5   using std::cin;
6   using std::endl;
7
8   int main()
9   {
10      int x, y, i, power;
11
12      i = 1;
13      power = 1;
14
15      cout << "Enter base as an integer: ";
16      cin >> x;
17
18      cout << "Enter exponent as an integer: ";
19      cin >> y;
20
21      while ( i <= y ) {
22         power *= x;
23         ++i;
24      }
25
26      cout << power << endl;
27      return 0;
28   }
```

2.9   a) Error: Missing the closing right brace of the **while** body.
Correction: Add closing right brace after the statement **++c;**.

b) Error: Used stream insertion instead of stream extraction.
Correction: Change **<<** to **>>**.

c) Error: Semicolon after **else** results in a logic error. The second output statement will always be executed.
Correction: Remove the semicolon after **else**.

2.10   The value of the variable **z** is never changed in the **while** structure. Therefore, if the loop-continuation condition **(z >= 0)** is **true**, an infinite loop is created. To prevent the infinite loop, **z** must be decremented so that it eventually becomes less than 0.

2.11   a) False. The **default** case is optional. If no default action is needed, then there is no need for a **default** case.

b) False. The **break** statement is used to exit the **switch** structure. The **break** statement is not required when the **default** case is the last case.

c) False. Both of the relational expressions must be **true** in order for the entire expression to be **true** when using the **&&** operator.

d) True.

2.12 a) ```
sum = 0;
for (count = 1; count <= 99; count += 2)
    sum += count;
```

b)  ```
cout << setiosflags(ios::fixed | ios::showpoint | ios::left)
    << setprecision( 1 ) << setw( 15 ) << 333.546372
    << setprecision( 2 ) << setw( 15 ) << 333.546372
    << setprecision( 3 ) << setw( 15 ) << 333.546372
    << endl;
```
Output is:

333.5   333.55   333.546

c) ```
cout << setiosflags(ios::fixed | ios::showpoint)
    << setprecision(2) << setw(10) << pow(2.5, 3)
    << endl;
```
Output is:

      15.63

d)  ```
x = 1;
while ( x <= 20 ) {
    cout << x;
    if ( x % 5 == 0 )
        cout << endl;
    else
        cout << '\t';
    x++;
}
```

e) ```
for (x = 1; x <= 20; x++) {
    cout << x;
    if (x % 5 == 0)
        cout << endl;
    else
        cout << '\t';
}
```

or

```
for ( x = 1; x <= 20; x++ )
    if ( x % 5 == 0 )
        cout << x << endl;
    else
        cout << x << '\t';
```

2.13 a) Error: The semicolon after the **while** header causes an infinite loop.
Correction: Replace the semicolon by a **{**, or remove both the **;** and the **}**.

b) Error: Using a floating-point number to control a **for** repetition structure.
Correction: Use an integer and perform the proper calculation in order to get the values you desire.

```
for ( y = 1; y != 10; y++ )
    cout << ( static_cast< double >( y ) / 10 ) << endl;
```
```

    c) Error: Missing **break** statement in the statements for the first **case**.
        Correction: Add a **break** statement at the end of the statements for the first **case**. Note
        that this is not necessarily an error if the programmer wants the statement of **case 2:** to
        execute every time the **case 1:** statement executes.
    d) Error: Improper relational operator used in the while repetition-continuation condition.
        Correction: Use **<=** rather than **<**, or change **10** to **11**.

EXERCISES

Exercises 2.14 through 2.38 correspond to Sections 2.1 through 2.12.
Exercises 2.39 through 2.63 correspond to Sections 2.13 through 2.21.

2.14   Identify and correct the error(s) in each of the following:

    a)
```
if ( age >= 65 );
    cout << "Age is greater than or equal to 65" << endl;
else
    cout << "Age is less than 65 << endl";
```

    b)
```
if ( age >= 65 )
    cout << "Age is greater than or equal to 65" << endl;
else;
    cout << "Age is less than 65 << endl";
```

    c)
```
int x = 1, total;
while ( x <= 10 ) {
    total += x;
    ++x;
}
```

    d)
```
While ( x <= 100 )
    total += x;
    ++x;
```

    e)
```
while ( y > 0 ) {
    cout << y << endl;
    ++y;
}
```

2.15   What does the following program print?

```
1   #include <iostream>
2
3   using std::cout;
4   using std::endl;
5
6   int main()
7   {
8       int y, x = 1, total = 0;
9
10      while ( x <= 10 ) {
11          y = x * x;
12          cout << y << endl;
13          total += y;
14          ++x;
15      }
```

```
16
17        cout << "Total is " << total << endl;
18        return 0;
19   }
```

For Exercises 2.16 to 2.19, perform each of these steps:
   a) Read the problem statement.
   b) Formulate the algorithm using pseudocode and top-down, stepwise refinement.
   c) Write a C++ program.
   d) Test, debug and execute the C++ program.

2.16   Drivers are concerned with the mileage obtained by their automobiles. One driver has kept track of several tankfuls of gasoline by recording miles driven and gallons used for each tankful. Develop a C++ program that will input the miles driven and gallons used for each tankful. The program should calculate and display the miles per gallon obtained for each tankful. After processing all input information, the program should calculate and print the combined miles per gallon obtained for all tankfuls.

```
Enter the gallons used (-1 to end): 12.8
Enter the miles driven: 287
The miles / gallon for this tank was 22.421875

Enter the gallons used (-1 to end): 10.3
Enter the miles driven: 200
The miles / gallon for this tank was 19.417475

Enter the gallons used (-1 to end): 5
Enter the miles driven: 120
The miles / gallon for this tank was 24.000000

Enter the gallons used (-1 to end): -1

The overall average miles/gallon was 21.601423
```

2.17   Develop a C++ program that will determine if a department store customer has exceeded the credit limit on a charge account. For each customer, the following facts are available:
   a) Account number (an integer)
   b) Balance at the beginning of the month
   c) Total of all items charged by this customer this month
   d) Total of all credits applied to this customer's account this month
   e) Allowed credit limit

   The program should input each of these facts, calculate the new balance (= beginning balance + charges – credits) and determine if the new balance exceeds the customer's credit limit. For those customers whose credit limit is exceeded, the program should display the customer's account number, credit limit, new balance and the message "Credit limit exceeded".

```
Enter account number (-1 to end): 100
Enter beginning balance: 5394.78
Enter total charges: 1000.00
Enter total credits: 500.00
Enter credit limit: 5500.00
Account:        100
Credit limit: 5500.00
Balance:        5894.78
Credit Limit Exceeded.

Enter account number (-1 to end): 200
Enter beginning balance: 1000.00
Enter total charges: 123.45
Enter total credits: 321.00
Enter credit limit: 1500.00

Enter account number (-1 to end): 300
Enter beginning balance: 500.00
Enter total charges: 274.73
Enter total credits: 100.00
Enter credit limit: 800.00

Enter account number (-1 to end): -1
```

2.18   One large chemical company pays its salespeople on a commission basis. The salespeople receive $200 per week plus 9 percent of their gross sales for that week. For example, a salesperson who sells $5000 worth of chemicals in a week receives $200 plus 9 percent of $5000, or a total of $650. Develop a C++ program that will input each salesperson's gross sales for last week and calculate and display that salesperson's earnings. Process one salesperson's figures at a time.

```
Enter sales in dollars (-1 to end): 5000.00
Salary is: $650.00

Enter sales in dollars (-1 to end): 6000.00
Salary is: $740.00

Enter sales in dollars (-1 to end): 7000.00
Salary is: $830.00

Enter sales in dollars (-1 to end): -1
```

2.19   Develop a C++ program that will determine the gross pay for each of several employees. The company pays "straight-time" for the first 40 hours worked by each employee and pays "time-and-a-half" for all hours worked in excess of 40 hours. You are given a list of the employees of the company, the number of hours each employee worked last week and the hourly rate of each employee. Your program should input this information for each employee and should determine and display the employee's gross pay.

```
Enter hours worked (-1 to end): 39
Enter hourly rate of the worker ($00.00): 10.00
Salary is $390.00

Enter hours worked (-1 to end): 40
Enter hourly rate of the worker ($00.00): 10.00
Salary is $400.00

Enter hours worked (-1 to end): 41
Enter hourly rate of the worker ($00.00): 10.00
Salary is $415.00

Enter hours worked (-1 to end): -1
```

2.20 The process of finding the largest number (i.e., the maximum of a group of numbers) is used frequently in computer applications. For example, a program that determines the winner of a sales contest would input the number of units sold by each salesperson. The salesperson who sells the most units wins the contest. Write a pseudocode program, then a C++ program that inputs a series of 10 numbers, and determines and prints the largest of the numbers. Hint: Your program should use three variables, as follows:

counter: A counter to count to 10 (i.e., to keep track of how many numbers have been input and to determine when all 10 numbers have been processed).
number: The current number input to the program.
largest: The largest number found so far.

2.21 Write a C++ program that utilizes looping and the tab escape sequence **\t** to print the following table of values:

N	10*N	100*N	1000*N
1	10	100	1000
2	20	200	2000
3	30	300	3000
4	40	400	4000
5	50	500	5000

2.22 Using an approach similar to Exercise 2.20, find the *two* largest values among the 10 numbers. Note: You must input each number only once.

2.23 Modify the program in Fig. 2.11 to validate its inputs. On any input, if the value entered is other than 1 or 2, keep looping until the user enters a correct value.

2.24 What does the following program print?

```
1   #include <iostream>
2
3   using std::cout;
4   using std::endl;
5
```

```
6   int main()
7   {
8      int count = 1;
9
10     while ( count <= 10 ) {
11        cout << (count % 2 ? "****" : "++++++++")
12              << endl;
13        ++count;
14     }
15
16     return 0;
17  }
```

2.25   What does the following program print?

```
1   #include <iostream>
2
3   using std::cout;
4   using std::endl;
5
6   int main()
7   {
8      int row = 10, column;
9
10     while ( row >= 1 ) {
11        column = 1;
12
13        while ( column <= 10 ) {
14           cout << (row % 2 ? "<" : ">");
15           ++column;
16        }
17
18        --row;
19        cout << endl;
20     }
21
22     return 0;
23  }
```

2.26   *(Dangling Else Problem)* Determine the output for each of the following when **x** is **9** and **y** is **11** and when **x** is **11** and **y** is **9**. Note that the compiler ignores the indentation in a C++ program. Also, the C++ compiler always associates an **else** with the previous **if** unless told to do otherwise by the placement of braces **{}**. Because, on first glance, the programmer may not be sure which **if** an **else** matches, this is referred to as the "dangling else" problem. We have eliminated the indentation from the following code to make the problem more challenging. (Hint: Apply indentation conventions you have learned.)

```
a)  if ( x < 10 )
    if ( y > 10 )
    cout << "*****" << endl;
    else
    cout << "#####" << endl;
    cout << "$$$$$" << endl;
```

b)
```
if ( x < 10 ) {
if ( y > 10 )
cout << "*****" << endl;
}
else {
cout << "#####" << endl;
cout << "$$$$$" << endl;
}
```

2.27   *(Another Dangling Else Problem)* Modify the following code to produce the output shown. Use proper indentation techniques. You must not make any changes other than inserting braces. The compiler ignores indentation in a C++ program. We have eliminated the indentation from the following code to make the problem more challenging. Note: It is possible that no modification is necessary.

```
if ( y == 8 )
if ( x == 5 )
cout << "@@@@@" << endl;
else
cout << "#####" << endl;
cout << "$$$$$" << endl;
cout << "&&&&&" << endl;
```

a) Assuming **x = 5** and **y = 8**, the following output is produced.

```
@@@@@
$$$$$
&&&&&
```

b) Assuming **x = 5** and **y = 8**, the following output is produced.

```
@@@@@
```

c) Assuming **x = 5** and **y = 8**, the following output is produced.

```
@@@@@
&&&&&
```

d) Assuming **x = 5** and **y = 7**, the following output is produced. Note: The last three output statements after the **else** are all part of a compound statement.

```
#####
$$$$$
&&&&&
```

2.28   Write a program that reads in the size of the side of a square and then prints a hollow square of that size out of asterisks and blanks. Your program should work for squares of all side sizes between 1 and 20. For example, if your program reads a size of 5, it should print

```
*****
*   *
*   *
*   *
*****
```

2.29   A palindrome is a number or a text phrase that reads the same backwards as forwards. For example, each of the following five-digit integers is a palindrome: 12321, 55555, 45554 and 11611. Write a program that reads in a five-digit integer and determines whether it is a palindrome. (Hint: Use the division and modulus operators to separate the number into its individual digits.)

2.30   Input an integer containing only 0s and 1s (i.e., a "binary" integer) and print its decimal equivalent. (Hint: Use the modulus and division operators to pick off the "binary" number's digits one at a time from right to left. Just as in the decimal number system where the rightmost digit has a positional value of 1 and the next digit left has a positional value of 10, then 100, then 1000, etc., in the binary number system, the rightmost digit has a positional value of 1, the next digit left has a positional value of 2, then 4, then 8, etc. Thus the decimal number 234 can be interpreted as 4 * 1 + 3 * 10 + 2 * 100. The decimal equivalent of binary 1101 is 1 * 1 + 0 * 2 + 1 * 4 + 1 * 8 or 1 + 0 + 4 + 8, or 13.)

2.31   Write a program that displays the following checkerboard pattern

```
* * * * * * * *
 * * * * * * * *
* * * * * * * *
 * * * * * * * *
* * * * * * * *
 * * * * * * * *
* * * * * * * *
 * * * * * * * *
```

Your program must use only three output statements, one of each of the following forms:

```
cout << "* ";
cout << ' ';
cout << endl;
```

2.32   Write a program that keeps printing the multiples of the integer 2, namely 2, 4, 8, 16, 32, 64, etc. Your loop should not terminate (i.e., you should create an infinite loop). What happens when you run this program?

2.33   Write a program that reads the radius of a circle (as a **double** value) and computes and prints the diameter, the circumference and the area. Use the value 3.14159 for π.

2.34   What's wrong with the following statement? Provide the correct statement to accomplish what the programmer was probably trying to do.

```
cout << ++( x + y );
```

2.35   Write a program that reads three nonzero **double** values and determines and prints if they could represent the sides of a triangle.

2.36   Write a program that reads three nonzero integers and determines and prints if they could be the sides of a right triangle.

2.37   A company wants to transmit data over the telephone, but they are concerned that their phones may be tapped. All of their data are transmitted as four-digit integers. They have asked you to write a program that encrypts their data so that it can be transmitted more securely. Your program should read a four-digit integer and encrypt it as follows: Replace each digit by *(the sum of that digit plus 7) modulus 10*. Then, swap the first digit with the third, swap the second digit with the fourth and print the encrypted integer. Write a separate program that inputs an encrypted four-digit integer and decrypts it to form the original number.

2.38   The factorial of a nonnegative integer n is written $n!$ (pronounced "n factorial") and is defined as follows:

$$n! = n \cdot (n-1) \cdot (n-2) \cdot \ldots \cdot 1 \quad \text{(for values of } n \text{ greater than or equal to 1)}$$

and

$$n! = 1 \quad \text{(for } n = 0\text{)}.$$

For example, $5! = 5 \cdot 4 \cdot 3 \cdot 2 \cdot 1$, which is 120.

   a) Write a program that reads a nonnegative integer and computes and prints its factorial.
   b) Write a program that estimates the value of the mathematical constant e by using the formula:

$$e = 1 + \frac{1}{1!} + \frac{1}{2!} + \frac{1}{3!} + \ldots$$

   c) Write a program that computes the value of e^x by using the formula

$$e^x = 1 + \frac{x}{1!} + \frac{x^2}{2!} + \frac{x^3}{3!} + \ldots$$

2.39   Find the error(s) in each of the following:

   a) ```
For (x = 100, x >= 1, x++)
    cout << x << endl;
```
   b)  The following code should print whether integer **value** is odd or even:
```
switch (value % 2) {
    case 0:
        cout << "Even integer" << endl;
    case 1:
        cout << "Odd integer" << endl;
}
```
   c)  The following code should output the odd integers from 19 to 1:
```
for (x = 19; x >= 1; x += 2)
    cout << x << endl;
```
   d)  The following code should output the even integers from 2 to 100:
```
counter = 2;

do {
    cout << counter << endl;
    counter += 2;
} While (counter < 100);
```
```

2.40   Write a program that sums a sequence of integers. Assume that the first integer read specifies the number of values remaining to be entered. Your program should read only one value per input statement. A typical input sequence might be

        5 100 200 300 400 500

where the **5** indicates that the subsequent **5** values are to be summed.

2.41   Write a program that calculates and prints the average of several integers. Assume the last value read is the sentinel **9999**. A typical input sequence might be

        10 8 11 7 9 9999

indicating that the average of all the values preceding **9999** is to be calculated.

2.42   What does the following program do?

```
1    #include <iostream>
2
3    using std::cout;
4    using std::cin;
5    using std::endl;
6
7    int main()
8    {
9       int x, y;
10
11      cout << "Enter two integers in the range 1-20: ";
12      cin >> x >> y;
13
14      for ( int i = 1; i <= y; i++ ) {
15
16         for ( int j = 1; j <= x; j++ )
17            cout << '@';
18
19         cout << endl;
20      }
21
22      return 0;
23   }
```

2.43   Write a program that finds the smallest of several integers. Assume that the first value read specifies the number of values remaining and that the first number is not one of the integers to compare.

2.44   Write a program that calculates and prints the product of the odd integers from 1 to 15.

2.45   The *factorial* function is used frequently in probability problems. The factorial of a positive integer *n* (written *n!* and pronounced "n factorial") is equal to the product of the positive integers from 1 to *n*. Write a program that evaluates the factorials of the integers from 1 to 5. Print the results in tabular format. What difficulty might prevent you from calculating the factorial of 20?

2.46   Modify the compound interest program of Section 2.15 to repeat its steps for interest rates of 5 percent, 6 percent, 7 percent, 8 percent, 9 percent and 10 percent. Use a **for** loop to vary the interest rate.

2.47   Write a program that prints the following patterns separately one below the other. Use **for** loops to generate the patterns. All asterisks (*) should be printed by a single statement of the form **cout << '*';** (this causes the asterisks to print side by side). Hint: The last two patterns require that each line begin with an appropriate number of blanks. Extra credit: Combine your code from the four separate problems into a single program that prints all four patterns side by side by making clever use of nested **for** loops.

```
(A)                  (B)                  (C)                  (D)
*                    **********           **********                    *
**                   *********             *********                   **
***                  ********               ********                  ***
****                 *******                 *******                 ****
*****                ******                   ******                *****
******               *****                     *****               ******
*******              ****                       ****               *******
********             ***                         ***               ********
*********            **                           **               *********
**********           *                             *               **********
```

2.48   One interesting application of computers is drawing graphs and bar charts (sometimes called "histograms"). Write a program that reads five numbers (each between 1 and 30). For each number read, your program should print a line containing that number of adjacent asterisks. For example, if your program reads the number seven, it should print *******.

2.49   A mail order house sells five different products whose retail prices are product 1 — $2.98, product 2—$4.50, product 3—$9.98, product 4—$4.49 and product 5—$6.87. Write a program that reads a series of pairs of numbers as follows:
   a) Product number
   b) Quantity sold for one day

Your program should use a **switch** statement to help determine the retail price for each product. Your program should calculate and display the total retail value of all products sold last week.

2.50   Modify the program of Fig. 2.22 so that it calculates the grade-point average for the class. A grade of 'A' is worth 4 points, 'B' is worth 3 points, etc.

2.51   Modify the program in Fig. 2.21 so it uses only integers to calculate the compound interest. (Hint: Treat all monetary amounts as integral numbers of pennies. Then "break" the result into its dollar portion and cents portion by using the division and modulus operations. Insert a period.)

2.52   Assume $i = 1$, $j = 2$, $k = 3$ and $m = 2$. What does each of the following statements print? Are the parentheses necessary in each case?
   a) **cout << (i == 1) << endl;**
   b) **cout << (j == 3) << endl;**
   c) **cout << (i >= 1 && j < 4) << endl;**
   d) **cout << (m <= 99 && k < m) << endl;**
   e) **cout << (j >= i || k == m) << endl;**
   f) **cout << (k + m < j || 3 - j >= k) << endl;**
   g) **cout << (!m) << endl;**
   h) **cout << (!(j - m)) << endl;**
   i) **cout << (!(k > m)) << endl;**

2.53   Write a program that prints a table of the binary, octal and hexadecimal equivalents of the decimal numbers in the range 1 through 256. If you are not familiar with these number systems, read Appendix C first.

2.54   Calculate the value of π from the infinite series

$$\pi = 4 - \frac{4}{3} + \frac{4}{5} - \frac{4}{7} + \frac{4}{9} - \frac{4}{11} + \cdots$$

Print a table that shows the value of π approximated by 1 term of this series, by two terms, by three terms, etc. How many terms of this series do you have to use before you first get 3.14? 3.141? 3.1415? 3.14159?

2.55   *(Pythagorean Triples)* A right triangle can have sides that are all integers. The set of three integer values for the sides of a right triangle is called a Pythagorean triple. These three sides must satisfy the relationship that the sum of the squares of two of the sides is equal to the square of the hypotenuse. Find all Pythagorean triples for **side1**, **side2** and **hypotenuse** all no larger than 500. Use a triple-nested **for**-loop that tries all possibilities. This is an example of "brute force" computing. You will learn in more advanced computer science courses that there are many interesting problems for which there is no known algorithmic approach other than using sheer brute force.

2.56   A company pays its employees as managers (who receive a fixed weekly salary), hourly workers (who receive a fixed hourly wage for up to the first 40 hours they work and "time-and-a-half," i.e., 1.5 times their hourly wage, for overtime hours worked), commission workers (who receive $250 plus 5.7% of their gross weekly sales), or pieceworkers (who receive a fixed amount of money per item for each of the items they produce—each pieceworker in this company works on only one type of item). Write a program to compute the weekly pay for each employee. You do not know the number of employees in advance. Each type of employee has its own pay code: Managers have paycode 1, hourly workers have code 2, commission workers have code 3 and pieceworkers have code 4. Use a **switch** to compute each employee's pay based on that employee's paycode. Within the **switch**, prompt the user (i.e., the payroll clerk) to enter the appropriate facts your program needs to calculate each employee's pay based on that employee's paycode.

2.57   *(De Morgan's Laws)* In this chapter, we discussed the logical operators **&&**, **||** and **!**. De Morgan's Laws can sometimes make it more convenient for us to express a logical expression. These laws state that the expression **!** (*condition1* **&&** *condition2*) is logically equivalent to the expression (**!***condition1* **||** **!***condition2*). Also, the expression **!** (*condition1* **||** *condition2*) is logically equivalent to the expression (**!***condition1* **&&** **!***condition2*). Use De Morgan's Laws to write equivalent expressions for each of the following, then write a program to show that both the original expression and the new expression in each case are equivalent:

    a) **!(x < 5) && !(y >= 7)**
    b) **!(a == b) || !(g != 5)**
    c) **!((x <= 8) && (y > 4))**
    d) **!((i > 4) || (j <= 6))**

2.58   Write a program that prints the following diamond shape. You may use output statements that print either a single asterisk (*****) or a single blank. Maximize your use of repetition (with nested **for** structures) and minimize the number of output statements.

```
    *
   ***
  *****
 *******
*********
 *******
  *****
   ***
    *
```

2.59   Modify the program you wrote in Exercise 2.58 to read an odd number in the range 1 to 19 to specify the number of rows in the diamond. Your program should then display a diamond of the appropriate size.

2.60   A criticism of the **break** statement and the **continue** statement is that each is unstructured. Actually **break** statements and **continue** statements can always be replaced by structured statements, although doing so can be awkward. Describe in general how you would remove any **break** statement from a loop in a program and replace that statement with some structured equivalent. (Hint: The **break** statement leaves a loop from within the body of the loop. The other way to leave is by failing the loop-continuation test. Consider using in the loop-continuation test a second test that indicates "early exit because of a 'break' condition.") Use the technique you developed here to remove the break statement from the program of Fig. 2.26.

2.61   What does the following program segment do?

```
1    for ( i = 1; i <= 5; i++ ) {
2       for ( j = 1; j <= 3; j++ ) {
3          for ( k = 1; k <= 4; k++ )
4             cout << '*';
5          cout << endl;
6       }
7       cout << endl;
8    }
```

2.62   Describe in general how you would remove any **continue** statement from a loop in a program and replace that statement with some structured equivalent. Use the technique you developed here to remove the **continue** statement from the program of Fig. 2.27.

2.63   *("The Twelve Days of Christmas" Song)* Write a program that uses repetition and **switch** structures to print the song "The Twelve Days of Christmas." One **switch** structure should be used to print the day (i.e., "First," "Second," etc.). A separate **switch** structure should be used to print the remainder of each verse.

Exercise 2.64 corresponds to Section 2.22, "Thinking About Objects."

2.64   Describe in 200 words or less what an automobile is and does. List the nouns and verbs separately. In the text, we stated that each noun might correspond to an object that will need to be built to implement a system, in this case a car. Pick five of the objects you listed, and, for each, list several attributes and several behaviors. Describe briefly how these objects interact with one another and other objects in your description. You have just performed several of the key steps in a typical object-oriented design.

2.65   *(Peter Minuit Problem)* Legend has it that in 1626 Peter Minuit purchased Manhattan for $24.00 in barter. Did he make a good investment? To answer this question, modify the compound interest program of Fig. 2.21 to begin with a principal of $24.00 and to calculate the amount of interest on deposit if that money had been kept on deposit until this year (374 years through 2000). Run the program with interest rates of 5%, 6%, 7%, 8%, 9% and 10% to observe the wonders of compound interest.

3

Functions

Objectives

- To understand how to construct programs modularly from small pieces called functions.
- To be able to create new functions.
- To understand the mechanisms used to pass information between functions.
- To introduce simulation techniques using random number generation.
- To understand how the visibility of identifiers is limited to specific regions of programs.
- To understand how to write and use functions that call themselves.

Form ever follows function.
Louis Henri Sullivan

E pluribus unum.
(One composed of many.)
Virgil

O! call back yesterday, bid time return.
William Shakespeare
Richard II

Call me Ishmael.
Herman Melville
Moby Dick

When you call me that, smile.
Owen Wister

Outline

3.1 Introduction

Most computer programs that solve real-world problems are much larger than the programs presented in the first few chapters. Experience has shown that the best way to develop and maintain a large program is to construct it from smaller pieces or components each, of which is more manageable than the original program. This technique is called *divide and conquer.* This chapter describes many key features of the C++ language that facilitate the design, implementation, operation and maintenance of large programs.

3.2 Program Components in C++

Modules in C++ are called *functions* and *classes.* C++ programs are typically written by combining new functions the programmer writes with "pre-packaged" functions available in the *C++ standard library* and by combining new classes the programmer writes with "pre-packaged" classes available in various class libraries. In this chapter, we concentrate on functions; we will discuss classes in detail beginning with Chapter 6.

The C++ standard library provides a rich collection of functions for performing common mathematical calculations, string manipulations, character manipulations, input/output, error checking and many other useful operations. This makes the programmer's job easier, because these functions provide many of the capabilities programmers need. The C++ standard library functions are provided as part of the C++ programming environment.

Good Programming Practice 3.1

Familiarize yourself with the rich collection of functions and classes in the C++ standard library.

Software Engineering Observation 3.1

Avoid reinventing the wheel. When possible, use C++ standard library functions instead of writing new functions. This reduces program development time.

Portability Tip 3.1

Using the functions in the C++ standard library helps make programs more portable.

Performance Tip 3.1

Do not try to rewrite existing library routines to make them more efficient. You usually will not be able to increase the performance of these routines.

The programmer can write functions to define specific tasks that could be used at many points in a program. These are sometimes referred to as *programmer-defined functions*. The actual statements defining the function are written only once, and these statements are hidden from other functions.

A function is *invoked* (i.e., made to perform its designated task) by a *function call*. The function call specifies the function name and provides information (as *arguments*) that the called function needs to do its job. A common analogy for this is the hierarchical form of management. A boss (the *calling function* or *caller*) asks a worker (the *called function*) to perform a task and *return* (i.e., report back) the results when the task is done. The boss function does not know *how* the worker function performs its designated tasks. The worker might call other worker functions, and the boss will be unaware of this. We will soon see how this "hiding" of implementation details promotes good software engineering. Figure 3.1 shows the **main** function communicating with several worker functions in a hierarchical manner. Note that **worker1** acts as a boss function to **worker4** and **worker5**. Relationships among functions may be other than the hierarchical structure shown in this figure.

3.3 Math Library Functions

Math library functions allow the programmer to perform certain common mathematical calculations. We use various math library functions here to introduce the concept of functions. Later in the book, we will discuss many of the other functions in the C++ standard library.

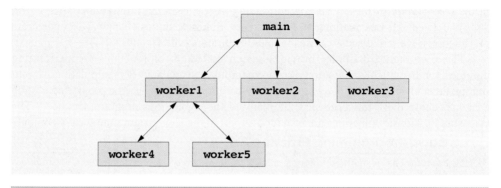

Fig. 3.1   Hierarchical boss function/worker function relationship.

Functions are normally called by writing the name of the function, followed by a left parenthesis, followed by the *argument* (or a comma-separated list of arguments) of the function, followed by a right parenthesis. For example, a programmer desiring to calculate and print the square root of **900.0** might write

```
cout << sqrt( 900.0 );
```

When this statement is executed, the math library function **sqrt** is called to calculate the square root of the number contained in the parentheses (**900.0**). The number **900.0** is the *argument* of the **sqrt** function. The preceding statement would print **30**. The **sqrt** function takes an argument of type **double** and returns a result of type **double**. All functions in the math library return the data type **double**. To use the math library functions, include the header file **<cmath>**.

Common Programming Error 3.1

Forgetting to include the math header file when using math library functions is a syntax error. A standard header file must be included for every standard library function used in a program.

Function arguments can be constants, variables, or expressions. If **c1 = 13.0, d = 3.0** and **f = 4.0**, then the statement

```
cout << sqrt( c1 + d * f );
```

calculates and prints the square root of **13.0 + 3.0 * 4.0 = 25.0**, namely **5** (because C++ does not ordinarily print trailing zeros or the decimal point in a floating-point number that has no fractional part).

Some math library functions are summarized in Fig. 3.2. In the figure, the variables **x** and **y** are of type **double**.

3.4 Functions

Functions allow the programmer to modularize a program. All variables declared in function definitions are *local variables*—they are known only in the function in which they are defined. Most functions have a list of *parameters* that provide the means for communicating information between functions. A function's parameters are also local variables.

Method	Description	Example
ceil(x)	rounds x to the smallest integer not less than x	ceil(9.2) is 10.0 ceil(-9.8) is -9.0
cos(x)	trigonometric cosine of x (x in radians)	cos(0.0) is 1.0
exp(x)	exponential function e^x	exp(1.0) is 2.71828 exp(2.0) is 7.38906
fabs(x)	absolute value of x	fabs(5.1) is 5.1 fabs(0.0) is 0.0 fabs(-8.76) is 8.76
floor(x)	rounds x to the largest integer not greater than x	floor(9.2) is 9.0 floor(-9.8) is -10.0
fmod(x, y)	remainder of x/y as a floating point number	fmod(13.657, 2.333) is 1.992
log(x)	natural logarithm of x (base e)	log(2.718282) is 1.0 log(7.389056) is 2.0
log10(x)	logarithm of x (base 10)	log10(10.0) is 1.0 log10(100.0) is 2.0
pow(x, y)	x raised to power y (x^y)	pow(2, 7) is 128 pow(9, .5) is 3
sin(x)	trigonometric sine of x (x in radians)	sin(0.0) is 0
sqrt(x)	square root of x	sqrt(900.0) is 30.0 sqrt(9.0) is 3.0
tan(x)	trigonometric tangent of x (x in radians)	tan(0.0) is 0

Fig. 3.2   Commonly used math library functions.

Software Engineering Observation 3.2

*In programs containing many functions, **main** should be implemented as a group of calls to functions that perform the bulk of the program's work.*

There are several motivations for "functionalizing" a program. The divide-and-conquer approach makes program development more manageable. Another motivation is *software reusability*—using existing functions as building blocks to create new programs. Software reusability is a major factor in object-oriented programming. With good function naming and definition, programs can be created from standardized functions that accomplish specific tasks, rather than being built by using customized code. A third motivation is to avoid repeating code in a program. Packaging code as a function allows the code to be executed from several locations in a program simply by calling the function.

Software Engineering Observation 3.3

Each function should be limited to performing a single, well-defined task, and the function name should effectively express that task. This promotes software reusability.

Software Engineering Observation 3.4

If you cannot choose a concise name that expresses what the function does, it is possible that your function is attempting to perform too many diverse tasks. It is usually best to break such a function into several smaller functions.

3.5 Function Definitions

Each program we have presented has consisted of a function called **main** that called standard library functions to accomplish its tasks. We now consider how programmers write their own customized functions.

Consider a program, with a user-defined function **square**, that calculates the squares of the integers from 1 to 10 (Fig. 3.3).

Good Programming Practice 3.2

Place a blank line between function definitions to separate the functions and enhance program readability.

Function **square** is *invoked* or *called* in **main** with the call

```
square( x )
```

Function **square** receives a copy of the value of **x** in the *parameter* **y**. Then **square** calculates **y * y**. The result is passed back to the point in **main** where **square** was invoked, and the result is displayed. Note that the value of **x** is not changed by the function call. This process is repeated ten times by using the **for** repetition structure.

```
1   // Fig. 3.3: fig03_03.cpp
2   // Creating and using a programmer-defined function
3   #include <iostream>
4
5   using std::cout;
6   using std::endl;
7
8   int square( int );    // function prototype
9
10  int main()
11  {
12     for ( int x = 1; x <= 10; x++ )
13        cout << square( x ) << "  ";
14
15     cout << endl;
16     return 0;
17  }
18
19  // Function definition
20  int square( int y )
21  {
22     return y * y;
23  }
```

Fig. 3.3   Creating and using a programmer-defined function (part 1 of 2).

```
1   4   9   16   25   36   49   64   81   100
```

Fig. 3.3   Creating and using a programmer-defined function (part 2 of 2).

The definition of **square** shows that it expects an integer parameter **y**. The keyword **int** preceding the function name indicates that **square** returns an integer result. The **return** statement in **square** passes the result of the calculation back to the calling function.

Line 8

```
int square( int );    // function prototype
```

is a *function prototype*. The data type **int** in parentheses informs the compiler that function **square** expects an integer value from the caller. The data type **int** to the left of the function name **square** informs the compiler that **square** returns an integer result to the caller. The compiler refers to the function prototype to check that calls to **square** contain the correct return type, the correct number of arguments and the correct argument types and that the arguments are in the correct order. The function prototype is not required if the definition of the function appears before the function's first use in the program. In such a case, the function definition also acts as the function prototype. If lines 20 through 23 in Fig. 3.3 were before **main**, the function prototype on line 8 would be unnecessary. Function prototypes are discussed in detail in Section 3.6.

The format of a function definition is

> *return-value-type function-name**(** parameter-list **)***
> **{**
>   *declarations and statements*
> **}**

The *function-name* is any valid identifier. The *return-value-type* is the data type of the result returned from the function to the caller. Return-value-type **void** indicates that a function does not return a value.

Common Programming Error 3.2
Omitting the return-value-type in a function definition is a syntax error.

Common Programming Error 3.3
Forgetting to return a value from a function that is supposed to return a value is a syntax error.

Common Programming Error 3.4
*Returning a value from a function whose return type has been declared **void** is a syntax error.*

The *parameter-list* is a comma-separated list containing the declarations of the parameters received by the function when it is called. If a function does not receive any values, *parameter-list* is **void** or simply left empty. A type must be listed explicitly for each parameter in the parameter list of a function.

Common Programming Error 3.5

Declaring function parameters of the same type as **float x, y** *instead of* **float x,**
float y*. The parameter declaration* **float x, y** *would actually report a compilation er-*
ror, because types are required for each parameter in the parameter list.

Common Programming Error 3.6

Placing a semicolon after the right parenthesis enclosing the parameter list of a function def-
inition is a syntax error.

Common Programming Error 3.7

Defining a function parameter again as a local variable in the function is a syntax error.

Good Programming Practice 3.3

Although it is not incorrect to do so, do not use the same names for the arguments passed to
a function and the corresponding parameters in the function definition. This helps avoid am-
biguity.

Common Programming Error 3.8

The **()** *in a function call is actually an operator in C++. It causes the function to be called.*
Forgetting the **()** *in a function call that takes no arguments is not a syntax error. The func-*
tion is not invoked when you probably intended it to be.

The *declarations* and *statements* in braces form the *function body.* The function body
is also referred to as a *block.* A block is simply a compound statement that includes declarations. Variables can be declared in any block, and blocks can be nested. *A function cannot*
be defined inside another function under any circumstances.

Common Programming Error 3.9

Defining a function inside another function is a syntax error.

Good Programming Practice 3.4

Choosing meaningful function names and meaningful parameter names makes programs
more readable and helps avoid excessive use of comments.

Software Engineering Observation 3.5

A function should fit in an editor window. Regardless of how long a function is, it should per-
form one task well. Small functions promote software reusability.

Software Engineering Observation 3.6

Programs should be written as collections of small functions. This makes programs easier to
write, debug, maintain and modify.

Software Engineering Observation 3.7

A function requiring a large number of parameters might be performing too many tasks. Con-
sider dividing the function into smaller functions that perform the separate tasks. The func-
tion header should fit on one line, if possible.

Common Programming Error 3.10

It is a syntax error if the function prototype, function header and function calls do not all agree
in the number, type and order of arguments and parameters and in the type of return value.

There are three ways to return control to the point at which a function was invoked. If the function does not return a result, control is returned simply when the function-ending right brace is reached, or by executing the statement

return;

If the function does return a result, the statement

return *expression***;**

returns the value of *expression* to the caller.

Our second example uses a programmer-defined function **maximum** to determine and return the largest of three integers (Fig. 3.4).

```cpp
1   // Fig. 3.4: fig03_04.cpp
2   // Finding the maximum of three integers
3   #include <iostream>
4
5   using std::cout;
6   using std::cin;
7   using std::endl;
8
9   int maximum( int, int, int );    // function prototype
10
11  int main()
12  {
13     int a, b, c;
14
15     cout << "Enter three integers: ";
16     cin >> a >> b >> c;
17
18     // a, b and c below are arguments to
19     // the maximum function call
20     cout << "Maximum is: " << maximum( a, b, c ) << endl;
21
22     return 0;
23  }
24
25  // Function maximum definition
26  // x, y and z below are parameters to
27  // the maximum function definition
28  int maximum( int x, int y, int z )
29  {
30     int max = x;
31
32     if ( y > max )
33        max = y;
34
35     if ( z > max )
36        max = z;
37
38     return max;
39  }
```

Fig. 3.4   Programmer-defined **maximum** function (part 1 of 2).

```
Enter three integers: 22 85 17
Maximum is: 85
```

```
Enter three integers: 92 35 14
Maximum is: 92
```

```
Enter three integers: 45 19 98
Maximum is: 98
```

Fig. 3.4   Programmer-defined **maximum** function (part 2 of 2).

The three integers are input. Next, the integers are passed to **maximum**, which determines the largest integer. This value is returned to **main** by the **return** statement in **maximum**. The value returned is then printed.

3.6 Function Prototypes

One of the most important features of C++ is the *function prototype*. A function prototype tells the compiler the name of the function, the type of data returned by the function, the number of parameters the function expects to receive, the types of the parameters and the order in which these parameters are expected. The compiler uses function prototypes to validate function calls. Early versions of C did not perform this kind of checking, so it was possible to call functions improperly without the compiler's detecting the errors. Such calls could result in fatal execution-time errors or nonfatal errors that caused subtle, difficult to detect logic errors. Function prototypes correct this deficiency.

Software Engineering Observation 3.8

*Function prototypes are required in C++. Use **#include** preprocessor directives to obtain function prototypes for the standard library functions from the header files for the appropriate libraries. Also use **#include** to obtain header files containing function prototypes used by you and/or your group members.*

Software Engineering Observation 3.9

A function prototype is not required if the definition of the function appears before the function's first use in the program. In such a case, the function definition also acts as the function prototype.

The function prototype for **maximum** in Fig. 3.4 is

```
int maximum( int, int, int );
```

This prototype states that **maximum** takes three arguments of type **int**, and returns a result of type **int**. Notice that this function prototype is the same as the header of the function definition of **maximum**, except the names of the parameters (**x**, **y** and **z**) are not included.

Good Programming Practice 3.5

Many programmers use parameter names in function prototypes for documentation purposes. The compiler ignores these names.

Common Programming Error 3.11

Forgetting the semicolon at the end of a function prototype is a syntax error.

The portion of a function prototype that includes the name of the function and the types of its arguments is called the *function signature* or simply the *signature*. The function signature does not include the return type of the function.

Common Programming Error 3.12

A function call that does not match the function prototype is a syntax error.

Common Programming Error 3.13

It is a syntax error if the function prototype and the function definition disagree.

As an example of the preceding Common Programming Error, in Fig. 3.4, if the function prototype had been written

```
void maximum( int, int, int );
```

the compiler would report an error, because the **void** return type in the function prototype would differ from the **int** return type in the function header.

Another important feature of function prototypes is the *coercion of arguments,* i.e., the forcing of arguments to the appropriate type. For example, the math library function **sqrt** can be called with an integer argument even though the function prototype in **<cmath>** specifies a **double** argument, and the function will still work correctly. The statement

```
cout << sqrt( 4 );
```

correctly evaluates **sqrt(4)**, and prints the value **2**. The function prototype causes the compiler to convert the integer argument value **4** to the **double** value **4.0** before the value is passed to **sqrt**. In general, argument values that do not correspond precisely to the parameter types in the function prototype are converted to the proper type before the function is called. These conversions can lead to incorrect results if C++'s *promotion rules* are not followed. The promotion rules specify how types can be converted to other types without losing data. In our **sqrt** example above, an **int** is automatically converted to a **double** without changing its value. However, a **double** converted to an **int** truncates the fractional part of the **double** value. Converting large integer types to small integer types (e.g., **long** to **short**) can also result in changed values.

The promotion rules apply to expressions containing values of two or more data types; such expressions are also referred to as *mixed-type expressions*. The type of each value in a mixed-type expression is promoted to the "highest" type in the expression (actually a temporary version of each value is created and used for the expression—the original values remain unchanged). Another common use of promotion is when the type of an argument to a function does not match the parameter type specified in the function definition. Figure 3.5 lists the built-in data types in order from "highest type" to "lowest type."

Converting values to lower types can result in incorrect values. Therefore, a value can be converted to a lower type only by explicitly assigning the value to a variable of lower type, or by using a cast operator. Function argument values are converted to the parameter types in a function prototype as if they are being assigned directly to variables of those types. If our **square** function that uses an integer parameter (Fig. 3.3) is called with a floating-point argument, the argument is converted to **int** (a lower type), and **square** usually returns an incorrect value. For example, **square(4.5)** would return **16**, not **20.25**.

Common Programming Error 3.14

Converting from a higher data type in the promotion hierarchy to a lower type can change the data value.

Common Programming Error 3.15

Forgetting a function prototype when a function is not defined before it is first invoked is a syntax error.

Software Engineering Observation 3.10

A function prototype placed outside any function definition applies to all calls to the function appearing after the function prototype in the file. A function prototype placed in a function applies only to calls made in that function.

3.7 Header Files

Each standard library has a corresponding *header file* containing the function prototypes for all the functions in that library and definitions of various data types and constants needed by those functions. Figure 3.6 lists some common C++ standard library header files that might be included in C++ programs. The term "macros" that is used several times in Fig. 3.6 is discussed in detail in Chapter 17, "Preprocessor." The header files ending in **.h** are "old-style" header files that have been superseded by the C++ standard library header files.

Data types		
long double		
double		
float		
unsigned long int	(synonymous with **unsigned long**)	
long int	(synonymous with **long**)	
unsigned int	(synonymous with **unsigned**)	
int		
unsigned short int	(synonymous with **unsigned short**)	
short int	(synonymous with **short**)	
unsigned char		
char		
bool	(**false** becomes 0, **true** becomes 1)	

Fig. 3.5   Promotion hierarchy for built-in data types.

Standard library header file	Explanation
\<cassert\>	Contains macros and information for adding diagnostics that aid program debugging. The old version of this header file is **assert.h**.
\<cctype\>	Contains function prototypes for functions that test characters for certain properties, and function prototypes for functions that can be used to convert lowercase letters to uppercase letters and vice versa. This header file replaces header file **ctype.h**.
\<cfloat\>	Contains the floating-point size limits of the system. This header file replaces header file **float.h**.
\<climits\>	Contains the integral size limits of the system. This header file replaces header file **limits.h**.
\<cmath\>	Contains function prototypes for math library functions. This header file replaces header file **math.h**.
\<cstdio\>	Contains function prototypes for the standard input/output library functions and information used by them. This header file replaces header file **stdio.h**.
\<cstdlib\>	Contains function prototypes for conversions of numbers to text, text to numbers, memory allocation, random numbers and various other utility functions. This header file replaces header file **stdlib.h**.
\<cstring\>	Contains function prototypes for C-style string processing functions. This header file replaces header file **string.h**.
\<ctime\>	Contains function prototypes and types for manipulating the time and date. This header file replaces header file **time.h**.
\<iostream\>	Contains function prototypes for the standard input and standard output functions. This header file replaces header file **iostream.h**.
\<iomanip\>	Contains function prototypes for the stream manipulators that enable formatting of streams of data. This header file replaces header file **iomanip.h**.
\<fstream\>	Contains function prototypes for functions that perform input from files on disk and output to files on disk (discussed in Chapter 14). This header file replaces header file **fstream.h**.
\<utility\>	Contains classes and functions that are used by many standard library header files.
\<vector\>, **\<list\>**, **\<deque\>**, **\<queue\>**, **\<stack\>**, **\<map\>**, **\<set\>**, **\<bitset\>**	The header files contain classes that implement the standard library containers. Containers are use to store data during a program's execution. We discuss these header files in the chapter entitled "The Standard Template Library."
\<functional\>	Contains classes and functions used by standard library algorithms.
\<memory\>	Contains classes and functions used by the standard library to allocate memory to the standard library containers.
\<iterator\>	Contains classes for accessing data in the standard library containers.

Fig. 3.6   Standard library header files (part 1 of 2).

Standard library header file	Explanation
<algorithm>	Contains functions for manipulating data in standard library containers.
<exception>, **<stdexcept>**	These header files contain classes that are used for exception handling (discussed in Chapter 13).
<string>	Contains the definition of class **string** from the standard library (discussed in Chapter 19, "Strings").
<sstream>	Contains function prototypes for functions that perform input from strings in memory and output to strings in memory (discussed in Chapter 14).
<locale>	Contains classes and functions normally used by stream processing to process data in the natural form for different languages (e.g., monetary formats, sorting strings, character presentation, etc.).
<limits>	Contains classes for defining the numerical data type limits on each computer platform.
<typeinfo>	Contains classes for run-time type identification (determining data types at execution time).

Fig. 3.6   Standard library header files (part 2 of 2).

The programmer can create custom header files. Programmer-defined header files should end in **.h**. A programmer-defined header file can be included by using the **#include** preprocessor directive. For example, the header file **square.h** can be included in our program by the directive

```
#include "square.h"
```

at the top of the program. Section 17.2 presents additional information on including header files.

3.8 Random Number Generation

We now take a brief and, it is hoped, entertaining diversion into a popular programming application, namely simulation and game playing. In this section and the next section, we will develop a nicely structured game-playing program that includes multiple functions. The program uses most of the control structures we have studied.

There is something in the air of a gambling casino that invigorates every type of person from the high-rollers at the plush mahogany-and-felt craps tables to the quarter-poppers at the one-armed bandits. It is the *element of chance*, the possibility that luck will convert a pocketful of money into a mountain of wealth. The element of chance can be introduced into computer applications by using the standard library function **rand**.

Consider the following statement:

```
i = rand();
```

The function **rand** generates an unsigned integer between 0 and **RAND_MAX** (a symbolic constant defined in the **<cstdlib>** header file). The value of **RAND_MAX** must be at least 32767—the maximum positive value for a two-byte (i.e., 16-bit) integer. If **rand** truly produces integers at random, every number between 0 and **RAND_MAX** has an equal *chance* (or *probability*) of being chosen each time **rand** is called.

The range of values produced directly by **rand** is often different than what is needed in a specific application. For example, a program that simulates coin tossing might require only 0 for "heads" and 1 for "tails." A program that simulates rolling a six-sided die would require random integers in range 1 to 6. A program that randomly predicts the next type of spaceship (out of four possibilities) that will fly across the horizon in a video game might require random integers in the range 1 through 4.

To demonstrate **rand**, let us develop a program to simulate 20 rolls of a six-sided die and print the value of each roll. The function prototype for the **rand** function can be found in **<cstdlib>**. To produce integers in the range 0 to 5, we use the modulus operator (**%**) in conjunction with **rand** as follows:

```
rand() % 6
```

This is called *scaling*. The number 6 is called the *scaling factor*. We then *shift* the range of numbers produced by adding 1 to our previous result. Figure 3.7 confirms that the results are in the range 1 to 6.

```cpp
// Fig. 3.7: fig03_07.cpp
// Shifted, scaled integers produced by 1 + rand() % 6
#include <iostream>

using std::cout;
using std::endl;

#include <iomanip>

using std::setw;

#include <cstdlib>

int main()
{
   for ( int i = 1; i <= 20; i++ ) {
      cout << setw( 10 ) << ( 1 + rand() % 6 );

      if ( i % 5 == 0 )
         cout << endl;
   }

   return 0;
}
```

5	5	3	5	5
2	4	2	5	5
5	3	2	2	1
5	1	4	6	4

Fig. 3.7   Shifted, scaled integers produced by **1 + rand() % 6**.

   To show that these numbers occur with approximately equal likelihood, let us simulate
6000 rolls of a die with the program of Fig. 3.8. Each integer from 1 to 6 should appear
approximately 1000 times.

```cpp
// Fig. 3.8: fig03_08.cpp
// Roll a six-sided die 6000 times
#include <iostream>

using std::cout;
using std::endl;

#include <iomanip>

using std::setw;

#include <cstdlib>

int main()
{
   int frequency1 = 0, frequency2 = 0,
       frequency3 = 0, frequency4 = 0,
       frequency5 = 0, frequency6 = 0,
       face;

   for ( int roll = 1; roll <= 6000; roll++ ) {
      face = 1 + rand() % 6;

      switch ( face ) {
         case 1:
            ++frequency1;
            break;
         case 2:
            ++frequency2;
            break;
         case 3:
            ++frequency3;
            break;
         case 4:
            ++frequency4;
            break;
         case 5:
            ++frequency5;
            break;
         case 6:
            ++frequency6;
            break;
         default:
            cout << "should never get here!";
      }
   }
```

Fig. 3.8   Rolling a six-sided die 6000 times (part 1 of 2).

```
48      cout << "Face" << setw( 13 ) << "Frequency"
49          << "\n   1" << setw( 13 ) << frequency1
50          << "\n   2" << setw( 13 ) << frequency2
51          << "\n   3" << setw( 13 ) << frequency3
52          << "\n   4" << setw( 13 ) << frequency4
53          << "\n   5" << setw( 13 ) << frequency5
54          << "\n   6" << setw( 13 ) << frequency6 << endl;
55
56      return 0;
57   }
```

Face	Frequency
1	987
2	984
3	1029
4	974
5	1004
6	1022

Fig. 3.8   Rolling a six-sided die 6000 times (part 2 of 2).

As the program output shows, by scaling and shifting, we have utilized the **rand** function to realistically simulate the rolling of a six-sided die. Note that the program should never get to the **default** case provided in the **switch** structure, but we nevertheless provide it as a matter of good practice. After we study arrays in Chapter 4, we will show how to replace the entire **switch** structure elegantly with a single-line statement.

Testing and Debugging Tip 3.1

*Provide a **default** case in a **switch** to catch errors even if you are absolutely, positively certain that you have no bugs!*

Executing the program of Fig. 3.7 again produces

5	5	3	5	5
2	4	2	5	5
5	3	2	2	1
5	1	4	6	4

Notice that exactly the same sequence of values was printed. How can these be random numbers? Ironically, this repeatability is an important characteristic of function **rand**. When debugging a program, this repeatability is essential for proving that corrections to a program work properly.

Function **rand** actually generates *pseudo-random numbers*. Calling **rand** repeatedly produces a sequence of numbers that appears to be random. However, the sequence repeats itself each time the program is executed. Once a program has been thoroughly debugged, it can be conditioned to produce a different sequence of random numbers for each execution. This is called *randomizing,* and is accomplished with the standard library function **srand**. Function **srand** takes an **unsigned** integer argument and *seeds* the **rand** function to produce a different sequence of random numbers for each execution of the program.

The use of **srand** is demonstrated in Fig. 3.9. In the program, we use the data type
unsigned, which is short for **unsigned int**. An **int** is stored in at least two bytes of
memory and can have positive and negative values. A variable of type **unsigned int** is
also stored in at least two bytes of memory. A two-byte **unsigned int** can have only
nonnegative values in the range 0 to 65535. A four-byte **unsigned int** can have only
nonnegative values in the range 0 to 4294967295. The **srand** function takes an
unsigned int value as an argument. The function prototype for the **srand** function is
in the header file **<cstdlib>**.

Let us run the program several times and observe the results. Notice that a *different*
sequence of random numbers is obtained each time the program is run, provided that a different seed is supplied.

If we wish to randomize without the need for entering a seed each time, we may use a
statement like

```cpp
1    // Fig. 3.9: fig03_09.cpp
2    // Randomizing die-rolling program
3    #include <iostream>
4
5    using std::cout;
6    using std::cin;
7    using std::endl;
8
9    #include <iomanip>
10
11   using std::setw;
12
13   #include <cstdlib>
14
15   int main()
16   {
17      unsigned seed;
18
19      cout << "Enter seed: ";
20      cin >> seed;
21      srand( seed );
22
23      for ( int i = 1; i <= 10; i++ ) {
24         cout << setw( 10 ) << 1 + rand() % 6;
25
26         if ( i % 5 == 0 )
27            cout << endl;
28      }
29
30      return 0;
31   }
```

```
Enter seed: 67
         1         6         5         1         4
         5         6         3         1         2
```

Fig. 3.9   Randomizing the die-rolling program (part 1 of 2).

Enter seed: 432				
4	2	6	4	3
2	5	1	4	4

Enter seed: 67				
1	6	5	1	4
5	6	3	1	2

Fig. 3.9   Randomizing the die-rolling program (part 2 of 2).

```
srand( time( 0 ) );
```

This causes the computer to read its clock to obtain the value for the seed automatically. The **time** function (with the argument **0** as written in the preceding statement) returns the current "calendar time" in seconds. This value is converted to an **unsigned** integer and used as the seed to the random number generator. The function prototype for **time** is in **<ctime>**.

Performance Tip 3.2

Function **srand** *need only be called once in a program to have the desired randomizing effect. Calling it more than once is redundant and hence reduces program performance.*

The values produced directly by **rand** are always in the range:

$$0 \leq \text{rand()} \leq \text{RAND\_MAX}$$

Previously we demonstrated how to write a single statement to simulate the rolling of a six-sided die with the statement:

```
face = 1 + rand() % 6;
```

which always assigns an integer (at random) to variable **face** in the range $1 \leq \text{face} \leq 6$. Note that the width of this range (i.e., the number of consecutive integers in the range) is 6 and the starting number in the range is 1. Referring to the preceding statement, we see that the width of the range is determined by the number used to scale **rand** with the modulus operator (i.e., 6), and the starting number of the range is equal to the number (i.e., 1) that is added to **rand % 6**. We can generalize this result as follows:

```
n = a + rand() % b;
```

where **a** is the *shifting value* (which is equal to the first number in the desired range of consecutive integers), and **b** is the scaling factor (which is equal to the width of the desired range of consecutive integers). In the exercises, we will see that it is possible to choose integers at random from sets of values other than ranges of consecutive integers.

Common Programming Error 3.16

Using **srand** *in place of* **rand** *to attempt to generate random numbers is a syntax error because function* **srand** *does not return a value.*

3.9 Example: A Game of Chance and Introducing enum

One of the most popular games of chance is a dice game known as "craps," which is played in casinos and back alleys throughout the world. The rules of the game are straightforward:

> *A player rolls two dice. Each die has six faces. These faces contain 1, 2, 3, 4, 5 and 6 spots. After the dice have come to rest, the sum of the spots on the two upward faces is calculated. If the sum is 7 or 11 on the first throw, the player wins. If the sum is 2, 3 or 12 on the first throw (called "craps"), the player loses (i.e., the "house" wins). If the sum is 4, 5, 6, 8, 9 or 10 on the first throw, then that sum becomes the player's "point." To win, you must continue rolling the dice until you "make your point." The player loses by rolling a 7 before making the point.*

The program in Fig. 3.10 simulates the game of craps. Figure 3.11 shows several sample executions.

Notice that the player must roll two dice on the first roll, and must do so later on all subsequent rolls. We define a function **rollDice** to roll the dice and compute and print their sum. Function **rollDice** is defined once, but it is called from two places in the program. Interestingly, **rollDice** takes no arguments, so we have indicated **void** in the parameter list. Function **rollDice** does return the sum of the two dice, so a return type of **int** is indicated in the function header.

The game is reasonably involved. The player may win or lose on the first roll, or may win or lose on any subsequent roll. The variable **gameStatus** is used to keep track of this. Variable **gameStatus** is declared to be of a type called **Status**. The line

```
enum Status { CONTINUE, WON, LOST };
```

creates a *user-defined type* called an *enumeration.* An enumeration, introduced by the keyword **enum** and followed by a *type name* (in this case, **Status**), is a set of integer constants represented by identifiers. The values of these *enumeration constants* start at **0**, unless specified otherwise, and are incremented by **1**. In the preceding enumeration, **CONTINUE** is assigned the value 0, **WON** is assigned the value 1 and **LOST** is assigned the value 2. The identifiers in an **enum** must be unique, but separate enumeration constants can have the same integer value.

Good Programming Practice 3.6

Capitalize the first letter of an identifier used as a user-defined type name.

Variables of user-defined type **Status** can only be assigned one of the three values declared in the enumeration. When the game is won, **gameStatus** is set to **WON**. When the game is lost, **gameStatus** is set to **LOST**. Otherwise, **gameStatus** is set to **CONTINUE** so the dice can be rolled again.

Common Programming Error 3.17

Assigning the integer equivalent of an enumeration constant to a variable of the enumeration type is a syntax error.

Another popular enumeration is

```
enum Months { JAN = 1, FEB, MAR, APR, MAY, JUN, JUL, AUG,
              SEP, OCT, NOV, DEC};
```

```cpp
1   // Fig. 3.10: fig03_10.cpp
2   // Craps
3   #include <iostream>
4
5   using std::cout;
6   using std::endl;
7
8   #include <cstdlib>
9
10  #include <ctime>
11
12  using std::time;
13
14  int rollDice( void );   // function prototype
15
16  int main()
17  {
18     enum Status { CONTINUE, WON, LOST };
19     int sum, myPoint;
20     Status gameStatus;
21
22     srand( time( 0 ) );
23     sum = rollDice();           // first roll of the dice
24
25     switch ( sum ) {
26        case 7:
27        case 11:                 // win on first roll
28           gameStatus = WON;
29           break;
30        case 2:
31        case 3:
32        case 12:                 // lose on first roll
33           gameStatus = LOST;
34           break;
35        default:                 // remember point
36           gameStatus = CONTINUE;
37           myPoint = sum;
38           cout << "Point is " << myPoint << endl;
39           break;                // optional
40     }
41
42     while ( gameStatus == CONTINUE ) {      // keep rolling
43        sum = rollDice();
44
45        if ( sum == myPoint )    // win by making point
46           gameStatus = WON;
47        else
48           if ( sum == 7 )       // lose by rolling 7
49              gameStatus = LOST;
50     }
51
52     if ( gameStatus == WON )
53        cout << "Player wins" << endl;
```

Fig. 3.10   Program to simulate the game of craps (part 1 of 2).

```
54        else
55            cout << "Player loses" << endl;
56
57        return 0;
58    }
59
60    int rollDice( void )
61    {
62        int die1, die2, workSum;
63
64        die1 = 1 + rand() % 6;
65        die2 = 1 + rand() % 6;
66        workSum = die1 + die2;
67        cout << "Player rolled " << die1 << " + " << die2
68            << " = " << workSum << endl;
69
70        return workSum;
71    }
```

Fig. 3.10   Program to simulate the game of craps (part 2 of 2).

```
Player rolled 6 + 5 = 11
Player wins
```

```
Player rolled 6 + 5 = 11
Player wins
```

```
Player rolled 4 + 6 = 10
Point is 10
Player rolled 2 + 4 = 6
Player rolled 6 + 5 = 11
Player rolled 3 + 3 = 6
Player rolled 6 + 4 = 10
Player wins
```

```
Player rolled 1 + 3 = 4
Point is 4
Player rolled 1 + 4 = 5
Player rolled 5 + 4 = 9
Player rolled 4 + 6 = 10
Player rolled 6 + 3 = 9
Player rolled 1 + 2 = 3
Player rolled 5 + 2 = 7
Player loses
```

Fig. 3.11   Sample outputs for the craps program.

which creates a user-defined type **Months** with enumeration constants representing the months of the year. Because the first value in the preceding enumeration is explicitly set to **1**, the remaining values are incremented from **1**, resulting in the values **1** through **12**. Any enumeration constant can be assigned an integer value in the enumeration definition, and subsequent enumeration constants will each have a value 1 higher than the preceding constant.

Common Programming Error 3.18

After an enumeration constant has been defined, attempting to assign another value to the enumeration constant is a syntax error.

Good Programming Practice 3.7

Use only uppercase letters in the names of enumeration constants. This makes these constants stand out in a program and reminds the programmer that enumeration constants are not variables.

Good Programming Practice 3.8

Using enumerations rather than integer constants can make programs clearer.

After the first roll, if the game is won, the body of the **while** structure is skipped because **gameStatus** is not equal to **CONTINUE**. The program proceeds to the **if/else** structure, which prints "**Player wins**" if **gameStatus** is equal to **WON** and "**Player loses**" if **gameStatus** is equal to **LOST**.

After the first roll, if the game is not over, **sum** is saved in **myPoint**. Execution proceeds with the **while** structure because **gameStatus** is equal to **CONTINUE**. Each time through the **while**, **rollDice** is called to produce a new **sum**. If **sum** matches **myPoint**, **gameStatus** is set to **WON**, the **while**-test fails, the **if/else** structure prints "**Player wins**" and execution terminates. If **sum** is equal to **7**, **gameStatus** is set to **LOST**, the **while**-test fails, the **if/else** statement prints "**Player loses**" and execution terminates.

Note the interesting use of the various program control mechanisms we have discussed. The craps program uses two functions—**main** and **rollDice**—and the **switch**, **while**, **if/else** and nested **if** structures. In the exercises, we investigate various interesting characteristics of the game of craps.

3.10 Storage Classes

In Chapters 1 through 3, we have used identifiers for variable names. The attributes of variables include name, type, size and value. In this chapter, we also use identifiers as names for user-defined functions. Actually, each identifier in a program has other attributes, including *storage class, scope* and *linkage*.

C++ provides five *storage class specifiers:* **auto**, **register**, **extern**, **mutable** and **static**. An identifier's storage class specifier helps determine its storage class, scope and linkage. This section discusses storage class specifiers **auto**, **register**, **extern** and **static**. Storage class specifier **mutable** (discussed in detail in Chapter 21) is used exclusively with C++ user-defined types called *classes* (introduced in Chapters 6 and 7).

An identifier's *storage class* determines the period during which that identifier exists in memory. Some identifiers exist briefly, some are repeatedly created and destroyed and others exist for the entire execution of a program. In this section, we discuss two storage classes: static and automatic.

An identifier's *scope* is where the identifier can be referenced in a program. Some identifiers can be referenced throughout a program; others can be referenced from only limited portions of a program. Section 3.11 discusses the scope of identifiers.

An identifier's *linkage* determines for a multiple-source-file program (a topic we will begin investigating in Chapter 6) whether an identifier is known only in the current source file or in any source file with proper declarations.

The storage class specifiers can be split into two storage classes: *automatic storage class* and *static storage class*. Keywords **auto** and **register** are used to declare variables of the automatic storage class. Such variables are created when the block in which they are declared is entered, they exist while the block is active, and they are destroyed when the block is exited.

Only variables can be of automatic storage class. A function's local variables and parameters normally are of automatic storage class. The storage class specifier **auto** explicitly declares variables of automatic storage class. For example, the following declaration indicates that **double** variables **x** and **y** are local variables of automatic storage class, i.e., they exist only in the body of the function in which the definition appears:

```
auto double x, y;
```

Local variables are of automatic storage class by default, so keyword **auto** is rarely used. For the remainder of the text, we will refer to variables of automatic storage class simply as automatic variables.

Performance Tip 3.3

Automatic storage is a means of conserving memory because automatic storage class variables are created when the block in which they are declared is entered and they are destroyed when the block is exited.

Software Engineering Observation 3.11

Automatic storage is an example of the principle of least privilege. Why have variables stored in memory and accessible when they are not needed?

Data in the machine-language version of a program are normally loaded into registers for calculations and other processing.

Performance Tip 3.4

*The storage class specifier **register** can be placed before an automatic variable declaration to suggest that the compiler maintain the variable in one of the computer's high-speed hardware registers rather than in memory. If intensely used variables such as counters or totals can be maintained in hardware registers, the overhead of repeatedly loading the variables from memory into the registers and storing the results back into memory can be eliminated.*

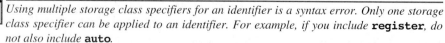

Common Programming Error 3.19

*Using multiple storage class specifiers for an identifier is a syntax error. Only one storage class specifier can be applied to an identifier. For example, if you include **register**, do not also include **auto**.*

The compiler might ignore **register** declarations. For example, there might not be a sufficient number of registers available for the compiler to use. The following declaration *suggests* that the integer variable **counter** be placed in one of the computer's registers; regardless of whether the compiler does this, **counter** is initialized to 1:

```
register int counter = 1;
```

The **register** keyword can be used only with local variables and function parameters.

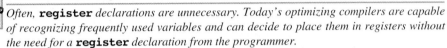

Performance Tip 3.5

Often, **register** *declarations are unnecessary. Today's optimizing compilers are capable of recognizing frequently used variables and can decide to place them in registers without the need for a* **register** *declaration from the programmer.*

Keywords **extern** and **static** are used to declare identifiers for variables and functions of the static storage class. Such variables exist from the point at which the program begins execution. For variables, storage is allocated and initialized once when the program begins execution. For functions, the name of the function exists when the program begins execution. However, even though the variables and the function names exist from the start of program execution, this does not mean that these identifiers can be used throughout the program. Storage class and scope (where a name can be used) are separate issues, as we will see in Section 3.11.

There are two types of identifiers with static storage class: external identifiers (such as global variables and function names), and local variables declared with the storage class specifier **static**. Global variables and function names default to storage class specifier **extern**. Global variables are created by placing variable declarations outside any function definition. Global variables retain their values throughout the execution of the program. Global variables and functions can be referenced by any function that follows their declarations or definitions in the source file.

Software Engineering Observation 3.12

Declaring a variable as global rather than local allows unintended side effects to occur when a function that does not need access to the variable accidentally or maliciously modifies it. In general, use of global variables should be avoided except in certain situations with unique performance requirements.

Software Engineering Observation 3.13

Variables used only in a particular function should be declared as local variables in that function rather than as global variables.

Local variables declared with the keyword **static** are still known only in the function in which they are defined, but, unlike automatic variables, **static** local variables retain their values when the function is exited. The next time the function is called, the **static** local variables contain the values they had when the function last exited. The following statement declares local variable **count** to be **static** and to be initialized to 1.

```
static int count = 1;
```

All numeric variables of the static storage class are initialized to zero if they are not explicitly initialized by the programmer. (Static pointer variables, discussed in Chapter 5, are also initialized to zero.)

Storage class specifiers **extern** and **static** have special meaning when they are explicitly applied to external identifiers. In Chapter 18, "Other Topics," we discuss the use of **extern** and **static** with external identifiers and multiple-source-file programs.

3.11 Scope Rules

The portion of the program where an identifier has meaning is known as its *scope*. For example, when we declare a local variable in a block, it can be referenced only in that block or in blocks nested within that block. The four scopes for an identifier are *function scope, file scope, block scope,* and *function-prototype scope.* Later we will see two other scopes— *class scope* (Chapter 6) and *namespace scope* (Chapter 21).

An identifier declared outside any function has *file scope.* Such an identifier is "known" in all functions from the point at which the identifier is declared until the end of the file. Global variables, function definitions and function prototypes placed outside a function all have file scope.

Labels (identifiers followed by a colon such as **start:**) are the only identifiers with *function scope.* Labels can be used anywhere in the function in which they appear, but cannot be referenced outside the function body. Labels are used in **switch** structures (as **case** labels) and in **goto** statements (see Chapter 18). Labels are implementation details that functions hide from one another. This hiding—more formally called *information hiding*—is one of the most fundamental principles of good software engineering.

Identifiers declared inside a block have *block scope.* Block scope begins at the identifier's declaration and ends at the terminating right brace (**}**) of the block. Local variables declared at the beginning of a function have block scope, as do function parameters, which are also local variables of the function. Any block can contain variable declarations. When blocks are nested and an identifier in an outer block has the same name as an identifier in an inner block, the identifier in the outer block is "hidden" until the inner block terminates. While executing in the inner block, the inner block sees the value of its own local identifier and not the value of the identically named identifier in the enclosing block. Local variables declared **static** still have block scope, even though they exist from the time the program begins execution. Storage duration does not affect the scope of an identifier.

The only identifiers with *function-prototype scope* are those used in the parameter list of a function prototype. As mentioned previously, function prototypes do not require names in the parameter list—only types are required. If a name is used in the parameter list of a function prototype, the compiler ignores the name. Identifiers used in a function prototype can be reused elsewhere in the program without ambiguity.

Common Programming Error 3.20

Accidentally using the same name for an identifier in an inner block that is used for an identifier in an outer block, when in fact the programmer wants the identifier in the outer block to be active for the duration of the inner block, is normally a logic error.

Good Programming Practice 3.9

Avoid variable names that hide names in outer scopes. This can be accomplished by avoiding the use of duplicate identifiers in a program.

The program of Fig. 3.12 demonstrates scoping issues with global variables, automatic local variables, and **static** local variables.

```
1   // Fig. 3.12: fig03_12.cpp
2   // A scoping example
3   #include <iostream>
4
5   using std::cout;
6   using std::endl;
7
8   void a( void );    // function prototype
9   void b( void );    // function prototype
10  void c( void );    // function prototype
11
12  int x = 1;         // global variable
13
14  int main()
15  {
16     int x = 5;      // local variable to main
17
18     cout << "local x in outer scope of main is " << x << endl;
19
20     {                // start new scope
21        int x = 7;
22
23        cout << "local x in inner scope of main is " << x << endl;
24     }                // end new scope
25
26     cout << "local x in outer scope of main is " << x << endl;
27
28     a();            // a has automatic local x
29     b();            // b has static local x
30     c();            // c uses global x
31     a();            // a reinitializes automatic local x
32     b();            // static local x retains its previous value
33     c();            // global x also retains its value
34
35     cout << "local x in main is " << x << endl;
36
37     return 0;
38  }
39
40  void a( void )
41  {
42     int x = 25;     // initialized each time a is called
43
44     cout << endl << "local x in a is " << x
45          << " after entering a" << endl;
46     ++x;
47     cout << "local x in a is " << x
48          << " before exiting a" << endl;
49  }
50
```

Fig. 3.12   A scoping example (part 1 of 2).

```
51   void b( void )
52   {
53       static int x = 50;   // Static initialization only
54                            // first time b is called.
55       cout << endl << "local static x is " << x
56            << " on entering b" << endl;
57       ++x;
58       cout << "local static x is " << x
59            << " on exiting b" << endl;
60   }
61
62   void c( void )
63   {
64       cout << endl << "global x is " << x
65            << " on entering c" << endl;
66       x *= 10;
67       cout << "global x is " << x << " on exiting c" << endl;
68   }
```

```
local x in outer scope of main is 5
local x in inner scope of main is 7
local x in outer scope of main is 5

local x in a is 25 after entering a
local x in a is 26 before exiting a

local static x is 50 on entering b
local static x is 51 on exiting b

global x is 1 on entering c
global x is 10 on exiting c

local x in a is 25 after entering a
local x in a is 26 before exiting a

local static x is 51 on entering b
local static x is 52 on exiting b

global x is 10 on entering c
global x is 100 on exiting c
local x in main is 5
```

Fig. 3.12   A scoping example (part 2 of 2).

A global variable **x** is declared and initialized to 1. This global variable is hidden in any block (or function) in which a variable named **x** is declared. In **main**, a local variable **x** is declared and initialized to 5. This variable is printed to show that the global **x** is hidden in **main**. Next, a new block is defined in **main** with another local variable **x** initialized to 7. This variable is printed to show that it hides **x** in the outer block of **main**. The variable **x** with value 7 is automatically destroyed when the block is exited, and the local variable **x** in the outer block of **main** is printed to show that it is no longer hidden. The program defines three functions—each takes no arguments and returns nothing. Function **a** defines automatic variable **x** and initializes it to 25. When **a** is called, the variable is printed, incremented, and printed again before exiting the function. Each time this function is called, automatic variable **x** is recreated and initialized to 25. Function **b** declares **static** variable **x** and initializes it to 50. Local variables declared as **static** retain their values even when they are out of scope. When **b** is called, **x** is printed, incremented, and printed again before exiting the function. In the next call to this function, **static** local variable **x** will contain the value 51. Function **c** does not declare any variables. Therefore, when it refers to variable **x**, the global **x** is used. When **c** is called, the global variable is printed, multiplied by 10, and printed again before exiting the function. The next time function **c** is called, the global variable has its modified value, 10. Finally, the program prints the local variable **x** in **main** again to show that none of the function calls modified the value of **x**, because the functions all referred to variables in other scopes.

3.12 Recursion

The programs we have discussed are generally structured as functions that call one another in a disciplined, hierarchical manner. For some problems, it is useful to have functions call themselves. A *recursive function* is a function that calls itself, either directly, or indirectly (through another function). Recursion is an important topic discussed at length in upper-level computer science courses. In this section and the next, simple examples of recursion are presented. This book contains an extensive treatment of recursion. Figure 3.17 (at the end of Section 3.14) summarizes the recursion examples and exercises in the book.

We first consider recursion conceptually and then examine several programs containing recursive functions. Recursive problem-solving approaches have a number of elements in common. A recursive function is called to solve a problem. The function actually knows how to solve only the simplest case(s), or so-called *base case(s)*. If the function is called with a base case, the function simply returns a result. If the function is called with a more complex problem, the function divides the problem into two conceptual pieces: a piece that the function knows how to do and a piece that the function does not know how to do. To make recursion feasible, the latter piece must resemble the original problem, but be a slightly simpler or slightly smaller version of the original problem. Because this new problem looks like the original problem, the function launches (calls) a fresh copy of itself to go to work on the smaller problem—this is referred to as a *recursive call* and is also called the *recursion step*. The recursion step also includes the keyword **return**, because its result will be combined with the portion of the problem the function knew how to solve to form a result that will be passed back to the original caller, possibly **main**.

The recursion step executes while the original call to the function is still open, i.e., it has not yet finished executing. The recursion step can result in many more such recursive calls as the function keeps dividing each new subproblem with which the function is called into two conceptual pieces. In order for the recursion to eventually terminate, each time the function calls itself with a slightly simpler version of the original problem this sequence of smaller and smaller problems must eventually converge on the base case. At that point, the function recognizes the base case, returns a result to the previous copy of the function, and a sequence of returns ensues all the way up the line until the original call of the function eventually returns the final result to **main**. All of this sounds quite exotic compared to the kind of conventional problem solving we have been using to this point. As an example of these concepts at work, let us write a recursive program to perform a popular mathematical calculation.

The factorial of a nonnegative integer n, written $n!$ (and pronounced "n factorial"), is the product

$$n \cdot (n - 1) \cdot (n - 2) \cdot \ldots \cdot 1$$

with 1! equal to 1, and 0! defined to be 1. For example, 5! is the product $5 \cdot 4 \cdot 3 \cdot 2 \cdot 1$, which is equal to 120.

The factorial of an integer, **number**, greater than or equal to 0, can be calculated *iteratively* (nonrecursively) by using **for** as follows:

```
factorial = 1;

for ( int counter = number; counter >= 1; counter-- )
    factorial *= counter;
```

A recursive definition of the factorial function is arrived at by observing the following relationship:

$$n! = n \cdot (n - 1)!$$

For example, 5! is clearly equal to 5 * 4! as is shown by the following:

$5! = 5 \cdot 4 \cdot 3 \cdot 2 \cdot 1$
$5! = 5 \cdot (4 \cdot 3 \cdot 2 \cdot 1)$
$5! = 5 \cdot (4!)$

The evaluation of 5! would proceed as shown in Fig. 3.13. Figure 3.13a shows how the succession of recursive calls proceeds until 1! is evaluated to be 1, which terminates the recursion. Figure 3.13b shows the values returned from each recursive call to its caller until the final value is calculated and returned.

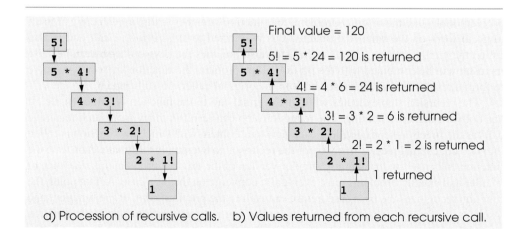

a) Procession of recursive calls.   b) Values returned from each recursive call.

Fig. 3.13   Recursive evaluation of *5!*.

The program of Fig. 3.14 uses recursion to calculate and print the factorials of the integers 0 to 10 (the choice of the data type **unsigned long** will be explained momentarily). The recursive function **factorial** first tests to see whether a terminating condition is **true**, i.e., is **number** less than or equal to 1. If **number** is indeed less than or equal to 1, **factorial** returns 1, no further recursion is necessary, and the program terminates. If **number** is greater than 1, the statement

```
return number * factorial( number - 1 );
```

```
1   // Fig. 3.14: fig03_14.cpp
2   // Recursive factorial function
3   #include <iostream>
4
5   using std::cout;
6   using std::endl;
7
8   #include <iomanip>
9
10  using std::setw;
11
12  unsigned long factorial( unsigned long );
13
14  int main()
15  {
16     for ( int i = 0; i <= 10; i++ )
17        cout << setw( 2 ) << i << "! = " << factorial( i ) << endl;
18
19     return 0;
20  }
21
22  // Recursive definition of function factorial
23  unsigned long factorial( unsigned long number )
24  {
25     if ( number <= 1 )    // base case
26        return 1;
27     else                  // recursive case
28        return number * factorial( number - 1 );
29  }
```

```
 0! = 1
 1! = 1
 2! = 2
 3! = 6
 4! = 24
 5! = 120
 6! = 720
 7! = 5040
 8! = 40320
 9! = 362880
10! = 3628800
```

Fig. 3.14   Calculating factorials with a recursive function .

expresses the problem as the product of **number** and a recursive call to **factorial** evaluating the factorial of **number – 1**. Note that **factorial(number – 1)** is a slightly simpler problem than the original calculation **factorial(number)**.

Function **factorial** has been declared to receive a parameter of type **unsigned long** and return a result of type **unsigned long**. This is shorthand notation for **unsigned long int**. The C++ language specification requires that a variable of type **unsigned long int** be stored in at least 4 bytes (32 bits), and thus it can hold a value at least in the range 0 to 4294967295. (The data type **long int** is also stored in at least 4 bytes and can hold a value at least in the range ±2147483647.) As can be seen in Fig. 3.14, factorial values become large quickly. We have chosen the data type **unsigned long** so that the program can calculate factorials greater than 7! on computers with small (such as 2-byte) integers. Unfortunately, function **factorial** produces large values so quickly that even **unsigned long** does not help us compute many factorial values before the size of an **unsigned long** variable is exceeded.

As we explore in the exercises, **double** could ultimately be needed by the user desiring to calculate factorials of larger numbers. This points to a weakness in most programming languages, namely that the languages are not easily extended to handle the unique requirements of various applications. As we will see in the section of the book on object-oriented programming, C++ is an extensible language that allows us to create arbitrarily large integers if we wish.

Common Programming Error 3.21

Forgetting to return a value from a recursive function when one is needed will cause most compilers to produce a warning message.

Common Programming Error 3.22

Either omitting the base case, or writing the recursion step incorrectly so that it does not converge on the base case, will cause "infinite" recursion, eventually exhausting memory. This is analogous to the problem of an infinite loop in an iterative (nonrecursive) solution. Infinite recursion can also be caused by providing an unexpected input.

3.13 Example Using Recursion: The Fibonacci Series

The Fibonacci series

0, 1, 1, 2, 3, 5, 8, 13, 21, …

begins with 0 and 1 and has the property that each subsequent Fibonacci number is the sum of the previous two Fibonacci numbers.

The series occurs in nature and, in particular, describes a form of spiral. The ratio of successive Fibonacci numbers converges on a constant value of 1.618…. This number, too, repeatedly occurs in nature and has been called the *golden ratio* or the *golden mean*. Humans tend to find the golden mean aesthetically pleasing. Architects often design windows, rooms, and buildings whose length and width are in the ratio of the golden mean. Postcards are often designed with a golden mean length/width ratio.

The Fibonacci series can be defined recursively as follows:

fibonacci(0) = 0
fibonacci(1) = 1
fibonacci(n) = fibonacci(n – 1) + fibonacci(n – 2)

The program of Fig. 3.15 calculates the ith Fibonacci number recursively by using function **fibonacci**. Notice that Fibonacci numbers tend to become large quickly. Therefore, we have chosen the data type **unsigned long** for the parameter type and the return type in function **fibonacci**. In Fig. 3.15, each pair of output lines shows a separate run of the program.

```cpp
1   // Fig. 3.15: fig03_15.cpp
2   // Recursive fibonacci function
3   #include <iostream>
4
5   using std::cout;
6   using std::cin;
7   using std::endl;
8
9   unsigned long fibonacci( unsigned long );
10
11  int main()
12  {
13      unsigned long result, number;
14
15      cout << "Enter an integer: ";
16      cin >> number;
17      result = fibonacci( number );
18      cout << "Fibonacci(" << number << ") = " << result << endl;
19      return 0;
20  }
21
22  // Recursive definition of function fibonacci
23  unsigned long fibonacci( unsigned long n )
24  {
25      if ( n == 0 || n == 1 )    // base case
26          return n;
27      else                       // recursive case
28          return fibonacci( n - 1 ) + fibonacci( n - 2 );
29  }
```

```
Enter an integer: 0
Fibonacci(0) = 0
```

```
Enter an integer: 1
Fibonacci(1) = 1
```

Fig. 3.15   Recursively generating Fibonacci numbers (part 1 of 2).

```
Enter an integer: 2
Fibonacci(2) = 1
```

```
Enter an integer: 3
Fibonacci(3) = 2
```

```
Enter an integer: 4
Fibonacci(4) = 3
```

```
Enter an integer: 5
Fibonacci(5) = 5
```

```
Enter an integer: 6
Fibonacci(6) = 8
```

```
Enter an integer: 10
Fibonacci(10) = 55
```

```
Enter an integer: 20
Fibonacci(20) = 6765
```

```
Enter an integer: 30
Fibonacci(30) = 832040
```

```
Enter an integer: 35
Fibonacci(35) = 9227465
```

Fig. 3.15   Recursively generating Fibonacci numbers (part 2 of 2).

The call to **fibonacci** from **main** is not a recursive call, but all subsequent calls to **fibonacci** are recursive. Each time **fibonacci** is invoked, it immediately tests for the base case—**n** equal to 0 or 1. If this is true, **n** is returned. Interestingly, if **n** is greater than 1, the recursion step generates *two* recursive calls, each of which is for a slightly simpler problem than the original call to **fibonacci**. Figure 3.16 shows how function **fibonacci** would evaluate **fibonacci(3)**—we abbreviate **fibonacci** simply as **f** to make the figure more readable.

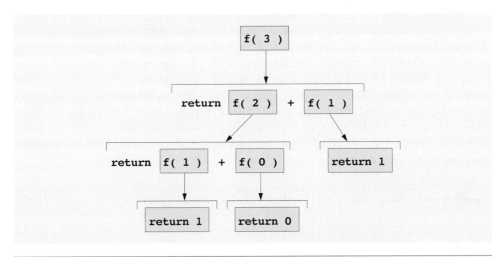

Fig. 3.16   Set of recursive calls to function **fibonacci**.

This figure raises some interesting issues about the order in which C++ compilers will evaluate the operands of operators. This is a different issue from the order in which operators are applied to their operands, namely the order dictated by the rules of operator precedence. From Fig. 3.16 it appears that while evaluating **f(3)**, two recursive calls will be made, namely **f(2)** and **f(1)**. But in what order will these calls be made?

Most programmers simply assume the operands will be evaluated left to right. Strangely, the C++ language does not specify the order in which the operands of most operators (including **+**) are to be evaluated. Therefore, the programmer must make no assumption about the order in which these calls will execute. The calls could in fact execute **f(2)** first and then **f(1)**, or the calls could execute in the reverse order, **f(1)** and then **f(2)**. In this program and in most other programs, it turns out the final result would be the same. But in some programs the evaluation of an operand can have *side effects* that could affect the final result of the expression.

The C++ language specifies the order of evaluation of the operands of only four operators—namely, **&&**, **||**, the comma (**,**) operator and **?:**. The first three of these are binary operators whose two operands are guaranteed to be evaluated left to right. The last operator is C++'s only ternary operator. Its leftmost operand is always evaluated first; if the leftmost operand evaluates to nonzero, the middle operand is evaluated next and the last operand is ignored; if the leftmost operand evaluates to zero, the third operand is evaluated next and the middle operand is ignored.

Common Programming Error 3.23

*Writing programs that depend on the order of evaluation of the operands of operators other than **&&**, **||**, **?:** and the comma (**,**) operator can lead to errors, because compilers might not necessarily evaluate the operands in the order the programmer expects.*

Portability Tip 3.2

*Programs that depend on the order of evaluation of the operands of operators other than **&&**, **||**, **?:** and the comma (**,**) operator can function differently on systems with different compilers.*

A word of caution is in order about recursive programs like the one we use here to generate Fibonacci numbers. Each level of recursion in function **fibonacci** has a doubling effect on the number of calls, i.e., the number of recursive calls that will be executed to calculate the nth Fibonacci number is on the order of 2^n. This rapidly gets out of hand. Calculating only the 20th Fibonacci number would require on the order of 2^{20} or about a million calls, calculating the 30th Fibonacci number would require on the order of 2^{30} or about a billion calls, and so on. Computer scientists refer to this as *exponential complexity*. Problems of this nature humble even the world's most powerful computers! Complexity issues in general, and exponential complexity in particular, are discussed in detail in the upper-level computer science curriculum course generally called "Algorithms."

Performance Tip 3.6

Avoid fibonacci-style recursive programs that result in an exponential "explosion" of calls.

3.14 Recursion vs. Iteration

In the previous sections, we studied two functions that can easily be implemented either recursively or iteratively. In this section, we compare the two approaches and discuss why the programmer might choose one approach over the other in a particular situation.

Both iteration and recursion are based on a control structure: Iteration uses a repetition structure; recursion uses a selection structure. Both iteration and recursion involve repetition: Iteration explicitly uses a repetition structure; recursion achieves repetition through repeated function calls. Iteration and recursion both involve a termination test: Iteration terminates when the loop-continuation condition fails; recursion terminates when a base case is recognized. Iteration with counter-controlled repetition and recursion both gradually approach termination: Iteration keeps modifying a counter until the counter assumes a value that makes the loop-continuation condition fail; recursion keeps producing simpler versions of the original problem until the base case is reached. Both iteration and recursion can occur infinitely: An infinite loop occurs with iteration if the loop-continuation test never becomes false; infinite recursion occurs if the recursion step does not reduce the problem each time in a manner that converges on the base case.

Recursion has many negatives. It repeatedly invokes the mechanism, and consequently the overhead, of function calls. This can be expensive in both processor time and memory space. Each recursive call causes another copy of the function (actually only the function's variables) to be created; this can consume considerable memory. Iteration normally occurs within a function, so the overhead of repeated function calls and extra memory assignment is omitted. So why choose recursion?

Software Engineering Observation 3.14

Any problem that can be solved recursively can also be solved iteratively (nonrecursively). A recursive approach is normally chosen in preference to an iterative approach when the recursive approach more naturally mirrors the problem and results in a program that is easier to understand and debug. Another reason to choose a recursive solution is that an iterative solution is not apparent.

Performance Tip 3.7

Avoid using recursion in performance situations. Recursive calls take time and consume additional memory.

Common Programming Error 3.24

Accidentally having a nonrecursive function call itself, either directly or indirectly (through another function), is a logic error.

Most programming textbooks introduce recursion much later than we have done here. We feel that recursion is a sufficiently rich and complex topic that it is better to introduce it earlier and spread the examples over the remainder of the text. Figure 3.17 summarizes the recursion examples and exercises in the text.

Chapter	Recursion Examples and Exercises
Chapter 3	Factorial function
	Fibonacci function
	Greatest common divisor
	Sum of two integers
	Multiply two integers
	Raising an integer to an integer power
	Towers of Hanoi
	Printing keyboard inputs in reverse
	Visualizing recursion
Chapter 4	Sum the elements of an array
	Print an array
	Print an array backwards
	Print a string backwards
	Check on whether a string is a palindrome
	Minimum value in an array
	Selection sort
	Eight Queens
	Linear search
	Binary search
Chapter 5	Quicksort
	Maze traversal
	Printing a string input at the keyboard backwards
Chapter 15	Linked-list insert
	Linked-list delete
	Search a linked list
	Print a linked list backwards
	Binary tree insert
	Preorder traversal of a binary tree
	Inorder traversal of a binary tree
	Postorder traversal of a binary tree

Fig. 3.17   Summary of recursion examples and exercises in the text.

Let us reconsider some observations that we make repeatedly throughout the book. Good software engineering is important. High performance is important. Unfortunately, these goals are often at odds with one another. Good software engineering is key to making more manageable the task of developing the larger and more complex software systems we need. High performance in these systems is key to realizing the systems of the future that will place ever greater computing demands on hardware. Where do functions fit in here?

Software Engineering Observation 3.15

Functionalizing programs in a neat, hierarchical manner promotes good software engineering, but it has a price.

Performance Tip 3.8

A heavily functionalized program—as compared to a monolithic (i.e., one-piece) program without functions—makes potentially large numbers of function calls, and these consume execution time and space on a computer's processor(s). But monolithic programs are difficult to program, test, debug, maintain and evolve.

So functionalize your programs judiciously, always keeping in mind the delicate balance between performance and good software engineering.

3.15 Functions with Empty Parameter Lists

In C++, an empty parameter list is specified by writing either **void** or nothing at all in parentheses. The prototype

```
void print();
```

specifies that function **print** does not take any arguments and does not return a value. Figure 3.18 demonstrates both C++ ways of declaring and using functions that do not take arguments.

```
1   // Fig. 3.18: fig03_18.cpp
2   // Functions that take no arguments
3   #include <iostream>
4
5   using std::cout;
6   using std::endl;
7
8   void function1();
9   void function2( void );
10
11  int main()
12  {
13     function1();
14     function2();
15
16     return 0;
17  }
```

Fig. 3.18   Two ways to declare and use functions that take no arguments (part 1 of 2).

```
18
19   void function1()
20   {
21       cout << "function1 takes no arguments" << endl;
22   }
23
24   void function2( void )
25   {
26       cout << "function2 also takes no arguments" << endl;
27   }
```

```
function1 takes no arguments
function2 also takes no arguments
```

Fig. 3.18   Two ways to declare and use functions that take no arguments (part 2 of 2).

Good Programming Practice 3.10

Always provide function prototypes, even though it is possible to omit them when functions are defined before they are used. Providing the prototypes avoids tying the code to the order in which functions are defined (which can easily change as a program evolves).

Portability Tip 3.3

The meaning of an empty function parameter list in C++ is dramatically different than in C. In C, it means all argument checking is disabled (i.e., the function call can pass any arguments it wants). In C++, it means that the function takes no arguments. Thus, C programs using this feature might report syntax errors when compiled in C++.

Now that we are discussing omitting things, it should be noted that a function defined in a file before any call to the function does not require a separate function prototype. In this case, the function header acts as the function prototype.

Common Programming Error 3.25

C++ programs do not compile unless function prototypes are provided for every function or each function is defined before it is called.

3.16 Inline Functions

Implementing a program as a set of functions is good from a software engineering stand-point, but function calls involve execution-time overhead. C++ provides *inline functions* to help reduce function-call overhead—especially for small functions. The qualifier **inline** before a function's return type in the function definition "advises" the compiler to generate a copy of the function's code in place (when appropriate) to avoid a function call. The trade-off is that multiple copies of the function code are inserted in the program (thus making the program larger) rather than having a single copy of the function to which control is passed each time the function is called. The compiler can ignore the **inline** qualifier and typically does so for all but the smallest functions.

Software Engineering Observation 3.16

*Any change to an **inline** function could require all clients of the function to be recompiled. This can be significant in some program development and maintenance situations.*

Good Programming Practice 3.11

The **inline** *qualifier should be used only with small, frequently used functions.*

Performance Tip 3.9

Using **inline** *functions can reduce execution time but increase program size.*

Figure 3.19 uses **inline** function **cube** to calculate the volume of a cube of side **s**. Keyword **const** in the parameter list of function **cube** tells the compiler that the function does not modify variable **s**. This ensures that the value of **s** is not changed by the function when the calculation is performed. Keyword **const** is discussed in detail in Chapters 4, 5 and 7.

Software Engineering Observation 3.17

Many programmers do not bother to declare value parameters as **const***, even though the called function should not be modifying the passed argument. Keyword* **const** *is only protecting a copy of the original argument, not the original argument itself.*

3.17 References and Reference Parameters

Two ways to invoke functions in many programming languages are *call-by-value* and *call-by-reference*. When an argument is passed call-by-value, a *copy* of the argument's value is made and passed to the called function. Changes to the copy do not affect the original variable's value in the caller. This prevents the accidental *side effects* that so greatly hinder the development of correct and reliable software systems. Each of the arguments that have been passed in the programs in this chapter so far has been passed call-by-value.

```
1   // Fig. 3.19: fig03_19.cpp
2   // Using an inline function to calculate
3   // the volume of a cube.
4   #include <iostream>
5
6   using std::cout;
7   using std::cin;
8   using std::endl;
9
10  inline double cube( const double s ) { return s * s * s; }
11
12  int main()
13  {
14     cout << "Enter the side length of your cube:  ";
15
16     double side;
17
18     cin >> side;
19     cout << "Volume of cube with side "
20          << side << " is " << cube( side ) << endl;
21
22     return 0;
23  }
```

Fig. 3.19   Using an **inline** function to calculate the volume of a cube.

```
Enter the side length of your cube:   3.5
Volume of cube with side 3.5 is 42.875
```

Fig. 3.19   Using an **inline** function to calculate the volume of a cube.

Performance Tip 3.10

One disadvantage of call-by-value is that, if a large data item is being passed, copying that data can take a considerable amount of execution time.

In this section we introduce *reference parameters*—the first of two means C++ provides for performing call-by-reference. With call-by-reference, the caller gives the called function the ability to access the caller's data directly, and to modify that data if the called function so chooses.

Performance Tip 3.11

Call-by-reference is good for performance reasons, because it eliminates the overhead of copying large amounts of data.

Software Engineering Observation 3.18

Call-by-reference can weaken security, because the called function can corrupt the caller's data.

We will show how to achieve the performance advantage of call-by-reference while simultaneously achieving the software engineering advantage of protecting the caller's data from corruption.

A reference parameter is an alias for its corresponding argument. To indicate that a function parameter is passed by reference, simply follow the parameter's type in the function prototype by an ampersand (**&**); use the same convention when listing the parameter's type in the function header. For example, the declaration

```
    int &count
```

in a function header may be pronounced "**count** is a reference to an **int**." In the function call, simply mention the variable by name, and it will be passed by reference. Then mentioning the variable by its parameter name in the body of the called function actually refers to the original variable in the calling function, and the original variable can be modified directly by the called function. As always, the function prototype and header must agree.

Figure 3.20 compares call-by-value and call-by-reference with reference parameters. The "styles" of the arguments in the calls to **squareByValue** and **squareByReference** are identical, i.e., both variables are simply mentioned by name. Without checking the function prototypes or function definitions, it is not possible to tell from the calls alone whether either function can modify its arguments. Because function prototypes are mandatory, however, the compiler has no trouble resolving the ambiguity.

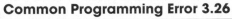

Common Programming Error 3.26

Because reference parameters are mentioned only by name in the body of the called function, the programmer might inadvertently treat reference parameters as call-by-value parameters. This can cause unexpected side effects if the original copies of the variables are changed by the calling function.

```cpp
1  // Fig. 3.20: fig03_20.cpp
2  // Comparing call-by-value and call-by-reference
3  // with references.
4  #include <iostream>
5
6  using std::cout;
7  using std::endl;
8
9  int squareByValue( int );
10 void squareByReference( int & );
11
12 int main()
13 {
14    int x = 2, z = 4;
15
16    cout << "x = " << x << " before squareByValue\n"
17         << "Value returned by squareByValue: "
18         << squareByValue( x ) << endl
19         << "x = " << x << " after squareByValue\n" << endl;
20
21    cout << "z = " << z << " before squareByReference" << endl;
22    squareByReference( z );
23    cout << "z = " << z << " after squareByReference" << endl;
24
25    return 0;
26 }
27
28 int squareByValue( int a )
29 {
30    return a *= a;    // caller's argument not modified
31 }
32
33 void squareByReference( int &cRef )
34 {
35    cRef *= cRef;    // caller's argument modified
36 }
```

```
x = 2 before squareByValue
Value returned by squareByValue: 4
x = 2 after squareByValue

z = 4 before squareByReference
z = 16 after squareByReference
```

Fig. 3.20   An example of call-by-reference.

In Chapter 5 we discuss pointers; we will see that pointers enable an alternate form of call-by-reference in which the style of the call clearly indicates call-by-reference (and the potential for modifying the caller's arguments).

Performance Tip 3.12

For passing large objects, use a constant reference parameter to simulate the appearance and security of call-by-value and avoid the overhead of passing a copy of the large object.

To specify a reference to a constant, place the **const** qualifier before the type specifier in the parameter declaration.

Note the placement of **&** in the parameter list of the **squareByReference** function. Some C++ programmers prefer to write **int& cRef** rather than **int &cRef**.

Software Engineering Observation 3.19

For the combined reasons of clarity and performance, many C++ programmers prefer that modifiable arguments be passed to functions by using pointers, small nonmodifiable arguments be passed call-by-value and large nonmodifiable arguments be passed to functions by using references to constants.

References can also be used as aliases for other variables within a function. For example, the code

```
int count = 1;       // declare integer variable count
int &cRef = count;   // create cRef as an alias for count
++cRef;              // increment count (using its alias)
```

increments variable **count** by using its alias **cRef**. Reference variables must be initialized in their declarations (see Fig. 3.21 and Fig. 3.22) and cannot be reassigned as aliases to other variables. Once a reference is declared as an alias for another variable, all operations supposedly performed on the alias (i.e., the reference) are actually performed on the original variable itself. The alias is simply another name for the original variable. Taking the address of a reference and comparing references do not cause syntax errors; rather, each operation actually occurs on the variable for which the reference is an alias. A reference argument must be an *lvalue*, not a constant or expression that returns an *rvalue*.

```cpp
1   // Fig. 3.21: fig03_21.cpp
2   // References must be initialized
3   #include <iostream>
4
5   using std::cout;
6   using std::endl;
7
8   int main()
9   {
10      int x = 3, &y = x;   // y is now an alias for x
11
12      cout << "x = " << x << endl << "y = " << y << endl;
13      y = 7;
14      cout << "x = " << x << endl << "y = " << y << endl;
15
16      return 0;
17  }
```

```
x = 3
y = 3
x = 7
y = 7
```

Fig. 3.21   Using an initialized reference.

Common Programming Error 3.27

*Declaring multiple references in one statement while assuming that the **&** distributes across a comma-separated list of variable names. To declare variables **x**, **y** and **z** all as references to integer, use the notation **int &x = a, &y = b, &z = c;** rather than the incorrect notation* **int& x = a, y = b, z = c;** *or the other common incorrect notation* **int &x, y, z;.**

Functions can return references, but this can be dangerous. When returning a reference to a variable declared in the called function, the variable should be declared **static** within that function. Otherwise the reference refers to an automatic variable that is discarded when the function terminates; such a variable is said to be "undefined" and the program's behavior would be unpredictable (some compilers issue warnings when this is done). References to undefined variables are called *dangling references*.

Common Programming Error 3.28

Not initializing a reference variable when it is declared is a syntax error.

Common Programming Error 3.29

Attempting to reassign a previously declared reference to be an alias to another variable is a logic error. The value of the other variable is simply assigned to the location for which the reference is already an alias.

```cpp
1  // Fig. 3.22: fig03_22.cpp
2  // References must be initialized
3  #include <iostream>
4
5  using std::cout;
6  using std::endl;
7
8  int main()
9  {
10     int x = 3, &y;    // Error: y must be initialized
11
12     cout << "x = " << x << endl << "y = " << y << endl;
13     y = 7;
14     cout << "x = " << x << endl << "y = " << y << endl;
15
16     return 0;
17  }
```

Borland C++ command-line compiler error message

```
Error E2304 Fig03_22.cpp 10: Reference variable 'y' must be initialized
in function main()
```

Microsoft Visual C++ compiler error message

```
Fig03_22.cpp(10) : error C2530: 'y' : references must be initialized
```

Fig. 3.22   Attempting to use an uninitialized reference.

Common Programming Error 3.30

Returning a pointer or reference to an automatic variable in a called function is a logic error. Some compilers will issue a warning when this occurs in a program.

3.18 Default Arguments

Function calls commonly pass a particular value of an argument. The programmer can specify that such an argument is a *default argument,* and the programmer can provide a default value for that argument. When a default argument is omitted in a function call, the default value of that argument is automatically inserted by the compiler and passed in the call.

Default arguments must be the rightmost (trailing) arguments in a function's parameter list. When one is calling a function with two or more default arguments, if an omitted argument is not the rightmost argument in the argument list, all arguments to the right of that argument also must be omitted. Default arguments should be specified with the first occurrence of the function name—typically, in the prototype. Default values can be constants, global variables or function calls. Default arguments also can be used with **inline** functions.

Figure 3.23 demonstrates using default arguments in calculating the volume of a box. The function prototype for **boxVolume** at line 8 specifies that all three arguments have been given default values of **1**. Note that the default values should be defined only in the function prototype. Also note that we provided variable names in the function prototype for readability. As always, variable names are not required in function prototypes.

```cpp
1   // Fig. 3.23: fig03_23.cpp
2   // Using default arguments
3   #include <iostream>
4
5   using std::cout;
6   using std::endl;
7
8   int boxVolume( int length = 1, int width = 1, int height = 1 );
9
10  int main()
11  {
12     cout << "The default box volume is: " << boxVolume()
13          << "\n\nThe volume of a box with length 10,\n"
14          << "width 1 and height 1 is: " << boxVolume( 10 )
15          << "\n\nThe volume of a box with length 10,\n"
16          << "width 5 and height 1 is: " << boxVolume( 10, 5 )
17          << "\n\nThe volume of a box with length 10,\n"
18          << "width 5 and height 2 is: " << boxVolume( 10, 5, 2 )
19          << endl;
20
21     return 0;
22  }
23
```

Fig. 3.23   Using default arguments (part 1 of 2).

```
24   // Calculate the volume of a box
25   int boxVolume( int length, int width, int height )
26   {
27      return length * width * height;
28   }
```

```
The default box volume is: 1

The volume of a box with length 10,
width 1 and height 1 is: 10

The volume of a box with length 10,
width 5 and height 1 is: 50

The volume of a box with length 10,
width 5 and height 2 is: 100
```

Fig. 3.23   Using default arguments (part 2 of 2).

The first call to **boxVolume** (line 12) specifies no arguments and thus uses all three default values. The second call (line 14) passes a **length** argument and thus uses default values for the **width** and **height** arguments. The third call (line 16) passes arguments for **length** and **width** and thus uses a default value for the **height** argument. The last call (line 18) passes arguments for **length**, **width** and **height**, thus using no default values.

Good Programming Practice 3.12

Using default arguments can simplify writing function calls. However, some programmers feel that explicitly specifying all arguments is clearer.

Common Programming Error 3.31

Specifying and attempting to use a default argument that is not a rightmost (trailing) argument (while not simultaneously defaulting all the rightmost arguments) is a syntax error.

3.19 Unary Scope Resolution Operator

It is possible to declare local and global variables of the same name. C++ provides the *unary scope resolution operator (::)* to access a global variable when a local variable of the same name is in scope. The unary scope resolution operator cannot be used to access a local variable of the same name in an outer block. A global variable can be accessed directly without the unary scope resolution operator if the name of the global variable is not the same as the name of a local variable in scope. In Chapter 6, we discuss the use of the *binary scope resolution operator* with classes.

Figure 3.24 demonstrates the unary scope resolution operator with local and global variables of the same name. To emphasize that the local and global versions of constant variable **PI** are distinct, the program declares one of the variables **double** and one **float**.

Common Programming Error 3.32

Attempting to access a nonglobal variable in an outer block by using the unary scope resolution operator is a syntax error if no global variable exists with the same name as the variable in the outer block and a logic error if one does.

```
1    // Fig. 3.24: fig03_24.cpp
2    // Using the unary scope resolution operator
3    #include <iostream>
4
5    using std::cout;
6    using std::endl;
7
8    #include <iomanip>
9
10   using std::setprecision;
11
12   const double PI = 3.14159265358979;
13
14   int main()
15   {
16      const float PI = static_cast< float >( ::PI );
17
18      cout << setprecision( 20 )
19           << "  Local float value of PI = " << PI
20           << "\nGlobal double value of PI = " << ::PI << endl;
21
22      return 0;
23   }
```

Borland C++ command-line compiler output

```
 Local float value of PI = 3.141592741012573242
Global double value of PI = 3.141592653589790007
```

Microsoft Visual C++ compiler output

```
 Local float value of PI = 3.1415927410125732
Global double value of PI = 3.14159265358979
```

Fig. 3.24   Using the unary scope resolution operator.

Good Programming Practice 3.13

Avoid using variables of the same name for different purposes in a program. Although this is allowed in various circumstances, it can be confusing.

3.20 Function Overloading

C++ enables several functions of the same name to be defined, as long as these functions have different sets of parameters (at least as far as their types are concerned). This capability is called *function overloading*. When an overloaded function is called, the C++ compiler selects the proper function by examining the number, types and order of the arguments in the call. Function overloading is commonly used to create several functions of the same name that perform similar tasks but on different data types.

Good Programming Practice 3.14

Overloading functions that perform closely related tasks can make programs more readable and understandable.

Figure 3.25 uses overloaded function **square** to calculate the square of an **int** and the square of a **double**. In Chapter 8, we discuss how to overload operators to define how they should operate on objects of user-defined data types. (In fact, we have been using many overloaded operators to this point, including the stream insertion operator **<<** and the stream extraction operator **>>**. We will say more about overloading **<<** and **>>** in Chapter 8.) Section 3.21 introduces function templates for automatically generating overloaded functions that perform identical tasks on different data types. Chapter 12 discusses function templates and class templates in detail.

Overloaded functions are distinguished by their *signatures*—a signature is a combination of a function's name and its parameter types. The compiler encodes each function identifier with the number and types of its parameters (sometimes referred to as *name mangling* or *name decoration*) to enable *type-safe linkage*. Type-safe linkage ensures that the proper overloaded function is called and that the arguments conform to the parameters. Linkage errors are detected and reported by the compiler. Figure 3.26 was compiled on the Borland C++ compiler. Rather than showing the execution output of the program (as we normally would), we show the mangled function names produced in assembly language by Borland C++. Each mangled name begins with **@** followed by the function name. The mangled parameter list begins with **$q**. In the parameter list for function **nothing2**, **c** represents a **char**, **i** represents an **int**, **pf** represents a **float *** and **pd** represents a **double ***. In the parameter list for function **nothing1**, **i** represents an **int**, **f** represents a **float**, **c** represents a **char** and **pi** represents an **int ***. The two **square** functions are distinguished by their parameter lists; one specifies **d** for double and the other specifies **i** for **int**. The return types of the functions are not specified in the mangled names. Function name mangling is compiler-specific. Overloaded functions can have different return types but must have different parameter lists.

```
1   // Fig. 3.25: fig03_25.cpp
2   // Using overloaded functions
3   #include <iostream>
4
5   using std::cout;
6   using std::endl;
7
8   int square( int x ) { return x * x; }
9
10  double square( double y ) { return y * y; }
11
12  int main()
13  {
14     cout << "The square of integer 7 is " << square( 7 )
15          << "\nThe square of double 7.5 is " << square( 7.5 )
16          << endl;
17
18     return 0;
19  }
```

Fig. 3.25   Using overloaded functions (part 1 of 2).

```
The square of integer 7 is 49
The square of double 7.5 is 56.25
```

Fig. 3.25   Using overloaded functions (part 2 of 2).

```
1    // Fig. 3.26: fig03_26.cpp
2    // Name mangling
3
4    int square( int x ) { return x * x; }
5
6    double square( double y ) { return y * y; }
7
8    void nothing1( int a, float b, char c, int *d )
9       { }  // empty function body
10
11   char *nothing2( char a, int b, float *c, double *d )
12      { return 0; }
13
14   int main()
15   {
16      return 0;
17   }
```

```
_main
@nothing2$qcipfpd
@nothing1$qifcpi
@square$qd
@square$qi
```

Fig. 3.26   Name mangling to enable type-safe linkage .

Common Programming Error 3.33

Creating overloaded functions with identical parameter lists and different return types is a syntax error.

The compiler uses only the parameter lists to distinguish between functions of the same name. Overloaded functions need not have the same number of parameters. Programmers should use caution when overloading functions with default parameters, because this may cause ambiguity.

Common Programming Error 3.34

A function with default arguments omitted might be called identically to another overloaded function; this is a syntax error. For example, having in a program both a function that explicitly takes no arguments and a function of the same name that contains all default arguments results in a syntax error when an attempt is made to use that function name in a call passing no arguments.

3.21 Function Templates

Overloaded functions are normally used to perform similar operations that involve different program logic on different data types. If the program logic and operations are identical for each data type, this may be performed more compactly and conveniently by using *function templates*. The programmer writes a single function template definition. Given the argument types provided in calls to this function, C++ automatically generates separate *template functions* to handle each type of call appropriately. Thus, defining a single function template defines a whole family of solutions.

All function template definitions begin with the **template** keyword followed by a list of formal type parameters to the function template enclosed in angle brackets (**<** and **>**). Every formal type parameter is preceded by either keyword **typename** or keyword **class**. The *formal type parameters* are built-in types or user-defined types used to specify the types of the arguments to the function, to specify the return type of the function and to declare variables within the body of the function definition. The function definition follows and is defined like any other function.

The following function template definition is also used in Fig. 3.27.

```
template < class T >    // or template< typename T >
T maximum( T value1, T value2, T value3 )
{
   T max = value1;

   if ( value2 > max )
      max = value2;

   if ( value3 > max )
      max = value3;

   return max;
}
```

This function template declares a single formal type parameter **T** as the type of the data to be tested by function **maximum**. When the compiler detects a **maximum** invocation in the program source code, the type of the data passed to **maximum** is substituted for **T** throughout the template definition, and C++ creates a complete function for determining the maximum of three values of the specified data type. Then, the newly created function is compiled. Thus, templates really are a means of code generation. In Fig. 3.27, three functions are created—one expects three **int** values, one expects three **double** values and one expects three **char** values. The function template created for type **int** is:

```
int maximum( int value1, int value2, int value3 )
{
   int max = value1;

   if ( value2 > max )
      max = value2;

   if ( value3 > max )
      max = value3;

   return max;
}
```

The name of a type parameter must be unique in the formal parameter list of a particular template definition. Figure 3.27 illustrates the use of the **maximum** template function
to determine the largest of three **int** values, three **double** values and three **char** values.

```cpp
1   // Fig. 3.27: fig03_27.cpp
2   // Using a function template
3   #include <iostream>
4
5   using std::cout;
6   using std::cin;
7   using std::endl;
8
9   template < class T >
10  T maximum( T value1, T value2, T value3 )
11  {
12     T max = value1;
13
14     if ( value2 > max )
15        max = value2;
16
17     if ( value3 > max )
18        max = value3;
19
20     return max;
21  }
22
23  int main()
24  {
25     int int1, int2, int3;
26
27     cout << "Input three integer values: ";
28     cin >> int1 >> int2 >> int3;
29     cout << "The maximum integer value is: "
30          << maximum( int1, int2, int3 );          // int version
31
32     double double1, double2, double3;
33
34     cout << "\nInput three double values: ";
35     cin >> double1 >> double2 >> double3;
36     cout << "The maximum double value is: "
37          << maximum( double1, double2, double3 ); // double version
38
39     char char1, char2, char3;
40
41     cout << "\nInput three characters: ";
42     cin >> char1 >> char2 >> char3;
43     cout << "The maximum character value is: "
44          << maximum( char1, char2, char3 )        // char version
45          << endl;
46
47     return 0;
48  }
```

Fig. 3.27 Using a function template (part 1 of 2).

```
Input three integer values: 1 2 3
The maximum integer value is: 3
Input three double values: 3.3 2.2 1.1
The maximum double value is: 3.3
Input three characters: A C B
The maximum character value is: C
```

Fig. 3.27   Using a function template (part 2 of 2).

 Common Programming Error 3.35

Not placing either keyword **class** *or keyword* **typename** *before every type parameter of a function template is a syntax error.*

3.22 (Optional Case Study) Thinking About Objects: Identifying a Class's Attributes

In the "Thinking About Objects" section at the end of Chapter 2, we began the first phase of an object-oriented design (OOD) for our elevator simulator—identifying the classes needed to implement the simulator. We began by listing the nouns in the problem statement, and we created a separate class for each category of nouns that performs an important duty in the elevator simulation. We then represented the classes and their relationships in a UML class diagram. Classes have *attributes* and *operations*. Class attributes are implemented in C++ programs as data; class operations are implemented as functions. In this section we will determine many of the class attributes needed to implement the elevator simulator. In Chapter 4, we determine the operations. In Chapter 5, we concentrate on the interactions, often called *collaborations*, between the objects in the elevator simulator.

Consider the attributes of some real-world objects. A person's attributes include height and weight. A radio's attributes include its station setting, its volume setting and whether it is set to AM or FM. A car's attributes include its speedometer and odometer readings, the amount of gas in its tank, what gear it is in, etc. A personal computer's attributes include manufacturer (e.g., Apple, IBM or Compaq), type of screen (e.g., monochrome or color), main memory size (in megabytes), hard disk size (in gigabytes), etc.

Attributes describe classes. We can identify the attributes of our system by looking for descriptive words and phrases in the problem statement. For each descriptive word or phrase we find, we create an attribute and assign that attribute to a class. We also create attributes to represent any data that a class may need. For example, class **Scheduler** needs to know the times to create the next person to step onto each of the floors. Figure 3.28 is a table that lists the words or phrases from the problem statement that describe each class.

Note that classes **Bell** and **Building** list no attributes. As we progress through this case study, we will continue to add, modify and delete information about each of the classes in our system.

Figure 3.29 is a class diagram that lists some of the attributes for each class in our system—these attributes are created from the descriptive words and phrases in Fig. 3.28. In the UML class diagram, a class's attributes are placed in the middle compartment of the class's rectangle. Consider the following attribute of class **Elevator**:

```
capacity : int = 1
```

Class	Descriptive words and phrases
Elevator	starts the day waiting...on floor 1 of the building alternates direction: moving up and moving down capacity of 1 takes 5 seconds to move from one floor to the other elevator moving
Clock	begins the day set to time 0
Scheduler	[schedules person arrival times for] a random integer between 5 and 20 seconds into the future from the current time (for each floor)
Person	person number (from output)
Floor	capacity of 1 is unoccupied / occupied
FloorButton	has been pressed
ElevatorButton	has been pressed
Door	door shut / door open
Bell	none in problem statement
Light	light off / on
Building	none in problem statement

Fig. 3.28   Descriptive words and phrases in problem statement.

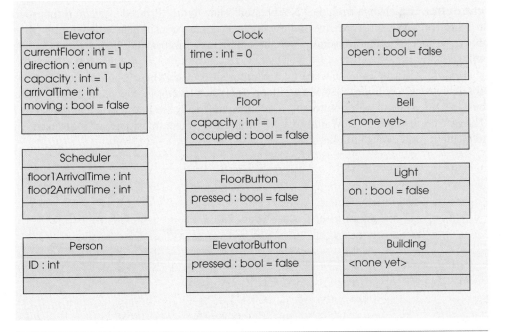

Fig. 3.29   Class diagram showing attributes.

This listing contains three pieces of information about the attribute. The attribute has a *name*—**capacity**. The attribute also has a *type*, **int**. The type depends on the language used to write the software system. In C++ for example, the value can be a primitive type, such as **int**, **char** or **float**, as well as a user-defined type like a class (we begin our study of classes in Chapter 6, where we will see that each new class is essentially a new data type).

We can also indicate an *initial value* for each attribute. The **capacity** attribute has an initial value of 1. If a particular attribute has no specified initial value, only its name and type (separated by a colon) are shown. For example, the **floor1ArrivalTime** attribute of class **Scheduler** is of type **int**. Here we show no initial value, because the value of this attribute is a random number that we do not yet know; the random number will be determined at execution time. For now we do not overly concern ourselves with the types or initial values of the attributes. We include only the information we can glean from the problem statement.

Statechart Diagrams

Objects in a system can have *states*. States describe the condition of an object at a given point in time. *Statechart diagrams* (also called *state* diagrams) give us a way to express how, and under what conditions, the objects in a system change state.

Figure 3.30 is a simple statechart diagram that models the states of an object of class **FloorButton** or of class **ElevatorButton**. Each state in a statechart diagram is represented as a rounded rectangle with the name of the state placed inside. A solid circle with an attached arrowhead points to the initial state (i.e., the "Not pressed" state). The solid lines with arrowheads indicate *transitions* between states. An object can transition from one state to another in response to an *event*. For example, classes **FloorButton** and **ElevatorButton** change from the "Not pressed" state to the "Pressed" state in response to a "button press" event. The name of the event that causes a transition is written near the line that corresponds to that transition (we can include more information about events, as we will see).

Figure 3.31 shows the statechart diagram for class **Elevator**. The elevator has three possible states: "Waiting," "Servicing Floor" (i.e., the elevator is stopped on a floor, but is busy resetting the elevator button or communicating with the floor, etc.) and "Moving." The elevator begins in the "Waiting" state. Events that trigger transitions are indicated next to the appropriate transition lines.

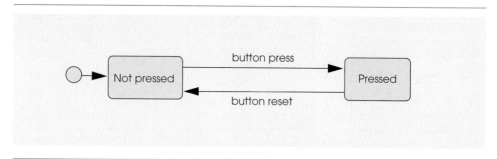

Fig. 3.30   Statechart diagram for classes **FloorButton** and **ElevatorButton**.

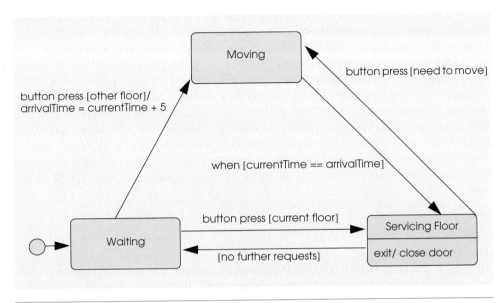

Fig. 3.31   Statechart diagram for class **Elevator**.

Let us examine the events in this statechart diagram. The text

    button press [need to move]

tells us that the "button press" event causes the elevator to transition from the "Servicing Floor" state to the "Moving" state. The *guard condition* in square brackets states that the transition occurs only if the elevator needs to move. The complete event text states that the elevator transitions from the "Servicing Floor" state to the "Moving" state in response to the "button press" event only if the elevator needs to move. Similarly, the elevator transitions from the "Waiting" state to the "Servicing Floor" state when a button is pressed on the elevator's current floor.

The text next to the transition line from the "Waiting" state to the "Moving" state indicates that this transition occurs in the event of a button press (if the button is pressed on the other floor). The forward slash ("/") indicates that an *action* accompanies this state change. The elevator performs the action of calculating and setting the time at which it will arrive at the other floor.[1]

A state transition can also occur on the event that a certain condition is **true**. The text

    when [currentTime == arrivalTime]

indicates that the elevator transitions from the "Moving" state to the "Servicing Floor" state *when* the current time of the simulation becomes equal to the time at which the elevator is scheduled to arrive on a floor.

---

1. In a real-world elevator system, a sensor on the elevator might cause it to stop on a floor. In our elevator simulator, we know that the elevator takes five seconds to move from one floor to another. Thus, in our simulation, the elevator can simply schedule its own arrival to a floor, and the elevator will stop at that scheduled time.

The text that accompanies the transition line from the "Servicing Floor" state to the "Waiting" state indicates that the elevator enters the "Waiting" state from the "Servicing Floor" state on the condition that no further requests for the elevator's service exist.[2]

An object can also perform actions while in a particular state. (see the "Servicing Floor" state in Fig. 3.31) We model these actions by splitting the appropriate state into two compartments. The top compartment contains the state name, and the bottom compartment contains the state actions. The UML defines a special *action-label* called *exit*. The *exit* action indicates an action that is performed when the object exits a state. In our model, the elevator must perform the "close door" action when it exits the "Servicing Floor" state. In other words, if the elevator needs to move, it must first close its door; or if the elevator has no more requests (button presses) to satisfy, it will close its door and enter the "Waiting" state.

Activity Diagrams

The *activity diagram* is a variation of the statechart diagram. The activity diagram focuses on the activities that an object performs; in other words, the activity diagram models what an object does during its lifetime.

The statechart diagram in the previous figure (Fig. 3.31) conveys no information about which state the elevator enters if two different people in the building press a button at the same time on different floors. It also contains no information on how the elevator decides if it needs to move. The activity diagram in Fig. 3.32 adds to the information presented in that statechart diagram by modeling the activities the elevator performs in response to a request for service.

Activities are represented as oval. The name of the activity is placed inside the oval. A solid line with an arrowhead connects two activities, indicating the order in which the activities are performed. As with statechart diagrams, the solid circle indicates the starting point of the sequence of activities. The sequence of activities modeled in this diagram is executed whenever a button is pressed (i.e., if either of the floor's buttons are currently in the "Pressed" state). When this condition is **true**, the elevator must make a decision (represented by the diamond).[3] The elevator chooses among different activities at this point, based on certain conditions. Each line (or path) extending from the diamond represents one of these different sets of activities. A guard condition placed next to each path indicates under what circumstances that path is executed.

In our diagram, the elevator performs one of three different sets of activities when a button is pressed. If the elevator is in motion (i.e., in the "Moving" state), the elevator cannot immediately perform any more activities, so the sequence of activities on the current path simply terminates. A solid circle surrounded by another circle (sometimes called a "bull's-eye") indicates the ending point of an activity diagram.

---

2. In a real-world elevator system, the elevator probably transitions between these states after a certain amount of time expires. We want to program a simulator, but we do not want to concern ourselves with the details of how the elevator will "know" when no further requests for its services exist. Therefore, we simply say that the elevator changes state in the event that no more requests exist.
3. This symbol should not be confused with the large diamond symbol used in flowchart diagrams like the ones presented in section 2.21.

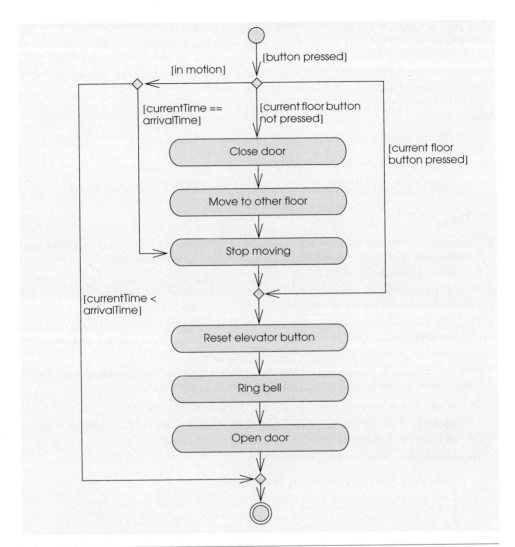

Fig. 3.32   Activity diagram modeling elevator's logic for responding to button presses.

If the floor button is pressed on the elevator's current floor, the elevator resets its button, rings its bell and opens its door. If the button on the elevator's current floor is not pressed, the elevator must first close its door, move to the other floor and then stop at the other floor before it can service the other floor. Notice that the UML models the merging of decision paths with another small diamond symbol. After the elevator opens its door, the sequence of activities terminates.

Conclusion
To recap, we have expanded our knowledge of the classes in our system (as we will continue to do in the next several chapters), and we represented this new knowledge in our class diagram. We have also used statechart and activity diagrams to gain more information

about how our system works. Even though we have not yet discussed the details of object-oriented programming in C++, we already have a significant amount of information about our system. In the "Thinking About Objects" sections at the ends of Chapters 4 and 5, we determine the operations associated with our classes and how our classes interact (i.e., collaborate) with one another.

Note

1. In this chapter, you learned how to implement "randomness." The statement

```
arrivalTime = currentTime + ( 5 + rand() % 16 );
```

can be used to schedule randomly the next arrival of a person on a floor.

SUMMARY

- The best way to develop and maintain a large program is to divide it into several smaller program modules, each of which is more manageable than the original program. Modules are written in C++ as classes and functions.

- A function is invoked by a function call. The function call mentions the function by name and provides information (as arguments) that the called function needs to perform its task.

- The purpose of information hiding is for functions to have access only to the information they need to complete their tasks. This is a means of implementing the principle of least privilege, one of the most important principles of good software engineering.

- Data type **double** is a floating-point type like **float**. A variable of type **double** can store a value of much greater magnitude and precision than **float** can store.

- Each argument of a function may be a constant, a variable, or an expression.

- A local variable is known only in a function definition. Functions are not allowed to know the implementation details of any other function (including local variables).

- The general format for a function definition is

    return-value-type   function-name **(** *parameter-list* **)**
    {
        declarations and statements
    }

- The *return-value-type* states the type of the value returned to the calling function. If a function does not return a value, the *return-value-type* is declared as **void**. The *function-name* is any valid identifier. The *parameter-list* is a comma-separated list containing the declarations of the variables that will be passed to the function. If a function does not receive any values, *parameter-list* is declared as **void**. The *function-body* is the set of declarations and statements that constitutes the function.

- The arguments passed to a function should match in number, type and order with the parameters in the function definition.

- When a program encounters a function call, control is transferred from the point of invocation to the called function, the function is executed and control returns to the caller.

- A called function can return control to the caller in one of three ways. If the function does not return a value, control is returned when the function-ending right brace is reached or by executing the statement

```
return;
```

If the function does return a value, the statement

    return *expression***;**

returns the value of *expression*.

- A function prototype declares the return-type of the function and declares the number, the types and order of the parameters the function expects to receive.
- Function prototypes enable the compiler to verify that functions are called correctly.
- The compiler ignores variable names mentioned in the function prototype.
- Each standard library has a corresponding header file containing the function prototypes for all the functions in that library, as well as definitions of symbolic constants needed by those functions.
- Programmers can and should create and include their own header files.
- When an argument is passed call-by-value, a copy of the variable's value is made, and the copy is passed to the called function. Changes to the copy in the called function do not affect the original variable's value.
- The **rand** function generates an integer between 0 and **RAND_MAX**, which is defined to be at least 32767.
- The function prototypes for **rand** and **srand** are contained in **<cstdlib>**.
- Values produced by **rand** can be scaled and shifted to produce values in a specific range.
- To randomize the output of **rand**, use the standard library function **srand**.
- The **srand** statement ordinarily is inserted in a program only after the program has been thoroughly debugged. While debugging, it is better to omit **srand**. This ensures repeatability, which is essential to proving that corrections to a random-number generation program work properly.
- To randomize without the need for entering a seed each time, we can use **srand(time(0))**. Function **time** normally returns "calendar time" in seconds. Function **time**'s prototype is located in the header **<ctime>**.
- The general equation for scaling and shifting a random number is

    n = a + rand() % b;

where **a** is the shifting value (which is equal to the first number in the desired range of consecutive integers) and **b** is the scaling factor (which is equal to the width of the desired range of consecutive integers).

- An enumeration, introduced by the keyword **enum** and followed by a type name, is a set of integer constants represented by identifiers.
- The values of these enumeration constants start at **0**, unless specified otherwise, and are incremented by **1**.
- The identifiers in an **enum** must be unique, but separate enumeration constants can have the same integer value.
- Any enumeration constant can be explicitly assigned an integer value in the enumeration.
- Each variable identifier has the attributes storage class, scope and linkage.
- C++ provides five storage class specifiers: **auto**, **register**, **extern**, **mutable** and **static**.
- An identifier's storage class determines when that identifier exists in memory.
- An identifier's scope is where the identifier can be referenced in a program.
- An identifier's linkage determines for a multiple-source-file program that an identifier is known either only in the current source file or in any source file with proper declarations.

- Variables of automatic storage class are created when the block in which they are declared is entered, exist while the block is active and are destroyed when the block is exited. A function's local variables normally are of automatic storage class by default.

- The storage class specifier **register** can be placed before an automatic variable declaration to suggest that the compiler maintain the variable in one of the computer's high-speed hardware registers. The compiler might ignore **register** declarations. Keyword **register** can be used only with variables of the automatic storage class.

- Keywords **extern** and **static** are used to declare identifiers for variables and functions of static storage class.

- Static storage class variables are allocated and initialized when the program begins execution.

- Two types of identifiers have static storage class: external identifiers, and local variables declared with the storage class specifier **static**.

- Global variables are created by placing variable declarations outside any function definition, and they retain their values throughout the execution of the program.

- Local variables declared **static** retain their value when the function in which they are declared is exited.

- All numeric variables of static storage class are initialized to zero if they are not explicitly initialized by the programmer.

- Identifier scopes include function scope, file scope, block scope and function-prototype scope.

- Labels are the only identifiers with function scope. Labels can be used anywhere in the function in which they appear, but cannot be referenced outside the function body.

- An identifier declared outside any function has file scope. Such an identifier is "known" from the point at which the identifier is declared until the end of the file.

- Identifiers declared inside a block have block scope. Block scope ends at the terminating right brace (**}**) of the block.

- Local variables declared at the beginning of a function have block scope, as do function parameters, which are considered local variables by the function.

- Any block can contain variable declarations. When blocks are nested, and an identifier in an outer block has the same name as an identifier in an inner block, the identifier in the outer block is "hidden" until the inner block terminates.

- The only identifiers with function-prototype scope are those used in the parameter list of a function prototype. Identifiers used in a function prototype can be reused elsewhere in the program without ambiguity.

- A recursive function is a function that calls itself either directly or indirectly.

- If a recursive function is called with a base case, the function simply returns a result. If the function is called with a more complex problem, the function divides the problem into two conceptual pieces: a piece that the function knows how to do, and a slightly smaller version of the original problem. Because this new problem looks like the original problem, the function launches a recursive call to work on the smaller problem.

- For recursion to terminate, each time the recursive function calls itself with a slightly simpler version of the original problem, the sequence of smaller and smaller problems must converge on the base case. When the function recognizes the base case, the result is returned to the previous function call, and a sequence of returns ensues all the way up the line until the original call of the function eventually returns the final result.

- The C++ standard does not specify the order in which the operands of most operators are to be evaluated. C++ specifies the order of evaluation of the operands of the operators **&&**, **||**, the comma (**,**) operator and **?:**. The first three are binary operators whose operands are evaluated left to right. The last operator is C++'s only ternary operator. Its leftmost operand is evaluated first; if it evaluates to nonzero, the middle operand is evaluated next, and the last operand is ignored; if it evaluates to zero, the third operand is evaluated next, and the middle operand is ignored.

- Both iteration and recursion are based on a control structure: Iteration uses a repetition structure; recursion uses a selection structure.

- Both iteration and recursion involve repetition: Iteration explicitly uses a repetition structure; recursion achieves repetition through repeated function calls.

- Iteration and recursion both involve a termination test: Iteration terminates when the loop-continuation condition fails; recursion terminates when a base case is recognized.

- Iteration and recursion can occur infinitely: An infinite loop occurs with iteration if the loop-continuation test never becomes false; infinite recursion occurs if the recursion step does not reduce the problem in a manner that converges on the base case.

- Recursion repeatedly invokes the mechanism, and consequently the overhead, of function calls. This can be expensive in both processor time and memory space.

- C++ programs do not compile unless a function prototype is provided for every function or a function is defined before it is first called.

- A function that does not return a value is declared with a **void** return type. An attempt to return a value from the function or to use the result of the function invocation in the calling function is a syntax error. An empty parameter list is specified with empty parentheses or **void** in parentheses.

- Inline functions eliminate function-call overhead. The programmer uses the keyword **inline** to advise the compiler to generate function code in line (when possible) to minimize function calls. The compiler could choose to ignore the **inline** advice.

- C++ offers a direct form of call-by-reference using reference parameters. To indicate that a function parameter is passed by reference, follow the parameter's type in the function prototype by an **&**. In the function call, mention the variable by name and it will be passed call-by-reference. In the called function, mentioning the variable by its local name actually refers to the original variable in the calling function. Thus, the original variable can be modified directly by the called function.

- Reference parameters can also be created for local use as aliases for other variables within a function. Reference variables must be initialized in their declarations, and they cannot be reassigned as aliases to other variables. Once a reference variable is declared as an alias for another variable, all operations supposedly performed on the alias are actually performed on the variable.

- C++ allows the programmer to specify default arguments and their default values. If a default argument is omitted in a call to a function, the default value of that argument is used. Default arguments must be the rightmost (trailing) arguments in a function's parameter list. Default arguments should be specified with the first occurrence of the function name. Default values can be constants, global variables, or function calls.

- The unary scope resolution operator (**::**) enables a program to access a global variable when a local variable of the same name is in scope.

- It is possible to define several functions with the same name but with different parameter types. This is called function overloading. When an overloaded function is called, the compiler selects the proper function by examining the number and types of arguments in the call.

- Overloaded functions can have different return values and must have different parameter lists. Two functions differing only by return type will result in a compilation error.

- Function templates enable the creation of functions that perform the same operations on different types of data, but the function template is defined only once.

TERMINOLOGY

ampersand (**&**) suffix
argument in a function call
auto storage class specifier
automatic storage
automatic storage class
automatic variable
base case in recursion
block
block scope
C++ standard library
call a function
call-by-reference
call-by-value
called function
caller
calling function
coercion of arguments
collaboration
component
const
constant variable
copy of a value
dangling reference
default function arguments
divide and conquer
element of chance
enum
enumeration
enumeration constant
extern storage class specifier
factorial function
file scope
function
function call
function declaration
function definition
function overloading
function prototype
function scope
function signature
global variable
header file
infinite recursion
information hiding
inline function
invoke a function
iteration
linkage
linkage specification
local variable

math library functions
mixed-type expression
modular program
mutable storage class specifier
name decoration
name mangling
named constant
optimizing compiler
overloading
parameter in a function definition
principle of least privilege
programmer-defined function
promotion hierarchy
rand
random number generation
randomize
RAND_MAX
read-only variable
recursion
recursive call
recursive function
reference parameter
reference type
register storage class specifier
return
return-value-type
scaling
scope
shifting
side effect
signature
simulation
software engineering
software reusability
srand
standard library header files
static storage class specifier
static storage duration
static variable
storage class specifier
storage class
template
template function
time
type-safe linkage
typename
unary scope resolution operator (**::**)
unsigned
void

"Thinking About Objects" Terminology

action
action-label
activity
activity diagram
arrowhead symbol in the UML
attribute
attribute initial value in the UML
attribute name in the UML

attribute type in the UML
"bull's-eye" symbol in UML activity diagram
descriptive words in problem statement
diamond symbol in UML activity diagram
event
"exit" action
guard condition
initial state

initial value of class attribute
oval symbol in UML activity diagram
rounded rectangle symbol in UML
   statechart diagram
solid line with arrowhead symbol in UML
   statechart and activity diagrams

starting point symbol in UML statechart and
   activity diagrams
state
statechart diagram
transition
"when" event

COMMON PROGRAMMING ERRORS

3.1   Forgetting to include the math header file when using math library functions is a syntax error. A standard header file must be included for every standard library function used in a program.

3.2   Omitting the return-value-type in a function definition is a syntax error.

3.3   Forgetting to return a value from a function that is supposed to return a value is a syntax error.

3.4   Returning a value from a function whose return type has been declared **void** is a syntax error.

3.5   Declaring function parameters of the same type as **float x, y** instead of **float x, float y**. The parameter declaration **float x, y** would actually report a compilation error, because types are required for each parameter in the parameter list.

3.6   Placing a semicolon after the right parenthesis enclosing the parameter list of a function definition is a syntax error.

3.7   Defining a function parameter again as a local variable in the function is a syntax error.

3.8   The **()** in a function call is actually an operator in C++. It causes the function to be called. Forgetting the **()** in a function call that takes no arguments is not a syntax error. The function is not invoked when you probably intended it to be.

3.9   Defining a function inside another function is a syntax error.

3.10   It is a syntax error if the function prototype, function header and function calls do not all agree in the number, type and order of arguments and parameters and in the type of return value.

3.11   Forgetting the semicolon at the end of a function prototype is a syntax error.

3.12   A function call that does not match the function prototype is a syntax error.

3.13   It is a syntax error if the function prototype and the function definition disagree.

3.14   Converting from a higher data type in the promotion hierarchy to a lower type can change the data value.

3.15   Forgetting a function prototype when a function is not defined before it is first invoked is a syntax error.

3.16   Using **srand** in place of **rand** to attempt to generate random numbers is a syntax error because function **srand** does not return a value.

3.17   Assigning the integer equivalent of an enumeration constant to a variable of the enumeration type is a syntax error.

3.18   After an enumeration constant has been defined, attempting to assign another value to the enumeration constant is a syntax error.

3.19   Using multiple storage class specifiers for an identifier is a syntax error. Only one storage class specifier can be applied to an identifier. For example, if you include **register**, do not also include **auto**.

3.20   Accidentally using the same name for an identifier in an inner block that is used for an identifier in an outer block, when in fact the programmer wants the identifier in the outer block to be active for the duration of the inner block, is normally a logic error.

3.21   Forgetting to return a value from a recursive function when one is needed will cause most compilers to produce a warning message.

3.22   Either omitting the base case, or writing the recursion step incorrectly so that it does not converge on the base case, will cause "infinite" recursion, eventually exhausting memory. This is analogous to the problem of an infinite loop in an iterative (nonrecursive) solution. Infinite recursion can also be caused by providing an unexpected input.

3.23   Writing programs that depend on the order of evaluation of the operands of operators other than **&&**, **||**, **?:** and the comma (**,**) operator can lead to errors, because compilers might not necessarily evaluate the operands in the order the programmer expects.

3.24   Accidentally having a nonrecursive function call itself, either directly or indirectly (through another function), is a logic error.

3.25   C++ programs do not compile unless function prototypes are provided for every function or each function is defined before it is called.

3.26   Because reference parameters are mentioned only by name in the body of the called function, the programmer might inadvertently treat reference parameters as call-by-value parameters. This can cause unexpected side effects if the original copies of the variables are changed by the calling function.

3.27   Declaring multiple references in one statement while assuming that the **&** distributes across a comma-separated list of variable names. To declare variables **x**, **y** and **z** all as references to integer, use the notation **int &x = a, &y = b, &z = c;** rather than the incorrect notation **int& x = a, y = b, z = c;** or the other common incorrect notation **int &x, y, z;**.

3.28   Not initializing a reference variable when it is declared is a syntax error.

3.29   Attempting to reassign a previously declared reference to be an alias to another variable is a logic error. The value of the other variable is simply assigned to the location for which the reference is already an alias.

3.30   Returning a pointer or reference to an automatic variable in a called function is a logic error. Some compilers will issue a warning when this occurs in a program.

3.31   Specifying and attempting to use a default argument that is not a rightmost (trailing) argument (while not simultaneously defaulting all the rightmost arguments) is a syntax error.

3.32   Attempting to access a nonglobal variable in an outer block by using the unary scope resolution operator is a syntax error if no global variable exists with the same name as the variable in the outer block and a logic error if one does.

3.33   Creating overloaded functions with identical parameter lists and different return types is a syntax error.

3.34   A function with default arguments omitted might be called identically to another overloaded function; this is a syntax error. For example, having in a program both a function that explicitly takes no arguments and a function of the same name that contains all default arguments results in a syntax error when an attempt is made to use that function name in a call passing no arguments.

3.35   Not placing either keyword **class** or keyword **typename** before every type parameter of a function template is a syntax error.

GOOD PROGRAMMING PRACTICES

3.1   Familiarize yourself with the rich collection of functions and classes in the C++ standard library.

3.2   Place a blank line between function definitions to separate the functions and enhance program readability.

3.3   Although it is not incorrect to do so, do not use the same names for the arguments passed to a function and the corresponding parameters in the function definition. This helps avoid ambiguity.

3.4   Choosing meaningful function names and meaningful parameter names makes programs more readable and helps avoid excessive use of comments.

3.5   Many programmers use parameter names in function prototypes for documentation purposes. The compiler ignores these names.

3.6   Capitalize the first letter of an identifier used as a user-defined type name.

3.7   Use only uppercase letters in the names of enumeration constants. This makes these constants stand out in a program and reminds the programmer that enumeration constants are not variables.

3.8   Using enumerations rather than integer constants can make programs clearer.

3.9   Avoid variable names that hide names in outer scopes. This can be accomplished by avoiding the use of duplicate identifiers in a program.

3.10   Always provide function prototypes, even though it is possible to omit them when functions are defined before they are used. Providing the prototypes avoids tying the code to the order in which functions are defined (which can easily change as a program evolves).

3.11   The **inline** qualifier should be used only with small, frequently used functions.

3.12   Using default arguments can simplify writing function calls. However, some programmers feel that specifying all arguments explicitly is clearer.

3.13   Avoid using variables of the same name for different purposes in a program. Although this is allowed in various circumstances, it can be confusing.

3.14   Overloading functions that perform closely related tasks can make programs more readable and understandable.

PERFORMANCE TIPS

3.1   Do not try to rewrite existing library routines to make them more efficient. You usually will not be able to increase the performance of these routines.

3.2   Function **srand** need only be called once in a program to have the desired randomizing effect. Calling it more than once is redundant and hence reduces program performance.

3.3   Automatic storage is a means of conserving memory because automatic storage class variables are created when the block in which they are declared is entered and they are destroyed when the block is exited.

3.4   The storage class specifier **register** can be placed before an automatic variable declaration to suggest that the compiler maintain the variable in one of the computer's high-speed hardware registers rather than in memory. If intensely used variables such as counters or totals can be maintained in hardware registers, the overhead of repeatedly loading the variables from memory into the registers and storing the results back into memory can be eliminated.

3.5   Often, **register** declarations are unnecessary. Today's optimizing compilers are capable of recognizing frequently used variables and can decide to place them in registers without the need for a **register** declaration from the programmer.

3.6   Avoid fibonacci-style recursive programs that result in an exponential "explosion" of calls.

3.7   Avoid using recursion in performance situations. Recursive calls take time and consume additional memory.

3.8   A heavily functionalized program—as compared to a monolithic (i.e., one-piece) program without functions—makes potentially large numbers of function calls, and these consume execution time and space on a computer's processor(s). But monolithic programs are difficult to program, test, debug, maintain and evolve.

3.9   Using **inline** functions can reduce execution time but increase program size.

3.10   One disadvantage of call-by-value is that, if a large data item is being passed, copying that data can take a considerable amount of execution time.

3.11   Call-by-reference is good for performance reasons, because it eliminates the overhead of copying large amounts of data.

3.12   For passing large objects, use a constant reference parameter to simulate the appearance and security of call-by-value and avoid the overhead of passing a copy of the large object.

PORTABILITY TIPS

3.1   Using the functions in the C++ standard library helps make programs more portable.

3.2   Programs that depend on the order of evaluation of the operands of operators other than **&&**, **||**, **?:** and the comma (**,**) operator can function differently on systems with different compilers.

3.3   The meaning of an empty function parameter list in C++ is dramatically different from in C. In C, it means all argument checking is disabled (i.e., the function call can pass any arguments it wants). In C++, it means that the function takes no arguments. Thus, C programs using this feature might report syntax errors when compiled in C++.

SOFTWARE ENGINEERING OBSERVATIONS

3.1   Avoid reinventing the wheel. When possible, use C++ standard library functions instead of writing new functions. This reduces program development time.

3.2   In programs containing many functions, **main** should be implemented as a group of calls to functions that perform the bulk of the program's work.

3.3   Each function should be limited to performing a single, well-defined task, and the function name should effectively express that task. This promotes software reusability.

3.4   If you cannot choose a concise name that expresses what the function does, it is possible that your function is attempting to perform too many diverse tasks. It is usually best to break such a function into several smaller functions.

3.5   A function should fit in an editor window. Regardless of how long a function is, it should perform one task well. Small functions promote software reusability.

3.6   Programs should be written as collections of small functions. This makes programs easier to write, debug, maintain and modify.

3.7   A function requiring a large number of parameters might be performing too many tasks. Consider dividing the function into smaller functions that perform the separate tasks. The function header should fit on one line, if possible.

3.8   Function prototypes are required in C++. Use **#include** preprocessor directives to obtain function prototypes for the standard library functions from the header files for the appropriate libraries. Also use **#include** to obtain header files containing function prototypes used by you and/or your group members.

3.9   A function prototype is not required if the definition of the function appears before the function's first use in the program. In such a case, the function definition also acts as the function prototype.

3.10   A function prototype placed outside any function definition applies to all calls to the function appearing after the function prototype in the file. A function prototype placed in a function applies only to calls made in that function.

3.11   Automatic storage is an example of the principle of least privilege. Why have variables stored in memory and accessible when they are not needed?

3.12   Declaring a variable as global rather than local allows unintended side effects to occur when a function that does not need access to the variable accidentally or maliciously modifies it. In general, use of global variables should be avoided except in certain situations with unique performance requirements.

3.13   Variables used only in a particular function should be declared as local variables in that function rather than as global variables.

3.14   Any problem that can be solved recursively can also be solved iteratively (nonrecursively). A recursive approach is normally chosen in preference to an iterative approach when the recursive approach more naturally mirrors the problem and results in a program that is easier to understand and debug. Another reason to choose a recursive solution is that an iterative solution is not apparent.

3.15   Functionalizing programs in a neat, hierarchical manner promotes good software engineering, but it has a price.

3.16   Any change to an **inline** function could require all clients of the function to be recompiled. This can be significant in some program development and maintenance situations.

3.17   Many programmers do not bother to declare value parameters as **const**, even though the called function should not be modifying the passed argument. Keyword **const** is only protecting a copy of the original argument, not the original argument itself.

3.18   Call-by-reference can weaken security, because the called function can corrupt the caller's data.

3.19   For the combined reasons of clarity and performance, many C++ programmers prefer that modifiable arguments be passed to functions by using pointers, small nonmodifiable arguments be passed call-by-value and large nonmodifiable arguments be passed to functions by using references to constants.

TESTING AND DEBUGGING TIP

3.1   Provide a **default** case in a **switch** to catch errors even if you are absolutely, positively certain that you have no bugs!

SELF-REVIEW EXERCISES

3.1   Answer each of the following:
  a) Program components in C++ are called _____ and_____.
  b) A function is invoked with a _____.
  c) A variable that is known only within the function in which it is defined is called a _____.
  d) The _____ statement in a called function is used to pass the value of an expression back to the calling function.
  e) The keyword _____ is used in a function header to indicate that a function does not return a value or to indicate that a function contains no parameters.
  f) The _____ of an identifier is the portion of the program in which the identifier can be used.
  g) The three ways to return control from a called function to a caller are _____, _____ and _____.
  h) A _____ allows the compiler to check the number, types and order of the arguments passed to a function.
  i) Function _____ is used to produce random numbers.
  j) Function _____ is used to set the random number seed to randomize a program.

k) The storage class specifiers are **mutable**, _____, _____, _____ and _____.

l) Variables declared in a block or in the parameter list of a function are assumed to be of storage class _____ unless specified otherwise.

m) Storage class specifier _____ is a recommendation to the compiler to store a variable in one of the computer's registers.

n) A variable declared outside any block or function is an _____ variable.

o) For a local variable in a function to retain its value between calls to the function, it must be declared with the _____ storage class specifier.

p) The four possible scopes of an identifier are _____, _____, _____ and _____.

q) A function that calls itself either directly or indirectly is a _____ function.

r) A recursive function typically has two components: one that provides a means for the recursion to terminate by testing for a _____ case, and one that expresses the problem as a recursive call for a slightly simpler problem than the original call.

s) In C++, it is possible to have various functions with the same name that operate on different types and/or numbers of arguments. This is called function _____.

t) The _____ enables access to a global variable with the same name as a variable in the current scope.

u) The _____ qualifier is used to declare read-only variables.

v) A function _____ enables a single function to be defined to perform a task on many different data types.

3.2   For the following program, state the scope (either function scope, file scope, block scope or function-prototype scope) of each of the following elements.

a) The variable **x** in **main**.

b) The variable **y** in **cube**.

c) The function **cube**.

d) The function **main**.

e) The function prototype for **cube**.

f) The identifier **y** in the function prototype for **cube**.

```cpp
1   // ex03_02.cpp
2   #include <iostream>
3
4   using std::cout;
5   using std::endl;
6
7   int cube( int y );
8
9   int main()
10  {
11      int x;
12
13      for ( x = 1; x <= 10; x++ )
14          cout << cube( x ) << endl;
15
16      return 0;
17  }
18
19  int cube( int y )
20  {
21      return y * y * y;
22  }
```

3.3   Write a program that tests whether the examples of the math library function calls shown in Fig. 3.2 actually produce the indicated results.

3.4   Give the function header for each of the following functions.
   a) Function **hypotenuse** that takes two double-precision, floating-point arguments, **side1** and **side2**, and returns a double-precision, floating-point result.
   b) Function **smallest** that takes three integers, **x**, **y**, **z** and returns an integer.
   c) Function **instructions** that does not receive any arguments and does not return a value. (Note: Such functions are commonly used to display instructions to a user.)
   d) Function **intToDouble** that takes an integer argument, **number**, and returns a single-precision, floating-point result.

3.5   Give the function prototype for each of the following:
   a) The function described in Exercise 3.4a.
   b) The function described in Exercise 3.4b.
   c) The function described in Exercise 3.4c.
   d) The function described in Exercise 3.4d.

3.6   Write a declaration for each of the following:
   a) Integer **count** that should be maintained in a register. Initialize **count** to **0**.
   b) Double-precision, floating-point variable **lastVal** that is to retain its value between calls to the function in which it is defined.
   c) External integer **number**, whose scope should be restricted to the remainder of the file in which it is defined.

3.7   Find the error in each of the following program segments and explain how the error can be corrected (see also Exercise 3.53):
   a)
```
int g( void ) {
    cout << "Inside function g" << endl;

    int h( void )
    {
        cout << "Inside function h" << endl;
    }
}
```
   b)
```
int sum( int x, int y )
{
    int result;

    result = x + y;
}
```
   c)
```
int sum( int n )
{
    if ( n == 0 )
        return 0;
    else
        n + sum( n - 1 );
}
```
   d)
```
void f( double a );
{
    float a;
    cout << a << endl;
}
```

e) **void product(void)**

```
{
    int a, b, c, result;
    cout << "Enter three integers: ";
    cin >> a >> b >> c;
    result = a * b * c;
    cout << "Result is " << result;
    return result;
}
```

3.8   Why would a function prototype contain a parameter type declaration such as **double &**?

3.9   (True/False) All calls in C++ are performed call-by-value.

3.10   Write a complete program that uses an **inline** function **sphereVolume** to prompt the user for the radius of a sphere and to calculate and print the volume of that sphere by using the assignment **volume = (4.0 / 3) * 3.14159 * pow(radius, 3)**.

ANSWERS TO SELF-REVIEW EXERCISES

3.1   a) Functions and classes. b) Function call. c) Local variable. d) **return**. e) **void** f) Scope.   g) **return;** or **return expression;** or encountering the closing right brace of a function.   h) Function prototype.   i) **rand** j) **srand**.   k) **auto**, **register**, **extern**, **static**.   l) **auto**.   m) **register**.   n) External, global.   o) **static**.   p) Function scope, file scope, block scope, function-prototype scope. q) Recursive.   r) Base.   s) Overloading.   t) Unary scope resolution operator (**::**).   u) **const**.   v) Template.

3.2   a) Block scope.   b) Block Scope.   c) File scope.   d) File scope.   e) File scope. f) Function-prototype scope.

3.3   See below..

```
1   // ex03_03.cpp
2   // Testing the math library functions
3   #include <iostream>
4
5   using std::cout;
6   using std::endl;
7   using std::ios;
8
9   #include <iomanip>
10
11  using std::setiosflags;
12  using std::fixed;
13  using std::setprecision;
14
15  #include <cmath>
16
17  int main()
18  {
19     cout << setiosflags( ios::fixed | ios::showpoint )
20         << setprecision( 1 )
21         << "sqrt(" << 900.0 << ") = " << sqrt( 900.0 )
22         << "\nsqrt(" << 9.0 << ") = " << sqrt( 9.0 )
23         << "\nexp(" << 1.0 << ") = " << setprecision( 6 )
```

```
24              << exp( 1.0 ) << "\nexp(" << setprecision( 1 ) << 2.0
25              << ") = " << setprecision( 6 ) << exp( 2.0 )
26              << "\nlog(" << 2.718282 << ") = " << setprecision( 1 )
27              << log( 2.718282 ) << "\nlog(" << setprecision( 6 )
28              << 7.389056 << ") = " << setprecision( 1 )
29              << log( 7.389056 ) << endl;
30      cout << "log10(" << 1.0 << ") = " << log10( 1.0 )
31              << "\nlog10(" << 10.0 << ") = " << log10( 10.0 )
32              << "\nlog10(" << 100.0 << ") = " << log10( 100.0 )
33              << "\nfabs(" << 13.5 << ") = " << fabs( 13.5 )
34              << "\nfabs(" << 0.0 << ") = " << fabs( 0.0 )
35              << "\nfabs(" << -13.5 << ") = " << fabs( -13.5 ) << endl;
36      cout << "ceil(" << 9.2 << ") = " << ceil( 9.2 )
37              << "\nceil(" << -9.8 << ") = " << ceil( -9.8 )
38              << "\nfloor(" << 9.2 << ") = " << floor( 9.2 )
39              << "\nfloor(" << -9.8 << ") = " << floor( -9.8 ) << endl;
40      cout << "pow(" << 2.0 << ", " << 7.0 << ") = "
41              << pow( 2.0, 7.0 ) << "\npow(" << 9.0 << ", "
42              << 0.5 << ") = " << pow( 9.0, 0.5 )
43              << setprecision(3) << "\nfmod("
44              << 13.675 << ", " << 2.333 << ") = "
45              << fmod( 13.675, 2.333 ) << setprecision( 1 )
46              << "\nsin(" << 0.0 << ") = " << sin( 0.0 )
47              << "\ncos(" << 0.0 << ") = " << cos( 0.0 )
48              << "\ntan(" << 0.0 << ") = " << tan( 0.0 ) << endl;
49      return 0;
50   }
```

```
sqrt(900.0) = 30.0
sqrt(9.0) = 3.0
exp(1.0) = 2.718282
exp(2.0) = 7.389056
log(2.718282) = 1.0
log(7.389056) = 2.0
log10(1.0) = 0.0
log10(10.0) = 1.0
log10(100.0) = 2.0
fabs(13.5) = 13.5
fabs(0.0) = 0.0
fabs(-13.5) = 13.5
ceil(9.2) = 10.0
ceil(-9.8) = -9.0
floor(9.2) = 9.0
floor(-9.8) = -10.0
pow(2.0, 7.0) = 128.0
pow(9.0, 0.5) = 3.0
fmod(13.675, 2.333) = 2.010
sin(0.0) = 0.0
cos(0.0) = 1.0
tan(0.0) = 0.0
```

3.4   a) **double hypotenuse(double side1, double side2)**
        b) **int smallest(int x, int y, int z)**

c) **void instructions(void) // in C++ (void) can be written ()**
d) **float intToDouble(int number)**

3.5   a) **double hypotenuse(double, double);**
b) **int smallest(int, int, int);**
c) **void instructions(void); // in C++ (void) can be written ()**
d) **float intToDouble(int);**

3.6   a) **register int count = 0;**
b) **static double lastVal;**
c) **static int number;**
   Note: This would appear outside any function definition.

3.7   a) Error: Function **h** is defined in function **g**.
   Correction: Move the definition of **h** out of the definition of **g**.
b) Error: The function is supposed to return an integer, but does not.
   Correction: Delete variable **result** and place the following statement in the function:

return x + y;

c) Error: The result of **n + sum(n – 1)** is not returned; **sum** returns an improper result.
   Correction: Rewrite the statement in the **else** clause as

return n + sum(n – 1);

d) Errors: Semicolon after the right parenthesis that encloses the parameter list, and re-defining the parameter **a** in the function definition.
   Corrections: Delete the semicolon after the right parenthesis of the parameter list, and delete the declaration **float a;**.
e) Error: The function returns a value when it is not supposed to.
   Correction: Eliminate the **return** statement.

3.8   Because the programmer is declaring a reference parameter of type "reference to" **double** to get access through call-by-reference to the original argument variable.

3.9   False. C++ allows direct call-by-reference via the use of reference parameters in addition to the use of pointers.

3.10   See below.

```
1   // ex03_10.cpp
2   // Inline function that calculates the volume of a sphere
3   #include <iostream>
4
5   using std::cout;
6   using std::cin;
7   using std::endl;
8
9   const double PI = 3.14159;
10
11  inline double sphereVolume( const double r )
12     { return 4.0 / 3.0 * PI * r * r * r; }
13
14  int main()
15  {
16     double radius;
```

```
17
18        cout << "Enter the length of the radius of your sphere: ";
19        cin >> radius;
20        cout << "Volume of sphere with radius " << radius <<
21                " is " << sphereVolume( radius ) << endl;
22        return 0;
23   }
```

EXERCISES

3.11   Show the value of **x** after each of the following statements is performed:
```
a) x = fabs( 7.5 )
b) x = floor( 7.5 )
c) x = fabs( 0.0 )
d) x = ceil( 0.0 )
e) x = fabs( -6.4 )
f) x = ceil( -6.4 )
g) x = ceil( -fabs( -8 + floor( -5.5 ) ) )
```

3.12   A parking garage charges a $2.00 minimum fee to park for up to three hours. The garage charges an additional $0.50 per hour for each hour *or part thereof* in excess of three hours. The maximum charge for any given 24-hour period is $10.00. Assume that no car parks for longer than 24 hours at a time. Write a program that will calculate and print the parking charges for each of 3 customers who parked their cars in this garage yesterday. You should enter the hours parked for each customer. Your program should print the results in a neat tabular format and should calculate and print the total of yesterday's receipts. The program should use the function **calculateCharges** to determine the charge for each customer. Your outputs should appear in the following format:

```
Car          Hours          Charge
1             1.5            2.00
2             4.0            2.50
3            24.0           10.00
TOTAL        29.5           14.50
```

3.13   An application of function **floor** is rounding a value to the nearest integer. The statement

```
y = floor( x + .5 );
```

will round the number **x** to the nearest integer and assign the result to **y**. Write a program that reads several numbers and uses the preceding statement to round each of these numbers to the nearest integer. For each number processed, print both the original number and the rounded number.

3.14   Function **floor** can be used to round a number to a specific decimal place. The statement

```
y = floor( x * 10 + .5 ) / 10;
```

rounds **x** to the tenths position (the first position to the right of the decimal point). The statement

```
y = floor( x * 100 + .5 ) / 100;
```

rounds **x** to the hundredths position (the second position to the right of the decimal point). Write a program that defines four functions to round a number **x** in various ways:

a) **roundToInteger(number)**
b) **roundToTenths(number)**
c) **roundToHundredths(number)**
d) **roundToThousandths(number)**

For each value read, your program should print the original value, the number rounded to the nearest integer, the number rounded to the nearest tenth, the number rounded to the nearest hundredth and the number rounded to the nearest thousandth.

3.15   Answer each of the following questions.
a) What does it mean to choose numbers "at random?"
b) Why is the **rand** function useful for simulating games of chance?
c) Why would you randomize a program by using **srand**? Under what circumstances is it desirable not to randomize?
d) Why is it often necessary to scale and/or shift the values produced by **rand**?
e) Why is computerized simulation of real-world situations a useful technique?

3.16   Write statements that assign random integers to the variable n in the following ranges:
a) $1 \le n \le 2$
b) $1 \le n \le 100$
c) $0 \le n \le 9$
d) $1000 \le n \le 1112$
e) $-1 \le n \le 1$
f) $-3 \le n \le 11$

3.17   For each of the following sets of integers, write a single statement that will print a number at random from the set.
a) 2, 4, 6, 8, 10.
b) 3, 5, 7, 9, 11.
c) 6, 10, 14, 18, 22.

3.18   Write a function **integerPower(base, exponent)** that returns the value of

base ^{exponent}

For example, **integerPower(3, 4) = 3 * 3 * 3 * 3**. Assume that **exponent** is a positive, nonzero integer and that **base** is an integer. The function **integerPower** should use **for** or **while** to control the calculation. Do not use any math library functions.

3.19   Define a function **hypotenuse** that calculates the length of the hypotenuse of a right triangle when the other two sides are given. Use this function in a program to determine the length of the hypotenuse for each of the following triangles. The function should take two arguments of type **double** and return the hypotenuse as a **double**.

Triangle	Side 1	Side 2
1	3.0	4.0
2	5.0	12.0
3	8.0	15.0

3.20   Write a function **multiple** that determines for a pair of integers whether the second integer is a multiple of the first. The function should take two integer arguments and return **true** if the second is a multiple of the first, **false** otherwise. Use this function in a program that inputs a series of pairs of integers.

3.21   Write a program that inputs a series of integers and passes them one at a time to function **even**, which uses the modulus operator to determine whether an integer is even. The function should take an integer argument and return **true** if the integer is even and **false** otherwise.

3.22   Write a function that displays at the left margin of the screen a solid square of asterisks whose side is specified in integer parameter **side**. For example, if **side** is **4**, the function displays

```
****
****
****
****
```

3.23   Modify the function created in Exercise 3.22 to form the square out of whatever character is contained in character parameter **fillCharacter**. Thus, if **side** is **5** and **fillCharacter** is "**#**," then this function should print

```
#####
#####
#####
#####
#####
```

3.24   Use techniques similar to those developed in Exercises 3.22 and 3.23 to produce a program that graphs a wide range of shapes.

3.25   Write program segments that accomplish each of the following:
   a) Calculate the integer part of the quotient when integer **a** is divided by integer **b**.
   b) Calculate the integer remainder when integer **a** is divided by integer **b**.
   c) Use the program pieces developed in a) and b) to write a function that inputs an integer between **1** and **32767** and prints it as a series of digits, each pair of which is separated by two spaces. For example, the integer **4562** should be printed as

```
4   5   6   2
```

3.26   Write a function that takes the time as three integer arguments (for hours, minutes and seconds), and returns the number of seconds since the last time the clock "struck 12." Use this function to calculate the amount of time in seconds between two times, both of which are within one 12-hour cycle of the clock.

3.27   Implement the following integer functions:
   a) Function **celsius** returns the Celsius equivalent of a Fahrenheit temperature.
   b) Function **fahrenheit** returns the Fahrenheit equivalent of a Celsius temperature.
   c) Use these functions to write a program that prints charts showing the Fahrenheit equivalents of all Celsius temperatures from 0 to 100 degrees, and the Celsius equivalents of all Fahrenheit temperatures from 32 to 212 degrees. Print the outputs in a neat tabular format that minimizes the number of lines of output while remaining readable.

3.28   Write a function that returns the smallest of three double-precision, floating-point numbers.

3.29   An integer number is said to be a *perfect number* if the sum of its factors, including 1 (but not the number itself), is equal to the number. For example, 6 is a perfect number, because 6 = 1 + 2 + 3. Write a function **perfect** that determines whether parameter **number** is a perfect number. Use this function in a program that determines and prints all the perfect numbers between 1 and 1000. Print the factors of each perfect number to confirm that the number is indeed perfect. Challenge the power of your computer by testing numbers much larger than 1000.

3.30   An integer is said to be *prime* if it is divisible by only 1 and itself. For example, 2, 3, 5 and 7 are prime, but 4, 6, 8 and 9 are not.
   a) Write a function that determines whether a number is prime.
   b) Use this function in a program that determines and prints all the prime numbers between 1 and 10,000. How many of these 10,000 numbers do you really have to test before being sure that you have found all the primes?
   c) Initially, you might think that $n/2$ is the upper limit for which you must test to see whether a number is prime, but you need only go as high as the square root of n. Why? Rewrite the program, and run it both ways. Estimate the performance improvement.

3.31   Write a function that takes an integer value and returns the number with its digits reversed. For example, given the number 7631, the function should return 1367.

3.32   The *greatest common divisor (GCD)* of two integers is the largest integer that evenly divides each of the numbers. Write a function **gcd** that returns the greatest common divisor of two integers.

3.33   Write a function **qualityPoints** that inputs a student's average and returns 4 if a student's average is 90–100, 3 if the average is 80–89, 2 if the average is 70–79, 1 if the average is 60–69 and 0 if the average is lower than 60.

3.34   Write a program that simulates coin tossing. For each toss of the coin, the program should print **Heads** or **Tails**. Let the program toss the coin 100 times and count the number of times each side of the coin appears. Print the results. The program should call a separate function **flip** that takes no arguments and returns **0** for tails and **1** for heads. *Note:* If the program realistically simulates the coin tossing, then each side of the coin should appear approximately half the time.

3.35   Computers are playing an increasing role in education. Write a program that will help an elementary school student learn multiplication. Use **rand** to produce two positive one-digit integers. It should then type a question such as:

How much is 6 times 7?

The student then types the answer. Your program checks the student's answer. If it is correct, print **"Very good!"**, and then ask another multiplication question. If the answer is wrong, print **"No. Please try again."** and then let the student try the same question again repeatedly until the student finally gets it right.

3.36   The use of computers in education is referred to as *computer-assisted instruction* (CAI). One problem that develops in CAI environments is student fatigue. This can be eliminated by varying the computer's dialogue to hold the student's attention. Modify the program of Exercise 3.35 so the various comments are printed for each correct answer and each incorrect answer as follows:

Responses to a correct answer

Very good!
Excellent!
Nice work!
Keep up the good work!

Responses to an incorrect answer

```
No. Please try again.
Wrong. Try once more.
Don't give up!
No. Keep trying.
```

Use the random number generator to choose a number from 1 to 4 to select an appropriate response to each answer. Use a **switch** structure to issue the responses.

3.37   More sophisticated computer-aided instruction systems monitor the student's performance over a period of time. The decision to begin a new topic is often based on the student's success with previous topics. Modify the program of Exercise 3.36 to count the number of correct and incorrect responses typed by the student. After the student types 10 answers, your program should calculate the percentage of correct responses. If the percentage is lower than 75 percent, your program should print **"Please ask your instructor for extra help"** and then terminate.

3.38   Write a program that plays the game of "guess the number" as follows: Your program chooses the number to be guessed by selecting an integer at random in the range 1 to 1000. The program then types:

```
I have a number between 1 and 1000.
Can you guess my number?
Please type your first guess.
```

The player then types a first guess. The program responds with one of the following:

```
1. Excellent! You guessed the number!
   Would you like to play again (y or n)?
2. Too low. Try again.
3. Too high. Try again.
```

If the player's guess is incorrect, your program should loop until the player finally gets the number right. Your program should keep telling the player **Too high** or **Too low** to help the player "zero in" on the correct answer.

3.39   Modify the program of Exercise 3.38 to count the number of guesses the player makes. If the number is 10 or fewer, print **Either you know the secret or you got lucky!** If the player guesses the number in 10 tries, then print **Ahah! You know the secret!** If the player makes more than 10 guesses, then print **You should be able to do better!** Why should it take no more than 10 guesses? Well, with each "good guess" the player should be able to eliminate half of the numbers. Now show why any number from 1 to 1000 can be guessed in 10 or fewer tries.

3.40   Write a recursive function **power(base, exponent)** that, when invoked, returns

$$base^{\,exponent}$$

For example, **power(3, 4) = 3 * 3 * 3 * 3**. Assume that **exponent** is an integer greater than or equal to 1. *Hint:* The recursion step would use the relationship

$$base^{\,exponent} = base \cdot base^{\,exponent - 1}$$

and the terminating condition occurs when **exponent** is equal to **1** because

$$base^1 = base$$

3.41   The Fibonacci series

0, 1, 1, 2, 3, 5, 8, 13, 21, …

begins with the terms 0 and 1 and has the property that each succeeding term is the sum of the two preceding terms. a) Write a *nonrecursive* function **fibonacci(n)** that calculates the *n*th Fibonacci number. b) Determine the largest Fibonacci number that can be printed on your system. Modify the program of part a) to use **double** instead of **int** to calculate and return Fibonacci numbers, and use this modified program to repeat part b).

3.42   *(Towers of Hanoi)* Every budding computer scientist must grapple with certain classic problems. The Towers of Hanoi (see Fig. 3.33) is one of the most famous of these. Legend has it that in a temple in the Far East, priests are attempting to move a stack of disks from one peg to another. The initial stack had 64 disks threaded onto one peg and arranged from bottom to top by decreasing size. The priests are attempting to move the stack from this peg to a second peg under the constraints that exactly one disk is moved at a time, and at no time may a larger disk be placed above a smaller disk. A third peg is available for temporarily holding disks. Supposedly, the world will end when the priests complete their task, so there is little incentive for us to facilitate their efforts.

Let us assume that the priests are attempting to move the disks from peg 1 to peg 3. We wish to develop an algorithm that will print the precise sequence of peg-to-peg disk transfers.

If we were to approach this problem with conventional methods, we would rapidly find ourselves hopelessly knotted up in managing the disks. Instead, if we attack the problem with recursion in mind, it immediately becomes tractable. Moving *n* disks can be viewed in terms of moving only *n* - 1 disks (hence, the recursion), as follows:

a)   Move *n* - 1 disks from peg 1 to peg 2, using peg 3 as a temporary holding area.
b)   Move the last disk (the largest) from peg 1 to peg 3.
c)   Move the *n* - 1 disks from peg 2 to peg 3, using peg 1 as a temporary holding area.

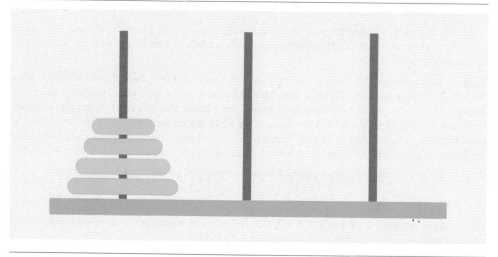

Fig. 3.33   The Towers of Hanoi for the case with four disks.

The process ends when the last task involves moving $n = 1$ disk, i.e., the base case. This is accomplished by trivially moving the disk without the need for a temporary holding area.

Write a program to solve the Towers of Hanoi problem. Use a recursive function with four parameters:

    a) The number of disks to be moved
    b) The peg on which these disks are initially threaded
    c) The peg to which this stack of disks is to be moved
    d) The peg to be used as a temporary holding area

Your program should print the precise instructions it will take to move the disks from the starting peg to the destination peg. For example, to move a stack of three disks from peg 1 to peg 3, your program should print the following series of moves:

    $1 \rightarrow 3$ (This means move one disk from peg 1 to peg 3.)
    $1 \rightarrow 2$
    $3 \rightarrow 2$
    $1 \rightarrow 3$
    $2 \rightarrow 1$
    $2 \rightarrow 3$
    $1 \rightarrow 3$

3.43 Any program that can be implemented recursively can be implemented iteratively, although sometimes with more difficulty and less clarity. Try writing an iterative version of the Towers of Hanoi. If you succeed, compare your iterative version with the recursive version you developed in Exercise 3.42. Investigate issues of performance, clarity and your ability to demonstrate the correctness of the programs.

3.44 (Visualizing Recursion) It is interesting to watch recursion "in action." Modify the factorial function of Fig. 3.14 to print its local variable and recursive call parameter. For each recursive call, display the outputs on a separate line and add a level of indentation. Do your utmost to make the outputs clear, interesting and meaningful. Your goal here is to design and implement an output format that helps a person understand recursion better. You may want to add such display capabilities to the many other recursion examples and exercises throughout the text.

3.45 The greatest common divisor of integers **x** and **y** is the largest integer that evenly divides both **x** and **y**. Write a recursive function **gcd** that returns the greatest common divisor of **x** and **y**. The **gcd** of **x** and **y** is defined recursively as follows: If **y** is equal to **0**, then **gcd(x, y)** is **x**; otherwise **gcd(x, y)** is **gcd(y, x % y)**, where % is the modulus operator.

3.46 Can **main** be called recursively? Write a program containing a function **main**. Include **static** local variable **count** and initialize it to 1. Postincrement and print the value of **count** each time **main** is called. Compile your program. What happens?

3.47 Exercises 3.35 through 3.37 developed a computer-assisted instruction program to teach an elementary school student multiplication. This exercise suggests enhancements to that program.

    a) Modify the program to allow the user to enter a grade-level capability. A grade level of 1 means to use only single-digit numbers in the problems, a grade level of two means to use numbers as large as two digits, etc.
    b) Modify the program to allow the user to pick the type of arithmetic problems he or she wishes to study. An option of 1 means addition problems only, 2 means subtraction problems only, 3 means multiplication problems only, 4 means division problems only, and 5 means to randomly intermix problems of all these types.

3.48 Write function **distance** that calculates the distance between two points *(x1, y1)* and *(x2, y2)*. All numbers and return values should be of type **double**.

3.49   What is wrong with the following program?

```cpp
// ex03_49.cpp
#include <iostream>

using std::cin;
using std::cout;

int main()
{
   int c;

   if ( ( c = cin.get() ) != EOF ) {
      main();
      cout << c;
   }

   return 0;
}
```

3.50   What does the following program do?

```cpp
// ex03_50.cpp
#include <iostream>

using std::cout;
using std::cin;
using std::endl;

int mystery( int, int );

int main()
{
   int x, y;

   cout << "Enter two integers: ";
   cin >> x >> y;
   cout << "The result is " << mystery( x, y ) << endl;
   return 0;
}

// Parameter b must be a positive
// integer to prevent infinite recursion
int mystery( int a, int b )
{
   if ( b == 1 )
      return a;
   else
      return a + mystery( a, b - 1 );
}
```

3.51   After you determine what the program of Exercise 3.50 does, modify the program to function properly after removing the restriction that the second argument be nonnegative.

3.52   Write a program that tests as many of the math library functions in Fig. 3.2 as you can. Exercise each of these functions by having your program print out tables of return values for a diversity of argument values.

3.53   Find the error in each of the following program segments and explain how to correct it:

a)
```
float cube( float );            // function prototype

double cube( float number )     // function definition
{
    return number * number * number;
}
```

b)
```
register auto int x = 7;
```

c)
```
int randomNumber = srand();
```

d)
```
float y = 123.45678;
int x;

x = y;
cout << static_cast< float >( x ) << endl;
```

e)
```
double square( double number )
{
    double number;
    return number * number;
}
```

f)
```
int sum( int n )
{
    if ( n == 0 )
        return 0;
    else
        return n + sum( n );
}
```

3.54   Modify the craps program of Fig. 3.10 to allow wagering. Package as a function the portion of the program that runs one game of craps. Initialize variable **bankBalance** to 1000 dollars. Prompt the player to enter a **wager**. Use a **while** loop to check that **wager** is less than or equal to **bankBalance** and, if not, prompt the user to reenter **wager** until a valid **wager** is entered. After a correct **wager** is entered, run one game of craps. If the player wins, increase **bankBalance** by **wager** and print the new **bankBalance**. If the player loses, decrease **bankBalance** by **wager**, print the new **bankBalance**, check on whether **bankBalance** has become zero and, if so, print the message **"Sorry. You busted!"** As the game progresses, print various messages to create some "chatter" such as **"Oh, you're going for broke, huh?"** or **"Aw cmon, take a chance!"**, or **"You're up big. Now's the time to cash in your chips!"**.

3.55   Write a C++ program that uses an **inline** function **circleArea** to prompt the user for the radius of a circle and to calculate and print the area of that circle.

3.56   Write a complete C++ program with the two alternate functions specified below, of which each simply triples the variable **count** defined in **main**. Then compare and contrast the two approaches. These two functions are

a) Function **tripleCallByValue** that passes a copy of **count** call-by-value, triples the copy and returns the new value.

b) Function **tripleByReference** that passes **count** with true call-by-reference via a reference parameter and triples the original copy of **count** through its alias (i.e., the reference parameter).

3.57   What is the purpose of the unary scope resolution operator?

3.58   Write a program that uses a function template called **min** to determine the smaller of two arguments. Test the program using integer, character and floating-point number pairs.

3.59   Write a program that uses a function template called **max** to determine the largest of three arguments. Test the program using integer, character and floating-point number pairs.

3.60   Determine whether the following program segments contain errors. For each error, explain how it can be corrected. Note: For a particular program segment, it is possible that no errors are present in the segment.

a)
```
template < class A >
int sum( int num1, int num2, int num3 )
{
    return num1 + num2 + num3;
}
```

b)
```
void printResults( int x, int y )
{
    cout << "The sum is " << x + y << '\n';
    return x + y;
}
```

c)
```
template < A >
A product( A num1, A num2, A num3 )
{
    return num1 * num2 * num3;
}
```

d)
```
double cube( int );
int cube( int );
```

4

Arrays

Objectives

- To introduce the array data structure.
- To understand the use of arrays to store, sort and search lists and tables of values.
- To understand how to declare an array, initialize an array and refer to individual elements of an array.
- To be able to pass arrays to functions.
- To understand basic sorting techniques.
- To be able to declare and manipulate multiple-subscript arrays.

With sobs and tears he sorted out
Those of the largest size ...
Lewis Carroll

Attempt the end, and never stand to doubt;
Nothing's so hard, but search will find it out.
Robert Herrick

Now go, write it before them in a table,
and note it in a book.
Isaiah 30:8

'Tis in my memory lock'd,
And you yourself shall keep the key of it.
William Shakespeare

Outline

4.1 Introduction

This chapter serves as an introduction to the important topic of data structures. *Arrays* are data structures consisting of related data items of the same type. In Chapter 6, we discuss the notions of *structures* and *classes*—each capable of holding related data items of possibly different types. Arrays and structures are "static" entities in that they remain the same size throughout program execution. (They may, of course, be of automatic storage class and hence created and destroyed each time the blocks in which they are defined are entered and exited.) In Chapter 15, we introduce dynamic data structures such as lists, queues, stacks, and trees that may grow and shrink as programs execute. The style of arrays we use in this chapter are C-style pointer-based arrays (we will study pointers in Chapter 5). Later in the text in Chapter 8 on "Operator Overloading" and in Chapter 20 on "The Standard Template Library," we will cover arrays as full-fledged objects using the techniques of object-oriented programming. We will discover that these object-based arrays are safer and more versatile than the C-like, pointer-based arrays we discuss here in Chapter 4.

4.2 Arrays

An array is a consecutive group of memory locations that all have the same name and the same type. To refer to a particular location or element in the array, we specify the name of the array and the *position number* of the particular element in the array.

Figure 4.1 shows an integer array called **c**. This array contains 12 *elements*. Any one of these elements may be referred to by giving the name of the array followed by the position number of the particular element in square brackets (**[ ]**). The first element in every array is the *zeroth element*. Thus, the first element of array **c** is referred to as **c[0]**, the second element of array **c** is referred to as **c[1]** (1 element from the beginning of the array), the seventh element of array **c** is referred to as **c[6]** (6 elements from the beginning of the array), and, in general, the *i*th element of array **c** is referred to as **c[i – 1]**. Array names follow the same conventions as other variable names.

The position number contained within square brackets is more formally called a *subscript* (this number specifies the number of elements from the beginning of the array). A subscript must be an integer or an integer expression (using any integral type). If a program uses an expression as a subscript, then the expression is evaluated to determine the subscript. For example, if we assume that variable **a** is equal to **5** and that variable **b** is equal to **6**, then the statement

```
c[ a + b ] += 2;
```

adds 2 to array element **c[11]**. Note that a subscripted array name is an *lvalue*—it can be used on the left side of an assignment.

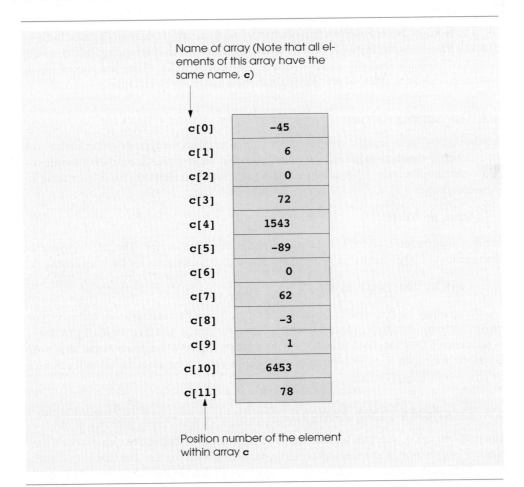

Name of array (Note that all elements of this array have the same name, **c**)

c[0]	−45
c[1]	6
c[2]	0
c[3]	72
c[4]	1543
c[5]	−89
c[6]	0
c[7]	62
c[8]	−3
c[9]	1
c[10]	6453
c[11]	78

Position number of the element within array **c**

Fig. 4.1   A 12-element array.

Let us examine array **c** in Fig. 4.1 more closely. The *name* of the entire array is **c**. Its 12 elements are named **c[0]**, **c[1]**, **c[2]**, ..., **c[11]**. The *value* of **c[0]** is **–45**, the value of **c[1]** is **6**, the value of **c[2]** is **0**, the value of **c[7]** is **62**, and the value of **c[11]** is **78**. To print the sum of the values contained in the first three elements of array **c**, we would write

```
cout << c[ 0 ] + c[ 1 ] + c[ 2 ] << endl;
```

To divide the value of the seventh element of array **c** by **2** and assign the result to the variable **x**, we would write

```
x = c[ 6 ] / 2;
```

Common Programming Error 4.1

It is important to note the difference between the "seventh element of the array" and "array element seven." Because array subscripts begin at 0, the "seventh element of the array" has a subscript of 6, while "array element seven" has a subscript of 7 and is actually the eighth element of the array. Unfortunately, this is a source of "off-by-one" errors.

The brackets used to enclose the subscript of an array are actually an operator in C++. Brackets have the same level of precedence as parentheses. The chart in Fig. 4.2 shows the precedence and associativity of the operators introduced so far. They are shown top to bottom in decreasing order of precedence with their associativity and type.

4.3 Declaring Arrays

Arrays occupy space in memory. The programmer specifies the type of each element and the number of elements required by each array so that the compiler may reserve the appropriate amount of memory. To tell the compiler to reserve 12 elements for integer array **c**, use the declaration

```
int c[ 12 ];
```

Memory may be reserved for several arrays with a single declaration. The following declaration reserves 100 elements for the integer array **b** and 27 elements for the integer array **x**.

```
int b[ 100 ], x[ 27 ];
```

Arrays may be declared to contain other data types. For example, an array of type **char** can be used to store a character string. Character strings and their similarity to arrays (a relationship C++ inherited from C) and the relationship between pointers and arrays are discussed in Chapter 5. After we introduce object-oriented programming, we will consider strings as full-fledged objects.

4.4 Examples Using Arrays

The program in Fig. 4.3 uses a **for** repetition structure to initialize the elements of a ten-element integer array **n** to zeros and prints the array in tabular format. The first output statement displays the column headings for the columns printed in the subsequent **for** structure. Remember that **setw** specifies the field width in which the *next* value is to be output.

Operators	Associativity	Type
() []	left to right	highest
++ -- static_cast<*type*>()	left to right	postfix
++ -- + - !	right to left	unary
* / %	left to right	multiplicative
+ -	left to right	additive
<< >>	left to right	insertion/extraction
< <= > >=	left to right	relational
== !=	left to right	equality
&&	left to right	logical AND
||	left to right	logical OR
?:	right to left	conditional
= += -= *= /= %=	right to left	assignment
,	left to right	comma

Fig. 4.2   Operator precedence and associativity.

```cpp
// Fig. 4.3: fig04_03.cpp
// initializing an array
#include <iostream>

using std::cout;
using std::endl;

#include <iomanip>

using std::setw;

int main()
{
   int i, n[ 10 ];

   for ( i = 0; i < 10; i++ )        // initialize array
      n[ i ] = 0;

   cout << "Element" << setw( 13 ) << "Value" << endl;

   for ( i = 0; i < 10; i++ )        // print array
      cout << setw( 7 ) << i << setw( 13 ) << n[ i ] << endl;

   return 0;
}
```

Fig. 4.3   Initializing the elements of an array to zeros (part 1 of 2).

Element	Value
0	0
1	0
2	0
3	0
4	0
5	0
6	0
7	0
8	0
9	0

Fig. 4.3   Initializing the elements of an array to zeros (part 2 of 2).

The elements of an array can also be initialized in the array declaration by following the declaration with an equals sign and a comma-separated list (enclosed in braces) of *initializers*. The program in Fig. 4.4 initializes an integer array with 10 values and prints the array in tabular format.

If there are fewer initializers than elements in the array, the remaining elements are automatically initialized to zero. For example, the elements of the array **n** in Fig. 4.3 could have been initialized to zero with the declaration

```
int n[ 10 ] = { 0 };
```

which explicitly initializes the first element to zero and implicitly initializes the remaining nine elements to zero, because there are fewer initializers than elements in the array. Remember that automatic arrays are not implicitly initialized to zero. The programmer must at least initialize the first element to zero for the remaining elements to be automatically zeroed. The method used in Fig. 4.3 can be performed repeatedly as a program executes.

The array declaration

```
int n[ 5 ] = { 32, 27, 64, 18, 95, 14 };
```

would cause a syntax error, because there are 6 initializers and only 5 array elements.

Common Programming Error 4.2

Forgetting to initialize the elements of an array whose elements should be initialized is a logic error.

Common Programming Error 4.3

Providing more initializers in an array initializer list than there are elements in the array is a syntax error.

If the array size is omitted from a declaration with an initializer list, the number of elements in the array will be the number of elements in the initializer list. For example,

```
int n[] = { 1, 2, 3, 4, 5 };
```

would create a five-element array.

Performance Tip 4.1

If, instead of initializing an array with execution-time assignment statements, you initialize the array at compile time with an array initializer list, your program will execute faster.

```
1   // Fig. 4.4: fig04_04.cpp
2   // Initializing an array with a declaration
3   #include <iostream>
4
5   using std::cout;
6   using std::endl;
7
8   #include <iomanip>
9
10  using std::setw;
11
12  int main()
13  {
14     int n[ 10 ] = { 32, 27, 64, 18, 95, 14, 90, 70, 60, 37 };
15
16     cout << "Element" << setw( 13 ) << "Value" << endl;
17
18     for ( int i = 0; i < 10; i++ )
19        cout << setw( 7 ) << i << setw( 13 ) << n[ i ] << endl;
20
21     return 0;
22  }
```

Element	Value
0	32
1	27
2	64
3	18
4	95
5	14
6	90
7	70
8	60
9	37

Fig. 4.4   Initializing the elements of an array with a declaration.

The program in Fig. 4.5 initializes the elements of a 10-element array **s** to the integers **2, 4, 6, …, 20** and prints the array in tabular format. These numbers are generated by multiplying each successive value of the loop counter by **2** and adding **2**.

```
1   // Fig. 4.5: fig04_05.cpp
2   // Initialize array s to the even integers from 2 to 20.
3   #include <iostream>
4
5   using std::cout;
6   using std::endl;
7
8   #include <iomanip>
9
10  using std::setw;
```

Fig. 4.5   Generating values to be placed into elements of an array (part 1 of 2).

```
11
12   int main()
13   {
14      const int arraySize = 10;
15      int j, s[ arraySize ];
16
17      for ( j = 0; j < arraySize; j++ )    // set the values
18         s[ j ] = 2 + 2 * j;
19
20      cout << "Element" << setw( 13 ) << "Value" << endl;
21
22      for ( j = 0; j < arraySize; j++ )    // print the values
23         cout << setw( 7 ) << j << setw( 13 ) << s[ j ] << endl;
24
25      return 0;
26   }
```

Element	Value
0	2
1	4
2	6
3	8
4	10
5	12
6	14
7	16
8	18
9	20

Fig. 4.5   Generating values to be placed into elements of an array (part 2 of 2).

Line 14

```
const int arraySize = 10;
```

uses the **const** qualifier to declare a so-called *constant variable* **arraySize** the value of which is **10**. Constant variables must be initialized with a constant expression when they are declared and cannot be modified thereafter (Fig. 4.6 and Fig. 4.7). Constant variables are also called *named constants*, or *read-only variables*. Note that the term "constant variable" is an oxymoron—a contradiction in terms like "jumbo shrimp" or "freezer burn." (Please send your favorite oxymorons to our email address listed in the Preface. Thanks!)

```
1   // Fig. 4.6: fig04_06.cpp
2   // Using a properly initialized constant variable
3   #include <iostream>
4
5   using std::cout;
6   using std::endl;
7
```

Fig. 4.6   Correctly initializing and using a constant variable.

```
8   int main()
9   {
10     const int x = 7;   // initialized constant variable
11
12     cout << "The value of constant variable x is: "
13          << x << endl;
14
15     return 0;
16  }
```

```
The value of constant variable x is: 7
```

Fig. 4.6   Correctly initializing and using a constant variable.

```
1   // Fig. 4.7: fig04_07.cpp
2   // A const object must be initialized
3
4   int main()
5   {
6      const int x;   // Error: x must be initialized
7
8      x = 7;         // Error: cannot modify a const variable
9
10     return 0;
11  }
```

Borland C++ command-line compiler error messages

```
Fig04_07.cpp:
Error E2304 Fig04_07.cpp 6: Constant variable 'x' must be
    initialized in function main()
Error E2024 Fig04_07.cpp 8: Cannot modify a const object in
    function main()
*** 2 errors in Compile ***
```

Microsoft Visual C++ compiler error messages

```
Compiling...
Fig04_07.cpp
d:\fig04_07.cpp(6) : error C2734:
    'x' : const object must be initialized if not extern
d:\fig04_07.cpp(8) : error C2166:
    l-value specifies const object
Error executing cl.exe.

test.exe - 2 error(s), 0 warning(s)
```

Fig. 4.7   A **const** object must be initialized.

Common Programming Error 4.4

Assigning a value to a constant variable in an executable statement is a syntax error.

Constant variables can be placed anywhere a constant expression is expected. In Fig. 4.5, constant variable **arraySize** is used to specify the size of array **s** in the declaration

```
int j, s[ arraySize ];
```

Common Programming Error 4.5

Only constants can be used to declare automatic and static arrays. Not using a constant for this purpose is a syntax error.

Using constant variables to specify array sizes makes programs more *scalable*. In Fig. 4.5, the first **for** loop could fill a 1000-element array by simply changing the value of **arraySize** in its declaration from **10** to **1000**. If the constant variable **arraySize** had not been used, we would have to change the program in three separate places to scale the program to handle 1000 array elements. As programs get larger, this technique becomes more useful for writing clear programs.

Software Engineering Observation 4.1

Defining the size of each array as a constant variable instead of a constant makes programs more scalable.

Good Programming Practice 4.1

Defining the size of an array as a constant variable instead of a literal constant makes programs clearer. This technique is used to get rid of so-called magic numbers*; i.e., repeatedly mentioning the size 10, for example, in array processing code for a 10-element array gives the number 10 an artificial significance and may unfortunately confuse the reader when the program includes other 10s that have nothing to do with the array size.*

The program in Fig. 4.8 sums the values contained in the 12-element integer array **a**. The statement in the body of the **for** loop does the totaling. It is important to remember that the values being supplied as initializers for array **a** normally would be read into the program from the user at the keyboard. For example, the **for** structure

```
for ( int j = 0; j < arraySize; j++ )
   cin >> a[ j ];
```

reads one value at a time from the keyboard and stores the value in element **a[j]**.

```
1   // Fig. 4.8: fig04_08.cpp
2   // Compute the sum of the elements of the array
3   #include <iostream>
4
5   using std::cout;
6   using std::endl;
7
```

Fig. 4.8   Computing the sum of the elements of an array (part 1 of 2).

```
 8   int main()
 9   {
10      const int arraySize = 12;
11      int a[ arraySize ] = { 1, 3, 5, 4, 7, 2, 99,
12                                 16, 45, 67, 89, 45 };
13      int total = 0;
14
15      for ( int i = 0; i < arraySize; i++ )
16         total += a[ i ];
17
18      cout << "Total of array element values is " << total << endl;
19      return 0;
20   }
```

```
Total of array element values is 383
```

Fig. 4.8   Computing the sum of the elements of an array (part 2 of 2).

Our next example uses arrays to summarize the results of data collected in a survey. Consider the following problem statement:

> *Forty students were asked to rate the quality of the food in the student cafeteria on a scale of 1 to 10 (1 meaning awful and 10 meaning excellent). Place the 40 responses in an integer array and summarize the results of the poll.*

This is a typical array application (see Fig. 4.9). We wish to summarize the number of responses of each type (i.e., 1 through 10). The array **responses** is a 40-element array of the students' responses. We use an 11-element array **frequency** to count the number of occurrences of each response. We ignore the first element, **frequency[0]**, because it is more logical to have the response 1 increment **frequency[1]** than **frequency[0]**. This allows us to use each response directly as a subscript on the **frequency** array.

```
 1   // Fig. 4.9: fig04_09.cpp
 2   // Student poll program
 3   #include <iostream>
 4
 5   using std::cout;
 6   using std::endl;
 7
 8   #include <iomanip>
 9
10   using std::setw;
11
12   int main()
13   {
14      const int responseSize = 40, frequencySize = 11;
15      int responses[ responseSize ] = { 1, 2, 6, 4, 8, 5, 9, 7, 8,
16          10, 1, 6, 3, 8, 6, 10, 3, 8, 2, 7, 6, 5, 7, 6, 8, 6, 7,
17          5, 6, 6, 5, 6, 7, 5, 6, 4, 8, 6, 8, 10 };
```

Fig. 4.9   A student poll analysis program (part 1 of 2).

```
18      int frequency[ frequencySize ] = { 0 };
19
20      for ( int answer = 0; answer < responseSize; answer++ )
21         ++frequency[ responses[answer] ];
22
23      cout << "Rating" << setw( 17 ) << "Frequency" << endl;
24
25      for ( int rating = 1; rating < frequencySize; rating++ )
26         cout << setw( 6 ) << rating
27              << setw( 17 ) << frequency[ rating ] << endl;
28
29      return 0;
30   }
```

Rating	Frequency
1	2
2	2
3	2
4	2
5	5
6	11
7	5
8	7
9	1
10	3

Fig. 4.9   A student poll analysis program (part 2 of 2).

Good Programming Practice 4.2

Strive for program clarity. It is sometimes worthwhile to trade off the most efficient use of memory or processor time in favor of writing clearer programs.

Performance Tip 4.2

Sometimes performance considerations far outweigh clarity considerations.

The first **for** loop (lines 20 and 21) takes the responses one at a time from the array **responses** and increments 1 of the 10 counters (**frequency[1]** through **frequency[10]**) in the **frequency** array. The key statement in the loop is

```
++frequency[ responses[ answer ] ];
```

This statement increments the appropriate **frequency** counter, depending on the value of **responses[answer]**. For example, when the counter **answer** is **0**, the value of **responses[answer]** is **1**, so **++frequency[responses[answer]];** is actually interpreted as

```
++frequency[ 1 ];
```

which increments array element one. When **answer** is **1**, **responses[answer]** is **2**, so **++frequency[responses[answer]];** is interpreted as

```
++frequency[ 2 ];
```

which increments array element two. When **answer** is **2**, **responses[answer]** is **6**, so **++frequency[responses[answer]];** is interpreted as

```
++frequency[ 6 ];
```

which increments array element six, and so on. Note that regardless of the number of responses processed in the survey, only an 11-element array is required (ignoring element zero) to summarize the results. If the data contained invalid values such as 13, the program would attempt to add **1** to **frequency[13]**. This would be outside the bounds of the array. *C++ has no array bounds checking to prevent the computer from referring to an element that does not exist.* Thus, an executing program can walk off either end of an array without warning. The programmer should ensure that all array references remain within the bounds of the array. C++ is an extensible language. In Chapter 8, we will extend C++ by implementing an array as a user-defined type with a class. Our new array definition will enable us to perform many operations that are not standard for C++'s built-in arrays. For example, we will be able to compare arrays directly, assign one array to another, input and output entire arrays with **cin** and **cout**, initialize arrays automatically, prevent access to out-of-range array elements and change the range of subscripts (and even their subscript type) so that the first element of an array is not required to be element 0.

Common Programming Error 4.6

Referring to an element outside the array bounds is an execution-time logic error. It is not a syntax error.

Testing and Debugging Tip 4.1

When looping through an array, the array subscript should never go below 0 and should always be less than the total number of elements in the array (one less than the size of the array). Make sure that the loop-terminating condition prevents accessing elements outside this range.

Testing and Debugging Tip 4.2

Programs should validate the correctness of all input values to prevent erroneous information from affecting a program's calculations.

Portability Tip 4.1

The (normally serious) effects of referencing elements outside the array bounds are system dependent. Often this results in changes to the value of an unrelated variable.

Testing and Debugging Tip 4.3

When we study classes (beginning with Chapter 6), we will see how to develop a "smart array," which automatically checks that all subscript references are in bounds at run time. Using such smart data types helps eliminate bugs.

Our next example (Fig. 4.10) reads numbers from an array and graphs the information in the form of a bar chart, or histogram—each number is printed, and then a bar consisting of that many asterisks is printed beside the number. The nested **for** loop actually draws the bars. Note the use of **endl** to end a histogram bar.

Common Programming Error 4.7

*Although it is possible to use the same counter variable in a **for** loop and a second **for** loop nested inside, this is normally a logic error.*

Testing and Debugging Tip 4.4

Although it is possible to modify a loop counter in a **for** *body, avoid doing so, because this often leads to subtle bugs.*

```cpp
1   // Fig. 4.10: fig04_10.cpp
2   // Histogram printing program
3   #include <iostream>
4
5   using std::cout;
6   using std::endl;
7
8   #include <iomanip>
9
10  using std::setw;
11
12  int main()
13  {
14     const int arraySize = 10;
15     int n[ arraySize ] = { 19, 3, 15, 7, 11, 9, 13, 5, 17, 1 };
16
17     cout << "Element" << setw( 13 ) << "Value"
18        << setw( 17 ) << "Histogram" << endl;
19
20     for ( int i = 0; i < arraySize; i++ ) {
21        cout << setw( 7 ) << i << setw( 13 )
22           << n[ i ] << setw( 9 );
23
24        for ( int j = 0; j < n[ i ]; j++ )    // print one bar
25           cout << '*';
26
27        cout << endl;
28     }
29
30     return 0;
31  }
```

```
Element          Value         Histogram
      0             19         *******************
      1              3         ***
      2             15         ***************
      3              7         *******
      4             11         ***********
      5              9         *********
      6             13         *************
      7              5         *****
      8             17         *****************
      9              1         *
```

Fig. 4.10   A program that prints histograms .

In Chapter 3, we stated that we would show a more elegant method of writing the dice-rolling program of Fig. 3.8. The problem was to roll a single six-sided die 6000 times to test whether the random-number generator actually produces random numbers. An array version of this program is shown in Fig. 4.11.

To this point, we have discussed only integer arrays. However, arrays may be of any type. We now discuss storing character strings in character arrays. So far, the only string-processing capability we introduced is outputting a string with **cout** and **<<**. A string such as "**hello**" is really an array of characters. Character arrays have several unique features.

```cpp
1   // Fig. 4.11: fig04_11.cpp
2   // Roll a six-sided die 6000 times
3   #include <iostream>
4
5   using std::cout;
6   using std::endl;
7
8   #include <iomanip>
9
10  using std::setw;
11
12  #include <cstdlib>
13  #include <ctime>
14
15  int main()
16  {
17     const int arraySize = 7;
18     int face, frequency[ arraySize ] = { 0 };
19
20     srand( time( 0 ) );
21
22     for ( int roll = 1; roll <= 6000; roll++ )
23        ++frequency[ 1 + rand() % 6 ]; // replaces 20-line switch
24                                       // of Fig. 3.8
25
26     cout << "Face" << setw( 13 ) << "Frequency" << endl;
27
28     // ignore element 0 in the frequency array
29     for ( face = 1; face < arraySize; face++ )
30        cout << setw( 4 ) << face
31             << setw( 13 ) << frequency[ face ] << endl;
32
33     return 0;
34  }
```

Face	Frequency
1	1037
2	987
3	1013
4	1028
5	952
6	983

Fig. 4.11   Dice-rolling program using arrays instead of **switch**.

A character array can be initialized using a string literal. For example, the declaration

```
char string1[] = "first";
```

initializes the elements of array **string1** to the individual characters in the string literal **"first"**. The size of array **string1** in the preceding declaration is determined by the compiler based on the length of the string. It is important to note that the string **"first"** contains five characters *plus* a special string termination character called the *null character*. Thus, array **string1** actually contains six elements. The character constant representation of the null character is **'\0'** (backslash followed by zero). All strings end with this character. A character array representing a string should always be declared large enough to hold the number of characters in the string and the terminating null character.

Character arrays also can be initialized with individual character constants in an initializer list. The preceding declaration is equivalent to the more tedious form

```
char string1[] = { 'f', 'i', 'r', 's', 't', '\0' };
```

Because a string is an array of characters, we can access individual characters in a string directly using array subscript notation. For example, **string1[0]** is the character **'f'** and **string1[3]** is the character **'s'**.

We also can input a string directly into a character array from the keyboard using **cin** and **>>**. For example, the declaration

```
char string2[ 20 ];
```

creates a character array capable of storing a string of 19 characters and a terminating null character. The statement

```
cin >> string2;
```

reads a string from the keyboard into **string2** and automatically appends the null character to the end of **string2**. Note in the preceding statement that only the name of the array is supplied; no information about the size of the array is provided. It is the programmer's responsibility to ensure that the array into which the string is read is capable of holding any string the user types at the keyboard. **cin** reads characters from the keyboard until the first whitespace character is encountered—it does not care how large the array is. Thus, inputting data with **cin** and **>>** can insert data beyond the end of the array (see Section 5.12 for information on preventing insertion beyond the end of a **char** array).

Common Programming Error 4.8

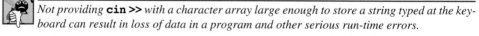

Not providing **cin >>** *with a character array large enough to store a string typed at the keyboard can result in loss of data in a program and other serious run-time errors.*

A character array representing a null-terminated string can be output with **cout** and **<<**. The array **string2** is printed with the statement

```
cout << string2 << endl;
```

Note that **cout <<**, like **cin >>**, does not care how large the character array is. The characters of the string are printed until a terminating null character is encountered.

Figure 4.12 demonstrates initializing a character array with a string literal, reading a string into a character array, printing a character array as a string, and accessing individual characters of a string.

```
1    // Fig. 4_12: fig04_12.cpp
2    // Treating character arrays as strings
3    #include <iostream>
4
5    using std::cout;
6    using std::cin;
7    using std::endl;
8
9    int main()
10   {
11      char string1[ 20 ], string2[] = "string literal";
12
13      cout << "Enter a string: ";
14      cin >> string1;
15      cout << "string1 is: " << string1
16           << "\nstring2 is: " << string2
17           << "\nstring1 with spaces between characters is:\n";
18
19      for ( int i = 0; string1[ i ] != '\0'; i++ )
20         cout << string1[ i ] << ' ';
21
22      cin >> string1;   // reads "there"
23      cout << "\nstring1 is: " << string1 << endl;
24
25      cout << endl;
26      return 0;
27   }
```

```
Enter a string: Hello there
string1 is: Hello
string2 is: string literal
string1 with spaces between characters is:
H e l l o
string1 is: there
```

Fig. 4.12   Treating character arrays as strings.

Figure 4.12 uses a **for** structure (lines 19 and 20) to loop through the **string1** array and print the individual characters separated by spaces. The condition in the **for** structure, **string1[i] != '\0'**, is true while the terminating null character has not been encountered in the string.

Chapter 3 discussed the storage class specifier **static**. A **static** local variable in a function definition exists for the duration of the program, but is only visible in the function body.

Performance Tip 4.3

We can apply **static** *to a local array declaration so the array is not created and initialized each time the function is called, and the array is not destroyed each time the function is exited in the program. This improves performance.*

Arrays that are declared **static** are initialized when the program is loaded. If a **static** array is not explicitly initialized by the programmer, that array is initialized to zero by the compiler when the array is created.

Figure 4.13 demonstrates function **staticArrayInit** with a local array declared **static** and function **automaticArrayInit** with an automatic local array. Function **staticArrayInit** is called twice. The **static** local array is initialized to zero by the compiler. The function prints the array, adds 5 to each element and prints the array again. The second time the function is called, the **static** array contains the values stored during the first function call. Function **automaticArrayInit** is also called twice. The elements of the automatic local array are initialized with the values 1, 2 and 3. The function prints the array, adds 5 to each element and prints the array again. The second time the function is called, the array elements are reinitialized to 1, 2 and 3, because the array has automatic storage class.

```cpp
1   // Fig. 4.13: fig04_13.cpp
2   // Static arrays are initialized to zero
3   #include <iostream>
4
5   using std::cout;
6   using std::endl;
7
8   void staticArrayInit( void );
9   void automaticArrayInit( void );
10
11  int main()
12  {
13     cout << "First call to each function:\n";
14     staticArrayInit();
15     automaticArrayInit();
16
17     cout << "\n\nSecond call to each function:\n";
18     staticArrayInit();
19     automaticArrayInit();
20     cout << endl;
21
22     return 0;
23  }
24
25  // function to demonstrate a static local array
26  void staticArrayInit( void )
27  {
28     static int array1[ 3 ];
29     int i;
30
31     cout << "\nValues on entering staticArrayInit:\n";
32
33     for ( i = 0; i < 3; i++ )
34        cout << "array1[" << i << "] = " << array1[ i ] << "  ";
35
36     cout << "\nValues on exiting staticArrayInit:\n";
37
```

Fig. 4.13   Comparing **static** array initialization and automatic array initialization (part 1 of 2).

```
38      for ( i = 0; i < 3; i++ )
39          cout << "array1[" << i << "] = "
40              << ( array1[ i ] += 5 ) << "   ";
41  }
42
43  // function to demonstrate an automatic local array
44  void automaticArrayInit( void )
45  {
46      int i, array2[ 3 ] = { 1, 2, 3 };
47
48      cout << "\n\nValues on entering automaticArrayInit:\n";
49
50      for ( i = 0; i < 3; i++ )
51          cout << "array2[" << i << "] = " << array2[ i ] << "   ";
52
53      cout << "\nValues on exiting automaticArrayInit:\n";
54
55      for ( i = 0; i < 3; i++ )
56          cout << "array2[" << i << "] = "
57              << ( array2[ i ] += 5 ) << "   ";
58  }
```

```
First call to each function:

Values on entering staticArrayInit:
array1[0] = 0   array1[1] = 0   array1[2] = 0
Values on exiting staticArrayInit:
array1[0] = 5   array1[1] = 5   array1[2] = 5

Values on entering automaticArrayInit:
array2[0] = 1   array2[1] = 2   array2[2] = 3
Values on exiting automaticArrayInit:
array2[0] = 6   array2[1] = 7   array2[2] = 8

Second call to each function:

Values on entering staticArrayInit:
array1[0] = 5   array1[1] = 5   array1[2] = 5
Values on exiting staticArrayInit:
array1[0] = 10   array1[1] = 10   array1[2] = 10

Values on entering automaticArrayInit:
array2[0] = 1   array2[1] = 2   array2[2] = 3
Values on exiting automaticArrayInit:
array2[0] = 6   array2[1] = 7   array2[2] = 8
```

Fig. 4.13   Comparing **static** array initialization and automatic array initialization (part 2 of 2).

Common Programming Error 4.9

*Assuming that elements of a function's local **static** array are initialized to zero every time the function is called can lead to logic errors in a program.*

4.5 Passing Arrays to Functions

To pass an array argument to a function, specify the name of the array without any brackets. For example, if array **hourlyTemperatures** has been declared as

```
int hourlyTemperatures[ 24 ];
```

the function call statement

```
modifyArray( hourlyTemperatures, 24 );
```

passes array **hourlyTemperatures** and its size to function **modifyArray**. When passing an array to a function, the array size is normally passed as well, so the function can process the specific number of elements in the array. (Otherwise, we would need to build this knowledge into the called function itself or, worse yet, place the array size in a global variable.) In Chapter 8, when we introduce the **Array** class, we will build the size of the array into the user-defined type—every **Array** object that we create will "know" its own size. Thus, when we pass an **Array** object into a function, we no longer will have to pass the size of the array as an argument.

C++ automatically passes arrays to functions using simulated call-by-reference—the called functions can modify the element values in the callers' original arrays. The value of the name of the array is the address of the first element of the array. Because the starting address of the array is passed, the called function knows precisely where the array is stored. Therefore, when the called function modifies array elements in its function body, it is modifying the actual elements of the array in their original memory locations.

Performance Tip 4.4

Passing arrays by simulated call-by-reference makes sense for performance reasons. If arrays were passed by call-by-value, a copy of each element would be passed. For large, frequently passed arrays, this would be time consuming and would consume considerable storage for the copies of the arrays.

Software Engineering Observation 4.2

It is possible to pass an array by value (by using a simple trick we explain in Chapter 16)— this is rarely done.

Although entire arrays are passed by simulated call-by-reference, individual array elements are passed by call-by-value exactly as simple variables are. Such simple single pieces of data are called *scalars* or *scalar quantities.* To pass an element of an array to a function, use the subscripted name of the array element as an argument in the function call. In Chapter 5, we show how to simulate call-by-reference for scalars (i.e., individual variables and array elements).

For a function to receive an array through a function call, the function's parameter list must specify that an array will be received. For example, the function header for function **modifyArray** might be written as

```
void modifyArray( int b[], int arraySize )
```

indicating that **modifyArray** expects to receive the address of an array of integers in parameter **b** and the number of array elements in parameter **arraySize**. The size of the array is not required between the array brackets. If it is included, the compiler will ignore it. Because arrays are passed by simulated call-by-reference, when the called function uses the array name **b**, it will in fact be referring to the actual array in the caller (array **hourly-Temperatures** in the preceding call). In Chapter 5, we introduce other notations for indicating that an array is being received by a function. As we will see, these notations are based on the intimate relationship between arrays and pointers.

Note the strange appearance of the function prototype for **modifyArray**

```
void modifyArray( int [], int );
```

This prototype could have been written

```
void modifyArray( int anyArrayName[], int anyVariableName )
```

but as we learned in Chapter 3, C++ compilers ignore variable names in prototypes.

Good Programming Practice 4.3

Some programmers include variable names in function prototypes to make programs clearer. The compiler ignores these names.

Remember, the prototype tells the compiler the number of arguments and the types of each argument (in the order in which the arguments are expected to appear).

The program in Fig. 4.14 demonstrates the difference between passing an entire array and passing an array element. The program first prints the five elements of integer array **a**. Next, **a** and its size are passed to function **modifyArray**, where each of **a**'s elements is multiplied by 2. Then **a** is reprinted in **main**. As the output shows, the elements of **a** are indeed modified by **modifyArray**. Now the program prints the value of **a[3]** and passes it to function **modifyElement**. Function **modifyElement** multiplies its argument by 2 and prints the new value. Note that when **a[3]** is reprinted in **main**, it has not been modified, because individual array elements are passed by call-by-value.

There may be situations in your programs in which a function should not be allowed to modify array elements. Because arrays are always passed by simulated call-by-reference, modification of values in an array is difficult to control. C++ provides the type qualifier **const** that can be used to prevent modification of array values in a function. When a function specifies an array parameter that is preceded by the **const** qualifier, the elements of the array become constant in the function body, and any attempt to modify an element of the array in the function body results in a syntax error. This enables the programmer to correct a program so it does not attempt to modify array elements.

```
1   // Fig. 4.14: fig04_14.cpp
2   // Passing arrays and individual array elements to functions
3   #include <iostream>
4
5   using std::cout;
6   using std::endl;
7
8   #include <iomanip>
```

Fig. 4.14   Passing arrays and individual array elements to functions (part 1 of 3).

```
9
10   using std::setw;
11
12   void modifyArray( int [], int );   // appears strange
13   void modifyElement( int );
14
15   int main()
16   {
17      const int arraySize = 5;
18      int i, a[ arraySize ] = { 0, 1, 2, 3, 4 };
19
20      cout << "Effects of passing entire array call-by-reference:"
21          << "\n\nThe values of the original array are:\n";
22
23      for ( i = 0; i < arraySize; i++ )
24         cout << setw( 3 ) << a[ i ];
25
26      cout << endl;
27
28      // array a passed call-by-reference
29      modifyArray( a, arraySize );
30
31      cout << "The values of the modified array are:\n";
32
33      for ( i = 0; i < arraySize; i++ )
34         cout << setw( 3 ) << a[ i ];
35
36      cout << "\n\n\n"
37          << "Effects of passing array element call-by-value:"
38          << "\n\nThe value of a[3] is " << a[ 3 ] << '\n';
39
40      modifyElement( a[ 3 ] );
41
42      cout << "The value of a[3] is " << a[ 3 ] << endl;
43
44      return 0;
45   }
46
47   // In function modifyArray, "b" points to the original
48   // array "a" in memory.
49   void modifyArray( int b[], int sizeOfArray )
50   {
51      for ( int j = 0; j < sizeOfArray; j++ )
52         b[ j ] *= 2;
53   }
54
55   // In function modifyElement, "e" is a local copy of
56   // array element a[ 3 ] passed from main.
57   void modifyElement( int e )
58   {
59      cout << "Value in modifyElement is "
60          << ( e *= 2 ) << endl;
61   }
```

Fig. 4.14   Passing arrays and individual array elements to functions (part 2 of 3).

```
Effects of passing entire array call-by-reference:

The values of the original array are:
  0  1  2  3  4
The values of the modified array are:
  0  2  4  6  8


Effects of passing array element call-by-value:

The value of a[3] is 6
Value in modifyElement is 12
The value of a[3] is 6
```

Fig. 4.14   Passing arrays and individual array elements to functions (part 3 of 3).

Figure 4.15 demonstrates the **const** qualifier. Function **tryToModifyArray** is defined with parameter **const int b[]**, which specifies that array **b** is constant and cannot be modified. Each of the three attempts by the function to modify array elements results in the syntax error "**Cannot modify a const object**." The **const** qualifier will be discussed again in Chapter 7.

```cpp
1   // Fig. 4.15: fig04_15.cpp
2   // Demonstrating the const type qualifier
3   #include <iostream>
4
5   using std::cout;
6   using std::endl;
7
8   void tryToModifyArray( const int [] );
9
10  int main()
11  {
12     int a[] = { 10, 20, 30 };
13  ssss
14     tryToModifyArray( a );
15     cout << a[ 0 ] << ' ' << a[ 1 ] << ' ' << a[ 2 ] << '\n';
16     return 0;
17  }
18
19  // In function tryToModifyArray, "b" cannot be used
20  // to modify the original array "a" in main.
21  void tryToModifyArray( const int b[] )
22  {
23     b[ 0 ] /= 2;    // error
24     b[ 1 ] /= 2;    // error
25     b[ 2 ] /= 2;    // error
26  }
```

Fig. 4.15   Demonstrating the **const** type qualifier (part 1 of 2).

Borland C++ command-line compiler error messages

```
Fig04_15.cpp:
Error E2024 Fig04_15.cpp 23: Cannot modify a const object in
    function tryToModifyArray(const int * const)
Error E2024 Fig04_15.cpp 24: Cannot modify a const object in
    function tryToModifyArray(const int * const)
Error E2024 Fig04_15.cpp 25: Cannot modify a const object in
    function tryToModifyArray(const int * const)
Warning W8057 Fig04_15.cpp 26: Parameter 'b' is never used in
    function tryToModifyArray(const int * const)
*** 3 errors in Compile ***
```

Microsoft Visual C++ compiler error messages

```
Compiling...
Fig04_15.cpp
D:\Fig04_15.cpp(23) : error C2166:
    l-value specifies const object
D:\Fig04_15.cpp(24) : error C2166:
    l-value specifies const object
D:\Fig04_15.cpp(25) : error C2166:
    l-value specifies const object
Error executing cl.exe.

test.exe - 3 error(s), 0 warning(s)
```

Fig. 4.15   Demonstrating the **const** type qualifier (part 2 of 2).

Common Programming Error 4.10

Forgetting that arrays are passed by reference and hence can be modified may result in a logic error.

Software Engineering Observation 4.3

*The **const** type qualifier can be applied to an array parameter in a function definition to prevent the original array from being modified in the function body. This is another example of the principle of least privilege. Functions should not be given the capability to modify an array unless it is absolutely necessary.*

4.6 Sorting Arrays

Sorting data (i.e., placing the data into some particular order such as ascending or descending) is one of the most important computing applications. A bank sorts all checks by account number so that it can prepare individual bank statements at the end of each month. Telephone companies sort their lists of accounts by last name and, within that, by first name to make it easy to find phone numbers. Virtually every organization must sort some data and, in many cases, massive amounts of data. Sorting data is an intriguing problem that has attracted some of the most intense research efforts in the field of computer science. In this chapter, we discuss the simplest known sorting scheme. In the exercises and in Chapter 15, we investigate more complex schemes that yield superior performance.

Performance Tip 4.5

Sometimes, the simplest algorithms perform poorly. Their virtue is that they are easy to write, test and debug. More complex algorithms are sometimes needed to realize maximum performance.

The program in Fig. 4.16 sorts the values of the 10-element array **a** into ascending order. The technique we use is called the *bubble sort,* or the *sinking sort*, because the smaller values gradually "bubble" their way upward to the top of the array like air bubbles rising in water, while the larger values sink to the bottom of the array. The technique makes several passes through the array. On each pass, successive pairs of elements are compared. If a pair is in increasing order (or the values are identical), we leave the values as they are. If a pair is in decreasing order, their values are swapped in the array.

```cpp
1   // Fig. 4.16: fig04_16.cpp
2   // This program sorts an array's values into
3   // ascending order
4   #include <iostream>
5
6   using std::cout;
7   using std::endl;
8
9   #include <iomanip>
10
11  using std::setw;
12
13  int main()
14  {
15     const int arraySize = 10;
16     int a[ arraySize ] = { 2, 6, 4, 8, 10, 12, 89, 68, 45, 37 };
17     int i, hold;
18
19     cout << "Data items in original order\n";
20
21     for ( i = 0; i < arraySize; i++ )
22        cout << setw( 4 ) << a[ i ];
23
24     for ( int pass = 0; pass < arraySize - 1; pass++ )  // passes
25
26        for ( i = 0; i < arraySize - 1; i++ )         // one pass
27
28           if ( a[ i ] > a[ i + 1 ] ) {         // one comparison
29              hold = a[ i ];                     // one swap
30              a[ i ] = a[ i + 1 ];
31              a[ i + 1 ] = hold;
32           }
33
34     cout << "\nData items in ascending order\n";
35
36     for ( i = 0; i < arraySize; i++ )
37        cout << setw( 4 ) << a[ i ];
38
```

Fig. 4.16   Sorting an array with bubble sort (part 1 of 2).

```
39        cout << endl;
40        return 0;
41  }
```

```
Data items in original order
    2   6   4   8  10  12  89  68  45  37
Data items in ascending order
    2   4   6   8  10  12  37  45  68  89
```

Fig. 4.16   Sorting an array with bubble sort (part 2 of 2).

First the program compares **a[0]** with **a[1]**, then **a[1]** with **a[2]**, then **a[2]** with **a[3]**, and so on until it completes the pass by comparing **a[8]** to **a[9]**. Although there are 10 elements, only nine comparisons are performed. Because of the way the successive comparisons are made, a large value may move down the array many positions on a single pass, but a small value may move up only one position. On the first pass, the largest value is guaranteed to sink to the bottom element of the array, **a[9]**. On the second pass, the second largest value is guaranteed to sink to **a[8]**. On the ninth pass, the ninth largest value sinks to **a[1]**. This leaves the smallest value in **a[0]**, so only nine passes are needed to sort a 10-element array.

The sorting is performed by the nested **for** loop. If a swap is necessary, it is performed by the three assignments

```
hold = a[ i ];
a[ i ] = a[ i + 1 ];
a[ i + 1 ] = hold;
```

where the extra variable **hold** temporarily stores one of the two values being swapped. The swap cannot be performed with only the two assignments

```
a[ i ] = a[ i + 1 ];
a[ i + 1 ] = a[ i ];
```

If, for example, **a[i]** is **7** and **a[i + 1]** is **5**, after the first assignment both values will be **5**, and the value **7** will be lost, hence the need for the extra variable **hold**.

The chief virtue of the bubble sort is that it is easy to program. However, the bubble sort runs slowly. This becomes apparent when sorting large arrays. In the exercises, we will develop more efficient versions of the bubble sort and investigate some far more efficient sorts than the bubble sort. More advanced courses investigate sorting and searching in greater depth.

4.7 Case Study: Computing Mean, Median and Mode Using Arrays

We now consider a larger example. Computers are commonly used to compile and analyze the results of surveys and opinion polls. The program in Fig. 4.17 uses array **response** initialized with 99 responses (represented by constant variable **responseSize**) to a survey. Each of the responses is a number from 1 to 9. The program computes the mean, median and mode of the 99 values.

```
1   // Fig. 4.17: fig04_17.cpp
2   // This program introduces the topic of survey data analysis.
3   // It computes the mean, median, and mode of the data.
4   #include <iostream>
5
6   using std::cout;
7   using std::endl;
8   using std::ios;
9
10  #include <iomanip>
11
12  using std::setw;
13  using std::setiosflags;
14  using std::setprecision;
15
16  void mean( const int [], int );
17  void median( int [], int );
18  void mode( int [], int [], int );
19  void bubbleSort( int[], int );
20  void printArray( const int[], int );
21
22  int main()
23  {
24     const int responseSize = 99;
25     int frequency[ 10 ] = { 0 },
26        response[ responseSize ] =
27           { 6, 7, 8, 9, 8, 7, 8, 9, 8, 9,
28             7, 8, 9, 5, 9, 8, 7, 8, 7, 8,
29             6, 7, 8, 9, 3, 9, 8, 7, 8, 7,
30             7, 8, 9, 8, 9, 8, 9, 7, 8, 9,
31             6, 7, 8, 7, 8, 7, 9, 8, 9, 2,
32             7, 8, 9, 8, 9, 8, 9, 7, 5, 3,
33             5, 6, 7, 2, 5, 3, 9, 4, 6, 4,
34             7, 8, 9, 6, 8, 7, 8, 9, 7, 8,
35             7, 4, 4, 2, 5, 3, 8, 7, 5, 6,
36             4, 5, 6, 1, 6, 5, 7, 8, 7 };
37
38     mean( response, responseSize );
39     median( response, responseSize );
40     mode( frequency, response, responseSize );
41
42     return 0;
43  }
44
45  void mean( const int answer[], int arraySize )
46  {
47     int total = 0;
48
49     cout << "********\n  Mean\n********\n";
50
51     for ( int j = 0; j < arraySize; j++ )
52        total += answer[ j ];
53
```

Fig. 4.17   Survey data analysis program (part 1 of 3).

```
54          cout << "The mean is the average value of the data\n"
55               << "items. The mean is equal to the total of\n"
56               << "all the data items divided by the number\n"
57               << "of data items (" << arraySize
58               << "). The mean value for\nthis run is: "
59               << total << " / " << arraySize << " = "
60               << setiosflags( ios::fixed | ios::showpoint )
61               << setprecision( 4 )
62               << static_cast< double >( total ) / arraySize << "\n\n";
63       }
64
65       void median( int answer[], int size )
66       {
67          cout << "\n********\n Median\n********\n"
68               << "The unsorted array of responses is";
69
70          printArray( answer, size );
71          bubbleSort( answer, size );
72          cout << "\n\nThe sorted array is";
73          printArray( answer, size );
74          cout << "\n\nThe median is element " << size / 2
75               << " of\nthe sorted " << size
76               << " element array.\nFor this run the median is "
77               << answer[ size / 2 ] << "\n\n";
78       }
79
80       void mode( int freq[], int answer[], int size )
81       {
82          int rating, largest = 0, modeValue = 0;
83
84          cout << "\n********\n  Mode\n********\n";
85
86          for ( rating = 1; rating <= 9; rating++ )
87             freq[ rating ] = 0;
88
89          for ( int j = 0; j < size; j++ )
90             ++freq[ answer[ j ] ];
91
92          cout << "Response"<< setw( 11 ) << "Frequency"
93               << setw( 19 ) << "Histogram\n\n" << setw( 55 )
94               << "1    1    2    2\n" << setw( 56 )
95               << "5    0    5    0    5\n\n";
96
97          for ( rating = 1; rating <= 9; rating++ ) {
98             cout << setw( 8 ) << rating << setw( 11 )
99                  << freq[ rating ] << "          ";
100
101          if ( freq[ rating ] > largest ) {
102             largest = freq[ rating ];
103             modeValue = rating;
104          }
105
```

Fig. 4.17   Survey data analysis program (part 2 of 3).

```
106          for ( int h = 1; h <= freq[ rating ]; h++ )
107             cout << '*';
108
109          cout << '\n';
110       }
111
112       cout << "The mode is the most frequent value.\n"
113            << "For this run the mode is " << modeValue
114            << " which occurred " << largest << " times." << endl;
115    }
116
117    void bubbleSort( int a[], int size )
118    {
119       int hold;
120
121       for ( int pass = 1; pass < size; pass++ )
122
123          for ( int j = 0; j < size - 1; j++ )
124
125             if ( a[ j ] > a[ j + 1 ] ) {
126                hold = a[ j ];
127                a[ j ] = a[ j + 1 ];
128                a[ j + 1 ] = hold;
129             }
130    }
131
132    void printArray( const int a[], int size )
133    {
134       for ( int j = 0; j < size; j++ ) {
135
136          if ( j % 20 == 0 )
137             cout << endl;
138
139          cout << setw( 2 ) << a[ j ];
140       }
141    }
```

Fig. 4.17   Survey data analysis program (part 3 of 3).

The mean is the arithmetic average of the 99 values. Function **mean** computes the mean by totaling the 99 elements and dividing the result by 99.

The median is the "middle value." Function **median** determines the median by calling **bubbleSort** to sort array **response** and picking the middle element, **answer[size / 2]**, of the sorted array. Note that when there is an even number of elements, the median should be calculated as the mean of the two middle elements. Function **median** does not provide this capability. Function **printArray** is called to output the **response** array.

The mode is the value that occurs most frequently among the 99 responses. Function **mode** counts the number of responses of each type and then selects the value with the greatest count. This version of function **mode** does not handle a tie (see Exercise 4.14). Function **mode** also produces a histogram to aid in determining the mode graphically. Fig. 4.18 contains a sample run of this program. This example includes most of the common manipulations usually required in array problems, including passing arrays to functions.

```
********
  Mean
********
The mean is the average value of the data
items. The mean is equal to the total of
all the data items divided by the number
of data items (99). The mean value for
this run is: 681 / 99 = 6.8788


********
  Median
********
The unsorted array of responses is
  6 7 8 9 8 7 8 9 8 9 7 8 9 5 9 8 7 8 7 8
  6 7 8 9 3 9 8 7 8 7 7 8 9 8 9 8 9 7 8 9
  6 7 8 7 8 7 9 8 9 2 7 8 9 8 9 8 9 7 5 3
  5 6 7 2 5 3 9 4 6 4 7 8 9 6 8 7 8 9 7 8
  7 4 4 2 5 3 8 7 5 6 4 5 6 1 6 5 7 8 7

The sorted array is
  1 2 2 2 3 3 3 3 4 4 4 4 4 5 5 5 5 5 5 5
  5 6 6 6 6 6 6 6 6 6 6 7 7 7 7 7 7 7 7 7
  7 7 7 7 7 7 7 7 7 7 7 7 7 8 8 8 8 8 8 8
  8 8 8 8 8 8 8 8 8 8 8 8 8 8 8 8 8 8 8 8
  9 9 9 9 9 9 9 9 9 9 9 9 9 9 9 9 9 9 9

The median is element 49 of
the sorted 99 element array.
For this run the median is 7


********
  Mode
********
Response  Frequency          Histogram

                           1     1     2     2
                       5   0     5     0     5

        1          1       *
        2          3       ***
        3          4       ****
        4          5       *****
        5          8       ********
        6          9       *********
        7         23       ***********************
        8         27       ***************************
        9         19       *******************
The mode is the most frequent value.
For this run the mode is 8 which occurred 27 times.
```

Fig. 4.18   Sample run for the survey data analysis program.

4.8 Searching Arrays: Linear Search and Binary Search

Often, a programmer will be working with large amounts of data stored in arrays. It may be necessary to determine whether an array contains a value that matches a certain *key value*. The process of finding a particular element of an array is called *searching*. In this section, we discuss two searching techniques—the simple *linear search* technique and the more efficient *binary search* technique. Exercises 4.33 and 4.34 at the end of this chapter ask you to implement recursive versions of the linear search and the binary search.

The linear search (Fig. 4.19) compares each element of the array with the *search key*. Since the array is not in any particular order, it is just as likely that the value will be found in the first element as the last. On average, therefore, the program must compare the search key with half the elements of the array for a value in the array. To determine that a value is not in the array, the program must compare the search key to every element in the array.

The linear searching method works well for small arrays or for unsorted arrays. However, for large arrays, linear searching is inefficient. If the array is sorted, the high-speed binary search technique can be used.

```cpp
1   // Fig. 4.19: fig04_19.cpp
2   // Linear search of an array
3   #include <iostream>
4
5   using std::cout;
6   using std::cin;
7   using std::endl;
8
9   int linearSearch( const int [], int, int );
10
11  int main()
12  {
13     const int arraySize = 100;
14     int a[ arraySize ], searchKey, element;
15
16     for ( int x = 0; x < arraySize; x++ )   // create some data
17        a[ x ] = 2 * x;
18
19     cout << "Enter integer search key:" << endl;
20     cin >> searchKey;
21     element = linearSearch( a, searchKey, arraySize );
22
23     if ( element != -1 )
24        cout << "Found value in element " << element << endl;
25     else
26        cout << "Value not found" << endl;
27
28     return 0;
29  }
30
```

Fig. 4.19   Linear search of an array (part 1 of 2).

```
31   int linearSearch( const int array[], int key, int sizeOfArray )
32   {
33      for ( int n = 0; n < sizeOfArray; n++ )
34         if ( array[ n ] == key )
35            return n;
36
37      return -1;
38   }
```

```
Enter integer search key:
36
Found value in element 18
```

```
Enter integer search key:
37
Value not found
```

Fig. 4.19   Linear search of an array (part 2 of 2).

The binary search algorithm eliminates one-half of the elements in the array being searched after each comparison. The algorithm locates the middle element of the array and compares it with the search key. If they are equal, the search key is found, and the array subscript of that element is returned. Otherwise, the problem is reduced to searching one-half of the array. If the search key is less than the middle element of the array, the first half of the array is searched; otherwise, the second half of the array is searched. If the search key is not the middle element in the specified subarray (piece of the original array), the algorithm is repeated on one-quarter of the original array. The search continues until the search key is equal to the middle element of a subarray or until the subarray consists of one element that is not equal to the search key (i.e., the search key is not found).

In a worst-case scenario, searching an array of 1024 elements will take only 10 comparisons using a binary search. Repeatedly dividing 1024 by 2 (because after each comparison, we are able to eliminate half of the array) yields the values 512, 256, 128, 64, 32, 16, 8, 4, 2 and 1. The number 1024 (2^{10}) is divided by 2 only 10 times to get the value 1. Dividing by 2 is equivalent to one comparison in the binary search algorithm. An array of 1048576 (2^{20}) elements takes a maximum of 20 comparisons to find the search key. An array of one billion elements takes a maximum of 30 comparisons to find the search key. This is a tremendous increase in performance over the linear search that required comparing the search key to an average of half the elements in the array. For a one-billion-element array, this is a difference between an average of 500 million comparisons and a maximum of 30 comparisons! The maximum number of comparisons needed for the binary search of any sorted array can be determined by finding the first power of 2 greater than the number of elements in the array.

Performance Tip 4.6

The tremendous performance gains of the binary search over the linear search do not come without a price. Sorting an array is an expensive operation compared with searching an entire array once for one item. The overhead of sorting an array becomes worthwhile when the array will need to be searched many times at high speed.

Figure 4.20 presents the iterative version of function **binarySearch**. The function receives four arguments—an integer array **b**, an integer **searchKey**, the **low** array subscript and the **high** array subscript. If the search key does not match the middle element of a subarray, the **low** subscript or **high** subscript is adjusted so a smaller subarray can be searched. If the search key is less than the middle element, the **high** subscript is set to **middle – 1**, and the search is continued on the elements from **low** to **middle – 1**. If the search key is greater than the middle element, the **low** subscript is set to **middle + 1**, and the search is continued on the elements from **middle + 1** to **high**. The program uses an array of 15 elements. The first power of 2 greater than the number of elements in this array is 16 (2^4), so a maximum of 4 comparisons are required to find the search key. Function **printHeader** outputs the array subscripts and function **printRow** outputs each subarray during the binary search process. The middle element in each subarray is marked with an asterisk (*) to indicate the element with which the search key is compared.

```
1   // Fig. 4.20: fig04_20.cpp
2   // Binary search of an array
3   #include <iostream>
4
5   using std::cout;
6   using std::cin;
7   using std::endl;
8
9   #include <iomanip>
10
11  using std::setw;
12
13  int binarySearch( const int [], int, int, int, int );
14  void printHeader( int );
15  void printRow( const int [], int, int, int, int );
16
17  int main()
18  {
19     const int arraySize = 15;
20     int a[ arraySize ], key, result;
21
22     for ( int i = 0; i < arraySize; i++ )
23        a[ i ] = 2 * i;     // place some data in array
24
25     cout << "Enter a number between 0 and 28: ";
26     cin >> key;
27
28     printHeader( arraySize );
29     result = binarySearch( a, key, 0, arraySize - 1, arraySize );
30
31     if ( result != -1 )
32        cout << '\n' << key << " found in array element "
33             << result << endl;
34     else
35        cout << '\n' << key << " not found" << endl;
36
```

Fig. 4.20   Binary search of a sorted array (part 1 of 3).

```
37        return 0;
38     }
39
40     // Binary search
41     int binarySearch( const int b[], int searchKey, int low, int high,
42                       int size )
43     {
44        int middle;
45
46        while ( low <= high ) {
47           middle = ( low + high ) / 2;
48
49           printRow( b, low, middle, high, size );
50
51           if ( searchKey == b[ middle ] )   // match
52              return middle;
53           else if ( searchKey < b[ middle ] )
54              high = middle - 1;             // search low end of array
55           else
56              low = middle + 1;              // search high end of array
57        }
58
59        return -1;   // searchKey not found
60     }
61
62     // Print a header for the output
63     void printHeader( int size )
64     {
65        int i;
66
67        cout << "\nSubscripts:\n";
68
69        for ( i = 0; i < size; i++ )
70           cout << setw( 3 ) << i << ' ';
71
72        cout << '\n';
73
74        for ( i = 1; i <= 4 * size; i++ )
75           cout << '-';
76
77        cout << endl;
78     }
79
80     // Print one row of output showing the current
81     // part of the array being processed.
82     void printRow( const int b[], int low, int mid, int high, int size )
83     {
84        for ( int i = 0; i < size; i++ )
85           if ( i < low || i > high )
86              cout << "    ";
87           else if ( i == mid )                // mark middle value
88              cout << setw( 3 ) << b[ i ] << '*';
```

Fig. 4.20   Binary search of a sorted array (part 2 of 3).

```
89              else
90                  cout << setw( 3 ) << b[ i ] << ' ';
91
92          cout << endl;
93      }
```

```
Enter a number between 0 and 28: 25
Subscripts:
   0    1    2    3    4    5    6    7    8    9   10   11   12   13   14
-------------------------------------------------------------------------
   0    2    4    6    8   10   12   14*  16   18   20   22   24   26   28
                                         16   18   20   22*  24   26   28
                                                             24   26*  28
                                                             24*

25 not found
```

```
Enter a number between 0 and 28: 8
Subscripts:
   0    1    2    3    4    5    6    7    8    9   10   11   12   13   14
-------------------------------------------------------------------------
   0    2    4    6    8   10   12   14*  16   18   20   22   24   26   28
   0    2    4    6*   8   10   12
                       8   10*  12
                       8*
8 found in array element 4
```

```
Enter a number between 0 and 28: 6
Subscripts:
   0    1    2    3    4    5    6    7    8    9   10   11   12   13   14
-------------------------------------------------------------------------
   0    2    4    6    8   10   12   14*  16   18   20   22   24   26   28
   0    2    4    6*   8   10   12
6 found in array element 3
```

Fig. 4.20   Binary search of a sorted array (part 3 of 3).

4.9 Multiple-Subscripted Arrays

Arrays in C++ can have multiple subscripts. A common use of multiple-subscripted arrays is to represent *tables* of values consisting of information arranged in *rows* and *columns*. To identify a particular table element, we must specify two subscripts: The first (by convention) identifies the element's row, and the second (by convention) identifies the element's column.

Tables or arrays that require two subscripts to identify a particular element are called *double-subscripted arrays*. Note that multiple-subscripted arrays can have more than two subscripts. C++ compilers support at least 12 array subscripts. Fig. 4.21 illustrates a double-subscripted array, **a**. The array contains three rows and four columns, so it is said to be a 3-by-4 array. In general, an array with *m* rows and *n* columns is called an *m-by-n array*.

Every element in array **a** is identified in Fig. 4.21 by an element name of the form **a[i][j]**; **a** is the name of the array, and **i** and **j** are the subscripts that uniquely identify each element in **a**. Notice that the names of the elements in the first row all have a first subscript of **0**; the names of the elements in the fourth column all have a second subscript of **3**.

Common Programming Error 4.11

*Referencing a double-subscripted array element **a[x][y]** incorrectly as **a[x, y]**. Actually, **a[x, y]** is treated as **a[y]**, because C++ evaluates the expression (containing a comma operator) **x, y** simply as **y** (the last of the comma-separated expressions).*

A multiple-subscripted array can be initialized in its declaration much like a single subscripted array. For example, a double-subscripted array **b[2][2]** could be declared and initialized with

```
int b[ 2 ][ 2 ] = { { 1, 2 }, { 3, 4 } };
```

The values are grouped by row in braces. So, **1** and **2** initialize **b[0][0]** and **b[0][1]**, and **3** and **4** initialize **b[1][0]** and **b[1][1]**. If there are not enough initializers for a given row, the remaining elements of that row are initialized to **0**. Thus, the declaration

```
int b[ 2 ][ 2 ] = { { 1 }, { 3, 4 } };
```

would initialize **b[0][0]** to **1**, **b[0][1]** to **0**, **b[1][0]** to **3** and **b[1][1]** to **4**.

Figure 4.22 demonstrates initializing double-subscripted arrays in declarations. The program declares three arrays, each with two rows and three columns. The declaration of **array1** provides six initializers in two sublists. The first sublist initializes the first row of the array to the values 1, 2 and 3; and the second sublist initializes the second row of the array to the values 4, 5 and 6. If the braces around each sublist are removed from the **array1** initializer list, the compiler automatically initializes the elements of the first row followed by the elements of the second row.

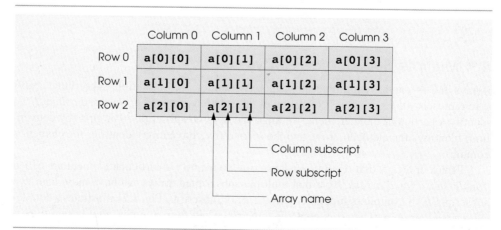

Fig. 4.21   A double-subscripted array with three rows and four columns.

```cpp
1   // Fig. 4.22: fig04_22.cpp
2   // Initializing multidimensional arrays
3   #include <iostream>
4
5   using std::cout;
6   using std::endl;
7
8   void printArray( int [][ 3 ] );
9
10  int main()
11  {
12     int array1[ 2 ][ 3 ] = { { 1, 2, 3 }, { 4, 5, 6 } },
13         array2[ 2 ][ 3 ] = { 1, 2, 3, 4, 5 },
14         array3[ 2 ][ 3 ] = { { 1, 2 }, { 4 } };
15
16     cout << "Values in array1 by row are:" << endl;
17     printArray( array1 );
18
19     cout << "Values in array2 by row are:" << endl;
20     printArray( array2 );
21
22     cout << "Values in array3 by row are:" << endl;
23     printArray( array3 );
24
25     return 0;
26  }
27
28  void printArray( int a[][ 3 ] )
29  {
30     for ( int i = 0; i < 2; i++ ) {
31
32        for ( int j = 0; j < 3; j++ )
33           cout << a[ i ][ j ] << ' ';
34
35        cout << endl;
36     }
37  }
```

```
Values in array1 by row are:
1 2 3
4 5 6
Values in array2 by row are:
1 2 3
4 5 0
Values in array3 by row are:
1 2 0
4 0 0
```

Fig. 4.22 Initializing multidimensional arrays.

The declaration of **array2** provides five initializers. The initializers are assigned to the first row and then the second row. Any elements that do not have an explicit initializer are initialized to zero automatically, so **array2[1][2]** is initialized to zero.

The declaration of **array3** provides three initializers in two sublists. The sublist for the first row explicitly initializes the first two elements of the first row to 1 and 2. The third element is automatically initialized to zero. The sublist for the second row explicitly initializes the first element to 4. The last two elements are automatically initialized to zero.

The program calls function **printArray** to output each array's elements. Notice that the function definition specifies the array parameter as **int a[ ][3]**. When we receive a single-subscripted array as an argument to a function, the array brackets are empty in the function's parameter list. The size of the first subscript of a multiple-subscripted array is not required either, but all subsequent subscript sizes are required. The compiler uses these sizes to determine the locations in memory of elements in multiple-subscripted arrays. All array elements are stored consecutively in memory, regardless of the number of subscripts. In a double-subscripted array, the first row is stored in memory followed by the second row.

Providing the subscript values in a parameter declaration enables the compiler to tell the function how to locate an element in the array. In a double-subscripted array, each row is a single-subscripted array. To locate an element in a particular row, the function must know exactly how many elements are in each row so it can skip the proper number of memory locations when accessing the array. Thus, when accessing **a[1][2]**, the function knows to skip the first row's three elements in memory to get to the second row (row 1). Then, the function accesses the third element of that row (element 2).

Many common array manipulations use **for** repetition structures. For example, the following **for** structure sets all the elements in the third row of array **a** in Fig. 4.21 to zero:

```
for ( column = 0; column < 4; column++ )
   a[ 2 ][ column ] = 0;
```

We specified the *third* row, and therefore we know that the first subscript is always **2**. (**0** is the first row subscript, and **1** is the second row subscript.) The **for** loop varies only the second subscript (i.e., the column subscript). The preceding **for** structure is equivalent to the following assignment statements:

```
a[ 2 ][ 0 ] = 0;
a[ 2 ][ 1 ] = 0;
a[ 2 ][ 2 ] = 0;
a[ 2 ][ 3 ] = 0;
```

The following nested **for** structure determines the total of all the elements in array **a**:

```
total = 0;

for ( row = 0; row < 3; row++ )
   for ( column = 0; column < 4; column++ )
      total += a[ row ][ column ];
```

The **for** structure totals the elements of the array one row at a time. The outer **for** structure begins by setting **row** (i.e., the row subscript) to **0**, so the elements of the first row may be totaled by the inner **for** structure. The outer **for** structure then increments **row** to **1**, so the elements of the second row can be totaled. Then, the outer **for** structure increments **row** to **2**, so the elements of the third row can be totaled. The result is printed when the nested **for** structure terminates.

The program of Fig. 4.23 performs several other common array manipulations on 3-by-4 array **studentGrades**. Each row of the array represents a student, and each column represents a grade on one of the four exams the students took during the semester. The array manipulations are performed by four functions. Function **minimum** determines the lowest grade of any student for the semester. Function **maximum** determines the highest grade of any student for the semester. Function **average** determines a particular student's semester average. Function **printArray** outputs the double-subscripted array in a neat, tabular format.

```cpp
1   // Fig. 4.23: fig04_23.cpp
2   // Double-subscripted array example
3   #include <iostream>
4
5   using std::cout;
6   using std::endl;
7   using std::ios;
8
9   #include <iomanip>
10
11  using std::setw;
12  using std::setiosflags;
13  using std::setprecision;
14
15  const int students = 3;   // number of students
16  const int exams = 4;      // number of exams
17
18  int minimum( int [][ exams ], int, int );
19  int maximum( int [][ exams ], int, int );
20  double average( int [], int );
21  void printArray( int [][ exams ], int, int );
22
23  int main()
24  {
25     int studentGrades[ students ][ exams ] =
26           { { 77, 68, 86, 73 },
27             { 96, 87, 89, 78 },
28             { 70, 90, 86, 81 } };
29
30     cout << "The array is:\n";
31     printArray( studentGrades, students, exams );
32     cout << "\n\nLowest grade: "
33          << minimum( studentGrades, students, exams )
34          << "\nHighest grade: "
35          << maximum( studentGrades, students, exams ) << '\n';
36
37     for ( int person = 0; person < students; person++ )
38        cout << "The average grade for student " << person << " is "
39             << setiosflags( ios::fixed | ios::showpoint )
40             << setprecision( 2 )
41             << average( studentGrades[ person ], exams ) << endl;
42
43     return 0;
44  }
```

Fig. 4.23　Example of using double-subscripted arrays (part 1 of 3).

```
45
46   // Find the minimum grade
47   int minimum( int grades[][ exams ], int pupils, int tests )
48   {
49      int lowGrade = 100;
50
51      for ( int i = 0; i < pupils; i++ )
52
53         for ( int j = 0; j < tests; j++ )
54
55            if ( grades[ i ][ j ] < lowGrade )
56               lowGrade = grades[ i ][ j ];
57
58      return lowGrade;
59   }
60
61   // Find the maximum grade
62   int maximum( int grades[][ exams ], int pupils, int tests )
63   {
64      int highGrade = 0;
65
66      for ( int i = 0; i < pupils; i++ )
67
68         for ( int j = 0; j < tests; j++ )
69
70            if ( grades[ i ][ j ] > highGrade )
71               highGrade = grades[ i ][ j ];
72
73      return highGrade;
74   }
75
76   // Determine the average grade for a particular student
77   double average( int setOfGrades[], int tests )
78   {
79      int total = 0;
80
81      for ( int i = 0; i < tests; i++ )
82         total += setOfGrades[ i ];
83
84      return static_cast< double >( total ) / tests;
85   }
86
87   // Print the array
88   void printArray( int grades[][ exams ], int pupils, int tests )
89   {
90      cout << "                     [0]  [1]  [2]  [3]";
91
92      for ( int i = 0; i < pupils; i++ ) {
93         cout << "\nstudentGrades[" << i << "] ";
94
95         for ( int j = 0; j < tests; j++ )
96            cout << setiosflags( ios::left ) << setw( 5 )
97               << grades[ i ][ j ];
```

Fig. 4.23   Example of using double-subscripted arrays (part 2 of 3).

```
98      }
99  }
```

```
The array is:
                [0]   [1]   [2]   [3]
studentGrades[0] 77    68    86    73
studentGrades[1] 96    87    89    78
studentGrades[2] 70    90    86    81

Lowest grade: 68
Highest grade: 96
The average grade for student 0 is 76.00
The average grade for student 1 is 87.50
The average grade for student 2 is 81.75
```

Fig. 4.23   Example of using double-subscripted arrays (part 3 of 3).

Functions **minimum**, **maximum** and **printArray** each receive three arguments—the **studentGrades** array (called **grades** in each function), the number of students (rows of the array) and the number of exams (columns of the array). Each function loops through array **grades** using nested **for** structures. The following nested **for** structure is from the function **minimum** definition:

```
for ( i = 0; i < pupils; i++ )
    for ( j = 0; j < tests; j++ )
        if ( grades[ i ][ j ] < lowGrade )
            lowGrade = grades[ i ][ j ];
```

The outer **for** structure begins by setting **i** (i.e., the row subscript) to **0**, so the elements of the first row can be compared with variable **lowGrade** in the body of the inner **for** structure. The inner **for** structure loops through the four grades of a particular row and compares each grade with **lowGrade**. If a grade is less than **lowGrade**, **lowGrade** is set to that grade. The outer **for** structure then increments the row subscript to **1**. The elements of the second row are compared with variable **lowGrade**. The outer **for** structure then increments the row subscript to **2**. The elements of the third row are compared with variable **lowGrade**. When execution of the nested structure is complete, **lowGrade** contains the smallest grade in the double-subscripted array. Function **maximum** works similarly to function **minimum**.

Function **average** takes two arguments—a single-subscripted array of test results for a particular student and the number of test results in the array. When **average** is called, the first argument is **studentGrades[student]**, which specifies that a particular row of the double-subscripted array **studentGrades** is to be passed to **average**. For example, the argument **studentGrades[1]** represents the four values (a single-subscripted array of grades) stored in the second row of the double-subscripted array **studentGrades**. A double-subscripted array could be considered an array with elements that are single-subscripted arrays. Function **average** calculates the sum of the array elements, divides the total by the number of test results and returns the floating-point result.

4.10 (Optional Case Study) Thinking About Objects: Identifying the Operations of a Class

In the "Thinking About Objects" sections at the ends of Chapters 2 and 3, we performed the first few steps of an object-oriented design for our elevator simulator. In Chapter 2, we identified the classes we need to implement, and we created a class diagram that models the structure of our system. In Chapter 3, we determined many of the attributes of our classes, we investigated the possible states of class **Elevator** and represented them in a statechart diagram and we modeled in an activity diagram the logic the elevator uses to respond to button presses.

In this section, we concentrate on determining the class *operations* (or behaviors) needed to implement the elevator simulator. In Chapter 5, we will concentrate on the collaborations (interactions) between objects of our classes.

An operation of a class is a service that the class provides to "clients" (users) of that class. Let us consider the operations of some real-world classes. A radio's operations include setting its station and volume (typically invoked by a listener adjusting the radio's controls). A car's operations include accelerating (invoked by pressing the accelerator pedal), decelerating (invoked by pressing the brake pedal), turning and shifting gears.

Objects do not ordinarily perform their operations spontaneously. Rather, a specific operation is normally invoked when a sending object (often called a *client object*) sends a *message* to a receiving object (often called a *server object*) requesting that the receiving object perform that specific operation. This sounds like a member function call—precisely how messages are sent to objects in C++. In this section, we will identify many of the operations our classes need to offer to their clients in our system.

We can derive many of the operations of each class directly from the problem statement. To do so, we examine the verbs and verb phrases from the problem statement. We then relate each of these phrases to a particular class in our system (see Fig. 4.24). Many of the verb phrases in the table in Fig. 4.24 will help determine the operations of our classes.

Class	Verb phrases
Elevator	moves, arrives at a floor, resets the elevator button, sounds the elevator bell, signals its arrival to a floor, opens its door, closes its door
Clock	ticks every second
Scheduler	randomly schedules times, creates a person, tells a person to step onto a floor, verifies that a floor is unoccupied, delays creating a person by one second
Person	steps onto floor, presses floor button, presses elevator button, enters elevator, exits elevator
Floor	resets floor button, turns off light, turns on light
FloorButton	summons elevator
ElevatorButton	signals elevator to move
Door	(opening of door) signals person to exit elevator, (opening of door) signals person to enter elevator

Fig. 4.24   Verb phrases for each class in simulator.

Class	Verb phrases
Bell	none in problem statement
Light	none in problem statement
Building	none in problem statement

Fig. 4.24   Verb phrases for each class in simulator.

To create operations from these verb phrases, we examine the verb phrases listed with each class. The "moves" verb listed with class **Elevator** refers to the activity in which the elevator moves between floors. Should "moves" be an operation of class **Elevator**? No message tells the elevator to move; rather, the elevator decides to move in response to a button press based on the condition that the door is closed. Therefore, "moves" does not correspond to an operation. The "arrives at a floor" phrase is also not an operation, because the elevator itself decides when to arrive on the floor, based on the time.

The "resets elevator button" phrase implies that the elevator sends a message to the elevator button telling the button to reset. Therefore, class **ElevatorButton** needs an operation to provide this service to the elevator. We place this operation in the bottom compartment of class **ElevatorButton** in our class diagram (Fig. 4.25). We represent the names of the operations as function names and include information about the return type:

```
resetButton() : void
```

The operation name is written first, followed by parentheses containing a comma-separated list of the parameters that the operation takes (in this case, none). A colon follows the parameter list, followed by the return type of the operation (in this case **void**). Note that most of our operations appear to have no parameters and to have a return type of **void**; this might change as our design and implementation processes proceed.

From the "sounds the elevator bell" phrase listed with class **Elevator**, we conclude that class **Bell** should have an operation that provides a service—ringing. We list the **ringBell** operation under class **Bell**.

When the elevator arrives at a floor, it "signals its arrival to a floor," and the floor responds by performing its various activities (i.e., resetting the floor button and turning on the light). Therefore, class **Floor** needs an operation that provides this service. We call this operation **elevatorArrived** and place the operation name in the bottom compartment of class **Floor** in Fig. 4.25.

The remaining two verb phrases listed with class **Elevator** state that the elevator needs to open and close its door. Therefore, class **Door** needs to provide these operations. We place the **openDoor** and **closeDoor** operations in the bottom compartment of class **Door**.

Class **Clock** lists the phrase "ticks every second." This phrase brings up an interesting point. Certainly "getting the time" is an operation that the clock provides, but is the ticking of the clock also an operation? To answer this question, we focus on our simulation will work.

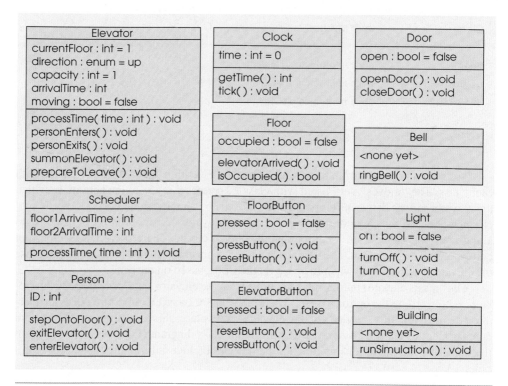

Fig. 4.25 Class diagram with attributes and operations.

The problem statement indicates that the scheduler needs to know the current time to decide whether the scheduler should create a new person to step onto a floor. The elevator needs the time to decide whether it is time to arrive at a floor. We also decided that the building bears the responsibility for running the simulation and for passing the time to the scheduler and to the elevator. We now begin to see how our simulation will run. The building repeats the following steps once per second for the duration of the simulation:

1. Get the time from the clock.

2. Give the time to the scheduler so that the scheduler can create a new person, if necessary.

3. Give the time to the elevator so that the elevator can decide to arrive at a floor, if the elevator is moving.

We decided that the building has full responsibility for running all parts of the simulation. Therefore, the building must also increment the clock. The clock should be incremented once per second; then the time should be passed on to the scheduler and to the elevator.

This leads us to create two operations—**getTime** and **tick**—and list them under class **Clock**. The **getTime** operation returns as an **int** the value of the clock's time attribute. In the preceding items 2 and 3, we see the phrases "Give the time to the scheduler" and "Give the time to the elevator." Thus we can add the operation **processTime** to classes **Scheduler** and **Elevator**. We can also add the operation **runSimulation** to class **Building**.

Class **Scheduler** lists the verb phrases "randomly schedules times" and "delays creating a person by one second." The scheduler decides to perform these actions itself and does not provide these services to clients. Therefore, these two phrases do not correspond to operations.

The phrase "creates person" listed with class **Scheduler** presents a special case. Although we can model an object of class **Scheduler** sending a "create" message, an object of class **Person** cannot respond to a "create" message because that object does not yet exist. The creation of objects is left to implementation details, and is not represented as an operation of a class. We discuss the creation of new objects when we discuss implementation in Chapter 7.

The phrase "tells a person to step onto a floor" listed in Fig. 4.24 means that class **Person** should have an operation that the scheduler can invoke to tell the person step onto a floor. We call this operation **stepOntoFloor** and list the operation under class **Person**.

The phrase "verifies that a floor is unoccupied" implies that class **Floor** needs to provide a service that allows objects in the system to know whether the floor is occupied or unoccupied. The operation we create for this service should return **true** if the floor is occupied and **false** if not. We place the operation

```
isOccupied( ) : bool
```

in the bottom compartment of class **Floor**.

Class **Person** lists the phrases "presses floor button" and "presses elevator button." We therefore place the **pressButton** operation under classes **FloorButton** and **ElevatorButton** in our UML class diagram (Fig. 4.25). Note that we have already dealt with the fact that a person "steps onto a floor" when we analyzed the verb phrases for class **Scheduler**, so we do not need to create any operations based on the "steps onto floor" phrase listed with class **Person**. The "enters elevator" and "exits elevator" phrases listed with class **Person** suggest that class **Elevator** needs operations that correspond to these actions.[1]

Class **Floor** also lists "resets floor button" in its verb phrases column, so we list the appropriate **resetButton** operation under class **FloorButton**. Class **Floor** also lists "turns off light" and "turns on light," so we create the **turnOff** and **turnOn** operations and list them under class **Light**.

The "summons elevator" phrase listed under class **FloorButton** implies that class **Elevator** needs a **summonElevator** operation. The phrase "signals elevator to move" listed with class **ElevatorButton** implies that class **Elevator** needs to provide a "move" service. Before the elevator can move, however, the elevator must close its door. Therefore, a **prepareToLeave** operation, wherein the elevator performs the necessary actions before moving, seems a more appropriate choice to list under class **Elevator**.

The phrases listed with class **Door** imply that the door sends a message to a person to tell it to exit the elevator or enter the elevator. We create two operations for class **Person** to cover these behaviors—**exitElevator** and **enterElevator**.

---

1. At this point, we can only guess what these operations do. For example, perhaps these operations model real-world elevators with a sensor that detects when passengers enter and exit. For now, we simply list these operations. We will discover what, if any, actions these operations perform when we concentrate on implementing our simulator in C++.

For now we do not overly concern ourselves with the parameters or return types; we are attempting only to gain a basic understanding of the operations of each class. As we continue our design process, the number of operations belonging to each class can vary—we might find that new operations are needed or that some current operations are unnecessary.

Sequence Diagrams

We can use the UML *sequence diagram* (see Fig. 4.26) to model our "simulation loop"— the steps from the preceding discussion that the building repeats for the duration of the simulation. The sequence diagram focuses on how messages are sent between objects over time.

Each object is represented by a rectangle at the top of the diagram. The name of the object is placed inside the rectangle. We write object names in the sequence diagram using the convention we introduced with the object diagram in the "Thinking About Objects" section at the end of Chapter 2 (Fig. 2.45). The dashed line that extends down from an object's rectangle is that object's *lifeline*. This lifeline represents the progression of time. Actions happen along an object's lifeline in chronological order from top to bottom—an action near the top of a lifeline happens before an action near the bottom.

A message between two objects in a sequence diagram is represented as a line with a solid arrowhead that extends from the object sending that message to the object receiving that message. The message invokes the corresponding operation in the receiving object. The arrowhead points to the lifeline of the object receiving the message. The name of the message appears above the message line and should include any parameters being passed. For example, the object of class **Building** sends the **processTime** message to the object of class **Elevator**. The name of the message appears above the message line, and the name of the parameter (**currentTime**) appears inside parentheses to the right of the message; each parameter name is followed by a colon and the parameter type.

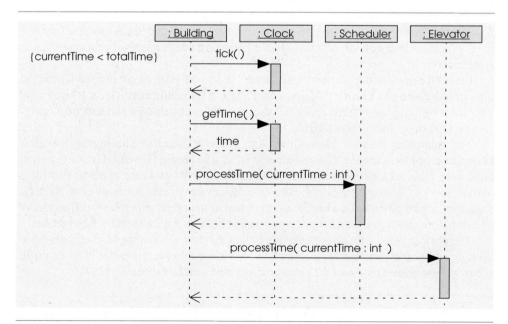

Fig. 4.26 Sequence diagram modeling simulation loop.

If an object returns the flow of control or if an object returns a value, a return message (represented as a dashed line with an arrowhead) extends from the object returning control to the object that initially sent the message. For example, the object of class **Clock** returns **time** in response to the **getTime** message received from the object of class **Building**.

The rectangles along the objects' lifelines—called *activations*—each represent the duration of an activity. An activation is initiated when an object receives a message and is denoted by a rectangle on that object's lifeline. The height of the rectangle corresponds to the duration of the activity or activities initiated by the message—the longer the duration of the activity, the taller the rectangle.

The text to the far left of the diagram in Fig. 4.26 indicates a timing constraint. While the current time is less than the total simulation time (**currentTime < totalTime**), the objects continue sending messages to one another in the sequence modeled in the diagram.

Figure 4.27 models how the scheduler handles the time and creates new people to walk onto floors. For this diagram, we assume the scheduler has scheduled a person to walk onto each of the two floors at a time that matches the time supplied by the building. Let us follow the flow of messages through this sequence diagram.

Object **building** first sends the **processTime** message to the **scheduler**, passing the current time. The **scheduler** object must then decide whether to create a new person to step onto the first floor (represented by the **floor1** object of class **Floor**). The problem statement tells us that the scheduler must first verify that the floor is unoccupied before it can create a new person to step onto that floor. The **scheduler** object therefore sends an **isOccupied** message to the **floor1** object, to accomplish this task.

The **floor1** object returns either **true** or **false** (indicated by the dashed return message line and the **bool** type). At this point, the **scheduler** object's lifeline splits into two parallel lifelines to represent each possible sequence of messages that the object can send, based on the value returned by the **floor1** object. An object's lifeline can split into two or more lifelines to indicate the *conditional execution of activities*. A condition must be supplied for each lifeline. The new lifeline(s) run parallel to the main lifeline, and the lifelines may converge at some later point.

If the **floor1** object returns **true** (i.e., the floor is occupied), the **scheduler** calls its own **delayArrival** function, passing a parameter indicating the **floor1** arrival time needs to be rescheduled. This function is not an operation of class **Scheduler** because it is not invoked by another object. The **delayArrival** function is simply an activity class **Scheduler** performs inside an operation. Notice that when the **scheduler** object sends a message to itself (i.e., invokes one of its own member functions), the activation bar for that message is centered on the right edge of the current activation bar.

If the **floor1** object returns **false** (i.e., the floor is unoccupied), the **scheduler** object creates a new object of class **Person**. In a sequence diagram, when a new object is created, the new object's rectangle is placed at a vertical position that corresponds to the time at which the object is created. An object that creates another object sends a message with the word "create" enclosed in guillemets (« »). The arrowhead of this message points to the new object's rectangle. A large "X" at the end of an object's lifetime denotes the destruction of that object. [Note: Our sequence diagram does not model the destruction of any objects of class **Person**; therefore, no "X" appears in the diagram. Creating and destroying objects dynamically, using C++'s **new** and **delete** operators, is discussed in Chapter 7.]

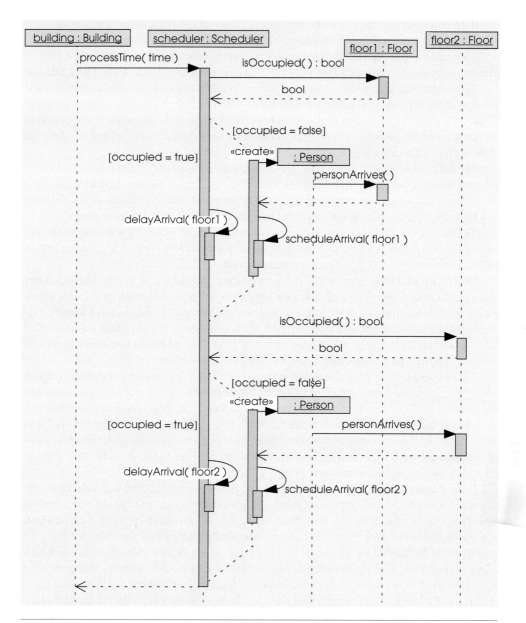

Fig. 4.27   Sequence diagram for scheduling process.

After the new object of class **Person** is created, the person must next step onto the first floor. Therefore, the new **Person** object sends a **personArrives** message to the **floor1** object. This message notifies the **floor1** object that a person is stepping onto it.

After the **scheduler** object has created a new object of class **Person**, it schedules a new arrival for **floor1**. The **scheduler** object invokes its own **scheduleArrival** function, and the activation bar for this call is centered on the right of the current activation bar. The **scheduleArrival** function is not an operation; it is an activity that class

Scheduler performs inside an operation. At this point, the two lifelines converge. The **scheduler** object then handles the second floor in the same manner as the first. When the scheduler has finished with **floor2**, the **scheduler** object returns control to the **building** object.

In this section, we have discussed the operations of classes and introduced the UML sequence diagram to illustrate these operations. In the "Thinking About Objects" section at the end of Chapter 5, we examine how objects in a system interact with one another to accomplish a specific task, and we begin implementing our elevator simulator in C++.

SUMMARY

- C++ stores lists of values in arrays. An array is a group of consecutive related memory locations. These locations are related by the fact that they all have the same name and the same type. To refer to a particular location or element within the array, we specify the name of the array and the subscript. The subscript indicates the number of elements from the beginning of the array.

- A subscript may be an integer or an integer expression. Subscript expressions are evaluated to determine the particular element of the array.

- It is important to note the difference when referring to the seventh element of the array as opposed to array element seven. The seventh element has a subscript of **6**, while array element seven has a subscript of **7** (actually the eighth element of the array). This is a source of "off-by-one" errors.

- Arrays occupy space in memory. To reserve 100 elements for integer array **b** and 27 elements for integer array **x**, the programmer writes

    ```
    int b[ 100 ], x[ 27 ];
    ```

- An array of type **char** can be used to store a character string.

- The elements of an array can be initialized by declaration, by assignment and by input.

- If there are fewer initializers than elements in the array, the remaining elements are initialized to zero.

- C++ does not prevent referencing elements beyond the bounds of an array.

- A character array can be initialized using a string literal.

- All strings end with the null character ('**\0**').

- Character arrays can be initialized with character constants in an initializer list.

- Individual characters in a string stored in an array can be accessed directly using array subscript notation.

- To pass an array to a function, the name of the array is passed. To pass a single element of an array to a function, simply pass the name of the array followed by the subscript (contained in square brackets) of the particular element.

- Arrays are passed to functions using simulated call-by-reference—the called functions can modify the element values in the callers' original arrays. The value of the name of the array is the address of the first element of the array. Because the starting address of the array is passed, the called function knows precisely where the array is stored.

- To receive an array argument, the function's parameter list must specify that an array will be received. The size of the array is not required in the brackets for a single-subscripted array parameter.

- C++ provides the type qualifier **const** that enables programs to prevent modification of array values in a function. When an array parameter is preceded by the **const** qualifier, the elements of the array become constant in the function body, and any attempt to modify an element of the array in the function body is a syntax error.

- An array can be sorted using the bubble-sort technique. Several passes of the array are made. On each pass, successive pairs of elements are compared. If a pair is in order (or the values are identical), it is left as is. If a pair is out of order, the values are swapped. For small arrays, the bubble sort is acceptable, but for larger arrays it is inefficient compared to other more sophisticated sorting algorithms.

- The linear search compares each element of the array with the search key. If the array is not in any particular order, it is just as likely that the value will be found in the first element as the last. On average, therefore, the program will have to compare the search key with half the elements of the array. The linear searching method works well for small arrays and is acceptable for unsorted arrays.

- The binary search eliminates from consideration half the elements in the array after each comparison by locating the middle element of the array and comparing it with the search key. If they are equal, the search key is found, and the array subscript of that element is returned. Otherwise, the problem is reduced to searching one-half of the array.

- In a worst-case scenario, searching an array of 1024 elements will take only 10 comparisons using a binary search.

- Arrays may be used to represent tables of values consisting of information arranged in rows and columns. To identify a particular element of a table, two subscripts are specified. The first (by convention) identifies the row in which the element is contained, and the second (by convention) identifies the column in which the element is contained. Tables or arrays that require two subscripts to identify a particular element are called double-subscripted arrays.

- When we receive a single-subscripted array as an argument to a function, the array brackets are empty in the function's parameter list. The size of the first subscript of a multiple-subscripted array is not required either, but all subsequent subscript sizes are required. The compiler uses these sizes to determine the locations in memory of elements in multiple-subscripted arrays.

- To pass one row of a double-subscripted array to a function that receives a single-subscripted array, simply pass the name of the array followed by the first subscript.

TERMINOLOGY

`a[ i ]`
`a[ i ][ j ]`
array
array initializer list
binary search of an array
bounds checking
bubble sort
column subscript
constant variable
const type qualifier
declare an array
double-subscripted array
element of an array
initialize an array
initializer
linear search of an array
magic number
m-by-*n* array
multiple-subscripted array
name of an array

named constant
null character (`'\0'`)
off-by-one error
passing arrays to functions
pass-by-reference
pass of a bubble sort
position number
row subscript
scalability
scalar
search an array
search key
simulated call-by-reference
single-subscripted array
sinking sort
sort an array
square brackets `[]`
string
subscript
table of values

tabular format

temporary area for exchange of values

triple-subscripted array

value of an element

"walk off" an array

zeroth element

"Thinking About Objects" Terminology

activation rectangle symbol in UML
   sequence diagram

behavior

client object

collaboration

conditional execution of activities

duration of activity

flow of messages in UML sequence diagram

guillemets

line with solid arrowhead in sequence diagram

message

object lifeline in UML sequence diagram

object rectangle symbol in UML sequence diagram

operation

return message symbol in UML sequence diagram

return type of an operation

sequence diagram

server object

service that an object provides

simulation loop

splitting an object's lifeline

verbs in a problem statement

COMMON PROGRAMMING ERRORS

4.1 It is important to note the difference between the "seventh element of the array" and "array element seven." Because array subscripts begin at 0, the "seventh element of the array" has a subscript of 6, while "array element seven" has a subscript of 7 and is actually the eighth element of the array. Unfortunately, this is a source of "off-by-one" errors.

4.2 Forgetting to initialize the elements of an array whose elements should be initialized is a logic error.

4.3 Providing more initializers in an array initializer list than there are elements in the array is a syntax error.

4.4 Assigning a value to a constant variable in an executable statement is a syntax error.

4.5 Only constants can be used to declare automatic and static arrays. Not using a constant for this purpose is a syntax error.

4.6 Referring to an element outside the array bounds is an execution-time logic error. It is not a syntax error.

4.7 Although it is possible to use the same counter variable in a **for** loop and a second **for** loop nested inside, this is normally a logic error.

4.8 Not providing **cin >>** with a character array large enough to store a string typed at the keyboard can result in loss of data in a program and other serious run-time errors.

4.9 Assuming that elements of a function's local **static** array are initialized to zero every time the function is called can lead to logic errors in a program.

4.10 Forgetting that arrays are passed by reference and hence can be modified may result in a logic error.

4.11 Referencing a double-subscripted array element **a[x][y]** incorrectly as **a[x, y]**. Actually, **a[x, y]** is treated as **a[y]**, because C++ evaluates the expression (containing a comma operator) **x, y** simply as **y** (the last of the comma-separated expressions).

GOOD PROGRAMMING PRACTICES

4.1 Defining the size of an array as a constant variable instead of a literal constant makes programs clearer. This technique is used to get rid of so-called *magic numbers*; i.e., repeatedly mentioning the size 10, for example, in array processing code for a 10-element array gives the number 10 an artificial significance and may unfortunately confuse the reader when the program includes other 10s that have nothing to do with the array size.

4.2   Strive for program clarity. It is sometimes worthwhile to trade off the most efficient use of memory or processor time in favor of writing clearer programs.

4.3   Some programmers include variable names in function prototypes to make programs clearer. The compiler ignores these names.

PERFORMANCE TIPS

4.1   If, instead of initializing an array with execution time assignment statements, you initialize the array at compile time with an array initializer list, your program will execute faster.

4.2   Sometimes performance considerations far outweigh clarity considerations.

4.3   We can apply **static** to a local array declaration so the array is not created and initialized each time the function is called, and the array is not destroyed each time the function is exited in the program. This improves performance.

4.4   Passing arrays by simulated call-by-reference makes sense for performance reasons. If arrays were passed by call-by-value, a copy of each element would be passed. For large, frequently passed arrays, this would be time consuming and would consume considerable storage for the copies of the arrays.

4.5   Sometimes, the simplest algorithms perform poorly. Their virtue is that they are easy to write, test and debug. More complex algorithms are sometimes needed to realize maximum performance.

4.6   The tremendous performance gains of the binary search over the linear search do not come without a price. Sorting an array is an expensive operation compared with searching an entire array once for one item. The overhead of sorting an array becomes worthwhile when the array will need to be searched many times at high speed.

PORTABILITY TIP

4.1   The (normally serious) effects of referencing elements outside the array bounds are system dependent. Often this results in changes to the value of an unrelated variable.

SOFTWARE ENGINEERING OBSERVATIONS

4.1   Defining the size of each array as a constant variable instead of a constant makes programs more scalable.

4.2   It is possible to pass an array by value (by using a simple trick we explain in Chapter 6)—this is rarely done.

4.3   The **const** type qualifier can be applied to an array parameter in a function definition to prevent the original array from being modified in the function body. This is another example of the principle of least privilege. Functions should not be given the capability to modify an array unless it is absolutely necessary.

TESTING AND DEBUGGING TIPS

4.1   When looping through an array, the array subscript should never go below 0 and should always be less than the total number of elements in the array (one less than the size of the array). Make sure that the loop-terminating condition prevents accessing elements outside this range.

4.2   Programs should validate the correctness of all input values to prevent erroneous information from affecting a program's calculations.

4.3   When we study classes (beginning with Chapter 6), we will see how to develop a "smart array," which automatically checks that all subscript references are in bounds at run time. Using such smart data types helps eliminate bugs.

4.4   Although it is possible to modify a loop counter in a **for** body, avoid doing so, because this often leads to subtle bugs.

SELF-REVIEW EXERCISES

4.1   Answer each of the following:
   a) Lists and tables of values are stored in _____.
   b) The elements of an array are related by the fact that they have the same _____ and _____.
   c) The number used to refer to a particular element of an array is called its _____.
   d) A _____ should be used to declare the size of an array, because it makes the program more scalable.
   e) The process of placing the elements of an array in order is called _____ the array.
   f) The process of determining if an array contains a certain key value is called _____ the array.
   g) An array that uses two subscripts is referred to as a _____ array.

4.2   State whether the following are *true* or *false*. If the answer is *false*, explain why.
   a) An array can store many different types of values.
   b) An array subscript should normally be of data type **float**.
   c) If there are fewer initializers in an initializer list than the number of elements in the array, the remaining elements are automatically initialized to the last value in the list of initializers.
   d) It is an error if an initializer list contains more initializers than there are elements in the array.
   e) An individual array element that is passed to a function and modified in that function will contain the modified value when the called function completes execution.

4.3   Answer the following questions regarding an array called **fractions**:
   a) Define a constant variable **arraySize** initialized to 10.
   b) Declare an array with **arraySize** elements of type **double**, and initialize the elements to **0**.
   c) Name the fourth element from the beginning of the array.
   d) Refer to array element 4.
   e) Assign the value **1.667** to array element 9.
   f) Assign the value **3.333** to the seventh element of the array.
   g) Print array elements 6 and 9 with two digits of precision to the right of the decimal point, and show the output that is actually displayed on the screen.
   h) Print all the elements of the array using a **for** repetition structure. Define the integer variable **x** as a control variable for the loop. Show the output.

4.4   Answer the following questions regarding an array called **table**:
   a) Declare the array to be an integer array and to have 3 rows and 3 columns. Assume that the constant variable **arraySize** has been defined to be 3.
   b) How many elements does the array contain?
   c) Use a **for** repetition structure to initialize each element of the array to the sum of its subscripts. Assume that the integer variables **x** and **y** are declared as control variables.
   d) Write a program segment to print the values of each element of an array table in tabular format with 3 rows and 3 columns. Assume that the array was initialized with the declaration

```
int table[ arraySize ][ arraySize ] =
      { { 1, 8 }, { 2, 4, 6 }, { 5 } };
```

and the integer variables **x** and **y** are declared as control variables. Show the output.

4.5   Find the error in each of the following program segments and correct the error:
   a) **#include <iostream>;**

b) `arraySize = 10;  // arraySize was declared const`
c) Assume that `int b[ 10 ] = { 0 };`
```
for ( int i = 0; i <= 10; i++ )
    b[ i ] = 1;
```
d) Assume that `int a[ 2 ][ 2 ] = { { 1, 2 }, { 3, 4 } };`
   `a[ 1, 1 ] = 5;`

ANSWERS TO SELF-REVIEW EXERCISES

4.1   a) Arrays.   b) Name, type.   c) Subscript.   d) Constant variable.   e) Sorting.
       f) Searching.   g) Double-subscripted.

4.2   a) False. An array can store only values of the same type.
       b) False. An array subscript should normally be an integer or an integer expression.
       c) False. The remaining elements are automatically initialized to zero.
       d) True.
       e) False. Individual elements of an array are passed by call-by-value. If the entire array is
           passed to a function, then any modifications will be reflected in the original.

4.3   a) `const int arraySize = 10;`
       b) `double fractions[ arraySize ] = { 0 };`
       c) `fractions[ 3 ]`
       d) `fractions[ 4 ]`
       e) `fractions[ 9 ] = 1.667;`
       f) `fractions[ 6 ] = 3.333;`
       g) `cout << setiosflags( ios::fixed | ios::showpoint )`
          `        << setprecision( 2 ) << fractions[ 6 ] << ' '`
          `        << fractions[ 9 ] << endl;`
          Output: `3.33 1.67.`
       h) `for ( int x = 0; x < arraySize; x++ )`
          `    cout << "fractions[" << x << "] = " << fractions[ x ]`
          `            << endl;`
          Output:
          `fractions[ 0 ] = 0`
          `fractions[ 1 ] = 0`
          `fractions[ 2 ] = 0`
          `fractions[ 3 ] = 0`
          `fractions[ 4 ] = 0`
          `fractions[ 5 ] = 0`
          `fractions[ 6 ] = 3.333`
          `fractions[ 7 ] = 0`
          `fractions[ 8 ] = 0`
          `fractions[ 9 ] = 1.667`

4.4   a) `int table[ arraySize ][ arraySize ];`
       b) Nine.
       c) `for ( x = 0; x < arraySize; x++ )`
          `    for ( y = 0; y < arraySize; y++ )`
          `        table[ x ][ y ] = x + y;`
       d) `cout << "      [0]   [1]   [2]" << endl;`
          `for ( int x = 0; x < arraySize; x++ ) {`
          `    cout << '[' << x << "] ";`
          `    for ( int y = 0; y < arraySize; y++ )`

```
        cout << setw( 3 ) << table[ x ][ y ] << "   ";
     cout << endl;
```

Output:

	[0]	[1]	[2]
[0]	1	8	0
[1]	2	4	6
[2]	5	0	0

4.5   a) Error: Semicolon at end of **#include** preprocessor directive.
Correction: Eliminate semicolon.

b) Error: Assigning a value to a constant variable using an assignment statement.
Correction: Assign a value to the constant variable in a **const int arraySize** declaration.

c) Error: Referencing an array element outside the bounds of the array (**b[10]**).
Correction: Change the final value of the control variable to **9**.

d) Error: Array subscripting done incorrectly.
Correction: Change the statement to **a[1][1] = 5;**

EXERCISES

4.6   Fill in the blanks in each of the following:
a) C++ stores lists of values in _____.
b) The elements of an array are related by the fact that they _____.
c) When referring to an array element, the position number contained within square brackets is called a _____.
d) The names of the four elements of array **p** are _____, _____, _____ and _____.
e) Naming an array, stating its type and specifying the number of elements in the array is called _____ the array.
f) The process of placing the elements of an array into either ascending or descending order is called _____.
g) In a double-subscripted array, the first subscript (by convention) identifies the _____ of an element, and the second subscript (by convention) identifies the _____ of an element.
h) An *m*-by-*n* array contains _____ rows, _____ columns and _____ elements.
i) The name of the element in row 3 and column 5 of array **d** is _____.

4.7   State which of the following are true and which are false; for those that are false, explain why they are false.
a) To refer to a particular location or element within an array, we specify the name of the array and the value of the particular element.
b) An array declaration reserves space for the array.
c) To indicate that 100 locations should be reserved for integer array **p**, the programmer writes the declaration

```
     p[ 100 ];
```

d) A C++ program that initializes the elements of a 15-element array to zero must contain at least one **for** statement.
e) A C++ program that totals the elements of a double-subscripted array must contain nested **for** statements.

4.8   Write C++ statements to accomplish each of the following:
   a) Display the value of the seventh element of character array **f**.
   b) Input a value into element 4 of single-subscripted floating-point array **b**.
   c) Initialize each of the 5 elements of single-subscripted integer array **g** to **8**.
   d) Total and print the elements of floating-point array **c** of 100 elements.
   e) Copy array **a** into the first portion of array **b**. Assume **double a[11], b[34];**
   f) Determine and print the smallest and largest values contained in 99-element floating-point array **w**.

4.9   Consider a 2-by-3 integer array **t**.
   a) Write a declaration for **t**.
   b) How many rows does **t** have?
   c) How many columns does **t** have?
   d) How many elements does **t** have?
   e) Write the names of all the elements in the second row of **t**.
   f) Write the names of all the elements in the third column of **t**.
   g) Write a single statement that sets the element of **t** in row 1 and column 2 to zero.
   h) Write a series of statements that initialize each element of **t** to zero. Do not use a loop.
   i) Write a nested **for** structure that initializes each element of **t** to zero.
   j) Write a statement that inputs the values for the elements of **t** from the terminal.
   k) Write a series of statements that determine and print the smallest value in array **t**.
   l) Write a statement that displays the elements of the first row of **t**.
   m) Write a statement that totals the elements of the fourth column of **t**.
   n) Write a series of statements that prints the array **t** in neat, tabular format. List the column subscripts as headings across the top and list the row subscripts at the left of each row.

4.10   Use a single-subscripted array to solve the following problem. A company pays its salespeople on a commission basis. The salespeople receive $200 per week plus 9 percent of their gross sales for that week. For example, a salesperson who grosses $5000 in sales in a week receives $200 plus 9 percent of $5000, or a total of $650. Write a program (using an array of counters) that determines how many of the salespeople earned salaries in each of the following ranges (assume that each salesperson's salary is truncated to an integer amount):
   a) $200–$299
   b) $300–$399
   c) $400–$499
   d) $500–$599
   e) $600–$699
   f) $700–$799
   g) $800–$899
   h) $900–$999
   i) $1000 and over

4.11   The bubble sort presented in Fig. 4.16 is inefficient for large arrays. Make the following simple modifications to improve the performance of the bubble sort:
   a) After the first pass, the largest number is guaranteed to be in the highest-numbered element of the array; after the second pass, the two highest numbers are "in place," and so on. Instead of making nine comparisons on every pass, modify the bubble sort to make eight comparisons on the second pass, seven on the third pass, and so on.
   b) The data in the array may already be in the proper order or near-proper order, so why make nine passes if fewer will suffice? Modify the sort to check at the end of each pass if any swaps have been made. If none have been made, then the data must already be in the proper order, so the program should terminate. If swaps have been made, then at least one more pass is needed.

4.12   Write single statements that perform the following single-subscripted array operations:
a) Initialize the 10 elements of integer array **counts** to zero.
b) Add 1 to each of the 15 elements of integer array **bonus**.
c) Read 12 values for **double** array **monthlyTemperatures** from the keyboard.
d) Print the 5 values of integer array **bestScores** in column format.

4.13   Find the error(s) in each of the following statements:
a) Assume that: **char str[5];**
```
cin >> str;      // User types hello
```
b) Assume that: **int a[3];**
```
cout << a[ 1 ] << " " << a[ 2 ] << " " << a[ 3 ] << endl;
```
c) **double f[3] = { 1.1, 10.01, 100.001, 1000.0001 };**
d) Assume that: **double d[2][10];**
```
d[ 1, 9 ] = 2.345;
```

4.14   Modify the program of Fig. 4.17 so function **mode** is capable of handling a tie for the mode value. Also modify function **median** so the two middle elements are averaged in an array with an even number of elements.

4.15   Use a single-subscripted array to solve the following problem. Read in 20 numbers, each of which is between 10 and 100, inclusive. As each number is read, print it only if it is not a duplicate of a number already read. Provide for the "worst case" in which all 20 numbers are different. Use the smallest possible array to solve this problem.

4.16   Label the elements of 3-by-5 double-subscripted array **sales** to indicate the order in which they are set to zero by the following program segment:
```
for ( row = 0; row < 3; row++ )
   for ( column = 0; column < 5; column++ )
      sales[ row ][ column ] = 0;
```

4.17   Write a program that simulates the rolling of two dice. The program should use **rand** to roll the first die and should use **rand** again to roll the second die. The sum of the two values should then be calculated. *Note:* Since each die can show an integer value from 1 to 6, then the sum of the two values will vary from 2 to 12, with 7 being the most frequent sum and 2 and 12 being the least frequent sums. Figure 4.28 shows the 36 possible combinations of the two dice. Your program should roll the two dice 36,000 times. Use a single-subscripted array to tally the numbers of times each possible sum appears. Print the results in a tabular format. Also, determine if the totals are reasonable (i.e., there are six ways to roll a 7, so approximately one sixth of all the rolls should be 7).

	1	2	3	4	5	6
1	2	3	4	5	6	7
2	3	4	5	6	7	8
3	4	5	6	7	8	9
4	5	6	7	8	9	10
5	6	7	8	9	10	11
6	7	8	9	10	11	12

Fig. 4.28   The 36 possible outcomes of rolling two dice.

4.18   What does the following program do?

```cpp
// ex04_18.cpp
#include <iostream>

using std::cout;
using std::endl;

int whatIsThis( int [], int );

int main()
{
   const int arraySize = 10;
   int a[ arraySize ] = { 1, 2, 3, 4, 5, 6, 7, 8, 9, 10 };

   int result = whatIsThis( a, arraySize );

   cout << "Result is " << result << endl;
   return 0;
}

int whatIsThis( int b[], int size )
{
   if ( size == 1 )
      return b[ 0 ];
   else
      return b[ size - 1 ] + whatIsThis( b, size - 1 );
}
```

4.19   Write a program that runs 1000 games of craps and answers the following questions:

a)   How many games are won on the 1st roll, 2nd roll, ..., 20th roll, and after the 20th roll?

b)   How many games are lost on the 1st roll, 2nd roll, ..., 20th roll, and after the 20th roll?

c)   What are the chances of winning at craps? (*Note:* You should discover that craps is one of the fairest casino games. What do you suppose this means?)

d)   What is the average length of a game of craps?

e)   Do the chances of winning improve with the length of the game?

4.20   (*Airline Reservations System*) A small airline has just purchased a computer for its new automated reservations system. You have been asked to program the new system. You are to write a program to assign seats on each flight of the airline's only plane (capacity: 10 seats).

Your program should display the following menu of alternatives—**Please type 1 for "First Class"** and **Please type 2 for "Economy"**. If the person types **1**, your program should assign a seat in the first class section (seats 1-5). If the person types **2**, your program should assign a seat in the economy section (seats 6-10). Your program should print a boarding pass indicating the person's seat number and whether it is in the first class or economy section of the plane.

Use a single-subscripted array to represent the seating chart of the plane. Initialize all the elements of the array to 0 to indicate that all seats are empty. As each seat is assigned, set the corresponding elements of the array to 1 to indicate that the seat is no longer available.

Your program should, of course, never assign a seat that has already been assigned. When the first class section is full, your program should ask the person if it is acceptable to be placed in the nonsmoking section (and vice versa). If yes, then make the appropriate seat assignment. If no, then print the message **"Next flight leaves in 3 hours."**

4.21   What does the following program do?

```
1   // ex04_21.cpp
2   #include <iostream>
3
4   using std::cout;
5   using std::endl;
6
7   void someFunction( int [], int );
8
9   int main()
10  {
11     const int arraySize = 10;
12     int a[ arraySize ] =
13         32, 27, 64, 18, 95, 14, 90, 70, 60, 37 };
14
15     cout << "The values in the array are:" << endl;
16     someFunction( a, arraySize );
17     cout << endl;
18     return 0;
19  }
20
21  void someFunction( int b[], int size )
22  {
23     if ( size > 0 ) {
24         someFunction( &b[ 1 ], size - 1 );
25         cout << b[ 0 ] << " ";
26     }
27  }
```

4.22   Use a double-subscripted array to solve the following problem. A company has four sales-people (1 to 4) who sell five different products (1 to 5). Once a day, each salesperson passes in a slip for each different type of product sold. Each slip contains the following:
   a) The salesperson number
   b) The product number
   c) The total dollar value of that product sold that day

Thus, each salesperson passes in between 0 and 5 sales slips per day. Assume that the information from all of the slips for last month is available. Write a program that will read all this information for last month's sales and summarize the total sales by salesperson by product. All totals should be stored in the double-subscripted array **sales**. After processing all the information for last month, print the results in tabular format with each of the columns representing a particular salesperson and each of the rows representing a particular product. Cross total each row to get the total sales of each product for last month; cross total each column to get the total sales by salesperson for last month. Your tab-ular printout should include these cross totals to the right of the totaled rows and to the bottom of the totaled columns.

4.23   (*Turtle Graphics*) The Logo language, which is particularly popular among personal comput-er users, made the concept of *turtle graphics* famous. Imagine a mechanical turtle that walks around the room under the control of a C++ program. The turtle holds a pen in one of two positions, up or down. While the pen is down, the turtle traces out shapes as it moves; while the pen is up, the turtle moves about freely without writing anything. In this problem, you will simulate the operation of the turtle and create a computerized sketchpad as well.

Use a 20-by-20 array **floor** that is initialized to zeros. Read commands from an array that contains them. Keep track of the current position of the turtle at all times and whether the pen is currently up or down. Assume that the turtle always starts at position 0,0 of the floor with its pen up. The set of turtle commands your program must process are as follows:

Command	Meaning
1	Pen up
2	Pen down
3	Turn right
4	Turn left
5,10	Move forward 10 spaces (or a number other than 10)
6	Print the 20-by-20 array
9	End of data (sentinel)

Suppose that the turtle is somewhere near the center of the floor. The following "program" would draw and print a 12-by-12 square and end with the pen in the up position:

```
2
5,12
3
5,12
3
5,12
3
5,12
1
6
9
```

As the turtle moves with the pen down, set the appropriate elements of array **floor** to **1**'s. When the **6** command (print) is given, wherever there is a **1** in the array, display an asterisk or some other character you choose. Wherever there is a zero, display a blank. Write a program to implement the turtle graphics capabilities discussed here. Write several turtle graphics programs to draw interesting shapes. Add other commands to increase the power of your turtle graphics language.

4.24 (*Knight's Tour*) One of the more interesting puzzlers for chess buffs is the Knight's Tour problem, originally proposed by the mathematician Euler. The question is this: Can the chess piece called the knight move around an empty chessboard and touch each of the 64 squares once and only once? We study this intriguing problem in depth here.

The knight makes L-shaped moves (over two in one direction and then over one in a perpendicular direction). Thus, from a square in the middle of an empty chessboard, the knight can make eight different moves (numbered 0 through 7) as shown in Fig. 4.29.

    a) Draw an 8-by-8 chessboard on a sheet of paper and attempt a Knight's Tour by hand. Put a **1** in the first square you move to, a **2** in the second square, a **3** in the third, etc. Before starting the tour, estimate how far you think you will get, remembering that a full tour consists of 64 moves. How far did you get? Was this close to your estimate?

    b) Now let us develop a program that will move the knight around a chessboard. The board is represented by an 8-by-8 double-subscripted array **board**. Each of the squares is initialized to zero. We describe each of the eight possible moves in terms of both their horizontal and vertical components. For example, a move of type 0, as shown in Fig. 4.25, consists of moving two squares horizontally to the right and one square vertically upward. Move 2 consists of moving one square horizontally to the left and two squares vertically upward. Horizontal moves to the left and vertical moves upward are indicated with negative numbers. The eight moves may be described by two single-subscripted arrays, **horizontal** and **vertical**, as follows:

```
horizontal[ 0 ] = 2
horizontal[ 1 ] = 1
horizontal[ 2 ] = -1
horizontal[ 3 ] = -2
horizontal[ 4 ] = -2
horizontal[ 5 ] = -1
horizontal[ 6 ] = 1
horizontal[ 7 ] = 2

vertical[ 0 ] = -1
vertical[ 1 ] = -2
vertical[ 2 ] = -2
vertical[ 3 ] = -1
vertical[ 4 ] = 1
vertical[ 5 ] = 2
vertical[ 6 ] = 2
vertical[ 7 ] = 1
```

Let the variables **currentRow** and **currentColumn** indicate the row and column of the knight's current position. To make a move of type **moveNumber**, where **moveNumber** is between 0 and 7, your program uses the statements

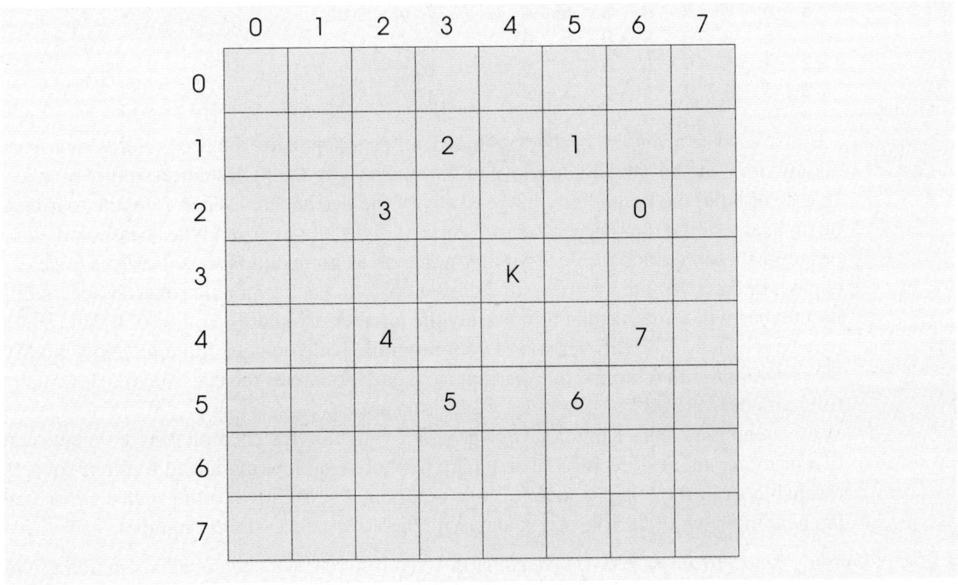

Fig. 4.29   The eight possible moves of the knight.

```
currentRow += vertical[ moveNumber ];
currentColumn += horizontal[ moveNumber ];
```

Keep a counter that varies from **1** to **64**. Record the latest count in each square the knight moves to. Remember to test each potential move to see if the knight has already visited that square, and, of course, test every potential move to make sure that the knight does not land off the chessboard. Now write a program to move the knight around the chessboard. Run the program. How many moves did the knight make?

c) After attempting to write and run a Knight's Tour program, you have probably developed some valuable insights. We will use these to develop a *heuristic* (or strategy) for moving the knight. Heuristics do not guarantee success, but a carefully developed heuristic greatly improves the chance of success. You may have observed that the outer squares are more troublesome than the squares nearer the center of the board. In fact, the most troublesome, or inaccessible, squares are the four corners.

   Intuition may suggest that you should attempt to move the knight to the most troublesome squares first and leave open those that are easiest to get to, so when the board gets congested near the end of the tour, there will be a greater chance of success.

   We may develop an "accessibility heuristic" by classifying each of the squares according to how accessible they are and then always moving the knight to the square (within the knight's L-shaped moves, of course) that is most inaccessible. We label a double-subscripted array **accessibility** with numbers indicating from how many squares each particular square is accessible. On a blank chessboard, each center square is rated as **8**, each corner square is rated as **2** and the other squares have accessibility numbers of **3**, **4** or **6** as follows:

```
2  3  4  4  4  4  3  2
3  4  6  6  6  6  4  3
4  6  8  8  8  8  6  4
4  6  8  8  8  8  6  4
4  6  8  8  8  8  6  4
4  6  8  8  8  8  6  4
3  4  6  6  6  6  4  3
2  3  4  4  4  4  3  2
```

   Now write a version of the Knight's Tour program using the accessibility heuristic. At any time, the knight should move to the square with the lowest accessibility number. In case of a tie, the knight may move to any of the tied squares. Therefore, the tour may begin in any of the four corners. (*Note:* As the knight moves around the chessboard, your program should reduce the accessibility numbers as more and more squares become occupied. In this way, at any given time during the tour, each available square's accessibility number will remain equal to precisely the number of squares from which that square may be reached.) Run this version of your program. Did you get a full tour? Now modify the program to run 64 tours, one starting from each square of the chessboard. How many full tours did you get?

d) Write a version of the Knight's Tour program which, when encountering a tie between two or more squares, decides what square to choose by looking ahead to those squares reachable from the "tied" squares. Your program should move to the square for which the next move would arrive at a square with the lowest accessibility number.

4.25 (*Knight's Tour: Brute-Force Approaches*) In Exercise 4.24, we developed a solution to the Knight's Tour problem. The approach used, called the "accessibility heuristic," generates many solutions and executes efficiently.

As computers continue increasing in power, we will be able to solve more problems with sheer computer power and relatively unsophisticated algorithms. Let us call this approach "brute force" problem solving.

      a) Use random-number generation to enable the knight to walk around the chessboard (in its legitimate L-shaped moves, of course) at random. Your program should run one tour and print the final chessboard. How far did the knight get?

      b) Most likely, the preceding program produced a relatively short tour. Now modify your program to attempt 1000 tours. Use a single-subscripted array to keep track of the number of tours of each length. When your program finishes attempting the 1000 tours, it should print this information in neat tabular format. What was the best result?

      c) Most likely, the preceding program gave you some "respectable" tours, but no full tours. Now "pull all the stops out" and simply let your program run until it produces a full tour. (*Caution:* This version of the program could run for hours on a powerful computer.) Once again, keep a table of the number of tours of each length, and print this table when the first full tour is found. How many tours did your program attempt before producing a full tour? How much time did it take?

      d) Compare the brute-force version of the Knight's Tour with the accessibility-heuristic version. Which required a more careful study of the problem? Which algorithm was more difficult to develop? Which required more computer power? Could we be certain (in advance) of obtaining a full tour with the accessibility heuristic approach? Could we be certain (in advance) of obtaining a full tour with the brute-force approach? Argue the pros and cons of brute-force problem solving in general.

4.26   (*Eight Queens*) Another puzzler for chess buffs is the Eight Queens problem. Simply stated: Is it possible to place eight queens on an empty chessboard so that no queen is "attacking" any other, i.e., no two queens are in the same row, the same column, or along the same diagonal? Use the thinking developed in Exercise 4.24 to formulate a heuristic for solving the Eight Queens problem. Run your program. (*Hint:* It is possible to assign a value to each square of the chessboard indicating how many squares of an empty chessboard are "eliminated" if a queen is placed in that square. Each of the corners would be assigned the value 22, as in Fig. 4.30.) Once these "elimination numbers" are placed in all 64 squares, an appropriate heuristic might be: Place the next queen in the square with the smallest elimination number. Why is this strategy intuitively appealing?

4.27   (*Eight Queens: Brute-Force Approaches*) In this exercise, you will develop several brute-force approaches to solving the Eight Queens problem introduced in Exercise 4.26.

      a) Solve the Eight Queens exercise, using the random brute-force technique developed in Exercise 4.25.

      b) Use an exhaustive technique, i.e., try all possible combinations of eight queens on the chessboard.

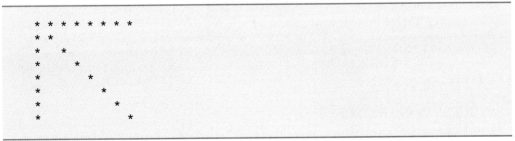

Fig. 4.30   The 22 squares eliminated by placing a queen in the upper-left corner.

c) Why do you suppose the exhaustive brute-force approach may not be appropriate for solving the Knight's Tour problem?

d) Compare and contrast the random brute-force and exhaustive brute-force approaches in general.

4.28 (*Knight's Tour: Closed-Tour Test*) In the Knight's Tour, a full tour occurs when the knight makes 64 moves touching each square of the chess board once and only once. A closed tour occurs when the 64th move is one move away from the location in which the knight started the tour. Modify the Knight's Tour program you wrote in Exercise 4.24 to test for a closed tour if a full tour has occurred.

4.29 (*The Sieve of Eratosthenes*) A prime integer is any integer that is evenly divisible only by itself and 1. The Sieve of Eratosthenes is a method of finding prime numbers. It operates as follows:

a) Create an array with all elements initialized to 1 (true). Array elements with prime sub scripts will remain 1. All other array elements will eventually be set to zero.

b) Starting with array subscript 2 (subscript 1 must be prime), every time an array element is found whose value is 1, loop through the remainder of the array and set to zero every element whose subscript is a multiple of the subscript for the element with value 1. For array subscript 2, all elements beyond 2 in the array that are multiples of 2 will be set to zero (subscripts 4, 6, 8, 10, etc.); for array subscript 3, all elements beyond 3 in the array that are multiples of 3 will be set to zero (subscripts 6, 9, 12, 15, etc.); and so on.

When this process is complete, the array elements that are still set to one indicate that the subscript is a prime number. These subscripts can then be printed. Write a program that uses an array of 1000 elements to determine and print the prime numbers between 1 and 999. Ignore element 0 of the array.

4.30 (*Bucket Sort*) A bucket sort begins with a single-subscripted array of positive integers to be sorted and a double-subscripted array of integers with rows subscripted from 0 to 9 and columns sub scripted from 0 to n - 1, where n is the number of values in the array to be sorted. Each row of the double-subscripted array is referred to as a bucket. Write a function **bucketSort** that takes an integer array and the array size as arguments and performs as follows:

a) Place each value of the single-subscripted array into a row of the bucket array based on the value's ones digit. For example, 97 is placed in row 7, 3 is placed in row 3 and 100 is placed in row 0. This is called a "distribution pass."

b) Loop through the bucket array row by row, and copy the values back to the original array. This is called a "gathering pass." The new order of the preceding values in the single-subscripted array is 100, 3 and 97.

c) Repeat this process for each subsequent digit position (tens, hundreds, thousands, etc.). On the second pass, 100 is placed in row 0, 3 is placed in row 0 (because 3 has no tens digit) and 97 is placed in row 9. After the gathering pass, the order of the values in the single-subscripted array is 100, 3 and 97. On the third pass, 100 is placed in row 1, 3 is placed in row zero and 97 is placed in row zero (after the 3). After the last gathering pass, the original array is now in sorted order.

Note that the double-subscripted array of buckets is 10 times the size of the integer array being sorted. This sorting technique provides better performance than a bubble sort, but requires much more memory. The bubble sort requires space for only one additional element of data. This is an example of the space–time trade-off: The bucket sort uses more memory than the bubble sort, but performs better. This version of the bucket sort requires copying all the data back to the original array on each pass. Another possibility is to create a second double-subscripted bucket array and repeatedly swap the data between the two bucket arrays.

RECURSION EXERCISES

4.31 (*Selection Sort*) A selection sort searches an array looking for the smallest element in the array. Then, the smallest element is swapped with the first element of the array. The process is repeated for the subarray beginning with the second element of the array. Each pass of the array results in one element being placed in its proper location. This sort performs comparably to the bubble sort—for an array of *n* elements, *n* - 1 passes must be made, and for each subarray, *n* - 1 comparisons must be made to find the smallest value. When the subarray being processed contains one element, the array is sorted. Write recursive function **selectionSort** to perform this algorithm.

4.32   (*Palindromes*) A palindrome is a string that is spelled the same way forwards and backwards. Some examples of palindromes are "radar," "able was i ere i saw elba" and (if blanks are ignored) "a man a plan a canal panama." Write a recursive function **testPalindrome** that returns **true** if the string stored in the array is a palindrome, and **false** otherwise. The function should ignore spaces and punctuation in the string.

4.33   (*Linear Search*) Modify the program in Fig. 4.19 to use recursive function **linearSearch** to perform a linear search of the array. The function should receive an integer array and the size of the array as arguments. If the search key is found, return the array subscript; otherwise, return –1.

4.34   (*Binary Search*) Modify the program of Fig. 4.20 to use a recursive function **binary-Search** to perform the binary search of the array. The function should receive an integer array and the starting subscript and ending subscript as arguments. If the search key is found, return the array subscript; otherwise, return –1.

4.35   (*Eight Queens*) Modify the Eight Queens program you created in Exercise 4.26 to solve the problem recursively.

4.36   (*Print an array*) Write a recursive function **printArray** that takes an array and the size of the array as arguments and returns nothing. The function should stop processing and return when it receives an array of size zero.

4.37   (*Print a string backwards*) Write a recursive function **stringReverse** that takes a character array containing a string as an argument, prints the string backwards and returns nothing. The function should stop processing and return when the terminating null character is encountered.

4.38   (*Find the minimum value in an array*) Write a recursive function **recursiveMinimum** that takes an integer array and the array size as arguments and returns the smallest element of the array. The function should stop processing and return when it receives an array of 1 element.

5

Pointers
and Strings

Objectives

- To be able to use pointers.
- To be able to use pointers to pass arguments to functions by call-by-reference.
- To understand the close relationships among pointers, arrays and strings.
- To understand the use of pointers to functions.
- To be able to declare and use arrays of strings.

Addresses are given to us to conceal our whereabouts.
Saki (H. H. Munro)

By indirections find directions out.
William Shakespeare, Hamlet

Many things, having full reference
To one consent, may work contrariously.
William Shakespeare, King Henry V

You will find it a very good practice always to verify your references, sir!
Dr. Routh

You can't trust code that you did not totally create yourself.
(Especially code from companies that employ people like me.)
Ken Thompson, 1983 Turing Award Lecture
Association for Computing Machinery, Inc.

Outline

5.1 Introduction

In this chapter, we discuss one of the most powerful features of the C++ programming language, the pointer. Pointers are among C++'s most difficult capabilities to master. In Chapter 3, we saw that references can be used to perform call-by-reference. Pointers enable programs to simulate call-by-reference and to create and manipulate dynamic data structures (i.e., data structures that can grow and shrink), such as linked lists, queues, stacks and trees. This chapter explains basic pointer concepts. This chapter also reinforces the intimate relationship among arrays, pointers and strings and includes a nice collection of string processing exercises.

Chapter 6 examines the use of pointers with structures. In Chapters 9 and 10, we will see that object-oriented programming is performed with pointers and references. Chapter 15 introduces dynamic memory management techniques and presents examples of creating and using dynamic data structures.

The view of arrays and strings as pointers derives from C. Later in the book we will discuss arrays and strings as full-fledged objects.

5.2 Pointer Variable Declarations and Initialization

Pointer variables contain memory addresses as their values. Normally, a variable directly contains a specific value. A pointer, on the other hand, contains an address of a variable that contains a specific value. In this sense, a variable name *directly* references a value, and a pointer *indirectly* references a value (Fig. 5.1). Referencing a value through a pointer is called *indirection*.

Pointers, like any other variables, must be declared before they can be used. The declaration

```
int *countPtr, count;
```

declares the variable **countPtr** to be of type **int *** (i.e., a pointer to an integer value) and is read, "**countPtr** is a pointer to **int**" or "**countPtr** points to an object of type integer." Also, variable **count** is declared to be an integer, not a pointer to an integer. The ***** only applies to **countPtr** in the declaration. Each variable being declared as a pointer must be preceded by an asterisk (*****). For example, the declaration

```
double *xPtr, *yPtr;
```

indicates that both **xPtr** and **yPtr** are pointers to **double** values. When ***** is used in this manner in a declaration, it indicates that the variable being declared is a pointer. Pointers can be declared to point to objects of any data type.

Common Programming Error 5.1

Assuming that the ***** *used to declare a pointer distributes to all pointer variable names in a comma-separated list of pointer variables in a declaration can lead to pointers being declared as nonpointers. Each pointer must be declared with the* ***** *prefixed to the name.*

Good Programming Practice 5.1

Although it is not required to do so, including the letters **Ptr** *in pointer variable names makes it clear that these variables are pointers and need to be handled appropriately.*

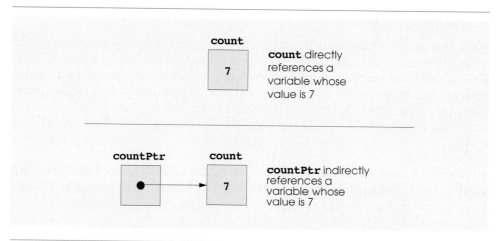

Fig. 5.1   Directly and indirectly referencing a variable.

Pointers should be initialized either when they are declared or in an assignment statement. A pointer may be initialized to **0**, **NULL**, or an address. A pointer with the value **0** or **NULL** points to nothing. Symbolic constant **NULL** is defined in header file **<iostream>** (and in several standard library header files). Initializing a pointer to **NULL** is equivalent to initializing a pointer to **0**, but in C++ **0** is preferred. When **0** is assigned, it is converted to a pointer of the appropriate type. The value **0** is the only integer value that can be assigned directly to a pointer variable without casting the integer to a pointer type first. Assigning a variable's address to a pointer is discussed in Section 5.3.

Testing and Debugging Tip 5.1

Initialize pointers to prevent pointing to unknown or uninitialized areas of memory.

5.3 Pointer Operators

The **&**, or *address, operator* is a unary operator that returns the address of its operand. For example, assuming the declarations

```
int y = 5;
int *yPtr;
```

the statement

```
yPtr = &y;
```

assigns the address of the variable **y** to pointer variable **yPtr**. Variable **yPtr** is then said to "point to" **y**. Figure 5.2 shows a schematic representation of memory after the preceding assignment is executed. In the figure, we show the "pointing relationship" by drawing an arrow from the pointer to the object it points to.

Figure 5.3 shows the representation of the pointer in memory, assuming that integer variable **y** is stored at location **600000** and that pointer variable **yPtr** is stored at location **500000**. The operand of the address operator must be an *lvalue* (i.e., something to which a value can be assigned, such as a variable name); the address operator cannot be applied to constants, to expressions that do not result in references or to variables declared with the storage class **register**.

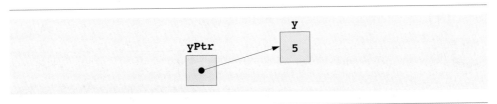

Fig. 5.2   Graphical representation of a pointer pointing to an integer variable in memory.

Fig. 5.3   Representation of **y** and **yPtr** in memory.

The *** *operator*, commonly referred to as the *indirection operator* or *dereferencing operator*, returns a synonym, alias or nickname for the object to which its operand (i.e., a pointer) points. For example (referring again to Fig. 5.2), the statement

```
cout << *yPtr << endl;
```

prints the value of variable **y**, namely, 5, in much the same way as the statement

```
cout << y << endl;
```

would. Using *** in this manner is called *dereferencing a pointer.* Note that a dereferenced pointer may also be used on the left side of an assignment statement, as in

```
*yPtr = 9;
```

which would assign **9** to **y** in Fig. 5.3. The dereferenced pointer may also be used to receive an input value as in

```
cin >> *yPtr;
```

The dereferenced pointer is an *lvalue*, or "left value."

Common Programming Error 5.2

Dereferencing a pointer that has not been properly initialize, or that has not been assigned to point to a specific location in memory could cause a fatal execution time error, or it could accidentally modify important data and allow the program to run to completion providing incorrect results.

Common Programming Error 5.3

An attempt to dereference a nonpointer is a syntax error.

Common Programming Error 5.4

*Dereferencing a **0** pointer is normally a fatal execution-time error.*

The program in Fig. 5.4 demonstrates the pointer operators. Memory locations are output in this example as hexadecimal integers by **<<**. (See Appendix C, "Number Systems," for more information on hexadecimal integers.)

Portability Tip 5.1

The format in which a pointer is output is machine dependent. Some systems output pointer values as hexadecimal integers, while others use decimal integers.

```
1   // Fig. 5.4: fig05_04.cpp
2   // Using the & and * operators
3   #include <iostream>
4
5   using std::cout;
6   using std::endl;
7
```

Fig. 5.4   The **&** and ***** pointer operators (part 1 of 2).

```
 8   int main()
 9   {
10      int a;         // a is an integer
11      int *aPtr;     // aPtr is a pointer to an integer
12
13      a = 7;
14      aPtr = &a;     // aPtr set to address of a
15
16      cout << "The address of a is " << &a
17           << "\nThe value of aPtr is " << aPtr;
18
19      cout << "\n\nThe value of a is " << a
20           << "\nThe value of *aPtr is " << *aPtr;
21
22      cout << "\n\nShowing that * and & are inverses of "
23           << "each other.\n&*aPtr = " << &*aPtr
24           << "\n*&aPtr = " << *&aPtr << endl;
25      return 0;
26   }
```

```
The address of a is 006AFDF4
The value of aPtr is 006AFDF4
The value of a is 7
The value of *aPtr is 7
Showing that * and & are inverses of each other.
&*aPtr = 006AFDF4
*&aPtr = 006AFDF4
```

Fig. 5.4   The & and * pointer operators (part 2 of 2).

Notice that the address of **a** and the value of **aPtr** are identical in the output, confirming that the address of **a** is indeed assigned to the pointer variable **aPtr**. The & and * operators are inverses of one another—when they are both applied consecutively to **aPtr** in either order, the same result is printed. Figure 5.5 lists the precedence and associativity of the operators introduced to this point.

Operators								Associativity	Type
() []								left to right	highest
++ -- static_cast<_type_>()								left to right	postfix
++ -- + - ! & *								right to left	unary
* / %								left to right	multiplicative
+ -								left to right	additive
<< >>								left to right	insertion/extraction
< <= > >=								left to right	relational

Fig. 5.5   Operator precedence and associativity (part 1 of 2).

Operators							Associativity	Type
==	!=						left to right	equality
&&							left to right	logical AND
||							left to right	logical OR
?:							right to left	conditional
=	+=	-=	*=	/=		%=	right to left	assignment
,							left to right	comma

Fig. 5.5   Operator precedence and associativity (part 2 of 2).

5.4 Calling Functions by Reference

There are three ways in C++ to pass arguments to a function—*by call-by-value, call-by-reference with reference arguments* and *call-by-reference with pointer arguments*. In Chapter 3, we compared and contrasted call-by-value and call-by-reference with reference arguments. In this chapter, we concentrate on call-by-reference with pointer arguments.

As we saw in Chapter 3, **return** can be used to return one value from a called function to a caller (or to return control from a called function without passing back a value). We also saw that arguments can be passed to a function using reference arguments to enable the function to modify the original values of the arguments (thus, more than one value can be "returned" from a function) or to pass large data objects to a function and avoid the overhead of passing the objects by call-by-value (which, of course, requires making a copy of the object). Pointers, like references, also can be used to modify one or more variables in the caller or to pass pointers to large data objects to avoid the overhead of passing the objects by call-by-value.

In C++, programmers can use pointers and the indirection operator to simulate call-by-reference (exactly as call-by-reference is accomplished in C programs). When calling a function with arguments that should be modified, the addresses of the arguments are passed. This is normally accomplished by applying the address operator (**&**) to the name of the variable whose value will be modified.

As we saw in Chapter 4, arrays are not passed using operator **&**, because the name of the array is the starting location in memory of the array. The name of an array is equivalent to **&arrayName[0]** (i.e., an array name is already a pointer). When the address of a variable is passed to a function, the indirection operator (*****) can be used in the function to form a synonym, alias or nickname for the name of the variable—this in turn can be used to modify the value (if the variable is not declared **const**) at that location in the caller's memory.

Figures 5.6 and 5.7 present two versions of a function that cubes an integer—**cubeByValue** and **cubeByReference**. Figure 5.6 passes variable **number** to function **cubeByValue** using call-by-value. Function **cubeByValue** cubes its argument and passes the new value back to **main** using a **return** statement. The new value is assigned to **number** in **main**. You have the opportunity to examine the result of the function call before modifying a variable's value. For example, in this program, we could have stored the result of **cubeByValue** in another variable, examined its value and assigned the result to **number** after checking the reasonableness of that value.

```
1   // Fig. 5.6: fig05_06.cpp
2   // Cube a variable using call-by-value
3   #include <iostream>
4
5   using std::cout;
6   using std::endl;
7
8   int cubeByValue( int );     // prototype
9
10  int main()
11  {
12     int number = 5;
13
14     cout << "The original value of number is " << number;
15     number = cubeByValue( number );
16     cout << "\nThe new value of number is " << number << endl;
17     return 0;
18  }
19
20  int cubeByValue( int n )
21  {
22     return n * n * n;     // cube local variable n
23  }
```

```
The original value of number is 5
The new value of number is 125
```

Fig. 5.6   Cube a variable using call-by-value.

Figure 5.7 passes the variable **number** using call-by-reference—the address of **number** is passed—to function **cubeByReference**. Function **cubeByReference** takes **nPtr** (a pointer to **int**) as an argument. The function dereferences the pointer and cubes the value to which **nPtr** points. This changes the value of **number** in **main**. Figures 5.8 and 5.9 analyze graphically the programs in Fig. 5.6 and Fig. 5.7, respectively.

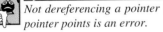

Common Programming Error 5.5

Not dereferencing a pointer when it is necessary to do so to obtain the value to which the pointer points is an error.

```
1   // Fig. 5.7: fig05_07.cpp
2   // Cube a variable using call-by-reference
3   // with a pointer argument
4   #include <iostream>
5
6   using std::cout;
7   using std::endl;
8
9   void cubeByReference( int * );     // prototype
10
```

Fig. 5.7   Cube a variable using call-by-reference with a pointer argument (part 1 of 2).

```
11   int main()
12   {
13      int number = 5;
14
15      cout << "The original value of number is " << number;
16      cubeByReference( &number );
17      cout << "\nThe new value of number is " << number << endl;
18      return 0;
19   }
20
21   void cubeByReference( int *nPtr )
22   {
23      *nPtr = *nPtr * *nPtr * *nPtr;   // cube number in main
24   }
```

```
The original value of number is 5
The new value of number is 125
```

Fig. 5.7   Cube a variable using call-by-reference with a pointer argument (part 2 of 2).

A function receiving an address as an argument must define a pointer parameter to receive the address. For example, the header for function **cubeByReference** is

```
void cubeByReference( int *nPtr )
```

The function header specifies that function **cubeByReference** receives the address of an integer variable (i.e., an integer pointer) as an argument, stores the address locally in **nPtr** and does not return a value.

The function prototype for **cubeByReference** contains **int *** in parentheses. As with other variable types, it is not necessary to include names of pointers in function prototypes. Parameter names included for documentation purposes are ignored by the compiler.

In the function header and in the prototype for a function that expects a single-subscripted array as an argument, the pointer notation in the parameter list of **cubeByReference** may be used. The compiler does not differentiate between a function that receives a pointer and a function that receives a single-subscripted array. This, of course, means that the function must "know" when it is receiving an array or simply a single variable for which it is to perform call-by-reference. When the compiler encounters a function parameter for a single-subscripted array of the form **int b[ ]**, the compiler converts the parameter to the pointer notation **int * const b** (pronounced "**b** is a constant pointer to an integer"— **const** is explained in Section 5.5). Both forms of declaring a function parameter as a single-subscripted array are interchangeable.

Good Programming Practice 5.2

Use call-by-value to pass arguments to a function unless the caller explicitly requires that the called function modify the value of the argument variable in the caller's environment. This is another example of the principle of least privilege.

Before **main** calls **cubeByValue**:

```
int main()                        number
{
    int number = 5;                  5

    number = cubeByValue( number );
}
```

```
int cubeByValue( int n )
{
    return n * n * n;
}
                                    n

                              undefined
```

After **cubeByValue** receives the call:

```
int main()                        number
{
    int number = 5;                  5

    number = cubeByValue( number );
}
```

```
int cubeByValue( int n )
{
    return n * n * n;
}
                                    n

                                    5
```

After **cubeByValue** cubes the parameter **n**:

```
int main()                        number
{
    int number = 5;                  5

    number = cubeByValue( number );
}
```

```
int cubeByValue( int n )
{                           125
    return n * n * n;
}
                                    n

                              undefined
```

After **cubeByValue** returns to **main**:

```
int main()                        number
{
    int number = 5;                  5
                     125
    number = cubeByValue( number );
}
```

```
int cubeByValue( int n )
{
    return n * n * n;
}
                                    n

                              undefined
```

After **main** completes the assignment to **number**:

```
int main()                        number
{
    int number = 5;                 125

    number = cubeByValue( number );
}
```

```
int cubeByValue( int n )
{
    return n * n * n;
}
                                    n

                              undefined
```

Fig. 5.8   Analysis of a typical call-by-value.

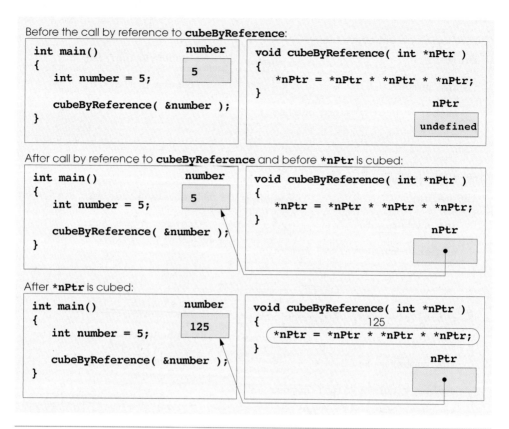

Before the call by reference to **cubeByReference**:

```
int main()                number
{                            5
    int number = 5;

    cubeByReference( &number );
}
```

```
void cubeByReference( int *nPtr )
{
    *nPtr = *nPtr * *nPtr * *nPtr;
}
                                    nPtr

                              undefined
```

After call by reference to **cubeByReference** and before ***nPtr** is cubed:

```
int main()                number
{                            5
    int number = 5;

    cubeByReference( &number );
}
```

```
void cubeByReference( int *nPtr )
{
    *nPtr = *nPtr * *nPtr * *nPtr;
}
                                    nPtr
```

After ***nPtr** is cubed:

```
int main()                number
{                           125
    int number = 5;

    cubeByReference( &number );
}
```

```
void cubeByReference( int *nPtr )
{                               125
    *nPtr = *nPtr * *nPtr * *nPtr;
}
                                    nPtr
```

Fig. 5.9   Analysis of a typical call-by-reference with a pointer argument.

5.5 Using the `const` Qualifier with Pointers

The **const** *qualifier* enables the programmer to inform the compiler that the value of a particular variable should not be modified.

Software Engineering Observation 5.1

The **const** *qualifier can be used to enforce the principle of least privilege. Using the principle of least privilege to properly design software can greatly reduce debugging time and improper side effects and can make a program easier to modify and maintain.*

Portability Tip 5.2

Although **const** *is well defined in ANSI C and C++, some compilers do not enforce it properly.*

Over the years, a large base of legacy code was written in early versions of C that did not use **const**, because it was not available. For this reason, there are great opportunities for improvement in the software engineering of old C code. Also, many programmers currently using ANSI C and C++ do not use **const** in their programs, because they began programming in early versions of C. These programmers are omitting many opportunities for good software engineering.

Six possibilities exist for using (or not using) **const** with function parameters—two with call-by-value parameter passing and four with call-by-reference parameter passing. How do you choose one of the six possibilities? Let the principle of least privilege be your guide. Always award a function enough access to the data in its parameters to accomplish its specified task, but no more.

In Chapter 3, we explained that when a function is called using call-by-value, a copy of the argument (or arguments) in the function call is made and passed to the function. If the copy is modified in the function, the original value is maintained in the caller without change. In many cases, a value passed to a function is modified so the function can accomplish its task. However, in some instances, the value should not be altered in the called function, even though the called function manipulates only a copy of the original value.

Consider a function that takes a single-subscripted array and its size as arguments and prints the array. Such a function should loop through the array and output each array element individually. The size of the array is used in the function body to determine the high subscript of the array so the loop can terminate when the printing is completed. The size of the array does not change in the function body.

Software Engineering Observation 5.2

If a value does not (or should not) change in the body of a function to which it is passed, the parameter should be declared **const** *to ensure that it is not accidentally modified.*

If an attempt is made to modify a **const** value, the compiler catches it and issues either a warning or an error depending on the particular compiler.

Software Engineering Observation 5.3

Only one value can be altered in a calling function when call-by-value is used. That value must be assigned from the return value of the function. To modify multiple values in a calling function, several arguments are passed by call-by-reference.

Good Programming Practice 5.3

Before using a function, check its function prototype to determine the parameters that it can modify.

There are four ways to pass a pointer to a function: a nonconstant pointer to nonconstant data, a nonconstant pointer to constant data, a constant pointer to non-constant data, and a constant pointer to constant data. Each combination provides a different level of access privileges.

The highest access is granted by a nonconstant pointer to nonconstant data—the data can be modified through the dereferenced pointer, and the pointer can be modified to point to other data. Declaration for nonconstant pointers to nonconstant data do not include **const**. Such a pointer can be used to receive a string in a function that uses pointer arithmetic to process (and possibly modify) each character in the string. Function **convert-ToUppercase** of Fig. 5.10 declares parameter **sPtr** (**char *sPtr**) to be a nonconstant pointer to nonconstant data. The function processes the string **s** one character at a time using pointer arithmetic. Function **islower** takes one character argument and returns true if the character is a lowercase letter and false otherwise. Characters in the range **'a'** through **'z'** are converted to their corresponding uppercase letters by function **toupper**; others remain unchanged. Function **toupper** takes one character as an argument. If the character is a lowercase letter, the corresponding uppercase letter is returned;

otherwise, the original character is returned. Function **toupper** and function **islower** are part of the character handling library **<cctype>** (see Chapter 16, "Characters, Strings, Structures, and Bit Manipulation").

A nonconstant pointer to constant data is a pointer that can be modified to point to any data item of the appropriate type, but the data to which it points cannot be modified through that pointer. Such a pointer might be used to receive an array argument to a function that will process each element of the array without modifying the data. For example, function **printCharacters** of Fig. 5.11 declares parameters **sPtr** to be of type **const char ***. The declaration is read from right to left as "**sPtr** is a pointer to a character constant." The body of the function uses a **for** structure to output each character in the string until the null character is encountered. After each character is printed, pointer **sPtr** is incremented to point to the next character in the string.

```cpp
1   // Fig. 5.10: fig05_10.cpp
2   // Converting lowercase letters to uppercase letters
3   // using a non-constant pointer to non-constant data
4   #include <iostream>
5
6   using std::cout;
7   using std::endl;
8
9   #include <cctype>
10
11  void convertToUppercase( char * );
12
13  int main()
14  {
15     char string[] = "characters and $32.98";
16
17     cout << "The string before conversion is: " << string;
18     convertToUppercase( string );
19     cout << "\nThe string after conversion is:  "
20          << string << endl;
21     return 0;
22  }
23
24  void convertToUppercase( char *sPtr )
25  {
26     while ( *sPtr != '\0' ) {
27
28        if ( islower( *sPtr ) )
29           *sPtr = toupper( *sPtr );  // convert to uppercase
30
31        ++sPtr;  // move sPtr to the next character
32     }
33  }
```

```
The string before conversion is: characters and $32.98
The string after conversion is:  CHARACTERS AND $32.98
```

Fig. 5.10   Converting a string to uppercase.

```
1   // Fig. 5.11: fig05_11.cpp
2   // Printing a string one character at a time using
3   // a non-constant pointer to constant data
4   #include <iostream>
5
6   using std::cout;
7   using std::endl;
8
9   void printCharacters( const char * );
10
11  int main()
12  {
13     char string[] = "print characters of a string";
14
15     cout << "The string is:\n";
16     printCharacters( string );
17     cout << endl;
18     return 0;
19  }
20
21  // In printCharacters, sPtr cannot modify the character
22  // to which it points. sPtr is a "read-only" pointer
23  void printCharacters( const char *sPtr )
24  {
25     for ( ; *sPtr != '\0'; sPtr++ )   // no initialization
26        cout << *sPtr;
27  }
```

```
The string is:
print characters of a string
```

Fig. 5.11   Printing a string one character at a time using a nonconstant pointer to constant data.

Figure 5.12 demonstrates the syntax error messages produced when attempting to compile a function that receives a nonconstant pointer to constant data and then tries to use that pointer to modify the data.

```
1   // Fig. 5.12: fig05_12.cpp
2   // Attempting to modify data through a
3   // non-constant pointer to constant data.
4   #include <iostream>
5
6   void f( const int * );
7
8   int main()
9   {
10     int y;
11
```

Fig. 5.12   Attempting to modify data through a nonconstant pointer to constant data (part 1 of 2).

```
12        f( &y );        // f attempts illegal modification
13
14        return 0;
15   }
16
17   // xPtr cannot modify the value of the variable
18   // to which it points
19   void f( const int *xPtr )
20   {
21        *xPtr = 100;   // cannot modify a const object
22   }
```

Borland C++ command-line compiler error message

```
Error E2024 Fig05_12.cpp 20: Cannot modify a const object in
function f(const int *)
Warning W8057 Fig05_12.cpp 21: Parameter 'xPtr' is never used in
function f(const int *)
```

Microsoft Visual C++ compiler error message

```
Fig05_12.cpp(20) : error C2166: l-value specifies const object
```

Fig. 5.12 Attempting to modify data through a nonconstant pointer to constant data (part 2 of 2).

As we know, arrays are aggregate data types that store related data items of the same type under one name. In Chapter 6, we discuss another form of aggregate data type called a *structure* (sometimes called a *record* in other languages). A structure is capable of storing related data items of different data types under one name (e.g., storing information about each employee of a company). When a function is called with an array as an argument, the array is automatically passed to the function by simulated call-by-reference. However, structures are always passed by call-by-value—a copy of the entire structure is passed. This requires the execution-time overhead of making a copy of each data item in the structure and storing it on the computer's function call stack (the place where the local variables used in the function call are stored while the function is executing). When structure data must be passed to a function, we can use a pointer to constant data (or a reference to constant data) to get the performance of call-by-reference and the protection of call-by-value. When a pointer to a structure is passed, only a copy of the address at which the structure is stored must be made. On a machine with 4-byte addresses, a copy of 4 bytes of memory is made rather than a copy of possibly hundreds or thousands of bytes of the structure.

Performance Tip 5.1

Pass large objects such as structures using pointers to constant data, or references to constant data, to obtain the performance benefits of call-by-reference and the security of call-by-value.

A constant pointer to nonconstant data is a pointer that always points to the same memory location, and the data at that location can be modified through the pointer. This is the default for an array name. An array name is a constant pointer to the beginning of the array. All data in the array can be accessed and changed by using the array name and array subscripting. A constant pointer to nonconstant data can be used to receive an array as an argument to a function that accesses array elements using array subscript notation. Pointers that are declared **const** must be initialized when they are declared (if the pointer is a function parameter, it is initialized with a pointer that is passed to the function). The program of Fig. 5.13 attempts to modify a constant pointer. Pointer **ptr** is declared to be of type **int * const**. The declaration in the figure is read from right to left as "**ptr** is a constant pointer to an integer." The pointer is initialized with the address of integer variable **x**. The program attempts to assign the address of **y** to **ptr**, but an error message is generated. Note that no error is produced when the value **7** is assigned to ***ptr**—the value to which **ptr** points can be modified using **ptr**.

Common Programming Error 5.6

Not initializing a pointer that is declared **const** *is a syntax error.*

The least amount of access privilege is granted by a constant pointer to constant data. Such a pointer always points to the same memory location, and the data at that memory location cannot be modified using the pointer. This is how an array should be passed to a function that only looks at the array using array subscript notation and does not modify the array. The program of Fig. 5.14 declares pointer variable **ptr** to be of type **const int * const**. This declaration is read from right to left as "**ptr** is a constant pointer to an integer constant." The figure shows the error messages generated when an attempt is made to modify the data to which **ptr** points and when an attempt is made to modify the address stored in the pointer variable. Note that no error is generated when we attempt to output the value to which **ptr** points, because nothing is being modified in the output statement.

```
1   // Fig. 5.13: fig05_13.cpp
2   // Attempting to modify a constant pointer to
3   // non-constant data
4   #include <iostream>
5
6   int main()
7   {
8      int x, y;
9
10     int * const ptr = &x;  // ptr is a constant pointer to an
11                            // integer. An integer can be modified
12                            // through ptr, but ptr always points
13                            // to the same memory location.
14     *ptr = 7;
15     ptr = &y;
16
17     return 0;
18  }
```

Fig. 5.13   Attempting to modify a constant pointer to nonconstant data (part 1 of 2).

Borland C++ command-line compiler error message

```
Error E2024 Fig05_13.cpp 15: Cannot modify a const object in function
main()
```

Microsoft Visual C++ compiler error message

```
Fig05_13.cpp(15) : error C2166: l-value specifies const object
```

Fig. 5.13   Attempting to modify a constant pointer to nonconstant data (part 2 of 2).

```
1    // Fig. 5.14: fig05_14.cpp
2    // Attempting to modify a constant pointer to
3    // constant data.
4    #include <iostream>
5
6    using std::cout;
7    using std::endl;
8
9    int main()
10   {
11      int x = 5, y;
12
13      const int *const ptr = &x;  // ptr is a constant pointer to a
14                                  // constant integer. ptr always
15                                  // points to the same location
16                                  // and the integer at that
17                                  // location cannot be modified.
18      cout << *ptr << endl;
19      *ptr = 7;
20      ptr = &y;
21
22      return 0;
23   }
```

Borland C++ command-line compiler error message

```
Error E2024 Fig05_14.cpp 19: Cannot modify a const object in
function main()
Error E2024 Fig05_14.cpp 20: Cannot modify a const object in
function main()
```

Microsoft Visual C++ compiler error message

```
Fig05_14.cpp(19) : error C2166: l-value specifies const object
Fig05_14.cpp(20) : error C2166: l-value specifies const object
```

Fig. 5.14   Attempting to modify a constant pointer to constant data .

5.6 Bubble Sort Using Call-by-reference

Let us modify the bubble sort program of Fig. 4.16 to use two functions—**bubbleSort** and **swap** (Fig. 5.15). Function **bubbleSort** performs the sort of the array. It calls function **swap** to exchange the array elements **array[j]** and **array[j + 1]**. Remember that C++ enforces information hiding between functions, so **swap** does not have access to individual array elements in **bubbleSort**. Because **bubbleSort** *wants* **swap** to have access to the array elements to be swapped, **bubbleSort** passes each of these elements by call-by-reference to **swap**—the address of each array element is passed explicitly. Although entire arrays are automatically passed by call-by-reference, individual array elements are scalars and are ordinarily passed by call-by-value. Therefore, **bubbleSort** uses the address operator (**&**) on each array element in the **swap** call as follows to effect call-by-reference:

```
swap( &array[ j ], &array[ j + 1 ] );
```

Function **swap** receives **&array[j]** in pointer variable **element1Ptr**. Because of information hiding, **swap** is not allowed to know the name **array[j]**, but **swap** can use ***element1Ptr** as a synonym for **array[j]**. Thus, when **swap** references ***element1Ptr**, it is actually referencing **array[j]** in **bubbleSort**. Similarly, when **swap** references ***element2Ptr**, it is actually referencing **array[j + 1]** in **bubbleSort**.

```cpp
1   // Fig. 5.15: fig05_15.cpp
2   // This program puts values into an array, sorts the values into
3   // ascending order, and prints the resulting array.
4   #include <iostream>
5
6   using std::cout;
7   using std::endl;
8
9   #include <iomanip>
10
11  using std::setw;
12
13  void bubbleSort( int *, const int );
14
15  int main()
16  {
17     const int arraySize = 10;
18     int a[ arraySize ] = { 2, 6, 4, 8, 10, 12, 89, 68, 45, 37 };
19     int i;
20
21     cout << "Data items in original order\n";
22
23     for ( i = 0; i < arraySize; i++ )
24        cout << setw( 4 ) << a[ i ];
25
26     bubbleSort( a, arraySize );          // sort the array
```

Fig. 5.15 Bubble sort with call-by-reference (part 1 of 2).

```
27          cout << "\nData items in ascending order\n";
28
29          for ( i = 0; i < arraySize; i++ )
30             cout << setw( 4 ) << a[ i ];
31
32          cout << endl;
33          return 0;
34       }
35
36       void bubbleSort( int *array, const int size )
37       {
38          void swap( int * const, int * const );
39
40          for ( int pass = 0; pass < size - 1; pass++ )
41
42             for ( int j = 0; j < size - 1; j++ )
43
44                if ( array[ j ] > array[ j + 1 ] )
45                   swap( &array[ j ], &array[ j + 1 ] );
46       }
47
48       void swap( int * const element1Ptr, int * const element2Ptr )
49       {
50          int hold = *element1Ptr;
51          *element1Ptr = *element2Ptr;
52          *element2Ptr = hold;
53       }
```

```
Data items in original order
   2   6   4   8  10  12  89  68  45  37
Data items in ascending order
   2   4   6   8  10  12  37  45  68  89
```

Fig. 5.15 Bubble sort with call-by-reference (part 2 of 2).

Even though **swap** is not allowed to say

```
hold = array[ j ];
array[ j ] = array[ j + 1 ];
array[ j + 1 ] = hold;
```

precisely the same effect is achieved by

```
hold = *element1Ptr;
*element1Ptr = *element2Ptr;
*element2Ptr = hold;
```

in the **swap** function of Fig. 5.15.

Several features of function **bubbleSort** should be noted. The function header declares **array** as **int *array**, rather than **int array[]**, to indicate that **bubble-Sort** receives a single-subscripted array as an argument (again, these notations are interchangeable). Parameter **size** is declared **const** to enforce the principle of least privilege. Although parameter **size** receives a copy of a value in **main** and modifying the copy

cannot change the value in **main**, **bubbleSort** does not need to alter **size** to accomplish its task. The array size remains fixed during the execution of **bubbleSort**. Therefore, **size** is declared **const** to ensure that it is not modified. If the size of the array is modified during the sorting process, the sorting algorithm would not run correctly.

The prototype for function **swap** is included in the body of function **bubbleSort**, because it is the only function that calls **swap**. Placing the prototype in **bubbleSort** restricts proper calls of **swap** to those made from **bubbleSort**. Other functions that attempt to call **swap** do not have access to a proper function prototype. This normally results in a syntax error, because C++ requires function prototypes.

Software Engineering Observation 5.4

Placing function prototypes in the definitions of other functions enforces the principle of least privilege by restricting function calls to the functions in which the prototypes appear.

Note that function **bubbleSort** receives the size of the array as a parameter. The function must know the size of the array to sort the array. When an array is passed to a function, the memory address of the first element of the array is received by the function. The array size must be passed separately to the function.

By defining function **bubbleSort** so it receives the array size as a parameter, we enable the function to be used by any program that sorts single-subscripted integer arrays of arbitrary size.

Software Engineering Observation 5.5

When passing an array to a function, also pass the size of the array (rather than building into the function knowledge of the array size). This helps make the function more general. General functions are often reusable in many programs.

The size of the array could have been programmed directly into the function. This restricts the use of the function to an array of a specific size and reduces its reusability. Only programs processing single-subscripted integer arrays of the specific size coded into the function can use the function.

C++ provides the *unary operator* **sizeof** to determine the size of an array (or of any other data type) in bytes during program compilation. When applied to the name of an array, as in Fig. 5.16, the **sizeof** operator returns the total number of bytes in the array as a value of type **size_t** which is usually **unsigned int**. The computer we used here stores variables of type **float** in 4 bytes of memory, and **array** is declared to have 20 elements, so **array** uses 80 bytes in memory. When applied to a pointer parameter in a function that receives an array as an argument, the **sizeof** operator returns the size of the pointer in bytes (4), not the size of the array.

Common Programming Error 5.7

*Using the **sizeof** operator in a function to find the size in bytes of an array parameter results in the size in bytes of a pointer, not the size in bytes of the array.*

```
1   // Fig. 5.16: fig05_16.cpp
2   // Sizeof operator when used on an array name
3   // returns the number of bytes in the array.
```

Fig. 5.16   The **sizeof** operator when applied to an array name returns the number of bytes in the array.

```
4    #include <iostream>
5
6    using std::cout;
7    using std::endl;
8
9    size_t getSize( double * );
10
11   int main()
12   {
13      double array[ 20 ];
14
15      cout << "The number of bytes in the array is "
16           << sizeof( array )
17           << "\nThe number of bytes returned by getSize is "
18           << getSize( array ) << endl;
19
20      return 0;
21   }
22
23   size_t getSize( double *ptr )
24   {
25      return sizeof( ptr );
26   }
```

```
The number of bytes in the array is 80
The number of bytes returned by getSize is 4
```

Fig. 5.16   The **sizeof** operator when applied to an array name returns the number of bytes in the array.

The number of elements in an array also can be determined using the results of two **sizeof** operations. For example, consider the following array declaration:

```
double realArray[ 22 ];
```

If variables of data type **double** are stored in 8 bytes of memory, array **realArray** contains a total of 176 bytes. To determine the number of elements in the array, the following expression can be used:

```
sizeof realArray / sizeof( double )
```

The expression determines the number of bytes in array **realArray** and divides that value by the number of bytes used in memory to store a **double** value.

The program of Fig. 5.17 uses the **sizeof** operator to calculate the number of bytes used to store each of the standard data types on the personal computer we were using.

 Portability Tip 5.3

*The number of bytes used to store a particular data type may vary between systems. When writing programs that depend on data type sizes, and that will run on several computer systems, use **sizeof** to determine the number of bytes used to store the data types.*

```cpp
1   // Fig. 5.17: fig05_17.cpp
2   // Demonstrating the sizeof operator
3   #include <iostream>
4
5   using std::cout;
6   using std::endl;
7
8   #include <iomanip>
9
10
11  int main()
12  {
13     char c;
14     short s;
15     int i;
16     long l;
17     float f;
18     double d;
19     long double ld;
20     int array[ 20 ], *ptr = array;
21
22     cout << "sizeof c = " << sizeof c
23          << "\tsizeof(char) = " << sizeof( char )
24          << "\nsizeof s = " << sizeof s
25          << "\tsizeof(short) = " << sizeof( short )
26          << "\nsizeof i = " << sizeof i
27          << "\tsizeof(int) = " << sizeof( int )
28          << "\nsizeof l = " << sizeof l
29          << "\tsizeof(long) = " << sizeof( long )
30          << "\nsizeof f = " << sizeof f
31          << "\tsizeof(float) = " << sizeof( float )
32          << "\nsizeof d = " << sizeof d
33          << "\tsizeof(double) = " << sizeof( double )
34          << "\nsizeof ld = " << sizeof ld
35          << "\tsizeof(long double) = " << sizeof( long double )
36          << "\nsizeof array = " << sizeof array
37          << "\nsizeof ptr = " << sizeof ptr
38          << endl;
39     return 0;
40  }
```

```
sizeof c = 1     sizeof(char) = 1
sizeof s = 2     sizeof(short) = 2
sizeof i = 4     sizeof(int) = 4
sizeof l = 4     sizeof(long) = 4
sizeof f = 4     sizeof(float) = 4
sizeof d = 8     sizeof(double) = 8
sizeof ld = 8    sizeof(long double) = 8
sizeof array = 80
sizeof ptr = 4
```

Fig. 5.17   Using the **sizeof** operator to determine standard data type sizes.

Operator **sizeof** can be applied to any variable name, type name or constant value. When applied to a variable name (which is not an array name) or a constant value, the number of bytes used to store the specific type of variable or constant is returned. Note that the parentheses used with **sizeof** are required if a type name is supplied as its operand. The parentheses used with **sizeof** are not required if a variable name is supplied as its operand. Remember, that **sizeof** is an operator, not a function.

Common Programming Error 5.8

Omitting the parentheses in a **sizeof** *operation when the operand is a type name is a syntax error.*

Performance Tip 5.2

sizeof *is a compile-time unary operator, not an execution-time function. Thus, using* **sizeof** *does not negatively impact execution performance.*

5.7 Pointer Expressions and Pointer Arithmetic

Pointers are valid operands in arithmetic expressions, assignment expressions and comparison expressions. However, not all the operators normally used in these expressions are valid with pointer variables. This section describes the operators that can have pointers as operands and how these operators are used.

A limited set of arithmetic operations may be performed on pointers. A pointer may be incremented (**++**) or decremented (**--**), an integer may be added to a pointer (**+** or **+=**), an integer may be subtracted from a pointer (**-** or **-=**) or one pointer may be subtracted from another.

Assume that array **int v[5]** has been declared and that its first element is at location **3000** in memory. Assume that pointer **vPtr** has been initialized to point to **v[0]** (i.e., that the value of **vPtr** is **3000**). Figure 5.18 diagrams this situation for a machine with 4-byte integers. Note that **vPtr** can be initialized to point to array **v** with either of the following statements:

```
vPtr = v;
vPtr = &v[ 0 ];
```

Portability Tip 5.4

Most computers today have 2-byte or 4-byte integers. Some of the newer machines use 8-byte integers. Because the results of pointer arithmetic depend on the size of the objects a pointer points to, pointer arithmetic is machine dependent.

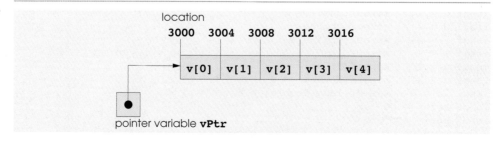

Fig. 5.18   The array **v** and a pointer variable **vPtr** that points to **v**.

In conventional arithmetic, the addition **3000 + 2** yields the value **3002**. This is normally not the case with pointer arithmetic. When an integer is added to or subtracted from a pointer, the pointer is not simply incremented or decremented by that integer, but by that integer times the size of the object to which the pointer refers. The number of bytes depends on the object's data type. For example, the statement

```
vPtr += 2;
```

would produce **3008** (**3000 + 2 * 4**), assuming that an integer is stored in 4 bytes of memory. In the array **v**, **vPtr** would now point to **v[2]** (Fig. 5.19). If an integer is stored in 2 bytes of memory, then the preceding calculation would result in memory location **3004** (**3000 + 2 * 2**). If the array were of a different data type, the preceding statement would increment the pointer by twice the number of bytes it takes to store an object of that data type. When performing pointer arithmetic on a character array, the results will be consistent with regular arithmetic, because each character is one byte long.

If **vPtr** had been incremented to **3016**, which points to **v[4]**, the statement

```
vPtr -= 4;
```

would set **vPtr** back to **3000**—the beginning of the array. If a pointer is being incremented or decremented by one, the increment (**++**) and decrement (**--**) operators can be used. Each of the statements

```
++vPtr;
vPtr++;
```

increments the pointer to point to the next location in the array. Each of the statements

```
--vPtr;
vPtr--;
```

decrements the pointer to point to the previous element of the array.

Pointer variables pointing to the same array may be subtracted from one another. For example, if **vPtr** contains the location **3000** and **v2Ptr** contains the address **3008**, the statement

```
x = v2Ptr - vPtr;
```

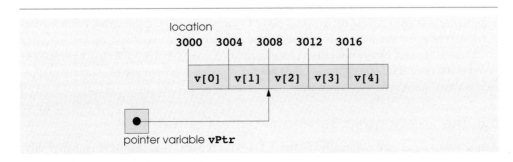

Fig. 5.19   The pointer **vPtr** after pointer arithmetic.

would assign to **x** the number of array elements from **vPtr** to **v2Ptr**, in this case, **2**. Pointer arithmetic is meaningless unless performed on an array. We cannot assume that two variables of the same type are stored contiguously in memory unless they are adjacent elements of an array.

Common Programming Error 5.9

Using pointer arithmetic on a pointer that does not refer to an array of values is normally a logic error.

Common Programming Error 5.10

Subtracting or comparing two pointers that do not refer to elements of the same array is normally a logic error.

Common Programming Error 5.11

Running off either end of an array when using pointer arithmetic is normally a logic error.

A pointer can be assigned to another pointer if both pointers are of the same type. Otherwise, a cast operator must be used to convert the value of the pointer on the right of the assignment to the pointer type on the left of the assignment. The exception to this rule is the pointer to **void** (i.e., **void ***), which is a generic pointer capable of representing any pointer type. All pointer types can be assigned a pointer to **void** without casting. However, a pointer to **void** cannot be assigned directly to a pointer of another type—the **void** pointer must first be cast to the proper pointer type.

A **void *** pointer cannot be dereferenced. For example, the compiler knows that a pointer to **int** refers to four bytes of memory on a machine with 4-byte integers, but a pointer to **void** simply contains a memory location for an unknown data type—the precise number of bytes to which the pointer refers is not known by the compiler. The compiler must know the data type to determine the number of bytes to be dereferenced for a particular pointer. For a pointer to **void**, this number of bytes cannot be determined from the type.

Common Programming Error 5.12

*Assigning a pointer of one type to a pointer of another (other than **void ***) without casting the first pointer to the type of the second pointer is a syntax error.*

Common Programming Error 5.13

*Dereferencing a **void *** pointer is a syntax error.*

Pointers can be compared using equality and relational operators, but such comparisons are meaningless unless the pointers point to members of the same array. Pointer comparisons compare the addresses stored in the pointers. A comparison of two pointers pointing to the same array could show, for example, that one pointer points to a higher numbered element of the array than the other pointer does. A common use of pointer comparison is determining whether a pointer is 0.

5.8 The Relationship Between Pointers and Arrays

Arrays and pointers are intimately related in C++ and may be used *almost* interchangeably. An array name can be thought of as a constant pointer. Pointers can be used to do any operation involving array subscripting.

Good Programming Practice 5.4

Use array notation instead of pointer notation when manipulating arrays. Although the program may take slightly longer to compile, it will probably be clearer.

Assume that integer array **b[5]** and integer pointer variable **bPtr** have been declared. Because the array name (without a subscript) is a pointer to the first element of the array, we can set **bPtr** to the address of the first element in array **b** with the statement

> **bPtr = b;**

This is equivalent to taking the address of the first element of the array as follows:

> **bPtr = &b[0];**

Array element **b[3]** can alternatively be referenced with the pointer expression

> ***(bPtr + 3)**

The **3** in the preceding expression is the *offset* to the pointer. When the pointer points to the beginning of an array, the offset indicates which element of the array should be referenced, and the offset value is identical to the array subscript. The preceding notation is referred to as *pointer/offset notation*. The parentheses are necessary, because the precedence of ***** is higher than the precedence of **+**. Without the parentheses, the above expression would add **3** to the value of the expression ***bPtr** (i.e., **3** would be added to **b[0]**, assuming that **bPtr** points to the beginning of the array). Just as the array element can be referenced with a pointer expression, the address

> **&b[3]**

can be written with the pointer expression

> **bPtr + 3**

The array name can be treated as a pointer and used in pointer arithmetic. For example, the expression

> ***(b + 3)**

also refers to the array element **b[3]**. In general, all subscripted array expressions can be written with a pointer and an offset. In this case, pointer/offset notation was used with the name of the array as a pointer. Note that the preceding statement does not modify the array name in any way; **b** still points to the first element in the array.

Pointers can be subscripted exactly as arrays can. For example, the expression

> **bPtr[1]**

refers to the array element **b[1]**; this expression is referred to as *pointer/subscript notation.*

Remember that an array name is essentially a constant pointer; it always points to the beginning of the array. Thus, the expression

> **b += 3**

is invalid, because it attempts to modify the value of the array name with pointer arithmetic.

Common Programming Error 5.14

Although array names are pointers to the beginning of the array and pointers can be modified in arithmetic expressions, array names cannot be modified in arithmetic expressions, because array names are constant pointers.

Figure 5.20 uses the four methods we have discussed for referring to array elements—array subscripting, pointer/offset with the array name as a pointer, pointer subscripting, and pointer/offset with a pointer—to print the four elements of the integer array **b**.

```cpp
1   // Fig. 5.20: fig05_20.cpp
2   // Using subscripting and pointer notations with arrays
3
4   #include <iostream>
5
6   using std::cout;
7   using std::endl;
8
9   int main()
10  {
11      int b[] = { 10, 20, 30, 40 }, i, offset;
12      int *bPtr = b;    // set bPtr to point to array b
13
14      cout << "Array b printed with:\n"
15           << "Array subscript notation\n";
16
17      for ( i = 0; i < 4; i++ )
18         cout << "b[" << i << "] = " << b[ i ] << '\n';
19
20
21      cout << "\nPointer/offset notation where\n"
22           << "the pointer is the array name\n";
23
24      for ( offset = 0; offset < 4; offset++ )
25         cout << "*(b + " << offset << ") = "
26              << *( b + offset ) << '\n';
27
28
29      cout << "\nPointer subscript notation\n";
30
31      for ( i = 0; i < 4; i++ )
32         cout << "bPtr[" << i << "] = " << bPtr[ i ] << '\n';
33
34      cout << "\nPointer/offset notation\n";
35
36      for ( offset = 0; offset < 4; offset++ )
37         cout << "*(bPtr + " << offset << ") = "
38              << *( bPtr + offset ) << '\n';
39
40      return 0;
41  }
```

Fig. 5.20   Using four methods of referencing array elements (part 1 of 2).

```
Array b printed with:
Array subscript notation
b[0] = 10
b[1] = 20
b[2] = 30
b[3] = 40

Pointer/offset notation where
the pointer is the array name
*(b + 0) = 10
*(b + 1) = 20
*(b + 2) = 30
*(b + 3) = 40

Pointer subscript notation
bPtr[0] = 10
bPtr[1] = 20
bPtr[2] = 30
bPtr[3] = 40

Pointer/offset notation
*(bPtr + 0) = 10
*(bPtr + 1) = 20
*(bPtr + 2) = 30
*(bPtr + 3) = 40
```

Fig. 5.20   Using four methods of referencing array elements (part 2 of 2).

To further illustrate the interchangeability of arrays and pointers, let us look at the two string copying functions—**copy1** and **copy2**—in the program of Fig. 5.21. Both functions copy a string into a character array. After a comparison of the function prototypes for **copy1** and **copy2**, the functions appear identical (because of the interchangeability of arrays and pointers). These functions accomplish the same task, but they are implemented differently.

```cpp
1   // Fig. 5.21: fig05_21.cpp
2   // Copying a string using array notation
3   // and pointer notation.
4   #include <iostream>
5
6   using std::cout;
7   using std::endl;
8
9   void copy1( char *, const char * );
10  void copy2( char *, const char * );
11
12  int main()
13  {
14      char string1[ 10 ], *string2 = "Hello",
15          string3[ 10 ], string4[] = "Good Bye";
```

Fig. 5.21   Copying a string using array notation and pointer notation (part 1 of 2).

```
16
17        copy1( string1, string2 );
18        cout << "string1 = " << string1 << endl;
19
20        copy2( string3, string4 );
21        cout << "string3 = " << string3 << endl;
22
23        return 0;
24   }
25
26   // copy s2 to s1 using array notation
27   void copy1( char *s1, const char *s2 )
28   {
29        for ( int i = 0; ( s1[ i ] = s2[ i ] ) != '\0'; i++ )
30           ;   // do nothing in body
31   }
32
33   // copy s2 to s1 using pointer notation
34   void copy2( char *s1, const char *s2 )
35   {
36        for ( ; ( *s1 = *s2 ) != '\0'; s1++, s2++ )
37           ;   // do nothing in body
38   }
```

```
string1 = Hello
string3 = Good Bye
```

Fig. 5.21   Copying a string using array notation and pointer notation (part 2 of 2).

Function **copy1** uses array subscript notation to copy the string in **s2** to the character array **s1**. The function declares an integer counter variable **i** to use as the array subscript. The **for** structure header performs the entire copy operation—its body is the empty statement. The header specifies that **i** is initialized to zero and incremented by one on each iteration of the loop. The condition in the **for**, (s1[i] = s2[i]) != '\0', performs the copy operation character by character from **s2** to **s1**. When the null character is encountered in **s2**, it is assigned to **s1**, and the loop terminates because the null character is equal to '\0'. Remember that the value of an assignment statement is the value assigned to the left argument.

Function **copy2** uses pointers and pointer arithmetic to copy the string in **s2** to the character array **s1**. Again, the **for** structure header performs the entire copy operation. The header does not include any variable initialization. As in function **copy1**, the condition (*s1 = *s2) != '\0' performs the copy operation. Pointer **s2** is dereferenced, and the resulting character is assigned to the dereferenced pointer **s1**. After the assignment in the condition, the pointers are incremented to point to the next element of array **s1** and the next character of string **s2**, respectively. When the null character is encountered in **s2**, it is assigned to the dereferenced pointer **s1** and the loop terminates.

Note that the first argument to both **copy1** and **copy2** must be an array large enough to hold the string in the second argument. Otherwise, an error may occur when an attempt is made to write into a memory location beyond the boundary of the array. Also, note that the second parameter of each function is declared as **const char *** (a constant string). In both functions, the second argument is copied into the first argument—characters are copied from the second argument one at a time, but the characters are never modified. Therefore, the second parameter is declared to point to a constant value, so the principle of least privilege is enforced. Neither function requires the ability to modify the second argument, so neither function is provided with the capability of modifying the second argument.

5.9 Arrays of Pointers

Arrays may contain pointers. A common use of such a data structure is to form an array of strings, referred to simply as a *string array*. Each entry in the array is a string, but in C++ a string is essentially a pointer to its first character. So each entry in an array of strings is actually a pointer to the first character of a string. Consider the declaration of string array **suit** that might be useful in representing a deck of cards:

```
const char *suit[ 4 ] = { "Hearts", "Diamonds",
                          "Clubs", "Spades" };
```

The **suit[4]** portion of the declaration indicates an array of 4 elements. The **char *** portion of the declaration indicates that each element of array **suit** is of type "pointer to **char**." The four values to be placed in the array are **"Hearts"**, **"Diamonds"**, **"Clubs"** and **"Spades"**. Each of these is stored in memory as a null-terminated character string that is one character longer than the number of characters between quotes. The four strings are 7, 9, 6 and 7 characters long, respectively. Although it appears as though these strings are being placed in the **suit** array, only pointers are actually stored in the array (Fig. 5.22). Each pointer points to the first character of its corresponding string. Thus, even though the **suit** array is fixed in size, it provides access to character strings of any length. This flexibility is one example of C++'s powerful data structuring capabilities.

The suit strings could be placed into a double-subscripted array in which each row represents one suit, and each column represents one of the letters of a suit name. Such a data structure must have a fixed number of columns per row, and that number must be as large as the largest string. Therefore, considerable memory is wasted when a large number of strings is stored with most strings shorter than the longest string. We use arrays of strings to help represent a deck of cards in the next section.

5.10 Case Study: A Card Shuffling and Dealing Simulation

In this section, we use random-number generation to develop a card shuffling and dealing simulation program. This program can then be used to implement programs that play specific card games. To reveal some subtle performance problems, we have intentionally used suboptimal shuffling and dealing algorithms. In the exercises, we develop more efficient algorithms.

Using the top-down, stepwise-refinement approach, we develop a program that will shuffle a deck of 52 playing cards and then deal each of the 52 cards. The top-down approach is particularly useful in attacking larger, more complex problems than we have seen in the early chapters.

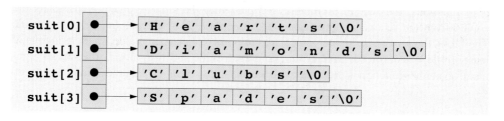

Fig. 5.22   A graphical representation of the **suit** array.

We use a 4-by-13 double-subscripted array **deck** to represent the deck of playing cards (Fig. 5.23). The rows correspond to the suits—row 0 corresponds to hearts, row 1 to diamonds, row 2 to clubs, and row 3 to spades. The columns correspond to the face values of the cards—columns 0 through 9 correspond to faces ace through 10, respectively, and columns 10 through 12 correspond to jack, queen and king, respectively. We shall load string array **suit** with character strings representing the four suits and string array **face** with character strings representing the 13 face values.

This simulated deck of cards may be shuffled as follows. First the array **deck** is cleared to zeros. Then, a **row** (0–3) and a **column** (0–12) are each chosen at random. The number 1 is inserted in array element **deck[row][column]** to indicate that this card is going to be the 1st one dealt from the shuffled deck. This process continues with the numbers 2, 3, …, 52 being randomly inserted in the **deck** array to indicate which cards are to be placed 2nd, 3rd, …, and 52nd in the shuffled deck. As the **deck** array begins to fill with card numbers, it is possible that a card will be selected twice (i.e., **deck[row][column]** will be nonzero when it is selected). This selection is simply ignored, and other **row**s and **column**s are repeatedly chosen at random until an unselected card is found. Eventually, the numbers 1 through 52 will occupy the 52 slots of the **deck** array. At this point, the deck of cards is fully shuffled.

This shuffling algorithm could execute for an indefinitely long period if cards that have already been shuffled are repeatedly selected at random. This phenomenon is known as *indefinite postponement*. In the exercises we discuss a better shuffling algorithm that eliminates the possibility of indefinite postponement.

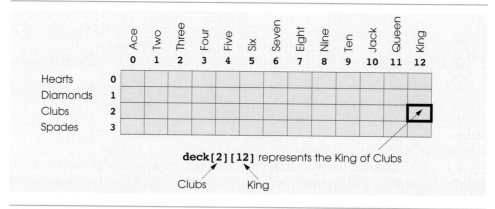

Fig. 5.23   Double-subscripted array representation of a deck of cards.

Performance Tip 5.3

Sometimes an algorithm that emerges in a "natural" way can contain subtle performance problems such as indefinite postponement. Seek algorithms that avoid indefinite postponement.

To deal the first card, we search the array for **deck[row][column]** matching **1**. This is accomplished with a nested **for** structure that varies **row** from 0 to 3 and **column** from 0 to 12. What card does that slot of the array correspond to? The **suit** array has been preloaded with the four suits, so to get the suit, we print the character string **suit[row]**. Similarly, to get the face value of the card, we print the character string **face[column]**. We also print the character string **" of "**. Printing this information in the proper order enables us to print each card in the form **"King of Clubs"**, **"Ace of Diamonds"** and so on.

Let us proceed with the top-down, stepwise-refinement process. The top is simply

> *Shuffle and deal 52 cards*

Our first refinement yields:

> *Initialize the suit array*
> *Initialize the face array*
> *Initialize the deck array*
> *Shuffle the deck*
> *Deal 52 cards*

"Shuffle the deck" may be expanded as follows:

> *For each of the 52 cards*
>   *Place card number in randomly selected unoccupied slot of deck*

"Deal 52 cards" may be expanded as follows:

> *For each of the 52 cards*
>   *Find card number in deck array and print face and suit of card*

Incorporating these expansions yields our complete second refinement:

> *Initialize the suit array*
> *Initialize the face array*
> *Initialize the deck array*
>
> *For each of the 52 cards*
>   *Place card number in randomly selected unoccupied slot of deck*
>
> *For each of the 52 cards*
>   *Find card number in deck array and print face and suit of card*

"Place card number in randomly selected unoccupied slot of deck" may be expanded as follows:

> *Choose slot of deck randomly*
>
> *While chosen slot of deck has been previously chosen*
>   *Choose slot of deck randomly*
>
> *Place card number in chosen slot of deck*

"Find card number in deck array and print face and suit of card" may be expanded as follows:

For each slot of the deck array
*   If slot contains card number*
*   Print the face and suit of the card*

Incorporating these expansions yields our third refinement:

Initialize the suit array
Initialize the face array
Initialize the deck array

For each of the 52 cards
*   Choose slot of deck randomly*

*   While slot of deck has been previously chosen*
*   Choose slot of deck randomly*

*   Place card number in chosen slot of deck*

For each of the 52 cards
*   For each slot of deck array*
*   If slot contains desired card number*
*   Print the face and suit of the card*

This completes the refinement process. Note that this program is more efficient if the shuffle and deal portions of the algorithm are combined, so that each card is dealt as it is placed in the deck. We have chosen to program these operations separately, because normally cards are dealt after they are shuffled (not as they are shuffled).

The card shuffling and dealing program is shown in Fig. 5.24, and a sample execution is shown in Fig. 5.25. Note the output formatting used in function **deal**:

```
cout << setw( 5 ) << setiosflags( ios::right )
     << wFace[ column ] << " of "
     << setw( 8 ) << setiosflags( ios::left )
     << wSuit[ row ]
     << ( card % 2 == 0 ? '\n' : '\t' );
```

The preceding output statement causes the face to be output right justified in a field of 5 characters and the suit to be output left justified in a field of 8 characters. The output is printed in two-column format. If the card being output is in the first column, a tab is output after the card to move to the second column; otherwise, a newline is output.

There is a weakness in the dealing algorithm. Once a match is found, even if it is found on the first try, the two inner **for** structures continue searching the remaining elements of **deck** for a match. In the exercises, we correct this deficiency.

```
1   // Fig. 5.24: fig05_24.cpp
2   // Card shuffling dealing program
3   #include <iostream>
4
```

Fig. 5.24   Card shuffling and dealing program (part 1 of 3).

```
 5   using std::cout;
 6   using std::ios;
 7
 8   #include <iomanip>
 9
10   using std::setw;
11   using std::setiosflags;
12
13   #include <cstdlib>
14   #include <ctime>
15
16   void shuffle( int [][ 13 ] );
17   void deal( const int [][ 13 ], const char *[], const char *[] );
18
19   int main()
20   {
21      const char *suit[ 4 ] =
22         { "Hearts", "Diamonds", "Clubs", "Spades" };
23      const char *face[ 13 ] =
24         { "Ace", "Deuce", "Three", "Four",
25           "Five", "Six", "Seven", "Eight",
26           "Nine", "Ten", "Jack", "Queen", "King" };
27      int deck[ 4 ][ 13 ] = { 0 };
28
29      srand( time( 0 ) );
30
31      shuffle( deck );
32      deal( deck, face, suit );
33
34      return 0;
35   }
36
37   void shuffle( int wDeck[][ 13 ] )
38   {
39      int row, column;
40
41      for ( int card = 1; card <= 52; card++ ) {
42         do {
43            row = rand() % 4;
44            column = rand() % 13;
45         } while( wDeck[ row ][ column ] != 0 );
46
47         wDeck[ row ][ column ] = card;
48      }
49   }
50
51   void deal( const int wDeck[][ 13 ], const char *wFace[],
52              const char *wSuit[] )
53   {
54      for ( int card = 1; card <= 52; card++ )
55
56         for ( int row = 0; row <= 3; row++ )
57
```

Fig. 5.24   Card shuffling and dealing program (part 2 of 3).

```
58            for ( int column = 0; column <= 12; column++ )
59
60                if ( wDeck[ row ][ column ] == card )
61                   cout << setw( 5 ) << setiosflags( ios::right )
62                        << wFace[ column ] << " of "
63                        << setw( 8 ) << setiosflags( ios::left )
64                        << wSuit[ row ]
65                        << ( card % 2 == 0 ? '\n' : '\t' );
66   }
```

Fig. 5.24   Card shuffling and dealing program (part 3 of 3).

```
   Six of Clubs          Seven of Diamonds
   Ace of Spades           Ace of Diamonds
   Ace of Hearts         Queen of Diamonds
 Queen of Clubs          Seven of Hearts
   Ten of Hearts         Deuce of Clubs
   Ten of Spades         Three of Spades
   Ten of Diamonds        Four of Spades
  Four of Diamonds         Ten of Clubs
   Six of Diamonds         Six of Spades
 Eight of Hearts         Three of Diamonds
  Nine of Hearts         Three of Hearts
 Deuce of Spades           Six of Hearts
  Five of Clubs          Eight of Clubs
 Deuce of Diamonds       Eight of Spades
  Five of Spades          King of Clubs
  King of Diamonds        Jack of Spades
 Deuce of Hearts         Queen of Hearts
   Ace of Clubs           King of Spades
 Three of Clubs           King of Hearts
  Nine of Clubs           Nine of Spades
  Four of Hearts         Queen of Spades
 Eight of Diamonds        Nine of Diamonds
  Jack of Diamonds       Seven of Clubs
  Five of Hearts          Five of Diamonds
  Four of Clubs           Jack of Hearts
  Jack of Clubs          Seven of Spades
```

Fig. 5.25   Sample run of card shuffling and dealing program.

5.11 Function Pointers

A pointer to a function contains the address of the function in memory. In Chapter 4, we saw that an array name is really the address in memory of the first element of the array. Similarly, a function name is really the starting address in memory of the code that performs the function's task. Pointers to functions can be passed to functions, returned from functions, stored in arrays and assigned to other function pointers.

To illustrate the use of pointers to functions, we have modified the bubble sort program of Fig. 5.15 to form the program of Fig. 5.26. Our new program consists of **main** and the functions **bubble**, **swap**, **ascending** and **descending**. Function **bubbleSort** receives a pointer to a function—either function **ascending** or function **descending**—as an argument in addition to an integer array and the size of the array. The program prompts the user to choose if the array should be sorted in ascending order or in descending order. If the user enters 1, a pointer to function **ascending** is passed to function **bubble**, causing the array to be sorted into increasing order. If the user enters 2, a pointer to function **descending** is passed to function **bubble**, causing the array to be sorted into decreasing order. The output of the program is shown in Fig. 5.27.

```cpp
1   // Fig. 5.26: fig05_26.cpp
2   // Multipurpose sorting program using function pointers
3   #include <iostream>
4
5   using std::cout;
6   using std::cin;
7   using std::endl;
8
9   #include <iomanip>
10
11  using std::setw;
12
13  void bubble( int [], const int, bool (*)( int, int ) );
14  bool ascending( int, int );
15  bool descending( int, int );
16
17  int main()
18  {
19     const int arraySize = 10;
20     int order,
21         counter,
22         a[ arraySize ] = { 2, 6, 4, 8, 10, 12, 89, 68, 45, 37 };
23
24     cout << "Enter 1 to sort in ascending order,\n"
25          << "Enter 2 to sort in descending order: ";
26     cin >> order;
27     cout << "\nData items in original order\n";
28
29     for ( counter = 0; counter < arraySize; counter++ )
30        cout << setw( 4 ) << a[ counter ];
31
32     if ( order == 1 ) {
33        bubble( a, arraySize, ascending );
34        cout << "\nData items in ascending order\n";
35     }
36     else {
37        bubble( a, arraySize, descending );
38        cout << "\nData items in descending order\n";
39     }
40
41     for ( counter = 0; counter < arraySize; counter++ )
42        cout << setw( 4 ) << a[ counter ];
43
```

Fig. 5.26   Multipurpose sorting program using function pointers (part 1 of 2).

```
44        cout << endl;
45        return 0;
46  }
47
48  void bubble( int work[], const int size,
49               bool (*compare)( int, int ) )
50  {
51      void swap( int * const, int * const );   // prototype
52
53      for ( int pass = 1; pass < size; pass++ )
54
55          for ( int count = 0; count < size - 1; count++ )
56
57              if ( (*compare)( work[ count ], work[ count + 1 ] ) )
58                  swap( &work[ count ], &work[ count + 1 ] );
59  }
60
61  void swap( int * const element1Ptr, int * const element2Ptr )
62  {
63      int temp;
64
65      temp = *element1Ptr;
66      *element1Ptr = *element2Ptr;
67      *element2Ptr = temp;
68  }
69
70  bool ascending( int a, int b )
71  {
72      return b < a;   // swap if b is less than a
73  }
74
75  bool descending( int a, int b )
76  {
77      return b > a;   // swap if b is greater than a
78  }
```

Fig. 5.26   Multipurpose sorting program using function pointers (part 2 of 2).

The following parameter appears in the function header for **bubble**:

```
bool ( *compare )( int, int )
```

This tells **bubble** to expect a parameter that is a pointer to a function that receives two integer parameters and returns a boolean result. Parentheses are needed around ***compare** because * has a lower precedence than the parentheses enclosing the function parameters. If we had not included the parentheses, the declaration would have been

```
bool *compare( int, int )
```

which declares a function that receives two integers as parameters and returns a pointer to a boolean.

```
Enter 1 to sort in ascending order,
Enter 2 to sort in descending order: 1

Data items in original order
   2    6    4    8   10   12   89   68   45   37
Data items in ascending order
   2    4    6    8   10   12   37   45   68   89
```

```
Enter 1 to sort in ascending order,
Enter 2 to sort in descending order: 2

Data items in original order
   2    6    4    8   10   12   89   68   45   37
Data items in descending order
  89   68   45   37   12   10    8    6    4    2
```

Fig. 5.27 The outputs of the bubble sort program in Fig. 5.26.

The corresponding parameter in the function prototype of **bubble** is

```
bool (*)( int, int )
```

Note that only types have been included, but for documentation purposes, the programmer can include names that the compiler will ignore.

The function passed to **bubble** is called in an **if** statement as follows:

```
if ( ( *compare )( work[ count ], work[ count + 1 ] ) )
```

Just as a pointer to a variable is dereferenced to access the value of the variable, a pointer to a function is dereferenced to execute the function.

The call to the function could have been made without dereferencing the pointer, as in

```
if ( compare( work[ count ], work[ count + 1 ] ) )
```

which uses the pointer directly as the function name. We prefer the first method of calling a function through a pointer because it explicitly illustrates that **compare** is a pointer to a function that is dereferenced to call the function. The second method of calling a function through a pointer makes it appear as though **compare** is an actual function. This may be confusing to a user of the program who would like to see the definition of function **compare** and finds that it is never defined in the file.

One use of function pointers is in menu-driven systems. A user is prompted to select an option from a menu (e.g., from 1 to 5). Each option is serviced by a different function. Pointers to each function are stored in an array of pointers to functions. The user's choice is used as a subscript into the array, and the pointer in the array is used to call the function.

The program of Fig. 5.28 provides a generic example of the mechanics of declaring and using an array of pointers to functions. Three functions are defined—**function1**, **function2** and **function3**— that each take an integer argument and return nothing. Pointers to these three functions are stored in array **f**, which is declared as follows:

```
void ( *f[ 3 ] )( int ) = { function1, function2, function3 };
```

The declaration is read beginning in the leftmost set of parentheses as, "**f** is an array of 3 pointers to functions that each take an **int** as an argument and return **void**." The array is initialized with the names of the three functions (which, again, are pointers). When the user enters a value between 0 and 2, the value is used as the subscript into the array of pointers to functions. The function call is made as follows:

```
(*f[ choice ])( choice );
```

In the call, **f[choice]** selects the pointer at location **choice** in the array. The pointer is dereferenced to call the function, and **choice** is passed as the argument to the function. Each function prints its argument's value and its function name to indicate that the function is called correctly. In the exercises, you will develop a menu-driven system.

```cpp
1   // Fig. 5.28: fig05_28.cpp
2   // Demonstrating an array of pointers to functions
3   #include <iostream>
4
5   using std::cout;
6   using std::cin;
7   using std::endl;
8
9   void function1( int );
10  void function2( int );
11  void function3( int );
12
13  int main()
14  {
15     void (*f[ 3 ])( int ) = { function1, function2, function3 };
16     int choice;
17
18     cout << "Enter a number between 0 and 2, 3 to end: ";
19     cin >> choice;
20
21     while ( choice >= 0 && choice < 3 ) {
22        (*f[ choice ])( choice );
23        cout << "Enter a number between 0 and 2, 3 to end: ";
24        cin >> choice;
25     }
26
27     cout << "Program execution completed." << endl;
28     return 0;
29  }
30
31  void function1( int a )
32  {
33     cout << "You entered " << a
34          << " so function1 was called\n\n";
35  }
36
```

Fig. 5.28   Demonstrating an array of pointers to functions (part 1 of 2).

```
37   void function2( int b )
38   {
39      cout << "You entered " << b
40           << " so function2 was called\n\n";
41   }
42
43   void function3( int c )
44   {
45      cout << "You entered " << c
46           << " so function3 was called\n\n";
47   }
```

```
Enter a number between 0 and 2, 3 to end: 0
You entered 0 so function1 was called

Enter a number between 0 and 2, 3 to end: 1
You entered 1 so function2 was called

Enter a number between 0 and 2, 3 to end: 2
You entered 2 so function3 was called

Enter a number between 0 and 2, 3 to end: 3
Program execution completed
```

Fig. 5.28   Demonstrating an array of pointers to functions (part 2 of 2).

5.12 Introduction to Character and String Processing

In this section, we introduce some common standard library functions that facilitate string processing. The techniques discussed here are appropriate for developing text editors, word processors, page layout software, computerized typesetting systems and other kinds of text-processing software. We use pointer-based strings here. Later in the book we include a full chapter on strings as full-fledged objects.

5.12.1 Fundamentals of Characters and Strings

Characters are the fundamental building blocks of C++ source programs. Every program is composed of a sequence of characters that—when grouped together meaningfully—is interpreted by the computer as a series of instructions used to accomplish a task. A program may contain *character constants*. A character constant is an integer value represented as a character in single quotes. The value of a character constant is the integer value of the character in the machine's character set. For example, `'z'` represents the integer value of **z** (122 in the ASCII character set), and `'\n'` represents the integer value of newline (10 in the ASCII character set).

A string is a series of characters treated as a single unit. A string may include letters, digits and various *special characters* such as **+**, **-**, *****, **/** and **$**. *String literals,* or *string constants,* in C++ are written in double quotation marks as follows:

```
"John Q. Doe"              (a name)
"9999 Main Street"         (a street address)
"Waltham, Massachusetts"   (a city and state)
"(201) 555-1212"           (a telephone number)
```

A string in C++ is an array of characters ending in the *null character ('\0')*. A string is accessed via a pointer to the first character in the string. The value of a string is the (constant) address of its first character. Thus, in C++, it is appropriate to say that *a string is a constant pointer*—in fact, a pointer to the string's first character. In this sense, strings are like arrays, because an array name is also a (constant) pointer to its first element.

A string may be assigned in a declaration to either a character array or a variable of type **char ***. The declarations

```
char color[] = "blue";
const char *colorPtr = "blue";
```

each initialize a variable to the string **"blue"**. The first declaration creates a 5-element array **color** containing the characters **'b'**, **'l'**, **'u'**, **'e'** and **'\0'**. The second declaration creates pointer variable **colorPtr** that points to the string **"blue"** somewhere in memory.

Portability Tip 5.5

*When a variable of type **char *** is initialized with a string literal, some compilers may place the string in a location in memory where the string cannot be modified. If you may need to modify a string literal, it should be stored in a character array to ensure modifiability on all systems.*

The declaration **char color[] = "blue";** could also be written

```
char color[] = { 'b', 'l', 'u', 'e', '\0' };
```

When declaring a character array to contain a string, the array must be large enough to store the string and its terminating null character. The preceding declaration determines the size of the array automatically based on the number of initializers provided in the initializer list.

Common Programming Error 5.15

Not allocating sufficient space in a character array to store the null character that terminates a string.

Common Programming Error 5.16

Creating or using a "string" that does not contain a terminating null character.

Good Programming Practice 5.5

When storing a string of characters in a character array, be sure that the array is large enough to hold the largest string that will be stored. C++ allows strings of any length to be stored. If a string is longer than the character array in which it is to be stored, characters beyond the end of the array will overwrite data in memory following the array.

A string can be assigned to an array using stream extraction with **cin**. For example, the following statement can be used to assign a string to character array **word[20]**:

```
cin >> word;
```

The string entered by the user is stored in **word**. The preceding statement reads characters until a space, tab, newline or end-of-file indicator is encountered. Note that the string should be no longer than 19 characters to leave room for the terminating null character. The **setw** stream manipulator introduced in Chapter 2 can be used to ensure that the string read into **word** does not exceed the size of the array. For example, the statement

```
cin >> setw( 20 ) >> word;
```

specifies that **cin** should read a maximum of 19 characters into array **word** and save the 20th location in the array to store the terminating null character for the string. The **setw** stream manipulator only applies to the next value being input.

In some cases, it is desirable to input an entire line of text into an array. For this purpose, C++ provides the function **cin.getline**. The **cin.getline** function takes three arguments—a character array in which the line of text will be stored, a length and a delimiter character. For example, the program segment

```
char sentence[ 80 ];
cin.getline( sentence, 80, '\n' );
```

declares array **sentence** of 80 characters, and then reads a line of text from the keyboard into the array. The function stops reading characters when the delimiter character '**\n**' is encountered, when the end-of-file indicator is entered or when the number of characters read so far is one less than the length specified in the second argument. (The last character in the array is reserved for the terminating null character.) If the delimiter character is encountered, it is read and discarded. The third argument to **cin.getline** has '**\n**' as a default value, so the preceding function call could have been written as follows:

```
cin.getline( sentence, 80 );
```

Chapter 11, "Stream Input/Output," provides a detailed discussion of **cin.getline** and other input/output functions.

Common Programming Error 5.17

Processing a single character as a string can lead to a fatal run-time error. A string is a pointer—probably a respectably large integer. However, a character is a small integer (ASCII values range 0–255). On many systems, this causes an error, because low memory addresses are reserved for special purposes such as operating system interrupt handlers—so "access violations" occur.

Common Programming Error 5.18

Passing a character as an argument to a function when a string is expected can lead to a fatal run-time error.

Common Programming Error 5.19

Passing a string as an argument to a function when a character is expected is a syntax error.

5.12.2 String Manipulation Functions of the String-handling Library

The string-handling library provides many useful functions for manipulating string data, comparing strings, searching strings for characters and other strings, tokenizing strings (separating strings into logical pieces) and determining the length of strings. This section presents some common string manipulation functions of the string-handling library (from the standard library). The functions are summarized in Fig. 5.29.

Note that several functions in Fig. 5.29 contain parameters with data type **size_t**. This type is defined in the header file **<cstddef>** (a header file from the standard library that is included in many other standard library header files, including **<cstring>**) to be an unsigned integral type such as **unsigned int** or **unsigned long**.

 Common Programming Error 5.20

Forgetting to include the **<cstring>** *header file when using functions from the string handling library.*

Function prototype	Function description
char *strcpy(char *s1, const char *s2);	Copies the string **s2** into the character array **s1**. The value of **s1** is returned.
char *strncpy(char *s1, const char *s2, size_t n);	Copies at most **n** characters of the string **s2** into the character array **s1**. The value of **s1** is returned.
char *strcat(char *s1, const char *s2);	Appends the string **s2** to the string **s1**. The first character of **s2** overwrites the terminating null character of **s1**. The value of **s1** is returned.
char *strncat(char *s1, const char *s2, size_t n);	Appends at most **n** characters of string **s2** to string **s1**. The first character of **s2** overwrites the terminating null character of **s1**. The value of **s1** is returned.
int strcmp(const char *s1, const char *s2);	Compares the string **s1** with the string **s2**. The function returns a value of zero, less than zero or greater than zero if **s1** is equal to, less than or greater than **s2**, respectively.
int strncmp(const char *s1, const char *s2, size_t n);	Compares up to **n** characters of the string **s1** with the string **s2**. The function returns zero, less than zero or greater than zero if **s1** is equal to, less than or greater than **s2**, respectively.
char *strtok(char *s1, const char *s2);	A sequence of calls to **strtok** breaks string **s1** into "tokens"—logical pieces such as words in a line of text—delimited by characters contained in string **s2**. The first call contains **s1** as the first argument, and subsequent calls to continue tokenizing the same string contain **NULL** as the first argument. A pointer to the current token is returned by each call. If there are no more tokens when the function is called, **NULL** is returned.

Fig. 5.29   *String manipulation functions of the string handling library (part 1 of 2).*

Function prototype	Function description

```
size_t strlen( const char *s );
```
>   Determines the length of string **s**. The number of characters preceding
>   the terminating null character is returned.

Fig. 5.29   String manipulation functions of the string handling library (part 2 of 2).

Function **strcpy** copies its second argument—a string—into its first argument—a character array that must be large enough to store the string and its terminating null character, which is also copied. Function **strncpy** is equivalent to **strcpy**, except that **strncpy** specifies the number of characters to be copied from the string into the array. Note that function **strncpy** does not necessarily copy the terminating null character of its second argument—a terminating null character is written only if the number of characters to be copied is at least one more than the length of the string. For example, if **"test"** is the second argument, a terminating null character is written only if the third argument to **strncpy** is at least **5** (4 characters in **"test"** plus 1 terminating null character). If the third argument is larger than **5**, null characters are appended to the array until the total number of characters specified by the third argument are written.

Common Programming Error 5.21

Not appending a terminating null character to the first argument of a **strncpy** *when the third argument is less than or equal to the length of the string in the second argument can cause fatal run-time errors.*

Figure 5.30 uses **strcpy** to copy the entire string in array **x** into array **y** and uses **strncpy** to copy the first **14** characters of array **x** into array **z**. A null character (**'\0'**) is appended to array **z**, because the call to **strncpy** in the program does not write a terminating null character. (The third argument is less than the string length of the second argument.)

```cpp
1   // Fig. 5.30: fig05_30.cpp
2   // Using strcpy and strncpy
3   #include <iostream>
4
5   using std::cout;
6   using std::endl;
7
8   #include <cstring>
9
10  int main()
11  {
12      char x[] = "Happy Birthday to You";
13      char y[ 25 ], z[ 15 ];
14
```

Fig. 5.30   Using **strcpy** and **strncpy** (part 1 of 2).

```
15        cout << "The string in array x is: " << x
16            << "\nThe string in array y is: " << strcpy( y, x )
17            << '\n';
18        strncpy( z, x, 14 );   // does not copy null character
19        z[ 14 ] = '\0';
20        cout << "The string in array z is: " << z << endl;
21
22        return 0;
23   }
```

```
The string in array x is: Happy Birthday to You
The string in array y is: Happy Birthday to You
The string in array z is: Happy Birthday
```

Fig. 5.30   Using **strcpy** and **strncpy** (part 2 of 2).

Function **strcat** appends its second argument—a string—to its first argument—a character array containing a string. The first character of the second argument replaces the null character (**'\0'**) that terminates the string in the first argument. The programmer must ensure that the array used to store the first string is large enough to store the combination of the first string, the second string and the terminating null character (copied from the second string). Function **strncat** appends a specified number of characters from the second string to the first string. A terminating null character is appended to the result. The program of Fig. 5.31 demonstrates function **strcat** and function **strncat**.

```
1   // Fig. 5.31: fig05_31.cpp
2   // Using strcat and strncat
3   #include <iostream>
4
5   using std::cout;
6   using std::endl;
7
8   #include <cstring>
9
10  int main()
11  {
12     char s1[ 20 ] = "Happy ";
13     char s2[] = "New Year ";
14     char s3[ 40 ] = "";
15
16     cout << "s1 = " << s1 << "\ns2 = " << s2;
17     cout << "\nstrcat(s1, s2) = " << strcat( s1, s2 );
18     cout << "\nstrncat(s3, s1, 6) = " << strncat( s3, s1, 6 );
19     cout << "\nstrcat(s3, s1) = " << strcat( s3, s1 ) << endl;
20
21     return 0;
22  }
```

Fig. 5.31   Using **strcat** and **strncat** (part 1 of 2).

```
s1 = Happy
s2 = New Year
strcat(s1, s2) = Happy New Year
strncat(s3, s1, 6) = Happy
strcat(s3, s1) = Happy Happy New Year
```

Fig. 5.31   Using **strcat** and **strncat** (part 2 of 2).

Figure 5.32 compares three strings using **strcmp** and **strncmp**. Function **strcmp** compares its first string argument to its second string argument character by character. The function returns zero if the strings are equal, a negative value if the first string is less than the second string and a positive value if the first string is greater than the second string. Function **strncmp** is equivalent to **strcmp**, except that **strncmp** compares up to a specified number of characters. Function **strncmp** does not compare characters following a null character in a string. The program prints the integer value returned by each function call.

Common Programming Error 5.22

*Assuming that **strcmp** and **strncmp** return one when their arguments are equal is a logic error. Both functions return zero (C++'s false value) for equality. Therefore, when testing two strings for equality, the result of the **strcmp** or **strncmp** function should be compared with zero to determine if the strings are equal.*

```
1   // Fig. 5.32: fig05_32.cpp
2   // Using strcmp and strncmp
3   #include <iostream>
4
5   using std::cout;
6   using std::endl;
7
8   #include <iomanip>
9
10  using std::setw;
11
12  #include <cstring>
13
14  int main()
15  {
16     char *s1 = "Happy New Year";
17     char *s2 = "Happy New Year";
18     char *s3 = "Happy Holidays";
19
20     cout << "s1 = " << s1 << "\ns2 = " << s2
21          << "\ns3 = " << s3 << "\n\nstrcmp(s1, s2) = "
22          << setw( 2 ) << strcmp( s1, s2 )
23          << "\nstrcmp(s1, s3) = " << setw( 2 )
24          << strcmp( s1, s3 ) << "\nstrcmp(s3, s1) = "
25          << setw( 2 ) << strcmp( s3, s1 );
26
```

Fig. 5.32   Using **strcmp** and **strncmp** (part 1 of 2).

```
27        cout << "\n\nstrncmp(s1, s3, 6) = " << setw( 2 )
28             << strncmp( s1, s3, 6 ) << "\nstrncmp(s1, s3, 7) = "
29             << setw( 2 ) << strncmp( s1, s3, 7 )
30             << "\nstrncmp(s3, s1, 7) = "
31             << setw( 2 ) << strncmp( s3, s1, 7 ) << endl;
32        return 0;
33    }
```

```
s1 = Happy New Year
s2 = Happy New Year
s3 = Happy Holidays

strcmp(s1, s2) =  0
strcmp(s1, s3) =  1
strcmp(s3, s1) = -1

strncmp(s1, s3, 6) =  0
strncmp(s1, s3, 7) =  1
strncmp(s3, s1, 7) = -1
```

Fig. 5.32   Using **strcmp** and **strncmp** (part 2 of 2).

To understand just what it means for one string to be "greater than" or "less than" another string, consider the process of alphabetizing a series of last names. The reader would, no doubt, place "Jones" before "Smith," because the first letter of "Jones" comes before the first letter of "Smith" in the alphabet. But the alphabet is more than just a list of 26 letters—it is an ordered list of characters. Each letter occurs in a specific position within the list. "Z" is more than just a letter of the alphabet; "Z" is specifically the 26th letter of the alphabet.

How does the computer know that one letter comes before another? All characters are represented inside the computer as numeric codes; when the computer compares two strings, it actually compares the numeric codes of the characters in the strings.

Portability Tip 5.6

The internal numeric codes used to represent characters may be different on different computers.

Portability Tip 5.7

Do not explicitly test for ASCII codes, as in **if (ch == 65)***; rather, use the corresponding character, constant as in* **if (ch == 'A')***.*

In an effort at standardizing character representations, most computer manufacturers have designed their machines to utilize one of two popular coding schemes—*ASCII* or *EBCDIC*. ASCII stands for "American Standard Code for Information Interchange," and EBCDIC stands for "Extended Binary Coded Decimal Interchange Code." There are other coding schemes, but these two are the most popular.

ASCII and EBCDIC are called *character codes,* or *character sets.* String and character manipulations actually involve the manipulation of the appropriate numeric codes and not the characters themselves. This explains the interchangeability of characters and small integers in C++. Since it is meaningful to say that one numeric code is greater than, less than or equal to another numeric code, it becomes possible to relate various characters or strings to one another by referring to the character codes. Appendix B contains the ASCII character codes.

Function **strtok** is used to break a string into a series of *tokens*. A token is a sequence of characters separated by *delimiting characters* (usually spaces or punctuation marks). For example, in a line of text, each word can be considered a token, and the spaces separating the words can be considered delimiters.

Multiple calls to **strtok** are required to break a string into tokens (assuming that the string contains more than one token). The first call to **strtok** contains two arguments, a string to be tokenized and a string containing characters that separate the tokens (i.e., delimiters). In the program of Fig. 5.33, the statement

```
tokenPtr = strtok( string, " " );
```

assigns **tokenPtr** a pointer to the first token in **string**. The second argument, " ", indicates that tokens in **string** are separated by spaces. Function **strtok** searches for the first character in **string** that is not a delimiting character (space). This begins the first token. The function then finds the next delimiting character in the string and replaces it with a null (**'\0'**) character. This terminates the current token. Function **strtok** saves a pointer to the next character following the token in **string** and returns a pointer to the current token.

Subsequent calls to **strtok** to continue tokenizing **string** contain **NULL** as the first argument. The **NULL** argument indicates that the call to **strtok** should continue tokenizing from the location in **string** saved by the last call to **strtok**. If no tokens remain when **strtok** is called, **strtok** returns **NULL**. The program of Fig. 5.33 uses **strtok** to tokenize the string **"This is a sentence with 7 tokens"**. Each token is printed separately. Note that **strtok** modifies the input string; therefore, a copy of the string should be made if the string will be used again in the program after the calls to **strtok**.

Common Programming Error 5.23

Not realizing that **strtok** *modifies the string being tokenized and then attempting to use that string as if it were the original unmodified string.*

```
1   // Fig. 5.33: fig05_33.cpp
2   // Using strtok
3   #include <iostream>
4
5   using std::cout;
6   using std::endl;
7
8   #include <cstring>
9
10  int main()
11  {
12     char string[] = "This is a sentence with 7 tokens";
13     char *tokenPtr;
14
15     cout << "The string to be tokenized is:\n" << string
16        << "\n\nThe tokens are:\n";
17
```

Fig. 5.33   Using **strtok** (part 1 of 2).

```
18        tokenPtr = strtok( string, " " );
19
20        while ( tokenPtr != NULL ) {
21           cout << tokenPtr << '\n';
22           tokenPtr = strtok( NULL, " " );
23        }
24
25        return 0;
26     }
```

```
The string to be tokenized is:
This is a sentence with 7 tokens

The tokens are:
This
is
a
sentence
with
7
tokens
```

Fig. 5.33   Using **strtok** (part 2 of 2).

Function **strlen** takes a string as an argument and returns the number of characters in the string—the terminating null character is not included in the length. The program of Fig. 5.34 demonstrates function **strlen**.

```
1   // Fig. 5.34: fig05_34.cpp
2   // Using strlen
3   #include <iostream>
4
5   using std::cout;
6   using std::endl;
7
8   #include <cstring>
9
10  int main()
11  {
12     char *string1 = "abcdefghijklmnopqrstuvwxyz";
13     char *string2 = "four";
14     char *string3 = "Boston";
15
16     cout << "The length of \"" << string1
17          << "\" is " << strlen( string1 )
18          << "\nThe length of \"" << string2
19          << "\" is " << strlen( string2 )
20          << "\nThe length of \"" << string3
21          << "\" is " << strlen( string3 ) << endl;
22
23     return 0;
24  }
```

Fig. 5.34   Using **strlen** (part 1 of 2).

```
The length of "abcdefghijklmnopqrstuvwxyz" is 26
The length of "four" is 4
The length of "Boston" is 6
```

Fig. 5.34   Using **strlen** (part 2 of 2).

5.13 (Optional Case Study) Thinking About Objects: Collaborations Among Objects

This is the last of our object-oriented design assignments before we begin our study of C++ object-oriented programming in Chapter 6. After we discuss collaborations among objects in this section and OOP techniques in Chapter 6, you will be prepared to begin coding the elevator simulator in C++. To complete the elevator simulator, you will also need the C++ techniques discussed in Chapters 7 and 9. We have included at the end of this section a list of Internet and World Wide Web UML resources and a bibliography of UML references.

In this section, we concentrate on the collaborations (interactions) between objects. When two objects communicate with one another in order to accomplish a task, they are said to *collaborate*—objects do this by sending and receiving messages. A *collaboration* consists of:

1. an object of one class

2. sending a particular message

3. to an object of another class

The message sent by the first class invokes an operation of the second class. In the "Thinking About Objects" section at the end of Chapter 4, we determined many of the operations of the classes in our system. In this section, we concentrate on the messages that invoke these operations. Figure 5.35 is the table of classes and verb phrases from section 4.10. We have removed all the verb phrases that do not correspond to operations. The remaining phrases are the collaborations in our system. We associate the phrases "provides the time to the scheduler" and "provides the time to the elevator" with class **Building** because we have decided that the building will control the simulation. We associate the phrases "increments the time" and "gets the time" with class **Building** for the same reason.

Class	Verb phrases
Elevator	resets the elevator button, sounds the elevator bell, signals its arrival to a floor, opens its door, closes its door
Clock	ticks every second
Scheduler	tells a person to step onto a floor, verifies that a floor is unoccupied
Person	presses floor button, presses elevator button, enters elevator, exits elevator
Floor	resets floor button, turns off light, turns on light

Fig. 5.35   Modified list of verb phrases for classes in the system.

Class	Verb phrases
FloorButton	summons elevator
ElevatorButton	signals elevator to prepare to leave
Door	(opening of door) signals person to exit elevator, (opening of door) signals person to enter elevator
Bell	
Light	
Building	increments the time, gets the time, provides the time to the scheduler, provides the time to the elevator

Fig. 5.35   Modified list of verb phrases for classes in the system.

We examine the list of verbs to determine the collaborations in our system. For example, class **Elevator** lists the phrase "resets the elevator button." To accomplish this task, an object of class **Elevator** must send the **resetButton** message to an object of class **ElevatorButton**, invoking the **resetButton** operation of that class. Figure 5.36 lists all the collaborations that can be gleaned from our table of verb phrases.

An object of class	Sends the message	To an object of class
Elevator	resetButton	ElevatorButton
	ringBell	Bell
	elevatorArrived	Floor
	openDoor	Door
	closeDoor	Door
Clock		
Scheduler	stepOntoFloor	Person
	isOccupied	Floor
Person	pressButton	FloorButton
	pressButton	ElevatorButton
	passengerEnters	Elevator
	passengerExits	Elevator
	personArrives	Floor
Floor	resetButton	FloorButton
	turnOff	Light
	turnOn	Light
FloorButton	summonElevator	Elevator
ElevatorButton	prepareToLeave	Elevator
Door	exitElevator	Person
	enterElevator	Person

Fig. 5.36   Collaborations in the elevator system.

An object of class	Sends the message	To an object of class
Bell		
Light		
Building	tick	Clock
	getTime	Clock
	processTime	Scheduler
	processTime	Elevator

Fig. 5.36   Collaborations in the elevator system.

Collaboration Diagrams

Now let us consider the objects that must interact so that people in our simulation can enter and exit the elevator when it arrives on a floor. The UML provides the *collaboration diagram* to model this interaction. Collaboration diagrams and sequence diagrams both provide information about how objects interact, but each diagram has a different emphasis. Sequence diagrams focus on *when* these interactions occur. Collaboration diagrams focus on *which objects participate* in the interactions.

Figure 5.37 shows a collaboration diagram that models the interactions among objects in the system as objects of class **Person** enter and exit the elevator. The collaboration begins when the elevator arrives on a floor. As in a sequence diagram, an object in a collaboration diagram is represented as a rectangle that encloses the object's name.

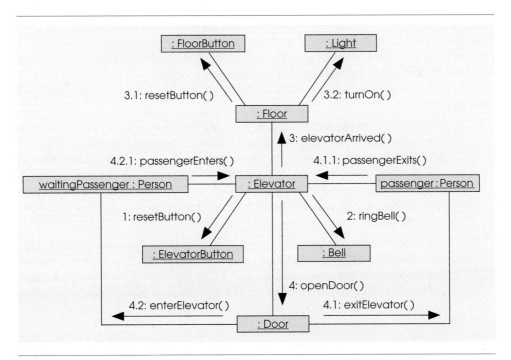

Fig. 5.37   Collaboration diagram for loading and unloading passengers.

Collaborating objects are connected with solid lines, and messages are passed between objects along these lines in the direction shown by the arrows. The name of the message appears next to the arrow.

The *sequence of messages* in a collaboration diagram progresses in numerical order from least to greatest. In this diagram, the numbering starts with message 1. The elevator sends this message (**resetButton**) to the elevator button to reset the button. The elevator then sends the **ringBell** message (message 2) to the bell. Then the elevator notifies the floor of its arrival (message 3), so that the floor can reset its button and turn on its light (messages 3.1 and 3.2, respectively).

After the floor has reset its button and turned on its light, the elevator opens its door (message 4). At this point, the door sends the **exitElevator** message (message 4.1) to the **passenger** object.[1] The **passenger** object notifies the elevator of its intent to exit via the **passengerExits** message (message 4.1.1).

After the person riding the elevator has exited, the person waiting on the floor (the **waitingPassenger** object) can enter the elevator. Notice that the door sends the **enterElevator** message (message 4.2) to the **waitingPassenger** object after the **passenger** object sends the **passengerExits** message to the elevator (message 4.1.1). This sequence ensures that a person on the floor will wait for a person in the elevator to exit before the person on the floor enters the elevator. The **waitingPassenger** object enters the elevator via the **passengerEnters** message (message 4.2.1).

Summary

We now have a reasonably complete listing of the classes that we will need to implement our elevator simulator, as well as the interactions among the objects of these classes. In the next chapter, we begin our study of object-oriented programming in C++. After reading Chapter 6, we will be ready to write a substantial portion of the elevator simulator in C++. After completing Chapter 7, we will implement a complete, working elevator simulator. In Chapter 9, we will discuss how to use inheritance to exploit commonality among classes to minimize the amount of software needed to implement a system.

Let us summarize the object-oriented design process we have used in Chapters 2 through 5.

0. In the analysis phase, meet with the clients (the people who want you to build their system) and gather as much information as possible about the system. With this information, create the use cases that describe the ways in which users interact with the system. (In our case study, we do not concentrate on the analysis phase. The results of this phase are represented in the problem statement, and the use case derived from this statement.) We note again that real-world systems often have many use cases.

1. Begin locating the classes in the system by listing the nouns in the problem statement. Filter the list by eliminating nouns that clearly represent attributes of classes and other nouns that are clearly not part of the software system being modeled. Create a class diagram that models the classes in the system and their relationships (associations).

---

1. In the real world, a person riding on the elevator will wait until the door opens to exit the elevator. We must model this behavior; therefore, we have the door send a message to the **passenger** object in the elevator. This message represents a visual cue to the person in the elevator. When the person receives the cue, the person can exit the elevator.

2. Extract the attributes of each class from the problem statement by listing words and phrases that describe each class in the system.

3. Learn more about the dynamic nature of the system. Create statechart diagrams to learn how the classes in the system change over time.

4. Examine verbs and verb phrases associated with each class. Use these phrases to extract the operations of the classes in our system. Activity diagrams can help model the details of these operations.

5. Examine the collaborations between various objects. Use sequence and collaboration diagrams to model these interactions. Add attributes and operations to the classes as the design process reveals the need for them.

6. At this point, our design probably still has a few missing pieces. These will become apparent as we implement our elevator simulator in C++ beginning in Chapter 6.

UML Resources on the Internet and World Wide Web

The following is a collection of Internet and World Wide Web resources for the UML. These resources include the UML 1.3 specifications and other reference materials, general resources, tutorials, FAQs, articles, whitepapers and software.

References

www.omg.org
Omg.org is the homesite for the Object Management Group (OMG). The OMG is the group responsible for overseeing maintenance and future revisions of the UML. Their Web site contains information about the UML and other object-oriented technologies.

www.rational.com
Rational Software Corporation initially developed the UML. Their Web site contains information about the UML and the creators of the UML—Grady Booch, James Rumbaugh and Ivar Jacobson.

www.omg.org/cgi-bin/doc?ad/99-06-09
This location contains PDF and ZIP versions of the official UML 1.3 specifications.

www.omg.org/techprocess/meetings/schedule/UML_1.4_RTF.html
The OMG maintains at this site information concerning the UML 1.4 specifications, expected to be available beginning in August 2000.

www.rational.com/uml/resources/quick/index.jtmpl
Rational Software Corporation's UML quick-reference guide.

www.holub.com/class/oo_design/uml.html
This site provides a detailed UML quick-reference card with additional commentary.

softdocwiz.com/UML.htm
Kendall Scott, an author of several UML resources, maintains a UML dictionary at this site.

Resources

www.omg.org/uml/
The OMG UML resource page.

www.rational.com/uml/index.jtmpl
Rational Software Corporation's UML resource page

www.platinum.com/corp/uml/uml.htm
UML Partners member Platinum Technology maintains a UML resource page at this location.

www.cetus-links.org/oo_uml.html
This site contains hundreds of links to UML sites, including information, tutorials and software.

www.uml-zone.com
This site contains a wealth of UML information, including articles and links to news groups and to other sites.

home.pacbell.net/ckobryn/uml.htm
This site is maintained by Cris Kobryn, a software architect with UML experience. It contains general information and links to important sites on the Web.

www.methods-tools.com/cgi-bin/DiscussionUML.cgi
This site contains the front page to a UML discussion group.

www.pols.co.uk/usecasezone/index.htm
This site provides resources and articles about applying use cases.

www.ics.uci.edu/pub/arch/uml/uml_books_and_tools.html
This site contains links to information about other books on the UML, as well as a list of tools that support UML notation.

home.earthlink.net/~salhir/
Sinan Si Alhir, author of *UML in a Nutshell*, maintains a site at this location that includes links to many UML resources.

Software

www.rational.com/products/rose/index.jtmpl
This site is the home page for Rational Software Corporation's UML visual modeling tool Rational Rose.™ You can download a trial version from this location and use it free of charge for a limited time period.

www.rosearchitect.com/
Rosearchitect.com is an online magazine, published by Rational Software Corporation, that covers UML modeling using Rational Rose.

www.advancedsw.com/
Advanced Software Technologies is the author of GDPro, a UML visual modeling tool. You can download a trial version from their Web site and use it free for a limited time period.

www.visualobject.com/
Visual Object Modelers has created a visual UML modeling tool. You can download a limited demonstration version from their Web site and use it free for a limited time period.

www.microgold.com/version2/stage/product.html
Microgold Software, Inc. has created *With*Class, a software design application that supports the UML notation.

www.lysator.liu.se/~alla/dia/dia.html
Dia is a gtk+ diagramming tool that can draw UML class diagrams. Dia runs under UNIX, but the Web site also includes a link to a Windows version.

dir.lycos.com/Computers/Software/Object_Oriented/Methodologies/ UML/Tools/
This site lists dozens of UML modeling tools and their home pages.

www.methods-tools.com/tools/modeling.html
This site contains a listing of many object modeling tools, including those that support the UML.

Articles and Whitepapers

www.omg.org/news/pr99/UML_2001_CACM_Oct99_p29-Kobryn.pdf
This article, written by Cris Kobryn, explores the past, present and future of the UML.

www.sdmagazine.com/uml/focus.rosenberg.htm
Here you will find an article with tips on how to incorporate the UML into your projects.

www.db.informatik.uni-bremen.de/umlbib/
The UML Bibliography provides names and authors of many UML-related articles. You can search articles by author or title.

usecasehelp.com/wp/white_papers.htm
This site maintains a list of whitepapers on applying use case modeling to system analysis and design.

www.ratio.co.uk/white.html
You can read a whitepaper that outlines a process for OOAD using the UML at this site. The paper also includes some implementation in C++.

www.tucs.fi/publications/techreports/TR234.pdf
This file contains an OOAD case study of a digital sound recorder using the UML.

www.conallen.com/whitepapers/webapps/ModelingWebApplications.htm
This site contains a case study that models web applications using the UML.

www.sdmagazine.com/
The Software Development Magazine Online site has a repository of many articles on the UML. You can search by subject or browse article titles.

Tutorials

www.qoses.com/education/
This site contains a bank of tutorials created by UML author Kendall Scott and maintained by Qoses.

www.qoses.com/education/tests/test02.html
You can take an on-line UML quiz at this location. The results are e-mailed to you.

www.rational.com/products/rose/tryit/tutorial/index.jtmpl
Rational Software Corporation provides a tutorial file for Rational Rose at this site.

FAQs

www.rational.com/uml/gstart/faq.jtmpl
This is the location of Rational Software Corporation's UML FAQ.

usecasehelp.com/faq/faq.htm
This site contains a small FAQ file maintained by *usecasehelp.com*.

www.jguru.com/jguru/faq/
Enter UML in the search box to access a this site's UML FAQ.

www.uml-zone.com/umlfaq.asp
This site contains a small UML FAQ maintained by *uml-zone.com*.

Bibliography

(Al98)   Alhir, S. *UML in a Nutshell*. Cambridge: O'Reily & Associates, Inc., 1998.

(Bo99)   Booch, G, Rumbaugh, J. and Jacobson, I. *The Unified Modeling Language User Guide*. Reading, MA: Addison-Wesley, 1999.

(Fi98)   Firesmith, D.G. and B. Henderson-Sellers. "Clarifying Specialized Forms of Association in UML and OML." *Journal of Object-oriented Programming* May 1998: 47–50.

(Fo97)   Fowler M. and Scott, K. *UML Distilled: Applying the Standard Object Modeling Language*. Reading, MA: Addison-Wesley, 1997.

(Jo00)   Johnson, L.J. "Model Behavior." *Enterprise Development* May 2000: 20–28.

(Mc98)   McLaughlin, M. and A. Moore. "Real-Time Extensions to the UML." *Dr. Dobb's Journal* December 1998: 82–93.

(Me98)   Melewski, D. "UML Gains Ground." *Application Development Trends* October 1998: 34–44.

(Me97)   Melewski, D. "UML: Ready for Prime Time?" *Application Development Trends* November 1997: 30–44.

(Me99)   Melewski, D. "Wherefore and what now, UML?" *Application Development Trends* December 1999: 61–68.

(Mu97)   Muller, P. *Instant UML*. Birmingham, UK: Wrox Press Ltd, 1997.

(Pe99)   Perry, P. "UML Steps to the Plate." *Application Development Trends* May 1999: 33–36.

(Ru99)   Rumbaugh, J, Jacobson, I. and Booch, G. *The Unified Modeling Language Reference Manual*. Reading, MA: Addison-Wesley, 1999.

(Sc99)   Schmuller, J. *Sam's Teach Yourself UML in 24 Hours*. Indianapolis: Macmillan Computer Publishing, 1999.

(UML99)   *The Unified Modeling Language Specification: Version 1.3*. Framingham, MA: Object Management Goup (OMG), 1999.

SUMMARY

- Pointers are variables that contain as their values addresses of other variables.
- The declaration

      int *ptr;

    declares **ptr** to be a pointer to a variable of type **int** and is read, "**ptr** is a pointer to **int**." The * as used here in a declaration indicates that the variable is a pointer.

- There are three values that can be used to initialize a pointer: **0**, **NULL** or an address of an object of the same type. Initializing a pointer to **0** and initializing that same pointer to **NULL** are identical.

- The only integer that can be assigned to a pointer without casting is zero.

- The **&** (address) operator returns the address of its operand.

- The operand of the address operator must be a variable name (or another **lvalue**); the address operator cannot be applied to constants, to expressions that do not return an **lvalue** or to variables declared with the storage class **register**.

- The * operator, referred to as the indirection, or dereferencing, operator, returns a synonym, alias or nickname for the name of the object that its operand points to in memory. This is called dereferencing the pointer.

- When calling a function with an argument that the caller wants the called function to modify, the address of the argument may be passed. The called function then uses the indirection operator (*) to modify the value of the argument in the calling function.

- A function receiving an address as an argument must have a pointer as its corresponding parameter.

- It is not necessary to include the names of pointers in function prototypes; it is only necessary to include the pointer types. Pointer names may be included for documentation reasons, but the compiler ignores them.

- The **const** qualifier enables the programmer to inform the compiler that the value of a particular variable should not be modified.
- If an attempt is made to modify a **const** value, the compiler catches it and issues either a warning or an error, depending on the particular compiler.
- There are four ways to pass a pointer to a function: a nonconstant pointer to nonconstant data, a nonconstant pointer to constant data, a constant pointer to nonconstant data, and a constant pointer to constant data.
- Arrays are automatically passed by reference using pointers, because the value of the array name is the address of the array's first element.
- To pass a single element of an array by call-by-reference using pointers, the address of the specific array element must be passed.
- C++ provides the special unary operator **sizeof** to determine the size of an array (or of any other data type) in bytes during program compilation.
- When applied to the name of an array, the **sizeof** operator returns the total number of bytes in the array as an integer.
- Operator **sizeof** can be applied to any variable name, type or constant.
- The arithmetic operations that may be performed on pointers are incrementing (**++**) a pointer, decrementing (**--**) a pointer, adding (**+** or **+=**) a pointer and an integer, subtracting (**-** or **-=**) a pointer and an integer and subtracting one pointer from another.
- When an integer is added or subtracted from a pointer, the pointer is incremented or decremented by that integer times the size of the object pointed to.
- Pointer arithmetic operations should only be performed on contiguous portions of memory such as an array. All elements of an array are stored contiguously in memory.
- When performing pointer arithmetic on a character array, the results are like regular arithmetic, because each character is stored in one byte of memory.
- Pointers can be assigned to one another if both pointers are of the same type. Otherwise, a cast must be used. The exception to this is a pointer to **void**, which is a generic pointer type that can hold pointers of any type. Pointers to **void** can be assigned pointers of other types. A void pointer can be assigned to a pointer of another type only with an explicit type cast.
- A pointer to **void** may not be dereferenced.
- Pointers can be compared using the equality and relational operators. Pointer comparisons are normally meaningful only if the pointers point to members of the same array.
- Pointers can be subscripted exactly as array names can.
- An array name is equivalent to a constant pointer to the first element of the array.
- In pointer/offset notation, the offset is the same as an array subscript.
- All subscripted array expressions can be written with a pointer and an offset using either the name of the array as a pointer or a separate pointer that points to the array.
- An array name is a constant pointer that always points to the same location in memory.
- Arrays may contain pointers.
- A pointer to a function is the address where the code for the function resides.
- Pointers to functions can be passed to functions, returned from functions, stored in arrays and assigned to other pointers.
- A common use of function pointers is in so called menu-driven systems. The function pointers are used to select which function to call for a particular menu item.

- Function **strcpy** copies its second argument—a string—into its first argument—a character array. The programmer must ensure that the target array is large enough to store the string and its terminating null character.

- Function **strncpy** is equivalent to **strcpy**, except that a call to **strncpy** specifies the number of characters to be copied from the string into the array. The terminating null character will only be copied if the number of characters to be copied is one more than the length of the string.

- Function **strcat** appends its second string argument—including the terminating null character—to its first string argument. The first character of the second string replaces the null (`'\0'`) character of the first string. The programmer must ensure that the target array used to store the first string is large enough to store both the first string and the second string.

- Function **strncat** appends a specified number of characters from the second string to the first string. A terminating null character is appended to the result.

- Function **strcmp** compares its first string argument with its second string argument character by character. The function returns zero if the strings are equal, a negative value if the first string is less than the second string and a positive value if the first string is greater than the second string.

- Function **strncmp** is equivalent to **strcmp**, except that **strncmp** compares a specified number of characters. If the number of characters in one of the strings is less than the number of characters specified, **strncmp** compares characters until the null character in the shorter string is encountered.

- A sequence of calls to **strtok** breaks a string into tokens that are separated by characters contained in a second string argument. The first call contains the string to be tokenized as the first argument, and subsequent calls to continue tokenizing the same string contain **NULL** as the first argument. A pointer to the current token is returned by each call. If there are no more tokens when **strtok** is called, **NULL** is returned.

- Function **strlen** takes a string as an argument and returns the number of characters in the string—the terminating null character is not included in the length of the string.

TERMINOLOGY

adding a pointer and an integer
address operator (**&**)
appending strings to other strings
array of pointers
array of strings
ASCII
call-by-reference
call-by-value
character code
character constant
character pointer
character set
classes, responsibilities and collaborations (CRC)
comparing strings
const
constant pointer
constant pointer to constant data
constant pointer to nonconstant data
copying strings
<cstring>

decrement a pointer
delimiter
dereference a pointer
dereferencing operator (*****)
directly reference a variable
EBCDIC
function pointer
increment a pointer
indefinite postponement
indirection
indirection operator (*****)
indirectly reference a variable
initialize a pointer
islower
length of a string
literal
nonconstant pointer to constant data
nonconstant pointer to nonconstant data
NULL pointer
numeric code of a character

offset
pointer
pointer arithmetic
pointer assignment
pointer comparison
pointer expression
pointer indexing
pointer/offset notation
pointer subscripting
pointer to a function
pointer to **void** (**void ***)
pointer types
principle of least privilege
simulated call-by-reference
sizeof
strcat
strcmp
strcpy

string
string concatenation
string constant
string literal
string processing
strlen
strncat
strncmp
strncpy
strtok
subtracting an integer from a pointer
subtracting two pointers
token
tokenizing strings
toupper
void * (pointer to **void**)
word processing

"Thinking About Objects" Terminology

collaboration
collaboration diagram
interaction among objects
message
numbers in UML collaboration diagram
objects that participate in interactions

rectangle symbol in UML collaboration diagram
sequence of messages
solid line symbol in UML collaboration diagram
solid line with arrowhead symbol in UML collaboration diagram
when interactions occur

COMMON PROGRAMMING ERRORS

5.1   Assuming that the * used to declare a pointer distributes to all pointer variable names in a comma-separated list of pointer variables in a declaration can lead to pointers being declared as nonpointers. Each pointer must be declared with the * prefixed to the name.

5.2   Dereferencing a pointer that has not been properly initialized or that has not been assigned to point to a specific location in memory could cause a fatal execution time error, or it could accidentally modify important data and allow the program to run to completion providing incorrect results.

5.3   An attempt to dereference a nonpointer is a syntax error.

5.4   Dereferencing a **0** pointer is normally a fatal execution-time error.

5.5   Not dereferencing a pointer when it is necessary to do so to obtain the value to which the pointer points is an error.

5.6   Not initializing a pointer that is declared **const** is a syntax error.

5.7   Using the **sizeof** operator in a function to find the size in bytes of an array parameter results in the size in bytes of a pointer, not the size in bytes of the array.

5.8   Omitting the parentheses in a **sizeof** operation when the operand is a type name is a syntax error.

5.9   Using pointer arithmetic on a pointer that does not refer to an array of values is normally a logic error.

5.10   Subtracting or comparing two pointers that do not refer to elements of the same array is normally a logic error.

5.11   Running off either end of an array when using pointer arithmetic is normally a logic error.

5.12 Assigning a pointer of one type to a pointer of another (other than **void ***) without casting the first pointer to the type of the second pointer is a syntax error.

5.13 Dereferencing a **void *** pointer is a syntax error.

5.14 Although array names are pointers to the beginning of the array and pointers can be modified in arithmetic expressions, array names cannot be modified in arithmetic expressions, because array names are constant pointers.

5.15 Not allocating sufficient space in a character array to store the null character that terminates a string.

5.16 Creating or using a "string" that does not contain a terminating null character.

5.17 Processing a single character as a string can lead to a fatal run-time error. A string is a pointer—probably a respectably large integer. However, a character is a small integer (ASCII values range 0–255). On many systems, this causes an error, because low memory addresses are reserved for special purposes such as operating system interrupt handlers—so, "access violations" occur.

5.18 Passing a character as an argument to a function when a string is expected can lead to a fatal run-time error.

5.19 Passing a string as an argument to a function when a character is expected is a syntax error.

5.20 Forgetting to include the **<cstring>** header file when using functions from the string handling library.

5.21 Not appending a terminating null character to the first argument of a **strncpy** when the third argument is less than or equal to the length of the string in the second argument can cause fatal run-time errors.

5.22 Assuming that **strcmp** and **strncmp** return one when their arguments are equal is a logic error. Both functions return zero (C++'s false value) for equality. Therefore, when testing two strings for equality, the result of the **strcmp** or **strncmp** function should be compared with zero to determine if the strings are equal.

5.23 Not realizing that **strtok** modifies the string being tokenized and then attempting to use that string as if it were the original unmodified string.

GOOD PROGRAMMING PRACTICES

5.1 Although it is not required to do so, including the letters **Ptr** in pointer variable names makes it clear that these variables are pointers and need to be handled appropriately.

5.2 Use call-by-value to pass arguments to a function unless the caller explicitly requires that the called function modify the value of the argument variable in the caller's environment. This is another example of the principle of least privilege.

5.3 Before using a function, check its function prototype to determine the parameters that it can modify.

5.4 Use array notation instead of pointer notation when manipulating arrays. Although the program may take slightly longer to compile, it will probably be clearer.

5.5 When storing a string of characters in a character array, be sure that the array is large enough to hold the largest string that will be stored. C++ allows strings of any length to be stored. If a string is longer than the character array in which it is to be stored, characters beyond the end of the array will overwrite data in memory following the array.

PERFORMANCE TIPS

5.1 Pass large objects such as structures using pointers to constant data, or references to constant data, to obtain the performance benefits of call-by-reference and the security of call-by-value.

5.2   **sizeof** is a compile-time unary operator, not an execution-time function. Thus, using **sizeof** does not negatively impact execution performance.

5.3   Sometimes an algorithm that emerges in a "natural" way can contain subtle performance problems such as indefinite postponement. Seek algorithms that avoid indefinite postponement.

PORTABILITY TIPS

5.1   The format in which a pointer is output is machine dependent. Some systems output pointer values as hexadecimal integers, while others use decimal integers.

5.2   Although **const** is well defined in ANSI C and C++, some compilers do not enforce it properly.

5.3   The number of bytes used to store a particular data type may vary between systems. When writing programs that depend on data type sizes and that will run on several computer systems, use **sizeof** to determine the number of bytes used to store the data types.

5.4   Most computers today have 2-byte or 4-byte integers. Some of the newer machines use 8-byte integers. Because the results of pointer arithmetic depend on the size of the objects a pointer points to, pointer arithmetic is machine dependent.

5.5   When a variable of type **char *** is initialized with a string literal, some compilers may place the string in a location in memory where the string cannot be modified. If you may need to modify a string literal, it should be stored in a character array to ensure modifiability on all systems.

5.6   The internal numeric codes used to represent characters may be different on different computers.

5.7   Do not explicitly test for ASCII codes, as in **if (ch == 65)**; rather, use the corresponding character constant, as in **if (ch == 'A')**.

SOFTWARE ENGINEERING OBSERVATIONS

5.1   The **const** qualifier can be used to enforce the principle of least privilege. Using the principle of least privilege to properly design software can greatly reduce debugging time and improper side effects and can make a program easier to modify and maintain.

5.2   If a value does not (or should not) change in the body of a function to which it is passed, the parameter should be declared **const** to ensure that it is not accidentally modified.

5.3   Only one value can be altered in a calling function when call-by-value is used. That value must be assigned from the return value of the function. To modify multiple values in a calling function, several arguments are passed by call-by-reference.

5.4   Placing function prototypes in the definitions of other functions enforces the principle of least privilege by restricting function calls to the functions in which the prototypes appear.

5.5   When passing an array to a function, also pass the size of the array (rather than building into the function knowledge of the array size). This helps make the function more general. General functions are often reusable in many programs.

TESTING AND DEBUGGING TIP

5.1   Initialize pointers to prevent pointing to unknown or uninitialized areas of memory.

SELF-REVIEW EXERCISES

5.1   Answer each of the following:
   a) A pointer is a variable that contains as its value the _____ of another variable.
   b) The three values that can be used to initialize a pointer are _____, _____ and _____.
   c) The only integer that can be assigned to a pointer is _____.

5.2   State whether the following are *true* or *false*. If the answer is *false*, explain why.
   a)   The address operator **&** can only be applied to constants, to expressions and to variables declared with the storage class **register**.
   b)   A pointer that is declared to be **void** can be dereferenced.
   c)   Pointers of different types may not be assigned to one another without a cast operation.

5.3   Answer each of the following. Assume that single-precision, floating-point numbers are stored in 4 bytes and that the starting address of the array is at location 1002500 in memory. Each part of the exercise should use the results of previous parts where appropriate.
   a)   Declare an array of type **double** called **numbers** with 10 elements, and initialize the elements to the values **0.0, 1.1, 2.2, ..., 9.9**. Assume that the symbolic constant **SIZE** has been defined as **10**.
   b)   Declare a pointer **nPtr** that points to a variable of type **double**.
   c)   Print the elements of array **numbers** using array subscript notation. Use a **for** structure, and assume that the integer control variable **i** has been declared. Print each number with one position of precision to the right of the decimal point.
   d)   Give two separate statements that assign the starting address of array **numbers** to the pointer variable **nPtr**.
   e)   Print the elements of array **numbers** using pointer/offset notation with pointer **nPtr**.
   f)   Print the elements of array **numbers** using pointer/offset notation with the array name as the pointer.
   g)   Print the elements of array **numbers** by subscripting pointer **nPtr**.
   h)   Refer to element 4 of array **numbers** using array subscript notation, pointer/offset notation with the array name as the pointer, pointer subscript notation with **nPtr** and pointer/offset notation with **nPtr**.
   i)   Assuming that **nPtr** points to the beginning of array **numbers**, what address is referenced by **nPtr + 8**? What value is stored at that location?
   j)   Assuming that **nPtr** points to **numbers[5]**, what address is referenced by **nPtr** after **nPtr -= 4** is executed? What is the value stored at that location?

5.4   For each of the following, write a single statement that performs the indicated task. Assume that floating-point variables **number1** and **number2** have been declared and that **number1** has been initialized to **7.3**. Also, assume that variable **ptr** is of type **char *** and arrays **s1[100]** and **s2[100]** are of type **char**.
   a)   Declare the variable **fPtr** to be a pointer to an object of type **double**.
   b)   Assign the address of variable **number1** to pointer variable **fPtr**.
   c)   Print the value of the object pointed to by **fPtr**.
   d)   Assign the value of the object pointed to by **fPtr** to variable **number2**.
   e)   Print the value of **number2**.
   f)   Print the address of **number1**.
   g)   Print the address stored in **fPtr**. Is the value printed the same as the address of **number1**?
   h)   Copy the string stored in array **s2** into array **s1**.
   i)   Compare the string in **s1** to the string in **s2**. Print the result.
   j)   Append the first 10 characters from the string in **s2** to the string in **s1**.
   k)   Determine the length of the string in **s1**. Print the result.
   l)   Assign to **ptr** the location of the first token in **s2**. Tokens in **s2** are separated by commas (**,**).

5.5   Do each of the following:
   a)   Write the function header for a function called **exchange** that takes two pointers to double-precision, floating-point numbers **x** and **y** as parameters and does not return a value.
   b)   Write the function prototype for the function in part (a).

c) Write the function header for a function called **evaluate** that returns an integer and that takes as parameters integer **x** and a pointer to function **poly**. Function **poly** takes an integer parameter and returns an integer.

d) Write the function prototype for the function in part (c).

e) Show two different methods of initializing character array **vowel** with the string of vowels, **"AEIOU"**.

5.6   Find the error in each of the following program segments. Assume the following declarations:

```
int *zPtr;          // zPtr will reference array z
int *aPtr = 0;
void *sPtr = 0;
int number, i;
int z[ 5 ] = { 1, 2, 3, 4, 5 };

sPtr = z;
```

a) ++zPtr;
b) // use pointer to get first value of array
   number = zPtr;
c) // assign array element 2 (the value 3) to number
   number = *zPtr[2];
d) // print entire array z
   for (i = 0; i <= 5; i++)
      cout << zPtr[i] << endl;
e) // assign the value pointed to by sPtr to number
   number = *sPtr;
f) ++z;
g) char s[10];
   cout << strncpy(s, "hello", 5) << endl;
h) char s[12];
   strcpy(s, "Welcome Home");
i) if (strcmp(string1, string2))
      cout << "The strings are equal" << endl;

5.7   What (if anything) prints when each of the following statements is performed? If the statement contains an error, describe the error and indicate how to correct it. Assume the following variable declarations:

```
char s1[ 50 ] = "jack", s2[ 50 ] = "jill", s3[ 50 ], *sptr;
```

a) cout << strcpy(s3, s2) << endl;
b) cout << strcat(strcat(strcpy(s3, s1), " and "), s2)
        << endl;
c) cout << strlen(s1) + strlen(s2) << endl;
d) cout << strlen(s3) << endl;

ANSWERS TO SELF-REVIEW EXERCISES

5.1   a) address. b) **0, NULL**, an address. c) **0**.

5.2   a) False. The address operator can only be applied to variables, and it cannot be applied to constants, expressions, or variables declared with storage class **register**.

b) False. A pointer to **void** cannot be dereferenced, because there is no way to know exactly how many bytes of memory should be dereferenced.

    c) False. Pointers of type **void** can be assigned pointers of other types. Pointers of type **void** can be assigned to pointers of other types only with an explicit type cast.

5.3   a) `double numbers[ SIZE ] = { 0.0, 1.1, 2.2, 3.3, 4.4, 5.5,`
                                     `6.6, 7.7, 8.8, 9.9 };`

    b) `double *nPtr;`

    c) `cout << setiosflags( ios::fixed | ios::showpoint )`
        `<< setprecision( 1 );`
     `for ( i = 0; i < SIZE; i++ )`
       `cout << numbers[ i ] << ' ';`

    d) `nPtr = numbers;`
     `nPtr = &numbers[ 0 ];`

    e) `cout << setiosflags( ios::fixed | ios::showpoint )`
        `<< setprecision( 1 );`
     `for ( i = 0; i < SIZE; i++ )`
       `cout << *( nPtr + i ) << ' ';`

    f) `cout << setiosflags( ios::fixed | ios::showpoint )`
        `<< setprecision( 1 );`
     `for ( i = 0; i < SIZE; i++ )`
       `cout << *( numbers + i ) << ' ';`

    g) `cout << setiosflags( ios::fixed | ios::showpoint )`
        `<< setprecision( 1 );`
     `for ( i = 0; i < SIZE; i++ )`
       `cout << nPtr[ i ] << ' ';`

    h) `numbers[ 3 ]`
     `*( numbers + 3 )`
     `nPtr[ 3 ]`
     `*( nPtr + 3 )`

    i) The address is **1002500 + 8 * 4 = 1002532**. The value is **8.8**.

    j) The address of **numbers[5]** is **1002500 + 5 * 4 = 1002520**. The address of **nPtr -= 4** is **1002520 – 4 * 4 = 1002504**. The value at that location is **1.1**.

5.4   a) `double *fPtr;`

    b) `fPtr = &number1;`

    c) `cout << "The value of *fPtr is " << *fPtr << endl;`

    d) `number2 = *fPtr;`

    e) `cout << "The value of number2 is " << number2 << endl;`

    f) `cout << "The address of number1 is " << &number1 << endl;`

    g) `cout << "The address stored in fPtr is " << fPtr << endl;`
     Yes, the value is the same.

    h) `strcpy( s1, s2 );`

    i) `cout << "strcmp(s1, s2) = " << strcmp( s1, s2 ) << endl;`

    j) `strncat( s1, s2, 10 );`

    k) `cout << "strlen(s1) = " << strlen( s1 ) << endl;`

    l) `ptr = strtok( s2, "," );`

5.5   a) `void exchange( double *x, double *y )`

    b) `void exchange( double *, double * );`

    c) `int evaluate( int x, int (*poly)( int ) )`

    d) `int evaluate( int, int (*)( int ) );`

    e) `char vowel[] = "AEIOU";`
     `char vowel[] = { 'A', 'E', 'I', 'O', 'U', '\0' };`

5.6   a) Error: **zPtr** has not been initialized.
            Correction: Initialize **zPtr** with **zPtr = z;**
        b) Error: The pointer is not dereferenced.
            Correction: Change the statement to **number = *zPtr;**
        c) Error: **zPtr[2]** is not a pointer and should not be dereferenced.
            Correction: Change ***zPtr[2]** to **zPtr[2]**.
        d) Error: Referring to an array element outside the array bounds with pointer subscripting.
            Correction: Change the relational operator in the **for** structure to **<** to avoid walking off
            the end of the array.
        e) Error: Dereferencing a void pointer.
            Correction: In order to dereference the pointer, it must first be cast to an integer pointer.
            Change the above statement to **number = *(int *)sPtr;**
        f) Error: Trying to modify an array name with pointer arithmetic.
            Correction: Use a pointer variable instead of the array name to accomplish pointer arith-
            metic, or subscript the array name to refer to a specific element.
        g) Error: Function **strncpy** does not write a terminating null character to array **s** because
            its third argument is equal to the length of the string **"hello"**.
            Correction: Make the third argument of **strncpy** **6** or assign **'\0'** to **s[5]** to ensure
            that the terminating null character is added to the string.
        h) Error: Character array **s** is not large enough to store the terminating null character.
            Correction: Declare the array with more elements.
        i) Error: Function **strcmp** will return 0 if the strings are equal; therefore, the condition in
            the **if** structure will be false, and the output statement will not be executed.
            Correction: Explicitly compare the result of **strcmp** with **0** in the condition of the **if**
            structure.

5.7   a) **jill**
        b) **jack and jill**
        c) **8**
        d) **13**

EXERCISES

5.8   State whether the following are *true* or *false*. If *false*, explain why.
        a) Two pointers that point to different arrays cannot be compared meaningfully.
        b) Because the name of an array is a pointer to the first element of the array, array names
            may be manipulated in precisely the same manner as pointers.

5.9   Answer each of the following. Assume that unsigned integers are stored in 2 bytes and that
the starting address of the array is at location 1002500 in memory.
        a) Declare an array of type **unsigned int** called **values** with 5 elements, and initialize
            the elements to the even integers from 2 to 10. Assume that the symbolic constant **SIZE**
            has been defined as **5**.
        b) Declare a pointer **vPtr** that points to an object of type **unsigned int**.
        c) Print the elements of array **values** using array subscript notation. Use a **for** structure
            and assume integer control variable **i** has been declared.
        d) Give two separate statements that assign the starting address of array **values** to pointer
            variable **vPtr**.
        e) Print the elements of array **values** using pointer/offset notation.
        f) Print the elements of array **values** using pointer/offset notation with the array name as
            the pointer.
        g) Print the elements of array **values** by subscripting the pointer to the array.

    h) Refer to the fifth element of **values** using array subscript notation pointer/offset notation with the array name as the pointer, pointer subscript notation, and pointer/offset notation.

    i) What address is referenced by **vPtr + 3**? What value is stored at that location?

    j) Assuming **vPtr** points to **values[4]**, what address is referenced by **vPtr -= 4**? What value is stored at that location?

5.10   For each of the following, write a single statement that performs the indicated task. Assume that long integer variables **value1** and **value2** have been declared and that **value1** has been initialized to **200000**.

    a) Declare the variable **lPtr** to be a pointer to an object of type **long**.

    b) Assign the address of variable **value1** to pointer variable **lPtr**.

    c) Print the value of the object pointed to by **lPtr**.

    d) Assign the value of the object pointed to by **lPtr** to variable **value2**.

    e) Print the value of **value2**.

    f) Print the address of **value1**.

    g) Print the address stored in **lPtr**. Is the value printed the same as the address of **value1**?

5.11   Do each of the following.

    a) Write the function header for function **zero** that takes a long integer array parameter **bigIntegers** and does not return a value.

    b) Write the function prototype for the function in part **(a)**.

    c) Write the function header for function **add1AndSum** that takes an integer array parameter **oneTooSmall** and returns an integer.

    d) Write the function prototype for the function described in part **(c)**.

Note: Exercises 5.12 through 5.15 are reasonably challenging. Once you have done these problems, you ought to be able to implement most popular card games easily.

5.12   Modify the program in Fig. 5.24 so that the card dealing function deals a five-card poker hand. Then write functions to accomplish each of the following:

    a) Determine if the hand contains a pair.

    b) Determine if the hand contains two pairs.

    c) Determine if the hand contains three of a kind (e.g., three jacks).

    d) Determine if the hand contains four of a kind (e.g., four aces).

    e) Determine if the hand contains a flush (i.e., all five cards of the same suit).

    f) Determine if the hand contains a straight (i.e., five cards of consecutive face values).

5.13   Use the functions developed in Exercise 5.12 to write a program that deals two five-card poker hands, evaluates each hand, and determines which is the better hand.

5.14   Modify the program developed in Exercise 5.13 so that it can simulate the dealer. The dealer's five-card hand is dealt "face down" so the player cannot see it. The program should then evaluate the dealer's hand, and, based on the quality of the hand, the dealer should draw one, two or three more cards to replace the corresponding number of unneeded cards in the original hand. The program should then reevaluate the dealer's hand. (*Caution:* This is a difficult problem!)

5.15   Modify the program developed in Exercise 5.14 so that it can handle the dealer's hand automatically, but the player is allowed to decide which cards of the player's hand to replace. The program should then evaluate both hands and determine who wins. Now use this new program to play 20 games against the computer. Who wins more games: you or the computer? Have one of your friends play 20 games against the computer. Who wins more games? Based on the results of these games, make appropriate modifications to refine your poker-playing program. (This, too, is a difficult problem.) Play 20 more games. Does your modified program play a better game?

5.16   In the card-shuffling and dealing program of Fig. 5.24, we intentionally used an inefficient shuffling algorithm that introduced the possibility of indefinite postponement. In this problem, you will create a high-performance shuffling algorithm that avoids indefinite postponement.

Modify Fig. 5.24 as follows. Initialize the **deck** array as shown in Fig. 5.38. Modify the **shuffle** function to loop row by row and column by column through the array touching every element once. Each element should be swapped with a randomly selected element of the array. Print the resulting array to determine if the deck is satisfactorily shuffled (as in Fig. 5.39, for example). You may want your program to call the **shuffle** function several times to ensure a satisfactory shuffle.

Note that although the approach in this problem improves the shuffling algorithm, the dealing algorithm still requires searching the **deck** array for card 1, then card 2, then card 3, and so on. Worse yet, even after the dealing algorithm locates and deals the card, the algorithm continues searching through the remainder of the deck. Modify the program of Fig. 5.24 so that once a card is dealt, no further attempts are made to match that card number, and the program immediately proceeds with dealing the next card.

5.17   (*Simulation: The Tortoise and the Hare*) In this problem you will re-create the classic race of the tortoise and the hare. You will use random-number generation to develop a simulation of this memorable event.

Our contenders begin the race at "square 1" of 70 squares. Each square represents a possible position along the race course. The finish line is at square 70. The first contender to reach or pass square 70 is rewarded with a pail of fresh carrots and lettuce. The course weaves its way up the side of a slippery mountain, so occasionally the contenders lose ground.

Unshuffled **deck** array												
	0	1	2	3	4	5	6	7	8	9	10	11	12
0	1	2	3	4	5	6	7	8	9	10	11	12	13
1	14	15	16	17	18	19	20	21	22	23	24	25	26
2	27	28	29	30	31	32	33	34	35	36	37	38	39
3	40	41	42	43	44	45	46	47	48	49	50	51	52

Fig. 5.38   Unshuffled **deck** array.

Sample shuffled **deck** array												
	0	1	2	3	4	5	6	7	8	9	10	11	12
0	19	40	27	25	36	46	10	34	35	41	18	2	44
1	13	28	14	16	21	30	8	11	31	17	24	7	1
2	12	33	15	42	43	23	45	3	29	32	4	47	26
3	50	38	52	39	48	51	9	5	37	49	22	6	20

Fig. 5.39   Sample shuffled **deck** array.

There is a clock that ticks once per second. With each tick of the clock, your program should adjust the position of the animals according to the following rules:

Animal	Move type	Percentage of the time	Actual move
Tortoise	Fast plod	50%	3 squares to the right
	Slip	20%	6 squares to the left
	Slow plod	30%	1 square to the right
Hare	Sleep	20%	No move at all
	Big hop	20%	9 squares to the right
	Big slip	10%	12 squares to the left
	Small hop	30%	1 square to the right
	Small slip	20%	2 squares to the left

Use variables to keep track of the positions of the animals (i.e., position numbers are 1–70). Start each animal at position 1 (i.e., the "starting gate"). If an animal slips left before square 1, move the animal back to square 1.

Generate the percentages in the preceding table by producing a random integer i in the range 1 $\leq i \leq$ 10. For the tortoise, perform a "fast plod" when $1 \leq i \leq 5$, a "slip" when $6 \leq i \leq 7$ or a "slow plod" when $8 \leq i \leq 10$. Use a similar technique to move the hare.

Begin the race by printing

```
BANG !!!!!
AND THEY'RE OFF !!!!!
```

For each tick of the clock (i.e., each repetition of a loop), print a 70-position line showing the letter **T** in the tortoise's position and the letter **H** in the hare's position. Occasionally, the contenders land on the same square. In this case, the tortoise bites the hare, and your program should print **OUCH!!!** beginning at that position. All print positions other than the **T**, the **H** or the **OUCH!!!** (in case of a tie) should be blank.

After printing each line, test if either animal has reached or passed square 70. If so, print the winner and terminate the simulation. If the tortoise wins, print **TORTOISE WINS!!! YAY!!!** If the hare wins, print **Hare wins. Yuch.** If both animals win on the same clock tick, you may want to favor the turtle (the "underdog"), or you may want to print **It's a tie**. If neither animal wins, perform the loop again to simulate the next tick of the clock. When you are ready to run your program, assemble a group of fans to watch the race. You'll be amazed how involved the audience gets!

SPECIAL SECTION: BUILDING YOUR OWN COMPUTER

In the next several problems, we take a temporary diversion away from the world of high-level-language programming. We "peel open" a computer and look at its internal structure. We introduce machine-language programming and write several machine-language programs. To make this an especially valuable experience, we then build a computer (through the technique of software-based *simulation*) on which you can execute your machine-language programs!

5.18   (*Machine-Language Programming*) Let us create a computer we will call the Simpletron. As its name implies, it is a simple machine, but, as we will soon see, a powerful one as well. The Simpletron runs programs written in the only language it directly understands; that is, Simpletron Machine Language, or SML for short.

The Simpletron contains an *accumulator*—a "special register" in which information is put before the Simpletron uses that information in calculations or examines it in various ways. All information in the Simpletron is handled in terms of *words*. A word is a signed four-digit decimal number, such as **+3364**, **–1293**, **+0007**, **–0001**, etc. The Simpletron is equipped with a 100-word memory, and these words are referenced by their location numbers **00, 01, …, 99**.

Before running an SML program, we must *load,* or place, the program into memory. The first instruction (or statement) of every SML program is always placed in location **00**. The simulator will start executing at this location.

Each instruction written in SML occupies one word of the Simpletron's memory. (Thus, instructions are signed four-digit decimal numbers.) We shall assume that the sign of an SML instruction is always plus, but the sign of a data word may be either plus or minus. Each location in the Simpletron's memory may contain an instruction, a data value used by a program or an unused (and hence undefined) area of memory. The first two digits of each SML instruction are the *operation code* that specifies the operation to be performed. SML operation codes are shown in Fig. 5.40.

Operation code	Meaning
Input/output operations:	
`const int READ = 10`	Read a word from the keyboard into a specific location in memory.
`const int WRITE = 11;`	Write a word from a specific location in memory to the screen.
Load and store operations:	
`const int LOAD = 20;`	Load a word from a specific location in memory into the accumulator.
`const int STORE = 21;`	Store a word from the accumulator into a specific location in memory.
Arithmetic operations:	
`const int ADD = 30;`	Add a word from a specific location in memory to the word in the accumulator (leave result in accumulator).
`const int SUBTRACT = 31;`	Subtract a word from a specific location in memory from the word in the accumulator (leave result in accumulator).
`const int DIVIDE = 32;`	Divide a word from a specific location in memory into the word in the accumulator (leave result in accumulator).
`const int MULTIPLY = 33;`	Multiply a word from a specific location in memory by the word in the accumulator (leave result in accumulator).

Fig. 5.40   Simpletron Machine Language (SML) operation codes (part 1 of 2).

Operation code	Meaning

Transfer of control operations:

`const int BRANCH = 40;`	Branch to a specific location in memory.
`const int BRANCHNEG = 41;`	Branch to a specific location in memory if the accumulator is negative.
`const int BRANCHZERO = 42;`	Branch to a specific location in memory if the accumulator is zero.
`const int HALT = 43;`	Halt—the program has completed its task.

Fig. 5.40 Simpletron Machine Language (SML) operation codes (part 2 of 2).

The last two digits of an SML instruction are the *operand*—the address of the memory location containing the word to which the operation applies.

Now let us consider several simple SML programs. The first SML program (Example 1) reads two numbers from the keyboard and computes and prints their sum. The instruction **+1007** reads the first number from the keyboard and places it into location **07** (which has been initialized to zero). Then instruction **+1008** reads the next number into location **08**. The *load* instruction, **+2007**, puts (copies) the first number into the accumulator, and the *add* instruction, **+3008**, adds the second number to the number in the accumulator. *All SML arithmetic instructions leave their results in the accumulator.* The *store* instruction, **+2109**, places (copies) the result back into memory location **09** from which the *write* instruction, **+1109**, takes the number and prints it (as a signed four-digit decimal number). The *halt* instruction, **+4300**, terminates execution.

Example 1 Location	Number	Instruction
00	+1007	(Read A)
01	+1008	(Read B)
02	+2007	(Load A)
03	+3008	(Add B)
04	+2109	(Store C)
05	+1109	(Write C)
06	+4300	(Halt)
07	+0000	(Variable A)
08	+0000	(Variable B)
09	+0000	(Result C)

The SML program in Example 2 reads two numbers from the keyboard and determines and prints the larger value. Note the use of the instruction **+4107** as a conditional transfer of control, much the same as C++'s **if** statement.

Example 2 Location	Number	Instruction
00	+1009	(Read A)
01	+1010	(Read B)
02	+2009	(Load A)
03	+3110	(Subtract B)
04	+4107	(Branch negative to 07)
05	+1109	(Write A)
06	+4300	(Halt)
07	+1110	(Write B)
08	+4300	(Halt)
09	+0000	(Variable A)
10	+0000	(Variable B)

Now write SML programs to accomplish each of the following tasks.

    a) Use a sentinel-controlled loop to read positive numbers and compute and print their sum. Terminate input when a negative number is entered.

    b) Use a counter-controlled loop to read seven numbers, some positive and some negative, and compute and print their average.

    c) Read a series of numbers and determine and print the largest number. The first number read indicates how many numbers should be processed.

5.19 (*A Computer Simulator*) It may at first seem outrageous, but in this problem, you are going to build your own computer. No, you will not be soldering components together. Rather, you will use the powerful technique of *software-based simulation* to create a *software model* of the Simpletron. You will not be disappointed. Your Simpletron simulator will turn the computer you are using into a Simpletron, and you will actually be able to run, test and debug the SML programs you wrote in Exercise 5.18.

When you run your Simpletron simulator, it should begin by printing

```
*** Welcome to Simpletron! ***

*** Please enter your program one instruction ***
*** (or data word) at a time. I will type the ***
*** location number and a question mark (?).  ***
*** You then type the word for that location. ***
*** Type the sentinel -99999 to stop entering ***
*** your program. ***
```

Simulate the memory of the Simpletron with a single-subscripted array **memory** that has 100 elements. Now assume that the simulator is running, and let us examine the dialog as we enter the program of Example 2 of Exercise 5.18:

```
00 ? +1009
01 ? +1010
02 ? +2009
03 ? +3110
04 ? +4107
```

```
05 ? +1109
06 ? +4300
07 ? +1110
08 ? +4300
09 ? +0000
10 ? +0000
11 ? -99999
```

```
*** Program loading completed ***
*** Program execution begins   ***
```

The SML program has now been placed (or loaded) in array **memory**. Now the Simpletron executes your SML program. Execution begins with the instruction in location **00** and, like C++, continues sequentially, unless directed to some other part of the program by a transfer of control.

Use the variable **accumulator** to represent the accumulator register. Use the variable
counter to keep track of the location in memory that contains the instruction being performed.
Use variable **operationCode** to indicate the operation currently being performed (i.e., the left
two digits of the instruction word). Use variable **operand** to indicate the memory location on
which the current instruction operates. Thus, **operand** is the rightmost two digits of the instruction
currently being performed. Do not execute instructions directly from memory. Rather, transfer the
next instruction to be performed from memory to a variable called **instructionRegister**.
Then "pick off" the left two digits and place them in **operationCode**, and "pick off" the right
two digits and place them in **operand**. When Simpletron begins execution, the special registers are
all initialized to zero.

Now let us "walk through" the execution of the first SML instruction, **+1009** in memory location **00**. This is called an *instruction execution cycle*.

The **counter** tells us the location of the next instruction to be performed. We *fetch* the contents of that location from **memory** by using the C++ statement

```
instructionRegister = memory[ counter ];
```

The operation code and operand are extracted from the instruction register by the statements

```
operationCode = instructionRegister / 100;
operand = instructionRegister % 100;
```

Now the Simpletron must determine that the operation code is actually a *read* (versus a *write*, a
load, etc.). A **switch** differentiates among the twelve operations of SML.

In the **switch** structure, the behavior of various SML instructions is simulated as follows (we
leave the others to the reader):

read:	`cin >> memory[ operand ];`
load:	`accumulator = memory[ operand ];`
add:	`accumulator += memory[ operand ];`
branch:	We will discuss the branch instructions shortly.
halt:	This instruction prints the message
	`*** Simpletron execution terminated ***`

It then prints the name and contents of each register, as well as the complete contents of memory.
Such a printout is often called a *computer dump* (and, no, a computer dump is not a place where old
computers go). To help you program your dump function, a sample dump format is shown in Fig.
5.41. Note that a dump after executing a Simpletron program would show the actual values of
instructions and data values at the moment execution terminated.

```
REGISTERS:
accumulator              +0000
counter                     00
instructionRegister      +0000
operationCode               00
operand                     00

MEMORY:
       0       1       2       3       4       5       6       7       8       9
 0 +0000  +0000  +0000  +0000  +0000  +0000  +0000  +0000  +0000  +0000
10 +0000  +0000  +0000  +0000  +0000  +0000  +0000  +0000  +0000  +0000
20 +0000  +0000  +0000  +0000  +0000  +0000  +0000  +0000  +0000  +0000
30 +0000  +0000  +0000  +0000  +0000  +0000  +0000  +0000  +0000  +0000
40 +0000  +0000  +0000  +0000  +0000  +0000  +0000  +0000  +0000  +0000
50 +0000  +0000  +0000  +0000  +0000  +0000  +0000  +0000  +0000  +0000
60 +0000  +0000  +0000  +0000  +0000  +0000  +0000  +0000  +0000  +0000
70 +0000  +0000  +0000  +0000  +0000  +0000  +0000  +0000  +0000  +0000
80 +0000  +0000  +0000  +0000  +0000  +0000  +0000  +0000  +0000  +0000
90 +0000  +0000  +0000  +0000  +0000  +0000  +0000  +0000  +0000  +0000
```

Fig. 5.41   A sample dump.

Let us proceed with the execution of our program's first instruction—**+1009** in location **00**. As we have indicated, the **switch** statement simulates this by performing the C++ statement

```
cin >> memory[ operand ];
```

A question mark (**?**) should be displayed on the screen before the **cin** is executed to prompt the user for input. The Simpletron waits for the user to type a value and then press the *Return key*. The value is then read into location **09**.

At this point, simulation of the first instruction is completed. All that remains is to prepare the Simpletron to execute the next instruction. Since the instruction just performed was not a transfer of control, we need merely increment the instruction counter register as follows:

```
++counter;
```

This completes the simulated execution of the first instruction. The entire process (i.e., the instruction execution cycle) begins anew with the fetch of the next instruction to be executed.

Now let us consider how the branching instructions—the transfers of control—are simulated. All we need to do is adjust the value in the instruction counter appropriately. Therefore, the unconditional branch instruction (**40**) is simulated within the **switch** as

```
counter = operand;
```

The conditional "branch if accumulator is zero" instruction is simulated as

```
if ( accumulator == 0 )
    counter = operand;
```

At this point you should implement your Simpletron simulator and run each of the SML programs you wrote in Exercise 5.18. You may embellish SML with additional features and provide for these in your simulator.

Your simulator should check for various types of errors. During the program loading phase, for example, each number the user types into the Simpletron's **memory** must be in the range **-9999** to

+9999. Your simulator should use a **while** loop to test that each number entered is in this range and, if not, keep prompting the user to reenter the number until the user enters a correct number.

During the execution phase, your simulator should check for various serious errors, such as attempts to divide by zero, attempts to execute invalid operation codes, accumulator overflows (i.e., arithmetic operations resulting in values larger than **+9999** or smaller than **−9999**) and the like. Such serious errors are called *fatal errors*. When a fatal error is detected, your simulator should print an error message such as

```
*** Attempt to divide by zero ***
*** Simpletron execution abnormally terminated ***
```

and should print a full computer dump in the format we have discussed previously. This will help the user locate the error in the program.

MORE POINTER EXERCISES

5.20   Modify the card-shuffling and dealing program of Fig. 5.24 so the shuffling and dealing operations are performed by the same function (**shuffleAndDeal**). The function should contain one nested looping structure that is similar to function **shuffle** in Fig. 5.24.

5.21   What does this program do?

```cpp
1   // ex05_21.cpp
2   #include <iostream>
3
4   using std::cout;
5   using std::cin;
6   using std::endl;
7
8   void mystery1( char *, const char * );
9
10  int main()
11  {
12     char string1[ 80 ], string2[ 80 ];
13
14     cout << "Enter two strings: ";
15     cin >> string1 >> string2;
16     mystery1( string1, string2 );
17     cout << string1 << endl;
18     return 0;
19  }
20
21  void mystery1( char *s1, const char *s2 )
22  {
23     while ( *s1 != '\0' )
24        ++s1;
25
26     for ( ; *s1 = *s2; s1++, s2++ )
27        ;    // empty statement
28  }
```

5.22   What does this program do?

```cpp
1   // ex05_22.cpp
2   #include <iostream>
3
4   using std::cout;
5   using std::cin;
6   using std::endl;
7
8   int mystery2( const char * );
9
10  int main()
11  {
12      char string[ 80 ];
13
14      cout << "Enter a string: ";
15      cin >> string;
16      cout << mystery2( string ) << endl;
17      return 0;
18  }
19
20  int mystery2( const char *s )
21  {
22      int x;
23
24      for ( x = 0; *s != '\0'; s++ )
25          ++x;
26
27      return x;
28  }
```

5.23   Find the error in each of the following program segments. If the error can be corrected, explain how.

a) ```cpp
int *number;
cout << number << endl;
```
b) ```cpp
double *realPtr;
long *integerPtr;
integerPtr = realPtr;
```
c) ```cpp
int * x, y;
x = y;
```
d) ```cpp
char s[] = "this is a character array";
for ( ; *s != '\0'; s++)
    cout << *s << ' ';
```
e) ```cpp
short *numPtr, result;
void *genericPtr = numPtr;
result = *genericPtr + 7;
```
f) ```cpp
double x = 19.34;
double xPtr = &x;
cout << xPtr << endl;
```
g) ```cpp
char *s;
cout << s << endl;
```
```

5.24   (*Quicksort*) In the examples and exercises of Chapter 4, we discussed the sorting techniques of the bubble sort, bucket sort, and selection sort. We now present the recursive sorting technique called Quicksort. The basic algorithm for a single-subscripted array of values is as follows:

   a) *Partitioning Step:* Take the first element of the unsorted array and determine its final location in the sorted array (i.e., all values to the left of the element in the array are less than the element, and all values to the right of the element in the array are greater than the element). We now have one element in its proper location and two unsorted subarrays.

   b) *Recursive Step:* Perform step 1 on each unsorted subarray.

Each time step 1 is performed on a subarray, another element is placed in its final location of the sorted array, and two unsorted subarrays are created. When a subarray consists of one element, it must be sorted, therefore that element is in its final location.

The basic algorithm seems simple enough, but how do we determine the final position of the first element of each subarray. As an example, consider the following set of values (the element in bold is the partitioning element—it will be placed in its final location in the sorted array):

   37   2   6   4   89   8   10   12   68   45

   a) Starting from the rightmost element of the array, compare each element with **37** until an element less than **37** is found. Then swap **37** and that element. The first element less than **37** is 12, so **37** and 12 are swapped. The new array is

   12   2   6   4   89   8   10   **37**   68   45

   Element 12 is in italic to indicate that it was just swapped with **37**.

   b) Starting from the left of the array, but beginning with the element after 12, compare each element with **37** until an element greater than **37** is found. Then swap **37** and that element. The first element greater than **37** is 89, so **37** and 89 are swapped. The new array is

   12   2   6   4   **37**   8   10   *89*   68   45

   c) Starting from the right, but beginning with the element before 89, compare each element with **37** until an element less than **37** is found. Then swap **37** and that element. The first element less than **37** is 10, so **37** and 10 are swapped. The new array is

   12   2   6   4   *10*   8   **37**   89   68   45

   d) Starting from the left, but beginning with the element after 10, compare each element with **37** until an element greater than **37** is found. Then swap **37** and that element. There are no more elements greater than **37**, so when we compare **37** with itself, we know that **37** has been placed in its final location of the sorted array.

Once the partition has been applied on the array, there are two unsorted subarrays. The subarray with values less than 37 contains 12, 2, 6, 4, 10 and 8. The subarray with values greater than 37 contains 89, 68 and 45. The sort continues with both subarrays being partitioned in the same manner as the original array.

Based on the preceding discussion, write recursive function **quickSort** to sort a single-subscripted integer array. The function should receive as arguments an integer array, a starting subscript and an ending subscript. Function **partition** should be called by **quickSort** to perform the partitioning step.

5.25   (*Maze Traversal*) The following grid of hashes (**#**) and dots (**.**) is a double-subscripted array representation of a maze:

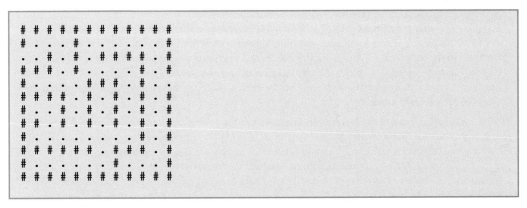

In the preceding double-subscripted array, the hashes (#), represent the walls of the maze and the dots represent squares in the possible paths through the maze. Moves can only be made to a location in the array that contains a dot.

There is a simple algorithm for walking through a maze that guarantees finding the exit (assuming that there is an exit). If there is not an exit, you will arrive at the starting location again. Place your right hand on the wall to your right and begin walking forward. Never remove your hand from the wall. If the maze turns to the right, you follow the wall to the right. As long as you do not remove your hand from the wall, eventually you will arrive at the exit of the maze. There may be a shorter path than the one you have taken, but you are guaranteed to get out of the maze if you follow the algorithm.

Write recursive function **mazeTraverse** to walk through the maze. The function should receive as arguments a 12-by-12 character array representing the maze and the starting location of the maze. As **mazeTraverse** attempts to locate the exit from the maze, it should place the character **X** in each square in the path. The function should display the maze after each move so the user can watch as the maze is solved.

5.26 (*Generating Mazes Randomly*) Write a function **mazeGenerator** that takes as an argument a double-subscripted 12-by-12 character array and randomly produces a maze. The function should also provide the starting and ending locations of the maze. Try your function **mazeTraverse** from Exercise 5.25 using several randomly generated mazes.

5.27 (*Mazes of Any Size*) Generalize functions **mazeTraverse** and **mazeGenerator** of Exercises 5.25 and 5.26 to process mazes of any width and height.

5.28 (*Arrays of Pointers to Functions*) Rewrite the program of Fig. 4.23 to use a menu-driven interface. The program should offer the user five options as follows (these should be displayed on the screen):

```
Enter a choice:
   0   Print the array of grades
   1   Find the minimum grade
   2   Find the maximum grade
   3   Print the average on all tests for each student
   4   End program
```

One restriction on using arrays of pointers to functions is that all the pointers must have the same type. The pointers must be to functions of the same return type that receive arguments of the same type. For this reason, the functions in Fig. 4.23 must be modified so they each return the same type and take the same parameters. Modify functions **minimum** and **maximum** to print the minimum or maximum value and return nothing. For option 3, modify function **average** of Fig. 4.23 to output the average for each student (not a specific student). Function **average** should return nothing and take the same parameters as **printArray**, **minimum** and **maximum**. Store the pointers to the four functions in array **processGrades**, and use the choice made by the user as the subscript into the array for calling each function.

5.29 (*Modifications to the Simpletron Simulator*) In Exercise 5.19, you wrote a software simulation of a computer that executes programs written in Simpletron Machine Language (SML). In this exercise, we propose several modifications and enhancements to the Simpletron Simulator. In Exercises 15.26 and 15.27, we propose building a compiler that converts programs written in a high-level programming language (a variation of BASIC) to SML. Some of the following modifications and enhancements may be required to execute the programs produced by the compiler. (*Note:* Some modifications may conflict with others and therefore must be done separately.)

   a) Extend the Simpletron Simulator's memory to contain 1000 memory locations to enable the Simpletron to handle larger programs.
   b) Allow the simulator to perform modulus calculations. This requires an additional Simpletron Machine Language instruction.
   c) Allow the simulator to perform exponentiation calculations. This requires an additional Simpletron Machine Language instruction.
   d) Modify the simulator to use hexadecimal values rather than integer values to represent Simpletron Machine Language instructions.
   e) Modify the simulator to allow output of a newline. This requires an additional Simpletron Machine Language instruction.
   f) Modify the simulator to process floating-point values in addition to integer values.
   g) Modify the simulator to handle string input. [*Hint:* Each Simpletron word can be divided into two groups, each holding a two-digit integer. Each two-digit integer represents the ASCII decimal equivalent of a character. Add a machine-language instruction that will input a string and store the string beginning at a specific Simpletron memory location. The first half of the word at that location will be a count of the number of characters in the string (i.e., the length of the string). Each succeeding half-word contains one ASCII character expressed as two decimal digits. The machine-language instruction converts each character into its ASCII equivalent and assigns it to a half-word.]
   h) Modify the simulator to handle output of strings stored in the format of part (g). [*Hint:* Add a machine language instruction that will print a string beginning at a certain Simpletron memory location. The first half of the word at that location is a count of the number of characters in the string (i.e., the length of the string). Each succeeding half-word contains one ASCII character expressed as two decimal digits. The machine-language instruction checks the length and prints the string by translating each two-digit number into its equivalent character.]
   i) Modify the simulator to include instruction **SML_DEBUG** that prints a memory dump after each instruction is executed. Give **SML_DEBUG** an operation code of **44**. The word **+4401** turns on debug mode and **+4400** turns off debug mode.

5.30 What does this program do?

```
1   // ex05_30.cpp
2   #include <iostream>
3
4   using std::cout;
```

```
 5   using std::cin;
 6   using std::endl;
 7
 8   bool mystery3( const char *, const char * );
 9
10   int main()
11   {
12      char string1[ 80 ], string2[ 80 ];
13
14      cout << "Enter two strings: ";
15      cin >> string1 >> string2;
16      cout << "The result is "
17           << mystery3( string1, string2 ) << endl;
18
19      return 0;
20   }
21
22   bool mystery3( const char *s1, const char *s2 )
23   {
24      for ( ; *s1 != '\0' && *s2 != '\0'; s1++, s2++ )
25
26         if ( *s1 != *s2 )
27            return false;
28
29      return true;
30   }
```

STRING MANIPULATION EXERCISES

5.31 Write a program that uses function **strcmp** to compare two strings input by the user. The program should state whether the first string is less than, equal to or greater than the second string.

5.32 Write a program that uses function **strncmp** to compare two strings input by the user. The program should input the number of characters to be compared. The program should state whether the first string is less than, equal to or greater than the second string.

5.33 Write a program that uses random-number generation to create sentences. The program should use four arrays of pointers to **char** called **article**, **noun**, **verb** and **preposition**. The program should create a sentence by selecting a word at random from each array in the following order: **article**, **noun**, **verb**, **preposition**, **article** and **noun**. As each word is picked, it should be concatenated to the previous words in an array that is large enough to hold the entire sentence. The words should be separated by spaces. When the final sentence is output, it should start with a capital letter and end with a period. The program should generate 20 such sentences.

The arrays should be filled as follows: the **article** array should contain the articles **"the"**, **"a"**, **"one"**, **"some"** and **"any"**; the **noun** array should contain the nouns **"boy"**, **"girl"**, **"dog"**, **"town"** and **"car"**; the **verb** array should contain the verbs **"drove"**, **"jumped"**, **"ran"**, **"walked"** and **"skipped"**; the **preposition** array should contain the prepositions **"to"**, **"from"**, **"over"**, **"under"** and **"on"**.

After the preceding program is written and working, modify the program to produce a short story consisting of several of these sentences. (How about the possibility of a random term paper writer!)

5.34 *(Limericks)* A limerick is a humorous five-line verse in which the first and second lines rhyme with the fifth, and the third line rhymes with the fourth. Using techniques similar to those developed in Exercise 5.33, write a C++ program that produces random limericks. Polishing this program to produce good limericks is a challenging problem, but the result will be worth the effort!

5.35   Write a program that encodes English language phrases into pig Latin. Pig Latin is a form of coded language often used for amusement. Many variations exist in the methods used to form pig Latin phrases. For simplicity, use the following algorithm:

> To form a pig-Latin phrase from an English-language phrase, tokenize the phrase into words with function **strtok**. To translate each English word into a pig-Latin word, place the first letter of the English word at the end of the English word, and add the letters "**ay**." Thus the word "**jump**" becomes "**umpjay**," the word "**the**" becomes "**hetay**" and the word "**computer**" becomes "**omputercay**." Blanks between words remain as blanks. Assume that the: the English phrase consists of words separated by blanks, there are no punctuation marks and all words have two or more letters. Function **printLatinWord** should display each word. (*Hint:* Each time a token is found in a call to **strtok**, pass the token pointer to function **printLatinWord**, and print the pig Latin word.)

5.36   Write a program that inputs a telephone number as a string in the form **(555) 555-5555**. The program should use function **strtok** to extract the area code as a token, the first three digits of the phone number as a token, and the last four digits of the phone number as a token. The seven digits of the phone number should be concatenated into one string. The program should convert the area code string to **int** and convert the phone number string to **long**. Both the area code and the phone number should be printed.

5.37   Write a program that inputs a line of text, tokenizes the line with function **strtok** and outputs the tokens in reverse order.

5.38   Use the string comparison functions discussed in Section 5.12.2 and the techniques for sorting arrays developed in Chapter 4 to write a program that alphabetizes a list of strings. Use the names of 10 or 15 towns in your area as data for your program.

5.39   Write two versions of each of the string copy and string concatenation functions in Fig. 5.29. The first version should use array subscripting, and the second version should use pointers and pointer arithmetic.

5.40   Write two versions of each string comparison function in Fig. 5.29. The first version should use array subscripting, and the second version should use pointers and pointer arithmetic.

5.41   Write two versions of function **strlen** in Fig. 5.29. The first version should use array subscripting, and the second version should use pointers and pointer arithmetic.

SPECIAL SECTION: ADVANCED STRING MANIPULATION EXERCISES

The preceding exercises are keyed to the text and designed to test the reader's understanding of fundamental string manipulation concepts. This section includes a collection of intermediate and advanced string manipulation exercises. The reader should find these problems challenging, yet enjoyable. The problems vary considerably in difficulty. Some require an hour or two of program writing and implementation. Others are useful for lab assignments that might require two or three weeks of study and implementation. Some are challenging term projects.

5.42   *(Text Analysis)* The availability of computers with string manipulation capabilities has resulted in some rather interesting approaches to analyzing the writings of great authors. Much attention has been focused on whether William Shakespeare ever lived. Some scholars believe there is substantial evidence indicating that Christopher Marlowe or other authors actually penned the masterpieces attributed to Shakespeare. Researchers have used computers to find similarities in the writings of these two authors. This exercise examines three methods for analyzing texts with a computer.

a) Write a program that reads several lines of text from the keyboard and prints a table indicating the number of occurrences of each letter of the alphabet in the text. For example, the phrase

To be, or not to be: that is the question:

contains one "a," two "b's," no "c's," etc.

b) Write a program that reads several lines of text and prints a table indicating the number of one-letter words, two-letter words, three-letter words, etc., appearing in the text. For example, the phrase

Whether 'tis nobler in the mind to suffer

contains

Word length	Occurrences
1	0
2	2
3	1
4	2 (including 'tis)
5	0
6	2
7	1

c) Write a program that reads several lines of text and prints a table indicating the number of occurrences of each different word in the text. The first version of your program should include the words in the table in the same order in which they appear in the text. For example, the lines

To be, or not to be: that is the question:
Whether 'tis nobler in the mind to suffer

d) contain the words "to" three times, the word "be" two times, the word "or" once, etc. A more interesting (and useful) printout should then be attempted in which the words are sorted alphabetically.

5.43   *(Word Processing)* One important function in word-processing systems is *type justification*—the alignment of words to both the left and right margins of a page. This generates a professional-looking document that gives the appearance of being set in type rather than prepared on a typewriter. Type justification can be accomplished on computer systems by inserting blank characters between each of the words in a line so that the rightmost word aligns with the right margin.

Write a program that reads several lines of text and prints this text in type-justified format. Assume that the text is to be printed on 8-1/2-inch-wide paper, and that one-inch margins are to be allowed on both the left and right sides of the printed page. Assume that the computer prints 10 characters to the horizontal inch. Therefore, your program should print 6 1/2 inches of text, or 65 characters per line.

5.44   *(Printing Dates in Various Formats)* Dates are commonly printed in several different formats in business correspondence. Two of the more common formats are

07/21/1955 and **July 21, 1955**

Write a program that reads a date in the first format and prints that date in the second format.

5.45   *(Check Protection)* Computers are frequently employed in check-writing systems such as payroll and accounts payable applications. Many strange stories circulate regarding weekly paychecks being printed (by mistake) for amounts in excess of $1 million. Weird amounts are printed by computerized check-writing systems, because of human error or machine failure. Systems designers build controls into their systems to prevent such erroneous checks from being issued.

Another serious problem is the intentional alteration of a check amount by someone who intends to cash a check fraudulently. To prevent a dollar amount from being altered, most computerized check-writing systems employ a technique called *check protection.*

Checks designed for imprinting by computer contain a fixed number of spaces in which the computer may print an amount. Suppose a paycheck contains eight blank spaces in which the computer is supposed to print the amount of a weekly paycheck. If the amount is large, then all eight of those spaces will be filled, for example,

```
1,230.60    (check amount)
--------
12345678    (position numbers)
```

On the other hand, if the amount is less than $1000, then several of the spaces would ordinarily be left blank. For example,

```
  99.87
--------
12345678
```

contains three blank spaces. If a check is printed with blank spaces, it is easier for someone to alter the amount of the check. To prevent a check from being altered, many check-writing systems insert *leading asterisks* to protect the amount as follows:

```
***99.87
--------
12345678
```

Write a program that inputs a dollar amount to be printed on a check and then prints the amount in check-protected format with leading asterisks if necessary. Assume that nine spaces are available for printing an amount.

5.46   *(Writing the Word Equivalent of a Check Amount)* Continuing the discussion of the previous example, we reiterate the importance of designing check-writing systems to prevent alteration of check amounts. One common security method requires that the check amount be written both in numbers, and "spelled out" in words as well. Even if someone is able to alter the numerical amount of the check, it is extremely difficult to change the amount in words.

Many computerized check-writing systems do not print the amount of the check in words. Perhaps the main reason for this omission is the fact that most high-level languages used in commercial applications do not contain adequate string manipulation features. Another reason is that the logic for writing word equivalents of check amounts is somewhat involved.

Write a program that inputs a numeric check amount and writes the word equivalent of the amount. For example, the amount 112.43 should be written as

ONE HUNDRED TWELVE and 43/100

5.47   *(Morse Code)* Perhaps the most famous of all coding schemes is the Morse code, developed by Samuel Morse in 1832 for use with the telegraph system. The Morse code assigns a series of dots and dashes to each letter of the alphabet, each digit and a few special characters (such as period, comma, colon and semicolon). In sound-oriented systems, the dot represents a short sound, and the dash represents a long sound. Other representations of dots and dashes are used with light-oriented systems and signal-flag systems.

Separation between words is indicated by a space, or, quite simply, the absence of a dot or dash. In a sound-oriented system, a space is indicated by a short period of time during which no sound is transmitted. The international version of the Morse code appears in Fig. 5.42.

Write a program that reads an English-language phrase and encodes the phrase into Morse code. Also write a program that reads a phrase in Morse code and converts the phrase into the English-language equivalent. Use one blank between each Morse-coded letter and three blanks between each Morse-coded word.

5.48 *(A Metric Conversion Program)* Write a program that will assist the user with metric conversions. Your program should allow the user to specify the names of the units as strings (i.e., centimeters, liters, grams, etc. for the metric system and inches, quarts, pounds, etc., for the English system) and should respond to simple questions such as

```
"How many inches are in 2 meters?"
"How many liters are in 10 quarts?"
```

Character	Code	Character	Code
A	.−	T	−
B	−...	U	..−
C	−.−.	V	...−
D	−..	W	.−−
E	.	X	−..−
F	..−.	Y	−.−−
G	−−.	Z	−−..
H	....		
I	..	*Digits*	
J	.−−−	1	.−−−−
K	−.−	2	..−−−
L	.−..	3	...−−
M	−−	4	....−
N	−.	5	.....
O	−−−	6	−....
P	.−−.	7	−−...
Q	−−.−	8	−−−..
R	.−.	9	−−−−.
S	...	0	−−−−−

Fig. 5.42 The letters of the alphabet as expressed in international Morse code.

Your program should recognize invalid conversions. For example, the question

    "How many feet in 5 kilograms?"

is not meaningful, because **"feet"** are units of length, while **"kilograms"** are units of weight.

A CHALLENGING STRING MANIPULATION PROJECT

5.49   *(A Crossword Puzzle Generator)* Most people have worked a crossword puzzle, but few have ever attempted to generate one. Generating a crossword puzzle is a difficult problem. It is suggested here as a string manipulation project requiring substantial sophistication and effort. There are many issues the programmer must resolve to get even the simplest crossword puzzle generator program working. For example, how does one represent the grid of a crossword puzzle inside the computer? Should one use a series of strings, or should double-subscripted arrays be used? The programmer needs a source of words (i.e., a computerized dictionary) that can be directly referenced by the program. In what form should these words be stored to facilitate the complex manipulations required by the program? The really ambitious reader will want to generate the "clues" portion of the puzzle in which the brief hints for each "across" word and each "down" word are printed for the puzzle worker. Merely printing a version of the blank puzzle itself is not a simple problem.

6

Classes and Data Abstraction

Objectives

- To understand the software engineering concepts of encapsulation and data hiding.
- To understand the notions of data abstraction and abstract data types (ADTs).
- To be able to create C++ ADTs, namely classes.
- To understand how to create, use, and destroy class objects.
- To be able to control access to object data members and member functions.
- To begin to appreciate the value of object orientation.

My object all sublime
I shall achieve in time.
W. S. Gilbert

Is it a world to hide virtues in?
William Shakespeare, Twelfth Night

Your public servants serve you right.
Adlai Stevenson

Private faces in public places
Are wiser and nicer
Than public faces in private places.
W. H. Auden

Outline

6.1 Introduction

Now we begin our introduction to object orientation in C++. Why have we deferred object-oriented programming in C++ until Chapter 6? The answer is that the objects we will build will be composed in part of structured program pieces, so we needed to establish a basis in structured programming first.

Through our "Thinking About Objects" sections at the ends of Chapters 1 through 5, we have introduced the basic concepts (i.e., "object think") and terminology (i.e., "object speak") of object-oriented programming in C++. In these special sections, we also discussed the techniques of *object-oriented design (OOD):* We analyzed a typical problem statement that required a system (an elevator simulator) to be built, determined what classes were needed to implement the systems, determined what attributes objects of these classes needed to have, determined what behaviors objects of these classes needed to exhibit, and specified how the objects needed to interact with one another to accomplish the overall goals of the system.

Let us briefly review some key concepts and terminology of object orientation. Object-oriented programming (OOP) *encapsulates* data (attributes) and functions (behavior) into packages called *classes;* the data and functions of a class are intimately tied together. A class is like a blueprint. Out of a blueprint, a builder can build a house. Out of a class, a programmer can create an object. One blueprint can be reused many times to make many houses. One class can be reused many times to make many objects of the same class. Classes have the property of *information hiding.* This means that although class objects may know how to communicate with one another across well-defined *interfaces,* classes normally are not allowed to know how other classes are implemented—implementation details are hidden within the classes themselves. Surely it is possible to drive a car effectively without knowing the details of how engines, transmissions and exhaust systems work internally. We will see why information hiding is so crucial to good software engineering.

In C and other *procedural programming languages,* programming tends to be *caction-oriented,* whereas ideally in C++ programming is *object-oriented.* In C, the unit of programming is the *function.* In C++, the unit of programming is the *class* from which objects are eventually *instantiated* (i.e., created).

C programmers concentrate on writing functions. Groups of actions that perform some task are formed into functions, and functions are grouped to form programs. Data are certainly important in C, but the view is that data exist primarily in support of the actions that functions perform. The *verbs* in a system specification help the C programmer determine the set of functions that will work together to implement the system.

C++ programmers concentrate on creating their own *user-defined types* called *classes.* Classes are also referred to as *programmer-defined types.* Each class contains data as well as the set of functions that manipulate the data. The data components of a class are called *data members.* The function components of a class are called *member functions* (or *methods* in other object-oriented languages). Just as an instance of a built-in type such as **int** is called a *variable,* an instance of a user-defined type (i.e., a class) is called an *object.* [In the C++ community, the terms variable and object are often used interchangeably.] The focus of attention in C++ is on classes rather than functions. The *nouns* in a system specification help the C++ programmer determine the set of classes that will be used to create the objects that will work together to implement the system.

Classes in C++ are a natural evolution of the C notion of **struct**. Before proceeding with the specifics of developing classes in C++, we discuss structures, and we build a user-defined type based on a structure. The weaknesses we expose in this approach will help motivate the notion of a class.

6.2 Structure Definitions

Structures are aggregate data types built using elements of other types including other **struct**s. Consider the following structure definition:

```
struct Time {
    int hour;       // 0–23
    int minute;     // 0–59
    int second;     // 0–59
};
```

Keyword **struct** introduces the structure definition. The identifier **Time** is the *structure tag* that names the structure definition and is used to declare variables of the *structure type.* In this example, the new type name is **Time**. The names declared in the braces of the structure definition are the structure's *members*. Members of the same structure must have unique names, but two different structures may contain members of the same name without conflict. Each structure definition must end with a semicolon. The preceding explanation is valid for classes also as we will soon see; structures and classes are quite similar in C++.

The definition of **Time** contains three members of type **int**—**hour**, **minute** and **second**. Structure members can be any type, and one structure can contain members of many different types. A structure cannot, however, contain an instance of itself. For example, a member of type **Time** cannot be declared in the structure definition for **Time**. A pointer to another **Time** structure, however, can be included. A structure containing a member that is a pointer to the same structure type is referred to as a *self-referential structure*. Self-referential structures are useful for forming linked data structures such as linked lists, queues, stacks and trees, as we will see in Chapter 15.

The preceding structure definition does not reserve any space in memory; rather, the definition creates a new data type that is used to declare variables. Structure variables are declared like variables of other types. The declaration

```
Time timeObject, timeArray[ 10 ], *timePtr,
    &timeRef = timeObject;
```

declares **timeObject** to be a variable of type **Time**, **timeArray** to be an array with 10 elements of type **Time**, **timePtr** to be a pointer to a **Time** object and **timeRef** to be a reference to a **Time** object that is initialized with **timeObject**.

6.3 Accessing Members of Structures

Members of a structure (or of a class) are accessed using the *member access operators*— the *dot operator* (**.**) and the *arrow operator* (**->**). The dot operator accesses a structure or class member via the variable name for the object or via a reference to the object. For example, to print member **hour** of structure **timeObject**, use the statement

```
cout << timeObject.hour;
```

To print member **hour** of the structure referenced by **timeRef**, use the statement

```
cout << timeRef.hour;
```

The arrow operator—consisting of a minus sign (**-**) and a greater than sign (**>**) with no intervening spaces—accesses a structure member or class member via a pointer to the object. Assume that the pointer **timePtr** has been declared to point to a **Time** object, and that the address of structure **timeObject** has been assigned to **timePtr**. To print member **hour** of structure **timeObject** with pointer **timePtr**, use the statements

```
timePtr = &timeObject;
cout << timePtr->hour;
```

The expression **timePtr->hour** is equivalent to **(*timePtr).hour**, which dereferences the pointer and accesses the member **hour** using the dot operator. The parentheses are needed here because the dot operator (**.**) has a higher precedence than the pointer dereferencing operator (*****). The arrow operator and dot operator, along with parentheses and brackets (**[ ]**), have the second highest operator precedence (after the scope resolution operator introduced in Chapter 3) and associate from left to right.

Common Programming Error 6.1

The expression **(*timePtr).hour** *refers to the* **hour** *member of the* **struct** *pointed to by* **timePtr**. *Omitting the parentheses, as in* ***timePtr.hour** *would be a syntax error because* **.** *has a higher precedence than* *****, *so the expression would execute as if parenthesized as* ***(timePtr.hour)**. *This would be a syntax error because with a pointer you must use the arrow operator to refer to a member.*

6.4 Implementing a User-Defined Type Time with a struct

Figure 6.1 creates the user-defined structure type **Time** with three integer members: **hour**, **minute** and **second**. The program defines a single **Time** structure called **dinnerTime** and uses the dot operator to initialize the structure members with the values **18** for **hour**, **30** for **minute** and **0** for **second**. The program then prints the time in military format (also called "universal format") and standard format. Note that the print functions receive references to constant **Time** structures. This causes **Time** structures to be passed to the print functions by reference—thus eliminating the copying overhead associated with passing structures to functions by value—and the use of **const** prevents the **Time** structure from being modified by the print functions. In Chapter 7, we discuss **const** objects and **const** member functions.

\

```
1   // Fig. 6.1: fig06_01.cpp
2   // Create a structure, set its members, and print it.
3   #include <iostream>
4
5   using std::cout;
6   using std::endl;
7
8   struct Time {        // structure definition
9       int hour;        // 0-23
10      int minute;      // 0-59
11      int second;      // 0-59
12  };
13
14  void printMilitary( const Time & );   // prototype
15  void printStandard( const Time & );   // prototype
16
17  int main()
18  {
19      Time dinnerTime;     // variable of new type Time
20
21      // set members to valid values
22      dinnerTime.hour = 18;
23      dinnerTime.minute = 30;
24      dinnerTime.second = 0;
25
26      cout << "Dinner will be held at ";
27      printMilitary( dinnerTime );
```

Fig. 6.1   Creating a structure, setting its members and printing the structure (part 1 of 2).

```
28          cout << " military time,\nwhich is ";
29          printStandard( dinnerTime );
30          cout << " standard time.\n";
31
32          // set members to invalid values
33          dinnerTime.hour = 29;
34          dinnerTime.minute = 73;
35
36          cout << "\nTime with invalid values: ";
37          printMilitary( dinnerTime );
38          cout << endl;
39          return 0;
40      }
41
42      // Print the time in military format
43      void printMilitary( const Time &t )
44      {
45          cout << ( t.hour < 10 ? "0" : "" ) << t.hour << ":"
46              << ( t.minute < 10 ? "0" : "" ) << t.minute;
47      }
48
49      // Print the time in standard format
50      void printStandard( const Time &t )
51      {
52          cout << ( ( t.hour == 0 || t.hour == 12 ) ?
53                  12 : t.hour % 12 )
54              << ":" << ( t.minute < 10 ? "0" : "" ) << t.minute
55              << ":" << ( t.second < 10 ? "0" : "" ) << t.second
56              << ( t.hour < 12 ? " AM" : " PM" );
57      }
```

```
Dinner will be held at 18:30 military time,
which is 6:30:00 PM standard time.

Time with invalid values: 29:73
```

Fig. 6.1   Creating a structure, setting its members and printing the structure (part 2 of 2).

Performance Tip 6.1

By default, structures are passed call-by-value. To avoid the overhead of copying a structure, pass the structure call-by-reference.

Software Engineering Observation 6.1

To avoid the overhead of call-by-value yet still gain the benefit that the caller's original data are protected from modification, pass large-size arguments as **const** *references.*

There are drawbacks to creating new data types with structures in this manner. Since initialization is not specifically required, it is possible to have uninitialized data and the consequent problems. Even if the data are initialized, they may not be initialized correctly.

Invalid values can be assigned to the members of a structure (as we did in Fig. 6.1) because the program has direct access to the data. In lines 33 and 34, the program was easily able to assign bad values to the **hour** and **minute** members of the **Time** object **dinner-Time**. If the implementation of the **struct** is changed (e.g., the time could be represented as the number of seconds since midnight), all programs that use the **struct** must be changed. This is because the programmer directly manipulates the data representation. There is no "interface" to it to ensure that the programmer uses the data type's services correctly and to ensure that the data remain in a consistent state.

Software Engineering Observation 6.2

It is important to write programs that are understandable and easy to maintain. Change is the rule rather than the exception. Programmers should anticipate that their code will be modified. As we will see, classes can facilitate program modifiability.

There are other problems associated with C-style structures. In C, structures cannot be printed as a unit; rather, their members must be printed and formatted one at a time. A function could be written to print the members of a structure in some appropriate format. Chapter 8, "Operator Overloading," illustrates how to overload the **<<** operator to enable objects of a structure type or class type to be printed easily. In C, structures may not be compared in their entirety; they must be compared member by member. Chapter 8 also illustrates how to overload equality operators and relational operators to compare objects of (C++) structure and class types.

The following section reimplements our **Time** structure as a C++ class and demonstrates some of the advantages to creating so-called *abstract data types* as classes. We will see that classes and structures can be used almost identically in C++. The difference between the two is in the default accessibility associated with the members of each. This will be explained shortly.

6.5 Implementing a `Time` Abstract Data Type with a `class`

Classes enable the programmer to model objects that have *attributes* (represented as *data members*) and *behaviors* or *operations* (represented as *member functions*). Types containing data members and member functions are defined in C++ using the keyword **class**.

Member functions are sometimes called *methods* in other object-oriented programming languages, and are invoked in response to *messages* sent to an object. A message corresponds to a member-function call sent from one object to another or sent from a function to an object.

Once a class has been defined, the class name can be used to declare objects of that class. Figure 6.2 contains a simple definition for class **Time**.

Our **Time** class definition begins with the keyword **class**. The *body* of the class definition is delineated with left and right braces (**{** and **}**). The class definition terminates with a semicolon. Our **Time** class definition and our **Time** structure definition each contain the three integer members **hour**, **minute** and **second**.

Common Programming Error 6.2

Forgetting the semicolon at the end of a class (or structure) definition is a syntax error.

```
1   class Time {
2   public:
3       Time();
4       void setTime( int, int, int );
5       void printMilitary();
6       void printStandard();
7   private:
8       int hour;        // 0 - 23
9       int minute;      // 0 - 59
10      int second;      // 0 - 59
11  };
```

Fig. 6.2   Simple definition of **class Time**.

The remaining parts of the class definition are new. The **public:** and **private:** labels are called *member access specifiers*. Any data member or member function declared after member access specifier **public** (and before the next member access specifier) is accessible wherever the program has access to an object of class **Time**. Any data member or member function declared after member access specifier **private** (and up to the next member access specifier) is accessible only to member functions of the class. Member access specifiers are always followed by a colon (**:**) and can appear multiple times and in any order in a class definition. For the remainder of the text, we will refer to the member access specifiers as **public** and **private** (without the colon). In Chapter 9 we introduce a third member access specifier, **protected**, as we study inheritance and the part it plays in object-oriented programming.

Good Programming Practice 6.1

*Use each member access specifier only once in a class definition for clarity and readability. Place **public** members first where they are easy to locate.*

The class definition contains prototypes for the following four member functions after the **public** member access specifier—**Time**, **setTime**, **printMilitary** and **printStandard**. These are the **public** *member functions* or **public** *services* or **public** *behaviors* or *interface* of the class. These functions will be used by *clients* (i.e., portions of a program that are users) of the class to manipulate the data of the class. The data members of the class support the delivery of the *services* the class provides to the clients of the class with its member functions. These services allow the client code to interact with an object of the class.

Notice the member function with the same name as the class; it is called a *constructor* function of that class. A constructor is a special member function that initializes the data members of a class object. A class constructor function is called automatically when an object of that class is created. We will see that it is common to have several constructors for a class; this is accomplished through function overloading. Note that no return type is specified for the constructor.

Common Programming Error 6.3

Specifying a return type and/or a return value for a constructor is a syntax error.

The three integer members appear after the **private** member access specifier. This indicates that these data members of the class are only accessible to member functions—and, as we will see in the next chapter, "friends"—of the class. Thus, the data members can only be accessed by the four functions whose prototypes appear in the class definition (or by friends of the class). Data members are normally listed in the **private** portion of a class and member functions are normally listed in the **public** portion. It is possible to have **private** member functions and **public** data, as we will see later; the latter is uncommon and is considered a poor programming practice.

Once the class has been defined, it can be used as a type in object, array and pointer definitions as follows:

```
Time sunset,             // object of type Time
     arrayOfTimes[ 5 ],  // array of Time objects
     *pointerToTime,     // pointer to a Time object
     &dinnerTime = sunset; // reference to a Time object
```

The class name becomes a new type specifier. There may be many objects of a class, just as there may be many variables of a type such as **int**. The programmer can create new class types as needed. This is one reason why C++ is said to be an *extensible language*.

Figure 6.3 uses the **Time** class. The program instantiates a single object of class **Time** called **t**. When the object is instantiated, the **Time** constructor is called automatically and initializes each **private** data member to **0**. The time is then printed in military and standard formats to confirm that the members have been initialized properly. The time is then set using the **setTime** member function and is printed again in both formats. Then **setTime** attempts to set the data members to invalid values, and the time is again printed in both formats.

```
1   // Fig. 6.3: fig06_03.cpp
2   // Time class.
3   #include <iostream>
4
5   using std::cout;
6   using std::endl;
7
8   // Time abstract data type (ADT) definition
9   class Time {
10  public:
11      Time();                        // constructor
12      void setTime( int, int, int ); // set hour, minute, second
13      void printMilitary();          // print military time format
14      void printStandard();          // print standard time format
15  private:
16      int hour;       // 0 - 23
17      int minute;     // 0 - 59
18      int second;     // 0 - 59
19  };
```

Fig. 6.3   Abstract data type **Time** implementation as a class (part 1 of 3).

```
20
21    // Time constructor initializes each data member to zero.
22    // Ensures all Time objects start in a consistent state.
23    Time::Time() { hour = minute = second = 0; }
24
25    // Set a new Time value using military time. Perform validity
26    // checks on the data values. Set invalid values to zero.
27    void Time::setTime( int h, int m, int s )
28    {
29       hour = ( h >= 0 && h < 24 ) ? h : 0;
30       minute = ( m >= 0 && m < 60 ) ? m : 0;
31       second = ( s >= 0 && s < 60 ) ? s : 0;
32    }
33
34    // Print Time in military format
35    void Time::printMilitary()
36    {
37       cout << ( hour < 10 ? "0" : "" ) << hour << ":"
38            << ( minute < 10 ? "0" : "" ) << minute;
39    }
40
41    // Print Time in standard format
42    void Time::printStandard()
43    {
44       cout << ( ( hour == 0 || hour == 12 ) ? 12 : hour % 12 )
45            << ":" << ( minute < 10 ? "0" : "" ) << minute
46            << ":" << ( second < 10 ? "0" : "" ) << second
47            << ( hour < 12 ? " AM" : " PM" );
48    }
49
50    // Driver to test simple class Time
51    int main()
52    {
53       Time t;   // instantiate object t of class Time
54
55       cout << "The initial military time is ";
56       t.printMilitary();
57       cout << "\nThe initial standard time is ";
58       t.printStandard();
59
60       t.setTime( 13, 27, 6 );
61       cout << "\n\nMilitary time after setTime is ";
62       t.printMilitary();
63       cout << "\nStandard time after setTime is ";
64       t.printStandard();
65
66       t.setTime( 99, 99, 99 );   // attempt invalid settings
67       cout << "\n\nAfter attempting invalid settings:"
68            << "\nMilitary time: ";
69       t.printMilitary();
70       cout << "\nStandard time: ";
71       t.printStandard();
72       cout << endl;
```

Fig. 6.3   Abstract data type **Time** implementation as a class (part 2 of 3).

```
73        return 0;
74   }
```

```
The initial military time is 00:00
The initial standard time is 12:00:00 AM

Military time after setTime is 13:27
Standard time after setTime is 1:27:06 PM

After attempting invalid settings:
Military time: 00:00
Standard time: 12:00:00 AM
```

Fig. 6.3   Abstract data type **Time** implementation as a class (part 3 of 3).

Again, note that the data members **hour**, **minute** and **second** are preceded by the **private** member access specifier. A class' **private** data members are normally not accessible outside the class. (Again, we will see in Chapter 7 that friends of a class may access the class' **private** members.) The philosophy here is that the actual data representation used within the class is of no concern to the class' clients. For example, it would be perfectly reasonable for the class to represent the time internally as the number of seconds since midnight. Clients could use the same **public** member functions and get the same results without being aware of this. In this sense, the implementation of a class is said to be *hidden* from its clients. Such *information hiding* promotes program modifiability and simplifies the client's perception of a class.

Software Engineering Observation 6.3

Clients of a class use the class without knowing the internal details of how the class is implemented. If the class implementation is changed (to improve performance, for example), provided the class' interface remains constant, the class' client source code need not change (although the client may need to be recompiled). This makes it much easier to modify systems.

In this program, the **Time** constructor initializes the data members to 0 (i.e., the military time equivalent of 12 AM). This ensures that the object is in a consistent state when it is created. Invalid values cannot be stored in the data members of a **Time** object because the constructor is automatically called when the **Time** object is created and all subsequent attempts by a client to modify the data members are scrutinized by function **setTime**.

Software Engineering Observation 6.4

Member functions are usually shorter than functions in non-object-oriented programs because the data stored in data members have ideally been validated by a constructor and/or by member functions that store new data. Because the data are already in the object, the member function calls often have no arguments or at least have fewer arguments than typical function calls in non-object-oriented languages. Thus, the calls are shorter, the function definitions are shorter and the function prototypes are shorter.

Note that the data members of a class cannot be initialized where they are declared in the class body. These data members should be initialized by the class' constructor, or they can be assigned values by "set" functions.

Common Programming Error 6.4

Attempting to initialize a data member of a class explicitly in the class definition is a syntax error.

A function with the same name as the class but preceded with a *tilde character (~)* is called the *destructor* of that class (this example does not explicitly include a destructor, so the system "plugs one in" for you). The destructor does "termination housekeeping" on each class object before the memory for the object is reclaimed by the system. Destructors cannot take arguments and hence cannot be overloaded. We will discuss constructors and destructors in more detail later in this chapter and in Chapter 7.

Note that the functions the class provides to the outside world are preceded by the **public** member access specifier. The **public** functions implement the behaviors or services the class provides to its clients—commonly referred to as the class' *interface* or **public** *interface*.

Software Engineering Observation 6.5

Clients have access to a class' interface but should not have access to a class' implementation.

The class definition contains declarations of the class' data members and the class' member functions. The member function declarations are the function prototypes we discussed in earlier chapters. Member functions can be defined inside a class, but it is a good programming practice to define the functions outside the class definition.

Software Engineering Observation 6.6

Declaring member functions inside a class definition (via their function prototypes) and defining those member functions outside that class definition separates the interface of a class from its implementation. This promotes good software engineering. Clients of a class cannot see the implementation of that class' member functions and need not recompile if that implementation changes.

Note the use of the *binary scope resolution operator (::)* in each member function definition following the class definition in Fig. 6.3. Once a class is defined and its member functions are declared, the member functions must be defined. Each member function of the class can be defined directly in the class body (rather than including the function prototype of the class), or the member function can be defined after the class body. When a member function is defined after its corresponding class definition, the function name is preceded by the class name and the binary scope resolution operator (::). Because different classes can have the same member names, the scope resolution operator "ties" the member name to the class name to uniquely identify the member functions of a particular class.

Common Programming Error 6.5

When defining a class' member functions outside that class, omitting the class name and scope resolution operator on the function name is an error.

Even though a member function declared in a class definition may be defined outside that class definition, that member function is still within that *class' scope,* i.e., its name is known only to other members of the class unless referred to via an object of the class, a reference to an object of the class or a pointer to an object of the class. We will say more about class scope shortly.

If a member function is defined in a class definition, the member function is automatically inlined. Member functions defined outside a class definition may be made inline by explicitly using the keyword **inline**. Remember that the compiler reserves the right not to inline any function.

Performance Tip 6.2

Defining a small member function inside the class definition automatically inlines the member function (if the compiler chooses to do so). This can improve performance, but it does not promote the best software engineering because clients of the class will be able to see the implementation of the function and their code must be recompiled if the inline function definition changes.

Software Engineering Observation 6.7

Only the simplest member functions and most stable member functions (i.e., the implementation is unlikely to change) should be defined in the class header.

It is interesting that the **printMilitary** and **printStandard** member functions take no arguments. This is because member functions implicitly know that they are to print the data members of the particular **Time** object for which they are invoked. This makes member function calls more concise than conventional function calls in procedural programming.

Testing and Debugging Tip 6.1

The fact that member function calls generally take either no arguments or substantially fewer arguments than conventional function calls in non-object-oriented languages reduces the likelihood of passing the wrong arguments, the wrong types of arguments and/or the wrong number of arguments.

Software Engineering Observation 6.8

Using an object-oriented programming approach can often simplify function calls by reducing the number of parameters to be passed. This benefit of object-oriented programming derives from the fact that encapsulation of data members and member functions within an object gives the member functions the right to access the data members.

Classes simplify programming because the client (or user of the class object) need only be concerned with the operations encapsulated or embedded in the object. Such operations are usually designed to be client-oriented rather than implementation-oriented. Clients need not be concerned with a class' implementation (although the client, of course, wants a correct and efficient implementation). Interfaces do change, but less frequently than implementations. When an implementation changes, implementation-dependent code must change accordingly. By hiding the implementation we eliminate the possibility of other program parts becoming dependent on the details of the class implementation.

Software Engineering Observation 6.9

A central theme of this book is "reuse, reuse, reuse." We will carefully discuss a number of techniques for "polishing" classes to encourage reuse. We focus on "crafting valuable classes" and creating valuable "software assets."

Often, classes do not have to be created "from scratch." Rather, they may be *derived* from other classes that provide attributes and behaviors the new classes can use. Or classes can include objects of other classes as members. Such *software reuse* can greatly enhance programmer productivity. Deriving new classes from existing classes is called *inheritance* and is discussed in detail in Chapter 9. Including class objects as members of other classes is called *composition* (or *aggregation*) and is discussed in Chapter 7.

People new to object-oriented programming often express concern at the fact that objects must be quite large because they contain data and functions. Logically, this is true—the programmer may think of objects as containing data and functions. Physically, however, this is not true.

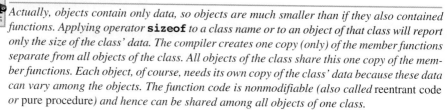

Performance Tip 6.3

Actually, objects contain only data, so objects are much smaller than if they also contained functions. Applying operator **sizeof** *to a class name or to an object of that class will report only the size of the class' data. The compiler creates one copy (only) of the member functions separate from all objects of the class. All objects of the class share this one copy of the member functions. Each object, of course, needs its own copy of the class' data because these data can vary among the objects. The function code is nonmodifiable (also called* reentrant code *or* pure procedure*) and hence can be shared among all objects of one class.*

6.6 Class Scope and Accessing Class Members

A class' data members (variables declared in the class definition) and member functions (functions declared in the class definition) belong to that *class' scope*. Nonmember functions are defined as *file scope*.

Within a class' scope, class members are immediately accessible by all of that class' member functions and can be referenced by name. Outside a class' scope, class members are referenced through one of the handles on an object—an object name, a reference to an object or a pointer to an object. [We will see in Chapter 7 that an implicit handle is inserted by the compiler on every reference to a data member or member function in an object.]

Member functions of a class can be overloaded, but only by other member functions of the class. To overload a member function, simply provide in the class definition a prototype for each version of the overloaded function, and provide a separate function definition for each version of the function.

Variables defined in a member function have *function scope*—they are known only to that function. If a member function defines a variable with the same name as a variable with class scope, the class-scope variable is hidden by the function-scope variable in the function scope. Such a hidden variable can be accessed by preceding the operator with the class name followed by the scope resolution operator (**::**). Hidden global variables can be accessed with the unary scope resolution operator (see Chapter 3).

The operators used to access class members are identical to the operators used to access structure members. The *dot member selection operator (.)* is combined with an object's name or with a reference to an object to access the object's members. The *arrow member selection operator (->)* is combined with a pointer to an object to access that object's members.

Figure 6.4 uses a simple class called **Count** with **public** data member **x** of type **int**, and **public** member function **print** to illustrate accessing the members of a class with the member selection operators. The program creates (defines) three variables related to type **Count**—**counter**, **counterRef** (a reference to a **Count** object) and **coun-**

terPtr (a pointer to a **Count** object). Variable **counterRef** is defined to reference **counter**, and variable **counterPtr** is defined to point to **counter**. *It is important to note that data member* **x** *has been made* **public** *here simply to demonstrate how* **public** *members are accessed off handles (i.e., a name, a reference or a pointer). As we have stated, data are typically made* **private**, *as we will do in most subsequent examples.* In Chapter 9, "Inheritance," we will sometimes make data **protected**.

```cpp
1   // Fig. 6.4: fig06_04.cpp
2   // Demonstrating the class member access operators . and ->
3   //
4   // CAUTION: IN FUTURE EXAMPLES WE AVOID PUBLIC DATA!
5   #include <iostream>
6
7   using std::cout;
8   using std::endl;
9
10  // Simple class Count
11  class Count {
12  public:
13      int x;
14      void print() { cout << x << endl; }
15  };
16
17  int main()
18  {
19      Count counter,                  // create counter object
20            *counterPtr = &counter,   // pointer to counter
21            &counterRef = counter;    // reference to counter
22
23      cout << "Assign 7 to x and print using the object's name: ";
24      counter.x = 7;          // assign 7 to data member x
25      counter.print();        // call member function print
26
27      cout << "Assign 8 to x and print using a reference: ";
28      counterRef.x = 8;       // assign 8 to data member x
29      counterRef.print();     // call member function print
30
31      cout << "Assign 10 to x and print using a pointer: ";
32      counterPtr->x = 10;     // assign 10 to data member x
33      counterPtr->print();    // call member function print
34      return 0;
35  }
```

```
Assign 7 to x and print using the object's name: 7
Assign 8 to x and print using a reference: 8
Assign 10 to x and print using a pointer: 10
```

Fig. 6.4   Accessing an object's data members and member functions through each type of object handle—through the object's name, through a reference and through a pointer to the object.

6.7 Separating Interface from Implementation

One of the fundamental principles of good software engineering is to separate interface from implementation. This makes it easier to modify programs. As far as clients of a class are concerned, changes in the class' implementation do not affect the client as long as the class' interface originally provided to the client is unchanged (the class' functionality could be expanded beyond the original interface).

Software Engineering Observation 6.10

Place the class declaration in a header file to be included by any client that wants to use the class. This forms the class' **public** *interface (and provides the client with the function prototypes it needs to be able to call the class' member functions). Place the definitions of the class member functions in a source file. This forms the implementation of the class.*

Software Engineering Observation 6.11

Clients of a class do not need access to the class' source code in order to use the class. The clients do, however, need to be able to link to the class' object code. This encourages independent software vendors (ISVs) to provide class libraries for sale or license. The ISVs provide in their products only the header files and the object modules. No proprietary information is revealed—as would be the case if source code were provided. The C++ user community benefits by having more ISV-produced class libraries available.

Actually, things are not quite this rosy. Header files do contain some portion of the implementation and hints about other portions of the implementation. Inline member functions, for example, need to be in a header file, so that when the compiler compiles a client, the client can include the **inline** function definition in place. Private members are listed in the class definition in the header file, so these members are visible to clients even though the clients may not access the **private** members. In Chapter 7, we show how to use a so-called *proxy class* to hide even the **private** data of a class from clients of the class.

Software Engineering Observation 6.12

Information important to the interface to a class should be included in the header file. Information that will be used only internally in the class and will not be needed by clients of the class should be included in the unpublished source file. This is yet another example of the principle of least privilege.

Figure 6.5 splits the program of Fig. 6.3 into multiple files. When building a C++ program, each class definition is normally placed in a *header file,* and that class' member function definitions are placed in *source-code files* of the same base name. The header files are included (via **#include**) in each file in which the class is used, and the source-code file is compiled and linked with the file containing the main program. See your compiler's documentation to determine how to compile and link programs consisting of multiple source files.

Figure 6.5 consists of the header file **time1.h** in which class **Time** is declared, the file **time1.cpp** in which the member functions of class **Time** are defined and the file **fig06_05.cpp** in which function **main** is defined. The output for this program is identical to the output of Fig. 6.3.

```cpp
1   // Fig. 6.5: time1.h
2   // Declaration of the Time class.
3   // Member functions are defined in time1.cpp
4
5   // prevent multiple inclusions of header file
6   #ifndef TIME1_H
7   #define TIME1_H
8
9   // Time abstract data type definition
10  class Time {
11  public:
12     Time();                          // constructor
13     void setTime( int, int, int );   // set hour, minute, second
14     void printMilitary();            // print military time format
15     void printStandard();            // print standard time format
16  private:
17     int hour;        // 0 - 23
18     int minute;      // 0 - 59
19     int second;      // 0 - 59
20  };
21
22  #endif
```

Fig. 6.5　　Separating **Time** class interface and implementation—**time1.h**.

```cpp
23  // Fig. 6.5: time1.cpp
24  // Member function definitions for Time class.
25  #include <iostream>
26
27  using std::cout;
28
29  #include "time1.h"
30
31  // Time constructor initializes each data member to zero.
32  // Ensures all Time objects start in a consistent state.
33  Time::Time() { hour = minute = second = 0; }
34
35  // Set a new Time value using military time. Perform validity
36  // checks on the data values. Set invalid values to zero.
37  void Time::setTime( int h, int m, int s )
38  {
39     hour   = ( h >= 0 && h < 24 ) ? h : 0;
40     minute = ( m >= 0 && m < 60 ) ? m : 0;
41     second = ( s >= 0 && s < 60 ) ? s : 0;
42  }
43
44  // Print Time in military format
45  void Time::printMilitary()
46  {
47     cout << ( hour < 10 ? "0" : "" ) << hour << ":"
```

Fig. 6.5　　Separating **Time** class interface and implementation—**time1.cpp** (part 1 of 2).

```
48             << ( minute < 10 ? "0" : "" ) << minute;
49   }
50
51   // Print time in standard format
52   void Time::printStandard()
53   {
54      cout << ( ( hour == 0 || hour == 12 ) ? 12 : hour % 12 )
55           << ":" << ( minute < 10 ? "0" : "" ) << minute
56           << ":" << ( second < 10 ? "0" : "" ) << second
57           << ( hour < 12 ? " AM" : " PM" );
58   }
```

Fig. 6.5   Separating **Time** class interface and implementation—**time1.cpp** (part 2 of 2).

```
59   // Fig. 6.5: fig06_05.cpp
60   // Driver for Time1 class
61   // NOTE: Compile with time1.cpp
62   #include <iostream>
63
64   using std::cout;
65   using std::endl;
66
67   #include "time1.h"
68
69   // Driver to test simple class Time
70   int main()
71   {
72      Time t;   // instantiate object t of class time
73
74      cout << "The initial military time is ";
75      t.printMilitary();
76      cout << "\nThe initial standard time is ";
77      t.printStandard();
78
79      t.setTime( 13, 27, 6 );
80      cout << "\n\nMilitary time after setTime is ";
81      t.printMilitary();
82      cout << "\nStandard time after setTime is ";
83      t.printStandard();
84
85      t.setTime( 99, 99, 99 );   // attempt invalid settings
86      cout << "\n\nAfter attempting invalid settings:\n"
87           << "Military time: ";
88      t.printMilitary();
89      cout << "\nStandard time: ";
90      t.printStandard();
91      cout << endl;
92      return 0;
93   }
```

Fig. 6.5   Separating **Time** class interface and implementation—**fig06_05.cpp** (part 1 of 2)

```
The initial military time is 00:00
The initial standard time is 12:00:00 AM

Military time after setTime is 13:27
Standard time after setTime is 1:27:06 PM

After attempting invalid settings:
Military time: 00:00
Standard time: 12:00:00 AM
```

Fig. 6.5　Separating **Time** class interface and implementation—**fig06_05.cpp** (part 2 of 2)

Note that the class declaration is enclosed in the following preprocessor code:

```
// prevent multiple inclusions of header file
#ifndef TIME1_H
#define TIME1_H
   ...
#endif
```

When we build larger programs, other definitions and declarations will also be placed in header files. The preceding preprocessor directives prevent the code between **#ifndef** (if not defined) and **#endif** from being included if the name **TIME1_H** has been defined. If the header has not been included previously in a file, the name **TIME1_H** is defined by the **#define** directive and the header file statements are included. If the header has been included previously, **TIME1_H** is defined already and the header file is not included again. Attempts to include a header file multiple times (inadvertently) typically occur in large programs with many header files that may themselves include other header files. Note: The convention we use for the symbolic constant name in the preprocessor directives is simply the header file name with the underscore character replacing the period.

Testing and Debugging Tip 6.2

Use **#ifndef**, **#define** *and* **#endif** *preprocessor directives to prevent header files from being included more than once in a program.*

Good Programming Practice 6.2

Use the name of the header file with the period replaced by an underscore in the **#ifndef** *and* **#define** *preprocessor directives of a header file.*

6.8 Controlling Access to Members

The member access specifiers **public** and **private** (and **protected**, as we will see in Chapter 9, "Inheritance") are used to control access to a class' data members and member functions. The default access mode for classes is **private** so all members after the class header and before the first member access specifier are **private**. After each member access specifier, the mode that was invoked by that member access specifier applies until the next member access specifier or until the terminating right brace (**}**) of the class definition. The member access specifiers **public**, **private** and **protected** may be repeated, but such usage is rare and can be confusing.

A class' **private** members can be accessed only by member functions (and **friend**s, as we will see in Chapter 7) of that class. The **public** members of a class may be accessed by any function in the program.

The primary purpose of **public** members is to present to the class' clients a view of the *services* (behaviors) the class provides. This set of services forms the **public** *interface* of the class. Clients of the class need not be concerned with how the class accomplishes its tasks. The **private** members of a class as well as the definitions of its **public** member functions are not accessible to the clients of a class. These components form the *implementation* of the class.

Software Engineering Observation 6.13

C++ encourages programs to be implementation independent. When the implementation of a class used by implementation-independent code changes, that code need not be modified. If any part of the interface of the class changes, the implementation-independent code must be recompiled.

Common Programming Error 6.6

*An attempt by a function, which is not a member of a particular class (or a **friend** of that class), to access a **private** member of that class is a syntax error.*

Figure 6.6 demonstrates that **private** class members are only accessible through the **public** class interface using **public** member functions. When this program is compiled, the compiler generates two errors stating that the **private** member specified in each statement is not accessible. Figure 6.6 includes **time1.h** and is compiled with **time1.cpp** from Fig. 6.5.

Good Programming Practice 6.3

*If you choose to list the **private** members first in a class definition, explicitly use the **private** member access specifier despite the fact that **private** is assumed by default. This improves program clarity. Our preference is to list the **public** members of a class first to emphasize the class' interface.*

```
1   // Fig. 6.6: fig06_06.cpp
2   // Demonstrate errors resulting from attempts
3   // to access private class members.
4   #include <iostream>
5
6   using std::cout;
7
8   #include "time1.h"
9
10  int main()
11  {
12      Time t;
13
14      // Error: 'Time::hour' is not accessible
15      t.hour = 7;
16
17      // Error: 'Time::minute' is not accessible
18      cout << "minute = " << t.minute;
```

Fig. 6.6   Erroneous attempt to access **private** members of a class (part 1 of 2).

```
19
20       return 0;
21   }
```

Borland C++ command-line compiler error messages

```
Time1.cpp:
Fig06_06.cpp:
Error E2247 Fig06_06.cpp 15:
  'Time::hour' is not accessible in function main()
Error E2247 Fig06_06.cpp 18:
  'Time::minute' is not accessible in function main()

*** 2 errors in Compile ***
```

Microsoft Visual C++ compiler error messages

```
Compiling...
Fig06_06.cpp
D:\Fig06_06.cpp(15) : error C2248: 'hour' : cannot access private
member declared in class 'Time'
D:\Fig6_06\time1.h(18) : see declaration of 'hour'
D:\Fig06_06.cpp(18) : error C2248: 'minute' : cannot access private
member declared in class 'Time'
D:\time1.h(19) : see declaration of 'minute'
Error executing cl.exe.

test.exe - 2 error(s), 0 warning(s)
```

Fig. 6.6   Erroneous attempt to access **private** members of a class (part 2 of 2).

Good Programming Practice 6.4

*Despite the fact that the **public** and **private** member access specifiers may be repeated and intermixed, list all the **public** members of a class first in one group and then list all the **private** members in another group. This focuses the client's attention on the class' **public** interface, rather than on the class' implementation.*

Software Engineering Observation 6.14

*Keep all the data members of a class **private**. Provide **public** member functions to set the values of **private** data members and to get the values of **private** data members. This architecture helps hide the implementation of a class from its clients, which reduces bugs and improves program modifiability.*

A client of a class may be a member function of another class or it may be a global function (i.e., a C-like "loose" or "free" function in the file that is not a member function of any class).

The default access for members of a class is **private**. Access to members of a class may be explicitly set to **public**, **protected** (as we will see in Chapter 9) or **private**. The default access for **struct** members is **public**. Access to members of a **struct** also may be explicitly set to **public**, **protected** or **private**.

Software Engineering Observation 6.15

Class designers use **private**, **protected** *and* **public** *members to enforce the notion of information hiding and the principle of least privilege.*

Just because class data is **private** does not necessarily mean that clients cannot effect changes to that data. The data can be changed by member functions or **friend**s of that class. As we will see, these functions should be designed to ensure the integrity of the data.

Access to a class' **private** data should be carefully controlled by the use of member functions, called *access functions* (also called *accessor methods*). For example, to allow clients to read the value of **private** data, the class can provide a *get* function. To enable clients to modify **private** data, the class can provide a *set* function. Such modification would seem to violate the notion of **private** data. But a *set* member function can provide data validation capabilities (such as range checking) to ensure that the value is set properly. A *set* function can also translate between the form of the data used in the interface and the form used in the implementation. A *get* function need not expose the data in "raw" format; rather, the *get* function can edit the data and limit the view of the data the client will see.

Software Engineering Observation 6.16

The class designer need not provide set *and/or* get *functions for each* **private** *data item; these capabilities should be provided only when appropriate. If the service is useful to the client code, that service should be provided in the class'* **public** *interface.*

Testing and Debugging Tip 6.3

Making the data members of a class **private** *and the member functions of the class* **public** *facilitates debugging because problems with data manipulations are localized to either the class' member functions or the* **friend**s *of the class.*

6.9 Access Functions and Utility Functions

Not all member functions need be made **public** to serve as part of the interface of a class. Some member functions remain **private** and serve as *utility functions* to the other functions of the class.

Software Engineering Observation 6.17

Member functions tend to fall into a number of different categories: functions that read and return the value of **private** *data members; functions that set the value of* **private** *data members; functions that implement the services of the class; and functions that perform various mechanical chores for the class such as initializing class objects, assigning class objects, converting between classes and built-in types or between classes and other classes and handling memory for class objects.*

Access functions can read or display data. Another common use for access functions is to test the truth or falsity of conditions—such functions are often called *predicate functions.* An example of a predicate function would be an **isEmpty** function for any container class—a class capable of holding many objects—such as a linked list, a stack or a queue. A program would test **isEmpty** before attempting to read another item from the container object. An **isFull** predicate function might test a container class object to determine if it has no additional room. A set of useful predicate functions for our **Time** class might be **isAM** and **isPM**.

Figure 6.7 demonstrates the notion of a *utility function* (also called a *helper function*). A utility function is not part of a class' interface; rather, it is a **private** member function that supports the operation of the class' **public** member functions. Utility functions are not intended to be used by clients of a class.

```cpp
1   // Fig. 6.7: salesp.h
2   // SalesPerson class definition
3   // Member functions defined in salesp.cpp
4   #ifndef SALESP_H
5   #define SALESP_H
6
7   class SalesPerson {
8   public:
9      SalesPerson();              // constructor
10     void getSalesFromUser(); // get sales figures from keyboard
11     void setSales( int, double ); // User supplies one month's
12                                 // sales figures.
13     void printAnnualSales();
14
15  private:
16     double totalAnnualSales();  // utility function
17     double sales[ 12 ];         // 12 monthly sales figures
18  };
19
20  #endif
```

Fig. 6.7　Using a utility function—**salesp.h**.

```cpp
21  // Fig. 6.7: salesp.cpp
22  // Member functions for class SalesPerson
23  #include <iostream>
24
25  using std::cout;
26  using std::cin;
27  using std::endl;
28
29  #include <iomanip>
30
31  using std::setprecision;
32  using std::setiosflags;
33  using std::ios;
34
35  #include "salesp.h"
36
37  // Constructor function initializes array
38  SalesPerson::SalesPerson()
39  {
40     for ( int i = 0; i < 12; i++ )
41        sales[ i ] = 0.0;
42  }
43
```

Fig. 6.7　Using a utility function—**salesp.cpp** (part 1 of 2)

```
44  // Function to get 12 sales figures from the user
45  // at the keyboard
46  void SalesPerson::getSalesFromUser()
47  {
48     double salesFigure;
49
50     for ( int i = 1; i <= 12; i++ ) {
51        cout << "Enter sales amount for month " << i << ": ";
52
53        cin >> salesFigure;
54        setSales( i, salesFigure );
55     }
56  }
57
58  // Function to set one of the 12 monthly sales figures.
59  // Note that the month value must be from 0 to 11.
60  void SalesPerson::setSales( int month, double amount )
61  {
62     if ( month >= 1 && month <= 12 && amount > 0 )
63        sales[ month - 1 ] = amount; // adjust for subscripts 0-11
64     else
65        cout << "Invalid month or sales figure" << endl;
66  }
67
68  // Print the total annual sales
69  void SalesPerson::printAnnualSales()
70  {
71     cout << setprecision( 2 )
72          << setiosflags( ios::fixed | ios::showpoint )
73          << "\nThe total annual sales are: $"
74          << totalAnnualSales() << endl;
75  }
76
77  // Private utility function to total annual sales
78  double SalesPerson::totalAnnualSales()
79  {
80     double total = 0.0;
81
82     for ( int i = 0; i < 12; i++ )
83        total += sales[ i ];
84
85     return total;
86  }
```

Fig. 6.7   Using a utility function—**salesp.cpp** (part 2 of 2)

Class **SalesPerson** has an array of 12 monthly sales figures initialized by the constructor to zero and set to user-supplied values by function **setSales**. Public member function **printAnnualSales** prints the total sales for the last 12 months. Utility function **totalAnnualSales** totals the 12 monthly sales figures for the benefit of **printAnnualSales**. Member function **printAnnualSales** edits the sales figures into dollar amount format.

```
87   // Fig. 6.7: fig06_07.cpp
88   // Demonstrating a utility function
89   // Compile with salesp.cpp
90   #include "salesp.h"
91
92   int main()
93   {
94       SalesPerson s;          // create SalesPerson object s
95
96       s.getSalesFromUser();   // note simple sequential code
97       s.printAnnualSales();   // no control structures in main
98       return 0;
99   }
```

```
Enter sales amount for month 1: 5314.76
Enter sales amount for month 2: 4292.38
Enter sales amount for month 3: 4589.83
Enter sales amount for month 4: 5534.03
Enter sales amount for month 5: 4376.34
Enter sales amount for month 6: 5698.45
Enter sales amount for month 7: 4439.22
Enter sales amount for month 8: 5893.57
Enter sales amount for month 9: 4909.67
Enter sales amount for month 10: 5123.45
Enter sales amount for month 11: 4024.97
Enter sales amount for month 12: 5923.92

The total annual sales are: $60120.59
```

Fig. 6.7   Using a utility function—**fig06_07.cpp**.

Note that **main** includes only a simple sequence of member function calls—there are no control structures.

Software Engineering Observation 6.18

A phenomenon of object-oriented programming is that once a class is defined, creating and manipulating objects of that class usually involves issuing only a simple sequence of member function calls—few, if any, control structures are needed. By contrast, it is common to have control structures in the implementation of a class' member functions.

6.10 Initializing Class Objects: Constructors

When a class object is created, its members can be initialized by that class' *constructor* function. A constructor is a class member function with the same name as the class. The programmer provides the constructor, which is then invoked automatically each time an object of that class is created (instantiated). Constructors may be overloaded to provide a variety of means for initializing objects of a class. Data members must either be initialized in a constructor of the class or their values may be *set* later after the object is created. However, it is considered a good programming and software engineering practice to ensure that an object is fully initialized before the client code invokes the object's member functions. In general, you should not rely on the client code to ensure that an object gets initialized properly.

Common Programming Error 6.7

Data members of a class cannot be initialized in the class definition.

Common Programming Error 6.8

Attempting to declare a return type for a constructor and/or attempting to return a value from a constructor are syntax errors.

Good Programming Practice 6.5

When appropriate (almost always), provide a constructor to ensure that every object is properly initialized with meaningful values. Pointer data members, in particular, should be initialized to some legitimate pointer value or to 0.

Testing and Debugging Tip 6.4

Every member function (and **friend***) that modifies the* **private** *data members of an object should ensure that the data remains in a consistent state.*

When an object of a class is declared, *initializers* can be provided in parentheses to the right of the object name and before the semicolon. These initializers are passed as arguments to the class' constructor. We will soon see several examples of these *constructor calls.* [Note: Although programmers do not explicitly call constructors, programmers can still provide data that get passed to constructors as arguments.]

6.11 Using Default Arguments with Constructors

The constructor from **time1.cpp** (Fig. 6.5) initialized **hour**, **minute** and **second** to **0** (i.e., 12 midnight in military time). Constructors can contain default arguments. Figure 6.8 redefines the **Time** constructor function to include default arguments of zero for each variable. By providing default arguments to the constructor, even if no values are provided in a constructor call, the object is still guaranteed to be initialized to a consistent state, due to the default arguments. A programmer-supplied constructor that defaults all its arguments (or explicitly requires no arguments) is also a *default constructor*, i.e., a constructor that can be invoked with no arguments. There can be only one default constructor per class.

In this program, the constructor calls member function **setTime** with the values passed to the constructor (or the default values) to ensure that the value supplied for **hour** is in the range 0 to 23, and that the values for **minute** and **second** are each in the range 0 to 59. If a value is out of range, it is set to zero by **setTime** (this is an example of ensuring that a data member remains in a consistent state).

Note that the **Time** constructor could be written to include the same statements as member function **setTime**. This may be slightly more efficient because the extra call to **setTime** is eliminated. However, coding the **Time** constructor and member function **setTime** identically makes maintenance of this program more difficult. If the implementation of member function **setTime** changes, the implementation of the **Time** constructor should change accordingly. Having the **Time** constructor call **setTime** directly requires any changes to the implementation of **setTime** to be made only once. This reduces the likelihood of a programming error when altering the implementation. Also, the performance of the **Time** constructor can be enhanced by explicitly declaring the constructor **inline** or by defining the constructor in the class definition (which implicitly **inline**s the function definition).

\

```
1   // Fig. 6.8: time2.h
2   // Declaration of the Time class.
3   // Member functions are defined in time2.cpp
4
5   // preprocessor directives that
6   // prevent multiple inclusions of header file
7   #ifndef TIME2_H
8   #define TIME2_H
9
10  // Time abstract data type definition
11  class Time {
12  public:
13     Time( int = 0, int = 0, int = 0 );  // default constructor
14     void setTime( int, int, int ); // set hour, minute, second
15     void printMilitary();          // print military time format
16     void printStandard();          // print standard time format
17  private:
18     int hour;      // 0 - 23
19     int minute;    // 0 - 59
20     int second;    // 0 - 59
21  };
22
23  #endif
```

Fig. 6.8   Using a constructor with default arguments—**time2.h**.

```
24  // Fig. 6.8: time2.cpp
25  // Member function definitions for Time class.
26  #include <iostream>
27
28  using std::cout;
29
30  #include "time2.h"
31
32  // Time constructor initializes each data member to zero.
33  // Ensures all Time objects start in a consistent state.
34  Time::Time( int hr, int min, int sec )
35     { setTime( hr, min, sec ); }
36
37  // Set a new Time value using military time. Perform validity
38  // checks on the data values. Set invalid values to zero.
39  void Time::setTime( int h, int m, int s )
40  {
41     hour   = ( h >= 0 && h < 24 ) ? h : 0;
42     minute = ( m >= 0 && m < 60 ) ? m : 0;
43     second = ( s >= 0 && s < 60 ) ? s : 0;
44  }
45
```

Fig. 6.8   Using a constructor with default arguments—**time2.cpp** (part 1 of 2).

```
1   // Print Time in military format
2   void Time::printMilitary()
3   {
4      cout << ( hour < 10 ? "0" : "" ) << hour << ":"
5           << ( minute < 10 ? "0" : "" ) << minute;
6   }
7
8   // Print Time in standard format
9   void Time::printStandard()
10  {
11     cout << ( ( hour == 0 || hour == 12 ) ? 12 : hour % 12 )
12          << ":" << ( minute < 10 ? "0" : "" ) << minute
13          << ":" << ( second < 10 ? "0" : "" ) << second
14          << ( hour < 12 ? " AM" : " PM" );
15  }
```

Fig. 6.8   Using a constructor with default arguments—**time2.cpp** (part 2 of 2).

```
16  // Fig. 6.8: fig06_08.cpp
17  // Demonstrating a default constructor
18  // function for class Time.
19  #include <iostream>
20
21  using std::cout;
22  using std::endl;
23
24  #include "time2.h"
25
26  int main()
27  {
28     Time t1,              // all arguments defaulted
29          t2(2),           // minute and second defaulted
30          t3(21, 34),      // second defaulted
31          t4(12, 25, 42),  // all values specified
32          t5(27, 74, 99);  // all bad values specified
33
34     cout << "Constructed with:\n"
35          << "all arguments defaulted:\n    ";
36     t1.printMilitary();
37     cout << "\n    ";
38     t1.printStandard();
39
40     cout << "\nhour specified; minute and second defaulted:"
41          << "\n    ";
42     t2.printMilitary();
43     cout << "\n    ";
44     t2.printStandard();
45
46     cout << "\nhour and minute specified; second defaulted:"
47          << "\n    ";
48     t3.printMilitary();
```

Fig. 6.8   Using a constructor with default arguments—**fig06_08.cpp** (part 1 of 2).

```
49        cout << "\n    ";
50        t3.printStandard();
51
52        cout << "\nhour, minute, and second specified:"
53            << "\n    ";
54        t4.printMilitary();
55        cout << "\n    ";
56        t4.printStandard();
57
58        cout << "\nall invalid values specified:"
59            << "\n    ";
60        t5.printMilitary();
61        cout << "\n    ";
62        t5.printStandard();
63        cout << endl;
64
65        return 0;
66    }
```

```
Constructed with:
all arguments defaulted:
   00:00
   12:00:00 AM
hour specified; minute and second defaulted:
   02:00
   2:00:00 AM
hour and minute specified; second defaulted:
   21:34
   9:34:00 PM
hour, minute, and second specified:
   12:25
   12:25:42 PM
all invalid values specified:
   00:00
   12:00:00 AM
```

Fig. 6.8   Using a constructor with default arguments—**fig06_08.cpp** (part 2 of 2).

Software Engineering Observation 6.19

If a member function of a class already provides all or part of the functionality required by a constructor (or other member function) of the class, call that member function from the constructor (or other member function). This simplifies the maintenance of the code and reduces the likelihood of an error if the implementation of the code is modified. As a general rule: Avoid repeating code.

Good Programming Practice 6.6

Declare default function argument values only in the function prototype within the class definition in the header file.

Common Programming Error 6.9

Specifying default initializers for the same member function in both a header file and in the member function definition.

Note: Any change to the default arguments of a method requires the client code to be recompiled. If it is likely that the default argument values will change, use overloaded functions instead. Thus, if the implementation of a member function changes, the client code need not be recompiled.

Figure 6.8 initializes five **Time** objects—one with all three arguments defaulted in the constructor call, one with one argument specified, one with two arguments specified, one with three arguments specified and one with three invalid arguments specified. The contents of each object's data members after instantiation and initialization are displayed.

If no constructor is defined for a class, the compiler creates a default constructor. Such a constructor does not perform any initialization, so when the object is created, it is not guaranteed to be in a consistent state.

Software Engineering Observation 6.20

It is possible for a class not to have a default constructor if any constructors are defined and none of them is explicitly a default constructor.

6.12 Using Destructors

A *destructor* is a special member function of a class. The name of the destructor for a class is the *tilde (~)* character followed by the class name. This naming convention has intuitive appeal, because as we will see in a later chapter, the tilde operator is the bitwise complement operator, and, in a sense, the destructor is the complement of the constructor.

A class' destructor is called when an object is destroyed—e.g., for automatic objects when program execution leaves the scope in which an object of that class was instantiated. The destructor itself does not actually destroy the object—it performs *termination housekeeping* before the system reclaims the object's memory so that memory may be reused to hold new objects.

A destructor receives no parameters and returns no value. A class may have only one destructor—destructor overloading is not allowed.

Common Programming Error 6.10

It is a syntax error to attempt to pass arguments to a destructor, to specify a return type for a destructor (even **void** *cannot be specified), to return values from a destructor or to overload a destructor.*

Notice that destructors have not been provided for the classes presented so far. We will soon see several examples of classes with useful destructors. In Chapter 8, we will see that destructors are appropriate for classes whose objects contain dynamically allocated memory (for arrays and strings, for example). In Chapter 7, we discuss how to dynamically allocate and deallocate storage.

Software Engineering Observation 6.21

As we will see (throughout the remainder of the book), constructors and destructors have much greater prominence in C++ and object-oriented programming than is possible to convey after only our brief introduction here.

6.13 When Constructors and Destructors Are Called

Constructors and destructors are called automatically. The order in which these function calls are made depends on the order in which execution enters and leaves the scope in which objects are instantiated. Generally, destructor calls are made in the reverse order of the constructor calls. However, as we will see in Fig. 6.9, the storage class of objects can alter the order in which the destructors are called.

Constructors are called for objects defined in global scope before any other function (including **main**) in that file begins execution (although the order of execution of global object constructors between files is not guaranteed). The corresponding destructors are called when **main** terminates or the **exit** function (see Chapter 18, "Other Topics," for more information on the function) is called. Destructors are not called for global objects if the program is terminated with a call to function **abort** (see Chapter 18, "Other Topics," for more information on this function).

Constructors are called for automatic local objects when execution reaches the point where the objects are defined. Corresponding destructors are called when the objects leave scope (i.e., the block in which they are defined exits). Constructors and destructors for automatic objects are called each time the objects enter and leave scope. Destructors are not called for automatic objects if the program is terminated with a call to functions **exit** or **abort**.

Constructors are called for **static** local objects only once when execution first reaches the point where the objects are defined. Corresponding destructors are called when **main** terminates or the **exit** function is called. Destructors are not called for **static** objects if the program is terminated with a call to function **abort**.

The program of Fig. 6.9 demonstrates the order in which constructors and destructors are called for objects of type **CreateAndDestroy** in several scopes. The program defines **first** in global scope. Its constructor is called as the program begins execution and its destructor is called at program termination after all other objects are destroyed.

Function **main** declares three objects. Objects **second** and **fourth** are local automatic objects, and object **third** is a **static** local object. The constructors for each of these objects are called when execution reaches the point where each object is declared. The destructors for objects **fourth** and **second** are called in that order when the end of **main** is reached. Because object **third** is **static**, it exists until program termination. The destructor for object **third** is called before the destructor for **first**, but after all other objects are destroyed.

```
1   // Fig. 6.9: create.h
2   // Definition of class CreateAndDestroy.
3   // Member functions defined in create.cpp.
4   #ifndef CREATE_H
5   #define CREATE_H
6
7   class CreateAndDestroy {
8   public:
9      CreateAndDestroy( int );   // constructor
10     ~CreateAndDestroy();       // destructor
11  private:
12     int data;
13  };
14
15  #endif
```

Fig. 6.9　Demonstrating the order in which constructors and destructors are called—**create.h**.

```
16  // Fig. 6.9: create.cpp
17  // Member function definitions for class CreateAndDestroy
18  #include <iostream>
19
20  using std::cout;
21  using std::endl;
22
23  #include "create.h"
24
25  CreateAndDestroy::CreateAndDestroy( int value )
26  {
27     data = value;
28     cout << "Object " << data << "    constructor";
29  }
30
31  CreateAndDestroy::~CreateAndDestroy()
32     { cout << "Object " << data << "    destructor " << endl; }
```

Fig. 6.9   Demonstrating the order in which constructors and destructors are called—
`create.cpp`.

```
33  // Fig. 6.9: fig06_09.cpp
34  // Demonstrating the order in which constructors and
35  // destructors are called.
36  #include <iostream>
37
38  using std::cout;
39  using std::endl;
40
41  #include "create.h"
42
43  void create( void );    // prototype
44
45  CreateAndDestroy first( 1 );  // global object
46
47  int main()
48  {
49     cout << "    (global created before main)" << endl;
50
51     CreateAndDestroy second( 2 );            // local object
52     cout << "    (local automatic in main)" << endl;
53
54     static CreateAndDestroy third( 3 );  // local object
55     cout << "    (local static in main)" << endl;
56
57     create();  // call function to create objects
58
59     CreateAndDestroy fourth( 4 );            // local object
60     cout << "    (local automatic in main)" << endl;
61     return 0;
62  }
```

Fig. 6.9   Demonstrating the order in which constructors and destructors are called—
`fig06_09.cpp` (part 1 of 2).

```
63
64    // Function to create objects
65    void create( void )
66    {
67       CreateAndDestroy fifth( 5 );
68       cout << "   (local automatic in create)" << endl;
69
70       static CreateAndDestroy sixth( 6 );
71       cout << "   (local static in create)" << endl;
72
73       CreateAndDestroy seventh( 7 );
74       cout << "   (local automatic in create)" << endl;
75    }
```

```
Object 1    constructor    (global created before main)
Object 2    constructor    (local automatic in main)
Object 3    constructor    (local static in main)
Object 5    constructor    (local automatic in create)
Object 6    constructor    (local static in create)
Object 7    constructor    (local automatic in create)
Object 7    destructor
Object 5    destructor
Object 4    constructor    (local automatic in main)
Object 4    destructor
Object 2    destructor
Object 6    destructor
Object 3    destructor
Object 1    destructor
```

Fig. 6.9   Demonstrating the order in which constructors and destructors are called—
fig06_09.cpp (part 2 of 2).

Function **create** declares three objects—**fifth** and **seventh** are local automatic objects, and **sixth** is a **static** local object. The destructors for objects **seventh** and **fifth** are called in that order when the end of **create** is reached. Because **sixth** is **static**, it exists until program termination. The destructor for **sixth** is called before the destructors for **third** and **first**, but after all other objects are destroyed.

6.14 Using Data Members and Member Functions

A class' **private** data members can be accessed only by member functions (and **friend**s) of the class. A typical manipulation might be the adjustment of a customer's bank balance (e.g., a **private** data member of a class **BankAccount**) by a member function **computeInterest**.

Classes often provide **public** member functions to allow clients of the class to *set* (i.e., write) or *get* (i.e., read) the values of **private** data members. These functions need not be called *set* and *get* specifically, but they often are. More specifically, a member function that *set*s data member **interestRate** would typically be named **setInterestRate**, and a member function that *get*s the **interestRate** would typically be called **getInterestRate**. Get functions are also commonly called "query" functions.

It may seem that providing both *set* and *get* capabilities is essentially the same as making the data members **public**. This is yet another subtlety of C++ that makes the language so desirable for software engineering. If a data member is **public**, then the data member may be read or written at will by any function in the program. If a data member is **private**, a **public** *get* function would certainly seem to allow other functions to read the data at will, but the *get* function could control the formatting and display of the data. A **public** *set* function could—and most likely would—carefully scrutinize any attempt to modify the value of the data member. This would ensure that the new value is appropriate for that data item. For example, an attempt to *set* the day of the month to 37 could be rejected, an attempt to *set* a person's weight to a negative value could be rejected, an attempt to *set* a numeric quantity to an alphabetic value could be rejected, an attempt to *set* a grade on an exam to 185 (when the proper range is zero to 100) could be rejected, etc.

Software Engineering Observation 6.22

Making data members **private** *and controlling access, especially write access, to those data members through* **public** *member functions helps ensure data integrity.*

Testing and Debugging Tip 6.5

The benefits of data integrity are not automatic simply because data members are made **private**—*the programmer must provide the validity checking. C++ does, however, provide a framework in which programmers can design better programs in a convenient manner.*

Good Programming Practice 6.7

Member functions that set *the values of private data should verify that the intended new values are proper; if they are not, the* set *functions should place the* **private** *data members into an appropriate consistent state.*

The client of a class should be notified when an attempt is made to assign an invalid value to a data member. A class' *set* functions are often written to return values indicating that an attempt was made to assign invalid data to an object of the class. This enables clients of the class to test the return values of *set* functions to determine if the object they are manipulating is a valid object and to take appropriate action if the object is not valid.

Figure 6.10 extends our **Time** class to include *get* and *set* functions for the **hour**, **minute** and **second private** data members. The *set* functions strictly control the setting of the data members. Attempts to *set* any data member to an incorrect value cause the data member to be set to zero (thus leaving the data member in a consistent state). Each *get* function simply returns the appropriate data member's value. The program first uses the *set* functions to *set* the **private** data members of **Time** object **t** to valid values, then uses the *get* functions to retrieve the values for output. Next the *set* functions attempt to *set* the **hour** and **second** members to invalid values and the **minute** member to a valid value, and then the *get* functions retrieve the values for output. The output confirms that invalid values cause the data members to be *set* to zero. Finally, the program *set*s the time to **11:58:00** and increments the minute value by 3 with a call to function **increment-Minutes**. Function **incrementMinutes** is a nonmember function that uses the *get* and *set* member functions to increment the **minute** member properly. Although this works, it incurs the performance burden of issuing multiple function calls. In the next chapter, we discuss the notion of **friend** functions as a means of eliminating this performance burden.

Common Programming Error 6.11

A constructor can call other member functions of the class such as set *or* get *functions, but because the constructor is initializing the object, the data members may not yet be in a consistent state. Using data members before they have been properly initialized can cause logic errors.*

```
1   // Fig. 6.10: time3.h
2   // Declaration of the Time class.
3   // Member functions defined in time3.cpp
4
5   // preprocessor directives that
6   // prevent multiple inclusions of header file
7   #ifndef TIME3_H
8   #define TIME3_H
9
10  class Time {
11  public:
12     Time( int = 0, int = 0, int = 0 );  // constructor
13
14     // set functions
15     void setTime( int, int, int );  // set hour, minute, second
16     void setHour( int );    // set hour
17     void setMinute( int );  // set minute
18     void setSecond( int );  // set second
19
20     // get functions
21     int getHour();          // return hour
22     int getMinute();        // return minute
23     int getSecond();        // return second
24
25     void printMilitary();   // output military time
26     void printStandard();   // output standard time
27
28  private:
29     int hour;               // 0 - 23
30     int minute;             // 0 - 59
31     int second;             // 0 - 59
32  };
33
34  #endif
```

Fig. 6.10   Using *set* and *get* functions—**tim3.h**.

```
35  // Fig. 6.10: time3.cpp
36  // Member function definitions for Time class.
37  #include <iostream>
38
39  using std::cout;
```

Fig. 6.10   Using set and get functions—**time3.cpp** (part 1 of 2).

```
40
41    #include "time3.h"
42
43    // Constructor function to initialize private data.
44    // Calls member function setTime to set variables.
45    // Default values are 0 (see class definition).
46    Time::Time( int hr, int min, int sec )
47       { setTime( hr, min, sec ); }
48
49    // Set the values of hour, minute, and second.
50    void Time::setTime( int h, int m, int s )
51    {
52       setHour( h );
53       setMinute( m );
54       setSecond( s );
55    }
56
57    // Set the hour value
58    void Time::setHour( int h )
59       { hour = ( h >= 0 && h < 24 ) ? h : 0; }
60
61    // Set the minute value
62    void Time::setMinute( int m )
63       { minute = ( m >= 0 && m < 60 ) ? m : 0; }
64
65    // Set the second value
66    void Time::setSecond( int s )
67       { second = ( s >= 0 && s < 60 ) ? s : 0; }
68
69    // Get the hour value
70    int Time::getHour() { return hour; }
71
72    // Get the minute value
73    int Time::getMinute() { return minute; }
74
75    // Get the second value
76    int Time::getSecond() { return second; }
77
78    // Print time is military format
79    void Time::printMilitary()
80    {
81       cout << ( hour < 10 ? "0" : "" ) << hour << ":"
82            << ( minute < 10 ? "0" : "" ) << minute;
83    }
84
85    // Print time in standard format
86    void Time::printStandard()
87    {
88       cout << ( ( hour == 0 || hour == 12 ) ? 12 : hour % 12 )
89            << ":" << ( minute < 10 ? "0" : "" ) << minute
90            << ":" << ( second < 10 ? "0" : "" ) << second
91            << ( hour < 12 ? " AM" : " PM" );
92    }
```

Fig. 6.10   Using set and get functions—**time3.cpp** (part 2 of 2).

```cpp
93   // Fig. 6.10: fig06_10.cpp
94   // Demonstrating the Time class set and get functions
95   #include <iostream>
96
97   using std::cout;
98   using std::endl;
99
100  #include "time3.h"
101
102  void incrementMinutes( Time &, const int );
103
104  int main()
105  {
106     Time t;
107
108     t.setHour( 17 );
109     t.setMinute( 34 );
110     t.setSecond( 25 );
111
112     cout << "Result of setting all valid values:\n"
113          << "  Hour: " << t.getHour()
114          << "  Minute: " << t.getMinute()
115          << "  Second: " << t.getSecond();
116
117     t.setHour( 234 );      // invalid hour set to 0
118     t.setMinute( 43 );
119     t.setSecond( 6373 ); // invalid second set to 0
120
121     cout << "\n\nResult of attempting to set invalid hour and"
122          << " second:\n  Hour: " << t.getHour()
123          << "  Minute: " << t.getMinute()
124          << "  Second: " << t.getSecond() << "\n\n";
125
126     t.setTime( 11, 58, 0 );
127     incrementMinutes( t, 3 );
128
129     return 0;
130  }
131
132  void incrementMinutes( Time &tt, const int count )
133  {
134     cout << "Incrementing minute " << count
135          << " times:\nStart time: ";
136     tt.printStandard();
137
138     for ( int i = 0; i < count; i++ ) {
139        tt.setMinute( ( tt.getMinute() + 1 ) % 60 );
140
141        if ( tt.getMinute() == 0 )
142           tt.setHour( ( tt.getHour() + 1 ) % 24 );
143
144        cout << "\nminute + 1: ";
```

Fig. 6.10   Using *set* and *get* functions—**fig06_10.cpp** (part 1 of 2).

```
145        tt.printStandard();
146    }
147
148    cout << endl;
149 }
```

```
Result of setting all valid values:
  Hour: 17  Minute: 34  Second: 25

Result of attempting to set invalid hour and second:
  Hour: 0  Minute: 43  Second: 0

Incrementing minute 3 times:
Start time: 11:58:00 AM
minute + 1: 11:59:00 AM
minute + 1: 12:00:00 PM
minute + 1: 12:01:00 PM
```

Fig. 6.10   Using *set* and *get* functions—**fig06_10.cpp** (part 2 of 2).

Using *set* functions is certainly important from a software engineering standpoint because they can perform validity checking. Both *set* and *get* functions have another important software engineering advantage.

Software Engineering Observation 6.23

Accessing **private** *data through* set *and* get *member functions not only protects the data members from receiving invalid values, but it also insulates clients of the class from the representation of the data members. Thus, if the representation of the data changes for some reason (typically to reduce the amount of storage required or to improve performance), only the member functions need to change—the clients need not change as long as the interface provided by the member functions remains the same. The clients may, however, need to be recompiled.*

6.15 A Subtle Trap: Returning a Reference to a **private** Data Member

A reference to an object is an alias for the *name* of the object and hence may be used on the left side of an assignment statement. In this context, the reference makes a perfectly acceptable *lvalue* that can receive a value. One way to use this capability (unfortunately!) is to have a **public** member function of a class return a non-**const** reference to a **private** data member of that class.

Figure 6.11 uses a simplified **Time** class to demonstrate returning a reference to a **private** data member. Such a return actually makes a call to function **badSetHour** an alias for the **private** data member **hour**! The function call can be used in any way that the **private** data member can be used, including as an *lvalue* in an assignment statement!

Good Programming Practice 6.8

Never have a **public** *member function return a non-***const** *reference (or a pointer) to a* **private** *data member. Returning such a reference violates the encapsulation of the class. In fact, returning any reference or pointer to* **private** *data still makes the client code dependent on the representation of the class' data. So, returning pointers or references to* **private** *data should be avoided.*

```
1    // Fig. 6.11: time4.h
2    // Declaration of the Time class.
3    // Member functions defined in time4.cpp
4
5    // preprocessor directives that
6    // prevent multiple inclusions of header file
7    #ifndef TIME4_H
8    #define TIME4_H
9
10   class Time {
11   public:
12      Time( int = 0, int = 0, int = 0 );
13      void setTime( int, int, int );
14      int getHour();
15      int &badSetHour( int );   // DANGEROUS reference return
16   private:
17      int hour;
18      int minute;
19      int second;
20   };
21
22   #endif
```

Fig. 6.11   Returning a reference to a **private** data member—**time4.h**.

```
23   // Fig. 6.11: time4.cpp
24   // Member function definitions for Time class.
25   #include "time4.h"
26
27   // Constructor function to initialize private data.
28   // Calls member function setTime to set variables.
29   // Default values are 0 (see class definition).
30   Time::Time( int hr, int min, int sec )
31      { setTime( hr, min, sec ); }
32
33   // Set the values of hour, minute, and second.
34   void Time::setTime( int h, int m, int s )
35   {
36      hour   = ( h >= 0 && h < 24 ) ? h : 0;
37      minute = ( m >= 0 && m < 60 ) ? m : 0;
38      second = ( s >= 0 && s < 60 ) ? s : 0;
39   }
40
41   // Get the hour value
42   int Time::getHour() { return hour; }
43
44   // POOR PROGRAMMING PRACTICE:
45   // Returning a reference to a private data member.
46   int &Time::badSetHour( int hh )
47   {
48      hour = ( hh >= 0 && hh < 24 ) ? hh : 0;
```

Fig. 6.11   Returning a reference to a **private** data member—**time4.cpp** (part 1 of 2).

```
49
50       return hour;   // DANGEROUS reference return
51   }
```

Fig. 6.11   Returning a reference to a **private** data member—**time4.cpp** (part 2 of 2).

```
52   // Fig. 6.11: fig06_11.cpp
53   // Demonstrating a public member function that
54   // returns a reference to a private data member.
55   // Time class has been trimmed for this example.
56   #include <iostream>
57
58   using std::cout;
59   using std::endl;
60
61   #include "time4.h"
62
63   int main()
64   {
65      Time t;
66      int &hourRef = t.badSetHour( 20 );
67
68      cout << "Hour before modification: " << hourRef;
69      hourRef = 30;   // modification with invalid value
70      cout << "\nHour after modification: " << t.getHour();
71
72      // Dangerous: Function call that returns
73      // a reference can be used as an lvalue!
74      t.badSetHour(12) = 74;
75      cout << "\n\n*********************************\n"
76           << "POOR PROGRAMMING PRACTICE!!!!!!!!\n"
77           << "badSetHour as an lvalue, Hour: "
78           << t.getHour()
79           << "\n*******************************" << endl;
80
81      return 0;
82   }
```

```
Hour before modification: 20
Hour after modification: 30

*********************************
POOR PROGRAMMING PRACTICE!!!!!!!!
badSetHour as an lvalue, Hour: 74
*********************************
```

Fig. 6.11   Returning a reference to a private data member—**fig06_11.cpp**.

The program begins by declaring **Time** object **t** and reference **hourRef** that is assigned the reference returned by the call **t.badSetHour(20)**. The program displays the value of the alias **hourRef**. Next, the alias is used to set the value of **hour** to 30 (an invalid value) and the value is displayed again. Finally, the function call itself is used as an *lvalue* and assigned the value 74 (another invalid value), and the value is displayed.

6.16 Assignment by Default Memberwise Copy

The assignment operator (=) can be used to assign an object to another object of the same type. Such assignment is by default performed by *memberwise copy*—each member of one object is copied (assigned) individually to the same member in another object (see Fig. 6.12). (Note: Memberwise copy can cause serious problems when used with a class whose data members contain dynamically allocated storage; in Chapter 8, "Operator Overloading," we will discuss these problems and show how to deal with them.)

Objects may be passed as function arguments and may be returned from functions. Such passing and returning is performed call-by-value by default—a copy of the object is passed or returned (we present several examples in Chapter 8, "Operator Overloading").

Performance Tip 6.4

*Passing an object call-by-value is good from a security standpoint because the called function has no access to the original object, but call-by-value can degrade performance when making a copy of a large object. An object can be passed call-by-reference by passing either a pointer or a reference to the object. Call-by-reference offers good performance but is weaker from a security standpoint because the called function is given access to the original object. Call-by-**const**-reference is a safe, good-performing alternative.*

```
1   // Fig. 6.12: fig06_12.cpp
2   // Demonstrating that class objects can be assigned
3   // to each other using default memberwise copy
4   #include <iostream>
5
6   using std::cout;
7   using std::endl;
8
9   // Simple Date class
10  class Date {
11  public:
12     Date( int = 1, int = 1, int = 1990 );  // default constructor
13     void print();
14  private:
15     int month;
16     int day;
17     int year;
18  };
19
20  // Simple Date constructor with no range checking
21  Date::Date( int m, int d, int y )
22  {
23     month = m;
24     day = d;
25     year = y;
26  }
27
```

Fig. 6.12   Assigning one object to another with default memberwise copy (part 1 of 2).

```
28    // Print the Date in the form mm-dd-yyyy
29    void Date::print()
30       { cout << month << '-' << day << '-' << year; }
31
32    int main()
33    {
34       Date date1( 7, 4, 1993 ), date2;   // d2 defaults to 1/1/90
35
36       cout << "date1 = ";
37       date1.print();
38       cout << "\ndate2 = ";
39       date2.print();
40
41       date2 = date1;   // assignment by default memberwise copy
42       cout << "\n\nAfter default memberwise copy, date2 = ";
43       date2.print();
44       cout << endl;
45
46       return 0;
47    }
```

```
date1 = 7-4-1993
date2 = 1-1-1990

After default memberwise copy, date2 = 7-4-1993
```

Fig. 6.12   Assigning one object to another with default memberwise copy (part 2 of 2).

6.17 Software Reusability

People who write object-oriented programs concentrate on implementing useful classes. There is a tremendous opportunity to capture and catalog classes so that they can be accessed by large segments of the programming community. Many *class libraries* exist and others are being developed worldwide. There are efforts to make these libraries broadly accessible. Software is increasingly being constructed from existing, well-defined, carefully tested, well-documented, portable, widely available components. This kind of software reusability speeds the development of powerful, high-quality software. *Rapid applications development (RAD)* through the mechanisms of reusable componentry has become an important field.

Significant problems must be solved, however, before the full potential of software reusability can be realized. We need cataloging schemes, licensing schemes, protection mechanisms to ensure that master copies of classes are not corrupted, description schemes so that designers of new systems can determine if existing objects meet their needs, browsing mechanisms to determine what classes are available and how closely they meet software developer requirement and the like. Many interesting research and development problems need to be solved. There is great motivation to solve these problems because the potential value of their solutions is enormous.

6.18 (Optional Case Study) Thinking About Objects: Starting to Program the Classes for the Elevator Simulator

In the "Thinking About Objects" sections in Chapters 1 through 5, we introduced the fundamentals of object orientation and developed an object-oriented design for an elevator simulator. In the body of Chapter 6, we introduced the details of programming with C++ classes. We now begin implementing our object-oriented design in C++. In this section, we will use our UML class diagram to outline the C++ header files that define our classes.

Implementation: Visibility

In the body of Chapter 6, we introduced the access specifiers **public** and **private**. Before we create the class header files, we must first consider which elements from our class diagram should be **public** and which elements should be **private**.

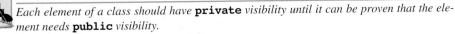

Software Engineering Observation 6.24

*Each element of a class should have **private** visibility until it can be proven that the element needs **public** visibility.*

In Chapter 6, we discussed how data members should generally be **private**, but what about member functions? The operations of a class are its member functions. These operations must be invoked by clients of that class; therefore, the member functions should be **public**. In the UML, **public** visibility is indicated by placing a plus sign (+) before a particular element (i.e., a member function or a data member); a minus sign (-) indicates **private** visibility. Figure 6.13 shows our updated class diagram with visibility notations included. (Note that we have added the **personArrives** operation to class **Floor** from our sequence diagram in Fig. 4.27.) As we write the C++ header files for the classes in our system, we automatically place the items designated with "+" into the **public** sections and items designated with "-" into the **private** sections of the class declarations.

Implementation: Handles

In order for an object of class A to communicate with an object of class B, the class A object must have a *handle* to the class B object. This means that either the class A object must know the name of the class B object, or the class A object must hold a reference (Section 3.17) or a pointer (Chapter 5) to the class B object.[1] Figure 5.36 contained a list of collaborations among objects in our system. The classes in the left column of the table need a handle to each of the classes in the right column of the table to send messages to those classes. Figure 6.14 lists the handles for each class based on the information displayed in the table from Figure 5.36.

In the body of Chapter 6, we discussed how to implement handles in C++ as references and pointers to classes (and, again, we will prefer references over pointers, where appropriate). These references then become attributes (data) of the class. Until we discuss composition in Chapter 7, we cannot represent every item from Fig. 6.14 in our class header files. We will discuss these special cases shortly.

---

1. In situations where the name of the class B object is not available to the class A object, we will prefer references over pointers (where appropriate), because references are inherently safer than pointers.

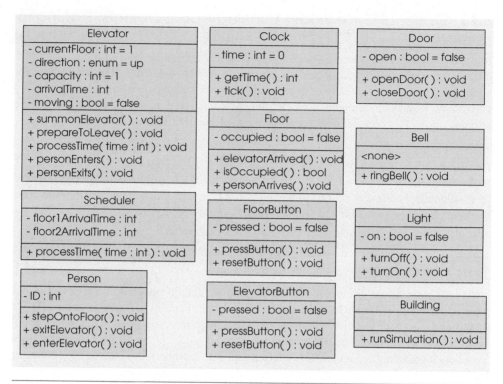

Fig. 6.13   Complete class diagram with visibility notations.

Class	Handles
Elevator	ElevatorButton, Bell, Floor, Door
Clock	
Scheduler	Person, Floor
Person	FloorButton, ElevatorButton, Elevator, Floor
Floor	FloorButton, Light
FloorButton	Elevator
ElevatorButton	Elevator
Door	Person
Bell	
Light	
Building	Clock, Scheduler, Elevator

Fig. 6.14   List of handles for each class.

Implementation: Class Header Files

Now that we have discussed programming C++ classes, we are ready to begin writing the code for our elevator simulator. In this section, we examine the header files for each class in our system. In the "Thinking About Objects" section at the end of Chapter 7, we present the complete, working C++ code for the simulator. In Chapter 9, we modify that code to incorporate inheritance.

To demonstrate the order in which constructors and destructors run, we will code a constructor and destructor for each of our classes that simply display messages indicating that these functions are running. We include the constructor and destructor prototypes in our header files; we include their implementations in the **.cpp** files presented in Chapter 7.

Figure 6.15 lists the header file for class **Bell**. Working from our class diagram (Fig. 6.13), we declare a constructor, a destructor (lines 8 and 9) and the member function **ring-Bell** (line 10); each of these member functions has **public** visibility. We have identified no other **public** or **private** elements for this class, so our header file is complete.

Figure 6.16 lists the header file for class **Clock**. We include a constructor and destructor (lines 8 and 9) and the **public** member functions **tick()** and **getTime()** (lines 10 and 11) from Fig. 6.13. We implement the **time** attribute in our class header file by declaring a **private** data member **time** of type **int** (line 13). Once per second in our simulation, an object of class **Building** invokes the **getTime** member function of an object of class **Clock** to get the current value of **time** and invokes the **tick** member function to increment **time**.

```
1   // bell.h
2   // Definition for class Bell.
3   #ifndef BELL_H
4   #define BELL_H
5
6   class Bell {
7   public:
8      Bell();                // constructor
9      ~Bell();               // destructor
10     void ringBell();       // ring the bell
11  };
12
13  #endif // BELL_H
```

Fig. 6.15   Class **Bell** header file.

```
1   // clock.h
2   // Definition for class Clock.
3   #ifndef CLOCK_H
4   #define CLOCK_H
5
6   class Clock {
7   public:
8      Clock();               // constructor
9      ~Clock();              // destructor
10     void tick();           // increment clock by one second
```

Fig. 6.16   Class **Clock** header file (part 1 of 2).

```
11       int getTime();           // returns clock's current time
12     private:
13       int time;                // clock's time
14   };
15
16   #endif // CLOCK_H
```

Fig. 6.16   Class **Clock** header file (part 2 of 2).

Figure 6.17 lists the header file for class **Person**. We declare the **ID** attribute (line 16) and (in lines 12–14) the operations **stepOntoFloor**, **enterElevator** and **exitElevator** from our class diagram (Fig. 6.13). We also declare a **public getID** member function (line 10) that returns the person's **ID** number. We will use this operation to keep track of the people in our simulation.

Objects of class **Person** are not created at the beginning of the simulation—they are randomly created dynamically as the simulation runs. For this reason, we must implement objects of class **Person** differently from objects of our other classes in our system. After we discuss how to create new objects dynamically in Chapter 7, we will add significant elements to the header file for class **Person**.

Figure 6.18 lists the header file for class **Door**. We declare a constructor and a destructor (lines 8 and 9)), the **public** member functions **openDoor** and **closeDoor** in lines 11 and 12. We declare the **private** class data member **open** in line 14. The table in Fig. 6.14 states that class **Door** needs a handle to class **Person**. However, because objects of class **Person** are created dynamically in our system, we are unsure at this point how to implement handles to objects of class **Person**. After we discuss dynamically created objects in Chapter 7, we will have a better idea of how to implement handles to class **Person**.

```
 1   // person.h
 2   // definition of class Person
 3   #ifndef PERSON_H
 4   #define PERSON_H
 5
 6   class Person {
 7   public:
 8      Person( int );           // constructor
 9      ~Person();               // destructor
10      int getID();             // returns person's ID
11
12      void stepOntoFloor();
13      void enterElevator();
14      void exitElevator()
15   private:
16      int ID;                  // person's unique ID #
17   };
18
19   #endif // PERSON_H
```

Fig. 6.17   Class **Person** header file.

```
1   // door.h
2   // Definition for class Door.
3   #ifndef DOOR_H
4   #define DOOR_H
5
6   class Door {
7   public:
8      Door();                          // constructor
9      ~Door();                         // destructor
10
11     void openDoor();
12     void closeDoor();
13  private:
14     bool open;                       // open or closed
15  };
16
17  #endif // DOOR_H
```

Fig. 6.18   Class **Door** header file.

We list the header file for class **Light** in Figure 6.19. The information from the class diagram in Fig. 6.13 leads us to declare **public** member functions **turnOn** and **turnOff** and **private** data member **on** of type **bool**. In this header file, we also introduce something new to our implementation—the need to distinguish between different objects of the same class in our system. We know that the simulation contains two objects of class **Light**: one object belongs to the first floor, and the other object belongs to the second floor. We want to be able to distinguish between these two objects for output purposes, so we need to give a name to each. Therefore, we add line 14

```
        char *name;       // whi\ch floor the light is on
```

to the **private** section of the class declaration. We also add a **char** * parameter to the constructor (line 8), so that it can initialize the name of each object of class **Light**.

```
1   // light.h
2   // Definition for class Light.
3   #ifndef LIGHT_H
4   #define LIGHT_H
5
6   class Light {
7   public:
8      Light( char * );                 // constructor
9      ~Light();                        // destructor
10     void turnOn();                   // turns light on
11     void turnOff();                  // turns light off
12  private:
13     bool on;                         // on or off
14     char *name;
15  };
16
17  #endif // LIGHT_H
```

Fig. 6.19   Class **Light** header file.

Figure 6.20 lists the header file for class **Building**. The **public** section of the class declaration includes a constructor, a destructor and the **runSimulation** member function from Fig. 6.13. When we first identified the **runSimulation** operation in Chapter 4, we did not know what object would invoke the function to begin the simulation. Now that we have discussed classes in C++, we know that an object of class **Building** needs to be declared in **main** and that **main** will then invoke **runSimulation**. The code in the main program is:

```
Building building;          // create the building object
building.runSimulation();   // invoke runSimulation
```

We also choose to include a parameter of type **int** in the **runSimulation** declaration. The **building** object will run the elevator simulation for the number of seconds passed to the object via this parameter. The preceding invocation of **runSimulation** would then include a number indicating the duration of the simulation. The table in Fig. 6.14 indicates that class **Building** needs handles to its composite objects. We cannot implement these handles at this point, because we have not discussed composition. Therefore, we delay the implementation of the component objects of class **Building** until Chapter 7 (see the comments in lines 14–18 in Fig. 6.20).

Figure 6.21 lists the header file for class **ElevatorButton**. We declare the **pressed** attribute, the **pressButton** and **resetButton** member functions (from the class diagram in Fig. 6.13) and the constructor and destructor. Figure 6.14 states that class **ElevatorButton** needs a handle to the elevator. In line 19

```
Elevator &elevatorRef;
```

we include this handle (notice that we use a reference to implement the handle). In Chapter 7, we discuss how to send messages to the elevator using this reference.

```
1   // building.h
2   // Definition for class Building.
3   #ifndef BUILDING_H
4   #define BUILDING_H
5
6   class Building {
7   public:
8      Building();              // constructor
9      ~Building();             // destructor
10
11     // runs simulation for specified amount of time
12     void runSimulation( int );
13  private:
14     // In Chapter 7, we show how to include:
15     //    one object of class Clock
16     //    one object of class Scheduler
17     //    one object of class Elevator
18     //    two objects of class Floor
19  };
20
21  #endif // BUILDING_H
```

Fig. 6.20   Class **Building** header file.

```
1   // elevatorButton.h
2   // Definition for class ElevatorButton.
3   #ifndef ELEVATORBUTTON_H
4   #define ELEVATORBUTTON_H
5
6   class Elevator;                         // forward declaration
7
8   class ElevatorButton {
9   public:
10      ElevatorButton( Elevator & );       // constructor
11      ~ElevatorButton();                  // destructor
12
13      void pressButton();                 // press the button
14      void resetButton();                 // reset the button
15   private:
16      bool pressed;                       // state of button
17
18      // reference to button's elevator
19      Elevator &elevatorRef;
20   };
21
22   #endif // ELEVATORBUTTON_H
```

Fig. 6.21   Class **ElevatorButton** header file.

A reference must be initialized when it is declared, but we are not allowed to assign a value to class data member in the header file. Therefore, a reference must be initialized in the constructor; we pass an **Elevator** reference to the constructor as a parameter in line 10.

Line 6

```
class Elevator;        // forward declaration
```

is a *forward declaration* of class **Elevator**. The forward declaration allows us to declare a reference to an object of class **Elevator** without needing to include the header file for class **Elevator** in the header file for class **ElevatorButton**.[2]

Figure 6.22 lists the header file for class **FloorButton**. This header file is identical to the header file for class **ElevatorButton**, except we declare a **private** data member **floorNumber** of type **int**. Objects of class **FloorButton** need to know to which floor they belong for simulator output purposes. The floor number is passed in as a constructor argument for initialization purposes (line 10).

Figure 6.23 lists the header file for class **Scheduler**. In lines 23 and 24

```
int floor1ArrivalTime;
int floor2ArrivalTime;
```

we declare the **private** data members of class **Scheduler** that correspond to the attributes we have identified for this class (Fig. 6.13). In line 12, we declare the **public** member function **processTime** that corresponds to the operation we identified in the "Thinking About Objects" section at the end of Chapter 4.

2. Using the forward declaration (where possible) instead of including the full header file helps avoid a preprocessor problem called a circular include. We discuss the circular include problem in more detail in Chapter 7.

```
1   // floorButton.h
2   // Definition for class FloorButton.
3   #ifndef FLOORBUTTON_H
4   #define FLOORBUTTON_H
5
6   class Elevator;                        // forward declaration
7
8   class FloorButton {
9   public:
10     FloorButton( int, Elevator & ); // constructor
11     ~FloorButton();                // destructor
12
13     void pressButton();            // press the button
14     void resetButton();            // reset the button
15  private:
16     int floorNumber;               // number of the button's floor
17     bool pressed;                  // state of button
18
19     // reference to button's elevator
20     Elevator &elevatorRef;
21  };
22
23  #endif // FLOORBUTTON_H
```

Fig. 6.22   Class **FloorButton** header file.

```
1   // scheduler.h
2   // definition for class Scheduler
3   #ifndef SCHEDULER_H
4   #define SCHEDULER_H
5
6   class Floor;                       // forward declaration
7
8   class Scheduler {
9   public:
10     Scheduler( Floor &, Floor & );   // constructor
11     ~Scheduler();                    // destructor
12     void processTime( int );         // set scheduler's time
13  private:
14
15     // method that schedules arrivals to a specified floor
16     void scheduleTime( Floor & );
17
18     // method that delays arrivals to a specified floor
19     void delayTime( Floor & );
20
21     Floor &floor1Ref;
22     Floor &floor2Ref;
23     int floor1ArrivalTime;
24     int floor2ArrivalTime;
25  };
```

Fig. 6.23   Class **Scheduler** header file (part 1 of 2).

```
26
27  #endif  // SCHEDULER_H
```

Fig. 6.23   Class **Scheduler** header file (part 2 of 2).

In lines 15–19 we declare the functions we identified in the sequence diagram in Fig. 4.27. Each of these functions takes as a parameter a reference to an object of class **Floor**. Note that we did not list these functions as operations (i.e., **public** member functions), because these methods are not invoked by client objects. Instead, these methods are used only by class **Scheduler** to perform its own internal actions. Therefore, we place these methods in the **private** section of the class declaration.

In lines 21 and 22, we declare the handles identified in Fig. 6.14. Again, we implement each handle as a reference to an object of class **Floor**. Class **Scheduler** needs these handles so that it can send the **isOccupied** message to the two floors in the simulation (see diagram in Fig. 4.27). We must also make a forward declaration of class **Floor** in line 6 so that we may declare the references.

Figure 6.24 contains the header file for class **Floor**. We declare the **public** member functions **elevatorArrived**, **isOccupied** and **personArrives** from Fig. 6.13. We also declare the **public** member function **elevatorLeaving** in line 26. We add this member function so the elevator can tell the floor when the elevator is preparing to leave. The elevator invokes the **elevatorLeaving** operation, and the floor responds by turning off its light.

```
1   // floor.h
2   // Definition for class Floor.
3   #ifndef FLOOR_H
4   #define FLOOR_H
5
6   class Elevator;                 // forward declaration
7
8   class Floor {
9   public:
10     Floor( int, Elevator & );   // constructor
11     ~Floor();                    // destructor
12
13     // return true if floor is occupied
14     bool isOccupied();
15
16     // return floor's number
17     int getNumber();
18
19     // pass a handle to new person coming on floor
20     void personArrives();
21
22     // notify floor that elevator has arrived
23     void elevatorArrived();
24
25     // notify floor that elevator is leaving
26     void elevatorLeaving();
```

Fig. 6.24   Class **Floor** header file.

```
27
28       // declaration of FloorButton component (see Chapter 7)
29
30    private:
31       int floorNumber;              // the floor's number
32       Elevator &elevatorRef;        // pointer to elevator
33       // declaration of Light component (see Chapter 7)
34    };
35
36    #endif // FLOOR_H
```

Fig. 6.24   Class **Floor** header file.

In line 31, we add a **private floorNumber** data member to the class—we add this value for output purposes, just as we did with the **floorNumber** data member of class **FloorButton**. We also add a parameter of type **int** to the constructor so the constructor can initialize that data member. We also declare the handle to class **Elevator** identified in Fig. 6.14. We defer declaration of the component members of class **Floor** (see lines 28 and 33) until Chapter 7.

We list the header file for class **Elevator** in Fig. 6.25. In the **public** section of the header file, we declare the **summonElevator**, **prepareToLeave** and **process-Time** operations listed in Fig. 6.13. To differentiate between people on the floor and people in the elevator, we rename the last two operations listed under class **Elevator**. We call these operations **passengerEnters** and **passengerExits**, and we declare them in the **public** section of the header file. We also declare a reference to each of the two floors (lines 38-39); the constructor (line 10) initializes these references.

```
1    // elevator.h
2    // Definition for class Elevator.
3    #ifndef ELEVATOR_H
4    #define ELEVATOR_H
5
6    class Floor;                            // forward declaration
7
8    class Elevator {
9    public:
10      Elevator( Floor &, Floor & );   // constructor
11      ~Elevator();                    // destructor
12
13      // request that elevator service a particluar floor
14      void summonElevator( int );
15
16      // prepare elevator to leave
17      void prepareToLeave();
18
19      // give time to elevator
20      void processTime( int );
21
22      // notify elevator that passenger is boarding
23      void passengerEnters();
```

Fig. 6.25   Class **Elevator** header file.

```
24
25     // notify elevator that passenger is exiting
26     void passengerExits();
27
28     // declaration of ElevatorButton component (see Chapter 7)
29  private:
30     bool moving;                    // elevator state
31     int direction;                  // current direction
32     int currentFloor;               // current location
33
34     // time for arrival at a floor
35     int arrivalTime;
36
37     // References to floors serviced by elevator
38     Floor &floor1Ref;
39     Floor &floor2Ref;
40
41     // declaration of Door component (see Chapter 7)
42     // declaration of Bell component (see Chapter 7)
43  };
44
45  #endif // ELEVATOR_H
```

Fig. 6.25   Class **Elevator** header file.

In the **private** section of the header file, we declare the **moving**, **direction**, **currentFloor** and **arrivalTime** attributes from Fig. 6.13. We do not need to declare the **capacity** attribute; instead, we will write our code to ensure that only one person may be on the elevator at a time.

Conclusion
In the next "Thinking About Objects" section, we present the full C++ code for our elevator simulation. We will use the concepts presented in the next chapter to implement composite relationships, dynamic creation of objects of class **Person** and **static** and **const** data members and functions. In the "Thinking About Objects" section at the end of Chapter 9, we use inheritance to further improve our object-oriented elevator simulator design and implementation.

SUMMARY
- Structures are aggregate data types built using data of other types.
- The keyword **struct** introduces a structure definition. The body of a structure is delineated by braces (**{** and **}**). Every structure definition must end with a semicolon.
- A structure tag name can be used to declare variables of a structure type.
- Structure definitions do not reserve space in memory; they create new data types that are used to declare variables.
- Members of a structure or a class are accessed using the member access operators—the dot operator (**.**) and the arrow operator (**->**). The dot operator accesses a structure member via the object's variable name or a reference to the object. The arrow operator accesses a structure member via a pointer to the object.

Classes and Data Abstraction

- Drawbacks to creating new data types with **struct**s are the possibility of having uninitialized data; improper initialization; all programs using a **struct** must be changed if the **struct** implementation changes and no protection is provided to ensure that data are kept in a consistent state with proper data values.

- Classes enable the programmer to model objects with attributes and behaviors. Class types can be defined in C++ using the keywords **class** and **struct**, but keyword **class** is normally used for this purpose.

- The class name can be used to declare objects of that class.

- Class definitions begin with the keyword **class**. The body of the class definition is delineated with braces (**{** and **}**). Class definitions terminate with a semicolon.

- Any data member or member function declared after **public:** in a class is visible to any function with access to an object of the class.

- Any data member or member function declared after **private:** is only visible to **friend**s and other members of the class.

- Member access specifiers always end with a colon (**:**) and can appear multiple times and in any order in a class definition.

- Private data are not accessible from outside the class.

- The implementation of a class should be hidden from its clients.

- A constructor is a special member function with the same name as the class that is used to initialize the members of a class object. The constructor is called when an object of that class is instantiated.

- The function with the same name as the class but preceded with a tilde character (~) is called a destructor.

- The set of **public** member functions of a class is called the class' interface or **public** interface.

- When a member function is defined outside the class definition, the function name is preceded by the class name and the binary scope resolution operator (**::**).

- Member functions defined using the scope resolution operator outside a class definition are within that class' scope.

- Member functions defined in a class definition are automatically **inlined**. The compiler reserves the right not to **inline** any function.

- Calling member functions is more concise than calling functions in procedural programming because most data used by the member function are directly accessible in the object.

- Within a class' scope, class members may be referenced simply by their names. Outside a class' scope, class members are referenced through either an object name, a reference to an object or a pointer to an object.

- Member selection operators **.** and **->** are used to access class members.

- A fundamental principle of good software engineering is separating interface from implementation.

- Class definitions are normally placed in header files and member function definitions are normally placed in source-code files of the same base name.

- The default access mode for classes is **private** so all members after the class header and before the first member access specifier are considered to be **private**.

- A class' **public** members present a view of the services the class provides to the class' clients.

- Access to a class' **private** data can be carefully controlled via member functions called access functions. If a class wants to allow clients to read **private** data, the class can provide a *get* function. To enable clients to modify **private** data, the class can provide a *set* function.

- Data members of a class are normally made **private** and member functions of a class are normally made **public**. Some member functions may be **private** and serve as utility functions to the other functions of the class.

- Data members of a class cannot be initialized in a class definition. They must be initialized in a constructor, or their values may be *set* after their object is created.

- Constructors can be overloaded.

- Once a class object is properly initialized, all member functions that manipulate the object should ensure that the object remains in a consistent state.

- When an object of a class is declared, initializers can be provided. These initializers are passed to the class' constructor.

- Constructors can specify default arguments.

- Constructors may not specify return types, nor may they attempt to return values.

- If no constructor is defined for a class, the compiler creates a default constructor. A default constructor supplied by the compiler does not perform any initialization, so when the object is created, it is not guaranteed to be in a consistent state.

- The destructor of an automatic object is called when the object goes out of scope. The destructor itself does not actually destroy the object, but it does perform termination housekeeping before the system reclaims the object's storage.

- Destructors do not receive parameters and do not return values. A class may have only one destructor (destructors cannot be overloaded).

- The assignment operator (**=**) is used to assign an object to another object of the same type. Such assignment is normally performed by default memberwise copy. Memberwise copy is not ideal for all classes.

TERMINOLOGY

& reference operator
abstract data type (ADT)
access function
arrow member selection operator (**->**)
attribute
behavior
binary scope resolution operator (**::**)
class
class definition
class member selector operator (**.**)
class scope
client of a class
consistent state for a data member
constructor
data member
data type
default constructor
destructor
dot member selection operator (**.**)
encapsulation
extensibility
file scope

get function
global object
header file
helper function
implementation of a class
information hiding
initialize a class object
inline member function
instance of a class
instantiate an object of a class
interface to a class
member access control
member access specifiers
member function
member initializer
member selection operator (**.** and **->**)
memberwise copy
message
nonmember function
nonstatic local object
object
object-oriented design (OOD)

object-oriented programming (OOP)
predicate function
principle of least privilege
private
procedural programming
programmer-defined type
protected
proxy class
public
public interface of a class
query function
rapid applications development (RAD)

reusable code
scope resolution operator (**::**)
self-referential structure
services of a class
set function
software reusability
source-code file
static local object
structure
tilde (~) in destructor name
user-defined type
utility function

"Thinking About Objects" Terminology

"+" symbol for **public** visibility
"-" symbol for **private** visibility
circular include problem
forward declaration
handle

private visibility
public visibility
references vs. pointers
visibility

COMMON PROGRAMMING ERRORS

6.1   The expression **(*timePtr).hour** refers to the **hour** member of the **struct** pointed to by **timePtr**. Omitting the parentheses, as in ***timePtr.hour** would be a syntax error because **.** has a higher precedence than *****, so the expression would execute as if parenthesized as ***(timePtr.hour)**. This would be a syntax error because with a pointer you must use the arrow operator to refer to a member.

6.2   Forgetting the semicolon at the end of a class (or structure) definition is a syntax error.

6.3   Specifying a return type and/or a return value for a constructor is a syntax error.

6.4   Attempting to initialize a data member of a class explicitly in the class definition is a syntax error.

6.5   When defining a class' member functions outside that class, omitting the class name and scope resolution operator on the function name is an error.

6.6   An attempt by a function, which is not a member of a particular class (or a **friend** of that class), to access a **private** member of that class is a syntax error.

6.7   Data members of a class cannot be initialized in the class definition.

6.8   Attempting to declare a return type for a constructor and/or attempting to return a value from a constructor are syntax errors.

6.9   Specifying default initializers for the same member function in both a header file and in the member function definition.

6.10   It is a syntax error to attempt to pass arguments to a destructor, to specify a return type for a destructor (even **void** cannot be specified), to return values from a destructor or to overload a destructor.

6.11   A constructor can call other member functions of the class such as *set* or *get* functions, but because the constructor is initializing the object, the data members may not yet be in a consistent state. Using data members before they have been properly initialized can cause logic errors.

GOOD PROGRAMMING PRACTICES

6.1   Use each member access specifier only once in a class definition for clarity and readability. Place **public** members first where they are easy to locate.

6.2   Use the name of the header file with the period replaced by an underscore in the **#ifndef** and **#define** preprocessor directives of a header file.

6.3   If you choose to list the **private** members first in a class definition, explicitly use the **private** member access specifier despite the fact that **private** is assumed by default. This improves program clarity. Our preference is to list the **public** members of a class first to emphasize the class' interface.

6.4   Despite the fact that the **public** and **private** member access specifiers may be repeated and intermixed, list all the **public** members of a class first in one group and then list all the **private** members in another group. This focuses the client's attention on the class' **public** interface, rather than on the class' implementation.

6.5   When appropriate (almost always), provide a constructor to ensure that every object is properly initialized with meaningful values. Pointer data members, in particular, should be initialized to some legitimate pointer value or to 0.

6.6   Declare default function argument values only in the function prototype within the class definition in the header file.

6.7   Member functions that *set* the values of private data should verify that the intended new values are proper; if they are not, the *set* functions should place the **private** data members into an appropriate consistent state.

6.8   Never have a **public** member function return a non-const reference (or a pointer) to a **private** data member. Returning such a reference violates the encapsulation of the class. In fact, returning any reference or pointer to **private** data still makes the client code dependent on the representation of the class' data. So, returning pointers or references to **private** data should be avoided.

PERFORMANCE TIPS

6.1   By default, structures are passed call-by-value. To avoid the overhead of copying a structure, pass the structure call-by-reference.

6.2   Defining a small member function inside the class definition automatically inlines the member function (if the compiler chooses to do so). This can improve performance, but it does not promote the best software engineering because clients of the class will be able to see the implementation of the function and their code must be recompiled if the inline function definition changes.

6.3   Actually, objects contain only data, so objects are much smaller than if they also contained functions. Applying operator **sizeof** to a class name or to an object of that class will report only the size of the class' data. The compiler creates one copy (only) of the member functions separate from all objects of the class. All objects of the class share this one copy of the member functions. Each object, of course, needs its own copy of the class' data because these data can vary among the objects. The function code is nonmodifiable (also called *reentrant code* or *pure procedure*) and hence can be shared among all objects of one class.

6.4   Passing an object call-by-value is good from a security standpoint because the called function has no access to the original object, but call-by-value can degrade performance when making a copy of a large object. An object can be passed call-by-reference by passing either a pointer or a reference to the object. Call-by-reference offers good performance but is weaker from a security standpoint because the called function is given access to the original object. Call-by-**const**-reference is a safe, good-performing alternative.

SOFTWARE ENGINEERING OBSERVATIONS

6.1   To avoid the overhead of call-by-value yet still gain the benefit that the caller's original data are protected from modification, pass large-size arguments as **const** references.

6.2   It is important to write programs that are understandable and easy to maintain. Change is the rule rather than the exception. Programmers should anticipate that their code will be modified. As we will see, classes can facilitate program modifiability.

6.3   Clients of a class use the class without knowing the internal details of how the class is implemented. If the class implementation is changed (to improve performance, for example), provided the class' interface remains constant, the class' client source code need not change (although the client may need to be recompiled). This makes it much easier to modify systems.

6.4   Member functions are usually shorter than functions in non-object-oriented programs because the data stored in data members have ideally been validated by a constructor and/or by member functions that store new data. Because the data are already in the object, the member function calls often have no arguments or at least have fewer arguments than typical function calls in non-object-oriented languages. Thus, the calls are shorter, the function definitions are shorter and the function prototypes are shorter.

6.5   Clients have access to a class' interface but should not have access to a class' implementation.

6.6   Declaring member functions inside a class definition (via their function prototypes) and defining those member functions outside that class definition separates the interface of a class from its implementation. This promotes good software engineering. Clients of a class cannot see the implementation of that class' member functions and need not recompile if that implementation changes.

6.7   Only the simplest member functions and most stable member functions (i.e., the implementation is unlikely to change) should be defined in the class header.

6.8   Using an object-oriented programming approach can often simplify function calls by reducing the number of parameters to be passed. This benefit of object-oriented programming derives from the fact that encapsulation of data members and member functions within an object gives the member functions the right to access the data members.

6.9   A central theme of this book is "reuse, reuse, reuse." We will carefully discuss a number of techniques for "polishing" classes to encourage reuse. We focus on "crafting valuable classes" and creating valuable "software assets."

6.10   Place the class declaration in a header file to be included by any client that wants to use the class. This forms the class' **public** interface (and provides the client with the function prototypes it needs to be able to call the class' member functions). Place the definitions of the class member functions in a source file. This forms the implementation of the class.

6.11   Clients of a class do not need access to the class' source code in order to use the class. The clients do, however, need to be able to link to the class' object code. This encourages independent software vendors (ISVs) to provide class libraries for sale or license. The ISVs provide in their products only the header files and the object modules. No proprietary information is revealed—as would be the case if source code were provided. The C++ user community benefits by having more ISV-produced class libraries available.

6.12   Information important to the interface to a class should be included in the header file. Information that will be used only internally in the class and will not be needed by clients of the class should be included in the unpublished source file. This is yet another example of the principle of least privilege.

6.13   C++ encourages programs to be implementation independent. When the implementation of a class used by implementation-independent code changes, that code need not be modified.

If any part of the interface of the class changes, the implementation-independent code must be recompiled.

6.14   Keep all the data members of a class **private**. Provide **public** member functions to *set* the values of **private** data members and to *get* the values of **private** data members. This architecture helps hide the implementation of a class from its clients, which reduces bugs and improves program modifiability.

6.15   Class designers use **private**, **protected** and **public** members to enforce the notion of information hiding and the principle of least privilege.

6.16   The class designer need not provide *set* and/or *get* functions for each **private** data item; these capabilities should be provided only when appropriate. If the service is useful to the client code, that service should be provided in the class's **public** interface.

6.17   Member functions tend to fall into a number of different categories: functions that read and return the value of **private** data members; functions that set the value of **private** data members; functions that implement the services of the class and functions that perform various mechanical chores for the class such as initializing class objects, assigning class objects, converting between classes and built-in types or between classes and other classes and handling memory for class objects.

6.18   A phenomenon of object-oriented programming is that once a class is defined, creating and manipulating objects of that class usually involves issuing only a simple sequence of member function calls—few, if any, control structures are needed. By contrast, it is common to have control structures in the implementation of a class' member functions.

6.19   If a member function of a class already provides all or part of the functionality required by a constructor (or other member function) of the class, call that member function from the constructor (or other member function). This simplifies the maintenance of the code and reduces the likelihood of an error if the implementation of the code is modified. As a general rule: Avoid repeating code.

6.20   It is possible for a class not to have a default constructor if any constructors are defined and none of them is explicitly a default constructor.

6.21   As we will see (throughout the remainder of the book), constructors and destructors have much greater prominence in C++ and object-oriented programming than is possible to convey after only our brief introduction here.

6.22   Making data members **private** and controlling access, especially write access, to those data members through **public** member functions helps ensure data integrity.

6.23   Accessing **private** data through *set* and *get* member functions not only protects the data members from receiving invalid values, but it also insulates clients of the class from the representation of the data members. Thus, if the representation of the data changes for some reason (typically to reduce the amount of storage required or to improve performance), only the member functions need to change—the clients need not change as long as the interface provided by the member functions remains the same. The clients may, however, need to be recompiled.

TESTING AND DEBUGGING TIPS

6.1   The fact that member function calls generally take either no arguments or substantially fewer arguments than conventional function calls in non-object-oriented languages reduces the likelihood of passing the wrong arguments, the wrong types of arguments and/or the wrong number of arguments.

6.2   Use **#ifndef**, **#define** and **#endif** preprocessor directives to prevent header files from being included more than once in a program.

6.3   Making the data members of a class **private** and the member functions of the class **public** facilitates debugging because problems with data manipulations are localized to either the class' member functions or the **friend**s of the class.

6.4   Every member function (and **friend**) that modifies the **private** data members of an object should ensure that the data remains in a consistent state.

6.5   The benefits of data integrity are not automatic simply because data members are made **private**—the programmer must provide the validity checking. C++ does, however, provide a framework in which programmers can design better programs in a convenient manner.

SELF-REVIEW EXERCISES

6.1   Fill in the blanks in each of the following:

a) The keyword _____ introduces a structure definition.

b) Class members are accessed via the _____ operator in conjunction with the name of an object of the class or via the _____ operator in conjunction with a pointer to an object of the class.

c) Members of a class specified as _____ are accessible only to member functions of the class and **friend**s of the class.

d) A _____ is a special member function used to initialize the data members of a class.

e) The default access for members of a class is _____.

f) A _____ function is used to assign values to **private** data members of a class.

g) _____ can be used to assign an object of a class to another object of the same class.

h) Member functions of a class are normally made _____ and data members of a class are normally made _____.

i) A _____ function is used to retrieve values of **private** data of a class.

j) The set of **public** member functions of a class is referred to as the class' _____.

k) A class implementation is said to be hidden from its clients or _____.

l) The keywords _____ and _____ can be used to introduce a class definition.

m) Members of a class specified as _____ are accessible anywhere an object of the class is in scope.

6.2   Find the error(s) in each of the following and explain how to correct it:

a) Assume the following prototype is declared in class **Time**:

```
void ~Time( int );
```

b) The following is a partial definition of class **Time**.

```
class Time {
public:
// function prototypes
private:
    int hour = 0;
    int minute = 0;
    int second = 0;
};
```

c) Assume the following prototype is declared in class **Employee**:

```
int Employee( const char *, const char * );
```

ANSWERS TO SELF-REVIEW EXERCISES

6.1   a) **struct**. b) dot (**.**), arrow (**->**). c) **private**. d) constructor. e) **private**. f) *set*. g) Default memberwise copy (performed by the assignment operator). h) **public**, **private**. i) *get*. j) interface. k) encapsulated. l) **class**, **struct**. m) **public**.

6.2   a) Error: Destructors are not allowed to return values or take arguments.
        Correction: Remove the return type **void** and the parameter **int** from the declaration.
    b) Error: Members cannot be explicitly initialized in the class definition.
        Correction: Remove the explicit initialization from the class definition and initialize the data members in a constructor.
    c) Error: Constructors are not allowed to return values.
        Correction: Remove the return type **int** from the declaration.

EXERCISES

6.3   What is the purpose of the scope resolution operator?

6.4   Compare and contrast the notions of **struct** and **class** in C++.

6.5   Provide a constructor that is capable of using the current time from the **time()** function—declared in the C Standard Library header **time.h**—to initialize an object of the **Time** class.

6.6   Create a class called **Complex** for performing arithmetic with complex numbers. Write a driver program to test your class.
    Complex numbers have the form

    realPart + imaginaryPart * i

where **i** is

$$\sqrt{-1}$$

Use **double** variables to represent the **private** data of the class. Provide a constructor function that enables an object of this class to be initialized when it is declared. The constructor should contain default values in case no initializers are provided. Provide **public** member functions for each of the following:
    a) Addition of two **Complex** numbers: The real parts are added together and the imaginary parts are added together.
    b) Subtraction of two **Complex** numbers: The real part of the right operand is subtracted from the real part of the left operand and the imaginary part of the right operand is subtracted from the imaginary part of the left operand.
    c) Printing **Complex** numbers in the form **(a, b)** where **a** is the real part and **b** is the imaginary part.

6.7   Create a class called **Rational** for performing arithmetic with fractions. Write a driver program to test your class.
    Use integer variables to represent the **private** data of the class—the numerator and the denominator. Provide a constructor function that enables an object of this class to be initialized when it is declared. The constructor should contain default values in case no initializers are provided and should store the fraction in reduced form (i.e., the fraction

$$\frac{2}{4}$$

would be stored in the object as 1 in the numerator and 2 in the denominator). Provide **public** member functions for each of the following:
    a) Addition of two **Rational** numbers. The result should be stored in reduced form.
    b) Subtraction of two **Rational** numbers. The result should be stored in reduced form.
    c) Multiplication of two **Rational** numbers. The result should be stored in reduced form.

d) Division of two **Rational** numbers. The result should be stored in reduced form.

e) Printing **Rational** numbers in the form **a/b** where **a** is the numerator and **b** is the denominator.

f) Printing **Rational** numbers in floating-point format.

6.8   Modify the **Time** class of Fig. 6.10 to include a **tick** member function that increments the
time stored in a **Time** object by one second. The **Time** object should always remain in a consistent
state. Write a driver program that tests the **tick** member function in a loop that prints the time in
standard format during each iteration of the loop to illustrate that the **tick** member function works
correctly. Be sure to test the following cases:

a) Incrementing into the next minute.

b) Incrementing into the next hour.

c) Incrementing into the next day (i.e., 11:59:59 PM to 12:00:00 AM).

6.9   Modify the **Date** class of Fig. 6.12 to perform error checking on the initializer values for
data members **month**, **day** and **year**. Also, provide a member function **nextDay** to increment the
day by one. The **Date** object should always remain in a consistent state. Write a driver program that
tests the **nextDay** function in a loop that prints the date during each iteration of the loop to illustrate
that the **nextDay** function works correctly. Be sure to test the following cases:

a) Incrementing into the next month.

b) Incrementing into the next year.

6.10   Combine the modified **Time** class of Exercise 6.8 and the modified **Date** class of Exercise
6.9 into one class called **DateAndTime** (in Chapter 9 we will discuss inheritance, which will enable
us to accomplish this task quickly without modifying the existing class definitions). Modify the
ticks function to call the **nextDay** function if the time is incremented into the next day. Modify
function **printStandard** and **printMilitary** to output the date in addition to the time. Write
a driver program to test the new class **DateAndTime**. Specifically, test incrementing the time into
the next day.

6.11   Modify the *set* functions in the program of Fig. 6.10 to return appropriate error values if an
attempt is made to *set* a data member of an object of class **Time** to an invalid value.

6.12   Create a class **Rectangle**. The class has attributes **length** and **width**, each of which defaults to 1. It has member functions that calculate the **perimeter** and the **area** of the rectangle. It
has *set* and *get* functions for both **length** and **width**. The *set* functions should verify that **length**
and **width** are each floating-point numbers larger than 0.0 and less than 20.0.

6.13   Create a more sophisticated **Rectangle** class than the one you created in Exercise 6.12.
This class stores only the Cartesian coordinates of the four corners of the rectangle. The constructor
calls a *set* function that accepts four sets of coordinates and verifies that each of these is in the first
quadrant with no single *x* or *y* coordinate larger than 20.0. The *set* function also verifies that the supplied coordinates do, in fact, specify a rectangle. Member functions calculate the **length**, **width**,
perimeter and **area**. The length is the larger of the two dimensions. Include a predicate function
square that determines if the rectangle is a square.

6.14   Modify the **Rectangle** class of Exercise 6.13 to include a **draw** function that displays the
rectangle inside a 25-by-25 box enclosing the portion of the first quadrant in which the rectangle resides. Include a **setFillCharacter** function to specify the character out of which the body of the
rectangle will be drawn. Include a **setPerimeterCharacter** function to specify the character
that will be used to draw the border of the rectangle. If you feel ambitious, you might include functions to scale the size of the rectangle, rotate it, and move it around within the designated portion of
the first quadrant.

6.15   Create a class **HugeInteger** that uses a 40-element array of digits to store integers as large
as 40-digits each. Provide member functions **inputHugeInteger**, **outputHugeInteger**,

addHugeIntegers and **substractHugeIntegers**. For comparing **HugeInteger** objects, provide functions **isEqualTo**, **isNotEqualTo**, **isGreaterThan**, **isLessThan**, **IsGreaterThanOrEqualTo** and **isLessThanOrEqualTo**—each of these is a "predicate" function that simply returns **true** if the relationship holds between the two huge integers and returns **false** if the relationship does not hold. Provide a predicate function **isZero**. If you feel ambitious, also provide member functions **multiplyHugeIntegers**, **divideHugeIntegers** and **modulusHugeIntegers**.

6.16 Create a class **TicTacToe** that will enable you to write a complete program to play the game of tic-tac-toe. The class contains as **private** data a 3-by-3 double array of integers. The constructor should initialize the empty board to all zeros. Allow two human players. Wherever the first player moves, place a 1 in the specified square; place a 2 wherever the second player moves. Each move must be to an empty square. After each move, determine if the game has been won or if the game is a draw. If you feel ambitious, modify your program so that the computer makes the moves for one of the players automatically. Also, allow the player to specify whether he or she wants to go first or second. If you feel exceptionally ambitious, develop a program that will play three-dimensional tic-tac-toe on a 4-by-4-by-4 board (Caution: This is an extremely challenging project that could take many weeks of effort!).

7

Classes: Part II

Objectives

- To be able to create and destroy objects dynamically.
- To be able to specify **const** (constant) objects and **const** member functions.
- To understand the purpose of **friend** functions and friend classes.
- To understand how to use **static** data members and member functions.
- To understand the concept of a container class.
- To understand the notion of iterator classes that walk through the elements of container classes.
- To understand the use of the **this** pointer.

But what, to serve our private ends,
Forbids the cheating of our friends?
Charles Churchill

Instead of this absurd division into sexes they ought to class people as static and dynamic.
Evelyn Waugh

This above all: to thine own self be true.
William Shakespeare, Hamlet

Have no friends not equal to yourself.
Confucius

Outline

7.1 Introduction

In this chapter we continue our study of classes and data abstraction. We discuss many more advanced topics and lay the groundwork for the discussion of classes and operator overloading in Chapter 8. The discussion in Chapters 6 through 8 encourages programmers to use objects, what we call *object-based programming (OBP)*. Then, Chapters 9 and 10 introduce inheritance and polymorphism—the techniques of truly *object-oriented programming (OOP)*. In this and several subsequent chapters, we use the C-style strings we introduced in Chapter 5. This will help the reader master the complex topic of C pointers and prepare for the professional world in which the reader will see a great deal of C legacy code that has been put in place over the last two decades. In Chapter 19, "Class **string**," we discuss the new style of strings, namely strings as full-fledged class objects. Thus, the reader will become familiar with the two most prevalent methods of creating and manipulating strings in C++.

7.2 `const` (Constant) Objects and `const` Member Functions

We have emphasized the *principle of least privilege* as one of the most fundamental principles of good software engineering. Let us see how this principle applies to objects.

Some objects need to be modifiable and some do not. The programmer may use the keyword **const** to specify that an object is not modifiable, and that any attempt to modify the object is a syntax error. For example,

```
const Time noon( 12, 0, 0 );
```

declares a **const** object **noon** of class **Time** and initializes it to 12 noon.

Software Engineering Observation 7.1

Declaring an object as **const** *helps enforce the principle of least privilege. Attempts to modify the object are caught at compile time rather than causing execution-time errors.*

Software Engineering Observation 7.2

Using **const** *is crucial to proper class design, program design and coding.*

Performance Tip 7.1

Declaring variables and objects **const** *is not only an effective software engineering practice—it can improve performance as well because today's sophisticated optimizing compilers can perform certain optimizations on constants that cannot be performed on variables.*

C++ compilers disallow any member function calls for **const** objects unless the member functions themselves are also declared **const**. This is true even for *get* member functions that do not modify the object. Member functions declared **const** cannot modify the object—the compiler disallows this.

A function is specified as **const** *both* in its prototype and in its definition by inserting the keyword **const** after the function's parameter list, and, in the case of the function definition, before the left brace that begins the function body. For example, the following member function of class **A**

```
int A::getValue() const { return privateDataMember };
```

simply returns the value of one of the object's data members, and is appropriately declared **const**.

Common Programming Error 7.1

Defining as **const** *a member function that modifies a data member of an object is a syntax error.*

Common Programming Error 7.2

Defining as **const** *a member function that calls a non-***const*** member function of the class on the same instance of the class is a syntax error.*

Common Programming Error 7.3

*Invoking a non-***const*** member function on a* **const** *object is a syntax error.*

Software Engineering Observation 7.3

A **const** *member function can be overloaded with a non-***const*** version. The choice of which overloaded member function to use is made by the compiler based on whether the object is* **const** *or not.*

An interesting problem arises here for constructors and destructors, each of which often needs to modify objects. The **const** declaration is not allowed for constructors and destructors of **const** objects. A constructor must be allowed to modify an object so that the object can be initialized properly. A destructor must be able to perform its termination housekeeping chores before an object is destroyed.

Common Programming Error 7.4

Attempting to declare a constructor or destructor **const** *is a syntax error.*

Figure 7.1 instantiates two **Time** objects—one non-**const** object and one **const** object. The program attempts to modify the **const** object **noon** with non-**const** member functions **setHour** (at line 102) and **printStandard** (at line 108). The program also illustrates the three other combinations of member function calls on objects—a non-**const** member function on a non-**const** object (line 100), a **const** member function on a non-**const** object (line 104) and a **const** member function on a **const** object (line 106 and 107). The messages generated by two popular compilers for non-**const** member functions called on a **const** object are shown in the output window.

Good Programming Practice 7.1

Declare as **const** *all member functions that do not need to modify the current object so that you can use them on a* **const** *object if you need to.*

Notice that even though a constructor must be a non-**const** member function, it can still be called for a **const** object. The definition of the **Time** constructor at lines 42 and 43

```
Time::Time( int hr, int min, int sec )
   { setTime( hr, min, sec ); }
```

shows that the **Time** constructor calls another non-**const** member function—**set-Time**—to perform the initialization of a **Time** object. Invoking a non-**const** member function from the constructor call for a **const** object is allowed. The **const**ness of an object is enforced from the time the constructor completes initialization of the object until that object's destructor is called.

Software Engineering Observation 7.4

A **const** *object cannot be modified by assignment so it must be initialized. When a data member of a class is declared* **const***, a* **member initializer** *must be used to provide the constructor with the initial value of the data member for an object of the class.*

Also notice that line 108 (line 20 in the source file)

```
noon.printStandard();  // non-const          const
```

generates a compiler error even though member function **printStandard** of class **Time** does not modify the object on which it is invoked. Not modifying an object is not sufficient to indicate a **const** method. The method must also explicitly be declared **const**.

```
1   // Fig. 7.1: time5.h
2   // Declaration of the class Time.
3   // Member functions defined in time5.cpp
4   #ifndef TIME5_H
5   #define TIME5_H
6
```

Fig. 7.1   Using a **Time** class with **const** objects and **const** member functions—**time5.h** (part 1 of 2).

```
7    class Time {
8    public:
9       Time( int = 0, int = 0, int = 0 );  // default constructor
10
11      // set functions
12      void setTime( int, int, int );  // set time
13      void setHour( int );       // set hour
14      void setMinute( int );     // set minute
15      void setSecond( int );     // set second
16
17      // get functions (normally declared const)
18      int getHour() const;       // return hour
19      int getMinute() const;     // return minute
20      int getSecond() const;     // return second
21
22      // print functions (normally declared const)
23      void printMilitary() const;  // print military time
24      void printStandard();        // print standard time
25   private:
26      int hour;                  // 0 - 23
27      int minute;                // 0 - 59
28      int second;                // 0 - 59
29   };
30
31   #endif
```

Fig. 7.1   Using a **Time** class with **const** objects and **const** member functions— **time5.h** (part 2 of 2).

```
32   // Fig. 7.1: time5.cpp
33   // Member function definitions for Time class.
34   #include <iostream>
35
36   using std::cout;
37
38   #include "time5.h"
39
40   // Constructor function to initialize private data.
41   // Default values are 0 (see class definition).
42   Time::Time( int hr, int min, int sec )
43      { setTime( hr, min, sec ); }
44
45   // Set the values of hour, minute, and second.
46   void Time::setTime( int h, int m, int s )
47   {
48      setHour( h );
49      setMinute( m );
50      setSecond( s );
51   }
52
```

Fig. 7.1   Using a **Time** class with **const** objects and **const** member functions— **time5.cpp** (part 1 of 2).

```
53   // Set the hour value
54   void Time::setHour( int h )
55      { hour = ( h >= 0 && h < 24 ) ? h : 0; }
56
57   // Set the minute value
58   void Time::setMinute( int m )
59      { minute = ( m >= 0 && m < 60 ) ? m : 0; }
60
61   // Set the second value
62   void Time::setSecond( int s )
63      { second = ( s >= 0 && s < 60 ) ? s : 0; }
64
65   // Get the hour value
66   int Time::getHour() const { return hour; }
67
68   // Get the minute value
69   int Time::getMinute() const { return minute; }
70
71   // Get the second value
72   int Time::getSecond() const { return second; }
73
74   // Display military format time: HH:MM
75   void Time::printMilitary() const
76   {
77      cout << ( hour < 10 ? "0" : "" ) << hour << ":"
78           << ( minute < 10 ? "0" : "" ) << minute;
79   }
80
81   // Display standard format time: HH:MM:SS AM (or PM)
82   void Time::printStandard()   // should be const
83   {
84      cout << ( ( hour == 12 ) ? 12 : hour % 12 ) << ":"
85           << ( minute < 10 ? "0" : "" ) << minute << ":"
86           << ( second < 10 ? "0" : "" ) << second
87           << ( hour < 12 ? " AM" : " PM" );
88   }
```

Fig. 7.1   Using a **Time** class with **const** objects and **const** member functions— **time5.cpp** (part 2 of 2).

```
89   // Fig. 7.1: fig07_01.cpp
90   // Attempting to access a const object with
91   // non-const member functions.
92   #include "time5.h"
93
94   int main()
95   {
96      Time wakeUp( 6, 45, 0 );          // non-constant object
97      const Time noon( 12, 0, 0 );      // constant object
98
```

Fig. 7.1   Using a **Time** class with **const** objects and **const** member functions— **fig07_01.cpp** (part 1 of 2).

```
99                                   // MEMBER FUNCTION   OBJECT
100      wakeUp.setHour( 18 );       // non-const          non-const
101
102      noon.setHour( 12 );         // non-const          const
103
104      wakeUp.getHour();           // const              non-const
105
106      noon.getMinute();           // const              const
107      noon.printMilitary();       // const              const
108      noon.printStandard();       // non-const          const
109      return 0;
110   }
```

Borland C++ command-line compiler warning messages

```
Fig07_01.cpp:
Warning W8037 Fig07_01.cpp 14: Non-const function Time::setHour(int)
   called for const object in function main()
Warning W8037 Fig07_01.cpp 20: Non-const function Time::printStandard()
   called for const object in function main()
Turbo Incremental Link 5.00 Copyright (c) 1997, 2000 Borland
```

Microsoft Visual C++ compiler error messages

```
Compiling...
Fig07_01.cpp
d:fig07_01.cpp(14) : error C2662: 'setHour' : cannot convert 'this'
pointer from 'const class Time' to 'class Time &'
Conversion loses qualifiers
d:\fig07_01.cpp(20) : error C2662: 'printStandard' : cannot convert
'this' pointer from 'const class Time' to 'class Time &'
Conversion loses qualifiers
Time5.cpp
Error executing cl.exe.

test.exe - 2 error(s), 0 warning(s)
```

Fig. 7.1   Using a **Time** class with **const** objects and **const** member functions—
fig07_01.cpp (part 2 of 2).

Figure 7.2 demonstrates the use of a member initializer to initialize **const** data member **increment** of class **Increment**. The constructor for **Increment** is modified as follows:

```
Increment::Increment( int c, int i )
   : increment( i )
{ count = c; }
```

The notation **: increment(i)** initializes **increment** to the value **i**. If multiple member initializers are needed, simply include them in a comma-separated list after the colon. All data members *can* be initialized using member initializer syntax, but **const**s and references *must* be initialized in this manner. Later in this chapter, we will see that member objects must be initialized this way. In Chapter 9 when we study inheritance, we will see that base class portions of derived classes also must be initialized this way.

```cpp
1   // Fig. 7.2: fig07_02.cpp
2   // Using a member initializer to initialize a
3   // constant of a built-in data type.
4   #include <iostream>
5
6   using std::cout;
7   using std::endl;
8
9   class Increment {
10  public:
11     Increment( int c = 0, int i = 1 );
12     void addIncrement() { count += increment; }
13     void print() const;
14
15  private:
16     int count;
17     const int increment;    // const data member
18  };
19
20  // Constructor for class Increment
21  Increment::Increment( int c, int i )
22     : increment( i )    // initializer for const member
23  { count = c; }
24
25  // Print the data
26  void Increment::print() const
27  {
28     cout << "count = " << count
29          << ", increment = " << increment << endl;
30  }
31
32  int main()
33  {
34     Increment value( 10, 5 );
35
36     cout << "Before incrementing: ";
37     value.print();
38
39     for ( int j = 0; j < 3; j++ ) {
40        value.addIncrement();
41        cout << "After increment " << j + 1 << ": ";
42        value.print();
43     }
44
45     return 0;
46  }
```

Fig. 7.2   Using a member initializer to initialize a constant of a built-in data type (part 1 of 2).

```
Before incrementing: count = 10, increment = 5
After increment 1: count = 15, increment = 5
After increment 2: count = 20, increment = 5
After increment 3: count = 25, increment = 5
```

Fig. 7.2   Using a member initializer to initialize a constant of a built-in data type (part 2 of 2).

Testing and Debugging Tip 7.1

*Always declare member functions **const** if they do not modify the object. This can help eliminate many bugs.*

Figure 7.3 illustrates the compiler errors issued by two popular C++ compilers for a program that attempts to initialize **increment** with an assignment statement rather than with a member initializer.

```cpp
1   // Fig. 7.3: fig07_03.cpp
2   // Attempting to initialize a constant of
3   // a built-in data type with an assignment.
4   #include <iostream>
5
6   using std::cout;
7   using std::endl;
8
9   class Increment {
10  public:
11     Increment( int c = 0, int i = 1 );
12     void addIncrement() { count += increment; }
13     void print() const;
14  private:
15     int count;
16     const int increment;
17  };
18
19  // Constructor for class Increment
20  Increment::Increment( int c, int i )
21  {             // Constant member 'increment' is not initialized
22     count = c;
23     increment = i;   // ERROR: Cannot modify a const object
24  }
25
26  // Print the data
27  void Increment::print() const
28  {
29     cout << "count = " << count
30          << ", increment = " << increment << endl;
31  }
32
```

Fig. 7.3   Erroneous attempt to initialize a constant of a built-in data type by assignment (part 1 of 2).

```
33   int main()
34   {
35      Increment value( 10, 5 );
36
37      cout << "Before incrementing: ";
38      value.print();
39
40      for ( int j = 0; j < 3; j++ ) {
41         value.addIncrement();
42         cout << "After increment " << j << ": ";
43         value.print();
44      }
45
46      return 0;
47   }
```

Borland C++ command-line compiler warning and error messages

```
Fig07_03.cpp:
Warning W8038 Fig07_03.cpp 21: Constant member 'Increment::increment'
   is not initialized in function Increment::Increment(int,int)
Error E2024 Fig07_03.cpp 23: Cannot modify a const object in function
   Increment::Increment(int,int)
Warning W8057 Fig07_03.cpp 24: Parameter 'i' is never used in function
   Increment::Increment(int,int)
*** 1 errors in Compile ***
```

Microsoft Visual C++ compiler error messages

```
Compiling...
Fig07_03.cpp
D:\Fig07_03.cpp(21) : error C2758: 'increment' : must be initialized in
constructor base/member initializer list
D:\Fig07_03.cpp(16) : see declaration of 'increment'
D:\Fig07_03.cpp(23) : error C2166: l-value specifies const object
Error executing cl.exe.

test.exe - 2 error(s), 0 warning(s)
```

Fig. 7.3   Erroneous attempt to initialize a constant of a built-in data type by assignment (part 2 of 2).

Common Programming Error 7.5

*Not providing a member initializer for a **const** data member is a syntax error.*

Software Engineering Observation 7.5

*Constant class members (**const** objects and **const** "variables") must be initialized with member initializer syntax; assignments are not allowed.*

Note that the **print** function at line 27 is declared **const**. It is reasonable, yet strange, to label this function **const** because we will probably never have a **const Increment** object.

Software Engineering Observation 7.6

It is good practice to declare all of a class' member functions that do not modify the object in which they operate as **const**. *Occasionally, this will be an anomaly because you will have no intention of creating* **const** *objects of that class. Declaring such member functions* **const** *does offer a benefit though. If you inadvertently modify the object in that member function, the compiler will issue a syntax error message.*

Testing and Debugging Tip 7.2

Languages like C++ are "moving targets" as they evolve. More keywords are likely to be added to the language. Avoid using "loaded" words like "object" as identifiers. Even though "object" is not currently a keyword in C++, it could become one, so future compiling with new compilers could "break" existing code.

C++ provides a keyword called **mutable** that affects the treatment of **const** objects in a program. We discuss keyword **mutable** in Chapter 21.

7.3 Composition: Objects as Members of Classes

An **AlarmClock** class object needs to know when it is supposed to sound its alarm, so why not include a **Time** object as a member of the **AlarmClock** object? Such a capability is called *composition*. A class can have objects of other classes as members.

Software Engineering Observation 7.7

The most common form of software reusability is composition, *in which a class has objects of other classes as members.*

When an object is created, its constructor is called automatically, so we need to specify how arguments are passed to member-object constructors. Member objects are constructed in the order in which they are declared (not in the order they are listed in the constructor's member initializer list) and before their enclosing class objects (sometimes called *host objects*) are constructed.

Figure 7.4 uses class **Employee** and class **Date** to demonstrate objects as members of other objects. Class **Employee** contains **private** data members **firstName**, **lastName**, **birthDate** and **hireDate**. Members **birthDate** and **hireDate** are **const** objects of class **Date**, which contains **private** data members **month**, **day** and **year**. The program instantiates an **Employee** object, and initializes and displays its data members. Note the syntax of the function header in the **Employee** constructor definition:

```
Employee::Employee( char *fname, char *lname,
                    int bmonth, int bday, int byear,
                    int hmonth, int hday, int hyear )
    : birthDate( bmonth, bday, byear ),
      hireDate( hmonth, hday, hyear )
```

The constructor takes eight arguments (**fname**, **lname**, **bmonth**, **bday**, **byear**, **hmonth**, **hday** and **hyear**). The colon (**:**) in the header separates the member initializers from the parameter list. The member initializers specify the **Employee** arguments being passed to the constructors of the member **Date** objects. Arguments **bmonth**, **bday** and **byear** are passed to object **birthDate**'s constructor, and arguments **hmonth**, **hday** and **hyear** are passed to object **hireDate**'s constructor. Multiple member initializers are separated by commas.

```
 1   // Fig. 7.4: date1.h
 2   // Declaration of the Date class.
 3   // Member functions defined in date1.cpp
 4   #ifndef DATE1_H
 5   #define DATE1_H
 6
 7   class Date {
 8   public:
 9      Date( int = 1, int = 1, int = 1900 ); // default constructor
10      void print() const;  // print date in month/day/year format
11      ~Date();   // provided to confirm destruction order
12   private:
13      int month;   // 1-12
14      int day;     // 1-31 based on month
15      int year;    // any year
16
17      // utility function to test proper day for month and year
18      int checkDay( int );
19   };
20
21   #endif
```

Fig. 7.4   Using member-object initializers—**date1.h** .

```
22   // Fig. 7.4: date1.cpp
23   // Member function definitions for Date class.
24   #include <iostream>
25
26   using std::cout;
27   using std::endl;
28
29   #include "date1.h"
30
31   // Constructor: Confirm proper value for month;
32   // call utility function checkDay to confirm proper
33   // value for day.
34   Date::Date( int mn, int dy, int yr )
35   {
36      if ( mn > 0 && mn <= 12 )           // validate the month
37         month = mn;
38      else {
39         month = 1;
40         cout << "Month " << mn << " invalid. Set to month 1.\n";
41      }
42
43      year = yr;                          // should validate yr
44      day = checkDay( dy );               // validate the day
45
46      cout << "Date object constructor for date ";
47      print();          // interesting: a print with no arguments
48      cout << endl;
49   }
```

Fig. 7.4   Using member-object initializers—**date1.cpp** (part 1 of 2).

```
50
51    // Print Date object in form  month/day/year
52    void Date::print() const
53       { cout << month << '/' << day << '/' << year; }
54
55    // Destructor: provided to confirm destruction order
56    Date::~Date()
57    {
58       cout << "Date object destructor for date ";
59       print();
60       cout << endl;
61    }
62
63    // Utility function to confirm proper day value
64    // based on month and year.
65    // Is the year 2000 a leap year?
66    int Date::checkDay( int testDay )
67    {
68       static const int daysPerMonth[ 13 ] =
69          {0, 31, 28, 31, 30, 31, 30, 31, 31, 30, 31, 30, 31};
70
71       if ( testDay > 0 && testDay <= daysPerMonth[ month ] )
72          return testDay;
73
74       if ( month == 2 &&          // February: Check for leap year
75            testDay == 29 &&
76            ( year % 400 == 0 ||
77            ( year % 4 == 0 && year % 100 != 0 ) ) )
78          return testDay;
79
80       cout << "Day " << testDay << " invalid. Set to day 1.\n";
81
82       return 1;   // leave object in consistent state if bad value
83    }
```

Fig. 7.4   Using member-object initializers—**date1.cpp** (part 2 of 2).

```
84    // Fig. 7.4: emply1.h
85    // Declaration of the Employee class.
86    // Member functions defined in emply1.cpp
87    #ifndef EMPLY1_H
88    #define EMPLY1_H
89
90    #include "date1.h"
91
92    class Employee {
93    public:
94       Employee( char *, char *, int, int, int, int, int, int );
95       void print() const;
96       ~Employee();   // provided to confirm destruction order
```

Fig. 7.4   Using member-object initializers—**emply1.h** (part 1 of 2).

```
97   private:
98      char firstName[ 25 ];
99      char lastName[ 25 ];
100     const Date birthDate;
101     const Date hireDate;
102  };
103
104  #endif
```

Fig. 7.4   Using member-object initializers—**emply1.h** (part 2 of 2).

```
105  // Fig. 7.4: emply1.cpp
106  // Member function definitions for Employee class.
107  #include <iostream>
108
109  using std::cout;
110  using std::endl;
111
112  #include <cstring>
113  #include "emply1.h"
114  #include "date1.h"
115
116  Employee::Employee( char *fname, char *lname,
117                      int bmonth, int bday, int byear,
118                      int hmonth, int hday, int hyear )
119     : birthDate( bmonth, bday, byear ),
120       hireDate( hmonth, hday, hyear )
121  {
122     // copy fname into firstName and be sure that it fits
123     int length = strlen( fname );
124     length = ( length < 25 ? length : 24 );
125     strncpy( firstName, fname, length );
126     firstName[ length ] = '\0';
127
128     // copy lname into lastName and be sure that it fits
129     length = strlen( lname );
130     length = ( length < 25 ? length : 24 );
131     strncpy( lastName, lname, length );
132     lastName[ length ] = '\0';
133
134     cout << "Employee object constructor: "
135          << firstName << ' ' << lastName << endl;
136  }
137
138  void Employee::print() const
139  {
140     cout << lastName << ", " << firstName << "\nHired: ";
141     hireDate.print();
142     cout << "  Birth date: ";
143     birthDate.print();
144     cout << endl;
145  }
```

Fig. 7.4   Using member-object initializers—**emply1.cpp** (part 1 of 2).

```
146
147   // Destructor: provided to confirm destruction order
148   Employee::~Employee()
149   {
150      cout << "Employee object destructor: "
151           << lastName << ", " << firstName << endl;
152   }
```

Fig. 7.4   Using member-object initializers—**empl y1.cpp** (part 2 of 2).

```
153   // Fig. 7.4: fig07_04.cpp
154   // Demonstrating composition: an object with member objects.
155   #include <iostream>
156
157   using std::cout;
158   using std::endl;
159
160   #include "empl y1.h"
161
162   int main()
163   {
164      Employee e( "Bob", "Jones", 7, 24, 1949, 3, 12, 1988 );
165
166      cout << '\n';
167      e.print();
168
169      cout << "\nTest Date constructor with invalid values:\n";
170      Date d( 14, 35, 1994 );  // invalid Date values
171      cout << endl;
172      return 0;
173   }
```

```
Date object constructor for date 7/24/1949
Date object constructor for date 3/12/1988
Employee object constructor: Bob Jones

Jones, Bob
Hired: 3/12/1988  Birth date: 7/24/1949

Test Date constructor with invalid values:
Month 14 invalid. Set to month 1.
Day 35 invalid. Set to day 1.
Date object constructor for date 1/1/1994

Date object destructor for date 1/1/1994
Employee object destructor: Jones, Bob
Date object destructor for date 3/12/1988
Date object destructor for date 7/24/1949
```

Fig. 7.4   Using member-object initializers—**fig07_04.cpp** .

Remember that **const** members and references are also initialized in the member initializer list (in Chapter 9, we will see that base class portions of derived classes are also initialized this way). Class **Date** and class **Employee** each include a destructor function that prints a message when a **Date** object or an **Employee** object is destroyed, respectively. This enables us to confirm in the program output that objects are constructed from the inside out and destructed in the reverse order from the outside in (i.e., the **Date** member objects are destroyed after the **Employee** object that contains them).

A member object does not need to be initialized explicitly through a member initializer. If a member initializer is not provided, the member object's default constructor will be called implicitly. Values, if any, established by the default constructor can be overridden by *set* functions. However, for complex initialization, this approach may require significant additional work and time.

Common Programming Error 7.6

Not providing a default constructor for the class of a member object when no member initializer is provided for that member object is a syntax error.

Performance Tip 7.2

Initialize member objects explicitly through member initializers. This eliminates the overhead of "doubly initializing" member objects—once when the member object's default constructor is called and again when set *functions are used to initialize the member object.*

Software Engineering Observation 7.8

*If a class has as a member an object of another class, making that member object **public** does not violate the encapsulation and hiding of that member object's **private** members.*

Notice the call to **Date** member function **print** at line 52. Many member functions of classes in C++ require no arguments. This is because each member function contains an implicit handle (in the form of a pointer) to the object on which it operates. We discuss the implicit pointer—called **this**—in Section 7.5.

In this first version of our **Employee** class (for ease of programming), we use two 25-character arrays to represent the first and last name of the **Employee**. These arrays may be a waste of space for names shorter than 24 characters (remember, one character in each array is for the terminating null character, **'\0'**, of the string). Also, names longer than 24 characters must be truncated to fit into these character arrays. Later in this chapter we will present another version of class **Employee** that dynamically creates the exact amount of space to hold the first and the last name. Also, we could use two **string** objects to represent the names. Standard library class **string** is presented in detail in Chapter 19.

7.4 **friend** Functions and **friend** Classes

A **friend** *function* of a class is defined outside that class' scope, yet has the right to access **private** (and as we will see in Chapter 9, "Inheritance," **protected**) members of the class. A function or an entire class may be declared to be a **friend** of another class.

Using **friend** functions can enhance performance. A mechanical example is shown here of how a **friend** function works. Later in the book, **friend** functions are used to overload operators for use with class objects and to create iterator classes. Objects of an iterator class are used to successively select items or perform an operation on items in a container class (see Section 7.9) object. Objects of container classes are capable of storing items. Using **friend**s is often appropriate when a member function cannot be used for certain operations as we will see in Chapter 8, "Operator Overloading."

To declare a function as a **friend** of a class, precede the function prototype in the class definition with the keyword **friend**. To declare class **ClassTwo** as a **friend** of class **ClassOne**, place a declaration of the form

```
friend class ClassTwo;
```

in the definition of class **ClassOne**.

Software Engineering Observation 7.9

*Even though the prototypes for **friend** functions appear in the class definition, **friend**s are still not member functions.*

Software Engineering Observation 7.10

*Member access notions of **private**, **protected** and **public** are not relevant to friendship declarations, so friendship declarations can be placed anywhere in the class definition.*

Good Programming Practice 7.2

Place all friendship declarations first in the class immediately after the class header and do not precede them with any member-access specifier.

Friendship is granted, not taken, i.e., for class B to be a **friend** of class A, class A must explicitly declare that class B is its **friend**. Also, friendship is neither symmetric nor transitive, i.e., if class A is a **friend** of class B, and class B is a **friend** of class C, you cannot infer that class B is a **friend** of class A (again, friendship is not symmetric), that class C is a **friend** of class B, or that class A is a **friend** of class C (again, friendship is not transitive).

Software Engineering Observation 7.11

Some people in the OOP community feel that "friendship" corrupts information hiding and weakens the value of the object-oriented design approach.

Figure 7.5 demonstrates the declaration and use of **friend** function **setX** for setting the **private** data member **x** of class **count**. Note that the **friend** declaration appears first (by convention) in the class declaration, even before **public** member functions are declared. The program of Fig. 7.6 demonstrates the messages produced by the compiler when non-**friend** function **cannotSetX** is called to modify **private** data member **x**. Figures 7.5 and 7.6 are intended to introduce the "mechanics" of using **friend** functions—practical examples of using **friend** functions appear in forthcoming chapters.

```
1   // Fig. 7.5: fig07_05.cpp
2   // Friends can access private members of a class.
3   #include <iostream>
4
5   using std::cout;
6   using std::endl;
7
```

Fig. 7.5   Friends can access **private** members of a class (part 1 of 2).

```
8    // Modified Count class
9    class Count {
10      friend void setX( Count &, int ); // friend declaration
11   public:
12      Count() { x = 0; }                  // constructor
13      void print() const { cout << x << endl; }  // output
14   private:
15      int x;   // data member
16   };
17
18   // Can modify private data of Count because
19   // setX is declared as a friend function of Count
20   void setX( Count &c, int val )
21   {
22      c.x = val;   // legal: setX is a friend of Count
23   }
24
25   int main()
26   {
27      Count counter;
28
29      cout << "counter.x after instantiation: ";
30      counter.print();
31      cout << "counter.x after call to setX friend function: ";
32      setX( counter, 8 );   // set x with a friend
33      counter.print();
34      return 0;
35   }
```

```
counter.x after instantiation: 0
counter.x after call to setX friend function: 8
```

Fig. 7.5   Friends can access **private** members of a class (part 2 of 2).

Note that function **setX** (line 20) is a C-style, stand-alone function—it is not a member function of class **Count**. For this reason, when **setX** is invoked for object **counter**, we use the statement at line 32

```
setX( counter, 8 );  // set x with a friend
```

that takes **counter** as an argument rather than using a handle (such as the name of the object) to call the function, as in

```
counter.setX( 8 );
```

As we mentioned, Fig. 7.5 is a mechanical example of the **friend** construct. It would normally be appropriate to define function **setX** as a member function of class **Count**.

Software Engineering Observation 7.12

Because C++ is a hybrid language, it is common to have a mix of two types of function calls in one program and often back to back—C-like calls that pass primitive data or objects to functions and C++ calls that pass functions (or messages) to objects.

```
1   // Fig. 7.6: fig07_06.cpp
2   // Non-friend/non-member functions cannot access
3   // private data of a class.
4   #include <iostream>
5
6   using std::cout;
7   using std::endl;
8
9   // Modified Count class
10  class Count {
11  public:
12     Count() { x = 0; }                        // constructor
13     void print() const { cout << x << endl; }  // output
14  private:
15     int x;   // data member
16  };
17
18  // Function tries to modify private data of Count,
19  // but cannot because it is not a friend of Count.
20  void cannotSetX( Count &c, int val )
21  {
22     c.x = val;   // ERROR: 'Count::x' is not accessible
23  }
24
25  int main()
26  {
27     Count counter;
28
29     cannotSetX( counter, 3 ); // cannotSetX is not a friend
30     return 0;
31  }
```

Borland C++ command-line compiler error messages

```
Borland C++ 5.5 for Win32 Copyright (c) 1993, 2000 Borland
Fig07_06.cpp:
Error E2247 Fig07_06.cpp 22: 'Count::x' is not accessible in
   function cannotSetX(Count &,int)
*** 1 errors in Compile ***
```

Microsoft Visual C++ compiler error messages

```
Compiling...
Fig07_06.cpp
D:\books\2000\cpphtp3\examples\Ch07\Fig07_06\Fig07_06.cpp(22) :
   error C2248: 'x' : cannot access private member declared in
   class 'Count'
        D:\books\2000\cpphtp3\examples\Ch07\Fig07_06\
        Fig07_06.cpp(15) : see declaration of 'x'
Error executing cl.exe.

test.exe - 1 error(s), 0 warning(s)
```

Fig. 7.6   Non-**friend**/non-member functions cannot access **private** members.

It is possible to specify overloaded functions as **friend**s of a class. Each overloaded function intended to be a **friend** must be explicitly declared in the class definition as a **friend** of the class.

7.5 Using the `this` Pointer

Every object has access to its own address through a pointer called **this**. An object's **this** pointer is not part of the object itself—i.e., the **this** pointer is not reflected in the result of a **sizeof** operation on the object. Rather, the **this** pointer is passed into the object (by the compiler) as an implicit first argument on every non-**static** member function call to the object (**static** members are discussed in Section 7.7).

The **this** pointer is implicitly used to reference both the data members and member functions of an object; it can also be used explicitly. The type of the **this** pointer depends on the type of the object and whether the member function in which **this** is used is declared **const**. In a non-constant member function of class **Employee**, the **this** pointer has type **Employee * const** (a constant pointer to an **Employee** object). In a constant member function of the class **Employee**, the **this** pointer has the data type **const Employee * const** (a constant pointer to an **Employee** object that is constant).

For now, we show a simple example of using the **this** pointer explicitly; later in this chapter and in Chapter 8, we show some substantial and subtle examples of using **this**. Every non-**static** member function has access to the **this** pointer to the object for which the member function is being invoked.

Performance Tip 7.3

For reasons of economy of storage, only one copy of each member function exists per class, and this member function is invoked by every object of that class. Each object, on the other hand, has its own copy of the class' data members.

Figure 7.7 demonstrates the explicit use of the **this** pointer to enable a member function of class **Test** to print the **private** data **x** of a **Test** object.

```
1   // Fig. 7.7: fig07_07.cpp
2   // Using the this pointer to refer to object members.
3   #include <iostream>
4
5   using std::cout;
6   using std::endl;
7
8   class Test {
9   public:
10     Test( int = 0 );            // default constructor
11     void print() const;
12  private:
13     int x;
14  };
15
16  Test::Test( int a ) { x = a; }  // constructor
```

Fig. 7.7   Using the **this** pointer.

```
17
18   void Test::print() const    // ( ) around *this required
19   {
20      cout << "          x = " << x
21           << "\n  this->x = " << this->x
22           << "\n(*this).x = " << ( *this ).x << endl;
23   }
24
25   int main()
26   {
27      Test testObject( 12 );
28
29      testObject.print();
30
31      return 0;
32   }
```

```
         x = 12
   this->x = 12
(*this).x = 12
```

Fig. 7.7   Using the **this** pointer.

For illustration purposes, the **print** member function in Fig. 7.7 first prints **x** directly. Then, **print** uses two different notations for accessing **x** through the **this** pointer—the arrow operator (**->**) off the **this** pointer and the dot operator (**.**) off the dereferenced **this** pointer.

Note the parentheses around ***this** when used with the dot member selection operator (**.**). The parentheses are needed because the dot operator has higher precedence than the ***** operator. Without the parentheses, the expression

*this.x

would be evaluated as if it were parenthesized as follows:

*(this.x)

which is a syntax error because the dot operator cannot be used with a pointer.

Common Programming Error 7.7

*Attempting to use the member selection operator (**.**) with a pointer to an object is a syntax error—the dot member selection operator may only be used with an object or with a reference to an object.*

One interesting use of the **this** pointer is to prevent an object from being assigned to itself. As we will see in Chapter 8, "Operator Overloading," self-assignment can cause serious errors when the objects contain pointers to dynamically allocated storage.

Another use of the **this** pointer is in enabling cascaded member function calls. Figure 7.8 illustrates returning a reference to a **Time** object to enable member function calls of class **Time** to be cascaded. Member functions **setTime**, **setHour**, **setMinute** and **setSecond** each return ***this** with a return type of **Time &**.

```
1    // Fig. 7.8: time6.h
2    // Cascading member function calls.
3
4    // Declaration of class Time.
5    // Member functions defined in time6.cpp
6    #ifndef TIME6_H
7    #define TIME6_H
8
9    class Time {
10   public:
11      Time( int = 0, int = 0, int = 0 );   // default constructor
12
13      // set functions
14      Time &setTime( int, int, int ); // set hour, minute, second
15      Time &setHour( int );      // set hour
16      Time &setMinute( int );    // set minute
17      Time &setSecond( int );    // set second
18
19      // get functions (normally declared const)
20      int getHour() const;       // return hour
21      int getMinute() const;     // return minute
22      int getSecond() const;     // return second
23
24      // print functions (normally declared const)
25      void printMilitary() const;  // print military time
26      void printStandard() const;  // print standard time
27   private:
28      int hour;                  // 0 - 23
29      int minute;                // 0 - 59
30      int second;                // 0 - 59
31   };
32
33   #endif
```

Fig. 7.8   Cascading member function calls—**time6.h** .

```
34   // Fig. 7.8: time.cpp
35   // Member function definitions for Time class.
36   #include <iostream>
37
38   using std::cout;
39
40   #include "time6.h"
41
42   // Constructor function to initialize private data.
43   // Calls member function setTime to set variables.
44   // Default values are 0 (see class definition).
45   Time::Time( int hr, int min, int sec )
46      { setTime( hr, min, sec ); }
```

Fig. 7.8   Cascading member function calls—**time6.cpp** (part 1 of 3).

```
47
48   // Set the values of hour, minute, and second.
49   Time &Time::setTime( int h, int m, int s )
50   {
51      setHour( h );
52      setMinute( m );
53      setSecond( s );
54      return *this;    // enables cascading
55   }
56
57   // Set the hour value
58   Time &Time::setHour( int h )
59   {
60      hour = ( h >= 0 && h < 24 ) ? h : 0;
61
62      return *this;    // enables cascading
63   }
64
65   // Set the minute value
66   Time &Time::setMinute( int m )
67   {
68      minute = ( m >= 0 && m < 60 ) ? m : 0;
69
70      return *this;    // enables cascading
71   }
72
73   // Set the second value
74   Time &Time::setSecond( int s )
75   {
76      second = ( s >= 0 && s < 60 ) ? s : 0;
77
78      return *this;    // enables cascading
79   }
80
81   // Get the hour value
82   int Time::getHour() const { return hour; }
83
84   // Get the minute value
85   int Time::getMinute() const { return minute; }
86
87   // Get the second value
88   int Time::getSecond() const { return second; }
89
90   // Display military format time: HH:MM
91   void Time::printMilitary() const
92   {
93      cout << ( hour < 10 ? "0" : "" ) << hour << ":"
94           << ( minute < 10 ? "0" : "" ) << minute;
95   }
96
97   // Display standard format time: HH:MM:SS AM (or PM)
98   void Time::printStandard() const
99   {
```

Fig. 7.8   Cascading member function calls—`time6.cpp` (part 2 of 3).

```
100    cout << ( ( hour == 0 || hour == 12 ) ? 12 : hour % 12 )
101         << ":" << ( minute < 10 ? "0" : "" ) << minute
102         << ":" << ( second < 10 ? "0" : "" ) << second
103         << ( hour < 12 ? " AM" : " PM" );
104 }
```

Fig. 7.8   Cascading member function calls—**time6.cpp** (part 3 of 3).

```
105 // Fig. 7.8: fig07_08.cpp
106 // Cascading member function calls together
107 // with the this pointer
108 #include <iostream>
109
110 using std::cout;
111 using std::endl;
112
113 #include "time6.h"
114
115 int main()
116 {
117    Time t;
118
119    t.setHour( 18 ).setMinute( 30 ).setSecond( 22 );
120    cout << "Military time: ";
121    t.printMilitary();
122    cout << "\nStandard time: ";
123    t.printStandard();
124
125    cout << "\n\nNew standard time: ";
126    t.setTime( 20, 20, 20 ).printStandard();
127    cout << endl;
128
129    return 0;
130 }
```

```
Military time: 18:30
Standard time: 6:30:22 PM

New standard time: 8:20:20 PM
```

Fig. 7.8   Cascading member function calls—**fig07_08.cpp**.

Why does the technique of returning ***this** as a reference work? The dot operator (**.**) associates from left to right, so the expression

        t.setHour(18).setMinute(30).setSecond(22);

first evaluates **t.setHour(18)** then returns a reference to object **t** as the value of this function call. The remaining expression is then interpreted as

        t.setMinute(30).setSecond(22);

The **t.setMinute(30)** call executes and returns the equivalent of **t**. The remaining expression is interpreted as

    t.setSecond(22);

Note the calls

    t.setTime(20, 20, 20).printStandard();

also use the cascading feature. These calls must appear in this order in this expression because **printStandard** as defined in the class does not return a reference to **t**. Placing the call to **printStandard** in the preceding statement before the call to **setTime** results in a syntax error.

7.6 Dynamic Memory Allocation with Operators `new` and `delete`

The **new** and **delete** operators provide a nicer means of performing dynamic memory allocation (for any built-in or user-defined type) than do C's **malloc** and **free** function calls. Consider the following code

    TypeName *typeNamePtr;

In ANSI C, to dynamically create an object of type **TypeName**, you would say

    typeNamePtr = malloc(sizeof(TypeName));

This requires a function call to **malloc** and explicit use of the **sizeof** operator. In versions of C prior to ANSI C, you would also have to cast the pointer returned by **malloc** with the cast **(TypeName *)**. Function **malloc** does not provide any method of initializing the allocated block of memory. In C++, you simply write

    typeNamePtr = new TypeName;

The **new** operator automatically creates an object of the proper size, calls the constructor for the object and returns a pointer of the correct type. If **new** is unable to find space, it returns a **0** pointer in versions of C++ prior to the ANSI/ISO standard. [Note: In Chapter 13, we will show you how to deal with **new** failures in the context of the ANSI/ISO C++ standard. In particular, we will show how **new** "throws" an "exception" and we will show how to "catch" that exception and deal with it.] To destroy the object and free the space for this object in C++ you must use the **delete** operator as follows:

    delete typeNamePtr;

C++ allows you to provide an *initializer* for a newly created object, as in

    double *thingPtr = new double(3.14159);

which initializes a newly created **double** object to **3.14159**.

A 10-element integer array can be created and assigned to **arrayPtr** as follows:

    int *arrayPtr = new int[10];

This array is deleted with the statement

    delete [] arrayPtr;

As we will see, using **new** and **delete** instead of **malloc** and **free** offers other benefits as well. In particular, **new** invokes the constructor and **delete** invokes the class' destructor.

Common Programming Error 7.8

*Mixing **new**-and-**delete**-style dynamic memory allocation with **malloc**-and-**free**-style dynamic memory allocation is a logic error: Space created by **malloc** cannot be freed by **delete**; objects created by **new** cannot be deleted by **free**.*

Common Programming Error 7.9

*Using **delete** instead of **delete []** for arrays can lead to runtime logic errors. To avoid problems, space created as an array should be deleted with the **delete []** operator and space created as an individual element should be deleted with the **delete** operator.*

Good Programming Practice 7.3

*Because C++ includes C, C++ programs can contain storage created by **malloc** and deleted by **free**, and objects created by **new** and deleted by **delete**. It is best to use only **new** and **delete**.*

7.7 **static** Class Members

Each object of a class has its own copy of all the data members of the class. In certain cases only one copy of a variable should be shared by all objects of a class. A **static** class variable is used for these and other reasons. A **static** class variable represents "class-wide" information (i.e., a property of the class, not of a specific object of the class). The declaration of a **static** member begins with the keyword **static**.

Let us motivate the need for **static** class-wide data with a video game example. Suppose we have a video game with **Martian**s and other space creatures. Each **Martian** tends to be brave and willing to attack other space creatures when the **Martian** is aware that there are at least five **Martian**s present. If fewer than five are present, each **Martian** becomes cowardly. So each **Martian** needs to know the **martianCount**. We could endow each instance of class **Martian** with **martianCount** as a data member. If we do this, then every **Martian** will have a separate copy of the data member and every time we create a new **Martian** we will have to update the data member **martianCount** in every **Martian** object. This wastes space with the redundant copies and wastes time in updating the separate copies. Instead, we declare **martianCount** to be **static**. This makes **martianCount** class-wide data. Every **Martian** can see the **martianCount** as if it were a data member of the **Martian**, but only one copy of the static **martianCount** is maintained by C++. This saves space. We save time by having the **Martian** constructor increment the static **martianCount**. Because there is only one copy, we do not have to increment separate copies of **martianCount** for each **Martian** object.

Performance Tip 7.4

*Use **static** data members to save storage when a single copy of the data will suffice.*

Although **static** data members may seem like global variables, **static** data members have class scope. **static** members can be **public**, **private** or **protected**. **static** data members *must* be initialized *once* (and only once) at file scope. A class's **public static** class members can be accessed through any object of that class, or they can be accessed through the class name using the binary scope resolution operator. A class's **private** and **protected static** members must be accessed through **public** member functions of the class or through **friend**s of the class. A class's **static** members exist even when no objects of that class exist. To access a **public static** class member when no objects of the class exist, simply prefix the class name and the binary scope resolution operator (**::**) to the name of the data member. To access a **private** or **protected static** class member when no objects of the class exist, a **public static** member function must be provided and the function must be called by prefixing its name with the class name and binary scope resolution operator.

The program of Fig. 7.9 demonstrates the use of a **private static** data member and a **public static** member function. The data member **count** is initialized to zero at file scope with the statement

```
int Employee::count = 0;
```

Data member **count** maintains a count of the number of objects of class **Employee** that have been instantiated. When objects of class **Employee** exist, member **count** can be referenced through any member function of an **Employee** object—in this example, **count** is referenced by both the constructor and the destructor.

Common Programming Error 7.10

It is a syntax error to include keyword **static** *in the definition of a* **static** *class variable at file scope.*

```
1   // Fig. 7.9: employ1.h
2   // An employee class
3   #ifndef EMPLOY1_H
4   #define EMPLOY1_H
5
6   class Employee {
7   public:
8      Employee( const char*, const char* );  // constructor
9      ~Employee();                            // destructor
10     const char *getFirstName() const;       // return first name
11     const char *getLastName() const;        // return last name
12
13     // static member function
14     static int getCount();  // return # objects instantiated
15
16  private:
17     char *firstName;
18     char *lastName;
19
20     // static data member
21     static int count;  // number of objects instantiated
22  };
23
24  #endif
```

Fig. 7.9   Using a **static** data member to maintain a count of the number of objects of a class—**employ1.h** .

```
25   // Fig. 7.9: employ1.cpp
26   // Member function definitions for class Employee
27   #include <iostream>
28
29   using std::cout;
30   using std::endl;
31
32   #include <cstring>
33   #include <cassert>
34   #include "employ1.h"
35
36   // Initialize the static data member
37   int Employee::count = 0;
38
39   // Define the static member function that
40   // returns the number of employee objects instantiated.
41   int Employee::getCount() { return count; }
42
43   // Constructor dynamically allocates space for the
44   // first and last name and uses strcpy to copy
45   // the first and last names into the object
46   Employee::Employee( const char *first, const char *last )
47   {
48      firstName = new char[ strlen( first ) + 1 ];
49      assert( firstName != 0 );     // ensure memory allocated
50      strcpy( firstName, first );
51
52      lastName = new char[ strlen( last ) + 1 ];
53      assert( lastName != 0 );      // ensure memory allocated
54      strcpy( lastName, last );
55
56      ++count;   // increment static count of employees
57      cout << "Employee constructor for " << firstName
58          << ' ' << lastName << " called." << endl;
59   }
60
61   // Destructor deallocates dynamically allocated memory
62   Employee::~Employee()
63   {
64      cout << "~Employee() called for " << firstName
65          << ' ' << lastName << endl;
66      delete [] firstName;   // recapture memory
67      delete [] lastName;    // recapture memory
68      --count;   // decrement static count of employees
69   }
70
71   // Return first name of employee
72   const char *Employee::getFirstName() const
73   {
74      // Const before return type prevents client from modifying
75      // private data. Client should copy returned string before
76      // destructor deletes storage to prevent undefined pointer.
```

Fig. 7.9   Using a **static** data member to maintain a count of the number of objects of a class—**employ1.cpp** (part 1 of 2).

```
77        return firstName;
78    }
79
80    // Return last name of employee
81    const char *Employee::getLastName() const
82    {
83        // Const before return type prevents client from modifying
84        // private data. Client should copy returned string before
85        // destructor deletes storage to prevent undefined pointer.
86        return lastName;
87    }
```

Fig. 7.9   Using a **static** data member to maintain a count of the number of objects of a class—**employ1.cpp** (part 2 of 2).

```
88    // Fig. 7.9: fig07_09.cpp
89    // Driver to test the employee class
90    #include <iostream>
91
92    using std::cout;
93    using std::endl;
94
95    #include "employ1.h"
96
97    int main()
98    {
99        cout << "Number of employees before instantiation is "
100            << Employee::getCount() << endl;    // use class name
101
102        Employee *e1Ptr = new Employee( "Susan", "Baker" );
103        Employee *e2Ptr = new Employee( "Robert", "Jones" );
104
105        cout << "Number of employees after instantiation is "
106            << e1Ptr->getCount();
107
108        cout << "\n\nEmployee 1: "
109            << e1Ptr->getFirstName()
110            << " " << e1Ptr->getLastName()
111            << "\nEmployee 2: "
112            << e2Ptr->getFirstName()
113            << " " << e2Ptr->getLastName() << "\n\n";
114
115        delete e1Ptr;    // recapture memory
116        e1Ptr = 0;
117        delete e2Ptr;    // recapture memory
118        e2Ptr = 0;
119
120        cout << "Number of employees after deletion is "
121            << Employee::getCount() << endl;
122
```

Fig. 7.9   Using a **static** data member to maintain a count of the number of objects of a class—**fig07_09.cpp** (part 1 of 2).

```
123      return 0;
124  }
```

```
Number of employees before instantiation is 0
Employee constructor for Susan Baker called.
Employee constructor for Robert Jones called.
Number of employees after instantiation is 2

Employee 1: Susan Baker
Employee 2: Robert Jones

~Employee() called for Susan Baker
~Employee() called for Robert Jones
Number of employees after deletion is 0
```

Fig. 7.9   Using a **static** data member to maintain a count of the number of objects of a class—**fig07_09.cpp** (part 2 of 2).

When no objects of class **Employee** exist, member **count** can still be referenced, but only through a call to **static** member function **getCount** as follows:

   Employee::getCount()

In this example, function **getCount** is used to determine the number of **Employee** objects currently instantiated. Note that when there are no objects instantiated in the program, the **Employee::getCount()** function call is issued. However, when there are objects instantiated, function **getCount** can be called through one of the objects as shown in the statement at lines 105 and 106

```
     cout << "Number of employees after instantiation is "
          << e1Ptr->getCount();
```

Note that the calls **e2Ptr->getCount()** and **Employee::getCount()** produce the same result.

Software Engineering Observation 7.13

*Some organizations have in their software engineering standards that all calls to **static** member functions be made using the class name and not the object handle.*

A member function may be declared **static** if it does not access non-**static** class data members and member functions. Unlike non-**static** member functions, a **static** member function has no **this** pointer because **static** data members and **static** member functions exist independent of any objects of a class.

Common Programming Error 7.11

*Referring to the **this** pointer within a **static** member function is a syntax error.*

Common Programming Error 7.12

*Declaring a **static** member function **const** is a syntax error.*

Software Engineering Observation 7.14

*A class' **static** data members and **static** member functions exist and can be used even if no objects of that class have been instantiated.*

Lines 102 and 103 use operator **new** to dynamically allocate two **Employee** objects. When each **Employee** object is allocated, its constructor is called. When **delete** is used at lines 115 and 117 to deallocate the two **Employee** objects, their destructors are called.

Good Programming Practice 7.4

*After deleting dynamically allocated memory, set the pointer that referred to that memory to **0**. This disconnects the pointer from the previously allocated space on the free store.*

Note the use of **assert** in the **Employee** constructor function. The **assert** "macro"—defined in the **cassert** header file—tests the value of a condition. If the value of the expression is **false**, then **assert** issues an error message and calls function **abort** (of the general utilities header file—**<cstdlib>**) to terminate program execution. This is a useful debugging tool for testing if a variable has a correct value. *Note:* Function **abort** immediately terminates program execution without running any destructors.

In this program, **assert** determines if the **new** operator was able to fulfill the request for memory to be allocated dynamically. For example, in the **Employee** constructor function, the following line (which is also called an *assertion*)

```
assert( firstName != 0 );
```

tests pointer **firstName** to determine if it is not equal to **0**. If the condition in the preceding assertion is **true**, the program continues without interruption. If the condition in the preceding assertion is **false**, an error message containing the line number, the condition being tested and the file name in which the assertion appears is printed, and the program terminates. The programmer may then concentrate on this area of the code to find the error. In Chapter 13, "Exception Handling," we will provide a better method of dealing with execution time errors.

Assertions do not have to be removed from the program when debugging is completed. When assertions are no longer needed for debugging purposes in a program, the line

```
#define NDEBUG
```

is inserted at the beginning of the program file (typically this can also be specified in the compiler options). This causes the preprocessor to ignore all assertions instead of the programmer having to delete each assertion manually.

Note that the implementations of functions **getFirstName** and **getLastName** return to the client of the class constant character pointers. In this implementation, if the client wishes to retain a copy of the first name or last name, the client is responsible for copying the dynamically allocated memory in the **Employee** object after obtaining the constant character pointer from the object. Note that it is also possible to implement **getFirstName** and **getLastName** so the client is required to pass a character array and the size of the array to each function. Then, the functions could copy the first or last name into the character array provided by the client. Once again, class **string** (Chapter 19) could be used here to return a copy of a **string** object to the caller.

7.8 Data Abstraction and Information Hiding

Classes normally hide their implementation details from the clients of the classes. This is called *information hiding*. As an example of information hiding, let us consider a data structure called a *stack*.

Think of a stack in terms of a pile of dishes. When a dish is placed on the pile, it is always placed at the top (referred to as *pushing onto the stack*), and when a dish is removed from the pile, it is always removed from the top (referred to as *popping off the stack*). Stacks are known as *last-in, first-out (LIFO) data structures*—the last item pushed (inserted) on the stack is the first item popped (removed) from the stack.

The programmer may create a stack class and hide from its clients the implementation of the stack. Stacks can easily be implemented with arrays (or linked lists; see Chapter 15, "Data Structures"). A client of a stack class need not know how the stack is implemented. The client simply requires that when data items are placed in the stack, the data items will be recalled in last-in, first-out order. Describing the functionality of a class independent of its implementation is called *data abstraction* and C++ classes define so-called *abstract data types (ADTs)*. Although users may happen to know the details of how a class is implemented, users should not write code that depends on these details. This means that the implementation of a particular class (such as one that implements a stack and its operations of *push* and *pop*) can be altered or replaced without affecting the rest of the system, as long as the **public** interface to that class does not change.

The job of a high-level language is to create a view convenient for programmers to use. There is no single accepted standard view—that is one reason why there are so many programming languages. Object-oriented programming in C++ presents yet another view.

Most programming languages emphasize actions. In these languages, data exist in support of the actions programs need to take. Data are viewed as being "less interesting" than actions, anyway. Data are "crude." There are only a few built-in data types, and it is difficult for programmers to create their own new data types.

This view changes with C++ and the object-oriented style of programming. C++ elevates the importance of data. The primary activity in C++ is creating new types (i.e., classes) and expressing the interactions among objects of those types.

To move in this direction, the programming-languages community needed to formalize some notions about data. The formalization we consider is the notion of abstract data types (ADTs). ADTs receive as much attention today as structured programming did over the last two decades. ADTs do not replace structured programming. Rather, they provide an additional formalization that can further improve the program development process.

What is an abstract data type? Consider the built-in type **int**. What comes to mind is the notion of an integer in mathematics, but **int** on a computer is not precisely what an integer is in mathematics. In particular, computer **int**s are normally quite limited in size. For example, **int** on a 32-bit machine may be limited approximately to the range –2 billion to +2 billion. If the result of a calculation falls outside this range, an "overflow" error occurs and the machine responds in some machine-dependent manner, including the possibility of "quietly" producing an incorrect result. Mathematical integers do not have this problem. So the notion of a computer **int** is really only an approximation to the notion of a real-world integer. The same is true with **double**.

Even **char** is an approximation; **char** values are normally eight-bit patterns of ones and zeros; these patterns look nothing like the characters they represent such as a capital **Z**, a lowercase **z**, a dollar sign (**$**), a digit (**5**), and so on. Values of type **char** on most computers are quite limited compared with the range of real-world characters. The seven-bit ASCII character set provides for 128 different character values. This is completely inadequate for representing languages such as Japanese and Chinese that require thousands of characters.

The point is that even the built-in data types provided with programming languages like C++ are really only approximations or models of real-world concepts and behaviors. We have taken **int** for granted until this point, but now you have a new perspective to consider. Types like **int**, **double**, **char** and others are all examples of abstract data types. They are essentially ways of representing real-world notions to some satisfactory level of precision within a computer system.

An abstract data type actually captures two notions, namely a *data representation* and the *operations* that are allowed on those data. For example, the notion of **int** defines addition, subtraction, multiplication, division and modulus operations in C++, but division by zero is undefined; and these allowed operations perform in a manner sensitive to machine parameters such as the fixed-word size of the underlying computer system. Another example is the notion of negative integers, whose operations and data representation are clear, but the operation of taking the square root of a negative integer is undefined. In C++, the programmer uses classes to more precisely implement abstract data types and their services. We create our own stack class in Chapter 12, "Templates," and we study the standard library **stack** class in Chapter 20, "Standard Template Library (STL)."

7.8.1 Example: Array Abstract Data Type

We discussed arrays in Chapter 4. An array is not much more than a pointer and some space. This primitive capability is acceptable for performing array operations if the programmer is cautious and undemanding. There are many operations that would be nice to perform with arrays, but that are not built into C++. With C++ classes, the programmer can develop an array ADT that is preferable to "raw" arrays. The array class can provide many helpful new capabilities such as

- Subscript range checking.
- An arbitrary range of subscripts instead of having to start with 0.
- Array assignment.
- Array comparison.
- Array input/output.
- Arrays that know their sizes.
- Arrays that expand dynamically to accomodate more elements.

We create our own array class in Chapter 8, "Operator Overloading," and we study the standard library class (called **vector**) in Chapter 20.

C++ has a small set of built-in types. Classes extend the base programming language.

 **Software Engineering Observation 7.15**

The programmer is able to create new types through the class mechanism. These new types can be designed to be used as conveniently as the built-in types. Thus, C++ is an extensible language. Although the language is easy to extend with these new types, the base language itself is not changeable.

New classes created in C++ environments can be proprietary to an individual, to small groups or to companies. Classes can also be placed in standard class libraries intended for wide distribution. This does not necessarily promote standards although de facto standards are emerging. The full value of C++ can be realized only when substantial and standardized class libraries are used to develop new applications. ANSI (the American National Standards Institute) and ISO (the International Standards Organization) have developed a standard version of C++ that includes a standard class library. The reader who learns C++ and object-oriented programming will be ready to take advantage of the new kinds of rapid, component-oriented software development made possible with increasingly abundant and rich libraries.

7.8.2 Example: String Abstract Data Type

C++ is an intentionally sparse language that provides programmers with only the raw capabilities needed to build a broad range of systems (consider it a tool for making tools). The language is designed to minimize performance burdens. C++ is appropriate for both applications programming and systems programming—the latter places extraordinary performance demands on programs. Certainly, it would have been possible to include a string data type among C++'s built-in data types. Instead, the language was designed to include mechanisms for creating and implementing string abstract data types through classes. We will develop our own string ADT in Chapter 8. The ANSI/ISO standard includes a **string** class that we discuss in detail in Chapter 19.

7.8.3 Example: Queue Abstract Data Type

Each of us stands in line from time to time. A waiting line is also called a *queue*. We wait in line at the supermarket checkout counter, we wait in line to get gasoline, we wait in line to board a bus, we wait in line to pay a toll on the highway and students know all too well about waiting in line during registration to get the courses they want. Computer systems use many waiting lines internally, so we need to write programs that simulate what queues are and do.

A queue is a good example of an abstract data type. A queue offers well-understood behavior to its clients. Clients put things in a queue one at a time—using an *enqueue* operation—and the clients get those things back one at a time on demand—using a *dequeue* operation. Conceptually, a queue can become infinitely long. A real queue, of course, is finite. Items are returned from a queue in *first-in, first-out (FIFO)* order—the first item inserted in the queue is the first item removed from the queue.

The queue hides an internal data representation that somehow keeps track of the items currently waiting in line, and it offers a set of operations to its clients, namely *enqueue* and *dequeue*. The clients are not concerned about the implementation of the queue. Clients merely want the queue to operate "as advertised." When a client enqueues a new item, the queue should accept that item and place it internally in some kind of first-in, first-out data structure. When the client wants the next item from the front of the queue, the queue should remove the item from its internal representation and should deliver the item to the outside world (i.e., to the *client* of the queue) in FIFO order, i.e., the item that has been in the queue the longest should be the next one returned by the next *dequeue* operation.

The queue ADT guarantees the integrity of its internal data structure. Clients may not manipulate this data structure directly. Only the queue member functions have access to its internal data. Clients may cause only allowable operations to be performed on the data representation; operations not provided in the ADT's **public** interface are rejected in some appropriate manner. This could mean issuing an error message, terminating execution or simply ignoring the operation request.

We create our own queue class in Chapter 15, "Data Structures," and we study the standard library **queue** class in Chapter 20.

7.9 Container Classes and Iterators

Among the most popular types of classes are *container classes* (also called *collection classes*), i.e., classes designed to hold collections of objects. Container classes commonly provide services such as insertion, deletion, searching, sorting, testing an item to determine if it is a member of the collection and the like. Arrays, stacks, queues, trees and linked lists are examples of container classes; we studied arrays in Chapter 4 and we will study each of these other data structures in Chapters 15 and 20.

It is common to associate *iterator objects*—or more simply *iterators*—with container classes. An iterator is an object that returns the next item of a collection (or performs some action on the next item of a collection). Once an iterator for a class has been written, obtaining the next element from the class can be expressed simply. Just as a book being shared by several people could have several bookmarks in it at once, a container class can have several iterators operating on it at once. Each iterator maintains its own "position" information. We will discuss containers and iterators in great detail in Chapter 20, "Standard Template Library (STL)."

7.10 Proxy Classes

It is desirable to hide the implementation details of a class to prevent access to proprietary information (including **private** data) and proprietary program logic in a class. Providing clients of your class with a *proxy class* that knows only the **public** interface to your class enables the clients to use your class' services without giving the client access to your class' implementation details.

Implementing a proxy class requires several steps (Fig. 7.10). First, we create the class definition and implementation files for the class whose **private** data we would like to hide. Our example class, which we call **Implementation**, is shown in Fig. 7.10, lines 1 through 12. The proxy class **Interface** is shown in Fig. 7.10, 13 through 41, and the test program and output are shown in Fig. 7.10, lines 42 through 61.

```
1   // Fig. 7.10: implementation.h
2   // Header file for class Implementation
3
4   class Implementation {
5      public:
6         Implementation( int v ) { value = v; }
7         void setValue( int v ) { value = v; }
8         int getValue() const { return value; }
9
10      private:
11         int value;
12   };
```

Fig. 7.10   Implementing a proxy class—**implementation.h** .

```
13  // Fig. 7.10: interface.h
14  // Header file for interface.cpp
15  class Implementation;    // forward class declaration
16
17  class Interface {
18     public:
19        Interface( int );
20        void setValue( int );   // same public interface as
21        int getValue() const;   // class Implementation
22        ~Interface();
23     private:
24        Implementation *ptr;    // requires previous
25                                // forward declaration
26  };
```

Fig. 7.10   Implementing a proxy class—**interface.h** .

```
27  // Fig. 7.10: interface.cpp
28  // Definition of class Interface
29  #include "interface.h"
30  #include "implementation.h"
31
32  Interface::Interface( int v )
33     : ptr ( new Implementation( v ) ) { }
34
35  // call Implementation's setValue function
36  void Interface::setValue( int v ) { ptr->setValue( v ); }
37
38  // call Implementation's getValue function
39  int Interface::getValue() const { return ptr->getValue(); }
40
41  Interface::~Interface() { delete ptr; }
```

Fig. 7.10   Implementing a proxy class—**interface.cpp** .

```
42  // Fig. 7.10: fig07_10.cpp
43  // Hiding a class's private data with a proxy class.
44  #include <iostream>
45
46  using std::cout;
47  using std::endl;
48
49  #include "interface.h"
50
51  int main()
52  {
53     Interface i( 5 );
54
55     cout << "Interface contains: " << i.getValue()
56          << " before setValue" << endl;
```

Fig. 7.10   Implementing a proxy class—**fig07_10.cpp** (part 1 of 2).

```
57      i.setValue( 10 );
58      cout << "Interface contains: " << i.getValue()
59          << " after setValue" << endl;
60      return 0;
61   }
```

```
Interface contains: 5 before setVal
Interface contains: 10 after setVal
```

Fig. 7.10   Implementing a proxy class—`fig07_10.cpp` (part 2 of 2).

Class **Implementation** provides a single **private** data member called **value** (these are the data we would like to hide from the client), a constructor to initialize **value** and functions **setValue** and **getValue**.

We create a proxy class definition with an identical **public** interface to that of class **Implementation**. The only **private** member of the proxy class is a pointer to an object of class **Implementation**. Using a pointer in this manner allows us to hide the implementation details of class **Implementation** from the client.

Class **Interface** in part 2 of Fig. 7.10 is the proxy class for class **Implementation**. Notice that the only mention in class **Interface** of the proprietary class **Implementation** is in the pointer declaration (line 24). When a class definition (such as class **Interface**) uses only a pointer to another class (such as to class **Implementation**), the class header file for that other class (which would ordinarily reveal the **private** data of that class) is not required to be included with **#include**. You can simply declare that other class as a data type with a *forward class declaration* (line 15) before the type is used in the file.

The implementation file containing the member functions for proxy class **Interface** (Fig. 7.10, part 3) is the only file that includes the header file **implementation.h** containing class **Implementation**. The file **interface.cpp** (Fig. 7.10, part 3) is provided to the client as a precompiled object file along with the header file **interface.h** that includes the function prototypes of the services provided by the proxy class. Because file **interface.cpp** is made available to the client only as compiled object code, the client is not able to see the interactions between the proxy class and the proprietary class.

The program in part 4 of Fig. 7.10 tests class **Interface**. Notice that only the header file for class **Interface** is included in **main**—there is no mention of the existence of a separate class called **Implementation**. Thus, the client never sees the **private** data of class **Implementation**, nor can the client code become dependent on the **Implementation** code.

7.10 (Optional Case Study) Thinking About Objects: Programming the Classes for the Elevator Simulator

In the "Thinking About Objects" sections at the ends of Chapters 2 through 5, we designed our elevator simulator, and, in Chapter 6, we began programming the simulator in C++. In the body of Chapter 7, we discussed the remaining C++ capabilities that we need to implement a complete, working elevator simulator. We discussed dynamic object management, using **new** and **delete** to create and destroy objects, respectively. We also discussed composition, a capability that allows us to create classes that have objects of other classes as data members. Composition enables us to create a **Building** class that contains a **Scheduler** object, a **Clock** object, an **Elevator** object and two **Floor** objects; an **Elevator** class that contains one object each of classes **ElevatorButton**, **Door** and **Bell**; and a **Floor** class that contains **FloorButton** and **Light** objects. We also discussed how to use **static** class members, **const** class members, and member-initialization syntax in constructors. In this section, we continue implementing our elevator system in C++ using these techniques. At the end of this section we present a complete elevator simulator C++ program (approximately 1000 lines of code) and a detailed code walkthrough. In the "Thinking About Objects" section at the end of Chapter 9, we complete our elevator simulator case study by incorporating inheritance into the elevator simulator; at that point we present only the additional C++ code it takes us to implement the inheritance.

An Overview of the Elevator Simulation Implementation

Our elevator simulation is controlled by an object of class **Building**, which contains two objects of class **Floor** and one object of classes **Elevator**, **Clock** and **Scheduler**. This composite relationship was shown in the UML class diagram (Fig. 2.44) presented in the "Thinking About Objects" section at the end of Chapter 2. The clock simply keeps track of the current time in seconds and is incremented once per second by the building. The scheduler is responsible for scheduling the arrival of people to each floor.

After each tick of the clock, the building updates the scheduler with the current time (via the **processTime** member function of class **Scheduler**). The scheduler checks this time against the next scheduled arrival times for people on each floor. If a person is scheduled to arrive on a floor, the scheduler checks to see whether the floor is unoccupied by calling the **isOccupied** member function of class **Floor**. If this call returns **true**, there is a person currently on the floor, so the scheduler invokes its **delayArrival** function to delay for one second the next arrival time for a person to that floor.

If the floor is empty (i.e., the call returns **false**), the scheduler creates a new object of class **Person**, and that person steps onto the appropriate floor. The person then invokes the **pressButton** member function of class **FloorButton**. The floor button, in turn, invokes the **summonElevator** method of class **Elevator**.

The building also updates the elevator with the current time in seconds after each tick of the clock. Upon receiving the updated time, the elevator first checks its current state (either "moving" or "not moving"). If the elevator is moving between floors, but is not scheduled to arrive at a floor at that time, the elevator simply outputs its direction of motion to the screen. If the elevator is moving, and the current time matches the next scheduled arrival time, the elevator stops, resets its elevator button, rings its bell and notifies the floor that the elevator has arrived (via the **elevatorArrived** member function of class **Floor**). In response, the floor resets its floor button and turns on its light. The elevator then opens its door, which allows the person in the elevator to exit and the person on the floor to enter. The elevator then closes its door and determines whether the other floor needs service. If the other floor needs service, the elevator begins moving to that floor.

If the elevator is not moving when it receives the updated time from the building, the elevator determines which floors need its service. If the current floor needs service (i.e., a person has pressed a button on the elevator's current floor), the elevator rings its bell, notifies the floor that the elevator has arrived, and opens the elevator door. The person on the floor enters the elevator and presses the elevator button to start the elevator moving to the other floor. If the other floor needs service (i.e., a person has pressed a button on the other floor), the elevator begins moving to that floor.

The Elevator Simulation Implementation

In the preceding "Thinking About Objects" sections we gathered much information about our system. We used this information to create an object-oriented design of our elevator simulation, and we represented this design using the UML. We have now discussed all the C++ object-oriented programming technology needed to implement a working simulation. The remainder of this section contains our C++ implementation and a detailed code walk-through.

Our driver program (Fig. 7.11) first prompts the user to enter the length of time for which the simulation should run (lines 15–16). The call to **cin.ignore** in line 17 instructs the **cin** stream to ignore the return character the user types after the integer at run time. This removes the return character from the input stream. The driver then creates the **building** object (line 19) and invokes its **runSimulation** member function, passing as a parameter the duration specified by the user (line 23). The driver also prints out messages, indicating to the user when the simulation begins (line 21) and ends (line 24).

```
1    // Figure 7.11
2    // Driver for the simulation.
3    #include <iostream>
4
5    using std::cout;
6    using std::cin;
7    using std::endl;
8
9    #include "building.h"
10
11   int main()
12   {
13       int duration;              // length of simulation in seconds
14
15       cout << "Enter run time: ";
16       cin >> duration;
17       cin.ignore();                              // ignore return char
18
19       Building building;                         // create the building
20
21       cout << endl << "*** ELEVATOR SIMULATION BEGINS ***"
22            << endl << endl;
23       building.runSimulation( duration );   // start simulation
24       cout << "*** ELEVATOR SIMULATION ENDS ***" << endl;
25
26       return 0;
27   }
```

Fig. 7.11   Driver for the elevator simulation.

According to our class diagram (Fig. 2.44), class **Building** is composed of objects from several other classes. The **Building** header file presented in Fig. 7.12 reflects this composition (lines 46–50). Class **Building** is composed of two **Floor** objects (**floor1** and **floor2**), an **Elevator** object (**elevator**), a **Clock** object (**clock**) and a **Scheduler** object (**scheduler**).

The implementation file for class **Building** is shown in Fig. 7.13. The constructor is in lines 64 through 69. In the member initialization list (lines 65–68), constructors for many of the objects of which class **Building** is composed are called with appropriate arguments. **FLOOR1** and **FLOOR2** (mentioned in lines 65–66) are constants defined in class **Floor** (lines 821–822).

```
28   // building.h
29   // Definition for class Building.
30   #ifndef BUILDING_H
31   #define BUILDING_H
32
33   #include "elevator.h"
34   #include "floor.h"
35   #include "clock.h"
36   #include "scheduler.h"
37
38   class Building {
39
40   public:
41      Building();                    // constructor
42      ~Building();                   // destructor
43      void runSimulation( int );     // run simulation for specified time
44
45   private:
46      Floor floor1;                  // floor1 object
47      Floor floor2;                  // floor2 object
48      Elevator elevator;             // elevator object
49      Clock clock;                   // clock object
50      Scheduler scheduler;           // scheduler object
51   };
52
53   #endif // BUILDING_H
```

Fig. 7.12   Class **Building** header file.

```
54   // building.cpp
55   // Member function definitions for class Building.
56   #include <iostream>
57
58   using std::cout;
59   using std::cin;
60   using std::endl;
61
62   #include "building.h"
63
```

Fig. 7.13   Class **Building** implementation file (part 1 of 2).

```
64   Building::Building() // constructor
65      : floor1( Floor::FLOOR1, elevator ),
66        floor2( Floor::FLOOR2, elevator ),
67        elevator( floor1, floor2 ),
68        scheduler( floor1, floor2 )
69   { cout << "building created" << endl; }
70
71   Building::~Building() // destructor
72   { cout << "building destroyed" << endl; }
73
74   // control the simulation
75   void Building::runSimulation( int totalTime )
76   {
77      int currentTime = 0;
78
79      while ( currentTime < totalTime ) {
80         clock.tick();
81         currentTime = clock.getTime();
82         cout << "TIME: " << currentTime << endl;
83         scheduler.processTime( currentTime );
84         elevator.processTime( currentTime );
85         cin.get(); // stop each second for user to view output
86      }
87   }
```

Fig. 7.13   Class **Building** implementation file (part 2 of 2).

The main functionality of class **Building** is in its **runSimulation** member function (lines 74–87), which loops until the specified amount of time has passed. On each iteration, the **building** instructs the **clock** to increment its time by one second by sending
clock the **tick** message (line 80). Then, the **building** retrieves the time from the
clock by calling the **getTime** member function (line 81). The **currentTime** is then
sent via the **processTime** messages to the **scheduler** and the **elevator** in lines 83
and 84, respectively. Finally, we add a call to **cin.get** (line 85) to allow the user to stop
output scrolling temporarily to view the simulation output for the next simulated second of
time, before pressing the enter key to resume output scrolling.

Clock is a simple class that is not composed of any other objects. The header file for
class **Clock** is shown in Fig. 7.14, and its implementation is in Fig. 7.15. An object of class
Clock can receive messages to increment **time** through the **tick** member function,
which is prototyped on line 98 and implemented on lines 122 and 123. The current time is
made available to other objects through the **getTime** member function on lines 99, 125
and 126. Notice that **getTime** is **const**.

```
88   // clock.h
89   // Definition for class Clock.
90   #ifndef CLOCK_H
91   #define CLOCK_H
92
```

Fig. 7.14   Class **Clock** header file (part 1 of 2).

```
93    class Clock {
94
95    public:
96       Clock();              // constructor
97       ~Clock();             // destructor
98       void tick();          // increment clock by one second
99       int getTime() const;  // returns clock's current time
100
101   private:
102      int time;             // clock's time
103   };
104
105   #endif // CLOCK_H
```

Fig. 7.14   Class **Clock** header file (part 2 of 2).

```
106   // clock.cpp
107   // Member function definitions for class Clock.
108   #include <iostream>
109
110   using std::cout;
111   using std::endl;
112
113   #include "clock.h"
114
115   Clock::Clock()              // constructor
116      : time( 0 )
117   { cout << "clock created" << endl; }
118
119   Clock::~Clock()             // destructor
120   { cout << "clock destroyed" << endl; }
121
122   void Clock::tick()          // increment time by 1
123   { time++; }
124
125   int Clock::getTime() const // return current time
126   { return time; }
```

Fig. 7.15   Class **Clock** implementation file.

Class **Scheduler** (Fig. 7.16) is responsible for creating objects of class **Person** at randomly generated times and for placing these objects on the appropriate floors. The **public** interface lists the **processTime** member function, which takes as its argument the current time (line 139). The header file also lists several **private** utility functions (which we discuss momentarily) that perform the tasks required by the **processTime** member function.

Figure 7.17 lists the implementation file for class **Scheduler**. The **processTime** member function (lines 222–232) delegates most of its responsibilities to smaller utility functions within the class. Class **Scheduler**'s constructor (lines 178–189) first seeds the pseudo-random number generator with a number based on the current real-world time (line 183). This causes the random-number generator to produce a different series of numbers each time the program is executed. Class **Scheduler** then calls the **scheduleTime** utility function (lines 194–207) once for each of the two floors (lines 187-188). This member function calculates a pseudo-random arrival time (in this case, a random number in the range 5 to 20, inclusive) for the first **Person** object on each floor.

```
127  // scheduler.h
128  // definition for class Scheduler
129  #ifndef SCHEDULER_H
130  #define SCHEDULER_H
131
132  class Floor;                          // forward declaration
133
134  class Scheduler {
135
136  public:
137     Scheduler( Floor &, Floor & );    // constructor
138     ~Scheduler();                      // destructor
139     void processTime( int );           // set scheduler's time
140
141  private:
142     // schedule arrival to a floor
143     void scheduleTime( const Floor & );
144
145     // delay arrival to a floor
146     void delayTime( const Floor & );
147
148     // create new person; place on floor
149     void createNewPerson( Floor & );
150
151     // handle person arrival on a floor
152     void handleArrivals( Floor &, int );
153
154     int currentClockTime;
155
156     Floor &floor1Ref;
157     Floor &floor2Ref;
158
159     int floor1ArrivalTime;
160     int floor2ArrivalTime;
161  };
162
163  #endif // SCHEDULER_H
```

Fig. 7.16   Class **Scheduler** header file.

```
164  // scheduler.cpp
165  // Member function definitions for class Scheduler.
166  #include <iostream>
167
168  using std::cout;
169  using std::endl;
170
```

Fig. 7.17   Class **Scheduler** implementation file (part 1 of 3).

```
171  #include <cstdlib>
172  #include <ctime>
173
174  #include "scheduler.h"
175  #include "floor.h"
176  #include "person.h"
177
178  // constructor
179  Scheduler::Scheduler( Floor &firstFloor, Floor &secondFloor )
180     : currentClockTime( 0 ), floor1Ref( firstFloor ),
181       floor2Ref( secondFloor )
182  {
183     srand( time( 0 ) ); // seed random number generator
184     cout << "scheduler created" << endl;
185
186     // schedule first arrivals for floor 1 and floor 2
187     scheduleTime( floor1Ref );
188     scheduleTime( floor2Ref );
189  }
190
191  Scheduler::~Scheduler() // destructor
192  { cout << "scheduler destroyed" << endl; }
193
194  // schedule arrival on a floor
195  void Scheduler::scheduleTime( const Floor &floor )
196  {
197     int floorNumber = floor.getNumber();
198     int arrivalTime = currentClockTime + ( 5 + rand() % 16 );
199
200     floorNumber == Floor::FLOOR1 ?
201        floor1ArrivalTime = arrivalTime :
202        floor2ArrivalTime = arrivalTime;
203
204     cout << "(scheduler schedules next person for floor "
205          << floorNumber << " at time " << arrivalTime << ')'
206          << endl;
207  }
208
209  // reschedule an arrival on a floor
210  void Scheduler::delayTime( const Floor &floor )
211  {
212     int floorNumber = floor.getNumber();
213
214     int arrivalTime = ( floorNumber == Floor::FLOOR1 ) ?
215        ++floor1ArrivalTime : ++floor2ArrivalTime;
216
217     cout << "(scheduler delays next person for floor "
218          << floorNumber << " until time " << arrivalTime << ')'
219          << endl;
220  }
221
```

Fig. 7.17   Class **Scheduler** implementation file (part 2 of 3).

```
222   // give time to scheduler
223   void Scheduler::processTime( int time )
224   {
225      currentClockTime = time;    // record time
226
227      // handle arrivals on floor 1
228      handleArrivals( floor1Ref, currentClockTime );
229
230      // handle arrivals on floor 2
231      handleArrivals( floor2Ref, currentClockTime );
232   }
233
234   // create new person and place it on specified floor
235   void Scheduler::createNewPerson( Floor &floor )
236   {
237      int destinationFloor =
238         floor.getNumber() == Floor::FLOOR1 ?
239            Floor::FLOOR2 : Floor::FLOOR1;
240
241      // create new person
242      Person *newPersonPtr = new Person( destinationFloor );
243
244      cout << "scheduler creates person "
245         << newPersonPtr->getID() << endl;
246
247      // place person on proper floor
248      newPersonPtr->stepOntoFloor( floor );
249
250      scheduleTime( floor ); // schedule next arrival
251   }
252
253   // handle arrivals for a specified floor
254   void Scheduler::handleArrivals( Floor &floor, int time )
255   {
256      int floorNumber = floor.getNumber();
257
258      int arrivalTime = ( floorNumber == Floor::FLOOR1 ) ?
259         floor1ArrivalTime : floor2ArrivalTime;
260
261      if ( arrivalTime == time ) {
262
263         if ( floor.isOccupied() ) // see if floor occupied
264            delayTime( floor );
265         else
266            createNewPerson( floor );
267      }
268   }
```

Fig. 7.17   Class **Scheduler** implementation file (part 3 of 3).

In our simulation, the **building** updates the **scheduler** every second with the current time via the **scheduler**'s **processTime** member function (lines 222–232). The sequence diagram in Fig. 4.27 modeled the sequence of activities that occur in response to this message, and our implementation reflects this model. When the **processTime** member function is invoked, **scheduler** calls the **handleArrivals** utility function for each floor (lines 228 and 231). This utility function compares the current **time** (as provided by **building**) to the next scheduled arrival time for the given floor (line 261). If the current time matches the arrival time for this floor, and if the floor is currently occupied (line 263), **scheduler** calls the **delayTime** utility function to delay the next scheduled arrival by one second (line 264). If the floor is unoccupied, the **scheduler** invokes utility function **createNewPerson** (line 266), which creates a new object of class **Person** by using the **new** operator (line 242). The **scheduler** then sends this new object of class **Person** the **stepOntoFloor** message (line 248). Once the person has stepped onto the floor, the **scheduler** calculates the next arrival time for a person on that floor by calling utility function **scheduleTime** (line 250).

We have examined the implementation for all the classes that compose the controller portion of the simulation; we now examine the classes that compose the world portion of the simulation. Class **Bell**, like class **Clock**, is not composed of other objects. Class **Bell**'s **public** interface, as defined in its header file in Fig. 7.18, consists of a constructor, a destructor and the **ringBell** member function. The implementations of these functions (lines 292–293, 295–296, and 298–299, respectively in Fig. 7.19) simply outputs messages to the screen.

```
269  // bell.h
270  // Definition for class Bell.
271  #ifndef BELL_H
272  #define BELL_H
273
274  class Bell {
275
276  public:
277     Bell();                   // constructor
278     ~Bell();                  // destructor
279     void ringBell() const;    // ring the bell
280  };
281
282  #endif // BELL_H
```

Fig. 7.18 Class **Bell** header file.

```
283  // bell.cpp
284  // Member function definitions for class Bell.
285  #include <iostream>
286
287  using std::cout;
288  using std::endl;
289
290  #include "bell.h"
291
292  Bell::Bell() // constructor
293  { cout << "bell created" << endl; }
294
```

Fig. 7.19 Class **Bell** implementation file (part 1 of 2).

```
295   Bell::~Bell() // destructor
296   { cout << "bell destroyed" << endl; }
297
298   void Bell::ringBell() const // ring bell
299   { cout << "elevator rings its bell" << endl; }
```

Fig. 7.19   Class **Bell** implementation file (part 2 of 2).

Class **Light** (Figs. 7.20 and 7.21) exposes two member functions in its **public** interface, in addition to the constructor and destructor. The **turnOn** member function simply turns the light on by setting the **on** data member to **true** (lines 335–339). The **turnOff** member function (lines 341–345) turns the light off by setting the **on** data member to **false**.

```
300   // light.h
301   // Definition for class Light.
302   #ifndef LIGHT_H
303   #define LIGHT_H
304
305   class Light {
306
307   public:
308      Light( const char * );   // constructor
309      ~Light();                // destructor
310      void turnOn();           // turns light on
311      void turnOff();          // turns light off
312
313   private:
314      bool on;                 // true if on; false if off
315      const char *name;        // which floor the light is on
316   };
317
318   #endif // LIGHT_H
```

Fig. 7.20   Class **Light** header file.

```
319   // light.cpp
320   // Member function definitions for class Light.
321   #include <iostream>
322
323   using std::cout;
324   using std::endl;
325
326   #include "light.h"
327
328   Light::Light( const char *string ) // constructor
329      : on( false ), name( string )
330   { cout << name << " light created" << endl; }
331
```

Fig. 7.21   Class **Light** implementation file.

```
332  Light::~Light()          // destructor
333  { cout << name << " light destroyed" << endl; }
334
335  void Light::turnOn()    // turn light on
336  {
337     on = true;
338     cout << name << " turns on its light" << endl;
339  }
340
341  void Light::turnOff()  // turn light off
342  {
343     on = false;
344     cout << name << " turns off its light" << endl;
345  }
```

Fig. 7.21   Class **Light** implementation file.

Class **Door** (Figs. 7.22 and 7.23) serves an important role in our elevator simulation. It is the **door** object that signals the elevator passenger to leave; the **door** also signals the person waiting on the floor to enter the **elevator**. These actions are accomplished by the **openDoor** member function of class **Door**. You will notice that the **openDoor** member function takes four arguments (lines 361–362 and 390–392). The first is a pointer to the object of class **Person** that occupies the **elevator**. The second argument is a pointer to the object of class **Person** waiting on the floor. The remaining two arguments are references to the appropriate object of class **Floor** and to the **elevator** object.

```
346  // door.h
347  // Definition for class Door.
348  #ifndef DOOR_H
349  #define DOOR_H
350
351  class Person;              // forward declaration
352  class Floor;               // forward declaration
353  class Elevator;            // forward declaration
354
355  class Door {
356
357  public:
358     Door();                 // constructor
359     ~Door();                // destructor
360
361     void openDoor( Person * const, Person * const,
362                    Floor &, Elevator & );
363     void closeDoor( const Floor & );
364
365  private:
366     bool open;              // open or closed
367  };
368
369  #endif // DOOR_H
```

Fig. 7.22   Class **Door** header file.

Class **Door** is a composite object of class **Elevator**; to implement this composition, the header file for class **Elevator** must contain the line

```
#include "door.h"
```

Class **Door** uses a reference to an object of class **Elevator** (line 362). To declare class **Elevator** to enable class **Door** to use this reference, we could place the following line in the header file for class **Door**:

```
#include "elevator.h"
```

Thus, the header file for class **Elevator** would include the header file for class **Door** and vice versa. The preprocessor would not be able to resolve such **#include** directives and would produce a fatal error because of this *circular include problem*.

To avoid this problem, we place a forward declaration of class **Elevator** in the header file for class **Door** (line 353). This forward declaration tells the preprocessor that we want to refer to objects of class **Elevator** in our file, but that the definition of class **Elevator** lies outside the file. Notice that we also make forward declarations to classes **Person** and **Floor** (lines 351–352), so we may use these classes in the prototype for the **openDoor** member function.

Figure 7.23 lists the implementation file for class **Door**. In lines 378–380, we include the header files for classes **Person**, **Floor** and **Elevator**. These **#include** directives correspond to our forward declarations in the header file; and the header files being included contain the mandatory function prototypes we need to be able to invoke the appropriate member functions of these classes.

When the **openDoor** member function (lines 389–409) is called, it first checks that the **door** is not already open. The **door** checks that the pointer to the person on the **elevator** (**passengerPtr**) is not zero (line 400). If this pointer is nonzero there is a person on the **elevator** that needs to exit. The person is told to exit the **elevator** via the **exitElevator** message (line 401). The **door** deletes the object of class **Person** object that was riding the **elevator** via the **delete** operator (line 402).

```
370  // door.cpp
371  // Member function definitions for class Door.
372  #include <iostream>
373
374  using std::cout;
375  using std::endl;
376
377  #include "door.h"
378  #include "person.h"
379  #include "floor.h"
380  #include "elevator.h"
381
```

Fig. 7.23   Class **Door** implementation file (part 1 of 2).

```
382  Door::Door() // constructor
383     : open( false )
384  { cout << "door created" << endl; }
385
386  Door::~Door() // destructor
387  { cout << "door destroyed" << endl; }
388
389  // open the door
390  void Door::openDoor( Person * const passengerPtr,
391                       Person * const nextPassengerPtr,
392                       Floor &currentFloor, Elevator &elevator )
393  {
394     if ( !open ) {
395        open = true;
396
397        cout << "elevator opens its door on floor "
398             << currentFloor.getNumber() << endl;
399
400        if ( passengerPtr != 0 ) {
401           passengerPtr->exitElevator( currentFloor, elevator );
402           delete passengerPtr; // passenger leaves simulation
403        }
404
405        if ( nextPassengerPtr != 0 )
406           nextPassengerPtr->enterElevator(
407              elevator, currentFloor );
408     }
409  }
410
411  // close the door
412  void Door::closeDoor( const Floor &currentFloor )
413  {
414     if ( open ) {
415        open = false;
416        cout << "elevator closes its door on floor "
417             << currentFloor.getNumber() << endl;
418     }
419  }
```

Fig. 7.23   Class **Door** implementation file (part 2 of 2).

Once the passenger has exited the **elevator**, the door checks the pointer to the person waiting on the floor (**nextPassengerPtr**) to see if that pointer is not (line 405). If the pointer is nonzero (i.e., there is a person waiting to enter the **elevator**), the person is allowed to enter the **elevator** via the **enterElevator** member function of class **Person** (lines 406–407). The **closeDoor** member function of class **Door** (lines 412–419) simply checks that the **Door** is open and, if so, closes it.

People in the system use an object of class **ElevatorButton** (Figs. 7.24, 7.25) to start the **elevator** moving to the other floor. The **pressButton** member function (lines 460–466) first sets the elevator button's **pressed** attribute to **true** then sends the **prepareToLeave** message to the **elevator**. The **resetButton** member function simply sets the **pressed** attribute to **false**.

```
420   // elevatorButton.h
421   // Definition for class ElevatorButton.
422   #ifndef ELEVATORBUTTON_H
423   #define ELEVATORBUTTON_H
424
425   class Elevator;                        // forward declaration
426
427   class ElevatorButton {
428
429   public:
430      ElevatorButton( Elevator & );       // constructor
431      ~ElevatorButton();                  // destructor
432
433      void pressButton();                 // press the button
434      void resetButton();                 // reset the button
435
436   private:
437      bool pressed;                       // state of button
438      Elevator &elevatorRef;              // reference to button's elevator
439   };
440
441   #endif // ELEVATORBUTTON_H
```

Fig. 7.24   Class **ElevatorButton** header file.

```
442   // elevatorButton.cpp:
443   // Member function definitions for class ElevatorButton.
444   #include <iostream>
445
446   using std::cout;
447   using std::endl;
448
449   #include "elevatorButton.h"
450   #include "elevator.h"
451
452   // constructor
453   ElevatorButton::ElevatorButton( Elevator &elevatorHandle )
454      : pressed( false ), elevatorRef( elevatorHandle )
455   { cout << "elevator button created" << endl; }
456
457   ElevatorButton::~ElevatorButton()    // destructor
458   { cout << "elevator button destroyed" << endl; }
459
460   void ElevatorButton::pressButton()   // press the button
461   {
462      pressed = true;
463      cout << "elevator button tells elevator to prepare to leave"
464         << endl;
465      elevatorRef.prepareToLeave( true );
466   }
467
```

Fig. 7.25   Class **ElevatorButton** implementation file (part 1 of 2).

```
468  void ElevatorButton::resetButton() // reset the button
469  { pressed = false; }
```

Fig. 7.25   Class **ElevatorButton** implementation file (part 2 of 2).

Class **FloorButton** (Figs. 7.26, 7.27) exposes the same member functions as class **ElevatorButton** through its **public** interface. The **public pressButton** member function summons the **elevator** via the **summonElevator** message. The floor button is reset through a call to the **resetButton** member function.

```
470  // floorButton.h
471  // Definition for class FloorButton.
472  #ifndef FLOORBUTTON_H
473  #define FLOORBUTTON_H
474
475  class Elevator;            // forward declaration
476
477  class FloorButton {
478
479  public:
480      FloorButton( const int, Elevator & ); // constructor
481      ~FloorButton();                        // destructor
482
483      void pressButton();     // press the button
484      void resetButton();     // reset the button
485
486  private:
487      const int floorNumber;   // number of the button's floor
488      bool pressed;            // state of button
489
490      // reference to button's elevator
491      Elevator &elevatorRef;
492  };
493
494  #endif // FLOORBUTTON_H
```

Fig. 7.26   Class **FloorButton** header file.

```
495  // floorButton.cpp
496  // Member function definitions for class FloorButton.
497  #include <iostream>
498
499  using std::cout;
500  using std::endl;
501
```

Fig. 7.27   Class **FloorButton** implementation file (part 1 of 2).

```
502  #include "floorButton.h"
503  #include "elevator.h"
504
505  // constructor
506  FloorButton::FloorButton( const int number,
507                            Elevator &elevatorHandle  )
508     : floorNumber( number ), pressed( false ),
509       elevatorRef( elevatorHandle )
510  {
511     cout << "floor " << floorNumber << " button created"
512        << endl;
513  }
514
515  FloorButton::~FloorButton() // destructor
516  {
517     cout << "floor " << floorNumber << " button destroyed"
518        << endl;
519  }
520
521  // press the button
522  void FloorButton::pressButton()
523  {
524     pressed = true;
525     cout << "floor " << floorNumber
526        << " button summons elevator" << endl;
527     elevatorRef.summonElevator( floorNumber );
528  }
529
530  // reset the button
531  void FloorButton::resetButton()
532  { pressed = false; }
```

Fig. 7.27   Class **FloorButton** implementation file (part 2 of 2).

The header file for class **Elevator** (Fig. 7.28) is the most complex in our simulation. Class **Elevator** exposes five member functions (in addition to its constructor and destructor) in its **public** interface. The **processTime** member function allows the building to send the updated clock **time** to the **elevator**. The **summonElevator** member function allows a **Person** object to send a message to the **elevator** to request its service. Member functions **passengerEnters** and **passengerExits** enable passengers to enter and exit the **elevator**, and the **prepareToLeave** member function enables the **elevator** to perform any necessary tasks before it begins moving to another floor. We declare object **elevatorButton public**, so that an object of class **Person** can directly access the **elevatorButton**. A person generally does not interface with the bell or the door (unless that person is an elevator technician). Therefore, we declare the **bell** and **door** objects in the **private** section of the class definition.

Utility functions are included in lines 558–561. Class **Elevator** also defines a series of **private static const** values (lines 564–566). These values are made **static** because they contain information that is used by all objects of class **Elevator**; these values should never be modified, so they are also declared **const**.

```
533  // elevator.h
534  // Definition for class Elevator.
535  #ifndef ELEVATOR_H
536  #define ELEVATOR_H
537
538  #include "elevatorButton.h"
539  #include "door.h"
540  #include "bell.h"
541
542  class Floor;                          // forward declaration
543  class Person;                         // forward declaration
544
545  class Elevator {
546
547  public:
548     Elevator( Floor &, Floor & );      // constructor
549     ~Elevator();                       // destructor
550     void summonElevator( int );        // request to service a  floor
551     void prepareToLeave( bool );       // prepare to leave
552     void processTime( int );           // give time to elevator
553     void passengerEnters( Person * const ); // board a passenger
554     void passengerExits();             // exit a passenger
555     ElevatorButton elevatorButton;     // note public object
556
557  private:
558     void processPossibleArrival();
559     void processPossibleDeparture();
560     void arriveAtFloor( Floor & );
561     void move();
562
563     // time to move between floors
564     static const int ELEVATOR_TRAVEL_TIME;
565     static const int UP;               // UP direction
566     static const int DOWN;             // DOWN direction
567
568     int currentBuildingClockTime;      // current time
569     bool moving;                       // elevator state
570     int direction;                     // current direction
571     int currentFloor;                  // current location
572     int arrivalTime;                   // time to arrive at a floor
573     bool floor1NeedsService;           // floor1 service flag
574     bool floor2NeedsService;           // floor2 service flag
575
576     Floor &floor1Ref;                  // reference to floor1
577     Floor &floor2Ref;                  // reference to floor2
578     Person *passengerPtr;              // pointer to current passenger
579
580     Door door;                         // door object
581     Bell bell;                         // bell object
582  };
583
584  #endif // ELEVATOR_H
```

Fig. 7.28   Class **Elevator** header file.

Lines 568–581 of the **Elevator** header file contain additional **private** data members. Note that reference handles are provided for each of the objects of class **Floor** (lines 576–577), whereas a pointer is used for the passenger object (line 578). We use a pointer for the passenger object because this handle will need to change every time an object of class **Person** enters or leaves the **elevator**. We prefer reference handles to the **Floor** objects.

We have used the UML to model many of the activities and collaborations associated with class **Elevator** (see Figs. 3.31, 3.32 and 5.37); our code for class **Elevator** (Fig. 7.29) implements the information contained in these models. The **Elevator** constructor has an extensive member initializer list (lines 602–607). You will remember from our definition of class **ElevatorButton** (Fig. 7.24) that an object that class requires a handle to an object of class **Elevator** as an argument to its constructor. We provide this handle in our member initialization list by dereferencing the **elevator**'s **this** pointer (line 602). Some compilers generate a warning on this line, because the **elevator** object has not yet been completely initialized.

```
585  // elevator.cpp
586  // Member function definitions for class Elevator.
587  #include <iostream>
588
589  using std::cout;
590  using std::endl;
591
592  #include "elevator.h"
593  #include "person.h"
594  #include "floor.h"
595
596  const int Elevator::ELEVATOR_TRAVEL_TIME = 5;
597  const int Elevator::UP = 0;
598  const int Elevator::DOWN = 1;
599
600  // constructor
601  Elevator::Elevator( Floor &firstFloor, Floor &secondFloor )
602     : elevatorButton( *this ), currentBuildingClockTime( 0 ),
603       moving( false ), direction( UP ),
604       currentFloor( Floor::FLOOR1 ), arrivalTime( 0 ),
605       floor1NeedsService( false ), floor2NeedsService( false ),
606       floor1Ref( firstFloor ), floor2Ref( secondFloor ),
607       passengerPtr( 0 )
608  { cout << "elevator created" << endl; }
609
610  Elevator::~Elevator() // destructor
611  { cout << "elevator destroyed" << endl; }
612
613  // give time to elevator
614  void Elevator::processTime( int time )
615  {
616     currentBuildingClockTime = time;
617
618     if ( moving )
619        processPossibleArrival();
```

Fig. 7.29   Class **Elevator** implementation file (part 1 of 4).

```
620      else
621         processPossibleDeparture();
622
623      if ( !moving )
624         cout << "elevator at rest on floor "
625             << currentFloor << endl;
626   }
627
628   // when elevator is moving, determine if it should stop
629   void Elevator::processPossibleArrival()
630   {
631      // if elevator arrives at destination floor
632      if ( currentBuildingClockTime == arrivalTime ) {
633
634         currentFloor =    // update current floor
635            ( currentFloor == Floor::FLOOR1 ?
636              Floor::FLOOR2 : Floor::FLOOR1 );
637
638         direction =       // update direction
639            ( currentFloor == Floor::FLOOR1 ? UP : DOWN );
640
641         cout << "elevator arrives on floor "
642             << currentFloor << endl;
643
644         arriveAtFloor( currentFloor == Floor::FLOOR1 ?
645              floor1Ref : floor2Ref );
646
647         return;
648      }
649
650      // elevator is moving
651      cout << "elevator moving "
652          << ( direction == UP ? "up" : "down" ) << endl;
653   }
654
655   // determine if elevator should move
656   void Elevator::processPossibleDeparture()
657   {
658      // this floor needs service?
659      bool currentFloorNeedsService =
660         currentFloor == Floor::FLOOR1 ?
661            floor1NeedsService : floor2NeedsService;
662
663      // other floor needs service?
664      bool otherFloorNeedsService =
665         currentFloor == Floor::FLOOR1 ?
666            floor2NeedsService : floor1NeedsService;
667
668      // service this floor (if needed)
669      if ( currentFloorNeedsService ) {
670         arriveAtFloor( currentFloor == Floor::FLOOR1 ?
671            floor1Ref : floor2Ref );
672
```

Fig. 7.29   Class **Elevator** implementation file (part 2 of 4).

```
673          return;
674      }
675
676      // service other floor (if needed)
677      else prepareToLeave( otherFloorNeedsService );
678  }
679
680  // arrive at a particular floor
681  void Elevator::arriveAtFloor( Floor& arrivalFloor )
682  {
683      moving = false;    // reset state
684
685      cout << "elevator resets its button" << endl;
686      elevatorButton.resetButton();
687
688      bell.ringBell();
689
690      // notify floor that elevator has arrived
691      Person *floorPersonPtr = arrivalFloor.elevatorArrived();
692
693      door.openDoor( passengerPtr, floorPersonPtr,
694                     arrivalFloor, *this );
695
696      // this floor needs service?
697      bool currentFloorNeedsService =
698        currentFloor == Floor::FLOOR1 ?
699            floor1NeedsService : floor2NeedsService;
700
701      // other floor needs service?
702      bool otherFloorNeedsService =
703        currentFloor == Floor::FLOOR1 ?
704            floor2NeedsService : floor1NeedsService;
705
706      // if this floor does not need service
707      // prepare to leave for the other floor
708      if ( !currentFloorNeedsService )
709          prepareToLeave( otherFloorNeedsService );
710      else   // otherwise, reset service flag
711          currentFloor == Floor::FLOOR1 ?
712              floor1NeedsService = false: floor2NeedsService = false;
713  }
714
715  // request service from elevator
716  void Elevator::summonElevator( int floor )
717  {
718      // set appropriate servicing flag
719      floor == Floor::FLOOR1 ?
720          floor1NeedsService = true : floor2NeedsService = true;
721  }
722
723  // accept a passenger
724  void Elevator::passengerEnters( Person * const personPtr )
725  {
```

Fig. 7.29   Class **Elevator** implementation file (part 3 of 4).

```
726      // board passenger
727      passengerPtr = personPtr;
728
729      cout << "person " << passengerPtr->getID()
730           << " enters elevator from floor "
731           << currentFloor << endl;
732  }
733
734  // notify elevator that passenger is exiting
735  void Elevator::passengerExits() { passengerPtr = 0; }
736
737  // prepare to leave a floor
738  void Elevator::prepareToLeave( bool leaving )
739  {
740      Floor &thisFloor =
741          currentFloor == Floor::FLOOR1 ? floor1Ref : floor2Ref;
742
743      // notify floor that elevator may be leaving
744      thisFloor.elevatorLeaving();
745
746      door.closeDoor( thisFloor );
747
748      if ( leaving )  // leave, if necessary
749          move();
750  }
751
752  void Elevator::move() // go to a particular floor
753  {
754      moving = true;  // change state
755
756      // schedule arrival time
757      arrivalTime = currentBuildingClockTime +
758          ELEVATOR_TRAVEL_TIME;
759
760      cout << "elevator begins moving "
761           << ( direction == DOWN ? "down " : "up ")
762           << "to floor "
763           << ( direction == DOWN ? '1' : '2' )
764           << " (arrives at time " << arrivalTime << ')'
765           << endl;
766  }
```

Fig. 7.29   Class **Elevator** implementation file (part 4 of 4).

The **building** invokes the **processTime** member function (lines 613–626) of class **Elevator**, passing as a parameter the current simulation **time**. This member function updates the **currentBuildingClockTime** data member with the current simulation **time** (line 616) and then checks the value of the **motion** data member (line 618). If the **elevator** is moving, the **elevator** invokes its **processPossibleArrival** utility function (line 619). If the **elevator** is not moving, the **elevator** invokes its **processPossibleDeparture** utility function (line 621). If the **elevator** is still not moving after determining whether it should arrive at the current floor or depart for the other floor, the **elevator** outputs a message to the screen indicating that it is at rest on the **currentFloor** (lines 623–625).

The **processPossibleArrival** function determines whether the **elevator** needs to stop moving by comparing the **currentBuildingClockTime** to the calculated **arrivalTime** (line 632). If it is time for the **elevator** to arrive at a particular floor, the **elevator** updates **currentFloor** (lines 634–636) and **direction** (lines 638–639). The **elevator** then calls its **arriveAtFloor** utility function to perform the necessary tasks upon arrival.

The **processPossibleDeparture** utility function determines whether or not the **elevator** needs to start moving to service another floor. The code determines whether the current floor or the other floor needs the **elevator**'s service (lines 658–666). If the current floor needs service, the **elevator** calls its **arriveAtFloor** utility function for the current floor (lines 670–671). Otherwise the **prepareToLeave** utility function is called (line 677), and the **elevator** will move to the other floor, if that floor needs service.

The **arriveAtFloor** utility function performs the tasks needed for the **elevator** to arrive at a particular floor. This utility function first stops the **elevator** by setting the **moving** member variable to **false** (line 683), then resets the **elevatorButton** (line 686) and rings the **bell** (line 688). A temporary pointer to an object of class **Person** is then declared, to store a handle to a **Person** object that might be waiting on the floor. This pointer receives the return value of the call to the floor's **elevatorArrived** member function (line 691).

The **elevator** opens its **door** by calling the **openDoor** member function of class **Door** passing as parameters a handle to the current passenger, a handle to the person waiting on the floor, a handle to the floor where the **elevator** has arrived and a handle to the **elevator** itself (lines 693–694). The **elevator** again determines whether either floor needs service (lines 696–704). If the current floor does not need the **elevator**'s service, the **elevator** prepares to leave for the other floor (line 709) and leaves if the other floor needs service. Otherwise, the **elevator** resets the service flag for the current floor (lines 711–712).

The **summonElevator** member function allows other objects to request service from the **elevator**. When invoked, the **summonElevator** member function takes a floor number as an argument and sets the appropriate service flag to **true** (lines 719 and 720).

The **passengerEnters** member function takes a pointer to an object of class **Person** as its only argument (line 724), and updates the **elevator**'s **passengerPtr** handle so that it points to the new passenger (line 727). The **passengerExits** member function simply sets the **passengerPtr** handle to zero, thus indicating that the passenger has left the **elevator** (line 735).

The **prepareToLeave** member function takes an argument of type **bool** that indicates whether the **elevator** is to leave the current floor (line 738). The **elevator** notifies the current floor that the **elevator** is leaving by sending the floor an **elevatorLeaving** message (line 744). The **elevator** then closes its **door** (line 746). Finally, the **elevator** checks whether it needs to leave the floor (line 748) and, if so, begins moving by calling the **move** utility function (line 749), which sets the **moving** data member to **true** (line 754). It then calculates the arrival time for the **elevator** at its destination by using the **static const** value **ELEVATOR_TRAVEL_TIME** (lines 757–758). Finally, it outputs the **direction** in which it is traveling, the destination floor, and the scheduled **arrivalTime** (lines 760–765).

Our class **Floor** definition (Fig. 7.30) contains a mixture of ways to associate objects of other classes with **Floor** objects. First, we use a reference as a handle to the **elevator** (line 804)—this is appropriate, because this handle always refers to the same **elevator**. We also have a pointer as a handle to a **Person** object (line 805)—this handle will change every time a person walks onto the floor or leaves the floor to enter the **elevator**. Finally, we have composite objects, including a **public floorButton** object (line 800) and a **private light** object (line 806). We declare the **floorButton public** to allow objects of class **Person** to access the **floorButton** object directly.[1] The definition for class **Floor** also contains the **static const** data members **FLOOR1** and **FLOOR2** (lines 798—799). We use these constants in place of actual floor numbers; we initialize these **const** data members in the implementation file (lines 821—822). Normally, **const** data members of a class must be initialized in the constructor member-initialization list. In the special case of **static const** data members, they are initialized at file scope.

```
767  // floor.h
768  // Definition for class Floor.
769  #ifndef FLOOR_H
770  #define FLOOR_H
771
772  #include "floorButton.h"
773  #include "light.h"
774
775  class Elevator;    // forward declaration
776  class Person;      // forward declaration
777
778  class Floor {
779
780  public:
781     Floor( int, Elevator & ); // constructor
782     ~Floor();                 // destructor
783     bool isOccupied() const;  // return true if floor occupied
784     int getNumber() const;    // return floor's number
785
786     // pass a handle to new person coming on floor
787     void personArrives( Person * const );
788
789     // notify floor that elevator has arrived
790     Person *elevatorArrived();
791
792     // notify floor that elevator is leaving
793     void elevatorLeaving();
794
795     // notify floor that person is leaving floor
796     void personBoardingElevator();
797
798     static const int FLOOR1;
799     static const int FLOOR2;
```

Fig. 7.30   Class **Floor** header file (part 1 of 2).

---

1. A person generally does not have permission to interface with the light on a floor (unless that person is a technician). Therefore, the **light** object is declared in the **private** section of the class definition.

```
800        FloorButton floorButton;    // floorButton object
801
802    private:
803        const int floorNumber;      // the floor's number
804        Elevator &elevatorRef;      // pointer to elevator
805        Person *occupantPtr;        // pointer to person on floor
806        Light light;                // light object
807    };
808
809    #endif // FLOOR_H
```

Fig. 7.30   Class **Floor** header file (part 2 of 2).

Figure 7.31 contains the implementation file for class **Floor**. The **isOccupied** member function of class **Floor** (lines 836–838) returns a **bool** value that indicates whether there is a person waiting on the floor. To determine whether a person is waiting, we check to see if the **occupantPtr** is not zero (line 838). If the **occupantPtr** is zero, there is no person waiting on the floor. The **getNumber** member function returns the value of the **floorNumber** member variable (line 841). The **personArrives** member function receives a pointer to the **Person** object walking onto the floor. This pointer is assigned to private data member **occupantPtr**.

```
810    // floor.cpp
811    // Member function definitions for class Floor.
812    #include <iostream>
813
814    using std::cout;
815    using std::endl;
816
817    #include "floor.h"
818    #include "person.h"
819    #include "elevator.h"
820
821    const int Floor::FLOOR1 = 1;
822    const int Floor::FLOOR2 = 2;
823
824    // constructor
825    Floor::Floor(int number, Elevator &elevatorHandle )
826       : floorButton( number, elevatorHandle ),
827         floorNumber( number ), elevatorRef( elevatorHandle ),
828         occupantPtr ( 0 ),
829         light( floorNumber == 1 ? "floor 1" : "floor 2" )
830    { cout << "floor " << floorNumber << " created" << endl; }
831
832    // destructor
833    Floor::~Floor()
834    { cout << "floor " << floorNumber << " destroyed" << endl; }
835
836    // determine if floor is occupied
837    bool Floor::isOccupied() const
838    { return ( occupantPtr != 0 ); }
```

Fig. 7.31   Class **Floor** implementation file (part 1 of 2).

```
839
840  // return this floor's number
841  int Floor::getNumber() const { return floorNumber; }
842
843  // pass person to floor
844  void Floor::personArrives( Person * const personPtr )
845  { occupantPtr = personPtr; }
846
847  // notify floor that elevator has arrived
848  Person *Floor::elevatorArrived()
849  {
850     // reset the button on floor, if necessary
851     cout << "floor " << floorNumber
852          << " resets its button" << endl;
853     floorButton.resetButton();
854
855     light.turnOn();
856
857     return occupantPtr;
858  }
859
860  // tell floor that the elevator is leaving
861  void Floor::elevatorLeaving() { light.turnOff(); }
862
863  // notifies floor that a person is leaving it
864  void Floor::personBoardingElevator() { occupantPtr = 0; }
```

Fig. 7.31   Class **Floor** implementation file (part 2 of 2).

The **elevatorArrived** member function (lines 847–858) resets the **floor**'s **floorButton** object (line 853), turns on the **light** and returns the **occupantPtr** handle (line 857). The **elevatorLeaving** member function turns off the **light** (line 861). Finally, the **personBoardingElevator** member function sets the **occupantPtr** to zero, indicating that the person has left the floor (line 864).

The elements of the header file for the **Person** class (Fig. 7.32) should appear familiar at this point. The **getID** member function returns the **Person** object's unique **ID**. The **stepOntoFloor**, **enterElevator** and **exitElevator** member functions form the remainder of the **Person**'s **public** interface. We use a **private static** class variable **personCount** to keep track of how many objects of class **Person** have been created. We also declare the **ID** and **destinationFloor** attributes as **private const** data members.

```
865  // person.h
866  // definition of class Person
867  #ifndef PERSON_H
868  #define PERSON_H
869
870  class Floor;      // forward declaration
871  class Elevator;   // forward declaration
872
```

Fig. 7.32   Class **Person** header file (part 1 of 2).

```
873  class Person {
874
875  public:
876     Person( const int );        // constructor
877     ~Person();                  // destructor
878     int getID() const;          // returns person's ID
879
880     void stepOntoFloor( Floor & );
881     void enterElevator( Elevator &, Floor & );
882     void exitElevator( const Floor &, Elevator & ) const;
883
884  private:
885     static int personCount;     // total number of persons
886     const int ID;               // person's unique ID #
887     const int destinationFloor; // destination floor #
888  };
889
890  #endif // PERSON_H
```

Fig. 7.32   Class **Person** header file (part 2 of 2).

The implementation of class **Person** (Fig. 7.33) begins with the constructor (lines 905–907), which takes a single **const int** as its argument. This represents the destination floor for the **Person** object. We use this value in our simulation outputs. The destructor (lines 909–914) displays a message indicating that a person has exited the **elevator**.

```
891  // person.cpp
892  // Member function definitions for class Person.
893  #include <iostream>
894
895  using std::cout;
896  using std::endl;
897
898  #include "person.h"
899  #include "floor.h"
900  #include "elevator.h"
901
902  // initialize static member personCount
903  int Person::personCount = 0;
904
905  Person::Person( const int destFloor ) // constructor
906     : ID( ++personCount ), destinationFloor( destFloor )
907  {}
908
909  Person::~Person() // destructor
910  {
911     cout << "person " << ID << " exits simulation on floor "
912          << destinationFloor << " (person destructor invoked)"
913          << endl;
914  }
915
916  int Person::getID() const { return ID; } // get the ID
```

Fig. 7.33   Class **Person** implementation file (part 1 of 2).

```
917
918   // person walks onto a floor
919   void Person::stepOntoFloor( Floor& floor )
920   {
921      // notify floor a person is coming
922      cout << "person " << ID << " steps onto floor "
923           << floor.getNumber() << endl;
924      floor.personArrives( this );
925
926      // press button on the floor
927      cout << "person " << ID
928           << " presses floor button on floor "
929           << floor.getNumber() << endl;
930      floor.floorButton.pressButton();
931   }
932
933   // person enters elevator
934   void Person::enterElevator( Elevator &elevator, Floor &floor )
935   {
936      floor.personBoardingElevator();    // person leaves floor
937
938      elevator.passengerEnters( this ); // person enters elevator
939
940      // press button on elevator
941      cout << "person " << ID
942           << " presses elevator button" << endl;
943      elevator.elevatorButton.pressButton();
944   }
945
946   // person exits elevator
947   void Person::exitElevator(
948      const Floor &floor, Elevator &elevator ) const
949   {
950      cout << "person " << ID << " exits elevator on floor "
951           << floor.getNumber() << endl;
952      elevator.passengerExits();
953   }
```

Fig. 7.33   Class **Person** implementation file (part 2 of 2).

Member function **stepOntoFloor** (lines 918–931) first notifies the floor that the person has arrived, by sending the floor a **personArrives** message (line 924). The person then calls **floorButton**'s **pressButton** method (line 930) which summons the **elevator**.

The **enterElevator** member function first notifies the floor that the person is boarding the **elevator**, by sending a **personBoardingElevator** message (line 936). The person sends the **passengerEnters** message to notify the **elevator** that the person is entering (line 938). The person then sends the **pressButton** message to the **elevatorButton** object, in order to start the **elevator** moving to the other floor (line 943). The **exitElevator** member function outputs a message, indicating that the person is exiting the **elevator**, then sends the **passengerExits** message to the **elevator**.

We have now completed a working implementation of the elevator simulation we introduced in Chapter 2. Chapter 8 does not contain a "Thinking About Objects" section. In Chapter 9, we discuss inheritance in C++, and apply it to our elevator.

SUMMARY

- The keyword **const** specifies that an object is not modifiable.
- The C++ compiler disallows non-**const** member function calls on **const** objects.
- An attempt by a **const** member function of a class to modify an object of that class is a syntax error.
- A function is specified as **const** both in its declaration and its definition.
- A **const** member function may be overloaded with a non-**const** version. The choice of which overloaded member function to use is made by the compiler based on whether the object has been declared **const** or not.
- A **const** object must be initialized—member initializers must be provided in the constructor of a class when that class contains **const** data members.
- Classes can be composed of objects of other classes.
- Member objects are constructed in the order in which they are listed in the class definition and before their enclosing class objects are constructed.
- If a member initializer is not provided for a member object, the member object's default constructor is called.
- A **friend** function of a class is a function defined outside that class and that has the right to access all members of the class.
- Friendship declarations can be placed anywhere in the class definition.
- The **this** pointer is implicitly used to reference both the non-**static** member functions and non-**static** data members of the object.
- Each non-**static** member function has access to its object's address via the **this** keyword.
- The **this** pointer may be used explicitly.
- The **new** operator allocates space for an object, runs the object's constructor and returns a pointer of the correct type. To free the space for this object, use the **delete** operator.
- An array of objects can be allocated dynamically with **new** as in

```
int *ptr = new int[100];
```

which allocates an array of 100 integers and assigns the starting location of the array to **ptr**. The preceding array of integers is deleted with the statement

```
delete [] ptr;
```

- A **static** data member represents "class-wide" information (i.e., a property of the class, not an object). The declaration of a **static** member begins with the keyword **static**.
- **static** data members have class scope.
- **static** members of a class can be accessed through an object of that class or through the class name using the scope resolution operator (if the member is **public**).
- A member function may be declared **static** if it does not access non-**static** class members. Unlike non-**static** member functions, a **static** member function has no **this** pointer. This is because **static** data members and **static** member functions exist independent of any objects of a class.

- Classes normally hide their implementation details from the clients of the classes. This is called information hiding.
- Stacks are known as last-in, first-out (LIFO) data structures—the last item pushed (inserted) on the stack is the first item popped (removed) from the stack.
- Describing the functionality of a class independent of its implementation is called data abstraction and C++ classes define so-called abstract data types (ADTs).
- C++ elevates the importance of data. The primary activity in C++ is creating new data types (i.e., classes) and expressing the interactions among objects of those data types.
- Abstract data types are ways of representing real-world notions to some satisfactory level of precision within a computer system.
- An abstract data type actually captures two notions, namely a data representation and the operations that are allowed on those data.
- C++ is an extensible language. Although the language is easy to extend with these new types, the base language itself is not changeable.
- C++ is an intentionally sparse language that provides programmers with only the raw capabilities needed to build a broad range of systems. The language is designed to minimize performance burdens.
- Items are returned from a queue in first-in, first-out (FIFO) order—the first item inserted in the queue is the first item removed from the queue.
- Container classes (also called collection classes) are designed to hold collections of objects. Container classes commonly provide services such as insertion, deletion, searching, sorting, testing an item for membership in the class and the like.
- It is common to associate iterator objects—or more simply iterators—with container classes. An iterator is an object that returns the next item of a collection (or performs some action on the next item of a collection).
- Providing clients of your class with a proxy class that knows only the **public** interface to your class enables the clients to use your class' services without giving the client access to your class' implementation details.
- The only **private** member of the proxy class is a pointer to an object of the class whose **private** data we would like to hide.
- When a class definition uses only a pointer to another class, the class header file for that other class (which would ordinarily reveal the **private** data of that class) is not required to be included with **#include**. You can simply declare that other class as a data type with a forward class declaration before the type is used in the file.
- The implementation file containing the member functions for the proxy class is the only file that includes the header file for the class whose **private** data we would like to hide.
- The implementation file is provided to the client as a precompiled object file along with the header file that includes the function prototypes of the services provided by the proxy class.

TERMINOLOGY

abstract data type (ADT)
binary scope resolution operator (`::`)
cascading member function calls
class scope
composition
const member function

const object
constructor
container
data representations
default constructor
default destructor

delete operator   member object constructor
delete[] operator   member selection operator (**.**)
dequeue (queue operation)   **new** operator
destructor   **new []** operator
dynamic objects   object-based programming
enqueue (queue operation)   operations in an ADT
extensible language   pointer member selection operator (**->**)
first-in-first-out (FIFO)   *pop* (stack operation)
forward class declaration   principle of least privilege
friend class   proxy class
friend function   *push* (stack operation)
host object   queue abstract data type
iterator   stack abstract data type
last-in-first-out (LIFO)   **static** data member
member access specifiers   **static** member function
member initializer   **this** pointer
member object

"Thinking About Objects" Terminology
circular include problem   forward declaration

COMMON PROGRAMMING ERRORS
7.1   Defining as **const** a member function that modifies a data member of an object is a syntax error.

7.2   Defining as **const** a member function that calls a non-**const** member function of the class on the same instance of the class is a syntax error.

7.3   Invoking a non-**const** member function on a **const** object is a syntax error.

7.4   Attempting to declare a constructor or destructor **const** is a syntax error.

7.5   Not providing a member initializer for a **const** data member is a syntax error.

7.6   Not providing a default constructor for the class of a member object when no member initializer is provided for that member object is a syntax error.

7.7   Attempting to use the member selection operator (**.**) with a pointer to an object is a syntax error—the dot member selection operator may only be used with an object or with a reference to an object.

7.8   Mixing **new**-and-**delete**-style dynamic memory allocation with **malloc**-and-**free**-style dynamic memory allocation is a logic error: Space created by **malloc** cannot be freed by **delete**; objects created by **new** cannot be deleted by **free**.

7.9   Using **delete** instead of **delete []** for arrays can lead to runtime logic errors. To avoid problems, space created as an array should be deleted with the **delete []** operator and space created as an individual element should be deleted with the **delete** operator.

7.10 It is a syntax error to include keyword **static** in the definition of a **static** class variable at file scope.

7.11 Referring to the **this** pointer within a **static** member function is a syntax error.

7.12 Declaring a **static** member function **const** is a syntax error.

GOOD PROGRAMMING PRACTICES
7.1   Declare as **const** all member functions that do not need to modify the current object so that you can use them on a **const** object if you need to.

7.2   Place all friendship declarations first in the class immediately after the class header and do not precede them with any member-access specifier.

7.3   Because C++ includes C, C++ programs can contain storage created by **malloc** and deleted by **free**, and objects created by **new** and deleted by **delete**. It is best to use only **new** and **delete**.

7.4   After deleting dynamically allocated memory, set the pointer that referred to that memory to **0**. This disconnects the pointer from the previously allocated space on the free store.

PERFORMANCE TIPS

7.1   Declaring variables and objects **const** is not only an effective software engineering practice—it can improve performance as well because today's sophisticated optimizing compilers can perform certain optimizations on constants that cannot be performed on variables.

7.2   Initialize member objects explicitly through member initializers. This eliminates the overhead of "doubly initializing" member objects—once when the member object's default constructor is called and again when *set* functions are used to initialize the member object.

7.3   For reasons of economy of storage, only one copy of each member function exists per class, and this member function is invoked by every object of that class. Each object, on the other hand, has its own copy of the class' data members.

7.4   Use **static** data members to save storage when a single copy of the data will suffice.

SOFTWARE ENGINEERING OBSERVATIONS

7.1   Declaring an object as **const** helps enforce the principle of least privilege. Attempts to modify the object are caught at compile time rather than causing execution-time errors.

7.2   Using **const** is crucial to proper class design, program design and coding.

7.3   A **const** member function can be overloaded with a non-**const** version. The choice of which overloaded member function to use is made by the compiler based on whether the object is **const** or not.

7.4   A **const** object cannot be modified by assignment so it must be initialized. When a data member of a class is declared **const**, a **member initializer** must be used to provide the constructor with the initial value of the data member for an object of the class.

7.5   Constant class members (**const** objects and **const** "variables") must be initialized with member initializer syntax; assignments are not allowed.

7.6   It is good practice to declare all of a class' member functions that do not modify the object in which they operate as **const**. Occasionally, this will be an anomaly because you will have no intention of creating **const** objects of that class. Declaring such member functions **const** does offer a benefit though. If you inadvertently modify the object in that member function, the compiler will issue a syntax error message.

7.7   The most common form of software reusability is *composition,* in which a class has objects of other classes as members.

7.8   If a class has as a member an object of another class, making that member object **public** does not violate the encapsulation and hiding of that member object's **private** members.

7.9   Even though the prototypes for **friend** functions appear in the class definition, **friend**s are still not member functions.

7.10   Member access notions of **private**, **protected** and **public** are not relevant to friendship declarations, so friendship declarations can be placed anywhere in the class definition.

7.11   Some people in the OOP community feel that "friendship" corrupts information hiding and weakens the value of the object-oriented design approach.

7.12   Because C++ is a hybrid language, it is common to have a mix of two types of function calls in one program and often back to back—C-like calls that pass primitive data or objects to functions and C++ calls that pass functions (or messages) to objects.

7.13   Some organizations have in their software engineering standards that all calls to **static** member functions be made using the class name and not the object handle.

7.14   A class' **static** data members and **static** member functions exist and can be used even if no objects of that class have been instantiated.

7.15   The programmer is able to create new types through the class mechanism. These new types can be designed to be used as conveniently as the built-in types. Thus, C++ is an extensible language. Although the language is easy to extend with these new types, the base language itself is not changeable.

TESTING AND DEBUGGING TIPS

7.1   Always declare member functions **const** if they do not modify the object. This can help eliminate many bugs.

7.2   Languages like C++ are "moving targets" as they evolve. More keywords are likely to be added to the language. Avoid using "loaded" words like "object" as identifiers. Even though "object" is not currently a keyword in C++, it could become one, so future compiling with new compilers could "break" existing code.

SELF-REVIEW EXERCISES

7.1   Fill in the blanks in each of the following:
a)   _____ syntax is used to initialize constant members of a class.
b)   A nonmember function must be declared as a _____ of a class to have access to that class' **private** data members.
c)   The _____ operator dynamically allocates memory for an object of a specified type and returns a _____ to that type.
d)   A constant object must be _____; it cannot be modified after it is created.
e)   A _____ data member represents class-wide information.
f)   An object's member functions have access to a "self pointer" to the object called the _____ pointer.
g)   The keyword _____ specifies that an object or variable is not modifiable after it is initialized.
h)   If a member initializer is not provided for a member object of a class, the object's _____ is called.
i)   A member function can be declared **static** if it does not access _____ class members.
j)   Member objects are constructed _____ their enclosing class object.
k)   The _____ operator reclaims memory previously allocated by **new**.

7.2   Find the error(s) in each of the following and explain how to correct it:
a)
```
class Example {
public:
    Example( int y = 10 ) { data = y; }
    int getIncrementedData() const { return ++data; }
    static int getCount()
    {
        cout << "Data is " << data << endl;
        return count;
    }
```

```
        private:
           int data;
           static int count;
     };
 b) char *string;
     string = new char[ 20 ];
     free( string );
```

ANSWERS TO SELF-REVIEW EXERCISES

7.1   a) Member initializer. b) **friend**. c) **new**, pointer. d) initialized. e) **static**. f) **this**.
g) **const**. h) default constructor. i) non-**static**. j) before. k) **delete**.

7.2   a) Error: The class definition for **Example** has two errors. The first occurs in function
           getIncrementedData. The function is declared **const**, but it modifies the object.
           Correction: To correct the first error, remove the **const** keyword from the definition of
           getIncrementedData.
           Error: The second error occurs in function **getCount**. This function is declared **stat-
           ic**, so it is not allowed to access any non-**static** member of the class.
           Correction: To correct the second error, remove the output line from the definition of
           getCount.
       b) Error: Memory dynamically allocated by **new** is deleted by the C Standard Library func-
           tion **free**.
           Correction: Use C++'s **delete** operator to reclaim the memory. C-style dynamic mem-
           ory allocation should not be mixed with C++'s **new** and **delete** operators.

EXERCISES

7.3   Compare and contrast dynamic memory allocation using the C++ operators **new** and **delete**, with dynamic memory allocation using the C Standard Library functions **malloc** and **free**.

7.4   Explain the notion of friendship in C++. Explain the negative aspects of friendship as described in the text.

7.5   Can a correct **Time** class definition include both of the following constructors? If not, explain why not.

```
     Time( int h = 0, int m = 0, int s = 0 );
     Time();
```

7.6   What happens when a return type, even **void**, is specified for a constructor or destructor?

7.7   Create a **Date** class with the following capabilities:
       a) Output the date in multiple formats such as

```
        DDD YYYY
        MM/DD/YY
        June 14, 1992
```

       b) Use overloaded constructors to create **Date** objects initialized with dates of the formats
           in part (a).
       c) Create a **Date** constructor that reads the system date using the standard library functions
           of the **<ctime>** header and sets the **Date** members.

In Chapter 8, we will be able to create operators for testing the equality of two dates and for comparing dates to determine if one date is prior to, or after, another.

7.8   Create a **SavingsAccount** class. Use a **static** data member to contain the **annualInterestRate** for each of the savers. Each member of the class contains a **private** data member **savingsBalance** indicating the amount the saver currently has on deposit. Provide a **calculateMonthlyInterest** member function that calculates the monthly interest by multiplying the **balance** by **annualInterestRate** divided by 12; this interest should be added to **savingsBalance**. Provide a **static** member function **modifyInterestRate** that sets the **static annualInterestRate** to a new value. Write a driver program to test class **SavingsAccount**. Instantiate two different **savingsAccount** objects, **saver1** and **saver2**, with balances of $2000.00 and $3000.00, respectively. Set **annualInterestRate** to 3%, then calculate the monthly interest and print the new balances for each of the savers. Then set the **annualInterestRate** to 4% and calculate the next month's interest and print the new balances for each of the savers.

7.9   Create a class called **IntegerSet**. Each object of class **IntegerSet** can hold integers in the range 0 through 100. A set is represented internally as an array of ones and zeros. Array element **a[i]** is 1 if integer i is in the set. Array element **a[j]** is 0 if integer j is not in the set. The default constructor initializes a set to the so-called "empty set," i.e., a set whose array representation contains all zeros.

Provide member functions for the common set operations. For example, provide a **unionOfIntegerSets** member function that creates a third set which is the set-theoretic union of two existing sets (i.e., an element of the third set's array is set to 1 if that element is 1 in either or both of the existing sets, and an element of the third set's array is set to 0 if that element is 0 in each of the existing sets).

Provide an **intersectionOfIntegerSets** member function that creates a third set which is the set-theoretic intersection of two existing sets (i.e., an element of the third set's array is set to 0 if that element is 0 in either or both of the existing sets, and an element of the third set's array is set to 1 if that element is 1 in each of the existing sets).

Provide an **insertElement** member function that inserts a new integer k into a set (by setting **a[k]** to 1). Provide a **deleteElement** member function that deletes integer m (by setting **a[m]** to 0).

Provide a **setPrint** member function that prints a set as a list of numbers separated by spaces. Print only those elements that are present in the set (i.e., their position in the array has a value of 1). Print **---** for an empty set.

Provide an **isEqualTo** member function that determines if two sets are equal.

Provide an additional constructor to take five integer arguments which can be used to initialize a set object. If you want to provide fewer than five elements in the set, use default arguments of -1 for the others.

Now write a driver program to test your **IntegerSet** class. Instantiate several **IntegerSet** objects. Test that all your member functions work properly.

7.10   It would be perfectly reasonable for the **Time** class of Fig. 7.8 to represent the time internally as the number of seconds since midnight rather than the three integer values **hour**, **minute** and **second**. Clients could use the same **public** methods and get the same results. Modify the **Time** class of Fig. 7.8 to implement the **Time** as the number of seconds since midnight and show that there is no visible change in functionality to the clients of the class.

8

Operator Overloading

Objectives

- To understand how to redefine (overload) operators to work with new types.
- To understand how to convert objects from one class to another class.
- To learn when to, and when not to, overload operators.
- To study several interesting classes that use overloaded operators.
- To create Array, String and Date classes.

The whole difference between construction and creation is exactly this: that a thing constructed can only be loved after it is constructed; but a thing created is loved before it exists.
Gilbert Keith Chesterton, Preface to Dickens, Pickwick Papers

The die is cast.
Julius Caesar

Our doctor would never really operate unless it was necessary. He was just that way. If he didn't need the money, he wouldn't lay a hand on you.
Herb Shriner

Outline

Summary • Terminology • Common Programming Errors • Good Programming Practices • Performance Tips • Software Engineering Observations • Testing and Debugging Tip • Self-Review Exercises • Answers to Self-Review Exercises • Exercises

8.1 Introduction

In Chapters 6 and 7, we introduced the basics of C++ classes and the notion of abstract data types (ADTs). Manipulations on class objects (i.e., instances of ADTs) were accomplished by sending messages (in the form of member function calls) to the objects. This function-call notation is cumbersome for certain kinds of classes, especially mathematical classes. For these kinds of classes it would be nice to use C++'s rich set of built-in operators to specify object manipulations. In this chapter, we show how to enable C++'s operators to work with class objects. This process is called *operator overloading*. It is straightforward and natural to extend C++ with these new capabilities. It also requires great care because when overloading is misused, it can make a program difficult to understand.

Operator **<<** has several purposes in C++—as the stream-insertion operator and as the bitwise left-shift operator. This is an example of operator overloading. Similarly, **>>** is also overloaded; it is used both as the stream-extraction operator and as the bitwise right-shift operator. [*Note:* The bitwise left-shift and bitwise right-shift operators are discussed in detail in Chapter 16.] Both of these operators are overloaded in the C++ class library. The C++ language itself overloads **+** and **–**. These operators perform differently depending on their context in integer arithmetic, floating-point arithmetic and pointer arithmetic.

C++ enables the programmer to overload most operators to be sensitive to the context in which they are used. The compiler generates the appropriate code based on the manner in which the operator is used. Some operators are overloaded frequently, especially the assignment operator and various arithmetic operators such as **+** and **–**. The job performed by overloaded operators can also be performed by explicit function calls, but operator notation is often clearer.

We will discuss when to use operator overloading and when not to use operator overloading. We show how to overload operators, and we present many complete programs using overloaded operators.

8.2 Fundamentals of Operator Overloading

C++ programming is a type-sensitive and type-focused process. Programmers can use built-in types and can define new types. The built-in types can be used with C++'s rich collection of operators. Operators provide programmers with a concise notation for expressing manipulations of objects of built-in types.

Programmers can use operators with user-defined types as well. Although C++ does not allow new operators to be created, it does allow most existing operators to be overloaded so that when these operators are used with class objects, the operators have meaning appropriate to the new types. This is one of C++'s most powerful features.

Software Engineering Observation 8.1

Operator overloading contributes to C++'s extensibility, one of the language's most appealing attributes.

Good Programming Practice 8.1

Use operator overloading when it makes a program clearer than accomplishing the same operations with explicit function calls.

Good Programming Practice 8.2

Avoid excessive or inconsistent use of operator overloading as this can make a program cryptic and difficult to read.

Although operator overloading may sound like an exotic capability, most programmers implicitly use overloaded operators regularly. For example, the addition operator (**+**) operates quite differently on integers, floats and doubles. But addition nevertheless works fine with variables of type **int**, **float**, **double** and a number of other built-in types because the addition operator (**+**) has been overloaded in the C++ language itself.

Operators are overloaded by writing a function definition (with a header and body) as you normally would, except that the function name now becomes the keyword **operator** followed by the symbol for the operator being overloaded. For example, the function name **operator+** would be used to overload the addition operator (**+**).

To use an operator on class objects, that operator *must* be overloaded—with two exceptions. The assignment operator (**=**) may be used with every class without explicit overloading. The default behavior of the assignment operator is a *memberwise assignment* of the data members of the class. We will soon see that such default memberwise assignment is dangerous for classes with pointer members; we will explicitly overload the assignment operator for such classes. The address operator (**&**) may also be used with objects of any class without overloading; it simply returns the address of the object in memory. The address operator can also be overloaded.

Overloading is most appropriate for mathematical classes. These often require that a substantial set of operators be overloaded to ensure consistency with the way these mathematical classes are handled in the real world. For example, it would be unusual to overload only addition for a complex number class because other arithmetic operators are also commonly used with complex numbers.

C++ is an operator-rich language. C++ programmers who understand the meaning and context of each operator are likely to make reasonable choices when it comes to overloading operators for new classes.

The point of operator overloading is to provide the same concise expressions for user-defined types that C++ provides with its rich collection of operators for built-in types. Operator overloading is not automatic, however; the programmer must write operator overloading functions to perform the desired operations. Sometimes these functions are best made member functions; sometimes they are best as **friend** functions and occasionally they can be made non-member, non-**friend** functions.

Extreme misuses of overloading are possible such as overloading operator **+** to perform subtraction-like operations or overloading operator **/** to perform multiplication-like operations. Such uses of overloading make a program extremely difficult to comprehend.

Good Programming Practice 8.3

Overload operators to perform the same function or similar functions on class objects as the operators perform on objects of built-in types. Avoid non-intuitive uses of operators.

Good Programming Practice 8.4

Before writing C++ programs with overloaded operators, consult the manuals for your compiler to become aware of restrictions and requirements unique to particular operators.

8.3 Restrictions on Operator Overloading

Most of C++'s operators can be overloaded. These are shown in Fig. 8.1. Figure 8.2 shows the operators that cannot be overloaded.

Common Programming Error 8.1

Attempting to overload a non-overloadable operator is a syntax error.

Operators that can be overloaded							
+	–	*	/	%	^	&	|
~	!	=	<	>	+=	–=	*=
/=	%=	^=	&=	|=	<<	>>	>>=
<<=	==	!=	<=	>=	&&	||	++
––	–>*	,	–>	[]	()	new	delete
new[]	delete[]						

Fig. 8.1   Operators that can be overloaded.

Operators that cannot be overloaded				
.	.*	::	?:	sizeof

Fig. 8.2   Operators that cannot be overloaded.

The precedence of an operator cannot be changed by overloading. This can lead to awkward situations in which an operator is overloaded in a manner for which its fixed precedence is inappropriate. However, parentheses can be used to force the order of evaluation of overloaded operators in an expression.

The associativity of an operator cannot be changed by overloading.

It is not possible to change the "arity" of an operator (i.e., the number of operands an operator takes): Overloaded unary operators remain as unary operators; overloaded binary operators remain as binary operators. C++'s only ternary operator (**? :**) cannot be overloaded (Fig. 8.2). Operators **&**, *****, **+** and **−** each have unary and binary versions; these unary and binary versions can be overloaded separately.

It is not possible to create new operators; only existing operators can be overloaded. Unfortunately, this prevents the programmer from using popular notations like the ****** operator used in FORTRAN and BASIC for exponentiation

Common Programming Error 8.2

Attempting to create new operators via operator overloading is a syntax error.

The meaning of how an operator works on objects of built-in types cannot be changed by operator overloading. The programmer cannot, for example, change the meaning of how **+** adds two integers. Operator overloading works only with objects of user-defined types or with a mixture of an object of a user-defined type and an object of a built-in type.

Common Programming Error 8.3

Attempting to modify how an operator works with objects of built-in types is a syntax error.

Software Engineering Observation 8.2

At least one argument of an operator function must be a class object or a reference to a class object. This prevents programmers from changing how operators work on built-in types.

Overloading an assignment operator and an addition operator to allow statements like

```
object2 = object2 + object1;
```

does not imply that the **+=** operator is also overloaded to allow statements such as

```
object2 += object1;
```

Such behavior can be achieved by explicitly overloading the **+=** operator for that class.

Common Programming Error 8.4

Assuming that overloading an operator such as + overloads related operators such as += or that overloading == overloads a related operator like !=. Operators can be overloaded only explicitly; there is no implicit overloading.

Common Programming Error 8.5

Attempting to change the "arity" of an operator via operator overloading is a syntax error.

Good Programming Practice 8.5

To ensure consistency among related operators, use one to implement the others (i.e., use an overloaded + operator to implement an overloaded += operator).

8.4 Operator Functions as Class Members vs. as `friend` Functions

Operator functions can be member functions or non-member functions; non-member functions are often made **friend**s for performance reasons. Member functions use the **this** pointer implicitly to obtain one of their class object arguments (the left argument for binary operators). Both class arguments must be explicitly listed in a non-member function call.

When overloading `()`, `[ ]`, `->` or any of the assignment operators, the operator overloading function must be declared as a class member. For the other operators, the operator overloading functions can be non-member functions.

Whether an operator function is implemented as a member function or as a non-member function, the operator is still used the same way in expressions. So which implementation is best?

When an operator function is implemented as a member function, the leftmost (or only) operand must be a class object (or a reference to a class object) of the operator's class. If the left operand must be an object of a different class or a built-in type, this operator function must be implemented as a non-member function (as we will do in Section 8.5 when overloading `<<` and `>>` as the stream-insertion and stream-extraction operators, respectively). A non-member operator function needs to be a **friend** if that function must access **private** or **protected** members of that class directly.

The overloaded `<<` operator must have a left operand of type **ostream &** (such as **cout** in the expression **cout << classObject**), so it must be a non-member function. Similarly, the overloaded `>>` operator must have a left operand of type **istream &** (such as **cin** in the expression **cin >> classObject**), so it, too, must be a non-member function. Also, each of these overloaded operator functions may require access to the **private** data members of the class object being output or input, so these overloaded operator functions are sometimes made **friend** functions of the class for performance reasons.

Performance Tip 8.1

*It is possible to overload an operator as a non-member, non-**friend** function, but such a function needing access to a class' **private** or **protected** data would need to use* set *or* get *functions provided in that class' **public** interface. The overhead of calling these functions could cause poor performance, so these functions can be **inlin**ed to improve performance.*

Operator member functions of a specific class are called only when the left operand of a binary operator is specifically an object of that class, or when the single operand of a unary operator is an object of that class.

Another reason why one might choose a non-member function to overload an operator is to enable the operator to be commutative. For example, suppose we have an object, **number**, of type **long int**, and an object **bigInteger1**, of class **HugeInteger** (a class in which integers may be arbitrarily large rather than being limited by the machine word size of the underlying hardware; class **HugeInteger** is developed in the chapter exercises). The addition operator (**+**) produces a temporary **HugeInteger** object as the sum of a **HugeInteger** and a **long int** (as in the expression **bigInteger1 + number**), or as the sum of a **long int** and a **HugeInteger** (as in the expression **number + bigInteger1**). Thus, we require the addition operator to be commutative (exactly as it is normally). The problem is that the class object must appear on the left of the addition operator if that operator is to be overloaded as a member function. So, we overload the operator as a non-member **friend** function to allow the **HugeInteger** to appear on the right of the addition. Function **operator+** that deals with the **HugeInteger** on the left can still be a member function. Remember that a non-member function need not necessarily be a **friend** if appropriate *set* and *get* functions exist in the class' **public** interface, and especially if the *set* and *get* functions are **inline**d.

8.5 Overloading Stream-Insertion and Stream-Extraction Operators

C++ is able to input and output the built-in data types using the stream-extraction operator **>>** and stream-insertion operator **<<**. These operators are overloaded (in the class libraries provided with C++ compilers) to process each built-in data type including C-like **char *** strings and pointers. The stream-insertion and stream-extraction operators also can be overloaded to perform input and output for user-defined types. Figure 8.3 demonstrates overloading the stream-extraction and stream-insertion operators to handle data of a user-defined telephone number class called **PhoneNumber**. This program assumes telephone numbers are input correctly. We leave it to the exercises to provide error-checking.

```
1   // Fig. 8.3: fig08_03.cpp
2   // Overloading the stream-insertion and
3   // stream-extraction operators.
4   #include <iostream>
5
6   using std::cout;
7   using std::cin;
8   using std::endl;
9   using std::ostream;
10  using std::istream;
11
12  #include <iomanip>
13
14  using std::setw;
15
16  class PhoneNumber {
17     friend ostream &operator<<( ostream&, const PhoneNumber & );
18     friend istream &operator>>( istream&, PhoneNumber & );
19
20  private:
21     char areaCode[ 4 ];   // 3-digit area code and null
22     char exchange[ 4 ];   // 3-digit exchange and null
23     char line[ 5 ];       // 4-digit line and null
24  };
25
26  // Overloaded stream-insertion operator (cannot be
27  // a member function if we would like to invoke it with
28  // cout << somePhoneNumber;).
29  ostream &operator<<( ostream &output, const PhoneNumber &num )
30  {
31     output << "(" << num.areaCode << ") "
32            << num.exchange << "-" << num.line;
```

Fig. 8.3   User-defined stream-insertion and stream-extraction operators (part 1 of 2).

```
33        return output;      // enables cout << a << b << c;
34     }
35
36     istream &operator>>( istream &input, PhoneNumber &num )
37     {
38        input.ignore();                      // skip (
39        input >> setw( 4 ) >> num.areaCode;  // input area code
40        input.ignore( 2 );                   // skip ) and space
41        input >> setw( 4 ) >> num.exchange;  // input exchange
42        input.ignore();                      // skip dash (-)
43        input >> setw( 5 ) >> num.line;      // input line
44        return input;       // enables cin >> a >> b >> c;
45     }
46
47     int main()
48     {
49        PhoneNumber phone;  // create object phone
50
51        cout << "Enter phone number in the form (123) 456-7890:\n";
52
53        // cin >> phone invokes operator>> function by
54        // issuing the call operator>>( cin, phone ).
55        cin >> phone;
56
57        // cout << phone invokes operator<< function by
58        // issuing the call operator<<( cout, phone ).
59        cout << "The phone number entered was: " << phone << endl;
60        return 0;
61     }
```

```
Enter phone number in the form (123) 456-7890:
(800) 555-1212
The phone number entered was: (800) 555-1212
```

Fig. 8.3   User-defined stream-insertion and stream-extraction operators (part 2 of 2).

The stream-extraction operator function **operator>>** (line 36) takes an **istream** reference called **input** and a **PhoneNumber** reference called **num** as arguments, and returns an **istream** reference. Operator function **operator>>** is used to input phone numbers of the form

    (800) 555-1212

into objects of class **PhoneNumber**. When the compiler sees the expression

    cin >> phone

in **main**, the compiler generates the function call

    operator>>(cin, phone);

When this call is executed, reference parameter **input** becomes an alias for **cin** and reference parameter **num** becomes an alias for **phone**. The operator function reads as strings the three parts of the telephone number into the **areaCode**, **exchange** and **line** members of the referenced **PhoneNumber** object (**num** in the operator function and **phone** in **main**). Stream manipulator **setw** limits the number of characters read into each character array. Remember that, when used with **cin**, **setw** restricts the number of characters read to one less than its argument (i.e., **setw(4)** allows three characters to be read and saves one position for a terminating null character). The parentheses, space and dash characters are skipped by calling **istream** member function **ignore**, which discards the specified number of characters in the input stream (one character by default). Function **operator>>** returns **istream** reference **input** (i.e., **cin**). This enables input operations on **PhoneNumber** objects to be cascaded with input operations on other **PhoneNumber** objects or on objects of other data types. For example, two **PhoneNumber** objects could be input as follows:

```
cin >> phone1 >> phone2;
```

First, the expression **cin >> phone1** would execute by making the call

```
operator>>( cin, phone1 );
```

This call would then return a reference to **cin** as the value of **cin >> phone1** so the remaining portion of the expression would be interpreted simply as **cin >> phone2**. This would execute by making the call

```
operator>>( cin, phone2 );
```

The stream-insertion operator takes an **ostream** reference (**output**) and a reference (**num**) to a user-defined type (**PhoneNumber**) as arguments, and returns an **ostream** reference. Function **operator<<** displays objects of type **PhoneNumber**. When the compiler sees the expression

```
cout << phone
```

in **main**, the compiler generates the non-member function call

```
operator<<( cout, phone );
```

Function **operator<<** displays the parts of the telephone number as strings because they are stored in string format.

Note that the functions **operator>>** and **operator<<** are declared in **class PhoneNumber** as non-member, **friend** functions. These operators must be non-members because the object of class **PhoneNumber** appears in each case as the right operand of the operator; the class operand must appear on the left of the operator to overload that operator as a member function. Overloaded input and output operators are declared as **friend**s if they need to access non-**public** class members directly for performance reasons. Also note that the **PhoneNumber** reference in **operator<<**'s parameter list is **const** (because the **PhoneNumber** will simply be output) and the **PhoneNumber** reference in **operator>>**'s parameter list is non-**const** (because the **PhoneNumber** object must be modified to store the input telephone number in the object).

Software Engineering Observation 8.3

*New input/output capabilities for user-defined types can be added to C++ without modifying the declarations or **private** data members for either the **ostream** class or the **istream** class. This is another example of the extensibility of the C++ programming language.*

8.6 Overloading Unary Operators

A unary operator for a class can be overloaded as a non-**static** member function with no arguments or as a non-member function with one argument; that argument must be either an object of the class or a reference to an object of the class. Member functions that implement overloaded operators must be non-**static** so they can access the non-**static** data of the class. Remember that **static** member functions can only access **static** data members of the class.

Later in this chapter, we will overload unary operator **!** to test if an object of our **String** class is empty and return a **bool** result. When overloading a unary operator such as **!** as a non-**static** member function with no arguments, if **s** is a **String** class object or a reference to a **String** class object, when the compiler sees the expression **!s**, the compiler generates the call **s.operator!()**. The operand **s** is the class object for which the **String** class member function **operator!** is being invoked. The function is declared in the class definition as follows:

```
class String {
public:
   bool operator!() const;
   ...
};
```

A unary operator such as **!** may be overloaded as a non-member function with one argument two different ways—either with an argument that is an object (this requires a copy of the object, so the side effects of the function are not applied to the original object), or with an argument that is a reference to an object (no copy of the original object is made, so all side effects of this function are applied to the original object). If **s** is a **String** class object (or a reference to a **String** class object), then **!s** is treated as if the call **operator!(s)** had been written, invoking the non-member **friend** function of class **String** declared below:

```
class String {
   friend bool operator!( const String & );
   ...
};
```

Good Programming Practice 8.6

*When overloading unary operators, it is preferable to make the operator functions class members instead of non-member **friend** functions. **friend** functions and **friend** classes should be avoided unless they are absolutely necessary. The use of **friend**s violates the encapsulation of a class.*

8.7 Overloading Binary Operators

A binary operator can be overloaded as a non-**static** member function with one argument, or as a non-member function with two arguments (one of those arguments must be either a class object or a reference to a class object).

Later in this chapter, we will overload **+=** to indicate concatenation of two string objects. When overloading binary operator **+=** as a non-**static** member function of a **String** class with one argument, if **y** and **z** are **String** class objects, then **y += z** is treated as if **y.operator+=(z)** had been written, invoking the **operator+=** member function declared below

```
class String {
public:
   const String &operator+=( const String & );
   ...
};
```

If binary operator **+=** is to be overloaded as a non-member function, it must take two arguments—one of which must be a class object or a reference to a class object. If **y** and **z** are **String** class objects or references to **String** class objects, then **y += z** is treated as if the call **operator+=(y, z)** had been written in the program, invoking non-member, **friend** function **operator+=** declared below

```
class String {
   friend const String &operator+=( String &,
                                    const String & );
   ...
};
```

8.8 Case Study: An **Array** Class

Array notation in C++ is just an alternative to pointers, so arrays have much potential for errors. For example, a program can easily "walk off" either end of an array because C++ does not check whether subscripts fall outside the range of an array. Arrays of size n must number their elements 0, ..., $n - 1$; alternate subscript ranges are not allowed. An entire non-**char** array cannot be input or output at once; each array element must be read or written individually. Two arrays cannot be meaningfully compared with equality operators or relational operators (because the array names are simply pointers to where the arrays begin in memory). When an array is passed to a general-purpose function designed to handle arrays of any size, the size of the array must be passed as an additional argument. One array cannot be assigned to another with the assignment operator(s) (because array names are **const** pointers and a constant pointer cannot be used on the left side of an assignment operator). These and other capabilities certainly seem like "naturals" for dealing with arrays, but C++ does not provide such capabilities. However, C++ does provide the means to implement such array capabilities through the mechanisms of operator overloading.

In this example, we develop an array class that performs range checking to ensure that subscripts remain within the bounds of the array. The class allows one array object to be assigned to another with the assignment operator. Objects of this array class know their size, so the size does not need to be passed separately as an argument when passing an array to a function. Entire arrays can be input or output with the stream-extraction and stream-insertion operators, respectively. Array comparisons can be made with the equality operators **==** and **!=**. Our array class uses a **static** member to keep track of the number of array objects that have been instantiated in the program.

This example will sharpen your appreciation of data abstraction. You will probably want to suggest many enhancements to this array class. Class development is an interesting, creative and intellectually challenging activity—always with the goal of "crafting valuable classes."

The program of Fig. 8.4 demonstrates class **Array** and its overloaded operators. First we walk through the driver program in **main**. Then we consider the class definition and each of the class' member function and **friend** function definitions.

```cpp
1   // Fig. 8.4: array1.h
2   // Simple class Array (for integers)
3   #ifndef ARRAY1_H
4   #define ARRAY1_H
5
6   #include <iostream>
7
8   using std::ostream;
9   using std::istream;
10
11  class Array {
12     friend ostream &operator<<( ostream &, const Array & );
13     friend istream &operator>>( istream &, Array & );
14  public:
15     Array( int = 10 );                      // default constructor
16     Array( const Array & );                 // copy constructor
17     ~Array();                               // destructor
18     int getSize() const;                    // return size
19     const Array &operator=( const Array & ); // assign arrays
20     bool operator==( const Array & ) const;  // compare equal
21
22     // Determine if two arrays are not equal and
23     // return true, otherwise return false (uses operator==).
24     bool operator!=( const Array &right ) const
25        { return ! ( *this == right ); }
26
27     int &operator[]( int );                 // subscript operator
28     const int &operator[]( int ) const;     // subscript operator
29     static int getArrayCount();             // Return count of
30                                             // arrays instantiated.
31  private:
32     int size; // size of the array
33     int *ptr; // pointer to first element of array
34     static int arrayCount;   // # of Arrays instantiated
35  };
36
37  #endif
```

Fig. 8.4   An **Array** class with operator overloading—**array1.h**.

```cpp
38   // Fig 8.4: array1.cpp
39   // Member function definitions for class Array
40   #include <iostream>
41
42   using std::cout;
43   using std::cin;
44   using std::endl;
```

Fig. 8.4   An **Array** class with operator overloading—**array1.cpp** (part 1 of 4).

```
45
46   #include <iomanip>
47
48   using std::setw;
49
50   #include <cstdlib>
51   #include <cassert>
52   #include "array1.h"
53
54   // Initialize static data member at file scope
55   int Array::arrayCount = 0;    // no objects yet
56
57   // Default constructor for class Array (default size 10)
58   Array::Array( int arraySize )
59   {
60      size = ( arraySize > 0 ? arraySize : 10 );
61      ptr = new int[ size ]; // create space for array
62      assert( ptr != 0 );     // terminate if memory not allocated
63      ++arrayCount;           // count one more object
64
65      for ( int i = 0; i < size; i++ )
66         ptr[ i ] = 0;          // initialize array
67   }
68
69   // Copy constructor for class Array
70   // must receive a reference to prevent infinite recursion
71   Array::Array( const Array &init ) : size( init.size )
72   {
73      ptr = new int[ size ]; // create space for array
74      assert( ptr != 0 );     // terminate if memory not allocated
75      ++arrayCount;           // count one more object
76
77      for ( int i = 0; i < size; i++ )
78         ptr[ i ] = init.ptr[ i ];  // copy init into object
79   }
80
81   // Destructor for class Array
82   Array::~Array()
83   {
84      delete [] ptr;          // reclaim space for array
85      --arrayCount;           // one fewer object
86   }
87
88   // Get the size of the array
89   int Array::getSize() const { return size; }
90
91   // Overloaded assignment operator
92   // const return avoids: ( a1 = a2 ) = a3
93   const Array &Array::operator=( const Array &right )
94   {
95      if ( &right != this ) {  // check for self-assignment
96
```

Fig. 8.4   An **Array** class with operator overloading—**array1.cpp** (part 2 of 4).

```
97           // for arrays of different sizes, deallocate original
98           // left side array, then allocate new left side array.
99           if ( size != right.size ) {
100             delete [] ptr;           // reclaim space
101             size = right.size;       // resize this object
102             ptr = new int[ size ];   // create space for array copy
103             assert( ptr != 0 );      // terminate if not allocated
104          }
105
106          for ( int i = 0; i < size; i++ )
107             ptr[ i ] = right.ptr[ i ];   // copy array into object
108       }
109
110       return *this;    // enables x = y = z;
111    }
112
113    // Determine if two arrays are equal and
114    // return true, otherwise return false.
115    bool Array::operator==( const Array &right ) const
116    {
117       if ( size != right.size )
118          return false;       // arrays of different sizes
119
120       for ( int i = 0; i < size; i++ )
121          if ( ptr[ i ] != right.ptr[ i ] )
122             return false; // arrays are not equal
123
124       return true;            // arrays are equal
125    }
126
127    // Overloaded subscript operator for non-const Arrays
128    // reference return creates an lvalue
129    int &Array::operator[]( int subscript )
130    {
131       // check for subscript out of range error
132       assert( 0 <= subscript && subscript < size );
133
134       return ptr[ subscript ]; // reference return
135    }
136
137    // Overloaded subscript operator for const Arrays
138    // const reference return creates an rvalue
139    const int &Array::operator[]( int subscript ) const
140    {
141       // check for subscript out of range error
142       assert( 0 <= subscript && subscript < size );
143
144       return ptr[ subscript ]; // const reference return
145    }
146
147    // Return the number of Array objects instantiated
148    // static functions cannot be const
149    int Array::getArrayCount() { return arrayCount; }
```

Fig. 8.4   An **Array** class with operator overloading—**array1.cpp** (part 3 of 4).

```
150
151  // Overloaded input operator for class Array;
152  // inputs values for entire array.
153  istream &operator>>( istream &input, Array &a )
154  {
155     for ( int i = 0; i < a.size; i++ )
156        input >> a.ptr[ i ];
157
158     return input;    // enables cin >> x >> y;
159  }
160
161  // Overloaded output operator for class Array
162  ostream &operator<<( ostream &output, const Array &a )
163  {
164     int i;
165
166     for ( i = 0; i < a.size; i++ ) {
167        output << setw( 12 ) << a.ptr[ i ];
168
169        if ( ( i + 1 ) % 4 == 0 ) // 4 numbers per row of output
170           output << endl;
171     }
172
173     if ( i % 4 != 0 )
174        output << endl;
175
176     return output;    // enables cout << x << y;
177  }
```

Fig. 8.4   An **Array** class with operator overloading—**array1.cpp** (part 4 of 4).

```
178  // Fig. 8.4: fig08_04.cpp
179  // Driver for simple class Array
180  #include <iostream>
181
182  using std::cout;
183  using std::cin;
184  using std::endl;
185
186  #include "array1.h"
187
188  int main()
189  {
190     // no objects yet
191     cout << "# of arrays instantiated = "
192          << Array::getArrayCount() << '\n';
193
194     // create two arrays and print Array count
195     Array integers1( 7 ), integers2;
196     cout << "# of arrays instantiated = "
197          << Array::getArrayCount() << "\n\n";
198
```

Fig. 8.4   An **Array** class with operator overloading—**fig08_04.cpp** (part 1 of 4).

```
199     // print integers1 size and contents
200     cout << "Size of array integers1 is "
201         << integers1.getSize()
202         << "\nArray after initialization:\n"
203         << integers1 << '\n';
204
205     // print integers2 size and contents
206     cout << "Size of array integers2 is "
207         << integers2.getSize()
208         << "\nArray after initialization:\n"
209         << integers2 << '\n';
210
211     // input and print integers1 and integers2
212     cout << "Input 17 integers:\n";
213     cin >> integers1 >> integers2;
214     cout << "After input, the arrays contain:\n"
215         << "integers1:\n" << integers1
216         << "integers2:\n" << integers2 << '\n';
217
218     // use overloaded inequality (!=) operator
219     cout << "Evaluating: integers1 != integers2\n";
220     if ( integers1 != integers2 )
221        cout << "They are not equal\n";
222
223     // create array integers3 using integers1 as an
224     // initializer; print size and contents
225     Array integers3( integers1 );
226
227     cout << "\nSize of array integers3 is "
228         << integers3.getSize()
229         << "\nArray after initialization:\n"
230         << integers3 << '\n';
231
232     // use overloaded assignment (=) operator
233     cout << "Assigning integers2 to integers1:\n";
234     integers1 = integers2;
235     cout << "integers1:\n" << integers1
236         << "integers2:\n" << integers2 << '\n';
237
238     // use overloaded equality (==) operator
239     cout << "Evaluating: integers1 == integers2\n";
240     if ( integers1 == integers2 )
241        cout << "They are equal\n\n";
242
243     // use overloaded subscript operator to create rvalue
244     cout << "integers1[5] is " << integers1[ 5 ] << '\n';
245
246     // use overloaded subscript operator to create lvalue
247     cout << "Assigning 1000 to integers1[5]\n";
248     integers1[ 5 ] = 1000;
249     cout << "integers1:\n" << integers1 << '\n';
250
```

Fig. 8.4   An **Array** class with operator overloading—**fig08_04.cpp** (part 2 of 4).

```
251      // attempt to use out of range subscript
252      cout << "Attempt to assign 1000 to integers1[15]" << endl;
253      integers1[ 15 ] = 1000;    // ERROR: out of range
254
255      return 0;
256 }
```

```
# of arrays instantiated = 0
# of arrays instantiated = 2

Size of array integers1 is 7
Array after initialization:
          0              0              0              0
          0              0              0

Size of array integers2 is 10
Array after initialization:
          0              0              0              0
          0              0              0              0
          0              0

Input 17 integers:
1 2 3 4 5 6 7 8 9 10 11 12 13 14 15 16 17
After input, the arrays contain:
integers1:
          1              2              3              4
          5              6              7
integers2:
          8              9             10             11
         12             13             14             15
         16             17

Evaluating: integers1 != integers2
They are not equal

Size of array integers3 is 7
Array after initialization:
          1              2              3              4
          5              6              7

Assigning integers2 to integers1:
integers1:
          8              9             10             11
         12             13             14             15
         16             17
integers2:
          8              9             10             11
         12             13             14             15
         16             17
```

Fig. 8.4   An **Array** class with operator overloading—**fig08_04.cpp** (part 3 of 4).

```
Evaluating: integers1 == integers2
They are equal

integers1[5] is 13
Assigning 1000 to integers1[5]
integers1:
            8           9          10          11
           12        1000          14          15
           16          17

Attempt to assign 1000 to integers1[15]
Assertion failed: 0 <= subscript && subscript < size, file Array1.cpp,
line 95 abnormal program termination
```

Fig. 8.4   An **Array** class with operator overloading—**fig08_04.cpp** (part 4 of 4).

The **static** class variable **arrayCount** of class **Array** contains the number of **Array** objects instantiated during program execution. The program begins by using **static** member function **getArrayCount** (line 192) to retrieve the number of arrays instantiated so far. Next, the program instantiates two objects of class **Array** (line 195)— **integers1** with seven elements and **integers2** with default size 10 elements (the default value specified by the **Array** default constructor). Line 197 calls function **getArrayCount** again to retrieve the value of class variable **arrayCount**. Lines 200 through 203 use member function **getSize** to determine the size of **Array integers1** and output **integers1** using the **Array** overloaded stream-insertion operator to confirm that the array elements were initialized correctly by the constructor. Next, lines 206 through 209 output the size of array **integers2** and output **integers2** using the **Array** overloaded stream-insertion operator.

The user is then prompted to input 17 integers. The **Array** overloaded stream-extraction operator is used to read these values into both arrays with line 213

```
cin >> integers1 >> integers2;
```

The first seven values are stored in **integers1** and the remaining 10 values are stored in **integers2**. In lines 214 through 216, the two arrays are output with the **Array** stream-insertion operator to confirm that the input was performed correctly.

Line 220 tests the overloaded inequality operator by evaluating the condition

```
integers1 != integers2
```

and the program reports that the arrays are indeed not equal.

Line 225 instantiates a third **Array** called **integers3** and initializes it with **Array integers1**. This invokes the **Array** *copy constructor* to copy the elements of **integers1** into **integers3**. We discuss the details of the copy constructor shortly.

Lines 227 through 230 output the size of **integers3** and output **integers3** using the **Array** overloaded stream-insertion operator to confirm that the array elements were initialized correctly by the constructor.

Next, line 234 tests the overloaded assignment operator (**=**) with the statement

```
integers1 = integers2;
```

Both **Array**s are printed in lines 235 and 236 to confirm that the assignment was success-ful. Note that **integers1** originally held 7 integers and needed to be resized to hold a copy of the 10 elements in **integers2**. As we will see, the overloaded assignment oper-ator performs this resizing in a manner transparent to the invoker of the operator.

Next, line 240 uses the overloaded equality operator (**==**) to confirm that objects **integers1** and **integers2** are indeed identical after the assignment.

Line 244 uses the overloaded subscript operator to refer to **integers1[5]**—an in-range element of **integers1**. This subscripted name is used as an *rvalue* to print the value in **integers1[5]**. Line 248, uses **integers1[5]** as an *lvalue* on the left side of an assignment statement to assign a new value, **1000**, to element **5** of **integers1**. Note that **operator[ ]** returns the reference to use as the *lvalue* after it determines that **5** is in range for **integers1**.

Line 253 attempts to assign the value **1000** to **integers1[15]**—an out-of-range element. The **Array** overloaded **[ ]** operator catches this error and program execution ter-minates abnormally.

Interestingly, the array subscript operator **[ ]** is not restricted for use only with arrays; it can be used to select elements from other kinds of ordered container classes such as linked lists, strings, dictionaries, and so on. Also, subscripts no longer have to be integers; characters, strings, floats or even objects of user-defined classes also could be used.

Now that we have seen how this program operates, let us walk through the class header and the member function definitions. Lines 32 through 34

```
int size; // size of the array
int *ptr; // pointer to first element of array
static int arrayCount;  // # of Arrays instantiated
```

represent the **private** data members of the class. The array consists of a **size** member indicating the number of elements in the array, an **int** pointer—**ptr**—that will point to the dynamically allocated array of integers stored in an **Array** object, and **static** mem-ber **arrayCount** indicating the number of array objects that have been instantiated.

Lines 12 and 13

```
friend ostream &operator<<( ostream &, const Array & );
friend istream &operator>>( istream &, Array & );
```

declare the overloaded stream-insertion operator and the overloaded stream-extraction op-erator to be **friend**s of class **Array**. When the compiler sees an expression like

```
cout << arrayObject
```

it invokes the **operator<<(ostream &, const Array &)** function by generating the call

```
operator<<( cout, arrayObject )
```

When the compiler sees an expression like

```
cin >> arrayObject
```

it invokes the **operator>>(istream &, Array &)** function by generating the call

```
operator>>( cin, arrayObject )
```

We note again that these stream-insertion and stream-extraction operator functions cannot be members of class **Array** because the **Array** object is always mentioned on the right side of a stream-insertion operator and a stream-extraction operator. If these operator functions were to be members of class **Array**, the following awkward statements would have to be used to output and input an **Array**:

```
arrayObject << cout;
arrayObject >> cin;
```

Function **operator<<** (defined at line 162) prints the number of elements indicated by the **size** from the array stored at **ptr**. Function **operator>>** (defined at line 153) inputs directly into the array pointed to by **ptr**. Each of these operator functions returns an appropriate reference to enable cascaded output or input statements, respectively.

Line 15

```
Array( int = 10 );                    // default constructor
```

declares the default constructor for the class and specifies that the array size defaults to 10 elements. When the compiler sees a declaration like

```
Array integers1( 7 );
```

or the equivalent form

```
Array integers1 = 7;
```

it invokes the default constructor (remember that the default constructor in this example actually receives a single **int** argument that has a default value of 10). The default constructor (defined at line 58) validates and assigns the argument to the **size** data member, uses **new** to obtain the space to hold the internal representation of this array and assigns the pointer returned by **new** to data member **ptr**, uses **assert** to test that **new** was successful, increments **arrayCount**, then uses a **for** loop to initialize all the elements of the array to zero. It is possible to have an **Array** class that does not initialize its members if, for example, these members are to be read at some later time. But this is considered to be a poor programming practice. **Array**s, and objects in general, should be maintained at all times in a properly initialized and consistent state.

Line 16

```
Array( const Array & );               // copy constructor
```

declares a *copy constructor* (defined at line 71) that initializes an **Array** by making a copy of an existing **Array** object. Such copying must be done carefully to avoid the pitfall of leaving both **Array** objects pointing to the same dynamically allocated storage, exactly the problem that would occur with default memberwise copy. Copy constructors are invoked whenever a copy of an object is needed, such as in call-by-value, when returning an object by value from a called function or when initializing an object to be a copy of another object of the same class. The copy constructor is called in a definition when an object of class **Array** is instantiated and initialized with another object of class **Array** as in the following declaration:

```
Array integers3( integers1 );
```

or the equivalent declaration

```
Array integers3 = integers1;
```

Common Programming Error 8.6

Note that the copy constructor must use call-by-reference not call-by-value. Otherwise, the copy constructor call results in infinite recursion (a fatal logic error) because, for call-by-value, a copy of the object passed to the copy constructor must be made, which results in the copy constructor being called recursively!

The copy constructor for **Array** uses a member initializer to copy the **size** of the array used for initialization into the **size** data member, uses **new** to obtain the space to hold the internal representation of this array and assigns the pointer returned by **new** to data member **ptr**, uses **assert** to test that **new** was successful, increments **arrayCount**, then uses a **for** loop to copy all the elements of the initializer array into this array.

Common Programming Error 8.7

*If the copy constructor simply copied the pointer in the source object to the target object's pointer, then both objects would point to the same dynamically allocated storage. The first destructor to execute would then delete the dynamically allocated storage, and the other object's **ptr** would then be undefined, a situation called a "dangling pointer" and likely to result in a serious run-time error.*

Software Engineering Observation 8.4

A constructor, a destructor, an overloaded assignment operator and a copy constructor are usually provided as a group for any class that uses dynamically allocated memory.

Line 17

```
~Array();                          // destructor
```

declares the destructor (defined at line 82) for the class. The destructor is invoked when the life of an object of class **Array** is terminated. The destructor uses **delete [ ]** to reclaim the dynamic storage allocated by **new** in the constructor and then decrements **array-Count**.

Line 18

```
int getSize() const;                    // return size
```

declares a function that reads the size of the array.

Line 19

```
const Array &operator=( const Array & ); // assign arrays
```

declares the overloaded assignment operator function for the class. When the compiler sees an expression like

```
integers1 = integers2;
```

it invokes the **operator=** function by generating the call

```
integers1.operator=( integers2 )
```

The **operator=** member function (defined at line 93) tests for *self assignment*. If a self assignment is being attempted, the assignment is skipped (i.e., the object already is itself;

in a moment we will see why self assignment is dangerous). If it is not a self assignment, then the member function determines if the sizes of the two arrays are identical—in which case the original array of integers in the left-side **Array** object is not reallocated. Otherwise, **operator=** uses **delete** to reclaim the space originally allocated in the target array, copies the **size** of the source array to the **size** of the target array, uses **new** to allocate that amount of space for the target array and places the pointer returned by **new** into the array's **ptr** member and uses **assert** to verify that **new** succeeded. Then, **operator=** uses a **for** loop to copy the array elements from the source array to the target array. Regardless of whether this is a self assignment or not, the member function then returns the current object (i.e., ***this**) as a constant reference; this enables cascaded **Array** assignments such as **x = y = z**.

Common Programming Error 8.8

Not providing an overloaded assignment operator and a copy constructor for a class when objects of that class contain pointers to dynamically allocated storage is a logic error.

Software Engineering Observation 8.5

It is possible to prevent one class object from being assigned to another. This is done by declaring the assignment operator as a **private** *member of the class.*

Software Engineering Observation 8.6

It is possible to prevent class objects from being copied; to do this, simply make both the overloaded assignment operator and the copy constructor **private**.

Line 20

```
bool operator==( const Array & ) const;   // compare equal
```

declares the overloaded equality operator (**==**) for the class. When the compiler sees the expression

```
integers1 == integers2
```

in **main**, the compiler invokes the **operator==** member function by generating the call

```
integers1.operator==( integers2 )
```

The **operator==** member function (defined at line 115) immediately returns **false** if the **size** members of the arrays are different. Otherwise, the member function compares each pair of elements. If they are all the same, **true** is returned. The first pair of elements to differ causes **false** to be returned immediately.

Lines 24 and 25

```
bool operator!=( const Array &right ) const
   { return ! ( *this == right ); }
```

define the overloaded inequality operator (**!=**) for the class. The **operator!=** member function is defined in terms of the overloaded equality operator. The function definition uses the overloaded **operator==** function to determine if one **Array** is equal to another, then returns the opposite of that result. Writing the **operator!=** function in this manner enables the programmer to reuse the **operator==** function and reduces the amount of code that must be written in the class. Also, note that the full function definition for **operator!=** is in the **Array** header file. This allows the compiler to **inline** the definition of **operator!=** to eliminate the overhead of the extra function call.

Lines 27 and 28

```
int &operator[]( int );          // subscript operator
const int &operator[]( int ) const;  // subscript operator
```

declare two overloaded subscript operators (defined at lines 129 and 139, respectively) for the class. When the compiler sees the expression

```
integers1[ 5 ]
```

in **main**, the compiler invokes the appropriate overloaded **operator[]** member function by generating the call

```
integers1.operator[]( 5 )
```

The compiler creates a call to the **const** version of **operator[]** when the subscript operator is used on a **const Array** object. For example, if **const** object **z** is instantiated with the statement

```
const Array z( 5 );
```

then a **const** version of **operator[]** is required when a statement such as

```
cout << z[ 3 ] << endl;
```

is executed. A **const** object can have only its **const** member functions called.

Each definition of **operator[]** tests if the subscript is in range, and, if it is not, the program terminates abnormally. If the subscript is in range, the appropriate element of the array is returned as a reference so that it may be used as an *lvalue* (for example, on the left side of an assignment statement) in the case of the non-**const** version of **operator[]**, or an *rvalue* in the case of the **const** version of **operator[]**.

Line 29

```
static int getArrayCount();       // return count of Arrays
```

declares **static** function **getArrayCount** that returns the value of **static** data member **arrayCount**, even if no objects of class **Array** exist.

8.9 Converting between Types

Most programs process information of a variety of types. Sometimes all the operations "stay within a type." For example, adding an integer to an integer produces an integer (as long as the result is not too large to be represented as an integer). But, it is often necessary to convert data of one type to data of another type. This can happen in assignments, in calculations, in passing values to functions and in returning values from functions. The compiler knows how to perform certain conversions among built-in types. Programmers can force conversions among built-in types by casting.

But what about user-defined types? The compiler cannot know how to convert among user-defined types and built-in types. The programmer must specify how such conversions are to occur. Such conversions can be performed with *conversion constructors*—single-argument constructors that turn objects of other types (including built-in types) into objects of a particular class. We will use a conversion constructor later in this chapter to convert ordinary **char *** strings into **String** class objects.

A *conversion operator* (also called a *cast operator*) can be used to convert an object of one class into an object of another class or into an object of a built-in type. Such a conversion operator must be a non-**static** member function; this kind of conversion operator cannot be a **friend** function.

The function prototype

```
A::operator char *() const;
```

declares an overloaded cast operator function for creating a temporary **char *** object out of an object of user-defined type **A**. An overloaded *cast operator function* does not specify a return type—the return type is the type to which the object is being converted. If **s** is a class object, when the compiler sees the expression **(char *) s** the compiler generates the call **s.operator char *()**. The operand **s** is the class object **s** for which the member function **operator char *** is being invoked.

Overloaded cast operator functions can be defined for converting objects of user-defined types into built-in types or into objects of other user-defined types. The prototypes

```
A::operator int() const;
A::operator otherClass() const;
```

declare overloaded cast operator functions for converting an object of user-defined type **A** into an integer and for converting an object of user-defined type **A** into an object of user-defined type **otherClass**.

One of the nice features of cast operators and conversion constructors is that, when necessary, the compiler can call these functions to create temporary objects. For example, if an object **s** of a user-defined **String** class appears in a program at a location where an ordinary **char *** is expected, such as

```
cout << s;
```

the compiler calls the overloaded cast operator function **operator char *** to convert the object into a **char *** and uses the resulting **char *** in the expression. With this cast operator provided for our **String** class, the stream-insertion operator does not have to be overloaded to output a **String** using **cout**.

8.10 Case Study: A **String** Class

As a capstone exercise to our study of overloading, we will build a class that handles the creation and manipulation of strings (Fig. 8.5). Class **string** is now part of the C++ standard libraries—we study class **string** in detail in Chapter 19. For now we will make extensive use of operator overloading to craft our own class **String**.

First, we present the header for class **String**. We discuss the **private** data used for representing **String** objects. Then we walk through the class' **public** interface, discussing each of the services the class provides. Next, we will walk through the driver program in **main**. We will discuss the coding style we "aspire to," i.e., the kinds of concise, operator-intensive expressions we would like to be able to write with objects of our new **String** class and with the class' collection of overloaded operators.

```
1   // Fig. 8.5: string1.h
2   // Definition of a String class
3   #ifndef STRING1_H
4   #define STRING1_H
5
6   #include <iostream>
7
8   using std::ostream;
9   using std::istream;
10
11  class String {
12     friend ostream &operator<<( ostream &, const String & );
13     friend istream &operator>>( istream &, String & );
14
15  public:
16     String( const char * = "" ); // conversion/default ctor
17     String( const String & );     // copy constructor
18     ~String();                    // destructor
19     const String &operator=( const String & );  // assignment
20     const String &operator+=( const String & ); // concatenation
21     bool operator!() const;                 // is String empty?
22     bool operator==( const String & ) const; // test s1 == s2
23     bool operator<( const String & ) const;  // test s1 < s2
24
25     // test s1 != s2
26     bool operator!=( const String & right ) const
27        { return !( *this == right ); }
28
29     // test s1 > s2
30     bool operator>( const String &right ) const
31        { return right < *this; }
32
33     // test s1 <= s2
34     bool operator<=( const String &right ) const
35        { return !( right < *this ); }
36
37     // test s1 >= s2
38     bool operator>=( const String &right ) const
39        { return !( *this < right ); }
40
41     char &operator[]( int );                // subscript operator
42     const char &operator[]( int ) const;    // subscript operator
43     String operator()( int, int );          // return a substring
44     int getLength() const;                  // return string length
45
46  private:
47     int length;                    // string length
48     char *sPtr;                    // pointer to start of string
49
50     void setString( const char * ); // utility function
51  };
52
53  #endif
```

Fig. 8.5   A **String** class with operator overloading—**string1.h**.

Then we discuss the member function definitions for the class **String**. For each of the overloaded operator functions, we show the code in the driver program that invokes the overloaded operator function, and we provide an explanation of how the overloaded operator function works.

```cpp
54   // Fig. 8.5: string1.cpp
55   // Member function definitions for class String
56   #include <iostream>
57
58   using std::cout;
59   using std::endl;
60
61   #include <iomanip>
62
63   using std::setw;
64
65   #include <cstring>
66   #include <cassert>
67   #include "string1.h"
68
69   // Conversion constructor: Convert char * to String
70   String::String( const char *s ) : length( strlen( s ) )
71   {
72      cout << "Conversion constructor: " << s << '\n';
73      setString( s );          // call utility function
74   }
75
76   // Copy constructor
77   String::String( const String &copy ) : length( copy.length )
78   {
79      cout << "Copy constructor: " << copy.sPtr << '\n';
80      setString( copy.sPtr ); // call utility function
81   }
82
83   // Destructor
84   String::~String()
85   {
86      cout << "Destructor: " << sPtr << '\n';
87      delete [] sPtr;          // reclaim string
88   }
89
90   // Overloaded = operator; avoids self assignment
91   const String &String::operator=( const String &right )
92   {
93      cout << "operator= called\n";
94
95      if ( &right != this ) {           // avoid self assignment
96         delete [] sPtr;                // prevents memory leak
97         length = right.length;         // new String length
98         setString( right.sPtr );       // call utility function
99      }
```

Fig. 8.5   A **String** class with operator overloading—**string1.cpp** (part 1 of 4).

```
100      else
101         cout << "Attempted assignment of a String to itself\n";
102
103      return *this;    // enables cascaded assignments
104   }
105
106   // Concatenate right operand to this object and
107   // store in this object.
108   const String &String::operator+=( const String &right )
109   {
110      char *tempPtr = sPtr;          // hold to be able to delete
111      length += right.length;        // new String length
112      sPtr = new char[ length + 1 ]; // create space
113      assert( sPtr != 0 );    // terminate if memory not allocated
114      strcpy( sPtr, tempPtr );        // left part of new String
115      strcat( sPtr, right.sPtr );    // right part of new String
116      delete [] tempPtr;              // reclaim old space
117      return *this;                   // enables cascaded calls
118   }
119
120   // Is this String empty?
121   bool String::operator!() const { return length == 0; }
122
123   // Is this String equal to right String?
124   bool String::operator==( const String &right ) const
125      { return strcmp( sPtr, right.sPtr ) == 0; }
126
127   // Is this String less than right String?
128   bool String::operator<( const String &right ) const
129      { return strcmp( sPtr, right.sPtr ) < 0; }
130
131   // Return a reference to a character in a String as an lvalue.
132   char &String::operator[]( int subscript )
133   {
134      // First test for subscript out of range
135      assert( subscript >= 0 && subscript < length );
136
137      return sPtr[ subscript ];   // creates lvalue
138   }
139
140   // Return a reference to a character in a String as an rvalue.
141   const char &String::operator[]( int subscript ) const
142   {
143      // First test for subscript out of range
144      assert( subscript >= 0 && subscript < length );
145
146      return sPtr[ subscript ];   // creates rvalue
147   }
148
149   // Return a substring beginning at index and
150   // of length subLength
151   String String::operator()( int index, int subLength )
152   {
```

Fig. 8.5   A **String** class with operator overloading—**string1.cpp** (part 2 of 4).

```
153     // ensure index is in range and substring length >= 0
154     assert( index >= 0 && index < length && subLength >= 0 );
155
156     // determine length of substring
157     int len;
158
159     if ( ( subLength == 0 ) || ( index + subLength > length ) )
160        len = length - index;
161     else
162        len = subLength;
163
164     // allocate temporary array for substring and
165     // terminating null character
166     char *tempPtr = new char[ len + 1 ];
167     assert( tempPtr != 0 ); // ensure space allocated
168
169     // copy substring into char array and terminate string
170     strncpy( tempPtr, &sPtr[ index ], len );
171     tempPtr[ len ] = '\0';
172
173     // Create temporary String object containing the substring
174     String tempString( tempPtr );
175     delete [] tempPtr;   // delete the temporary array
176
177     return tempString;   // return copy of the temporary String
178  }
179
180  // Return string length
181  int String::getLength() const { return length; }
182
183  // Utility function to be called by constructors and
184  // assignment operator.
185  void String::setString( const char *string2 )
186  {
187     sPtr = new char[ length + 1 ]; // allocate storage
188     assert( sPtr != 0 );  // terminate if memory not allocated
189     strcpy( sPtr, string2 );      // copy literal to object
190  }
191
192  // Overloaded output operator
193  ostream &operator<<( ostream &output, const String &s )
194  {
195     output << s.sPtr;
196     return output;    // enables cascading
197  }
198
199  // Overloaded input operator
200  istream &operator>>( istream &input, String &s )
201  {
202     char temp[ 100 ];    // buffer to store input
203
204     input >> setw( 100 ) >> temp;
205     s = temp;        // use String class assignment operator
```

Fig. 8.5   A **String** class with operator overloading—**string1.cpp** (part 3 of 4).

```
206     return input;    // enables cascading
207 }
```

Fig. 8.5   A **String** class with operator overloading—**string1.cpp** (part 4 of 4).

```
208 // Fig. 8.5: fig08_05.cpp
209 // Driver for class String
210 #include <iostream>
211
212 using std::cout;
213 using std::endl;
214
215 #include "string1.h"
216
217 int main()
218 {
219    String s1( "happy" ), s2( " birthday" ), s3;
220
221    // test overloaded equality and relational operators
222    cout << "s1 is \"" << s1 << "\"; s2 is \"" << s2
223        << "\"; s3 is \"" << s3 << '\"'
224        << "\nThe results of comparing s2 and s1:"
225        << "\ns2 == s1 yields "
226        << ( s2 == s1 ? "true" : "false" )
227        << "\ns2 != s1 yields "
228        << ( s2 != s1 ? "true" : "false" )
229        << "\ns2 >  s1 yields "
230        << ( s2 > s1 ? "true" : "false" )
231        << "\ns2 <  s1 yields "
232        << ( s2 < s1 ? "true" : "false" )
233        << "\ns2 >= s1 yields "
234        << ( s2 >= s1 ? "true" : "false" )
235        << "\ns2 <= s1 yields "
236        << ( s2 <= s1 ? "true" : "false" );
237
238    // test overloaded String empty (!) operator
239    cout << "\n\nTesting !s3:\n";
240    if ( !s3 ) {
241       cout << "s3 is empty; assigning s1 to s3;\n";
242       s3 = s1;                // test overloaded assignment
243       cout << "s3 is \"" << s3 << "\"";
244    }
245
246    // test overloaded String concatenation operator
247    cout << "\n\ns1 += s2 yields s1 = ";
248    s1 += s2;                // test overloaded concatenation
249    cout << s1;
250
251    // test conversion constructor
252    cout << "\n\ns1 += \" to you\" yields\n";
253    s1 += " to you";         // test conversion constructor
254    cout << "s1 = " << s1 << "\n\n";
```

Fig. 8.5   A **String** class with operator overloading—**fig08_05.cpp** (part 1 of 3).

```
255
256        // test overloaded function call operator () for substring
257        cout << "The substring of s1 starting at\n"
258            << "location 0 for 14 characters, s1(0, 14), is:\n"
259            << s1( 0, 14 ) << "\n\n";
260
261        // test substring "to-end-of-String" option
262        cout << "The substring of s1 starting at\n"
263            << "location 15, s1(15, 0), is: "
264            << s1( 15, 0 ) << "\n\n";   // 0 is "to end of string"
265
266        // test copy constructor
267        String *s4Ptr = new String( s1 );
268        cout << "*s4Ptr = " << *s4Ptr << "\n\n";
269
270        // test assignment (=) operator with self-assignment
271        cout << "assigning *s4Ptr to *s4Ptr\n";
272        *s4Ptr = *s4Ptr;              // test overloaded assignment
273        cout << "*s4Ptr = " << *s4Ptr << '\n';
274
275        // test destructor
276        delete s4Ptr;
277
278        // test using subscript operator to create lvalue
279        s1[ 0 ] = 'H';
280        s1[ 6 ] = 'B';
281        cout << "\ns1 after s1[0] = 'H' and s1[6] = 'B' is: "
282            << s1 << "\n\n";
283
284        // test subscript out of range
285        cout << "Attempt to assign 'd' to s1[30] yields:" << endl;
286        s1[ 30 ] = 'd';        // ERROR: subscript out of range
287
288        return 0;
289    }
```

```
Conversion constructor: happy
Conversion constructor:  birthday
Conversion constructor:
s1 is "happy"; s2 is " birthday"; s3 is ""
The results of comparing s2 and s1:
s2 == s1 yields false
s2 != s1 yields true
s2 >  s1 yields false
s2 <  s1 yields true
s2 >= s1 yields false
s2 <= s1 yields true

Testing !s3:
s3 is empty; assigning s1 to s3;
operator= called
s3 is "happy"
```

Fig. 8.5   A **String** class with operator overloading—**fig08_05.cpp** (part 2 of 3).

```
s1 += s2 yields s1 = happy birthday

s1 += " to you" yields
Conversion constructor:  to you
Destructor:  to you
s1 = happy birthday to you

Conversion constructor: happy birthday
Copy constructor: happy birthday
Destructor: happy birthday
The substring of s1 starting at
location 0 for 14 characters, s1(0, 14), is:
happy birthday

Destructor: happy birthday
Conversion constructor: to you
Copy constructor: to you
Destructor: to you
The substring of s1 starting at
location 15, s1(15, 0), is: to you

Destructor: to you
Copy constructor: happy birthday to you
*s4Ptr = happy birthday to you

assigning *s4Ptr to *s4Ptr
operator= called
Attempted assignment of a String to itself
*s4Ptr = happy birthday to you
Destructor: happy birthday to you

s1 after s1[0] = 'H' and s1[6] = 'B' is: Happy Birthday to you

Attempt to assign 'd' to s1[30] yields:

Assertion failed: subscript >= 0 && subscript < length, file
string1.cpp, line 82

Abnormal program termination
```

Fig. 8.5   A **String** class with operator overloading—**fig08_05.cpp** (part 3 of 3).

We begin with the internal representation of a **String**. Lines 47 and 48

```
int length;          // string length
char *sPtr;          // pointer to start of string
```

declare the **private** data members of the class. Our implementation of a **String** object has a **length** field, which represents the number of characters in the string not including the null character at the end of the character string, and has a pointer **sPtr** to its dynamically allocated storage representing the character string.

Now we walk through the **String** class header file in Fig. 8.5. Lines 12 and 13

```
friend ostream &operator<<( ostream &, const String & );
friend istream &operator>>( istream &, String & );
```

declare the overloaded stream-insertion operator function **operator<<** (defined at line 193) and the overloaded stream-extraction operator function **operator>>** (defined at line 200) as **friend**s of the class. The implementation of these is straightforward.
Line 16

```
String( const char * = "" ); // conversion/default ctor
```

declares a *conversion constructor*. This constructor (defined at line 70) takes a **const char *** argument (that defaults to the empty string) and instantiates a **String** object which includes that same character string. Any *single-argument constructor* can be thought of as a conversion constructor. As we will see, such constructors are helpful when we are doing any **String** operation using **char *** arguments. The conversion constructor converts the **char *** string into a **String** object which is then assigned to the target **String** object. The availability of this conversion constructor means that it is not necessary to supply an overloaded assignment operator for specifically assigning character strings to **String** objects. The compiler invokes the conversion constructor to create a temporary **String** object containing the character string. Then, the overloaded assignment operator is invoked to assign the temporary **String** object to another **String** object.

Software Engineering Observation 8.7

When a conversion constructor is used to perform an implicit conversion, C++ can only apply a single implicit constructor call to try to match the needs of another overloaded operator. It is not possible to match an overloaded operator's needs by performing a series of implicit, user-defined conversions.

The **String** conversion constructor could be invoked in a declaration such as **String s1("happy")**. The conversion constructor calculates the length of the character string and assigns it to **private** data member **length** in the member initializer list, then calls **private** utility function **setString**. Function **setString** (defined at line 185) uses **new** to attach a sufficient amount of space to **private** data member **sPtr**, uses **assert** to test that **new** succeeded and, if it did, uses **strcpy** to copy the character string into the object.
Line 17

```
String( const String & );      // copy constructor
```

is a copy constructor (defined at line 77) that initializes a **String** object by making a copy of an existing **String** object. Such copying must be done carefully to avoid the pitfall of leaving both **String** objects pointing to the same dynamically allocated storage, exactly the problem that would occur with *default memberwise copy*. The copy constructor operates similarly to the conversion constructor except that it simply copies the **length** member from the source **String** object to the target **String** object. Note that the copy constructor creates new space for the target object's internal character string. If it simply copied the **sPtr** in the source object to the target object's **sPtr**, then both objects would point to the same dynamically allocated storage. The first destructor to execute would then delete the dynamically allocated storage and the other object's **sPtr** would then be undefined (i.e., **sPtr** would be a *dangling pointer*), a situation likely to cause a serious run-time error.

Line 18

```
~String();                              // destructor
```

declares the destructor (defined at line 84) for class **String**. The destructor uses **delete** to reclaim the dynamic storage obtained by **new** to provide the space for the character string.

Line 19

```
const String &operator=( const String & );  // assignment
```

declares the overloaded assignment operator function **operator=** (defined at line 91). When the compiler sees an expression like **string1 = string2**, the compiler generates the function call

```
string1.operator=( string2 );
```

The overloaded assignment operator function **operator=** tests for self-assignment. If this is a self-assignment, the function returns because the object is already itself. If this test were omitted, the function would immediately delete the space in the target object and thus lose the character string—a classic example of a *memory leak*. If there is no self-assignment, the function does delete the space, copies the **length** field of the source object to the target object and calls **setString** (line 185) to create new space for the target object, determine if **new** succeeded and use **strcpy** to copy the character string from the source object to the target object. Whether or not this is a self-assignment, ***this** is returned to enable cascaded assignments.

Line 20

```
const String &operator+=( const String & ); // concatenation
```

declares the overloaded string concatenation operator (defined at line 108). When the compiler sees the expression **s1 += s2** in **main**, the function call **s1.operator+=(s2)** is generated. Function **operator+=** creates a temporary pointer to hold the current object's character string until the character string's memory can be deleted, calculates the combined length of the concatenated string, uses **new** to reserve space for the string, uses **assert** to test that **new** succeeded, uses **strcpy** to copy the original string into the newly allocated space, uses **strcat** to concatenate the source object's character string to the newly allocated space, uses **delete** to reclaim the space occupied by this object's original character string and returns ***this** as a **String &** to enable cascading of **+=** operators.

Do we need a second overloaded concatenation operator to allow concatenation of a **String** and a **char ***? No. The **const char *** conversion constructor converts a conventional string into a temporary **String** object which then matches the existing overloaded concatenation operator. Again, C++ can perform such conversions only one level deep to facilitate a match. C++ can also perform an implicit compiler-defined conversion between built-in types before it performs the conversion between a built-in type and a class. Note that when a temporary **String** object is created, the conversion constructor and the destructor are called (see the output resulting from **s1 += " to you"** in Fig. 8.5). This is an example of function call overhead that is hidden from the client of the class when temporary class objects are created and destroyed during implicit conversions. Similar overhead is generated by copy constructors in call-by-value parameter passing and returning class objects by value.

Performance Tip 8.2

Having the overloaded **+=** *concatenation operator that takes a single argument of type* **const char *** *executes more efficiently than having to do the implicit conversion first, then the concatenation. Implicit conversions require less code and cause fewer errors.*

Line 21

```
bool operator!() const;                    // is String empty?
```

declares the overloaded negation operator (defined at line 121). This operator is commonly used with string classes to test if a string is empty. For example, when the compiler sees the expression **!string1**, it generates the function call

```
string1.operator!()
```

This function simply returns the result of testing if **length** is equal to zero.
The lines

```
bool operator==( const String & ) const;  // test s1 == s2
bool operator<( const String & ) const;   // test s1 < s2
```

declare the overloaded equality operator (defined at line 124) and the overloaded less than operator (defined at line 128) for the **String** class. These are all similar, so let us discuss one example, namely overloading the **==** operator. When the compiler sees the expression **string1 == string2**, the compiler generates the function call

```
string1.operator==( string2 )
```

which returns **true** if **string1** is equal to **string2**. Each of these operators uses **strcmp** to compare the character strings in the **String** objects. Note that we use the function **strcmp** from **<cstring>**. Many C++ programmers advocate using some of the overloaded operator functions to implement others. So, the **!=**, **>**, **<=** and **>=** operators are implemented (lines 26 through 39) in terms of **operator==** and **operator<**. For example, overloaded function **operator>=** is implemented at line 38 in the header file as follows:

```
bool operator>=( const String &right ) const
    { return !( *this < right ); }
```

The preceding **operator>=** definition uses the overloaded **<** operator to determine if one **String** object is greater than or equal to another. Note that the operator functions for **!=**, **>**, **<=** and **>=** are defined in the header file. The compiler **inline**s these definitions to eliminate the overhead of the extra function calls.

Software Engineering Observation 8.8

By implementing member functions using previously defined member functions, the programmer reuses code to reduce the amount of code that must be written.

Lines 41 and 42

```
char &operator[]( int );           // subscript operator
const char &operator[]( int ) const; // subscript operator
```

declare two overloaded subscript operators (defined at lines 132 and 141)—one for non-**const Strings** and one for **const Strings**. When the compiler sees an expression like **string1[0]**, the compiler generates the call **string1.operator[](0)** (using the appropriate version of **operator[]** based on whether or not the **String** is **const**). Function **operator[]** first uses **assert** to perform a range check on the subscript; if the subscript is out of range, the program will print an error message and terminate abnormally. If the subscript is in range, the non-**const** version of **operator[]** returns as a **char &** to the appropriate character of the **String** object; this **char &** may be used as an *lvalue* to modify the designated character of the **String** object. The **const** version of **operator[]** returns **const char &** to the appropriate character of the **String** object; this **char &** may be used as an *rvalue* to read the value of the character.

Testing and Debugging Tip 8.1

*Returning a **char** reference from an overloaded subscript operator in a **String** class is dangerous. For example, the client could use this reference to insert a null (* **'\0'** *) anywhere in the string.*

Line 43

```
String operator()( int, int ); // return a substring
```

declares the *overloaded function-call operator* (defined at line 151). In string classes, it is common to overload this operator to select a substring from a **String**. The two integer parameters specify the start location and the length of the substring being selected from the **String**. If the start location is out of range or the substring length is negative, an error message is generated. If the substring length is 0, then the substring is selected to the end of the **String** object. For example, suppose **string1** is a **String** object containing the character string **"AEIOU"**. When the compiler sees the expression **string1(2, 2)**, it generates the call **string1.operator()(2, 2)**. When this call executes, it produces and **return**s a new dynamically allocated **String** object containing the string **"IO"**.

Overloading the function call operator **()** is powerful because functions can take arbitrarily long and complex parameter lists. So we can use this capability for many interesting purposes. One such use of the function call operator is an alternate array subscripting notation: Instead of using C's awkward double square bracket notation for double arrays, such as in **a[b][c]**, some programmers prefer to overload the function call operator to enable the notation **a(b, c)**. The overloaded function call operator can only be a non-**static** member function. This operator is used only when the "function name" is an object of class **String**.

Line 44

```
inline int getLength() const;       // return string length
```

declares a function that returns the length of the **String**. Note that this function (defined at line 181) obtains the length by returning the value of the **String**'s **private** data.

At this point, the reader should now step through the code in **main**, examine the output window and check each use of an overloaded operator.

8.11 Overloading ++ and --

The increment and decrement operators—preincrement, postincrement, predecrement and postdecrement—can all be overloaded. We will see how the compiler distinguishes between the prefix version and the postfix version of an increment or decrement operator.

To overload the increment operator to allow both preincrement and postincrement usage, each overloaded operator function must have a distinct signature so the compiler will be able to determine which version of **++** is intended. The prefix versions are overloaded exactly as any other prefix unary operator would be.

Suppose, for example, that we want to add 1 to the day in **Date** object **d1**. When the compiler sees the preincrementing expression

    ++d1

the compiler generates the member function call

    d1.operator++()

whose prototype would be

    Date &operator++();

If the preincrementing is implemented as a non-member function, when the compiler sees the expression

    ++d1

the compiler generates the function call

    operator++(d1)

whose prototype would be declared in the **Date** class as

    friend Date &operator++(Date &);

Overloading the postincrementing operator presents a bit of a challenge because the compiler must be able to distinguish between the signatures of the overloaded preincrement and postincrement operator functions. The convention that has been adopted in C++ is that when the compiler sees the postincrementing expression

    d1++

it will generate the member-function call

    d1.operator++(0)

whose prototype is

    Date operator++(int)

The 0 is strictly a "dummy value" to make the argument list of **operator++**, used for postincrementing, distinguishable from the argument list of **operator++**, used for preincrementing.

If the postincrementing is implemented as a non-member function, when the compiler sees the expression

d1++

the compiler generates the function call

operator++(d1, 0)

whose prototype would be

friend Date operator++(Date &, int);

Once again, the **0** argument is used by the compiler so the argument list of **operator++**, used for postincrementing, is distinguishable from the argument list for preincrementing.

Everything stated in this section for overloading preincrement and postincrement operators applies to overloading predecrement and postdecrement operators. Next, we examine a **Date** class with overloaded preincrement and postincrement operators.

8.12 Case Study: A **Date** Class

Figure 8.6 illustrates a **Date** class. The class uses overloaded preincrement and postincrement operators to add 1 to the day in a **Date** object, while causing appropriate increments to the month and year if necessary.

```
1   // Fig. 8.6: date1.h
2   // Definition of class Date
3   #ifndef DATE1_H
4   #define DATE1_H
5   #include <iostream>
6
7   using std::ostream;
8
9   class Date {
10      friend ostream &operator<<( ostream &, const Date & );
11
12  public:
13      Date( int m = 1, int d = 1, int y = 1900 ); // constructor
14      void setDate( int, int, int ); // set the date
15      Date &operator++();             // preincrement operator
16      Date operator++( int );         // postincrement operator
17      const Date &operator+=( int ); // add days, modify object
18      bool leapYear( int ) const;     // is this a leap year?
19      bool endOfMonth( int ) const;   // is this end of month?
20
21  private:
22      int month;
23      int day;
24      int year;
25
26      static const int days[];        // array of days per month
27      void helpIncrement();           // utility function
28  };
29
30  #endif
```

Fig. 8.6   **Date** with overloaded increment operators—**date1.h**.

```cpp
31   // Fig. 8.6: date1.cpp
32   // Member function definitions for Date class
33   #include <iostream>
34   #include "date1.h"
35
36   // Initialize static member at file scope;
37   // one class-wide copy.
38   const int Date::days[] = { 0, 31, 28, 31, 30, 31, 30,
39                              31, 31, 30, 31, 30, 31 };
40
41   // Date constructor
42   Date::Date( int m, int d, int y ) { setDate( m, d, y ); }
43
44   // Set the date
45   void Date::setDate( int mm, int dd, int yy )
46   {
47      month = ( mm >= 1 && mm <= 12 ) ? mm : 1;
48      year = ( yy >= 1900 && yy <= 2100 ) ? yy : 1900;
49
50      // test for a leap year
51      if ( month == 2 && leapYear( year ) )
52         day = ( dd >= 1 && dd <= 29 ) ? dd : 1;
53      else
54         day = ( dd >= 1 && dd <= days[ month ] ) ? dd : 1;
55   }
56
57   // Preincrement operator overloaded as a member function.
58   Date &Date::operator++()
59   {
60      helpIncrement();
61      return *this;  // reference return to create an lvalue
62   }
63
64   // Postincrement operator overloaded as a member function.
65   // Note that the dummy integer parameter does not have a
66   // parameter name.
67   Date Date::operator++( int )
68   {
69      Date temp = *this;
70      helpIncrement();
71
72      // return non-incremented, saved, temporary object
73      return temp;    // value return; not a reference return
74   }
75
76   // Add a specific number of days to a date
77   const Date &Date::operator+=( int additionalDays )
78   {
79      for ( int i = 0; i < additionalDays; i++ )
80         helpIncrement();
81
82      return *this;    // enables cascading
83   }
```

Fig. 8.6   **Date** with overloaded increment operators—**date1.cpp** (part 1 of 2).

```
84
85   // If the year is a leap year, return true;
86   // otherwise, return false
87   bool Date::leapYear( int y ) const
88   {
89      if ( y % 400 == 0 || ( y % 100 != 0 && y % 4 == 0 ) )
90         return true;    // a leap year
91      else
92         return false;   // not a leap year
93   }
94
95   // Determine if the day is the end of the month
96   bool Date::endOfMonth( int d ) const
97   {
98      if ( month == 2 && leapYear( year ) )
99         return d == 29; // last day of Feb. in leap year
100     else
101        return d == days[ month ];
102  }
103
104  // Function to help increment the date
105  void Date::helpIncrement()
106  {
107     if ( endOfMonth( day ) && month == 12 ) {   // end year
108        day = 1;
109        month = 1;
110        ++year;
111     }
112     else if ( endOfMonth( day ) ) {             // end month
113        day = 1;
114        ++month;
115     }
116     else            // not end of month or year; increment day
117        ++day;
118  }
119
120  // Overloaded output operator
121  ostream &operator<<( ostream &output, const Date &d )
122  {
123     static char *monthName[ 13 ] = { "", "January",
124        "February", "March", "April", "May", "June",
125        "July", "August", "September", "October",
126        "November", "December" };
127
128     output << monthName[ d.month ] << ' '
129           << d.day << ", " << d.year;
130
131     return output;   // enables cascading
132  }
```

Fig. 8.6   **Date** with overloaded increment operators—**date1.cpp** (part 2 of 2).

Date's **public** interface includes an overloaded stream-insertion operator, a default
constructor, a **setDate** function, an overloaded preincrement operator, an overloaded

postincrement operator, an overloaded addition assignment operator (**+=**), a function to test for leap years and a function to determine if a day is the last day of the month.

The driver program in **main** creates the date objects **d1**, which is initialized by default to January 1, 1900; **d2**, which is initialized to December 27, 1992 and **d3**, which the program attempts to initialize to an invalid date. The **Date** constructor calls **setDate** to validate the month, day and year specified. If the month is invalid, it is set to 1. An invalid year is set to 1900. An invalid day is set to 1.

The driver program outputs each of the constructed **Date** objects using the overloaded stream-insertion operator. The overloaded operator **+=** is used to add seven days to **d2**. Then the **setDate** function is used to set **d3** to February 28, 1992. Next, a new **Date** object, **d4**, is set to March 18, 1969. Then **d4** is incremented by 1 with the overloaded preincrement operator. The date is printed before and after the preincrementing to confirm that it worked correctly. Finally, **d4** is incremented with the overloaded postincrement operator. The date is printed before and after the postincrementing to confirm that it worked correctly.

```
133  // Fig. 8.6: fig08_06.cpp
134  // Driver for class Date
135  #include <iostream>
136
137  using std::cout;
138  using std::endl;
139
140  #include "date1.h"
141
142  int main()
143  {
144     Date d1, d2( 12, 27, 1992 ), d3( 0, 99, 8045 );
145     cout << "d1 is " << d1
146          << "\nd2 is " << d2
147          << "\nd3 is " << d3 << "\n\n";
148
149     cout << "d2 += 7 is " << ( d2 += 7 ) << "\n\n";
150
151     d3.setDate( 2, 28, 1992 );
152     cout << "  d3 is " << d3;
153     cout << "\n++d3 is " << ++d3 << "\n\n";
154
155     Date d4( 3, 18, 1969 );
156
157     cout << "Testing the preincrement operator:\n"
158          << "  d4 is " << d4 << '\n';
159     cout << "++d4 is " << ++d4 << '\n';
160     cout << "  d4 is " << d4 << "\n\n";
161
162     cout << "Testing the postincrement operator:\n"
163          << "  d4 is " << d4 << '\n';
164     cout << "d4++ is " << d4++ << '\n';
165     cout << "  d4 is " << d4 << endl;
166
```

Fig. 8.6   **Date** with overloaded increment operators—**fig08_06.cpp** (part 1 of 2).

```
167       return 0;
168   }
```

```
d1 is January 1, 1900
d2 is December 27, 1992
d3 is January 1, 1900

d2 += 7 is January 3, 1993

  d3 is February 28, 1992
++d3 is February 29, 1992

Testing the preincrement operator:
  d4 is March 18, 1969
++d4 is March 19, 1969
  d4 is March 19, 1969

Testing the postincrement operator:
  d4 is March 19, 1969
d4++ is March 19, 1969
  d4 is March 20, 1969
```

Fig. 8.6   **Date** with overloaded increment operators—**fig08_06.cpp** (part 2 of 2).

Overloading the preincrementing operator is straightforward. The preincrementing operator calls **private** utility function **helpIncrement** to increment the date. This function deals with "wraparounds" or "carries" that occur when we increment the last day of the month. These carries require incrementing the month. If the month is already 12, then the year must also be incremented. Function **helpIncrement** uses functions **leap-Year** and **endOfMonth** to increment the day correctly.

The overloaded preincrement operator returns a reference to the current **Date** object (i.e., the one that was just incremented). This occurs because the current object, ***this**, is returned as a **Date &**.

Overloading the postincrement operator is a bit trickier. To emulate the effect of the postincrement, we must return an unincremented copy of the **Date** object. On entry to **operator++**, we save the current object (***this**) in **temp**. Next, we call **helpIncrement** to increment the current **Date** object. Then, we return the unincremented copy of the object previously stored in **temp**. Note that this function cannot return a reference to the local **Date** object **temp** because local variables are destroyed when the function in which they are declared is exited. Thus, declaring the return type to this function as **Date &** would return a reference to an object that no longer exists. Returning a reference to a local variable is a common error for which most compilers will issue a warning.

SUMMARY

• Operator **<<** is used for multiple purposes in C++—as the stream-insertion operator and as the left-shift operator. This is an example of operator overloading. Similarly, **>>** is also overloaded; it is used both as the stream-extraction operator and as the right-shift operator.

- C++ enables the programmer to overload most operators to be sensitive to the context in which they are used. The compiler generates the appropriate code based on the operator's use.
- Operator overloading contributes to C++'s extensibility.
- To overload an operator, write a function definition; the function name must be the keyword **operator** followed by the symbol for the operator being overloaded.
- To use an operator on class objects, that operator *must* be overloaded—with two exceptions. The assignment operator (**=**) may be used with two objects of the same class to perform a default memberwise copy without overloading. The address operator (**&**) may also be used with objects of any class without overloading; it returns the address of the object in memory.
- Operator overloading provides the same concise expressions for user-defined types that C++ provides with its rich collection of operators that work on built-in types.
- The precedence and associativity of an operator cannot be changed by overloading.
- It is not possible to change the number of operands an operator takes: Overloaded unary operators remain as unary operators; overloaded binary operators remain as binary operators. C++'s only ternary operator, **?:**, cannot be overloaded.
- It is not possible to create symbols for new operators; only existing operators may be overloaded.
- The meaning of how an operator works on built-in types cannot be changed by overloading.
- When overloading **()**, **[]**, **->** or any assignment operator, the operator overloading function must be declared as a class member.
- Operator functions can be member functions or non-member functions.
- When an operator function is implemented as a member function, the leftmost operand must be a class object (or a reference to a class object) of the operator's class.
- If the left operand must be an object of a different class, this operator function must be implemented as a non-member function.
- Operator member functions are called only when the left operand of a binary operator is an object of that class, or when the single operand of a unary operator is an object of that class.
- One might choose a non-member function to overload an operator in order to enable the operator to be commutative (i.e., given the proper overloaded operator definitions, the left argument of an operator can be an object of another data type).
- A unary operator can be overloaded as a non-**static** member function with no arguments or as a non-member function with one argument; that argument must be either an object of a user-defined type or a reference to an object of a user-defined type.
- A binary operator can be overloaded as a non-**static** member function with one argument, or as a non-member function with two arguments (one of those arguments must be either a class object or a reference to a class object).
- Array subscript operator **[]** is not restricted for use only with arrays; it can be used to select elements from other kinds of ordered container classes such as linked lists, strings, dictionaries etc. Also, subscripts no longer have to be integers; characters or strings could be used, for example.
- A copy constructor is used to initialize an object with another object of the same class. Copy constructors are also invoked whenever a copy of an object is needed, such as in call-by-value, and when returning a value from a called function. In a copy constructor, the object being copied must be passed in by reference.
- The compiler does not know how to convert between user-defined types and built-in types—the programmer must explicitly specify how such conversions are to occur. Such conversions can be performed with conversion constructors (i.e., single-argument constructors) that simply turn objects of other types into objects of a particular class.

- A conversion operator (or cast operator) can be used to convert an object of one class into an object of another class or into an object of a built-in type. Such a conversion operator must be a non-**static** member function; this kind of conversion operator cannot be a **friend** function.
- A conversion constructor is a single-argument constructor used to convert the argument into an object of the constructor's class. The compiler can call such a constructor implicitly.
- The assignment operator is the most frequently overloaded operator. It is normally used to assign an object to another object of the same class, but through the use of conversion constructors, it can also be used to assign between different classes.
- If an overloaded assignment operator is not defined, assignment is still allowed, but it defaults to a memberwise copy of each data member. In some cases this is acceptable. For objects that contain pointers to dynamically allocated storage, memberwise copy results in two different objects pointing to the same dynamically allocated storage. When the destructor for either of these objects is called, the dynamically allocated storage is released. If the other object then refers to that storage, the result is undefined.
- To overload the increment operator to allow both preincrement and postincrement usage, each overloaded operator function must have a distinct signature so the compiler will be able to determine which version of **++** is intended. The prefix versions are overloaded exactly as any other prefix unary operator. Providing a unique signature to the postincrement operator function is achieved by providing a second argument—which must be of type **int**. Actually, the user does not supply a value for this special integer argument. It is there simply to help the compiler distinguish between prefix and postfix versions of increment and decrement operators.

TERMINOLOGY

cascaded overloaded operators
cast operator function
class **Array**
class **Date**
class **HugeInteger**
class **PhoneNumber**
class **String**
conversion constructor
conversion function
conversion operator
conversions between built-in types and classes
conversions between class types
copy constructor
dangling pointer
default memberwise copy
explicit type conversions (with casts)
friend overloaded operator function
function call operator
implicit type conversions
member function overloaded operator
memory leak
non-overloadable operators
operator char *
operator int
operator keyword
operator overloading

operator!
operator!=
operator()
operator+
operator++
operator++(int)
operator+=
operator--
operator<
operator<<
operator<=
operator=
operator==
operator>
operator>=
operator>>
operator[]
operators implemented as functions
overloadable operators
overloaded **!=** operator
overloaded **+** operator
overloaded **++** operator
overloaded **+=** operator
overloaded **--** operator
overloaded **<** operator
overloaded **<<** operator

overloaded **<=** operator
overloaded **=** operator
overloaded **==** operator
overloaded **>** operator
overloaded **>=** operator
overloaded **>>** operator
overloaded assignment (**=**) operator
overloaded **[ ]** operator
overloading
overloading a binary operator

overloading a unary operator
postfix unary operator overloading
prefix unary operator overloading
self assignment
single-argument constructor
string concatenation
substring
user-defined conversion
user-defined type

COMMON PROGRAMMING ERRORS

8.1   Attempting to overload a nonoverloadable operator is a syntax error.

8.2   Attempting to create new operators via operator overloading is a syntax error.

8.3   Attempting to modify how an operator works with objects of built-in types is a syntax error.

8.4   Assuming that overloading an operator such as **+** overloads related operators such as **+=** or that overloading **==** overloads a related operator like **!=**. Operators can be overloaded only explicitly; there is no implicit overloading.

8.5   Attempting to change the "arity" of an operator via operator overloading is a syntax error.

8.6   Note that the copy constructor *must* use call-by-reference, not call-by-value. Otherwise, the copy constructor call results in infinite recursion (a fatal logic error) because, for call-by-value, a copy of the object passed to the copy constructor must be made, which results in the copy constructor being called recursively!

8.7   If the copy constructor simply copied the pointer in the source object to the target object's pointer, then both objects would point to the same dynamically allocated storage. The first destructor to execute would then delete the dynamically allocated storage, and the other object's **ptr** would then be undefined, a situation called a *"dangling pointer"* and likely to result in a serious run-time error.

8.8   Not providing an overloaded assignment operator and a copy constructor for a class when objects of that class contain pointers to dynamically allocated storage is a logic error.

GOOD PROGRAMMING PRACTICES

8.1   Use operator overloading when it makes a program clearer than accomplishing the same operations with explicit function calls.

8.2   Avoid excessive or inconsistent use of operator overloading as this can make a program cryptic and difficult to read.

8.3   Overload operators to perform the same function or similar functions on class objects as the operators perform on objects of built-in types. Avoid non-intuitive uses of operators.

8.4   Before writing C++ programs with overloaded operators, consult the manuals for your compiler to become aware of restrictions and requirements unique to particular operators.

8.5   To ensure consistency among related operators, use one to implement the others (i.e., use an overloaded **+** operator to implement an overloaded **+=** operator).

8.6   When overloading unary operators, it is preferable to make the operator functions class members instead of non-member **friend** functions. **friend** functions and **friend** classes should be avoided unless they are absolutely necessary. The use of **friend**s violates the encapsulation of a class.

PERFORMANCE TIPS

8.1 It is possible to overload an operator as a non-member, non-**friend** function, but such a function needing access to a class' **private** or **protected** data would need to use *set* or *get* functions provided in that class' **public** interface. The overhead of calling these functions could cause poor performance, so these functions can be **inline**d to improve performance.

8.2 Having the overloaded **+=** concatenation operator that takes a single argument of type **const char *** executes more efficiently than having to do the implicit conversion first, then the concatenation. Implicit conversions require less code and cause fewer errors.

SOFTWARE ENGINEERING OBSERVATIONS

8.1 Operator overloading contributes to C++'s extensibility, one of the language's most appealing attributes.

8.2 At least one argument of an operator function must be a class object or a reference to a class object. This prevents programmers from changing how operators work on built-in types.

8.3 New input/output capabilities for user-defined types can be added to C++ without modifying the declarations or **private** data members for either the **ostream** class or the **istream** class. This is another example of the extensibility of the C++ programming language.

8.4 A constructor, a destructor, an overloaded assignment operator and a copy constructor are usually provided as a group for any class that uses dynamically allocated memory.

8.5 It is possible to prevent one class object from being assigned to another. This is done by declaring the assignment operator as a **private** member of the class.

8.6 It is possible to prevent class objects from being copied; to do this, simply make both the overloaded assignment operator and the copy constructor **private**.

8.7 When a conversion constructor is used to perform an implicit conversion, C++ can only apply a single implicit constructor call to try to match the needs of another overloaded operator. It is not possible to match an overloaded operator's needs by performing a series of implicit, user-defined conversions.

8.8 By implementing member functions using previously defined member functions, the programmer reuses code to reduce the amount of code that must be written.

TESTING AND DEBUGGING TIP

8.1 Returning a **char** reference from an overloaded subscript operator in a **String** class is dangerous. For example, the client could use this reference to insert a null (**'\0'**) anywhere in the string.

SELF-REVIEW EXERCISES

8.1 Fill in the blanks in each of the following:
   a) Suppose **a** and **b** are integer variables and we form the sum **a + b**. Now suppose **c** and **d** are floating-point variables and we form the sum **c + d**. The two **+** operators here are clearly being used for different purposes. This is an example of _____.
   b) Keyword _____ introduces an overloaded operator function definition.
   c) To use operators on class objects, they must be overloaded, with the exception of the operators _____ and _____.
   d) The _____, _____ and _____ of an operator cannot be changed by overloading the operator.

8.2 Explain the multiple meanings of the operators **<<** and **>>** in C++.

8.3   In what context might the name **operator/** be used in C++?

8.4   (True/False) In C++, only existing operators can be overloaded.

8.5   How does the precedence of an overloaded operator in C++ compare with the precedence of the original operator?

ANSWERS TO SELF-REVIEW EXERCISES

8.1   a) operator overloading. b) **operator**. c) assignment (**=**), address(**&**). d) precedence, associativity, "arity."

8.2   Operator **>>** is both the right-shift operator and the stream-extraction operator depending, on its context. Operator **<<** is both the left-shift operator and the stream-insertion operator depending, on its context.

8.3   For operator overloading: It would be the name of a function that would provide an overloaded version of the **/** operator.

8.4   True.

8.5   Identical.

EXERCISES

8.6   Give as many examples as you can of operator overloading implicit in C++. Give a reasonable example of a situation in which you might want to overload an operator explicitly in C++.

8.7   The C++ operators that cannot be overloaded are _____, _____, _____, _____ and _____.

8.8   String concatenation requires two operands—the two strings that are to be concatenated. In the text we showed how to implement an overloaded concatenation operator that concatenates the second **String** object to the right of the first **String** object, thus modifying the first **String** object. In some applications, it is desirable to produce a concatenated **String** object without modifying the **String** arguments. Implement **operator+** to allow operations such as

```
string1 = string2 + string3;
```

8.9   *(Ultimate operator overloading exercise)* To appreciate the care that should go into selecting operators for overloading, list each of C++'s overloadable operators, and for each, list a possible meaning (or several, if appropriate) for each of several classes you have studied in this course. We suggest you try:
   a) Array
   b) Stack
   c) String

After doing this, comment on which operators seem to have meaning for a wide variety of classes. Which operators seem to be of little value for overloading? Which operators seem ambiguous?

8.10   Now work the process described in the previous problem in reverse. List each of C++'s overloadable operators. For each, list what you feel is perhaps the "ultimate operation" the operator should be used to represent. If there are several excellent operations, list them all.

8.11   *(Project)* C++ is an evolving language, and new languages are always being developed. What additional operators would you recommend adding to C++ or to a future language like C++ that would support both procedural programming and object-oriented programming? Write a careful justification. You might consider sending your suggestions to the ANSI C++ Committee or the newsgroup **comp.std.c++**.

8.12   One nice example of overloading the function call operator **()** is to allow the more common form of double-array subscripting. Instead of saying

```
chessBoard[ row ][ column ]
```

for an array of objects, overload the function call operator to allow the alternate form

```
chessBoard( row, column )
```

8.13   Create a class **DoubleSubscriptedArray** that has similar features to class **Array** in Fig. 8.4. At construction time, the class should be able to create an array of any number of rows and any number of columns. The class should supply **operator()** to perform double-subscripting operations. For example, in a 3-by-5 **DoubleSubscriptedArray** called **a**, the user could write **a(1, 3)** to access the element at row **1** and column **3**. Remember that **operator()** can receive any number of arguments (see class **String** in Fig. 18.5 for an example of **operator()**). The underlying representation of the double-subscripted array should be a single-subscripted array of integers with *rows * columns* number of elements. Function **operator()** should perform the proper pointer arithmetic to access each element of the array. There should be two versions of **operator()**—one that returns **int &** so an element of a **DoubleSubscriptedArray** can be used as an *lvalue* and one that returns **const int &** so an element of a **const DoubleSubscripted-Array** can be used as an *rvalue*. The class should also provide the following operators: **==, !=, =,** **<<** (for outputting the array in row and column format) and **>>** (for inputting the entire array contents).

8.14   Overload the subscript operator to return the largest element of a collection, the second largest, the third largest, etc.

8.15   Consider class **Complex** shown in Fig. 8.7. The class enables operations on so-called *complex numbers*. These are numbers of the form **realPart + imaginaryPart * i** where *i* has the value:

$$\sqrt{-1}$$

a) Modify the class to enable input and output of complex numbers through the overloaded **>>** and **<<** operators, respectively (you should remove the **print** function from the class).

b) Overload the multiplication operator to enable multiplication of two complex numbers as in algebra.

c) Overload the **==** and **!=** operators to allow comparisons of complex numbers.

```
1   // Fig. 8.7: complex1.h
2   // Definition of class Complex
3   #ifndef COMPLEX1_H
4   #define COMPLEX1_H
5
6   class Complex {
7   public:
8      Complex( double = 0.0, double = 0.0 );      // constructor
9      Complex operator+( const Complex & ) const;  // addition
10     Complex operator-( const Complex & ) const;  // subtraction
11     const Complex &operator=( const Complex & ); // assignment
12     void print() const;                          // output
```

Fig. 8.7   A complex number class—**complex1.h** (part 1 of 2).

```
13   private:
14      double real;          // real part
15      double imaginary;     // imaginary part
16   };
17
18   #endif
```

Fig. 8.7   A complex number class—`complex1.h` (part 2 of 2).

```
19   // Fig. 8.7: complex1.cpp
20   // Member function definitions for class Complex
21   #include <iostream>
22
23   using std::cout;
24
25   #include "complex1.h"
26
27   // Constructor
28   Complex::Complex( double r, double i )
29      : real( r ), imaginary( i ) { }
30
31   // Overloaded addition operator
32   Complex Complex::operator+( const Complex &operand2 ) const
33   {
34      return Complex( real + operand2.real,
35                      imaginary + operand2.imaginary );
36   }
37
38   // Overloaded subtraction operator
39   Complex Complex::operator-( const Complex &operand2 ) const
40   {
41      return Complex( real - operand2.real,
42                      imaginary - operand2.imaginary );
43   }
44
45   // Overloaded = operator
46   const Complex& Complex::operator=( const Complex &right )
47   {
48      real = right.real;
49      imaginary = right.imaginary;
50      return *this;   // enables cascading
51   }
52
53   // Display a Complex object in the form: (a, b)
54   void Complex::print() const
55      { cout << '(' << real << ", " << imaginary << ')'; }
```

Fig. 8.7   A complex number class—`complex1.cpp` .

```
56   // Fig. 8.7: fig08_07.cpp
57   // Driver for class Complex
```

Fig. 8.7   A complex number class—`fig08_07.cpp` (part 1 of 2).

```
58    #include <iostream>
59
60    using std::cout;
61    using std::endl;
62
63    #include "complex1.h"
64
65    int main()
66    {
67        Complex x, y( 4.3, 8.2 ), z( 3.3, 1.1 );
68
69        cout << "x: ";
70        x.print();
71        cout << "\ny: ";
72        y.print();
73        cout << "\nz: ";
74        z.print();
75
76        x = y + z;
77        cout << "\n\nx = y + z:\n";
78        x.print();
79        cout << " = ";
80        y.print();
81        cout << " + ";
82        z.print();
83
84        x = y - z;
85        cout << "\n\nx = y - z:\n";
86        x.print();
87        cout << " = ";
88        y.print();
89        cout << " - ";
90        z.print();
91        cout << endl;
92
93        return 0;
94    }
```

```
x: (0, 0)
y: (4.3, 8.2)
z: (3.3, 1.1)

x = y + z:
(7.6, 9.3) = (4.3, 8.2) + (3.3, 1.1)

x = y - z:
(1, 7.1) = (4.3, 8.2) - (3.3, 1.1)
```

Fig. 8.7   A complex number class—**fig08_07.cpp** (part 2 of 2).

8.16   A machine with 32-bit integers can represent integers in the range of approximately –2 billion to +2 billion. This fixed-size restriction is rarely troublesome. But there are applications in which we would like to be able to use a much wider range of integers. This is what C++ was built to do, namely create powerful new data types. Consider class **HugeInt** of Fig. 8.8. Study the class carefully, then

    a) Describe precisely how it operates.

    b) What restrictions does the class have?

    c) Overload the * multiplication operator.

    d) Overload the / division operator.

    e) Overload all the relational and equality operators.

```
1   // Fig. 8.8: hugeint1.h
2   // Definition for class HugeInt
3   #ifndef HUGEINT1_H
4   #define HUGEINT1_H
5
6   #include <iostream>
7
8   using std::ostream;
9
10  class HugeInt {
11     friend ostream &operator<<( ostream &, const HugeInt & );
12  public:
13     HugeInt( long = 0 );          // conversion/default constructor
14     HugeInt( const char * );           // conversion constructor
15     HugeInt operator+( const HugeInt & ); // add another HugeInt
16     HugeInt operator+( int );          // add an int
17     HugeInt operator+( const char * ); // add an int in a char *
18  private:
19     short integer[ 30 ];
20  };
21
22  #endif
```

Fig. 8.8   A huge integer class—**hugeint1.h** .

```
23  // Fig. 8.8: hugeint1.cpp
24  // Member and friend function definitions for class HugeInt
25  #include <cstring>
26  #include "hugeint1.h"
27
28  // Conversion constructor
29  HugeInt::HugeInt( long val )
30  {
31     int i;
32
33     for ( i = 0; i <= 29; i++ )
34        integer[ i ] = 0;   // initialize array to zero
35
36     for ( i = 29; val != 0 && i >= 0; i-- ) {
37        integer[ i ] = val % 10;
38        val /= 10;
39     }
40  }
```

Fig. 8.8   A huge integer class—**hugeint1.cpp** (part 1 of 3).

```
41
42   HugeInt::HugeInt( const char *string )
43   {
44      int i, j;
45
46      for ( i = 0; i <= 29; i++ )
47         integer[ i ] = 0;
48
49      for ( i = 30 - strlen( string ), j = 0; i <= 29; i++, j++ )
50         if ( isdigit( string[ j ] ) )
51            integer[ i ] = string[ j ] - '0';
52   }
53
54   // Addition
55   HugeInt HugeInt::operator+( const HugeInt &op2 )
56   {
57      HugeInt temp;
58      int carry = 0;
59
60      for ( int i = 29; i >= 0; i-- ) {
61         temp.integer[ i ] = integer[ i ] +
62                             op2.integer[ i ] + carry;
63
64         if ( temp.integer[ i ] > 9 ) {
65            temp.integer[ i ] %= 10;
66            carry = 1;
67         }
68         else
69            carry = 0;
70      }
71
72      return temp;
73   }
74
75   // Addition
76   HugeInt HugeInt::operator+( int op2 )
77      { return *this + HugeInt( op2 ); }
78
79   // Addition
80   HugeInt HugeInt::operator+( const char *op2 )
81      { return *this + HugeInt( op2 ); }
82
83   ostream& operator<<( ostream &output, const HugeInt &num )
84   {
85      int i;
86
87      for ( i = 0; ( num.integer[ i ] == 0 ) && ( i <= 29 ); i++ )
88         ; // skip leading zeros
89
90      if ( i == 30 )
91         output << 0;
92      else
```

Fig. 8.8   A huge integer class—**hugeint1.cpp** (part 2 of 3).

```
93        for ( ; i <= 29; i++ )
94            output << num.integer[ i ];
95
96    return output;
97  }
```

Fig. 8.8   A huge integer class—**hugeint1.cpp** (part 3 of 3).

```
98   // Fig. 8.8: fig08_08.cpp
99   // Test driver for HugeInt class
100  #include <iostream>
101
102  using std::cout;
103  using std::endl;
104
105  #include "hugeint1.h"
106
107  int main()
108  {
109     HugeInt n1( 7654321 ), n2( 7891234 ),
110            n3( "99999999999999999999999999999" ),
111            n4( "1" ), n5;
112
113     cout << "n1 is " << n1 << "\nn2 is " << n2
114         << "\nn3 is " << n3 << "\nn4 is " << n4
115         << "\nn5 is " << n5 << "\n\n";
116
117     n5 = n1 + n2;
118     cout << n1 << " + " << n2 << " = " << n5 << "\n\n";
119
120     cout << n3 << " + " << n4 << "\n= " << ( n3 + n4 )
121         << "\n\n";
122
123     n5 = n1 + 9;
124     cout << n1 << " + " << 9 << " = " << n5 << "\n\n";
125
126     n5 = n2 + "10000";
127     cout << n2 << " + " << "10000" << " = " << n5 << endl;
128
129     return 0;
130  }
```

```
n1 is 7654321
n2 is 7891234
n3 is 99999999999999999999999999999
n4 is 1
n5 is 0

7654321 + 7891234 = 15545555

99999999999999999999999999999 + 1
= 100000000000000000000000000000
```

Fig. 8.8   A huge integer class—**fig08_08.cpp** (part 1 of 2).

```
7654321 + 9 = 7654330

7891234 + 10000 = 7901234
```

Fig. 8.8   A huge integer class—`fig08_08.cpp` (part 2 of 2).

8.17   Create a class **RationalNumber** (fractions) with the following capabilities:
   a)   Create a constructor that prevents a 0 denominator in a fraction, reduces or simplifies
        fractions that are not in reduced form and avoids negative denominators.
   b)   Overload the addition, subtraction, multiplication and division operators for this class.
   c)   Overload the relational and equality operators for this class.

8.18   Study the C string-handling library functions and implement each of the functions as part of
the **String** class. Then, use these functions to perform text manipulations.

8.19   Develop class **Polynomial**. The internal representation of a **Polynomial** is an array of
terms. Each term contains a coefficient and an exponent. The term

$$2x^4$$

has a coefficient of 2 and an exponent of 4. Develop a full class containing proper constructor and
destructor functions as well as *set* and *get* functions. The class should also provide the following
overloaded operator capabilities:
   a)   Overload the addition operator (**+**) to add two **Polynomials**.
   b)   Overload the subtraction operator (**-**) to subtract two **Polynomials**.
   c)   Overload the assignment operator to assign one **Polynomial** to another.
   d)   Overload the multiplication operator (*****) to multiply two **Polynomials**.
   e)   Overload the addition assignment operator (**+=**), the subtraction assignment operator
        (**-=**), and the multiplication assignment operator (***=**).

8.20   The program of Fig. 8.3 contains the comment

```
// Overloaded stream-insertion operator (cannot be
// a member function if we would like to invoke it with
// cout << somePhoneNumber;)
```

Actually, it cannot be a member function of class **ostream**, but it can be a member function of
class **PhoneNumber** if we were willing to invoke it in either of the following ways:

```
somePhoneNumber.operator<<( cout );
```

or

```
somePhoneNumber << cout;
```

Rewrite the program of Fig. 8.3 with the overloaded stream-insertion **operator<<** as a member
function and try the two preceding statements in the program to prove that they work.

Inheritance

Objectives

- To be able to create new classes by inheriting from existing classes.
- To understand how inheritance promotes software reusability.
- To understand the notions of base classes and derived classes.
- To be able to use multiple inheritance to derive a class from several base classes.

Say not you know another entirely, till you have divided an inheritance with him.
Johann Kasper Lavater

This method is to define as the number of a class the class of all classes similar to the given class.
Bertrand Russell

A deck of cards was built like the purest of hierarchies, with every card a master to those below it, a lackey to those above it.
Ely Culbertson

Good as it is to inherit a library, it is better to collect one.
Augustine Birrell

Save base authority from others' books.
William Shakespeare, Love's Labours Lost

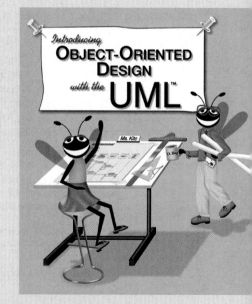

Outline

9.1 Introduction[1]

In this and the next chapter we discuss two of the most important capabilities of object-oriented programming—*inheritance* and *polymorphism*. Inheritance is a form of software reusability in which new classes are created from existing classes by absorbing their attributes and behaviors, and overriding or embellishing these with capabilities the new classes require. Software reusability saves time in program development. It encourages the reuse of proven and debugged high-quality software, thus reducing problems after a system becomes functional. These are exciting possibilities. Polymorphism enables us to write programs in a general fashion to handle a wide variety of existing and yet-to-be-specified related classes. Inheritance and polymorphism are effective techniques for managing software complexity.

When creating a new class, instead of writing completely new data members and member functions, the programmer can designate that the new class is to *inherit* the data members and member functions of a previously defined *base class*. The new class is referred to as a *derived class*. Each derived class itself becomes a candidate to be a base

---

1. Note: A number of the techniques described here and in Chapter 10 will be changing as the C++ community gradually begins adopting new techniques as specified in the C++ standard. We discuss the new techniques, such as run-time type identification (RTTI), in Chapter 21.

class for some future derived class. With *single inheritance,* a class is derived from one base class. With *multiple inheritance,* a derived class inherits from multiple (possibly unrelated) base classes. Single inheritance is straightforward—we show several examples that should enable the reader to become proficient quickly. Multiple inheritance is complex and error prone—we show only a simple example and issue a strong caution urging the reader to pursue further study before using this powerful capability.

A derived class can add data members and member functions of its own, so a derived class can be larger than its base class. A derived class is more specific than its base class and represents a smaller group of objects. With single inheritance, the derived class starts out essentially the same as the base class. The real strength of inheritance comes from the ability to define in the derived class additions, replacements or refinements to the features inherited from the base class.

C++ offers three kinds of inheritance—**public**, **protected** and **private**. In this chapter we concentrate on **public** inheritance and briefly explain the other two kinds. In Chapter 15 we show how **private** inheritance can be used as an alternate form of composition. The third form, **protected** inheritance, is a relatively recent addition to C++ and is rarely used. With **public** inheritance, every object of a derived class may also be treated as an object of that derived class' base class. However, the converse is not true—base-class objects are not objects of that base class' derived classes. We will take advantage of this "derived-class-object-is-a-base-class-object" relationship to perform some interesting manipulations. For example, we can thread a wide variety of different objects related through inheritance into a linked list of base-class objects. This allows a variety of objects to be processed in a general way. As we will see in the next chapter, this capability—called polymorphism—is a key thrust of object-oriented programming.

We add a new form of member access control in this chapter, namely **protected** access. Derived classes and their **friend**s can access **protected** base-class members, whereas non-**friend**, non-derived-class-member functions cannot.

Experience in building software systems indicates that significant portions of the code deal with closely related special cases. It becomes difficult in such systems to see the "big picture" because the designer and the programmer become preoccupied with the special cases. Object-oriented programming provides several ways of "seeing the forest through the trees"—a process called *abstraction.*

If a program is loaded with closely related special cases, then it is common to see **switch** statements that distinguish among the special cases and provide the processing logic to deal with each case individually. In Chapter 10, we show how to use inheritance and polymorphism to replace such **switch** logic with simpler logic.

We distinguish between *"is a" relationships* and *"has a" relationships.* "Is a" is inheritance. In an "is a" relationship, an object of a derived-class type may also be treated as an object of the base-class type. "Has a" is composition (see Fig. 7.4). In a "has a" relationship, a class object *has* one or more objects of other classes as members.

A derived class cannot access the **private** members of its base class; allowing this would violate the encapsulation of the base class. A derived class can, however, access the **public** and **protected** members of its base class. Base-class members that should not be accessible to a derived class via inheritance are declared **private** in the base class. A derived class can access **private** members of the base class only through access functions provided in the base class' **public** and **protected** interfaces.

One problem with inheritance is that a derived class can inherit **public** member function implementations that it does not need to have or should expressly not have. When a base-class member implementation is inappropriate for a derived class, that member can be overridden in the derived class with an appropriate implementation. In some cases, **public** inheritance is simply inappropriate.

Perhaps most exciting is the notion that new classes can inherit from existing *class libraries.* Organizations develop their own class libraries and take advantage of other libraries available worldwide. Eventually, software will be constructed predominantly from *standardized reusable components* just as hardware is often constructed today. This will help to meet the challenges of developing the ever more powerful software we will need in the future.

9.2 Inheritance: Base Classes and Derived Classes

Often an object of one class really "is an" object of another class as well. A rectangle certainly *is a* quadrilateral (as is a square, a parallelogram and a trapezoid). Thus, class **Rectangle** can be said to *inherit* from class **Quadrilateral**. In this context, class **Quadrilateral** is called a *base class* and class **Rectangle** is called a *derived class.* A rectangle *is a* specific type of quadrilateral, but it is incorrect to claim that a quadrilateral *is a* rectangle (the quadrilateral could, for example, be a parallelogram). Figure 9.1 shows several simple inheritance examples.

Other object-oriented programming languages such as Smalltalk and Java use different terminology: In inheritance, the base class is called the *superclass* (represents a superset of objects) and the derived class is called the *subclass* (represents a subset of objects). Because inheritance normally produces derived classes with *more* features than their base classes, the terms superclass and subclass can be confusing; we will avoid these terms. Because derived class objects may be thought of as objects of their base classes, this implies that more objects are associated with base classes and fewer objects are associated with derived classes, so it is reasonable to call base classes "superclasses" and derived classes "subclasses."

Base class	Derived classes
Student	GraduateStudent UndergraduateStudent
Shape	Circle Triangle Rectangle
Loan	CarLoan HomeImprovementLoan MortgageLoan
Employee	FacultyMember StaffMember
Account	CheckingAccount SavingsAccount

Fig. 9.1   Some simple inheritance examples.

Inheritance forms tree-like hierarchical structures. A base class exists in a hierarchical relationship with its derived classes. A class can certainly exist by itself, but it is when a class is used with the mechanism of inheritance that the class becomes either a base class that supplies attributes and behaviors to other classes, or the class becomes a derived class that inherits attributes and behaviors.

Let us develop a simple inheritance hierarchy. A typical university community has thousands of people who are community members. These people consist of employees, students and alumni. Employees are either faculty members or staff members. Faculty members are either administrators (such as deans and department chairpersons) or teaching faculty. This yields the inheritance hierarchy shown in Fig. 9.2. Note that some administrators also teach classes, so we have used multiple inheritance to form class **AdministratorTeacher**. Because students often work for their universities, and because employees often take courses, it would also be reasonable to use multiple inheritance to create a class called **EmployeeStudent**.

Another substantial inheritance hierarchy is the **Shape** hierarchy of Fig. 9.3. A common observation among students learning object-oriented programming is that there are abundant examples of hierarchies in the real world. It is just that these students are not accustomed to categorizing the real world in this manner, so it takes some adjustment in their thinking.

Let us consider the syntax for indicating inheritance. To specify that class **CommissionWorker** is derived from class **Employee**, class, **CommissionWorker** would typically be defined as follows:

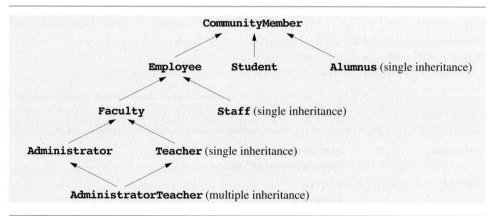

Fig. 9.2   An inheritance hierarchy for university community members.

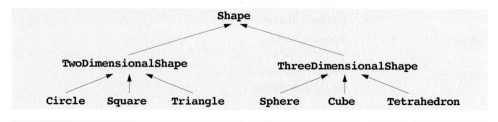

Fig. 9.3   A portion of a **Shape** class hierarchy.

```
class CommissionWorker : public Employee {
   ...
};
```

This is called **public** *inheritance* and is the most commonly used type of inheritance. We will also discuss **private** *inheritance* and **protected** *inheritance*. With **public** inheritance, the **public** and **protected** members of the base class are inherited as **public** and **protected** members of the derived class, respectively. Remember that **private** members of a base class are not accessible from that class' derived classes. Note that **friend** functions are not inherited.

It is possible to treat base-class objects and derived-class objects similarly; that commonality is expressed in the attributes and behaviors of the base class. Objects of any class derived with **public** inheritance from a common base class can all be treated as objects of that base class. We will consider many examples in which we can take advantage of this relationship with an ease of programming not available in non-object-oriented languages, such as C.

9.3 Protected Members

A base class' **public** members are accessible by all functions in the program. A base class' **private** members are accessible only by member functions and **friend**s of the base class.

We introduced **protected** access as an intermediate level of protection between **public** access and **private** access. A base class' **protected** members may be accessed only by members and **friend**s of the base class and by members and **friend**s of derived classes. Derived-class members can refer to **public** and **protected** members of the base class simply by using the member names. Note that **protected** data "breaks" encapsulation—a change to **protected** members of a base class may require modification of all derived classes.

Software Engineering Observation 9.1

*In general, declare data members of a class **private** and use **protected** only as a "last resort" when systems need to be tuned to meet unique performance requirements.*

9.4 Casting Base-Class Pointers to Derived-Class Pointers

An object of a publicly derived class can also be treated as an object of its corresponding base class. This makes possible some interesting manipulations. For example, despite the fact that objects of a variety of classes derived from a particular base class may be quite different from one another, we can still create a linked list of them—again, as long as we treat them as base-class objects. But the reverse is not true: A base-class object is not also automatically a derived-class object.

Common Programming Error 9.1

Treating a base-class object as a derived-class object can cause errors.

The programmer may, however, use an explicit cast to convert a base-class pointer to a derived-class pointer. This process is often called *downcasting a pointer*. But be careful— if such a pointer is to be dereferenced, then the programmer should be sure that the type of the pointer matches the type of the object to which it points. Our treatment in this section uses techniques widely available in most compilers. In Chapter 21, we revisit many of these topics in the context of the latest compilers that conform to recent features of the C++ standard, such as run-time type identification (RTTI), **dynamic_cast** and **typeid**.

Common Programming Error 9.2

Explicitly casting a base-class pointer that points to a base-class object into a derived-class pointer and then referring to derived-class members that do not exist in that object can lead to run-time logic errors.

Our first example is shown in Fig. 9.4. Lines 1 through 43 show the **Point** class definition and **Point** member function definitions. Lines 44 through 106 show the **Circle** class definition and **Circle** member function definitions. Lines 107 through 147 show a driver program in which we demonstrate assigning derived-class pointers to base-class pointers (often called *upcasting a pointer*) and casting base-class pointers to derived-class pointers.

```cpp
1   // Fig. 9.4: point.h
2   // Definition of class Point
3   #ifndef POINT_H
4   #define POINT_H
5
6   #include <iostream>
7
8   using std::ostream;
9
10  class Point {
11     friend ostream &operator<<( ostream &, const Point & );
12  public:
13     Point( int = 0, int = 0 );       // default constructor
14     void setPoint( int, int );       // set coordinates
15     int getX() const { return x; }   // get x coordinate
16     int getY() const { return y; }   // get y coordinate
17  protected:          // accessible by derived classes
18     int x, y;        // x and y coordinates of the Point
19  };
20
21  #endif
```

Fig. 9.4   Casting base-class pointers to derived-class pointers—**point.h** .

```cpp
22  // Fig. 9.4: point.cpp
23  // Member functions for class Point
24  #include <iostream>
25  #include "point.h"
26
27  // Constructor for class Point
28  Point::Point( int a, int b ) { setPoint( a, b ); }
29
```

Fig. 9.4   Casting base-class pointers to derived-class pointers—**point.cpp** (part 1 of 2).

```
30    // Set x and y coordinates of Point
31    void Point::setPoint( int a, int b )
32    {
33       x = a;
34       y = b;
35    }
36
37    // Output Point (with overloaded stream insertion operator)
38    ostream &operator<<( ostream &output, const Point &p )
39    {
40       output << '[' << p.x << ", " << p.y << ']';
41
42       return output;    // enables cascaded calls
43    }
```

Fig. 9.4   Casting base-class pointers to derived-class pointers—**point.cpp** (part 2 of 2).

```
44    // Fig. 9.4: circle.h
45    // Definition of class Circle
46    #ifndef CIRCLE_H
47    #define CIRCLE_H
48
49    #include <iostream>
50
51    using std::ostream;
52
53    #include <iomanip>
54
55    using std::ios;
56    using std::setiosflags;
57    using std::setprecision;
58
59    #include "point.h"
60
61    class Circle : public Point {   // Circle inherits from Point
62       friend ostream &operator<<( ostream &, const Circle & );
63    public:
64       // default constructor
65       Circle( double r = 0.0, int x = 0, int y = 0 );
66
67       void setRadius( double );    // set radius
68       double getRadius() const;    // return radius
69       double area() const;         // calculate area
70    protected:
71       double radius;
72    };
73
74    #endif
```

Fig. 9.4   Casting base-class pointers to derived-class pointers—**circle.h** .

```
75   // Fig. 9.4: circle.cpp
76   // Member function definitions for class Circle
77   #include "circle.h"
78
79   // Constructor for Circle calls constructor for Point
80   // with a member initializer then initializes radius.
81   Circle::Circle( double r, int a, int b )
82      : Point( a, b )        // call base-class constructor
83   { setRadius( r ); }
84
85   // Set radius of Circle
86   void Circle::setRadius( double r )
87      { radius = ( r >= 0 ? r : 0 ); }
88
89   // Get radius of Circle
90   double Circle::getRadius() const { return radius; }
91
92   // Calculate area of Circle
93   double Circle::area() const
94      { return 3.14159 * radius * radius; }
95
96   // Output a Circle in the form:
97   // Center = [x, y]; Radius = #.##
98   ostream &operator<<( ostream &output, const Circle &c )
99   {
100     output << "Center = " << static_cast< Point >( c )
101            << "; Radius = "
102            << setiosflags( ios::fixed | ios::showpoint )
103            << setprecision( 2 ) << c.radius;
104
105     return output;    // enables cascaded calls
106  }
```

Fig. 9.4   Casting base-class pointers to derived-class pointers—`circle.cpp`.

```
107  // Fig. 9.4: fig09_04.cpp
108  // Casting base-class pointers to derived-class pointers
109  #include <iostream>
110
111  using std::cout;
112  using std::endl;
113
114  #include <iomanip>
115
116  #include "point.h"
117  #include "circle.h"
118
119  int main()
120  {
121     Point *pointPtr = 0, p( 30, 50 );
122     Circle *circlePtr = 0, c( 2.7, 120, 89 );
```

Fig. 9.4   Casting base-class pointers to derived-class pointers—`fig09_04.cpp`
(part 1 of 2).

```
123
124    cout << "Point p: " << p << "\nCircle c: " << c << '\n';
125
126    // Treat a Circle as a Point (see only the base class part)
127    pointPtr = &c;    // assign address of Circle to pointPtr
128    cout << "\nCircle c (via *pointPtr): "
129         << *pointPtr << '\n';
130
131    // Treat a Circle as a Circle (with some casting)
132    // cast base-class pointer to derived-class pointer
133    circlePtr = static_cast< Circle * >( pointPtr );
134    cout << "\nCircle c (via *circlePtr):\n" << *circlePtr
135         << "\nArea of c (via circlePtr): "
136         << circlePtr->area() << '\n';
137
138    // DANGEROUS: Treat a Point as a Circle
139    pointPtr = &p;    // assign address of Point to pointPtr
140
141    // cast base-class pointer to derived-class pointer
142    circlePtr = static_cast< Circle * >( pointPtr );
143    cout << "\nPoint p (via *circlePtr):\n" << *circlePtr
144         << "\nArea of object circlePtr points to: "
145         << circlePtr->area() << endl;
146    return 0;
147 }
```

```
Point p: [30, 50]
Circle c: Center = [120, 89]; Radius = 2.70

Circle c (via *pointPtr): [120, 89]

Circle c (via *circlePtr):
Center = [120, 89]; Radius = 2.70
Area of c (via circlePtr): 22.90

Point p (via *circlePtr):
Center = [30, 50]; Radius = 0.00
Area of object circlePtr points to: 0.00
```

Fig. 9.4   Casting base-class pointers to derived-class pointers—`fig09_04.cpp`
(part 2 of 2).

Let us first examine the **Point** class definition. The **public** interface to **Point**
includes member functions **setPoint**, **getX** and **getY**. The data members **x** and **y** of
Point are specified as **protected**. This prevents clients of **Point** objects from directly
accessing the data, but enables classes derived from **Point** to access the inherited data
members directly. If the data were **private**, the **public** member functions of **Point**
would need to be used to access the data, even by derived classes. Note that the **Point**
overloaded stream-insertion operator function is able to reference variables **x** and **y** directly
because the overloaded stream-insertion operator function is a **friend** of class **Point**.
Note also that it is necessary to reference **x** and **y** through objects as in **p.x** and **p.y**. This
is because the overloaded stream-insertion operator function is not a member function of

the class **Point** so we must use an explicit handle so the compiler knows what object we are referencing. Note that this class offers inlined **public** member functions **getX** and **getY** so **operator<<** does not need to be a **friend** to achieve good performance. However, needed **public** member functions may not be provided in the **public** interface of every class, so friendship is often appropriate.

Class **Circle** inherits from class **Point** with **public** inheritance. This is specified in the first line of the class definition:

```
class Circle : public Point {  // Circle inherits from Point
```

The colon (**:**) in the header of the class definition indicates inheritance. The keyword **public** indicates the type of inheritance. (In Section 9.7 we will discuss **protected** and **private** inheritance.) All the **public** and **protected** members of class **Point** are inherited as **public** and **protected** members, respectively, into class **Circle**. This means that the **public** interface to **Circle** includes the **Point public** members as well as the **Circle public** members **area**, **setRadius** and **getRadius**.

The **Circle** constructor must invoke the **Point** constructor to initialize the **Point** base-class portion of a **Circle** object. This is accomplished with a member initializer (introduced in Chapter 7) as follows:

```
Circle::Circle( double r, int a, int b )
   : Point( a, b )        // call base-class constructor
```

The second line of the constructor function header invokes the **Point** constructor by name. Values **a** and **b** are passed from the **Circle** constructor to the **Point** constructor to initialize the base-class members **x** and **y**. If the **Circle** constructor did not invoke the **Point** constructor explicitly, the default **Point** constructor would be invoked implicitly with the default values for **x** and **y** (i.e., 0 and 0). If in this case the **Point** class did not provide a default constructor, the compiler would issue a syntax error. Note that the **Circle** overloaded **operator<<** function is able to output the **Point** part of the **Circle** by casting the **Circle** reference **c** to a **Point**. This results in a call to **operator<<** for **Point** and outputs the **x** and **y** coordinates using the proper **Point** formatting.

The driver program creates **pointPtr** as a pointer to a **Point** object and instantiates **Point** object **p**, then creates **circlePtr** as a pointer to a **Circle** object and instantiates **Circle** object **c**. The objects **p** and **c** are output using their overloaded stream-insertion operators to show that they were initialized correctly. Next, the driver assigns a derived-class pointer (the address of object **c**) to base-class pointer **pointPtr** and outputs the **Circle** object **c** using **operator<<** for **Point** and the dereferenced pointer ***pointPtr**. Note that only the **Point** portion of the **Circle** object **c** is displayed. With **public** inheritance, it is always valid to assign a derived-class pointer to a base-class pointer because a derived-class object *is a* base-class object. The base-class pointer "sees" only the base-class part of the derived-class object. The compiler performs an implicit conversion of the derived-class pointer to a base-class pointer.

Then, the driver program demonstrates casting **pointPtr** back to a **Circle ***. The result of the cast operation is assigned to **circlePtr**. The **Circle** object **c** is output using the overloaded stream-insertion operator for **Circle** and the dereferenced pointer ***circlePtr**. The area of **Circle** object **c** is output via **circlePtr**. This results in a valid area value because the pointers are always pointing to a **Circle** object.

A base-class pointer cannot be assigned directly to a derived-class pointer because this is an inherently dangerous assignment—derived-class pointers expect to be pointing to derived-class objects. The compiler does not perform an implicit conversion in this case. Using an explicit cast informs the compiler that the programmer knows this type of pointer conversion is dangerous—the programmer assumes responsibility for using the pointer appropriately, so the compiler is willing to allow the dangerous conversion.

Next, the driver assigns a base-class pointer (the address of object **p**) to base-class pointer **pointPtr** and casts **pointPtr** back to a **Circle ***. The result of the cast operation is assigned to **circlePtr**. **Point** object **p** is output using **operator<<** for **Circle** and the dereferenced pointer ***circlePtr**. Note the zero value output for the radius member (which actually does not exist because **circlePtr** is really aimed at a **Point** object). Outputting a **Point** as a **Circle** results in an undefined value (in this case it happens to be zero) for the **radius** because the pointers are always pointing to a **Point** object. A **Point** object does not have a **radius** member. Therefore, the program outputs whatever value happens to be in memory at the location that **circlePtr** expects the **radius** data member to be. The area of the object pointed to by **circlePtr** (**Point** object **p**) is also output via **circlePtr**. Note that the value for the area is 0.00 because this calculation is based on the "undefined" value of the **radius**. Obviously, accessing data members that are not there is dangerous. Calling member functions that do not exist can crash a program.

In this section we have shown the mechanics of pointer conversions. This material establishes the foundation we will need for our deeper treatment of object-oriented programming with polymorphism in the next chapter.

9.5 Using Member Functions

A derived class' member functions may need to access certain base class data members and member functions.

 Software Engineering Observation 9.2

A derived class cannot directly access **private** *members of its base class.*

This is a crucial aspect of software engineering in C++. If a derived class could access the base class' **private** members, this would violate the encapsulation of the base class. Hiding **private** members is a huge help in testing, debugging and correctly modifying systems. If a derived class could access its base class' **private** members, it would then be possible for classes derived from that derived class to access that data as well, and so on. This would propagate access to what is supposed to be **private** data, and the benefits of encapsulation would be lost throughout the class hierarchy.

9.6 Overriding Base-Class Members in a Derived Class

A derived class can override a base-class member function by supplying a new version of that function with the same signature (if the signature were different, this would be function overloading rather than function overriding). When that function is mentioned by name in the derived class, the derived-class version is automatically selected. The scope-resolution operator may be used to access the base-class version from the derived class.

Common Programming Error 9.3

When a base-class member function is overridden in a derived class, it is common to have the derived-class version call the base-class version and do some additional work. Not using the scope-resolution operator to reference the base class' member function causes infinite recursion because the derived-class member function actually calls itself. This will eventually cause the system to exhaust memory, a fatal execution-time error.

Consider a simplified class **Employee**. It stores the employee's **firstName** and **lastName**. This information is common to all employees including classes derived from class **Employee**. From class **Employee** now derive classes **HourlyWorker**, **PieceWorker**, **Boss** and **CommissionWorker**. The **HourlyWorker** gets paid by the hour with "time-and-a-half" for overtime hours in excess of 40 hours per week. The **PieceWorker** gets paid a fixed rate per item produced—for simplicity, assume this person makes only one type of item, so the **private** data members are number of items produced and rate per item. The **Boss** gets a fixed wage per week. The **CommissionWorker** gets a small fixed weekly base salary plus a fixed percentage of that person's gross sales for the week. For simplicity, we study only class **Employee** and derived class **HourlyWorker**.

Our next example is shown in Fig. 9.5. Lines 1 through 50 show the **Employee** class definition and **Employee** member function definitions. Lines 51 through 106 show the **HourlyWorker** class definition and **HourlyWorker** member function definition. Lines 107 through 117 show a driver program for the **Employee/HourlyWorker** inheritance hierarchy that simply instantiates an **HourlyWorker** object, initializes it and calls **HourlyWorker** member function **print** to output the object's data.

```
1   // Fig. 9.5: employ.h
2   // Definition of class Employee
3   #ifndef EMPLOY_H
4   #define EMPLOY_H
5
6   class Employee {
7   public:
8      Employee( const char *, const char * );  // constructor
9      void print() const;  // output first and last name
10     ~Employee();  // destructor
11  private:
12     char *firstName;  // dynamically allocated string
13     char *lastName;   // dynamically allocated string
14  };
15
16  #endif
```

Fig. 9.5   Overriding base-class members in a derived class—**employ.h**.

```
17  // Fig. 9.5: employ.cpp
18  // Member function definitions for class Employee
19  #include <iostream>
20
```

Fig. 9.5   Overriding base-class members in a derived class—**employ.cpp** (part 1 of 2).

```
21   using std::cout;
22
23   #include <cstring>
24   #include <cassert>
25   #include "employ.h"
26
27   // Constructor dynamically allocates space for the
28   // first and last name and uses strcpy to copy
29   // the first and last names into the object.
30   Employee::Employee( const char *first, const char *last )
31   {
32      firstName = new char[ strlen( first ) + 1 ];
33      assert( firstName != 0 ); // terminate if not allocated
34      strcpy( firstName, first );
35
36      lastName = new char[ strlen( last ) + 1 ];
37      assert( lastName != 0 );  // terminate if not allocated
38      strcpy( lastName, last );
39   }
40
41   // Output employee name
42   void Employee::print() const
43      { cout << firstName << ' ' << lastName; }
44
45   // Destructor deallocates dynamically allocated memory
46   Employee::~Employee()
47   {
48      delete [] firstName;   // reclaim dynamic memory
49      delete [] lastName;    // reclaim dynamic memory
50   }
```

Fig. 9.5   Overriding base-class members in a derived class—**employ.cpp** (part 2 of 2).

```
51   // Fig. 9.5: hourly.h
52   // Definition of class HourlyWorker
53   #ifndef HOURLY_H
54   #define HOURLY_H
55
56   #include "employ.h"
57
58   class HourlyWorker : public Employee {
59   public:
60      HourlyWorker( const char*, const char*, double, double );
61      double getPay() const;   // calculate and return salary
62      void print() const;      // overridden base-class print
63   private:
64      double wage;             // wage per hour
65      double hours;            // hours worked for week
66   };
67
68   #endif
```

Fig. 9.5   Overriding base-class members in a derived class—**hourly.h** .

```
69    // Fig. 9.5: hourly.cpp
70    // Member function definitions for class HourlyWorker
71    #include <iostream>
72
73    using std::cout;
74    using std::endl;
75
76    #include <iomanip>
77
78    using std::ios;
79    using std::setiosflags;
80    using std::setprecision;
81
82    #include "hourly.h"
83
84    // Constructor for class HourlyWorker
85    HourlyWorker::HourlyWorker( const char *first,
86                                const char *last,
87                                double initHours, double initWage )
88       : Employee( first, last )   // call base-class constructor
89    {
90       hours = initHours;   // should validate
91       wage = initWage;     // should validate
92    }
93
94    // Get the HourlyWorker's pay
95    double HourlyWorker::getPay() const { return wage * hours; }
96
97    // Print the HourlyWorker's name and pay
98    void HourlyWorker::print() const
99    {
100      cout << "HourlyWorker::print() is executing\n\n";
101      Employee::print();   // call base-class print function
102
103      cout << " is an hourly worker with pay of $"
104           << setiosflags( ios::fixed | ios::showpoint )
105           << setprecision( 2 ) << getPay() << endl;
106   }
```

Fig. 9.5   Overriding base-class members in a derived class—**hourly.cpp**.

```
107   // Fig. 9.5: fig09_05.cpp
108   // Overriding a base-class member function in a
109   // derived class.
110   #include "hourly.h"
111
112   int main()
113   {
114      HourlyWorker h( "Bob", "Smith", 40.0, 10.00 );
```

Fig. 9.5   Overriding base-class members in a derived class—**fig09_05.cpp** (part 1 of 2).

```
115      h.print();
116      return 0;
117  }
```

```
HourlyWorker::print() is executing

Bob Smith is an hourly worker with pay of $400.00
```

Fig. 9.5   Overriding base-class members in a derived class—`fig09_05.cpp` (part 2 of 2).

The **Employee** class definition consists of two private **char *** data members—**firstName** and **lastName**—and three member functions—a constructor, a destructor and **print**. The constructor function receives two strings and dynamically allocates character arrays to store the strings. Note that the **assert** macro (discussed in Chapter 18, "Other Topics") is used to determine if memory was allocated to **firstName** and **lastName**. If not, the program terminates with an error message indicating the condition tested, the line number on which the condition appears and the file in which the condition is located. [Note, once again, that in the C++ standard, **new** "throws" an exception if insufficient memory is available; we discuss this in Chapter 13.] Because the data of **Employee** are **private**, the only access to the data is through member function **print** which simply outputs the first name and last name of the employee. The destructor function returns the dynamically allocated memory to the system (to avoid a "memory leak").

Class **HourlyWorker** inherits from class **Employee** with **public** inheritance. Again, this is specified in the first line of the class definition using the colon (**:**) notation as follows:

```
class HourlyWorker : public Employee
```

The **public** interface to **HourlyWorker** includes the **Employee print** function and **HourlyWorker** member functions **getPay** and **print**. Note that class **HourlyWorker** defines its own **print** function with the same prototype as **Employee::print()**—this is an example of function overriding. Therefore, class **HourlyWorker** has access to two **print** functions. Class **HourlyWorker** also contains **private** data members **wage** and **hours** for calculating the employee's weekly salary.

The **HourlyWorker** constructor uses member initializer syntax to pass the strings **first** and **last** to the **Employee** constructor so the base-class members can be initialized, then initializes members **hours** and **wage**. Member function **getPay** calculates the salary of the **HourlyWorker**.

HourlyWorker member function **print** overrides the **Employee print** member function. Often, base-class member functions are overridden in a derived class to provide more functionality. The overridden functions sometimes call the base-class version of the function to perform part of the new task. In this example, the derived-class **print** function calls the base-class **print** function to output the employee's name (the base-class **print** is the only function with access to the **private** data of the base class). The derived-class **print** function also outputs the employee's pay. Note how the base-class version of **print** is called

```
Employee::print();
```

Because the base-class function and the derived-class function have the same name and signature, the base-class function must be preceded by its class name and the scope resolution operator. Otherwise, the derived-class version of the function would be called causing infinite recursion (i.e., the **HourlyWorker print** function would call itself).

9.7 **public**, **protected** and **private** Inheritance

When deriving a class from a base class, the base class may be inherited as **public**, **protected** or **private**. Use of **protected** and **private** inheritance is rare and each should be used only with great care; we normally use **public** inheritance in this book (Chapter 15 demonstrates **private** inheritance as another form of composition). Figure 9.6 summarizes for each type of inheritance the accessibility of base-class members in a derived class. The first column contains the base-class member-access specifiers.

When deriving a class from a **public** base class, **public** members of the base class become **public** members of the derived class and **protected** members of the base class become **protected** members of the derived class. A base class' **private** members are never directly accessible from a derived class, but can be accessed through calls to the **public** and **protected** members of the base class.

Base class member access specifier	Type of inheritance		
	public inheritance	**protected** inheritance	**private** inheritance
public	**public** in derived class. Can be accessed directly by any non-**static** member functions, **friend** functions and non-member functions.	**protected** in derived class. Can be accessed directly by all non-**static** member functions and **friend** functions.	**private** in derived class. Can be accessed directly by all non-**static** member functions and **friend** functions.
protected	**protected** in derived class. Can be accessed directly by all non-**static** member functions and **friend** functions.	**protected** in derived class. Can be accessed directly by all non-**static** member functions and **friend** functions.	**private** in derived class. Can be accessed directly by all non-**static** member functions and **friend** functions.
private	Hidden in derived class. Can be accessed by non-**static** member functions and **friend** functions through **public** or **protected** member functions of the base class.	Hidden in derived class. Can be accessed by non-**static** member functions and **friend** functions through **public** or **protected** member functions of the base class.	Hidden in derived class. Can be accessed by non-**static** member functions and **friend** functions through **public** or **protected** member functions of the base class.

Fig. 9.6   Summary of base-class member accessibility in a derived class.

When deriving from a **protected** base class, **public** and **protected** members of the base class become **protected** members of the derived class. When deriving from a **private** base class, **public** and **protected** members of the base class become **private** members (e.g., the functions become utility functions) of the derived class. **Private** and **protected** inheritance are not "is a" relationships.

9.8 Direct Base Classes and Indirect Base Classes

A base class may be a *direct base class* of a derived class, or a base class may be an *indirect base class* of a derived class. A direct base class of a derived class is explicitly listed in that derived class' header with the colon (**:**) notation when that derived class is declared. An indirect base class is not explicitly listed in the derived class' header; rather the indirect base class is inherited from two or more levels up the class hierarchy.

9.9 Using Constructors and Destructors in Derived Classes

Because a derived class inherits its base class' members, when an object of a derived class is instantiated, the base class' constructor must be called to initialize the base-class members of the derived-class object. A *base-class initializer* (which uses the member-initializer syntax we have seen) can be provided in the derived-class constructor to call the base-class constructor explicitly; otherwise, the derived class' constructor will call the base class' default constructor implicitly.

Base-class constructors and base-class assignment operators are not inherited by derived classes. Derived-class constructors and assignment operators, however, can call base-class constructors and assignment operators.

A derived-class constructor always calls the constructor for its base class first to initialize the derived class' base-class members. If the derived-class constructor is omitted, the derived class' default constructor calls the base-class' default constructor. Destructors are called in the reverse order of constructor calls, so a derived-class destructor is called before its base-class destructor.

Software Engineering Observation 9.3

Suppose we create an object of a derived class where both the base class and the derived class contain objects of other classes. When an object of that derived class is created, first the constructors for the base class' member objects execute, then the base-class constructor executes, then the constructors for the derived class' member objects execute, then the derived class' constructor executes. Destructors are called in the reverse of the order in which their corresponding constructors are called.

Software Engineering Observation 9.4

The order in which member objects are constructed is the order in which those objects are declared within the class definition. The order in which the member initializers are listed does not affect the order of construction.

Software Engineering Observation 9.5

In inheritance, base-class constructors are called in the order in which inheritance is specified in the derived-class definition. The order in which the base-class constructors are specified in the derived-class member initializer list does not affect the order of construction.

Figure 9.7 demonstrates the order in which base-class and derived-class constructors and destructors are called. Lines 1 through 39 show a simple **Point** class containing a constructor, a destructor and **protected** data members **x** and **y**. The constructor and destructor both print the **Point** object for which they are invoked.

```
1   // Fig. 9.7: point2.h
2   // Definition of class Point
3   #ifndef POINT2_H
4   #define POINT2_H
5
6   class Point {
7   public:
8      Point( int = 0, int = 0 );  // default constructor
9      ~Point();      // destructor
10  protected:        // accessible by derived classes
11     int x, y;      // x and y coordinates of Point
12  };
13
14  #endif
```

Fig. 9.7   Order in which base-class and derived-class constructors and destructors are called—**point2.h** .

```
15  // Fig. 9.7: point2.cpp
16  // Member function definitions for class Point
17  #include <iostream>
18
19  using std::cout;
20  using std::endl;
21
22  #include "point2.h"
23
24  // Constructor for class Point
25  Point::Point( int a, int b )
26  {
27     x = a;
28     y = b;
29
30     cout << "Point   constructor: "
31          << '[' << x << ", " << y << ']' << endl;
32  }
33
34  // Destructor for class Point
35  Point::~Point()
36  {
37     cout << "Point   destructor:   "
38          << '[' << x << ", " << y << ']' << endl;
39  }
```

Fig. 9.7   Order in which base-class and derived-class constructors and destructors are called—**point2.cpp** .

```
40   // Fig. 9.7: circle2.h
41   // Definition of class Circle
42   #ifndef CIRCLE2_H
43   #define CIRCLE2_H
44
45   #include "point2.h"
46
47   class Circle : public Point {
48   public:
49      // default constructor
50      Circle( double r = 0.0, int x = 0, int y = 0 );
51
52      ~Circle();
53   private:
54      double radius;
55   };
56
57   #endif
```

Fig. 9.7 Order in which base-class and derived-class constructors and destructors are called—`circle2.h`.

```
58   // Fig. 9.7: circle2.cpp
59   // Member function definitions for class Circle
60   #include <iostream>
61
62   using std::cout;
63   using std::endl;
64
65   #include "circle2.h"
66
67   // Constructor for Circle calls constructor for Point
68   Circle::Circle( double r, int a, int b )
69      : Point( a, b )   // call base-class constructor
70   {
71      radius = r;  // should validate
72      cout << "Circle constructor: radius is "
73           << radius << " [" << x << ", " << y << ']' << endl;
74   }
75
76   // Destructor for class Circle
77   Circle::~Circle()
78   {
79      cout << "Circle destructor:  radius is "
80           << radius << " [" << x << ", " << y << ']' << endl;
81   }
```

Fig. 9.7 Order in which base-class and derived-class constructors and destructors are called—`circle2.cpp`.

```
82   // Fig. 9.7: fig09_07.cpp
83   // Demonstrate when base-class and derived-class
84   // constructors and destructors are called.
85   #include <iostream>
86
87   using std::cout;
88   using std::endl;
89
90   #include "point2.h"
91   #include "circle2.h"
92
93   int main()
94   {
95      // Show constructor and destructor calls for Point
96      {
97         Point p( 11, 22 );
98      }
99
100     cout << endl;
101     Circle circle1( 4.5, 72, 29 );
102     cout << endl;
103     Circle circle2( 10, 5, 5 );
104     cout << endl;
105     return 0;
106  }
```

```
Point   constructor: [11, 22]
Point   destructor:  [11, 22]

Point   constructor: [72, 29]
Circle constructor: radius is 4.5 [72, 29]

Point   constructor: [5, 5]
Circle constructor: radius is 10 [5, 5]

Circle destructor:  radius is 10 [5, 5]
Point   destructor:  [5, 5]
Circle destructor:  radius is 4.5 [72, 29]
Point   destructor:  [72, 29]
```

Fig. 9.7   Order in which base-class and derived-class constructors and destructors are called—**fig09_07.cpp** .

Lines 40 through 81 show a simple **Circle** class derived from **Point** with **public** inheritance. Class **Circle** provides a constructor, a destructor and a **private** data member **radius**. The constructor and destructor both print the **Circle** object for which they are invoked. The **Circle** constructor also invokes the **Point** constructor using member initializer syntax and passes the values **a** and **b** so the base-class data members **x** and **y** can be initialized.

Lines 82 through 106 are the driver program for this **Point/Circle** hierarchy. The program begins by instantiating a **Point** object in a scope inside **main**. The object goes in and out of scope immediately, so the **Point** constructor and destructor are both called. Next, the program instantiates **Circle** object **circle1**. This invokes the **Point** constructor to perform output with values passed from the **Circle** constructor, then performs the output specified in the **Circle** constructor. **Circle** object **circle2** is instantiated next. Again, the **Point** and **Circle** constructors are both called. Note that the body of the **Point** constructor is performed before the body of the **Circle** constructor. The end of **main** is reached, so the destructors are called for objects **circle1** and **circle2**. Destructors are called in the reverse order of their corresponding constructors. Therefore, the **Circle** destructor and **Point** destructor are called in that order for object **circle2**, then the **Circle** and **Point** destructors are called in that order for object **circle1**.

9.10 Implicit Derived-Class Object to Base-Class Object Conversion

Despite the fact that a derived-class object also "is a" base-class object, the derived-class type and the base-class type are different. Under **public** inheritance, derived-class objects can be treated as base-class objects. This makes sense because the derived class has members corresponding to each of the base-class members—remember that the derived class can have more members than the base class. Assignment in the other direction is not allowed because assigning a base-class object to a derived-class object would leave the additional derived-class members undefined. Although such assignment is not "naturally" allowed, it could be made legitimate by providing a properly overloaded assignment operator and/or conversion constructor (see Chapter 8). Note that what we say about pointers in the remainder of this section also applies to references.

Common Programming Error 9.4

Assigning a derived-class object to an object of a corresponding base class, then attempting to reference derived-class-only members in the new base-class object is a syntax error.

With **public** inheritance, a pointer to a derived-class object may be implicitly converted into a pointer to a base-class object, because a derived-class object is a base-class object.

There are four possible ways to mix and match base-class pointers and derived-class pointers with base-class objects and derived-class objects:

1. Referring to a base-class object with a base-class pointer is straightforward.

2. Referring to a derived-class object with a derived-class pointer is straightforward.

3. Referring to a derived-class object with a base-class pointer is safe because the derived-class object is an object of its base class as well. Such code can only refer to base-class members. If this code refers to derived-class-only members through the base-class pointer, the compiler will report a syntax error.

4. Referring to a base-class object with a derived-class pointer is a syntax error. The derived-class pointer must first be cast to a base-class pointer.

Common Programming Error 9.5

Casting a base-class pointer to a derived-class pointer can cause errors if that pointer is then used to reference a base-class object that does not have the desired derived-class members.

As convenient as it may be to treat derived-class objects as base-class objects, and to do this by manipulating all these objects with base-class pointers, there is a problem. In a payroll system, for example, we would like to be able to walk through a linked list of employees and calculate the weekly pay for each person. But using base-class pointers enables the program to call only the base-class payroll calculation routine (if indeed there were such a routine in the base class). We need a way to invoke the proper payroll calculation routine for each object, whether it is a base-class object or a derived-class object, and to do this simply by using the base-class pointer. The solution is to use **virtual** functions and polymorphism, as will be discussed in Chapter 10.

9.11 Software Engineering with Inheritance

We can use inheritance to customize existing software. We inherit the attributes and behaviors of an existing class, then add attributes and behaviors (or override base-class behaviors) to customize the class to meet our needs. This is done in C++ without the derived class having access to the base class' source code, but the derived class does need to be able to link to the base class' object code. This powerful capability is attractive to independent software vendors (ISVs). The ISVs can develop proprietary classes for sale or license and make these classes available to users in object-code format. Users can then derive new classes from these library classes rapidly and without accessing the ISVs' proprietary source code. All the ISVs need to supply with the object code are the header files.

Software Engineering Observation 9.6

In theory, users do not need to see the source code of classes from which they inherit. In practice, people who license classes tell us that the customers often demand the source code. Programmers still seem reluctant to incorporate code into their programs when this code has been written by other people.

Performance Tip 9.1

When performance is a major concern, programmers may want to see source code of classes they are inheriting from so they can tune the code to meet their performance requirements.

It can be difficult for students to appreciate the problems faced by designers and implementors on large-scale software projects. People experienced on such projects will invariably state that a key to improving the software development process is software reuse. Object-oriented programming in general, and C++ in particular, certainly do this.

The availability of substantial and useful class libraries delivers the maximum benefits of software reuse through inheritance. As interest in C++ grows, interest in class libraries is growing exponentially. Just as shrink-wrapped software produced by independent software vendors became an explosive growth industry with the arrival of the personal computer, so, too, is the creation and sale of class libraries. Application designers build their applications with these libraries, and library designers are being rewarded by having their libraries wrapped with the applications. Libraries currently being shipped with C++ compilers tend to be rather general-purpose and limited in scope. What is coming is a massive worldwide commitment to the development of class libraries for a huge variety of applications arenas.

Software Engineering Observation 9.7

Creating a derived class does not affect its base class' source code or object code; the integrity of a base class is preserved by inheritance.

A base class specifies commonality—all classes derived from a base class inherit the capabilities of that base class. In the object-oriented design process, the designer looks for commonality and "factors it out" to form desirable base classes. Derived classes are then customized beyond the capabilities inherited from the base class.

Software Engineering Observation 9.8

In an object-oriented system, classes are often closely related. "Factor out" common attributes and behaviors and place these in a base class. Then use inheritance to form derived classes.

Just as the designer of non-object-oriented systems seeks to avoid unnecessary proliferation of functions, the designer of object-oriented systems should avoid unnecessary proliferation of classes. Such a proliferation of classes creates management problems and can hinder software reusability simply because it is more difficult for a potential reuser of a class to locate that class in a huge collection. The trade-off is to create fewer classes, each providing substantial additional functionality. Such classes might be too rich for certain reusers; they can mask the excessive functionality, thus "toning down" the classes to meet their needs.

Performance Tip 9.2

If classes produced through inheritance are larger than they need to be, memory and processing resources may be wasted. Inherit from the class "closest" to what you need.

Note that reading a set of derived-class declarations can be confusing because inherited members are not shown, but they are nevertheless present in the derived classes. A similar problem can exist in the documentation of derived classes.

Software Engineering Observation 9.9

A derived class contains the attributes and behaviors of its base class. A derived class can also contain additional attributes and behaviors. With inheritance, the base class can be compiled independently of the derived class. Only the derived class' incremental attributes and behaviors need to be compiled to be able to combine these with the base class to form the derived class.

Software Engineering Observation 9.10

Modifications to a base class do not require derived classes to change as long as the **public** *and* **protected** *interfaces to the base class remain unchanged. Derived classes may, however, need to be recompiled.*

9.12 Composition vs. Inheritance

We have discussed *is a* relationships, which are supported by **public** inheritance. We have also discussed *has a* relationships (and seen examples in preceding chapters) in which a class may have other classes as members—such relationships create new classes by *composition* of existing classes. For example, given the classes **Employee**, **BirthDate** and **TelephoneNumber**, it is improper to say that an **Employee** *is a* **BirthDate** or that an **Employee** *is a* **TelephoneNumber**. But it is certainly appropriate to say that an **Employee** *has a* **BirthDate** and that an **Employee** *has a* **TelephoneNumber**.

Software Engineering Observation 9.11

Program modifications to a class that is a member of another class do not require the enclosing class to change as long as the **public** *interface to the member class remains unchanged. Note that the composite class may, however, need to be recompiled.*

9.13 "Uses A" and "Knows A" Relationships

Inheritance and composition each encourage software reuse by creating new classes that have much in common with existing classes. There are other ways to use the services of classes. Although a person object is not a car and a person object does not contain a car, a person object certainly *uses a* car. A function uses an object simply by calling a non-**private** member function of that object using a pointer, reference or the object name itself.

An object can be *aware of* another object. Knowledge networks frequently have such relationships. One object can contain a pointer handle or a reference handle to another object to be aware of that object. In this case, one object is said to have a *knows a* relationship with the other object; this is sometimes called an *association*.

9.14 Case Study: Point, Circle, Cylinder

Now let us consider the capstone exercise for this chapter. We consider a point, circle, cylinder hierarchy. First we develop and use class **Point** (Fig. 9.8). Then we present an example in which we derive class **Circle** from class **Point** (Fig. 9.9). Finally, we present an example in which we derive class **Cylinder** from class **Circle** (Fig. 9.10).

Figure 9.8 shows class **Point**. Lines 1 through 42 are the class **Point** header file and implementation file. Note that **Point**'s data members are **protected**. Thus, when class **Circle** is derived from class **Point**, the member functions of class **Circle** will be able to directly reference coordinates **x** and **y** rather than using access functions. This may result in better performance.

Lines 43 through 64 are the driver program for class **Point**. Note that **main** must use the access functions **getX** and **getY** to read the values of **protected** data members **x** and **y**; remember that **protected** data members are accessible only to members and **friend**s of their class and members and **friend**s of their derived classes.\

```
1   // Fig. 9.8: point2.h
2   // Definition of class Point
3   #ifndef POINT2_H
4   #define POINT2_H
5
6   #include <iostream>
7
8   using std::ostream;
9
10  class Point {
11     friend ostream &operator<<( ostream &, const Point & );
12  public:
13     Point( int = 0, int = 0 );      // default constructor
14     void setPoint( int, int );      // set coordinates
15     int getX() const { return x; }  // get x coordinate
16     int getY() const { return y; }  // get y coordinate
17  protected:            // accessible to derived classes
18     int x, y;          // coordinates of the point
19  };
20
21  #endif
```

Fig. 9.8   Demonstrating class **Point**—**point2.h**.

```
22   // Fig. 9.8: point2.cpp
23   // Member functions for class Point
24   #include "point2.h"
25
26   // Constructor for class Point
27   Point::Point( int a, int b ) { setPoint( a, b ); }
28
29   // Set the x and y coordinates
30   void Point::setPoint( int a, int b )
31   {
32      x = a;
33      y = b;
34   }
35
36   // Output the Point
37   ostream &operator<<( ostream &output, const Point &p )
38   {
39      output << '[' << p.x << ", " << p.y << ']';
40
41      return output;              // enables cascading
42   }
```

Fig. 9.8   Demonstrating class **Point**—**point2.cpp** .

```
43   // Fig. 9.8: fig09_08.cpp
44   // Driver for class Point
45   #include <iostream>
46
47   using std::cout;
48   using std::endl;
49
50   #include "point2.h"
51
52   int main()
53   {
54      Point p( 72, 115 );    // instantiate Point object p
55
56      // protected data of Point inaccessible to main
57      cout << "X coordinate is " << p.getX()
58           << "\nY coordinate is " << p.getY();
59
60      p.setPoint( 10, 10 );
61      cout << "\n\nThe new location of p is " << p << endl;
62
63      return 0;
64   }
```

```
X coordinate is 72
Y coordinate is 115

The new location of p is [10, 10]
```

Fig. 9.8   Demonstrating class **Point**—**fig09_08.cpp** .

Our next example is shown in Fig. 9.9. The **Point** class definition and the member function definitions from Fig. 9.8 are reused here. Lines 1 through 62 show the **Circle** class definition and **Circle** member function definitions. Lines 63 through 90 are the driver program for class **Circle**. Note that class **Circle** inherits from class **Point** with **public** inheritance. This means that the **public** interface to **Circle** includes the **Point** member functions as well as the **Circle** member functions **setRadius**, **getRadius** and **area**.

```
1   // Fig. 9.9: circle2.h
2   // Definition of class Circle
3   #ifndef CIRCLE2_H
4   #define CIRCLE2_H
5
6   #include <iostream>
7
8   using std::ostream;
9
10  #include "point2.h"
11
12  class Circle : public Point {
13     friend ostream &operator<<( ostream &, const Circle & );
14  public:
15     // default constructor
16     Circle( double r = 0.0, int x = 0, int y = 0 );
17     void setRadius( double );       // set radius
18     double getRadius() const;       // return radius
19     double area() const;            // calculate area
20  protected:              // accessible to derived classes
21     double radius;       // radius of the Circle
22  };
23
24  #endif
```

Fig. 9.9   Demonstrating class **Circle—circle2.h**.

```
25  // Fig. 9.9: circle2.cpp
26  // Member function definitions for class Circle
27  #include <iomanip>
28
29  using std::ios;
30  using std::setiosflags;
31  using std::setprecision;
32
33  #include "circle2.h"
34
35  // Constructor for Circle calls constructor for Point
36  // with a member initializer and initializes radius
37  Circle::Circle( double r, int a, int b )
38     : Point( a, b )         // call base-class constructor
39  { setRadius( r ); }
```

Fig. 9.9   Demonstrating class **Circle—circle2.cpp** (part 1 of 2).

```
40
41   // Set radius
42   void Circle::setRadius( double r )
43      { radius = ( r >= 0 ? r : 0 ); }
44
45   // Get radius
46   double Circle::getRadius() const { return radius; }
47
48   // Calculate area of Circle
49   double Circle::area() const
50      { return 3.14159 * radius * radius; }
51
52   // Output a circle in the form:
53   // Center = [x, y]; Radius = #.##
54   ostream &operator<<( ostream &output, const Circle &c )
55   {
56      output << "Center = " << static_cast< Point > ( c )
57             << "; Radius = "
58             << setiosflags( ios::fixed | ios::showpoint )
59             << setprecision( 2 ) << c.radius;
60
61      return output;    // enables cascaded calls
62   }
```

Fig. 9.9   Demonstrating class **Circle**—**circle2.cpp** (part 2 of 2).

```
63   // Fig. 9.9: fig09_09.cpp
64   // Driver for class Circle
65   #include <iostream>
66
67   using std::cout;
68   using std::endl;
69
70   #include "point2.h"
71   #include "circle2.h"
72
73   int main()
74   {
75      Circle c( 2.5, 37, 43 );
76
77      cout << "X coordinate is " << c.getX()
78           << "\nY coordinate is " << c.getY()
79           << "\nRadius is " << c.getRadius();
80
81      c.setRadius( 4.25 );
82      c.setPoint( 2, 2 );
83      cout << "\n\nThe new location and radius of c are\n"
84           << c << "\nArea " << c.area() << '\n';
85
```

Fig. 9.9   Demonstrating class **Circle**—**fig09_09.cpp** (part 1 of 2).

```
86        Point &pRef = c;
87        cout << "\nCircle printed as a Point is: " << pRef << endl;
88
89        return 0;
90  }
```

```
X coordinate is 37
Y coordinate is 43
Radius is 2.5

The new location and radius of c are
Center = [2, 2]; Radius = 4.25
Area 56.74

Circle printed as a Point is: [2, 2]
```

Fig. 9.9   Demonstrating class **Circle**—**fig09_09.cpp** (part 2 of 2).

Note that the **Circle** overloaded **operator<<** function which, is a **friend** of class **Circle** is able to output the **Point** part of the **Circle** by casting the **Circle** reference **c** to a **Point**. This results in a call to **operator<<** for **Point** and outputs the **x** and **y** coordinates using the proper **Point** formatting.

The driver program instantiates an object of class **Circle** then uses *get* functions to obtain the information about the **Circle** object. Again, **main** is neither a member function nor a **friend** of class **Circle** so it cannot directly reference the **protected** data of class **Circle**. The driver program then uses *set* functions **setRadius** and **set-Point** to reset the radius and coordinates of the center of the circle. Finally, the driver initializes reference variable **pRef** of type "reference to **Point** object" (**Point &**) to **Circle** object **c**. The driver then prints **pRef**, which, despite the fact that it is initialized with a **Circle** object, "thinks" it is a **Point** object, so the **Circle** object actually prints as a **Point** object.

Our last example is shown in Fig. 9.10. The **Point** class and **Circle** class definitions, and their member function definitions from Fig. 9.8 and Fig. 9.9 are reused here. Lines 1 through 65 show the **Cylinder** class definition and **Cylinder** member function definitions. Lines 66 through 109 are the driver program for class **Cylinder**. Note that class **Cylinder** inherits from class **Circle** with **public** inheritance. This means that the **public** interface to **Cylinder** includes the **Circle** member functions and **Point** member functions as well as the **Cylinder** member functions **setHeight**, **getH-eight**, **area** (overridden from **Circle**) and **volume**. Note that the **Cylinder** constructor is required to invoke the constructor for its direct base class **Circle**, but not for its indirect base class **Point**. Each derived class constructor is only responsible for calling the constructors of that class' immediate base class (or classes, in the case of multiple inheritance). Also, note that the **Cylinder** overloaded **operator<<** function, which is a **friend** of class **Cylinder** is able to output the **Circle** part of the **Cylinder** by casting the **Cylinder** reference **c** to a **Circle**. This results in a call to **operator<<** for **Circle** and outputs the **x** and **y** coordinates and the **radius** using the proper **Circle** formatting.

The driver program instantiates an object of class **Cylinder** then uses *get* functions to obtain the information about the **Cylinder** object. Again, **main** is neither a member function nor a **friend** of class **Cylinder** so it cannot directly reference the **protected** data of class **Cylinder**. The driver program then uses *set* functions **setHeight**, **setRadius** and **setPoint** to reset the height, radius and coordinates of the cylinder. Finally, the driver initializes reference variable **pRef** of type "reference to **Point** object" (**Point &**) to **Cylinder** object **cyl**. It then prints **pRef**, which, despite the fact that it is initialized with a **Cylinder** object, "thinks" it is a **Point** object, so the **Cylinder** object actually prints as a **Point** object. The driver then initializes reference variable **circleRef** of type "reference to **Circle** object" (**Circle &**) to **Cylinder** object **cyl**. The driver program then prints **circleRef**, which, despite the fact that it is initialized with a **Cylinder** object, "thinks" it is a **Circle** object, so the **Cylinder** object actually prints as a **Circle** object. The area of the **Circle** is also output.

This example nicely demonstrates **public** inheritance and defining and referencing **protected** data members. The reader should now be confident with the basics of inheritance. In the next chapter, we show how to program with inheritance hierarchies in a general manner using polymorphism. Data abstraction, inheritance and polymorphism are the crux of object-oriented programming.

```cpp
1    // Fig. 9.10: cylindr2.h
2    // Definition of class Cylinder
3    #ifndef CYLINDR2_H
4    #define CYLINDR2_H
5
6    #include <iostream>
7
8    using std::ostream;
9
10   #include "circle2.h"
11
12   class Cylinder : public Circle {
13      friend ostream &operator<<( ostream &, const Cylinder & );
14
15   public:
16      // default constructor
17      Cylinder( double h = 0.0, double r = 0.0,
18                int x = 0, int y = 0 );
19
20      void setHeight( double );      // set height
21      double getHeight() const;      // return height
22      double area() const;           // calculate and return area
23      double volume() const;         // calculate and return volume
24
25   protected:
26      double height;                 // height of the Cylinder
27   };
28
29   #endif
```

Fig. 9.10   Demonstrating class **Cylinder**—**cylindr2.h**.

```
30   // Fig. 9.10: cylindr2.cpp
31   // Member and friend function definitions
32   // for class Cylinder.
33   #include "cylindr2.h"
34
35   // Cylinder constructor calls Circle constructor
36   Cylinder::Cylinder( double h, double r, int x, int y )
37      : Circle( r, x, y )    // call base-class constructor
38   { setHeight( h ); }
39
40   // Set height of Cylinder
41   void Cylinder::setHeight( double h )
42      { height = ( h >= 0 ? h : 0 ); }
43
44   // Get height of Cylinder
45   double Cylinder::getHeight() const { return height; }
46
47   // Calculate area of Cylinder (i.e., surface area)
48   double Cylinder::area() const
49   {
50      return 2 * Circle::area() +
51             2 * 3.14159 * radius * height;
52   }
53
54   // Calculate volume of Cylinder
55   double Cylinder::volume() const
56      { return Circle::area() * height; }
57
58   // Output Cylinder dimensions
59   ostream &operator<<( ostream &output, const Cylinder &c )
60   {
61      output << static_cast< Circle >( c )
62             << "; Height = " << c.height;
63
64      return output;    // enables cascaded calls
65   }
```

Fig. 9.10   Demonstrating class **Cylinder**—**cylindr2.cpp** .

```
66   // Fig. 9.10: fig09_10.cpp
67   // Driver for class Cylinder
68   #include <iostream>
69
70   using std::cout;
71   using std::endl;
72
73   #include "point2.h"
74   #include "circle2.h"
75   #include "cylindr2.h"
76
77   int main()
78   {
```

Fig. 9.10   Demonstrating class **Cylinder**—**fig09_10.cpp** (part 1 of 2).

```
79        // create Cylinder object
80        Cylinder cyl( 5.7, 2.5, 12, 23 );
81
82        // use get functions to display the Cylinder
83        cout << "X coordinate is " << cyl.getX()
84             << "\nY coordinate is " << cyl.getY()
85             << "\nRadius is " << cyl.getRadius()
86             << "\nHeight is " << cyl.getHeight() << "\n\n";
87
88        // use set functions to change the Cylinder's attributes
89        cyl.setHeight( 10 );
90        cyl.setRadius( 4.25 );
91        cyl.setPoint( 2, 2 );
92        cout << "The new location, radius, and height of cyl are:\n"
93             << cyl << '\n';
94
95        cout << "The area of cyl is:\n"
96             << cyl.area() << '\n';
97
98        // display the Cylinder as a Point
99        Point &pRef = cyl;    // pRef "thinks" it is a Point
100       cout << "\nCylinder printed as a Point is: "
101            << pRef << "\n\n";
102
103       // display the Cylinder as a Circle
104       Circle &circleRef = cyl;  // circleRef thinks it is a Circle
105       cout << "Cylinder printed as a Circle is:\n" << circleRef
106            << "\nArea: " << circleRef.area() << endl;
107
108       return 0;
109   }
```

```
X coordinate is 12
Y coordinate is 23
Radius is 2.5
Height is 5.7

The new location, radius, and height of cyl are:
Center = [2, 2]; Radius = 4.25; Height = 10.00
The area of cyl is:
380.53
Cylinder printed as a Point is: [2, 2]

Cylinder printed as a Circle is:
Center = [2, 2]; Radius = 4.25
Area: 56.74
```

Fig. 9.10   Demonstrating class **Cylinder**—**fig09_10.cpp** (part 2 of 2).

9.15 Multiple Inheritance

So far in this chapter, we have discussed single inheritance in which each class is derived from exactly one base class. A class may be derived from more than one base class; such derivation is called *multiple inheritance*. Multiple inheritance means that a derived class inherits the members of several base classes. This powerful capability encourages interesting forms of software reuse, but can cause a variety of ambiguity problems.

Good Programming Practice 9.1

Multiple inheritance is a powerful capability when used properly. Multiple inheritance should be used when an "is a" relationship exists between a new type and two or more existing types (i.e., type A "is a" type B and type A "is a" type C).

Consider the multiple inheritance example in Fig. 9.11. Class **Base1** contains one **protected** data member—**int value**. **Base1** contains a constructor that sets **value** and **public** member function **getData** that returns **value**.

Class **Base2** is similar to class **Base1** except that its **protected** data is **char letter**. **Base2** also has a **public** member function **getData**, but this function returns the value of **char letter**.

Class **Derived** is inherited from both class **Base1** and class **Base2** through multiple inheritance. **Derived** has **private** data member **double real** and has **public** member function **getReal** that reads the value of **double real**.

```
1   // Fig. 9.11: base1.h
2   // Definition of class Base1
3   #ifndef BASE1_H
4   #define BASE1_H
5
6   class Base1 {
7   public:
8      Base1( int x ) { value = x; }
9      int getData() const { return value; }
10  protected:       // accessible to derived classes
11     int value;    // inherited by derived class
12  };
13
14  #endif
```

Fig. 9.11   Demonstrating multiple inheritance—**base1.h** .

```
15  // Fig. 9.11: base2.h
16  // Definition of class Base2
17  #ifndef BASE2_H
18  #define BASE2_H
19
20  class Base2 {
21  public:
22     Base2( char c ) { letter = c; }
23     char getData() const { return letter; }
24  protected:        // accessible to derived classes
25     char letter;   // inherited by derived class
26  };
27
28  #endif
```

Fig. 9.11   Demonstrating multiple inheritance—**base2.h** ..

```
29   // Fig. 9.11: derived.h
30   // Definition of class Derived which inherits
31   // multiple base classes (Base1 and Base2).
32   #ifndef DERIVED_H
33   #define DERIVED_H
34
35   #include <iostream>
36
37   using std::ostream;
38
39   #include "base1.h"
40   #include "base2.h"
41
42   // multiple inheritance
43   class Derived : public Base1, public Base2 {
44      friend ostream &operator<<( ostream &, const Derived & );
45
46   public:
47      Derived( int, char, double );
48      double getReal() const;
49
50   private:
51      double real;    // derived class's private data
52   };
53
54   #endif
```

Fig. 9.11   Demonstrating multiple inheritance—**derived.h**..

```
55   // Fig. 9.11: derived.cpp
56   // Member function definitions for class Derived
57   #include "derived.h"
58
59   // Constructor for Derived calls constructors for
60   // class Base1 and class Base2.
61   // Use member initializers to call base-class constructors
62   Derived::Derived( int i, char c, double f )
63      : Base1( i ), Base2( c ), real ( f ) { }
64
65   // Return the value of real
66   double Derived::getReal() const { return real; }
67
68   // Display all the data members of Derived
69   ostream &operator<<( ostream &output, const Derived &d )
70   {
71      output << "    Integer: " << d.value
72             << "\n  Character: " << d.letter
73             << "\nReal number: " << d.real;
74
75      return output;    // enables cascaded calls
76   }
```

Fig. 9.11   Demonstrating multiple inheritance—**derived.cpp** ..

```
77   // Fig. 9.11: fig09_11.cpp
78   // Driver for multiple inheritance example
79   #include <iostream>
80
81   using std::cout;
82   using std::endl;
83
84   #include "base1.h"
85   #include "base2.h"
86   #include "derived.h"
87
88   int main()
89   {
90      Base1 b1( 10 ), *base1Ptr = 0;   // create Base1 object
91      Base2 b2( 'Z' ), *base2Ptr = 0;  // create Base2 object
92      Derived d( 7, 'A', 3.5 );        // create Derived object
93
94      // print data members of base class objects
95      cout << "Object b1 contains integer " << b1.getData()
96          << "\nObject b2 contains character " << b2.getData()
97          << "\nObject d contains:\n" << d << "\n\n";
98
99      // print data members of derived class object
100     // scope resolution operator resolves getData ambiguity
101     cout << "Data members of Derived can be"
102         << " accessed individually:"
103         << "\n    Integer: " << d.Base1::getData()
104         << "\n  Character: " << d.Base2::getData()
105         << "\nReal number: " << d.getReal() << "\n\n";
106
107     cout << "Derived can be treated as an "
108         << "object of either base class:\n";
109
110     // treat Derived as a Base1 object
111     base1Ptr = &d;
112     cout << "base1Ptr->getData() yields "
113         << base1Ptr->getData() << '\n';
114
115     // treat Derived as a Base2 object
116     base2Ptr = &d;
117     cout << "base2Ptr->getData() yields "
118         << base2Ptr->getData() << endl;
119
120     return 0;
121  }
```

```
Object b1 contains integer 10
Object b2 contains character Z
Object d contains:
    Integer: 7
  Character: A
Real number: 3.5
```

Fig. 9.11   Demonstrating multiple inheritance—**fig09_11.cpp** (part 1 of 2).

```
Data members of Derived can be accessed individually:
    Integer: 7
  Character: A
Real number: 3.5

Derived can be treated as an object of either base class:
base1Ptr->getData() yields 7
base2Ptr->getData() yields A
```

Fig. 9.11   Demonstrating multiple inheritance—**fig09_11.cpp** (part 2 of 2).

Note how straightforward it is to indicate multiple inheritance by following the colon
(**:**) after **class Derived** with a comma-separated list of base classes. Note also that constructor **Derived** explicitly calls base-class constructors for each of its base classes,
Base1 and **Base2**, through the member-initializer syntax. Again, base-class constructors
are called in the order that the inheritance is specified, not in the order in which their constructors are mentioned. And if the base-class constructors are not explicitly called in the
member initializer list, their default constructors will be called implicitly.

The overloaded stream-insertion operator for **Derived** uses dot notation off the
derived object **d** to print **value**, **letter** and **real**. This operator function is a **friend**
of **Derived**, so **operator<<** can directly access **private** data member **real** of
Derived. Also, because this operator is a **friend** of a derived class, it can access the
protected members **value** and **letter** of **Base1** and **Base2**, respectively.

Now let us examine the driver program in **main**. We create object **b1** of class **Base1**
and initialize it to **int** value **10**. We create object **b2** of class **Base2** and initialize it to
char value **'Z'**. Then, we create object **d** of class **Derived** and initialize it to contain
int value **7**, **char** value **'A'** and **double** value **3.5**.

The contents of each of the base-class objects is printed by calling the **getData**
member function for each object. Even though there are two **getData** functions, the calls
are not ambiguous because they refer directly to the object **b1** version of **getData** and the
object **b2** version of **getData**.

Next we print the contents of **Derived** object **d** with static binding. But we do have
an ambiguity problem because this object contains two **getData** functions, one inherited
from **Base1** and one inherited from **Base2**. This problem is easy to solve by using the
binary scope resolution operator as in **d.Base1::getData()** to print the **int** in
value and **d.Base2::getData()** to print the **char** in **letter**. The **double** value
in **real** is printed without ambiguity with the call **d.getReal()**. Next we demonstrate
that the *is a* relationships of single inheritance also apply to multiple inheritance. We assign
the address of derived object **d** to base-class pointer **base1Ptr** and we print **int value**
by invoking **Base1** member function **getData** off **base1Ptr**. We then assign the
address of derived object **d** to base-class pointer **base2Ptr** and we print **char letter**
by invoking **Base2** member function **getData** off **base2Ptr**.

This example showed the mechanics of multiple inheritance in a simple example and
introduced a simple ambiguity problem. Multiple inheritance is a complex topic dealt with
in more detail in advanced C++ texts.

Software Engineering Observation 9.12

Multiple inheritance is a powerful feature, but it can introduce complexity into a system. Great care is required in the design of a system to use multiple inheritance properly; it should not be used when single inheritance will do the job.

9.16 (Optional Case Study) Thinking About Objects: Incorporating Inheritance into the Elevator Simulation

We now examine our simulation design to see whether it might benefit from inheritance. In the previous chapters, we have been treating **ElevatorButton** and **FloorButton** as separate classes. In fact, these classes have much in common; each is a *kind of* a button. To apply inheritance, we first look for commonality between these classes. We then extract this commonality, place it into base class **Button** and derive classes **ElevatorButton** and **FloorButton** from **Button**.

Let us now examine the similarities between classes **ElevatorButton** and **FloorButton**. Figure 9.12 shows the attributes and operations of both classes, as declared in their header files from Chapter 7 (Figs. 7.24 and 7.26, respectively). The classes have one attribute (**pressed**) and two operations (**pressButton** and **resetButton**) in common. We place these three elements in base class **Button**, then **Elevator-Button** and **FloorButton** inherit the attributes and operations of **Button**. In our previous implementation, **ElevatorButton** and **FloorButton** each declared a reference to an object of class **Elevator**—class **Button** should also contain this reference.

Figure 9.13 models our new elevator simulator design incorporating inheritance. Notice that class **Floor** is composed of one object of class **FloorButton** and one object of class **Light**; class **Elevator** is composed of one object of class **ElevatorButton**, one object of class **Door** and one object of **Bell**. A solid line with a hollow arrowhead extends from each of the derived classes to the base class—this line indicates that classes **FloorButton** and **ElevatorButton** inherit from class **Button**.

One question remains: do the derived classes need to override any of the base class member functions? If we compare the **public** member functions of each class (Figs. 7.25 and 7.27), we notice that the **resetButton** member function is identical for both classes. This function does not need to be overridden. The **pressButton** member function, however, is different for each class. Class **ElevatorButton** contains the **pressButton** code

```
pressed = true;
cout << "elevator button tells elevator to prepare to leave"
    << endl;
elevatorRef.prepareToLeave( true );
```

while class **FloorButton** contains the **pressButton** code

```
pressed = true;
cout << "floor " << floorNumber
    << " button summons elevator" << endl;
elevatorRef.summonElevator( floorNumber );
```

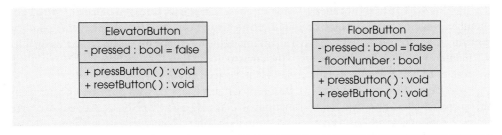

Fig. 9.12 Attributes and operations of classes **ElevatorButton** and **FloorButton**.

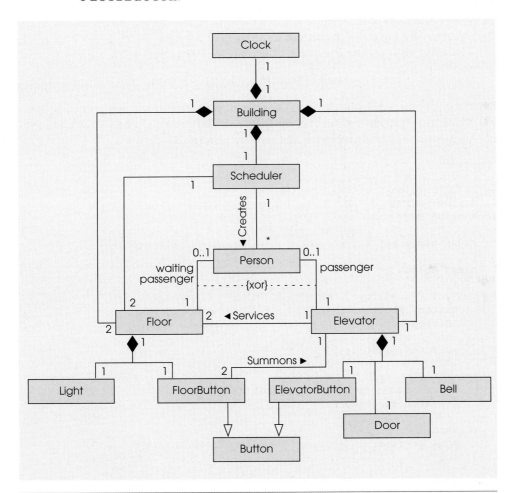

Fig. 9.13 Full elevator simulator class diagram indicating inheritance from class **Button**.

The first line of each block of code is identical, but the remaining sections of the two blocks are different. Therefore, each derived class needs to override the base class **Button** member function **pressButton**.

Figure 9.14 lists the header file for the base class **Button**.[2] We declare **public** member functions **pressButton** and **resetButton** and **private** data member **pressed** of type **bool**. Notice the declaration of the reference to class **Elevator** in line 18 and the corresponding parameter to the constructor in line 11. We show how to initialize the reference when we discuss the code for the derived classes.

The derived classes perform two different actions. Class **ElevatorButton** invokes the **prepareToLeave** member function of class **Elevator**; class **FloorButton** invokes the **summonElevator** member function. Thus, both classes need access to the **elevatorRef** data member of the base class; however, this data member should not be available to non-**Button** objects. Therefore, we place the **elevatorRef** data member in the **protected** section of **Button**. The **pressed** data member is declared **private**, because it is manipulated only through the base class member functions; derived classes do not need to access **pressed** directly.

Figure 9.15 lists the implementation file for class **Button**. Line 12

```
: elevatorRef( elevatorHandle ), pressed( false )
```

initializes the reference to the elevator. The constructor and destructor simply display messages indicating that they are running, and the **pressButton** and **resetButton** member functions manipulate **private** data member **pressed**.

```cpp
1   // button.h
2   // Definition for class Button.
3   #ifndef BUTTON_H
4   #define BUTTON_H
5
6   class Elevator;                    // forward declaration
7
8   class Button {
9
10  public:
11     Button( Elevator & );           // constructor
12     ~Button();                      // destructor
13     void pressButton();             // sets button on
14     void resetButton();             // resets button off
15
16  protected:
17     // reference to button's elevator
18     Elevator &elevatorRef;
19
20  private:
21     bool pressed;                   // state of button
22  };
23
24  #endif // BUTTON_H
```

Fig. 9.14   Class **Button** header file.

---

2. The beauty of encapsulation is that no other files in our elevator simulation need to be changed. We simply substitute the new **elevatorButton** and **floorButton .h** and **.cpp** files for the old ones and add the files for class **Button**. We then compile the new **.cpp** files and link the resulting object files with those already created from the existing simulator files.

```
1   // button.cpp
2   // Member function definitions for class Button.
3   #include <iostream>
4
5   using std::cout;
6   using std::endl;
7
8   #include "button.h"
9
10  // constructor
11  Button::Button( Elevator &elevatorHandle )
12     : elevatorRef( elevatorHandle ), pressed( false )
13  { cout << "button created" << endl; }
14
15  // destructor
16  Button::~Button()
17  { cout << "button destroyed" << endl; }
18
19  // press the button
20  void Button::pressButton() { pressed = true; }
21
22  // reset the button
23  void Button::resetButton() { pressed = false; }
```

Fig. 9.15   Class **Button** implementation file.

Figure 9.16 contains the header file for class **ElevatorButton**. We inherit from class **Button** in line 10. This inheritance means that class **ElevatorButton** contains the **protected elevatorRef** data member and the **public pressButton** and **resetButton** member functions of the base class. In line 15, we provide a function prototype for **pressButton** to signal our intent to override that member function in the **.cpp** file. We will discuss the implementation of **pressButton** momentarily.

```
1   // elevatorButton.h
2   // Definition for class ElevatorButton.
3   #ifndef ELEVATORBUTTON_H
4   #define ELEVATORBUTTON_H
5
6   #include "button.h"
7
8   class Elevator;                        // forward declaration
9
10  class ElevatorButton : public Button {
11
12  public:
13     ElevatorButton( Elevator & );       // constructor
14     ~ElevatorButton();                  // destructor
15     void pressButton();                 // press the button
16  };
17
18  #endif // ELEVATORBUTTON_H
```

Fig. 9.16   Class **ElevatorButton** header file.

The constructor takes as a parameter a reference to class **Elevator** (line 13). We will discuss the necessity for this parameter when we discuss the implementation file for this class. Notice, however, that we must still make a forward declaration of class **Elevator** (line 8), so that we may include the parameter in the constructor declaration.

The implementation file for class **ElevatorButton** is listed in Fig. 9.17. The constructors and destructors of this class display messages to indicate that these functions are executing. Line 14:

```
: Button( elevatorHandle )
```

passes the **Elevator** reference up to the base class constructor.

Our **pressButton** member function override first calls the **pressButton** member function in the base class (line 24); this call sets the **pressed** attribute of class **Button** to **true**. In line 27, we invoke the **elevator**'s **prepareToLeave** member function with an argument of **true** to tell the elevator to move to the other floor.

Figure 9.18 lists the header file for class **FloorButton**. The only difference between this file and that for class **ElevatorButton** is the addition in line 19 of the **floorNumber** data member. We use this data member to distinguish the floors in the simulation output messages. We include a parameter of type **int** in the constructor declaration (line 13), so we can initialize **floorNumber**.

```cpp
1   // elevatorButton.cpp:
2   // Member function definitions for class ElevatorButton.
3   #include <iostream>
4
5   using std::cout;
6   using std::endl;
7
8   #include "elevatorButton.h"
9   #include "elevator.h"
10
11  // constructor
12  ElevatorButton::ElevatorButton(
13     Elevator &elevatorHandle )
14     : Button( elevatorHandle )
15  { cout << "elevator button created" << endl; }
16
17  // destructor
18  ElevatorButton::~ElevatorButton()
19  { cout << "elevator button destroyed" << endl; }
20
21  // press the button
22  void ElevatorButton::pressButton()
23  {
24     Button::pressButton();
25     cout << "elevator button tells elevator to prepare to leave"
26        << endl;
27     elevatorRef.prepareToLeave( true );
28  }
```

Fig. 9.17   Class **ElevatorButton** implementation file.

```
1    // floorButton.h
2    // Definition for class FloorButton.
3    #ifndef FLOORBUTTON_H
4    #define FLOORBUTTON_H
5
6    #include "button.h"
7
8    class Elevator;                      // forward declaration
9
10   class FloorButton : public Button{
11
12   public:
13       FloorButton( int, Elevator & ); // constructor
14       ~FloorButton();                  // destructor
15
16       void pressButton();        // press the button
17
18   private:
19       int floorNumber;          // number of the button's floor
20   };
21
22   #endif // FLOORBUTTON_H
```

Fig. 9.18   Class **FloorButton** header file.

Figure 9.19 contains the implementation file for class **FloorButton**. In line 14, we pass the **Elevator** reference up to the base class **Button** constructor and initialize the **floorNumber** data member. The constructor and destructor print appropriate messages, using the **floorNumber** data member. The **pressButton** member function override (lines 27-34) begins by calling **pressButton** in the base class, then invokes the elevator's **summonElevator** member function, passing **floorNumber** to indicate the floor that is summoning the elevator.

```
1    // floorButton.cpp
2    // Member function definitions for class FloorButton.
3    #include <iostream>
4
5    using std::cout;
6    using std::endl;
7
8    #include "floorButton.h"
9    #include "elevator.h"
10
11   // constructor
12   FloorButton::FloorButton( int number,
13                             Elevator &elevatorHandle )
14       : Button( elevatorHandle ), floorNumber( number )
15   {
16       cout << "floor " << floorNumber << " button created"
17           << endl;
18   }
```

Fig. 9.19   Class **FloorButton** implementation file (part 1 of 2).

```
19
20    // destructor
21    FloorButton::~FloorButton()
22    {
23       cout << "floor " << floorNumber << " button destroyed"
24          << endl;
25    }
26
27    // press the button
28    void FloorButton::pressButton()
29    {
30       Button::pressButton();
31       cout << "floor " << floorNumber
32          << " button summons elevator" << endl;
33       elevatorRef.summonElevator( floorNumber );
34    }
```

Fig. 9.19   Class **FloorButton** implementation file (part 2 of 2).

We have now completed the implementation for the elevator simulator case study that we began in Chapter 2. One significant architectural opportunity remains. You may have noticed that classes **Button**, **Door** and **Light** have much in common. Each of these classes contains a "state" attribute and corresponding "set on" and "set off" operations. Class **Bell** also bears some similarity to these other classes. Object-oriented thinking tells us that we should place commonalities in one or more base classes, from which we should then use inheritance to form appropriate derived classes. We leave the implementation of this inheritance to the reader as an exercise. We suggest that you begin by modifying the class diagram in Fig. 9.13. [Hint: **Button**, **Door** and **Light** are essentially "toggle" classes—they each have "state," "set on" and "set off" capabilities; **Bell** is a "thinner" class, with only a single operation and no state.]

We sincerely hope that this elevator simulation case study was a challenging and meaningful experience for you. We employed a carefully developed, incremental object-oriented process to produce a UML-based design for our elevator simulator. From this design, we produced a substantial working C++ implementation using key programming notions, including classes, objects, encapsulation, visibility, composition and inheritance. In the remaining chapters of the book, we present many additional key C++ technologies. We would be most grateful if you would take a moment to send your comments, criticisms and suggestions for improving this case study to us at **deitel@deitel.com**.

SUMMARY

- One of the keys to the power of object-oriented programming is achieving software reusability through inheritance.

- The programmer can designate that the new class is to inherit the data members and member functions of a previously defined base class. In this case, the new class is referred to as a derived class.

- With single inheritance, a class is derived from only one base class. With multiple inheritance, a derived class inherits from multiple (possibly unrelated) base classes.

- A derived class normally adds data members and member functions of its own, so a derived class generally has a larger definition than its base class. A derived class is more specific than its base class and normally represents fewer objects.

- A derived class cannot access the **private** members of its base class; allowing this would violate the encapsulation of the base class. A derived class can, however, access the **public** and **protected** members of its base class.
- A derived-class constructor always calls the constructor for its base class first to create and initialize the derived class' base-class members.
- Destructors are called in the reverse order of constructor calls, so a derived-class destructor is called before its base-class destructor.
- Inheritance enables software reusability, which saves time in development and encourages the use of previously proven and debugged high-quality software.
- Inheritance can be accomplished from existing class libraries. Someday most software will be constructed from standardized reusable components exactly as most hardware is constructed today.
- The implementor of a derived class does not need access to the source code of a base class, but does need the interface to the base class and the base class' object code.
- An object of a derived class can be treated as an object of its corresponding public base class. However, the reverse is not true.
- A base class exists in a hierarchical relationship with its singly derived classes.
- A class can exist by itself. When that class is used with the mechanism of inheritance, it becomes either a base class that supplies attributes and behaviors to other classes, or the class becomes a derived class that inherits those attributes and behaviors.
- An inheritance hierarchy can be arbitrarily deep within the physical limitations of a particular system.
- Hierarchies are useful tools for understanding and managing complexity. With software becoming increasingly complex, C++ provides mechanisms for supporting hierarchical structures through inheritance and polymorphism.
- An explicit cast can be used to convert a base-class pointer to a derived-class pointer. Such a pointer should not be dereferenced unless it actually points to an object of the derived class type.
- **Protected** access serves as an intermediate level of protection between **public** access and **private** access. **Protected** members of a base class may be accessed by members and **friend**s of the base class and by members and **friend**s of derived classes; no other functions can access the **protected** members of a base class.
- **Protected** members are used to extend privileges to derived classes while denying those privileges to nonclass, non-**friend** functions.
- Multiple inheritance is indicated by placing a colon (**:**) after the derived-class name and following the colon with a comma-separated list of base classes. Member initializer syntax is used in the derived-class constructor to call base-class constructors.
- When deriving a class from a base class, the base class may be declared as either **public, protected** or **private**.
- When deriving a class from a **public** base class, **public** members of the base class become **public** members of the derived class, and **protected** members of the base class become **protected** members of the derived class.
- When deriving a class from a **protected** base class, **public** and **protected** members of the base class become **protected** members of the derived class.
- When deriving a class from a **private** base class, **public** and **protected** members of the base class become **private** members of the derived class.
- A base class may be either a direct base class of a derived class or an indirect base class of a derived class. A direct base class is explicitly listed where the derived class is declared. An indirect base class is not explicitly listed; rather it is inherited from several levels up the class hierarchy tree.

- When a base-class member is inappropriate for a derived class, we may simply redefine that member in the derived class.
- It is important to distinguish between "is a" relationships and "has a" relationships. In a "has a" relationship, a class object has an object of another class as a member. In an "is a" relationship, an object of a derived-class type may also be treated as an object of the base-class type. "Is a" is inheritance. "Has a" is composition.
- A derived-class object can be assigned to a base-class object. This kind of assignment makes sense because the derived class has members corresponding to each of the base-class members.
- A pointer to a derived-class object can be implicitly converted into a pointer for a base-class object.
- It is possible to convert a base-class pointer to a derived-class pointer by using an explicit cast. The target should be a derived-class object.
- A base class specifies commonality. All classes derived from a base class inherit the capabilities of that base class. In the object-oriented design process, the designer looks for commonality and factors it out to form desirable base classes. Derived classes are then customized beyond the capabilities inherited from the base class.
- Reading a set of derived-class declarations can be confusing because not all the members of the derived class are present in these declarations. In particular, inherited members are not listed in the derived-class declarations, but these members are indeed present in the derived classes.
- "Has a" relationships are examples of creating new classes by composition of existing classes.
- "Knows a" relationships are examples of objects containing pointers or references to other objects so they can be aware of those objects.
- Member object constructors are called in the order in which the objects are declared. In inheritance, base-class constructors are called in the order in which inheritance is specified and before the derived-class constructor.
- For a derived-class object, first the base-class constructor is called, then the derived-class constructor is called (which may call member object constructors).
- When the derived-class object is destroyed, the destructors are called in the reverse order of the constructors—first the derived-class destructor is called, then the base-class destructor is called.
- A class may be derived from more than one base class; such derivation is called multiple inheritance.
- Indicate multiple inheritance by following the colon (:) inheritance indicator with a comma-separated list of base classes.
- The derived-class constructor calls base-class constructors for each of its base classes through the member-initializer syntax. Base-class constructors are called in the order in which the base classes are declared during inheritance.

TERMINOLOGY

abstraction
ambiguity in multiple inheritance
association
base class
base-class constructor
base class default constructor
base-class destructor
base-class initializer
base-class pointer
class hierarchy

class libraries
client of a class
composition
customize software
derived class
derived-class constructor
derived-class destructor
derived-class pointer
direct-base class
downcasting a pointer

friend of a base class
friend of a derived class
function overriding
has a relationship
hierarchical relationship
indirect base class
infinite recursion error
inheritance
is a relationship
knows a relationship
member access control
member class
member object
multiple inheritance
object-oriented programming (OOP)
override a base-class member function
pointer to a base-class object

pointer to a derived-class object
private base class
private inheritance
protected base class
protected inheritance
protected keyword
protected member of a class
public base class
public inheritance
single inheritance
software reusability
standardized software components
subclass
superclass
upcasting a pointer
uses a relationship

COMMON PROGRAMMING ERRORS

9.1   Treating a base-class object as a derived-class object can cause errors.

9.2   Explicitly casting a base-class pointer that points to a base-class object into a derived-class pointer and then referring to derived-class members that do not exist in that object can lead to run-time logic errors.

9.3   When a base-class member function is overridden in a derived class, it is common to have the derived-class version call the base-class version and do some additional work. Not using the scope-resolution operator to reference the base class' member function causes infinite recursion because the derived-class member function actually calls itself. This will eventually cause the system to exhaust memory, a fatal execution-time error.

9.4   Assigning a derived-class object to an object of a corresponding base class, then attempting to reference derived-class-only members in the new base-class object is a syntax error.

9.5   Casting a base-class pointer to a derived-class pointer can cause errors if that pointer is then used to reference a base-class object that does not have the desired derived-class members.

GOOD PROGRAMMING PRACTICE

9.1   Multiple inheritance is a powerful capability when used properly. Multiple inheritance should be used when an "is a" relationship exists between a new type and two or more existing types (i.e., type A "is a" type B and type A "is a" type C).

PERFORMANCE TIPS

9.1   When performance is a major concern, programmers may want to see source code of classes they are inheriting from so they can tune the code to meet their performance requirements.

9.2   If classes produced through inheritance are larger than they need to be, memory and processing resources may be wasted. Inherit from the class "closest" to what you need.

SOFTWARE ENGINEERING OBSERVATIONS

9.1   In general, declare data members of a class **private** and use **protected** only as a "last resort" when systems need to be tuned to meet unique performance requirements.

9.2   A derived class cannot directly access **private** members of its base class.

9.3   Suppose we create an object of a derived class where both the base class and the derived class contain objects of other classes. When an object of that derived class is created, first the constructors for the base class' member objects execute, then the base-class constructor executes, then the constructors for the derived class' member objects execute, then the derived class' constructor executes. Destructors are called in the reverse of the order in which their corresponding constructors are called.

9.4   The order in which member objects are constructed is the order in which those objects are declared within the class definition. The order in which the member initializers are listed does not affect the order of construction.

9.5   In inheritance, base-class constructors are called in the order in which inheritance is specified in the derived-class definition. The order in which the base-class constructors are specified in the derived-class member initializer list does not affect the order of construction.

9.6   In theory, users do not need to see the source code of classes from which they inherit. In practice, people who license classes tell us that the customers often demand the source code. Programmers still seem reluctant to incorporate code into their programs when this code has been written by other people.

9.7   Creating a derived class does not affect its base class' source code or object code; the integrity of a base class is preserved by inheritance.

9.8   In an object-oriented system, classes are often closely related. "Factor out" common attributes and behaviors and place these in a base class. Then use inheritance to form derived classes.

9.9   A derived class contains the attributes and behaviors of its base class. A derived class can also contain additional attributes and behaviors. With inheritance, the base class can be compiled independently of the derived class. Only the derived class' incremental attributes and behaviors need to be compiled to be able to combine these with the base class to form the derived class.

9.10   Modifications to a base class do not require derived classes to change as long as the **public** and **protected** interfaces to the base class remain unchanged. Derived classes may, however, need to be recompiled.

9.11   Program modifications to a class that is a member of another class do not require the enclosing class to change as long as the **public** interface to the member class remains unchanged. Note that the composite class may, however, need to be recompiled.

9.12   Multiple inheritance is a powerful feature, but it can introduce complexity into a system. Great care is required in the design of a system to use multiple inheritance properly; it should not be used when single inheritance will do the job.

SELF-REVIEW EXERCISES

9.1   Fill in the blanks in each of the following:
   a) If the class **Alpha** inherits from the class **Beta**, class **Alpha** is called the _____ class and class **Beta** is called the _____ class.
   b) C++ provides for _____, which allows a derived class to inherit from many base classes, even if these base classes are unrelated.
   c) Inheritance enables _____, which saves time in development and encourages using previously proven and high-quality software.
   d) An object of a _____ class can be treated as an object of its corresponding _____ class.
   e) To convert a base-class pointer to a derived-class pointer, a _____ must be used because the compiler considers this a dangerous operation.

f) The three member access specifiers are _____, _____ and _____.

g) When deriving a class from a base class with **public** inheritance, **public** members of the base class become _____ members of the derived class, and **protected** members of the base class become _____ members of the derived class.

h) When deriving a class from a base class with **protected** inheritance, **public** members of the base class become _____ members of the derived class, and **protected** members of the base class become _____ members of the derived class.

i) A "has a" relationship between classes represents _____ and an "is a" relationship between classes represents _____.

ANSWERS TO SELF-REVIEW EXERCISES

9.1   a) derived, base. b) multiple inheritance. c) software reusability. d) derived, base. e) cast. f) **public**, **protected**, **private**. g) **public**, **protected**. h) **protected**, **protected**. i) composition, inheritance.

EXERCISES

9.2   Consider the class **Bicycle**. Given your knowledge of some common components of bicycles, show a class hierarchy in which the class **Bicycle** inherits from other classes, which, in turn, inherit from yet other classes. Discuss the instantiation of various objects of class **Bicycle**. Discuss inheritance from class **Bicycle** for other closely related derived classes.

9.3   Briefly define each of the following terms: inheritance, multiple inheritance, base class and derived class.

9.4   Discuss why converting a base-class pointer to a derived-class pointer is considered dangerous by the compiler.

9.5   Distinguish between single inheritance and multiple inheritance.

9.6   (True/False) A derived class is often called a subclass because it represents a subset of its base class (i.e., a derived class is generally smaller than its base class).

9.7   (True/False) A derived-class object is also an object of that derived class' base class.

9.8   Some programmers prefer not to use **protected** access because it breaks the encapsulation of the base class. Discuss the relative merits of using **protected** access vs. insisting on using **private** access in base classes.

9.9   Many programs written with inheritance could be solved with composition instead, and vice versa. Discuss the relative merits of these approaches in the context of the **Point**, **Circle**, **Cylinder** class hierarchy in this chapter. Rewrite the program of Fig. 9.10 (and the supporting classes) to use composition rather than inheritance. After you do this, reassess the relative merits of the two approaches both for the **Point**, **Circle**, **Cylinder** problem and for object-oriented programs in general.

9.10   Rewrite the **Point**, **Circle**, **Cylinder** program of Fig. 9.10 as a **Point**, **Square**, **Cube** program. Do this two ways—once with inheritance and once with composition.

9.11   In the chapter, we stated, "When a base-class member is inappropriate for a derived class, that member can be overridden in the derived class with an appropriate implementation." If this is done, does the derived-class-is-a-base-class-object relationship still hold? Explain your answer.

9.12   Study the inheritance hierarchy of Fig. 9.2. For each class, indicate some common attributes and behaviors consistent with the hierarchy. Add some other classes (e.g., **UndergraduateStudent**, **GraduateStudent**, **Freshman**, **Sophomore**, **Junior**, **Senior**, etc.) to enrich the hierarchy.

9.13   Write an inheritance hierarchy for class **Quadrilateral**, **Trapezoid**, **Parallelogram**, **Rectangle** and **Square**. Use **Quadrilateral** as the base class of the hierarchy. Make the hierarchy as deep (i.e., as many levels) as possible. The **private** data of **Quadrilateral** should be the (*x, y*) coordinate pairs for the four endpoints of the **Quadrilateral**. Write a driver program that instantiates and displays objects of each of these classes.

9.14   Write down all the shapes you can think of—both two-dimensional and three-dimensional—and form those shapes into a shape hierarchy. Your hierarchy should have base class **Shape** from which class **TwoDimensionalShape** and class **ThreeDimensionalShape** are derived. Once you have developed the hierarchy, define each of the classes in the hierarchy. We will use this hierarchy in the exercises of Chapter 10 to process all shapes as objects of base-class **Shape**. This is a technique called polymorphism.

10

Virtual Functions and Polymorphism

Objectives

- To understand the notion of polymorphism.
- To understand how to declare and use **virtual** functions to effect polymorphism.
- To understand the distinction between abstract classes and concrete classes.
- To learn how to declare pure **virtual** functions to create abstract classes.
- To appreciate how polymorphism makes systems extensible and maintainable.
- To understand how C++ implements **virtual** functions and dynamic binding "under the hood."

One Ring to rule them all, One Ring to find them,
One Ring to bring them all and in the darkness bind them.
John Ronald Reuel Tolkien, *The Fellowship of the Ring*

The silence often of pure innocence
Persuades when speaking fails.
William Shakespeare, The Winter's Tale

General propositions do not decide concrete cases.
Oliver Wendell Holmes

A philosopher of imposing stature doesn't think in a vacuum.
Even his most abstract ideas are, to some extent, conditioned
by what is or is not known in the time when he lives.
Alfred North Whitehead

10.1 Introduction

With *virtual functions* and *polymorphism,* it is possible to design and implement systems that are more easily *extensible*. Programs can be written to generically process—as base-class objects—objects of all existing classes in a hierarchy. Classes that do not exist during program development can be added with little or no modifications to the generic part of the program—as long as those classes are part of the hierarchy that is being processed generically. The only parts of a program that will need modification are those parts that require direct knowledge of the particular class that is added to the hierarchy.

10.2 Type Fields and `switch` Statements

One means of dealing with objects of different types is to use a **switch** statement to take an appropriate action on each object based on that object's type. For example, in a hierarchy of shapes in which each shape specifies its type as a data member, a **switch** structure could determine which **print** function to call based on the type of the particular object.

There are many problems with using **switch** logic. The programmer might forget to make such a type test when one is warranted. The programmer may forget to test all possible cases in a **switch**. If a **switch**-based system is modified by adding new types, the programmer might forget to insert the new cases in all existing **switch** statements. Every addition or deletion of a class to handle new types demands that every **switch** statement in the system be modified; tracking these down can be time consuming and prone to error.

As we will see, **virtual** functions and polymorphic programming can eliminate the need for **switch** logic. The programmer can use the **virtual** function mechanism to perform the equivalent logic automatically, thus avoiding the kinds of errors typically associated with **switch** logic.

Software Engineering Observation 10.1

An interesting consequence of using **virtual** *functions and polymorphism is that programs take on a simplified appearance. They contain less branching logic in favor of simpler sequential code. This facilitates testing, debugging, program maintenance and bug avoidance.*

10.3 `virtual` Functions

Suppose a set of shape classes such as **Circle**, **Triangle**, **Rectangle**, **Square**, etc. are all derived from base class **Shape**. In object-oriented programming, each of these classes might be endowed with the ability to draw itself. Although each class has its own **draw** function, the **draw** function for each shape is quite different. When drawing a shape, whatever that shape may be, it would be nice to be able to treat all these shapes generically as objects of the base class **Shape**. Then to draw any shape, we could simply call function **draw** of base class **Shape** and let the program determine *dynamically* (i.e., at run time) which derived class **draw** function to use.

To enable this kind of behavior, we declare **draw** in the base class as a **virtual** *function* and we *override* **draw** in each of the derived classes to draw the appropriate shape. A virtual function is declared by preceding the function's prototype with the keyword **virtual** in the base class. For example,

```
virtual void draw() const;
```

may appear in base class **Shape**. The preceding prototype declares that function **draw** is a constant function that takes no arguments, returns nothing and is a **virtual** function.

Software Engineering Observation 10.2

Once a function is declared **virtual**, *it remains* **virtual** *all the way down the inheritance hierarchy from that point even if it is not declared* **virtual** *when a class overrides it.*

Good Programming Practice 10.1

Even though certain functions are implicitly **virtual** *because of a declaration made higher in the class hierarchy, explicitly declare these functions* **virtual** *at every level of the hierarchy to promote program clarity.*

Software Engineering Observation 10.3

When a derived class chooses not to define a **virtual** *function, the derived class simply inherits its immediate base class'* **virtual** *function definition.*

If function **draw** in the base class has been declared **virtual**, and if we then use a base-class pointer or reference to point to the derived-class object and invoke the **draw** function using this pointer (e.g., **shapePtr->draw()**) or reference, the program will choose the correct derived class' **draw** function dynamically (i.e., at run time) based on the object type—not the pointer or reference type. Such *dynamic binding* will be illustrated in the case studies in Sections 10.6 and 10.9.

When a **virtual** function is called by referencing a specific object by name and using the dot member selection operator (e.g., **squareObject.draw()**), the reference is resolved at compile time (this is called *static binding*) and the **virtual** function that is called is the one defined for (or inherited by) the class of that particular object.

10.4 Abstract Base Classes and Concrete Classes

When we think of a class as a type, we assume that objects of that type will be instantiated. However, there are cases in which it is useful to define classes for which the programmer never intends to instantiate any objects. Such classes are called *abstract classes*. Because these are used as base classes in inheritance situations, we normally will refer to them as *abstract base classes*. No objects of an abstract base class can be instantiated.

The sole purpose of an abstract class is to provide an appropriate base class from which classes may inherit interface and/or implementation. Classes from which objects can be instantiated are called *concrete classes*.

We could have an abstract base class **TwoDimensionalShape** and derive concrete classes such as **Square**, **Circle**, **Triangle**, etc. We could also have an abstract base class **ThreeDimensionalShape** and derive concrete classes such as **Cube**, **Sphere**, **Cylinder**, etc. Abstract base classes are too generic to define real objects; we need to be more specific before we can think of instantiating objects. That is what concrete classes do; they provide the specifics that make it reasonable to instantiate objects.

A class is made abstract by declaring one or more of its **virtual** functions to be "pure." A *pure* **virtual** *function* is one with an *initializer of* **= 0** in its declaration as in

```
virtual double earnings() const = 0;    // pure virtual
```

Software Engineering Observation 10.4

*If a class is derived from a class with a pure **virtual** function, and if no definition is supplied for that pure **virtual** function in the derived class, then that **virtual** function remains pure in the derived class. Consequently, the derived class is also an abstract class.*

Common Programming Error 10.1

*Attempting to instantiate an object of an abstract class (i.e., a class that contains one or more pure **virtual** functions) is a syntax error.*

A hierarchy does not need to contain any abstract classes, but as we will see, many good object-oriented systems have class hierarchies headed by an abstract base class. In some cases, abstract classes constitute the top few levels of the hierarchy. A good example of this is a shape hierarchy. The hierarchy could be headed by abstract base class **Shape**. On the next level down, we can have two more abstract base classes, namely **TwoDimensionalShape** and **ThreeDimensionalShape**. The next level down would start defining concrete classes for two-dimensional shapes such as circles and squares, and concrete classes for three-dimensional shapes such as spheres and cubes.

10.5 Polymorphism

C++ enables *polymorphism*—the ability for objects of different classes related by inheritance to respond differently to the same message (i.e., member function call). The same message sent to many different types of objects takes on "many forms"—hence the term polymorphism. If, for example, class **Rectangle** is derived from class **Quadrilateral**, then a **Rectangle** object *is a* more specific version of a **Quadrilateral** object. An operation (such as calculating the perimeter or the area) that can be performed on an **Quadrilateral** object also can be performed on a **Rectangle** object.

Polymorphism is implemented via **virtual** functions. When a request is made through a base-class pointer (or reference) to use a **virtual** function, C++ chooses the correct overridden function in the appropriate derived class associated with the object.

Sometimes a non-**virtual** member function is defined in a base class and overridden in a derived class. If such a member function is called through a base-class pointer to the derived-class object, the base-class version is used. If the member function is called through a derived-class pointer, the derived-class version is used. This is non-polymorphic behavior.

Consider the following example using the **Employee** base class and **Hourly-Worker** derived class of Fig. 9.5:

```
Employee e, *ePtr = &e;
HourlyWorker h, *hPtr = &h;
ePtr->print();      // call base-class print function
hPtr->print();      // call derived-class print function
ePtr = &h;          // allowable implicit conversion
ePtr->print();      // still calls base-class print
```

Our **Employee** base class and **HourlyWorker** derived class both have their own **print** functions defined. Because the functions were not declared **virtual** and they have the same signature, calling the **print** function through an **Employee** pointer results in **Employee::print()** being called (regardless of whether the **Employee** pointer is pointing to a base-class **Employee** object or a derived-class **HourlyWorker** object) and calling the **print** function through an **HourlyWorker** pointer results in **Hourly-Worker::print()** being called. The base-class **print** function is also available to the derived class, but to call the base-class **print** for a derived-class object through a pointer to a derived-class object, for example, the function must be called explicitly as follows:

```
hPtr->Employee::print();   // call base-class print function
```

This specifies that the base-class **print** should be called explicitly.

Through the use of **virtual** functions and polymorphism, one member function call can cause different actions to occur depending on the type of the object receiving the call (we will see that a small amount of execution-time overhead is required). This gives the programmer tremendous expressive capability. We will see examples of the power of polymorphism and **virtual** functions in the next several sections.

Software Engineering Observation 10.5

*With **virtual** functions and polymorphism, the programmer can deal in generalities and let the execution-time environment concern itself with the specifics. The programmer can command a wide variety of objects to behave in manners appropriate to those objects without even knowing the types of those objects.*

Software Engineering Observation 10.6

Polymorphism promotes extensibility: Software written to invoke polymorphic behavior is written independently of the types of the objects to which messages are sent. Thus, new types of objects that can respond to existing messages can be added into such a system without modifying the base system. Except for client code that instantiates new objects, programs need not be recompiled.

Software Engineering Observation 10.7

*An abstract class defines an interface for the various members of a class hierarchy. The abstract class contains pure **virtual** functions that will be defined in the derived classes. All functions in the hierarchy can use this same interface through polymorphism.*

Although we cannot instantiate objects of abstract base classes, we *can* declare pointers and references to abstract base classes. Such pointers and references can then be used to enable polymorphic manipulations of derived-class objects when such objects are instantiated from concrete classes.

Let us consider applications of polymorphism and **virtual** functions. A screen manager needs to display many objects of different classes, including new object types that will be added to the system even after the screen manager is written. The system may need to display various shapes (i.e., base class is **Shape**) such as squares, circles, triangles, rectangles, points, lines and the like (each shape class is derived from the base class **Shape**). The screen manager uses base-class pointers or references (to **Shape**) to manage all the objects to be displayed. To draw any object (regardless of the level at which that object appears in the inheritance hierarchy), the screen manager uses a base-class pointer (or reference) to the object and simply sends a **draw** message to the object. Function **draw** has been declared pure **virtual** in base class **Shape** and has been overridden in each of the derived classes. Each **Shape** object knows how to draw itself. The screen manager does not have to worry about what type each object is or whether the object is of a type the screen manager has seen before—the screen manager simply tells each object to **draw** itself.

Polymorphism is particularly effective for implementing layered software systems. In operating systems, for example, each type of physical device may operate differently from the others. Regardless of this, commands to *read* or *write* data from and to devices can have a certain uniformity. The *write* message sent to a device-driver object needs to be interpreted specifically in the context of that device driver and how that device driver manipulates devices of a specific type. However, the *write* call itself is really no different from the *write* to any other device in the system—it simply places some number of bytes from memory onto that device. An object-oriented operating system might use an abstract base class to provide an interface appropriate for all device drivers. Then, through inheritance from that abstract base class, derived classes are formed that all operate similarly. The capabilities (i.e., the **public** interface) offered by the device drivers are provided as pure **virtual** functions in the abstract base class. Implementations of these **virtual** functions are provided in the derived classes that correspond to the specific types of device drivers.

With polymorphic programming, a program might walk through a container, such as an array of pointers to objects from various levels of a class hierarchy. The pointers in such an array would all be base-class pointers to derived-class objects. For example, an array of objects of class **TwoDimensionalShape** could contain **TwoDimensionalShape *** pointers to objects from the derived classes **Square**, **Circle**, **Triangle**, **Rectangle**, **Line**, etc. Sending a message to draw each object in the array would, using polymorphism, draw the correct picture on the screen.

10.6 Case Study: A Payroll System Using Polymorphism

Let us use **virtual** functions and polymorphism to perform payroll calculations based on the type of an employee (Fig. 10.1). We use a base class **Employee**. The derived classes of **Employee** are **Boss** who gets paid a fixed weekly salary regardless of the number of hours worked, **CommissionWorker** who gets a flat base salary plus a percentage of sales, **PieceWorker** who gets paid by the number of items produced, and **Hourly-Worker** who gets paid by the hour and receives overtime pay.

An **earnings** function call certainly applies generically to all employees. But the way each person's earnings are calculated depends on the class of the employee, and these classes are all derived from the base class **Employee**. So **earnings** is declared pure **virtual** in base class **Employee** and appropriate implementations of **earnings** are provided for each of the derived classes. Then, to calculate any employee's earnings, the program simply uses a base-class pointer (or reference) to that employee's object and invokes the **earnings** function. In a real payroll system, the various employee objects might be pointed to by individual elements in an array (or list) of pointers of type **Employee ***. The program would simply walk through the array one element at a time using the **Employee *** pointers to invoke the **earnings** function of each object.

```
1   // Fig. 10.1: employ2.h
2   // Abstract base class Employee
3   #ifndef EMPLOY2_H
4   #define EMPLOY2_H
5
6   class Employee {
7   public:
8      Employee( const char *, const char * );
9      ~Employee();   // destructor reclaims memory
10     const char *getFirstName() const;
11     const char *getLastName() const;
12
13     // Pure virtual function makes Employee abstract base class
14     virtual double earnings() const = 0;   // pure virtual
15     virtual void print() const;            // virtual
16   private:
17     char *firstName;
18     char *lastName;
19   };
20
21   #endif
```

Fig. 10.1 Demonstrating polymorphism with the **Employee** class hierarchy— **employ2.h**.

```
22  // Fig. 10.1: employ2.cpp
23  // Member function definitions for
24  // abstract base class Employee.
25  // Note: No definitions given for pure virtual functions.
```

Fig. 10.1 Demonstrating polymorphism with the **Employee** class hierarchy— **employ2.cpp** (part 1 of 2)

```
26  #include <iostream>
27
28  using std::cout;
29
30  #include <cstring>
31  #include <cassert>
32  #include "employ2.h"
33
34  // Constructor dynamically allocates space for the
35  // first and last name and uses strcpy to copy
36  // the first and last names into the object.
37  Employee::Employee( const char *first, const char *last )
38  {
39     firstName = new char[ strlen( first ) + 1 ];
40     assert( firstName != 0 );     // test that new worked
41     strcpy( firstName, first );
42
43     lastName = new char[ strlen( last ) + 1 ];
44     assert( lastName != 0 );     // test that new worked
45     strcpy( lastName, last );
46  }
47
48  // Destructor deallocates dynamically allocated memory
49  Employee::~Employee()
50  {
51     delete [] firstName;
52     delete [] lastName;
53  }
54
55  // Return a pointer to the first name
56  // Const return type prevents caller from modifying private
57  // data. Caller should copy returned string before destructor
58  // deletes dynamic storage to prevent undefined pointer.
59  const char *Employee::getFirstName() const
60  {
61     return firstName;     // caller must delete memory
62  }
63
64  // Return a pointer to the last name
65  // Const return type prevents caller from modifying private
66  // data. Caller should copy returned string before destructor
67  // deletes dynamic storage to prevent undefined pointer.
68  const char *Employee::getLastName() const
69  {
70     return lastName;     // caller must delete memory
71  }
72
73  // Print the name of the Employee
74  void Employee::print() const
75     { cout << firstName << ' ' << lastName; }
```

Fig. 10.1 Demonstrating polymorphism with the **Employee** class hierarchy—
employ2.cpp (part 2 of 2)

```
76   // Fig. 10.1: boss1.h
77   // Boss class derived from Employee
78   #ifndef BOSS1_H
79   #define BOSS1_H
80   #include "employ2.h"
81
82   class Boss : public Employee {
83   public:
84      Boss( const char *, const char *, double = 0.0 );
85      void setWeeklySalary( double );
86      virtual double earnings() const;
87      virtual void print() const;
88   private:
89      double weeklySalary;
90   };
91
92   #endif
```

Fig. 10.1   Demonstrating polymorphism with the **Employee** class hierarchy—
           `boss1.h`.

```
93   // Fig. 10.1: boss1.cpp
94   // Member function definitions for class Boss
95   #include <iostream>
96
97   using std::cout;
98
99   #include "boss1.h"
100
101  // Constructor function for class Boss
102  Boss::Boss( const char *first, const char *last, double s )
103     : Employee( first, last )   // call base-class constructor
104  { setWeeklySalary( s ); }
105
106  // Set the Boss's salary
107  void Boss::setWeeklySalary( double s )
108     { weeklySalary = s > 0 ? s : 0; }
109
110  // Get the Boss's pay
111  double Boss::earnings() const { return weeklySalary; }
112
113  // Print the Boss's name
114  void Boss::print() const
115  {
116     cout << "\n             Boss: ";
117     Employee::print();
118  }
```

Fig. 10.1   Demonstrating polymorphism with the **Employee** class hierarchy—
           `boss1.cpp`.

```
119   // Fig. 10.1: commis1.h
120   // CommissionWorker class derived from Employee
121   #ifndef COMMIS1_H
122   #define COMMIS1_H
123   #include "employ2.h"
124
125   class CommissionWorker : public Employee {
126   public:
127      CommissionWorker( const char *, const char *,
128                        double = 0.0, double = 0.0,
129                        int = 0 );
130      void setSalary( double );
131      void setCommission( double );
132      void setQuantity( int );
133      virtual double earnings() const;
134      virtual void print() const;
135   private:
136      double salary;        // base salary per week
137      double commission;    // amount per item sold
138      int quantity;         // total items sold for week
139   };
140
141   #endif
```

Fig. 10.1   Demonstrating polymorphism with the **Employee** class hierarchy—
             `commis1.h`.

```
142   // Fig. 10.1: commis1.cpp
143   // Member function definitions for class CommissionWorker
144   #include <iostream>
145
146   using std::cout;
147
148   #include "commis1.h"
149
150   // Constructor for class CommissionWorker
151   CommissionWorker::CommissionWorker( const char *first,
152         const char *last, double s, double c, int q )
153      : Employee( first, last )  // call base-class constructor
154   {
155      setSalary( s );
156      setCommission( c );
157      setQuantity( q );
158   }
159
160   // Set CommissionWorker's weekly base salary
161   void CommissionWorker::setSalary( double s )
162      { salary = s > 0 ? s : 0; }
163
```

Fig. 10.1   Demonstrating polymorphism with the **Employee** class hierarchy—
             `commis1.cpp` (part 1 of 2).

```
164   // Set CommissionWorker's commission
165   void CommissionWorker::setCommission( double c )
166     { commission = c > 0 ? c : 0; }
167
168   // Set CommissionWorker's quantity sold
169   void CommissionWorker::setQuantity( int q )
170     { quantity = q > 0 ? q : 0; }
171
172   // Determine CommissionWorker's earnings
173   double CommissionWorker::earnings() const
174     { return salary + commission * quantity; }
175
176   // Print the CommissionWorker's name
177   void CommissionWorker::print() const
178   {
179      cout << "\nCommission worker: ";
180      Employee::print();
181   }
```

Fig. 10.1   Demonstrating polymorphism with the **Employee** class hierarchy—
             commis1.cpp (part 2 of 2).

```
182   // Fig. 10.1: piece1.h
183   // PieceWorker class derived from Employee
184   #ifndef PIECE1_H
185   #define PIECE1_H
186   #include "employ2.h"
187
188   class PieceWorker : public Employee {
189   public:
190      PieceWorker( const char *, const char *,
191                   double = 0.0, int = 0);
192      void setWage( double );
193      void setQuantity( int );
194      virtual double earnings() const;
195      virtual void print() const;
196   private:
197      double wagePerPiece; // wage for each piece output
198      int quantity;        // output for week
199   };
200
201   #endif
```

Fig. 10.1   Demonstrating polymorphism with the **Employee** class hierarchy—
             piece1.h.

```
202   // Fig. 10.1: piece1.cpp
203   // Member function definitions for class PieceWorker
204   #include <iostream>
205
```

Fig. 10.1   Demonstrating polymorphism with the **Employee** class hierarchy—
             piece1.cpp (part 1 of 2).

```
206  using std::cout;
207
208  #include "piece1.h"
209
210  // Constructor for class PieceWorker
211  PieceWorker::PieceWorker( const char *first, const char *last,
212                            double w, int q )
213     : Employee( first, last )   // call base-class constructor
214  {
215     setWage( w );
216     setQuantity( q );
217  }
218
219  // Set the wage
220  void PieceWorker::setWage( double w )
221     { wagePerPiece = w > 0 ? w : 0; }
222
223  // Set the number of items output
224  void PieceWorker::setQuantity( int q )
225     { quantity = q > 0 ? q : 0; }
226
227  // Determine the PieceWorker's earnings
228  double PieceWorker::earnings() const
229     { return quantity * wagePerPiece; }
230
231  // Print the PieceWorker's name
232  void PieceWorker::print() const
233  {
234     cout << "\n     Piece worker: ";
235     Employee::print();
236  }
```

Fig. 10.1   Demonstrating polymorphism with the **Employee** class hierarchy— **piece1.cpp** (part 2 of 2).

```
237  // Fig. 10.1: hourly1.h
238  // Definition of class HourlyWorker
239  #ifndef HOURLY1_H
240  #define HOURLY1_H
241  #include "employ2.h"
242
243  class HourlyWorker : public Employee {
244  public:
245     HourlyWorker( const char *, const char *,
246                   double = 0.0, double = 0.0);
247     void setWage( double );
248     void setHours( double );
249     virtual double earnings() const;
250     virtual void print() const;
```

Fig. 10.1   Demonstrating polymorphism with the **Employee** class hierarchy— **hourly1.h** (part 1 of 2).

```
251  private:
252     double wage;    // wage per hour
253     double hours;   // hours worked for week
254  };
255
256  #endif
```

Fig. 10.1 Demonstrating polymorphism with the **Employee** class hierarchy—
hourly1.h (part 2 of 2).

```
257  // Fig. 10.1: hourly1.cpp
258  // Member function definitions for class HourlyWorker
259  #include <iostream>
260
261  using std::cout;
262
263  #include "hourly1.h"
264
265  // Constructor for class HourlyWorker
266  HourlyWorker::HourlyWorker( const char *first,
267                              const char *last,
268                              double w, double h )
269     : Employee( first, last )    // call base-class constructor
270  {
271     setWage( w );
272     setHours( h );
273  }
274
275  // Set the wage
276  void HourlyWorker::setWage( double w )
277     { wage = w > 0 ? w : 0; }
278
279  // Set the hours worked
280  void HourlyWorker::setHours( double h )
281     { hours = h >= 0 && h < 168 ? h : 0; }
282
283  // Get the HourlyWorker's pay
284  double HourlyWorker::earnings() const
285  {
286     if ( hours <= 40 ) // no overtime
287        return wage * hours;
288     else               // overtime is paid at wage * 1.5
289        return 40 * wage + ( hours - 40 ) * wage * 1.5;
290  }
291
292  // Print the HourlyWorker's name
293  void HourlyWorker::print() const
294  {
295     cout << "\n    Hourly worker: ";
296     Employee::print();
297  }
```

Fig. 10.1 Demonstrating polymorphism with the **Employee** class hierarchy—
hourly1.cpp.

```
298   // Fig. 10.1: fig10_01.cpp
299   // Driver for Employee hierarchy
300   #include <iostream>
301
302   using std::cout;
303   using std::endl;
304
305   #include <iomanip>
306
307   using std::ios;
308   using std::setiosflags;
309   using std::setprecision;
310
311   #include "employ2.h"
312   #include "boss1.h"
313   #include "commis1.h"
314   #include "piece1.h"
315   #include "hourly1.h"
316
317   void virtualViaPointer( const Employee * );
318   void virtualViaReference( const Employee & );
319
320   int main()
321   {
322      // set output formatting
323      cout << setiosflags( ios::fixed | ios::showpoint )
324           << setprecision( 2 );
325
326      Boss b( "John", "Smith", 800.00 );
327      b.print();                               // static binding
328      cout << " earned $" << b.earnings();     // static binding
329      virtualViaPointer( &b );                 // uses dynamic binding
330      virtualViaReference( b );                // uses dynamic binding
331
332      CommissionWorker c( "Sue", "Jones", 200.0, 3.0, 150 );
333      c.print();                               // static binding
334      cout << " earned $" << c.earnings();     // static binding
335      virtualViaPointer( &c );                 // uses dynamic binding
336      virtualViaReference( c );                // uses dynamic binding
337
338      PieceWorker p( "Bob", "Lewis", 2.5, 200 );
339      p.print();                               // static binding
340      cout << " earned $" << p.earnings();     // static binding
341      virtualViaPointer( &p );                 // uses dynamic binding
342      virtualViaReference( p );                // uses dynamic binding
343
344      HourlyWorker h( "Karen", "Price", 13.75, 40 );
345      h.print();                               // static binding
346      cout << " earned $" << h.earnings();     // static binding
347      virtualViaPointer( &h );                 // uses dynamic binding
348      virtualViaReference( h );                // uses dynamic binding
349      cout << endl;
```

Fig. 10.1   Demonstrating polymorphism with the **Employee** class hierarchy—
         `fig10_01.cpp` (part 1 of 2).

```
350     return 0;
351 }
352
353 // Make virtual function calls off a base-class pointer
354 // using dynamic binding.
355 void virtualViaPointer( const Employee *baseClassPtr )
356 {
357     baseClassPtr->print();
358     cout << " earned $" << baseClassPtr->earnings();
359 }
360
361 // Make virtual function calls off a base-class reference
362 // using dynamic binding.
363 void virtualViaReference( const Employee &baseClassRef )
364 {
365     baseClassRef.print();
366     cout << " earned $" << baseClassRef.earnings();
367 }
```

```
           Boss: John Smith earned $800.00
           Boss: John Smith earned $800.00
           Boss: John Smith earned $800.00
Commission worker: Sue Jones earned $650.00
Commission worker: Sue Jones earned $650.00
Commission worker: Sue Jones earned $650.00
      Piece worker: Bob Lewis earned $500.00
      Piece worker: Bob Lewis earned $500.00
      Piece worker: Bob Lewis earned $500.00
     Hourly worker: Karen Price earned $550.00
     Hourly worker: Karen Price earned $550.00
     Hourly worker: Karen Price earned $550.00
```

Fig. 10.1   Demonstrating polymorphism with the **Employee** class hierarchy—
            fig10_01.cpp (part 2 of 2).

Let us consider the **Employee** class (lines 1–75). The **public** member functions include a constructor that takes the first name and last name as arguments; a destructor that reclaims dynamically allocated memory; a *get* function that returns the first name; a *get* function that returns the last name; a pure **virtual** function **earnings** and a **virtual** function **print**. Why is **earnings** pure **virtual**? The answer is that it does not make sense to provide an implementation of this function in the **Employee** class. We cannot calculate the earnings for a generic employee—we must first know what kind of employee it is. By making this function pure **virtual** we are indicating that we will provide an implementation of this function in each derived class, but not in the base class itself. The programmer never intends to call this pure **virtual** function in the abstract base class **Employee**; all derived classes will override **earnings** with appropriate implementations for those classes.

Class **Boss** (lines 76–118) is derived from **Employee** with **public** inheritance. The **public** member functions include a constructor that takes a first name, a last name and a weekly salary as arguments and passes the first name and last name to the **Employee** constructor to initialize the **firstName** and **lastName** members of the base-class part of the derived-class object; a *set* function to assign a new value to **private** data member **weeklySalary**; a virtual **earnings** function defining how to calculate a **Boss**' earnings and a **virtual print** function that outputs the type of the employee then calls **Employee::print()** to output the employee's name.

Class **CommissionWorker** (lines 119–181) is derived from **Employee** with **public** inheritance. The **public** member functions include a constructor that takes a first name, a last name, a salary, a commission and a quantity of items sold as arguments, and passes the first name and last name to the **Employee** constructor; *set* functions to assign new values to **private** data members **salary**, **commission** and **quantity**; a **virtual earnings** function defining how to calculate a **CommissionWorker**'s earnings and a **virtual print** function that outputs the type of the employee then calls **Employee::print()** to output the employee's name.

Class **PieceWorker** (lines 182–236) is derived from **Employee** with **public** inheritance. The **public** member functions include a constructor that takes a first name, a last name, a wage per piece and a quantity of items produced as arguments, and passes the first name and last name to the **Employee** constructor; *set* functions to assign new values to private data members **wagePerPiece** and **quantity**; a **virtual earnings** function defining how to calculate a **PieceWorker**'s earnings and a **virtual print** function that outputs the type of the employee then calls **Employee::print()** to output the employee's name.

Class **HourlyWorker** (lines 237–297) is derived from **Employee** with **public** inheritance. The **public** member functions include a constructor that takes a first name, a last name, a wage and the number of hours worked as arguments and passes the first name and last name to the **Employee** constructor to initialize the **firstName** and **lastName** members of the base-class part of the derived-class object; *set* functions to assign new values to **private** data members **wage** and **hours**; a **virtual earnings** function defining how to calculate an **HourlyWorker**'s earnings and a **virtual print** function that outputs the type of the employee then calls **Employee::print()** to output the employee's name.

The driver program is shown in lines 298–367. Each of the four code segments in **main** is similar, so we discuss only the first segment, which deals with a **Boss** object.
Line 326

```
Boss b( "John", "Smith", 800.00 );
```

instantiates derived-class object **b** of class **Boss** and provides the constructor arguments, including the first name, the last name and the fixed weekly salary.
Line 327

```
b.print();                              // static binding\
```

explicitly invokes the **Boss** version of member function **print** by using the dot member selection operator off the specific **Boss** object **b**. This is an example of static binding because the type of the object for which the function is being called is known at compile time. This call is included for comparison purposes to illustrate that the correct **print** function is invoked using dynamic binding.
Line 328

```
cout << " earned $" << b.earnings();    // static binding
```

explicitly invokes the **Boss** version of member function **earnings** by using the dot member selection operator off the specific **Boss** object **b**. This is also an example of static binding. This call is also included for comparison purposes, this time to illustrate that the correct **earnings** function is invoked using dynamic binding.

Line 329

```
virtualViaPointer( &b );            // uses dynamic binding
```

invokes function **virtualViaPointer** (line 355) with the address of derived-class object **b**. The function receives this address in its parameter **baseClassPtr,** which is declared as a **const Employee ***. This is precisely how to effect polymorphic behavior.

Line 357

```
baseClassPtr->print();
```

invokes member function **print** of the object pointed to by **baseClassPtr**. Because **print** is declared **virtual** in the base class, the system invokes the derived class object's **print** function—precisely what is called polymorphic behavior. This function call is an example of dynamic binding—the **virtual** function is invoked through a base-class pointer, so the decision as to what function to invoke is deferred until run time.

Line 358

```
cout << " earned $" << baseClassPtr->earnings();
```

invokes the **earnings** member function of the object pointed to by **baseClassPtr**. Because **earnings** is declared as a **virtual** function in the base class, the system invokes the derived-class object's **earnings** function. This, too, is dynamic binding.

Line 330

```
virtualViaReference( b );           // uses dynamic binding
```

invokes function **virtualViaReference** (line 363) to demonstrate that polymorphism can also be accomplished with **virtual** functions called off base-class references. The function receives object **b** in parameter **baseClassRef,** which is declared as a **const Employee &**. This is precisely how to effect polymorphic behavior with references.

Line 365

```
baseClassRef.print();
```

invokes the **print** member function of the object referred to by **baseClassRef**. Because **print** is declared as a **virtual** function in the base class, the system invokes the derived class object's **print** function. This function call is also an example of dynamic binding—the function is invoked through a base-class reference, so the decision as to what function to invoke is deferred until run time.

Line 366

```
cout << " earned $" << baseClassRef.earnings();
```

invokes the **earnings** member function of the object referred to by **baseClassRef**. Because **earnings** is declared as a **virtual** function in the base class, the system invokes the derived-class object's **earnings** function. This, too, is dynamic binding.

10.7 New Classes and Dynamic Binding

Polymorphism and **virtual** functions work nicely when all possible classes are not known in advance. But they also work when new kinds of classes are added to systems. New classes are accommodated by dynamic binding (also called *late binding*). An object's type need not be known at compile time for a **virtual** function call to be compiled. At run time, the **virtual** function call is matched with the appropriate member function of the called object.

A screen manager program can now display new kinds of objects as they are added to the system without the screen manager needing to be recompiled. The **draw** function call remains the same. The new objects themselves contain the actual drawing capabilities. This makes it easy to add new capabilities to systems with minimal impact. It also promotes software reuse.

Dynamic binding enables independent software vendors (ISVs) to distribute software without revealing proprietary secrets. Software distributions can consist of only header files and object files. No source code needs to be revealed. Software developers can then use inheritance to derive new classes from those provided by the ISVs. Software that works with the classes the ISVs provide will continue to work with the derived classes and will use (via dynamic binding) the overridden **virtual** functions provided in these classes.

In Section 10.9, we present an additional comprehensive polymorphism case study. In Section 10.10, we describe in depth precisely how polymorphism, virtual functions and dynamic binding are implemented in C++.

10.8 virtual Destructors

A problem can occur when using polymorphism to process dynamically allocated objects of a class hierarchy. If an object (with a non-**virtual** destructor) is destroyed explicitly by applying the **delete** operator to a base-class pointer to the object, the base-class destructor function (matching the pointer type) is called on the object. This occurs regardless of the type of the object to which the base-class pointer is pointing and regardless of the fact that each class's destructor has a different name.

There is a simple solution to this problem—declare a **virtual** base-class destructor. This makes all derived-class destructors **virtual** even though they do not have the same name as the base-class destructor. Now, if an object in the hierarchy is destroyed explicitly by applying the **delete** operator to a base-class pointer to a derived-class object, the destructor for the appropriate class is called. Remember, when a derived-class object is destroyed, the base-class part of the derived-class object is also destroyed—the base-class destructor automatically executes after the derived-class destructor.

Good Programming Practice 10.2

If a class has **virtual** *functions, provide a* **virtual** *destructor, even if one is not required for the class. Classes derived from this class may contain destructors that must be called properly.*

Common Programming Error 10.2

Constructors cannot be **virtual**. *Declaring a constructor as a* **virtual** *function is a syntax error.*

10.9 Case Study: Inheriting Interface and Implementation

Our next example (Fig. 10.2) re-examines the **Point**, **Circle**, **Cylinder** hierarchy from the previous chapter except that we now head the hierarchy with abstract base class **Shape**. **Shape** has two pure **virtual** functions—**printShapeName** and **print**—so **Shape** is an abstract base class. **Shape** contains two other **virtual** functions, **area** and **volume**, each of which has a default implementation that returns a value of zero. **Point** inherits these implementations from **Shape**. This makes sense because both the area and volume of a point are zero. **Circle** inherits the **volume** function from **Point**, but **Circle** provides its own implementation for the **area** function. **Cylinder** provides its own implementations for both the **area** function and the **volume** function.

Note that although **Shape** is an abstract base class, it still contains implementations of certain member functions, and these implementations are inheritable. The **Shape** class provides an inheritable interface in the form of four **virtual** functions that all members of the hierarchy will contain. Class **Shape** also provides some implementations that derived classes in the first few levels of the hierarchy will use.

Software Engineering Observation 10.8

A class can inherit interface and/or implementation from a base class. Hierarchies designed for implementation inheritance *tend to have their functionality high in the hierarchy—each new derived class inherits one or more member functions that were defined in a base class, and the new derived class uses the base-class definitions. Hierarchies designed for* interface inheritance *tend to have their functionality lower in the hierarchy—a base class specifies one or more functions that should be defined for each class in the hierarchy (i.e., they have the same signature), but the individual derived classes provide their own implementations of the function(s).*

Base class **Shape** (lines 1–16) consists of four **public virtual** functions and does not contain any data. Functions **printShapeName** and **print** are pure **virtual**, so they are overridden in each of the derived classes. Functions **area** and **volume** are defined to return **0.0**. These functions are overridden in derived classes when it is appropriate for those classes to have a different **area** calculation and/or a different **volume** calculation. Note that **Shape** is an abstract class and it contains some "impure" **virtual** functions (**area** and **volume**). Abstract classes can also include non-**virtual** functions and data, which will be inherited by derived classes.

Class **Point** (lines 17–54) is derived from **Shape** with **public** inheritance. A **Point** has an area of **0.0** and a volume of **0.0**, so the base-class member functions **area** and **volume** are not overridden here—they are simply inherited as defined in **Shape**. Functions **printShapeName** and **print** are implementations of **virtual** functions that were defined as pure **virtual** in the base class—if we did not override these functions in class **Point**, then **Point** would also be an abstract class and we would not be able to instantiate **Point** objects. Other member functions include a *set* function to assign new **x** and **y** coordinates to a **Point** and *get* functions to return the **x** and **y** coordinates of a **Point**.

Class **Circle** (lines 55–99) is derived from **Point** with **public** inheritance. A **Circle** has a volume of **0.0**, so base-class member function **volume** is not overridden here—it is inherited from **Point,** which previously inherited **volume** from **Shape**. A **Circle** has nonzero area, so the **area** function is overridden in this class. Functions

printShapeName and **print** are implementations of **virtual** functions that were defined as pure **virtual** in the **Shape** class. If these functions are not overridden here, the **Point** versions of these functions would be inherited. Other member functions include a *set* function to assign a new **radius** to a **Circle** and a *get* function to return the **radius** of a **Circle**.

```
1   // Fig. 10.2: shape.h
2   // Definition of abstract base class Shape
3   #ifndef SHAPE_H
4   #define SHAPE_H
5
6   class Shape {
7   public:
8      virtual double area() const { return 0.0; }
9      virtual double volume() const { return 0.0; }
10
11     // pure virtual functions overridden in derived classes
12     virtual void printShapeName() const = 0;
13     virtual void print() const = 0;
14  };
15
16  #endif
```

Fig. 10.2   Demonstrating interface inheritance with the **Shape** class hierarchy—
          shape.h.

```
17  // Fig. 10.2: point1.h
18  // Definition of class Point
19  #ifndef POINT1_H
20  #define POINT1_H
21
22  #include <iostream>
23
24  using std::cout;
25
26  #include "shape.h"
27
28  class Point : public Shape {
29  public:
30     Point( int = 0, int = 0 );   // default constructor
31     void setPoint( int, int );
32     int getX() const { return x; }
33     int getY() const { return y; }
34     virtual void printShapeName() const { cout << "Point: "; }
35     virtual void print() const;
36  private:
37     int x, y;   // x and y coordinates of Point
38  };
39
40  #endif
```

Fig. 10.2   Demonstrating interface inheritance with the **Shape** class hierarchy—
          point1.h.

Class **Cylinder** (lines 100–154) is derived from **Circle** with **public** inheritance. A **Cylinder** has area and volume different from those of **Circle**, so the **area** and **volume** functions are both overridden in this class. Functions **printShapeName** and **print** are implementations of **virtual** functions that were defined as pure **virtual** in the **Shape** class. If these functions are not overridden here, the **Circle** versions of these functions would be inherited. Other member functions include *set* and *get* functions to assign a new **height** and return the **height** of a **Cylinder**, respectively.

```
41   // Fig. 10.2: point1.cpp
42   // Member function definitions for class Point
43   #include "point1.h"
44
45   Point::Point( int a, int b ) { setPoint( a, b ); }
46
47   void Point::setPoint( int a, int b )
48   {
49      x = a;
50      y = b;
51   }
52
53   void Point::print() const
54      { cout << '[' << x << ", " << y << ']'; }
```

Fig. 10.2   Demonstrating interface inheritance with the **Shape** class hierarchy— **point1.cpp**.

```
55   // Fig. 10.2: circle1.h
56   // Definition of class Circle
57   #ifndef CIRCLE1_H
58   #define CIRCLE1_H
59   #include "point1.h"
60
61   class Circle : public Point {
62   public:
63      // default constructor
64      Circle( double r = 0.0, int x = 0, int y = 0 );
65
66      void setRadius( double );
67      double getRadius() const;
68      virtual double area() const;
69      virtual void printShapeName() const { cout << "Circle: "; }
70      virtual void print() const;
71   private:
72      double radius;    // radius of Circle
73   };
74
75   #endif
```

Fig. 10.2   Demonstrating interface inheritance with the **Shape** class hierarchy— **circle1.h**.

```
76   // Fig. 10.2: circle1.cpp
77   // Member function definitions for class Circle
78   #include <iostream>
79
80   using std::cout;
81
82   #include "circle1.h"
83
84   Circle::Circle( double r, int a, int b )
85      : Point( a, b )  // call base-class constructor
86   { setRadius( r ); }
87
88   void Circle::setRadius( double r ) { radius = r > 0 ? r : 0; }
89
90   double Circle::getRadius() const { return radius; }
91
92   double Circle::area() const
93      { return 3.14159 * radius * radius; }
94
95   void Circle::print() const
96   {
97      Point::print();
98      cout << "; Radius = " << radius;
99   }
```

Fig. 10.2   Demonstrating interface inheritance with the **Shape** class hierarchy—
`circle1.cpp`.

```
100  // Fig. 10.2: cylindr1.h
101  // Definition of class Cylinder
102  #ifndef CYLINDR1_H
103  #define CYLINDR1_H
104  #include "circle1.h"
105
106  class Cylinder : public Circle {
107  public:
108     // default constructor
109     Cylinder( double h = 0.0, double r = 0.0,
110              int x = 0, int y = 0 );
111
112     void setHeight( double );
113     double getHeight();
114     virtual double area() const;
115     virtual double volume() const;
116     virtual void printShapeName() const { cout << "Cylinder: "; }
117     virtual void print() const;
118  private:
119     double height;   // height of Cylinder
120  };
121
122  #endif
```

Fig. 10.2   Demonstrating interface inheritance with the **Shape** class hierarchy—
`cylindr1.h`.

```
123  // Fig. 10.2: cylindr1.cpp
124  // Member and friend function definitions for class Cylinder
125  #include <iostream>
126
127  using std::cout;
128
129  #include "cylindr1.h"
130
131  Cylinder::Cylinder( double h, double r, int x, int y )
132     : Circle( r, x, y )   // call base-class constructor
133  { setHeight( h ); }
134
135  void Cylinder::setHeight( double h )
136     { height = h > 0 ? h : 0; }
137
138  double Cylinder::getHeight() { return height; }
139
140  double Cylinder::area() const
141  {
142     // surface area of Cylinder
143     return 2 * Circle::area() +
144            2 * 3.14159 * getRadius() * height;
145  }
146
147  double Cylinder::volume() const
148     { return Circle::area() * height; }
149
150  void Cylinder::print() const
151  {
152     Circle::print();
153     cout << "; Height = " << height;
154  }
```

Fig. 10.2　Demonstrating interface inheritance with the **Shape** class hierarchy—
`cylindr1.cpp`.

```
155  // Fig. 10.2: fig10_02.cpp
156  // Driver for shape, point, circle, cylinder hierarchy
157  #include <iostream>
158
159  using std::cout;
160  using std::endl;
161
162  #include <iomanip>
163
164  using std::ios;
165  using std::setiosflags;
166  using std::setprecision;
167
168  #include "shape.h"
169  #include "point1.h"
```

Fig. 10.2　Demonstrating interface inheritance with the **Shape** class hierarchy—
`fig10_02.cpp` (part 1 of 3).

```
170   #include "circle1.h"
171   #include "cylindr1.h"
172
173   void virtualViaPointer( const Shape * );
174   void virtualViaReference( const Shape & );
175
176   int main()
177   {
178      cout << setiosflags( ios::fixed | ios::showpoint )
179         << setprecision( 2 );
180
181      Point point( 7, 11 );                    // create a Point
182      Circle circle( 3.5, 22, 8 );             // create a Circle
183      Cylinder cylinder( 10, 3.3, 10, 10 );    // create a Cylinder
184
185      point.printShapeName();    // static binding
186      point.print();             // static binding
187      cout << '\n';
188
189      circle.printShapeName();   // static binding
190      circle.print();            // static binding
191      cout << '\n';
192
193      cylinder.printShapeName(); // static binding
194      cylinder.print();          // static binding
195      cout << "\n\n";
196
197      Shape *arrayOfShapes[ 3 ];   // array of base-class pointers
198
199      // aim arrayOfShapes[0] at derived-class Point object
200      arrayOfShapes[ 0 ] = &point;
201
202      // aim arrayOfShapes[1] at derived-class Circle object
203      arrayOfShapes[ 1 ] = &circle;
204
205      // aim arrayOfShapes[2] at derived-class Cylinder object
206      arrayOfShapes[ 2 ] = &cylinder;
207
208      // Loop through arrayOfShapes and call virtualViaPointer
209      // to print the shape name, attributes, area, and volume
210      // of each object using dynamic binding.
211      cout << "Virtual function calls made off "
212         << "base-class pointers\n";
213
214      for ( int i = 0; i < 3; i++ )
215         virtualViaPointer( arrayOfShapes[ i ] );
216
217      // Loop through arrayOfShapes and call virtualViaReference
218      // to print the shape name, attributes, area, and volume
219      // of each object using dynamic binding.
220      cout << "Virtual function calls made off "
221         << "base-class references\n";
```

Fig. 10.2 Demonstrating interface inheritance with the **Shape** class hierarchy—
fig10_02.cpp (part 2 of 3).

```
222
223      for ( int j = 0; j < 3; j++ )
224         virtualViaReference( *arrayOfShapes[ j ] );
225
226      return 0;
227   }
228
229   // Make virtual function calls off a base-class pointer
230   // using dynamic binding.
231   void virtualViaPointer( const Shape *baseClassPtr )
232   {
233      baseClassPtr->printShapeName();
234      baseClassPtr->print();
235      cout << "\nArea = " << baseClassPtr->area()
236           << "\nVolume = " << baseClassPtr->volume() << "\n\n";
237   }
238
239   // Make virtual function calls off a base-class reference
240   // using dynamic binding.
241   void virtualViaReference( const Shape &baseClassRef )
242   {
243      baseClassRef.printShapeName();
244      baseClassRef.print();
245      cout << "\nArea = " << baseClassRef.area()
246           << "\nVolume = " << baseClassRef.volume() << "\n\n";
247   }
```

```
Point: [7, 11]
Circle: [22, 8]; Radius = 3.50
Cylinder: [10, 10]; Radius = 3.30; Height = 10.00
Virtual function calls made off base-class pointers
Point: [7, 11]
Area = 0.00
Volume = 0.00
Circle: [22, 8]; Radius = 3.50
Area = 38.48
Volume = 0.00
Cylinder: [10, 10]; Radius = 3.30; Height = 10.00
Area = 275.77
Volume = 342.12
Virtual function calls made off base-class references
Point: [7, 11]
Area = 0.00
Volume = 0.00
Circle: [22, 8]; Radius = 3.50
Area = 38.48
Volume = 0.00
Cylinder: [10, 10]; Radius = 3.30; Height = 10.00
Area = 275.77
Volume = 342.12
```

Fig. 10.2 Demonstrating interface inheritance with the **Shape** class hierarchy—
fig10_02.cpp (part 3 of 3).

The driver program (lines 155–247) begins by instantiating **Point** object **point**, **Circle** object **circle** and **Cylinder** object **cylinder**. Functions **printShapeName** and **print** are invoked for each object to print the name of the object and to illustrate that the objects are initialized correctly. Each call to **printShapeName** and **print** in lines 185 through 194 uses static binding—at compile time the compiler knows the type of each object for which **printShapeName** and **print** are called.

Next, array **arrayOfShapes**, each element of which is of type **Shape ***, is declared. This array of base-class pointers is used to point to each of the derived-class objects. The address of object **point** is assigned to **arrayOfShapes[0]** (line 200), the address of object **circle** is assigned to **arrayOfShapes[1]** (line 203) and the address of object **cylinder** is assigned to **arrayOfShapes[2]** (line 206).

Next, a **for** structure (line 214) walks through the array **arrayOfShapes** and invokes function **virtualViaPointer** (line 215)

```
virtualViaPointer( arrayOfShapes[ i ] );
```

for each element of the array. Function **virtualViaPointer** receives in parameter **baseClassPtr** (of type **const Shape ***) the address stored in an element of **arrayOfShapes**. Each time **virtualViaPointer** executes, the following four **virtual** function calls are made

```
baseClassPtr->printShapeName()
baseClassPtr->print()
baseClassPtr->area()
baseClassPtr->volume()
```

Each of these calls invokes a **virtual** function on the object to which **baseClassPtr** points at run time—an object whose type cannot be determined here at compile time. The output illustrates that the appropriate functions for each class are invoked. First, the string **"Point: "** and the coordinates of the object **point** are output; the area and volume are both **0.00**. Next, the string **"Circle: "**, the coordinates of the center of object **circle** and the radius of object **circle** are output; the area of **circle** is calculated and the volume is returned as **0.00**. Finally, the string **"Cylinder: "**, the coordinates of the center of the base of object **cylinder**, the radius of object **cylinder** and the height of object **cylinder** are output; the area of **cylinder** is calculated and the volume of **cylinder** is calculated. All the **virtual** function calls to **printShapeName**, **print**, **area** and **volume** are resolved at run-time with dynamic binding.

Finally, a **for** structure (line 223) walks through **arrayOfShapes** and invokes function **virtualViaReference** (line 224)

```
virtualViaReference( *arrayOfShapes[ j ] );
```

for each element of the array. Function **virtualViaReference** receives in its parameter **baseClassRef** (of type **const Shape &**), a reference formed by dereferencing the address stored in an element of the array. During each call to **virtualViaReference**, the following **virtual** function calls are made

```
baseClassRef.printShapeName()
baseClassRef.print()
```

```
baseClassRef.area()
baseClassRef.volume()
```

Each of the preceding calls invokes these functions on the object to which **baseClass-Ref** refers. The output produced using base-class references is identical to the output produced using base-class pointers.

10.10 Polymorphism, `virtual` Functions and Dynamic Binding "Under the Hood"

C++ makes polymorphism easy to program. It is certainly possible to program for polymorphism in non-object-oriented languages such as C, but doing so requires complex and potentially dangerous pointer manipulations. In this section we discuss how C++ implements polymorphism, **virtual** functions and dynamic binding internally. This will give you a solid understanding of how these capabilities really work. More importantly, it will help you appreciate the overhead of polymorphism—in additional memory consumption and processor time. This will help you determine when to use polymorphism and when to avoid it. As you will see in Chapter 20, "Standard Template Library (STL)," the STL components were implemented without polymorphism and **virtual** functions—this was done to avoid execution-time overhead and achieve optimal performance to meet the unique requirements of the STL.

First, we will explain the data structures the C++ compiler builds at compile time to support polymorphism at run time. Then, we will show how an executing program uses these data structures to execute **virtual** functions and achieve the dynamic binding associated with polymorphism.

When C++ compiles a class that has one or more **virtual** functions, it builds a **virtual** *function table (vtable)* for that class. The *vtable* is used by the executing program to select the proper function implementations each time a **virtual** function of that class is to be executed. Figure 10.3 illustrates the **virtual** function tables for classes **Shape**, **Point**, **Circle** and **Cylinder**.

In the *vtable* for class **Shape**, the first function pointer points to the implementation of the **area** function for that class, namely a function that returns an area of **0.0**. The second function pointer points to the **volume,** function which also returns **0.0**. The **printShapeName** and **print** functions are each pure **virtual**—they lack implementations so their function pointers are each set to **0**. Any class that has one or more **0** pointers in its *vtable* is an abstract class. Classes without any **0** *vtable* pointers (as **Point, Circle** and **Cylinder**) are concrete classes.

Class **Point** inherits the **area** and **volume** functions of class **Shape**, so the compiler simply sets these two pointers in the *vtable* for class **Point** to be copies of the **area** and **volume** pointers in class **Shape**. Class **Point** overrides function **printShapeName** to print **"Point: "** so the function pointer points to the **printShapeName** function of class **Point**. **Point** also overrides **print** so the corresponding function pointer points to the **Point** class function that prints **[x, y]**.

The **Circle area** function pointer in the *vtable* for class **Circle** points to the **Circle area** function that returns πr^2. The **volume** function pointer is simply copied from the **Point** class—that pointer was previously copied into **Point** from **Shape**. The **printShapeName** function pointer points to the **Circle** version of the function that prints "**Circle:** ". The **print** function pointer points to **Circle**'s **print** function that prints **[x, y] r**.

The **Cylinder area** function pointer in the *vtable* for class **Cylinder** points to the **Cylinder area** function that calculates the surface area of the **Cylinder**, namely $2\pi r^2 + 2\pi rh$. The **Cylinder volume** function pointer points to a **volume** function that returns $\pi r^2 h$. The **Cylinder printShapeName** function pointer points to a function that prints "**Cylinder:** ". The **Cylinder print** function pointer points to its function that prints **[x, y] r h**.

Polymorphism is accomplished through a complex data structure involving three levels of pointers. We have discussed one level—the function pointers in the *vtable*. These pointers point to the actual functions to be executed when a **virtual** function is invoked.

Now we consider the second level of pointers. Whenever an object of a class with **virtual** functions is instantiated, the compiler attaches to the front of the object a pointer to the *vtable* for that class. [Note: This pointer is normally at the front of the object, but it is not required to be implemented that way.]

The third level of pointer is simply the handle on the object that is receiving the **virtual** function call (this handle may also be a reference).

Now let us see how a typical **virtual** function call is executed. Consider the call

> **baseClassPtr->printShapeName()**

in function **virtualViaPointer**. Assume for the following discussion that **baseClassPtr** contains the address in **arrayOfShapes[1]** (i.e., the address of object **circle**). When the compiler compiles this statement, it determines that the call is indeed being made off a base-class pointer and that **printShapeName** is a **virtual** function.

Next, the compiler determines that **printShapeName** is the third entry in each of the *vtables*. To locate this entry, the compiler notes that it will need to skip the first two entries. Thus, the compiler compiles an *offset* or *displacement* of 8 bytes (4 bytes for each pointer on today's popular 32-bit machines) into the machine language object code that will execute the **virtual** function call.

Then, the compiler generates code that will (Note: The numbers in the list below correspond to the circled numbers in Fig. 10.3):

1. Select the *ith* entry from **arrayOfShapes** (in this case the address of object **circle**) and pass it to **virtualViaPointer**. This sets **baseClassPtr** to point to **circle**.

2. Dereference that pointer to get to the **circle** object—which as you recall, begins with a pointer to the **Circle** *vtable*.

3. Dereference **circle**'s *vtable* pointer to get to the **Circle** *vtable*.

4. Skip the offset of 8 bytes to pick up the **printShapeName** function pointer.

5. Dereference the **printShapeName** function pointer to form the name of the actual function to be executed and use the function call operator **()** to execute the appropriate **printShapeName** function and print the character string "**Circle:** ".

The data structures of Fig. 10.3 may appear to be complex, but most of this complexity is managed by the compiler and hidden from the programmer, making polymorphic programming straightforward in C++.

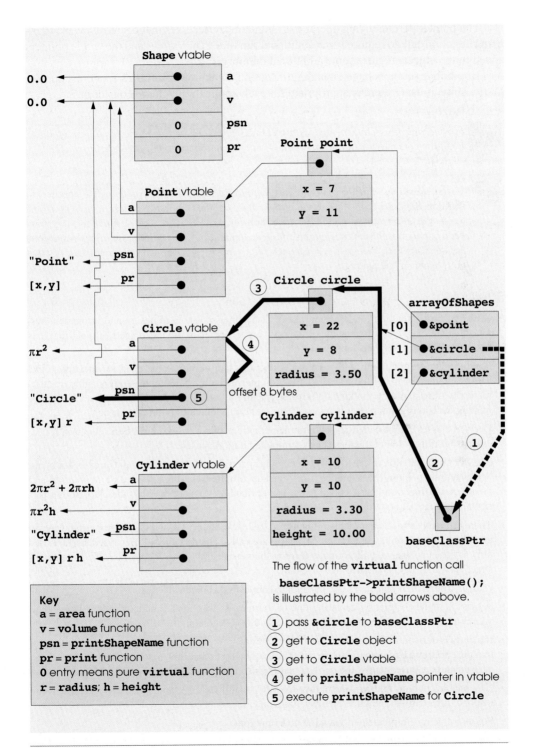

Fig. 10.3　Flow of control of a **virtual** function call.

The pointer dereferencing operations and memory accesses that occur on every **virtual** function call do require some additional run time. The *vtables* and the *vtable* pointers added to the objects require some additional memory.

Hopefully, you now have enough information about how **virtual** functions operate to determine if using them is appropriate for each application you are considering.

Performance Tip 10.1

Polymorphism as implemented with **virtual** *functions and dynamic binding is efficient. Programmers may use these capabilities with nominal impact on system performance.*

Performance Tip 10.2

Virtual functions and dynamic binding enable polymorphic programming as opposed to **switch** *logic programming. C++ optimizing compilers normally generate code that runs at least as efficiently as hand-coded* **switch***-based logic. One way or the other, the overhead of polymorphism is acceptable for most applications. But in some situations—real-time applications with stringent performance requirements, for example—the overhead of polymorphism may be too high.*

SUMMARY

- With **virtual** functions and polymorphism, it becomes possible to design and implement systems that are more easily extensible. Programs can be written to process objects of types that may not exist when the program is under development.

- Polymorphic programming with **virtual** functions can eliminate the need for **switch** logic. The programmer can use the **virtual** function mechanism to perform the equivalent logic automatically, thus avoiding the kinds of errors typically associated with **switch** logic. Client code making decisions about object types and representations indicates poor class design.

- Derived classes can provide their own implementations of a base class **virtual** function if necessary, but if they do not, the base class's implementation is used.

- If a **virtual** function is called by referencing a specific object by name and using the dot member selection operator, the reference is resolved at compile time (this is called *static binding*) and the **virtual** function that is called is the one defined for (or inherited by) the class of that particular object.

- There are many situations in which it is useful to define classes for which the programmer never intends to instantiate any objects. Such classes are called abstract classes. Because these are used only as base classes, we will normally refer to them as abstract base classes. No objects of an abstract class may be instantiated in a program.

- Classes from which objects can be instantiated are called concrete classes.

- A class is made abstract by declaring one or more of its **virtual** functions to be pure. A pure **virtual** function is one with an initializer of **= 0** in its declaration.

- If a class is derived from a class with a pure **virtual** function without supplying a definition for that pure **virtual** function in the derived class, then that **virtual** function remains pure in the derived class. Consequently, the derived class is also an abstract class.

- C++ enables polymorphism—the ability for objects of different classes related by inheritance to respond differently to the same member function call.

- Polymorphism is implemented via **virtual** functions.

- When a request is made through a base-class pointer or reference to use a **virtual** function, C++ chooses the correct overridden function in the appropriate derived class associated with the object.

- Through the use of **virtual** functions and polymorphism, one member function call can cause different actions depending on the type of the object receiving the call.

- Although we cannot instantiate objects of abstract base classes, we can declare pointers to abstract base classes. Such pointers can be used to enable polymorphic manipulations of derived-class objects when such objects are instantiated from concrete classes.

- New kinds of classes are regularly added to systems. New classes are accommodated by dynamic binding (also called late binding). The type of an object need not be known at compile time for a **virtual** function call to be compiled. At run time, the **virtual** function call is matched with the member function of the receiving object.

- Dynamic binding enables independent software vendors (ISVs) to distribute software without revealing proprietary secrets. Software distributions can consist of only header files and object files. No source code needs to be revealed. Software developers can then use inheritance to derive new classes from those provided by the ISVs. The software that works with the classes the ISVs provide will continue to work with the derived classes and will use (via dynamic binding) the overridden **virtual** functions provided in these classes.

- Dynamic binding requires that at run time, the call to a **virtual** member function be routed to the **virtual** function version appropriate for the class. A **virtual** function table called the *vtable* is implemented as an array containing function pointers. Each class with **virtual** functions has a *vtable*. For each **virtual** function in the class, the *vtable* has an entry containing a function pointer to the version of the **virtual** function to use for an object of that class. The **virtual** function to use for a particular class could be the function defined in that class, or it could be a function inherited either directly or indirectly from a base class higher in the hierarchy.

- When a base class provides a **virtual** member function, derived classes can override the **virtual** function, but they do not have to override it. Thus, a derived class can use a base class' version of a **virtual** member function, and this would be indicated in the *vtable*.

- Each object of a class with **virtual** functions contains a pointer to the *vtable* for that class. The appropriate function pointer in the *vtable* is obtained and dereferenced to complete the call at run time. This *vtable* lookup and pointer dereferencing require nominal run time overhead, usually less than the best possible client code.

- Declare the base-class destructor **virtual** if the class contains **virtual** functions. This makes all derived-class destructors **virtual** even though they do not have the same name as the base-class destructor. If an object in the hierarchy is destroyed explicitly by applying the **delete** operator to a base-class pointer to a derived-class object, the destructor for the appropriate class is called.

- Any class that has one or more **0** pointers in its *vtable* is an abstract class. Classes without any **0** *vtable* pointers (like **Point**, **Circle** and **Cylinder**) are concrete classes.

TERMINOLOGY

abstract base class
abstract class
base-class **virtual** function
class hierarchy
concrete class
convert derived-class pointer to base-class pointer
derived class
derived-class constructor
direct base class
displacement into *vtable*

dynamic binding
override a pure **virtual** function
override a **virtual** function
pointer to a base class
pointer to a derived class
pointer to an abstract class
polymorphism
programming "in the general"
programming "in the specific"
pure **virtual** function (= **0**)

reference to a base class	offset into *vtable*
early binding	reference to a derived class
eliminating **switch** statements	reference to an abstract class
explicit pointer conversion	software reusability
extensibility	static binding
implementation inheritance	**switch** logic
independent software vendor (ISV)	**virtual** destructor
indirect base class	**virtual** function
inheritance	**virtual** function table
interface inheritance	*vtable*
late binding	*vtable* pointer

COMMON PROGRAMMING ERRORS

10.1 Attempting to instantiate an object of an abstract class (i.e., a class that contains one or more pure **virtual** functions) is a syntax error.

10.2 Constructors cannot be **virtual**. Declaring a constructor as a **virtual** function is a syntax error.

GOOD PROGRAMMING PRACTICES

10.1 Even though certain functions are implicitly **virtual** because of a declaration made higher in the class hierarchy, explicitly declare these functions **virtual** at every level of the hierarchy to promote program clarity.

10.2 If a class has **virtual** functions, provide a **virtual** destructor, even if one is not required for the class. Classes derived from this class may contain destructors that must be called properly.

PERFORMANCE TIPS

10.1 Polymorphism as implemented with **virtual** functions and dynamic binding is efficient. Programmers may use these capabilities with nominal impact on system performance.

10.2 Virtual functions and dynamic binding enable polymorphic programming as opposed to **switch** logic programming. C++ optimizing compilers normally generate code that runs at least as efficiently as hand-coded **switch**-based logic. One way or the other, the overhead of polymorphism is acceptable for most applications. But in some situations—real-time applications with stringent performance requirements, for example—the overhead of polymorphism may be too high.

SOFTWARE ENGINEERING OBSERVATIONS

10.1 An interesting consequence of using **virtual** functions and polymorphism is that programs take on a simplified appearance. They contain less branching logic in favor of simpler sequential code. This facilitates testing, debugging, program maintenance and bug avoidance.

10.2 Once a function is declared **virtual**, it remains **virtual** all the way down the inheritance hierarchy from that point even if it is not declared **virtual** when a class overrides it.

10.3 When a derived class chooses not to define a **virtual** function, the derived class simply inherits its immediate base class' **virtual** function definition.

10.4 If a class is derived from a class with a pure **virtual** function, and if no definition is supplied for that pure **virtual** function in the derived class, then that **virtual** function remains pure in the derived class. Consequently, the derived class is also an abstract class.

10.5   With **virtual** functions and polymorphism, the programmer can deal in generalities and let the execution-time environment concern itself with the specifics. The programmer can command a wide variety of objects to behave in manners appropriate to those objects without even knowing the types of those objects.

10.6   Polymorphism promotes extensibility: Software written to invoke polymorphic behavior is written independently of the types of the objects to which messages are sent. Thus, new types of objects that can respond to existing messages can be added into such a system without modifying the base system. Except for client code that instantiates new objects, programs need not be recompiled.

10.7   An abstract class defines an interface for the various members of a class hierarchy. The abstract class contains pure **virtual** functions that will be defined in the derived classes. All functions in the hierarchy can use this same interface through polymorphism.

10.8   A class can inherit interface and/or implementation from a base class. Hierarchies designed for implementation inheritance tend to have their functionality high in the hierarchy—each new derived class inherits one or more member functions that were defined in a base class, and the new derived class uses the base-class definitions. Hierarchies designed for interface inheritance tend to have their functionality lower in the hierarchy—a base class specifies one or more functions that should be defined for each class in the hierarchy (i.e., they have the same signature), but the individual derived classes provide their own implementations of the function(s).

SELF-REVIEW EXERCISE

10.1   Fill in the blanks in each of the following:
  a) Using inheritance and polymorphism helps eliminate _____ logic.
  b) A pure **virtual** function is specified by placing _____ at the end of its prototype in the class definition.
  c) If a class contains one or more pure **virtual** functions, it is an _____.
  d) A function call resolved at compile time is referred to as _____ binding.
  e) A function call resolved at run time is referred to as _____ binding.

ANSWERS TO SELF-REVIEW EXERCISE

10.1   a) **switch**. b) **= 0**. c) abstract base class. d) static or early. e) dynamic or late.

EXERCISES

10.2   What are **virtual** functions? Describe a circumstance in which **virtual** functions would be appropriate.

10.3   Given that constructors cannot be **virtual**, describe a scheme for how you might achieve a similar effect.

10.4   How is it that polymorphism enables you to program "in the general" rather than "in the specific." Discuss the key advantages of programming "in the general."

10.5   Discuss the problems of programming with **switch** logic. Explain why polymorphism is an effective alternative to using **switch** logic.

10.6   Distinguish between static binding and dynamic binding. Explain the use of **virtual** functions and the vtable in dynamic binding.

10.7   Distinguish between inheriting interface and inheriting implementation. How do inheritance hierarchies designed for inheriting interface differ from those designed for inheriting implementation?

10.8   Distinguish between **virtual** functions and pure **virtual** functions.

10.9   (True/False) All **virtual** functions in an abstract base class must be declared as pure **virtual** functions.

10.10   Suggest one or more levels of abstract base classes for the **Shape** hierarchy discussed in this chapter (the first level is **Shape** and the second level consists of the classes **TwoDimensionalShape** and **ThreeDimensionalShape**).

10.11   How does polymorphism promote extensibility?

10.12   You have been asked to develop a flight simulator that will have elaborate graphical outputs. Explain why polymorphic programming would be especially effective for a problem of this nature.

10.13   Develop a basic graphics package. Use the **Shape** class inheritance hierarchy from Chapter 9. Limit yourself to two-dimensional shapes such as squares, rectangles, triangles and circles. Interact with the user. Let the user specify the position, size, shape and fill characters to be used in drawing each shape. The user can specify many items of the same shape. As you create each shape, place a **Shape *** pointer to each new **Shape** object into an array. Each class has its own **draw** member function. Write a polymorphic screen manager that walks through the array (preferably using an iterator) sending **draw** messages to each object in the array to form a screen image. Redraw the screen image each time the user specifies an additional shape.

10.14   Modify the payroll system of Fig. 10.1 to add private data members **birthDate** (a **Date** object) and **departmentCode** (an **int**) to class **Employee**. Assume this payroll is processed once per month. Then, as your program calculates the payroll for each **Employee** (polymorphically), add a $100.00 bonus to the person's payroll amount if this is the month in which the **Employee**'s birthday occurs.

10.15   In Exercise 9.14, you developed a **Shape** class hierarchy and defined the classes in the hierarchy. Modify the hierarchy so that class **Shape** is an abstract base class containing the interface to the hierarchy. Derive **TwoDimensionalShape** and **ThreeDimensionalShape** from class **Shape**—these classes should also be abstract. Use a **virtual print** function to output the type and dimensions of each class. Also include **virtual area** and **volume** functions so these calculations can be performed for objects of each concrete class in the hierarchy. Write a driver program that tests the **Shape** class hierarchy.

11

C++ Stream
Input/Output

Objectives

- To understand how to use C++ object-oriented stream input/output.
- To be able to format inputs and outputs.
- To understand the stream I/O class hierarchy.
- To understand how to input/output objects of user-defined types.
- To be able to create user-defined stream manipulators.
- To be able to determine the success or failure of input/output operations.
- To be able to tie output streams to input streams.

Consciousness ... does not appear to itself chopped up in bits ... A "river" or a "stream" are the metaphors by which it is most naturally described.
William James

All the news that's fit to print.
Adolph S. Ochs

Outline

Summary • Terminology • Common Programming Errors • Good Programming Practices • Performance Tip • Portability Tip • Software Engineering Observations • Self-Review Exercises • Answers to Self-Review Exercises • Exercises

11.1 Introduction

The C++ standard libraries provide an extensive set of input/output capabilities. This chapter discusses a range of capabilities sufficient for performing most common I/O operations and overviews the remaining capabilities. Some of the features presented here were discussed earlier in the text, but this chapter provides a more complete discussion of the input/output capabilities of C++.

Many of the I/O features described here are object-oriented. The reader should find it interesting to see how such capabilities are implemented. This style of I/O makes use of other C++ features, such as references, function overloading and operator overloading.

As we will see, C++ uses *type safe I/O*. Each I/O operation is automatically performed in a manner sensitive to the data type. If an I/O function has been properly defined to handle a particular data type, then that function is called to handle that data type. If there is no match between the type of the actual data and a function for handling that data type, a compiler error indication is set. Thus, improper data cannot sneak through the system (as can occur in C—a hole in C that allows for some rather subtle and often bizarre errors).

Users may specify I/O of user-defined types as well as standard types. This *extensibility* is one of the most valuable features of C++.

Good Programming Practice 11.1

Use the C++ form of I/O exclusively in C++ programs, despite the fact that C-style I/O is available to C++ programmers.

Software Engineering Observation 11.1

C++ style I/O is type safe.

Software Engineering Observation 11.2

C++ enables a common treatment of I/O of predefined types and user-defined types. This kind of commonality facilitates software development in general and software reuse in particular.

11.2 Streams

C++ I/O occurs in *streams* of bytes. A stream is simply a sequence of bytes. In input operations, the bytes flow from a device (e.g., a keyboard, a disk drive, a network connection) to main memory. In output operations, bytes flow from main memory to a device (e.g., a display screen, a printer, a disk drive, a network connection).

The application associates meaning with bytes. The bytes may represent ASCII characters, internal format raw data, graphics images, digital speech, digital video or any other kind of information an application may require.

The job of the system I/O mechanisms is to move bytes from devices to memory and vice versa in a consistent and reliable manner. Such transfers often involve mechanical motion such as the rotation of a disk or a tape, or typing keystrokes at a keyboard. The time these transfers take is normally huge compared to the time the processor takes to manipulate data internally. Thus, I/O operations require careful planning and tuning to ensure maximum performance.

C++ provides both "low-level" and "high-level" I/O capabilities. Low-level I/O capabilities (i.e., unformatted I/O) typically specify that some number of bytes should simply be transferred device-to-memory or memory-to-device. In such transfers, the individual byte is the item of interest. Such low-level capabilities do provide high-speed, high-volume transfers, but these capabilities are not particularly convenient for people.

People prefer a higher-level view of I/O (i.e., *formatted I/O*), in which bytes are grouped into meaningful units such as integers, floating-point numbers, characters, strings and user-defined types. These type-oriented capabilities are satisfactory for most I/O other than high-volume file processing.

Performance Tip 11.1

Use unformatted I/O for the best performance in high-volume file processing.

11.2.1 Iostream Library Header Files

The C++ **iostream** library provides hundreds of I/O capabilities. Several header files contain portions of the library interface.

Most C++ programs include the **<iostream>** header file, which declares basic services required for all stream-I/O operations. The **<iostream>** header file defines the **cin**, **cout**, **cerr** and **clog** objects which correspond to the standard input stream, the standard output stream, the unbuffered standard error stream and the buffered standard error stream, respectively. Both unformatted- and formatted-I/O services are provided.

The **<iomanip>** header declares services useful for performing formatted I/O with so-called *parameterized stream manipulators*.

The **<fstream>** header declares services important for user-controlled file processing operations. We use this header in the file processing programs of Chapter 14.

C++ implementations generally contain other I/O-related libraries that provide system-specific capabilities such as controlling special-purpose devices for audio and video I/O.

11.2.2 Stream Input/Output Classes and Objects

The **iostream** library contains many classes for handling a wide variety of I/O operations. The **istream** class supports stream-input operations. The **ostream** class supports stream-output operations. The **iostream** class supports both stream-input and stream-output operations.

The **istream** class and the **ostream** class are each derived through single inheritance from the **ios** base class. The **iostream** class is derived through multiple inheritance from both the **istream** class and the **ostream** class. These inheritance relationships are summarized in Fig. 11.1.

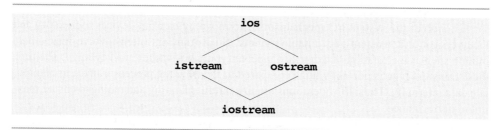

Fig. 11.1   Portion of the stream I/O class hierarchy.

Operator overloading provides a convenient notation for performing input/output. The left shift operator (**<<**) is overloaded to designate stream output and is referred to as the *stream-insertion operator*. The right shift operator (**>>**) is overloaded to designate stream input and is referred to as the *stream-extraction operator*. These operators are used with the standard stream objects **cin**, **cout**, **cerr** and **clog**, and commonly with user-defined stream objects.

The predefined object **cin** is an instance of the **istream** class and is said to be "tied to" (or connected to) the standard input device, normally the keyboard. The stream-extraction operator (**>>**) as used in the following statement causes a value for the integer variable **grade** (assuming that **grade** has been declared as an **int** variable) to be input from **cin** to memory:

```
      cin >> grade;   // data "flows" in the direction of the arrows
                      // to the right
```

Note that the stream-extraction operation is "smart enough" to "know" what the type of the data is. Assuming that **grade** has been properly declared, no additional type information needs to be specified for use with the stream-extraction operator (as is the case, incidentally, in C-style I/O).

The predefined object **cout** is an instance of the **ostream** class and is said to be "tied to" the standard output device, normally the display screen. The stream-insertion operator (**<<**) as used in the following statement causes the value of the integer variable **grade** (assuming that **grade** has been declared as an **int** variable) to be output from memory to the standard output device:

```
      cout << grade; // data "flows" in the direction of the arrows
                     // to the left
```

Note that the stream-insertion operator is "smart enough" to "know" the type of **grade** (assuming it has been properly declared), so no additional type information needs to be specified for use with the stream-insertion operator.

The predefined object **cerr** is an instance of the **ostream** class and is said to be "tied to" the standard error device. Outputs to object **cerr** are unbuffered. This means that each stream insertion to **cerr** causes its output to appear immediately; this is appropriate for promptly notifying a user about errors.

The predefined object **clog** is an instance of the **ostream** class and is also said to be "tied to" the standard error device. Outputs to **clog** are buffered. This means that each insertion to **clog** could cause its output to be held in a buffer until the buffer is filled or until the buffer is flushed.

C++ file processing uses the classes **ifstream** to perform file input operations, **ofstream** for file output operations and **fstream** for file input/output operations. The **ifstream** class inherits from **istream**, the **ofstream** class inherits from **ostream** and the **fstream** class inherits from **iostream**. The various inheritance relationships of the I/O-related classes are summarized in Fig. 11.2. There are many more classes in the full stream-I/O class hierarchy supported at most installations, but the classes shown here provide the vast majority of the capabilities most programmers will need. See the class library reference for your C++ system for more file processing information.

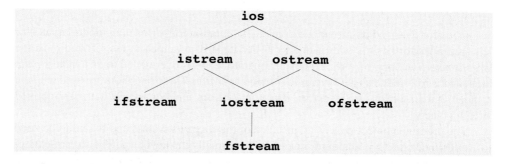

Fig. 11.2 Portion of stream-I/O class hierarchy with key file-processing classes.

11.3 Stream Output

The C++ **ostream** class provides the ability to perform formatted and unformatted output. Capabilities for output include output of standard data types with the stream-insertion operator; output of characters with the **put** member function; unformatted output with the **write** member function (Section 11.5); output of integers in decimal, octal and hexadecimal formats (Section 11.6.1); output of floating-point values with various precisions (Section 11.6.2), with forced decimal points (Section 11.7.2), in scientific notation and in fixed notation (Section 11.7.6); output of data justified in fields of designated field widths (Section 11.7.3); output of data in fields padded with specified characters (Section 11.7.4); and output of uppercase letters in scientific notation and hexadecimal notation (Section 11.7.7).

11.3.1 Stream-Insertion Operator

Stream output may be performed with the stream-insertion operator (i.e., the overloaded **<<** operator). The **<<** operator is overloaded to output data items of built-in types, to output strings and to output pointer values. Section 11.9 shows how to overload **<<** to output data items of user-defined types. Figure 11.3 demonstrates output of a string using a single stream-insertion statement. Multiple insertion statements may be used as in Fig. 11.4. When this program is run, it produces the same output as the previous program.

```
1  // Fig. 11.3: fig11_03.cpp
2  // Outputting a string using stream insertion.
3  #include <iostream>
4
5  using std::cout;
6
7  int main()
8  {
9     cout << "Welcome to C++!\n";
10
11     return 0;
12 }
```

```
Welcome to C++!
```

Fig. 11.3 Outputting a string using stream insertion.

```
1   // Fig. 11.4: fig11_04.cpp
2   // Outputting a string using two stream insertions.
3   #include <iostream>
4
5   using std::cout;
6
7   int main()
8   {
9       cout << "Welcome to ";
10      cout << "C++!\n";
11
12      return 0;
13  }
```

```
Welcome to C++!
```

Fig. 11.4   Outputting a string using two stream insertions.

The effect of the **\n** (newline) escape sequence is also achieved by the **endl** (end line) *stream manipulator*, as in Fig. 11.5. The **endl** stream manipulator issues a newline character and, in addition, flushes the output buffer (i.e., causes the output buffer to be output immediately even if it is not full). The output buffer may also be flushed simply by

```
cout << flush;
```

Stream manipulators are discussed in detail in Section 11.6.

Expressions can be output as shown in Fig. 11.6.

Good Programming Practice 11.2

When outputting expressions, place them in parentheses to prevent operator precedence problems between the operators in the expression and the **<<** *operator.*

```
1   // Fig. 11.5: fig11_05.cpp
2   // Using the endl stream manipulator.
3   #include <iostream>
4
5   using std::cout;
6   using std::endl;
7
8   int main()
9   {
10      cout << "Welcome to ";
11      cout << "C++!";
12      cout << endl;     // end line stream manipulator
13
14      return 0;
15  }
```

```
Welcome to C++!
```

Fig. 11.5   Using the **endl** stream manipulator.

```
1    // Fig. 11.6: fig11_06.cpp
2    // Outputting expression values.
3    #include <iostream>
4
5    using std::cout;
6    using std::endl;
7
8    int main()
9    {
10      cout << "47 plus 53 is ";
11
12      // parentheses not needed; used for clarity
13      cout << ( 47 + 53 );        // expression
14      cout << endl;
15
16      return 0;
17   }
```

```
47 plus 53 is 100
```

Fig. 11.6   Outputting expression values.

11.3.2 Cascading Stream-Insertion/Extraction Operators

The overloaded **<<** and **>>** operators may each be used in a *cascaded form* as shown in Fig. 11.7.

The multiple stream insertions in Fig. 11.7 are executed as if they had been written

$$(\; (\; (\; \texttt{cout} \; \texttt{<<} \; \texttt{"47 plus 53 is "} \;) \; \texttt{<<} \; (\; \texttt{47} \; \texttt{+} \; \texttt{53} \;) \;) \; \texttt{<<} \; \texttt{endl} \;);$$

(i.e., **<<** associates from left to right). This kind of cascading of stream-insertion operators is allowed because the overloaded **<<** operator returns a reference to its left-operand object, (i.e., **cout**). Thus the leftmost parenthesized expression

```
1    // Fig. 11.7: fig11_07.cpp
2    // Cascading the overloaded << operator.
3    #include <iostream>
4
5    using std::cout;
6    using std::endl;
7
8    int main()
9    {
10      cout << "47 plus 53 is " << ( 47 + 53 ) << endl;
11
12      return 0;
13   }'
```

```
47 plus 53 is 100
```

Fig. 11.7   Cascading the overloaded **<<** operator.

```
( cout << "47 plus 53 is " )
```

outputs the specified character string and returns a reference to **cout**. This allows the middle parenthesized expression to be evaluated as

```
( cout << ( 47 + 53 ) )
```

which outputs the integer value **100** and returns a reference to **cout**. The rightmost parenthesized expression is then evaluated as

```
cout << endl
```

which outputs a newline, flushes **cout** and returns a reference to **cout**. This last return is not used.

11.3.3 Output of **char *** Variables

In C-style I/O, it is necessary for the programmer to supply type information. C++ determines data types automatically—a nice improvement over C. But sometimes this "gets in the way." For example, we know that a character string is of type **char ***. Suppose we want to print the value of that pointer, i.e., the memory address of the first character of that string. But the **<<** operator has been overloaded to print data of type **char *** as a null-terminated string. The solution is to cast the pointer to **void *** (this should be done to any pointer variable the programmer wishes to output as an address). Figure 11.8 demonstrates printing a **char *** variable in both string and address formats. Note that the address prints as a hexadecimal (base 16) number. We say more about controlling the bases of numbers in Sections 11.6.1, 11.7.4, 11.7.5 and 11.7.7. *Note:* The output of the program in Fig. 11.8 may differ from compiler to compiler.

```
1   // Fig. 11.8: fig11_08.cpp
2   // Printing the address stored in a char* variable
3   #include <iostream>
4
5   using std::cout;
6   using std::endl;
7
8   int main()
9   {
10      char *string = "test";
11
12      cout << "Value of string is: " << string
13           << "\nValue of static_cast< void * >( string ) is: "
14           << static_cast< void * >( string ) << endl;
15      return 0;
16  }
```

```
Value of string is: test
Value of static_cast< void *>( string ) is: 0046C070
```

Fig. 11.8   Printing the address stored in a **char *** variable.

11.3.4 Character Output with Member Function `put`; Cascading `puts`

The **put** member function outputs one character as in

```
cout.put( 'A' );
```

which displays **A** on the screen. Calls to **put** may be cascaded as in

```
cout.put( 'A' ).put( '\n' );
```

which outputs the letter **A** followed by a newline character. As with **<<**, the preceding statement executes in this manner because the dot operator (**.**) associates from left to right and the **put** member function returns a reference to the **ostream** object that received the **put** message (function call). The **put** function may also be called with an ASCII-valued expression, as in **cout.put(65),** which also outputs **A**.

11.4 Stream Input

Now let us consider stream input. This may be performed with the stream-extraction operator, i.e., the overloaded **>>** operator. This operator normally skips *whitespace characters* (such as blanks, tabs and newlines) in the input stream. Later we will see how to change this behavior. The stream-extraction operator returns zero (false) when end-of-file is encountered on a stream; otherwise, the stream-extraction operator returns a reference to the object that received the extraction message (e.g., **cin** in the expression **cin >> grade**). Each stream contains a set of *state bits* used to control the state of the stream (i.e., formatting, setting error states, etc.). Stream extraction causes the stream's **failbit** to be set if data of the wrong type are input and causes the stream's **badbit** to be set if the operation fails. We will soon see how to test these bits after an I/O operation. Sections 11.7 and 11.8 discuss the stream state bits in detail.

11.4.1 Stream-Extraction Operator

To read two integers, use the **cin** object and the overloaded **>>** stream-extraction operator as in Fig. 11.9. Note that stream-extraction operations can also be cascaded.

```
1   // Fig. 11.9: fig11_09.cpp
2   // Calculating the sum of two integers input from the keyboard
3   // with cin and the stream-extraction operator.
4   #include <iostream>
5
6   using std::cout;
7   using std::cin;
8   using std::endl;
9
10  int main()
11  {
12      int x, y;
13
```

Fig. 11.9   Calculating the sum of two integers input from the keyboard with **cin** and the stream-extraction operator (part 1 of 2).

```
1         cout << "Enter two integers: ";
2         cin >> x >> y;
3         cout << "Sum of " << x << " and " << y << " is: "
4              << ( x + y ) << endl;
5
6         return 0;
7  }
```

```
Enter two integers: 30 92
Sum of 30 and 92 is: 122
```

Fig. 11.9   Calculating the sum of two integers input from the keyboard with **cin** and the stream-extraction operator (part 2 of 2).

The relatively high precedence of the **>>** and **<<** operators can cause problems. For example, the program of Fig. 11.10 will not compile properly without the parentheses around the conditional expression. The reader should verify this.

```
1   // Fig. 11.10: fig11_10.cpp
2   // Avoiding a precedence problem between the stream-insertion
3   // operator and the conditional operator.
4   // Need parentheses around the conditional expression.
5   #include <iostream>
6
7   using std::cout;
8   using std::cin;
9   using std::endl;
10
11  int main()
12  {
13     int x, y;
14
15     cout << "Enter two integers: ";
16     cin >> x >> y;
17     cout << x << ( x == y ? " is" : " is not" )
18          << " equal to " << y << endl;
19
20     return 0;
21  }
```

```
Enter two integers: 7 5
7 is not equal to 5
```

```
Enter two integers: 8 8
8 is equal to 8
```

Fig. 11.10   Avoiding a precedence problem between the stream-insertion operator and the conditional operator .

Common Programming Error 11.1

Attempting to read from an **ostream** *(or from any other output-only stream).*

Common Programming Error 11.2

Attempting to write to an istream (or to any other input-only stream).

Common Programming Error 11.3

Not providing parentheses to force proper precedence when using the relatively high precedence stream-insertion operator **<<** *or stream-extraction operator* **>>**.

A popular way to input a series of values is to use the stream-extraction operation in the loop-continuation condition of a **while** loop. The extraction returns false (0) when end-of-file is encountered. Consider the program of Fig. 11.11, which finds the highest grade on an exam. Assume that the number of grades is not known in advance and that the user will type end-of-file to indicate that all the grades have been entered. The **while** condition, **(cin >> grade)**, becomes 0 (interpreted as **false**) when the user enters end-of-file.

```cpp
1   // Fig. 11.11: fig11_11.cpp
2   // Stream-extraction operator returning false on end-of-file.
3   #include <iostream>
4
5   using std::cout;
6   using std::cin;
7   using std::endl;
8
9   int main()
10  {
11      int grade, highestGrade = -1;
12
13      cout << "Enter grade (enter end-of-file to end): ";
14      while ( cin >> grade ) {
15         if ( grade > highestGrade )
16            highestGrade = grade;
17
18         cout << "Enter grade (enter end-of-file to end): ";
19      }
20
21      cout << "\n\nHighest grade is: " << highestGrade << endl;
22      return 0;
23  }
```

```
Enter grade (enter end-of-file to end): 67
Enter grade (enter end-of-file to end): 87
Enter grade (enter end-of-file to end): 73
Enter grade (enter end-of-file to end): 95
Enter grade (enter end-of-file to end): 34
Enter grade (enter end-of-file to end): 99
Enter grade (enter end-of-file to end): ^Z
Highest grade is: 99
```

Fig. 11.11 Stream-extraction operator returning **false** on end-of-file.

Portability Tip 11.1

When prompting the user on how to end input from the keyboard, ask the user to "enter end-of-file to end input" rather than prompting for <ctrl>-d (UNIX and Macintosh) or <ctrl>-z (PC and VAX).

In Fig. 11.11, **cin >> grade** can be used as a condition because the base class **ios** (from which **istream** is inherited) provides an overloaded cast operator that converts a stream into a pointer of type **void ***. The value of the returned pointer is 0 (**false**) if an error occurred while attempting to read a value or the end-of-file indicator was encountered. The compiler is able to use the **void *** cast operator implicitly.

11.4.2 get and getline Member Functions

The **get** member function with no arguments inputs one character from the designated stream (even if this is whitespace) and returns this character as the value of the function call. This version of **get** returns **EOF** when end-of-file on the stream is encountered.

Figure 11.12 demonstrates the use of member functions **eof** and **get** on input stream **cin** and member function **put** on output stream **cout**. The program first prints the value of **cin.eof()**, i.e., **false** (**0** on the output) to show that end-of-file has not occurred on **cin**. The user enters a line of text and presses *Enter* followed by end-of-file (*<ctrl>-z* on IBM PC-compatible systems, *<ctrl>-d* on UNIX and Macintosh systems). The program reads each character and outputs it to **cout** using member function **put**. When the end-of-file is encountered, the **while** ends and **cin.eof()**—now **true**—is printed again (**1** on the output) to show that end-of-file has been set on **cin**. Note that this program uses the version of **istream** member function **get** that takes no arguments and returns the character being input.

```
1   // Fig. 11.12: fig11_12.cpp
2   // Using member functions get, put and eof.
3   #include <iostream>
4
5   using std::cout;
6   using std::cin;
7   using std::endl;
8
9   int main()
10  {
11     char c;
12
13     cout << "Before input, cin.eof() is " << cin.eof()
14         << "\nEnter a sentence followed by end-of-file:\n";
15
16     while ( ( c = cin.get() ) != EOF )
17        cout.put( c );
18
19     cout << "\nEOF in this system is: " << c;
20     cout << "\nAfter input, cin.eof() is " << cin.eof() << endl;
21     return 0;
22  }
```

Fig. 11.12 Using member functions **get**, **put** and **eof** (part 1 of 2).

```
Before input, cin.eof() is 0
Enter a sentence followed by end-of-file:
Testing the get and put member functions^Z
Testing the get and put member functions
EOF in this system is: -1
After input cin.eof() is 1
```

Fig. 11.12 Using member functions **get**, **put** and **eof** (part 2 of 2).

The **get** member function with a character reference argument inputs the next character from the input stream (even if this is a whitespace character) and stores it in the character argument. This version of **get** returns 0 when end-of-file is encountered; otherwise this version of **get** returns a reference to the **istream** object for which the **get** member function is being invoked.

A third version of the **get** member function takes three arguments—a character array, a size limit and a delimiter (with default value **'\n'**). This version reads characters from the input stream. It reads up to one less than the specified maximum number of characters and terminates, or terminates as soon as the delimiter is read. A null character is inserted to terminate the input string in the character array used as a buffer by the program. The delimiter is not placed in the character array, but does remain in the input stream (the delimiter will be the next character read). Thus, the result of a second consecutive **get** is an empty line unless the delimiter character is flushed from the input stream. Figure 11.13 compares input using **cin** with stream extraction (which reads characters until a whitespace character is encountered) and input with **cin.get**. Note that the call to **cin.get** does not specify a delimiter character, so the default **'\n'** is used.

```
1   // Fig. 11.13: fig11_13.cpp
2   // Contrasting input of a string with cin and cin.get.
3   #include <iostream>
4
5   using std::cout;
6   using std::cin;
7   using std::endl;
8
9   int main()
10  {
11     const int SIZE = 80;
12     char buffer1[ SIZE ], buffer2[ SIZE ];
13
14     cout << "Enter a sentence:\n";
15     cin >> buffer1;
16     cout << "\nThe string read with cin was:\n"
17          << buffer1 << "\n\n";
18
19     cin.get( buffer2, SIZE );
20     cout << "The string read with cin.get was:\n"
21          << buffer2 << endl;
```

Fig. 11.13 Contrasting input of a string using **cin** with stream extraction and input with **cin.get** (part 1 of 2).

```
22
23    return 0;
24  }
```

```
Enter a sentence:
Contrasting string input with cin and cin.get

The string read with cin was:
Contrasting

The string read with cin.get was:
 string input with cin and cin.get
```

Fig. 11.13 Contrasting input of a string using **cin** with stream extraction and input with **cin.get** (part 2 of 2).

The **getline** member function operates like the third version of the **get** member function and inserts a null character after the line in the character array. The **getline** function removes the delimiter from the stream (i.e., reads the character and discards it), but does not store it in the character array. The program of Fig. 11.14 demonstrates the use of the **getline** member function to input a line of text.

```
1   // Fig. 11.14: fig11_14.cpp
2   // Character input with member function getline.
3   #include <iostream>
4
5   using std::cout;
6   using std::cin;
7   using std::endl;
8
9   int main()
10  {
11     const SIZE = 80;
12     char buffer[ SIZE ];
13
14     cout << "Enter a sentence:\n";
15     cin.getline( buffer, SIZE );
16
17     cout << "\nThe sentence entered is:\n" << buffer << endl;
18     return 0;
19  }
```

```
Enter a sentence:
Using the getline member function

The sentence entered is:
Using the getline member function
```

Fig. 11.14 Character input with member function **getline**.

11.4.3 `istream` Member Functions `peek`, `putback` and `ignore`

The **ignore** member function skips over a designated number of characters (the default is one character) or terminates upon encountering a designated delimiter (the default delimiter is **EOF,** which causes **ignore** to skip to the end of the file when reading from a file).

The **putback** member function places the previous character obtained by a **get** from an input stream back onto that stream. This function is useful for applications that scan an input stream looking for a field beginning with a specific character. When that character is input, the application puts the character back on the stream so that the character can be included in the data about to be input.

The **peek** member function returns the next character from an input stream, but does not remove the character from the stream.

11.4.4 Type-Safe I/O

C++ offers *type-safe I/O*. The **<<** and **>>** operators are overloaded to accept data items of specific types. If unexpected data are processed, various error flags are set which the user may test to determine if an I/O operation succeeded or failed. In this manner, the program "stays in control." We discuss these error flags in Section 11.8.

11.5 Unformatted I/O with `read`, `gcount` and `write`

Unformatted input/output is performed with the **read** and **write** member functions. Each of these inputs or outputs some number of bytes to or from a character array in memory. These bytes are not formatted in any way. They are simply input or output as raw bytes. For example, the call

```
char buffer[] = "HAPPY BIRTHDAY";
cout.write( buffer, 10 );
```

outputs the first 10 bytes of **buffer** (including null characters that would cause output with **cout** and **<<** to terminate). Since a character string evaluates to the address of its first character, the call

```
cout.write( "ABCDEFGHIJKLMNOPQRSTUVWXYZ", 10 );
```

displays the first 10 characters of the alphabet.

The **read** member function inputs a designated number of characters into a character array. If fewer than the designated number of characters are read, **failbit** is set. We will soon see how to determine if **failbit** has been set (see Section 11.8). Member function **gcount** reports the number of characters read by the last input operation.

Figure 11.15 demonstrates **istream** member functions **read** and **gcount** and **ostream** member function **write**. The program inputs 20 characters (from a longer input sequence) into character array **buffer** with **read**, determines the number of characters input with **gcount** and outputs the characters in **buffer** with **write**.

```
1   // Fig. 11.15: fig11_15.cpp
2   // Unformatted I/O with read, gcount and write.
```

Fig. 11.15 Unformatted I/O with the **read**, **gcount** and **write** member functions (part 1 of 2).

```
3    #include <iostream>
4
5    using std::cout;
6    using std::cin;
7    using std::endl;
8
9    int main()
10   {
11      const int SIZE = 80;
12      char buffer[ SIZE ];
13
14      cout << "Enter a sentence:\n";
15      cin.read( buffer, 20 );
16      cout << "\nThe sentence entered was:\n";
17      cout.write( buffer, cin.gcount() );
18      cout << endl;
19      return 0;
20   }
```

```
Enter a sentence:
Using the read, write, and gcount member functions
The sentence entered was:
Using the read, writ
```

Fig. 11.15 Unformatted I/O with the **read**, **gcount** and **write** member functions (part 2 of 2).

11.6 Stream Manipulators

C++ provides various *stream manipulators* that perform formatting tasks. The stream manipulators provide capabilities such as setting field widths, setting precisions, setting and unsetting format flags, setting the fill character in fields, flushing streams, inserting a newline in the output stream and flushing the stream, inserting a null character in the output stream and skipping whitespace in the input stream. These features are described in the following sections.

11.6.1 Integral Stream Base: dec, oct, hex and setbase

Integers are normally interpreted as decimal (base 10) values. To change the base in which integers are interpreted on a stream, insert the manipulator **hex** to set the base to hexadecimal (base 16) or insert the manipulator **oct** to set the base to octal (base 8). Insert the **dec** stream manipulator to reset the stream base to decimal.

The base of a stream may also be changed by the stream manipulator **setbase**, which takes one integer argument of **10**, **8**, or **16** to set the base. Because **setbase** takes an argument, it is called a *parameterized stream manipulator*. Using **setbase** or any other parameterized manipulator requires the inclusion of the **<iomanip>** header file. The stream base remains the same until it is explicitly changed. Figure 11.16 shows the use of the **hex**, **oct**, **dec** and **setbase** stream manipulators.

```
1   // Fig. 11.16: fig11_16.cpp
2   // Using hex, oct, dec and setbase stream manipulators.
3   #include <iostream>
4
5   using std::cout;
6   using std::cin;
7   using std::endl;
8
9   #include <iomanip>
10
11  using std::hex;
12  using std::dec;
13  using std::oct;
14  using std::setbase;
15
16  int main()
17  {
18     int n;
19
20     cout << "Enter a decimal number: ";
21     cin >> n;
22
23     cout << n << " in hexadecimal is: "
24          << hex << n << '\n'
25          << dec << n << " in octal is: "
26          << oct << n << '\n'
27          << setbase( 10 ) << n << " in decimal is: "
28          << n << endl;
29
30     return 0;
31  }
```

```
Enter a decimal number: 20
20 in hexadecimal is: 14
20 in octal is: 24
20 in decimal is: 20
```

Fig. 11.16   Using the **hex**, **oct**, **dec** and **setbase** stream manipulators .

11.6.2 Floating-Point Precision (precision, setprecision)

We can control the *precision* of floating-point numbers, i.e., the number of digits to the right of the decimal point, by using either the **setprecision** stream manipulator or the **precision** member function. A call to either of these sets the precision for all subsequent output operations until the next precision-setting call. The **precision** member function with no argument returns the current precision setting. The program of Fig. 11.17 uses both the **precision** member function and the **setprecision** manipulator to print a table showing the square root of **2** with precisions varying from **0** through **9**.

```cpp
1   // Fig. 11.17: fig11_17.cpp
2   // Controlling precision of floating-point values
3   #include <iostream>
4
5   using std::cout;
6   using std::cin;
7   using std::endl;
8
9   #include <iomanip>
10
11  using std::ios;
12  using std::setiosflags;
13  using std::setprecision;
14
15  #include <cmath>
16
17  int main()
18  {
19     double root2 = sqrt( 2.0 );
20     int places;
21
22     cout << setiosflags( ios::fixed )
23         << "Square root of 2 with precisions 0-9.\n"
24         << "Precision set by the "
25         << "precision member function:" << endl;
26
27     for ( places = 0; places <= 9; places++ ) {
28        cout.precision( places );
29        cout << root2 << '\n';
30     }
31
32     cout << "\nPrecision set by the "
33         << "setprecision manipulator:\n";
34
35     for ( places = 0; places <= 9; places++ )
36        cout << setprecision( places ) << root2 << '\n';
37
38     return 0;
39  }
```

```
Square root of 2 with precisions 0-9.
Precision set by the precision member function:
1
1.4
1.41
1.414
1.4142
1.41421
1.414214
1.4142136
1.41421356
1.414213562
```

(continued next page)

Fig. 11.17   Controlling precision of floating-point values (part 1 of 2).

```
Precision set by the setprecision manipulator:
1
1.4
1.41
1.414
1.4142
1.41421
1.414214
1.4142136
1.41421356
1.414213562
```

Fig. 11.17 Controlling precision of floating-point values (part 2 of 2).

11.6.3 Field Width (`setw`, `width`)

The **ios width** member function sets the field width (i.e., the number of character positions in which a value should be output or the number of characters that should be input) and returns the previous width. If values processed are smaller than the field width, *fill characters* are inserted as *padding*. A value wider than the designated width will not be truncated—the full number will be printed.

Common Programming Error 11.4

The width setting applies only for the next insertion or extraction; afterward, the width is implicitly set to **0** *(i.e., output values will simply be as wide as they need to be). The* **width** *function with no argument returns the current setting. It is a logic error to assume that the width setting applies to all subsequent outputs.*

Common Programming Error 11.5

When not providing a sufficiently wide field to handle outputs, the outputs print as wide as they need to be, possibly causing difficult-to-read outputs.

Figure 11.18 demonstrates the use of the **width** member function on both input and output. Note that on input into a **char** array, a maximum of one fewer characters than the width will be read because provision is made for the null character to be placed in the input string. Remember that stream extraction terminates when nonleading whitespace is encountered. The **setw** stream manipulator also may be used to set the field width. Note: When the user is prompted for inpuft, the user should enter a line of text and press *Enter* followed by end-of-file (*<ctrl>-z* on IBM PC-compatible systems, *<ctrl>-d* on UNIX and Macintosh systems). Note: When inputting anything other than a **char** array, **width** and **setw** are ignored.

```
1   // fig11_18.cpp
2   // Demonstrating the width member function
3   #include <iostream>
4
5   using std::cout;
6   using std::cin;
7   using std::endl;
```

Fig. 11.18 Demonstrating the **width** member function (part 1 of 2).

```
8
9   int main()
10  {
11      int w = 4;
12      char string[ 10 ];
13
14      cout << "Enter a sentence:\n";
15      cin.width( 5 );
16
17      while ( cin >> string ) {
18          cout.width( w++ );
19          cout << string << endl;
20          cin.width( 5 );
21      }
22
23      return 0;
24  }
```

```
Enter a sentence:
This is a test of the width member function
This
   is
    a
 test
    of
    the
    widt
       h
     memb
        er
     func
      tion
```

Fig. 11.18 Demonstrating the **width** member function (part 2 of 2).

11.6.4 User-Defined Manipulators

Users may create their own stream manipulators. Figure 11.19 shows the creation and use of new stream manipulators **bell**, **ret** (carriage return), **tab** and **endLine**. Users may also create their own parameterized stream manipulators—consult your installation's manuals for instructions on how to do this.

```
1   // Fig. 11.19: fig11_19.cpp
2   // Creating and testing user-defined, nonparameterized
3   // stream manipulators.
4   #include <iostream>
5
6   using std::ostream;
7   using std::cout;
8   using std::flush;
```

Fig. 11.19 Creating and testing user-defined, nonparameterized stream manipulators
(part 1 of 2).

```
9
10    // bell manipulator (using escape sequence \a)
11    ostream& bell( ostream& output ) { return output << '\a'; }
12
13    // ret manipulator (using escape sequence \r)
14    ostream& ret( ostream& output ) { return output << '\r'; }
15
16    // tab manipulator (using escape sequence \t)
17    ostream& tab( ostream& output ) { return output << '\t'; }
18
19    // endLine manipulator (using escape sequence \n
20    // and the flush member function)
21    ostream& endLine( ostream& output )
22    {
23       return output << '\n' << flush;
24    }
25
26    int main()
27    {
28       cout << "Testing the tab manipulator:" << endLine
29            << 'a' << tab << 'b' << tab << 'c' << endLine
30            << "Testing the ret and bell manipulators:"
31            << endLine << "..........";
32       cout << bell;
33       cout << ret << "-----" << endLine;
34       return 0;
35    }
```

```
Testing the tab manipulator:
a         b         c
Testing the ret and bell manipulators:
-----.....
```

Fig. 11.19 Creating and testing user-defined, nonparameterized stream manipulators (part 2 of 2).

11.7 Stream Format States

Various *format flags* specify the kinds of formatting to be performed during stream I/O operations. The **setf**, **unsetf** and **flags** member functions control the flag settings.

11.7.1 Format State Flags

Each of the format state flags shown in Fig. 11.20 (and some that are not shown) is defined as an enumeration in class **ios** and is explained in the next several sections.

These flags can be controlled by the **flags**, **setf** and **unsetf** member functions, but many C++ programmers prefer to use stream manipulators (see Section 11.7.8). The programmer may use the bitwise-or operation, |, to combine various options into a single **long** value (see Fig. 11.23). Calling the **flags** member function for a stream and specifying these "or-ed" options sets the options on that stream and returns a **long** value containing the prior options. This value is often saved so that **flags** may be called with this saved value to restore the previous stream options.

Format state flag	Description
`ios::skipws`	Skip whitespace characters on an input stream.
`ios::left`	Left justify output in a field. Padding characters appear to the right if necessary.
`ios::right`	Right justify output in a field. Padding characters appear to the left if necessary.
`ios::internal`	Indicate that a number's sign should be left justified in a field and a number's magnitude should be right justified in that same field (i.e., padding characters appear between the sign and the number).
`ios::dec`	Specify that integers should be treated as decimal (base 10) values.
`ios::oct`	Specify that integers should be treated as octal (base 8) values.
`ios::hex`	Specify that integers should be treated as hexadecimal (base 16) values.
`ios::showbase`	Specify that the base of a number is to be output ahead of the number (a leading **0** for octals; a leading **0x** or **0X** for hexadecimals).
`ios::showpoint`	Specify that floating-point numbers should be output with a decimal point. This is normally used with `ios::fixed` to guarantee a certain number of digits to the right of the decimal point.
`ios::uppercase`	Specify that uppercase letters (i.e., **X** and **A** through **F**) should be used in the hexadecimal integer and that uppercase **E** should be used when representing a floating-point value in scientific notation.
`ios::showpos`	Specify that positive and negative numbers should be preceded by a **+** or **−** sign, respectively.
`ios::scientific`	Specify output of a floating-point value in scientific notation.
`ios::fixed`	Specify output of a floating-point value in fixed-point notation with a specific number of digits to the right of the decimal point.

Fig. 11.20 Format state flags .

The **flags** function must specify a value representing the settings of all the flags. The one-argument **setf** function, on the other hand, specifies one or more "or-ed" flags and "ors" them with the existing flag settings to form a new format state.

The **setiosflags** parameterized stream manipulator performs the same functions as the **setf** member function. The **resetiosflags** stream manipulator performs the same functions as the **unsetf** member function. To use either of these stream manipulators, be sure to #include **<iomanip>**.

The **skipws** flag indicates that **>>** should skip whitespace on an input stream. The default behavior of **>>** is to skip whitespace. To change this, use the call **unsetf(ios::skipws)**. The **ws** stream manipulator also may be used to specify that whitespace should be skipped.

11.7.2 Trailing Zeros and Decimal Points (`ios::showpoint`)

The **showpoint** flag is set to force a floating-point number to be output with its decimal point and trailing zeros. A floating-point value of **79.0** will print as **79** without **showpoint** set and as **79.000000** (or as many trailing zeros as are specified by the current precision) with **showpoint** set. The program in Fig. 11.21 shows the use of the **setf** member function to set the **showpoint** flag to control trailing zeros and the printing of the decimal point for floating-point values.

11.7.3 Justification (ios::left, ios::right, ios::internal)

The **left** and **right** flags enable fields to be left-justified with padding characters to the right, or right-justified with padding characters to the left, respectively. The character to be used for padding is specified by the **fill** member function or the **setfill** parameterized stream manipulator (see Section 11.7.4). Figure 11.22 shows the use of the **setw**, **setiosflags** and **resetiosflags** manipulators and the **setf** and **unsetf** member functions to control the left- and right-justification of integer data in a field.

```
1   // Fig. 11.21: fig11_21.cpp
2   // Controlling the printing of trailing zeros and decimal
3   // points for floating-point values.
4   #include <iostream>
5
6   using std::cout;
7   using std::endl;
8
9   #include <iomanip>
10
11  using std::ios;
12
13  #include <cmath>
14
15  int main()
16  {
17     cout << "Before setting the ios::showpoint flag\n"
18          << "9.9900 prints as: " << 9.9900
19          << "\n9.9000 prints as: " << 9.9000
20          << "\n9.0000 prints as: " << 9.0000
21          << "\n\nAfter setting the ios::showpoint flag\n";
22     cout.setf( ios::showpoint );
23     cout << "9.9900 prints as: " << 9.9900
24          << "\n9.9000 prints as: " << 9.9000
25          << "\n9.0000 prints as: " << 9.0000 << endl;
26     return 0;
27  }
```

```
Before setting the ios::showpoint flag
9.9900 prints as: 9.99
9.9000 prints as: 9.9
9.0000 prints as: 9

After setting the ios::showpoint flag
9.9900 prints as: 9.99000
9.9000 prints as: 9.90000
9.0000 prints as: 9.00000
```

Fig. 11.21   Controlling the printing of trailing zeros and decimal points with **float** values.

```
1   // Fig. 11.22: fig11_22.cpp
2   // Left-justification and right-justification.
3   #include <iostream>
4
5   using std::cout;
6   using std::endl;
7
8   #include <iomanip>
9
10  using std::ios;
11  using std::setw;
12  using std::setiosflags;
13  using std::resetiosflags;
14
15  int main()
16  {
17     int x = 12345;
18
19     cout << "Default is right justified:\n"
20          << setw(10) << x << "\n\nUSING MEMBER FUNCTIONS"
21          << "\nUse setf to set ios::left:\n" << setw(10);
22
23     cout.setf( ios::left, ios::adjustfield );
24     cout << x << "\nUse unsetf to restore default:\n";
25     cout.unsetf( ios::left );
26     cout << setw( 10 ) << x
27          << "\n\nUSING PARAMETERIZED STREAM MANIPULATORS"
28          << "\nUse setiosflags to set ios::left:\n"
29          << setw( 10 ) << setiosflags( ios::left ) << x
30          << "\nUse resetiosflags to restore default:\n"
31          << setw( 10 ) << resetiosflags( ios::left )
32          << x << endl;
33     return 0;
34  }
```

```
Default is right justified:
     12345

USING MEMBER FUNCTIONS
Use setf to set ios::left:
12345
Use unsetf to restore default:
     12345

USING PARAMETERIZED STREAM MANIPULATORS
Use setiosflags to set ios::left:
12345
Use resetiosflags to restore default:
     12345
```

Fig. 11.22 Left-justification and right-justification .

The **internal** flag indicates that a number's sign (or base when the **ios::show-base** flag is set; see Section 11.7.5) should be left-justified within a field, the number's magnitude should be right-justified and intervening spaces should be padded with the fill character. The **left**, **right** and **internal** flags are contained in static data member **ios::adjustfield**. The **ios::adjustfield** argument must be provided as the second argument to **setf** when setting the **left**, **right** or **internal** justification flags. This enables **setf** to ensure that only one of the three justification flags is set (they are mutually exclusive). Figure 11.23 shows the use of the **setiosflags** and **setw** stream manipulators to specify internal spacing. Note the use of the **ios::showpos** flag to force the printing of the plus sign.

11.7.4 Padding (fill, setfill)

The **fill** *member function* specifies the fill character to be used with adjusted fields; if no value is specified, spaces are used for padding. The **fill** function returns the prior padding character. The **setfill** *manipulator* also sets the padding character. Figure 11.24 demonstrates the use of the **fill** member function and the **setfill** manipulator to control the setting and resetting of the fill character.

```
1   // Fig. 11.23: fig11_23.cpp
2   // Printing an integer with internal spacing and
3   // forcing the plus sign.
4   #include <iostream>
5
6   using std::cout;
7   using std::endl;
8
9   #include <iomanip>
10
11  using std::ios;
12  using std::setiosflags;
13  using std::setw;
14
15  int main()
16  {
17     cout << setiosflags( ios::internal | ios::showpos )
18        << setw( 10 ) << 123 << endl;
19     return 0;
20  }
```

```
+        123
```

Fig. 11.23 Printing an integer with internal spacing and forcing the plus sign.

```
1   // Fig. 11.24: fig11_24.cpp
2   // Using the fill member function and the setfill
3   // manipulator to change the padding character for
4   // fields larger than the values being printed.
```

Fig. 11.24 Using the **fill** member function and the **setfill** manipulator to change the padding character for fields larger than the values being printed (part 1 of 2).

```
5    #include <iostream>
6
7    using std::cout;
8    using std::endl;
9
10   #include <iomanip>
11
12   using std::ios;
13   using std::setw;
14   using std::hex;
15   using std::dec;
16   using std::setfill;
17
18   int main()
19   {
20      int x = 10000;
21
22      cout << x << " printed as int right and left justified\n"
23           << "and as hex with internal justification.\n"
24           << "Using the default pad character (space):\n";
25      cout.setf( ios::showbase );
26      cout << setw( 10 ) << x << '\n';
27      cout.setf( ios::left, ios::adjustfield );
28      cout << setw( 10 ) << x << '\n';
29      cout.setf( ios::internal, ios::adjustfield );
30      cout << setw( 10 ) << hex << x;
31
32      cout << "\n\nUsing various padding characters:\n";
33      cout.setf( ios::right, ios::adjustfield );
34      cout.fill( '*' );
35      cout << setw( 10 ) << dec << x << '\n';
36      cout.setf( ios::left, ios::adjustfield );
37      cout << setw( 10 ) << setfill( '%' ) << x << '\n';
38      cout.setf( ios::internal, ios::adjustfield );
39      cout << setw( 10 ) << setfill( '^' ) << hex << x << endl;
40      return 0;
41   }
```

```
10000 printed as int right and left justified
and as hex with internal justification.
Using the default pad character (space):
     10000
10000
0x    2710

Using various padding characters:
*****10000
10000%%%%%
0x^^^^2710
```

Fig. 11.24 Using the `fill` member function and the `setfill` manipulator to change the padding character for fields larger than the values being printed (part 2 of 2).

11.7.5 Integral Stream Base (`ios::dec`, `ios::oct`, `ios::hex`, `ios::showbase`)

The `ios::basefield` *static member* (used similarly to `ios::adjustfield` with `setf`) includes the `ios::oct`, `ios::hex` and `ios::dec` flag bits to specify that integers are to be treated as octal, hexadecimal and decimal values, respectively. Stream insertions default to decimal if none of these bits is set. The default for stream extractions is to process the data in the form in which it is supplied—integers starting with **0** are treated as octal values, integers starting with **0x** or **0X** are treated as hexadecimal values and all other integers are treated as decimal values. Once a particular base is specified for a stream, all integers on that stream are processed with that base until a new base is specified or until the end of the program.

Set the **showbase** flag to force the base of an integral value to be output. Decimal numbers are output normally, octal numbers are output with a leading **0** and hexadecimal numbers are output with either a leading **0x** or a leading **0X** (the **uppercase** flag determines which option is chosen; see Section 11.7.7). Figure 11.25 demonstrates the use of the **showbase** flag to force an integer to print in decimal, octal and hexadecimal formats.

```cpp
// Fig. 11.25: fig11_25.cpp
// Using the ios::showbase flag
#include <iostream>

using std::cout;
using std::endl;

#include <iomanip>

using std::ios;
using std::setiosflags;
using std::oct;
using std::hex;

int main()
{
   int x = 100;

   cout << setiosflags( ios::showbase )
        << "Printing integers preceded by their base:\n"
        << x << '\n'
        << oct << x << '\n'
        << hex << x << endl;
   return 0;
}
```

```
Printing integers preceded by their base:
100
0144
0x64
```

Fig. 11.25 Using the `ios::showbase` flag.

11.7.6 Floating-Point Numbers; Scientific Notation (`ios::scientific`, `ios::fixed`)

The `ios::scientific` *flag* and the `ios::fixed` *flag* are contained in the *static data member* `ios::floatfield` (these flags are used similarly to `ios::adjustfield` and `ios::basefield` in `setf`). These flags control the output format of floating-point numbers. The `scientific` flag forces the output of a floating-point number in scientific format. The `fixed` flag forces a floating-point number to display a specific number of digits (as specified by the `precision` member function) to the right of the decimal point. Without these flags set, the value of the floating-point number determines the output format.

The call `cout.setf(0, ios::floatfield)` restores the default format for outputting floating-point numbers. Figure 11.26 demonstrates displaying floating-point numbers in fixed and scientific formats using the two-argument `setf` with `ios::floatfield`. The exponent format in scientific notation may differ between compilers.

```
1   // Fig. 11.26: fig11_26.cpp
2   // Displaying floating-point values in system default,
3   // scientific, and fixed formats.
4   #include <iostream>
5
6   using std::cout;
7   using std::endl;
8   using std::ios;
9
10  int main()
11  {
12      double x = .001234567, y = 1.946e9;
13
14      cout << "Displayed in default format:\n"
15           << x << '\t' << y << '\n';
16      cout.setf( ios::scientific, ios::floatfield );
17      cout << "Displayed in scientific format:\n"
18           << x << '\t' << y << '\n';
19      cout.unsetf( ios::scientific );
20      cout << "Displayed in default format after unsetf:\n"
21           << x << '\t' << y << '\n';
22      cout.setf( ios::fixed, ios::floatfield );
23      cout << "Displayed in fixed format:\n"
24           << x << '\t' << y << endl;
25      return 0;
26  }
```

```
Displayed in default format:
0.00123457      1.946e+009
Displayed in scientific format:
1.234567e-003   1.946000e+009
Displayed in default format after unsetf:
0.00123457      1.946e+009
Displayed in fixed format:
0.001235        1946000000.000000
```

Fig. 11.26   Displaying floating-point values in system default, scientific and fixed format.

11.7.7 Uppercase/Lowercase Control (`ios::uppercase`)

The **`ios::uppercase`** flag forces an uppercase **X** or **E** to be output with hexadecimal integers or with scientific notation floating-point values, respectively (Fig. 11.27). When set, the **`ios::uppercase`** flag causes all letters in a hexadecimal value to be uppercase.

11.7.8 Setting and Resetting the Format Flags (`flags`, `setiosflags`, `resetiosflags`)

The **`flags`** member function without an argument simply returns (as a **`long`** value) the current settings of the format flags. The **`flags`** member function with a **`long`** argument sets the format flags as specified by the argument and returns the prior flag settings. Any format flags not specified in the argument to **`flags`** are reset. Note that the initial settings of the flags on each system may differ. The program of Fig. 11.28 demonstrates the use of the **`flags`** member function to set a new format state and save the previous format state, then restore the original format settings.

```
1   // Fig. 11.27: fig11_27.cpp
2   // Using the ios::uppercase flag
3   #include <iostream>
4
5   using std::cout;
6   using std::endl;
7
8   #include <iomanip>
9
10  using std::setiosflags;
11  using std::ios;
12  using std::hex;
13
14  int main()
15  {
16     cout << setiosflags( ios::uppercase )
17          << "Printing uppercase letters in scientific\n"
18          << "notation exponents and hexadecimal values:\n"
19          << 4.345e10 << '\n' << hex << 123456789 << endl;
20     return 0;
21  }
```

```
Printing uppercase letters in scientific
notation exponents and hexadecimal values:
4.345E+010
75BCD15
```

Fig. 11.27 Using the **`ios::uppercase`** flag.

```
1   // Fig. 11.28: fig11_28.cpp
2   // Demonstrating the flags member function.
3   #include <iostream>
```

Fig. 11.28 Demonstrating the **`flags`** member function (part 1 of 2).

```
4
5   using std::cout;
6   using std::endl;
7   using std::ios;
8
9
10  int main()
11  {
12     int i = 1000;
13     double d = 0.0947628;
14
15     cout << "The value of the flags variable is: "
16          << cout.flags()
17          << "\nPrint int and double in original format:\n"
18          << i << '\t' << d << "\n\n";
19     long originalFormat =
20          cout.flags( ios::oct | ios::scientific );
21     cout << "The value of the flags variable is: "
22          << cout.flags()
23          << "\nPrint int and double in a new format\n"
24          << "specified using the flags member function:\n"
25          << i << '\t' << d << "\n\n";
26     cout.flags( originalFormat );
27     cout << "The value of the flags variable is: "
28          << cout.flags()
29          << "\nPrint values in original format again:\n"
30          << i << '\t' << d << endl;
31     return 0;
32  }
```

```
The value of the flags variable is: 0
Print int and double in original format:
1000    0.0947628

The value of the flags variable is: 4040
Print int and double in a new format
specified using the flags member function:
1750    9.476280e-002

The value of the flags variable is: 0
Print values in original format again:
1000    0.0947628
```

Fig. 11.28 Demonstrating the **flags** member function (part 2 of 2).

The **setf** member function sets the format flags provided in its argument and returns the previous flag settings as a **long** value as in

```
long previousFlagSettings =
        cout.setf( ios::showpoint | ios::showpos );
```

The **setf** member function with two **long** arguments as in

```
cout.setf( ios::left, ios::adjustfield );
```

first clears the bits of **ios::adjustfield** and then sets the **ios::left** flag. This version of **setf** is used with the bit fields associated with **ios::basefield** (represented by **ios::dec**, **ios::oct** and **ios::hex**), **ios::floatfield** (represented by **ios::scientific** and **ios::fixed**) and **ios::adjustfield** (represented by **ios::left**, **ios::right** and **ios::internal**).

The **unsetf** member function resets the designated flags and returns the value of the flags prior to being reset.

11.8 Stream Error States

The state of a stream may be tested through bits in class **ios**—the base class for the classes **istream**, **ostream** and **iostream** we are using for I/O.

The **eofbit** is set for an input stream after end-of-file is encountered. A program can use the **eof** member function to determine if end-of-file has been encountered on a stream after an attempt to extract data beyond the end of the stream. The call

```
cin.eof()
```

returns true if end-of-file has been encountered on **cin** and false otherwise.

The **failbit** is set for a stream when a format error occurs on the stream. For example, a format error occurs when the program is inputting integers and a nondigit character is encountered in the input stream. When such an error occurs, the characters are not lost. The **fail** member function reports if a stream operation has failed; it is normally possible to recover from such errors.

The **badbit** is set for a stream when an error occurs that results in the loss of data. The **bad** member function reports if a stream operation has failed. Such serious failures are normally nonrecoverable.

The **goodbit** is set for a stream if none of the bits **eofbit**, **failbit** or **badbit** are set for the stream.

The **good** member function returns **true** if the **bad**, **fail** and **eof** functions would all return false. I/O operations should only be performed on "good" streams.

The **rdstate** member function returns the error state of the stream. A call to **cout.rdstate**, for example, would return the state of the stream, which could then be tested by a **switch** statement that examines **ios::eofbit**, **ios::badbit**, **ios::failbit** and **ios::goodbit**. The preferred means of testing the state of a stream is to use the member functions **eof**, **bad**, **fail** and **good**—using these functions does not require the programmer to be familiar with particular status bits.

The **clear** member function is normally used to restore a stream's state to "good" so that I/O may proceed on that stream. The default argument for **clear** is **ios::goodbit**, so the statement

```
cin.clear();
```

clears **cin** and sets **goodbit** for the stream. The statement

```
cin.clear( ios::failbit )
```

sets the **failbit**. The user might want to do this when performing input on **cin** with a user-defined type and encountering a problem. The name **clear** seems inappropriate in this context, but it is correct.

The program of Fig. 11.29 illustrates the use of the **rdstate**, **eof**, **fail**, **bad**, **good** and **clear** member functions. *Note:* The actual values output may differ from compiler to compiler.

```cpp
1   // Fig. 11.29: fig11_29.cpp
2   // Testing error states.
3   #include <iostream>
4
5   using std::cout;
6   using std::endl;
7   using std::cin;
8
9   int main()
10  {
11     int x;
12     cout << "Before a bad input operation:"
13          << "\ncin.rdstate(): " << cin.rdstate()
14          << "\n    cin.eof(): " << cin.eof()
15          << "\n   cin.fail(): " << cin.fail()
16          << "\n    cin.bad(): " << cin.bad()
17          << "\n   cin.good(): " << cin.good()
18          << "\n\nExpects an integer, but enter a character: ";
19     cin >> x;
20
21     cout << "\nAfter a bad input operation:"
22          << "\ncin.rdstate(): " << cin.rdstate()
23          << "\n    cin.eof(): " << cin.eof()
24          << "\n   cin.fail(): " << cin.fail()
25          << "\n    cin.bad(): " << cin.bad()
26          << "\n   cin.good(): " << cin.good() << "\n\n";
27
28     cin.clear();
29
30     cout << "After cin.clear()"
31          << "\ncin.fail(): " << cin.fail()
32          << "\ncin.good(): " << cin.good() << endl;
33     return 0;
34  }
```

```
Before a bad input operation:
cin.rdstate(): 0
    cin.eof(): 0
   cin.fail(): 0
    cin.bad(): 0
   cin.good(): 1

Expects an integer, but enter a character: A

After a bad input operation:
cin.rdstate(): 2
    cin.eof(): 0
```

(continued next page)

Fig. 11.29 Testing error states (part 1 of 2).

```
   cin.fail(): 0
    cin.bad(): 0
   cin.good(): 1

After cin.clear()
cin.fail(): 0
cin.good(): 1
```

Fig. 11.29 Testing error states (part 2 of 2).

The **operator!** member function returns **true** if either the **badbit** is set, the **failbit** is set or both are set. The **operator void*** member function returns **false** (0) if either the **badbit** is set, the **failbit** is set or both are set. These functions are useful in file processing when a true/false condition is being tested under the control of a selection structure or repetition structure.

11.9 Tying an Output Stream to an Input Stream

Interactive applications generally involve an **istream** for input and an **ostream** for output. When a prompting message appears on the screen, the user responds by entering the appropriate data. Obviously, the prompt needs to appear before the input operation proceeds. With output buffering, outputs appear only when the buffer fills, when outputs are flushed explicitly by the program or automatically at the end of the program. C++ provides member function **tie** to synchronize (i.e., "tie together") the operation of an **istream** and an **ostream** to ensure that outputs appear before their subsequent inputs. The call

```
    cin.tie( &cout );
```

ties **cout** (an **ostream**) to **cin** (an **istream**). Actually, this particular call is redundant because C++ performs this operation automatically to create a user's standard input/output environment. The user would, however, explicitly tie together other **istream/ostream** pairs. To untie an input stream, **inputStream**, from an output stream, use the call

```
    inputStream.tie( 0 );
```

SUMMARY

- I/O operations are performed in a manner sensitive to the type of the data.
- C++ I/O occurs in streams of bytes. A stream is simply a sequence of bytes.
- I/O mechanisms of the system move bytes from devices to memory and vice versa in an efficient and reliable manner.
- C++ provides "low-level" and "high-level" I/O capabilities. Low-level I/O-capabilities specify that some number of bytes should be transferred device-to-memory or memory-to-device. High-level I/O is performed with bytes grouped into meaningful units such as integers, floats, characters, strings and user-defined types.
- C++ provides both unformatted I/O and formatted I/O operations. Unformatted I/O transfers are fast, but process raw data that are difficult for people to use. Formatted I/O processes data in meaningful units, but requires extra processing time that can negatively impact high-volume data transfers.

- Most C++ programs include the **<iostream>** header file that declares all stream I/O operations.
- Header **<iomanip>** declares the formatted input/output with parameterized stream manipulators.
- The **<fstream>** header declares file processing operations.
- The **istream** class supports stream input operations.
- The **ostream** class supports stream output operations.
- The **iostream** class supports both stream input and stream output operations.
- The **istream** class and the **ostream** class are each derived through single inheritance from the **ios** base class.
- The **iostream** class is derived through multiple inheritance from both the **istream** class and the **ostream** class.
- The left shift operator (**<<**) is overloaded to designate stream output and is referred to as the stream-insertion operator.
- The right shift operator (**>>**) is overloaded to designate stream input and is referred to as the stream-extraction operator.
- The **istream** object **cin** is tied to the standard input device, normally the keyboard.
- The **ostream** class object **cout** is tied to the standard output device, normally the screen.
- The **ostream** class object **cerr** is tied to the standard error device. Outputs to **cerr** are unbuffered; each insertion to **cerr** appears immediately.
- Stream manipulator **endl** issues a newline character and flushes the output buffer.
- The C++ compiler determines data types automatically for input and output.
- Addresses are displayed in hexadecimal format by default.
- To print the address in a pointer variable, cast the pointer to **void***.
- Member function **put** outputs one character. Calls to **put** may be cascaded.
- Stream input is performed with the stream-extraction operator **>>**. This operator automatically skips whitespace characters in the input stream.
- The **>>** operator returns **false** after end-of-file is encountered on a stream.
- Stream extraction causes **failbit** to be set for improper input and **badbit** to be set if the operation fails.
- A series of values can be input using the stream-extraction operation in a **while** loop header. The extraction returns 0 when end-of-file is encountered.
- The **get** member function with no arguments inputs one character and returns the character; **EOF** is returned if end-of-file is encountered on the stream.
- Member function **get** with an argument of type **char** reference inputs one character. **EOF** is returned when end-of-file is encountered; otherwise, the **istream** object for which the **get** member function is being invoked is returned.
- Member function **get** with three arguments—a character array, a size limit and a delimiter (with default value newline)—reads characters from the input stream up to a maximum of limit - 1 characters and terminates, or terminates when the delimiter is read. The input string is terminated with a null character. The delimiter is not placed in the character array, but remains in the input stream.
- The **getline** member function operates like the three-argument **get** member function. The **getline** function removes the delimiter from the input stream, but does not store it in the string.
- Member function **ignore** skips the specified number of characters (the default is 1) in the input stream; it terminates if the specified delimiter is encountered (the default delimiter is **EOF**).

- The **putback** member function places the previous character obtained by a **get** on a stream back onto that stream.

- The **peek** member function returns the next character from an input stream, but does not extract (remove) the character from the stream.

- C++ offers type-safe I/O. If unexpected data are processed by the **<<** and **>>** operators, various error flags are set which the user may test to determine if an I/O operation succeeded or failed.

- Unformatted I/O is performed with member functions **read** and **write**. These input or output some number of bytes to or from memory beginning at a designated memory address. They are input or output as raw bytes with no formatting.

- The **gcount** member function returns the number of characters input by the previous **read** operation on that stream.

- Member function **read** inputs a specified number of characters into a character array. **failbit** is set if fewer than the specified number of characters are read.

- To change the base in which integers output, use the manipulator **hex** to set the base to hexadecimal (base 16) or **oct** to set the base to octal (base 8). Use manipulator **dec** to reset the base to decimal. The base remains the same until explicitly changed.

- The parameterized stream manipulator **setbase** also sets the base for integer output. **setbase** takes one integer argument of **10**, **8** or **16** to set the base.

- Floating-point precision can be controlled using either the **setprecision** stream manipulator or the **precision** member function. Both set the precision for all subsequent output operations until the next precision-setting call. The **precision** member function with no argument returns the current precision value.

- Parameterized manipulators require the inclusion of the **<iomanip>** header file.

- Member function **width** sets the field width and returns the previous width. Values smaller than the field are padded with fill characters. The field width setting applies only for the next insertion or extraction; the field width is implicitly set to **0** afterward (subsequent values will be output as large as they need to be). Values larger than a field are printed in their entirety. Function **width** with no argument returns the current width setting. Manipulator **setw** also sets the width.

- For input, the **setw** stream manipulator establishes a maximum string size; if a larger string is entered, the larger line is broken into pieces no larger than the designated size.

- Users may create their own stream manipulators.

- Member functions **setf**, **unsetf** and **flags** control the flag settings.

- The **skipws** flag indicates that **>>** should skip whitespace on an input stream. The **ws** stream manipulator also skips over leading whitespace in an input stream.

- Format flags are defined as an enumeration in class **ios**.

- Format flags are controlled by the **flags** and **setf** member functions, but many C++ programmers prefer to use stream manipulators. The bitwise-or operation, **|**, can be used to combine various options into a single **long** value. Calling the **flags** member function for a stream and specifying these "or-ed" options sets the options on that stream and returns a **long** value containing the prior options. This value is often saved so **flags** may be called with this saved value to restore the previous stream options.

- The **flags** function must specify a value representing the total settings of all the flags. The **setf** function with one argument, on the other hand, automatically "ors" the specified flags with the existing flag settings to form a new format state.

- The **showpoint** flag is set to force a floating-point number to be output with a decimal point and number of significant digits specified by the precision.

- The **left** and **right** flags cause fields to be left-justified with padding characters to the right, or right-justified with padding characters to the left.

- The **internal** flag indicates that a number's sign (or base when the flag **ios::showbase** is set) should be left-justified within a field, magnitude should be right-justified and intervening spaces should be padded with the fill character.

- **ios::adjustfield** contains the flags **left**, **right** and **internal**.

- Member function **fill** specifies the fill character to be used with **left**, **right** and **internal** adjusted fields (space is the default); the prior padding character is returned. Stream manipulator **setfill** also sets the fill character.

- Static member **ios::basefield** has **oct**, **hex** and **dec** bits to specify that integers are to be treated as octal, hexadecimal and decimal values, respectively. Integer output defaults to decimal if none of these bits is set; stream extractions process the data in the form the data is supplied.

- Set the **showbase** flag to force the base of an integral value to be output.

- Static data member **ios::floatfield** contains the flags **scientific** and **fixed**. Set the **scientific** flag to output a floating-point number in scientific format. Set the **fixed** flag to output a floating-point number with the precision specified by the **precision** member function.

- The call **cout.setf(0, ios::floatfield)** restores the default format for displaying floating-point numbers.

- Set the **uppercase** flag to force an uppercase **X** or **E** to be output with hexadecimal integers or with scientific notation floating-point values, respectively. When set, the **ios::uppercase** flag causes all letters in a hexadecimal value to be uppercase.

- Member function **flags** with no argument returns the **long** value of the current settings of the format flags. Member function **flags** with a **long** argument sets the format flags specified by the argument and returns the prior flag settings.

- Member function **setf** sets the format flags in its argument and returns the previous flag settings as a **long** value.

- Member function **setf(long setBits, long resetBits)** clears the bits of the **reset-Bits**, then sets the bit in **setBits**.

- Member function **unsetf** resets the designated flags and returns the value of the flags prior to being reset.

- Parameterized stream manipulator **setiosflags** performs the same functions as member function **flags**.

- Parameterized stream manipulator **resetiosflags** performs the same functions as member function **unsetf**.

- The state of a stream may be tested through bits in class **ios**.

- The **eofbit** is set for an input stream after end-of-file is encountered during an input operation. The **eof** member function reports if the **eofbit** has been set.

- The **failbit** is set for a stream when a format error occurs on the stream. No characters are lost. The **fail** member function reports if a stream operation has failed; it is normally possible to recover from such errors.

- The **badbit** is set for a stream when an error occurs that results in data loss. The **bad** member function reports if a stream operation failed. Such serious failures are normally nonrecoverable.

- The **good** member function returns true if the **bad**, **fail** and **eof** functions would all return false. I/O operations should only be performed on "good" streams.

- The **rdstate** member function returns the error state of the stream.

- Member function **clear** is normally used to restore a stream's state to "good" so that I/O may proceed on that stream.

- C++ provides the **tie** member function to synchronize **istream** and **ostream** operations to ensure that outputs appear before subsequent inputs.

TERMINOLOGY

bad member function
badbit
cerr
cin
clear member function
clog
cout
dec stream manipulator
default fill character (space)
default precision
end-of-file
endl
eof member function
eofbit
fail member function
failbit
field width
fill character
fill member function
flags member function
flush member function
flush stream manipulator
format flags
format states
formatted I/O
fstream class
gcount member function
get member function
getline member function
good member function
hex stream manipulator
ifstream class
ignore member function
in-memory formatting
<iomanip> standard header file
ios class
ios::adjustfield
ios::basefield
ios::fixed
ios::floatfield
ios::internal
ios::scientific
ios::showbase
ios::showpoint

ios::showpos
iostream class
istream class
leading **0** (octal)
leading **0x** or **0X** (hexadecimal)
left-justified
oct stream manipulator
ofstream class
operator void* member function
operator! member function
ostream class
padding
parameterized stream manipulator
peek member function
precision member function
predefined streams
put member function
putback member function
rdstate member function
read member function
resetiosflags stream manipulator
right-justified
setbase stream manipulator
setf member function
setfill stream manipulator
setiosflags stream manipulator
setprecision stream manipulator
setw stream manipulator
skipws
stream input
stream manipulator
stream output
stream-extraction operator (**>>**)
stream-insertion operator (**<<**)
tie member function
type-safe I/O
unformatted I/O
unsetf member function
uppercase
user-defined streams
whitespace characters
width
write member function
ws member function

COMMON PROGRAMMING ERRORS

11.1 Attempting to read from an ostream (or from any other output-only stream).

11.2 Attempting to write to an istream (or to any other input-only stream).

11.3 Not providing parentheses to force proper precedence when using the relatively high precedence stream-insertion operator **<<** or stream-extraction operator **>>**.

11.4 The width setting applies only for the next insertion or extraction; afterward, the width is implicitly set to **0** (i.e., output values will simply be as wide as they need to be). The **width** function with no argument returns the current setting. It is a logic error to assume that the width setting applies to all subsequent outputs.

11.5 When not providing a sufficiently wide field to handle outputs, the outputs print as wide as they need to be, possibly causing difficult-to-read outputs.

GOOD PROGRAMMING PRACTICES

11.1 Use the C++ form of I/O exclusively in C++ programs, despite the fact that C-style I/O is available to C++ programmers.

11.2 When outputting expressions, place them in parentheses to prevent operator precedence problems between the operators in the expression and the **<<** operator.

PERFORMANCE TIP

11.1 Use unformatted I/O for the best performance in high-volume file processing.

PORTABILITY TIP

11.1 When prompting the user on how to end input from the keyboard, ask the user to "enter end-of-file to end input" rather than prompting for *<ctrl>-d* (UNIX and Macintosh) or *<ctrl>-z* (PC and VAX).

SOFTWARE ENGINEERING OBSERVATIONS

11.1 C++ style I/O is type safe.

11.2 C++ enables a common treatment of I/O of predefined types and user-defined types. This kind of commonality facilitates software development in general and software reuse in particular.

SELF-REVIEW EXERCISES

11.1 Answer each of the following:
a) Overloaded stream operators are often defined as _____ functions of a class.
b) The format justification bits that can be set include _____, _____ and _____.
c) Input/output in C++ occurs as _____ of bytes.
d) Parameterized stream manipulators _____ and _____ can be used to set and reset format state flags.
e) Most C++ programs should include the _____ header file that contains the declarations required for all stream I/O operations.
f) Member functions _____ and _____ set and reset format state flags.
g) Header file _____ contains the declarations required for performing "in-memory" formatting.
h) When using parameterized manipulators, the header file _____ must be included.
i) Header file _____ contains the declarations required for user-controlled file processing.

j) The _____ stream manipulator inserts a newline character in the output stream and flushes the output stream.

k) Header file _____ is used in programs that mix C-style and C++-style I/O.

l) The **ostream** member function _____ is used to perform unformatted output.

m) Input operations are supported by the _____ class.

n) Outputs to the standard error stream are directed to either the _____ or the _____ stream object.

o) Output operations are supported by the _____ class.

p) The symbol for the stream-insertion operator is _____.

q) The four objects that correspond to the standard devices on the system include _____, _____, _____ and _____.

r) The symbol for the stream-extraction operator is _____.

s) The stream manipulators _____, _____ and _____ specify that integers should be displayed in octal, hexadecimal and decimal formats, respectively.

t) The default precision for displaying floating-point values is _____.

u) When set, the _____ flag causes positive numbers to display with a plus sign.

11.2   State whether the following are true or false. If the answer is false, explain why.

a) The stream member function **flags()** with a long argument sets the **flags** state variable to its argument and returns its previous value.

b) The stream-insertion operator **<<** and the stream-extraction operator **>>** are overloaded to handle all standard data types—including strings and memory addresses (stream-insertion only)—and all user-defined data types.

c) The stream member function **flags()** with no arguments resets all the flag bits in the **flags** state variable.

d) The stream-extraction operator **>>** can be overloaded with an operator function that takes an **istream** reference and a reference to a user-defined type as arguments and returns an **istream** reference.

e) The **ws** stream manipulator skips leading whitespace in an input stream.

f) The stream-insertion operator **<<** can be overloaded with an operator function that takes an **istream** reference and a reference to a user-defined type as arguments and returns an **istream** reference.

g) Input with the stream-extraction operator **>>** always skips leading whitespace characters in the input stream.

h) The input and output features are provided as part of C++.

i) The stream member function **rdstate()** returns the current state of the stream.

j) The **cout** stream is normally connected to the display screen.

k) The stream member function **good()** returns true if the **bad()**, **fail()** and **eof()** member functions all return false.

l) The **cin** stream is normally connected to the display screen.

m) If a nonrecoverable error occurs during a stream operation, the **bad** member function will return true.

n) Output to **cerr** is unbuffered and output to **clog** is buffered.

o) When the **ios::showpoint** flag is set, floating-point values are forced to print with the default six digits of precision—provided that the precision value has not been changed, in which case floating-point values print with the specified precision.

p) The **ostream** member function **put** outputs the specified number of characters.

q) The stream manipulators **dec**, **oct** and **hex** only affect the next integer output operation.

r) When output, memory addresses are displayed as **long** integers by default.

11.3   For each of the following, write a single statement that performs the indicated task.

a) Output the string **"Enter your name: "**.

b) Set a flag to cause the exponent in scientific notation and the letters in hexadecimal values to print in capital letters.
c) Output the address of the variable **string** of type **char ***.
d) Set a flag so that floating-point values print in scientific notation.
e) Output the address of the variable **integerPtr** of type **int ***.
f) Set a flag so that when integer values are output, the integer base for octal and hexadecimal values is displayed.
g) Output the value pointed to by **floatPtr** of type **float ***.
h) Use a stream member function to set the fill character to **'*'** for printing in field widths larger than the values being output. Write a separate statement to do this with a stream manipulator.
i) Output the characters **'O'** and **'K'** in one statement with **ostream** function **put**.
j) Get the value of the next character in the input stream without extracting it from the stream.
k) Input a single character into variable **c** of type **char** using the **istream** member function **get** in two different ways.
l) Input and discard the next six characters in the input stream.
m) Use the **istream** member function **read** to input 50 characters into array **line** of type **char**.
n) Read 10 characters into character array **name**. Stop reading characters if the **'.'** delimiter is encountered. Do not remove the delimiter from the input stream. Write another statement that performs this task and removes the delimiter from the input.
o) Use the **istream** member function **gcount** to determine the number of characters input into character array **line** by the last call to **istream** member function **read** and output that number of characters using **ostream** member function **write**.
p) Write separate statements to flush the output stream using a member function and a stream manipulator.
q) Output the following values: **124, 18.376, 'Z', 1000000** and **"String"**.
r) Print the current precision setting using a member function.
s) Input an integer value into **int** variable **months** and a floating-point value into **float** variable **percentageRate**.
t) Print **1.92, 1.925** and **1.9258** with **3** digits of precision using a manipulator.
u) Print integer **100** in octal, hexadecimal and decimal using stream manipulators.
v) Print integer **100** in decimal, octal and hexadecimal using a single stream manipulator to change the base.
w) Print **1234** right-justified in a **10**-digit field.
x) Read characters into character array **line** until the character **'z'** is encountered up to a limit of **20** characters (including a terminating null character). Do not extract the delimiter character from the stream.
y) Use integer variables **x** and **y** to specify the field width and precision used to display the **double** value **87.4573** and display the value.

11.4 Identify the error in each of the following statements and explain how to correct it.
a) `cout << "Value of x <= y is: " << x <= y;`
b) The following statement should print the integer value of **'c'**.
`cout << 'c';`
c) `cout << ""A string in quotes"";`

11.5 For each of the following, show the output.
a) `cout << "12345" << endl;`
`cout.width( 5 );`
`cout.fill( '*' );`
`cout << 123 << endl << 123;`

```
b) cout << setw( 10 ) << setfill( '$' ) << 10000;
c) cout << setw( 8 ) << setprecision( 3 ) << 1024.987654;
d) cout << setiosflags( ios::showbase ) << oct << 99
        << endl << hex << 99;
e) cout << 100000 << endl
        << setiosflags( ios::showpos ) << 100000;
f) cout << setw( 10 ) << setprecision( 2 ) <<
        << setiosflags( ios::scientific ) << 444.93738;
```

ANSWERS TO SELF-REVIEW EXERCISES

11.1   a) **friend**   b) **ios::left, ios::right** and **ios::internal**.   c) streams.
d) **setiosflags, resetiosflags**.   e) **iostream**.   f) **setf, unsetf**.   g) **strstream**.
h) **iomanip**.   i) **fstream**.   j) **endl**.   k) **stdiostream**.   l) **write**.   m) **istream**.   n) **cerr** or
clog.   o) **ostream**.   p) <<.   q) **cin, cout, cerr** and **clog**.   r) >>.   s) **oct, hex** and **dec**.   t) six
digits of precision.   u) **ios::showpos**.

11.2   a) True.
       b) False. The stream-insertion and stream-extraction operators are not overloaded for all
          user-defined types. The programmer of a class must specifically provide the overloaded
          operator functions to overload the stream operators for use with each user-defined type.
       c) False. The stream member function **flags()** with no arguments simply returns the cur-
          rent value of the **flags** state variable.
       d) True.
       e) True.
       f) False. To overload the stream-insertion operator <<, the overloaded operator function
          must take an **ostream** reference and a reference to a user-defined type as arguments and
          return an **ostream** reference.
       g) True. Unless **ios::skipws** is off.
       h) False. The I/O features of C++ are provided as part of the C++ Standard Library. The
          C++ language does not contain capabilities for input, output or file processing.
       i) True.
       j) True.
       k) True.
       l) False. The **cin** stream is connected to the standard input of the computer, which is nor-
          mally the keyboard.
       m) True.
       n) True.
       o) True.
       p) False. The **ostream** member function **put** outputs its single-character argument.
       q) False. The stream manipulators **dec, oct** and **hex** set the output format state for inte-
          gers to the specified base until the base is changed again or the program terminates.
       r) False. Memory addresses are displayed in hexadecimal format by default. To display ad-
          dresses as **long** integers, the address must be cast to a **long** value.

11.3   a) **cout << "Enter your name: ";**
       b) **cout.setf(ios::uppercase);**
       c) **cout << (void *) string;**
       d) **cout.setf(ios::scientific, ios::floatfield);**
       e) **cout << integerPtr;**
       f) **cout << setiosflags(ios::showbase);**
       g) **cout << *floatPtr;**

h) `cout.fill( '*' );`
   `cout << setfill( '*' );`
i) `cout.put( 'O' ).put( 'K' );`
j) `cin.peek();`
k) `c = cin.get();`
   `cin.get( c );`
l) `cin.ignore( 6 );`
m) `cin.read( line, 50 );`
n) `cin.get( name, 10, '.' );`
   `cin.getline( name, 10, '.' );`
o) `cout.write( line, cin.gcount() );`
p) `cout.flush();`
   `cout << flush;`
q) `cout << 124 << 18.376 << 'Z' << 1000000 << "String";`
r) `cout << cout.precision();`
s) `cin >> months >> percentageRate;`
t) `cout << setprecision( 3 ) << 1.92 << '\t'`
   `        << 1.925 << '\t' << 1.9258;`
u) `cout << oct << 100 << hex << 100 << dec << 100;`
v) `cout << 100 << setbase( 8 ) << 100 << setbase( 16 ) << 100;`
w) `cout << setw( 10 ) << 1234;`
x) `cin.get( line, 20, 'z' );`
y) `cout << setw( x ) << setprecision( y ) << 87.4573;`

11.4 a) Error: The precedence of the **<<** operator is higher than the precedence of **<=**, which causes the statement to be evaluated improperly and also causes a compiler error.
Correction: To correct the statement, add parentheses around the expression **x <= y**. This problem will occur with any expression that uses operators of lower precedence than the **<<** operator if the expression is not placed in parentheses.

b) Error: In C++, characters are not treated as small integers, as they are in C.
    Correction: To print the numerical value for a character in the computer's character set, the character must be cast to an integer value as in the following:
    `cout << int('c');`

c) Error: Quote characters cannot be printed in a string unless an escape sequence is used.
    Correction: Print the string in one of the following ways:
    `cout << '"' << "A string in quotes" << '"';`
    `cout << "\"A string in quotes\"";`

11.5 a) `12345`
    `**123`
    `123`
b) `$$$$$10000`
c) `1024.988`
d) `0143`
    `0x63`
e) `100000`
    `+100000`
f) `  4.45e+02`

EXERCISES

11.6 Write a statement for each of the following:

a) Print integer **40000** left-justified in a **15**-digit field.

b) Read a string into character array variable **state**.

c) Print **200** with and without a sign.

d) Print the decimal value **100** in hexadecimal form preceded by **0x**.

e) Read characters into array **s** until the character **'p'** is encountered up to a limit of 10 characters (including the terminating null character). Extract the delimiter from the input stream and discard it.

f) Print **1.234** in a **9**-digit field with preceding zeros.

g) Read a string of the form **"characters"** from the standard input. Store the string in character array **s**. Eliminate the quotation marks from the input stream. Read a maximum of 50 characters (including the terminating null character).

11.7   Write a program to test inputting integer values in decimal, octal and hexadecimal format. Output each integer read by the program in all three formats. Test the program with the following input data: 10, 010, 0x10.

11.8   Write a program that prints pointer values using casts to all the integer data types. Which ones print strange values? Which ones cause errors?

11.9   Write a program to test the results of printing the integer value **12345** and the floating-point value **1.2345** in various-size fields. What happens when the values are printed in fields containing fewer digits than the values?

11.10   Write a program that prints the value **100.453627** rounded to the nearest digit, tenth, hundredth, thousandth and ten thousandth.

11.11   Write a program that inputs a string from the keyboard and determines the length of the string. Print the string using twice the length as the field width.

11.12   Write a program that converts integer Fahrenheit temperatures from **0** to **212** degrees to floating-point Celsius temperatures with **3** digits of precision. Use the formula

```
celsius = 5.0 / 9.0 * ( fahrenheit - 32 );
```

to perform the calculation. The output should be printed in two right-justified columns and the Celsius temperatures should be preceded by a sign for both positive and negative values.

11.13   In some programming languages, strings are entered surrounded by either single or double quotation marks. Write a program that reads the three strings **suzy**, **"suzy"** and **'suzy'**. Are the single and double quotes ignored or read as part of the string?

11.14   In Fig. 8.3, the stream-extraction and -insertion operators were overloaded for input and output of objects of the **PhoneNumber** class. Rewrite the stream-extraction operator to perform the following error checking on input. The **operator>>** function will need to be entirely recoded.

a) Input the entire phone number into an array. Test that the proper number of characters has been entered. There should be a total of 14 characters read for a phone number of the form **(800) 555-1212**. Use the stream member function **clear** to set **ios::failbit** for improper input.

b) The area code and exchange do not begin with **0** or **1**. Test the first digit of the area code and exchange portions of the phone number to be sure that neither begins with **0** or **1**. Use stream member function **clear** to set **ios::failbit** for improper input.

c) The middle digit of an area code used to always be **0** or **1** (although this has changed recently). Test the middle digit for a value of **0** or **1**. Use the stream member function **clear** to set **ios::failbit** for improper input. If none of the above operations results in **ios::failbit** being set for improper input, copy the three parts of the telephone number into the **areaCode**, **exchange** and **line** members of the

PhoneNumber object. In the main program, if **ios::failbit** has been set on the input, have the program print an error message and end rather than print the phone number.

11.15 Write a program that accomplishes each of the following:
   a) Create the user-defined class **Point** that contains the private integer data members **xCoordinate** and **yCoordinate** and declares stream-insertion and stream-extraction overloaded operator functions as **friend**s of the class.
   b) Define the stream-insertion and stream-extraction operator functions. The stream-extraction operator function should determine if the data entered are valid data, and if not, it should set the **ios::failbit** to indicate improper input. The stream-insertion operator should not be able to display the point after an input error occurred.
   c) Write a **main** function that tests input and output of user-defined class **Point** using the overloaded stream-extraction and stream-insertion operators.

11.16 Write a program that accomplishes each of the following:
   a) Create the user-defined class **Complex** that contains the private integer data members **real** and **imaginary**, and declares stream-insertion and stream-extraction overloaded operator functions as **friend**s of the class.
   b) Define the stream-insertion and -extraction operator functions. The stream-extraction operator function should determine if the data entered are valid, and if not, it should set **ios::failbit** to indicate improper input. The input should be of the form

   ```
   3 + 8i
   ```
   c) The values can be negative or positive, and it is possible that one of the two values is not provided. If a value is not provided, the appropriate data member should be set to 0. The stream-insertion operator should not be able to display the point if an input error occurred. The output format should be identical to the input format shown above. For negative imaginary values, a minus sign should be printed rather than a plus sign.
   d) Write a **main** function that tests input and output of user-defined class **Complex** using the overloaded stream-extraction and stream-insertion operators.

11.17 Write a program that uses a **for** structure to print a table of ASCII values for the characters in the ASCII character set from **33** to **126**. The program should print the decimal value, octal value, hexadecimal value and character value for each character. Use the stream manipulators **dec**, **oct** and **hex** to print the integer values.

11.18 Write a program to show that the **getline** and three-argument **get istream** member functions each end the input string with a string-terminating null character. Also, show that **get** leaves the delimiter character on the input stream while **getline** extracts the delimiter character and discards it. What happens to the unread characters in the stream?

11.19 Write a program that creates the user-defined manipulator **skipwhite** to skip leading whitespace characters in the input stream. The manipulator should use the **isspace** function from the **<cctype>** library to test if the character is a whitespace character. Each character should be input using the **istream** member function **get**. When a nonwhitespace character is encountered, the **skipwhite** manipulator finishes its job by placing the character back on the input stream and returning an **istream** reference.

Test the manipulator by creating a **main** function in which the **ios::skipws** flag is unset so that the stream-extraction operator does not automatically skip whitespace. Then test the manipulator on the input stream by entering a character preceded by whitespace as input. Print the character that was input to confirm that a whitespace character was not input.

12

Templates

Objectives

- To be able to use function templates to create a group of related (overloaded) functions.
- To be able to distinguish between function templates and template functions.
- To be able to use class templates to create a group of related types.
- To be able to distinguish between class templates and template classes.
- To understand how to overload template functions.
- To understand the relationships among templates, friends, inheritance and static members.

Behind that outside pattern
the dim shapes get clearer every day.
It is always the same shape, only very numerous.
Charlotte Perkins Gilman
The Yellow Wallpaper

If you are able to slip through the parameters
of the skies and the earth, then do so.
The Koran

A Mighty Maze! but not without a plan.
Alexander Pope

Outline

12.1 Introduction

In this chapter we discuss one of C++'s more powerful features, namely templates. Templates enable us to specify, with a single code segment, an entire range of related (overloaded) functions—called *template functions*—or an entire range of related classes—called *template classes*.

We might write a single *function template* for an array sort function and then have C++ generate separate template functions that will sort an **int** array, sort a **float** array, sort an array of strings and so on.

We discussed function templates in Chapter 3. For the benefit of those readers who skipped that treatment, we present an additional discussion and example in this chapter.

We might write a single *class template* for a stack class and then have C++ generate separate template classes such as a stack-of-**int** class, a stack-of-**float** class, a stack-of-**string** class and so on.

Note the distinction between function templates and template functions: Function templates and class templates are like stencils out of which we trace shapes; template functions and template classes are like the separate tracings that all have the same shape but could be drawn in different colors, for example.

Software Engineering Observation 12.1

Templates are one of C++'s most powerful capabilities for software reuse.

In this chapter, we will present examples of a function template and a class template. We will also consider the relationships between templates and other C++ features such as overloading, inheritance, **friend**s and **static** members.

The design and details of the template mechanisms discussed here are based on the work of Bjarne Stroustrup as presented in his paper, *Parameterized Types for C++*, and published in the *Proceedings of the USENIX C++ Conference* held in Denver, Colorado, in October 1988.

This chapter is meant to serve only as a brief introduction to the rich and complex topic of templates. Chapter 20, "Standard Template Library (STL)," the largest chapter in this book, presents an in-depth treatment of the template container classes, iterators and algorithms of the STL. Chapter 20 contains dozens of live-code template-based examples illustrating more sophisticated template programming techniques than those used here in Chapter 12.

12.2 Function Templates

Overloaded functions are normally used to perform *similar* operations on different types of data. If the operations are *identical* for each type, this may be performed more compactly and conveniently using *function templates*. The programmer writes a single function template definition. Based on the argument types provided explicitly or inferred from calls to this function, the compiler generates separate object-code functions to handle each type of call appropriately. In C, this task can be performed using macros created with the preprocessor directive **#define** (see Chapter 17, "The Preprocessor"). However, *macros* present the possibility for serious side effects and do not enable the compiler to perform type checking. Function templates provide a compact solution like macros, but enable full type checking.

Testing and Debugging Tip 12.1

Function templates, like macros, enable software reuse. But unlike macros, function templates help eliminate many types of errors because of the scrutiny of full C++ type checking.

All function template definitions begin with the keyword **template** followed by a list of formal type parameters to the function template enclosed in *angle brackets (< and >)*; each formal type parameter must be preceded by the keyword **class** or **typename** as in

```
template< class T >
```

or

```
template< typename ElementType >
```

or

```
template< class BorderType, class FillType >
```

The formal type parameters of a template definition are used (as they would be with arguments of built-in types or user-defined types) to specify the *types* of the arguments to the function, to specify the return type of the function and to declare variables within the function. The function definition follows and is defined like any other function. Note that the keyword **class** or **typename** used to specify function template type parameters actually means "any built-in type or user-defined type."

Common Programming Error 12.1

Not placing **class** *(or* **typename***) before every formal type parameter of a function template.*

Let us examine the **printArray** function template in Fig. 12.1. The function template is used in the complete program of Fig. 12.2.

```
1   template< class T >
2   void printArray( const T *array, const int count )
3   {
4       for ( int i = 0; i < count; i++ )
5           cout << array[ i ] << " ";
6
7       cout << endl;
8   }
```

Fig. 12.1 A function template.

The **printArray** function template declares a single formal type parameter **T** (**T** could be any valid identifier) for the type of the array to be printed by function **print-Array**; **T** * is referred to as a *type parameter*. When the compiler detects a **printArray** function invocation in the program source code, the type of **printArray**'s first argument is substituted for **T** throughout the template definition and C++ creates a complete template function for printing an array of the specified data type. Then, the newly created function is compiled. In Fig. 12.2, three **printArray** functions are instantiated—one expects an **int** array, one expects a **double** array and one expects a **char** array. For example, the instantiation for type **int** is:

```
void printArray( const int *array, const int count )
{
    for ( int i = 0; i < count; i++ )
        cout << array[ i ] << " ";

    cout << endl;
}
```

Every formal type parameter in a function template definition should normally appear in the function's parameter list at least once. The name of a formal type parameter can be used only once in the parameter list of a template header. Formal type parameter names among template functions need not be unique.

Fig. 12.2 illustrates the use of the **printArray** function template. The program begins by instantiating **int** array **a**, **double** array **b**, and **char** array **c**, of sizes 5, 7 and 6, respectively. Then each of the arrays is printed by calling **printArray**—once with a first argument **a** of type **int** *, once with a first argument **b** of type **double** * and once with a first argument **c** of type **char** *. The call

```
printArray( a, aCount );
```

for example, causes the compiler to infer that **T** is **int** and to instantiate a **printArray** template function for which type parameter **T** is **int**. The call

```
printArray( b, bCount );
```

causes the compiler to infer that **T** is **double** and to instantiate a second **printArray** template function for which type parameter **T** is **double**. The call

```
printArray( c, cCount );
```

causes the compiler to infer that **T** is **char** and to instantiate a third **printArray** template function for which type parameter **T** is **char**.

```cpp
1   // Fig 12.2: fig12_02.cpp
2   // Using template functions
3   #include <iostream>
4
5   using std::cout;
6   using std::endl;
7
8   template< class T >
9   void printArray( const T *array, const int count )
10  {
11     for ( int i = 0; i < count; i++ )
12        cout << array[ i ] << " ";
13
14     cout << endl;
15  }
16
17  int main()
18  {
19     const int aCount = 5, bCount = 7, cCount = 6;
20     int a[ aCount ] = { 1, 2, 3, 4, 5 };
21     double b[ bCount ] = { 1.1, 2.2, 3.3, 4.4, 5.5, 6.6, 7.7 };
22     char c[ cCount ] = "HELLO";   // 6th position for null
23
24     cout << "Array a contains:" << endl;
25     printArray( a, aCount );   // integer template function
26
27     cout << "Array b contains:" << endl;
28     printArray( b, bCount );   // double template function
29
30     cout << "Array c contains:" << endl;
31     printArray( c, cCount );   // character template function
32
33     return 0;
34  }
```

```
Array a contains:
1 2 3 4 5
Array b contains:
1.1 2.2 3.3 4.4 5.5 6.6 7.7
Array c contains:
H E L L O
```

Fig. 12.2   Using template functions .

In this example, the template mechanism saves the programmer from having to write three separate overloaded functions with prototypes

```cpp
void printArray( const int *, const int );
void printArray( const double *, const int );
void printArray( const char *, const int );
```

that all use the same code, except for type **T**.

Performance Tip 12.1

Templates certainly offer the benefits of software reusability. But keep in mind that multiple copies of template functions and template classes are still instantiated in a program despite the fact that the template is written only once. These copies can consume considerable memory.

12.3 Overloading Template Functions

Template functions and overloading are intimately related. The related functions generated from a function template all have the same name, so the compiler uses overloading resolution to invoke the proper function.

A function template itself may be overloaded in several ways. We can provide other function templates that specify the same function name but different function parameters. For example, the **printArray** function template of Fig. 12.2 could be overloaded with another **printArray** function template with additional parameters **lowSubscript** and **highSubscript** to specify the portion of the array to be printed (see Exercise 12.4).

A function template can also be overloaded by providing other non-template functions with the same function name but different function arguments. For example, the **printArray** function template of Fig. 12.2 could be overloaded with a non-template version that specifically prints an array of character strings in neat, tabular, column format (see Exercise 12.5).

Common Programming Error 12.2

If a template is invoked with a user-defined class type and if that template uses operators (like ==, +, <=, etc.) with objects of that class type, then those operators must be overloaded! Forgetting to overload such operators causes errors because the compiler, of course, still generates calls to the appropriate overloaded operator functions despite the fact that these functions are not present.

The compiler performs a matching process to determine what function to call when a function is invoked. First the compiler tries to find and use a precise match in which the function names and argument types match perfectly with those of the function call. If this fails, the compiler checks if a function template is available that can be used to generate a template function with a precise match of function name and argument types. If such a function template is found, the compiler generates and uses the appropriate template function.

Common Programming Error 12.3

The compiler performs a matching process to determine what function to call when a function is invoked. If no match can be found, or if the matching process produces multiple matches, a compiler error is generated.

12.4 Class Templates

It is possible to understand what a stack is (a data structure into which we insert items in one order and retrieve them in last-in-first-out order) independent of the type of the items being placed in the stack. But when it comes to actually instantiating a stack, a data type must be specified. This creates a wonderful opportunity for software reusability. We need the means for describing the notion of a stack generically and instantiating classes that are type-specific versions of this generic class. This capability is provided by *class templates* in C++.

Software Engineering Observation 12.2

Class templates encourage software reusability by enabling type-specific versions of generic classes to be instantiated.

Class templates are called *parameterized types* because they require one or more type parameters to specify how to customize a "generic class" template to form a specific template class.

The programmer who wishes to produce a variety of template classes simply writes one class template definition. Each time the programmer needs a new type-specific instantiation, the programmer uses a concise, simple notation and the compiler writes the source code for the template class the programmer requires. One **Stack** class template, for example, could thus become the basis for creating many **Stack** classes (such as "**Stack** of **double**," "**Stack** of **int**," "**Stack** of **char**," "**Stack** of **Employee**," etc.) used in a program.

Note the definition of the **Stack** class template in Fig. 12.3. It looks like a conventional class definition except that it is preceded by the header (line 6)

```
template< class T >
```

to specify that this is a class template definition with type parameter **T** indicating the type of the **Stack** class to be created. The programmer need not specifically use identifier **T**—any identifier can be used. The type of element to be stored on this **Stack** is mentioned only generically as **T** throughout the **Stack** class header and member function definitions. We will show momentarily how **T** becomes associated with a specific type, such as **double** or **int**. There are two constraints for non-primitive data types used with this **Stack**: They must have a default constructor and they must support the assignment operator. If an object of the class used with this **Stack** contains dynamically allocated memory, the assignment operator should be overloaded for that type as shown in Chapter 8.

```
1   // Fig. 12.3: tstack1.h
2   // Class template Stack
3   #ifndef TSTACK1_H
4   #define TSTACK1_H
5
6   template< class T >
7   class Stack {
8   public:
9      Stack( int = 10 );      // default constructor (stack size 10)
10     ~Stack() { delete [] stackPtr; } // destructor
11     bool push( const T& ); // push an element onto the stack
12     bool pop( T& );         // pop an element off the stack
13  private:
14     int size;              // # of elements in the stack
15     int top;               // location of the top element
16     T *stackPtr;           // pointer to the stack
17
18     bool isEmpty() const { return top == -1; }     // utility
19     bool isFull() const { return top == size - 1; } // functions
20  };
```

Fig. 12.3   Demonstrating class template **Stack**—**tstack1.h** (part 1 of 2).

```
21
22    // Constructor with default size 10
23    template< class T >
24    Stack< T >::Stack( int s )
25    {
26       size = s > 0 ? s : 10;
27       top = -1;               // Stack is initially empty
28       stackPtr = new T[ size ]; // allocate space for elements
29    }
30
31    // Push an element onto the stack
32    // return 1 if successful, 0 otherwise
33    template< class T >
34    bool Stack< T >::push( const T &pushValue )
35    {
36       if ( !isFull() ) {
37          stackPtr[ ++top ] = pushValue; // place item in Stack
38          return true;   // push successful
39       }
40       return false;      // push unsuccessful
41    }
42
43    // Pop an element off the stack
44    template< class T >
45    bool Stack< T >::pop( T &popValue )
46    {
47       if ( !isEmpty() ) {
48          popValue = stackPtr[ top-- ];   // remove item from Stack
49          return true;   // pop successful
50       }
51       return false;      // pop unsuccessful
52    }
53
54    #endif
```

Fig. 12.3   Demonstrating class template **Stack—tstack1.h** (part 2 of 2).

```
55    // Fig. 12.3: fig12_03.cpp
56    // Test driver for Stack template
57    #include <iostream>
58
59    using std::cout;
60    using std::cin;
61    using std::endl;
62
63    #include "tstack1.h"
64
65    int main()
66    {
67       Stack< double > doubleStack( 5 );
68       double f = 1.1;
69       cout << "Pushing elements onto doubleStack\n";
```

Fig. 12.3   Demonstrating class template **Stack—fig12_03.cpp** (part 1 of 2).

```
70
71      while ( doubleStack.push( f ) ) { // success true returned
72         cout << f << ' ';
73         f += 1.1;
74      }
75
76      cout << "\nStack is full. Cannot push " << f
77             << "\n\nPopping elements from doubleStack\n";
78
79      while ( doubleStack.pop( f ) )  // success true returned
80         cout << f << ' ';
81
82      cout << "\nStack is empty. Cannot pop\n";
83
84      Stack< int > intStack;
85      int i = 1;
86      cout << "\nPushing elements onto intStack\n";
87
88      while ( intStack.push( i ) ) { // success true returned
89         cout << i << ' ';
90         ++i;
91      }
92
93      cout << "\nStack is full. Cannot push " << i
94             << "\n\nPopping elements from intStack\n";
95
96      while ( intStack.pop( i ) )  // success true returned
97         cout << i << ' ';
98
99      cout << "\nStack is empty. Cannot pop\n";
100     return 0;
101  }
```

```
Pushing elements onto doubleStack
1.1 2.2 3.3 4.4 5.5
Stack is full. Cannot push 6.6

Popping elements from doubleStack
5.5 4.4 3.3 2.2 1.1
Stack is empty. Cannot pop

Pushing elements onto intStack
1 2 3 4 5 6 7 8 9 10
Stack is full. Cannot push 11

Popping elements from intStack
10 9 8 7 6 5 4 3 2 1
Stack is empty. Cannot pop
```

Fig. 12.3   Demonstrating class template **Stack**—**fig12_03.cpp** (part 2 of 2).

Now let us consider the driver (function **main**) that exercises the **Stack** class template (see the output in Fig. 12.3). The driver begins by instantiating object **doubleStack** of size 5. This object is declared to be of class **Stack< double >** (pronounced "**Stack** of **double**"). The compiler associates type **double** with type parameter **T** in the template to produce the source code for a **Stack** class of type **double**. Although the programmer does not see this source code, it is included in the source code and compiled.

The driver then successively **push**es the **double** values 1.1, 2.2, 3.3, 4.4 and 5.5 onto **doubleStack**. The **push** loop terminates when the driver attempts to **push** a sixth value onto **doubleStack** (which is already full because it was created to hold a maximum of five elements).

The driver now **pop**s the five values off the stack (note in Fig. 12.3, that the values do **pop** off in last-in-first-out order). The driver attempts to **pop** a sixth value, but **doubleStack** is now empty, so the **pop** loop terminates.

Next, the driver instantiates integer stack **intStack** with the declaration

```
Stack< int > intStack;
```

(pronounced "**intStack** is a **Stack** of **int**"). Because no size is specified, the size defaults to 10 as specified in the default constructor (line 24). Once again, the driver loops **push**ing values onto **intStack** until it is full, then loops **pop**ping values off **intStack** until it is empty. Once again, the values **pop** off in last-in-first-out order.

The member function definitions outside the class each begin with the header (line 23)

```
template< class T >
```

Then each definition resembles a conventional function definition except that the **Stack** element type is always listed generically as type parameter **T**. The binary scope resolution operator is used with the class template name **Stack< T >** to tie each member function definition to the class template's scope. In this case, the class name is **Stack< T >**. When **doubleStack** is instantiated to be of type **Stack< double >**, the **Stack** constructor uses **new** to create an array of elements of type **double** to represent the stack (line 28). The statement

```
stackPtr = new T[ size ];
```

in the **Stack** class template definition is generated by the compiler in the **Stack< double >** template class as

```
stackPtr = new double[ size ];
```

Notice that the code in function **main** of Fig. 12.3 is almost identical for both the **doubleStack** manipulations in the top half of **main** and the **intStack** manipulations in the bottom half of **main**. This presents us with another opportunity to use a function template. Figure 12.4 uses function template **testStack** to perform the same tasks as **main** in Fig. 12.3—**push** a series of values onto a **Stack< T >** and **pop** the values off a **Stack< T >**. Function template **testStack** uses formal type parameter **T** to represent the data type stored in the **Stack< T >**. The function template takes four arguments—a reference to an object of type **Stack< T >**, a value of type **T** that will be the first value **push**ed onto the **Stack< T >**, a value of type **T** used to increment the values **push**ed onto the **Stack< T >** and a character string of type **const char *** that represents the name of the **Stack< T >** object for output purposes. Function **main** now simply instantiates an object of type **Stack< double >** called **doubleStack** and an object of type **Stack< int >** called **intStack** and uses these objects in lines 42 and 43

```
      testStack( doubleStack, 1.1, 1.1, "doubleStack" );
      testStack( intStack, 1, 1, "intStack" );
```

Note that the output of Fig. 12.4 precisely matches the output of Fig. 12.3.

```
1   // Fig. 12.4: fig12_04.cpp
2   // Test driver for Stack template.
3   // Function main uses a function template to manipulate
4   // objects of type Stack< T >.
5   #include <iostream>
6
7   using std::cout;
8   using std::cin;
9   using std::endl;
10
11  #include "tstack1.h"
12
13  // Function template to manipulate Stack< T >
14  template< class T >
15  void testStack(
16     Stack< T > &theStack,    // reference to the Stack< T >
17     T value,                 // initial value to be pushed
18     T increment,             // increment for subsequent values
19     const char *stackName )  // name of the Stack < T > object
20  {
21     cout << "\nPushing elements onto " << stackName << '\n';
22
23     while ( theStack.push( value ) ) { // success true returned
24        cout << value << ' ';
25        value += increment;
26     }
27
28     cout << "\nStack is full. Cannot push " << value
29          << "\n\nPopping elements from " << stackName << '\n';
30
31     while ( theStack.pop( value ) )   // success true returned
32        cout << value << ' ';
33
34     cout << "\nStack is empty. Cannot pop\n";
35  }
36
37  int main()
38  {
39     Stack< double > doubleStack( 5 );
40     Stack< int > intStack;
41
42     testStack( doubleStack, 1.1, 1.1, "doubleStack" );
43     testStack( intStack, 1, 1, "intStack" );
44
45     return 0;
46  }
```

Fig. 12.4   Passing a **Stack** template object to a function template (part 1 of 2).

```
Pushing elements onto doubleStack
1.1 2.2 3.3 4.4 5.5
Stack is full. Cannot push 6.6

Popping elements from doubleStack
5.5 4.4 3.3 2.2 1.1
Stack is empty. Cannot pop

Pushing elements onto intStack
1 2 3 4 5 6 7 8 9 10
Stack is full. Cannot push 11

Popping elements from intStack
10 9 8 7 6 5 4 3 2 1
Stack is empty. Cannot pop
```

Fig. 12.4   Passing a **Stack** template object to a function template (part 2 of 2).

12.5 Class Templates and Nontype Parameters

The **Stack** class template of the previous section used only type parameters in the template header. It is also possible to use *nontype parameters*; a nontype parameter can have a default argument and the nontype parameter is treated as **const**. For example, the template header could be modified to take an **int elements** parameter as follows:

> **template< class T, int elements >   // note non-type parameter**

Then, a declaration such as

> **Stack< double, 100 > mostRecentSalesFigures;**

would instantiate (at compile time) a 100-element **Stack** template class named **mostRecentSalesFigures** of **double** values; this template class would be of type **Stack< double, 100 >**. The class header might then contain a **private** data member with an array declaration such as

> **T stackHolder[elements];   // array to hold stack contents**

Performance Tip 12.2

*When it is possible to do so, specifying the size of a container class (such as an array class or a stack class) at compile time (possibly through a non-type template size parameter) eliminates the execution time overhead of creating the space dynamically with **new**.*

Software Engineering Observation 12.3

*When it is possible to do so, specifying the size of a container at compile time (possibly through a non-type template size parameter) avoids the possibility of a potentially fatal execution-time error if **new** is unable to obtain the needed memory.*

In the exercises, you will be asked to use a non-type parameter to create a template for the **Array** class developed in Chapter 8, "Operator Overloading." This template will enable **Array** objects to be instantiated with a specified number of elements of a specified type at compile time, rather than dynamically creating space for the **Array** objects at execution time.

A class for a specific type that does not match a common class template can be provided to override the class template for that type. For example, an **Array** class template can be used to instantiate an array of any type. The programmer may choose to take control of instantiating the **Array** class of a specific type, such as **Martian**. This is done simply by forming the new class with a class name of **Array<Martian>**.

12.6 Templates and Inheritance

Templates and inheritance relate in several ways:

- A class template can be derived from a template class.
- A class template can be derived from a non-template class.
- A template class can be derived from a class template.
- A non-template class can be derived from a class template.

12.7 Templates and `friends`

We have seen that functions and entire classes can be declared as **friend**s of non-template classes. With class templates, the obvious kinds of friendship arrangements can be declared. Friendship can be established between a class template and a global function, a member function of another class (possibly a template class), or even an entire class (possibly a template class). The notations required to establish these friendship relationships can be cumbersome.

Inside a class template for class **X** that has been declared with

```
template< class T > class X
```

a friendship declaration of the form

```
friend void f1();
```

makes function **f1** a **friend** of every template class instantiated from the preceding class template.

Inside a class template for class **X** that has been declared with

```
template< class T > class X
```

a friendship declaration of the form

```
friend void f2( X< T > & );
```

for a particular type **T** such as **float** makes function **f2(X< float > &)** a **friend** of **X< float >** only.

Inside a class template, you can declare that a member function of another class is a **friend** of any template class generated from the class template. Simply name the member function of the other class using the class name and the binary scope-resolution operator. For example, inside a class template for class **X** that has been declared with

```
template< class T > class X
```

a friendship declaration of the form

```
friend void A::f4();
```

makes member function **f4** of class **A** a **friend** of every template class instantiated from the preceding class template.

Inside a class template for class **X** that has been declared with

```
template< class T > class X
```

a friendship declaration of the form

```
friend void C< T >::f5( X< T > & );
```

for a particular type **T** such as **float** makes member function

```
C< float >::f5( X< float > & )
```

a **friend** function of *only* template class **X< float >**.

Inside a class template for class **X** that has been declared with

```
template< class T > class X
```

a second class **Y** can be declared with

```
friend class Y;
```

making every member function of class **Y** a **friend** of every template class produced from the class template for **X**.

Inside a class template for class **X** that has been declared with

```
template< class T > class X
```

a second class **Z** can be declared with

```
friend class Z< T >;
```

then when a template class is instantiated with a particular type for **T** such as **float**, all members of **class Z< float >** become **friend**s of template class **X< float >**.

12.8 Templates and static Members

What about **static** data members? Remember that with a non-template class, one copy of a **static** data member is shared among all objects of the class and the **static** data member must be initialized at file scope.

Each template class instantiated from a class template has its own copy of each **static** data member of the class template; all objects of that template class share that one **static** data member. And as with **static** data members of non-template classes, **static** data members of template classes must be initialized at file scope. Each template class gets its own copy of the class template's **static** member functions.

SUMMARY

- Templates enable us to specify a range of related (overloaded) functions—called template functions—or a range of related classes—called template classes.

- To use function templates, the programmer writes a single function template definition. Based on the argument types provided in calls to this function, C++ generates separate functions to handle each type of call appropriately. These are compiled along with the rest of a program's source code.

- All function template definitions begin with the keyword **template** followed by formal type parameters to the function template enclosed in angle brackets (**<** and **>**); each formal type parameter must be preceded by the keyword **class** (or **typename**). Keyword **class** (or **typename**) used to specify function template type parameters means "any built-in type or user-defined type."

- Template definition formal type parameters are used to specify the types of the arguments to the function, the return type of the function and to declare variables in the function.

- The name of a formal type parameter can be used only once in the type parameter list of a template header. Formal type parameter names among template functions need not be unique.

- A function template itself may be overloaded in several ways. We can provide other function templates that specify the same function name but different function parameters. A function template can also be overloaded by providing other non-template functions with the same function name but different function parameters.

- Class templates provide the means for describing a class generically and instantiating classes that are type-specific versions of this generic class.

- Class templates are called parameterized types; they require type parameters to specify how to customize a generic class template to form a specific template class.

- The programmer who wishes to use template classes writes one class template. When the programmer needs a new type-specific class, the programmer uses a concise notation and the compiler writes the source code for the template class.

- A class template definition looks like a conventional class definition except that it is preceded by **template< class T >** (or **template< typename T >**) to indicate this is a class template definition with type parameter **T** indicating the type of the class to be created. The type **T** is mentioned throughout the class header and member function definitions as a generic type name.

- The member function definitions outside the class each begin with the header **template< class T >** (or **template< typename T >**). Then each function definition resembles a conventional function definition except that the generic data in the class are always listed generically as type parameter **T**. The binary scope resolution operator is used with the class template name to tie each member function definition to the class template's scope as in **ClassName< T >**.

- It is possible to use nontype parameters in the header of a class template.

- A class for a specific type can be provided to override the class template for that type.

- A class template can be derived from a template class. A class template can be derived from a non-template class. A template class can be derived from a class template. A non-template class can be derived from a class template.

- Functions and entire classes can be declared as **friend**s of non-template classes. With class templates, the obvious kinds of friendship arrangements can be declared. Friendship can be established between a class template and a global function, a member function of another class (possibly a template class) or even an entire class (possibly a template class).

- Each template class instantiated from a class template has its own copy of each **static** data member of the class template; all objects of that template class share that one **static** data member. And as with **static** data members of non-template classes, **static** data members of template classes must be initialized at file scope.

- Each template class gets a copy of the class template's **static** member functions.

TERMINOLOGY

angle brackets (**<** and **>**)
class template
class template name
formal type parameter in a template header
friend of a template
function template
function template declaration
function template definition
keyword **class** in a template type parameter
keyword **template**
nontype parameter in a template header
overloading a template function
parameterized type

static data member of a class template
static data member of a template class
static member function of a class template
static member function of a template class
template argument
template class
template class member function
template function
template name
template parameter
template< class T >
type parameter in a template header
typename

COMMON PROGRAMMING ERRORS

12.1   Not placing **class** (or **typename**) before every formal type parameter of a function template.

12.2   If a template is invoked with a user-defined class type and if that template uses operators (like **==, +, <=,** etc.) with objects of that class type, then those operators must be overloaded! Forgetting to overload such operators causes errors because the compiler, of course, still generates calls to the appropriate overloaded operator functions despite the fact that these functions are not present.

12.3   The compiler performs a matching process to determine what function to call when a function is invoked. If no match can be found, or if the matching process produces multiple matches, a compiler error is generated.

PERFORMANCE TIPS

12.1   Templates certainly offer the benefits of software reusability. But keep in mind that multiple copies of template functions and template classes are still instantiated in a program despite the fact that the template is written only once. These copies can consume considerable memory.

12.2   When it is possible to do so, specifying the size of a container class (such as an array class or a stack class) at compile time (possibly through a nontype template size parameter) eliminates the execution time overhead of creating the space dynamically with **new**.

SOFTWARE ENGINEERING OBSERVATIONS

12.1   Templates are one of C++'s most powerful capabilities for software reuse.

12.2   Class templates encourage software reusability by enabling type-specific versions of generic classes to be instantiated.

12.3   When it is possible to do so, specifying the size of a container at compile time (possibly through a nontype template size parameter) avoids the possibility of a potentially fatal execution-time error if **new** is unable to obtain the needed memory.

TESTING AND DEBUGGING TIP

12.1   Function templates, like macros, enable software reuse. But unlike macros, function templates help eliminate many types of errors because of the scrutiny of full C++ type checking.

SELF-REVIEW EXERCISES

12.1   Answer each of the following true or false. For those that are false, state why.
   a) A **friend** function of a function template must be a template function.
   b) If several template classes are generated from a single class template with a single **static** data member, each of the template classes shares a single copy of the class template's **static** data member.
   c) A template function can be overloaded by another template function with the same function name.
   d) The name of a formal type parameter can be used only once in the formal type parameter list of the template definition. Formal type parameter names among template definitions must be unique.
   e) Keywords **class** and **typename** as used with a template type parameter specifically mean "any user-defined class type."

12.2   Fill in the blanks in each of the following:
   a) Templates enable us to specify, with a single code segment, an entire range of related functions called _____, or an entire range of related classes called _____.
   b) All function template definitions begin with the keyword _____ followed by a list of formal type parameters to the function template enclosed in _____.
   c) The related functions generated from a function template all have the same name, so the compiler uses _____ resolution to invoke the proper function.
   d) Class templates are also called _____ types.
   e) The _____ operator is used with a template class name to tie each member function definition to the class template's scope.
   f) As with **static** data members of non-template classes, **static** data members of template classes must also be initialized at _____ scope.

ANSWERS TO SELF-REVIEW EXERCISES

12.1   a) False. It could be a non-template function. b) False. Each template class will have a copy of the **static** data member. c) True. d) False. Formal type parameter names among template functions need not be unique. e) False. Keywords **class** and **typename** in this context also allow for a type parameter of a built-in type.

12.2   a) template functions, template classes.   b) **template**, angle brackets (**<** and **>**). c) overloading. d) parameterized. e) binary scope resolution. f) file.

EXERCISES

12.3   Write a function template **bubbleSort** based on the sort program of Fig. 5.15. Write a driver program that inputs, sorts and outputs an **int** array and a **float** array.

12.4   Overload function template **printArray** of Fig. 12.2 so that it takes two additional integer arguments, namely **int lowSubscript** and **int highSubscript**. A call to this function will print only the designated portion of the array. Validate **lowSubscript** and **highSubscript**; if either is out-of-range or if **highSubscript** is less than or equal to **lowSubscript**, the overloaded **printArray** function should return 0; otherwise, **printArray** should return the number of elements printed. Then modify **main** to exercise both versions of **printArray** on arrays **a**, **b** and **c**. Be sure to test all capabilities of both versions of **printArray**.

12.5   Overload function template **printArray** of Fig. 12.2 with a non-template version that specifically prints an array of character strings in neat, tabular, column format.

12.6   Write a simple function template for predicate function **isEqualTo** that compares its two arguments with the equality operator (**==**) and returns **true** if they are equal and **false** if they are not equal. Use this function template in a program that calls **isEqualTo** only with a variety of built-in types. Now write a separate version of the program that calls **isEqualTo** with a user-defined class type, but does not overload the equality operator. What happens when you attempt to run this program? Now overload the equality operator (with operator function **operator==**). Now what happens when you attempt to run this program?

12.7   Use a nontype parameter **numberOfElements** and a type parameter **elementType** to help create a template for the **Array** class we developed in Chapter 8, "Operator Overloading." This template will enable **Array** objects to be instantiated with a specified number of elements of a specified element type at compile time.

12.8   Write a program with class template **Array**. The template can instantiate an **Array** of any element type. Override the template with a specific definition for an **Array** of **float** elements (**class Array< float >**). The driver should demonstrate the instantiation of an **Array** of **int** through the template and should show that an attempt to instantiate an **Array** of **float** uses the definition provided in **class Array< float >**.

12.9   Distinguish between the terms "function template" and "template function."

12.10   Which is more like a stencil—a class template or a template class? Explain your answer.

12.11   What is the relationship between function templates and overloading?

12.12   Why might you choose to use a function template instead of a macro?

12.13   What performance problem can result from using function templates and class templates?

12.14   The compiler performs a matching process to determine which template function to call when a function is invoked. Under what circumstances does an attempt to make a match result in a compile error?

12.15   Why is it appropriate to call a class template a parameterized type?

12.16   Explain why you might use the statement

```
Array< Employee > workerList( 100 );
```

in a C++ program.

12.17   Review your answer to Exercise 12.16. Now, why might you use the statement

```
Array< Employee > workerList;
```

in a C++ program?

12.18   Explain the use of the following notation in a C++ program:

```
template< class T > Array< T >::Array( int s )
```

12.19   Why might you typically use a nontype parameter with a class template for a container such as an array or stack?

12.20   Describe how to provide a class for a specific type to override the class template for that type.

12.21   Describe the relationship between class templates and inheritance.

12.22   Suppose a class template has the header

```
template< class T1 > class C1
```

Describe the friendship relationships established by placing each of the following friendship declarations inside this class template header. Identifiers beginning with "**f**" are functions, identifiers beginning with "**C**" are classes and identifiers beginning with "**T**" can represent any type (i.e., built-in types or class types).

    a) `friend void f1();`
    b) `friend void f2( C1< T1 > &);`
    c) `friend void C2::f4();`
    d) `friend void C3< T1 >::f5( C1< T1 > & );`
    e) `friend class C5;`
    f) `friend class C6< T1 >;`

12.23 Suppose class template **Employee** has a **static** data member **count**. Suppose three template classes are instantiated from the class template. How many copies of the **static** data member will exist? How will the use of each be constrained (if at all)?

Exception Handling

Objectives

- To use **try**, **throw** and **catch** to watch for, indicate and handle exceptions, respectively.
- To process uncaught and unexpected exceptions.
- To be able to process **new** failures.
- To use **auto_ptr** to prevent memory leaks.
- To understand the standard exception hierarchy.

I never forget a face, but in your case I'll make an exception.
Groucho (Julius Henry) Marx

No rule is so general, which admits not some exception.
Robert Burton, The Anatomy of Melancholy

It is common sense to take a method and try it. If it fails, admit it frankly and try another. But above all, try something.
Franklin Delano Roosevelt

O! throw away the worser part of it,
And live the purer with the other half.
William Shakespeare

If they're running and they don't look where they're going
I have to come out from somewhere and catch them.
Jerome David Salinger

And oftentimes excusing of a fault
Doth make the fault the worse by the excuse.
William Shakespeare

To err is human, to forgive divine.
Alexander Pope, An Essay on Criticism

13.1 Introduction

In this chapter, we introduce *exception handling*. The extensibility of C++ can increase substantially the number and kinds of errors that can occur. The features presented here enable programmers to write clearer, more robust, more fault-tolerant programs. Recent systems developed with these and/or similar techniques have reported positive results. We also mention when exception handling should not be used.

The style and details of exception handling presented in this chapter are based on the work of Andrew Koenig and Bjarne Stroustrup as presented in their paper, "Exception Handling for C++ (revised)," published in the *Proceedings of the USENIX C++ Conference* held in San Francisco in April, 1990.

Error-handling code varies in nature and amount among software systems depending on the application and whether or not the software is a product for release. Commercial products tend to contain far more error-handling code than "casual" software.

There are many popular means of dealing with errors. Most commonly, error-handling code is interspersed throughout a system's code. Errors are dealt with at the places in the code where the errors can occur. The advantage to this approach is that a programmer reading code can see the error processing in the immediate vicinity of the code and determine if the proper error checking has been implemented.

The problem with this scheme is that the code in a sense becomes "polluted" with the error processing. It becomes more difficult for a programmer concerned with the application itself to read the code and determine if the code is functioning correctly. This makes it more difficult to understand and to maintain the code.

Some common examples of exceptions are failure of **new** to obtain a requested amount of memory, an out-of-bounds array subscript, arithmetic overflow, division by zero, and invalid function parameters.

C++'s exception-handling features enable the programmer to remove the error-handling code from the "main line" of a program's execution. This improves program readability and modifiability. With the C++ style of exception handling, it is possible to catch all kinds of exceptions, to catch all exceptions of a certain type or to catch all exceptions of related types. This makes programs more robust by reducing the likelihood that errors will not be caught by a program. Exception handling is provided to enable programs to catch and handle errors rather than letting them occur and suffering the consequences. If the programmer does not provide a means of handling a fatal error, the program terminates.

Exception handling is designed for dealing with *synchronous errors* such as an attempt to divide by zero (that occurs as the program executes the divide instruction). With exception handling, before the program executes the division, it checks the denominator and "throws" (issues) an exception if the denominator is zero.

Exception handling is not designed to deal with asynchronous situations such as disk I/O completions, network message arrivals, mouse clicks and the like; these are best handled through other means, such as interrupt processing.

Exception handling is used in situations in which the system can recover from the error causing the exception. The recovery procedure is called an *exception handler*. Exception handling is typically used when the error will be dealt with by a different part of the program (i.e., a different scope) from that which detected the error. A program that carries on an interactive dialog with a user should not use exceptions to process input errors.

Exception handling is especially appropriate for situations in which the program will not be able to recover, but needs to provide orderly cleanup, then shut down "gracefully."

Good Programming Practice 13.1

Use exceptions for errors that must be processed in a different scope from that in which they occur. Use other means of error handling for errors that will be processed in the scope in which they occur.

Good Programming Practice 13.2

Avoid using exception handling for purposes other than error handling, because this can reduce program clarity.

There is another reason to avoid using exception-handling techniques for conventional program control. Exception handling is designed for error processing, which is an infrequent activity that is often used because a program is about to terminate. Given this, it is not required that C++ compiler writers implement exception handling for the kind of optimal performance that might be expected of regular application code.

Performance Tip 13.1

Although it is possible to use exception handling for purposes other than error handling, this can reduce program performance.

Performance Tip 13.2

Exception handling is generally implemented in compilers in such a manner that when an exception does not occur, little or no overhead is imposed by the presence of exception-handling code. When exceptions happen, they do incur execution-time overhead. Certainly the presence of exception-handling code makes the program consume more memory.

Software Engineering Observation 13.1

Flow of control with conventional control structures is generally clearer and more efficient than with exceptions.

Common Programming Error 13.1

Another reason exceptions can be dangerous as an alternative to normal flow of control is that the stack is unwound and resources allocated prior to the occurrence of the exception may not be freed. This problem can be avoided by careful programming.

Exception handling helps improve a program's fault tolerance. It becomes "more pleasant" to write error-processing code, so programmers are more likely to provide it. It also becomes possible to catch exceptions in a variety of ways such as by type, or even to specify that exceptions of any type are to be caught.

The majority of programs written today support only a single thread of execution. Multithreading is receiving great attention in recent operating systems like Windows NT, OS/2, and various versions of UNIX. The techniques discussed in this chapter apply even for multithreaded programs, although we do not discuss multithreaded programs specifically.

We will show how to deal with "uncaught" exceptions. We will consider how unexpected exceptions are handled. We will show how related exceptions can be represented by exception classes derived from a common base exception class.

The exception-handling features of C++ are becoming widely used as a result of the C++ standard. Standardization is especially important on large software projects where dozens or even hundreds of people work on separate components of a system and these components need to interact for the overall system to function properly.

Software Engineering Observation 13.2

Exception handling is well suited to systems of separately developed components. Exception handling makes it easier to combine the components. Each component can perform its own exception detection separate from the handling of the exceptions in another scope.

Exception handling can be viewed as another means of returning control from a function or exiting a block of code. Normally, when an exception occurs, it will be handled by a caller of the function generating the exception, by a caller of that caller or however far back in the call chain it becomes necessary to go to find a handler for that exception.

13.2 When Exception Handling Should Be Used

Exception handling should be used to process only exceptional situations, despite the fact that there is nothing to prevent the programmer from using exceptions as an alternative to program control; to process exceptions for program components that are not geared to handling those exceptions directly; to process exceptions from software components such as functions, libraries and classes that are likely to be widely used, and where it does not make sense for those components to handle their own exceptions; and on large projects to handle error processing in a uniform manner project wide.

Good Programming Practice 13.3

Use conventional error-handling techniques rather than exception handling for straightforward, local error processing in which a program is easily able to deal with its own errors.

Software Engineering Observation 13.3

When dealing with libraries, the caller of the library function will likely have unique error processing in mind for an exception generated in the library function. It is unlikely that a library function will perform error processing that would meet the unique needs of all users. Therefore, exceptions are an appropriate means for dealing with errors produced by library functions.

13.3 Other Error-Handling Techniques

We have presented a variety of ways of dealing with exceptional situations prior to this chapter. The following summarizes these and other useful techniques:

- Use **assert** to test for coding and design errors. If an assertion is **false**, the program terminates and the code must be corrected. This is useful at debugging time.

- Simply ignore the exceptions. This would be devastating for software products released to the general public, or for special-purpose software needed for mission-critical situations. But for your own software developed for your own purposes, it is quite common to ignore many kinds of errors.

- Abort the program. This, of course, prevents a program from running to completion and producing incorrect results. Actually, for many types of errors this is appropriate, especially for nonfatal errors that enable a program to run to completion, perhaps misleading the programmer to think that the program functioned correctly. Here, too, such a strategy is inappropriate for mission-critical applications. Resource issues are also important here. If a program obtains a resource, the program should normally return that resource before program termination.

Common Programming Error 13.2

Aborting a program could leave a resource in a state in which other programs would not be able to acquire the resource; hence the program would have a so-called "resource leak."

- Set some error indicator. The problem with this is that programs may not check these error indicators at all points at which the errors could be troublesome.

- Test for the error condition, issue an error message and call **exit** to pass an appropriate error code to the program's environment.

- **setjump** and **longjump**. These **<csetjmp>** library functions enable the programmer to specify an immediate jump out of deeply nested function calls back to an error handler. Without **setjump/longjump**, a program must execute several returns to get out of the deeply nested function calls. These could be used to jump to some error handler. But they are dangerous in because they unwind the stack without calling destructors for automatic objects. This can lead to serious problems.

- Certain specific kinds of errors have dedicated capabilities for handling them. For example, when **new** fails to allocate memory, it can cause a **new_handler** function to execute to deal with the error. This function can be varied by supplying a function name as the argument to **set_new_handler**. We discuss function **set_new_handler** in detail in Section 13.14.

13.4 Basics of C++ Exception Handling: `try`, `throw`, `catch`

C++ exception handling is geared to situations in which the function that detects an error is unable to deal with it. Such a function will **throw** *an exception*. There is no guarantee that there will be "anything out there"—i.e., an *exception handler* specifically geared to processing that kind of exception. If there is, the exception will be *caught* and *handled*. If there is no exception handler for that particular kind of exception, the program terminates.

The programmer encloses in a **try** *block* the code that may generate an error that will produce an exception. The **try** block is followed by one or more **catch** *blocks*. Each **catch** block specifies the type of exception it can catch and handle. Each **catch** block contains an exception handler. If the exception matches the type of the parameter in one of the **catch** blocks, the code for that **catch** block is executed. If no handler is found, function **terminate** is called, which by default calls function **abort**.

Program control on a thrown exception leaves the **try** block and searches the **catch** blocks in order for an appropriate handler. (We will soon discuss what makes a handler "appropriate".) If no exceptions are thrown in the **try** block, the exception handlers for that block are skipped and the program resumes execution after the last **catch** block.

We can specify the exceptions a function **throw**s. As an option, we can specify that a function shall not **throw** any exceptions at all.

The exception is thrown in a **try** block in the function, or the exception is thrown from a function called directly or indirectly from the **try** block. The point at which the **throw** is executed is called the **throw** *point*. This term is also used to describe the **throw** expression itself. Once an exception is thrown, control cannot return to the **throw** point.

When an exception occurs, it is possible to communicate information to the exception handler from the point of the exception. That information is the type of the thrown object itself or information placed in the thrown object.

The thrown object is typically a character string (for an error message) or a class object. The thrown object conveys information to the exception handler that will process that exception.

Software Engineering Observation 13.4

A key to exception handling is that the portion of a program or system that will handle the exception can be quite different or distant from the portion of the program that detected and generated the exceptional situation.

13.5 A Simple Exception-Handling Example: Divide by Zero

Now let us consider a simple example of exception handling. Figure 13.1 uses **try**, **throw** and **catch** to detect a division by zero, indicate a divide-by-zero exception and handle a divide-by-zero exception.

```
1   // Fig. 13.1: fig13_01.cpp
2   // A simple exception handling example.
3   // Checking for a divide-by-zero exception.
4   #include <iostream>
5
```

Fig. 13.1   A simple exception-handling example with divide by zero (part 1 of 3).

```
6    using std::cout;
7    using std::cin;
8    using std::endl;
9
10   // Class DivideByZeroException to be used in exception
11   // handling for throwing an exception on a division by zero.
12   class DivideByZeroException {
13   public:
14      DivideByZeroException()
15         : message( "attempted to divide by zero" ) { }
16      const char *what() const { return message; }
17   private:
18      const char *message;
19   };
20
21   // Definition of function quotient. Demonstrates throwing
22   // an exception when a divide-by-zero exception is encountered.
23   double quotient( int numerator, int denominator )
24   {
25      if ( denominator == 0 )
26         throw DivideByZeroException();
27
28      return static_cast< double > ( numerator ) / denominator;
29   }
30
31   // Driver program
32   int main()
33   {
34      int number1, number2;
35      double result;
36
37      cout << "Enter two integers (end-of-file to end): ";
38
39      while ( cin >> number1 >> number2 ) {
40
41         // the try block wraps the code that may throw an
42         // exception and the code that should not execute
43         // if an exception occurs
44         try {
45            result = quotient( number1, number2 );
46            cout << "The quotient is: " << result << endl;
47         }
48         catch ( DivideByZeroException ex ) { // exception handler
49            cout << "Exception occurred: " << ex.what() << '\n';
50         }
51
52         cout << "\nEnter two integers (end-of-file to end): ";
53      }
54
55      cout << endl;
56      return 0;         // terminate normally
57   }
```

Fig. 13.1   A simple exception-handling example with divide by zero (part 2 of 3).

```
Enter two integers (end-of-file to end): 100 7
The quotient is: 14.2857

Enter two integers (end-of-file to end): 100 0
Exception occurred: attempted to divide by zero

Enter two integers (end-of-file to end): 33 9
The quotient is: 3.66667

Enter two integers (end-of-file to end):
```

Fig. 13.1   A simple exception-handling example with divide by zero (part 3 of 3).

Now consider the driver program in **main**. Note the "localized" declaration of **number1** and **number2**.

The program contains a **try** block (line 44) which wraps the code that may **throw** an exception. Note that the actual division that may cause the error is not explicitly listed inside the **try** block. Rather, the call to function **quotient** contains the code that attempts the actual division. Function **quotient** (defined on line 23) actually **throw**s the divide-by-zero exception object, as we will see momentarily. In general, errors may surface through explicitly mentioned code in the **try** block, through calls to a function or even through deeply nested function calls initiated by code in the **try** block.

The **try** block is immediately followed by a **catch** block containing the exception handler for the divide-by-zero error. In general, when an exception is thrown within a **try** block, the exception is caught by a **catch** block which specifies the appropriate type that matches the thrown exception. In Fig. 13.1, the **catch** block specifies that it will catch exception objects of type **DivideByZeroException**; this type matches the type of the object thrown in function **quotient**. The body of this exception handler prints the error message returned by calling function **what**. Exception handlers can be much more elaborate than this.

If, when executed, the code in a **try** block does not **throw** an exception, then all the **catch** handlers immediately following the **try** block are skipped and execution resumes with the first line of code after the **catch** handlers; in Fig. 13.1 a **return** statement is executed that **return**s **0**, indicating normal termination.

Now let us examine the definitions of class **DivideByZeroException** and function **quotient**. In function **quotient**, when the **if** statement determines that the denominator is zero, the body of the **if** statement issues a **throw** statement which specifies the name of the constructor for the exception object. This causes an object of class **DivideByZeroException** to be created. This object will be caught by the **catch** statement (specifying type **DivideByZeroException**) after the **try** block. The constructor for class **DivideByZeroException** simply points data member **message** at the string **"attempted to divide by zero"**. The **throw**n object is received in the parameter specified in the **catch** handler (in this case, parameter **ex**), and the message is printed there through a call to function **what**.

Good Programming Practice 13.4

Associating each type of execution-time error with an appropriately named exception object improves program clarity.

13.6 Throwing an Exception

Keyword **throw** is used to indicate that an exception has occurred. This is called *throwing an exception*. A **throw** normally specifies one operand. (A special case we will discuss specifies no operands.) The operand of a **throw** can be of any type. If the operand is an object, we call it an *exception object*. The value of any expression can be **throw**n instead of an object. It is possible to **throw** objects not intended for error handling.

Where is an exception caught? Upon being thrown, the exception will be caught by the closest exception handler (for the **try** block from which the exception was thrown) specifying an appropriate type. The exception handlers for a **try** block are listed immediately following the **try** block.

As part of throwing an exception, a temporary copy of the **throw** operand is created and initialized. This object then initializes the parameter in the exception handler. The temporary object is destroyed when the exception handler completes execution and exits.

Software Engineering Observation 13.5

If it is necessary to pass information about the error that caused an exception, such information can be placed in the thrown object. The **catch** *handler will then contain a parameter name through which that information could be referenced.*

Software Engineering Observation 13.6

An object can be thrown without containing information to be passed; in this case, mere knowledge that an exception of this type has been thrown may provide sufficient information for the handler to do its job correctly.

When an exception is thrown, control exits the current **try** block and proceeds to an appropriate **catch** handler (if one exists) after that **try** block. It is possible that the **throw** point could be in a deeply nested scope within a **try** block; control will still proceed to the **catch** handler. It is also possible that the **throw** point could be in a deeply nested function call; still, control will proceed to the **catch** handler.

A **try** block may appear to contain no error checking and include no **throw** statements, but code referenced in the **try** block could certainly cause error-checking code in constructors to execute. Code in a **try** block could perform array subscripting on an array class object whose **operator[]** member function is overloaded to **throw** an exception on a subscript-out-of-range error. Any function call can invoke code that might **throw** an exception or call another function that **throw**s an exception.

Although an exception can terminate program execution, it is not required to do so. However, an exception does terminate the block in which the exception occurred.

Common Programming Error 13.3

Exceptions should be thrown only within a **try** *block. An exception thrown outside a* **try** *block causes a call to* **terminate***.*

Common Programming Error 13.4

It is possible to **throw** *a conditional expression. But be careful because promotion rules may cause the value returned by the conditional expression to be of a different type than you may expect. For example, when throwing an* **int** *or a* **double** *from the same conditional expression, the conditional expression will convert the* **int** *to a* **double**. *Therefore the result will always be caught by a* **catch** *with a* **double** *argument rather than sometimes catching* **double** *(for the actual* **double***) and sometimes catching* **int***.*

13.7 Catching an Exception

Exception handlers are contained in **catch** blocks. Each **catch** block starts with the keyword **catch** followed by parentheses containing a type (indicating the type of exception this catch block handles) and an optional parameter name. This is followed by braces delineating the exception-handling code. When an exception is caught, the code in the **catch** block is executed.

The **catch** handler defines its own scope. A **catch** specifies in parentheses the type of the object to be caught. The parameter in a **catch** handler can be named or unnamed. If the parameter is named, the parameter can be referenced in the handler. If the parameter is unnamed, i.e., only a type is listed for purposes of matching with the thrown object type, then information is not conveyed from the **throw** point to the handler; only control passes from the **throw** point to the handler. For many exceptions, this is acceptable.

Common Programming Error 13.5

*Specifying a comma-separated list of **catch** arguments is a syntax error.*

An exception whose thrown object's type matches the type of the argument in the **catch** header causes the **catch** block, i.e., the exception handler for exceptions of that type, to execute.

The **catch** handler that catches an exception is the first one listed after the currently active **try** block that matches the type of the thrown object. The matching rules are discussed shortly.

An exception that is not caught causes a call to **terminate,** which by default terminates a program by calling **abort**. It is possible to specify customized behavior by designating another function to be executed by providing that function's name as the argument in a **set_terminate** function call.

A **catch** followed by parentheses enclosing an ellipsis

```
catch( ... )
```

means to catch all exceptions.

Common Programming Error 13.6

*Placing **catch(...)** before other **catch** blocks would prevent those blocks from ever being executed; **catch(...)** must be placed last in the list of handlers following a **try** block.*

Software Engineering Observation 13.7

*A weakness with catching exceptions with **catch(...)** is that you normally cannot be sure what the exception type is. Another weakness is that without a named parameter, there is no way to refer to the exception object inside the exception handler.*

It is possible that no handler will match a particular thrown object. This causes the search for a match to continue in the next enclosing try block. As this process continues, it may eventually be determined that there is no handler in the program that matches the type of the thrown object; in this case function **terminate** is called, which by default calls function **abort**.

The exception handlers are searched in order for an appropriate match. The first handler that yields a match is executed. When that handler finishes executing, control resumes with the first statement after the last **catch** block, i.e., the first statement after the last exception handler for that **try** block.

It is possible that several exception handlers will provide an acceptable match to the type of the exception that was thrown. In this case, the first exception handler that matches the exception type is executed. If several handlers match, and if each of these handles the exception differently, then the order of the handlers will affect the manner in which the exception is handled.

It is possible that several **catch** handlers could contain a class type that would match the type of a particular thrown object. This can happen for several reasons. First, there can be a "catch-all" handler **catch(...)** that will catch any exception. Second, because of inheritance hierarchies, it is possible that a derived-class object can be caught either by a handler specifying the derived-class type, or by handlers specifying the types of any base classes of that derived class.

Common Programming Error 13.7

*Placing a **catch** that catches a base-class object before a **catch** that catches an object of a class derived from that base class is a logic error. The base-class **catch** will catch all objects of classes derived from that base class, so the derived-class **catch** will never be executed.*

Testing and Debugging Tip 13.1

*The programmer determines the order in which the exception handlers are listed. This order can affect how exceptions originating in that **try** block are handled. If you are getting unexpected behavior in your program's handling of exceptions, it may be because an early **catch** block is intercepting and handling the exceptions before they reach your intended **catch** handler.*

Sometimes a program may process many closely related types of exceptions. Instead of providing separate exception classes and **catch** handlers for each, a programmer can provide a single exception class and **catch** handler for a group of exceptions. As each exception occurs, the exception object can be created with different **private** data. The **catch** handler can examine this **private** data to distinguish the type of the exception.

When does a match occur? The type of the **catch** handler parameter matches the type of the thrown object if

- they are indeed of the same type.

- the **catch** handler parameter type is a **public** base class of the class of the thrown object.

- the handler parameter is of a base-class pointer or reference type and the thrown object is of a derived-class pointer or reference type.

- the **catch** handler is of the form **catch(...)**.

Common Programming Error 13.8

*Placing an exception handler with a **void *** argument type before exception handlers with other pointer types causes a logic error. The **void *** handler would catch all exceptions of pointer types, so the other handlers would never execute. Only **catch (...)** should follow **catch (void *)**.*

An exact type match is required. No promotions or conversions are performed when looking for a handler except for derived-class-to-base-class conversions.

It is possible to **throw const** objects. In this case, the **catch** handler argument type must also be declared **const**.

If no handler is found for an exception, the program terminates. Although this may seem like the right thing to do, it is not what programmers are used to doing. Rather, errors often simply happen then program execution continues, possibly only "hobbling" along.

A **try** block followed by several **catch**es resembles a **switch** statement. It is not necessary to use **break** to exit an exception handler in a manner that skips over the remaining exception handlers. Each **catch** block defines a distinct scope, whereas all the cases in a **switch** statement are contained within the scope of the **switch**.

Common Programming Error 13.9

*Placing a semicolon after a **try** block or after any **catch** handler (other than the last* ***catch**) following a **try** block is a syntax error.*

An exception handler cannot access automatic objects defined within its **try** block, because, when an exception occurs, the **try** block terminates and all the automatic objects inside the **try** block are destroyed before the handler begins executing.

What happens when an exception occurs in an exception handler? The original exception that was caught is officially handled when the exception handler begins executing. So exceptions occurring in an exception handler need to be processed outside the **try** block in which the original exception was thrown.

Exception handlers can be written in a variety of ways. They could take a closer look at an error and decide to call **terminate**. They could *rethrow* an exception (Section 13.8). They could convert one type of exception into another by throwing a different exception. They could perform any necessary recovery and resume execution after the last exception handler. They could look at the situation causing the error, remove the cause of the error and retry by calling the original function that caused an exception. (This would not create infinite recursion.) They could return some status value to their environment, etc.

Software Engineering Observation 13.8

It is best to incorporate your exception-handling strategy into a system from the inception of the design process. It is difficult to add effective exception handling after a system has been implemented.

When a **try** block does not **throw** exceptions and the **try** block completes normal execution, control passes to the first statement after the last **catch** following the **try**.

It is not possible to return to the **throw** point by issuing a **return** statement in a **catch** handler. Such a **return** simply returns to the function that called the function containing the **catch** block.

Common Programming Error 13.10

*Assuming that after an exception is processed, control will return to the first statement after the **throw** is a logic error.*

Software Engineering Observation 13.9

*Another reason not to use exceptions for conventional flow of control is that these "additional" exceptions can get in the way of genuine error-type exceptions. It becomes more difficult for the programmer to keep track of the number of exception cases. For example, when a program processes an excessive variety of exceptions, can we really be sure of just what is being caught by a **catch(...)**? Exceptional situations should be rare, not commonplace.*

When an exception is caught, it is possible that resources may have been allocated but not yet released in the **try** block. The **catch** handler, if possible, should release these resources. For example, the **catch** handler should **delete** space allocated by **new** and should close any files opened in the **try** block that threw the exception.

A **catch** block can process the error in a manner that enables the program to continue executing correctly. Or the **catch** block can terminate the program.

A **catch** handler itself can discover an error and **throw** an exception. Such an exception will not be processed by **catch** handlers associated with the same **try** block as the **catch** handler throwing the exception. Rather, the thrown exception will be caught, if possible, by a **catch** handler associated with the next outer **try** block.

Common Programming Error 13.11

*Assuming that an exception thrown from a **catch** handler will be processed by that handler or any other handler associated with the **try** block that threw the exception which caused the original **catch** handler to execute is a logic error.*

13.8 Rethrowing an Exception

It is possible that the handler that catches an exception may decide that it cannot process the exception, or it may simply want to release resources before letting someone else handle it. In this case, the handler can simply rethrow the exception with the statement

```
throw;
```

Such a **throw** with no arguments rethrows the exception. If no exception was thrown to begin with, then the rethrow causes a call to **terminate**.

Common Programming Error 13.12

*Placing an empty **throw** statement outside a **catch** handler; executing such a **throw** causes a call to **terminate**.*

Even if a handler can process an exception, and regardless of whether it does any processing on that exception, the handler can still rethrow the exception for further processing outside the handler.

A rethrown exception is detected by the next enclosing **try** block and is handled by an exception handler listed after that enclosing **try** block.

Software Engineering Observation 13.10

*Use **catch(...)** to perform recovery that does not depend on the type of the exception, such as releasing common resources. The exception can be rethrown to alert more specific enclosing **catch** blocks.*

The program of Fig. 13.2 demonstrates rethrowing an exception. In the **try** block of **main**, function **throwException** is called at line 31. In the **try** block of function **throwException**, the **throw** statement at line 17 **throw**s an instance of standard library class **exception** (defined in header file **<exception>**). This exception is caught immediately in the **catch** handler at line 19, which prints an error message and then rethrows the exception. This terminates function **throwException** and returns control to the **try/catch** block in **main**. The exception is caught again at line 34 and an error message is printed.

```
1    // Fig. 13.2: fig13_02.cpp
2    // Demonstration of rethrowing an exception.
3    #include <iostream>
4
5    using std::cout;
6    using std::endl;
7
8    #include <exception>
9
10   using std::exception;
11
12   void throwException()
13   {
14      // Throw an exception and immediately catch it.
15      try {
16         cout << "Function throwException\n";
17         throw exception();   // generate exception
18      }
19      catch( exception e )
20      {
21         cout << "Exception handled in function throwException\n";
22         throw;   // rethrow exception for further processing
23      }
24
25      cout << "This also should not print\n";
26   }
27
28   int main()
29   {
30      try {
31         throwException();
32         cout << "This should not print\n";
33      }
34      catch ( exception e )
35      {
36         cout << "Exception handled in main\n";
37      }
38
39      cout << "Program control continues after catch in main"
40         << endl;
41      return 0;
42   }
```

```
Function throwException
Exception handled in function throwException
Exception handled in main
Program control continues after catch in main
```

Fig. 13.2   Rethrowing an exception.

13.9 Exception Specifications

An *exception specification* enumerates a list of exceptions that can be thrown by a function to be specified:

```
int g( double h ) throw ( a, b, c )
{
    // function body
}
```

It is possible to restrict the exception types thrown from a function. The exception types are specified in the function declaration as an *exception specification* (also called a **throw** *list*). The exception specification lists the exceptions that may be thrown. A function may **throw** the indicated exceptions or derived types. Despite this supposed guarantee that other exception types will not be thrown, it is possible to do so. If an exception not listed in the exception specification is thrown, function **unexpected** is called.

Placing **throw()** (i.e., an *empty exception specification*) after a function's parameter list states that the function will not **throw** any exceptions. Such a function could, in fact, **throw** an exception; this, too, would generate a call to **unexpected**.

Common Programming Error 13.13

Throwing an exception not in a function's exception specification causes a call to **unexpected***.*

A function with no exception specification can **throw** any exception:

```
void g();      // this function can throw any exception
```

The meaning of the **unexpected** function can be redefined by calling function **set_unexpected**.

One interesting aspect of exception handling is that the compiler will not consider it a syntax error if a function contains a **throw** expression for an exception not listed in the function's exception specification. The function must attempt to **throw** that exception at execution time before the error will be caught.

If a function **throw**s an exception of a particular class type, that function can also **throw** exceptions of all classes derived from that class with **public** inheritance.

13.10 Processing Unexpected Exceptions

Function **unexpected** calls the function specified with the **set_unexpected** function. If no function has been specified in this manner, **terminate** is called by default.

Function **terminate** can be called explicitly if a thrown exception cannot be caught, if the stack is corrupted during exception handling, as the default action on a call to **unexpected**, and if during stack unwinding initiated by an exception, an attempt by a destructor to **throw** an exception causes **terminate** to be called.

Function **set_terminate** can specify the function that will be called when **terminate** is called. Otherwise, **terminate** calls **abort**.

Prototypes for functions **set_terminate** and **set_unexpected** are located in header file **<exception>**.

Function **set_terminate** and function **set_unexpected** each return a pointer to the last function called by **terminate** and **unexpected**. This enables the programmer to save the function pointer so it can be restored later.

Functions **set_terminate** and **set_unexpected** take pointers to functions as arguments. Each argument must point to a function with **void** return type and no arguments.

If the last action of a user-defined termination function is not to exit a program, function **abort** will automatically be called to end program execution after the other statements of the user-defined termination function are executed.

13.11 Stack Unwinding

When an exception is thrown but not caught in a particular scope, the function-call stack is unwound and an attempt is made to **catch** the exception in the next outer **try/catch** block. Unwinding the function-call stack means that the function in which the exception was not caught terminates, all local variables in that function are destroyed and control returns to the point at which that function was called. If that point in the program is in a **try** block, an attempt is made to **catch** the exception. If that point in the program is not in a **try** block or the exception is not caught, stack unwinding occurs again. As mentioned in the previous section, if the exception is not caught in the program, function **terminate** is called to terminate the program. The program of Fig. 13.3 demonstrates stack unwinding.

```cpp
1   // Fig. 13.3: fig13_03.cpp
2   // Demonstrating stack unwinding.
3   #include <iostream>
4
5   using std::cout;
6   using std::endl;
7
8   #include <stdexcept>
9
10  using std::runtime_error;
11
12  void function3() throw ( runtime_error )
13  {
14     throw runtime_error( "runtime_error in function3" );
15  }
16
17  void function2() throw ( runtime_error )
18  {
19     function3();
20  }
21
22  void function1() throw ( runtime_error )
23  {
24     function2();
25  }
26
```

Fig. 13.3   Demonstration of stack unwinding (part 1 of 2).

```
27   int main()
28   {
29      try {
30         function1();
31      }
32      catch ( runtime_error e )
33      {
34         cout << "Exception occurred: " << e.what() << endl;
35      }
36
37      return 0;
38   }
```

```
Exception occurred: runtime_error in function3
```

Fig. 13.3   Demonstration of stack unwinding (part 2 of 2).

In **main**, the **try** block at line 30 calls **function1**. Next, **function1** (defined at line 22) calls **function2**. Then, **function2** (defined at line 17) calls **function3**. Line 14 of **function3 throw**s an **exception** object. Because line 14 is not in a **try** block, stack unwinding occurs—**function3** terminates at line 19 and control returns to **function2**. Because line 19 is not in a **try** block, stack unwinding occurs again—**function2** terminates at line 24 and control returns to **function1**. Because line 24 is not in a **try** block, stack unwinding occurs one more time—**function1** terminates at line 30 and control returns to **main**. Because line 30 is in a **try** block, the exception can be caught and processed in the first matching **catch** handler after the **try** block (at line 32).

13.12 Constructors, Destructors and Exception Handling

First, let us deal with an issue we have mentioned, but that has yet to be satisfactorily re-solved: What happens when an error is detected in a constructor? For example, how should a **String** constructor respond when **new** fails and indicates that it was unable to obtain the space needed to hold the **String**'s internal representation? The problem is that a con-structor cannot return a value, so how do we let the outside world know that the object has not been properly constructed? One scheme is simply to return the improperly constructed object and hope that anyone using the object would make appropriate tests to determine that the object was in fact bad. Another scheme is to set some variable outside the constructor. A thrown exception passes to the outside world the information about the failed constructor and the responsibility to deal with the failure.

To **catch** an exception, the exception handler must have access to a copy constructor for the thrown object. (Default memberwise copy is also valid.)

Exceptions thrown in constructors cause destructors to be called for any objects built as part of the object being constructed before the exception is thrown.

Destructors are called for every automatic object constructed in a **try** block before an exception is thrown. An exception is handled at the moment the handler begins executing; stack unwinding is guaranteed to have been completed at that point. If a destructor invoked as a result of stack unwinding **throw**s an exception, **terminate** is called.

If an object has member objects and if an exception is thrown before the outer object is fully constructed, then destructors will be executed for the member objects that have been fully constructed prior to the occurrence of the exception.

If an array of objects has been partially constructed when an exception occurs, only the destructors for the constructed array elements will be called.

An exception could preclude the operation of code that would normally release a resource, thus causing a *resource leak*. One technique to resolve this problem is to initialize a local object when the resource is acquired. When an exception occurs, the destructor will be invoked and can free the resource.

It is possible to **catch** exceptions thrown from destructors by enclosing the function that calls the destructor in a **try** block and providing a **catch** handler with the proper type. The thrown object's destructor executes after an exception handler completes execution.

13.13 Exceptions and Inheritance

Various exception classes can be derived from a common base class. If a **catch** catches a pointer or reference to an exception object of a base-class type, it can also **catch** a pointer or reference to all objects of classes derived from that base class. This can allow for polymorphic processing of related errors.

Testing and Debugging Tip 13.2

Using inheritance with exceptions enables an exception handler to **catch** *related errors with a rather concise notation. One could certainly* **catch** *each type of pointer or reference to a derived-class exception object individually, but it is more concise to* **catch** *pointers or references to base-class exception objects instead. Also, catching pointers or references to derived-class exception objects individually is subject to error if the programmer forgets to explicitly test for one or more of the derived-class pointer or reference types.*

13.14 Processing **new** Failures

There are several methods of dealing with **new** failures. To this point, we have used macro **assert** to test the value returned from **new**. If that value is **0**, the **assert** macro terminates the program. This is not a robust mechanism for dealing with **new** failures—it does not allow us to recover from the failure in any way. The C++ standard specifies that when **new** fails, it **throw**s a **bad_alloc** exception (defined in header file **<new>**). However, some compilers may not be compliant with the C++ standard and therefore use the version of **new** that returns **0** on failure. In this section we present three examples of **new** failing. The first example returns **0** when **new** fails. The second and third examples use the version of **new** that **throw**s a **bad_alloc** exception when **new** fails.

Figure 13.4 demonstrates **new** returning **0** on failure to allocate the requested amount of memory. The **for** structure at line 12 is supposed to loop 50 times and allocate an array of 5,000,000 **double** values (i.e., 40,000,000 bytes, because a **double** is normally 8 bytes) each time through the loop. The **if** structure at line 15 tests the result of each **new** operation to determine if the memory was allocated. If **new** fails and returns **0**, the message **"Memory allocation failed"** is printed and the loop terminates.

The output shows that only four iterations of the loop were performed before **new** failed and the loop terminated. Your output may differ based on the physical memory, disk space available for virtual memory on your system and the compiler used to compile the program.

```
1   // Fig. 13.4: fig13_04.cpp
2   // Demonstrating new returning 0
3   // when memory is not allocated
4   #include <iostream>
5
6   using std::cout;
7
8   int main()
9   {
10      double *ptr[ 50 ];
11
12      for ( int i = 0; i < 50; i++ ) {
13         ptr[ i ] = new double[ 5000000 ];
14
15         if ( ptr[ i ] == 0 ) { // new failed to allocate memory
16            cout << "Memory allocation failed for ptr[ "
17                 << i << " ]\n";
18            break;
19         }
20         else
21            cout << "Allocated 5000000 doubles in ptr[ "
22                 << i << " ]\n";
23      }
24
25      return 0;
26   }
```

```
Allocated 5000000 doubles in ptr[ 0 ]
Allocated 5000000 doubles in ptr[ 1 ]
Allocated 5000000 doubles in ptr[ 2 ]
Allocated 5000000 doubles in ptr[ 3 ]
Memory allocation failed for ptr[ 4 ]
```

Fig. 13.4   Demonstrating **new** returning 0 on failure.

Figure 13.5 demonstrates **new** throwing **bad_alloc** when it fails to allocate the requested memory. The **for** structure at line 18 inside the **try** block is supposed to loop 50 times and on each pass allocate an array of 5,000,000 **double** values (i.e., 40,000,000 bytes, because a **double** is normally 8 bytes). If **new** fails and **throws** a **bad_alloc** exception, the loop terminates and the program continues in the exception-handling flow of control at line 24, where the exception is caught and processed. The message **"Exception occurred: "** is printed, followed by the string (containing the exception-specific message **"Allocation Failure"**) returned from **exception.what()**. The output shows that only four iterations of the loop were performed before **new** failed and threw the **bad_alloc** exception. Your output may differ based on the physical memory, disk space available for virtual memory on your system and the compiler you use to compile the program.

```
1   // Fig. 13.5: fig13_05.cpp
2   // Demonstrating new throwing bad_alloc
3   // when memory is not allocated
4   #include <iostream>
5
6   using std::cout;
7   using std::endl;
8
9   #include <new>
10
11  using std::bad_alloc;
12
13  int main()
14  {
15     double *ptr[ 50 ];
16
17     try {
18        for ( int i = 0; i < 50; i++ ) {
19           ptr[ i ] = new double[ 5000000 ];
20           cout << "Allocated 5000000 doubles in ptr[ "
21              << i << " ]\n";
22        }
23     }
24     catch ( bad_alloc exception ) {
25        cout << "Exception occurred: "
26           << exception.what() << endl;
27     }
28
29     return 0;
30  }
```

```
Allocated 5000000 doubles in ptr[ 0 ]
Allocated 5000000 doubles in ptr[ 1 ]
Allocated 5000000 doubles in ptr[ 2 ]
Allocated 5000000 doubles in ptr[ 3 ]
Exception occurred: Allocation Failure
```

Fig. 13.5   Demonstrating **new** throwing **bad_alloc** on failure.

Compilers vary in their support for **new** failure handling. Many C++ compilers return **0** by default when **new** fails. Some of these compilers support **new** throwing an exception if the header file **<new>** (or **<new.h>**) is included. Other compilers **throw bad_alloc** by default whether or not you include header file **<new>**. Read the documentation for your compiler to determine your compiler's support for **new** failure handling.

The C++ standard specifies that standard-compliant compilers can still use a version of **new** that returns **0** when it fails. For this purpose, the header file **<new>** defines **nothrow** (of type **nothrow_t**), which is used as follows:

```
double *ptr = new( nothrow ) double[ 5000000 ];
```

The preceding statement indicates that the version of **new** that does not **throw bad_alloc** exceptions (i.e., **nothrow**) should be used to allocate an array of 5,000,000 **double**s.

Software Engineering Observation 13.11

The C++ standard recommends that to make programs more robust, programmers should use the version of **new** *that* **throws** *bad_alloc exceptions on failure.*

There is an additional feature that can be used to perform handling of **new** failures. Function **set_new_handler** (prototyped in header file **<new>**) takes as its argument a function pointer for a function that takes no arguments and returns **void**. The function pointer is registered as the function to call when **new** fails. This provides the programmer with a uniform method of processing every **new** failure regardless of where the failure occurs in the program. Once a **new** *handler* is registered in the program with **set_new_handler**, **new** will not throw **bad_alloc** on failure.

Operator **new** is actually a loop that attempts to acquire memory. If the memory is allocated, **new** returns a pointer to that memory. If **new** fails to allocate memory and no **new** handler function has been registered with **set_new_handler**, new throws a **bad_alloc** exception. If **new** fails to allocate memory and a **new** handler function has been registered, the **new** handler function is called. The C++ standard specifies that the **new** handler function should perform one of the following tasks:

1. Make more memory available by deleting other dynamically allocated memory and return to the loop in operator **new** to attempt to allocate the memory again.

2. Throw an exception of type **bad_alloc**.

3. Call function **abort** or **exit** (both from header file **<cstdlib>**) to terminate the program.

The program of Fig. 13.6 demonstrates **set_new_handler**. The function **customNewHandler** simply prints an error message and terminates the program with a call to **abort**. The output shows that only four iterations of the loop were performed before **new** failed and threw the **bad_alloc** exception. Your output may differ based on the physical memory, disk space available for virtual memory on your system and the compiler you use to compile the program.

```
1   // Fig. 13.6: fig13_06.cpp
2   // Demonstrating set_new_handler
3   #include <iostream>
4
5   using std::cout;
6   using std::cerr;
7
8   #include <new>
9   #include <cstdlib>
10
11  using std::set_new_handler;
12
13  void customNewHandler()
14  {
15     cerr << "customNewHandler was called";
16     abort();
17  }
```

Fig. 13.6   Demonstrating **set_new_handler** (part 1 of 2).

```
18
19   int main()
20   {
21      double *ptr[ 50 ];
22      set_new_handler( customNewHandler );
23
24      for ( int i = 0; i < 50; i++ ) {
25         ptr[ i ] = new double[ 5000000 ];
26
27         cout << "Allocated 5000000 doubles in ptr[ "
28              << i << " ]\n";
29      }
30
31      return 0;
32   }
```

```
Allocated 5000000 doubles in ptr[ 0 ]
Allocated 5000000 doubles in ptr[ 1 ]
Allocated 5000000 doubles in ptr[ 2 ]
Allocated 5000000 doubles in ptr[ 3 ]
customNewHandler was called
```

Fig. 13.6   Demonstrating **set_new_handler** (part 2 of 2).

13.15 Class **auto_ptr** and Dynamic Memory Allocation

A common programming practice is to allocate dynamic memory (possibly an object) on the free store, assign the address of that memory to a pointer, use the pointer to manipulate the memory and deallocate the memory with **delete** when the memory is no longer needed. If an exception occurs after the memory has been allocated and before the **delete** statement is executed, a memory leak could occur. The C++ standard provides class template **auto_ptr** in header file **<memory>** to deal with this situation.

An object of class **auto_ptr** maintains a pointer to dynamically allocated memory. When an **auto_ptr** object goes out of scope, it performs a **delete** operation on its pointer data member. Class template **auto_ptr** provides operators * and -> so an **auto_ptr** object can be used like a regular pointer variable. Figure 13.7 demonstrates an **auto_ptr** object that points to an object of class **Integer** (defined at lines 12–22).

```
1    // Fig. 13.7: fig13_07.cpp
2    // Demonstrating auto_ptr
3    #include <iostream>
4
5    using std::cout;
6    using std::endl;
7
8    #include <memory>
9
10   using std::auto_ptr;
```

Fig. 13.7   Demonstrating **auto_ptr** (part 1 of 2).

```
11
12   class Integer {
13   public:
14      Integer( int i = 0 ) : value( i )
15         { cout << "Constructor for Integer " << value << endl; }
16      ~Integer()
17         { cout << "Destructor for Integer " << value << endl; }
18      void setInteger( int i ) { value = i; }
19      int getInteger() const { return value; }
20   private:
21      int value;
22   };
23
24   int main()
25   {
26      cout << "Creating an auto_ptr object that points "
27           << "to an Integer\n";
28
29      auto_ptr< Integer > ptrToInteger( new Integer( 7 ) );
30
31      cout << "Using the auto_ptr to manipulate the Integer\n";
32      ptrToInteger->setInteger( 99 );
33      cout << "Integer after setInteger: "
34           << ( *ptrToInteger ).getInteger()
35           << "\nTerminating program" << endl;
36
37      return 0;
38   }
```

```
Creating an auto_ptr object that points to an Integer
Constructor for Integer 7
Using the auto_ptr to manipulate the Integer
Integer after setInteger: 99
Terminating program
Destructor for Integer 99
```

Fig. 13.7   Demonstrating **auto_ptr** (part 2 of 2).

Line 29

```
auto_ptr< Integer > ptrToInteger( new Integer( 7 ) );
```

creates **auto_ptr** object **ptrToInteger** and initializes it with a pointer to a dynamically allocated **Integer** object containing the value 7.

Line 32

```
ptrToInteger->setInteger( 99 );
```

uses the **auto_ptr** overloaded **->** operator and the function call operator **()** to call function **setInteger** on the **Integer** object pointed to by **ptrToInteger**.

The call

```
( *ptrToInteger ).getInteger()
```

in line 34 uses the **auto_ptr** overloaded * operator to dereference **ptrToInteger** and then uses the dot (.) operator and the function call operator **()** to call function **getInteger** on the **Integer** object pointed to by **ptrToInteger**.

Because **ptrToInteger** is a local automatic variable in **main**, **ptrToInteger** is destroyed when **main** terminates. This forces a **delete** of the **Integer** object pointed to by **ptrToInteger**, which, of course, forces a call to the **Integer** class destructor. Most importantly, this technique can prevent memory leaks.

13.16 Standard Library Exception Hierarchy

Experience has shown that exceptions fall nicely into a number of categories. The C++ standard includes a hierarchy of exception classes. This hierarchy is headed by base class **exception** (defined in header file **<exception>**), which contains function **what()** that is overridden in each derived class to issue an appropriate error message.

From base class **exception**, some of the immediate derived classes are **runtime_error** and **logic_error** (both defined in header **<stdexcept>**), each of which has several derived classes.

Also derived from **exception** are the exceptions thrown by C++ language features—for example, **bad_alloc** is thrown by **new** (Section 13.14), **bad_cast** is thrown by **dynamic_cast** (Chapter 21) and **bad_typeid** is thrown by **typeid** (Chapter 21). By including **std::bad_exception** in the **throw** list of a function, if an unexpected exception occurs, **unexpected()** can throw **bad_exception** instead of terminating (by default) or instead of calling another function specified with **set_unexpected**.

Class **logic_error** is the base class of several standard exception classes that indicate errors in program logic that can often be prevented by writing proper code. Descriptions of some of these classes follow. Class **invalid_argument** indicates that an invalid argument was passed to a function. (Proper coding can, of course, prevent invalid arguments from reaching a function.) Class **length_error** indicates that a length larger than the maximum size allowed for the object being manipulated was used for that object. (We throw **length_error**s in Chapter 19 when we deal with **string**s.) Class **out_of_range** indicates that a value such as a subscript into an array or **string** was out of range.

Class **runtime_error** is the base class of several other standard exception classes that indicate errors in a program and that can only be detected at execution time. Class **overflow_error** indicates that an arithmetic overflow error occurred. Class **underflow_error** indicates that an arithmetic underflow error occurred.

Software Engineering Observation 13.12

*The standard **exception** hierarchy is meant to serve as a starting point. Users can **throw** standard exceptions, **throw** exceptions derived from the standard exceptions or **throw** their own exceptions not derived from the standard exceptions.*

Common Programming Error 13.14

*User-defined exception classes need not be derived from class **exception**. Thus, writing **catch(exception e)** is not guaranteed to **catch** all exceptions a program may encounter.*

Testing and Debugging Tip 13.3

*To **catch** all exceptions that might be thrown in a **try** block, use **catch(...)**.*

SUMMARY

- Some common examples of exceptions are an out-of-bounds array subscript, arithmetic overflow, division by zero, invalid function parameters and determining that there is insufficient memory to satisfy an allocation request by **new**.

- The spirit behind exception handling is to enable programs to **catch** and handle errors rather than letting them occur and simply suffering the consequences. With exception handling, if the programmer does not provide a means of handling a fatal error, the program will **terminate**; nonfatal errors normally allow a program to continue executing, but produce incorrect results.

- Exception handling is designed for dealing with synchronous errors, i.e., errors that occur as the result of a program's execution.

- Exception handling is not designed to deal with asynchronous situations such as network message arrivals, disk I/O completions, mouse clicks, and the like; these are best handled through other means, such as interrupt processing.

- Exception handling is typically used in situations in which the error will be dealt with by a different part of the program (i.e., a different scope) from that which detected the error.

- Exceptions should not be used as a mechanism for specifying flow of control. Flow of control with conventional control structures is generally clearer and more efficient than with exceptions.

- Exception handling should be used to process exceptions for program components that are not geared to handling those exceptions directly.

- Exception handling should be used to process exceptions from software components such as functions, libraries, and classes that are likely to be widely used, and where it does not make sense for those components to handle their own exceptions.

- Exception handling should be used on large projects to handle error processing in a uniform manner for the entire project.

- C++ exception handling is geared to situations in which the function that detects an error is unable to deal with it. Such a function will **throw** an exception. If the exception matches the type of the parameter in one of the **catch** blocks, the code for that **catch** block is executed. Otherwise, function **terminate** is called, which by default calls function **abort**.

- The programmer encloses in a **try** block the code that may generate an error that will produce an exception. The **try** block is immediately followed by one or more **catch** blocks. Each **catch** block specifies the type of exception it can **catch** and handle. Each **catch** block contains an exception handler.

- Program control on a thrown exception leaves the **try** block and searches the **catch** blocks in order for an appropriate handler. If no exceptions are thrown in the **try** block, the exception handlers for that block are skipped and the program resumes execution after the last **catch** block.

- Exceptions are thrown in a **try** block in a function or from a function called directly or indirectly from the **try** block.

- Once an exception is thrown, control cannot return directly to the **throw** point.

- It is possible to communicate information to the exception handler from the point of the exception. That information is the type of thrown object or information placed in the thrown object.

- A popular exception type thrown is **char ***. It is common to simply include an error message as the operand of the **throw**.

- The exceptions thrown by a particular function can be specified with an exception specification. An empty exception specification states that the function will not **throw** any exceptions.

- Exceptions are caught by the closest exception handler (for the **try** block from which the exception was thrown) specifying an appropriate type.

- As part of throwing an exception, a temporary copy of the **throw** operand is created and initialized. This temporary object then initializes the proper variable in the exception handler. The temporary object is destroyed when the exception handler is exited.

- Errors are not always checked explicitly. A **try** block, for example, may appear to contain no error checking and include no **throw** statements. But code referenced in the **try** block could certainly cause error-checking code to execute.

- An exception terminates the block in which the exception occurred.

- Exception handlers are contained in **catch** blocks. Each **catch** block starts with the keyword **catch**, followed by parentheses containing a type and an optional parameter name. This is followed by braces delineating the exception-handling code. When an exception is caught, the code in the **catch** block is executed. The **catch** handler defines its own scope.

- The parameter in a **catch** handler can be named or unnamed. If the parameter is named, the parameter can be referenced in the handler. If the parameter is unnamed, i.e., only a type is listed for the purpose of matching with the thrown object type or an ellipsis for all types, then the handler will ignore the thrown object. The handler may rethrow the object to an outer **try** block.

- It is possible to specify customized behavior to replace function **terminate** by designating another function to be executed and providing that function's name as the argument in a **set_terminate** function call.

- **catch(...)** means to **catch** all exceptions.

- It is possible that no handler will match a particular thrown object. This causes the search for a match to continue in an enclosing **try** block.

- The exception handlers are searched in order for an appropriate match. The first handler that yields a match is executed. When that handler finishes executing, control resumes with the first statement after the last **catch** block.

- The order of the exception handlers affects how an exception is handled.

- A derived-class object can be caught either by a handler specifying the derived-class type or by handlers specifying the types of any base classes of that derived class.

- Sometimes a program may process many closely related types of exceptions. Instead of providing separate exception classes and **catch** handlers for each, a programmer can provide a single exception class and **catch** handler for a group of exceptions. As each exception occurs, the exception object can be created with different **private** data. The **catch** handler can examine these **private** data to distinguish the type of the exception.

- It is possible that even though a precise match is available, a match requiring standard conversions will be made because that handler appears before the one that would result in a precise match.

- By default, if no handler is found for an exception, the program terminates.

- An exception handler cannot directly access variables in the scope of its **try** block. Information the handler needs is normally passed in the thrown object.

- Exception handlers can take a closer look at an error and decide to call **terminate**. They can rethrow an exception. They can convert one type of exception into another by throwing a different exception. They can perform any necessary recovery and resume execution after the last exception handler. They can look at the situation causing the error, remove the cause of the error and retry by calling the original function that caused an exception. (This would not create infinite recursion.) They can simply return some status value to their environment, etc.

- A handler that catches a derived-class object should be placed before a handler that catches a base-class object. If the base-class handler were first, it would catch both the base-class objects and the object of classes derived from that base class.

- When an exception is caught, it is possible that resources may have been allocated but not yet released in the **try** block. The **catch** handler should release these resources.

- It is possible that a **catch** handler may decide that it cannot process the exception. In this case, the handler can simply rethrow the exception. A **throw** with no arguments rethrows the exception. If no exception was thrown to begin with, then the rethrow causes a call to **terminate**.

- Even if a handler can process an exception, and regardless of whether it does any processing on that exception, the handler can rethrow the exception for further processing outside the handler. A rethrown exception is detected by the next enclosing **try** block and is handled by an exception handler listed after that enclosing **try** block.

- A function with no exception specification can **throw** any exception.

- Function **unexpected** calls a function specified with function **set_unexpected**. If no function has been specified in this manner, **terminate** is called by default.

- Function **terminate** can be called in various ways: explicitly; if a thrown exception cannot be caught; if the stack is corrupted during exception handling; as the default action on a call to **unexpected**; or if, during stack unwinding initiated by an exception, an attempt by a destructor to **throw** an exception causes **terminate** to be called.

- Prototypes for functions **set_terminate** and **set_unexpected** are found in header file **<exception>**.

- Functions **set_terminate** and **set_unexpected** return pointers to the last function called by **terminate** and **unexpected**. This enables the programmer to save the function pointer so it can be restored later.

- Functions **set_terminate** and **set_unexpected** take pointers to functions as arguments. Each argument must point to a function with **void** return type and no arguments.

- If the last action of a user-defined termination function is not to exit a program, function **abort** will automatically be called to end program execution after the other statements of the user-defined termination function are executed.

- An exception thrown outside a **try** block will cause the program to terminate.

- If a handler cannot be found after a **try** block, stack unwinding continues until an appropriate handler is found. If a handler is ultimately not found, then **terminate** is called, which by default aborts the program with **abort**.

- Exception specifications list the exceptions that may be thrown from a function. A function may **throw** the indicated exceptions, or it may **throw** derived types. If an exception not listed in the exception specification is thrown, **unexpected** is called.

- If a function **throws** an exception of a particular class type, that function can also **throw** exceptions of all classes derived from that class with **public** inheritance.

- To **catch** an exception, the handler must have access to a copy constructor for the thrown object.

- Exceptions thrown from constructors cause destructors to be called for all completed base-class objects and member objects of the object being constructed before the exception is thrown.

- If an array of objects has been partially constructed when an exception occurs, only the destructors for the fully constructed array elements will be called.

- Exceptions thrown from destructors can be caught by enclosing the function that calls the destructor in a **try** block and provide a **catch** handler with the proper type.

- A powerful reason for using inheritance with exceptions is to create the ability to **catch** a variety of related errors easily with concise notation. One could certainly **catch** each type of derived-class exception object individually, but if all derived exceptions are handled the same, it is much more concise to simply catch the base-class exception object.

- The C++ standard specifies that when **new** fails, it **throws** a **bad_alloc** exception (**bad_alloc** is defined in header file **<new>**).
- Some compilers are not compliant with the C++ standard and still use the version of **new** that returns **0** on failure.
- Function **set_new_handler** (prototyped in header file **<new>**) takes as its argument a function pointer to a function that takes no arguments and returns **void**. The function pointer is registered as the function to call when **new** fails. Once a **new** handler is registered with **set_new_handler**, **new** will not throw **bad_alloc** on failure.
- An object of class **auto_ptr** maintains a pointer to dynamically allocated memory. When an **auto_ptr** object goes out of scope, it automatically performs a **delete** operation on its pointer data member. Class template **auto_ptr** provides operators ***** and **->** so an **auto_ptr** object can be used like a regular pointer variable.
- The C++ standard includes a hierarchy of exception classes headed by base class **exception** (defined in header file **<exception>**), which offers the service **what()** that is overridden in each derived class to issue an appropriate error message.
- By including **std::bad_exception** in the **throw** list of a function definition, if an unexpected exception occurs, **unexpected()** will throw **bad_exception** instead of terminating (by default) or instead of calling another function specified with **set_unexpected**.

TERMINOLOGY

abort()
assert macro
auto_ptr
bad_alloc
bad_cast
bad_typeid
catch(...)
catch a group of exceptions
catch an exception
catch argument
catch block
catch(void *)
dynamic_cast
empty exception specification
empty **throw** specification
enclosing **try** block
exception
exception declaration
exception handler
<exception> header file
exception list
exception object
exception specification
exceptional condition
exit()
fault tolerance
function with no exception specification
handle an exception

handler for a base class
handler for a derived class
invalid_argument
length_error
logic_error
<memory> header file
mission-critical application
nested exception handlers
new_handler
<new> header file
nothrow
out_of_range
overflow_error
rethrow an exception
robustness
runtime_error
set_new_handler()
set_terminate()
set_unexpected()
stack unwinding
std::bad_exception
<stdexcept> header file
terminate()
throw an exception
throw an unexpected exception
throw expression
throw list
throw point

throw without arguments
throw()
try block

uncaught exception
underflow_error
unexpected()

COMMON PROGRAMMING ERRORS

13.1   Another reason exceptions can be dangerous as an alternative to normal flow of control is that the stack is unwound and resources allocated prior to the occurrence of the exception may not be freed. This problem can be avoided by careful programming.

13.2   Aborting a program could leave a resource in a state in which other programs would not be able to acquire the resource; hence the program would have a so-called "resource leak."

13.3   Exceptions should be thrown only within a **try** block. An exception thrown outside a **try** block causes a call to **terminate**.

13.4   It is possible to **throw** a conditional expression. But be careful because promotion rules may cause the value returned by the conditional expression to be of a different type than you may expect. For example, when throwing an **int** or a **double** from the same conditional expression, the conditional expression will convert the **int** to a **double**. Therefore the result will always be caught by a **catch** with a **double** argument rather than sometimes catching **double** (for the actual **double**) and sometimes catching **int**.

13.5   Specifying a comma-separated list of **catch** arguments is a syntax error.

13.6   Placing **catch(...)** before other **catch** blocks would prevent those blocks from ever being executed; **catch(...)** must be placed last in the list of handlers following a **try** block.

13.7   Placing a **catch** that catches a base-class object before a **catch** that catches an object of a class derived from that base class is a logic error. The base-class **catch** will catch all objects of classes derived from that base class, so the derived-class **catch** will never be executed.

13.8   Placing an exception handler with a **void *** argument type before exception handlers with other pointer types causes a logic error. The **void *** handler would catch all exceptions of pointer types, so the other handlers would never execute. Only **catch (...)** should follow **catch (void *)**.

13.9   Placing a semicolon after a **try** block or after any **catch** handler (other than the last **catch**) following a **try** block is a syntax error.

13.10 Assuming that after an exception is processed, control will return to the first statement after the **throw** is a logic error.

13.11 Assuming that an exception thrown from a **catch** handler will be processed by that handler or any other handler associated with the **try** block that threw the exception which caused the original **catch** handler to execute is a logic error.

13.12 Placing an empty **throw** statement outside a **catch** handler; executing such a **throw** causes a call to **terminate**.

13.13 Throwing an exception not in a function's exception specification causes a call to **unexpected**.

13.14 User-defined exception classes need not be derived from class **exception**. Thus, writing **catch(exception e)** is not guaranteed to **catch** all exceptions a program may encounter.

GOOD PROGRAMMING PRACTICES

13.1   Use exceptions for errors that must be processed in a different scope from where they occur. Use other means of error handling for errors that will be processed in the scope in which they occur.

13.2   Avoid using exception handling for purposes other than error handling, because this can reduce program clarity.

13.3   Use conventional error-handling techniques rather than exception handling for straightforward, local error processing in which a program is easily able to deal with its own errors.

13.4   Associating each type of execution-time error with an appropriately named exception object improves program clarity.

PERFORMANCE TIPS

13.1   Although it is possible to use exception handling for purposes other than error handling, this can reduce program performance.

13.2   Exception handling is generally implemented in compilers in such a manner that when an exception does not occur, little or no overhead is imposed by the presence of exception-handling code. When exceptions happen, they do incur execution-time overhead. Certainly the presence of exception-handling code makes the program consume more memory.

SOFTWARE ENGINEERING OBSERVATIONS

13.1   Flow of control with conventional control structures is generally clearer and more efficient than with exceptions.

13.2   Exception handling is well suited to systems of separately developed components. Exception handling makes it easier to combine the components. Each component can perform its own exception detection separate from the handling of the exceptions in another scope.

13.3   When dealing with libraries, the caller of the library function will likely have unique error processing in mind for an exception generated in the library function. It is unlikely that a library function will perform error processing that would meet the unique needs of all users. Therefore, exceptions are an appropriate means for dealing with errors produced by library functions.

13.4   A key to exception handling is that the portion of a program or system that will handle the exception can be quite different or distant from the portion of the program that detected and generated the exceptional situation.

13.5   If it is necessary to pass information about the error that caused an exception, such information can be placed in the thrown object. The **catch** handler will then contain a parameter name through which that information could be referenced.

13.6   An object can be thrown without containing information to be passed; in this case, mere knowledge that an exception of this type has been thrown may provide sufficient information for the handler to do its job correctly.

13.7   A weakness with catching exceptions with **catch(...)** is that you normally cannot be sure what the exception type is. Another weakness is that without a named parameter, there is no way to refer to the exception object inside the exception handler.

13.8   It is best to incorporate your exception-handling strategy into a system from the inception of the design process. It is difficult to add effective exception handling after a system has been implemented.

13.9   Another reason not to use exceptions for conventional flow of control is that these "additional" exceptions can get in the way of genuine error-type exceptions. It becomes more difficult for the programmer to keep track of the number of exception cases. For example, when a program processes an excessive variety of exceptions, can we really be sure of just what is being caught by a **catch(...)**? Exceptional situations should be rare, not commonplace.

13.10 Use **catch(...)** to perform recovery that does not depend on the type of the exception, such as releasing common resources. The exception can be rethrown to alert more specific enclosing **catch** blocks.

13.11 The C++ standard recommends that to make programs more robust, programmers should use the version of **new** that **throws** **bad_alloc** exceptions on failure.

13.12 The standard **exception** hierarchy is meant to serve as a starting point. Users can **throw** standard exceptions, **throw** exceptions derived from the standard exceptions or **throw** their own exceptions not derived from the standard exceptions.

TESTING AND DEBUGGING TIPS

13.1 The programmer determines the order in which the exception handlers are listed. This order can affect how exceptions originating in that **try** block are handled. If you are getting unexpected behavior in your program's handling of exceptions, it may be because an early **catch** block is intercepting and handling the exceptions before they reach your intended **catch** handler.

13.2 Using inheritance with exceptions enables an exception handler to **catch** related errors with a rather concise notation. One could certainly **catch** each type of pointer or reference to a derived-class exception object individually, but it is more concise to **catch** pointers or references to base-class exception objects instead. Also, catching pointers or references to derived-class exception objects individually is subject to error if the programmer forgets to explicitly test for one or more of the derived-class pointer or reference types.

13.3 To **catch** all exceptions that might be thrown in a **try** block, use **catch(...)**.

SELF-REVIEW EXERCISES

13.1 List five common examples of exceptions.

13.2 Give several reasons why exception-handling techniques should not be used for conventional program control.

13.3 Why are exceptions appropriate for dealing with errors produced by library functions?

13.4 What is a "resource leak?"

13.5 If no exceptions are thrown in a **try** block, where does control proceed to after the **try** block completes execution?

13.6 What happens if an exception is thrown outside a **try** block?

13.7 Give a key advantage and a key disadvantage of using **catch(...)**.

13.8 What happens if no **catch** handler matches the type of a thrown object?

13.9 What happens if several handlers match the type of the thrown object?

13.10 Why would a programmer specify a base-class type as the type of a **catch** handler and then **throw** objects of derived-class types?

13.11 How might a **catch** handler be written to process related types of errors without using inheritance among exception classes?

13.12 What pointer type is used in a **catch** handler to catch any exception of any pointer type?

13.13 Suppose a **catch** handler with a precise match to an exception object type is available. Under what circumstances might a different handler be executed for exception objects of that type?

13.14 Must throwing an exception cause program termination?

13.15 What happens when a **catch** handler **throws** an exception?

13.16 What does the statement **throw;** do?

13.17 How does the programmer restrict the exception types that can be thrown from a function?

13.18   What happens if a function does **throw** an exception of a type not allowed by the exception specification for the function?

13.19   What happens to the automatic objects that have been constructed in a **try** block when that block **throw**s an exception?

ANSWERS TO SELF-REVIEW EXERCISES

13.1   Insufficient memory to satisfy a **new** request, array subscript out of bounds, arithmetic overflow, division by zero, invalid function parameters.

13.2   (a) Exception handling is designed to handle infrequently occurring situations that often result in program termination, so compiler writers are not required to implement exception handling to perform optimally.   (b) Flow of control with conventional control structures is generally clearer and more efficient than with exceptions.   (c) Problems can occur because the stack is unwound when an exception occurs and resources allocated prior to the exception may not be freed.   (d) The "additional" exceptions can get in the way of genuine error-type exceptions. It becomes more difficult for the programmer to keep track of the larger number of exception cases. What does a **catch(...)** really catch?

13.3   It is unlikely that a library function will perform error processing that will meet the unique needs of all users.

13.4   An aborting program could leave a resource in a state in which other programs would not be able to acquire the resource.

13.5   The exception handlers (in the **catch** blocks) for that **try** block are skipped and the program resumes execution after the last **catch** block.

13.6   An exception thrown outside a **try** block causes a call to **terminate**.

13.7   The form **catch(...)** catches any type of error thrown in a **try** block. An advantage is that no thrown error can slip by. A disadvantage is that the **catch** has no parameter, so it cannot reference information in the thrown object and cannot know the cause of the error.

13.8   This causes the search for a match to continue in the next enclosing **try** block. As this process continues, it may eventually be determined that there is no handler in the program that matches the type of the thrown object; in this case **terminate** is called, which by default calls **abort**. An alternate **terminate** function can be provided as an argument to **set_terminate**.

13.9   The first matching exception handler after the **try** block is executed.

13.10   This is a nice way to **catch** related types of exceptions.

13.11   Provide a single exception class and **catch** handler for a group of exceptions. As each exception occurs, the exception object can be created with different **private** data. The **catch** handler can examine these **private** data to distinguish the type of the exception.

13.12   **void ***.

13.13   A handler requiring standard conversions may appear before one with a precise match.

13.14   No, but it does terminate the block in which the exception is thrown.

13.15   The exception will be processed by a **catch** handler (if one exists) associated with the **try** block (if one exists) enclosing the **catch** handler that caused the exception.

13.16   It rethrows the exception.

13.17   Provide an exception specification listing the exception types that can be thrown from the function.

13.18   Function **unexpected** is called.

13.19   Through the process of stack unwinding, destructors are called for each of these objects.

EXERCISES

13.20   List the various exceptional conditions that have occurred in programs throughout this text. List as many additional exceptional conditions as you can. For each of these, describe briefly how a program would typically handle the exception using the exception-handling techniques discussed in this chapter. Some typical exceptions are division by zero, arithmetic overflow, array subscript out of bounds, exhaustion of the free store, etc.

13.21   Under what circumstances would the programmer not provide a parameter name when defining the type of the object that will be caught by a handler?

13.22   A program contains the statement

```
throw;
```

Where would you normally expect to find such a statement? What if that statement appeared in a different part of the program?

13.23   Under what circumstances would you use the following statement?

```
catch(...) { throw; }
```

13.24   Compare and contrast exception handling with the various other error-processing schemes discussed in the text.

13.25   List the advantages of exception handling over conventional means of error processing.

13.26   Provide reasons why exceptions should not be used as an alternate form of program control.

13.27   Describe a technique for handling related exceptions.

13.28   Until this chapter, we have found that dealing with errors detected by constructors is a bit awkward. Exception handling gives us a much better means of dealing with such errors. Consider a constructor for a **String** class. The constructor uses **new** to obtain space from the free store. Suppose **new** fails. Show how you would deal with this without exception handling. Discuss the key issues. Show how you would deal with such memory exhaustion with exception handling. Explain why the exception handling method is superior.

13.29   Suppose a program **throw**s an exception and the appropriate exception handler begins executing. Now suppose that the exception handler itself **throw**s the same exception. Does this create an infinite recursion? Write a program to check your observation.

13.30   Use inheritance to create a base exception class and various derived exception classes. Then show that a **catch** handler specifying the base class can **catch** derived-class exceptions.

13.31   Show a conditional expression that returns either a **double** or an **int**. Provide an **int** **catch** handler and a **double catch** handler. Show that only the **double catch** handler executes regardless of whether the **int** or the **double** is returned.

13.32   Write a program designed to generate and handle a memory exhaustion error. Your program should loop on a request to create dynamic storage through operator **new**.

13.33   Write a program which shows that all destructors for objects constructed in a block are called before an exception is thrown from that block.

13.34   Write a program which shows that member object destructors are called for only those member objects that were constructed before an exception occurred.

13.35 Write a program that demonstrates how any exception is caught with **catch(...)**.

13.36 Write a program which shows that the order of exception handlers is important. The first matching handler is the one that executes. Compile and run your program two different ways to show that two different handlers execute with two different effects.

13.37 Write a program that shows a constructor passing information about constructor failure to an exception handler after a **try** block.

13.38 Write a program that uses a multiple inheritance hierarchy of exception classes to create a situation in which the order of exception handlers matters.

13.39 Using **setjmp/longjmp**, a program can transfer control immediately to an error routine from a deeply nested function invocation. Unfortunately, as the stack is unwound, destructors are not called for the automatic objects that were created during the sequence of nested function calls. Write a program which demonstrates that these destructors are, in fact, not called.

13.40 Write a program that illustrates rethrowing an exception.

13.41 Write a program that uses **set_unexpected** to set a user-defined function for **unexpected**, uses **set_unexpected** again, and then resets **unexpected** back to its previous function. Write a similar program to test **set_terminate** and **terminate**.

13.42 Write a program which shows that a function with its own **try** block does not have to catch every possible error generated within the **try**. Some exceptions can slip through to, and be handled in, outer scopes.

13.43 Write a program that **throws** an error from a deeply nested function call and still has the **catch** handler following the **try** block enclosing the call chain catch the exception.

14

File Processing

Objectives

- To be able to create, read, write and update files.
- To become familiar with sequential access file processing.
- To become familiar with random-access file processing.
- To be able to specify high-performance unformatted I/O operations.
- To understand the differences between formatted and raw data file processing.
- To build a transaction processing program with random-access file processing.

I read part of it all the way through.
Samuel Goldwyn

I can only assume that a "Do Not File" document is filed in a "Do Not File" file.
Senator Frank Church
Senate Intelligence Subcommittee Hearing, 1975

14.1 Introduction

Storage of data in variables and arrays is temporary. *Files* are used for permanent retention of large amounts of data. Computers store files on *secondary storage devices* such as magnetic disks, optical disks and tapes. In this chapter, we explain how data files are created, updated, and processed by C++ programs. We consider both sequential access files and random-access files. We compare formatted data file processing and raw data file processing. We examine techniques for input of data from, and output of data to, **string**s rather than files in Chapter 19.

14.2 The Data Hierarchy

Ultimately, all data items processed by digital computers are reduced to combinations of zeros and ones. This occurs because it is simple and economical to build electronic devices that can assume two stable states—one state represents **0** and the other state represents **1**. It is remarkable that the impressive functions performed by computers involve only the most fundamental manipulations of **0**s and **1**s.

The smallest data item in a computer can assume the value **0** or the value **1**. Such a data item is called a *bit* (short for "*b*inary dig*it*"—a digit that can assume one of two values). Computer circuitry performs various simple bit manipulations such as examining the value of a bit, setting the value of a bit, and reversing a bit (from **1** to **0** or from **0** to **1**).

It is cumbersome for programmers to work with data in the low-level form of bits. Instead, programmers prefer to work with data in forms such as *decimal digits* (i.e., 0, 1, 2, 3, 4, 5, 6, 7, 8, and 9), *letters* (i.e., A through Z, and a through z), and *special symbols* (i.e., $, @, %, &, *, (,), -, +, ", :, ?, /, and many others). Digits, letters, and special symbols are referred to as *characters*. The set of all characters used to write programs and represent data items on a particular computer is called that computer's *character set*. Since computers can process only **1**s and **0**s, every character in a computer's character set is represented as a sequence of **1**s and **0**s (called a *byte*). Bytes are most commonly composed of eight bits. Programmers create programs and data items with characters; computers manipulate and process these characters as patterns of bits.

Just as characters are composed of bits, *fields* are composed of characters (or bytes). A field is a group of characters that conveys meaning. For example, a field consisting solely of uppercase and lowercase letters can be used to represent a person's name.

Data items processed by computers form a *data hierarchy* in which data items become larger and more complex in structure as we progress from bits, to characters (bytes), to fields, and so on.

A *record* (i.e., a **struct** or a **class** in C++) is composed of several fields (called members in C++). In a payroll system, for example, a record for a particular employee might consist of the following fields:

1. Employee identification number

2. Name

3. Address

4. Hourly salary rate

5. Number of exemptions claimed

6. Year-to-date earnings

7. Amount of federal taxes withheld, etc.

Thus, a record is a group of related fields. In the preceding example, each of the fields belongs to the same employee. Of course, a particular company may have many employees, and will have a payroll record for each one. A *file* is a group of related records. A company's payroll file normally contains one record for each employee. Thus, a payroll file for a small company might contain only 22 records, whereas a payroll file for a large company might contain 100,000 records. It is not unusual for a company to have many files, each containing millions of characters of information. Figure 14.1 illustrates the *data hierarchy*.

To facilitate the retrieval of specific records from a file, at least one field in each record is chosen as a *record key*. A record key identifies a record as belonging to a particular person or entity that is distinct from all other records in the file. In the payroll record described previously, the employee identification number would normally be chosen as the record key.

There are many ways to organize records in a file. In the most common type of organization, called a *sequential file,* records are typically stored in order by the record key field. In a payroll file, records are usually placed in order by employee identification number. The first employee record in the file contains the lowest employee identification number and subsequent records contain increasingly higher employee identification numbers.

Most businesses utilize many different files to store data. For example, companies may have payroll files, accounts receivable files (listing money due from clients), accounts payable files (listing money due to suppliers), inventory files (listing facts about all the items handled by the business) and many other types of files. A group of related files is sometimes called a *database*. A collection of programs designed to create and manage databases is called a *database management system* (DBMS).

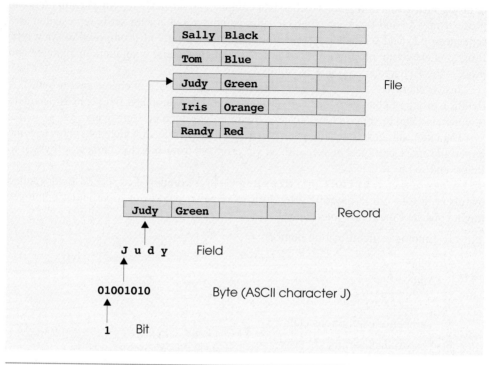

Fig. 14.1   The data hierarchy.

14.3 Files and Streams

C++ views each file simply as a sequence of bytes (Fig. 14.2). Each file ends either with an *end-of-file marker* or at a specific byte number recorded in a system-maintained, administrative data structure. When a file is *opened*, an object is created and a stream is associated with the object. In Chapter 11, we saw that four objects are created for us—**cin**, **cout**, **cerr** and **clog** when **<iostream>** is included. The streams associated with these objects provide communication channels between a program and a particular file or device. For example, the **cin** object (standard input stream object) enables a program to input data from the keyboard or other devices, the **cout** object (standard output stream object) enables a program to output data to the screen or other devices, and the **cerr** and **clog** objects (standard error stream objects) enable a program to output error messages to the screen or other devices.

To perform file processing in C++, the header files **<iostream>** and **<fstream>** must be included. The header **<fstream>** includes the definitions for the stream classes **ifstream** (for input from a file), **ofstream** (for output to a file), and **fstream** (for input to and output from a file). Files are opened by creating objects of these stream classes. These stream classes are derived from (i.e., inherit the functionality of) classes **istream**, **ostream** and **iostream**, respectively. Thus, the member functions, operators and manipulators described in Chapter 11, "C++ Stream Input/Output," can all be applied to file streams as well. The inheritance relationships of the I/O classes discussed to this point are summarized in Fig. 14.3.

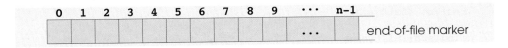

Fig. 14.2   C++'s view of a file of **n** bytes.

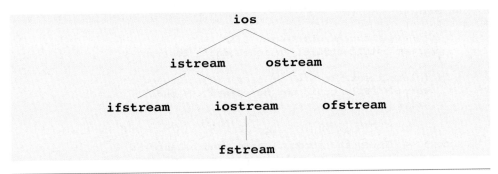

Fig. 14.3   Portion of stream I/O class hierarchy.

14.4 Creating a Sequential Access File

C++ imposes no structure on a file. Thus, notions like "record" do not exist in C++ files. Therefore, the programmer must structure files to meet the requirements of applications. In the following example, we see how the programmer can impose a simple record structure on a file. First we present the program, then we analyze it in detail.

Figure 14.4 creates a simple sequential access file that might be used in an accounts receivable system to help manage the money owed by a company's credit clients. For each client, the program obtains an account number, the client's name and the client's balance (i.e., the amount the client still owes the company for goods and services received in the past). The data obtained for each client constitutes a record for that client. The account number is used as the record key in this application; that is, the file will be created and maintained in account number order. This program assumes the user enters the records in account number order. In a comprehensive accounts receivable system, a sorting capability would be provided so the user could enter the records in any order—the records would then be sorted and written to the file.

```
1   // Fig. 14.4: fig14_04.cpp
2   // Create a sequential file
3   #include <iostream>
4
5   using std::cout;
6   using std::cin;
7   using std::ios;
8   using std::cerr;
9   using std::endl;
10
```

Fig. 14.4   Creating a sequential file (part 1 of 2).

```
11   #include <fstream>
12
13   using std::ofstream;
14
15   #include <cstdlib>
16
17   int main()
18   {
19      // ofstream constructor opens file
20      ofstream outClientFile( "clients.dat", ios::out );
21
22      if ( !outClientFile ) {   // overloaded ! operator
23         cerr << "File could not be opened" << endl;
24         exit( 1 );       // prototype in cstdlib
25      }
26
27      cout << "Enter the account, name, and balance.\n"
28           << "Enter end-of-file to end input.\n? ";
29
30      int account;
31      char name[ 30 ];
32      double balance;
33
34      while ( cin >> account >> name >> balance ) {
35         outClientFile << account << ' ' << name
36                            << ' ' << balance << '\n';
37         cout << "? ";
38      }
39
40      return 0;   // ofstream destructor closes file
41   }
```

```
Enter the account, name, and balance.
Enter EOF to end input.
? 100 Jones 24.98
? 200 Doe 345.67
? 300 White 0.00
? 400 Stone -42.16
? 500 Rich 224.62
? ^z
```

Fig. 14.4   Creating a sequential file (part 2 of 2).

Now let us examine this program. As stated previously, files are opened by creating objects of stream classes **ifstream**, **ofstream** or **fstream**. In Fig. 14.4, the file is to be opened for output, so an **ofstream** object is created. Two arguments are passed to the object's constructor—the *filename* and the *file open mode*. For an **ofstream** object, the file open mode can be either **ios::out** to output data to a file or **ios::app** to append data to the end of a file (without modifying any data already in the file). Existing files opened with mode **ios::out** are *truncated*—all data in the file is discarded. If the specified file does not yet exist, then a file is created with that filename.

The declaration

```
ofstream outClientFile( "clients.dat", ios::out );
```

on line 20 creates an **ofstream** object named **outClientFile** associated with the file **clients.dat** that is opened for output. The arguments **"clients.dat"** and **ios::out** are passed to the **ofstream** constructor, which opens the file. This establishes a "line of communication" with the file. By default, **ofstream** objects are opened for output, so the statement

```
ofstream outClientFile( "clients.dat" );
```

could have been used to open **clients.dat** for output. Figure 14.5 lists the file open modes.

Common Programming Error 14.1

*Opening an existing file for output (**ios::out**) when, in fact, the user wants to preserve the file; the contents of the file are discarded without warning.*

Common Programming Error 14.2

*Using an incorrect **ofstream** object to refer to a file.*

An **ofstream** object can be created without opening a specific file—a file can be attached to the object later. For example, the declaration

```
ofstream outClientFile;
```

creates an **ofstream** object named **outClientFile**. The **ofstream** member function **open** opens a file and attaches it to an existing **ofstream** object as follows:

```
outClientFile.open( "clients.dat", ios::out );
```

Common Programming Error 14.3

Not opening a file before attempting to reference it in a program.

Mode	Description
ios::app	Write all output to the end of the file.
ios::ate	Open a file for output and move to the end of the file (normally used to append data to a file). Data can be written anywhere in the file.
ios::in	Open a file for input.
ios::out	Open a file for output.
ios::trunc	Discard the file's contents if it exists (this is also the default action for **ios::out**)
ios::binary	Open a file for binary (i.e., non-text) input or output.

Fig. 14.5   File open modes.

After creating an **ofstream** object and attempting to open it, the program tests whether the open operation was successful. The **if** structure at lines 22 through 25

```
if ( !outClientFile ) {
   cerr << "File could not be opened" << endl;
   exit( 1 );
}
```

uses the overloaded **ios** operator member function **operator!** to determine if the open operation succeeded. The condition returns a nonzero (true) value if either the **failbit** or the **badbit** is set for the stream on the **open** operation. Some possible errors are attempting to open a nonexistent file for reading, attempting to open a file for reading without permission and opening a file for writing when no disk space is available.

When the condition indicates that the open attempt was unsuccessful, the error message "**File could not be opened**" is output and function **exit** terminates the program. The argument to **exit** is returned to the environment from which the program was invoked. Argument **0** indicates that the program terminated normally; any other value indicates that the program terminated due to an error. The calling environment (most likely the operating system) uses the value returned by **exit** to respond appropriately to the error.

Another overloaded **ios** operator member function—**operator void***—converts the stream to a pointer so it can be tested as **0** (the null pointer) or nonzero (any other pointer value). If the **failbit** or **badbit** (see Chapter 11) has been set for the stream, **0** (false) is returned. The condition in the following **while** header (line 34) implicitly invokes the **operator void*** member function:

```
while ( cin >> account >> name >> balance )
```

The condition remains **true** as long as neither the **failbit** nor the **badbit** has been set for **cin**. Entering the end-of-file indicator sets the **failbit** for **cin**. The **operator void *** function can be used to test an input object for end-of-file instead of explicitly calling the **eof** member function on the input object.

If the file is opened successfully, the program begins processing data. The following statement (lines 27 and 28) prompts the user to enter the various fields for each record, or to enter end-of-file when data entry is complete:

```
cout << "Enter the account, name, and balance.\n"
     << "Enter EOF to end input.\n? ";
```

Figure 14.6 lists the keyboard combinations for entering end-of-file for various computer systems.

Computer system	Keyboard combination
UNIX systems	*<ctrl> d* (on a line by itself)
IBM PC and compatibles	*<ctrl> z* (sometimes followed by pressing *Enter*)
Macintosh	*<ctrl> d*
VAX (VMS)	*<ctrl> z*

Fig. 14.6   End-of-file key combinations for various popular computer systems.

Line 34

```
while ( cin >> account >> name >> balance )
```

extracts each set of data and determines if end-of-file has been entered. When end-of-file or bad data is entered, the stream-extraction operation **>>** on **cin** returns **0** (normally **operator void*** returns true) and the **while** structure terminates. The user enters end-of-file to inform the program that there is no more data to be processed. The end-of-file indicator is set when the end-of-file key combination is entered by the user. The **while** structure continues looping as long as the end-of-file indicator has not been entered.

Lines 35 and 36

```
outClientFile << account << ' ' << name
              << ' ' << balance << '\n';
```

write a set of data to the file **"clients.dat"** using the stream-insertion operator **<<** and the **outClientFile** object associated with the file at the beginning of the program. The data may be retrieved by a program designed to read the file (see Section 14.5). Note that the file created in Fig. 14.4 is a text file. It can be read by any text editor.

Once the end-of-file indicator is entered, **main** terminates. This causes the **outClientFile** object to be destroyed thus invoking its destructor function which closes the file **clients.dat**. An **ofstream** object can explicitly be closed by the programmer using member function **close** as follows:

```
outClientFile.close();
```

Performance Tip 14.1

Explicitly close each file as soon as it is known that the program will not reference the file again. This can reduce resource usage in a program that will continue executing after it no longer needs a particular file. This practice also improves program clarity.

In the sample execution for the program of Fig. 14.4, the user enters information for five accounts, and then signals that data entry is complete by entering end-of-file (**^z** appears on screens of IBM PC compatibles). This dialog window does not show how the data records actually appear in the file. To verify that the file has been created successfully, in the next section we create a program to read the file and print its contents.

14.5 Reading Data from a Sequential Access File

Data is stored in files so that it may be retrieved for processing when needed. The previous section demonstrated how to create a file for sequential access. In this section, we discuss how to read data sequentially from a file.

Figure 14.7 reads records from the file **"clients.dat"** created by the program of Fig. 14.4 and prints the contents of the records. Files are opened for input by creating an **ifstream** class object. Two arguments are passed to the object—the filename and the file open mode. The declaration

```
ifstream inClientFile( "clients.dat", ios::in );
```

in line 29 creates an **ifstream** object called **inClientFile** and associates with it the file **clients.dat** that is to be opened for input. The arguments in parentheses are passed to the **ifstream** constructor function which opens the file and establishes a "line of communication" with the file.

```cpp
1    // Fig. 14.7: fig14_07.cpp
2    // Reading and printing a sequential file
3    #include <iostream>
4
5    using std::cout;
6    using std::cin;
7    using std::ios;
8    using std::cerr;
9    using std::endl;
10
11   #include <fstream>
12
13   using std::ifstream;
14
15   #include <iomanip>
16
17   using std::setiosflags;
18   using std::resetiosflags;
19   using std::setw;
20   using std::setprecision;
21
22   #include <cstdlib>
23
24   void outputLine( int, const char * const, double );
25
26   int main()
27   {
28      // ifstream constructor opens the file
29      ifstream inClientFile( "clients.dat", ios::in );
30
31      if ( !inClientFile ) {
32         cerr << "File could not be opened\n";
33         exit( 1 );
34      }
35
36      int account;
37      char name[ 30 ];
38      double balance;
39
40      cout << setiosflags( ios::left ) << setw( 10 ) << "Account"
41         << setw( 13 ) << "Name" << "Balance\n"
42         << setiosflags( ios::fixed | ios::showpoint );
43
44      while ( inClientFile >> account >> name >> balance )
45         outputLine( account, name, balance );
46
47      return 0;   // ifstream destructor closes the file
48   }
49
```

Fig. 14.7   Reading and printing a sequential file (part 1 of 2).

```
50   void outputLine( int acct, const char * const name, double bal )
51   {
52      cout << setiosflags( ios::left ) << setw( 10 ) << acct
53          << setw( 13 ) << name << setw( 7 ) << setprecision( 2 )
54          << resetiosflags( ios::left )
55          << bal << '\n';
56   }
```

```
Account   Name          Balance
100       Jones           24.98
200       Doe            345.67
300       White            0.00
400       Stone          -42.16
500       Rich           224.62
```

Fig. 14.7   Reading and printing a sequential file (part 2 of 2).

Objects of class **ifstream** are opened for input by default, so the statement

    ifstream inClientFile("clients.dat");

could have been used to open **clients.dat** for input. Just as with an **ofstream** object, an **ifstream** object can be created without opening a specific file and a file can be attached to it later.

Good Programming Practice 14.1

*Open a file for input only (using **ios::in**) if the contents of the file should not be modified. This prevents unintentional modification of the file's contents. This is an example of the principle of least privilege.*

The program uses the condition **!inClientFile** to determine whether the file was opened successfully before attempting to retrieve data from the file. Line 44

    while (inClientFile >> account >> name >> balance)

reads a set of data (i.e., a record) from the file. After the preceding line is executed the first time, **account** has the value **100**, **name** has the value **"Jones"**, and **balance** has the value **24.98**. Each time the line is executed, another record is read from the file into the variables **account**, **name** and **balance**. The records are displayed using function **outputLine** which uses parameterized stream manipulators to format the data for display. When the end of the file has been reached, the implicit call to **operator void*** in the **while** structure returns **0** (normally **operator void*** returns true), the file is closed by the **ifstream** destructor function, and the program terminates.

To retrieve data sequentially from a file, programs normally start reading from the beginning of the file, and read all the data consecutively until the desired data is found. It may be necessary to process the file sequentially several times (from the beginning of the file) during the execution of a program. Both the **istream** class and the **ostream** class provide member functions for repositioning the *file position pointer* (the byte number of the next byte in the file to be read or written). These member functions are **seekg** ("seek get") for the **istream** class and **seekp** ("seek put") for the **ostream** class. Each **istream** object has a "get pointer" that indicates the byte number in the file from which the next input is to occur, and each **ostream** object has a "put pointer" that indicates the byte number in the file at which the next output is to be placed. The statement

```
inClientFile.seekg( 0 );
```

repositions the file position pointer to the beginning of the file (location **0**) attached to **in-ClientFile**. The argument to **seekg** is normally a **long** integer. A second argument can be specified to indicate the *seek direction*. The seek direction can be **ios::beg** (the default) for positioning relative to the beginning of a stream, **ios::cur** for positioning relative to the current position in a stream or **ios::end** for positioning relative to the end of a stream. The file position pointer is an integer value that specifies the location in the file as a number of bytes from the starting location of the file (this is sometimes referred to as the *offset* from the beginning of the file). Some examples of positioning the "get" file position pointer are

```
// position to the nth byte of fileObject
// assumes ios::beg
fileObject.seekg( n );

// position n bytes forward in fileObject
fileObject.seekg( n, ios::cur );

// position y bytes back from end of fileObject
fileObject.seekg( y, ios::end );

// position at end of fileObject
fileObject.seekg( 0, ios::end );
```

The same operations can be performed with **ostream** member function **seekp**. Member functions **tellg** and **tellp** are provided to return the current locations of the "get" and "put" pointers, respectively. The following statement assigns the "get" file position pointer value to variable **location** of type **long**:

```
location = fileObject.tellg();
```

Figure 14.8 enables a credit manager to display the account information for those customers with zero balances (i.e., customers who do not owe the company any money), credit balances (i.e., customers to whom the company owes money), and debit balances (i.e., customers who owe the company money for goods and services received in the past). The program displays a menu and allows the credit manager to enter one of three options to obtain credit information. Option 1 produces a list of accounts with zero balances. Option 2 produces a list of accounts with credit balances. Option 3 produces a list of accounts with debit balances. Option 4 terminates program execution. Entering an invalid option simply displays the prompt to enter another choice. Program output is shown in Fig. 14.9.

```
1   // Fig. 14.8: fig14_08.cpp
2   // Credit inquiry program
3   #include <iostream>
4
```

Fig. 14.8   Credit inquiry program (part 1 of 4).

```
 5    using std::cout;
 6    using std::cin;
 7    using std::ios;
 8    using std::cerr;
 9    using std::endl;
10
11    #include <fstream>
12
13    using std::ifstream;
14
15    #include <iomanip>
16
17    using std::setiosflags;
18    using std::resetiosflags;
19    using std::setw;
20    using std::setprecision;
21
22    #include <cstdlib>
23
24    enum RequestType { ZERO_BALANCE = 1, CREDIT_BALANCE,
25                       DEBIT_BALANCE, END };
26    int getRequest();
27    bool shouldDisplay( int, double );
28    void outputLine( int, const char * const, double );
29
30    int main()
31    {
32       // ifstream constructor opens the file
33       ifstream inClientFile( "clients.dat", ios::in );
34
35       if ( !inClientFile ) {
36          cerr << "File could not be opened" << endl;
37          exit( 1 );
38       }
39
40       int request, account;
41       char name[ 30 ];
42       double balance;
43
44       cout << "Enter request\n"
45            << " 1 - List accounts with zero balances\n"
46            << " 2 - List accounts with credit balances\n"
47            << " 3 - List accounts with debit balances\n"
48            << " 4 - End of run"
49            << setiosflags( ios::fixed | ios::showpoint );
50       request = getRequest();
51
52       while ( request != END ) {
53
54          switch ( request ) {
55             case ZERO_BALANCE:
56                cout << "\nAccounts with zero balances:\n";
57                break;
```

Fig. 14.8   Credit inquiry program (part 2 of 4).

```
58              case CREDIT_BALANCE:
59                 cout << "\nAccounts with credit balances:\n";
60                 break;
61              case DEBIT_BALANCE:
62                 cout << "\nAccounts with debit balances:\n";
63                 break;
64           }
65
66           inClientFile >> account >> name >> balance;
67
68           while ( !inClientFile.eof() ) {
69              if ( shouldDisplay( request, balance ) )
70                 outputLine( account, name, balance );
71
72              inClientFile >> account >> name >> balance;
73           }
74
75           inClientFile.clear();     // reset eof for next input
76           inClientFile.seekg( 0 );  // move to beginning of file
77           request = getRequest();
78        }
79
80        cout << "End of run." << endl;
81
82        return 0;    // ifstream destructor closes the file
83     }
84
85     int getRequest()
86     {
87        int request;
88
89        do {
90           cout << "\n? ";
91           cin >> request;
92        } while( request < ZERO_BALANCE && request > END );
93
94        return request;
95     }
96
97     bool shouldDisplay( int type, double balance )
98     {
99        if ( type == CREDIT_BALANCE && balance < 0 )
100          return true;
101
102       if ( type == DEBIT_BALANCE && balance > 0 )
103          return true;
104
105       if ( type == ZERO_BALANCE && balance == 0 )
106          return true;
107
108       return false;
109    }
110
```

Fig. 14.8   Credit inquiry program (part 3 of 4).

```
111  void outputLine( int acct, const char * const name, double bal )
112  {
113     cout << setiosflags( ios::left ) << setw( 10 ) << acct
114          << setw( 13 ) << name << setw( 7 ) << setprecision( 2 )
115          << resetiosflags( ios::left )
116          << bal << '\n';
117  }
```

Fig. 14.8   Credit inquiry program (part 4 of 4).

```
Enter request
 1 - List accounts with zero balances
 2 - List accounts with credit balances
 3 - List accounts with debit balances
 4 - End of run
? 1

Accounts with zero balances:
300        White             0.00
? 2

Accounts with credit balances:
400        Stone            -42.16
? 3

Accounts with debit balances:
100        Jones             24.98
200        Doe              345.67
500        Rich             224.62

? 4
End of run.
```

Fig. 14.9   Sample program output for Fig. 14.8.

14.6 Updating Sequential Access Files

Data that are formatted and written to a sequential access file as shown in Section 14.4 cannot be modified without the risk of destroying other data in the file. For example, if the name "**White**" needs to be changed to "**Worthington**," the old name cannot simply be overwritten. The record for **White** was written to the file as

> **300 White 0.00**

If this record were rewritten beginning at the same location in the file using the longer name, the record would be

> **300 Worthington 0.00**

The new record contains six more characters than the original record. Therefore, the characters beyond the second "**o**" in "**Worthington**" would overwrite the beginning of the next sequential record in the file. The problem here is that in the formatted input/output model using the insertion operator **<<** and the extraction operator **>>** fields—and hence records—can vary in size. For example, 7, 14, –117, 2074, and 27383 are all **int**s and each is stored in the same number of "raw data" bytes internally, but when these integers are output as formatted text (character sequences) to the screen or to a file on disk, they become different-sized fields. Therefore, the formatted input/output model is not usually used to update records in place.

Such updating can be done, but it is awkward. For example, to make the preceding name change, the records before **300 White 0.00** in a sequential access file could be copied to a new file, the updated record would then be written to the new file, and the records after **300 White 0.00** would be copied to the new file. This requires processing every record in the file to update one record. If many records are being updated in one pass of the file, then this technique can be acceptable.

14.7 Random-Access Files

So far, we have seen how to create sequential access files and to search through them to locate particular information. Sequential access files are inappropriate for so-called *instant-access applications* in which a particular record of information must be located immediately. Common instant-access applications are airline reservation systems, banking systems, point-of-sale systems, automated teller machines and other kinds of *transaction processing systems* that require rapid access to specific data. The bank at which you have your account may have hundreds of thousands or even millions of other customers, yet when you use an automated teller machine, your account is checked for sufficient funds in seconds. This kind of instant access is possible with *random-access files*. Individual records of a random-access file can be accessed directly (and quickly) without searching through other records.

As we have said, C++ does not impose structure on a file. So the application that wants to use random-access files must create them. A variety of techniques can be used to create random-access files. Perhaps the simplest is to require that all records in a file be of the same fixed length. Using fixed-length records makes it easy for a program to calculate (as a function of the record size and the record key) the exact location of any record relative to the beginning of the file. We will soon see how this facilitates immediate access to specific records, even in large files.

Figure 14.10 illustrates C++'s view of a random-access file composed of fixed-length records (each record is 100 bytes long). A random-access file is like a railroad train with many cars—some empty and some with contents.

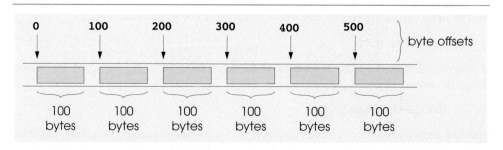

Fig. 14.10   C++'s view of a random-access file.

Data can be inserted in a random-access file without destroying other data in the file. Data stored previously also can be updated or deleted without rewriting the entire file. In the following sections we explain how to create a random-access file, enter data, read the data both sequentially and randomly, update the data, and delete data no longer needed.

14.8 Creating a Random-Access File

The **ostream** member function **write** outputs a fixed number of bytes beginning at a specific location in memory to the specified stream. When the stream is associated with a file, the data is written beginning at the location in the file specified by the "put" file position pointer. The **istream** member function **read** inputs a fixed number of bytes from the specified stream to an area in memory beginning at a specified address. If the stream is associated with a file, the bytes are input beginning at the location in the file specified by the "get" file position pointer.

Now, when writing an integer **number** to a file, instead of using

```
    outFile << number;
```

which could print as few as 1 digit or as many as 11 digits (10 digits plus a sign, each of which requires 1 byte of storage) for a 4-byte integer, we can use

```
    outFile.write( reinterpret_cast<const char *>( &number ),
                   sizeo\f( number ) );
```

which always writes 4 bytes (on a machine with 4-byte integers). Function **write** expects data type **const char *** as its first argument, hence we use operator **reinterpret_cast<const char *>** to convert the address of **number** to a **const char *** pointer. The second argument of **write** is an integer of type **size_t** specifying the number of bytes to be written. As we will see, **istream** function **read** can then be used to read the 4 bytes back into integer variable **number**.

If a program is going to read unformatted data (written by **write**), it must be compiled and executed on a system that is compatible with the program that wrote the data.

Random-access file processing programs rarely write a single field to a file. Normally, they write one **struct** or **class** object at a time, as we show in the following examples.

Consider the following problem statement:

> *Create a credit processing program capable of storing up to 100 fixed-length records for a company that can have up to 100 customers. Each record should consist of an account number that will be used as the record key, a last name, a first name and a balance. The program should be able to update an account, insert a new account, delete an account, and list all the account records in a formatted text file for printing.*

The next several sections introduce the techniques necessary to create this credit processing program. Figure 14.11 illustrates opening a random-access file, defining the record format using a **struct** (defined in header file **clntdata.h**) and writing data to the disk in binary format (binary mode is specified on line 33). This program initializes all 100 records of the file **"credit.dat"** with empty **struct**s using function **write**. Each empty **struct** contains **0** for the account number, the null string (represented by empty quotation marks) for the last name, the null string for the first name and **0.0** for the balance. Each record is initialized with the amount of empty space in which the account data will be stored, and to determine in subsequent programs if a record is empty or contains data.

```
1   // clntdata.h
2   // Definition of struct clientData used in
3   // Figs. 14.11, 14.12, 14.14 and 14.15.
4   #ifndef CLNTDATA_H
5   #define CLNTDATA_H
6
7   struct clientData {
8      int accountNumber;
9      char lastName[ 15 ];
10     char firstName[ 10 ];
11     double balance;
12  };
13
14  #endif
```

Fig. 14.11 Header file `clntdata.h`.

```
15  // Fig. 14.11: fig14_11.cpp
16  // Creating a randomly accessed file sequentially
17  #include <iostream>
18
19  using std::cerr;
20  using std::endl;
21  using std::ios;
22
23  #include <fstream>
24
25  using std::ofstream;
26  .
27  #include <cstdlib>
28
29  #include "clntdata.h"
30
31  int main()
32  {
33     ofstream outCredit( "credit.dat", ios::binary );
34
35     if ( !outCredit ) {
36        cerr << "File could not be opened." << endl;
37        exit( 1 );
38     }
39
40     clientData blankClient = { 0, "", "", 0.0 };
41
42     for ( int i = 0; i < 100; i++ )
43        outCredit.write(
44           reinterpret_cast<const char *>( &blankClient ),
45           sizeof( clientData ) );
46     return 0;
47  }
```

Fig. 14.11 Creating a random-access file sequentially.

In Fig. 14.11, the statement at lines 43 through 45

```
outCredit.write(
    reinterpret_cast<const char *>( &blankClient ),
    sizeof( clientData ) );
```

causes the structure **blankClient** of size **sizeof(clientData)** to be written to the **credit.dat** file associated with **ofstream** object **outCredit**. Remember that operator **sizeof** returns the size in bytes of the object contained in parentheses (see Chapter 5). Note that the first argument to function **write** on line 43 must be of type **const char ***. However, the data type of **&blankClient** is **clientData ***. To convert **&blankClient** to the appropriate pointer type, the expression

```
reinterpret_cast<const char *>( &blankClient )
```

uses the cast operator **reinterpret_cast** to convert the address of **blankClient** to a **const char *** so the call to **write** compiles without issuing a syntax error.

14.9 Writing Data Randomly to a Random-Access File

Figure 14.12 writes data to the file **"credit.dat"**. It uses the combination of **ostream** functions **seekp** and **write** to store data at exact locations in the file. Function **seekp** sets the "put" file position pointer to a specific position in the file, then **write** outputs the data. A sample execution is shown in Fig. 14.13. Note that the program of Fig. 14.12 includes (line 16) the header file **clntdata.h** defined in Fig. 14.11.

```
1   // Fig. 14.12: fig14_12.cpp
2   // Writing to a random access file
3   #include <iostream>
4
5   using std::cerr;
6   using std::endl;
7   using std::cout;
8   using std::cin;
9   using std::ios;
10
11  #include <fstream>
12
13  using std::ofstream;
14
15  #include <cstdlib>
16  #include "clntdata.h"
17
18  int main()
19  {
20     ofstream outCredit( "credit.dat", ios::binary );
21
22     if ( !outCredit ) {
23        cerr << "File could not be opened." << endl;
24        exit( 1 );
25     }
```

Fig. 14.12 Creating a random-access file sequentially (part 1 of 2).

```
26
27        cout << "Enter account number "
28            << "(1 to 100, 0 to end input)\n? ";
29
30        clientData client;
31        cin >> client.accountNumber;
32
33        while ( client.accountNumber > 0 &&
34                client.accountNumber <= 100 ) {
35          cout << "Enter lastname, firstname, balance\n? ";
36          cin >> client.lastName >> client.firstName
37              >> client.balance;
38
39          outCredit.seekp( ( client.accountNumber - 1 ) *
40                            sizeof( clientData ) );
41          outCredit.write(
42            reinterpret_cast<const char *>( &client ),
43            sizeof( clientData ) );
44
45          cout << "Enter account number\n? ";
46          cin >> client.accountNumber;
47        }
48
49        return 0;
50    }
```

Fig. 14.12 Creating a random-access file sequentially (part 2 of 2).

```
Enter account number (1 to 100, 0 to end input)
? 37
Enter lastname, firstname, balance
? Barker Doug 0.00
Enter account number
? 29
Enter lastname, firstname, balance
? Brown Nancy -24.54
Enter account number
? 96
Enter lastname, firstname, balance
? Stone Sam 34.98
Enter account number
? 88
Enter lastname, firstname, balance
? Smith Dave 258.34
Enter account number
? 33
Enter lastname, firstname, balance
? Dunn Stacey 314.33
Enter account number
? 0
```

Fig. 14.13 Sample execution of the program in Fig. 14.12.

Lines 39 and 40

```
outCredit.seekp( ( client.accountNumber - 1 ) *
                 sizeof( clientData ) );
```

position the "put" file position pointer for object **outCredit** to the byte location calculated by **(client.accountNumber - 1) * sizeof(clientData)**. Because the account number is between 1 and 100, 1 is subtracted from the account number when calculating the byte location of the record. Thus, for record 1, the file position pointer is set to byte 0 of the file. Note that the **ofstream** object **outCredit** is opened with file open mode **ios::binary**.

14.10 Reading Data Sequentially from a Random-Access File

In the previous sections, we created a random-access file and wrote data to that file. In this section, we develop a program that reads through the file sequentially and prints only those records containing data. These programs produce an additional benefit. See if you can determine what it is; we will reveal it at the end of this section.

The **istream** function **read** inputs a specified number of bytes from the current position in the specified stream into an object. For example, lines 43 and 44

```
inCredit.read( reinterpret_cast<char *>( &client ),
               sizeof( clientData ) );
```

from Fig. 14.14 read the number of bytes specified by **sizeof(clientData)** from the file associated with **ifstream** object **inCredit** and store the data in the structure **client**. Note that function **read** requires a first argument of type **char ***. Since **&client** is of type **clientData ***, **&client** must be cast to **char *** with the cast operator **reinterpret_cast**. Note that the program of Fig. 14.14 includes the header file **clntdata.h** defined in Fig. 14.11.

Figure 14.14 reads sequentially through every record in the **"credit.dat"** file, checks each record to see if it contains data, and displays formatted outputs for records containing data. The condition in line 46

```
while ( inCredit && !inCredit.eof() ) {
```

uses the **ios** member function **eof** to determine when the end of the file is reached and causes execution of the **while** structure to terminate. Also, if there is an error reading from the file, the loop will terminate because **inCredit** will evaluate to **false**. The data input from the file is output by **outputLine**, which takes two arguments—an **ostream** object and a **clientData** structure to be output. The **ostream** parameter type is interesting because any **ostream** object (such as **cout**) or any object of a derived class of **ostream** (such as an object of type **ofstream**) can be supplied as the argument. This means that the same function can be used, for example, to perform output to the standard output stream and to a file stream without writing separate functions.

What about that additional benefit we promised? If you examine the output window, you will notice that the records are listed in sorted order (by account number). This is a simple consequence of the way we stored these records in the file using direct access techniques. Compared to the bubble sort we have seen (Chapter 4), sorting with direct access techniques is blazingly fast. The speed is achieved by making the file large enough to hold every possible record that might be created. This of course means that the file could be sparsely occupied most of the time, a waste of storage. So here is yet another example of the space-time trade-off: By using large amounts of space, we are able to develop a much faster sorting algorithm.

```cpp
1   // Fig. 14.14: fig14_14.cpp
2   // Reading a random access file sequentially
3   #include <iostream>
4
5   using std::cout;
6   using std::endl;
7   using std::ios;
8   using std::cerr;
9
10  #include <iomanip>
11
12  using std::setprecision;
13  using std::setiosflags;
14  using std::resetiosflags;
15  using std::setw;
16
17  #include <fstream>
18
19  using std::ifstream;
20  using std::ostream;
21
22  #include <cstdlib>
23  #include "clntdata.h"
24
25  void outputLine( ostream&, const clientData & );
26
27  int main()
28  {
29     ifstream inCredit( "credit.dat", ios::in );
30
31     if ( !inCredit ) {
32        cerr << "File could not be opened." << endl;
33        exit( 1 );
34     }
35
36     cout << setiosflags( ios::left ) << setw( 10 ) << "Account"
37          << setw( 16 ) << "Last Name" << setw( 11 )
38          << "First Name" << resetiosflags( ios::left )
39          << setw( 10 ) << "Balance" << endl;
40
41     clientData client;
42
43     inCredit.read( reinterpret_cast<char *>( &client ),
44                 sizeof( clientData ) );
45
```

Fig. 14.14   Reading a random-access file sequentially (part 1 of 2).

```
46          while ( inCredit && !inCredit.eof() ) {
47
48              if ( client.accountNumber != 0 )
49                  outputLine( cout, client );
50
51              inCredit.read( reinterpret_cast<char *>( &client ),
52                             sizeof( clientData ) );
53          }
54
55          return 0;
56      }
57
58      void outputLine( ostream &output, const clientData &c )
59      {
60          output << setiosflags( ios::left ) << setw( 10 )
61                 << c.accountNumber << setw( 16 ) << c.lastName
62                 << setw( 11 ) << c.firstName << setw( 10 )
63                 << setprecision( 2 ) << resetiosflags( ios::left )
64                 << setiosflags( ios::fixed | ios::showpoint )
65                 << c.balance << '\n';
66      }
```

Account	Last Name	First Name	Balance
29	Brown	Nancy	-24.54
33	Dunn	Stacey	314.33
37	Barker	Doug	0.00
88	Smith	Dave	258.34
96	Stone	Sam	34.98

Fig. 14.14   Reading a random-access file sequentially (part 2 of 2).

14.11 Example: A Transaction Processing Program

We now present a substantial transaction processing program (Fig. 14.15) using a random-access file to achieve "instant" access processing. The program maintains a bank's account information. The program updates existing accounts, adds new accounts, deletes accounts and stores a formatted listing of all the current accounts in a text file for printing. We assume that the program of Fig. 14.11 has been executed to create the file **credit.dat** and that the program of Fig. 14.12 has been executed to insert the initial data.

The program has five options (option 5 is to terminate the program). Option 1 calls function **textFile** to store a formatted list of all the account information in a text file called **print.txt** that may be printed later. Function **textFile** takes an **fstream** object as an argument to be used to input data from the **credit.dat** file. Function **textFile** uses **istream** member function **read** and the sequential file access techniques of Fig. 14.14 to input data from **credit.dat**. Function **outputLine**, discussed in Section 14.10 is used to output the data to file **print.txt**. Note that **textFile** uses **istream** member function **seekg** to ensure that the file position pointer is at the beginning of the file. After choosing Option 1 the file **print.txt** contains

```
Account     Last Name       First Name     Balance
29          Brown           Nancy           -24.54
33          Dunn            Stacey          314.33
37          Barker          Doug              0.00
88          Smith           Dave            258.34
96          Stone           Sam              34.98
```

Option 2 calls the function **updateRecord** to update an account. The function will only update an existing record, so the function first determines if the specified record is empty. The record is read into structure **client** with **istream** member function **read**, then **client.accountNumber** is compared to zero to determine if the record contains information. If **client.accountNumber** is zero, a message is printed stating that the record is empty and the menu choices are displayed. If the record contains information, function **updateRecord** displays the record on the screen using function **outputLine**, inputs the transaction amount, calculates the new balance and rewrites the record to the file. A typical output for Option 2 is

```
Enter account to update (1 - 100): 37
37          Barker          Doug              0.00

Enter charge (+) or payment (-): +87.99
37          Barker          Doug             87.99
```

Option 3 calls the function **newRecord** to add a new account to the file. If the user enters an account number for an existing account, **newRecord** displays a message that the account exists, and displays the menu choices. This function adds a new account in the same manner as the program of Fig. 14.12. A typical output for Option 3 is

```
Enter new account number (1 - 100): 22
Enter lastname, firstname, balance
? Johnston Sarah 247.45
```

Option 4 calls function **deleteRecord** to delete a record from the file. The user is prompted to enter the account number. Only an existing record may be deleted, so if the specified account is empty, an error message is issued. If the account exists, it is reinitialized by copying an empty record (**blankClient**) to the file. A message is displayed to inform the user that the record has been deleted. A typical output for Option 4 is

```
Enter account to delete (1 - 100): 29
Account #29 deleted.
```

The file **"credit.dat"** is opened by creating an **fstream** object for reading and writing using modes **ios::in** and **ios::out** "or-ed" together.

```
1    // Fig. 14.15: fig14_15.cpp
2    // This program reads a random access file sequentially,
3    // updates data already written to the file, creates new
4    // data to be placed in the file, and deletes data
5    // already in the file.
6    #include <iostream>
7
8    using std::cout;
9    using std::cerr;
10   using std::cin;
11   using std::endl;
12   using std::ios;
13
14   #include <fstream>
15
16   using std::ofstream;
17   using std::ostream;
18   using std::fstream;
19
20   #include <iomanip>
21
22   using std::setiosflags;
23   using std::resetiosflags;
24   using std::setw;
25   using std::setprecision;
26
27   #include <cstdlib>
28   #include "clntdata.h"
29
30   int enterChoice();
31   void textFile( fstream& );
32   void updateRecord( fstream& );
33   void newRecord( fstream& );
34   void deleteRecord( fstream& );
35   void outputLine( ostream&, const clientData & );
36   int getAccount( const char * const );
37
38   enum Choices { TEXTFILE = 1, UPDATE, NEW, DELETE, END };
39
40   int main()
41   {
42      fstream inOutCredit( "credit.dat", ios::in | ios::out );
43
44      if ( !inOutCredit ) {
45         cerr << "File could not be opened." << endl;
46         exit ( 1 );
47      }
48
49      int choice;
50
```

Fig. 14.15 Bank account program (part 1 of 5).

```
51        while ( ( choice = enterChoice() ) != END ) {
52
53           switch ( choice ) {
54              case TEXTFILE:
55                 textFile( inOutCredit );
56                 break;
57              case UPDATE:
58                 updateRecord( inOutCredit );
59                 break;
60              case NEW:
61                 newRecord( inOutCredit );
62                 break;
63              case DELETE:
64                 deleteRecord( inOutCredit );
65                 break;
66              default:
67                 cerr << "Incorrect choice\n";
68                 break;
69           }
70
71           inOutCredit.clear();  // resets end-of-file indicator
72        }
73
74        return 0;
75     }
76
77     // Prompt for and input menu choice
78     int enterChoice()
79     {
80        cout << "\nEnter your choice" << endl
81             << "1 - store a formatted text file of accounts\n"
82             << "    called \"print.txt\" for printing\n"
83             << "2 - update an account\n"
84             << "3 - add a new account\n"
85             << "4 - delete an account\n"
86             << "5 - end program\n? ";
87
88        int menuChoice;
89        cin >> menuChoice;
90        return menuChoice;
91     }
92
93     // Create formatted text file for printing
94     void textFile( fstream &readFromFile )
95     {
96        ofstream outPrintFile( "print.txt", ios::out );
97
98        if ( !outPrintFile ) {
99           cerr << "File could not be opened." << endl;
100          exit( 1 );
101       }
102
```

Fig. 14.15   Bank account program (part 2 of 5).

```
103     outPrintFile << setiosflags( ios::left ) << setw( 10 )
104        << "Account" << setw( 16 ) << "Last Name" << setw( 11 )
105        << "First Name" << resetiosflags( ios::left )
106        << setw( 10 ) << "Balance" << endl;
107     readFromFile.seekg( 0 );
108
109     clientData client;
110     readFromFile.read( reinterpret_cast<char *>( &client ),
111                        sizeof( clientData ) );
112
113     while ( !readFromFile.eof() ) {
114        if ( client.accountNumber != 0 )
115           outputLine( outPrintFile, client );
116
117        readFromFile.read( reinterpret_cast<char *>( &client ),
118                           sizeof( clientData ) );
119     }
120  }
121
122  // Update an account's balance
123  void updateRecord( fstream &updateFile )
124  {
125     int account = getAccount( "Enter account to update" );
126
127     updateFile.seekg( ( account - 1 ) * sizeof( clientData ) );
128
129     clientData client;
130     updateFile.read( reinterpret_cast<char *>( &client ),
131                      sizeof( clientData ) );
132
133     if ( client.accountNumber != 0 ) {
134        outputLine( cout, client );
135        cout << "\nEnter charge (+) or payment (-): ";
136
137        double transaction;    // charge or payment
138        cin >> transaction;    // should validate
139        client.balance += transaction;
140        outputLine( cout, client );
141        updateFile.seekp( ( account-1 ) * sizeof( clientData ) );
142        updateFile.write(
143           reinterpret_cast<const char *>( &client ),
144           sizeof( clientData ) );
145     }
146     else
147        cerr << "Account #" << account
148           << " has no information." << endl;
149  }
150
151  // Create and insert new record
152  void newRecord( fstream &insertInFile )
153  {
154     int account = getAccount( "Enter new account number" );
```

Fig. 14.15 Bank account program (part 3 of 5).

```
155
156      insertInFile.seekg( ( account-1 ) * sizeof( clientData ) );
157
158      clientData client;
159      insertInFile.read( reinterpret_cast<char *>( &client ),
160                         sizeof( clientData ) );
161
162      if ( client.accountNumber == 0 ) {
163         cout << "Enter lastname, firstname, balance\n? ";
164         cin >> client.lastName >> client.firstName
165            >> client.balance;
166         client.accountNumber = account;
167         insertInFile.seekp( ( account - 1 ) *
168                            sizeof( clientData ) );
169         insertInFile.write(
170            reinterpret_cast<const char *>( &client ),
171            sizeof( clientData ) );
172      }
173      else
174         cerr << "Account #" << account
175              << " already contains information." << endl;
176   }
177
178   // Delete an existing record
179   void deleteRecord( fstream &deleteFromFile )
180   {
181      int account = getAccount( "Enter account to delete" );
182
183      deleteFromFile.seekg( (account-1) * sizeof( clientData ) );
184
185      clientData client;
186      deleteFromFile.read( reinterpret_cast<char *>( &client ),
187                           sizeof( clientData ) );
188
189      if ( client.accountNumber != 0 ) {
190         clientData blankClient = { 0, "", "", 0.0 };
191
192         deleteFromFile.seekp( ( account - 1) *
193                              sizeof( clientData ) );
194         deleteFromFile.write(
195            reinterpret_cast<const char *>( &blankClient ),
196            sizeof( clientData ) );
197         cout << "Account #" << account << " deleted." << endl;
198      }
199      else
200         cerr << "Account #" << account << " is empty." << endl;
201   }
202
203   // Output a line of client information
204   void outputLine( ostream &output, const clientData &c )
205   {
206      output << setiosflags( ios::left ) << setw( 10 )
207             << c.accountNumber << setw( 16 ) << c.lastName
```

Fig. 14.15 Bank account program (part 4 of 5).

```
208              << setw( 11 ) << c.firstName << setw( 10 )
209              << setprecision( 2 ) << resetiosflags( ios::left )
210              << setiosflags( ios::fixed | ios::showpoint )
211              << c.balance << '\n';
212  }
213
214  // Get an account number from the keyboard
215  int getAccount( const char * const prompt )
216  {
217     int account;
218
219     do {
220        cout << prompt << " (1 - 100): ";
221        cin >> account;
222     } while ( account < 1 || account > 100 );
223
224     return account;
225  }
```

Fig. 14.15 Bank account program (part 5 of 5).

14.12 Input/Output of Objects

In this chapter and Chapter 11 we discussed C++'s object-oriented style of input/output. But our examples concentrated on I/O of traditional data types rather than objects of user-defined classes. In Chapter 8, we showed how to input and output class objects using operator overloading. We accomplished object input by overloading the stream-extraction operator **>>** for the appropriate **istream** classes. We accomplished object output by overloading the stream-insertion operator **<<** for the appropriate **ostream** classes. In both cases only an object's data members were input or output, and, in each case, in a form meaningful for objects of that particular abstract data type. An object's member functions are available internally in the computer and are combined with the data values as these data are input via the overloaded stream-insertion operator.

When object data members are output to a disk file, we lose the object's type information. We only have data bytes, not type information, on a disk. If the program that is going to read this data knows what object type it corresponds to, then the data is simply read into objects of that type.

An interesting problem occurs when we store objects of different types in the same file. How can we distinguish them (or their collections of data members) as we read them into a program? The problem, of course, is that objects typically do not have type fields (we studied this issue carefully in Chapter 10, "Virtual Functions and Polymorphism").

One approach would be to have each overloaded output operator output a type code preceding each collection of data members that represents one object. Then object input would always begin by reading the type-code field and using a **switch** statement to invoke the proper overloaded function. Although this solution lacks the elegance of polymorphic programming, it provides a workable mechanism for retaining objects in files and retrieving them as needed.

SUMMARY

- All data items processed by a computer are reduced to combinations of zeros and ones.

- The smallest data item in a computer can assume the value **0** or the value **1**. Such a data item is called a bit.

- Digits, letters and special symbols are referred to as characters. The set of all characters that may be used to write programs and represent data items on a particular computer is called that computer's character set. Every character in the computer's character set is represented as a pattern of eight **1**s and **0**s (called a byte).

- A field is a group of characters (or bytes) that conveys meaning.

- A record is a group of related fields.

- At least one field in a record is chosen as a record key to identify a record as belonging to a particular person or entity that is distinct from all other records in the file.

- Sequential access is the simplest method of accessing data in a file.

- A collection of programs designed to create and manage databases is called a database management system (DBMS).

- C++ views each file as a sequential stream of bytes.

- Each file ends in some machine-dependent form of end-of-file marker.

- Streams provide communication channels between files and programs.

- The header files **<iostream>** and **<fstream>** must be included in a program to perform a C++ file I/O. Header **<fstream>** includes the definitions for the stream classes **ifstream**, **ofstream** and **fstream**.

- Files are opened by instantiating objects of stream classes **ifstream**, **ofstream** and **fstream**.

- C++ imposes no structure on a file. Thus, notions like "record" do not exist in C++. The programmer must structure a file to meet the requirements of a particular application.

- Files are opened for output by creating an **ofstream** class object. Two arguments are passed to the object—the filename and the file open mode. For an **ofstream** object, the file open mode can be either **ios::out** to output data to a file or **ios::app** to append data to the end of a file. Existing files opened with mode **ios::out** are truncated. If the file does not exist, it is created.

- The **ios** operator member function **operator!** returns a true value if either the **failbit** or the **badbit** has been set for a stream on the **open** operation.

- The **ios** operator member function **operator void*** converts the stream to a pointer for comparison with **0** (the null pointer). If either the **failbit** or the **badbit** has been set for the stream, **0** (false) is returned.

- Programs may process no files, one file or several files. Each file has a unique name and is associated with an appropriate file stream object. All file processing functions must refer to a file with the appropriate object.

- A "get pointer" indicates the position in the file from which the next input is to occur, and a "put pointer" indicates the position in the file at which the next output is to be placed. Both the **istream** class and the **ostream** class provide member functions for repositioning the file position pointer. The functions are **seekg** ("seek get") for class **istream** and **seekp** ("seek put") for class **ostream**.

- Member functions **tellp** and **tellg** return the current locations of the "put" and "get" pointers.

- A convenient way to implement random-access files is by using only fixed-length records. Using this technique, a program can quickly calculate the exact location of a record relative to the beginning of the file.

- Data can be inserted in a random-access file without destroying other data in the file. Data can be updated or deleted without rewriting the entire file.

- The **ostream** member function **write** outputs to a specified stream some number of bytes beginning at a designated location in memory. When the stream is associated with a file, the data is written at the location specified by the "put" file position pointer.

- The **istream** member function **read** extracts some number of bytes from the specified stream to an area in memory beginning with a designated address. The bytes are extracted beginning at the location specified by the "get" file position pointer. Function **read** requires a first argument of type **char***.

- Function **write** expects a first argument of type **const char***, so this argument must be cast to **const char*** if it is of some other pointer type. The second argument is an integer that specifies the number of bytes to be written.

- The compile-time, unary operator **sizeof** returns the size in bytes of the object contained in parentheses; **sizeof** returns an unsigned integer.

- The **ios** member function **eof** reports if the end-of-file indicator has been set for the designated stream. End-of-file is set after an attempted read fails.

TERMINOLOGY

alphabetic field
binary digit
bit
byte
cerr (standard error unbuffered)
character field
character set
cin (standard input)
clog (standard error buffered)
close a file
close member function
cout (standard output)
database
data hierarchy
database management system (DBMS)
decimal digit
end-of-file
end-of-file marker
ends stream manipulator
field
file
file name
file position pointer
fstream class
<fstream> header file
ifstream class
in-core I/O
in-memory I/O
input stream

ios::app file open mode
ios::ate file open mode
ios::beg seek starting point
ios::binary file open mode
ios::cur seek starting point
ios::end seek starting point
ios::in file open mode
ios::out file open mode
ios::trunc file open mode
istream class
numeric field
ofstream class
open a file
open member function
operator! member function
operator void* member function
ostream class
output stream
random-access file
record
record key
seekg istream member function
seekp ostream member function
sequential access file
special symbol
stream
tellg istream member function
tellp ostream member function
truncate an existing file

COMMON PROGRAMMING ERRORS

14.1 Opening an existing file for output (**ios::out**) when, in fact, the user wants to preserve the file; the contents of the file are discarded without warning.

14.2 Using an incorrect **ofstream** object to refer to a file.

14.3 Not opening a file before attempting to reference it in a program.

GOOD PROGRAMMING PRACTICE

14.1 Open a file for input only (using **ios::in**) if the contents of the file should not be modified. This prevents unintentional modification of the file's contents. This is an example of the principle of least privilege.

PERFORMANCE TIP

14.1 Explicitly close each file as soon as it is known that the program will not reference the file again. This can reduce resource usage in a program that will continue executing after it no longer needs a particular file. This practice also improves program clarity.

SELF-REVIEW EXERCISES

14.1 Fill in the blanks in each of the following:

a) Ultimately, all data items processed by a computer are reduced to combinations of _____ and _____.

b) The smallest data item a computer can process is called a _____.

c) A _____ is a group of related records.

d) Digits, letters and special symbols are referred to as _____.

e) A group of related files is called a _____.

f) Member function _____ of the file stream classes **fstream**, **ifstream** and **ofstream** closes a file.

g) The **istream** member function _____ reads a character from the specified stream.

h) The **istream** member functions _____ and _____ read a line from the specified stream.

i) Member function _____ of the file stream classes **fstream**, **ifstream** and **ofstream** opens a file.

j) The **istream** member function _____ is normally used when reading data from a file in random access applications.

k) Member functions _____ and _____ of classes **istream** and **ostream** set the position pointer to a specific location in an input or output stream, respectively.

14.2 State which of the following are *true* and which are *false*. If *false*, explain why.

a) Member function **read** cannot be used to read data from the input object **cin**.

b) The programmer must explicitly create the **cin**, **cout**, **cerr** and **clog** objects.

c) A program must explicitly call function **close** to close a file associated with an **ifstream**, **ofstream** or **fstream** object.

d) If the file position pointer points to a location in a sequential file other than the beginning of the file, the file must be closed and reopened to read from the beginning of the file.

e) The **ostream** member function **write** can write to standard output stream **cout**.

f) Data in sequential access files is always updated without overwriting nearby data.

g) It is not necessary to search through all the records in a random-access file to find a specific record.

h) Records in random-access files must be of uniform length.

i) Member functions **seekp** and **seekg** must seek relative to the beginning of a file.

14.3   Assume that each of the following statements applies to the same program.
   a)   Write a statement that opens file **"oldmast.dat"** for input; use **ifstream** object
        inOldMaster.
   b)   Write a statement that opens file **"trans.dat"** for input; use **ifstream** object **in-
        Transaction**.
   c)   Write a statement that opens file **"newmast.dat"** for output (and creation); use **of-
        stream** object **outNewMaster**.
   d)   Write a statement that reads a record from the file **"oldmast.dat"**. The record con-
        sists of integer **accountNum**, string **name** and floating-point **currentBalance**; use
        ifstream object **inOldMaster**.
   e)   Write a statement that reads a record from the file **"trans.dat"**. The record consists
        of integer **accountNum** and floating-point **dollarAmount**; use **ifstream** object
        inTransaction.
   f)   Write a statement that writes a record to the file **"newmast.dat"**. The record consists
        of integer **accountNum**, string **name**, and floating-point **currentBalance**; use
        ofstream object **outNewMaster**.

14.4   Find the error(s) and show how to correct it (them) in each of the following.
   a)   File **"payables.dat"** referred to by **ofstream** object **outPayable** has not been
        opened.

              outPayable << account << company << amount << endl;

   b)   The following statement should read a record from the file **"payables.dat"**. The
        ifstream object **inPayable** refers to this file, and **istream** object **inReceiv-
        able** refers to the file **"receivables.dat"**.

              inReceivable >> account >> company >> amount;

   c)   The file **"tools.dat"** should be opened to add data to the file without discarding the
        current data.

              ofstream outTools("tools.dat", ios::out);

ANSWERS TO SELF-REVIEW EXERCISES

14.1   a) 1s, 0s. b) Bit. c) File. d) Characters. e) Database. f) **close**. g) **get**. h) **get**,
        getline. i) **open**. j) **read**. k) **seekg**, **seekp**.

14.2   a)   False. Function **read** can read from any input stream object derived from **istream**.
   b)   False. These four streams are created automatically for the programmer. The **<ios-
        tream>** header file must be included in a file to use them. This header includes decla-
        rations of each of these stream objects.
   c)   False. The files will be closed when destructors for **ifstream**, **ofstream** or
        fstream objects are executed when the stream objects go out of scope or before pro-
        gram execution terminates, but it is a good programming practice to close all files explic-
        itly with **close** once they are no longer needed.
   d)   False. Member function **seekp** or **seekg** can be used to reposition the put or get file
        position pointer to the beginning of the file.
   e)   True.
   f)   False. In most cases, sequential file records are not of uniform length. Therefore, it is pos-
        sible that updating a record will cause other data to be overwritten.
   g)   True.
   h)   False. Records in a random-access file are normally of uniform length.
   i)   False. It is possible to seek from the beginning of the file, from the end of the file, and
        from the current position in the file.

14.3 a) `ifstream inOldMaster( "oldmast.dat", ios::in );`
   b) `ifstream inTransaction( "trans.dat", ios::in );`
   c) `ofstream outNewMaster( "newmast.dat", ios::out );`
   d) `inOldMaster >> accountNum >> name >> currentBalance;`
   e) `inTransaction >> accountNum >> dollarAmount;`
   f) `outNewMaster << accountNum << name << currentBalance;`

14.4 a) Error: The file **"payables.dat"** has not been opened before the attempt is made to output data to the stream.
   Correction: Use **ostream** function **open** to open **"payables.dat"** for output.
   b) Error: The incorrect **istream** object is being used to read a record from file **"payables.dat"**.
   Correction: Use **istream** object **inPayable** to refer to **"payables.dat"**.
   c) Error: The contents of the file are discarded because the file is opened for output (**ios::out**).
   Correction: To add data to the file, either open the file for updating (**ios::ate**) or open the file for appending (**ios::app**).

EXERCISES

14.5 Fill in the blanks in each of the following:
   a) Computers store large amounts of data on secondary storage devices as _____.
   b) A _____ is composed of several fields.
   c) A field that may contain only digits, letters and blanks is called an _____ field.
   d) To facilitate the retrieval of specific records from a file, one field in each record is chosen as a _____.
   e) The vast majority of information stored in computer systems is stored in _____ files.
   f) A group of related characters that conveys meaning is called a _____.
   g) The standard stream objects declared by header file **<iostream>** are _____, _____, _____ and _____.
   h) **ostream** member function _____ outputs a character to the specified stream.
   i) **ostream** member function _____ is generally used to write data to a randomly accessed file.
   j) **istream** member function _____ repositions the file position pointer in a file.

14.6 State which of the following are *true* and which are *false*. If *false*, explain why.
   a) The impressive functions performed by computers essentially involve the manipulation of zeros and ones.
   b) People prefer to manipulate bits instead of characters and fields because bits are more compact.
   c) People specify programs and data items as characters; computers then manipulate and process these characters as groups of zeros and ones.
   d) A person's 5-digit zip code is an example of a numeric field.
   e) A person's street address is generally considered to be an alphabetic field in computer applications.
   f) Data items represented in computers form a data hierarchy in which data items become larger and more complex as we progress from fields to characters to bits, etc.
   g) A record key identifies a record as belonging to a particular field.
   h) Most organizations store all information in a single file to facilitate computer processing.
   i) Each statement that processes a file in a C++ program explicitly refers to that file by name.
   j) When a program creates a file, the file is automatically retained by the computer for future reference.

14.7   Exercise 14.3 asked the reader to write a series of single statements. Actually, these statements form the core of an important type of file processing program, namely, a file-matching program. In commercial data processing, it is common to have several files in each application system. In an accounts receivable system, for example, there is generally a master file containing detailed information about each customer such as the customer's name, address, telephone number, outstanding balance, credit limit, discount terms, contract arrangements, and possibly a condensed history of recent purchases and cash payments.

As transactions occur (e.g., sales are made and cash payments arrive), they are entered into a file. At the end of each business period (a month for some companies, a week for others, and a day in some cases) the file of transactions (called `"trans.dat"` in Exercise 14.3) is applied to the master file (called `"oldmast.dat"` in Exercise 14.3), thus updating each account's record of purchases and payments. During an updating run, the master file is rewritten as a new file (`"newmast.dat"`), which is then used at the end of the next business period to begin the updating process again.

File-matching programs must deal with certain problems that do not exist in single-file programs. For example, a match does not always occur. A customer on the master file may not have made any purchases or cash payments in the current business period, and therefore no record for this customer will appear on the transaction file. Similarly, a customer who did make some purchases or cash payments may have just moved to this community, and the company may not have had a chance to create a master record for this customer.

Use the statements from Exercise 14.3 as a basis for writing a complete file-matching accounts receivable program. Use the account number on each file as the record key for matching purposes. Assume that each file is a sequential file with records stored in increasing order by account number.

When a match occurs (i.e., records with the same account number appear on both the master and transaction files), add the dollar amount on the transaction file to the current balance on the master file, and write the `"newmast.dat"` record. (Assume purchases are indicated by positive amounts on the transaction file and payments are indicated by negative amounts.) When there is a master record for a particular account but no corresponding transaction record, merely write the master record to `"newmast.dat"`. When there is a transaction record but no corresponding master record, print the message `"Unmatched transaction record for account number ..."` (fill in the account number from the transaction record).

14.8   After writing the program of Exercise 14.7, write a simple program to create some test data for checking out the program. Use the following sample account data:

Master file Account number	Name	Balance
100	Alan Jones	348.17
300	Mary Smith	27.19
500	Sam Sharp	0.00
700	Suzy Green	-14.22

Transaction file Account number	Transaction amount
100	27.14
300	62.11
400	100.56
900	82.17

14.9   Run the program of Exercise 14.7 using the files of test data created in Exercise 14.8. Print the new master file. Check that the accounts have been updated correctly.

14.10   It is possible (actually common) to have several transaction records with the same record key. This occurs because a particular customer might make several purchases and cash payments during a business period. Rewrite your accounts receivable file-matching program of Exercise 14.7 to provide for the possibility of handling several transaction records with the same record key. Modify the test data of Exercise 14.8 to include the following additional transaction records:

Account number	Dollar amount
300	83.89
700	80.78
700	1.53

14.11   Write a series of statements that accomplish each of the following. Assume the structure

```
struct Person {
   char lastName[ 15 ];
   char firstName[ 15 ];
   char age[ 4 ];
};
```

has been defined, and that the random-access file has been opened properly.
  a) Initialize the file **"nameage.dat"** with 100 records containing **lastName = "un-assigned"**, **firstName = ""** and **age = "0"**.
  b) Input 10 last names, first names and ages, and write them to the file.
  c) Update a record that has information in it, and if there is none, tell the user "No info."
  d) Delete a record that has information by reinitializing that particular record.

14.12   You are the owner of a hardware store and need to keep an inventory that can tell you what different tools you have, how many of each you have on hand and the cost of each one. Write a program that initializes the random-access file **"hardware.dat"** to one hundred empty records, lets you input the data concerning each tool, enables you to list all your tools, lets you delete a record for a tool that you no longer have and lets you update *any* information in the file. The tool identification number should be the record number. Use the following information to start your file:

Record #	Tool name	Quantity	Cost
3	Electric sander	7	57.98
17	Hammer	76	11.99
24	Jig saw	21	11.00
39	Lawn mower	3	79.50
56	Power saw	18	99.99
68	Screwdriver	106	6.99
77	Sledge hammer	11	21.50
83	Wrench	34	7.50

14.13   Modify the telephone number word-generating program you wrote in Chapter 4 so that it writes its output to a file. This allows you to read the file at your convenience. If you have a computerized dictionary available, modify your program to look up the thousands of seven-letter words in the dictionary. Some of the interesting seven-letter combinations created by this program may consist of two or more words. For example, the phone number 8432677 produces "THEBOSS." Modify your program to use the computerized dictionary to check each possible seven-letter word to see if it is a valid one-letter word followed by a valid six-letter word, a valid two-letter word followed by a valid five-letter word, etc.

14.14   Write a program that uses the **sizeof** operator to determine the sizes in bytes of the various data types on your computer system. Write the results to the file **"datasize.dat"** so you may print the results later. The format for the results in the file should be

Data type	Size
char	1
unsigned char	1
short int	2
unsigned short int	2
int	4
unsigned int	4
long int	4
unsigned long int	4
float	4
double	8
long double	16

Note: The sizes of the built-in data types on your computer may differ from those listed above.

15

Data Structures

Objectives

- To be able to form linked data structures using pointers, self-referential classes and recursion.
- To be able to create and manipulate dynamic data structures such as linked lists, queues, stacks and binary trees.
- To understand various important applications of linked data structures.
- To understand how to create reusable data structures with class templates, inheritance and composition.

Much that I bound, I could not free;
Much that I freed returned to me.
Lee Wilson Dodd

'Will you walk a little faster?' said a whiting to a snail,
'There's a porpoise close behind us, and he's treading on my tail.'
Lewis Carroll

There is always room at the top.
Daniel Webster

Push on — keep moving.
Thomas Morton

I think that I shall never see
A poem lovely as a tree.
Joyce Kilmer

Outline

15.1 Introduction

We have studied fixed-size *data structures* such as single-subscripted arrays, double-subscripted arrays and **struct**s. This chapter introduces *dynamic data structures* that grow and shrink during execution. *Linked lists* are collections of data items "lined up in a row"—insertions and removals are made anywhere in a linked list. *Stacks* are important in compilers and operating systems—insertions and removals are made only at one end of a stack—its *top*. *Queues* represent waiting lines; insertions are made at the back (also referred to as the *tail*) of a queue, and removals are made from the front (also referred to as the *head*) of a queue. *Binary trees* facilitate high-speed searching and sorting of data, efficient elimination of duplicate data items, representing file system directories and compiling expressions into machine language. These data structures have many other interesting applications.

We will discuss the major types of data structures and implement programs that create and manipulate these data structures. We use classes, class templates, inheritance and composition to create and package these data structures for reusability and maintainability.

Studying this chapter is solid preparation for Chapter 20, "Standard Template Library (STL)." The STL is a major portion of the C++ Standard Library. The STL provides containers, iterators for traversing those containers and algorithms for processing the elements of those containers. You will see that the STL has taken each of the data structures we discuss here in Chapter 15 and packaged them into templatized classes. The STL code is carefully written to be portable, efficient and extensible. Once you understand the principles and construction of data structures as presented in Chapter 15, you will be able to make the best use of the prepackaged data structures, iterators and algorithms in the STL. The STL is by far the single most important enhancement in the C++ standard. It is a world-class set of components for helping realize the vision of reuse, reuse, reuse.

The chapter examples are practical programs that you will be able to use in more advanced courses and in industry applications. The programs are especially heavy on pointer manipulation. The exercises include a rich collection of useful applications.

We encourage you to attempt the major project described in the special section entitled "Building Your Own Compiler." You have been using a compiler to translate your C++ programs to machine language so that you could execute these programs on your computer.

In this project, you will actually build your own compiler. It will read a file of statements written in a simple, yet powerful, high-level language similar to early versions of the popular language BASIC. Your compiler will translate these statements into a file of Simpletron Machine Language (SML) instructions—SML is the language you learned in the Chapter 5 special section, "Building Your Own Computer." Your Simpletron Simulator program will then execute the SML program produced by your compiler! Implementing this project using a heavily object-oriented approach will give you a wonderful opportunity to exercise most of what you have learned in this course. The special section carefully walks you through the specifications of the high-level language and describes the algorithms you will need to convert each type of high-level language statement into machine language instructions. If you enjoy being challenged, you might attempt the many enhancements to both the compiler and the Simpletron Simulator suggested in the Exercises.

15.2 Self-Referential Classes

A *self-referential class* contains a pointer member that points to a class object of the same class type. For example, the definition

```
class Node {
public:
   Node( int );
   void setData( int );
   int getData() const;
   void setNextPtr( Node * );
   const Node *getNextPtr() const;
private:
   int data;
   Node *nextPtr;
};
```

defines a type, **Node**. Type **Node** has two **private** data members—integer member **data** and pointer member **nextPtr**. Member **nextPtr** points to an object of type **Node**—an object of the same type as the one being declared here, hence the term "self-referential class." Member **nextPtr** is referred to as a *link*—i.e., **nextPtr** can be used to "tie" an object of type **Node** to another object of the same type. Type **Node** also has five member functions: a constructor that receives an integer to initialize member **data**, a **setData** function to set the value of member **data**, a **getData** function to return the value of member **data**, a **setNextPtr** function to set the value of member **nextPtr** and a **getNextPtr** function to return the value of member **nextPtr**.

Self-referential class objects can be linked together to form useful data structures such as lists, queues, stacks and trees. Figure 15.1 illustrates two self-referential class objects linked together to form a list. Note that a slash—representing a null (**0**) pointer—is placed in the link member of the second self-referential class object to indicate that the link does not point to another object. The slash is only for illustration purposes; it does not correspond to the backslash character in C++. A null pointer normally indicates the end of a data structure just as the null character (`'\0'`) indicates the end of a string.

Common Programming Error 15.1
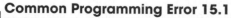
*Not setting the link in the last node of a list to null (**0**).*

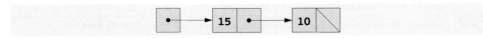

Fig. 15.1   Two self-referential class objects linked together.

15.3 Dynamic Memory Allocation

Creating and maintaining dynamic data structures requires *dynamic memory allocation*—the ability of a program to obtain more memory space at execution time to hold new nodes and to release space no longer needed. The limit for dynamic memory allocation can be as large as the amount of available physical memory in the computer or the amount of available virtual memory in a virtual memory system. Often, the limits are much smaller because available memory must be shared among many users.

Operators **new** and **delete** are essential to dynamic memory allocation. Operator **new** takes as an argument the type of the object being dynamically allocated and returns a pointer to an object of that type. For example, the statement

```
Node *newPtr = new Node( 10 );
```

allocates **sizeof(Node)** bytes, runs the **Node** constructor and stores a pointer to this memory in **newPtr**. If no memory is available, **new** throws a **bad_alloc** exception. The **10** is the node object's data.

The **delete** operator runs the **Node** destructor and deallocates memory allocated with **new**—the memory is returned to the system so that the memory can be reallocated in the future. To free memory dynamically allocated by the preceding **new**, use the statement

```
delete newPtr;
```

Note that **newPtr** itself is not deleted; rather the space **newPtr** points to is deleted. If **newPtr** has the value **0** (indicating a pointer to nothing), the preceding statement has no effect.

The following sections discuss lists, stacks, queues and trees. These data structures are created and maintained with dynamic memory allocation and self-referential classes.

Portability Tip 15.1

A class object's size is not necessarily the sum of the sizes of its data members. This is because of various machine-dependent boundary alignment requirements (see Chapter 16) and other reasons. Use operator **sizeof** *to determine an object's size.*

Common Programming Error 15.2

Assuming that the size of a class object is the sum of the sizes of its data members.

Common Programming Error 15.3

Not returning dynamically allocated memory when it is no longer needed can cause the system to run out of memory prematurely. This is sometimes called a "memory leak."

Good Programming Practice 15.1

When memory that was dynamically allocated with **new** *is no longer needed, use* **delete** *to return the memory to the system immediately.*

Common Programming Error 15.4

*Deleting memory with **delete** that was not allocated dynamically with **new**.*

Common Programming Error 15.5

Referring to memory that has been deleted.

Common Programming Error 15.6

Trying to delete memory that has already been deleted can lead to unpredictable results at execution time.

15.4 Linked Lists

A *linked list* is a linear collection of self-referential class objects, called *nodes,* connected by pointer *links*—hence, the term "linked" list. A linked list is accessed via a pointer to the first node of the list. Subsequent nodes are accessed via the link-pointer member stored in each node. By convention, the link pointer in the last node of a list is set to null (zero) to mark the end of the list. Data are stored in a linked list dynamically—each node is created as necessary. A node can contain data of any type, including objects of other classes. If nodes contain base-class pointers or base-class references to base-class and derived-class objects related by inheritance, we can have a linked list of such nodes and use **virtual** function calls to process these objects polymorphically. Stacks and queues are also linear data structures and, as we will see, are constrained versions of linked lists. Trees are non-linear data structures.

Lists of data can be stored in arrays, but linked lists provide several advantages. A linked list is appropriate when the number of data elements to be represented in the data structure at once is unpredictable. Linked lists are dynamic, so the length of a list can increase or decrease as necessary. The size of a "conventional" C++ array, however, cannot be altered, because the array size is fixed at compile time. "Conventional" arrays can become full. Linked lists become full only when the system has insufficient memory to satisfy dynamic storage allocation requests.

Performance Tip 15.1

An array can be declared to contain more elements than the number of items expected, but this can waste memory. Linked lists can provide better memory utilization in these situations. Linked lists allow the program to adapt at run time.

Linked lists can be maintained in sorted order by inserting each new element at the proper point in the list. Existing list elements do not need to be moved.

Performance Tip 15.2

Insertion and deletion in a sorted array can be time-consuming—all the elements following the inserted or deleted element must be shifted appropriately.

Performance Tip 15.3

The elements of an array are stored contiguously in memory. This allows immediate access to any array element because the address of any element can be calculated directly based on its position relative to the beginning of the array. Linked lists do not afford such immediate "direct access" to their elements.

Linked list nodes are normally not stored contiguously in memory. Logically, however, the nodes of a linked list appear to be contiguous. Figure 15.2 illustrates a linked list with several nodes.

Performance Tip 15.4

Using dynamic memory allocation (instead of arrays) for data structures that grow and shrink at execution time can save memory. Keep in mind, however, that pointers occupy space, and that dynamic memory allocation incurs the overhead of function calls.

The program of Fig. 15.3 (whose output is shown in Fig. 15.4) uses a **List** class template (see Chapter 12, "Templates") to manipulate a list of integer values and a list of floating-point values. The driver program (**fig15_03.cpp**) provides five options: 1) insert a value at the beginning of the list (function **insertAtFront**), 2) insert a value at the end of the list (function **insertAtBack**), 3) delete a value from the front of the list (function **removeFromFront**), 4) delete a value from the end of the list (function **removeFromBack**) and 5) terminate the list processing. A detailed discussion of the program follows. Exercise 15.20 asks you to implement a recursive function that prints a linked list backwards, and Exercise 15.21 asks you to implement a recursive function that searches a linked list for a particular data item.

Figure 15.3 consists of two class templates—**ListNode** and **List**. Encapsulated in each **List** object is a linked list of **ListNode** objects. The **ListNode** class template consists of private members **data** and **nextPtr**. **ListNode** member **data** stores a value of type **NODETYPE**, the type parameter passed to the class template. **ListNode** member **nextPtr** stores a pointer to the next **ListNode** object in the linked list.

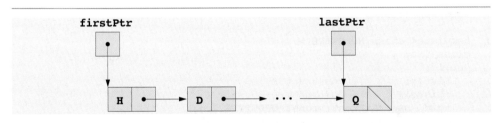

Fig. 15.2   A graphical representation of a list.

```
1    // Fig. 15.3: listnd.h
2    // ListNode template definition
3    #ifndef LISTND_H
4    #define LISTND_H
5
6    template< class NODETYPE > class List;  // forward declaration
7
8    template<class NODETYPE>
9    class ListNode {
10       friend class List< NODETYPE >; // make List a friend
11   public:
12      ListNode( const NODETYPE & ); // constructor
13      NODETYPE getData() const;      // return data in the node
```

Fig. 15.3   Manipulating a linked list—**listnd.h** (part 1 of 2).

```
14   private:
15      NODETYPE data;                     // data
16      ListNode< NODETYPE > *nextPtr;  // next node in the list
17   };
18
19   // Constructor
20   template<class NODETYPE>
21   ListNode< NODETYPE >::ListNode( const NODETYPE &info )
22      : data( info ), nextPtr( 0 ) { }
23
24   // Return a copy of the data in the node
25   template< class NODETYPE >
26   NODETYPE ListNode< NODETYPE >::getData() const { return data; }
27
28   #endif
```

Fig. 15.3   Manipulating a linked list—`listnd.h` (part 2 of 2).

```
29   // Fig. 15.3: list.h
30   // Template List class definition
31   #ifndef LIST_H
32   #define LIST_H
33
34   #include <iostream>
35   #include <cassert>
36   #include "listnd.h"
37
38   using std::cout;
39
40   template< class NODETYPE >
41   class List {
42   public:
43      List();         // constructor
44      ~List();        // destructor
45      void insertAtFront( const NODETYPE & );
46      void insertAtBack( const NODETYPE & );
47      bool removeFromFront( NODETYPE & );
48      bool removeFromBack( NODETYPE & );
49      bool isEmpty() const;
50      void print() const;
51   private:
52      ListNode< NODETYPE > *firstPtr;   // pointer to first node
53      ListNode< NODETYPE > *lastPtr;    // pointer to last node
54
55      // Utility function to allocate a new node
56      ListNode< NODETYPE > *getNewNode( const NODETYPE & );
57   };
58
59   // Default constructor
60   template< class NODETYPE >
61   List< NODETYPE >::List() : firstPtr( 0 ), lastPtr( 0 ) { }
62
```

Fig. 15.3   Manipulating a linked list—`list.h` (part 1 of 4)..

```
63   // Destructor
64   template< class NODETYPE >
65   List< NODETYPE >::~List()
66   {
67      if ( !isEmpty() ) {      // List is not empty
68         cout << "Destroying nodes ...\n";
69
70         ListNode< NODETYPE > *currentPtr = firstPtr, *tempPtr;
71
72         while ( currentPtr != 0 ) {   // delete remaining nodes
73            tempPtr = currentPtr;
74            cout << tempPtr->data << '\n';
75            currentPtr = currentPtr->nextPtr;
76            delete tempPtr;
77         }
78      }
79
80      cout << "All nodes destroyed\n\n";
81   }
82
83   // Insert a node at the front of the list
84   template< class NODETYPE >
85   void List< NODETYPE >::insertAtFront( const NODETYPE &value )
86   {
87      ListNode< NODETYPE > *newPtr = getNewNode( value );
88
89      if ( isEmpty() )   // List is empty
90         firstPtr = lastPtr = newPtr;
91      else {             // List is not empty
92         newPtr->nextPtr = firstPtr;
93         firstPtr = newPtr;
94      }
95   }
96
97   // Insert a node at the back of the list
98   template< class NODETYPE >
99   void List< NODETYPE >::insertAtBack( const NODETYPE &value )
100  {
101     ListNode< NODETYPE > *newPtr = getNewNode( value );
102
103     if ( isEmpty() )   // List is empty
104        firstPtr = lastPtr = newPtr;
105     else {             // List is not empty
106        lastPtr->nextPtr = newPtr;
107        lastPtr = newPtr;
108     }
109  }
110
111  // Delete a node from the front of the list
112  template< class NODETYPE >
113  bool List< NODETYPE >::removeFromFront( NODETYPE &value )
114  {
```

Fig. 15.3   Manipulating a linked list—**list.h** (part 2 of 4)..

```
115    if ( isEmpty() )                    // List is empty
116       return return;                   // delete unsuccessful
117    else {
118       ListNode< NODETYPE > *tempPtr = firstPtr;
119
120       if ( firstPtr == lastPtr )
121          firstPtr = lastPtr = 0;
122       else
123          firstPtr = firstPtr->nextPtr;
124
125       value = tempPtr->data;   // data being removed
126       delete tempPtr;
127       return return;                   // delete successful
128    }
129 }
130
131 // Delete a node from the back of the list
132 template< class NODETYPE >
133 bool List< NODETYPE >::removeFromBack( NODETYPE &value )
134 {
135    if ( isEmpty() )
136       return return;   // delete unsuccessful
137    else {
138       ListNode< NODETYPE > *tempPtr = lastPtr;
139
140       if ( firstPtr == lastPtr )
141          firstPtr = lastPtr = 0;
142       else {
143          ListNode< NODETYPE > *currentPtr = firstPtr;
144
145          while ( currentPtr->nextPtr != lastPtr )
146             currentPtr = currentPtr->nextPtr;
147
148          lastPtr = currentPtr;
149          currentPtr->nextPtr = 0;
150       }
151
152       value = tempPtr->data;
153       delete tempPtr;
154       return return;   // delete successful
155    }
156 }
157
158 // Is the List empty?
159 template< class NODETYPE >
160 bool List< NODETYPE >::isEmpty() const
161    { return firstPtr == 0; }
162
163 // return a pointer to a newly allocated node
164 template< class NODETYPE >
165 ListNode< NODETYPE > *List< NODETYPE >::getNewNode(
166                                      const NODETYPE &value )
167 {
```

Fig. 15.3   Manipulating a linked list—**list.h** (part 3 of 4)..

```
168    ListNode< NODETYPE > *ptr =
169       new ListNode< NODETYPE >( value );
170    assert( ptr != 0 );
171    return ptr;
172 }
173
174 // Display the contents of the List
175 template< class NODETYPE >
176 void List< NODETYPE >::print() const
177 {
178    if ( isEmpty() ) {
179       cout << "The list is empty\n\n";
180       return;
181    }
182
183    ListNode< NODETYPE > *currentPtr = firstPtr;
184
185    cout << "The list is: ";
186
187    while ( currentPtr != 0 ) {
188       cout << currentPtr->data << ' ';
189       currentPtr = currentPtr->nextPtr;
190    }
191
192    cout << "\n\n";
193 }
194
195 #endif
```

Fig. 15.3   Manipulating a linked list—**list.h** (part 4 of 4)..

```
196 // Fig. 15.3: fig15_03.cpp
197 // List class test
198 #include <iostream>
199 #include "list.h"
200
201 using std::cin;
202 using std::endl;
203
204 // Function to test an integer List
205 template< class T >
206 void testList( List< T > &listObject, const char *type )
207 {
208    cout << "Testing a List of " << type << " values\n";
209
210    instructions();
211    int choice;
212    T value;
213
214    do {
215       cout << "? ";
216       cin >> choice;
```

Fig. 15.3   Manipulating a linked list.

```
217
218        switch ( choice ) {
219            case 1:
220                cout << "Enter " << type << ": ";
221                cin >> value;
222                listObject.insertAtFront( value );
223                listObject.print();
224                break;
225            case 2:
226                cout << "Enter " << type << ": ";
227                cin >> value;
228                listObject.insertAtBack( value );
229                listObject.print();
230                break;
231            case 3:
232                if ( listObject.removeFromFront( value ) )
233                    cout << value << " removed from list\n";
234
235                listObject.print();
236                break;
237            case 4:
238                if ( listObject.removeFromBack( value ) )
239                    cout << value << " removed from list\n";
240
241                listObject.print();
242                break;
243        }
244    } while ( choice != 5 );
245
246    cout << "End list test\n\n";
247 }
248
249 void instructions()
250 {
251    cout << "Enter one of the following:\n"
252        << "  1 to insert at beginning of list\n"
253        << "  2 to insert at end of list\n"
254        << "  3 to delete from beginning of list\n"
255        << "  4 to delete from end of list\n"
256        << "  5 to end list processing\n";
257 }
258
259 int main()
260 {
261    List< int > integerList;
262    testList( integerList, "integer" ); // test integerList
263
264    List< double > doubleList;
265    testList( doubleList, "double" );      // test doubleList
266
267    return 0;
268 }
```

Fig. 15.3   Manipulating a linked list.

```
Testing a List of integer values
Enter one of the following:
   1 to insert at beginning of list
   2 to insert at end of list
   3 to delete from beginning of list
   4 to delete from end of list
   5 to end list processing
? 1
Enter integer: 1
The list is: 1

? 1
Enter integer: 2
The list is: 2 1

? 2
Enter integer: 3
The list is: 2 1 3

? 2
Enter integer: 4
The list is: 2 1 3 4

? 3
2 removed from list
The list is: 1 3 4

? 3
1 removed from list
The list is: 3 4

? 4
4 removed from list
The list is: 3

? 4
3 removed from list
The list is empty

? 5
End list test

Testing a List of double values
Enter one of the following:
   1 to insert at beginning of list
   2 to insert at end of list
   3 to delete from beginning of list
   4 to delete from end of list
   5 to end list processing
? 1
Enter double: 1.1
The list is: 1.1
```

Fig. 15.4   Sample output for the program of Fig. 15.3 (part 1 of 2).

```
? 1
Enter double: 2.2
The list is: 2.2 1.1

? 2
Enter double: 3.3
The list is: 2.2 1.1 3.3

? 2
Enter double: 4.4
The list is: 2.2 1.1 3.3 4.4

? 3
2.2 removed from list
The list is: 1.1 3.3 4.4

? 3
1.1 removed from list
The list is: 3.3 4.4

? 4
4.4 removed from list
The list is: 3.3

? 4
3.3 removed from list
The list is empty

? 5
End list test

All nodes destroyed

All nodes destroyed
```

Fig. 15.4   Sample output for the program of Fig. 15.3 (part 2 of 2).

The **List** class template consists of **private** members **firstPtr** (a pointer to the first **ListNode** in a **List** object) and **lastPtr** (a pointer to the last **ListNode** in a **List** object). The default constructor initializes both pointers to **0** (null). The destructor ensures that all **ListNode** objects in a **List** object are destroyed when that **List** object is destroyed. The primary functions of the **List** class template are **insertAtFront**, **insertAtBack**, **removeFromFront**, and **removeFromBack**.

Function **isEmpty** is called a *predicate function*—it does not alter the **List**; rather, it determines if the **List** is empty (i.e., the pointer to the first node of the **List** is null). If the **List** is empty, **true** is returned; otherwise, **false** is returned. Function **print** displays the **List**'s contents.

Good Programming Practice 15.2

Assign null (zero) to the link member of a new node. Pointers should be initialized before they are used.

Over the next several pages, we discuss each of the member functions of the **List** class in detail. Function **insertAtFront** (Fig. 15.5) places a new node at the front of the list. The function consists of several steps:

1. Call function **getNewNode**, passing it **value**, which is a constant reference to the node value to be inserted.

2. Function **getNewNode** uses operator **new** to create a new list node and return a pointer to this list node. If this pointer is nonzero, **getNewNode** returns a pointer to this newly allocated node to **newPtr** in **insertAtFront**.

3. If the list is empty, then both **firstPtr** and **lastPtr** are set to **newPtr**.

4. If the list is not empty, then the node pointed to by **newPtr** is threaded into the list by copying **firstPtr** to **newPtr->nextPtr** so that the new node points to what used to be the first node of the list, and copying **newPtr** to **firstPtr** so that **firstPtr** now points to the new first node of the list.

Figure 15.5 illustrates function **insertAtFront**. Part a) of the figure shows the list and the new node before the **insertAtFront** operation. The dotted arrows in part b) illustrate the steps 2 and 3 of the **insertAtFront** operation that enable the node containing **12** to become the new list front.

Function **insertAtBack** (Fig. 15.6) places a new node at the back of the list. The function consists of several steps:

1. Call function **getNewNode**, passing it **value**, which is a constant reference to the node value to be inserted.

2. Function **getNewNode** uses operator **new** to create a new list node and return a pointer to this list node. If this pointer is nonzero, **getNewNode** returns a pointer to this newly allocated node to **newPtr** in **insertAtBack**.

3. If the list is empty, then both **firstPtr** and **lastPtr** are set to **newPtr**.

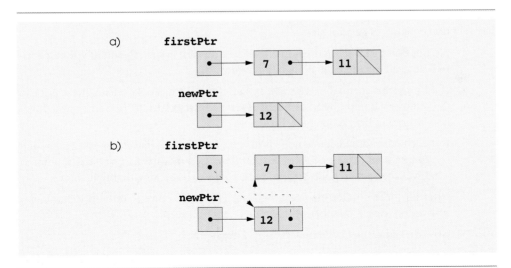

Fig. 15.5   The **insertAtFront** operation.

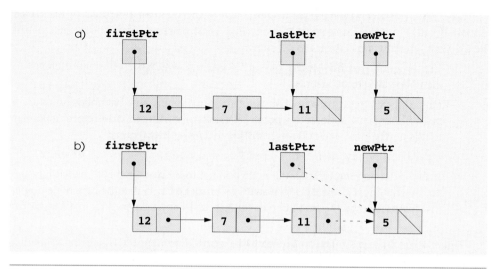

Fig. 15.6   A graphical representation of the **insertAtBack** operation.

4. If the list is not empty, then the node pointed to by **newPtr** is threaded into the list by copying **newPtr** into **lastPtr->nextPtr** so that the new node is pointed to by what used to be the last node of the list, and copying **newPtr** to **lastPtr** so that **lastPtr** now points to the new last node of the list.

Figure 15.6 illustrates an **insertAtBack** operation. Part a) of the figure shows the list and the new node before the operation. The dotted arrows in part b) illustrate the steps of function **insertAtBack** that enable a new node to be added to the end of a list that is not empty.

Function **removeFromFront** (Fig. 15.7) removes the front node of the list and copies the node value to the reference parameter. The function returns **false** if an attempt is made to remove a node from an empty list, and returns **true** if the removal is successful. The function consists of several steps:

1. Assign **tempPtr** the address to which **firstPtr** points. Eventually, **tempPtr** will be used to delete the node being removed.

2. If **firstPtr** is equal to **lastPtr**, i.e., if the list has only one element prior to the removal attempt, then set **firstPtr** and **lastPtr** to zero to dethread that node from the list (leaving the list empty).

3. If the list has more than one node prior to removal, then leave **lastPtr** as is and set **firstPtr** to **firstPtr->nextPtr**, i.e., modify **firstPtr** to point to what was the second node prior to removal (and is the new first node now).

4. After all these pointer manipulations are complete, copy to reference parameter **value** the **data** member of the node being removed.

5. Now **delete** the node pointed to by **tempPtr**.

6. Return **true**, indicating successful removal.

Figure 15.7 illustrates function **removeFromFront**. Part a) illustrates the list before the removal operation. Part b) shows actual pointer manipulations.

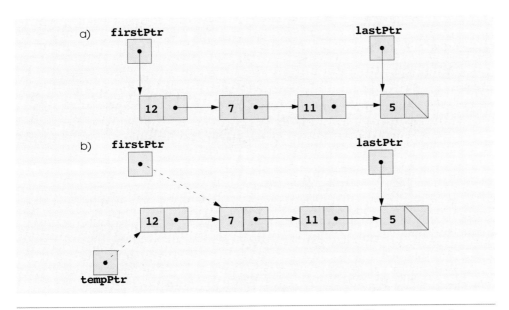

Fig. 15.7   A graphical representation of the **removeFromFront** operation.

Function **removeFromBack** (Fig. 15.8) removes the back node of the list and copies the node value to the reference parameter. The function returns **false** if an attempt is made to remove a node from an empty list, and returns **true** if the removal is successful. The function consists of several steps:

1. Assign **tempPtr** the address to which **lastPtr** points. Eventually, **tempPtr** will be used to delete the node being removed.

2. If **firstPtr** is equal to **lastPtr**, i.e., if the list has only one element prior to the removal attempt, then set **firstPtr** and **lastPtr** to zero to dethread that node from the list (leaving the list empty).

3. If the list has more than one node prior to removal, then assign **currentPtr** the address to which **firstPtr** points.

4. Now "walk the list" with **currentPtr** until it points to the node before the last node. This is done with a **while** loop that keeps replacing **currentPtr** by **currentPtr->nextPtr** while **currentPtr->nextPtr** is not **lastPtr**.

5. Assign **lastPtr** to the address to which **currentPtr** points to dethread the back node from the list.

6. Set the **currentPtr->nextPtr** to zero in the new last node of the list.

7. After all the pointer manipulations are complete, copy to reference parameter **value** the **data** member of the node being removed.

8. Now **delete** the node pointed to by **tempPtr**.

9. Return **true**, indicating successful removal.

Figure 15.8 illustrates function **removeFromBack**. Part a) of the figure illustrates the list before the removal operation. Part b) of the figure shows the actual pointer manipulations.

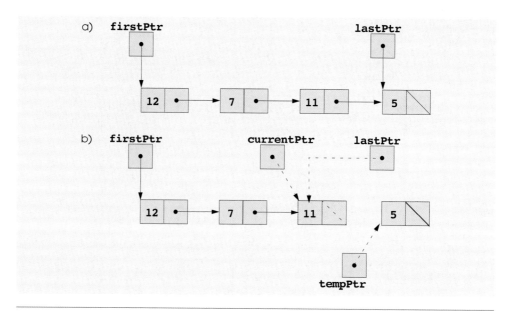

Fig. 15.8 A graphical representation of the **removeFromBack** operation.

Function **print** first determines if the list is empty. If so, **print** prints **"The list is empty"** and returns. Otherwise, it prints the data in the list. The function initializes **currentPtr** as a copy of **firstPtr** and then prints the string **"The list is: "**. While **currentPtr** is not null, **currentPtr->data** is printed and the value of **currentPtr->nextPtr** is assigned to **currentPtr**. Note that if the link in the last node of the list is not null, the printing algorithm will erroneously print past the end of the list. The printing algorithm is identical for linked lists, stacks and queues.

The kind of linked list we have been discussing is a *singly linked list*—the list begins with a pointer to the first node, and each node contains a pointer to the next node "in sequence." This list terminates with a node whose pointer member is 0. A singly linked list may be traversed in only one direction.

A *circular, singly linked list* begins with a pointer to the first node, and each node contains a pointer to the next node. The "last node" does not contain a 0 pointer; rather, the pointer in the last node points back to the first node, thus closing the "circle."

A *doubly linked list* allows traversals both forwards and backwards. Such a list is often implemented with two "start pointers"—one that points to the first element of the list to allow front-to-back traversal of the list, and one that points to the last element of the list to allow back-to-front traversal of the list. Each node has both a forward pointer to the next node in the list in the forward direction and a backward pointer to the next node in the list in the backward direction. If your list contains an alphabetized telephone directory, for example, searching for someone whose name begins with a letter near the front of the alphabet might begin from the front of the list. Searching for someone whose name begins with a letter near the end of the alphabet might begin from the back of the list.

In a *circular, doubly linked list*, the forward pointer of the last node points to the first node, and the backward pointer of the first node points to the last node, thus closing the "circle."

15.5 Stacks

In Chapter 12, "Templates," we explained the notion of a stack class template with an underlying array implementation. In this section, we use an underlying pointer-based linked-list implementation. We also discuss stacks in Chapter 20, "Standard Template Library (STL)."

A *stack* is a constrained version of a linked list—new nodes can be added to a stack and removed from a stack only at the top. For this reason, a stack is referred to as a *last-in, first-out (LIFO)* data structure. The link member in the last node of the stack is set to null (zero) to indicate the bottom of the stack.

Common Programming Error 15.7

Not setting the link in the bottom node of a stack to null (zero).

The primary member functions used to manipulate a stack are **push** and **pop**. Function **push** adds a new node to the top of the stack. Function **pop** removes a node from the top of the stack, stores the popped value in a reference variable that is passed to the calling function and returns **true** if the **pop** operation was successful (**false** otherwise).

Stacks have many interesting applications. For example, when a function call is made, the called function must know how to return to its caller, so the return address is pushed onto a stack. If a series of function calls occurs, the successive return values are pushed onto the stack in last-in, first-out order so that each function can return to its caller. Stacks support recursive function calls in the same manner as conventional nonrecursive calls.

Stacks contain the space created for automatic variables on each invocation of a function. When the function returns to its caller or throws an exception, the destructor (if any) for each local object is called, the space for that function's automatic variables is popped off the stack and those variables are no longer known to the program.

Stacks are used by compilers in the process of evaluating expressions and generating machine language code. The exercises explore several applications of stacks, including using them to develop a complete working compiler.

We will take advantage of the close relationship between lists and stacks to implement a stack class primarily by reusing a list class. We use two different forms of reusability. First, we implement the stack class through private inheritance of the list class. Then we implement an identically performing stack class through composition by including a list class as a private member of a stack class. Of course, all of the data structures in this chapter, including these two stack classes, are implemented as templates (see Chapter 12, "Templates") to encourage further reusability.

The program of Fig. 15.9 (whose output is shown in Fig. 15.10) creates a **Stack** class template primarily through **private** inheritance of the **List** class template of Fig. 15.3. We want the **Stack** to have member functions **push**, **pop**, **isStackEmpty** and **printStack**. Note that these are essentially the **insertAtFront**, **removeFrom-Front**, **isEmpty** and **print** functions of the **List** class template. Of course, the **List** class template contains other member functions (i.e., **insertAtBack** and **remove-FromBack**) that we would not want to make accessible through the **public** interface to the **Stack** class. So when we indicate that the **Stack** class template is to inherit the **List** class template, we specify **private** inheritance. This makes all the **List** class template's member functions **private** in the **Stack** class template. When we implement the

Stack's member functions, we then have each of these call the appropriate member function of the **List** class—**push** calls **insertAtFront**, **pop** calls **removeFromFront**, **isStackEmpty** calls **isEmpty** and **printStack** calls **print**.

```cpp
1   // Fig. 15.9: stack.h
2   // Stack class template definition
3   // Derived from class List
4   #ifndef STACK_H
5   #define STACK_H
6
7   #include "list.h"
8
9   template< class STACKTYPE >
10  class Stack : private List< STACKTYPE > {
11  public:
12     void push( const STACKTYPE &d ) { insertAtFront( d ); }
13     bool pop( STACKTYPE &d ) { return removeFromFront( d ); }
14     bool isStackEmpty() const { return isEmpty(); }
15     void printStack() const { print(); }
16  };
17
18  #endif
```

Fig. 15.9   A simple stack program—**stack.h**.

```cpp
19  // Fig. 15.9: fig15_09.cpp
20  // Driver to test the template Stack class
21  #include <iostream>
22  #include "stack.h"
23
24  using std::endl;
25
26  int main()
27  {
28     Stack< int > intStack;
29     int popInteger, i;
30     cout << "processing an integer Stack" << endl;
31
32     for ( i = 0; i < 4; i++ ) {
33        intStack.push( i );
34        intStack.printStack();
35     }
36
37     while ( !intStack.isStackEmpty() ) {
38        intStack.pop( popInteger );
39        cout << popInteger << " popped from stack" << endl;
40        intStack.printStack();
41     }
42
43     Stack< double > doubleStack;
44     double val = 1.1, popdouble;
45     cout << "processing a double Stack" << endl;
```

Fig. 15.9   A simple stack program—**fig15_09.cpp** (part 1 of 2).

```
46
47      for ( i = 0; i < 4; i++ ) {
48         doubleStack.push( val );
49         doubleStack.printStack();
50         val += 1.1;
51      }
52
53      while ( !doubleStack.isStackEmpty() ) {
54         doubleStack.pop( popdouble );
55         cout << popdouble << " popped from stack" << endl;
56         doubleStack.printStack();
57      }
58      return 0;
59   }
```

Fig. 15.9   A simple stack program—**fig15_09.cpp** (part 2 of 2).

```
processing an integer Stack
The list is: 0

The list is: 1 0

The list is: 2 1 0

The list is: 3 2 1 0

3 popped from stack
The list is: 2 1 0

2 popped from stack
The list is: 1 0

1 popped from stack
The list is: 0

0 popped from stack
The list is empty

processing a double Stack
The list is: 1.1

The list is: 2.2 1.1

The list is: 3.3 2.2 1.1

The list is: 4.4 3.3 2.2 1.1

4.4 popped from stack
The list is: 3.3 2.2 1.1
```

Fig. 15.10   Sample output from the program of Fig. 15.9 (part 1 of 2).

```
3.3 popped from stack
The list is: 2.2 1.1

2.2 popped from stack
The list is: 1.1

1.1 popped from stack
The list is empty

All nodes destroyed

All nodes destroyed
```

Fig. 15.10 Sample output from the program of Fig. 15.9 (part 2 of 2).

The stack class template is used in **main** to instantiate integer stack **intStack** of type **Stack< int >**. Integers 0 through 3 are pushed onto **intStack** and then popped off **intStack**. The stack class template is then used to instantiate stack **doubleStack** of type **Stack< double >**. Values 1.1, 2.2, 3.3 and 4.4 are pushed onto **doubleStack** and then popped off **doubleStack**.

Another way to implement a **Stack** class template is by reusing a **List** class template through composition. The program of Fig. 15.11 uses the files **list.h** and **listnd.h** from the **List** program. It also uses the same driver program as the previous **Stack** program, except the new header file—**stack_c.h**—is included and replaces **stack.h**. The output is also the same. The **Stack** class template definition now includes member object **s** of type **List< STACKTYPE >**.

```cpp
1   // Fig. 15.11: stack_c.h
2   // Definition of Stack class composed of List object
3   #ifndef STACK_C
4   #define STACK_C
5   #include "list.h"
6
7   template< class STACKTYPE >
8   class Stack {
9   public:
10     // no constructor; List constructor does initialization
11     void push( const STACKTYPE &d ) { s.insertAtFront( d ); }
12     bool pop( STACKTYPE &d ) { return s.removeFromFront( d ); }
13     bool isStackEmpty() const { return s.isEmpty(); }
14     void printStack() const { s.print(); }
15   private:
16     List< STACKTYPE > s;
17   };
18
19   #endif
```

Fig. 15.11 A simple stack program using composition—**stack_c.h**.

15.6 Queues

A *queue* is similar to a supermarket checkout line—the first person in line is serviced first, and other customers enter the line at the end and wait to be serviced. Queue nodes are removed only from the *head* of the queue and are inserted only at the *tail* of the queue. For this reason, a queue is referred to as a *first-in, first-out (FIFO)* data structure. The insert and remove operations are known as **enqueue** and **dequeue**.

Queues have many applications in computer systems. Most computers have only a single processor, so only one user at a time can be served. Entries for the other users are placed in a queue. Each entry gradually advances to the front of the queue as users receive service. The entry at the front of the queue is the next to receive service.

Queues are also used to support print spooling. A multiuser environment may have only a single printer. Many users may be generating outputs to be printed. If the printer is busy, other outputs may still be generated. These are "spooled" to disk (much as thread is wound onto a spool) where they wait in a queue until the printer becomes available.

Information packets also wait in queues in computer networks. Each time a packet arrives at a network node, it must be routed to the next node on the network along the path to the packet's final destination. The routing node routes one packet at a time, so additional packets are enqueued until the router can route them.

A file server in a computer network handles file access requests from many clients throughout the network. Servers have a limited capacity to service requests from clients. When that capacity is exceeded, client requests wait in queues.

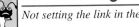

Common Programming Error 15.8

Not setting the link in the last node of a queue to null (zero).

Figure 15.12 (whose output is shown in Fig. 15.13) creates a **Queue** class template primarily through **private** inheritance of the **List** class template of Fig. 15.3. We want the **Queue** to have member functions **enqueue**, **dequeue**, **isQueueEmpty** and **printQueue**. We note that these are essentially the **insertAtBack**, **removeFromFront**, **isEmpty** and **print** functions of the **List** class template. Of course, the **List** class template contains other member functions (i.e., **insertAtFront** and **removeFromBack**) that we would not want to make accessible through the **public** interface to the **Queue** class. So when we indicate that the **Queue** class template is to inherit the **List** class template, we specify **private** inheritance. This makes all the **List** class template's member functions **private** in the **Queue** class template. When we implement the **Queue**'s member functions, we have each of these call the appropriate member function of the list class—**enqueue** calls **insertAtBack**, **dequeue** calls **removeFromFront**, **isQueueEmpty** calls **isEmpty** and **printQueue** calls **print**.

```
1   // Fig. 15.12: queue.h
2   // Queue class template definition
3   // Derived from class List
4   #ifndef QUEUE_H
5   #define QUEUE_H
6
```

Fig. 15.12   Processing a queue—**queue.h** (part 1 of 2).

```
7   #include "list.h"
8
9   template< class QUEUETYPE >
10  class Queue: private List< QUEUETYPE > {
11  public:
12     void enqueue( const QUEUETYPE &d ) { insertAtBack( d ); }
13     bool dequeue( QUEUETYPE &d )
14        { return removeFromFront( d ); }
15     bool isQueueEmpty() const { return isEmpty(); }
16     void printQueue() const { print(); }
17  };
18
19  #endif
```

Fig. 15.12   Processing a queue—**queue.h** (part 2 of 2).

```
20  // Fig. 15.12: fig15_12.cpp
21  // Driver to test the template Queue class
22  #include <iostream>
23  #include "queue.h"
24
25  using std::endl;
26
27  int main()
28  {
29     Queue< int > intQueue;
30     int dequeueInteger, i;
31     cout << "processing an integer Queue" << endl;
32
33     for ( i = 0; i < 4; i++ ) {
34        intQueue.enqueue( i );
35        intQueue.printQueue();
36     }
37
38     while ( !intQueue.isQueueEmpty() ) {
39        intQueue.dequeue( dequeueInteger );
40        cout << dequeueInteger << " dequeued" << endl;
41        intQueue.printQueue();
42     }
43
44     Queue< double > doubleQueue;
45     double val = 1.1, dequeuedouble;
46
47     cout << "processing a double Queue" << endl;
48
49     for ( i = 0; i < 4; i++ ) {
50        doubleQueue.enqueue( val );
51        doubleQueue.printQueue();
52        val += 1.1;
53     }
54
```

Fig. 15.12   Processing a queue—**fig15_12.cpp** (part 1 of 2).

```
55        while ( !doubleQueue.isQueueEmpty() ) {
56           doubleQueue.dequeue( dequeuedouble );
57           cout << dequeuedouble << " dequeued" << endl;
58           doubleQueue.printQueue();
59        }
60
61        return 0;
62    }
```

Fig. 15.12   Processing a queue—**fig15_12.cpp** (part 2 of 2).

```
processing an integer Queue
The list is: 0

The list is: 0 1

The list is: 0 1 2

The list is: 0 1 2 3

0 dequeued
The list is: 1 2 3

1 dequeued
The list is: 2 3

2 dequeued
The list is: 3

3 dequeued
The list is empty

processing a double Queue
The list is: 1.1

The list is: 1.1 2.2

The list is: 1.1 2.2 3.3

The list is: 1.1 2.2 3.3 4.4

1.1 dequeued
The list is: 2.2 3.3 4.4

2.2 dequeued
The list is: 3.3 4.4

3.3 dequeued
The list is: 4.4
```

Fig. 15.13   Sample output from the program in Fig. 15.12 (part 1 of 2).

```
4.4 dequeued
The list is empty

All nodes destroyed

All nodes destroyed
```

Fig. 15.13 Sample output from the program in Fig. 15.12 (part 2 of 2).

The queue class template is used in **main** to instantiate integer queue **intQueue** of type **Queue< int >**. Integers 0 through 3 are enqueued to **intQueue** then dequeued from **intQueue** in first-in, first-out order. The queue class template is then used to instantiate queue **doubleQueue** of type **Queue< double >**. Values 1.1, 2.2, 3.3 and 4.4 are enqueued to **doubleQueue** then dequeued from **doubleQueue** in first-in, first-out order.

15.7 Trees

Linked lists, stacks and queues are *linear data structures*. A tree is a nonlinear, two-dimensional data structure with special properties. Tree nodes contain two or more links. This section discusses *binary trees* (Fig. 15.14)—trees whose nodes all contain two links (none, one or both of which may be null). The *root node* is the first node in a tree. Each link in the root node refers to a *child*. The *left child* is the root node of the *left subtree,* and the *right child* is the root node of the *right subtree.* The children of a single node are called *siblings.* A node with no children is called a *leaf node.* Computer scientists normally draw trees from the root node down—exactly the opposite of trees in nature.

In this section, a special binary tree called a *binary search tree* is created. A binary search tree (with no duplicate node values) has the characteristic that the values in any left subtree are less than the value in its parent node, and the values in any right subtree are greater than the value in its parent node. Figure 15.15 illustrates a binary search tree with 12 values. Note that the shape of the binary search tree that corresponds to a set of data can vary, depending on the order in which the values are inserted into the tree.

 Common Programming Error 15.9

Not setting to null (zero) the links in leaf nodes of a tree.

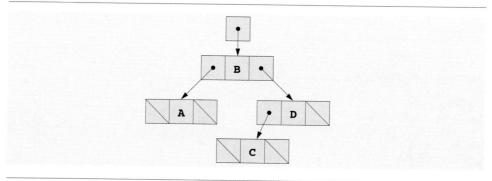

Fig. 15.14 A graphical representation of a binary tree.

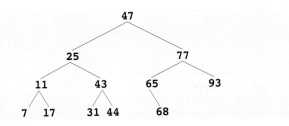

Fig. 15.15 A binary search tree.

The program of Fig. 15.16 (whose output is shown in Fig. 15.17) creates a binary search tree and traverses it (i.e., walks through all its nodes) three ways—using recursive *inorder, preorder* and *postorder traversals.*

```
1    // Fig. 15.16: treenode.h
2    // Definition of class TreeNode
3    #ifndef TREENODE_H
4    #define TREENODE_H
5
6    template< class NODETYPE > class Tree;    // forward declaration
7
8    template< class NODETYPE >
9    class TreeNode {
10       friend class Tree< NODETYPE >;
11   public:
12      TreeNode( const NODETYPE &d )
13         : leftPtr( 0 ), data( d ), rightPtr( 0 ) { }
14      NODETYPE getData() const { return data; }
15   private:
16      TreeNode< NODETYPE > *leftPtr;    // pointer to left subtree
17      NODETYPE data;
18      TreeNode< NODETYPE > *rightPtr;   // pointer to right subtree
19   };
20
21   #endif
```

Fig. 15.16 Creating and traversing a binary tree—**treenode.h**.

```
22   // Fig. 15.16: tree.h
23   // Definition of template class Tree
24   #ifndef TREE_H
25   #define TREE_H
26
27   #include <iostream>
28   #include <cassert>
29   #include "treenode.h"
30
31   using std::endl;
32
```

Fig. 15.16 Creating and traversing a binary tree—**tree.h** (part 1 of 3).

```
33  template< class NODETYPE >
34  class Tree {
35  public:
36     Tree();
37     void insertNode( const NODETYPE & );
38     void preOrderTraversal() const;
39     void inOrderTraversal() const;
40     void postOrderTraversal() const;
41  private:
42     TreeNode< NODETYPE > *rootPtr;
43
44     // utility functions
45     void insertNodeHelper(
46             TreeNode< NODETYPE > **, const NODETYPE & );
47     void preOrderHelper( TreeNode< NODETYPE > * ) const;
48     void inOrderHelper( TreeNode< NODETYPE > * ) const;
49     void postOrderHelper( TreeNode< NODETYPE > * ) const;
50  };
51
52  template< class NODETYPE >
53  Tree< NODETYPE >::Tree() { rootPtr = 0; }
54
55  template< class NODETYPE >
56  void Tree< NODETYPE >::insertNode( const NODETYPE &value )
57     { insertNodeHelper( &rootPtr, value ); }
58
59  // This function receives a pointer to a pointer so the
60  // pointer can be modified.
61  template< class NODETYPE >
62  void Tree< NODETYPE >::insertNodeHelper(
63          TreeNode< NODETYPE > **ptr, const NODETYPE &value )
64  {
65     if ( *ptr == 0 ) {                    // tree is empty
66        *ptr = new TreeNode< NODETYPE >( value );
67        assert( *ptr != 0 );
68     }
69     else                                  // tree is not empty
70        if ( value < ( *ptr )->data )
71           insertNodeHelper( &( ( *ptr )->leftPtr ), value );
72        else
73           if ( value > ( *ptr )->data )
74              insertNodeHelper( &( ( *ptr )->rightPtr ), value );
75           else
76              cout << value << " dup" << endl;
77  }
78
79  template< class NODETYPE >
80  void Tree< NODETYPE >::preOrderTraversal() const
81     { preOrderHelper( rootPtr ); }
82
83  template< class NODETYPE >
84  void Tree< NODETYPE >::preOrderHelper(
85                             TreeNode< NODETYPE > *ptr ) const
```

Fig. 15.16 Creating and traversing a binary tree—**tree.h** (part 2 of 3).

```
86   {
87      if ( ptr != 0 ) {
88         cout << ptr->data << ' ';
89         preOrderHelper( ptr->leftPtr );
90         preOrderHelper( ptr->rightPtr );
91      }
92   }
93
94   template< class NODETYPE >
95   void Tree< NODETYPE >::inOrderTraversal() const
96      { inOrderHelper( rootPtr ); }
97
98   template< class NODETYPE >
99   void Tree< NODETYPE >::inOrderHelper(
100                          TreeNode< NODETYPE > *ptr ) const
101  {
102     if ( ptr != 0 ) {
103        inOrderHelper( ptr->leftPtr );
104        cout << ptr->data << ' ';
105        inOrderHelper( ptr->rightPtr );
106     }
107  }
108
109  template< class NODETYPE >
110  void Tree< NODETYPE >::postOrderTraversal() const
111     { postOrderHelper( rootPtr ); }
112
113  template< class NODETYPE >
114  void Tree< NODETYPE >::postOrderHelper(
115                          TreeNode< NODETYPE > *ptr ) const
116  {
117     if ( ptr != 0 ) {
118        postOrderHelper( ptr->leftPtr );
119        postOrderHelper( ptr->rightPtr );
120        cout << ptr->data << ' ';
121     }
122  }
123
124  #endif
```

Fig. 15.16   Creating and traversing a binary tree—**tree.h** (part 3 of 3).

```
125  // Fig. 15.16: fig15_16.cpp
126  // Driver to test class Tree
127  #include <iostream>
128  #include <iomanip>
129  #include "tree.h"
130
131  using std::cout;
132  using std::cin;
133  using std::setiosflags;
134  using std::ios;
```

Fig. 15.16   Creating and traversing a binary tree—**fig15_16.cpp**.

```cpp
135  using std::setprecision;
136
137  int main()
138  {
139     Tree< int > intTree;
140     int intVal, i;
141
142     cout << "Enter 10 integer values:\n";
143     for ( i = 0; i < 10; i++ ) {
144        cin >> intVal;
145        intTree.insertNode( intVal );
146     }
147
148     cout << "\nPreorder traversal\n";
149     intTree.preOrderTraversal();
150
151     cout << "\nInorder traversal\n";
152     intTree.inOrderTraversal();
153
154     cout << "\nPostorder traversal\n";
155     intTree.postOrderTraversal();
156
157     Tree< double > doubleTree;
158     double doubleVal;
159
160     cout << "\n\n\nEnter 10 double values:\n"
161          << setiosflags( ios::fixed | ios::showpoint )
162          << setprecision( 1 );
163     for ( i = 0; i < 10; i++ ) {
164        cin >> doubleVal;
165        doubleTree.insertNode( doubleVal );
166     }
167
168     cout << "\nPreorder traversal\n";
169     doubleTree.preOrderTraversal();
170
171     cout << "\nInorder traversal\n";
172     doubleTree.inOrderTraversal();
173
174     cout << "\nPostorder traversal\n";
175     doubleTree.postOrderTraversal();
176
177     return 0;
178  }
```

Fig. 15.16 Creating and traversing a binary tree—**fig15_16.cpp**.

Function **main** begins by instantiating integer tree **intTree** of type **Tree<int>**. The program prompts for 10 integers, each of which is inserted in the binary tree through a call to **insertNode**. The program then performs preorder, inorder and postorder traversals (these are explained shortly) of **intTree**. The program then instantiates floating-point tree **doubleTree** of type **Tree<double>**. The program prompts for 10 **double** values, each of which is inserted in the binary tree through a call to **insertNode**. The program then performs preorder, inorder and postorder traversals of **doubleTree**.

```
Enter 10 integer values:
50 25 75 12 33 67 88 6 13 68

Preorder traversal
50 25 12 6 13 33 75 67 68 88
Inorder traversal
6 12 13 25 33 50 67 68 75 88
Postorder traversal
6 13 12 33 25 68 67 88 75 50


Enter 10 double values:
39.2 16.5 82.7 3.3 65.2 90.8 1.1 4.4 89.5 92.5

Preorder traversal
39.2 16.5 3.3 1.1 4.4 82.7 65.2 90.8 89.5 92.5
Inorder traversal
1.1 3.3 4.4 16.5 39.2 65.2 82.7 89.5 90.8 92.5
Postorder traversal
1.1 4.4 3.3 16.5 65.2 89.5 92.5 90.8 82.7 39.2
```

Fig. 15.17 Sample output from the program of Fig. 15.16.

Now we discuss the class template definitions. We begin with the **TreeNode** class template that declares as its friend the **Tree** class template. Class **TreeNode** has as **private** data the node's **data** value, and pointers **leftPtr** (to the node's left subtree) and **rightPtr** (to the node's right subtree). The constructor sets **data** to the value supplied as a constructor argument, and sets pointers **leftPtr** and **rightPtr** to zero (thus initializing this node to be a leaf node). Member function **getData** returns the **data** value.

The **Tree** class has as **private** data **rootPtr**, a pointer to the root node of the tree. The class has public member functions **insertNode** (that inserts a new node in the tree,) and **preorderTraversal**, **inorderTraversal** and **postorderTraversal**, each of which walks the tree in the designated manner. Each of these member functions calls its own separate recursive utility function to perform the appropriate operations on the internal representation of the tree. The **Tree** constructor initializes **rootPtr** to zero to indicate that the tree is initially empty.

The **Tree** class' utility function **insertNodeHelper** recursively inserts a node into the tree. *A node can only be inserted as a leaf node in a binary search tree.* If the tree is empty, a new **TreeNode** is created, initialized and inserted in the tree.

If the tree is not empty, the program compares the value to be inserted with the **data** value in the root node. If the insert value is smaller, the program recursively calls **insertNodeHelper** to insert the value in the left subtree. If the insert value is larger, the program recursively calls **insertNodeHelper** to insert the value in the right subtree. If the value to be inserted is identical to the data value in the root node, the program prints the message **" dup"** and returns without inserting the duplicate value into the tree.

Each of the member functions **inOrderTraversal**, **preOrderTraversal** and **postOrderTraversal** traverse the tree (Fig. 15.18) and print the node values.

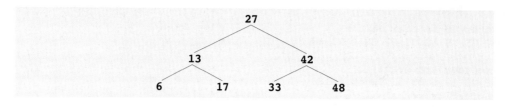

Fig. 15.18 A binary search tree.

The steps for an **inOrderTraversal** are:

1. Traverse the left subtree with an **inOrderTraversal**.
2. Process the value in the node (i.e., print the node value).
3. Traverse the right subtree with an **inOrderTraversal**.

The value in a node is not processed until the values in its left subtree are processed. The **inOrderTraversal** of the tree in Fig. 15.18 is:

   6 13 17 27 33 42 48

Note that the **inOrderTraversal** of a binary search tree prints the node values in ascending order. The process of creating a binary search tree actually sorts the data—and thus this process is called the *binary tree sort*.

The steps for a **preOrderTraversal** are:

1. Process the value in the node.
2. Traverse the left subtree with a **preOrderTraversal**.
3. Traverse the right subtree with a **preOrderTraversal**.

The value in each node is processed as the node is visited. After the value in a given node is processed, the values in the left subtree are processed, and then the values in the right subtree are processed. The **preOrderTraversal** of the tree in Fig. 15.18 is:

   27 13 6 17 42 33 48

The steps for a **postOrderTraversal** are:

1. Traverse the left subtree with a **postOrderTraversal**.
2. Traverse the right subtree with a **postOrderTraversal**.
3. Process the value in the node.

The value in each node is not printed until the values of its children are printed. The **postOrderTraversal** of the tree in Fig. 15.18 is:

   6 17 13 33 48 42 27

The binary search tree facilitates *duplicate elimination*. As the tree is being created, an attempt to insert a duplicate value will be recognized because a duplicate will follow the same "go left" or "go right" decisions on each comparison as the original value did. Thus, the duplicate will eventually be compared with a node containing the same value. The duplicate value may be discarded at this point.

Searching a binary tree for a value that matches a key value is also fast. If the tree is balanced, then each level contains about twice as many elements as the previous level. So a binary search tree with n elements would have a maximum of $\log_2 n$ levels, and thus a maximum of $\log_2 n$ comparisons would have to be made either to find a match or to determine that no match exists. This means, for example, that when searching a (balanced) 1000-element binary search tree, no more than 10 comparisons need to be made because $2^{10} >$ 1000. When searching a (balanced) 1,000,000-element binary search tree, no more than 20 comparisons need to be made because $2^{20} > 1,000,000$.

In the exercises, algorithms are presented for several other binary tree operations such as deleting an item from a binary tree, printing a binary tree in a two-dimensional tree format and performing a level-order traversal of a binary tree. The level-order traversal of a binary tree visits the nodes of the tree row by row, starting at the root node level. On each level of the tree, the nodes are visited from left to right. Other binary tree exercises include allowing a binary search tree to contain duplicate values, inserting string values in a binary tree and determining how many levels are contained in a binary tree.

SUMMARY

- Self-referential classes contain members called links that point to objects of the same class type.
- Self-referential classes enable many objects to be linked together in stacks, queues lists and trees.
- Dynamic memory allocation reserves a block of bytes in memory to store an object during program execution.
- A linked list is a linear collection of self-referential class objects.
- A linked list is a dynamic data structure—the length of the list increases or decreases as necessary.
- Linked lists can continue to grow until memory is exhausted.
- Linked lists provide a mechanism for insertion and deletion of data by pointer manipulation.
- A singly linked list begins with a pointer to the first node, and each node contains a pointer to the next node "in sequence." This list terminates with a node whose pointer member is 0. A singly linked list may be traversed in only one direction.
- A circular, singly linked list begins with a pointer to the first node, and each node contains a pointer to the next node. The pointer in the last node points to the first node, thus closing the "circle."
- A doubly linked list allows traversals both forwards and backwards. Each node has both a forward pointer to the next node in the list in the forward direction, and a backward pointer to the next node in the list in the backward direction.
- In a circular, doubly linked list, the forward pointer of the last node points to the first node, and the backward pointer of the first node points to the last node, thus closing the "circle."
- Stacks and queues are constrained versions of linked lists.
- New stack nodes are added to a stack and are removed from a stack only at the top of the stack. For this reason, a stack is referred to as a last-in, first-out (LIFO) data structure.
- The link member in the last node of the stack is set to null (zero) to indicate the bottom of the stack.
- The two primary operations used to manipulate a stack are **push** and **pop**. The **push** operation creates a new node and places it on the top of the stack. The **pop** operation removes a node from the top of the stack, deletes the memory that was allocated to that node and returns the popped value.
- In a queue data structure, nodes are removed from the head and added to the tail. For this reason, a queue is referred to as a first-in, first-out (FIFO) data structure. The add and remove operations are known as **enqueue** and **dequeue**.

- Trees are two-dimensional data structures requiring two or more links per node.
- Binary trees contain two links per node.
- The root node is the first node in the tree.
- Each of the pointers in the root node refers to a child. The left child is the first node in the left subtree, and the right child is the first node in the right subtree. The children of a node are called siblings. Any tree node that does not have any children is called a leaf node.
- A binary search tree has the characteristic that the value in the left child of a node is less than the value in its parent node, and the value in the right child of a node is greater than or equal to the value in its parent node. If there are no duplicate data values, the value in the right child is greater than the value in its parent node.
- An inorder traversal of a binary tree traverses the left subtree inorder, processes the value in the root node and then traverses the right subtree inorder. The value in a node is not processed until the values in its left subtree are processed.
- A preorder traversal processes the value in the root node, traverses the left subtree preorder and then traverses the right subtree preorder. The value in each node is processed as the node is encountered.
- A postorder traversal traverses the left subtree postorder, traverses the right subtree postorder then processes the value in the root node. The value in each node is not processed until the values in both its subtrees are processed.

TERMINOLOGY

binary search tree
binary tree
binary tree sort
child node
children
circular, doubly linked list
circular, singly linked list
deleting a node
dequeue
double indirection
doubly linked list
duplicate elimination
dynamic data structures
dynamic memory allocation
enqueue
FIFO (first-in, first-out)
head of a queue
inorder traversal of a binary tree
inserting a node
leaf node
left child
left subtree
level-order traversal of a binary tree
LIFO (last-in, first-out)
linear data structure
linked list

node
nonlinear data structure
null pointer
parent node
pointer to a pointer
pop
postorder traversal of a binary tree
predicate function
preorder traversal of a binary tree
push
queue
right child
right subtree
root node
self-referential structure
siblings
singly linked list
sizeof
stack
subtree
tail of a queue
top
traversal
tree
visit a node

15.2   It is possible to insert a node anywhere in a linked list and remove a node from anywhere in a linked list. Nodes in a stack may only be inserted at the top of the stack and removed from the top of a stack.

15.3   A queue has pointers to both its head and its tail so that nodes may be inserted at the tail and deleted from the head. A stack has a single pointer to the top of the stack, where both insertion and deletion of nodes are performed.

15.4   a) Classes allow us to instantiate as many data structure objects of a certain type (i.e., class) as we wish.

   b) Class templates enable us to instantiate related classes—each based on different type parameters—we can then generate as many objects of each template class as we like.

   c) Inheritance enables us to reuse code from a base class in a derived class so that the derived-class data structure is also a base-class data structure (with public inheritance, that is).

   d) Private inheritance enables us to reuse portions of the code from a base class to form a derived-class data structure; because the inheritance is **private**, all **public** base-class member functions become **private** in the derived class. This enables us to prevent clients of the derived-class data structure from accessing base-class member functions that do not apply to the derived class.

   e) Composition enables us to reuse code by making a class object data structure a member of a composed class; if we make the class object a **private** member of the composed class, then the class object's **public** member functions are not available through the composed object's interface.

15.5   The inorder traversal is:

   11 18 19 28 32 40 44 49 69 71 72 83 92 97 99

The preorder traversal is:

   49 28 18 11 19 40 32 44 83 71 69 72 97 92 99

The postorder traversal is:

   11 19 18 32 44 40 28 69 72 71 92 99 97 83 49

EXERCISES

15.6   Write a program that concatenates two linked list objects of characters. The program should include function **concatenate**, which takes references to both list objects as arguments and concatenates the second list to the first list.

15.7   Write a program that merges two ordered list objects of integers into a single ordered list object of integers. Function **merge** should receive references to each of the list objects to be merged, and should return an object containing the merged list.

15.8   Write a program that inserts 25 random integers from 0 to 100 in order in a linked list object. The program should calculate the sum of the elements and the floating-point average of the elements.

15.9   Write a program that creates a linked list object of 10 characters and then creates a second list object containing a copy of the first list, but in reverse order.

15.10   Write a program that inputs a line of text and uses a stack object to print the line reversed.

15.11   Write a program that uses a stack object to determine if a string is a palindrome (i.e., the string is spelled identically backwards and forwards). The program should ignore spaces and punctuation.

15.12 Stacks are used by compilers to help in the process of evaluating expressions and generating machine language code. In this and the next exercise, we investigate how compilers evaluate arithmetic expressions consisting only of constants, operators and parentheses.

Humans generally write expressions like **3 + 4** and **7 / 9** in which the operator (**+** or **/** here) is written between its operands—this is called *infix notation*. Computers "prefer" *postfix notation* in which the operator is written to the right of its two operands. The preceding infix expressions would appear in postfix notation as **3 4 +** and **7 9 /**, respectively.

To evaluate a complex infix expression, a compiler would first convert the expression to postfix notation and then evaluate the postfix version of the expression. Each of these algorithms requires only a single left-to-right pass of the expression. Each algorithm uses a stack object in support of its operation, and in each algorithm the stack is used for a different purpose.

In this exercise, you will write a C++ version of the infix-to-postfix conversion algorithm. In the next exercise, you will write a C++ version of the postfix expression evaluation algorithm. Later in the chapter, you will discover that code you write in this exercise can help you implement a complete working compiler.

Write a program that converts an ordinary infix arithmetic expression (assume a valid expression is entered) with single-digit integers such as

(6 + 2) * 5 - 8 / 4

to a postfix expression. The postfix version of the preceding infix expression is

6 2 + 5 * 8 4 / -

The program should read the expression into character array **infix**, and use modified versions of the stack functions implemented in this chapter to help create the postfix expression in character array **postfix**. The algorithm for creating a postfix expression is as follows:

1) Push a left parenthesis ' **(** ' onto the stack.
2) Append a right parenthesis ' **)** ' to the end of **infix**.
3) While the stack is not empty, read **infix** from left to right and do the following:

      If the current character in **infix** is a digit, copy it to the next element of **postfix**.

      If the current character in **infix** is a left parenthesis, push it onto the stack.

      If the current character in **infix** is an operator,

            Pop operators (if there are any) at the top of the stack while they have equal or higher precedence than the current operator, and insert the popped operators in **postfix**.

      Push the current character in **infix** onto the stack.

      If the current character in **infix** is a right parenthesis

            Pop operators from the top of the stack and insert them in **postfix** until a left parenthesis is at the top of the stack.

      Pop (and discard) the left parenthesis from the stack.

The following arithmetic operations are allowed in an expression:

    +   addition
    –   subtraction
    *   multiplication
    /   division
    ^   exponentiation
    %   modulus

The stack should be maintained with stack nodes that each contain a data member and a pointer to the next stack node.

Some of the functional capabilities you may want to provide are:

a) Function **convertToPostfix** that converts the infix expression to postfix notation.

b) Function **isOperator** that determines if **c** is an operator.

c) Function **precedence** that determines if the precedence of **operator1** is less than, equal to or greater than the precedence of **operator2**. The function returns -1, 0 and 1, respectively.

d) Function **push** that pushes a value onto the stack.

e) Function **pop** that pops a value off the stack.

f) Function **stackTop** that returns the top value of the stack without popping the stack.

g) Function **isEmpty** that determines if the stack is empty.

h) Function **printStack** that prints the stack.

15.13   Write a program that evaluates a postfix expression (assume it is valid) such as

6 2 + 5 * 8 4 / –

The program should read a postfix expression consisting of digits and operators into a character array. Using modified versions of the stack functions implemented earlier in this chapter, the program should scan the expression and evaluate it. The algorithm is as follows:

1) Append the null character (**'\0'**) to the end of the postfix expression. When the null character is encountered, no further processing is necessary.

2) While **'\0'** has not been encountered, read the expression from left to right.

> If the current character is a digit,

>> Push its integer value onto the stack (the integer value of a digit character is its value in the computer's character set minus the value of **'0'** in the computer's character set).

> Otherwise, if the current character is an *operator*,

>> Pop the two top elements of the stack into variables **x** and **y**.

>> Calculate **y** *operator* **x**.

>> Push the result of the calculation onto the stack.

3) When the null character is encountered in the expression, pop the top value of the stack. This is the result of the postfix expression.

Note: In step 2) above, if the operator is **'/'**, the top of the stack is **2** and the next element in the stack is **8**, then pop **2** into **x**, pop **8** into **y**, evaluate **8 / 2** and push the result, **4**, back onto the stack. This note also applies to operator **'–'**. The arithmetic operations allowed in an expression are:

+ addition

– subtraction

* multiplication

/ division

^ exponentiation

% modulus

The stack should be maintained with stack nodes that contain an **int** data member and a pointer to the next stack node. You may want to provide the following functional capabilities:

a) Function **evaluatePostfixExpression** that evaluates the postfix expression.

b) Function **calculate** that evaluates the expression **op1 operator op2**.

c) Function **push** that pushes a value onto the stack.

d) Function **pop** that pops a value off the stack.

e) Function **isEmpty** that determines if the stack is empty.

f) Function **printStack** that prints the stack.

15.14   Modify the postfix evaluator program of Exercise 15.13 so that it can process integer operands larger than 9.

15.15 *(Supermarket simulation)* Write a program that simulates a checkout line at a supermarket. The line is a queue object. Customers (i.e., customer objects) arrive in random integer intervals of 1 to 4 minutes. Also, each customer is served in random integer intervals of 1 to 4 minutes. Obviously, the rates need to be balanced. If the average arrival rate is larger than the average service rate, the queue will grow infinitely. Even with "balanced" rates, randomness can still cause long lines. Run the supermarket simulation for a 12-hour day (720 minutes) using the following algorithm:

1) Choose a random integer between 1 and 4 to determine the minute at which the first customer arrives.

2) At the first customer's arrival time:
   Determine customer's service time (random integer from 1 to 4);
   Begin servicing the customer;
   Schedule arrival time of next customer (random integer 1 to 4 added to the current time).

3) For each minute of the day:
   If the next customer arrives,
       Say so,
       Enqueue the customer;
       Schedule the arrival time of the next customer;
   If service was completed for the last customer;
       Say so
       Dequeue next customer to be serviced
       Determine customer's service completion time
           (random integer from 1 to 4 added to the current time).

Now run your simulation for 720 minutes and answer each of the following:

a) What is the maximum number of customers in the queue at any time?

b) What is the longest wait any one customer experiences?

c) What happens if the arrival interval is changed from 1-to-4 minutes to 1-to-3 minutes?

15.16 Modify the program of Fig. 15.16 to allow the binary tree object to contain duplicates.

15.17 Write a program based on Fig. 15.16 that inputs a line of text, tokenizes the sentence into separate words (you may want to use the **strtok** library function), inserts the words in a binary search tree and prints the inorder, preorder and postorder traversals of the tree. Use an OOP approach.

15.18 In this chapter, we saw that duplicate elimination is straightforward when creating a binary search tree. Describe how you would perform duplicate elimination using only a single-subscripted array. Compare the performance of array-based duplicate elimination with the performance of binary-search-tree-based duplicate elimination.

15.19 Write a function **depth** that receives a binary tree and determines how many levels it has.

15.20 *(Recursively print a list backwards)* Write a member function **printListBackwards** that recursively outputs the items in a linked list object in reverse order. Write a test program that creates a sorted list of integers and prints the list in reverse order.

15.21 *(Recursively search a list)* Write a member function **searchList** that recursively searches a linked list object for a specified value. The function should return a pointer to the value if it is found; otherwise, null should be returned. Use your function in a test program that creates a list of integers. The program should prompt the user for a value to locate in the list.

15.22 *(Binary tree delete)* In this exercise, we discuss deleting items from binary search trees. The deletion algorithm is not as straightforward as the insertion algorithm. There are three cases that are encountered when deleting an item—the item is contained in a leaf node (i.e., it has no children), the item is contained in a node that has one child or the item is contained in a node that has two children.

If the item to be deleted is contained in a leaf node, the node is deleted and the pointer in the parent node is set to null.

If the item to be deleted is contained in a node with one child, the pointer in the parent node is set to point to the child node and the node containing the data item is deleted. This causes the child node to take the place of the deleted node in the tree.

The last case is the most difficult. When a node with two children is deleted, another node in the tree must take its place. However, the pointer in the parent node cannot be assigned to point to one of the children of the node to be deleted. In most cases, the resulting binary search tree would not adhere to the following characteristic of binary search trees (with no duplicate values): *The values in any left subtree are less than the value in the parent node, and the values in any right subtree are greater than the value in the parent node.*

Which node is used as a *replacement node* to maintain this characteristic? Either the node containing the largest value in the tree less than the value in the node being deleted, or the node containing the smallest value in the tree greater than the value in the node being deleted. Let us consider the node with the smaller value. In a binary search tree, the largest value less than a parent's value is located in the left subtree of the parent node and is guaranteed to be contained in the rightmost node of the subtree. This node is located by walking down the left subtree to the right until the pointer to the right child of the current node is null. We are now pointing to the replacement node, which is either a leaf node or a node with one child to its left. If the replacement node is a leaf node, the steps to perform the deletion are as follows:

1) Store the pointer to the node to be deleted in a temporary pointer variable (this pointer is used to delete the dynamically allocated memory)
2) Set the pointer in the parent of the node being deleted to point to the replacement node
3) Set the pointer in the parent of the replacement node to null
4) Set the pointer to the right subtree in the replacement node to point to the right subtree of the node to be deleted
5) Delete the node to which the temporary pointer variable points.

The deletion steps for a replacement node with a left child are similar to those for a replacement node with no children, but the algorithm also must move the child in to the replacement node's position in the tree. If the replacement node is a node with a left child, the steps to perform the deletion are as follows:

1) Store the pointer to the node to be deleted in a temporary pointer variable
2) Set the pointer in the parent of the node being deleted to point to the replacement node
3) Set the pointer in the parent of the replacement node to point to the left child of the replacement node
4) Set the pointer to the right subtree in the replacement node to point to the right subtree of the node to be deleted
5) Delete the node to which the temporary pointer variable points.

Write member function **deleteNode**, which takes as its arguments a pointer to the root node of the tree object and the value to be deleted. The function should locate in the tree the node containing the value to be deleted and use the algorithms discussed here to delete the node. If the value is not found in the tree, the function should print a message that indicates whether or not the value is deleted. Modify the program of Fig. 15.16 to use this function. After deleting an item, call the **inOrder**, **preOrder** and **postOrder** traversal functions to confirm that the delete operation was performed correctly.

15.23 (*Binary tree search*) Write member function **binaryTreeSearch**, which attempts to locate a specified value in a binary search tree object. The function should take as arguments a pointer to the root node of the binary tree and a search key to be located. If the node containing the search key is found, the function should return a pointer to that node; otherwise, the function should return a null pointer.

15.24 (*Level-order binary tree traversal*) The program of Fig. 15.16 illustrated three recursive methods of traversing a binary tree—inorder, preorder and postorder traversals. This exercise presents the *level-order traversal* of a binary tree in which the node values are printed level by level, starting at the root node level. The nodes on each level are printed from left to right. The level-order traversal is not a recursive algorithm. It uses a queue object to control the output of the nodes. The algorithm is as follows:

    1) Insert the root node in the queue
    2) While there are nodes left in the queue,

            Get the next node in the queue
            Print the node's value
            If the pointer to the left child of the node is not null
                  Insert the left child node in the queue
            If the pointer to the right child of the node is not null
                  Insert the right child node in the queue.

Write member function **levelOrder** to perform a level-order traversal of a binary tree object. Modify the program of Fig 15.16 to use this function. (Note: You will also need to modify and incorporate the queue-processing functions of Fig. 15.12 in this program.)

15.25 (*Printing trees*) Write a recursive member function **outputTree** to display a binary tree object on the screen. The function should output the tree row by row, with the top of the tree at the left of the screen and the bottom of the tree toward the right of the screen. Each row is output vertically. For example, the binary tree illustrated in Fig. 15.19 is output as follows:

Note that the rightmost leaf node appears at the top of the output in the rightmost column and the root node appears at the left of the output. Each column of output starts five spaces to the right of the previous column. Function **outputTree** should receive an argument **totalSpaces** representing the number of spaces preceding the value to be output (this variable should start at zero so the root node is output at the left of the screen). The function uses a modified inorder traversal to output the tree—it starts at the rightmost node in the tree and works back to the left. The algorithm is as follows:

      While the pointer to the current node is not null

            Recursively call **outputTree** with the right subtree of the current node and
                totalSpaces + 5
            Use a **for** structure to count from 1 to **totalSpaces** and output spaces
            Output the value in the current node
            Set the pointer to the current node to point to the left subtree of the current node
            Increment **totalSpaces** by 5.

SPECIAL SECTION—BUILDING YOUR OWN COMPILER

In Exercises 5.18 and 5.19, we introduced Simpletron Machine Language (SML) and you implemented a Simpletron computer simulator to execute programs written in SML. In this section, we build a compiler that converts programs written in a high-level programming language to SML. This section "ties" together the entire programming process. You will write programs in this new high-level language, compile these programs on the compiler you build and run the programs on the simulator you built in Exercise 7.19. You should make every effort to implement your compiler in an object-oriented manner.

15.26 (*The Simple Language*) Before we begin building the compiler, we discuss a simple, yet powerful, high-level language similar to early versions of the popular language BASIC. We call the language *Simple*. Every Simple *statement* consists of a *line number* and a Simple *instruction*. Line numbers must appear in ascending order. Each instruction begins with one of the following Simple *commands*: **rem**, **input**, **let**, **print**, **goto**, **if/goto** and **end** (see Fig. 15.20). All commands except **end** can be used repeatedly. Simple evaluates only integer expressions using the **+**, **-**, ***** and **/** operators. These operators have the same precedence as in C. Parentheses can be used to change the order of evaluation of an expression.

Our Simple compiler recognizes only lowercase letters. All characters in a Simple file should be lowercase (uppercase letters result in a syntax error unless they appear in a **rem** statement, in which case they are ignored). A *variable name* is a single letter. Simple does not allow descriptive variable names, so variables should be explained in remarks to indicate their use in a program. Simple uses only integer variables. Simple does not have variable declarations—merely mentioning a variable name in a program causes the variable to be declared and initialized to zero automatically. The syntax of Simple does not allow string manipulation (reading a string, writing a string, comparing strings, etc.). If a string is encountered in a Simple program (after a command other than **rem**), the compiler generates a syntax error. The first version of our compiler will assume that Simple programs are entered correctly. Exercise 15.29 asks the student to modify the compiler to perform syntax error checking.

Command	Example statement	Description
rem	50 rem this is a remark	Text following **rem** is for documentation purposes and is ignored by the compiler.
input	30 input x	Display a question mark to prompt the user to enter an integer. Read that integer from the keyboard and store the integer in **x**.
let	80 let u = 4 * (j - 56)	Assign **u** the value of **4 * (j - 56)**. Note that an arbitrarily complex expression can appear to the right of the equals sign.
print	10 print w	Display the value of **w**.
goto	70 goto 45	Transfer program control to line **45**.
if/goto	35 if i == z goto 80	Compare **i** and **z** for equality and transfer control to line **80** if the condition is true; otherwise, continue execution with the next statement.
end	99 end	Terminate program execution.

Fig. 15.20   Simple commands.

Simple uses the conditional **if/goto** statement and the unconditional **goto** statement to alter the flow of control during program execution. If the condition in the **if/goto** statement is true, control is transferred to a specific line of the program. The following relational and equality operators are valid in an **if/goto** statement: <, >, <=, >=, == and !=. The precedence of these operators is the same as in C++.

Let us now consider several programs that demonstrate Simple's features. The first program (Fig. 15.21) reads two integers from the keyboard, stores the values in variables **a** and **b** and computes and prints their sum (stored in variable **c**).

The program of Fig. 15.22 determines and prints the larger of two integers. The integers are input from the keyboard and stored in **s** and **t**. The **if/goto** statement tests the condition **s >= t**. If the condition is true, control is transferred to line **90** and **s** is output; otherwise, **t** is output and control is transferred to the **end** statement in line **99** where the program terminates.

Simple does not provide a repetition structure (such as C++'s **for**, **while** or **do/while**). However, Simple can simulate each of C++'s repetition structures using the **if/goto** and **goto** statements. Figure 15.23 uses a sentinel-controlled loop to calculate the squares of several integers. Each integer is input from the keyboard and stored in variable **j**. If the value entered is the sentinel **-9999**, control is transferred to line **99**, where the program terminates. Otherwise, **k** is assigned the square of **j**, **k** is output to the screen and control is passed to line **20**, where the next integer is input.

```
1    10 rem     determine and print the sum of two integers
2    15 rem
3    20 rem     input the two integers
4    30 input a
5    40 input b
6    45 rem
7    50 rem     add integers and store result in c
8    60 let c = a + b
9    65 rem
10   70 rem     print the result
11   80 print c
12   90 rem     terminate program execution
13   99 end
```

Fig. 15.21   Simple program that determines the sum of two integers .

```
1    10 rem     determine the larger of two integers
2    20 input s
3    30 input t
4    32 rem
5    35 rem     test if s >= t
6    40 if s >= t goto 90
7    45 rem
8    50 rem     t is greater than s, so print t
9    60 print t
10   70 goto 99
11   75 rem
12   80 rem     s is greater than or equal to t, so print s
13   90 print s
14   99 end
```

Fig. 15.22   Simple program that finds the larger of two integers .

```
1   10 rem    calculate the squares of several integers
2   20 input j
3   23 rem
4   25 rem    test for sentinel value
5   30 if j == -9999 goto 99
6   33 rem
7   35 rem    calculate square of j and assign result to k
8   40 let k = j * j
9   50 print k
10  53 rem
11  55 rem    loop to get next j
12  60 goto 20
13  99 end
```

Fig. 15.23 Calculate the squares of several integers .

Using the sample programs of Fig. 15.21, Fig. 15.22 and Fig. 15.23 as your guide, write a Simple program to accomplish each of the following:

a) Input three integers, determine their average and print the result.

b) Use a sentinel-controlled loop to input 10 integers and compute and print their sum.

c) Use a counter-controlled loop to input 7 integers, some positive and some negative, and compute and print their average.

d) Input a series of integers and determine and print the largest. The first integer input indicates how many numbers should be processed.

e) Input 10 integers and print the smallest.

f) Calculate and print the sum of the even integers from 2 to 30.

g) Calculate and print the product of the odd integers from 1 to 9.

15.27 (*Building A Compiler; Prerequisite: Complete Exercises 5.18, 5.19, 15.12, 15.13 and 15.26*) Now that the Simple language has been presented (Exercise 15.26), we discuss how to build a Simple compiler. First, we consider the process by which a Simple program is converted to SML and executed by the Simpletron simulator (see Fig. 15.24). A file containing a Simple program is read by the compiler and converted to SML code. The SML code is output to a file on disk, in which SML instructions appear one per line. The SML file is then loaded into the Simpletron simulator, and the results are sent to a file on disk and to the screen. Note that the Simpletron program developed in Exercise 5.19 took its input from the keyboard. It must be modified to read from a file so it can run the programs produced by our compiler.

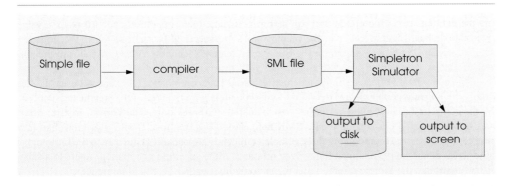

Fig. 15.24 Writing, compiling and executing a Simple language program.

The Simple compiler performs two *passes* of the Simple program to convert it to SML. The first pass constructs a *symbol table* (object) in which every *line number* (object), *variable name* (object) and *constant* (object) of the Simple program is stored with its type and corresponding location in the final SML code (the symbol table is discussed in detail below). The first pass also produces the corresponding SML instruction object(s) for each of the Simple statements (object, etc.). As we will see, if the Simple program contains statements that transfer control to a line later in the program, the first pass results in an SML program containing some "unfinished" instructions. The second pass of the compiler locates and completes the unfinished instructions, and outputs the SML program to a file.

First Pass

The compiler begins by reading one statement of the Simple program into memory. The line must be separated into its individual *tokens* (i.e., "pieces" of a statement) for processing and compilation (standard library function **strtok** can be used to facilitate this task). Recall that every statement begins with a line number followed by a command. As the compiler breaks a statement into tokens, if the token is a line number, a variable or a constant, it is placed in the symbol table. A line number is placed in the symbol table only if it is the first token in a statement. The **symbolTable** object is an array of **tableEntry** objects representing each symbol in the program. There is no restriction on the number of symbols that can appear in the program. Therefore, the **symbolTable** for a particular program could be large. Make the **symbolTable** a 100-element array for now. You can increase or decrease its size once the program is working.

Each **tableEntry** object contains three members. Member **symbol** is an integer containing the ASCII representation of a variable (remember that variable names are single characters), a line number or a constant. Member **type** is one of the following characters indicating the symbol's type: **'C'** for constant, **'L'** for line number and **'V'** for variable. Member **location** contains the Simpletron memory location (**00** to **99**) to which the symbol refers. Simpletron memory is an array of 100 integers in which SML instructions and data are stored. For a line number, the location is the element in the Simpletron memory array at which the SML instructions for the Simple statement begin. For a variable or constant, the location is the element in the Simpletron memory array in which the variable or constant is stored. Variables and constants are allocated from the end of Simpletron's memory backwards. The first variable or constant is stored in location at **99**, the next in location at **98**, etc.

The symbol table plays an integral part in converting Simple programs to SML. We learned in Chapter 5 that an SML instruction is a four-digit integer composed of two parts—the *operation code* and the *operand*. The operation code is determined by commands in Simple. For example, the simple command **input** corresponds to SML operation code **10** (read), and the Simple command **print** corresponds to SML operation code **11** (write). The operand is a memory location containing the data on which the operation code performs its task (e.g., operation code **10** reads a value from the keyboard and stores it in the memory location specified by the operand). The compiler searches **symbolTable** to determine the Simpletron memory location for each symbol so the corresponding location can be used to complete the SML instructions.

The compilation of each Simple statement is based on its command. For example, after the line number in a **rem** statement is inserted in the symbol table, the remainder of the statement is ignored by the compiler because a remark is for documentation purposes only. The **input**, **print**, **goto** and **end** statements correspond to the SML *read*, *write*, *branch* (to a specific location) and *halt* instructions. Statements containing these Simple commands are converted directly to SML (note that a **goto** statement may contain an unresolved reference if the specified line number refers to a statement further into the Simple program file; this is sometimes called a *forward reference*).

When a **goto** statement is compiled with an unresolved reference, the SML instruction must be *flagged* to indicate that the second pass of the compiler must complete the instruction. The flags are stored in 100-element array **flags** of type **int** in which each element is initialized to **-1**. If the memory location to which a line number in the Simple program refers is not yet known (i.e., it is not in the symbol table), the line number is stored in array **flags** in the element with the same subscript as the incomplete instruction. The operand of the incomplete instruction is set to **00** temporarily. For example, an unconditional branch instruction (making a forward reference) is left as **+4000** until the second pass of the compiler. The second pass of the compiler is described shortly.

Compilation of **if/goto** and **let** statements is more complicated than other statements—they are the only statements that produce more than one SML instruction. For an **if/goto**, the compiler produces code to test the condition and to branch to another line if necessary. The result of the branch could be an unresolved reference. Each of the relational and equality operators can be simulated using SML's *branch zero* and *branch negative* instructions (or a combination of both).

For a **let** statement, the compiler produces code to evaluate an arbitrarily complex arithmetic expression consisting of integer variables and/or constants. Expressions should separate each operand and operator with spaces. Exercises 15.12 and 15.13 presented the infix-to-postfix conversion algorithm and the postfix evaluation algorithm used by compilers to evaluate expressions. Before proceeding with your compiler, you should complete each of these exercises. When a compiler encounters an expression, it converts the expression from infix notation to postfix notation and then evaluates the postfix expression.

How is it that the compiler produces the machine language to evaluate an expression containing variables? The postfix evaluation algorithm contains a "hook" where the compiler can generate SML instructions rather than actually evaluating the expression. To enable this "hook" in the compiler, the postfix evaluation algorithm must be modified to search the symbol table for each symbol it encounters (and possibly insert it), determine the symbol's corresponding memory location and *push the memory location onto the stack (instead of the symbol).* When an operator is encountered in the postfix expression, the two memory locations at the top of the stack are popped and machine language for effecting the operation is produced using the memory locations as operands. The result of each subexpression is stored in a temporary location in memory and pushed back onto the stack so the evaluation of the postfix expression can continue. When postfix evaluation is complete, the memory location containing the result is the only location left on the stack. This is popped and SML instructions are generated to assign the result to the variable at the left of the **let** statement.

Second Pass

The second pass of the compiler performs two tasks: resolve any unresolved references and output the SML code to a file. Resolution of references occurs as follows:

    a) Search the **flags** array for an unresolved reference (i.e., an element with a value other than **-1**).

    b) Locate the object in array **symbolTable**, containing the symbol stored in the **flags** array (be sure that the type of the symbol is **'L'** for line number).

    c) Insert the memory location from member **location** into the instruction with the unresolved reference (remember that an instruction containing an unresolved reference has operand **00**).

    d) Repeat steps 1, 2 and 3 until the end of the **flags** array is reached.

After the resolution process is complete, the entire array containing the SML code is output to a disk file with one SML instruction per line. This file can be read by the Simpletron for execution (after the simulator is modified to read its input from a file). Compiling your first Simple program into an SML file and then executing that file should give you a real sense of personal accomplishment.

A Complete Example

The following example illustrates a complete conversion of a Simple program to SML as it will be performed by the Simple compiler. Consider a Simple program that inputs an integer and sums the values from 1 to that integer. The program and the SML instructions produced by the first pass of the Simple compiler are illustrated in Fig. 15.25. The symbol table constructed by the first pass is shown in Fig. 15.26.

Simple program	SML location and instruction	Description
5 rem sum 1 to x	*none*	**rem** ignored
10 input x	00 +1099	read **x** into location **99**
15 rem check y == x	*none*	**rem** ignored
20 if y == x goto 60	01 +2098	load **y** (**98**) into accumulator
	02 +3199	sub **x** (**99**) from accumulator
	03 +4200	branch zero to unresolved location
25 rem increment y	*none*	**rem** ignored
30 let y = y + 1	04 +2098	load **y** into accumulator
	05 +3097	add **1** (**97**) to accumulator
	06 +2196	store in temporary location **96**
	07 +2096	load from temporary location **96**
	08 +2198	store accumulator in **y**
35 rem add y to total	*none*	**rem** ignored
40 let t = t + y	09 +2095	load **t** (**95**) into accumulator
	10 +3098	add **y** to accumulator
	11 +2194	store in temporary location **94**
	12 +2094	load from temporary location **94**
	13 +2195	store accumulator in **t**
45 rem loop y	*none*	**rem** ignored
50 goto 20	14 +4001	branch to location **01**
55 rem output result	*none*	**rem** ignored
60 print t	15 +1195	output **t** to screen
99 end	16 +4300	terminate execution

Fig. 15.25 SML instructions produced after the compiler's first pass.

Symbol	Type	Location
5	L	00
10	L	00
'x'	V	99

Fig. 15.26 Symbol table for program of Fig. 15.25 (part 1 of 2).

Symbol	Type	Location
15	L	01
20	L	01
'y'	V	98
25	L	04
30	L	04
1	C	97
35	L	09
40	L	09
't'	V	95
45	L	14
50	L	14
55	L	15
60	L	15
99	L	16

Fig. 15.26 Symbol table for program of Fig. 15.25 (part 2 of 2).

Most Simple statements convert directly to single SML instructions. The exceptions in this program are remarks, the **if/goto** statement in line **20** and the **let** statements. Remarks do not translate into machine language. However, the line number for a remark is placed in the symbol table in case the line number is referenced in a **goto** statement or an **if/goto** statement. Line **20** of the program specifies that if the condition **y == x** is true, program control is transferred to line **60**. Because line **60** appears later in the program, the first pass of the compiler has not as yet placed **60** in the symbol table (statement line numbers are placed in the symbol table only when they appear as the first token in a statement). Therefore, it is not possible at this time to determine the operand of the SML *branch zero* instruction at location **03** in the array of SML instructions. The compiler places **60** in location **03** of the **flags** array to indicate that the second pass completes this instruction.

We must keep track of the next instruction location in the SML array because there is not a one-to-one correspondence between Simple statements and SML instructions. For example, the **if/goto** statement of line **20** compiles into three SML instructions. Each time an instruction is produced, we must increment the *instruction counter* to the next location in the SML array. Note that the size of Simpletron's memory could present a problem for Simple programs with many statements, variables and constants. It is conceivable that the compiler will run out of memory. To test for this case, your program should contain a *data counter* to keep track of the location at which the next variable or constant will be stored in the SML array. If the value of the instruction counter is larger than the value of the data counter, the SML array is full. In this case, the compilation process should terminate and the compiler should print an error message indicating that it ran out of memory during compilation. This serves to emphasize that although the programmer is freed from the burdens of managing memory by the compiler, the compiler itself must carefully determine the placement of instructions and data in memory, and must check for such errors as memory being exhausted during the compilation process.

A Step-by-Step View of the Compilation Process

Let us now walk through the compilation process for the Simple program in Fig. 15.25. The compiler reads the first line of the program

5 rem sum 1 to x

into memory. The first token in the statement (the line number) is determined using **strtok** (see Chapters 5 and 16 for a discussion of C++'s string manipulation functions). The token returned by **strtok** is converted to an integer using **atoi** so the symbol **5** can be located in the symbol table. If the symbol is not found, it is inserted in the symbol table. Since we are at the beginning of the program and this is the first line, no symbols are in the table yet. So, **5** is inserted into the symbol table as type **L** (line number) and assigned the first location in SML array (**00**). Although this line is a remark, a space in the symbol table is still allocated for the line number (in case it is referenced by a **goto** or an **if/goto**). No SML instruction is generated for a **rem** statement, so the instruction counter is not incremented.

The statement

10 input x

is tokenized next. The line number **10** is placed in the symbol table as type **L** and assigned the first location in the SML array (**00** because a remark began the program so the instruction counter is currently **00**). The command **input** indicates that the next token is a variable (only a variable can appear in an **input** statement). Because **input** corresponds directly to an SML operation code, the compiler has to determine the location of **x** in the SML array. Symbol **x** is not found in the symbol table. So, it is inserted into the symbol table as the ASCII representation of **x**, given type **V**, and assigned location **99** in the SML array (data storage begins at **99** and is allocated backwards). SML code can now be generated for this statement. Operation code **10** (the SML read operation code) is multiplied by 100, and the location of **x** (as determined in the symbol table) is added to complete the instruction. The instruction is then stored in the SML array at location **00**. The instruction counter is incremented by 1 because a single SML instruction was produced.

The statement

15 rem   check y == x

is tokenized next. The symbol table is searched for line number **15** (which is not found). The line number is inserted as type **L** and assigned the next location in the array, **01** (remember that **rem** statements do not produce code, so the instruction counter is not incremented).

The statement

20 if y == x goto 60

is tokenized next. Line number **20** is inserted in the symbol table and given type **L** with the next location in the SML array **01**. The command **if** indicates that a condition is to be evaluated. The variable **y** is not found in the symbol table, so it is inserted and given the type **V** and the SML location **98**. Next, SML instructions are generated to evaluate the condition. Since there is no direct equivalent in SML for the **if/goto**, it must be simulated by performing a calculation using **x** and **y** and branching based on the result. If **y** is equal to **x**, the result of subtracting **x** from **y** is zero, so the *branch zero* instruction can be used with the result of the calculation to simulate the **if/goto** statement. The first step requires that **y** be loaded (from SML location **98**) into the accumulator. This produces the instruction **01 +2098**. Next, **x** is subtracted from the accumulator. This produces the instruction **02 +3199**. The value in the accumulator may be zero, positive or negative. Since the operator is **==**, we want to *branch zero*. First, the symbol table is searched for the branch location (**60** in this case), which is not found. So, **60** is placed in the **flags** array at location **03**, and the instruction **03 +4200** is generated (we cannot add the branch location, because we have not assigned a location to line **60** in the SML array yet). The instruction counter is incremented to **04**.

The compiler proceeds to the statement

> **25 rem   increment y**

The line number **25** is inserted in the symbol table as type **L** and assigned SML location **04**. The instruction counter is not incremented.

When the statement

> **30 let y = y + 1**

is tokenized, the line number **30** is inserted in the symbol table as type **L** and assigned SML location **04**. Command **let** indicates that the line is an assignment statement. First, all the symbols on the line are inserted in the symbol table (if they are not already there). The integer **1** is added to the symbol table as type **C** and assigned SML location **97**. Next, the right side of the assignment is converted from infix to postfix notation. Then the postfix expression (**y 1 +**) is evaluated. Symbol **y** is located in the symbol table and its corresponding memory location is pushed onto the stack. Symbol **1** is also located in the symbol table and its corresponding memory location is pushed onto the stack. When the operator **+** is encountered, the postfix evaluator pops the stack into the right operand of the operator, pops the stack again into the left operand of the operator and then produces the SML instructions

> **04 +2098**   *(load **y**)*
> **05 +3097**   *(add **1**)*

The result of the expression is stored in a temporary location in memory (**96**) with instruction

> **06 +2196**   *(store temporary)*

and the temporary location is pushed on the stack. Now that the expression has been evaluated, the result must be stored in **y** (i.e., the variable on the left side of **=**). So, the temporary location is loaded into the accumulator and the accumulator is stored in **y** with the instructions

> **07 +2096**   *(load temporary)*
> **08 +2198**   *(store **y**)*

The reader will immediately notice that SML instructions appear to be redundant. We will discuss this issue shortly.

When the statement

> **35 rem   add y to total**

is tokenized, line number **35** is inserted in the symbol table as type **L** and assigned location **09**.

The statement

> **40 let t = t + y**

is similar to line **30**. The variable **t** is inserted in the symbol table as type **V** and assigned SML location **95**. The instructions follow the same logic and format as line **30**, and the instructions **09 +2095, 10 +3098, 11 +2194, 12 +2094** and **13 +2195** are generated. Note that the result of **t**

+ y is assigned to temporary location **94** before being assigned to **t** (**95**). Once again, the reader will note that the instructions in memory locations **11** and **12** appear to be redundant. Again, we will discuss this shortly.

The statement

```
45 rem    loop y
```

is a remark, so line **45** is added to the symbol table as type **L** and assigned SML location **14**.

The statement

```
50 goto 20
```

transfers control to line **20**. Line number **50** is inserted in the symbol table as type **L** and assigned SML location **14**. The equivalent of **goto** in SML is the *unconditional branch* (**40**) instruction that transfers control to a specific SML location. The compiler searches the symbol table for line **20** and finds that it corresponds to SML location **01**. The operation code (**40**) is multiplied by 100, and location **01** is added to it to produce the instruction **14 +4001**.

The statement

```
55 rem    output result
```

is a remark, so line **55** is inserted in the symbol table as type **L** and assigned SML location **15**.

The statement

```
60 print t
```

is an output statement. Line number **60** is inserted in the symbol table as type **L** and assigned SML location **15**. The equivalent of **print** in SML is operation code **11** (*write*). The location of **t** is determined from the symbol table and added to the result of the operation code multiplied by 100.

The statement

```
99 end
```

is the final line of the program. Line number **99** is stored in the symbol table as type **L** and assigned SML location **16**. The **end** command produces the SML instruction **+4300** (**43** is *halt* in SML), which is written as the final instruction in the SML memory array.

This completes the first pass of the compiler. We now consider the second pass. The **flags** array is searched for values other than **−1**. Location **03** contains **60**, so the compiler knows that instruction **03** is incomplete. The compiler completes the instruction by searching the symbol table for **60**, determining its location and adding the location to the incomplete instruction. In this case, the search determines that line **60** corresponds to SML location **15**, so the completed instruction **03 +4215** is produced, replacing **03 +4200**. The Simple program has now been compiled successfully.

To build the compiler, you will have to perform each of the following tasks:

a) Modify the Simpletron simulator program you wrote in Exercise 5.19 to take its input from a file specified by the user (see Chapter 14). The simulator should output its results to a disk file in the same format as the screen output. Convert the simulator to be an object-oriented program. In particular, make each part of the hardware an object. Arrange the instruction types into a class hierarchy using inheritance. Then execute the program polymorphically by telling each instruction to execute itself with an **executeInstruction** message.

b) Modify the infix-to-postfix conversion algorithm of Exercise 15.12 to process multi-digit integer operands and single-letter variable name operands. (Hint: Standard library function **strtok** can be used to locate each constant and variable in an expression, and constants can be converted from strings to integers using standard library function **atoi**.) (Note: The data representation of the postfix expression must be altered to support variable names and integer constants.)

c) Modify the postfix evaluation algorithm to process multidigit integer operands and variable name operands. Also, the algorithm should now implement the "hook" discussed above so that SML instructions are produced rather than directly evaluating the expression. (Hint: Standard library function **strtok** can be used to locate each constant and variable in an expression, and constants can be converted from strings to integers using standard library function **atoi**.) (*Note:* The data representation of the postfix expression must be altered to support variable names and integer constants.)

d) Build the compiler. Incorporate parts (b) and (c) for evaluating expressions in **let** statements. Your program should contain a function that performs the first pass of the compiler and a function that performs the second pass of the compiler. Both functions can call other functions to accomplish their tasks. Make your compiler as object oriented as possible.

15.28 (*Optimizing the Simple Compiler*) When a program is compiled and converted into SML, a set of instructions is generated. Certain combinations of instructions often repeat themselves, usually in triplets called *productions*. A production normally consists of three instructions such as *load*, *add* and *store*. For example, Fig. 15.27 illustrates five of the SML instructions that were produced in the compilation of the program in Fig. 15.25 The first three instructions are the production that adds **1** to **y**. Note that instructions **06** and **07** store the accumulator value in temporary location **96** and then load the value back into the accumulator so instruction **08** can store the value in location **98**. Often a production is followed by a load instruction for the same location that was just stored. This code can be *optimized* by eliminating the store instruction and the subsequent load instruction that operate on the same memory location, thus enabling the Simpletron to execute the program faster. Figure 15.28 illustrates the optimized SML for the program of Fig. 15.25. Note that there are four fewer instructions in the optimized code—a memory-space savings of 25%.

Modify the compiler to provide an option for optimizing the Simpletron Machine Language code it produces. Manually compare the nonoptimized code with the optimized code, and calculate the percentage reduction.

15.29 (*Modifications to the Simple compiler*) Perform the following modifications to the Simple compiler. Some of these modifications may also require modifications to the Simpletron Simulator program written in Exercise 5.19.

a) Allow the modulus operator (**%**) to be used in **let** statements. Simpletron Machine Language must be modified to include a modulus instruction.

b) Allow exponentiation in a **let** statement using ^ as the exponentiation operator. Simpletron Machine Language must be modified to include an exponentiation instruction.

1	04	+2098	*(load)*
2	05	+3097	*(add)*
3	06	+2196	*(store)*
4	07	+2096	*(load)*
5	08	+2198	*(store)*

Fig. 15.27 Nonoptimized code from the program of Fig. 15.25.

Simple program	SML location and instruction	Description
5 rem sum 1 to x	*none*	**rem** ignored
10 input x	00 +1099	read **x** into location **99**
15 rem check y == x	*none*	**rem** ignored
20 if y == x goto 60	01 +2098	load **y** (**98**) into accumulator
	02 +3199	sub **x** (**99**) from accumulator
	03 +4211	branch to location **11** if zero
25 rem increment y	*none*	**rem** ignored
30 let y = y + 1	04 +2098	load **y** into accumulator
	05 +3097	add **1** (**97**) to accumulator
	06 +2198	store accumulator in **y** (**98**)
35 rem add y to total	*none*	**rem** ignored
40 let t = t + y	07 +2096	load **t** from location (**96**)
	08 +3098	add **y** (**98**) accumulator
	09 +2196	store accumulator in **t** (**96**)
45 rem loop y	*none*	**rem** ignored
50 goto 20	10 +4001	branch to location **01**
55 rem output result	*none*	**rem** ignored
60 print t	11 +1196	output **t** (**96**) to screen
99 end	12 +4300	terminate execution

Fig. 15.28 Optimized code for the program of Fig. 15.25.

   c) Allow the compiler to recognize uppercase and lowercase letters in Simple statements (e.g., `'A'` is equivalent to `'a'`). No modifications to the Simulator are required.

   d) Allow **input** statements to read values for multiple variables such as **input x, y**. No modifications to the Simpletron Simulator are required.

   e) Allow the compiler to output multiple values in a single **print** statement such as **print a, b, c**. No modifications to the Simpletron Simulator are required.

   f) Add syntax-checking capabilities to the compiler so error messages are output when syntax errors are encountered in a Simple program. No modifications to the Simpletron Simulator are required.

   g) Allow arrays of integers. No modifications to the Simpletron Simulator are required.

   h) Allow subroutines specified by the Simple commands **gosub** and **return**. Command **gosub** passes program control to a subroutine, and command **return** passes control back to the statement after the **gosub**. This is similar to a function call in C++. The same subroutine can be called from many **gosub** commands distributed throughout a program. No modifications to the Simpletron Simulator are required.

   i) Allow repetition structures of the form

```
for x = 2 to 10 step 2
    Simple statements
next
```

This **for** statement loops from **2** to **10** with an increment of **2**. The **next** line marks the end of the body of the **for** line. No modifications to the Simpletron Simulator are required.

j) Allow repetition structures of the form

```
for x = 2 to 10
    Simple statements
next
```

This **for** statement loops from **2** to **10** with a default increment of **1**. No modifications to the Simpletron Simulator are required.

k) Allow the compiler to process string input and output. This requires the Simpletron Simulator to be modified to process and store string values. (Hint: Each Simpletron word can be divided into two groups, each holding a two-digit integer. Each two-digit integer represents the ASCII decimal equivalent of a character. Add a machine language instruction that will print a string beginning at a certain Simpletron memory location. The first half of the word at that location is a count of the number of characters in the string (i.e., the length of the string). Each succeeding half word contains one ASCII character expressed as two decimal digits. The machine language instruction checks the length and prints the string by translating each two-digit number into its equivalent character.)

l) Allow the compiler to process floating-point values in addition to integers. The Simpletron Simulator must also be modified to process floating-point values.

15.30 (*A Simple interpreter*) An interpreter is a program that reads a high-level language program statement, determines the operation to be performed by the statement and executes the operation immediately. The high-level language program is not converted into machine language first. Interpreters execute slowly because each statement encountered in the program must first be deciphered. If statements are contained in a loop, the statements are deciphered each time they are encountered in the loop. Early versions of the BASIC programming language were implemented as interpreters.

Write an interpreter for the Simple language discussed in Exercise 15.26. The program should use the infix-to-postfix converter developed in Exercise 15.12 and the postfix evaluator developed in Exercise 15.13 to evaluate expressions in a **let** statement. The same restrictions placed on the Simple language in Exercise 15.26 should be adhered to in this program. Test the interpreter with the Simple programs written in Exercise 15.26. Compare the results of running these programs in the interpreter with the results of compiling the Simple programs and running them in the Simpletron Simulator built in Exercise 5.19.

15.31 (*Insert/Delete Anywhere in a Linked List*) Our linked list class template allowed insertions and deletions at only the front and the back of the linked list. These capabilities were convenient for us when we used private inheritance and composition to produce a stack class template and a queue class template with a minimal amount of code by reusing the list class template. Actually, linked lists are more general that those we provided. Modify the linked list class template we developed in this chapter to handle insertions and deletions anywhere in the list.

15.32 (*List and Queues without Tail Pointers*) Our implementation of a linked list (Fig. 15.3) used both a **firstPtr** and a **lastPtr**. The **lastPtr** was useful for the **insertAtBack** and **removeFromBack** member functions of the **List** class. The **insertAtBack** function corresponds to the **enqueue** member function of the **Queue** class. Rewrite the **List** class so that it does not use a **lastPtr**. Thus, any operations on the tail of a list must begin searching the list from the front. Does this affect our implementation of the **Queue** class (Fig. 15.12)?

15.33 Use the composition version of the stack program (Fig. 15.11) to form a complete working stack program. Modify this program to **inline** the member functions. Compare the two approaches. Summarize the advantages and disadvantages of inlining member functions.

15.34 *(Performance of Binary Tree Sorting and Searching)* One problem with the binary tree sort is that the order in which the data are inserted affects the shape of the tree—for the same collection of data, different orderings can yield binary trees of dramatically different shapes. The performance of the binary tree sorting and searching algorithms is sensitive to the shape of the binary tree. What shape would a binary tree have if its data were inserted in increasing order? in decreasing order? What shape should the tree have to achieve maximal searching performance?

15.35 *(Indexed Lists)* As presented in the text, linked lists must be searched sequentially. For large lists, this can result in poor performance. A common technique for improving list searching performance is to create and maintain an index to the list. An index is a set of pointers to various key places in the list. For example, an application that searches a large list of names could improve performance by creating an index with 26 entries—one for each letter of the alphabet. A search operation for a last name beginning with 'Y' would then first search the index to determine where the 'Y' entries begin, and then "jump into" the list at that point and search linearly until the desired name is found. This would be much faster than searching the linked list from the beginning. Use the **List** class of Fig. 15.3 as the basis of an **IndexedList** class. Write a program that demonstrates the operation of indexed lists. Be sure to include member functions **insertInIndexedList**, **searchIndexedList** and **deleteFromIndexedList**.

Bits, Characters, Strings and Structures

Objectives

- To be able to create and use structures.
- To be able to pass structures to functions by call-by-value and call-by-reference.
- To manipulate data with the bitwise operators and to create bit fields for storing data compactly.
- To be able to use the functions of the character handling library (**cctype**).
- To be able to use the string conversion functions of the general utilities library (**cstdlib**).
- To be able to use the string processing functions of the string-handling library (**cstring**).
- To appreciate the power of function libraries as a means of achieving software reusability.

The same old charitable lie
Repeated as the years scoot by
Perpetually makes a hit—
"You really haven't changed a bit!"
Margaret Fishback

The chief defect of Henry King
Was chewing little bits of string.
Hilaire Belloc

Vigorous writing is concise. A sentence should contain no unnecessary words, a paragraph no unnecessary sentences.
William Strunk, Jr.

16.1 Introduction

In this chapter, we say more about structures and then discuss the manipulation of bits, characters and strings. Many of the techniques we present are C-like and are included for the benefit of the C++ programmer who will work with C legacy code.

Structures may contain variables of many different data types—in contrast to arrays that contain only elements of the same data type. This fact, and most of what we say about structures in the next several pages, applies to classes as well. Again, the major difference between structures and classes in C++ is that structure members default to **public** access and class members default to **private** access. Structures are commonly used to define data records to be stored in files (see Chapter 14, "File Processing and String Stream I/O"). Pointers and structures facilitate the formation of more complex data structures such as linked lists, queues, stacks and trees (see Chapter 15, "Data Structures"). We discuss how to declare structures, initialize them and pass them to functions. Then, we present a high-performance card-shuffling and dealing simulation.

16.2 Structure Definitions

Consider the following structure definition:

```
struct Card {
   char *face;
   char *suit;
};
```

Keyword **struct** introduces the definition for structure **Card**. The identifier **Card** is the *structure name* and is used in C++ to declare variables of the *structure type* (in C, the type

name of the preceding structure is **struct Card**). In this example, the structure type is
Card. Data (and possibly functions—just as with classes) declared within the braces of the
structure definition are the structure's *members*. Members of the same structure must have
unique names, but two different structures may contain members of the same name without
conflict. Each structure definition must end with a semicolon.

Common Programming Error 16.1

Forgetting the semicolon that terminates a structure definition.

The definition of **Card** contains two members of type **char ***—**face** and **suit**.
Structure members can be variables of the basic data types (e.g., **int**, **double**, etc.) or
aggregates, such as arrays and other structures. As we saw in Chapter 4, each element of an
array must be of the same type. Data members of a structure, however, can be of a variety
of data types. For example, an **Employee** structure might contain character string members for the first and last names, an **int** member for the employee's age, a **char** member
containing **'M'** or **'F'** for the employee's gender, a **double** member for the employee's
hourly salary, and so on.

A structure cannot contain an instance of itself. For example, a structure variable **Card**
cannot be declared in the definition for structure **Card**. A pointer to a **Card** structure, however, can be included. A structure containing a member that is a pointer to the same structure type is referred to as a *self-referential structure*. Self-referential structures are used in
Chapter 15 to build various kinds of linked data structures.

The preceding structure definition does not reserve any space in memory; rather, the
definition creates a new data type that is used to declare structure variables. Structure variables are declared like variables of other types. The declaration

```
Card oneCard, deck[ 52 ], *cPtr;
```

declares **oneCard** to be a structure variable of type **Card**, **deck** to be an array with 52
elements of type **Card** and **cPtr** to be a pointer to a **Card** structure. Variables of a given
structure type may also be declared by placing a comma-separated list of the variable names
between the closing brace of the structure definition and the semicolon that ends the structure definition. For example, the preceding declaration could have been incorporated into
the **Card** structure definition as follows:

```
struct Card {
   char *face;
   char *suit;
} oneCard, deck[ 52 ], *cPtr;
```

The structure name is optional. If a structure definition does not contain a structure
name, variables of the structure type may be declared only in the structure definition—not
in a separate declaration.

Good Programming Practice 16.1

*Provide a structure name when creating a structure type. The structure name is convenient
for declaring new variables of the structure type later in the program and is required if the
structure will be passed as a parameter to a function.*

The only valid built-in operations that may be performed on structures are assigning a
structure to a structure of the same type, taking the address (**&**) of a structure, accessing the

members of a structure (see Chapter 6, "Classes and Data Abstraction") and using the **sizeof** operator to determine the size of a structure. As with classes, most operators can be overloaded to work with objects of a structure type.

Structure members are not necessarily stored in consecutive bytes of memory. Sometimes there are "holes" in a structure, because computers may store specific data types only on certain memory boundaries such as half-word, word or double-word boundaries. A word is a standard memory unit used to store data in a computer—usually 2 bytes or 4 bytes. Consider the following structure definition in which structure variables (objects really) **sample1** and **sample2** of type **Example** are declared:

```
struct Example {
   char c;
   int i;
} sample1, sample2;
```

A computer with 2-byte words may require that each of the members of **Example** be aligned on a word boundary, i.e., at the beginning of a word (this is machine dependent). Figure 16.1 shows a sample storage alignment for an object of type **Example** that has been assigned the character **'a'** and the integer **97** (the bit representations of the values are shown). If the members are stored beginning at word boundaries, there is a 1-byte hole (byte **1** in the figure) in the storage for objects of type **Example**. The value in the 1-byte hole is undefined. If the member values of **sample1** and **sample2** are in fact equal, the structures do not necessarily compare equally, because the undefined 1-byte holes are not likely to contain identical values.

Common Programming Error 16.2

Comparing structures is a syntax error because of the different alignment requirements on various systems.

Portability Tip 16.1

Because the size of data items of a particular type is machine dependent, and because storage alignment considerations are machine dependent, so too is the representation of a structure.

16.3 Initializing Structures

Structures can be initialized using initializer lists, as is done with arrays. To initialize a structure, follow the variable name in the structure declaration with an equals sign and a brace-enclosed, comma-separated list of initializers. For example, the declaration

```
Card oneCard = { "Three", "Hearts" };
```

creates variable **oneCard** to be a **Card** structure (as defined previously) and initializes member **face** to **"Three"** and member **suit** to **"Hearts"**. If there are fewer initializers in the list than members in the structure, the remaining members are initialized to **0**. Structure variables declared outside a function definition (i.e., externally) are initialized to **0** if they are not explicitly initialized in the external declaration. Structure variables may also be initialized in assignment statements by assigning a structure variable of the same type or by assigning values to the individual data members of the structure.

Byte	0	1	2	3
	01100001		00000000	01100001

Fig. 16.1   A possible storage alignment for a variable of type **Example** showing an undefined area in memory.

16.4 Using Structures with Functions

There are two ways to pass the information in structures to functions. You can either pass the entire structure, or you can pass the individual members of a structure. By default, the data (except individual array members) passes by call-by-value. Structures and their members can also be passed by call-by-reference by passing either references or pointers.

To pass a structure by call-by-reference, pass the address of the structure variable or a reference to the structure variable. Arrays of structures—like all other arrays—are passed by call-by-reference.

In Chapter 4, we stated that an array could be passed by call-by-value by using a structure. To pass an array by call-by-value, create a structure (or a class) with the array as a member. Since structures are passed by call-by-value, the array is passed by call-by-value.

Common Programming Error 16.3

Assuming that structures, like arrays, are passed by call-by-reference and trying to modify the caller's structure values in the called function.

Performance Tip 16.1

Passing structures (and especially large structures) by call-by-reference is more efficient than passing structures by call-by-value (which requires the entire structure to be copied).

16.5 typedef

Keyword **typedef** provides a mechanism for creating synonyms (or aliases) for previously defined data types. Names for structure types are often defined with **typedef** to create shorter or more readable type names. For example, the statement

        typedef Card *CardPtr;

defines the new type name **CardPtr** as a synonym for type **Card ***.

Good Programming Practice 16.2

*Capitalize **typedef** names to emphasize that these names are synonyms for other type names.*

Creating a new name with **typedef** does not create a new data type; **typedef** simply creates a new type name that may then be used in the program as an alias for an existing type name.

Synonyms for built-in data types can be created with **typedef**. For example, a program requiring 4-byte integers may use type **int** on one system and type **long int** on another system that has 2-byte integers. Programs designed for portability can use **typedef** to create an alias such as **Integer** for 4-byte integers. **Integer** can then be aliased to **int** on systems with 4-byte integers and can be aliased to **long int** on systems with 2-byte integers where **long int** values occupy 4 bytes. Then, to write portable programs, the programmer simply declares all 4-byte integer variables to be of type **Integer**.

Portability Tip 16.2

Using **typedef** *can help make a program more portable.*

16.6 Example: High-Performance Card-shuffling and Dealing Simulation

The program in Fig. 16.2 is based on the card-shuffling and dealing simulation discussed in Chapter 5. The program represents the deck of cards as an array of structures and uses high-performance shuffling and dealing algorithms. The output is shown in Fig. 16.3.

```cpp
1    // Fig. 16.2: fig16_02.cpp
2    // Card shuffling and dealing program using structures
3    #include <iostream>
4
5    using std::cout;
6    using std::cin;
7    using std::endl;
8    using std::ios;
9
10   #include <iomanip>
11
12   using std::setiosflags;
13   using std::setw;
14
15   #include <cstdlib>
16   #include <ctime>
17
18   struct Card {
19      char *face;
20      char *suit;
21   };
22
23   void fillDeck( Card * const, char *[], char *[] );
24   void shuffle( Card * const );
25   void deal( Card * const );
26
27   int main()
28   {
29      Card deck[ 52 ];
30      char *face[] = { "Ace", "Deuce", "Three", "Four",
31                       "Five", "Six", "Seven", "Eight",
32                       "Nine", "Ten", "Jack", "Queen",
33                       "King" };
34      char *suit[] = { "Hearts", "Diamonds",
35                       "Clubs", "Spades" };
36
37      srand( time( 0 ) );              // randomize
38      fillDeck( deck, face, suit );
39      shuffle( deck );
40      deal( deck );
```

Fig. 16.2   High-performance card-shuffling and dealing simulation (part 1 of 2).

```
41      return 0;
42  }
43
44  void fillDeck( Card * const wDeck, char *wFace[],
45                  char *wSuit[] )
46  {
47     for ( int i = 0; i < 52; i++ ) {
48        wDeck[ i ].face = wFace[ i % 13 ];
49        wDeck[ i ].suit = wSuit[ i / 13 ];
50     }
51  }
52
53  void shuffle( Card * const wDeck )
54  {
55     for ( int i = 0; i < 52; i++ ) {
56        int j = rand() % 52;
57        Card temp = wDeck[ i ];
58        wDeck[ i ] = wDeck[ j ];
59        wDeck[ j ] = temp;
60     }
61  }
62
63  void deal( Card * const wDeck )
64  {
65     for ( int i = 0; i < 52; i++ )
66        cout << setiosflags( ios::right )
67             << setw( 5 ) << wDeck[ i ].face << " of "
68             << setiosflags( ios::left )
69             << setw( 8 ) << wDeck[ i ].suit
70             << ( ( i + 1 ) % 2 ? '\t' : '\n' );
71  }
```

Fig. 16.2   High-performance card-shuffling and dealing simulation (part 2 of 2).

In the program, function **fillDeck** initializes the **Card** array in order with character strings representing Ace through King of each suit. The **Card** array is passed to function **shuffle** where the high-performance shuffling algorithm is implemented. Function **shuffle** takes an array of 52 **Card** structures as an argument. The function loops through all 52 cards (array subscripts 0 to 51). For each card, a number between 0 and 51 is picked randomly. Next, the current **Card** structure and the randomly selected **Card** structure are swapped in the array. A total of 52 swaps are made in a single pass of the entire array, and the array of **Card** structures is shuffled! This algorithm does not suffer from indefinite postponement like the shuffling algorithm presented in Chapter 5. Because the **Card** structures were swapped in place in the array, the high-performance dealing algorithm implemented in function **deal** requires only one pass of the array to deal the shuffled cards.

Common Programming Error 16.4

Forgetting to include the array subscript when referring to individual structures in an array of structures.

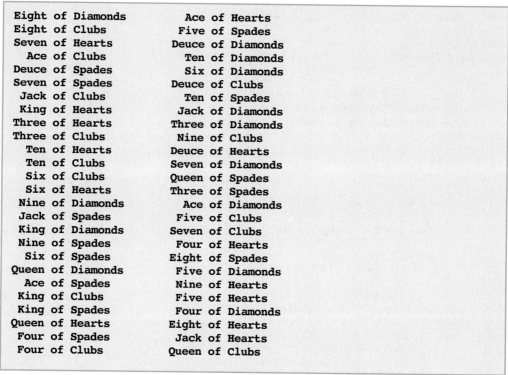

Eight of Diamonds	Ace of Hearts
Eight of Clubs	Five of Spades
Seven of Hearts	Deuce of Diamonds
Ace of Clubs	Ten of Diamonds
Deuce of Spades	Six of Diamonds
Seven of Spades	Deuce of Clubs
Jack of Clubs	Ten of Spades
King of Hearts	Jack of Diamonds
Three of Hearts	Three of Diamonds
Three of Clubs	Nine of Clubs
Ten of Hearts	Deuce of Hearts
Ten of Clubs	Seven of Diamonds
Six of Clubs	Queen of Spades
Six of Hearts	Three of Spades
Nine of Diamonds	Ace of Diamonds
Jack of Spades	Five of Clubs
King of Diamonds	Seven of Clubs
Nine of Spades	Four of Hearts
Six of Spades	Eight of Spades
Queen of Diamonds	Five of Diamonds
Ace of Spades	Nine of Hearts
King of Clubs	Five of Hearts
King of Spades	Four of Diamonds
Queen of Hearts	Eight of Hearts
Four of Spades	Jack of Hearts
Four of Clubs	Queen of Clubs

Fig. 16.3   Output for the high-performance card-shuffling and dealing simulation.

16.7 Bitwise Operators

C++ provides extensive bit manipulation capabilities for programmers who need to get down to the so-called "bits-and-bytes" level. Operating systems, test equipment software, networking software and many other kinds of software require that the programmer communicate "directly with the hardware." In this and the next several sections, we discuss C++'s bit manipulation capabilities. We introduce each of C++'s many bitwise operators, and we discuss how to save memory by using bit fields.

All data are represented internally by computers as sequences of bits. Each bit can assume the value **0** or the value **1**. On most systems, a sequence of 8 bits forms a *byte*—the standard storage unit for a variable of type **char**. Other data types are stored in larger numbers of bytes. Bitwise operators are used to manipulate the bits of integral operands (**char**, **short**, **int** and **long**; both **signed** and **unsigned**). Unsigned integers are normally used with the bitwise operators.

Portability Tip 16.3

Bitwise data manipulations are machine dependent.

Note that the bitwise operator discussions in this section show the binary representations of the integer operands. (For a detailed explanation of the binary (also called base-2) number system, see Appendix C, "Number Systems"). Because of the machine-dependent nature of bitwise manipulations, some of these programs may not work on your system.

The bitwise operators are: *bitwise AND* (**&**), *bitwise inclusive OR* (**|**), *bitwise exclusive OR* (**^**), *left shift* (**<<**), *right shift* (**>>**) and *complement* (**~**). (Note that we have been using **&**, **<<**, and **>>** for other purposes. This is a classic example of operator overloading.) The bitwise AND, bitwise inclusive OR, and bitwise exclusive OR operators compare their two operands bit by bit. The bitwise AND operator sets each bit in the result to 1 if the corresponding bit in both operands is 1. The bitwise inclusive-OR operator sets each bit in the result to 1 if the corresponding bit in either (or both) operand(s) is 1. The bitwise exclusive-OR operator sets each bit in the result to 1 if the corresponding bit in exactly one operand is 1. The left-shift operator shifts the bits of its left operand to the left by the number of bits specified in its right operand. The right-shift operator shifts the bits in its left operand to the right by the number of bits specified in its right operand. The bitwise complement operator sets all **0** bits in its operand to **1** in the result and sets all **1** bits to **0** in the result. Detailed discussions of each bitwise operator appear in the following examples. The bitwise operators are summarized in Fig. 16.4.

When using the bitwise operators, it is useful to print values in their binary representation to illustrate the precise effects of these operators. Figure 16.5 prints an **unsigned** integer in its binary representation in groups of eight bits each. Function **displayBits** uses the bitwise AND operator to combine variable **value** with constant **MASK**. Often, the bitwise AND operator is used with an operand called a *mask*—an integer value with specific bits set to **1**. Masks are used to hide some bits in a value while selecting other bits. In **displayBits**, mask constant **MASK** is assigned the value

```
1 << SHIFT
```

Constant **SHIFT** is assigned the result of

```
8 * sizeof( unsigned ) - 1
```

Operator	Name	Description
&	bitwise AND	The bits in the result are set to **1** if the corresponding bits in the two operands are both **1**.
|	bitwise inclusive OR	The bits in the result are set to **1** if at least one of the corresponding bits in the two operands is **1**.
^	bitwise exclusive OR	The bits in the result are set to **1** if exactly one of the corresponding bits in the two operands is **1**.
<<	left shift	Shifts the bits of the first operand left by the number of bits specified by the second operand; fill from right with **0** bits.
>>	right shift with sign extension	Shifts the bits of the first operand right by the number of bits specified by the second operand; the method of filling from the left is machine dependent.
~	one's complement	All **0** bits are set to **1** and all **1** bits are set to **0**.

Fig. 16.4   The bitwise operators.

```cpp
1   // Fig. 16.5: fig16_05.cpp
2   // Printing an unsigned integer in bits
3   #include <iostream>
4
5   using std::cout;
6   using std::cin;
7
8   #include <iomanip>
9
10  using std::setw;
11  using std::endl;
12
13  void displayBits( unsigned );
14
15  int main()
16  {
17      unsigned x;
18
19      cout << "Enter an unsigned integer: ";
20      cin >> x;
21      displayBits( x );
22      return 0;
23  }
24
25  void displayBits( unsigned value )
26  {
27      const int SHIFT = 8 * sizeof( unsigned ) - 1;
28      const unsigned MASK = 1 << SHIFT;
29
30      cout << setw( 7 ) << value << " = ";
31
32      for ( unsigned c = 1; c <= SHIFT + 1; c++ ) {
33          cout << ( value & MASK ? '1' : '0' );
34          value <<= 1;
35
36          if ( c % 8 == 0 )
37              cout << ' ';
38      }
39
40      cout << endl;
41  }
```

```
Enter an unsigned integer: 65000
  65000 = 00000000 00000000 11111101 11101000
```

Fig. 16.5   Printing an unsigned integer in bits.

This expression multiplies the number of bytes an **unsigned** requires by **8** to get the total number of bits then subtracts 1. The bit representation of **1 << SHIFT** is

10000000 00000000 00000000 00000000

The left-shift operator shifts the value **1** from the low order (rightmost) bit to the high-order (leftmost) bit in **MASK**, and fills in **0** bits from the right. The statement

```
cout << ( value & MASK ? '1' : '0' );
```

determines whether a **1** or a **0** should be printed for the current leftmost bit of variable **value**. Assume that variable **value** contains **65000** (**00000000 00000000 11111101 11101000**). When **value** and **MASK** are combined using **&**, all the bits except the high-order bit in variable **value** are "masked off" (hidden), because any bit "ANDed" with **0** yields **0**. If the leftmost bit is **1**, **value & MASK** evaluates to

```
00000000 00000000 11111101 11101000    (value)
10000000 00000000 00000000 00000000    (MASK)
-----------------------------------
00000000 00000000 00000000 00000000    (value & MASK)
```

which is interpreted as **false**, and **0** is printed. Variable **value** is then left shifted one bit by the expression **value <<= 1** (this is equivalent to the assignment **value = value << 1**). These steps are repeated for each bit variable **value**. Eventually, a bit with a value of **1** is shifted into the leftmost bit position, and the bit manipulation is as follows:

```
11111101 11101000 00000000 00000000    (value)
10000000 00000000 00000000 00000000    (MASK)
-----------------------------------
10000000 00000000 00000000 00000000    (value & MASK)
```

Because both left bits are **1**s, a value of **1** is printed. Figure 16.6 summarizes the results of combining two bits with the bitwise AND operator.

Common Programming Error 16.5

*Using the logical AND operator (**&&**) for the bitwise AND operator (**&**) and vice versa.*

The program of Fig. 16.7 demonstrates the use of the bitwise AND operator, the bitwise inclusive OR operator, the bitwise exclusive OR operator, and the bitwise complement operator. Function **displayBits** prints the **unsigned** integer values. The output is shown in Fig. 16.8.

Bit 1	Bit 2	Bit 1 & Bit 2
0	0	0
1	0	0
0	1	0
1	1	1

Fig. 16.6   Results of combining two bits with the bitwise AND operator (**&**).

```cpp
1   // Fig. 16.7: fig16_07.cpp
2   // Using the bitwise AND, bitwise inclusive OR, bitwise
3   // exclusive OR, and bitwise complement operators.
4   #include <iostream>
5
6   using std::cout;
7   using std::cin;
8
9   #include <iomanip>
10
11  using std::endl;
12  using std::setw;
13
14  void displayBits( unsigned );
15
16  int main()
17  {
18      unsigned number1, number2, mask, setBits;
19
20      number1 = 2179876355;
21      mask = 1;
22      cout << "The result of combining the following\n";
23      displayBits( number1 );
24      displayBits( mask );
25      cout << "using the bitwise AND operator & is\n";
26      displayBits( number1 & mask );
27
28      number1 = 15;
29      setBits = 241;
30      cout << "\nThe result of combining the following\n";
31      displayBits( number1 );
32      displayBits( setBits );
33      cout << "using the bitwise inclusive OR operator | is\n";
34      displayBits( number1 | setBits );
35
36      number1 = 139;
37      number2 = 199;
38      cout << "\nThe result of combining the following\n";
39      displayBits( number1 );
40      displayBits( number2 );
41      cout << "using the bitwise exclusive OR operator ^ is\n";
42      displayBits( number1 ^ number2 );
43
44      number1 = 21845;
45      cout << "\nThe one's complement of\n";
46      displayBits( number1 );
47      cout << "is" << endl;
48      displayBits( ~number1 );
49
50      return 0;
51  }
```

Fig. 16.7   Using the bitwise AND, bitwise inclusive-OR, bitwise exclusive-OR and bitwise complement operators (part 1 of 2).

```
52
53   void displayBits( unsigned value )
54   {
55      const int SHIFT = 8 * sizeof( unsigned ) - 1;
56      const unsigned MASK = 1 << SHIFT;
57
58      cout << setw( 10 ) << value << " = ";
59
60      for ( unsigned c = 1; c <= SHIFT + 1; c++ ) {
61         cout << ( value & MASK ? '1' : '0' );
62         value <<= 1;
63
64         if ( c % 8 == 0 )
65            cout << ' ';
66      }
67
68      cout << endl;
69   }
```

Fig. 16.7   Using the bitwise AND, bitwise inclusive-OR, bitwise exclusive-OR and bitwise complement operators (part 2 of 2).

```
The result of combining the following
2179876355 = 10000001 11101110 01000110 00000011
         1 = 00000000 00000000 00000000 00000001
using the bitwise AND operator & is
         1 = 00000000 00000000 00000000 00000001

The result of combining the following
        15 = 00000000 00000000 00000000 00001111
       241 = 00000000 00000000 00000000 11110001
using the bitwise inclusive OR operator | is
       255 = 00000000 00000000 00000000 11111111

The result of combining the following
       139 = 00000000 00000000 00000000 10001011
       199 = 00000000 00000000 00000000 11000111
using the bitwise exclusive OR operator ^ is
        76 = 00000000 00000000 00000000 01001100

The one's complement of
     21845 = 00000000 00000000 01010101 01010101
is
4294945450 = 11111111 11111111 10101010 10101010
```

Fig. 16.8   Output for the program of Fig. 16.7.

In Fig. 16.7, variable **mask** is assigned the value **1** (**00000000 00000000 00000000 00000001**), and variable **number1** is assigned value **2179876355** (**10000001 11101110 01000110 00000011**). When **mask** and **number1** are combined using the bitwise AND operator (**&**) in the expression **number1 & mask**, the result is **00000000 00000000 00000000 00000001**. All the bits except the low-order bit in variable **number1** are "masked off" (hidden) by "ANDing" with constant **MASK**.

The bitwise inclusive-OR operator is used to set specific bits to 1 in an operand. In Fig. 16.7, variable **number1** is assigned **15** (**00000000 00000000 00000000 00001111**), and variable **setBits** is assigned **241** (**00000000 00000000 00000000 11110001**). When **number1** and **setBits** are combined using the bitwise OR operator in the expression **number1 | setBits**, the result is **255** (**00000000 00000000 00000000 11111111**). Figure 16.9 summarizes the results of combining two bits with the bitwise inclusive-OR operator.

Common Programming Error 16.6

Using the logical OR operator (| |) for the bitwise OR operator (|) and vice versa.

The bitwise exclusive OR operator (^) sets each bit in the result to 1 if *exactly* one of the corresponding bits in its two operands is 1. In Fig. 16.7, variables **number1** and **number2** are assigned the values **139** (**00000000 00000000 00000000 10001011**) and **199** (**00000000 00000000 00000000 11000111**), respectively. When these variables are combined with the exclusive-OR operator in the expression **number1 ^ number2**, the result is **00000000 00000000 00000000 01001100**. Figure 16.10 summarizes the results of combining two bits with the bitwise exclusive-OR operator.

The *bitwise* complement operator (~) sets all **1** bits in its operand to **0** in the result and sets all **0** bits to **1** in the result—otherwise referred to as "taking the *one's complement* of the value." In Fig. 16.7, variable **number1** is assigned the value **21845** (**00000000 00000000 01010101 01010101**). When the expression **~number1** is evaluated, the result is (**11111111 11111111 10101010 10101010**).

Bit 1	Bit 2	Bit 1 | Bit 2
0	0	0
1	0	1
0	1	1
1	1	1

Fig. 16.9   Results of combining two bits with the bitwise inclusive-OR operator (|) .

Bit 1	Bit 2	Bit 1 ^ Bit 2
0	0	0
1	0	1
0	1	1
1	1	0

Fig. 16.10   Results of combining two bits with the bitwise exclusive-OR operator (^).

The program of Fig. 16.11 demonstrates the left-shift operator (**<<**) and the right-shift operator (**>>**). Function **displayBits** is used to print the **unsigned** integer values.

```cpp
1   // Fig. 16.11: fig16_11.cpp
2   // Using the bitwise shift operators
3   #include <iostream>
4
5   using std::cout;
6   using std::cin;
7   using std::endl;
8
9   #include <iomanip>
10
11  using std::setw;
12
13  void displayBits( unsigned );
14
15  int main()
16  {
17     unsigned number1 = 960;
18
19     cout << "The result of left shifting\n";
20     displayBits( number1 );
21     cout << "8 bit positions using the left "
22        << "shift operator is\n";
23     displayBits( number1 << 8 );
24     cout << "\nThe result of right shifting\n";
25     displayBits( number1 );
26     cout << "8 bit positions using the right "
27        << "shift operator is\n";
28     displayBits( number1 >> 8 );
29     return 0;
30  }
31
32  void displayBits( unsigned value )
33  {
34     const int SHIFT = 8 * sizeof( unsigned ) - 1;
35     const unsigned MASK = 1 << SHIFT;
36
37     cout << setw( 7 ) << value << " = ";
38
39     for ( unsigned c = 1; c <= SHIFT + 1; c++ ) {
40        cout << ( value & MASK ? '1' : '0' );
41        value <<= 1;
42
43        if ( c % 8 == 0 )
44           cout << ' ';
45     }
46
47     cout << endl;
48  }
```

Fig. 16.11 Using the bitwise shift operators (part 1 of 2).

```
The result of left shifting
    960 = 00000000 00000000 00000011 11000000
8 bit positions using the left shift operator is
 245760 = 00000000 00000011 11000000 00000000

The result of right shifting
    960 = 00000000 00000000 00000011 11000000
8 bit positions using the right shift operator is
      3 = 00000000 00000000 00000000 00000011
```

Fig. 16.11   Using the bitwise shift operators (part 2 of 2).

The left-shift operator (**<<**) shifts the bits of its left operand to the left by the number of bits specified in its right operand. Bits vacated to the right are replaced with **0**s; bits shifted off the left are lost. In the program of Fig. 16.11, variable **number1** is assigned the value **960** (**00000000 00000000 00000011 11000000**). The result of left shifting variable **number1** 8 bits in the expression **number1 << 8** is **245760** (**00000000 00000011 11000000 00000000**).

The right-shift operator (**>>**) shifts the bits of its left operand to the right by the number of bits specified in its right operand. Performing a right shift on an **unsigned** integer causes the vacated bits at the left to be replaced by 0s; bits shifted off the right are lost. In the program of Fig. 16.11, the result of right shifting **number1** in the expression **number1 >> 8** is **3** (**00000000 00000000 00000000 00000011**).

Common Programming Error 16.7

The result of shifting a value is undefined if the right operand is negative or if the right operand is larger than the number of bits in which the left operand is stored.

Portability Tip 16.4

The result of right shifting a signed value is machine dependent. Some machines fill with zeros and others use the sign bit.

Each bitwise operator (except the bitwise complement operator) has a corresponding assignment operator. These *bitwise assignment operators* are shown in Fig. 16.12 and are used in a similar manner to the arithmetic assignment operators introduced in Chapter 2.

Bitwise assignment operators	
&=	Bitwise AND assignment operator.
|=	Bitwise inclusive-OR assignment operator.
^=	Bitwise exclusive-OR assignment operator.
<<=	Left-shift assignment operator.
>>=	Right-shift with sign extension assignment operator.

Fig. 16.12   The bitwise assignment operators.

Figure 16.13 shows the precedence and associativity of the various operators introduced to this point in the text. They are shown top to bottom in decreasing order of precedence.

16.8 Bit Fields

C++ provides the ability to specify the number of bits in which an **unsigned** or **int** member of a class or a structure (or a **union**—see Chapter 18, "Other Topics") is stored. Such a member is referred to as a *bit field*. Bit fields enable better memory utilization by storing data in the minimum number of bits required. Bit field members *must* be declared as **int** or **unsigned**.

Performance Tip 16.2

Bit fields help conserve storage.

Consider the following structure definition:

```
struct BitCard {
    unsigned face : 4;
    unsigned suit : 2;
    unsigned color : 1;
};
```

Operators	Associativity	Type
:: (unary; right to left) **::** (binary; left to right)	left to right	highest
() **[]** **.** **->** **++** **--** static_cast<*type*>()	left to right	postfix expression
++ **--** **+** **-** **!** **delete** **sizeof** *** & new**	right to left	unary
* **/** **%**	left to right	multiplicative
+ **-**	left to right	additive
<< **>>**	left to right	shifting
< **<=** **>** **>=**	left to right	relational
== **!=**	left to right	equality
&	left to right	bitwise AND
^	left to right	bitwise XOR
|	left to right	bitwise OR
&&	left to right	logical AND
||	left to right	logical OR
?:	right to left	conditional
= **+=** **-=** ***=** **/=** **%=** **&=** **|=** **^=** **<<=** **>>=**	right to left	assignment
,	left to right	comma

Fig. 16.13 Operator precedence and associativity.

The definition contains three **unsigned** bit fields—**face**, **suit** and **color**—used to represent a card from a deck of 52 cards. A bit field is declared by following an **unsigned** or **int** member with a colon (**:**) and an integer constant representing the *width* of the field (i.e., the number of bits in which the member is stored). The width must be an integer constant between zero and the total number of bits used to store an **int** on your system.

The preceding structure definition indicates that member **face** is stored in 4 bits, member **suit** is stored in 2 bits and member **color** is stored in 1 bit. The number of bits is based on the desired range of values for each structure member. Member **face** stores values between **0** (Ace) and **12** (King)—4 bits can store a value between 0 and 15. Member **suit** stores values between **0** and **3** (**0** = Diamonds, **1** = Hearts, **2** = Clubs, **3** = Spades)— 2 bits can store a value between **0** and **3**. Finally, member **color** stores either **0** (Red) or **1** (Black)—1 bit can store either **0** or **1**.

The program in Fig. 16.14 (output shown in Fig. 16.15) creates array **deck** containing 52 **BitCard** structures. Function **fillDeck** inserts the 52 cards in the **deck** array, and function **deal** prints the 52 cards. Notice that bit field members of structures are accessed exactly as any other structure member. The member **color** is included as a means of indicating the card color on a system that allows color displays.

```cpp
1   // Fig. 16.14: fig16_14.cpp
2   // Example using a bit field
3   #include <iostream>
4
5   using std::cout;
6   using std::endl;
7
8   #include <iomanip>
9
10  using std::setw;
11
12  struct BitCard {
13     unsigned face : 4;    // 4 bits; 0-15
14     unsigned suit : 2;    // 2 bits; 0-3
15     unsigned color : 1;   // 1 bit; 0-1
16  };
17
18  void fillDeck( BitCard * const );
19  void deal( const BitCard * const );
20
21  int main()
22  {
23     BitCard deck[ 52 ];
24
25     fillDeck( deck );
26     deal( deck );
27     return 0;
28  }
29
```

Fig. 16.14 Using bit fields to store a deck of cards (part 1 of 2).

```
30    void fillDeck( BitCard * const wDeck )
31    {
32       for ( int i = 0; i <= 51; i++ ) {
33          wDeck[ i ].face = i % 13;
34          wDeck[ i ].suit = i / 13;
35          wDeck[ i ].color = i / 26;
36       }
37    }
38
39    // Output cards in two column format. Cards 0-25 subscripted
40    // with k1 (column 1). Cards 26-51 subscripted k2 in (column 2.)
41    void deal( const BitCard * const wDeck )
42    {
43       for ( int k1 = 0, k2 = k1 + 26; k1 <= 25; k1++, k2++ ) {
44          cout << "Card:" << setw( 3 ) << wDeck[ k1 ].face
45               << "  Suit:" << setw( 2 ) << wDeck[ k1 ].suit
46               << "  Color:" << setw( 2 ) << wDeck[ k1 ].color
47               << "    " << "Card:" << setw( 3 ) << wDeck[ k2 ].face
48               << "  Suit:" << setw( 2 ) << wDeck[ k2 ].suit
49               << "  Color:" << setw( 2 ) << wDeck[ k2 ].color
50               << endl;
51       }
52    }
```

Fig. 16.14   Using bit fields to store a deck of cards (part 2 of 2).

```
Card:  0  Suit: 0  Color: 0    Card:  0  Suit: 2  Color: 1
Card:  1  Suit: 0  Color: 0    Card:  1  Suit: 2  Color: 1
Card:  2  Suit: 0  Color: 0    Card:  2  Suit: 2  Color: 1
Card:  3  Suit: 0  Color: 0    Card:  3  Suit: 2  Color: 1
Card:  4  Suit: 0  Color: 0    Card:  4  Suit: 2  Color: 1
Card:  5  Suit: 0  Color: 0    Card:  5  Suit: 2  Color: 1
Card:  6  Suit: 0  Color: 0    Card:  6  Suit: 2  Color: 1
Card:  7  Suit: 0  Color: 0    Card:  7  Suit: 2  Color: 1
Card:  8  Suit: 0  Color: 0    Card:  8  Suit: 2  Color: 1
Card:  9  Suit: 0  Color: 0    Card:  9  Suit: 2  Color: 1
Card: 10  Suit: 0  Color: 0    Card: 10  Suit: 2  Color: 1
Card: 11  Suit: 0  Color: 0    Card: 11  Suit: 2  Color: 1
Card: 12  Suit: 0  Color: 0    Card: 12  Suit: 2  Color: 1
Card:  0  Suit: 1  Color: 0    Card:  0  Suit: 3  Color: 1
Card:  1  Suit: 1  Color: 0    Card:  1  Suit: 3  Color: 1
Card:  2  Suit: 1  Color: 0    Card:  2  Suit: 3  Color: 1
Card:  3  Suit: 1  Color: 0    Card:  3  Suit: 3  Color: 1
Card:  4  Suit: 1  Color: 0    Card:  4  Suit: 3  Color: 1
Card:  5  Suit: 1  Color: 0    Card:  5  Suit: 3  Color: 1
Card:  6  Suit: 1  Color: 0    Card:  6  Suit: 3  Color: 1
Card:  7  Suit: 1  Color: 0    Card:  7  Suit: 3  Color: 1
Card:  8  Suit: 1  Color: 0    Card:  8  Suit: 3  Color: 1
Card:  9  Suit: 1  Color: 0    Card:  9  Suit: 3  Color: 1
Card: 10  Suit: 1  Color: 0    Card: 10  Suit: 3  Color: 1
Card: 11  Suit: 1  Color: 0    Card: 11  Suit: 3  Color: 1
Card: 12  Suit: 1  Color: 0    Card: 12  Suit: 3  Color: 1
```

Fig. 16.15   Output of the program in Fig. 16.14.

It is possible to specify an *unnamed bit field*, in which case the field is used as *padding* in the structure. For example, the structure definition uses an unnamed 3-bit field as padding—nothing can be stored in those three bits. Member **b** is stored in another storage unit.

```
struct Example {
    unsigned a : 13;
    unsigned   : 3;
    unsigned b : 4;
};
```

An *unnamed bit field with a zero width* is used to align the next bit field on a new storage unit boundary. For example, the structure definition

```
struct Example {
    unsigned a : 13;
    unsigned   : 0;
    unsigned b : 4;
};
```

uses an unnamed **0**-bit field to skip the remaining bits (as many as there are) of the storage unit in which **a** is stored and align **b** on the next storage unit boundary.

Portability Tip 16.5

Bit-field manipulations are machine dependent. For example, some computers allow bit fields to cross word boundaries, whereas others do not.

Common Programming Error 16.8

Attempting to access individual bits of a bit field as if they were elements of an array. Bit fields are not "arrays of bits."

Common Programming Error 16.9

*Attempting to take the address of a bit field (the **&** operator may not be used with bit fields because they do not have addresses).*

Performance Tip 16.3

Although bit fields save space, using them can cause the compiler to generate slower executing machine-language code. This occurs because it takes extra machine-language operations to access only portions of an addressable storage unit. This is one of many examples of the kinds of space–time trade-offs that occur in computer science.

16.9 Character-handling Library

Most data are entered into computers as characters—including letters, digits and various special symbols. In this section, we discuss C++'s capabilities for examining and manipulating individual characters. In the remainder of the chapter, we continue the discussion of character-string manipulation that we began in Chapter 5.

The character-handling library includes several functions that perform useful tests and manipulations of character data. Each function receives a character—represented as an

int—or **EOF** as an argument. Characters are often manipulated as integers. Remember that **EOF** normally has the value **−1** and that some hardware architectures do not allow negative values to be stored in **char** variables. Therefore, the character-handling functions manipulate characters as integers. Figure 16.16 summarizes the functions of the character-handling library. When using functions from the character-handling library, be sure to include the **<cctype>** header file.

Figure 16.17 demonstrates functions **isdigit**, **isalpha**, **isalnum** and **isxdigit**. Function **isdigit** determines whether its argument is a digit (**0–9**). Function **isalpha** determines whether its argument is an uppercase letter (**A–Z**) or a lowercase letter (**a–z**). Function **isalnum** determines whether its argument is an uppercase letter, a lowercase letter or a digit. Function **isxdigit** determines whether its argument is a hexadecimal digit (**A–F**, **a–f**, **0–9**).

Prototype	Description
`int isdigit( int c )`	Returns **true** if **c** is a digit and **false** otherwise.
`int isalpha( int c )`	Returns **true** if **c** is a letter and **false** otherwise.
`int isalnum( int c )`	Returns **true** if **c** is a digit or a letter and **false** otherwise.
`int isxdigit( int c )`	Returns **true** if **c** is a hexadecimal digit character and **false** otherwise. (See Appendix C, "Number Systems," for a detailed explanation of binary numbers, octal numbers, decimal numbers and hexadecimal numbers.)
`int islower( int c )`	Returns **true** if **c** is a lowercase letter and **false** otherwise.
`int isupper( int c )`	Returns **true** if **c** is an uppercase letter; **false** otherwise.
`int tolower( int c )`	If **c** is an uppercase letter, **tolower** returns **c** as a lowercase letter. Otherwise, **tolower** returns the argument unchanged.
`int toupper( int c )`	If **c** is a lowercase letter, **toupper** returns **c** as an uppercase letter. Otherwise, **toupper** returns the argument unchanged.
`int isspace( int c )`	Returns **true** if **c** is a white-space character—newline (`'\n'`), space (`' '`), form feed (`'\f'`), carriage return (`'\r'`), horizontal tab (`'\t'`), or vertical tab (`'\v'`)—and **false** otherwise
`int iscntrl( int c )`	Returns **true** if **c** is a control character and **false** otherwise.
`int ispunct( int c )`	Returns **true** if **c** is a printing character other than a space, a digit, or a letter and **false** otherwise.
`int isprint( int c )`	Returns **true** value if **c** is a printing character including space (`' '`) and **false** otherwise.
`int isgraph( int c )`	Returns **true** if **c** is a printing character other than space (`' '`) and **false** otherwise.

Fig. 16.16 Summary of the character handling library functions.

The program of Fig. 16.17 uses the conditional operator (**?:**) with each function to determine whether the string " **is a** " or the string " **is not a** " should be printed in the output for each character tested. For example, the expression

```
isdigit( '8' ) ? "8 is a " : "8 is not a "
```

```
1    // Fig. 16.17: fig16_17.cpp
2    // Using functions isdigit, isalpha, isalnum and isxdigit
3    #include <iostream>
4
5    using std::cout;
6    using std::endl;
7
8    #include <cctype>
9
10   int main()
11   {
12      cout << "According to isdigit:\n"
13           << ( isdigit( '8' ) ? "8 is a" : "8 is not a" )
14           << " digit\n"
15           << ( isdigit( '#' ) ? "# is a" : "# is not a" )
16           << " digit\n";
17      cout << "\nAccording to isalpha:\n"
18           << ( isalpha( 'A' ) ? "A is a" : "A is not a" )
19           << " letter\n"
20           << ( isalpha( 'b' ) ? "b is a" : "b is not a" )
21           << " letter\n"
22           << ( isalpha( '&' ) ? "& is a" : "& is not a" )
23           << " letter\n"
24           << ( isalpha( '4' ) ? "4 is a" : "4 is not a" )
25           << " letter\n";
26      cout << "\nAccording to isalnum:\n"
27           << ( isalnum( 'A' ) ? "A is a" : "A is not a" )
28           << " digit or a letter\n"
29           << ( isalnum( '8' ) ? "8 is a" : "8 is not a" )
30           << " digit or a letter\n"
31           << ( isalnum( '#' ) ? "# is a" : "# is not a" )
32           << " digit or a letter\n";
33      cout << "\nAccording to isxdigit:\n"
34           << ( isxdigit( 'F' ) ? "F is a" : "F is not a" )
35           << " hexadecimal digit\n"
36           << ( isxdigit( 'J' ) ? "J is a" : "J is not a" )
37           << " hexadecimal digit\n"
38           << ( isxdigit( '7' ) ? "7 is a" : "7 is not a" )
39           << " hexadecimal digit\n"
40           << ( isxdigit( '$' ) ? "$ is a" : "$ is not a" )
41           << " hexadecimal digit\n"
42           << ( isxdigit( 'f' ) ? "f is a" : "f is not a" )
43           << " hexadecimal digit" << endl;
44      return 0;
45   }
```

Fig. 16.17 Using **isdigit**, **isalpha**, **isalnum** and **isxdigit** (part 1 of 2).

```
According to isdigit:
8 is a digit
# is not a digit

According to isalpha:
A is a letter
b is a letter
& is not a letter
4 is not a letter

According to isalnum:
A is a digit or a letter
8 is a digit or a letter
# is not a digit or a letter

According to isxdigit:
F is a hexadecimal digit
J is not a hexadecimal digit
7 is a hexadecimal digit
$ is not a hexadecimal digit
f is a hexadecimal digit
```

Fig. 16.17 Using `isdigit`, `isalpha`, `isalnum` and `isxdigit` (part 2 of 2).

indicates that if `'8'` is a digit (i.e., if `isdigit` returns a true (nonzero) value), the string `"8 is a "` is printed, and if `'8'` is not a digit (i.e., if `isdigit` returns `0`), the string `"8 is not a "` is printed.

The program of Fig. 16.18 demonstrates functions `islower`, `isupper`, `tolower` and `toupper`. Function `islower` determines whether its argument is a lowercase letter (`a–z`). Function `isupper` determines whether its argument is an uppercase letter (`A–Z`). Function `tolower` converts an uppercase letter to a lowercase letter, and returns the lowercase letter. If the argument is not an uppercase letter, `tolower` returns the argument unchanged. Function `toupper` converts a lowercase letter to an uppercase letter, and returns the uppercase letter. If the argument is not a lowercase letter, `toupper` returns the argument unchanged.

```cpp
1   // Fig. 16.18: fig16_18.cpp
2   // Using functions islower, isupper, tolower and toupper
3   #include <iostream>
4
5   using std::cout;
6   using std::endl;
7
8   #include <cctype>
9
10  int main()
11  {
12     cout << "According to islower:\n"
13          << ( islower( 'p' ) ? "p is a" : "p is not a" )
14          << " lowercase letter\n"
```

Fig. 16.18 Using `islower`, `isupper`, `tolower` and `toupper` (part 1 of 2).

```
15                << ( islower( 'P' ) ? "P is a" : "P is not a" )
16                << " lowercase letter\n"
17                << ( islower( '5' ) ? "5 is a" : "5 is not a" )
18                << " lowercase letter\n"
19                << ( islower( '!' ) ? "! is a" : "! is not a" )
20                << " lowercase letter\n";
21        cout << "\nAccording to isupper:\n"
22                << ( isupper( 'D' ) ? "D is an" : "D is not an" )
23                << " uppercase letter\n"
24                << ( isupper( 'd' ) ? "d is an" : "d is not an" )
25                << " uppercase letter\n"
26                << ( isupper( '8' ) ? "8 is an" : "8 is not an" )
27                << " uppercase letter\n"
28                << ( isupper('$') ? "$ is an" : "$ is not an" )
29                << " uppercase letter\n";
30        cout << "\nu converted to uppercase is "
31                << static_cast< char >( toupper( 'u' ) )
32                << "\n7 converted to uppercase is "
33                << static_cast< char >( toupper( '7' ) )
34                << "\n$ converted to uppercase is "
35                << static_cast< char >( toupper( '$' ) )
36                << "\nL converted to lowercase is "
37                << static_cast< char >( tolower( 'L' ) ) << endl;
38
39        return 0;
40    }
```

```
According to islower:
p is a lowercase letter
P is not a lowercase letter
5 is not a lowercase letter
! is not a lowercase letter

According to isupper:
D is an uppercase letter
d is not an uppercase letter
8 is not an uppercase letter
$ is not an uppercase letter

u converted to uppercase is U
7 converted to uppercase is 7
$ converted to uppercase is $
L converted to lowercase is l
```

Fig. 16.18 Using **islower**, **isupper**, **tolower** and **toupper** (part 2 of 2).

Figure 16.19 demonstrates functions **isspace**, **iscntrl**, **ispunct**, **isprint** and **isgraph**. Function **isspace** determines if its argument is a white-space character such as space (' '), form feed ('\f'), newline ('\n'), carriage return ('\r'), horizontal tab ('\t') or vertical tab ('\v'). Function **iscntrl** determines if its argument is a control character such as horizontal tab, vertical tab, form feed, alert ('\a'), backspace ('\b'), carriage return or newline. Function **ispunct** determines if its argument is a printing character other than a space, digit or letter such as $, #, (,), [,], {, }, ;, :, %, etc. Function **isprint** determines if its argument is a character that can be displayed on the screen (including the space character). Function **isgraph** tests for the same characters as **isprint**; however, the space character is not included.

```cpp
 1   // Fig. 16.19: fig16_19.cpp
 2   // Using functions isspace, iscntrl, ispunct, isprint, isgraph
 3   #include <iostream>
 4
 5   using std::cout;
 6   using std::endl;
 7
 8   #include <cctype>
 9
10   int main()
11   {
12      cout << "According to isspace:\nNewline "
13           << ( isspace( '\n' ) ? "is a" : "is not a" )
14           << " whitespace character\nHorizontal tab "
15           << ( isspace( '\t' ) ? "is a" : "is not a" )
16           << " whitespace character\n"
17           << ( isspace( '%' ) ? "% is a" : "% is not a" )
18           << " whitespace character\n";
19
20      cout << "\nAccording to iscntrl:\nNewline "
21           << ( iscntrl( '\n' ) ? "is a" : "is not a" )
22           << " control character\n"
23           << ( iscntrl( '$' ) ? "$ is a" : "$ is not a" )
24           << " control character\n";
25
26      cout << "\nAccording to ispunct:\n"
27           << ( ispunct( ';' ) ? "; is a" : "; is not a" )
28           << " punctuation character\n"
29           << ( ispunct( 'Y' ) ? "Y is a" : "Y is not a" )
30           << " punctuation character\n"
31           << ( ispunct('#') ? "# is a" : "# is not a" )
32           << " punctuation character\n";
33
34      cout << "\nAccording to isprint:\n"
35           << ( isprint( '$' ) ? "$ is a" : "$ is not a" )
36           << " printing character\nAlert "
37           << ( isprint( '\a' ) ? "is a" : "is not a" )
38           << " printing character\n";
39
40      cout << "\nAccording to isgraph:\n"
41           << ( isgraph( 'Q' ) ? "Q is a" : "Q is not a" )
42           << " printing character other than a space\nSpace "
43           << ( isgraph(' ') ? "is a" : "is not a" )
44           << " printing character other than a space" << endl;
45
46      return 0;
47   }
```

Fig. 16.19 Using **isspace**, **iscntrl**, **ispunct**, **isprint** and **isgraph** (part 1 of 2).

```
According to isspace:
Newline is a whitespace character
Horizontal tab is a whitespace character
% is not a whitespace character

According to iscntrl:
Newline is a control character
$ is not a control character

According to ispunct:
; is a punctuation character
Y is not a punctuation character
# is a punctuation character

According to isprint:
$ is a printing character
Alert is not a printing character

According to isgraph:
Q is a printing character other than a space
Space is not a printing character other than a space
```

Fig. 16.19   Using `isspace`, `iscntrl`, `ispunct`, `isprint` and `isgraph` (part 2 of 2).

16.10 String Conversion Functions

In Chapter 5, we discussed several of C++'s most popular character string manipulation functions. In the next several sections, we cover the remaining functions, including functions for converting strings to numeric values, functions for searching strings and functions for manipulating, comparing and searching blocks of memory.

This section presents the *string conversion functions* from the *general utilities library* `<cstdlib>`. These functions convert strings of digits to integer and floating-point values. Figure 16.20 summarizes the string conversion functions. Note the use of `const` to declare variable `nPtr` in the function headers (read from right to left as "`nPtr` is a pointer to a character constant"); `const` declares that the argument value will not be modified. When using functions from the general utilities library, be sure to include the `<cstdlib>` header file.

Prototype	Description
`double atof( const char *nPtr )`	Converts the string `nPtr` to `double`.
`int atoi( const char *nPtr )`	Converts the string `nPtr` to `int`.
`long atol( const char *nPtr )`	Converts the string `nPtr` to long `int`.
`double strtod( const char *nPtr, char **endPtr )`	
	Converts the string `nPtr` to `double`.

Fig. 16.20   Summary of the string conversion functions of the general utilities library (part 1 of 2).

Prototype	Description
`long strtol( const char *nPtr, char **endPtr, int base )`	
	Converts the string **nPtr** to **long**.
`unsigned long strtoul( const char *nPtr, char **endPtr, int base )`	
	Converts the string **nPtr** to **unsigned long**.

Fig. 16.20 Summary of the string conversion functions of the general utilities library (part 2 of 2).

Function **atof** (Fig. 16.21) converts its argument—a string that represents a floating-point number—to a **double** value. The function returns the **double** value. If the string cannot be converted—for example, if the first character of the string is not a digit—function **atof** returns zero.

Function **atoi** (Fig. 16.22) converts its argument—a string of digits that represents an integer—to an **int** value. The function returns the **int** value. If the string cannot be converted, function **atoi** returns zero.

```
1   // Fig. 16.21: fig16_21.cpp
2   // Using atof
3   #include <iostream>
4
5   using std::cout;
6   using std::endl;
7
8   #include <cstdlib>
9
10  int main()
11  {
12     double d = atof( "99.0" );
13
14     cout << "The string \"99.0\" converted to double is "
15          << d << "\nThe converted value divided by 2 is "
16          << d / 2.0 << endl;
17     return 0;
18  }
```

```
The string "99.0" converted to double is 99
The converted value divided by 2 is 49.5
```

Fig. 16.21 Using **atof**.

```
1   // Fig. 16.22: fig16_22.cpp
2   // Using atoi
3   #include <iostream>
4
```

Fig. 16.22 Using **atoi** (part 1 of 2).

```
5    using std::cout;
6    using std::endl;
7
8    #include <cstdlib>
9
10   int main()
11   {
12      int i = atoi( "2593" );
13
14      cout << "The string \"2593\" converted to int is " << i
15           << "\nThe converted value minus 593 is " << i - 593
16           << endl;
17      return 0;
18   }
```

```
The string "2593" converted to int is 2593
The converted value minus 593 is 2000
```

Fig. 16.22   Using **atoi** (part 2 of 2).

Function **atol** (Fig. 16.23) converts its argument—a string of digits representing a long integer—to a **long** value. The function returns the **long** value. If the string cannot be converted, function **atol** returns zero. If **int** and **long** are both stored in 4 bytes, function **atoi** and function **atol** work identically.

```
1    // Fig. 16.23: fig16_23.cpp
2    // Using atol
3    #include <iostream>
4
5    using std::cout;
6    using std::endl;
7
8    #include <cstdlib>
9
10   int main()
11   {
12      long x = atol( "1000000" );
13
14      cout << "The string \"1000000\" converted to long is " << x
15           << "\nThe converted value divided by 2 is " << x / 2
16           << endl;
17      return 0;
18   }
```

```
The string "1000000" converted to long int is 1000000
The converted value divided by 2 is 500000
```

Fig. 16.23   Using **atol**.

Function **strtod** (Fig. 16.24) converts a sequence of characters representing a floating-point value to **double**. Function **strtod** receives two arguments—a string (**char ***) and a pointer to a string (i.e., a **char ****). The string contains the character sequence to be converted to **double**. The second argument is assigned the location of the first character after the converted portion of the string. The statement

```
d = strtod( string, &stringPtr );
```

from the program of Fig. 16.24 indicates that **d** is assigned the **double** value converted from **string**, and **&stringPtr** is assigned the location of the first character after the converted value (**51.2**) in **string**.

Function **strtol** (Fig. 16.25) converts to **long** a sequence of characters representing an integer. The function receives three arguments—a string (**char ***), a pointer to a string and an integer. The string contains the character sequence to be converted. The second argument is assigned the location of the first character after the converted portion of the string. The integer specifies the *base* of the value being converted. The statement

```
x = strtol( string, &remainderPtr, 0 );
```

indicates that **x** is assigned the **long** value converted from **string**. The second argument, **&remainderPtr**, is assigned the remainder of **string** after the conversion. Using **NULL** for the second argument causes the remainder of the string to be ignored. The third argument, **0**, indicates that the value to be converted can be in octal (base 8), decimal (base 10) or hexadecimal (base 16).

```cpp
1   // Fig. 16.24: fig16_24.cpp
2   // Using strtod
3   #include <iostream>
4
5   using std::cout;
6   using std::endl;
7
8   #include <cstdlib>
9
10  int main()
11  {
12     double d;
13     const char *string = "51.2% are admitted";
14     char *stringPtr;
15
16     d = strtod( string, &stringPtr );
17     cout << "The string \"" << string
18        << "\" is converted to the\ndouble value " << d
19        << " and the string \"" << stringPtr << "\"" << endl;
20     return 0;
21  }
```

```
The string "51.2% are admitted" is converted to the
double value 51.2 and the string "% are admitted"
```

Fig. 16.24　Using **strtod**.

In a call to function **strtol**, the base can be specified as zero or any value between 2 and 36. (See Appendix C, "Number Systems," for a detailed explanation of the octal, decimal, hexadecimal and binary number systems). Numeric representations of integers from base 11 to base 36 use the characters A–Z to represent the values 10 to 35. For example, hexadecimal values can consist of the digits 0–9 and the characters A–F. A base-11 integer can consist of the digits 0–9 and the character A. A base-24 integer can consist of the digits 0–9 and the characters A–N. A base-36 integer can consist of the digits 0–9 and the characters A–Z.

Function **strtoul** (Fig. 16.26) converts to **unsigned long** a sequence of characters representing an **unsigned long** integer. The function works identically to function **strtol**. The statement

```
x = strtoul( string, &remainderPtr, 0 );
```

in the program of Fig. 16.26 indicates that **x** is assigned the **unsigned long** value converted from **string**. The second argument, **&remainderPtr**, is assigned the remainder of **string** after the conversion. The third argument, **0**, indicates that the value to be converted can be in octal, decimal or hexadecimal format.

```cpp
1   // Fig. 16.25: fig16_25.cpp
2   // Using strtol
3   #include <iostream>
4
5   using std::cout;
6   using std::endl;
7
8   #include <cstdlib>
9
10  int main()
11  {
12     long x;
13     const char *string = "-1234567abc";
14     char *remainderPtr;
15
16     x = strtol( string, &remainderPtr, 0 );
17     cout << "The original string is \"" << string
18          << "\"\nThe converted value is " << x
19          << "\nThe remainder of the original string is \""
20          << remainderPtr
21          << "\"\nThe converted value plus 567 is "
22          << x + 567 << endl;
23     return 0;
24  }
```

```
The original string is "-1234567abc"
The converted value is -1234567
The remainder of the original string is "abc"
The converted value plus 567 is -1234000
```

Fig. 16.25 Using **strtol**.

```
1   // Fig. 16.26: fig16_26.cpp
2   // Using strtoul
3   #include <iostream>
4
5   using std::cout;
6   using std::endl;
7
8   #include <cstdlib>
9
10  int main()
11  {
12     unsigned long x;
13     const char *string = "1234567abc";
14     char *remainderPtr;
15
16     x = strtoul( string, &remainderPtr, 0 );
17     cout << "The original string is \"" << string
18          << "\"\nThe converted value is " << x
19          << "\nThe remainder of the original string is \""
20          << remainderPtr
21          << "\"\nThe converted value minus 567 is "
22          << x - 567 << endl;
23     return 0;
24  }
```

```
The original string is "1234567abc"
The converted value is 1234567
The remainder of the original string is "abc"
The converted value minus 567 is 1234000
```

Fig. 16.26 Using `strtoul`.

16.11 Search Functions of the String-handling Library

This section presents the functions of the string-handling library used to search strings for characters and other strings. The functions are summarized in Fig. 16.27. Note that functions `strcspn` and `strspn` specify return type `size_t`. Type `size_t` is a type defined by the standard as the integral type of the value returned by operator `sizeof`.

Prototype	Description
`char *strchr( const char *s, int c )`	
	Locates the first occurrence of character **c** in string **s**. If **c** is found, a pointer to **c** in **s** is returned. Otherwise, a **NULL** pointer is returned.
`char *strrchr( const char *s, int c )`	
	Locates the last occurrence of **c** in string **s**. If **c** is found, a pointer to **c** in string **s** is returned. Otherwise, a **NULL** pointer is returned.

Fig. 16.27 Search functions of the string-handling library (part 1 of 2).

Prototype	Description

size_t strspn(const char *s1, const char *s2)

Determines and returns the length of the initial segment of string **s1** consisting only of characters contained in string **s2**.

char *strpbrk(const char *s1, const char *s2)

Locates the first occurrence in string **s1** of any character in string **s2**. If a character from string **s2** is found, a pointer to the character in string **s1** is returned. Otherwise, a **NULL** pointer is returned.

size_t strcspn(const char *s1, const char *s2)

Determines and returns the length of the initial segment of string **s1** consisting of characters not contained in string **s2**.

char *strstr(const char *s1, const char *s2)

Locates the first occurrence in string **s1** of string **s2**. If the string is found, a pointer to the string in **s1** is returned. Otherwise, a **NULL** pointer is returned.

Fig. 16.27 Search functions of the string-handling library (part 2 of 2).

Portability Tip 16.6

*Type **size_t** is a system-dependent synonym for either type **unsigned long** or type **unsigned int**.*

Function **strchr** searches for the first occurrence of a character in a string. If the character is found, **strchr** returns a pointer to the character in the string; otherwise, **strchr** returns **NULL**. The program of Fig. 16.28 uses **strchr** to search for the first occurrences of **'a'** and **'z'** in the string **"This is a test"**.

```
1   // Fig. 16.28: fig16_28.cpp
2   // Using strchr
3   #include <iostream>
4
5   using std::cout;
6   using std::endl;
7
8   #include <cstring>
9
10  int main()
11  {
12     const char *string = "This is a test";
13     char character1 = 'a', character2 = 'z';
14
15     if ( strchr( string, character1 ) != NULL )
16        cout << '\'' << character1 << "' was found in \""
17             << string << "\".\n";
```

Fig. 16.28 Using **strchr** (part 1 of 2).

```
18        else
19           cout << '\'' << character1 << "' was not found in \""
20                << string << "\".\n";
21
22        if ( strchr( string, character2 ) != NULL )
23           cout << '\'' << character2 << "' was found in \""
24                << string << "\".\n";
25        else
26           cout << '\'' << character2 << "' was not found in \""
27                << string << "\"." << endl;
28        return 0;
29     }
```

```
'a' was found in "This is a test".
'z' was not found in "This is a test".
```

Fig. 16.28   Using **strchr** (part 2 of 2).

Function **strcspn** (Fig. 16.29) determines the length of the initial part of the string in its first argument that does not contain any characters from the string in its second argument. The function returns the length of the segment.

```
1   // Fig. 16.29: fig16_29.cpp
2   // Using strcspn
3   #include <iostream>
4
5   using std::cout;
6   using std::endl;
7
8   #include <cstring>
9
10  int main()
11  {
12     const char *string1 = "The value is 3.14159";
13     const char *string2 = "1234567890";
14
15     cout << "string1 = " << string1 << "\nstring2 = " << string2
16          << "\n\nThe length of the initial segment of string1"
17          << "\ncontaining no characters from string2 = "
18          << strcspn( string1, string2 ) << endl;
19     return 0;
20  }
```

```
string1 = The value is 3.14159
string2 = 1234567890

The length of the initial segment of string1
containing no characters from string2 = 13
```

Fig. 16.29   Using **strcspn**.

Function **strpbrk** searches for the first occurrence in its first string argument of any character in its second string argument. If a character from the second argument is found, **strpbrk** returns a pointer to the character in the first argument; otherwise, **strpbrk** returns **NULL**. The program of Fig. 16.30 locates the first occurrence in **string1** of any character from **string2**.

Function **strrchr** searches for the last occurrence of the specified character in a string. If the character is found, **strrchr** returns a pointer to the character in the string; otherwise, **strrchr** returns **0**. The program of Fig. 16.31 searches for the last occurrence of the character **'z'** in the string **"A zoo has many animals including zebras"**.

```
1   // Fig. 16.30: fig16_30.cpp
2   // Using strpbrk
3   #include <iostream>
4
5   using std::cout;
6   using std::endl;
7
8   #include <cstring>
9
10  int main()
11  {
12     const char *string1 = "This is a test";
13     const char *string2 = "beware";
14
15     cout << "Of the characters in \"" << string2 << "\"\n'"
16          << *strpbrk( string1, string2 ) << '\''
17          << " is the first character to appear in\n\""
18          << string1 << '\"' << endl;
19     return 0;
20  }
```

```
Of the characters in "beware"
'a' is the first character to appear in
"This is a test"
```

Fig. 16.30 Using **strpbrk**.

```
1   // Fig. 16.31: fig16_31.cpp
2   // Using strrchr
3   #include <iostream>
4
5   using std::cout;
6   using std::endl;
7
8   #include <cstring>
9
10  int main()
11  {
12     const char *string1 = "A zoo has many animals "
13                           "including zebras";
```

Fig. 16.31 Using **strrchr** (part 1 of 2).

```
14        int c = 'z';
15
16        cout << "The remainder of string1 beginning with the\n"
17             << "last occurrence of character '"
18             << static_cast< char >( c )
19             << "' is: \"" << strrchr( string1, c ) << '\"' << endl;
20        return 0;
21    }
```

```
The remainder of string1 beginning with the
last occurrence of character 'z' is: "zebras"
```

Fig. 16.31 Using **strrchr** (part 2 of 2).

Function **strspn** (Fig. 16.32) determines the length of the initial part of the string in its first argument that contains only characters from the string in its second argument. The function returns the length of the segment.

Function **strstr** searches for the first occurrence of its second string argument in its first string argument. If the second string is found in the first string, a pointer to the location of the string in the first argument is returned. The program of Fig. 16.33 uses **strstr** to find the string **"def"** in the string **"abcdefabcdef"**.

```
1   // Fig. 16.32: fig16_32.cpp
2   // Using strspn
3   #include <iostream>
4
5   using std::cout;
6   using std::endl;
7
8   #include <cstring>
9
10  int main()
11  {
12      const char *string1 = "The value is 3.14159";
13      const char *string2 = "aehils Tuv";
14
15      cout << "string1 = " << string1
16           << "\nstring2 = " << string2
17           << "\n\nThe length of the initial segment of string1\n"
18           << "containing only characters from string2 = "
19           << strspn( string1, string2 ) << endl;
20      return 0;
21  }
```

```
string1 = The value is 3.14159
string2 = aehils Tuv

The length of the initial segment of string1
containing only characters from string2 = 13
```

Fig. 16.32 Using **strspn**.

```
1   // Fig. 16.33: fig16_33.cpp
2   // Using strstr
3   #include <iostream>
4
5   using std::cout;
6   using std::endl;
7
8   #include <cstring>
9
10  int main()
11  {
12     const char *string1 = "abcdefabcdef";
13     const char *string2 = "def";
14
15     cout << "string1 = " << string1 << "\nstring2 = " << string2
16          << "\n\nThe remainder of string1 beginning with the\n"
17          << "first occurrence of string2 is: "
18          << strstr( string1, string2 ) << endl;
19     return 0;
20  }
```

```
string1 = abcdefabcdef
string2 = def

The remainder of string1 beginning with the
first occurrence of string2 is: defabcdef
```

Fig. 16.33   Using strstr.

16.12 Memory Functions of the String-handling Library

The string-handling library functions presented in this section facilitate manipulating, comparing and searching blocks of memory. The functions treat blocks of memory as character arrays. These functions can manipulate any block of data. Figure 16.34 summarizes the memory functions of the string-handling library. In the function discussions, "object" refers to a block of data.

The pointer parameters to these functions are declared **void ***. In Chapter 5, we saw that a pointer to any data type can be assigned directly to a pointer of type **void ***. For this reason, these functions can receive pointers to any data type. Remember that a pointer of type **void *** cannot be assigned directly to a pointer to any data type. Because a **void *** pointer cannot be dereferenced, each function receives a size argument that specifies the number of characters (bytes) the function will process. For simplicity, the examples in this section manipulate character arrays (blocks of characters).

Function **memcpy** copies a specified number of characters (bytes) from the object pointed to by its second argument into the object pointed to by its first argument. The function can receive a pointer to any type of object. The result of this function is undefined if the two objects overlap in memory(i.e., they are parts of the same object). The program of Fig. 16.35 uses **memcpy** to copy the string in array **s2** to array **s1**.

```
1   // Fig. 16.37: fig16_37.cpp
2   // Using memcmp
3   #include <iostream>
4
5   using std::cout;
6   using std::endl;
7
8   #include <iomanip>
9
10  using std::setw;
11
12  #include <cstring>
13
14  int main()
15  {
16     char s1[] = "ABCDEFG", s2[] = "ABCDXYZ";
17
18     cout << "s1 = " << s1 << "\ns2 = " << s2 << endl
19          << "\nmemcmp(s1, s2, 4) = " << setw( 3 )
20          << memcmp( s1, s2, 4 ) << "\nmemcmp(s1, s2, 7) = "
21          << setw( 3 ) << memcmp( s1, s2, 7 )
22          << "\nmemcmp(s2, s1, 7) = " << setw( 3 )
23          << memcmp( s2, s1, 7 ) << endl;
24     return 0;
25  }
```

```
s1 = ABCDEFG
s2 = ABCDXYZ

memcmp(s1, s2, 4) =   0
memcmp(s1, s2, 7) = -1
memcmp(s2, s1, 7) =  1
```

Fig. 16.37　Using memcmp.

Function **memchr** searches for the first occurrence of a byte, represented as **unsigned char**, in the specified number of bytes of an object. If the byte is found, a pointer to the byte in the object is returned; otherwise, **NULL** is returned. The program of Fig. 16.38 searches for the character (byte) `'r'` in the string `"This is a string"`.

```
1   // Fig. 16.38: fig16_38.cpp
2   // Using memchr
3   #include <iostream>
4
5   using std::cout;
6   using std::endl;
7
8   #include <cstring>
9
```

Fig. 16.38　Using memchr.

```
10   int main()
11   {
12      char s[] = "This is a string";
13
14      cout << "The remainder of s after character 'r' "
15           << "is found is \""
16           << static_cast<char *>( memchr( s, 'r', 16 ) )
17           << '\"' << endl;
18      return 0;
19   }
```

```
The remainder of s after character 'r' is found is "ring"
```

Fig. 16.38   Using **memchr**.

Function **memset** copies the value of the byte in its second argument into a specified number of bytes of the object pointed to by its first argument. The program in Fig. 16.39 uses **memset** to copy **'b'** into the first 7 bytes of **string1**.

16.13 Another Function of the String-handling Library

The remaining function of the string-handling library is **strerror**. Figure 16.40 summarizes function **strerror**. Function **strerror** takes an error number and creates an error message string. A pointer to the string is returned. The program of Fig. 16.41 demonstrates **strerror**.

```
1   // Fig. 16.39: fig16_39.cpp
2   // Using memset
3   #include <iostream>
4
5   using std::cout;
6   using std::endl;
7
8   #include <cstring>
9
10  int main()
11  {
12     char string1[ 15 ] = "BBBBBBBBBBBBBB";
13
14     cout << "string1 = " << string1 << endl;
15     cout << "string1 after memset = "
16          << static_cast<char *>( memset( string1, 'b', 7 ) )
17          << endl;
18     return 0;
19  }
```

```
string1 = BBBBBBBBBBBBBB
string1 after memset = bbbbbbbBBBBBBB
```

Fig. 16.39   Using **memset**.

Prototype	Description

`char *strerror( int errornum )`

Maps **errornum** into a full text string in a system dependent manner.
A pointer to the string is returned.

Fig. 16.40 Another string manipulation function of the string-handling library.

```
1   // Fig. 16.41: fig16_41.cpp
2   // Using strerror
3   #include <iostream>
4
5   using std::cout;
6   using std::endl;
7
8   #include <cstring>
9
10  int main()
11  {
12     cout << strerror( 2 ) << endl;
13     return 0;
14  }
```

No such file or directory

Fig. 16.41 Using **strerror**.

Portability Tip 16.7

The message generated by **strerror** *is system dependent.*

SUMMARY

- Structures are collections of related variables, sometimes referred to as aggregates, under one name.
- Structures can contain variables of different data types.
- Keyword **struct** begins every structure definition. Within the braces of the structure definition are the structure member declarations.
- Members of the same structure must have unique names.
- A structure definition creates a new data type that can be used to declare variables.
- A structure can be initialized with an initializer list by following the variable in the declaration with an equal sign and a comma-separated list of initializers enclosed in braces. If there are fewer initializers in the list than members in the structure, the remaining members are initialized to zero (or **NULL** for pointer members).
- Entire structure variables may be assigned to structure variables of the same type.
- A structure variable may be initialized with a structure variable of the same type.
- Structures variables and individual structure members are passed to functions by call-by-value. Array members are, of course, passed by call-by-reference.

- To pass a structure by call-by-reference, pass the address of the structure variable. An array of structures is passed by call-by-reference. To pass an array by call-by-value, create a structure with the array as a member.

- Creating a new type name with **typedef** does not create a new type; it creates a name that is synonymous to a type defined previously.

- The bitwise AND operator (**&**) takes two integral operands. A bit in the result is set to one if the corresponding bits in each of the operands are one.

- Masks are used to hide some bits while preserving others.

- The bitwise inclusive OR operator (**|**) takes two operands. A bit in the result is set to one if the corresponding bit in either operand is set to one.

- Each of the bitwise operators (except complement) has a corresponding assignment operator.

- The bitwise exclusive-OR operator (**^**) takes two operands. A bit in the result is set to one if exactly one of the corresponding bits in the two operands is set to 1.

- The left-shift operator (**<<**) shifts the bits of its left operand left by the number of bits specified by its right operand. Bits vacated to the right are replaced with **0**s.

- The right-shift operator (**>>**) shifts the bits of its left operand right by the number of bits specified in its right operand. Performing a right shift on an unsigned integer causes bits vacated at the left to be replaced by zeros. Vacated bits in signed integers can be replaced with zeros or ones—this is machine dependent.

- The bitwise complement operator (**~**) takes one operand and reverses its bits—this produces the one's complement of the operand.

- Bit fields reduce storage use by storing data in the minimum number of bits required. Bit field members must be declared as **int** or **unsigned**.

- A bit field is declared by following an **unsigned** or **int** member name with a colon and the width of the bit field.

- The bit field width must be an integer constant between zero and the total number of bits used to store an **int** variable on your system

- If a bit field is specified without a name, the field is used as padding in the structure.

- An unnamed bit field with width **0** aligns the next bit field on a new machine word boundary.

- Function **islower** determines whether its argument is a lowercase letter (**a–z**). Function **isupper** determines if its argument is an uppercase letter (**A–Z**).

- Function **isdigit** determines whether its argument is a digit (**0–9**).

- Function **isalpha** determines if its argument is an uppercase (**A–Z**) or lowercase letter (**a–z**).

- Function **isalnum** determines whether its argument is an uppercase letter (**A–Z**), a lowercase letter (**a–z**), or a digit (**0–9**).

- Function **isxdigit** determines whether its argument is a hexadecimal digit (**A–F**, **a–f**, **0–9**).

- Function **toupper** converts a lowercase letter to an uppercase letter. Function **tolower** converts an uppercase letter to a lowercase letter.

- Function **isspace** determines whether its argument is one of the following white-space characters: **' '** (space), **'\f'**, **'\n'**, **'\r'**, **'\t'** or **'\v'**.

- Function **iscntrl** determines whether its argument is one of the following control characters: **'\t'**, **'\v'**, **'\f'**, **'\a'**, **'\b'**, **'\r'** or **'\n'**.

- Function **ispunct** determines whether its argument is a printing character other than a space, a digit or a letter.

- Function **isprint** determines if its argument is any printing character including space.

- Function **isgraph** determines if its argument is a printing character other than space.

- Function **atof** converts its argument—a string beginning with a series of digits that represents a floating-point number—to a **double** value.

- Function **atoi** converts its argument—a string beginning with a series of digits that represents an integer—to an **int** value.

- Function **atol** converts its argument—a string beginning with a series of digits that represents a long integer—to a **long** value.

- Function **strtod** converts a sequence of characters representing a floating-point value to **double**. The function receives two arguments—a string (**char ***) and a pointer to **char ***. The string contains the character sequence to be converted, and the pointer to **char *** is assigned the remainder of the string after the conversion.

- Function **strtol** converts a sequence of characters representing an integer to **long**. The function receives three arguments—a string (**char ***), a pointer to **char *** and an integer. The string contains the character sequence to be converted, the pointer to **char *** is assigned the remainder of the string after the conversion and the integer specifies the base of the value being converted.

- Function **strtoul** converts a sequence of characters representing an integer to **unsigned long**. The function receives three arguments—a string (**char ***), a pointer to **char *** and an integer. The string contains the character sequence to be converted, the pointer to **char *** is assigned the remainder of the string after the conversion and the integer specifies the base of the value being converted.

- Function **strchr** searches for the first occurrence of a character in a string. If the character is found, **strchr** returns a pointer to the character in the string; otherwise, **strchr** returns **NULL**.

- Function **strcspn** determines the length of the initial part of the string in its first argument that does not contain any characters from the string in its second argument. The function returns the length of the segment.

- Function **strpbrk** searches for the first occurrence in its first argument of any character that appears in its second argument. If a character from the second argument is found, **strpbrk** returns a pointer to the character; otherwise, **strpbrk** returns **NULL**.

- Function **strrchr** searches for the last occurrence of a character in a string. If the character is found, **strrchr** returns a pointer to the character in the string; otherwise, it returns **NULL**.

- Function **strspn** determines the length of the initial part of the string in its first argument that contains only characters from the string in its second argument. The function returns the length of the segment.

- Function **strstr** searches for the first occurrence of its second string argument in its first string argument. If the second string is found in the first string, a pointer to the location of the string in the first argument is returned.

- Function **memcpy** copies a specified number of characters from the object to which its second argument points into the object to which its first argument points. The function can receive a pointer to any type of object. The pointers are received by **memcpy** as **void** pointers and converted to **char** pointers for use in the function. Function **memcpy** manipulates the bytes of the argument as characters.

- Function **memmove** copies a specified number of bytes from the object pointed to by its second argument to the object pointed to by its first argument. Copying is accomplished as if the bytes are copied from the second argument to a temporary character array, and then copied from the temporary array to the first argument.

- Function **memcmp** compares the specified number of characters of its first and second arguments.

- Function **memchr** searches for the first occurrence of a byte, represented as **unsigned char**, in the specified number of bytes of an object. If the byte is found, a pointer to the byte is returned; otherwise, a **NULL** pointer is returned.

- Function **memset** copies its second argument, treated as an **unsigned char**, to a specified number of bytes of the object pointed to by the first argument.

- Function **strerror** maps an integer error number into a full text string in a system-dependent manner. A pointer to the string is returned.

TERMINOLOGY

^ bitwise exclusive-OR operator

^= bitwise exclusive-OR assignment operator

| bitwise inclusive-OR operator

|= bitwise inclusive-OR assignment operator

~ one's-complement operator

& bitwise AND operator

&= bitwise AND assignment operator

<< left-shift operator

<<= left-shift assignment operator

>> right-shift operator

>>= right shift assignment operator

array of structures

ASCII

atof

atoi

atol

bit field

bitwise operators

character code

character constant

character set

complementing

control character

<cctype>

<cstdlib>

<cstring>

delimiter

general utilities library

hexadecimal digits

initialization of structures

isalnum

isalpha

iscntrl

isdigit

isgraph

islower

isprint

ispunct

isspace

isupper

isxdigit

left shift

literal

mask

masking off bits

memchr

memcmp

memcpy

memmove

memset

one's complement

padding

pointer to a structure

printing character

record

right shift

search string

self-referential structure

shifting

space–time trade-offs

strchr

strcspn

strerror

string

string constant

string conversion functions

string literal

string processing

strpbrk

strrchr

strspn

strstr

strtod

strtol

strtoul

struct

structure assignment

structure initialization

structure type

tolower

toupper
typedef
unnamed bit field
white-space characters

width of a bit field
word processing
zero-width bit field

COMMON PROGRAMMING ERRORS

16.1   Forgetting the semicolon that terminates a structure definition.

16.2   Comparing structures is a syntax error because of the different alignment requirements on various systems.

16.3   Assuming that structures, like arrays, are passed by call-by-reference and trying to modify the caller's structure values in the called function.

16.4   Forgetting to include the array subscript when referring to individual structures in an array of structures.

16.5   Using the logical AND operator (**&&**) for the bitwise AND operator (**&**) and vice versa.

16.6   Using the logical OR operator (**||**) for the bitwise OR operator (**|**) and vice versa.

16.7   The result of shifting a value is undefined if the right operand is negative or if the right operand is larger than the number of bits in which the left operand is stored.

16.8   Attempting to access individual bits of a bit field as if they were elements of an array. Bit fields are not "arrays of bits."

16.9   Attempting to take the address of a bit field (the **&** operator may not be used with bit fields because they do not have addresses).

16.10 String manipulation functions other than **memmove** that copy characters have undefined results when copying takes place between parts of the same string.

GOOD PROGRAMMING PRACTICES

16.1   Provide a structure name when creating a structure type. The structure name is convenient for declaring new variables of the structure type later in the program and is required if the structure will be passed as a parameter to a function.

16.2   Capitalize **typedef** names to emphasize that these names are synonyms for other type names.

PERFORMANCE TIPS

16.1   Passing structures (and especially large structures) by call-by-reference is more efficient than passing structures by call-by-value (which requires the entire structure to be copied).

16.2   Bit fields help conserve storage.

16.3   Although bit fields save space, using them can cause the compiler to generate slower executing machine language code. This occurs because it takes extra machine language operations to access only portions of an addressable storage unit. This is one of many examples of the kinds of space–time trade-offs that occur in computer science.

PORTABILITY TIPS

16.1   Because the size of data items of a particular type is machine dependent, and because storage alignment considerations are machine dependent, so too is the representation of a structure.

16.2   Using **typedef** can help make a program more portable.

16.3   Bitwise data manipulations are machine dependent.

16.4   The result of right shifting a signed value is machine dependent. Some machines fill with zeros and others use the sign bit.

16.5   Bit-field manipulations are machine dependent. For example, some computers allow bit fields to cross word boundaries, whereas others do not.

16.6   Type **size_t** is a system-dependent synonym for either type **unsigned long** or type **unsigned int**.

16.7   The message generated by **strerror** is system dependent.

SELF-REVIEW EXERCISES

16.1   Fill in the blanks in each of the following:
  a) A _____ is a collection of related variables under one name.
  b) The bits in the result of an expression using the _____ operator are set to one if the corresponding bits in each operand are set to one. Otherwise, the bits are set to zero.
  c) The variables declared in a structure definition are called its _____.
  d) The bits in the result of an expression using the _____ operator are set to one if at least one of the corresponding bits in either operand is set to one. Otherwise, the bits are set to zero.
  e) Keyword _____ introduces a structure declaration.
  f) Keyword _____ is used to create a synonym for a previously defined data type.
  g) The bits in the result of an expression using the _____ operator are set to one if exactly one of the corresponding bits in either operand is set to one. Otherwise, the bits are set to zero.
  h) The bitwise AND operator **&** is often used to _____ bits, (i.e., to select certain bits from a bit string while zeroing others.
  i) The name of the structure is referred to as the structure _____.
  j) A structure member is accessed with either operator _____ or _____.
  k) The _____ and _____ operators are used to shift the bits of a value to the left or to the right, respectively.

16.2   State whether each of the following is *true* or *false*. If *false*, explain why.
  a) Structures may contain only one data type.
  b) Members of different structures must have unique names.
  c) Keyword **typedef** is used to define new data types.
  d) Structures are always passed to functions by call-by-reference.

16.3   Write a single statement or a set of statements to accomplish each of the following:
  a) Define a structure called **Part** containing **int** variable **partNumber** and **char** array **partName** whose values may be as long as 25 characters.
  b) Define **PartPtr** to be a synonym for the type **Part ***.
  c) Declare variable **a** to be of type **Part**, array **b[10]** to be of type **Part** and variable **ptr** to be of type pointer to **Part**.
  d) Read a part number and a part name from the keyboard into the members of variable **a**.
  e) Assign the member values of variable **a** to element three of array **b**.
  f) Assign the address of array **b** to the pointer variable **ptr**.
  g) Print the member values of element three of array **b** using the variable **ptr** and the structure pointer operator to refer to the members.

16.4   Find the error in each of the following:
  a) Assume that **struct Card** has been defined containing two pointers to type **char**, namely, **face** and **suit**. Also, the variable **c** has been declared to be of type **Card**, and the variable **cPtr** has been declared to be of type pointer to **Card**. Variable **cPtr** has been assigned the address of **c**.

```
cout << *cPtr.face << endl;
```

b) Assume that **struct Card** has been defined containing two pointers to type **char**, namely, **face** and **suit**. Also, the array **hearts[13]** has been declared to be of type **Card**. The following statement should print the member **face** of element 10 of the array.

```
cout << hearts.face << endl;
```

c)
```
struct Person {
    char lastName[ 15 ];
    char firstName[ 15 ];
    int age;
}
```

d) Assume that variable **p** has been declared as type **Person** and that variable **c** has been declared as type **Card**.

```
p = c;
```

16.5   Write a single statement to accomplish each of the following. Assume that variables **c** (which stores a character), **x**, **y** and **z** are of type **int**; variables **d**, **e** and **f** are of type **double**; variable **ptr** is of type **char *** and arrays **s1[100]** and **s2[100]** are of type **char**.

a) Convert the character stored in variable **c** to an uppercase letter. Assign the result to variable **c**.

b) Determine if the value of variable **c** is a digit. Use the conditional operator as shown in Figs. 16.17, 16.18 and 16.19 to print " **is a** " or " **is not a** " when the result is displayed.

c) Convert the string **"1234567"** to **long**, and print the value.

d) Determine if the value of variable **c** is a control character. Use the conditional operator to print " **is a** " or " **is not a** " when the result is displayed.

e) Assign **ptr** the location of the last occurrence of **c** in **s1**.

f) Convert the string **"8.63582"** to **double**, and print the value.

g) Determine if the value of **c** is a letter. Use the conditional operator to print " **is a** " or " **is not a** " when the result is displayed.

h) Assign **ptr** the location of the first occurrence of **s2** in **s1**.

i) Determine if the value of variable **c** is a printing character. Use the conditional operator to print " **is a** " or " **is not a** " when the result is displayed.

j) Assign **ptr** the location of the first occurrence in **s1** of any character from **s2**.

k) Assign **ptr** the location of the first occurrence of **c** in **s1**.

l) Convert the string **"-21"** to **int**, and print the value.

ANSWERS TO SELF-REVIEW EXERCISES

16.1   a) structure. b) bitwise AND (**&**). c) members. d) bitwise inclusive-OR (**|**). e) **struct**. f) **typedef**. g) bitwise exclusive-OR (**^**). h) mask. i) tag. j) structure member (**.**), structure pointer (**->**). k) left-shift operator (**<<**), right-shift operator (**>>**).

16.2   a) False. A structure can contain many data types.
b) False. The members of separate structures can have the same names, but the members of the same structure must have unique names.
c) False. **typedef** is used to define aliases for previously defined data types.
d) False. Structures are always passed to functions by call-by-value.

16.3   a)
```
struct Part {
    int partNumber;
    char partName[26];
};
```

896   Bits, Characters, Strings and Structures   Chapter 16

b) `typedef Part * PartPtr;`
c) `Part a, b[ 10 ], *ptr;`
d) `cin >> a.partNumber >> a.partName;`
e) `b[ 3 ] = a;`
f) `ptr = b;`
g) `cout << ( ptr + 3 )->partNumber << ' '`
        `<< ( ptr + 3 )->partName << endl;`

16.4   a) Error: The parentheses that should enclose `*cPtr` have been omitted, causing the order of evaluation of the expression to be incorrect.

b) Error: The array subscript has been omitted. The expression should be `hearts[ 10 ].face`.

c) Error: A semicolon is required to end a structure definition.

d) Error: Variables of different structure types cannot be assigned to one another.

16.5   a) `c = toupper( c );`
b) `cout << '\'' << c << "\' "`
        `<< ( isdigit( c ) ? "is a" : "is not a" )`
        `<< " digit" << endl;`
c) `cout << atol( "1234567" ) << endl;`
d) `cout << '\'' << c << "\' "`
        `<< ( iscntrl( c ) ? "is a" : "is not a" )`
        `<< " control character" << endl;`
e) `ptr = strrchr( s1, c );`
f) `out << atof( "8.63582" ) << endl;`
g) `cout << '\'' << c << "\' "`
        `<< ( isalpha( c ) ? "is a" : "is not a" )`
        `<< " letter" << endl;`
h) `ptr = strstr( s1, s2 );`
i) `cout << '\'' << c << "\' "`
        `<< ( isprint( c ) ? "is a" : "is not a" )`
        `<< " printing character" << endl;`
j) `ptr = strpbrk( s1, s2 );`
k) `ptr = strchr( s1, c );`
l) `cout << atoi( "-21" ) << endl;`

EXERCISES

16.6   Provide the definition for each of the following structures and unions:

a) Structure **Inventory** containing character array **partName[30]**, integer **partNumber**, floating-point **price**, integer **stock** and integer **reorder**.

b) A structure called **Address** that contains character arrays **streetAddress[25]**, **city[20]**, **state[3]** and **zipCode[6]**.

c) Structure **Student** that contains arrays **firstName[15]** and **lastName[15]**, and variable **homeAddress** of type **struct Address** from part (b).

d) Structure **Test** containing 16 bit fields with widths of 1 bit. The names of the bit fields are the letters **a** to **p**.

16.7   Consider the following structure definitions and variable declarations,

```
struct Customer {
   char lastName[ 15 ];
   char firstName[ 15 ];
   int customerNumber;
```

```
    struct {
        char phoneNumber[ 11 ];
        char address[ 50 ];
        char city[ 15 ];
        char state[ 3 ];
        char zipCode[ 6 ];
    } personal;
} customerRecord, *customerPtr;
```

```
customerPtr = &customerRecord;
```

Write a separate expression that accesses the structure members in each of the following parts:

   a) Member **lastName** of structure **customerRecord**.
   b) Member **lastName** of the structure pointed to by **customerPtr**.
   c) Member **firstName** of structure **customerRecord**.
   d) Member **firstName** of the structure pointed to by **customerPtr**.
   e) Member **customerNumber** of structure **customerRecord**.
   f) Member **customerNumber** of the structure pointed to by **customerPtr**.
   g) Member **phoneNumber** of member **personal** of structure **customerRecord**.
   h) Member **phoneNumber** of member **personal** of the structure pointed to by **customerPtr**.
   i) Member **address** of member **personal** of structure **customerRecord**.
   j) Member **address** of member **personal** of the structure pointed to by **customerPtr**.
   k) Member **city** of member **personal** of structure **customerRecord**.
   l) Member **city** of member **personal** of the structure pointed to by **customerPtr**.
   m) Member **state** of member **personal** of structure **customerRecord.**
   n) Member **state** of member **personal** of the structure pointed to by **customerPtr**.
   o) Member **zipCode** of member **personal** of structure **customerRecord**.
   p) Member **zipCode** of member **personal** of the structure pointed to by **customerPtr**.

16.8   Modify the program of Fig. 16.14 to shuffle the cards using a high-performance shuffle as shown in Fig. 16.2. Print the resulting deck in two column format as in Fig. 16.3. Precede each card with its color.

16.9   Write a program that right shifts an integer variable 4 bits. The program should print the integer in bits before and after the shift operation. Does your system place zeros or ones in the vacated bits?

16.10   If your computer uses 4-byte integers, modify the program of Fig. 16.5 so that it works with 4-byte integers.

16.11   Left shifting an **unsigned** integer by 1 bit is equivalent to multiplying the value by 2. Write function **power2** that takes two integer arguments **number** and **pow** and calculates

$$number * 2^{pow}$$

Use a shift operator to calculate the result. The program should print the values as integers and as bits.

16.12   The left-shift operator can be used to pack two character values into a 2-byte unsigned integer variable. Write a program that inputs two characters from the keyboard and passes them to function **packCharacters**. To pack two characters into an **unsigned** integer variable, assign the first character to the **unsigned** variable, shift the **unsigned** variable left by 8 bit positions and combine the **unsigned** variable with the second character using the bitwise inclusive-OR operator. The program should output the characters in their bit format before and after they are packed into the **unsigned** integer to prove that the characters are in fact packed correctly in the **unsigned** variable.

16.13   Using the right-shift operator, the bitwise AND operator and a mask, write function **unpackCharacters** that takes the **unsigned** integer from Exercise 16.12 and unpacks it into two characters. To unpack two characters from an **unsigned** 2-byte integer, combine the unsigned integer with the mask **65280** (**11111111 00000000**) and right shift the result 8 bits. Assign the resulting value to a **char** variable. Then, combine the **unsigned** integer with the mask **255** (**00000000 11111111**). Assign the result to another **char** variable. The program should print the **unsigned** integer in bits before it is unpacked, and then print the characters in bits to confirm that they were unpacked correctly.

16.14   If your system uses 4-byte integers, rewrite the program of Exercise 16.12 to pack 4 characters.

16.15   If your system uses 4-byte integers, rewrite the function **unpackCharacters** of Exercise 16.13 to unpack 4 characters. Create the masks you need to unpack the 4 characters by left shifting the value 255 in the mask variable by 8 bits 0, 1, 2 or 3 times (depending on the byte you are unpacking).

16.16   Write a program that reverses the order of the bits in an **unsigned** integer value. The program should input the value from the user and call function **reverseBits** to print the bits in reverse order. Print the value in bits both before and after the bits are reversed to confirm that the bits are reversed properly.

16.17   Write a program that demonstrates passing an array by value. (Hint: use a **struct**). Prove that a copy was passed by modifying the array copy in the called function.

16.18   Write a program that inputs a character from the keyboard and tests the character with each of the functions in the character handling library. The program should print the value returned by each function.

16.19   The following program uses function **multiple** to determine if the integer entered from the keyboard is a multiple of some integer **X**. Examine function **multiple**, and then determine the value of **X**.

```
1    // ex16_19.cpp
2    // This program determines if a value is a multiple of X
3    #include <iostream>
4
5    using std::cout;
6    using std::cin;
7    using std::endl;
8
9    bool multiple( int );
10
11   int main()
12   {
13      int y;
14
15      cout << "Enter an integer between 1 and 32000: ";
16      cin >> y;
17
18      if ( multiple( y ) )
19         cout << y << " is a multiple of X" << endl;
```

```
20        else
21           cout << y << " is not a multiple of X" << endl;
22
23        return 0;
24   }
25
26   bool multiple( int num )
27   {
28      bool mult = true;
29
30      for ( int i = 0, mask = 1; i < 10; i++, mask <<= 1 )
31         if ( ( num & mask ) != 0 ) {
32            mult = false;
33            break;
34         }
35
36      return mult;
37   }
```

16.20   What does the following program do?

```
1    // ex16_20.cpp
2    #include <iostream>
3
4    using std::cout;
5    using std::cin;
6    using std::endl;
7
8    int mystery( unsigned );
9
10   int main()
11   {
12      unsigned x;
13
14      cout << "Enter an integer: ";
15      cin >> x;
16      cout << "The result is " << mystery( x ) << endl;
17      return 0;
18   }
19
20   int mystery( unsigned bits )
21   {
22      const int SHIFT = 8 * sizeof( unsigned ) - 1;
23      const unsigned MASK = 1 << SHIFT;
24      unsigned total = 0;
25
26      for ( int i = 0; i < SHIFT + 1; i++, bits <<= 1 )
27         if ( ( bits & MASK ) == MASK )
28            ++total;
29
30      return !( total % 2 );
31   }
```

16.21 Write a program that inputs a line of text with **istream** member function **getline** (see Chapter 11) into character array **s[100]**. Output the line in uppercase letters and lowercase letters.

16.22 Write a program that inputs four strings that represent integers, converts the strings to integers sums the values, and prints the total of the four values.

16.23 Write a program that inputs four strings that represent floating-point values, converts the strings to double values, sums the values and prints the total of the four values.

16.24 Write a program that inputs a line of text and a search string from the keyboard. Using function **strstr**, locate the first occurrence of the search string in the line of text, and assign the location to variable **searchPtr** of type **char ***. If the search string is found, print the remainder of the line of text beginning with the search string. Then, use **strstr** again to locate the next occurrence of the search string in the line of text. If a second occurrence is found, print the remainder of the line of text beginning with the second occurrence. {Hint: The second call to **strstr** should contain the expression **searchPtr + 1** as its first argument.)

16.25 Write a program based on the program of Exercise 16.24 that inputs several lines of text and a search string, and uses function **strstr** to determine the total number of occurrences of the string in the lines of text. Print the result.

16.26 Write a program that inputs several lines of text and a search character and uses function **strchr** to determine the total number of occurrences of the character in the lines of text.

16.27 Write a program based on the program of Exercise 16.26 that inputs several lines of text and uses function **strchr** to determine the total number of occurrences of each letter of the alphabet in the text. Uppercase and lowercase letters should be counted together. Store the totals for each letter in an array, and print the values in tabular format after the totals have been determined.

16.28 The chart in Appendix B shows the numeric code representations for the characters in the ASCII character set. Study this chart, and then state whether each of the following is *true* or *false*:
   a) The letter "**A**" comes before the letter "**B**".
   b) The digit "**9**" comes before the digit "**0**".
   c) The commonly used symbols for addition, subtraction, multiplication and division all come before any of the digits.
   d) The digits come before the letters.
   e) If a sort program sorts strings into ascending sequence, then the program will place the symbol for a right parenthesis before the symbol for a left parenthesis.

16.29 Write a program that reads a series of strings and prints only those strings beginning with the letter "**b**".

16.30 Write a program that reads a series of strings and prints only those strings that end with the letters "**ED**".

16.31 Write a program that inputs an ASCII code and prints the corresponding character. Modify this program so that it generates all possible three-digit codes in the range 000 to 255 and attempts to print the corresponding characters. What happens when this program is run?

16.32 Using the ASCII character chart in Appendix B as a guide, write your own versions of the character handling functions in Fig. 16.16.

16.33 Write your own versions of the functions in Fig. 16.20 for converting strings to numbers.

16.34 Write your own versions of the functions in Fig. 16.27 for searching strings.

16.35 Write your own versions of the functions in Fig. 16.34 for manipulating blocks of memory.

16.36 *(Project: A Spelling Checker)* Many popular word-processing software packages have built-in spell checkers. We used spell-checking capabilities in preparing this book and discovered that no matter how careful we thought we were in writing a chapter, the software was always able to find a few more spelling errors than we were able to catch manually.

In this project, you are asked to develop your own spell-checker utility. We make suggestions to help get you started. You should then consider adding more capabilities. You may find it helpful to use a computerized dictionary as a source of words.

Why do we type so many words with incorrect spellings? In some cases, it is because we simply do not know the correct spelling, so we make a "best guess." In some cases, it is because we transpose two letters (e.g., "defualt" instead of "default"). Sometimes we double type a letter accidentally (e.g., "hanndy" instead of "handy"). Sometimes we type a nearby key instead of the one we intended (e.g., "biryhday" instead of "birthday"). And so on.

Design and implement a spell-checker program. Your program maintains an array **wordList** of character strings. You can either enter these strings or obtain them from a computerized dictionary.

Your program asks a user to enter a word. The program then looks up that word in the **wordList** array. If the word is present in the array, your program should print "**Word is spelled correctly.**"

If the word is not present in the array, your program should print "**Word is not spelled correctly.**" Then your program should try to locate other words in **wordList** that might be the word the user intended to type. For example, you can try all possible single transpositions of adjacent letters to discover that the word "default" is a direct match to a word in **wordList**. Of course, this implies that your program will check all other single transpositions, such as "edfault," "dfeault," "deafult," "defalut" and "defautl." When you find a new word that matches one in **wordList**, print that word in a message such as "**Did you mean "default?"**."

Implement other tests such as replacing each double letter with a single letter and any other tests you can develop to improve the value of your spell checker.

17

The Preprocessor

Objectives

- To be able to use **#include** for developing large programs.
- To be able to use **#define** to create macros and macros with arguments.
- To understand conditional compilation.
- To be able to display error messages during conditional compilation.
- To be able to use assertions to test if the values of expressions are correct.

Hold thou the good; define it well.
Alfred, Lord Tennyson

I have found you an argument; but I am not obliged to find you an understanding.
Samuel Johnson

A good symbol is the best argument, and is a missionary to persuade thousands.
Ralph Waldo Emerson

Conditions are fundamentally sound.
Herbert Hoover [December 1929]

The partisan, when he is engaged in a dispute, cares nothing about the rights of the question, but is anxious only to convince his hearers of his own assertions.
Plato

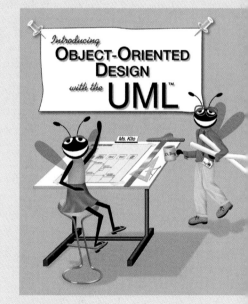

17.1 Introduction

This chapter introduces the *preprocessor.* Preprocessing occurs before a program is compiled. Some possible actions are: inclusion of other files in the file being compiled, definition of *symbolic constants* and *macros, conditional compilation* of program code and *conditional execution of preprocessor directives.* All preprocessor directives begin with **#**, and only whitespace characters may appear before a preprocessor directive on a line. Preprocessor directives are not C++ statements, so they do not end in a semicolon (**;**). Preprocessor directives are processed fully before compilation begins.

Common Programming Error 17.1

Placing a semicolon at the end of a preprocessor directive can lead to a variety of errors depending on the type of preprocessor directive.

Software Engineering Observation 17.1

Many preprocessor features (especially macros) are more appropriate for C programmers than for C++ programmers. C++ programmers should familiarize themselves with the preprocessor because they may need to work with C legacy code.

17.2 The `#include` Preprocessor Directive

The **#include** *preprocessor directive* has been used throughout this text. The **#include** directive causes a copy of a specified file to be included in place of the directive. The two forms of the **#include** directive are:

```
#include <filename>
#include "filename"
```

The difference between these is the location the preprocessor searches for the file to be included. If the file name is enclosed in angle brackets (**<** and **>**)—used for *standard library* *header files*—the preprocessor searches for the specified file in an implementation-dependent manner, normally through predesignated directories. If the file name is enclosed in quotes, the preprocessor searches first in the same directory as the file being compiled, then in the same implementation-dependent manner as a file name enclosed in angle brackets. This method is normally used to include programmer-defined header files.

The **#include** directive is normally used to include standard header files such as **<iostream>** and **<iomanip>**. The **#include** directive is also used with programs consisting of several source files that are to be compiled together. A *header file* containing declarations and definitions common to the separate program files is often created and included in the file. Examples of such declarations and definitions are classes, structures, unions, enumerations and function prototypes.

17.3 The #define Preprocessor Directive: Symbolic Constants

The **#define** *preprocessor directive* creates *symbolic constants*—constants represented as symbols—and *macros*—operations defined as symbols. The **#define** preprocessor directive format is

> **#define** *identifier replacement-text*

When this line appears in a file, all subsequent occurrences (except those inside a string) of *identifier* in that file will be replaced by *replacement-text* before the program is compiled. For example,

> **#define PI 3.14159**

replaces all subsequent occurrences of the symbolic constant **PI** with the numeric constant **3.14159**. Symbolic constants enable the programmer to create a name for a constant and use the name throughout the program. If the constant needs to be modified throughout the program, it can be modified once in the **#define** preprocessor directive—and when the program is recompiled, all occurrences of the constant in the program will be modified Note: *Everything to the right of the symbolic constant name replaces the symbolic constant.* For example, **#define PI = 3.14159** causes the preprocessor to replace every occurrence of **PI** with **= 3.14159**. This is the cause of many subtle logic and syntax errors. Redefining a symbolic constant with a new value is also an error. Note that **const** variables in C++ are preferred over symbolic constants. Constant variables have a specific data type and are visible by name to a debugger. Once a symbolic constant is replaced with its replacement text, only the replacement text is visible to a debugger. A disadvantage of **const** variables is they may require a memory location of their data type size—symbolic constants do not require any additional memory.

Common Programming Error 17.2

Using symbolic constants in a file other than the file in which the symbolic constants are defined is a syntax error.

Good Programming Practice 17.1

Using meaningful names for symbolic constants helps make programs more self-documenting.

17.4 The `#define` Preprocessor Directive: Macros

[Note: This section is included for the benefit of C++ programmers who will need to work with legacy C code. In C++, macros have been replaced by templates and inline functions.] A *macro* is an operation defined in a **#define** preprocessor directive. As with symbolic constants, the *macro-identifier* is replaced with the *replacement text* before the program is compiled. Macros may be defined with or without *arguments*. A macro without arguments is processed like a symbolic constant. In a macro with arguments, the arguments are substituted in the replacement text, then the macro is *expanded*—i.e., the replacement text replaces the macro-identifier and argument list in the program. (*Note:* There is no data type checking for macro arguments. A macro is used simply for text substitution.)

Consider the following macro definition with one argument for the area of a circle:

```
#define CIRCLE_AREA( x ) ( PI * ( x ) * ( x ) )
```

Wherever **CIRCLE_AREA(x)** appears in the file, the value of **x** is substituted for **x** in the replacement text, the symbolic constant **PI** is replaced by its value (defined previously) and the macro is expanded in the program. For example, the statement

```
area = CIRCLE_AREA( 4 );
```

is expanded to

```
area = ( 3.14159 * ( 4 ) * ( 4 ) );
```

Since the expression consists only of constants, at compile time the value of the expression is evaluated and the result is assigned to **area** at run time. The parentheses around each **x** in the replacement text and around the entire expression force the proper order of evaluation when the macro argument is an expression. For example, the statement

```
area = CIRCLE_AREA( c + 2 );
```

is expanded to

```
area = ( 3.14159 * ( c + 2 ) * ( c + 2 ) );
```

which evaluates correctly because the parentheses force the proper order of evaluation. If the parentheses are omitted, the macro expansion is

```
area = 3.14159 * c + 2 * c + 2;
```

which evaluates incorrectly as

```
area = ( 3.14159 * c ) + ( 2 * c ) + 2;
```

because of the rules of operator precedence.

Common Programming Error 17.3

Forgetting to enclose macro arguments in parentheses in the replacement text is a syntax error.

Macro **CIRCLE_AREA** could be defined as a function. Function **circleArea**

```
double circleArea( double x ) { return 3.14159 * x * x; }
```

performs the same calculation as **CIRCLE_AREA**, but the overhead of a function call is associated with function **circleArea**. The advantages of **CIRCLE_AREA** are that macros insert code directly in the program—avoiding function overhead—and the program remains readable because **CIRCLE_AREA** is defined separately and named meaningfully. A disadvantage is that its argument is evaluated twice. Also, every time a macro appears in a program, the macro is expanded. If the macro is large, this produces an increase in program size. Thus, there is a trade-off between execution speed and program size (disk space may be low). Note that **inline** functions (see Chapter 3) are preferred to obtain the performance of macros and the software engineering benefits of functions.

Performance Tip 17.1

Macros can sometimes be used to replace a function call with **inline** *code prior to execution time. This eliminates the overhead of a function call. Inline functions are preferable to macros because they offer the type-checking services of functions.*

The following is a macro definition with two arguments for the area of a rectangle:

```
#define RECTANGLE_AREA( x, y )  ( ( x ) * ( y ) )
```

Wherever **RECTANGLE_AREA(x, y)** appears in the program, the values of **x** and **y** are substituted in the macro replacement text, and the macro is expanded in place of the macro name. For example, the statement

```
rectArea = RECTANGLE_AREA( a + 4, b + 7 );
```

is expanded to

```
rectArea = ( ( a + 4 ) * ( b + 7 ) );
```

The value of the expression is evaluated and assigned to variable **rectArea**.

The replacement text for a macro or symbolic constant is normally any text on the line after the identifier in the **#define** directive. If the replacement text for a macro or symbolic constant is longer than the remainder of the line, a backslash (\) must be placed at the end of the line, indicating that the replacement text continues on the next line.

Symbolic constants and macros can be discarded using the **#undef** *preprocessor directive*. Directive **#undef** "undefines" a symbolic constant or macro name. The *scope* of a symbolic constant or macro is from its definition until it is undefined with **#undef**, or until the end of the file. Once undefined, a name can be redefined with **#define**.

Functions in the standard library sometimes are defined as macros based on other library functions. A macro commonly defined in the **<cstdio>** header file is

```
#define getchar() getc( stdin )
```

The macro definition of **getchar** uses function **getc** to get one character from the standard input stream. Function **putchar** of the **<cstdio>** header and the character handling functions of the **<cctype>** header often are implemented as macros as well. Note that expressions with side effects (i.e., variable values are modified) should not be passed to a macro because macro arguments may be evaluated more than once.

17.5 Conditional Compilation

Conditional compilation enables the programmer to control the execution of preprocessor directives and the compilation of program code. Each of the conditional preprocessor directives evaluates a constant integer expression that will determine if the code will be compiled. Cast expressions, **sizeof** expressions and enumeration constants cannot be evaluated in preprocessor directives.

The conditional preprocessor construct is much like the **if** selection structure. Consider the following preprocessor code:

```
#if !defined( NULL )
    #define NULL 0
#endif
```

These directives determine if the symbolic constant **NULL** is already defined. The expression **defined(NULL)** evaluates to **1** if **NULL** is defined; **0** otherwise. If the result is **0**, **!defined(NULL)** evaluates to **1**, and **NULL** is defined. Otherwise, the **#define** directive is skipped. Every **#if** construct ends with **#endif**. Directives **#ifdef** and **#ifndef** are shorthand for **#if defined(** *name* **)** and **#if !defined(** *name* **)**. A multiple-part conditional preprocessor construct may be tested using the **#elif** (the equivalent of **else if** in an **if** structure) and the **#else** (the equivalent of **else** in an **if** structure) directives.

During program development, programmers often find it helpful to "comment out" large portions of code to prevent it from being compiled. If the code contains C-style comments, **/*** and ***/** cannot be used to accomplish this task. Instead, the programmer can use the following preprocessor construct:

```
#if 0
    code prevented from compiling
#endif
```

To enable the code to be compiled, simply replace the value **0** in the preceding construct with the value **1**.

Conditional compilation is commonly used as a debugging aid. Output statements are often used to print variable values and to confirm the flow of control. These output statements can be enclosed in conditional preprocessor directives so the statements are only compiled until the debugging process is completed. For example,

```
#ifdef DEBUG
    cerr << "Variable x = " << x << endl;
#endif
```

causes the **cerr** statement to be compiled in the program if the symbolic constant **DEBUG** has been defined (**#define DEBUG**) before directive **#ifdef DEBUG**. When debugging is completed, the **#define** directive is removed from the source file and the output statements inserted for debugging purposes are ignored during compilation. In larger programs, it may be desirable to define several different symbolic constants that control the conditional compilation in separate sections of the source file.

Common Programming Error 17.4

Inserting conditionally compiled output statements for debugging purposes in locations where C++ currently expects a single statement can lead to syntax errors and logic errors. In this case, the conditionally compiled statement should be enclosed in a compound statement. Thus, when the program is compiled with debugging statements, the flow of control of the program is not altered.

17.6 The #error and #pragma Preprocessor Directives

The **#error** *directive*

> **#error** *tokens*

prints an implementation-dependent message including the *tokens* specified in the directive. The tokens are sequences of characters separated by spaces. For example,

> **#error 1 - Out of range error**

contains six tokens. In one popular C++ compiler, for example, when a **#error** directive is processed, the tokens in the directive are displayed as an error message, preprocessing stops and the program does not compile.

The **#pragma** *directive*

> **#pragma** *tokens*

causes an implementation-defined action. A pragma not recognized by the implementation is ignored. A particular C++ compiler, for example, might recognize pragmas that enable the programmer to take advantage of that compiler's specific capabilities. For more information on **#error** and **#pragma**, see the documentation for your C++ implementation.

17.7 The # and ## Operators

The **#** and **##** preprocessor operators are available in C++ and ANSI C. The **#** operator causes a replacement text token to be converted to a string surrounded by quotes. Consider the following macro definition:

> **#define HELLO(x) cout << "Hello, " #x << endl;**

When **HELLO(John)** appears in a program file, it is expanded to

> **cout << "Hello, " "John" << endl;**

The string **"John"** replaces **#x** in the replacement text. Strings separated by whitespace are concatenated during preprocessing, so the above statement is equivalent to

> **cout << "Hello, John" << endl;**

Note that the **#** operator must be used in a macro with arguments because the operand of **#** refers to an argument of the macro.

The **##** operator concatenates two tokens. Consider the following macro definition:

> **#define TOKENCONCAT(x, y)   x ## y**

When **TOKENCONCAT** appears in the program, its arguments are concatenated and used to replace the macro. For example, **TOKENCONCAT(O, K)** is replaced by **OK** in the program. The **##** operator must have two operands.

17.8 Line Numbers

The **#line** *preprocessor directive* causes the subsequent source code lines to be renumbered starting with the specified constant integer value. The directive

> **#line 100**

starts line numbering from **100** beginning with the next source code line. A file name can be included in the **#line** directive. The directive

```
#line 100 "file1.cpp"
```

indicates that lines are numbered from **100** beginning with the next source code line, and that the name of the file for the purpose of any compiler messages is **"file1.cpp"**. The directive normally is used to help make the messages produced by syntax errors and compiler warnings more meaningful. The line numbers do not appear in the source file.

17.9 Predefined Symbolic Constants

There are four *predefined symbolic constants* (Fig. 17.1). The identifiers for each predefined symbolic constant begin and end with *two* underscores. These identifiers and the **defined** identifier (Section 17.5) cannot be used in **#define** or **#undef** directives.

17.10 Assertions

The **assert** *macro*—defined in the **<cassert>** header file—tests the value of an expression. If the value of the expression is **0** (false), then **assert** prints an error message and calls function **abort** (of the general utilities library—**<cstdlib>**) to terminate program execution. This is a useful debugging tool for testing if a variable has a correct value. For example, suppose variable **x** should never be larger than **10** in a program. An assertion may be used to test the value of **x** and print an error message if the value of **x** is incorrect. The statement would be:

```
assert( x <= 10 );
```

If **x** is greater than **10** when the preceding statement is encountered in a program, an error message containing the line number and file name is printed, and the program terminates. The programmer may then concentrate on this area of the code to find the error. If the symbolic constant **NDEBUG** is defined, subsequent assertions will be ignored. Thus, when assertions are no longer needed (i.e., when debugging is complete), the line

```
#define NDEBUG
```

is inserted in the program file rather than deleting each assertion manually.

Symbolic constant	Description
__LINE__	The line number of the current source code line (an integer constant).
__FILE__	The presumed name of the source file (a string).
__DATE__	The date the source file is compiled (a string of the form **"Mmm dd yyyy"** such as **"Jan 19 2001"**).
__TIME__	The time the source file is compiled (a string literal of the form **"hh:mm:ss"**).

Fig. 17.1   The predefined symbolic constants.

Most C++ compilers now include exception handling. C++ programmers prefer using exceptions rather than assertions. But assertions are still valuable for C++ programmers who work with C legacy code.

SUMMARY

- All preprocessor directives begin with **#** and are processed before the program is compiled.
- Only whitespace characters may appear before a preprocessor directive on a line.
- The **#include** directive includes a copy of the specified file. If the file name is enclosed in quotes, the preprocessor begins searching in the same directory as the file being compiled for the file to be included. If the file name is enclosed in angle brackets (**<** and **>**), the search is performed in an implementation-defined manner.
- The **#define** preprocessor directive is used to create symbolic constants and macros.
- A symbolic constant is a name for a constant.
- A macro is an operation defined in a **#define** preprocessor directive. Macros may be defined with or without arguments.
- The replacement text for a macro or symbolic constant is any text remaining on the line after the identifier in the **#define** directive. If the replacement text for a macro or symbolic constant is too long to fit clearly on one line, a backslash (****) is placed at the end of the line, indicating that the replacement text continues on the next line.
- Symbolic constants and macros can be discarded using the **#undef** preprocessor directive. Directive **#undef** "undefines" the symbolic constant or macro name.
- The scope of a symbolic constant or macro is from its definition until it is undefined with **#undef**, or until the end of the file.
- Conditional compilation enables the programmer to control the execution of preprocessor directives and the compilation of program code.
- The conditional preprocessor directives evaluate constant integer expressions. Cast expressions, size of expressions and enumeration constants cannot be evaluated in preprocessor directives.
- Every **#if** construct ends with **#endif**.
- Directives **#ifdef** and **#ifndef** are provided as shorthand for **#if defined(**name**)** and **#if !defined(**name**)**.
- A multiple-part conditional preprocessor construct is tested using the **#elif** and **#else** directives.
- The **#error** directive prints an implementation-dependent message that includes the tokens specified in the directive and terminates preprocessing and compiling.
- The **#pragma** directive causes an implementation-defined action. If the pragma is not recognized by the implementation, the pragma is ignored.
- The **#** operator causes a replacement text token to be converted to a string surrounded by quotes. The **#** operator must be used in a macro with arguments because the operand of **#** must be an argument of the macro.
- The **##** operator concatenates two tokens. The **##** operator must have two operands.
- The **#line** preprocessor directive causes the subsequent source code lines to be renumbered starting with the specified constant integer value.
- There are four predefined symbolic constants. Constant **__LINE__** is the line number of the current source code line (an integer). Constant **__FILE__** is the presumed name of the file (a string). Constant **__DATE__** is the date the source file is compiled (a string). Constant

__**TIME**__ is the time the source file is compiled (a string). Note that each of the predefined symbolic constants begins and ends with two underbars.

- The **assert** macro—defined in the **<cassert>** header file—tests the value of an expression. If the value of the expression is **0** (false), then **assert** prints an error message and calls function **abort** to terminate program execution.

TERMINOLOGY

#define	convert-to-string preprocessor
#elif	**<cstdio>**
#else	**<cstdlib>**
#endif	debugger
#error	expand a macro
#if	header file
#ifdef	macro
#ifndef	macro with arguments
#include "filename"	operator **#**
#include <filename>	predefined symbolic constants
#line	preprocessing directive
#pragma	preprocessor
#undef	replacement text
abort	scope of a symbolic constant or macro
argument	standard library header files
assert	symbolic constant
cassert	\ (backslash) continuation character
concatenation preprocessor operator **##**	__**DATE**__
conditional compilation	__**FILE**__
conditional execution of preprocessor	__**LINE**__
directives	__**TIME**__

COMMON PROGRAMMING ERRORS

17.1 Placing a semicolon at the end of a preprocessor directive can lead to a variety of errors depending on the type of preprocessor directive.

17.2 Using symbolic constants in a file other than the file in which the symbolic constants are defined is a syntax error.

17.3 Forgetting to enclose macro arguments in parentheses in the replacement text is a syntax error.

17.4 Inserting conditionally compiled output statements for debugging purposes in locations where C++ currently expects a single statement can lead to syntax errors and logic errors. In this case, the conditionally compiled statement should be enclosed in a compound statement. Thus, when the program is compiled with debugging statements, the flow of control of the program is not altered.

GOOD PROGRAMMING PRACTICE

17.1 Using meaningful names for symbolic constants helps make programs more self-documenting.

PERFORMANCE TIP

17.1   Macros can sometimes be used to replace a function call with **inline** code prior to execution time. This eliminates the overhead of a function call. Inline functions are preferable to macros because they offer the type-checking services of functions.

SOFTWARE ENGINEERING OBSERVATION

17.1   Many preprocessor features (especially macros) are more appropriate for C programmers than for C++ programmers. C++ programmers should familiarize themselves with the preprocessor because they may need to work with C legacy code.

SELF-REVIEW EXERCISES

17.1   Fill in the blanks in each of the following:
   a) Every preprocessor directive must begin with _____.
   b) The conditional compilation construct may be extended to test for multiple cases by using the _____ and the _____ directives.
   c) The _____ directive creates macros and symbolic constants.
   d) Only _____ characters may appear before a preprocessor directive on a line.
   e) The _____ directive discards symbolic constant and macro names.
   f) The _____ and _____ directives are provided as shorthand notation for **#if defined(**_name_**)** and **#if !defined(**_name_**)**.
   g) _____ enables the programmer to control the execution of preprocessor directives and the compilation of program code.
   h) The _____ macro prints a message and terminates program execution if the value of the expression the macro evaluates is **0**.
   i) The _____ directive inserts a file in another file.
   j) The _____ operator concatenates its two arguments.
   k) The _____ operator converts its operand to a string.
   l) The character _____ indicates that the replacement text for a symbolic constant or macro continues on the next line.
   m) The _____ directive causes the source code lines to be numbered from the indicated value beginning with the next source code line.

17.2   Write a program to print the values of the predefined symbolic constants listed in Fig. 17.1.

17.3   Write a preprocessor directive to accomplish each of the following:
   a) Define symbolic constant **YES** to have the value **1**.
   b) Define symbolic constant **NO** to have the value **0**.
   c) Include the header file **common.h.** The header is found in the same directory as the file being compiled.
   d) Renumber the remaining lines in the file beginning with line number **3000**.
   e) If symbolic constant **TRUE** is defined, undefine it, and redefine it as **1**. Do not use **#ifdef**.
   f) If symbolic constant **TRUE** is defined, undefine it, and redefine it as **1**. Use the **#ifdef** preprocessor directive.
   g) If symbolic constant **ACTIVE** is not equal to **0**, define symbolic constant **INACTIVE** as **0**. Otherwise define **INACTIVE** as **1**.
   h) Define macro **CUBE_VOLUME** that computes the volume of a cube (takes one argument).

ANSWERS TO SELF-REVIEW EXERCISES

17.1   a) **#**. b) **#elif**, **#else**. c) **#define**. d) whitespace. e) **#undef**. f) **#ifdef**, **#ifndef**. g) Conditional compilation. h) **assert**. i) **#include**. j) **##**. k) **#**. l) ****. m) **#line**.

17.2   (See below.)

```
1   #include <iostream>
2   using std::cout;
3   using std::endl;
4   int main()
5   {
6       cout << "__LINE__ = " << __LINE__ << endl;
7       cout << "__FILE__ = " << __FILE__ << endl;
8       cout << "__DATE__ = " << __DATE__ << endl;
9       cout << "__TIME__ = " << __TIME__ << endl;
10      return 0;
11  }
```

```
__LINE__ = 6
__FILE__ = C:\ex17_02.cpp
__DATE__ = Apr 28 2000
__TIME__ = 13:48:58
```

17.3   a) `#define YES 1`
        b) `#define NO 0`
        c) `#include "common.h"`
        d) `#line 3000`
        e) `#if defined(TRUE)`
                `#undef TRUE`
                `#define TRUE 1`
            `#endif`
        f) `#ifdef TRUE`
                `#undef TRUE`
                `#define TRUE 1`
            `#endif`
        g) `#if ACTIVE`
                `#define INACTIVE 0`
            `#else`
                `#define INACTIVE 1`
            `#endif`
        h) `#define CUBE_VOLUME( x )  ( ( x ) * ( x ) * ( x ) )`

EXERCISES

17.4   Write a program that defines a macro with one argument to compute the volume of a sphere. The program should compute the volume for spheres of radius 1 to 10, and print the results in tabular format. The formula for the volume of a sphere is

$$(4.0 / 3) * \pi * r^3$$

where π is 3.14159.

17.5   Write a program that produces the following output:

```
The sum of x and y is 13
```

The program should define macro **SUM** with two arguments, **x** and **y**, and use **SUM** to produce the output.

17.6   Write a program that uses macro **MINIMUM2** to determine the smallest of two numeric values. Input the values from the keyboard.

17.7   Write a program that uses macro **MINIMUM3** to determine the smallest of three numeric values. Macro **MINIMUM3** should use macro **MINIMUM2** defined in Exercise 17.6 to determine the smallest number. Input the values from the keyboard.

17.8   Write a program that uses macro **PRINT** to print a string value.

17.9   Write a program that uses macro **PRINTARRAY** to print an array of integers. The macro should receive the array and the number of elements in the array as arguments.

17.10 Write a program that uses macro **SUMARRAY** to sum the values in a numeric array. The macro should receive the array and the number of elements in the array as arguments.

17.11 Rewrite the solutions to Exercises 17.4 to 17.10 as **inline** functions.

17.12 For each of the following macros, identify the possible problems (if any) when the preprocessor expands the macros:

a) `#define SQR( x ) x * x`
b) `#define SQR( x ) ( x * x )`
c) `#define SQR( x ) ( x ) * ( x )`
d) `#define SQR( x ) ( ( x ) * ( x ) )`

18

C Legacy
Code Topics

Objectives

- To be able to redirect keyboard input to come from a file and redirect screen output into a file.
- To be able to write functions that use variable-length argument lists.
- To be able to process command-line arguments.
- To be able to process unexpected events within a program.
- To be able to allocate memory dynamically for arrays using C-style dynamic memory allocation.
- To be able to resize memory dynamically allocated using C-style dynamic memory allocation.

We'll use a signal I have tried and found far-reaching and easy to yell. Waa-hoo!
Zane Grey

Use it up, wear it out; make it do, or do without.
Anonymous

It is quite a three-pipe problem.
Sir Arthur Conan Doyle

But yet an union in partition
William Shakespeare

I could never make out what those damned dots meant.
Winston Churchill

18.1 Introduction

This chapter presents several advanced topics not ordinarily covered in introductory courses. Many of the capabilities discussed here are specific to particular operating systems, especially UNIX and/or DOS. Much of the material is for the benefit of C++ programmers who will need to work with older C legacy code.

18.2 Redirecting Input/Output on UNIX and DOS Systems

Normally the input to a program is from the keyboard (standard input), and the output is from a program is displayed on the screen (standard output). On most computer systems—UNIX and DOS systems in particular—it is possible to *redirect* inputs to come from a file, and redirect outputs to be placed in a file. Both forms of redirection can be accomplished without using the file-processing capabilities of the standard library.

There are several ways to redirect input and output from the UNIX command line. Consider the executable file **sum** that inputs integers one at a time and keeps a running total of the values until the end-of-file indicator is set, and then prints the result. Normally the user inputs integers from the keyboard and enters the end-of-file key combination to indicate that no further values will be input. With input redirection, the input can be stored in a file. For example, if the data are stored in file **input**, the command line

```
$ sum < input
```

causes program **sum** to be executed; the *redirect input symbol (<)* indicates that the data in file **input** (instead of the keyboard) are to be used as input by the program. Redirecting input on a DOS system is performed identically.

Note that **$** is the UNIX command-line prompt. (Some UNIX systems use a **%** prompt.) Students often find it difficult to understand that redirection is an operating system function, not another C++ feature.

The second method of redirecting input is *piping*. A *pipe (|)* causes the output of one program to be redirected as the input to another program. Suppose program **random** outputs a series of random integers; the output of **random** can be "piped" directly to program **sum** using the UNIX command line

```
$ random | sum
```

This causes the sum of the integers produced by **random** to be calculated. Piping can be performed in UNIX and DOS.

Program output can be redirected to a file by using the *redirect output symbol (>)*. (The same symbol is used for UNIX and DOS.) For example, to redirect the output of program **random** to file **out**, use

```
$ random > out
```

Finally, program output can be appended to the end of an existing file by using the *append output symbol (>>)* (the same symbol is used for UNIX and DOS). For example, to append the output from program **random** to file **out** created in the preceding command line, use the command line

```
$ random >> out
```

18.3 Variable-Length Argument Lists

[Note: This material is included for the benefit of C++ programmers who will work with C legacy code. In C++, programmers use function overloading to accomplish much of what C programmers accomplish with variable-length argument lists.] It is possible to create functions that receive an unspecified number of arguments. An ellipsis (**. . .**) in a function's prototype indicates that the function receives a variable number of arguments of any type. Note that the ellipsis must always be placed at the end of the parameter list, and there must be at least one named parameter. The macros and definitions of the *variable arguments header* **<cstdarg>** (Fig. 18.1) provide the capabilities necessary to build functions with variable-length argument lists.

Identifier	Description
va_list	A type suitable for holding information needed by macros **va_start**, **va_arg** and **va_end**. To access the arguments in a variable-length argument list, an object of type **va_list** must be declared.
va_start	A macro that is invoked before the arguments of a variable-length argument list can be accessed. The macro initializes the object declared with **va_list** for use by the **va_arg** and **va_end** macros.

Fig. 18.1   The type and the macros defined in header **cstdarg** (part 1 of 2).

Identifier	Description
va_arg	A macro that expands to an expression of the value and type of the next argument in the variable-length argument list. Each invocation of **va_arg** modifies the object declared with **va_list** so that the object points to the next argument in the list.
va_end	A macro that facilitates a normal return from a function whose variable-length argument list was referred to by the **va_start** macro.

Fig. 18.1   The type and the macros defined in header **cstdarg** (part 2 of 2).

Figure 18.2 demonstrates function **average** that receives a variable number of arguments. The first argument of **average** is always the number of values to be averaged.

```cpp
1   // Fig. 18.2: fig18_02.cpp
2   // Using variable-length argument lists
3   #include <iostream>
4
5   using std::cout;
6   using std::endl;
7   using std::ios;
8
9   #include <iomanip>
10
11  using std::setw;
12  using std::setprecision;
13  using std::setiosflags;
14
15  #include <cstdarg>
16
17  double average( int, ... );
18
19  int main()
20  {
21     double w = 37.5, x = 22.5, y = 1.7, z = 10.2;
22
23     cout << setiosflags( ios::fixed | ios::showpoint )
24        << setprecision( 1 ) << "w = " << w << "\nx = " << x
25        << "\ny = " << y << "\nz = " << z << endl;
26     cout << setprecision( 3 ) << "\nThe average of w and x is "
27        << average( 2, w, x )
28        << "\nThe average of w, x, and y is "
29        << average( 3, w, x, y )
30        << "\nThe average of w, x, y, and z is "
31        << average( 4, w, x, y, z ) << endl;
32     return 0;
33  }
34
```

Fig. 18.2   Using variable-length argument lists (part 1 of 2).

```
35   double average( int i, ... )
36   {
37      double total = 0;
38      va_list ap;
39
40      va_start( ap, i );
41
42      for ( int j = 1; j <= i; j++ )
43         total += va_arg( ap, double );
44
45      va_end( ap );
46
47      return total / i;
48   }
```

```
w = 37.5
x = 22.5
y = 1.7
z = 10.2

The average of w and x is 30.000
The average of w, x, and y is 20.567
The average of w, x, y, and z is 17.975
```

Fig. 18.2   Using variable-length argument lists (part 2 of 2).

Function **average** uses all the definitions and macros of header **<cstdarg>**. Object **ap**, of type **va_list**, is used by macros **va_start**, **va_arg** and **va_end** to process the variable-length argument list of function **average**. The function invokes **va_start** to initialize object **ap** for use in **va_arg** and **va_end**. The macro receives two arguments—object **ap** and the identifier of the rightmost argument in the argument list before the ellipsis—**i** in this case (**va_start** uses **i** here to determine where the variable-length argument list begins). Next, function **average** repeatedly adds the arguments in the variable-length argument list to the **total**. The value to be added to **total** is retrieved from the argument list by invoking macro **va_arg**. Macro **va_arg** receives two arguments—object **ap** and the type of the value expected in the argument list (**double** in this case)—and returns the value of the argument. Function **average** invokes macro **va_end** with object **ap** as an argument to facilitate a normal return to **main** from **average**. Finally, the average is calculated and returned to **main**. Note that we used only **double** arguments for the variable-length portion of the argument list. Actually, any data type or a mixture of data types can be used as long as the proper type is specified each time **va_arg** is used.

Common Programming Error 18.1

Placing an ellipsis in the middle of a function parameter list. An ellipsis may only be placed at the end of the parameter list.

18.4 Using Command-Line Arguments

On many systems—DOS and UNIX in particular—it is possible to pass arguments to **main** from a command line by including parameters **int argc** and **char *argv[]** in the parameter list of **main**. Parameter **argc** receives the number of command-line arguments. Parameter **argv** is an array of strings in which the actual command-line arguments are stored. Common uses of command-line arguments include printing the arguments, passing options to a program and passing filenames to a program.

Figure 18.3 copies a file into another file one character at a time. The executable file for the program is called **copy**. A typical command line for the **copy** program on a UNIX system is

```
$ copy input output
```

This command line indicates that file **input** is to be copied to file **output**. When the program executes, if **argc** is not **3** (**copy** counts as one of the arguments), the program prints an error message and terminates. Otherwise, array **argv** contains the strings **"copy"**, **"input"** and **"output"**. The second and third arguments on the command line are used as file names by the program. The files are opened by creating **ifstream** object **inFile** and **ofstream** object **outFile**. If both files are opened successfully, characters are read from file **input** with member function **get** and written to file **output** with member function **put** until the end-of-file indicator for file **input** is set. Then the program terminates. The result is an exact copy of file **input**. Note that not all computer systems support command-line arguments as easily as UNIX and DOS. Macintosh and VMS systems, for example, require special settings for processing command-line arguments. See the manuals for your system for more information on command-line arguments.

```cpp
1   // Fig. 18.3: fig18_03.cpp
2   // Using command-line arguments
3   #include <iostream>
4
5   using std::cout;
6   using std::endl;
7   using std::ios;
8
9   #include <fstream>
10
11  using std::ifstream;
12  using std::ofstream;
13
14  int main( int argc, char *argv[] )
15  {
16     if ( argc != 3 )
17        cout << "Usage: copy infile outfile" << endl;
18     else {
19        ifstream inFile( argv[ 1 ], ios::in );
20
21        if ( !inFile ) {
22           cout << argv[ 1 ] << " could not be opened" << endl;
23           return -1;
24        }
25
26        ofstream outFile( argv[ 2 ], ios::out );
27
```

Fig. 18.3   Using command-line arguments (part 1 of 2).

```
28          if ( !outFile ) {
29              cout << argv[ 2 ] << " could not be opened" << endl;
30              inFile.close();
31              return -2;
32          }
33
34          while ( !inFile.eof() )
35              outFile.put( static_cast< char >( inFile.get() ) );
36
37          inFile.close();
38          outFile.close();
39      }
40
41      return 0;
42  }
```

Fig. 18.3   Using command-line arguments (part 2 of 2).

18.5 Notes on Compiling Multiple-Source-File Programs

As stated earlier in the text, it is possible to build programs that consist of multiple source files (see Chapter 6, "Classes and Data Abstraction"). There are several considerations when creating programs in multiple files. For example, the definition of a function must be entirely contained in one file—it cannot span two or more files.

In Chapter 3, we introduced the concepts of storage class and scope. We learned that variables declared outside any function definition are of storage class **static** by default and are referred to as global variables. Global variables are accessible to any function defined in the same file after the variable is declared. Global variables also are accessible to functions in other files; however, the global variables must be declared in each file in which they are used. For example, if we define global integer variable **flag** in one file, and refer to it in a second file, the second file must contain the declaration

extern int flag;

prior to the variable's use in that file. In the preceding declaration, the storage class specifier **extern** indicates to the compiler that variable **flag** is defined either later in the same file or in a different file. The compiler informs the linker that unresolved references to variable **flag** appear in the file. (The compiler does not know where the **flag** is defined, so it lets the linker attempt to find **flag**.) If the linker cannot locate a definition of **flag**, a linker error is reported, and no executable file is produced. If a proper global definition is located, the linker resolves the references by indicating where **flag** is located.

Performance Tip 18.1

Global variables increase performance because they can be accessed directly by any function—the overhead of passing data to functions is eliminated.

Software Engineering Observation 18.1

Global variables should be avoided unless application performance is critical, because they violate the principle of least privilege, and they make software difficult to maintain.

Just as **extern** declarations can be used to declare global variables to other program files, function prototypes can extend the scope of a function beyond the file in which it is defined. (The **extern** specifier is not required in a function prototype.) This is accomplished by including the function prototype in each file in which the function is invoked, and compiling the files together (see Section 17.2). Function prototypes indicate to the compiler that the specified function is defined either later in the same file or in a different file. The compiler does not attempt to resolve references to such a function—that task is left to the linker. If the linker cannot locate a function definition, an error is generated.

As an example of using function prototypes to extend the scope of a function, consider any program containing the preprocessor directive **#include <cstring>**. This directive includes in a file the function prototypes for functions such as **strcmp** and **strcat**. Other functions in the file can use **strcmp** and **strcat** to accomplish their tasks. The **strcmp** and **strcat** functions are defined for us separately. We do not need to know where they are defined. We are simply reusing the code in our programs. The linker resolves our references to these functions. This process enables us to use the functions in the standard library.

Software Engineering Observation 18.2

Creating programs in multiple source files facilitates software reusability and good software engineering. Functions may be common to many applications. In such instances, those functions should be stored in their own source files, and each source file should have a corresponding header file containing function prototypes. This enables programmers of different applications to reuse the same code by including the proper header file and compiling their application with the corresponding source file.

Portability Tip 18.1

Some systems do not support global variable names or function names of more than 6 characters. This should be considered when writing programs that will be ported to multiple platforms.

It is possible to restrict the scope of a global variable or function to the file in which it is defined. The storage class specifier **static**, when applied to a global variable or a function, prevents it from being used by any function that is not defined in the same file. This is referred to as *internal linkage*. Global variables and functions that are not preceded by **static** in their definitions have *external linkage*—they can be accessed in other files if those files contain proper declarations and/or function prototypes.

The global variable declaration

```
static double pi = 3.14159;
```

creates variable **pi** of type **double**, initializes it to **3.14159** and indicates that **pi** is known only to functions in the file in which it is defined.

The **static** specifier is commonly used with utility functions that are called only by functions in a particular file. If a function is not required outside a particular file, the principle of least privilege should be enforced by using **static**. If a function is defined before it is used in a file, **static** should be applied to the function definition. Otherwise, **static** should be applied to the function prototype.

When building large programs in multiple source files, compiling the program becomes tedious if small changes are made to one file, and the entire program must be recompiled. Many systems provide special utilities that recompile only the modified program file. On UNIX systems the utility is called **make**. Utility **make** reads a file called **makefile** that contains instructions for compiling and linking the program. Systems such as Borland C++ and Microsoft Visual C++ for PCs provide **make** utilities and "projects." For more information on **make** utilities, see the manual for your particular system.

18.6 Program Termination with `exit` and `atexit`

The general utilities library (**cstdlib**) provides methods of terminating program execution other than a conventional return from function **main**. Function **exit** forces a program to terminate as if it executed normally. The function often is used to terminate a program when an error is detected in the input, or if a file to be processed by the program cannot be opened. Function **atexit** *registers* a function in the program to be called upon successful termination of the program—i.e., either when the program terminates by reaching the end of **main**, or when **exit** is invoked.

Function **atexit** takes a pointer to a function (i.e., the function name) as an argument. Functions called at program termination cannot have arguments and cannot return a value. Up to 32 functions may be registered for execution at program termination.

Function **exit** takes one argument. The argument is normally the symbolic constant **EXIT_SUCCESS** or **EXIT_FAILURE**. If **exit** is called with **EXIT_SUCCESS**, the implementation-defined value for successful termination is returned to the calling environment. If **exit** is called with **EXIT_FAILURE**, the implementation-defined value for unsuccessful termination is returned. When function **exit** is invoked, any functions previously registered with **atexit** are invoked in the reverse order of their registration, all streams associated with the program are flushed and closed, and control returns to the host environment. Figure 18.4 tests functions **exit** and **atexit**. The program prompts the user to determine whether the program should be terminated with **exit** or by reaching the end of **main**. Note that function **print** is executed at program termination in each case.

```
1   // Fig. 18.4: fig18_04.cpp
2   // Using the exit and atexit functions
3   #include <iostream>
4
5   using std::cout;
6   using std::endl;
7   using std::cin;
8
9   #include <cstdlib>
10
11  void print( void );
12
13  int main()
14  {
15     atexit( print );        // register function print
16     cout << "Enter 1 to terminate program with function exit"
17        << "\nEnter 2 to terminate program normally\n";
18
```

Fig. 18.4   Using functions **exit** and **atexit** (part 1 of 2).

```
19        int answer;
20        cin >> answer;
21
22        if ( answer == 1 ) {
23           cout << "\nTerminating program with function exit\n";
24           exit( EXIT_SUCCESS );
25        }
26
27        cout << "\nTerminating program by reaching the end of main"
28             << endl;
29
30        return 0;
31    }
32
33    void print( void )
34    {
35        cout << "Executing function print at program termination\n"
36             << "Program terminated" << endl;
37    }
```

```
Enter 1 to terminate program with function exit
Enter 2 to terminate program normally
: 1

Terminating program with function exit
Executing function print at program termination
Program terminated
```

```
Enter 1 to terminate program with function exit
Enter 2 to terminate program normally
: 2

Terminating program by reaching the end of main
Executing function print at program termination
Program terminated
```

Fig. 18.4   Using functions **exit** and **atexit** (part 2 of 2).

18.7 The `volatile` Type Qualifier

The **volatile** type qualifier is applied to a definition of a variable that may be altered from outside the program (i.e., the variable is not completely under the control of the program). Thus, the compiler cannot perform optimizations (such as speeding program execution or reducing memory consumption, for example) that depend on "knowing that a variable's behavior is influenced only by program activities the compiler can observe."

18.8 Suffixes for Integer and Floating-Point Constants

C++ provides integer and floating-point suffixes for specifying the types of integer and floating-point constants. The integer suffixes are: **u** or **U** for an **unsigned** integer, **l** or **L** for a **long** integer, and **ul** or **UL** for an **unsigned long** integer. The following constants are of type **unsigned**, **long** and **unsigned long**, respectively:

```
174u
8358L
28373ul
```

If an integer constant is not suffixed, its type is determined by the first type capable of storing a value of that size (first **int**, then **long int**, and then **unsigned long int**).

The floating-point suffixes are **f** or **F** for a **float** and **l** or **L** for a **long double**. The following constants are of type **long double** and **float**, respectively:

```
3.14159L
1.28f
```

A floating-point constant that is not suffixed is of type **double**. A constant without a proper suffix results in either a compiler warning or error.

18.9 Signal Handling

An unexpected event, or *signal,* can terminate a program prematurely. Some unexpected events include *interrupts* (pressing *Ctrl c* on a UNIX or DOS system), *illegal instructions, segmentation violations, termination orders from the operating system* and *floating-point exceptions* (division by zero or multiplying large floating-point values). The *signal-handling library* provides function **signal** to *trap* unexpected events. Function **signal** receives two arguments—an integer signal number and a pointer to the signal-handling function. Signals can be generated by function **raise**, which takes an integer signal number as an argument. Figure 18.5 summarizes the standard signals defined in header file **<csignal>**. Figure 18.6 demonstrates functions **signal** and **raise**.

Signal	Explanation
SIGABRT	Abnormal termination of the program (such as a call to **abort**).
SIGFPE	An erroneous arithmetic operation, such as a divide by zero or an operation resulting in overflow.
SIGILL	Detection of an illegal instruction.
SIGINT	Receipt of an interactive attention signal.
SIGSEGV	An invalid access to storage.
SIGTERM	A termination request sent to the program.

Fig. 18.5   The signals defined in header **csignal**.

Figure 18.6 traps an interactive signal (**SIGINT**) with function **signal**. The program calls **signal** with **SIGINT** and a pointer to function **signal_handler**. (Remember that the name of a function is a pointer to the function.) Now, when a signal of type **SIGINT** occurs, function **signal_handler** is called, a message is printed and the user is given the option to continue normal execution of the program. If the user wishes to continue execution, the signal handler is reinitialized by calling **signal** again (some systems require the signal handler to be reinitialized), and control returns to the point in the program at which the signal was detected. In this program, function **raise** is used to simulate an interactive signal. A random number between **1** and **50** is chosen. If the number is **25**, then **raise** is called to generate the signal. Normally, interactive signals are initiated outside the program. For example, pressing *Ctrl-c* during program execution on a UNIX or DOS system generates an interactive signal that terminates program execution. Signal handling can be used to trap the interactive signal and prevent the program from terminating.

```cpp
1   // Fig. 18.6: fig18_06.cpp
2   // Using signal handling
3   #include <iostream>
4
5   using std::cout;
6   using std::cin;
7   using std::endl;
8
9   #include <iomanip>
10
11  using std::setw;
12
13  #include <csignal>
14  #include <cstdlib>
15  #include <ctime>
16
17  void signal_handler( int );
18
19  int main()
20  {
21     signal( SIGINT, signal_handler );
22     srand( time( 0 ) );
23
24     for ( int i = 1; i < 101; i++ ) {
25        int x = 1 + rand() % 50;
26
27        if ( x == 25 )
28           raise( SIGINT );
29
30        cout << setw( 4 ) << i;
31
32        if ( i % 10 == 0 )
33           cout << endl;
34     }
35
36     return 0;
37  }
```

Fig. 18.6   Using signal handling (part 1 of 2).

```
38
39   void signal_handler( int signalValue )
40   {
41      cout << "\nInterrupt signal (" << signalValue
42           << ") received.\n"
43           << "Do you wish to continue (1 = yes or 2 = no)? ";
44
45      int response;
46      cin >> response;
47
48      while ( response != 1 && response != 2 ) {
49         cout << "(1 = yes or 2 = no)? ";
50         cin >> response;
51      }
52
53      if ( response == 1 )
54         signal( SIGINT, signal_handler );
55      else
56         exit( EXIT_SUCCESS );
57   }
```

```
  1   2   3   4   5   6   7   8   9  10
 11  12  13  14  15  16  17  18  19  20
 21  22  23  24  25  26  27  28  29  30
 31  32  33  34  35  36  37  38  39  40
 41  42  43  44  45  46  47  48  49  50
 51  52  53  54  55  56  57  58  59  60
 61  62  63  64  65  66  67  68  69  70
 71  72  73  74  75  76  77  78  79  80
 81  82  83  84  85  86  87  88
Interrupt signal (4) received.
Do you wish to continue (1 = yes or 2 = no)? 1
 89  90
 91  92  93  94  95  96  97  98  99 100
```

Fig. 18.6   Using signal handling (part 2 of 2).

18.10 Dynamic Memory Allocation with `calloc` and `realloc`

In Chapter 7, when we discussed C++-style dynamic memory allocation with **new** and **delete**, we compared **new** and **delete** with the C functions **malloc** and **free**. C++ programmers should use **new** and **delete**, not **malloc** and **free**. However, most C++ programmers will find themselves reading a great deal of C legacy code, and therefore we include this additional discussion on C-style dynamic memory allocation.

The general utilities library (**<cstdlib>**) provides two other functions for dynamic memory allocation—**calloc** and **realloc**. These functions can be used to create and modify *dynamic arrays*. As shown in Chapter 5, "Pointers and Strings," a pointer to an array can be subscripted like an array. Thus, a pointer to a contiguous portion of memory created by **calloc** can be manipulated as an array. Function **calloc** dynamically allocates memory for an array and automatically initializes the memory to zeroes. The prototype for **calloc** is

```
void *calloc( size_t nmemb, size_t size );
```

It receives two arguments—the number of elements (**nmemb**) and the size of each element (**size**)—and initializes the elements of the array to zero. The function returns a pointer to the allocated memory or a null pointer (**0**) if the memory is not allocated.

Function **realloc** changes the size of an object allocated by a previous call to **malloc**, **calloc** or **realloc**. The original object's contents are not modified, provided that the memory allocated is larger than the amount allocated previously. Otherwise, the contents are unchanged up to the size of the new object. The prototype for **realloc** is

```
void *realloc( void *ptr, size_t size );
```

Function **realloc** takes two arguments—a pointer to the original object (**ptr**) and the new size of the object (**size**). If **ptr** is **0**, **realloc** works identically to **malloc**. If **size** is **0** and **ptr** is not **0**, the memory for the object is freed. Otherwise, if **ptr** is not **0** and size is greater than zero, **realloc** tries to allocate a new block of memory. If the new space cannot be allocated, the object pointed to by **ptr** is unchanged. Function **realloc** returns either a pointer to the reallocated memory or a null pointer.

18.11 The Unconditional Branch: `goto`

Throughout the text we have stressed the importance of using structured programming techniques to build reliable software that is easy to debug, maintain and modify. In some cases, performance is more important than strict adherence to structured programming techniques. In these cases, some unstructured programming techniques may be used. For example, we can use **break** to terminate execution of a repetition structure before the loop continuation condition becomes false. This saves unnecessary repetitions of the loop if the task is completed before loop termination.

Another instance of unstructured programming is the **goto** *statement*—an unconditional branch. The result of the **goto** statement is a change in the flow of control of the program to the first statement after the *label* specified in the **goto** statement. A label is an identifier followed by a colon. A label must appear in the same function as the **goto** statement that refers to it. Figure 18.7 uses **goto** statements to loop 10 times and print the counter value each time. After initializing **count** to **1**, the program tests **count** to determine whether it is greater than **10**. (The label **start** is skipped, because labels do not perform any action.) If so, control is transferred from the **goto** to the first statement after the label **end**. Otherwise, **count** is printed and incremented, and control is transferred from the **goto** to the first statement after the label **start**.

In Chapter 2, we stated that only three control structures are required to write any program—sequence, selection and repetition. When the rules of structured programming are followed, it is possible to create deeply nested control structures from which it is difficult to efficiently escape. Some programmers use **goto** statements in such situations as a quick exit from a deeply nested structure. This eliminates the need to test multiple conditions to escape from a control structure.

Performance Tip 18.2

*The **goto** statement can be used to exit deeply nested control structures efficiently.*

```
1   // Fig. 18.7: fig18_07.cpp
2   // Using goto
3   #include <iostream>
4
5   using std::cout;
6   using std::endl;
7
8   int main()
9   {
10     int count = 1;
11
12     start:                    // label
13        if ( count > 10 )
14           goto end;
15
16        cout << count << "   ";
17        ++count;
18        goto start;
19
20     end:                      // label
21        cout << endl;
22
23     return 0;
24   }
```

```
1   2   3   4   5   6   7   8   9   10
```

Fig. 18.7   Using **goto**.

Software Engineering Observation 18.3

*The **goto** statement should be used only in performance-oriented applications. The **goto** statement is unstructured and can lead to programs that are more difficult to debug, maintain and modify.*

18.12 Unions

A *union* (defined with keyword **union**) is a region of memory that, over time, can contain objects of a variety of types. However, at any moment, a **union** can contain a maximum of one object, because the members of a **union** share the same storage space. It is the programmer's responsibility to ensure that the data in a **union** is referenced with a member name of the proper data type.

Common Programming Error 18.2

*The result of referencing a **union** member other than the last one stored is undefined. It treats the stored data as a different type.*

Portability Tip 18.2

*If data are stored in a **union** as one type and referenced as another type, the results are implementation-dependent.*

At different times during a program's execution, some objects may not be relevant, while one other object is—so a **union** shares the space instead of wasting storage on objects that are not being used. The number of bytes used to store a **union** must be at least enough to hold the largest member.

Performance Tip 18.3

*Using **union**s conserves storage.*

Portability Tip 18.3

*The amount of storage required to store a **union** is implementation-dependent.*

Portability Tip 18.4

*Some **union**s may not port easily to other computer systems. Whether a **union** is portable or not often depends on the storage alignment requirements for the **union** member data types on a given system.*

A **union** is declared in the same format as a **struct** or a **class**. For example,

```
union Number {
    int x;
    double y;
};
```

indicates that **Number** is a **union** type with members **int x** and **double y**. The **union** definition normally precedes **main** in a program, so the definition can be used to declare variables in all the program's functions.

Software Engineering Observation 18.4

*As with a **struct** or a **class** declaration, a **union** declaration simply creates a new type. Placing a **union** or **struct** declaration outside any function does not create a global variable.*

The only valid built-in operations that can be performed on a **union** are assigning a **union** to another **union** of the same type, taking the address (**&**) of a **union** and accessing **union** members using the structure member operator (**.**) and the structure pointer operator (**->**). **union**s may not be compared, for the same reasons that structures cannot be compared.

Common Programming Error 18.3

*Comparing **union**s is a syntax error, because the compiler does not know which member of each is active and hence which member of one to compare to which member of the other.*

A **union** is similar to a class in that it can have a constructor to initialize any of its members. A **union** that has no constructor can be initialized with another **union** of the same type, with an expression of the type of the first member of the **union** or with an initializer (enclosed in braces) of the type of the first member of the **union**. **union**s can have other member functions, such as destructors, but a **union**'s member functions cannot be declared **virtual**. The members of a **union** are **public** by default.

Common Programming Error 18.4

*Initializing a **union** in a declaration with a value or an expression whose type is different from the type of the **union**'s first member.*

A **union** cannot be used as a base class in inheritance (i.e., classes may not be derived from **union**s). **union**s can have objects as members only if these objects do not have a constructor, a destructor or an overloaded assignment operator. None of a **union**'s data members can be declared **static**.

The program in Fig. 18.8 uses the variable **value** of type **union number** to display the value stored in the **union** as both an **int** and a **double**. The program output is implementation-dependent. The program output shows that the internal representation of a **double** value can be quite different from the representation of an **int**.

An *anonymous* **union** is a **union** without a type name that does not attempt to define objects or pointers before its terminating semicolon. Such a **union** does not create a type, but does create an unnamed object. An anonymous **union**'s members may be accessed

```
1   // Fig. 18.8: fig18_08.cpp
2   // An example of a union
3   #include <iostream>
4
5   using std::cout;
6   using std::endl;
7
8   union Number {
9      int x;
10     double y;
11  };
12
13  int main()
14  {
15     Number value;
16
17     value.x = 100;
18     cout << "Put a value in the integer member\n"
19          << "and print both members.\nint:    "
20          << value.x << "\ndouble: " << value.y << "\n\n";
21
22     value.y = 100.0;
23     cout << "Put a value in the floating member\n"
24          << "and print both members.\nint:    "
25          << value.x << "\ndouble: " << value.y << endl;
26     return 0;
27  }
```

```
Put a value in the integer member
and print both members.
int:    100
double: -9.25596e+061

Put a value in the floating member
and print both members.
int:    0
double: 100
```

Fig. 18.8   Printing the value of a **union** in both member data types.

directly in the scope in which the anonymous **union** is declared just as any other local variable—there is no need to use the dot (**.**) or arrow (**->**) operators.

Anonymous **union**s have some restrictions. Anonymous **union**s can contain only data members. All members of an anonymous **union** must be **public**. And an anonymous **union** declared globally (i.e., at file scope) must be explicitly declared **static**. Figure 18.9 illustrates the use of an anonymous **union**.

```cpp
1   // Fig. 18.9: fig18_09.cpp
2   // Using an anonymous union
3   #include <iostream>
4
5   using std::cout;
6   using std::endl;
7
8   int main()
9   {
10      // Declare an anonymous union.
11      // Note that members b, d, and fPtr share the same space.
12      union {
13         int b;
14         double d;
15         char *fPtr;
16      };
17
18      // Declare conventional local variables
19      int a = 1;
20      double c = 3.3;
21      char *ePtr = "Anonymous";
22
23      // Assign a value to each union member
24      // successively and print each.
25      cout << a << ' ';
26      b = 2;
27      cout << b << endl;
28
29      cout << c << ' ';
30      d = 4.4;
31      cout << d << endl;
32
33      cout << ePtr << ' ';
34      fPtr = "union";
35      cout << fPtr << endl;
36
37      return 0;
38   }
```

```
1 2
3.3 4.4
Anonymous union
```

Fig. 18.9   Using an anonymous **union**.

18.13 Linkage Specifications

It is possible from a C++ program to call functions written and compiled with a C compiler. As stated in Section 3.20, C++ specially encodes function names for type-safe linkage. C, however, does not encode its function names. Thus, a function compiled in C will not be recognized when an attempt is made to link C code with C++ code, because the C++ code expects a specially encoded function name. C++ enables the programmer to provide *linkage specifications* to inform the compiler that a function was compiled on a C compiler and to prevent the name of the function from being encoded by the C++ compiler. Linkage specifications are useful when large libraries of specialized functions have been developed, and the user either does not have access to the source code for recompilation into C++ or does not have time to convert the library functions from C to C++.

To inform the compiler that one or several functions have been compiled in C, write the function prototypes as follows:

```
extern "C" function prototype    // single function

extern "C"    // multiple functions
{
    function prototypes
}
```

These declarations inform the compiler that the specified functions are not compiled in C++, so name encoding should not be performed on the functions listed in the linkage specification. These functions can then be linked properly with the program. C++ environments normally include the standard C libraries and do not require the programmer to use linkage specifications for those functions.

SUMMARY

- On many systems—UNIX and DOS systems in particular—it is possible to redirect input to a program and output from a program. Input is redirected from the UNIX and DOS command lines using the redirect input symbol (**<**) or using a pipe (**|**). Output is redirected from the UNIX and DOS command lines using the redirect output symbol (**>**) or the append output symbol (**>>**). The redirect output symbol simply stores the program output in a file and the append output symbol appends the output to the end of a file.

- The macros and definitions of the variable arguments header **cstdarg** provide the capabilities necessary to build functions with variable-length argument lists.

- An ellipsis (**...**) in a function prototype indicates that the function receives a variable number of arguments.

- Type **va_list** is suitable for holding information needed by macros **va_start**, **va_arg** and **va_end**. To access the arguments in a variable-length argument list, an object of type **va_list** must be declared.

- Macro **va_start** is invoked before the arguments of a variable-length argument list can be accessed. The macro initializes the object declared with **va_list** for use by the **va_arg** and **va_end** macros.

- Macro **va_arg** expands to an expression of the value and type of the next argument in the variable-length argument list. Each invocation of **va_arg** modifies the object declared with **va_list** so that the object points to the next argument in the list.

- Macro **va_end** facilitates a normal return from a function whose variable argument list was referred to by the **va_start** macro.

- On many systems—DOS and UNIX in particular—it is possible to pass command-line arguments to **main** by including in **main**'s parameter list the parameters **int argc** and **char *argv[]**. Parameter **argc** is the number of command-line arguments. Parameter **argv** is an array of strings containing the command-line arguments.

- The definition of a function must be entirely contained in one file—it cannot span two or more files.

- Global variables must be declared in each file in which they are used.

- Function prototypes can extend the scope of a function beyond the file in which it is defined. (The **extern** specifier is not required in a function prototype.) This is accomplished by including the function prototype in each file in which the function is invoked and compiling the files together.

- The storage class specifier **static**, when applied to a global variable or a function, prevents it from being used by any function that is not defined in the same file. This is referred to as internal linkage. Global variables and functions that are not preceded by **static** in their definitions have external linkage—they can be accessed in other files if those files contain proper declarations and/or function prototypes.

- The **static** specifier is commonly used with utility functions that are called only by functions in a particular file. If a function is not required outside a particular file, the principle of least privilege should be enforced by using **static**.

- When building large programs in multiple source files, compiling the program becomes tedious if small changes are made to one file, and the entire program must be recompiled. Many systems provide special utilities that recompile only the modified program file. On UNIX systems the utility is called **make**. Utility **make** reads a file called **makefile** that contains instructions for compiling and linking the program.

- Function **exit** forces a program to terminate as if it executed normally.

- Function **atexit** registers a function in a program to be called upon normal termination of the program—i.e., either when the program terminates by reaching the end of **main** or when **exit** is invoked.

- Function **atexit** takes a pointer to a function (i.e., a function name) as an argument. Functions called at program termination cannot have arguments and cannot return a value. Up to 32 functions may be registered for execution at program termination.

- Function **exit** takes one argument. The argument is normally the symbolic constant **EXIT_SUCCESS** or the symbolic constant **EXIT_FAILURE**. If **exit** is called with **EXIT_SUCCESS**, the implementation-defined value for successful termination is returned to the calling environment. If **exit** is called with **EXIT_FAILURE**, the implementation-defined value for unsuccessful termination is returned.

- When function **exit** is invoked, any functions registered with **atexit** are invoked in the reverse order of their registration, all streams associated with the program are flushed and closed and control returns to the host environment.

- The **volatile** qualifier is used to prevent optimizations of a variable, because it can be modified from outside the program's scope.

- C++ provides integer and floating-point suffixes for specifying the types of integer and floating-point constants. The integer suffixes are **u** or **U** for an **unsigned** integer, **l** or **L** for a **long** integer and **ul** or **UL** for an **unsigned long** integer. If an integer constant is not suffixed, its type is determined by the first type capable of storing a value of that size (first **int**, then **long int** and then **unsigned long int**). The floating-point suffixes are **f** or **F** for a **float** and **l** or **L** for a **long double**. A floating-point constant that is not suffixed is of type **double**.

- The signal-handling library provides the capability to register a function to trap unexpected events with function **signal**. Function **signal** receives two arguments—an integer signal number and a pointer to the signal handling function.

- Signals can also be generated with function **raise** and an integer argument.

- The general utilities library (**cstdlib**) provides functions **calloc** and **realloc** for dynamic memory allocation. These functions can be used to create dynamic arrays.

- Function **calloc** receives two arguments—the number of elements (**nmemb**) and the size of each element (**size**)—and initializes the elements of the array to zero. The function returns either a pointer to the allocated memory, or a **NULL** pointer if the memory is not allocated.

- Function **realloc** changes the size of an object allocated by a previous call to **malloc**, **calloc** or **realloc**. The original object's contents are not modified, provided that the amount of memory allocated is larger than the amount allocated previously.

- Function **realloc** takes two arguments—a pointer to the original object (**ptr**) and the new size of the object (**size**). If **ptr** is **NULL**, **realloc** works identically to **malloc**. If **size** is **0** and the pointer received is not **NULL**, the memory for the object is freed. Otherwise, if **ptr** is not **NULL** and **size** is greater than zero, **realloc** tries to allocate a new block of memory for the object. If the new space cannot be allocated, the object pointed to by **ptr** is unchanged. Function **realloc** returns either a pointer to the reallocated memory, or a **NULL** pointer.

- The result of the **goto** statement is a change in the program's flow of control. Program execution continues at the first statement after the label in the **goto** statement.

- A label is an identifier followed by a colon. A label must appear in the same function as the **goto** statement that refers to it.

- A **union** is a derived data type whose members share the same storage space. The members can be any type. The storage reserved for a **union** is large enough to store its largest member. In most cases, **union**s contain two or more data types. Only one member, and thus one data type, can be referenced at a time.

- A **union** is declared in the same format as a structure.

- A **union** can be initialized only with a value of the type of its first member.

- C++ enables the programmer to provide linkage specifications to inform the compiler that a function was compiled on a C compiler and to prevent the name of the function from being encoded by the C++ compiler.

- To inform the compiler that one or several functions have been compiled in C, write the function prototypes as follows:

```
extern "C" function prototype    // single function

extern "C"    // multiple functions
{
    function prototypes
}
```

- These declarations inform the compiler that the specified functions are not compiled in C++, so name encoding should not be performed on the functions listed in the linkage specification. These functions can then be linked properly with the program.

- C++ environments normally include the standard C libraries and do not require the programmer to use linkage specifications for those functions.

TERMINOLOGY

append output symbol **>>**
argv
atexit
calloc
csignal
command-line arguments
const
cstdarg
dynamic arrays
event
exit
EXIT_FAILURE
EXIT_SUCCESS
extern "C"
extern storage class specifier
external linkage
float suffix (**f** or **F**)
floating-point exception
goto statement
I/O redirection
illegal instruction
internal linkage
interrupt
long double suffix (**l** or **L**)

long integer suffix (**l** or **L**)
make
makefile
pipe **|**
piping
raise
realloc
redirect input symbol **<**
redirect output symbol **>**
segmentation violation
signal
signal-handling library
static storage class specifier
trap
union
unsigned integer suffix (**u** or **U**)
unsigned long integer suffix (**ul** or **UL**)
variable-length argument list
va_arg
va_end
va_list
va_start
volatile

COMMON PROGRAMMING ERRORS

18.1 Placing an ellipsis in the middle of a function parameter list. An ellipsis may only be placed at the end of the parameter list.

18.2 The result of referencing a **union** member other than the last one stored is undefined. It treats the stored data as a different type.

18.3 Comparing **union**s is a syntax error, because the compiler does not know which member of each is active and hence which member of one to compare to which member of the other.

18.4 Initializing a **union** in a declaration with a value or an expression whose type is different from the type of the **union**'s first member.

PERFORMANCE TIPS

18.1 Global variables increase performance because they can be accessed directly by any function—the overhead of passing data to functions is eliminated.

18.2 The **goto** statement can be used to exit deeply nested control structures efficiently.

18.3 Using **union**s conserves storage.

PORTABILITY TIPS

18.1 Some systems do not support global variable names or function names of more than 6 characters. This should be considered when writing programs that will be ported to multiple platforms.

18.2 If data are stored in a **union** as one type and referenced as another type, the results are implementation-dependent.

18.3   The amount of storage required to store a **union** is implementation-dependent.

18.4   Some **union**s may not port easily to other computer systems. Whether a **union** is portable or not often depends on the storage alignment requirements for the **union** member data types on a given system.

SOFTWARE ENGINEERING OBSERVATIONS

18.1   Global variables should be avoided unless application performance is critical, because they violate the principle of least privilege, and they make software difficult to maintain.

18.2   Creating programs in multiple source files facilitates software reusability and good software engineering. Functions may be common to many applications. In such instances, those functions should be stored in their own source files, and each source file should have a corresponding header file containing function prototypes. This enables programmers of different applications to reuse the same code by including the proper header file and compiling their application with the corresponding source file.

18.3   The **goto** statement should be used only in performance-oriented applications. The **goto** statement is unstructured and can lead to programs that are more difficult to debug, maintain and modify.

18.4   As with a **struct** or a **class** declaration, a **union** declaration simply creates a new type. Placing a **union** or **struct** declaration outside any function does not create a global variable.

SELF-REVIEW EXERCISES

18.1   Fill in the blanks in each of the following:

a) Symbol _____ redirects input data from the keyboard to come from a file.

b) The _____ symbol is used to redirect the screen output to be placed in a file.

c) The _____ symbol is used to append the output of a program to the end of a file.

d) A _____ is used to direct the output of a program as the input of another program.

e) An _____ in the parameter list of a function indicates that the function can receive a variable number of arguments.

f) Macro _____ must be invoked before the arguments in a variable-length argument list can be accessed.

g) Macro _____ is used to access the individual arguments of a variable-length argument list.

h) Macro _____ facilitates a normal return from a function whose variable argument list was referred to by macro **va_start**.

i) Argument _____ of **main** receives the number of arguments in a command line.

j) Argument _____ of **main** stores command-line arguments as character strings.

k) The UNIX utility _____ reads a file called _____ that contains instructions for compiling and linking a program consisting of multiple source files. The utility only recompiles a file if the file has been modified since it was last compiled.

l) Function _____ forces a program to terminate execution.

m) Function _____ registers a function to be called upon normal termination of the program.

n) Type qualifier _____ indicates that an object should not be modified after it is initialized.

o) An integer or floating-point _____ can be appended to an integer or floating-point constant to specify the exact type of the constant.

p) Function _____ can be used to register a function to trap unexpected events.

q) Function _____ generates a signal from within a program.

r) Function _____ dynamically allocates memory for an array and initializes the elements to zero.

s) Function _____ changes the size of a block of dynamically allocated memory.

t) A _____ is a class containing a collection of variables that occupy the same memory, but at different times.

u) The _____ keyword is used to introduce a union definition.

ANSWERS TO SELF-REVIEW EXERCISES

18.1   a) redirect input. (**<**).   b) redirect output. (**>**).   c) append output (**>>**).   d) pipe (**|**). e) ellipsis (**...**).   f) **va_start**.   g) **va_arg**.   h) **va_end**.   i) **argc**.   j) **argv**.   k) **make, makefile**.   l) **exit**.   m) **atexit**.   n) **const**.   o) suffix.   p) **signal**.   q) **raise**.   r) **calloc**. s) **realloc**. t) union. u) **union**.

EXERCISES

18.2   Write a program that calculates the product of a series of integers that are passed to function **product** using a variable-length argument list. Test your function with several calls, each with a different number of arguments.

18.3   Write a program that prints the command-line arguments of the program.

18.4   Write a program that sorts an integer array into ascending order or descending order. The program should use command-line arguments to pass either argument **–a** for ascending order or **–d** for descending order. (Note: This is the standard format for passing options to a program in UNIX.)

18.5   Read the manuals for your system to determine what signals are supported by the signal-handling library (**csignal**). Write a program with signal handlers for the signals **SIGABRT** and **SIGINT**. The program should test the trapping of these signals by calling function **abort** to generate a signal of type **SIGABRT** and by pressing *Ctrl c* to generate a signal of type **SIGINT**.

18.6   Write a program that dynamically allocates an array of integers. The size of the array should be input from the keyboard. The elements of the array should be assigned values input from the keyboard. Print the values of the array. Next, reallocate the memory for the array to half of the current number of elements. Print the values remaining in the array to confirm that they match the first half of the values in the original array.

18.7   Write a program that takes two file names as command-line arguments, reads the characters from the first file one at a time and writes the characters in reverse order to the second file.

18.8   Write a program that uses **goto** statements to simulate a nested looping structure that prints a square of asterisks as follows:

```
*****
*   *
*   *
*   *
*****
```

The program should use only the following three output statements:

```
cout << '*';
cout << ' ';
cout << endl;
```

18.9 Provide the definition for **union Data** containing **char c, short s, long l, float f** and **double d**.

18.10 Create **union Integer** with members **char c, short s, int i** and **long l**. Write a program that inputs values of type **char, short, int** and **long** and stores the values in **union** variables of type **union Integer**. Each **union** variable should be printed as a **char**, a **short**, an **int** and a **long**. Do the values always print correctly?

18.11 Create **union FloatingPoint** with members **float f, double d** and **long double l**. Write a program that inputs value of type **float, double** and **long double** and stores the values in **union** variables of type **union FloatingPoint**. Each **union** variable should be printed as a **float**, a **double** and a **long double**. Do the values always print correctly?

18.12 Given the **union**

```
union A {
    double y;
    char *z;
};
```

which of the following are correct statements for initializing the **union**?
   a) **A p = B;   // B is of same type as A**
   b) **A q = x;   // x is a double**
   c) **A r = 3.14159;**
   d) **A s = { 79.63 };**
   e) **A t = { "Hi There!" };**
   f) **A u = { 3.14159, "Pi" };**

19

Class **string** and String Stream Processing

Objectives

- To use class **string** from the C++ standard library to treat **string**s as full-fledged objects.
- To be able to assign, concatenate, compare, search and swap **string**s.
- To be able to determine **string** characteristics.
- To be able to find, replace and insert characters in a **string**.
- To be able to convert **string**s to C-style strings.
- To be able to use **string** iterators.
- To be able to perform input from and output to **string**s in memory.

The difference between the almost-right word & the right word is really a large matter — it's the difference between the lightning bug and the lightning.
Mark Twain, Letter to George Bainton [October 15, 1888]

I have made this letter longer than usual, because I lack the time to make it short.
Blaise Pascal

Mum's the word.
Miguel de Cervantes, Don Quixote de la Mancha

Suit the action to the word, the word to the action; with this special observance, that you o'erstep not the modesty of nature.
William Shakespeare, Hamlet

19.1 Introduction

The C++ template class **`basic_string`** provides typical string manipulation operations such as copying, searching, etc. The template definition and all support facilities are defined in **`namespace std`**; these include the **`typedef`** statement

```
typedef basic_string< char > string;
```

that creates the alias type **`string`** for **`basic_string< char >`**. A **`typedef`** is also provided for the **`wchar_t`** type. Type **`wchar_t`** stores characters (e.g., 2-byte characters, 4-byte characters, etc.) for supporting other character sets. We use **`string`** exclusively throughout this chapter. To use **`string`**s include C++ standard library header file **`<string>`**. [Note: Type **`wchar_t`** is commonly used to represent Unicode, which does have 16-bit characters, but the size of **`wchar_t`** is not fixed by the standard.]

A **`string`** object can be initialized with a constructor argument such as

```
string s1( "Hello" );  // creates string from const char *
```

which creates a **`string`** containing the characters in **`"Hello"`** except, perhaps, the terminating **`'\0'`**, or with two constructor arguments as in

```
string s2( 8, 'x' );  // string of 8 'x' characters
```

which creates a **`string`** containing eight **`'x'`** characters. Class **`string`** also provides a default constructor and a copy constructor.

A **`string`** can also be initialized via the alternate construction syntax in the definition of a **`string`** as in

```
string month = "March";  // same as: string month( "March" );
```

Remember that operator **=** in the preceding declaration is not an assignment; rather it is a call to the **string** class constructor, which implicitly does the conversion.

Note that class **string** provides no conversions from **int** or **char** to **string** in a **string** definition. For example, the definitions

```
string error1 = 'c';
string error2( 'u' );
string error3 = 22;
string error4( 8 );
```

result in syntax errors. Note that assigning a single character to a **string** object is permitted in an assignment statement as in

```
s = 'n';
```

Common Programming Error 19.1

*Attempting to convert an **int** or **char** to a **string** via an assignment in a declaration or via a constructor argument is a syntax error.*

Common Programming Error 19.2

*Constructing a **string** that is too long to be represented throws a **length_error** exception.*

Unlike C-style **char *** strings, **string**s are not necessarily null terminated. The length of a **string** is stored in the **string** object and can be retrieved with member function **length**. The subscript operator, **[ ]**, can be used with **string**s to access individual characters. Like C-style strings, **string**s have a first subscript of **0** and a last subscript of **length–1**. Note that a string is not a pointer—the expression **&s[0]** is not equivalent to **s** when **s** is a **string**.

Most **string** member functions take as arguments a starting subscript location and the number of characters on which to operate.

Attempting to pass a **string** member function a value larger than the length of the **string** (for the number of characters to process) results in the value being set to the difference between the value and length. For example, passing 2 (starting subscript) and 100 (number of characters) to a function that operates on a **string** of size 50 results in 48 (50 -2) being used for the number of characters.

The stream extraction operator (**>>**) is overloaded to support **string**s. The statement

```
string stringObject;
cin >> stringObject;
```

reads a **string** from the standard input device. Input is delimited by whitespace characters. Function **getline** (from header file **<string>**) is also overloaded for **string**s. The statement

```
string s;
getline( cin, s );
```

reads a **string** from the keyboard into **s**. Input is delimited by a newline (**'\n'**).

19.2 string Assignment and Concatenation

The program of Fig. 19.1 demonstrates **string** assignment and concatenation.

```cpp
1   // Fig. 19.1: fig19_01.cpp
2   // Demonstrating string assignment and concatenation
3   #include <iostream>
4
5   using std::cout;
6   using std::endl;
7
8   #include <string>
9
10  using std::string;
11
12  int main()
13  {
14     string s1( "cat" ), s2, s3;
15
16     s2 = s1;              // assign s1 to s2 with =
17     s3.assign( s1 );  // assign s1 to s3 with assign()
18     cout << "s1: " << s1 << "\ns2: " << s2 << "\ns3: "
19         << s3 << "\n\n";
20
21     // modify s2 and s3
22     s2[ 0 ] = s3[ 2 ] = 'r';
23
24     cout << "After modification of s2 and s3:\n"
25         << "s1: " << s1 << "\ns2: " << s2 << "\ns3: ";
26
27     // demonstrating member function at()
28     int len = s3.length();
29     for ( int x = 0; x < len; ++x )
30        cout << s3.at( x );
31
32     // concatenation
33     string s4( s1 + "apult" ), s5;  // declare s4 and s5
34
35     // overloaded +=
36     s3 += "pet";           // create "carpet"
37     s1.append( "acomb" );     // create "catacomb"
38
39     // append subscript locations 4 thru the end of s1 to
40     // create the string "comb" (s5 was initially empty)
41     s5.append( s1, 4, s1.size() );
42
43     cout << "\n\nAfter concatcenation:\n" << "s1: " << s1
44         << "\ns2: " << s2 << "\ns3: " << s3 << "\ns4: " << s4
45         << "\ns5: " << s5 << endl;
46
47     return 0;
48  }
```

Fig. 19.1   Demonstrating **string** assignment and concatenation (part 1 of 2).

```
s1: cat
s2: cat
s3: cat

After modification of s2 and s3:
s1: cat
s2: rat
s3: car

After concatenation:
s1: catacomb
s2: rat
s3: carpet
s4: catapult
s5: comb
```

Fig. 19.1   Demonstrating **string** assignment and concatenation (part 2 of 2).

Line 8 includes header **string** for class **string**. Three **string**s **s1**, **s2** and **s3** are created at line 14. Line 16

```
s2 = s1;            // assign s1 to s2 with =
```

assigns **string s1** to **s2**. After the assignment takes place, **s2** is a copy of **s1**, but **s2** is not tied to **s1** in any way. Line 17

```
s3.assign( s1 );  // assign s1 to s3 with assign()
```

uses member function **assign** to copy **s1** into **s3**. A separate copy is made (i.e., **s1** and **s3** are independent objects). Class **string** also provides an overloaded version of function **assign** that copies a specified number of characters as in

```
myString.assign( s, start, numberOfChars );
```

where **s** is the **string** to be copied, **start** is the starting subscript and **numberOf-Chars** is the number of characters to copy.

Line 22

```
s2[ 0 ] = s3[ 2 ] = 'r';
```

uses the subscript operator to assign **'r'** to **s3[2]** (forming **"car"**) and to assign **'r'** to **s2[0]** (forming **"rat"**). The **string**s are then output.

Lines 28 through 30

```
int len = s3.length();
for ( int x = 0; x < len; ++x )
   cout << s3.at( x );
```

use a **for** loop to output the contents of **s3** one character at a time using function **at**. Function **at** provides *checked access* (or *range checking*), i.e., going past the end of the **string** throws an **out_of_range** exception (see Chapter 13 for a detailed discussion of exception handling). Note that the subscript operator, **[ ]**, does not provide checked access. This is consistent with its use on arrays.

Common Programming Error 19.3

*Accessing a **string** subscript outside the bounds of the **string** using function **at** throws an **out_of_range** exception.*

Common Programming Error 19.4

*Accessing an element beyond the size of the **string** using the subscript operator is a logic error.*

String **s4** is declared (line 33) and initialized to the result of concatenating **s1** and **"apult"** using the overloaded addition operator, **+**, which for class **string** denotes concatenation. Line 36

```
s3 += "pet";              // create "carpet"
```

uses the addition assignment operator, **+=**, to concatenate **s3** and **"pet"**.
    Line 37

```
s1.append( "acomb" );     // create "catacomb"
```

uses function **append** to concatenate **s1** and **"acomb"**. Line 41

```
s5.append( s1, 4, s1.size() );
```

appends characters from **s1** to **s5**. The characters from the fourth element to the last element of **s1** are concatenated to **s5**. Function **size** returns the number of characters in **string s1**.

19.3 Comparing `strings`

Class **string** provides functions for comparing **string**s. The program of Fig. 19.2 demonstrates **string** comparison capabilities.

```cpp
1   // Fig. 19.2: fig19_02.cpp
2   // Demonstrating string comparison capabilities
3   #include <iostream>
4
5   using std::cout;
6   using std::endl;
7
8   #include <string>
9
10  using std::string;
11
12  int main()
13  {
14     string s1( "Testing the comparison functions." ),
15            s2("Hello" ), s3( "stinger" ), z1( s2 );
16
17     cout << "s1: " << s1 << "\ns2: " << s2
18          << "\ns3: " << s3 << "\nz1: " << z1 << "\n\n";
19
```

Fig. 19.2 Comparing **string**s (part 1 of 2).

```
20        // comparing s1 and z1
21        if ( s1 == z1 )
22           cout << "s1 == z1\n";
23        else { // s1 != z1
24           if ( s1 > z1 )
25              cout << "s1 > z1\n";
26           else // s1 < z1
27              cout << "s1 < z1\n";
28        }
29
30        // comparing s1 and s2
31        int f = s1.compare( s2 );
32
33        if ( f == 0)
34           cout << "s1.compare( s2 ) == 0\n";
35        else if ( f > 0 )
36           cout << "s1.compare( s2 ) > 0\n";
37        else // f < 0
38           cout << "s1.compare( s2 ) < 0\n";
39
40        // comparing s1 (elements 2 - 5) and s3 (elements 0 - 5)
41        f = s1.compare( 2, 5, s3, 0, 5 );
42
43        if ( f == 0 )
44           cout << "s1.compare( 2, 5, s3, 0, 5 ) == 0\n";
45        else if ( f > 0 )
46           cout << "s1.compare( 2, 5, s3, 0, 5 ) > 0\n";
47        else  // f < 0
48           cout << "s1.compare( 2, 5, s3, 0, 5 ) < 0\n";
49
50        // comparing s2 and z1
51        f = z1.compare( 0, s2.size(), s2 );
52
53        if ( f == 0 )
54           cout << "z1.compare( 0, s2.size(), s2 ) == 0" << endl;
55        else if ( f > 0 )
56           cout << "z1.compare( 0, s2.size(), s2 ) > 0" << endl;
57        else  // f < 0
58           cout << "z1.compare( 0, s2.size(), s2 ) < 0" << endl;
59
60        return 0;
61     }
```

```
s1: Testing the comparison functions.
s2: Hello
s3: stinger
z1: Hello

s1 > z1
s1.compare( s2 ) > 0
s1.compare( 2, 5, s3, 0, 5 ) == 0
z1.compare( 0, s2.size(), s2 ) == 0
```

Fig. 19.2   Comparing **string**s (part 2 of 2).

The program declares four **string**s with lines 14 and 15

```
string s1( "Testing the comparison functions." ),
       s2( "Hello" ), s3( "stinger" ), z1( s2 );
```

and outputs each **string** (lines 17 and 18). The condition

```
s1 == z1
```

in line 21 tests **s1** against **z1** for equality. If the condition is **true**, "**s1 == z1**" is output. If the condition is **false**, the condition

```
s1 > z1
```

in line 24 is tested. All the overloaded operator functions demonstrated here as well as those not demonstrated here (**!=**, **<**, **>=** and **<=**) return **bool** values.

Line 31

```
int f = s1.compare( s2 );
```

uses **string** function **compare** to test **string s1** against **s2**. Variable **f** is declared and assigned **0** if the **string**s are equivalent, a positive number if **s1** is *lexicographically* greater than **s2** or a negative number if **s1** is lexicographically less than **s2**.

Line 41

```
f = s1.compare( 2, 5, s3, 0, 5 );
```

uses an overloaded version of function **compare** to compare portions of **s1** and **s3**. The first two arguments (**2** and **5**) specify the starting subscript and length of the portion of **s1** to compare with **s3**. The third argument is the comparison **string**. The last two arguments (**0** and **5**) are the starting subscript and length of the portion of the comparison **string** being compared. The value assigned to **f** is **0** for equality, a positive number if **s1** is lexicographically greater than **s3** or a negative number if **s1** is lexicographically less than **s3**. A **string** is then printed based on the value of **f**.

Line 51

```
f = z1.compare( 0, s2.size(), s2 );
```

uses another overloaded version of function **compare** to compare **z1** and **s2**. The first argument specifies the beginning subscript of **z1** used in the comparison. The second argument specifies the length of the portion of **z1** used in the comparison. Function **size** returns the number of characters in the specified **string**. The last argument is the comparison **string**. The value assigned to **f** is either a **0** for equality, a positive number if **z1** is lexicographically greater than **s2** or a negative number if **z1** is lexicographically less than **s2**. A **string** is then printed based on the value of **f**.

19.4 Substrings

Class **string** provides function **substr** for retrieving a substring from a **string**. The program of Fig. 19.3 demonstrates **substr**.

```
1   // Fig. 19.3: fig19_03.cpp
2   // Demonstrating function substr
3   #include <iostream>
4
5   using std::cout;
6   using std::endl;
7
8   #include <string>
9
10  using std::string;
11
12  int main()
13  {
14     string s( "The airplane flew away." );
15
16     // retrieve the substring "plane" which
17     // begins at subscript 7 and consists of 5 elements
18     cout << s.substr( 7, 5 ) << endl;
19
20     return 0;
21  }
```

```
plane
```

Fig. 19.3   Demonstrating function **substr**.

The program declares and initializes a **string** on line 18. The line

```
cout << s.substr( 7, 5 ) << endl;
```

uses function **substr** to retrieve a substring from **s**. The first argument specifies the beginning subscript of the substring. The last argument specifies the number of characters to extract.

19.5 Swapping strings

Class **string** provides function **swap** for swapping **string**s. The program of Fig. 19.4 swaps two **string**s.

```
1   // Fig. 19.4: fig19_04.cpp
2   // Using the swap function to swap two strings
3   #include <iostream>
4
5   using std::cout;
6   using std::endl;
7
8   #include <string>
9
10  using std::string;
11
```

Fig. 19.4   Using function **swap** to swap two **string**s (part 1 of 2).

```
12   int main()
13   {
14      string first( "one" ), second( "two" );
15
16      cout << "Before swap:\n first: " << first
17           << "\nsecond: " << second;
18      first.swap( second );
19      cout << "\n\nAfter swap:\n first: " << first
20           << "\nsecond: " << second << endl;
21
22      return 0;
23   }
```

```
Before swap:
 first: one
second: two

After swap:
 first: two
second: one
```

Fig. 19.4   Using function **swap** to swap two **string**s (part 2 of 2).

Line 14 declares and initializes **string**s **first** and **second**. Each **string** is then output. Line 18

```
first.swap( second );
```

uses function **swap** to swap the values of **first** and **second**. The two **string**s are printed again to confirm that they were indeed swapped.

19.6 `string` Characteristics

Class **string** provides functions for gathering information about a **string**'s size, length, capacity, maximum length and other characteristics. A **string**'s *size* or *length* is the number of characters currently stored in the **string**. A **string**'s *capacity* is the total number of elements that can be stored in the **string** without increasing the memory capacity of the **string**. The *maximum size* is the size of the largest possible **string** that can be stored in a **string** object. The program of Fig. 19.5 demonstrates **string** class functions for finding a **string**'s size, length and other characteristics.

The program declares empty **string s** (line 17) and passes it to function **print-Stats** (line 20). An *empty* **string** is a **string** that does not contain any characters. The string **"tomato"** is input from the keyboard. Note that **string**s are delimited by whitespace characters, which prevents the remaining characters from being input.

Function **printStats** takes a reference to a **const string** as an argument and outputs the capacity (using function **capacity**), maximum size (using function **max_size**), size (using function **size**), length (using function **length**) and whether or not the **string** is empty (using function **empty**). The initial call to **printStats** indicates that the initial values for the capacity, size and length of **s** are 0. Because the capacity is 0, when characters are placed in **s**, memory is allocated to accommodate the new characters. The size and length of 0 indicate that there are currently no characters stored in **s**. The size and length are always identical. The maximum size is 4294967293 for this implementation. String **s** is an empty **string**, so function **empty** returns **true**.

```cpp
1   // Fig. 19.5: fig19_05.cpp
2   // Demonstrating functions related to size and capacity
3   #include <iostream>
4
5   using std::cout;
6   using std::endl;
7   using std::cin;
8
9   #include <string>
10
11  using std::string;
12
13  void printStats( const string & );
14
15  int main()
16  {
17     string s;
18
19     cout << "Stats before input:\n";
20     printStats( s );
21
22     cout << "\n\nEnter a string: ";
23     cin >> s;   // delimited by whitespace
24     cout << "The string entered was: " << s;
25
26     cout << "\nStats after input:\n";
27     printStats( s );
28
29     s.resize( s.length() + 10 );
30     cout << "\n\nStats after resizing by (length + 10):\n";
31     printStats( s );
32
33     cout << endl;
34     return 0;
35  }
36
37  void printStats( const string &str )
38  {
39     cout << "capacity: " << str.capacity()
40          << "\nmax size: " << str.max_size()
41          << "\nsize: " << str.size()
42          << "\nlength: " << str.length()
43          << "\nempty: " << ( str.empty() ? "true": "false" );
44  }
```

Fig. 19.5   Printing **string** characteristics (part 1 of 2).

```
Stats before input:
capacity: 0
max size: 4294967293
size: 0
length: 0
empty: true

Enter a string: tomato soup
The string entered was: tomato
Stats after input:
capacity: 31
max size: 4294967293
size: 6
length: 6
empty: false

Stats after resizing by (length + 10):
capacity: 31
max size: 4294967293
size: 16
length: 16
empty: false
```

Fig. 19.5　Printing **string** characteristics (part 2 of 2).

Line 23 inputs a **string** into **s**. Note that the stream extraction operator, **>>**, is used. Line 29

```
s.resize( s.length() + 10 );
```

uses function **resize** to increase the length of **s** by 10 characters.

19.7 Finding Characters in a `string`

Class **string** provides functions for finding strings and characters in a **string**. The program of Fig. 19.6 demonstrates the *find* functions. All find functions are **const**.

```cpp
1   // Fig. 19.6: fig19_06.cpp
2   // Demonstrating the string find functions
3   #include <iostream>
4
5   using std::cout;
6   using std::endl;
7
8   #include <string>
9
10  using std::string;
11
```

Fig. 19.6　Demonstrating the **string find** functions (part 1 of 2).

```
12   int main()
13   {
14       // compiler concatenates all parts into one string literal
15       string s( "The values in any left subtree"
16                 "\nare less than the value in the"
17                 "\nparent node and the values in"
18                 "\nany right subtree are greater"
19                 "\nthan the value in the parent node" );
20
21       // find "subtree" at locations 23 and 102
22       cout << "Original string:\n" << s
23            << "\n\n(find) \"subtree\" was found at: "
24            << s.find( "subtree" )
25            << "\n(rfind) \"subtree\" was found at: "
26            << s.rfind( "subtree" );
27
28       // find 'p' in parent at locations 62 and 144
29       cout << "\n(find_first_of) character from \"qpxz\" at: "
30            << s.find_first_of( "qpxz" )
31            << "\n(find_last_of) character from \"qpxz\" at: "
32            << s.find_last_of( "qpxz" );
33
34       // find 'b' at location 25
35       cout << "\n(find_first_not_of) first character not\n"
36            << "   contained in \"heTv lusinodrpayft\": "
37            << s.find_first_not_of( "heTv lusinodrpayft" );
38
39       // find '\n' at location 121
40       cout << "\n(find_last_not_of) first character not\n"
41            << "   contained in \"heTv lusinodrpayft\": "
42            << s.find_last_not_of( "heTv lusinodrpayft" ) << endl;
43
44       return 0;
45   }
```

```
Original string:
The values in any left subtree
are less than the value in the
parent node and the values in
any right subtree are greater
than the value in the parent node

(find) "subtree" was found at: 23
(rfind) "subtree" was found at: 102
(find_first_of) character from "qpxz" at: 62
(find_last_of) character from "qpxz" at: 144
(find_first_not_of) first character not
   contained in "heTv lusinodrpayft": 25
(find_last_not_of) first character not
   contained in "heTv lusinodrpayft": 121
```

Fig. 19.6   Demonstrating the **string find** functions (part 2 of 2).

String **s** is declared on line 15 and initialized. The compiler concatenates all five string literals into one string literal. To avoid syntax errors, the end of each string must be closed with double quotes before going to the next line and beginning another string.

Common Programming Error 19.5

Not terminating a string with double quotes is a syntax error.

Line 24, a part of the insertion operation,

```
s.find( "subtree" )
```

attempts to find the **string "subtree"** in the **string s** using function **find**. If the **string** is found, the subscript of the starting location of that **string** is returned. If the **string** is not found, the value **string::npos** (a **public static** constant defined in class **string**) is returned. This value is returned by the **string find**-related functions to indicate that a substring or character was not found in the **string**.

The last item output with the stream insertion on line 26

```
s.rfind( "subtree" )     // reverse find
```

uses function **rfind** to search **string s** backwards. If the search **string** is found, the subscript location is returned. If the **string** is not found, **string::npos** is returned. (*Note:* The rest of the **find** functions presented in this section return the same value type unless otherwise noted.) Note that constant **string::npos** is also used in a different context—to indicate all elements of a **string**.

The call

```
s.find_first_of( "qpxz" )
```

on line 30 uses function **find_first_of** to find the first occurrence in **string s** of any character in **"qpxz"**. The searching is done from the beginning of **s**. The character **'p'** is found in position 62.

The call

```
s.find_last_of( "qpxz" );
```

on line 32 uses function **find_last_of** to find the last occurrence in **string s** of any character in **"qpxz"**. The searching is done from the end of **s**. The character **'p'** is found in position 144.

The call

```
s.find_first_not_of( "heTv lusinodrpayft" );
```

on line 37 uses function **find_first_not_of** to find the first character in **string s** not contained in **"heTv lusinodrpayft"**. Searching is done from the beginning of **s**.

The call

```
s.find_last_not_of( "heTv lusinodrpayft" );
```

on line 42 uses function **find_last_not_of** to find the first character not contained in **"heTv lusinodrpayft"**. Searching is done from the end of **s**.

19.8 Replacing Characters in a `string`

Figure 19.7 demonstrates **string** functions for replacing and erasing characters.

```
1   // Fig. 19.7: fig19_07.cpp
2   // Demonstrating functions erase and replace
3   #include <iostream>
4
5   using std::cout;
6   using std::endl;
7
8   #include <string>
9
10  using std::string;
11
12  int main()
13  {
14     // compiler concatenates all parts into one string
15     string s( "The values in any left subtree"
16                "\nare less than the value in the"
17                "\nparent node and the values in"
18                "\nany right subtree are greater"
19                "\nthan the value in the parent node" );
20
21     // remove all characters from location 62
22     // through the end of s
23     s.erase( 62 );
24
25     // output the new string
26     cout << "Original string after erase:\n" << s
27         << "\n\nAfter first replacement:\n";
28
29     // replace all spaces with a period
30     int x = s.find( " " );
31     while ( x < string::npos ) {
32        s.replace( x, 1, "." );
33        x = s.find( " ", x + 1 );
34     }
35
36     cout << s << "\n\nAfter second replacement:\n";
37
38     // replace all periods with two semicolons
39     // NOTE: this will overwrite characters
40     x = s.find( "." );
41     while ( x < string::npos ) {
42        s.replace( x, 2, "xxxxx;;yyy", 5, 2 );
43        x = s.find( ".", x + 1 );
44     }
45
46     cout << s << endl;
47     return 0;
48  }
```

Fig. 19.7   Demonstrating functions **erase** and **replace** (part 1 of 2).

```
Original string after erase:
The values in any left subtree
are less than the value in the

After first replacement:
The.values.in.any.left.subtree
are.less.than.the.value.in.the

After second replacement:
The;;alues;;n;;ny;;eft;;ubtree
are;;ess;;han;;he;;alue;;n;;he
```

Fig. 19.7   Demonstrating functions **erase** and **replace** (part 2 of 2).

The program declares and initializes **string s**. Line 23

```
s.erase( 62 );
```

uses function **erase** to erase everything from element 62 to the end of **s**.
Lines 30 through 34

```
int x = s.find( " " );
while ( x < string::npos ) {
   s.replace( x, 1, "." );
   x = s.find( " ", x + 1 );
}
```

use function **find** to find each occurrence of the space character. Each space is then replaced with a period by a call to function **replace**. Function **replace** takes three arguments: the beginning subscript, the number of characters to replace and the replacement
string. The constant **string::npos** represents the maximum string length. Function
find returns **string::npos** when the end of **s** is reached.
Lines 40 through 44

```
x = s.find( "." );
while ( x < string::npos ) {
   s.replace( x, 2, "xxxxx;;yyy", 5, 2 );
   x = s.find( ".", x + 1 );
}
```

use function **find** to find every period and function **replace** to replace every period and
its following character with two semicolons. The arguments passed to **replace** are the
subscript of the element where the replace operation begins, the number of characters to
replace, a replacement character string from which a substring is used to replace characters,
the element in the character string where the replacement substring begins and the number
of characters in the replacement character string to use.

19.9 Inserting Characters into a `string`

Class **string** provides functions for inserting characters into a **string**. The program of
Fig. 19.8 demonstrates the **string insert** capabilities.

```cpp
1   // Fig. 19.8: fig19_08.cpp
2   // Demonstrating the string insert functions.
3   #include <iostream>
4
5   using std::cout;
6   using std::endl;
7
8   #include <string>
9
10  using std::string;
11
12  int main()
13  {
14     string s1( "beginning end" ),
15            s2( "middle " ), s3( "12345678" ), s4( "xx" );
16
17     cout << "Initial strings:\ns1: " << s1
18          << "\ns2: " << s2 << "\ns3: " << s3
19          << "\ns4: " << s4 << "\n\n";
20
21     // insert "middle" at location 10
22     s1.insert( 10, s2 );
23
24     // insert "xx" at location 3 in s3
25     s3.insert( 3, s4, 0, string::npos );
26
27     cout << "Strings after insert:\ns1: " << s1
28          << "\ns2: " << s2 << "\ns3: " << s3
29          << "\ns4: " << s4 << endl;
30
31     return 0;
32  }
```

```
Initial strings:
s1: beginning end
s2: middle
s3: 12345678
s4: xx

Strings after insert:
s1: beginning middle end
s2: middle
s3: 123xx45678
s4: xx
```

Fig. 19.8   Demonstrating the **string insert** functions.

The program declares and initializes four **string**s **s1**, **s2**, **s3** and **s4**. Each **string** is then output. Line 22

```cpp
s1.insert( 10, s2 );
```

uses function **insert** to insert **string s2** before element 10.

Line 25

```
s3.insert( 3, s4, 0, string::npos );
```

uses **insert** to insert **s4** before **s3**'s third element. The last two arguments specify the starting element of **s4** and the number of characters from **s4** that should be inserted.

Performance Tip 19.1

Insert operations can result in additional memory management operations that decrease performance.

19.10 Conversion to C-Style `char *` Strings

Class **string** provides functions for converting **string**s to C-style strings. As mentioned earlier, unlike C-style strings, **string**s are not necessarily null terminated. These conversion functions are useful when a given function takes a C-style string as an argument. The program of Fig. 19.9 demonstrates conversion of **string**s to C-style strings.

```
1   // Fig. 19.9: fig19_09.cpp
2   // Converting to C-style strings.
3   #include <iostream>
4
5   using std::cout;
6   using std::endl;
7
8   #include <string>
9
10  using std::string;
11
12  int main()
13  {
14     string s( "STRINGS" );
15     const char *ptr1 = 0;
16     int len = s.length();
17     char *ptr2 = new char[ len + 1 ]; // including null
18
19     // copy characters out of string into allocated memory
20     s.copy( ptr2, len, 0 );
21     ptr2[ len ] = 0;   // add null terminator
22
23     // output
24     cout << "string s is " << s
25          << "\ns converted to a C-Style string is "
26          << s.c_str() << "\nptr1 is ";
27
28     // Assign to pointer ptr1 the const char * returned by
29     // function data(). NOTE: this is a potentially dangerous
30     // assignment. If the string is modified, the pointer
31     // ptr1 can become invalid. .
32     ptr1 = s.data();
33
```

Fig. 19.9   Converting **string**s to C-style strings and character arrays (part 1 of 2).

```
34        for ( int k = 0; k < len; ++k )
35           cout << *( ptr1 + k );     // use pointer arithmetic
36
37        cout << "\nptr2 is " << ptr2 << endl;
38        delete [] ptr2;
39        return 0;
40   }
```

```
string s is STRINGS
s converted to a C-Style string is STRINGS
ptr1 is STRINGS
ptr2 is STRINGS
```

Fig. 19.9   Converting **string**s to C-style strings and character arrays (part 2 of 2).

The program declares a **string**, an **int** and two pointers. The **string s** is initialized to **"STRINGS"**, **ptr1** is initialized to **0** and **len** is initialized to the length of **s**. Memory is dynamically allocated and attached to pointer **ptr2**.

Line 20

```
    s.copy( ptr2, len, 0 );
```

uses function **copy** to copy **s** into the array pointed to by **ptr2**. The conversion from **string** to C-style character string is implicit. Line 21 places a terminating null character in array **ptr3**.

The first stream insertion of line 26

```
    << s.c_str()
```

displays the null-terminated **const char *** returned from **c_str** when **string s** is converted.

Line 32

```
    ptr1 = s.data();
```

assigns a **const char *** non-null terminated C-style character array returned by **data** to **ptr1**. Note that we do not modify **string s** in this example. If **s** were to be modified, **ptr1** could become invalid—which could lead to unpredictable results.

Note that the character array returned by **data** and the C-style string returned by **c_str** have a limited lifetime. They are owned by **class string** and should not be **delete**d.

Lines 34 and 35 use pointer arithmetic to output the array pointed to by **ptr1**. In lines 37 and 38, the C-style string pointed to by **ptr2** is output and the memory allocated for **ptr2** is deleted to avoid a memory leak.

Common Programming Error 19.6

Not terminating with a null character the character array returned by **data** *or* **copy** *can lead to execution-time errors.*

Good Programming Practice 19.1

Whenever possible, use the more robust **string**s *rather than C-style strings.*

Common Programming Error 19.7

*Converting a **string** that contains one or more null characters to a C-style string can cause logic errors. The null characters are interpreted as terminators for C-style strings.*

19.11 Iterators

Class **string** provides *iterators* for forwards and backwards traversal of **string**s. Iterators provide access to individual characters with syntax that is similar to pointer operations. Iterators are not range checked. Note that in this section we provide "mechanical examples" to demonstrate the use of iterators. We discuss more robust uses of iterators in the next chapter. The program of Fig. 19.10 demonstrates iterators.

Lines 14 and 15

```
string s = "Testing iterators";
string::const_iterator i1 = s.begin();
```

declare **string s** and **string::const_iterator i1**. A **const_iterator** is an iterator that cannot modify the container—in this case the string—through which it is iterating. Iterator **i1** is initialized to the beginning of **s** with the **string** class function **begin**. Two versions of **begin** exist, one version that returns an **iterator** for iterating through a non-**const string** and a **const** version that returns a **const_iterator** for iterating through a **const string**. String **s** is then output.

```cpp
1   // Fig. 19.10: fig19_10.cpp
2   // Using an iterator to output a string.
3   #include <iostream>
4
5   using std::cout;
6   using std::endl;
7
8   #include <string>
9
10  using std::string;
11
12  int main()
13  {
14     string s( "Testing iterators" );
15     string::const_iterator i1 = s.begin();
16
17     cout << "s = " << s
18        << "\n(Using iterator i1) s is: ";
19
20     while ( i1 != s.end() ) {
21        cout << *i1;        // dereference iterator to get char
22        ++i1;               // advance iterator to next char
23     }
24
25     cout << endl;
26     return 0;
27  }
```

Fig. 19.10   Using an iterator to output a **string** (part 1 of 2).

```
s = Testing iterators
(Using iterator i1) s is: Testing iterators
```

Fig. 19.10   Using an iterator to output a **string** (part 2 of 2).

Lines 20 through 23

```
while ( i1 != s.end() ) {
   cout << *i1;
   ++i1;
}
```

use the iterator **i1** to "walk through" **s**. Function **end** returns an iterator at the first position after the last element of **s**. The contents of each location are printed by first dereferencing the iterator much as you would dereference a pointer, and the iterator is advanced one position using operator **++**.

Class **string** provides member functions **rend** and **rbegin** for accessing individual **string** characters in reverse from the end of a **string** towards the beginning of a **string**. Member functions **rend** and **rbegin** can return **reverse_iterator**s and **const_reverse_iterator**s (based on whether the **string** is non-**const** or **const**). We ask the reader to demonstrate these in the exercises. We will use iterators and reverse iterators more in Chapter 20.

Testing and Debugging Tip 19.1

Use **string** *member function* **at** *(rather than iterators) when you want the benefit of range checking.*

19.12 String Stream Processing

In addition to standard stream I/O and file stream I/O, C++ stream I/O includes capabilities for inputting from **string**s in memory and outputting to **string**s in memory. These capabilities are often referred to as *in-memory I/O* or *string stream processing*.

Input from a **string** is supported by class **istringstream**. Output to a **string** is supported by class **ostringstream**. The class names **istringstream** and **ostringstream** are actually aliases. These names are defined with the **typedef**s

```
typedef basic_istringstream< char > istringstream;
typedef basic_ostringstream< char > ostringstream;
```

Classes **basic_istringstream** and **basic_ostringstream** provide the same functionality as classes **istream** and **ostream** plus other member functions specific to in-memory formatting. Programs that use in-memory formatting must include the **<sstream>** and **<iostream>** header files.

One application of these techniques is data validation. A program can read an entire line at a time from the input stream into a **string**. Next, a validation routine can scrutinize the contents of the **string** and correct (or repair) the data, if necessary. Then, the program can proceed to input from the **string**, knowing that the input data are in the proper format.

Outputting to a **string** is a nice way to take advantage of the powerful output formatting capabilities of C++ streams. Data can be prepared in a **string** to mimic the edited screen format. That **string** could be written to a disk file to preserve the screen image.

An **ostringstream** object uses a **string** object to store the data that are output. The **ostringstream** member function **str** returns a **string** copy of the **string**.

Figure 19.11 demonstrates an **ostringstream** object. The program creates **ostringstream** object **outputString** (line 18) and uses the stream-insertion operator to output a series of **string**s and numerical values to the object.

Line 27

```
outputString << s1 << s2 << s3 << d << s4 << i << s5 << &i;
```

outputs **string s1**, **string s2**, **string s3**, **double d**, **string s4**, **int i**, **string s5** and the address of **int i**, all to **outputString** in memory. Line 28

```
1    // Fig. 19.11: fig19_11.cpp
2    // Using a dynamically allocated ostringstream object.
3    #include <iostream>
4
5    using std::cout;
6    using std::endl;
7
8    #include <string>
9
10   using std::string;
11
12   #include <sstream>
13
14   using std::ostringstream;
15
16   int main()
17   {
18      ostringstream outputString;
19      string s1( "Output of several data types " ),
20             s2( "to an ostringstream object:" ),
21             s3( "\n           double: " ),
22             s4( "\n             int: " ),
23             s5( "\naddress of int: " );
24      double d = 123.4567;
25      int i = 22;
26
27      outputString << s1 << s2 << s3 << d << s4 << i << s5 << &i;
28      cout << "outputString contains:\n" << outputString.str();
29
30      outputString << "\nmore characters added";
31      cout << "\n\nafter additional stream insertions,\n"
32           << "outputString contains:\n" << outputString.str()
33           << endl;
34
35      return 0;
36   }
```

Fig. 19.11 Using a dynamically allocated **ostringstream** object (part 1 of 2).

```
outputString contains:
Output of several data types to an ostringstream object:
        double: 123.457
           int: 22
address of int: 0068FD0C

after additional stream insertions,
outputString contains:
Output of several data types to an ostringstream object:
        double: 123.457
           int: 22
address of int: 0068FD0C
more characters added
```

Fig. 19.11 Using a dynamically allocated **ostringstream** object (part 2 of 2).

```
cout << "outputString contains:\n" << outputString.str();
```

uses the call **outputString.str()** to output a copy of the **string** created in line 27. Line 30 demonstrates that more data can be appended to the **string** in memory by simply issuing another stream insertion operation to **outputString**. Line 32 outputs **string outputString** after appending additional characters.

An **istringstream** object inputs data from a **string** in memory to program variables. The data is stored in an **istringstream** object as characters. Input from the **istringstream** object works identically to input from any file, in general, or from standard input, in particular. The end of the **string** is interpreted by the **istringstream** object as end-of-file.

Figure 19.12 demonstrates input from an **istringstream** object.

```
1   // Fig. 19.12: fig19_12.cpp
2   // Demonstrating input from an istringstream object.
3   #include <iostream>
4
5   using std::cout;
6   using std::endl;
7
8   #include <string>
9
10  using std::string;
11
12  #include <sstream>
13
14  using std::istringstream;
15
16  int main()
17  {
18      string input( "Input test 123 4.7 A" );
19      istringstream inputString( input );
```

Fig. 19.12 Demonstrating input from an **istringstream** object (part 1 of 2).

```
20        string string1, string2;
21        int i;
22        double d;
23        char c;
24
25        inputString >> string1 >> string2 >> i >> d >> c;
26
27        cout << "The following items were extracted\n"
28             << "from the istringstream object:"
29             << "\nstring: " << string1
30             << "\nstring: " << string2
31             << "\n    int: " << i
32             << "\ndouble: " << d
33             << "\n   char: " << c;
34
35        // attempt to read from empty stream
36        long x;
37
38        inputString >> x;
39
40        if ( inputString.good() )
41           cout << "\n\nlong value is: " << x << endl;
42        else
43           cout << "\n\ninputString is empty" << endl;
44
45        return 0;
46     }
```

```
The following items were extracted
from the istringstream object:
String: Input
String: test
   int: 123
double: 4.7
  char: A
inputString is empty
```

Fig. 19.12 Demonstrating input from an **istringstream** object (part 2 of 2).

Lines 18 and 19

```
string input( "Input test 123 4.7 A" );
istringstream inputString( input );
```

create **string input** containing the data and **istringstream** object **input-String** constructed to contain the data in **string input**. The **string input** contains the data

```
Input test 123 4.7 A
```

which when read as input to the program consist of two strings ("**Input**" and "**test**"), an **int** value (**123**), a **double** value (**4.7**) and a **char** value ('**A**'). These characters are extracted to variables **string1**, **string2**, **i**, **d** and **c**, respectively, in line 25

```
inputString >> string1 >> string2 >> i >> d >> c;
```

The data are then output in lines 27 through 33. The program attempts to read from **inputString** again in line 38. Because no data remain, the **if** condition (line 40) evaluates as **false** and the **else** part of the **if/else** structure is executed.

SUMMARY

- C++ template class **basic_string** provides typical string manipulation operations such as copying, searching, etc.
- The **typedef** statement

```
typedef basic_string< char > string;
```

  creates the type **string** for **basic_string< char >**. A **typedef** is also provided for the **wchar_t** type. Type **wchar_t** normally stores two-byte (16-bit) characters for supporting other character sets. The size of **wchar_t** is not fixed by the standard.
- To use **string**s include C++ standard library header file **<string>**.
- Class **string** provides no conversions from **int** or **char** to **string**.
- Assigning a single character to a **string** object is permitted in an assignment statement.
- **string**s are not necessarily null terminated.
- The length of a **string** is stored in the **string** object and can be retrieved with member function **length** or **size**.
- Most **string** member functions take as arguments a starting subscript location and the number of characters on which to operate.
- Attempting to pass to a **string** member function a value larger than the length of the **string** for the number of characters to process results in the value being set to the length of the remainder of the **string**.
- Class **string** provides overloaded **operator=** and member function **assign** for **string** assignments.
- The subscript operator, **[ ]**, provides direct access to any element of a **string**.
- Function **at** provides checked access—going past either end of the **string** throws an **out_of_range** exception. The subscript operator (**[ ]**) does not provide checked access.
- Class **string** provides the overloaded **+** and **+=** operators and member function **append** to perform **string** concatenation.
- Class **string** provides overloaded **==**, **!=**, **<**, **>**, **<=** and **>=** operators for **string** comparisons.
- **string** function **compare** compares two **string**s (or substrings) and returns **0** if the **string**s are equal, a positive number if the first **string** is lexicographically greater than the second or a negative number if the first string is lexicographically less than the second.
- Function **substr** retrieves a substring from a **string**.
- Function **swap** swaps the contents of two **string**s.
- Functions **size** and **length** return the size or length of a **string** (i.e., the number of characters currently stored in the **string**).
- Function **capacity** returns the total number of elements that can be stored in the **string** without increasing the memory requirements of the **string**.
- Function **max_size** returns size of the largest possible **string** that can be stored.
- Function **resize** changes the length of a **string**.

- Class **string** find functions **find**, **rfind**, **find_first_of**, **find_last_of**, **find_first_not_of** and **find_last_not_of** find strings or characters in a **string**.
- The value **string::npos** is often used to indicate processing of all the elements of a **string** in functions that require a number of characters to be processed.
- Function **erase** erases elements of a **string**.
- Function **replace** replaces characters in a **string**.
- Function **insert** inserts characters in a **string**.
- Function **c_str** returns a **const char *** pointing to a null-terminated C-style character string that contains all the characters in a **string**.
- Function **data** returns a **const char *** pointing to a non-null-terminated C-style character array that contains all the characters in a **string**.
- Class **string** provides member functions **end** and **begin** to access individual characters.
- Class **string** provides member functions **rend** and **rbegin** for accessing individual **string** characters in reverse from the end of a **string** towards the beginning of a **string**.
- Input from a **string** is supported by type **istringstream**. Output to a **string** is supported by type **ostringstream**.
- Programs that use in-core formatting must include header files **<sstream>** and **<iostream>**.
- The **ostringstream** member function **str** returns a **string** copy of a **string**.

TERMINOLOGY

access function
at function
capacity
capacity function
checked access
compare function
const_iterator
const_reverse_iterator
copy function
c_str function
data function
empty function
empty string
equality operators: **==**, **!=**
erase function
find function
find functions
find_first_not_of function
find_first_of function
find_last_not_of function
find_last_of function
getline function
in-core I/O
in-memory I/O
insert function
istringstream class
iterator

length function
length of a **string**
length_error exception
maximum size of a **string**
max_size function
namespace std
operators: **+**, **+=**, **<<**, **>>**, **[]**
ostringstream class
out_of_range exception
range_error exception
rbegin function
relational operators: **>**, **<**, **>=**, **<=**
rend function
replace function
resize function
reverse_iterator
size function
str string-stream member function
<sstream> header file
<string> header file
string class
subscript operator, **[]**
substr function
swap function
typedef basic_string<char> string
wchar_t type
wide characters

COMMON PROGRAMMING ERRORS

19.1   Attempting to convert an **int** or **char** to a **string** via an assignment in a declaration or via a constructor argument is a syntax error.

19.2   Constructing a **string** that is too long to be represented throws a **length_error** exception.

19.3   Accessing a **string** subscript outside the bounds of the **string** using function **at** throws an **out_of_range** exception.

19.4   Accessing an element beyond the size of the **string** using the subscript operator is a logic error.

19.5   Not terminating a string with double quotes is a syntax error.

19.6   Not terminating with a null character the character array returned by **data** or **copy** can lead to execution-time errors.

19.7   Converting a **string** that contains one or more null characters to a C-style string can cause logic errors. The null characters are interpreted as terminators for C-style strings.

GOOD PROGRAMMING PRACTICE

19.1   Whenever possible, use the more robust **string**s rather than C-style strings.

PERFORMANCE TIP

19.1   Insert operations can result in additional memory management operations that decrease performance.

TESTING AND DEBUGGING TIP

19.1   Use **string** member function **at** (rather than iterators) when you want the benefit of range checking.

SELF-REVIEW EXERCISES

19.1   Fill in the blanks in each of the following:
a) Header _____ must be included for class **string**.
b) Class **string** belongs to the _____ **namespace**.
c) Function _____ erases characters from a **string**.
d) Function _____ finds the first occurrence of any character from a series of characters.

19.2   State which of the following statements are *true* and which are *false*. If a statement is *false*, explain why.
a) Concatenation can be performed with the addition operator, **+=**.
b) Characters within a **string** begin at element 0.
c) The assignment operator, **=**, copies a **string**.
d) C-style string is a **string**.

19.3   Find the error(s) in each of the following and explain how to correct it (them):
a) ```
    string sv(28);   // construct sv
    string bc('z'); // construct bc
    ```
b)  ```
    // assume std namespace is known
    const char *ptr = name.data();   // name is "joe bob"
    ptr[ 3 ] = '-';
    cout << ptr << endl;
    ```

ANSWERS TO SELF-REVIEW EXERCISES

19.1 a) **string**. b) **std**. c) **erase**. d) **find_first_of**.

19.2 a) True.
   b) True.
   c) True.
   d) False. A **string** is an object that provides many different services. A C-style string does not provide any services. C-style strings are null terminated and **string**s are not.

19.3 a) Constructors do not exist for the arguments passed. Other valid constructors should be used—converting the arguments to **string**s if need be.
   b) Function **data** does not add a null terminator. Use **c_str** instead.

EXERCISES

19.4 Fill in the blanks in each of the following:
   a) Functions _____, _____ and _____ convert **string**s to C-style strings.
   b) Function _____ is used for assignment.
   c) _____ is the return type of function **rbegin**.
   d) Function _____ is used to retrieve a substring.

19.5 State which of the following statements are true and which are false. If a statement is false, explain why.
   a) **string**s are null terminated.
   b) Function **max_size** returns the maximum size for a **string**.
   c) Function **at** is capable of throwing an **out_of_range** exception.
   d) Function **begin** returns an **iterator**.
   e) **string**s are passed by reference by default.

19.6 Find any error(s) in each of the following and explain how to correct it (them):
   a) `std::cout << s.data() << std::endl;   // s is "hello"`
   b) `erase( s.rfind( "x" ), 1 );  // s is "xenon"`
   c)
```
string& foo( void )
{
    string s( "Hello" );
    ...    // other statements of function
    return;
}
```

19.7 (*Simple Encryption*) Some information on the Internet may be encrypted with a simple algorithm known as "rot13"—which rotates each character by 13 positions in the alphabet. Thus, `'a'` corresponds to `'n'`, and `'x'` corresponds to `'k'`. rot13 is an example of *symmetric key encryption*. With symmetric key encryption, both the encrypter and decrypter use the same key.
   a) Write a program that encrypts a message using rot13.
   b) Write a program that decrypts the scrambled message using 13 as the key.
   c) After writing the programs of part (a) and part (b) briefly answer the following question: If you did not know the key for part (b), how difficult do you think it would be to break the code using any resources available? What if you had access to substantial computing power (e.g., Cray supercomputers)? In Exercise 19.27 we ask you to write a program to accomplish this.

19.8 Write a program using iterators that demonstrates the use of functions **rbegin** and **rend**.

19.9 Write your own versions of functions **data** and **c_str**.

19.10   Write a program that reads in several **string**s and prints only those ending in "**r**" or "**ay**". Only lowercase letters should be considered.

19.11   Write a program that demonstrates passing a **string** both by reference and by value.

19.12   Write a program that separately inputs a first name and a last name and then concatenates the two into a new **string**.

19.13   Write a program that plays the game of hangman. The program should pick a word (which is either coded directly into the program or read from a text file) and display the following:

   Guess the word: XXXXXX

Each **X** represents a letter. If the user guesses correctly, the program should display:

   Congratulations!!! You guessed my word. Play again? yes/no

The appropriate response **yes** or **no** should be input. If the user guesses incorrectly, display the appropriate body part.

   After seven incorrect guesses, the user should be hanged. The display should look like

After each guess you want to display all their guesses.

19.14   Write a program that inputs a **string** and prints the **string** backwards. Convert all uppercase characters to lowercase and all lowercase characters to uppercase.

19.15   Write a program that uses the comparison capabilities introduced in this chapter to alphabetize a series of animal names. Only uppercase letters should be used for the comparisons.

19.16   Write a program that creates a cryptogram out of a **string**. A cryptogram is a message or word where each letter is replaced with another letter. For example the **string**

   The birds name was squawk

might be scrambled to form

   xms kbypo zhqs fho obrhfu

Note that spaces are not scrambled. In this particular case, '**T**' was replaced with '**x**', each '**a**' was replaced with '**h**', etc. Uppercase letters and lowercase letters should be treated the same. Use techniques similar to those in Exercise 19.7.

19.17   Modify the previous exercise to allow a user to solve the cryptogram by inputting two characters. The first character specifies the letter in the cryptogram and the second letter specifies the user's guess. For example, if the user inputs **r g**, then the user is guessing that the letter **r** is really a **g**.

19.18   Write a program that inputs a sentence and counts the number of palindromes in the sentence. A palindrome is a word that reads the same backwards and forwards. For example, **"tree"** is not a palindrome but **"noon"** is.

19.19   Write a program that counts the total number of vowels in a sentence. Output the frequency of each vowel.

19.20   Write a program that inserts the characters **"******"** in the exact middle of a **string**.

19.21   Write a program that erases the sequences **"by"** and **"BY"** from a **string**.

19.22   Write a program that inputs a line of text, replaces all punctuation marks with spaces and then uses the C-string library function **strtok** to tokenize the **string** into individual words.

19.23   Write a program that inputs a line of text and prints the text backwards. Use iterators in your solution.

19.24   Write a recursive version of Exercise 19.23.

19.25   Write a program that demonstrates the use of the **erase** functions that take **iterator** arguments.

19.26   Write a program that generates from the **string "abcdefghijklmnopqrstuvwx-yz{"** the following:

```
             a
            bcb
           cdedc
          defgfed
         efghihgfe
        fghijkjihgf
       ghijklmlkjihg
      hijklmnonmlkjih
     ijklmnopqponmlkji
    jklmnopqrsrqponmlkj
   klmnopqrstutsrqponmlk
  lmnopqrstuvwvutsrqponml
 mnopqrstuvwxyxwvutsrqponm
nopqrstuvwxyz{zyxwvutsrqpon
```

19.27   In Exercise 19.7 we asked you to write a simple encryption algorithm. Write a program that will attempt to decrypt a "rot13" message using simple frequency substitution (assume you do not know the key). The most frequent letters in the encrypted phrase should be substituted with the most commonly used English letters (a, e, i, o, u, s, t, r, etc.). Write the possibilities to a file. What made the code breaking easy? How can the encryption mechanism be improved?

19.28   Write a version of the bubble sort routine that sorts **string**s. Use function **swap** in your solution.

20

Standard Template Library (STL)

Objectives

- To be able to use the template STL containers, container adapters and "near containers."
- To be able to program with the dozens of STL algorithms.
- To understand how algorithms use iterators to access the elements of STL containers.
- To become familiar with the STL resources available on the Internet and the World Wide Web.

The shapes a bright container can contain!
Theodore Roethke

Journey over all the universe in a map.
Miguel de Cervantes

O! thou hast damnable iteration, and art indeed able to corrupt a saint.
William Shakespeare

That great dust heap called "history."
Augustine Birrell

The historian is a prophet in reverse.
Friedrich von Schlegel

Attempt the end, and never stand to doubt; Nothing's so hard but search will find it out.
Robert Herrick

Push on — keep moving.
Thomas Morton

Outline

Summary • Terminology • Common Programming Errors • Good Programming Practices • Performance Tips • Portability Tips • Software Engineering Observations • Testing and Debugging Tips • Self-Review Exercises • Answers to Self-Review Exercises • Exercises • STL Resources on the Internet and the World Wide Web • STL Bibliography

20.1 Introduction to the Standard Template Library (STL)

Besides maintainability and understandability, the great promise of object orientation is reuse, reuse, reuse. The C++ standard includes a Standard Library of many reusable components. In this chapter we introduce the *Standard Template Library (STL)*. We discuss the three key components of the STL—*containers* (popular templatized data structures), *iterators* and *algorithms*.

The STL was developed by Alexander Stepanov and Meng Lee at Hewlett-Packard. It is based on their research in the field of generic programming, with significant contributions from David Musser. The STL is expected to become widely used now that it has been accepted as part of the C++ standard.

STL is large. Our challenge was to present it with the goal that the reader would be able to begin using the STL effectively after reading this chapter. We present a large portion of STL's capabilities in three dozen "live-code" example programs. The reader will see STL "in action."

Chapter 15 presented an introduction to data structures. Data structures are containers (aggregations) of data. In an object-oriented world, data structures are objects that contain objects. The **Array** class we developed in Chapter 8 contained objects of primitive data type **int**. After studying Chapter 12, "Templates," we can "templatize" the **Array** class to be **Array< T >** from which we can instantiate an "infinite" variety of **Array** classes such as **Array< int >**, **Array< char >**, **Array< double >**, or even arrays of non-primitive class objects such as **Array< Employee >**, **Array< SpaceCreature >**, **Array< InventoryItem >**, etc.

What about other popular data structures such as lists, stacks, queues, priority queues, and the like? If we were to develop our own versions of each of these, would programs we write based on these class templates interoperate easily with other programs developed by programmers implementing their own versions of these popular data structures? Probably not. Thus, there is great motivation for developing a standardized library of templatized object containers—exactly what has been realized with the Standard Template Library (STL). Using STL can save considerable time and effort, and result in higher quality programs—precisely the benefits of a "world of reuse."

Performance Tip 20.1

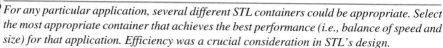

For any particular application, several different STL containers could be appropriate. Select the most appropriate container that achieves the best performance (i.e., balance of speed and size) for that application. Efficiency was a crucial consideration in STL's design.

Performance Tip 20.2

Standard Library capabilities are implemented to operate efficiently across a wide variety of applications. For some applications with unique performance requirements, it may be necessary to write your own customized implementations.

Software Engineering Observation 20.1

The STL approach allows general programs to be written so that the code does not depend on the underlying container. Such a programming style is called generic programming.

In the 1970s, the components we used were control structures and functions. In the 1980s, we used classes primarily from a variety of platform-dependent class libraries. In the late 1990s with STL, we see the next level of componentry, namely *platform-independent class libraries*. We anticipate an exponential explosion in the number of such classes that will become available in the next decade.

The STL is a major portion of the C++ standard, so the STL will be implemented by every major C++ compiler vendor. It is certain to be widely used.

In C and in "raw C++" we access elements of an array with pointers. In C++ STL, we access elements of containers via iterator objects that have the "feel" of pointers, but "behave" more "intelligently," as we will see. Iterator classes are designed to be used generically on any container.

Containers encapsulate some primitive operations, but the STL algorithms are implemented independently of the containers.

STL avoids **new** and **delete** in favor of *allocators* for storage allocation and deallocation. The programmer can supply allocators to customize how a container handles storage management, but the default allocators supplied by STL are sufficient for most applications. Custom allocators are an advanced topic that is beyond the scope of this text.

This is meant to be an introduction to the STL. It is by no means complete or comprehensive. However, it is a friendly, accessible chapter that should convince you of the value of the STL and encourage further study. We use the same "live-code approach" that we have used throughout the book. This may be one of the most important chapters in the book for you in terms of your appreciation of reuse, reuse, reuse. The STL containers include the most commonly used and most valuable data structures. They are all "templatized" so that you can tailor them to hold the type of data relevant to your particular applications.

In Chapter 15, we studied data structures. We built linked lists, queues, stacks and trees. We carefully wove link objects together with pointers. Pointer-based code is complex, and the slighest omission or oversight can lead to serious memory-access violations and memory-leak errors with no compiler complaints. Implementing additional data structures such as deques, priority queues, sets, maps, etc. would require substantial additional work.

Software Engineering Observation 20.2

Avoid reinventing the wheel; program with the reusable components of the C++ Standard Library. STL includes many of the most popular data structures as containers and provides various popular algorithms programs use to process data in these containers.

Testing and Debugging Tip 20.1

When programming pointer-based data structures and algorithms, we must do our own debugging and testing to be sure our data structures, classes and algorithms function properly. It is easy to make errors when manipulating pointers at this low a level. Memory leaks and memory-access violations are common in such custom code. For most programmers, and for most of the applications they will need to write, the prepackaged, templatized data structures of the STL are sufficient. Using the STL's code can avoid a great deal of testing and debugging time. One caution is that for large projects, template compile time can be significant.

Each STL container has associated member functions. Some functionality applies to all STL containers. Other functionality is unique to particular containers. We illustrate most of the common functionality with class templates **vector**, **list** and **deque**. We introduce container-specific functionality in examples for each of the other STL containers.

We have done an extensive search for Internet/World Wide Web resources and have included these for you at the back of this chapter. We also provide an extensive bibliography of STL-related articles.

20.1.1 Introduction to Containers

The STL container types are shown in Fig. 20.1. The containers are divided into three major categories—*sequence containers*, *associative containers* and *container adapters*. The sequence containers are sometimes referred to as *sequential containers*; we will normally use the term sequence containers. The sequence containers and associative containers are collectively referred to as the *first-class containers*. There are four other container types that are considered "near-containers"—C-like arrays (discussed in Chapter 4), **string** (discussed in Chapter 19), **bitset** for maintaining sets of **1/0** flag values and **valarray** for performing high-speed mathematical vector operations (this class is optimized for computation performance and is not as flexible as the first-class containers). These four types are considered "near-containers" because they exhibit similar capabilities to the first-class containers, but do not support all the capabilities of first-class containers.

Standard Library container class	Description
Sequence Containers	
vector	rapid insertions and deletions at back
	direct access to any element
deque	rapid insertions and deletions at front or back
	direct access to any element
list	doubly linked list, rapid insertion and deletion anywhere
Associative Containers	
set	rapid lookup, no duplicates allowed
multiset	rapid lookup, duplicates allowed
map	one-to-one mapping, no duplicates allowed, rapid key-based lookup
multimap	one-to-many mapping, duplicates allowed, rapid key-based lookup
Container Adapters	
stack	last-in-first-out (LIFO)
queue	first-in-first-out (FIFO)
priority_queue	highest priority element is always the first element out

Fig. 20.1   Standard Library container classes.

STL has been carefully designed so that the containers provide similar functionality. There are many generic operations such as function **size** that apply to all containers, and other operations that apply to subsets of similar containers. This encourages extensibility of the STL with new classes. Functions common to all Standard Library containers are illustrated in Fig. 20.2. [*Note:* Overloaded operator functions **operator<**, **operator<=**, **operator>**, **operator>=**, **operator==** and **operator!=** are not provided for **priority_queue**s.]

Common member functions for all STL containers	Description
default constructor	A constructor to provide a default initialization of the container. Normally, each container has several constructors that provide a variety of initialization methods for the container.
copy constructor	A constructor that initializes the container to be a copy of an existing container of the same type.
destructor	Destructor function for cleanup after a container is no longer needed.
empty	Returns **true** if there are no elements in the container; otherwise, returns **false**.
max_size	Returns the maximum number of elements for a container.
size	Returns the number of elements currently in the container.
operator=	Assigns one container to another.
operator<	Returns **true** if the first container is less than the second container; otherwise, returns **false**.
operator<=	Returns **true** if the first container is less than or equal to the second container; otherwise, returns **false**.
operator>	Returns **true** if the first container is greater than the second container; otherwise, returns **false**.
operator>=	Returns **true** if the first container is greater than or equal to the second container; otherwise, returns **false**.
operator==	Returns **true** if the first container is equal to the second container; otherwise, returns **false**.
operator!=	Returns **true** if the first container is not equal to the second container; otherwise, returns **false**.
swap	Swaps the elements of two containers.
Functions that are only found in first-class containers	
begin	The two versions of this function return either an **iterator** or a **const_iterator** that refers to the first element of the container.
end	The two versions of this function return either an **iterator** or a **const_iterator** that refers to the next position after the end of the container.

Fig. 20.2   Common functions for all STL containers (part 1 of 2).

Common member functions for all STL containers	Description
rbegin	The two versions of this function return either a **reverse_iterator** or a **const_reverse_iterator** that refers to the last element of the container.
rend	The two versions of this function return either a **reverse_iterator** or a **const_reverse_iterator** that refers to the position before the first element of the container.
erase	Erases one or more elements from the container.
clear	Erases all elements from the container.

Fig. 20.2   Common functions for all STL containers (part 2 of 2).

The header files for each of the Standard Library containers are shown in Fig. 20.3. The contents of these header files are all in **namespace std**. [*Note:* Some C++ compilers do not support the new-style header files. Many of these compilers provide their own version of the header file names. See your compiler documentation for more information on the STL support your compiler provides.]

Figure 20.4 shows the common **typedef**s (to create synonyms or aliases for lengthy type names) found in first-class containers. These **typedef**s are used in generic declarations of variables, parameters to functions and return values from functions. For example, **value_type** in each container is always a **typedef** that represents the type of value stored in the container.

Performance Tip 20.3

STL generally avoids inheritance and **virtual** *functions in favor of using generic programming with templates to achieve better execution-time performance.*

Standard Library container header files	
<vector>	
<list>	
<deque>	
<queue>	Contains both **queue** and **priority_queue**.
<stack>	
<map>	Contains both **map** and **multimap**.
<set>	Contains both **set** and **multiset**.
<bitset>	

Fig. 20.3   Standard Library container header files.

typedef	Description
value_type	The type of element stored in the container.
reference	A reference to the type of element stored in the container.
const_reference	A constant reference to the type of element stored in the container. Such a reference can only be used for *reading* elements in the container and for performing **const** operations.
pointer	A pointer to the type of element stored in the container.
iterator	An iterator that points to the type of element stored in the container.
const_iterator	A constant iterator that points to the type of element stored in the container and can only be used to *read* elements.
reverse_iterator	A reverse iterator that points to the type of element stored in the container. This type of iterator is for iterating through a container in reverse.
const_reverse_iterator	A constant reverse iterator to the type of element stored in the container and can only be used to *read* elements. This type of iterator is for iterating through a container in reverse.
difference_type	The type of the result of subtracting two iterators that refer to the same container (**operator-** is not defined for iterators of **list**s and associative containers).
size_type	The type used to count items in a container and index through a sequence container (cannot index through a **list**).

Fig. 20.4   Common **typedef**s found in first-class containers.

Portability Tip 20.1

STL is certain to become the favored means of programming with containers. Programming with STL will enhance the portability of your code.

Performance Tip 20.4
Know your STL components. Choosing the most appropriate container for a given problem can maximize performance and minimize memory requirements.

When preparing to use an STL container, it is important to ensure that the type of element being stored in the container supports a minimum set of functionality. When an element is inserted into a container, a copy of that element is made. For this reason, the element type should provide its own copy constructor and assignment operator. [*Note:* This is only required if default memberwise copy does not perform a proper copy operation for the element type.] Also, the associative containers and many algorithms require elements to be compared. For this reason, the element type should provide an equality operator (**==**) and a less than operator (**<**).

Software Engineering Observation 20.3

The equality and less than operators are technically not required for the elements stored in a container unless the elements need to be compared. However, when creating code from a template, some compilers require all parts of the template to be defined whereas other compilers require only the parts of the template that are actually used in the program.

20.1.2 Introduction to Iterators

Iterators have many features in common with pointers and are used to point to the elements of first-class containers (and for a few other purposes, as we will see). Iterators hold state information sensitive to the particular containers on which they operate: thus iterators are implemented appropriately for each type of container. Nevertheless, certain iterator operations are uniform across containers. For example, the dereferencing operator (*****) dereferences an iterator so you can use the element to which it points. The **++** operation on an iterator moves the iterator to the next element of the container (much as incrementing a pointer into an array aims the pointer at the next element of the array).

STL first-class containers provide member functions **begin()** and **end()**. Function **begin()** returns an iterator pointing to the first element of the container. Function **end()** returns an iterator pointing to the first element past the end of the container (an element that doesn't exist). If iterator **i** points to a particular element, then **++i** points to the "next" element and ***i** refers to the element pointed to by **i**. The iterator resulting from **end()** can be used only in an equality or inequality comparison to determine if the "moving iterator" (**i** in this case) has reached the end of the container.

We use an object of type **iterator** to refer to a container element that can be modified. We use an object of type **const_iterator** to refer to a container element that cannot be modified.

We use iterators with *sequences* (also called *ranges*). These sequences may be in containers, or they may be *input sequences* or *output sequences*. The program of Fig. 20.5 demonstrates input from the standard input (a sequence of data for input into a program) using an **istream_iterator** and output to the standard output (a sequence of data for output from a program) using an **ostream_iterator**. The program inputs two integers from the user at the keyboard and displays the sum of the integers. [*Note:* The examples in this chapter precede each use of an STL function and each definition of an STL container object with the "**std::**" prefix rather than placing the **using** statements at the beginning of the program as shown in most prior examples. Due to the differences in compilers and the complex code generated when using STL, it is difficult to construct the proper set of **using** statements that enable the programs to compile without errors. To allow these programs to compile on the widest variety of platforms, we chose the "**std::**" prefix approach.]

```
1   // Fig. 20.5: fig20_05.cpp
2   // Demonstrating input and output with iterators.
3   #include <iostream>
4
5   using std::cout;
6   using std::cin;
7   using std::endl;
```

Fig. 20.5 Demonstrating input and output stream iterators (part 1 of 2).

```
8
9    #include <iterator>
10
11   int main()
12   {
13      cout << "Enter two integers: ";
14
15      std::istream_iterator< int > inputInt( cin );
16      int number1, number2;
17
18      number1 = *inputInt;   // read first int from standard input
19      ++inputInt;            // move iterator to next input value
20      number2 = *inputInt;   // read next int from standard input
21
22      cout << "The sum is: ";
23
24      std::ostream_iterator< int > outputInt( cout );
25
26      *outputInt = number1 + number2;   // output result to cout
27      cout << endl;
28      return 0;
29   }
```

```
Enter two integers: 12 25
The sum is: 37
```

Fig. 20.5   Demonstrating input and output stream iterators (part 2 of 2).

Line 15

```
std::istream_iterator< int > inputInt( cin );
```

creates an **istream_iterator** that is capable of extracting (inputting) **int** values in a type-safe manner from the standard input object **cin**. Line 18

```
number1 = *inputInt;   // read first int from standard input
```

dereferences iterator **inputInt** to read the first integer from **cin** and assigns that integer to **number1**. Notice the use of the dereferencing operator * to get the value from the stream associated with **inputInt**; this is similar to dereferencing a pointer. Line 19

```
++inputInt;            // move iterator to next input value
```

positions iterator **inputInt** to the next value in the input stream. Line 20

```
number2 = *inputInt;   // read next int from standard input
```

inputs the next integer from **inputInt** and assigns it to **number2**.

Line 24

```
std::ostream_iterator< int > outputInt( cout );
```

creates an **ostream_iterator** that is capable of inserting (outputting) **int** values in the standard output object **cout**. Line 26

```
*outputInt = number1 + number2;   // output result
```

outputs an integer to **cout** by assigning to ***outputInt** the sum of **number1** and **number2**. Notice the use of the dereferencing operator ***** to use ***outputInt** as an *lvalue* in the assignment statement. If you want to output another value using **outputInt**, the iterator must be incremented with **++** (both preincrement and postincrement can be used).

Testing and Debugging Tip 20.2

*The * (dereferencing) operator of any **const** iterator returns a **const** reference to the container element, thus disallowing the use of non-**const** member functions.*

Common Programming Error 20.1

*Attempting to dereference an iterator positioned outside its container is a run-time logic error. In particular, the iterator returned by **end()** cannot be dereferenced or incremented.*

Common Programming Error 20.2

*Attempting to create a non-**const** iterator for a **const** container is a syntax error.*

Figure 20.6 shows the categories of iterators used by the STL. Each category provides a specific set of functionality.

Figure 20.7 illustrates the hierarchy of iterator categories. As you follow the hierarchy from top to bottom, each iterator category supports all the functionality of the categories above it in the figure. Thus the "weakest" iterator types are at the top and the most powerful iterator type is at the bottom. Note that this is not an inheritance hierarchy.

Category	Description
input	Used to read an element from a container. An input iterator can move only in the forward direction (i.e., from the beginning of the container to the end of the container) one element at a time. Input iterators support only one-pass algorithms—the same input iterator cannot be used to pass through a sequence twice.
output	Used to write an element to a container. An output iterator can move only in the forward direction one element at a time. Output iterators support only one-pass algorithms—the same output iterator cannot be used to pass through a sequence twice.
forward	Combines the capabilities of input and output iterators and retains their position in the container (as state information).
bidirectional	Combines the capabilities of a forward iterator with the ability to move in the backward direction (i.e., from the end of the container toward the beginning of the container). Forward iterators support multi-pass algorithms.
random access	Combines the capabilities of a bidirectional iterator with the ability to directly access any element of the container, i.e., to jump forward or backward by an arbitrary number of elements.

Fig. 20.6   Iterator categories.

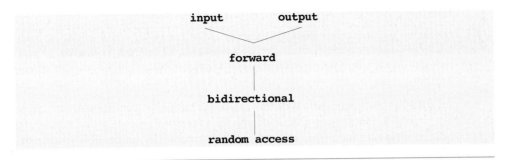

Fig. 20.7 Iterator category hierarchy.

The category of iterator supported by each container determines whether that container can be used with specific algorithms in the STL. Containers that support random-access iterators can be used with all algorithms in the STL. As we will see, pointers into arrays may be used in place of iterators in most STL algorithms, including those that require random-access iterators. Figure 20.8 shows the category of iterator supported by each of the STL containers. Note that only **vector**s, **deque**s, **list**s, **set**s, **multiset**s, **map**s and **multimap**s (i.e., the first-class containers) are traversable with iterators.

Software Engineering Observation 20.4

Using the "weakest iterator" that yields acceptable performance helps produce maximally reusable components.

Figure 20.9 shows the predefined iterator **typedef**s that are found in the class definitions of the STL containers. Not every **typedef** is defined for every container. We use **const** versions of the iterators for traversing read-only containers. We use reverse iterators to traverse containers in the reverse direction.

Container	Type of iterator supported
Sequence containers	
vector	random access
deque	random access
list	bidirectional
Associative containers	
set	bidirectional
multiset	bidirectional
map	bidirectional
multimap	bidirectional
Container adapters	
stack	no iterators supported
queue	no iterators supported
priority_queue	no iterators supported

Fig. 20.8 Iterator types supported by each Standard Library container.

Testing and Debugging Tip 20.3

Operations performed on a **const_iterator** *return* **const** *references to prevent modification to elements of the container being manipulated. Use* **const_iterator**s *in preference to* **iterator**s *where appropriate. This is another example of the principle of least privilege.*

Figure 20.10 shows some operations that can be performed on each iterator type. Note that the operations for each iterator type include all operations preceding that type in the figure. Note also that for input iterators and output iterators it is not possible to save the iterator, then use the saved value later.

Predefined **typedef**s for iterator types	Direction of ++	Capability
iterator	forward	read/write
const_iterator	forward	read
reverse_iterator	backward	read/write
const_reverse_iterator	backward	read

Fig. 20.9   Predefined iterator **typedef**s.

Iterator operation	Description
All iterators	
++p	preincrement an iterator
p++	postincrement an iterator
Input iterators	
*p	dereference an iterator for use as an *rvalue*
p = p1	assign one iterator to another
p == p1	compare iterators for equality
p != p1	compare iterators for inequality
Output iterators	
*p	dereference an iterator (for use as an *lvalue*)
p = p1	assign one iterator to another
Forward iterators	Forward iterators provide all the functionality of both input iterators and output iterators.

Fig. 20.10   Some Iterator operations for each type of iterator (part 1 of 2).

Iterator operation	Description
Bidirectional iterators	
--p	predecrement an iterator
p--	postdecrement an iterator
Random-access iterators	
p += i	Increment the iterator **p** by **i** positions.
p -= i	Decrement the iterator **p** by **i** positions.
p + i	Results in an iterator positioned at **p** incremented by **i** positions.
p - i	Results in an iterator positioned at **p** decremented by **i** positions.
p[i]	Return a reference to the element offset from **p** by **i** positions
p < p1	Return **true** if iterator **p** is less than iterator **p1** (i.e., iterator **p** is before iterator **p1** in the container); otherwise, return **false**.
p <= p1	Return **true** if iterator **p** is less than or equal to iterator **p1** (i.e., iterator **p** is before iterator **p1** or at the same location as iterator **p1** in the container); otherwise, return **false**.
p > p1	Return **true** if iterator **p** is greater than iterator **p1** (i.e., iterator **p** is after iterator **p1** in the container); otherwise, return **false**.
p >= p1	Return **true** if iterator **p** is greater than or equal to iterator **p1** (i.e., iterator **p** is after iterator **p1** or at the same location as iterator **p1** in the container); otherwise, return **false**.

Fig. 20.10 Some Iterator operations for each type of iterator (part 2 of 2).

20.1.3 Introduction to Algorithms

A crucial aspect of the STL is that it provides algorithms that can be used generically across a variety of containers. STL provides many algorithms you will use frequently to manipulate containers. Inserting, deleting, searching, sorting and others are appropriate for some or all of the STL containers.

STL includes approximately 70 standard algorithms. We provide live-code examples of most of these and summarize the others in tables. The algorithms operate on the elements of containers only indirectly through iterators. Many algorithms operate on sequences of elements defined by pairs of iterators—a first iterator pointing to the first element of the sequence and a second iterator pointing to one element past the last element of the sequence. Also, it is possible to create your own new algorithms that operate in a similar fashion so they can be used with the STL containers and iterators.

Container member function **begin()** returns an iterator to the first element of a container; **end()** returns an iterator to the first position past the last element of a container. Algorithms often return iterators.

An algorithm like **find()** for example, locates an element and returns an iterator to that element. If the element is not found, **find()** returns the **end()** iterator, which may be tested to determine if an element was not found (the return of **end()** assumes a search of the entire container). The **find()** algorithm can be used with any STL container.

Software Engineering Observation 20.5

STL is implemented concisely. Until now, class designers would have associated the algorithms with the containers by making the algorithms member functions of the containers. STL takes a different approach. The algorithms are separated from the containers and operate on elements of the containers only indirectly through iterators. This separation makes it easier to write generic algorithms applicable to many other container classes.

STL algorithms create yet another opportunity for reuse. Using the rich collection of popular algorithms can save programmers much time and effort.

If an algorithm uses less powerful iterators, it may also be used with containers that support more powerful iterators. Some algorithms demand powerful iterators; e.g., **sort** demands random-access iterators.

Software Engineering Observation 20.6

STL is extensible. It is straightforward to add new algorithms and to do so without changes to STL containers.

Software Engineering Observation 20.7

STL algorithms can operate on STL containers and on pointer-based, C-like arrays.

Portability Tip 20.2

Because STL algorithms process containers only indirectly through iterators, one algorithm can often be used with many different containers.

Figure 20.11 shows many of the *mutating-sequence algorithms*—i.e., the algorithms that result in modifications of the containers to which the algorithms are applied.

Figure 20.12 shows many of the non-mutating-sequence algorithms—i.e., the algorithms that do not result in modifications of the containers to which the algorithms are applied.

Figure 20.13 shows the numerical algorithms of the header file **<numeric>**.

Mutating-sequence algorithms		
`copy()`	`remove()`	`reverse_copy()`
`copy_backward()`	`remove_copy()`	`rotate()`
`fill()`	`remove_copy_if()`	`rotate_copy()`
`fill_n()`	`remove_if()`	`stable_partition()`
`generate()`	`replace()`	`swap()`
`generate_n()`	`replace_copy()`	`swap_ranges()`
`iter_swap()`	`replace_copy_if()`	`transform()`
`partition()`	`replace_if()`	`unique()`
`random_shuffle()`	`reverse()`	`unique_copy()`

Fig. 20.11 Mutating-sequence algorithms.

Non-mutating-sequence algorithms		
`adjacent_find()`	`find()`	`find_if()`
`count()`	`find_each()`	`mismatch()`
`count_if()`	`find_end()`	`search()`
`equal()`	`find_first_of()`	`search_n()`

Fig. 20.12 Non-mutating sequence algorithms.

Numerical algorithms from header file `<numeric>`
`accumulate()`
`inner_product()`
`partial_sum()`
`adjacent_difference()`

Fig. 20.13 Numerical algorithms from header file `<numeric>`.

20.2 Sequence Containers

The C++ Standard Template Library provides three sequence containers—**vector, list** and **deque**. Class **vector** and class **deque** both are based on arrays. Class **list** implements a linked-list data structure similar to our **List** class presented in Chapter 15, but more robust.

One of the most popular containers in the STL is **vector**. Class **vector** is a refinement of the kind of "smart" **Array** class we created in Chapter 8. A **vector** can change size dynamically. Unlike C and C++ "raw" arrays (see Chapter 4), **vector**s can be assigned to one another. This is not possible with pointer-based, C-like arrays because those array names are constant pointers and cannot be the targets of assignments. Just as with C arrays, **vector** subscripting does not perform automatic range checking, but class **vector** does provide this capability (as we will see) via member function **at**.

Performance Tip 20.5

Insertion at the back of a **vector** *is efficient. The* **vector** *simply grows if necessary to accommodate the new item. It is expensive to insert (or delete) an element in the middle of a* **vector**—*the entire portion of the* **vector** *after the insertion (or deletion) point must be moved, because* **vector** *elements occupy contiguous cells in memory just like a C or C++ "raw" array.*

Figure 20.2 presented the operations common to all the STL containers. Beyond these operations, each container typically provides a variety of other capabilities. Many of these capabilities are common to several containers. However, these operations are not always equally efficient for each container. Programmers must often choose the container most appropriate for their application.

Performance Tip 20.6

*Applications that require frequent insertions and deletions at both ends of a container normally use a **deque** rather than a **vector**. Although we can insert and delete elements at the front and back of both a **vector** and a **deque**, class **deque** is more efficient than **vector** for doing insertions and deletions at the front.*

Performance Tip 20.7

*Applications with frequent insertions and deletions in the middle and/or at the extremes of a container normally use a **list**, due to its efficient implementation of insertion and deletion anywhere in the data structure.*

In addition to the common operations described in Fig. 20.2, the sequence containers have several other common operations—**front** to return a reference to the first element in the container, **back** to return a reference to the last element in the container, **push_back** to insert a new element at the end of the container and **pop_back** to remove the last element of the container.

20.2.1 **vector** Sequence Container

Class **vector** provides a data structure with contiguous memory locations. This enables efficient, direct access to any element of a vector via the subscript operator **[ ]**, exactly like a C or C++ "raw" array. Class **vector** is most commonly used when the data in the container must be sorted and easily accessible via a subscript. When a **vector**'s memory is exhausted, the **vector** allocates a larger contiguous area of memory, copies the original elements into the new memory and deallocates the old memory.

Performance Tip 20.8

*Choose the **vector** container for the best random-access performance.*

Performance Tip 20.9

*Objects of class **vector** provide rapid indexed access with the overloaded subscript operator **[ ]** because they are stored in contiguous storage like a C or C++ raw array.*

Performance Tip 20.10

It is faster to insert many elements at once than one at a time

An important part of every container is the type of iterator it supports. This determines which algorithms can be applied to the container. A **vector** supports random-access iterators—i.e., all iterator operations shown in Fig. 20.10 can be applied to a **vector** iterator. All STL algorithms can operate on a **vector**. The iterators for a **vector** are normally implemented as pointers to elements of the **vector**. Each of the STL algorithms that take iterator arguments requires those iterators to provide a minimum level of functionality. If an algorithm requires a forward iterator, for example, that algorithm can operate on any container that provides forward iterators, bidirectional iterators or random-access iterators. As long as the container supports the algorithm's minimum iterator functionality, the algorithm can operate on the container.

Figure 20.14 illustrates several functions of the **vector** class template. Many of these functions are available in every Standard Library first-class container. You must include header file **<vector>** to use class **vector**.

```
1   // Fig. 20.14: fig20_14.cpp
2   // Testing Standard Library vector class template
3   #include <iostream>
4
5   using std::cout;
6   using std::cin;
7   using std::endl;
8
9   #include <vector>
10
11  template < class T >
12  void printVector( const std::vector< T > &vec );
13
14  int main()
15  {
16     const int SIZE = 6;
17     int a[ SIZE ] = { 1, 2, 3, 4, 5, 6 };
18     std::vector< int > v;
19
20     cout << "The initial size of v is: " << v.size()
21         << "\nThe initial capacity of v is: " << v.capacity();
22     v.push_back( 2 );   // method push_back() is in
23     v.push_back( 3 );   // every sequence collection
24     v.push_back( 4 );
25     cout << "\nThe size of v is: " << v.size()
26         << "\nThe capacity of v is: " << v.capacity();
27     cout << "\n\nContents of array a using pointer notation: ";
28
29     for ( int *ptr = a; ptr != a + SIZE; ++ptr )
30        cout << *ptr << ' ';
31
32     cout << "\nContents of vector v using iterator notation: ";
33     printVector( v );
34
35     cout << "\nReversed contents of vector v: ";
36
37     std::vector< int >::reverse_iterator p2;
38
39     for ( p2 = v.rbegin(); p2 != v.rend(); ++p2 )
40        cout << *p2 << ' ';
41
42     cout << endl;
43     return 0;
44  }
45
46  template < class T >
47  void printVector( const std::vector< T > &vec )
48  {
49     std::vector< T >::const_iterator p1;
50
51     for ( p1 = vec.begin(); p1 != vec.end(); p1++ )
52        cout << *p1 << ' ';
53  }
```

Fig. 20.14 Demonstrating Standard Library **vector** class template (part 1 of 2).

```
The initial size of v is: 0
The initial capacity of v is: 0
The size of v is: 3
The capacity of v is: 4

Contents of array a using pointer notation: 1 2 3 4 5 6
Contents of vector v using iterator notation: 2 3 4
Reversed contents of vector v: 4 3 2
```

Fig. 20.14 Demonstrating Standard Library **vector** class template (part 2 of 2).

Line 18

```
std::vector< int > v;
```

defines an instance called **v** of class **vector** that stores **int** values. When this object is instantiated, an empty **vector** is created with a size of 0 (i.e., the number of elements stored in the **vector**) and a capacity of 0 (i.e., the number of elements that can be stored without allocating more memory to the **vector**).

Lines 20 and 21

```
cout << "The initial size of v is: " << v.size()
     << "\nThe initial capacity of v is: " << v.capacity();
```

demonstrate the **size** and **capacity** functions that both initially return 0 for **vector v** in this example. Function **size**—available in every container—returns the number of elements currently stored in the container. Function **capacity** returns the number of elements that can be stored in the **vector** before the **vector** dynamically resizes itself to accommodate more elements.

Lines 22 through 24

```
v.push_back( 2 );  // method push_back() is in
v.push_back( 3 );  // every sequence container
v.push_back( 4 );
```

use function **push_back**—available in all sequence containers—to add an element to the end of the **vector**. If an element is added to a full **vector**, the **vector** increases its size—some STL implementations have the **vector** double its size.

Performance Tip 20.11

It may be wasteful to double the size of a **vector** *when more space is needed. For example, a full* **vector** *of 1,000,000 elements resizes to accommodate 2,000,000 elements when a new element is added. This leaves 999,999 elements unused. Programmers may use* **resize()** *to better control space usage.*

Lines 25 and 26 use **size** and **capacity** to illustrate the new size and capacity of the **vector** after the **push_back** operations. Function **size** returns 3—the number of elements added to the **vector**. Function **capacity** returns 4, indicating that we can add one more element without allocating more memory for the **vector**. When we added the first element, the size of **v** became 1 and the capacity of **v** became 1. When we added the second element, the size of **v** became 2 and the capacity of **v** became 2. When we added the third element, the size of **v** became 3 and the capacity of **v** became 4. If we add two more elements, the size of **v** would be 5 and the capacity would be 8. The capacity doubles each time the total space allocated to the **vector** is full and another element is added.

Lines 29 and 30 demonstrate how to output the contents of an array using pointers and pointer arithmetic. Line 33 calls function **printVector** to output the contents of a **vector** using iterators. The definition of function template **printVector** begins at line 46. The function receives a **const** reference to a **vector** as its argument. Line 49

```
std::vector< T >::const_iterator p1;
```

defines a **const_iterator** called **p1** that iterates through the **vector** and outputs its contents. A **const_iterator** enables the program to read the elements of the **vector**, but does not allow the program to modify the elements. The **for** structure at lines 51 and 52

```
for ( p1 = vec.begin(); p1 != vec.end(); p1++ )
   cout << *p1 << ' ';
```

initializes **p1** using **vector** member function **begin** that returns a **const_iterator** to the first element in the **vector** (there is another version of **begin** that returns an **iterator** that can be used for non-**const** containers). The loop continues as long as **p1** is not past the end of the **vector**. This is determined by comparing **p1** to the result of **vec.end()** that returns a **const_iterator** (as with **begin**, there is another version of **end** that returns an **iterator**) indicating the location after the last element of the **vector**. If **p1** is equal to this value, the end of the **vector** has been reached. Functions **begin** and **end** are available for all first-class containers. The body of the loop dereferences iterator **p1** to get the value in the current element of the **vector**. The expression **p1++** positions the iterator to the next element of the **vector**.

Testing and Debugging Tip 20.4

Only random-access iterators support **<**. *It is better to use* **!=** *and* **end()** *to test for end of container.*

Line 37

```
std::vector< int >::reverse_iterator p2;
```

declares a **reverse_iterator** that can be used to iterate through a **vector** backwards. All first-class containers support this type of iterator.

Lines 39 and 40

```
for ( p2 = v.rbegin(); p2 != v.rend(); p2++ )
   cout << *p2 << ' ';
```

use a **for** structure similar to that in function **printVector** to iterate through the **vector**. In this loop, functions **rbegin** (i.e., the iterator for the starting point for iterating in reverse through the container) and **rend** (i.e., the iterator for the ending point for iterating in reverse through the container) delineate the range of elements to output in reverse. As with functions **begin** and **end**, **rbegin** and **rend** can return a **const_reverse_iterator** or a **reverse_iterator** based on whether or not the container is constant.

Figure 20.15 illustrates functions that enable retrieval and manipulation of the elements of a **vector**. Line 16

```
std::vector< int > v( a, a + SIZE );
```

uses an overloaded **vector** constructor that takes two iterators as arguments. Remember that pointers into an array can be used as iterators. This statement creates integer **vector** **v** and initializes it with the contents of integer array **a** from location **a** up to—but not including—location **a + SIZE**.

```cpp
1   // Fig. 20.15: fig20_15.cpp
2   // Testing Standard Library vector class template
3   // element-manipulation functions
4   #include <iostream>
5
6   using std::cout;
7   using std::endl;
8
9   #include <vector>
10  #include <algorithm>
11
12  int main()
13  {
14     const int SIZE = 6;
15     int a[ SIZE ] = { 1, 2, 3, 4, 5, 6 };
16     std::vector< int > v( a, a + SIZE );
17     std::ostream_iterator< int > output( cout, " " );
18     cout << "Vector v contains: ";
19     std::copy( v.begin(), v.end(), output );
20
21     cout << "\nFirst element of v: " << v.front()
22          << "\nLast element of v: " << v.back();
23
24     v[ 0 ] = 7;         // set first element to 7
25     v.at( 2 ) = 10;     // set element at position 2 to 10
26     v.insert( v.begin() + 1, 22 );  // insert 22 as 2nd element
27     cout << "\nContents of vector v after changes: ";
28     std::copy( v.begin(), v.end(), output );
29
30     try {
31        v.at( 100 ) = 777;    // access element out of range
32     }
33     catch ( std::out_of_range e ) {
34        cout << "\nException: " << e.what();
35     }
36
37     v.erase( v.begin() );
38     cout << "\nContents of vector v after erase: ";
39     std::copy( v.begin(), v.end(), output );
40     v.erase( v.begin(), v.end() );
41     cout << "\nAfter erase, vector v "
42          << ( v.empty() ? "is" : "is not" ) << " empty";
43
```

Fig. 20.15 Demonstrating Standard Library **vector** class template element-manipulation functions (part 1 of 2).

```
44      v.insert( v.begin(), a, a + SIZE );
45      cout << "\nContents of vector v before clear: ";
46      std::copy( v.begin(), v.end(), output );
47      v.clear();  // clear calls erase to empty a collection
48      cout << "\nAfter clear, vector v "
49          << ( v.empty() ? "is" : "is not" ) << " empty";
50
51      cout << endl;
52      return 0;
53  }
```

```
Vector v contains: 1 2 3 4 5 6
First element of v: 1
Last element of v: 6
Contents of vector v after changes: 7 22 2 10 4 5 6
Exception: invalid vector<T> subscript
Contents of vector v after erase: 22 2 10 4 5 6
After erase, vector v is empty
Contents of vector v before clear: 1 2 3 4 5 6
After clear, vector v is empty
```

Fig. 20.15 Demonstrating Standard Library **vector** class template element-manipulation functions (part 2 of 2).

Line 17

```
std::ostream_iterator< int > output( cout, " " );
```

defines an **ostream_iterator** called **output** that can be used to output integers separated by single spaces via **cout**. An **ostream_iterator** is a type-safe output mechanism that will output only values of type **int** or a compatible type. The first argument to the constructor specifies the output stream, and the second argument is a string specifying separator characters for the values output—in this case a space character. We will use the **ostream_iterator** to output the contents of the **vector** in this example.

Line 19

```
std::copy( v.begin(), v.end(), output );
```

uses algorithm **copy** from the Standard Library to output the entire contents of **vector v** to the standard output. Algorithm **copy** copies each element in the container starting with the location specified by the iterator in its first argument and up to—but not including—the location specified by the iterator in its second argument. The first and second arguments must satisfy input iterator requirements—i.e., they must be iterators through which values can be read from a container. Also, applying **++** to the first iterator must eventually cause the first iterator to reach the second iterator argument in the container. The elements are copied to the location specified by the output iterator (i.e., an iterator through which a value can be stored or output) specified as the last argument. In this case, the output iterator is **ostream_iterator output** that is attached to **cout**, so the elements are copied to the standard output. To use the algorithms of the Standard Library, you must include the header file **<algorithm>**.

Lines 21 and 22 use functions **front** and **back** (available for all sequence containers) to determine the first and last element of the **vector**, respectively.

 Common Programming Error 20.3

The **vector** *must not be empty; otherwise, results of the* **front** *and* **back** *functions are undefined.*

Lines 24 and 25

```
v[ 0 ] = 7;        // set first element to 7
v.at( 2 ) = 10;    // set element at position 2 to 10
```

illustrate two ways to subscript through a **vector** (these also can be used with the **deque** containers). Line 24 uses the subscript operator that is overloaded to return either a reference to the value at the specified location or a constant reference to that value depending on whether or not the container is constant. Function **at** performs the same operation with one additional feature—bounds checking. Function **at** first checks the value supplied as an argument and determines if it is in the bounds of the **vector**. If not, function **at** throws an **out_of_bounds** exception (as demonstrated in lines 30 through 35). Some of the STL exception types are shown in Fig. 20.16 (the Standard Library exception types are discussed in Chapter 13, "Exception Handling").

Line 26

```
v.insert( v.begin() + 1, 22 );  // insert 22 as 2nd element
```

uses one of the three **insert** functions that are available to each sequence container. The preceding statement inserts the value 22 before the element at the location specified by the iterator in the first argument. In this example, the iterator is pointing to the second element of the **vector**, so 22 is inserted as the second element and the original second element becomes the third element of the **vector**. The other versions of **insert** allow inserting multiple copies of the same value starting at a particular position in the container or inserting a range of values from another container (or array) starting at a particular position in the original container.

Lines 37 and 40

```
v.erase( v.begin() );
v.erase( v.begin(), v.end() );
```

STL exception types	Description
out_of_range	Indicates when subscript is out of range—e.g., when an invalid subscript is specified to **vector** member function **at**.
invalid_argument	Indicates an invalid argument was passed to a function.
length_error	Indicates an attempt to create too long a container, **string**, etc.
bad_alloc	Indicates that an attempt to allocate memory with **new** (or with an allocator) failed because not enough memory was available.

Fig. 20.16 STL exception types.

use the two **erase** functions that are available in all first-class containers. Line 37 indicates that the element at the location specified by the iterator argument should be removed from the container (in this example the element at the beginning of the **vector**). Line 40 specifies that all elements in the range starting with the location of the first argument up to—but not including—the location of the second argument should be erased from the container. In this example, all the elements are erased from the **vector**. Line 42 uses function **empty** (available for all containers including the adapters) to confirm that the **vector** is empty.

Common Programming Error 20.4

Erasing an element that contains a pointer to a dynamically allocated object does not de-lete the object.

Line 44

```
v.insert( v.begin(), a, a + SIZE );
```

uses the version of function **insert** that uses the second and third arguments to specify the starting location and ending location in a sequence of values (possibly from another container, but in this case from integer array **a**) that should be inserted into the **vector**. Remember that the ending location specifies the position in the sequence after the last element to be inserted; copying is performed up to—but not including—this location.

Finally, line 47

```
v.clear();  // clear calls erase to empty a container
```

uses function **clear** (available in all first-class containers) to empty the **vector**. This function calls the version of **erase** used in line 40 to actually perform the operation.

[*Note:* There are other functions that are common to all containers and common to all sequence containers that have not been covered yet. We will cover most of these in the next few sections. We will also cover many functions that are specific to each container.]

20.2.2 **list** Sequence Container

The **list** sequence container provides an efficient implementation for insertion and deletion operations at any location in the container. If most of the insertions and deletions occur at the ends of the container, the **deque** data structure (Section 20.2.3) provides a more efficient implementation. Class **list** is implemented as a doubly linked list—i.e., every node in the **list** contains a pointer to the previous node in the **list** and the next node in the **list**. This enables class **list** to support bidirectional iterators that allow the container to be traversed both forwards and backwards. Any algorithm that requires input, output, forward or bidirectional iterators can operate on a **list**. Many of the **list** member functions manipulate the elements of the container as an ordered set of elements.

In addition to the member functions of all STL containers in Fig. 20.2 and the common member functions of all sequence containers discussed in Section 20.5, class **list** provides eight other member functions—**splice**, **push_front**, **pop_front**, **remove**, **unique**, **merge**, **reverse** and **sort**. Figure 20.17 demonstrates several features of class **list**. Remember that many of the functions presented in Figs. 20.14 and 20.15 can be used with class **list**. Header file **<list>** must be included to use class **list**.

```cpp
1    // Fig. 20.17: fig20_17.cpp
2    // Testing Standard Library class list
3    #include <iostream>
4
5    using std::cout;
6    using std::endl;
7
8    #include <list>
9    #include <algorithm>
10
11   template < class T >
12   void printList( const std::list< T > &listRef );
13
14   int main()
15   {
16      const int SIZE = 4;
17      int a[ SIZE ] = { 2, 6, 4, 8 };
18      std::list< int > values, otherValues;
19
20      values.push_front( 1 );
21      values.push_front( 2 );
22      values.push_back( 4 );
23      values.push_back( 3 );
24
25      cout << "values contains: ";
26      printList( values );
27      values.sort();
28      cout << "\nvalues after sorting contains: ";
29      printList( values );
30
31      otherValues.insert( otherValues.begin(), a, a + SIZE );
32      cout << "\notherValues contains: ";
33      printList( otherValues );
34      values.splice( values.end(), otherValues );
35      cout << "\nAfter splice values contains: ";
36      printList( values );
37
38      values.sort();
39      cout << "\nvalues contains: ";
40      printList( values );
41      otherValues.insert( otherValues.begin(), a, a + SIZE );
42      otherValues.sort();
43      cout << "\notherValues contains: ";
44      printList( otherValues );
45      values.merge( otherValues );
46      cout << "\nAfter merge:\n    values contains: ";
47      printList( values );
48      cout << "\n    otherValues contains: ";
49      printList( otherValues );
50
51      values.pop_front();
52      values.pop_back();    // all sequence containers
```

Fig. 20.17   Demonstrating Standard Library **list** class template (part 1 of 3).

```
53        cout << "\nAfter pop_front and pop_back values contains:\n";
54        printList( values );
55
56        values.unique();
57        cout << "\nAfter unique values contains: ";
58        printList( values );
59
60        // method swap is available in all containers
61        values.swap( otherValues );
62        cout << "\nAfter swap:\n   values contains: ";
63        printList( values );
64        cout << "\n   otherValues contains: ";
65        printList( otherValues );
66
67        values.assign( otherValues.begin(), otherValues.end() );
68        cout << "\nAfter assign values contains: ";
69        printList( values );
70
71        values.merge( otherValues );
72        cout << "\nvalues contains: ";
73        printList( values );
74        values.remove( 4 );
75        cout << "\nAfter remove( 4 ) values contains: ";
76        printList( values );
77        cout << endl;
78        return 0;
79    }
80
81    template < class T >
82    void printList( const std::list< T > &listRef )
83    {
84        if ( listRef.empty() )
85            cout << "List is empty";
86        else {
87            std::ostream_iterator< T > output( cout, " " );
88            std::copy( listRef.begin(), listRef.end(), output );
89        }
90    }
```

```
values contains: 2 1 4 3
values after sorting contains: 1 2 3 4
otherValues contains: 2 6 4 8
After splice values contains: 1 2 3 4 2 6 4 8
values contains: 1 2 2 3 4 4 6 8
otherValues contains: 2 4 6 8
After merge:
   values contains: 1 2 2 2 3 4 4 4 6 6 8 8
   otherValues contains: List is empty
After pop_front and pop_back values contains:
2 2 2 3 4 4 6 6 8
After unique values contains: 2 3 4 6 8
```
                                          (continued at top of next page)

Fig. 20.17   Demonstrating Standard Library **list** class template (part 2 of 3).

```
                                          (continued from bottom of previous page)
After swap:
   values contains: List is empty
   otherValues contains: 2 3 4 6 8
After assign values contains: 2 3 4 6 8
values contains: 2 2 3 3 4 4 6 6 8 8
After remove( 4 ) values contains: 2 2 3 3 6 6 8 8
```

Fig. 20.17 Demonstrating Standard Library `list` class template (part 3 of 3).

Line 18

```
std::list< int > values, otherValues;
```

instantiates two **list** objects capable of storing integers. Lines 20 and 21 use function **push_front** to insert integers at the beginning of **values**. Function **push_front** is specific to classes **list** and **deque** (not to **vector**). Lines 22 and 23 use function **push_back** to insert integers at the end of **values**. Remember that function **push_back** is common to all sequence containers.

Line 27

```
values.sort();
```

uses **list** member function **sort** to arrange the elements in the **list** in ascending order. [*Note:* This is different from the **sort** in the STL algorithms.] There is a second version of function **sort** that allows the programmer to supply a binary predicate function that takes two arguments (values in the list), performs a comparison and returns a **bool** value indicating the result. This function determines the order in which the elements of the **list** are sorted. This version could be particularly useful for a **list** that stores pointers rather than values. [*Note:* We demonstrate a unary predicate function in Fig. 20.28. A unary predicate function takes a single argument, performs a comparison using that argument and returns a **bool** value indicating the result.]

Line 34

```
values.splice( values.end(), otherValues );
```

uses **list** function **splice** to remove the elements in **otherValues** and insert them into **values** before the iterator position specified as the first argument. There are two other versions of this function. Function **splice** with three arguments allows one element to be removed from the container specified as the second argument from the location specified by the iterator in the third argument. Function **splice** with four arguments uses the last two arguments to specify a range of locations that should be removed from the container in the second argument and placed at the location specified in the first argument.

After inserting more elements in **list otherValues** and sorting both **values** and **otherValues**, line 45

```
values.merge( otherValues );
```

uses **list** member function **merge** to remove all elements of **otherValues** and insert them in sorted order into **values**. Both **list**s must be sorted in the same order before this operation is performed. A second version of **merge** enables the programmer to supply a predicate function that takes two arguments (values in the list) and returns a **bool** value. The predicate function specifies the sorting order used by **merge**.

Line 51 uses **list** function **pop_front** to remove the first element in the **list**. Line 52 uses function **pop_back** (available for all sequence containers) to remove the last element in the **list**.

Line 56

```
values.unique();
```

uses **list** function **unique** to remove duplicate elements in the **list**. The **list** should be in sorted order (so that all duplicates are side by side) before this operation is performed, to guarantee that all duplicates are eliminated. A second version of **unique** enables the programmer to supply a predicate function that takes two arguments (values in the list) and returns a **bool** value. The predicate function specifies if two elements are equal.

Line 61

```
values.swap( otherValues );
```

uses function **swap** (available to all containers) to exchange the contents of **values** with the contents of **otherValues**.

Line 67

```
values.assign( otherValues.begin(), otherValues.end() );
```

uses **list** function **assign** to replace the contents of **values** with the contents of **otherValues** in the range specified by the two iterator arguments. A second version of **assign** replaces the original contents with copies of the value specified in the second argument. The first argument of the function specifies the number of copies.

Line 74

```
values.remove( 4 );
```

uses **list** function **remove** to delete all copies of the value **4** from the **list**.

20.2.3 deque Sequence Container

Class **deque** provides many of the benefits of a **vector** and a **list** in one container. The term **deque** (pronounced "deek") is short for "double-ended queue." Class **deque** is implemented to provide efficient indexed access (using subscripting) for reading and modifying its elements much like a **vector**. Class **deque** is also implemented for efficient insertion and deletion operations at its front and back much like a **list** (although a **list** is also capable of efficient insertions and deletions in the middle of the **list**). Class **deque** provides support for random-access iterators, so **deque**s can be used with all STL algorithms. One of the most common uses of a **deque** is to maintain a first-in-first-out queue of elements.

Additional storage for a **deque** can be allocated at either end of the **deque** in blocks of memory that are typically maintained as an array of pointers to those blocks. Due to the noncontiguous memory layout of a **deque**, a **deque** iterator must be more intelligent than the pointers that are used to iterate through **vector**s or pointer-based arrays.

Performance Tip 20.12

Once a storage block is allocated for a **deque***, in several implementations the block is not deallocated until* **deque** *is destroyed. This makes the operation of a* **deque** *more efficient than if memory were repeatedly allocated, deallocated and reallocated. But this means that the* **deque** *is more likely to use memory inefficiently (than a* **vector***, for example).*

Performance Tip 20.13

Insertions and deletions in the middle of a **deque** *are optimized to minimize the number of elements copied to maintain the illusion that the elements of the* **deque** *are contiguous.*

Class **deque** provides the same basic operations as class **vector**, but adds member functions **push_front** and **pop_front** to allow insertion and deletion at the beginning of the **deque**, respectively.

Figure 20.18 demonstrates features of class **deque**. Remember that many of the functions presented in Figs. 20.14, 20.15 and 20.17 also can be used with class **deque**. Header file **<deque>** must be included to use class **deque**.

```cpp
1   // Fig. 20.18: fig20_18.cpp
2   // Testing Standard Library class deque
3   #include <iostream>
4
5   using std::cout;
6   using std::endl;
7
8   #include <deque>
9   #include <algorithm>
10
11  int main()
12  {
13     std::deque< double > values;
14     std::ostream_iterator< double > output( cout, " " );
15
16     values.push_front( 2.2 );
17     values.push_front( 3.5 );
18     values.push_back( 1.1 );
19
20     cout << "values contains: ";
21
22     for ( int i = 0; i < values.size(); ++i )
23        cout << values[ i ] << ' ';
24
25     values.pop_front();
26     cout << "\nAfter pop_front values contains: ";
27     std::copy ( values.begin(), values.end(), output );
28
29     values[ 1 ] = 5.4;
30     cout << "\nAfter values[ 1 ] = 5.4 values contains: ";
31     std::copy ( values.begin(), values.end(), output );
32     cout << endl;
33     return 0;
34  }
```

Fig. 20.18 Demonstrating Standard Library **deque** class template (part 1 of 2).

```
values contains: 3.5 2.2 1.1
After pop_front values contains: 2.2 1.1
After values[ 1 ] = 5.4 values contains: 2.2 5.4
```

Fig. 20.18 Demonstrating Standard Library **deque** class template (part 2 of 2).

Line 13

```
std::deque< double > values;
```

instantiates a **deque** that can store **double** values. Lines 16 through 18 use functions **push_front** and **push_back** to insert elements at the beginning and end of the **deque**, respectively. Remember that **push_back** is available for all sequence containers, but **push_front** is only available for class **list** and class **deque**.

The **for** structure at line 22

```
for ( int i = 0; i < values.size(); i++ )
    cout << values[ i ] << ' ';
```

uses the subscript operator to retrieve the value in each element of the **deque** for output. Note the use of function **size** in the condition to ensure that we do not attempt to access an element outside the bounds of the **deque**.

Line 25 uses function **pop_front** to demonstrate removing the first element of the **deque**. Remember that **pop_front** is only available for class **list** and class **deque** (not for class **vector**).

Line 29

```
values[ 1 ] = 5.4;
```

uses the subscript operator to create an *lvalue*. This enables values to be assigned directly to any element of the **deque**.

20.3 Associative Containers

The associative containers of the STL are designed to provide direct access to store and retrieve elements via *keys* (often called *search keys*). The four associative containers are **multiset**, **set**, **multimap** and **map**. In each container, the keys are maintained in sorted order. Iterating through an associative container traverses it in the sort order for that container. Classes **multiset** and **set** provide operations for manipulating sets of values where the values are the keys—i.e., there is not a separate value associated with each key. The main difference between a **multiset** and a **set** is that a **multiset** allows duplicate keys and a **set** does not. Classes **multimap** and **map** provide operations for manipulating values associated with keys (these values are sometimes referred to as *mapped values*). The main difference between a **multimap** and a **map** is that a **multimap** allows duplicate keys with associated values to be stored and a **map** allows only unique keys with associated values. In addition to the common member functions of all containers presented in Fig. 20.2, all associative containers also support several other member functions, including **find**, **lower_bound**, **upper_bound** and **count**. Examples of each of the associative containers and the common associative container member functions are presented in the next several subsections.

20.3.1 multiset Associative Container

The **multiset** associative container provides fast storage and retrieval of keys. A **multiset** allows duplicate keys. The ordering of the elements is determined by a *comparator function object*. For example, in an integer **multiset**, elements can be sorted in ascending order by ordering the keys with comparator function object **less< int >**. The data type of the keys in all associative containers must support comparison properly based on the comparator function object specified—keys sorted with **less< int >** must support comparison with **operator<**. If the keys used in the associative containers are of programmer-defined data types, those types must supply the appropriate comparison operators. A **multiset** supports bidirectional iterators (but not random-access iterators).

Performance Tip 20.14

*For performance reasons, **multiset**s and **set**s are typically implemented as so-called red–black binary search trees. With this internal representation, the binary search tree tends to be balanced, thus minimizing average search times.*

Figure 20.19 demonstrates the **multiset** associative container for a **multiset** of integers sorted in ascending order. Header file **<set>** must be included to use class **multiset**. Containers **multiset** and **set** provide the same member functions.

```cpp
1   // Fig. 20.19: fig20_19.cpp
2   // Testing Standard Library class multiset
3   #include <iostream>
4
5   using std::cout;
6   using std::endl;
7
8   #include <set>
9   #include <algorithm>
10
11  int main()
12  {
13      const int SIZE = 10;
14      int a[ SIZE ] = { 7, 22, 9, 1, 18, 30, 100, 22, 85, 13 };
15      typedef std::multiset< int, std::less< int > > ims;
16      ims intMultiset;      // ims for "integer multiset"
17      std::ostream_iterator< int > output( cout, " " );
18
19      cout << "There are currently " << intMultiset.count( 15 )
20           << " values of 15 in the multiset\n";
21      intMultiset.insert( 15 );
22      intMultiset.insert( 15 );
23      cout << "After inserts, there are "
24           << intMultiset.count( 15 )
25           << " values of 15 in the multiset\n";
26
27      ims::const_iterator result;
28
29      result = intMultiset.find( 15 );   // find returns iterator
30
```

Fig. 20.19 Demonstrating Standard Library **multiset** class template (part 1 of 2).

```
31      if ( result != intMultiset.end() ) // if iterator not at end
32         cout << "Found value 15\n";      // found search value 15
33
34      result = intMultiset.find( 20 );
35
36      if ( result == intMultiset.end() )     // will be true hence
37         cout << "Did not find value 20\n"; // did not find 20
38
39      intMultiset.insert( a, a + SIZE ); // add array a to multiset
40      cout << "After insert intMultiset contains:\n";
41      std::copy( intMultiset.begin(), intMultiset.end(), output );
42
43      cout << "\nLower bound of 22: "
44            << *( intMultiset.lower_bound( 22 ) );
45      cout << "\nUpper bound of 22: "
46            << *( intMultiset.upper_bound( 22 ) );
47
48      std::pair< ims::const_iterator, ims::const_iterator > p;
49
50      p = intMultiset.equal_range( 22 );
51      cout << "\nUsing equal_range of 22"
52            << "\n    Lower bound: " << *( p.first )
53            << "\n    Upper bound: " << *( p.second );
54      cout << endl;
55      return 0;
56   }
```

```
There are currently 0 values of 15 in the multiset
After inserts, there are 2 values of 15 in the multiset
Found value 15
Did not find value 20
After insert intMultiset contains:
1 7 9 13 15 15 18 22 22 30 85 100
Lower bound of 22: 22
Upper bound of 22: 30
Using equal_range of 22
   Lower bound: 22
   Upper bound: 30
```

Fig. 20.19 Demonstrating Standard Library **multiset** class template (part 2 of 2).

Lines 15 and 16

```
typedef std::multiset< int, std::less< int > > ims;
ims intMultiset;    // ims for "integer multiset"
```

use a **typedef** to create a new type name (alias) for a **multiset** of integers ordered in ascending order using the function object **less< int >**. This new type is then used to instantiate an integer **multiset** object, **intMultiset**.

Good Programming Practice 20.1

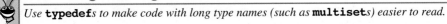

Use **typedef***s to make code with long type names (such as* **multiset***s) easier to read.*

The output statement at line 19

```
cout << "There are currently " << intMultiset.count( 15 )
    << " values of 15 in the multiset\n";
```

uses function **count** (available to all associative containers) to count the number of occurrences of the value **15** currently in the **multiset**.

Lines 21 and 22

```
intMultiset.insert( 15 );
intMultiset.insert( 15 );
```

use one of the three versions of function **insert** to add the value **15** to the **multiset** twice. A second version of **insert** takes an iterator and a value as arguments and begins the search for the insertion point from the iterator position specified. A third version of **insert** takes two iterators as arguments that specify a range of values to add to the **multiset** from another container.

Line 29

```
result = intMultiset.find( 15 );  // find returns iterator
```

uses function **find** (available to all associative containers) to locate the value **15** in the **multiset**. Function **find** returns an **iterator** or a **const_iterator** pointing to the earliest location at which the value is found. If the value is not found, **find** returns an **iterator** or a **const_iterator** equal to the value returned by a call to **end**.

Line 39

```
intMultiset.insert( a, a + SIZE ); // add array a to multiset
```

uses function **insert** to insert the elements of array **a** into the **multiset**. At line 41, the **copy** algorithm copies the elements of the **multiset** to the standard output. Note that the elements are displayed in ascending order.

Lines 43 through 46

```
cout << "\nLower bound of 22: "
    << *( intMultiset.lower_bound( 22 ) );
cout << "\nUpper bound of 22: "
    << *( intMultiset.upper_bound( 22 ) );
```

use functions **lower_bound** and **upper_bound** (available in all associative containers) to determine the location of the earliest occurrence of the value **22** in the **multiset** and the location of the element *after* the last occurrence of the value **22** in the **multiset**. Both functions return **iterator**s or **const_iterator**s pointing to the appropriate location or the iterator returned by **end** if the value is not in the **multiset**.

Line 48

```
std::pair< ims::const_iterator, ims::const_iterator > p;
```

instantiates an instance of class **pair** called **p**. Objects of class **pair** are used to associate pairs of values. In this example, the contents of a **pair** are two **const_iterator**s for our integer-based **multiset**. The purpose of **p** is to store the return value of **multiset** function **equal_range** that returns a **pair** containing the results of both a **lower_bound** and an **upper_bound** operation. Type **pair** contains two **public** data members called **first** and **second**.

Line 50

```
p = intMultiset.equal_range( 22 );
```

uses function **equal_range** to determine the **lower_bound** and **upper_bound** of **22** in the **multiset**. Lines 52 and 53 use **p.first** and **p.second**, respectively, to access the **lower_bound** and **upper_bound**. We dereferenced the iterators to output the values at the locations returned from **equal_range**.

20.3.2 set Associative Container

The **set** associative container is used for fast storage and retrieval of unique keys. The implementation of a **set** is identical to that of a **multiset** except that a **set** must have unique keys. Therefore, if an attempt is made to insert a duplicate key into a **set**, the duplicate is ignored; because this is the intended mathematical behavior of a set, we do not identify it as a common programming error. A **set** supports bidirectional iterators (but not random-access iterators). Figure 20.20 demonstrates a **set** of **double**s. Header file **<set>** must be included to use class **set**.

```cpp
1   // Fig. 20.20: fig20_20.cpp
2   // Testing Standard Library class set
3   #include <iostream>
4
5   using std::cout;
6   using std::endl;
7
8   #include <set>
9   #include <algorithm>
10
11  int main()
12  {
13     typedef std::set< double, std::less< double > > double_set;
14     const int SIZE = 5;
15     double a[ SIZE ] = { 2.1, 4.2, 9.5, 2.1, 3.7 };
16     double_set doubleSet( a, a + SIZE );;
17     std::ostream_iterator< double > output( cout, " " );
18
19     cout << "doubleSet contains: ";
20     std::copy( doubleSet.begin(), doubleSet.end(), output );
21
22     std::pair< double_set::const_iterator, bool > p;
23
24     p = doubleSet.insert( 13.8 );  // value not in set
25     cout << '\n' << *( p.first )
26        << ( p.second ? " was" : " was not" ) << " inserted";
27     cout << "\ndoubleSet contains: ";
28     std::copy( doubleSet.begin(), doubleSet.end(), output );
29
30     p = doubleSet.insert( 9.5 );   // value already in set
31     cout << '\n' << *( p.first )
32        << ( p.second ? " was" : " was not" ) << " inserted";
```

Fig. 20.20 Demonstrating Standard Library **set** class template (part 1 of 2).

```
33        cout << "\ndoubleSet contains: ";
34        std::copy( doubleSet.begin(), doubleSet.end(), output );
35
36        cout << endl;
37        return 0;
38    }
```

```
doubleSet contains: 2.1 3.7 4.2 9.5
13.8 was inserted
doubleSet contains: 2.1 3.7 4.2 9.5 13.8
9.5 was not inserted
doubleSet contains: 2.1 3.7 4.2 9.5 13.8
```

Fig. 20.20 Demonstrating Standard Library **set** class template (part 2 of 2).

Line 13

```
typedef std::set< double, std::less< double > > double_set;
```

uses **typedef** to create a new type name (alias) for a set of **double** values ordered in ascending order using the function object **less< double >**.

Line 16

```
double_set doubleSet( a, a + SIZE );
```

uses the new type **double_set** to instantiate object **doubleSet**. The constructor call takes the elements in array **a** between **a** and **a + SIZE** (i.e., the entire array) and inserts them into the **set**. Line 20 uses algorithm **copy** to output the contents of the **set**. Notice that the value **2.1**—which appeared twice in array **a**—only appears once in **doubleSet**. This is because container **set** does not allow duplicates.

Line 22

```
std::pair< double_set::const_iterator, bool > p;
```

defines a **pair** consisting of a **const_iterator** for a **double_set** and a **bool** value. This object stores the result of a call to **set** function **insert**.

Line 24

```
p = doubleSet.insert( 13.8 ); // value not in set
```

uses function **insert** to place the value **13.8** in the **set**. The returned **pair**, **p**, contains an iterator **p.first** pointing to the value **13.8** in the **set** and a **bool** value that is **true** if the value was inserted and **false** if the value was not inserted (because it was already in the **set**).

20.3.3 **multimap** Associative Container

The **multimap** associative container is used for fast storage and retrieval of keys and associated values (often called *key/value pairs*). Many of the methods used with **multiset**s and **set**s are also used with **multimap**s and **map**s. The elements of **multimap**s and **map**s are **pair**s of keys and values instead of individual values. When inserting into a **multimap** or **map**, a **pair** object that contains the key and the value is used. The ordering of the keys is determined by a comparator function object. For example, in a **multimap** that uses integers as the key type, keys can be sorted in ascending order by ordering the keys with comparator function object **less< int >**. Duplicate keys are allowed in a **multimap**, so multiple values can be associated with a single key. This is often called a one-to-many relationship. For example, in a credit-card transaction-processing system, one credit card account can have many associated transactions; in a university, one student can take many courses and one professor can teach many students; in the military, one rank (like "private") has many people. A **multimap** supports bidirectional iterators (but not random-access iterators). As with **multiset**s and **set**s, **multimap**s are typically implemented as a red–black binary search tree in which the nodes of the tree are key/value **pair**s. Figure 20.21 demonstrates the **multimap** associative container. Header file **<map>** must be included to use class **multimap**.

```
1   // Fig. 20.21: fig20_21.cpp
2   // Testing Standard Library class multimap
3   #include <iostream>
4
5   using std::cout;
6   using std::endl;
7
8   #include <map>
9
10  int main()
11  {
12     typedef std::multimap< int, double, std::less< int > > mmid;
13     mmid pairs;
14
15     cout << "There are currently " << pairs.count( 15 )
16        << " pairs with key 15 in the multimap\n";
17     pairs.insert( mmid::value_type( 15, 2.7 ) );
18     pairs.insert( mmid::value_type( 15, 99.3 ) );
19     cout << "After inserts, there are "
20        << pairs.count( 15 )
21        << " pairs with key 15\n";p
22     pairs.insert( mmid::value_type( 30, 111.11 ) );
23     pairs.insert( mmid::value_type( 10, 22.22 ) );
24     pairs.insert( mmid::value_type( 25, 33.333 ) );
25     pairs.insert( mmid::value_type( 20, 9.345 ) );
26     pairs.insert( mmid::value_type( 5, 77.54 ) );
27     cout << "Multimap pairs contains:\nKey\tValue\n";
28
29     for ( mmid::const_iterator iter = pairs.begin();
30          iter != pairs.end(); ++iter )
31       cout << iter->first << '\t'
32          << iter->second << '\n';
33
34     cout << endl;
35     return 0;
36  }
```

Fig. 20.21 Demonstrating Standard Library **multimap** class template (part 1 of 2).

```
There are currently 0 pairs with key 15 in the multimap
After inserts, there are 2 pairs with key 15
Multimap pairs contains:
Key      Value
5        77.54
10       22.22
15       2.7
15       99.3
20       9.345
25       33.333
30       111.11
```

Fig. 20.21 Demonstrating Standard Library **multimap** class template (part 2 of 2).

Performance Tip 20.15

A **multimap** *is implemented to efficiently locate all values paired with a given key.*

Line 12

```
typedef std::multimap< int, double, std::less< int > > mmid;
```

uses **typedef** to define an alias for a **multimap** type where the key type is **int**, the type of an associated value is **double** and the elements are ordered in ascending order. Line 13 uses the new type to instantiate a **multimap** called **pairs**.

Lines 15 and 16

```
cout << "There are currently " << pairs.count( 15 )
     << " pairs with key 15\n";
```

use function **count** to determine the number of key/value pairs with a key of **15**.

Line 17

```
pairs.insert( mmid::value_type( 15, 2.7 ) );
```

uses function **insert** to add a new key/value pair to the **multimap**. The expression **mmid::value_type(15, 2.7)** creates a **pair** object in which **first** is the key (**15**) of type **int** and **second** is the value (**2.7**) of type **double**. The type **mmid::value_type** is defined in line 12 as part of the **typedef** for the **multimap**.

The **for** structure at line 29 outputs the contents of the **multimap** including both keys and values. Lines 31 and 32

```
cout << iter->first << '\t'
     << iter->second << '\n';
```

use the **const_iterator** called **iter** to access the members of the **pair** in each element of the **multimap**. Notice in the output that the keys are in ascending order.

20.3.4 map Associative Container

The **map** associative container is used for fast storage and retrieval of unique keys and associated values. Duplicate keys are not allowed in a **map**, so only a single value can be associated with each key. This is called a *one-to-one mapping*. For example, a company that uses unique employee numbers such as a 100, 200 and 300 might have a **map** that associates employee numbers with their telephone extensions 4321, 4115 and 5217, respectively. With a **map** you specify the key and get back the associated data quickly. A **map** is commonly called an *associative array*. Providing the key in a **map**'s subscript operator **[ ]** locates the value associated with that key in the **map**. Insertions and deletions may be made anywhere in a **map**.

Figure 20.22 demonstrates the **map** associative container. Figure 20.22 uses the same features as Fig. 20.21 except for the subscript operator. Header file **<map>** must be included to use class **map**. Lines 31 and 32

```
pairs[ 25 ] = 9999.99;   // change existing value for 25
pairs[ 40 ] = 8765.43;   // insert new value for 40
```

use the subscript operator of class **map**. When the subscript is a key that is already in the **map**, the operator returns a reference to the associated value. When the subscript is a key that is not in the **map**, the operator inserts the key in the **map** and returns a reference that can be used to associate a value with that key. Line 31 replaces the value for the key **25** (previously **33.333** as specified in line 19) with a new value of **9999.99**. Line 32 inserts a new key/value **pair** (called *creating an association*) in the **map**.

```cpp
1    // Fig. 20.22: fig20_22.cpp
2    // Testing Standard Library class map
3    #include <iostream>
4
5    using std::cout;
6    using std::endl;
7
8    #include <map>
9
10   int main()
11   {
12       typedef std::map< int, double, std::less< int > > mid;
13       mid pairs;
14
15       pairs.insert( mid::value_type( 15, 2.7 ) );
16       pairs.insert( mid::value_type( 30, 111.11 ) );
17       pairs.insert( mid::value_type( 5, 1010.1 ) );
18       pairs.insert( mid::value_type( 10, 22.22 ) );
19       pairs.insert( mid::value_type( 25, 33.333 ) );
20       pairs.insert( mid::value_type( 5, 77.54 ) ); // dupe ignored
21       pairs.insert( mid::value_type( 20, 9.345 ) );
22       pairs.insert( mid::value_type( 15, 99.3 ) ); // dupe ignored
23       cout << "pairs contains:\nKey\tValue\n";
24
25       mid::const_iterator iter;
26
27       for ( iter = pairs.begin(); iter != pairs.end(); ++iter )
28           cout << iter->first << '\t'
29                << iter->second << '\n';
30
```

Fig. 20.22 Demonstrating Standard Library **map** class template (part 1 of 2).

```
31        pairs[ 25 ] = 9999.99;   // change existing value for 25
32        pairs[ 40 ] = 8765.43;   // insert new value for 40
33        cout << "\nAfter subscript operations, pairs contains:"
34             << "\nKey\tValue\n";
35
36        for ( iter = pairs.begin(); iter != pairs.end(); ++iter )
37           cout << iter->first << '\t'
38                << iter->second << '\n';
39
40        cout << endl;
41        return 0;
42    }
```

```
pairs contains:
Key     Value
5       1010.1
10      22.22
15      2.7
20      9.345
25      33.333
30      111.11

After subscript operations, pairs contains:
Key     Value
5       1010.1
10      22.22
15      2.7
20      9.345
25      9999.99
30      111.11
40      8765.43
```

Fig. 20.22 Demonstrating Standard Library **map** class template (part 2 of 2).

20.4 Container Adapters

The STL provides three so-called *container adapters*—**stack**, **queue** and **priority_queue**. Adapters are not first-class containers, because they do not provide the actual data structure implementation in which elements can be stored and because adapters do not support iterators. The benefit of an adapter class is that the programmer can choose an appropriate underlying data structure. All three adapter classes provide member functions **push** and **pop** that implement the proper method of inserting an element into each adapter data structure and the proper method of removing an element from each adapter data structure. The next several subsections provide examples of the adapter classes.

20.4.1 **stack** Adapter

Class **stack** provides functionality that enables insertions into and deletions from the underlying data structure at one end (commonly referred to as a *last-in-first-out* data structure). A **stack** can be implemented with any of the sequence containers: **vector**, **list** and **deque**. This example creates three integer stacks using each of the sequence containers of the Standard Library as the underlying data structure to represent the **stack**. By default, a **stack** is implemented with a **deque**. The **stack** operations are **push** to insert an element at the top of the **stack** (implemented by calling function **push_back** of the underlying container), **pop** to remove the top element of the **stack** (implemented by calling function **pop_back** of the underlying container), **top** to get a reference to the top element of the **stack** (implemented by calling function **back** of the underlying container), **empty** to determine if the **stack** is empty (implemented by calling function **empty** of the underlying container) and **size** to get the number of elements in the **stack** (implemented by calling function **size** of the underlying container).

Performance Tip 20.16

 Each of the common operations of a **stack** *is implemented as an* **inline** *function that calls the appropriate function of the underlying container. This avoids the overhead of a second function call.*

Performance Tip 20.17

 For the best performance, use class **deque** *or* **vector** *as the underlying container for a* **stack***.*

Figure 20.23 demonstrates the **stack** adapter class. Header file **<stack>** must be included to use class **stack**.

```
1   // Fig. 20.23: fig20_23.cpp
2   // Testing Standard Library class stack
3   #include <iostream>
4
5   using std::cout;
6   using std::endl;
7
8   #include <stack>
9   #include <vector>
10  #include <list>
11
12  template< class T >
13  void popElements( T &s );
14
15  int main()
16  {
17     std::stack< int > intDequeStack;    // deque-based stack
18     std::stack< int, std::vector< int > > intVectorStack;
19     std::stack< int, std::list< int > > intListStack;
20
21     for ( int i = 0; i < 10; ++i ) {
22        intDequeStack.push( i );
23        intVectorStack.push( i );
24        intListStack.push( i );
25     }
26
27     cout << "Popping from intDequeStack: ";
28     popElements( intDequeStack );
```

Fig. 20.23   Demonstrating Standard Library **stack** adapter class (part 1 of 2).

```
29          cout << "\nPopping from intVectorStack: ";
30          popElements( intVectorStack );
31          cout << "\nPopping from intListStack: ";
32          popElements( intListStack );
33
34          cout << endl;
35          return 0;
36      }
37
38      template< class T >
39      void popElements( T &s )
40      {
41          while ( !s.empty() ) {
42              cout << s.top() << ' ';
43              s.pop();
44          }
45      }
```

```
Popping from intDequeStack: 9 8 7 6 5 4 3 2 1 0
Popping from intVectorStack: 9 8 7 6 5 4 3 2 1 0
Popping from intListStack: 9 8 7 6 5 4 3 2 1 0
```

Fig. 20.23 Demonstrating Standard Library **stack** adapter class (part 2 of 2).

Lines 17 through 19

```
std::stack< int > intDequeStack; // default is deque-based
std::stack< int, std::vector< int > > intVectorStack;
std::stack< int, std::list< int > > intListStack;
```

instantiate three integer stacks. Line 17 specifies a **stack** of integers that uses the default **deque** container as its underlying data structure. Line 18 specifies a **stack** of integers that uses a **vector** of integers as its underlying data structure. Line 19 specifies a **stack** of integers that uses a **list** of integers as its underlying data structure.

Lines 22 through 24 each use function **push** (available in each adapter class) to place an integer on top of each **stack**.

Function **popElements** at line 38 pops the elements off each **stack**. Line 42 uses **stack** function **top** to retrieve the top element of the **stack** for output. Function **top** does not remove the top element. Line 43 uses function **pop** (available in each adapter class) to remove the top element of the **stack**. Function **pop** does not return a value.

20.4.2 **queue** Adapter

Class **queue** enables insertions at the back of the underlying data structure and deletions from the front of the underlying data structure (commonly referred to as a *first-in-first-out* data structure). A **queue** can be implemented with STL data structures **list** and **deque**. By default, a **queue** is implemented with a **deque**. The common **queue** operations are **push** to insert an element at the back of the **queue** (implemented by calling function **push_back** of the underlying container), **pop** to remove the element at the front of the **queue** (implemented by calling function **pop_front** of the underlying container),

front to get a reference to the first element in the **queue** (implemented by calling function **front** of the underlying container), **back** to get a reference to the last element in the **queue** (implemented by calling function **back** of the underlying container), **empty** to determine if the **queue** is empty (implemented by calling function **empty** of the underlying container) and **size** to get the number of elements in the **queue** (implemented by calling function **size** of the underlying container).

Performance Tip 20.18

Each of the common operations of a **queue** *is implemented as an* **inline** *function that calls the appropriate function of the underlying container. This avoids the overhead of a second function call.*

Performance Tip 20.19

For the best performance, use class **deque** *as the underlying container for a* **queue***.*

Figure 20.24 demonstrates the **queue** adapter class. Header file **<queue>** must be included to use a **queue**.

```cpp
1   // Fig. 20.24: fig20_24.cpp
2   // Testing Standard Library adapter class template queue
3   #include <iostream>
4
5   using std::cout;
6   using std::endl;
7
8   #include <queue>
9
10  int main()
11  {
12      std::queue< double > values;
13
14      values.push( 3.2 );
15      values.push( 9.8 );
16      values.push( 5.4 );
17
18      cout << "Popping from values: ";
19
20      while ( !values.empty() ) {
21         cout << values.front() << ' ';   // does not remove
22         values.pop();                     // removes element
23      }
24
25      cout << endl;
26      return 0;
27  }
```

```
Popping from values: 3.2 9.8 5.4
```

Fig. 20.24 Demonstrating Standard Library **queue** adapter class templates.

Line 12

```
std::queue< double > values;
```

instantiates a **queue** that stores **double** values. Lines 14 through 16 use function **push** to add elements to the **queue**. The **while** structure at line 20 uses function **empty** (available in all containers) to determine if the **queue** is empty.

While there are more elements in the **queue**, line 21 uses **queue** function **front** to read (but not remove) the first element in the **queue** for output. Line 22 removes the first element in the **queue** with function **pop** (available in all adapter classes).

20.4.3 `priority_queue` Adapter

Class **priority_queue** provides functionality that enables insertions in sorted order into the underlying data structure and deletions from the front of the underlying data structure. A **priority_queue** can be implemented with STL data structures **vector** and **deque**. By default, a **priority_queue** is implemented with a **vector** as the underlying data structure. When adding elements to a **priority_queue**, the elements are inserted in priority order such that the highest priority element (i.e., the largest value) will be the first element removed from the **priority_queue**. This is usually accomplished by using a sorting technique called *heapsort* that always maintains the largest value (i.e., highest priority) at the front of the data structure—such a data structure is called a *heap*. The comparison of elements is performed with comparator function object **less< T >** by default, but the programmer can supply a different comparator.

The common **priority_queue** operations are **push** to insert an element at the appropriate location based on priority order of the **priority_queue** (implemented by calling function **push_back** of the underlying container then reordering the elements using heapsort), **pop** to remove the highest priority element of the **priority_queue** (implemented by calling function **pop_back** of the underlying container after removing the top element of the heap), **top** to get a reference to the top element of the **priority_queue** (implemented by calling function **front** of the underlying container), **empty** to determine if the **priority_queue** is empty (implemented by calling function **empty** of the underlying container) and **size** to get the number of elements in the **priority_queue** (implemented by calling function **size** of the underlying container).

Performance Tip 20.20

Each of the common operations of a **priority_queue** *is implemented as an* **inline** *function that calls the appropriate function of the underlying container. This avoids the overhead of a second function call.*

Performance Tip 20.21

For the best performance, use class **vector** *as the underlying container for a* **priority_queue**.

Figure 20.25 demonstrates the **priority_queue** adapter class. Header file **<queue>** must be included to use class **priority_queue**.

```
1   // Fig. 20.25: fig20_25.cpp
2   // Testing Standard Library class priority_queue
3   #include <iostream>
4
5   using std::cout;
6   using std::endl;
7
8   #include <queue>
9
10  int main()
11  {
12     std::priority_queue< double > priorities;
13
14     priorities.push( 3.2 );
15     priorities.push( 9.8 );
16     priorities.push( 5.4 );
17
18     cout << "Popping from priorities: ";
19
20     while ( !priorities.empty() ) {
21        cout << priorities.top() << ' ';
22        priorities.pop();
23     }
24
25     cout << endl;
26     return 0;
27  }
```

```
Popping from priorities: 9.8 5.4 3.2
```

Fig. 20.25 Demonstrating Standard Library **priority_queue** adapter class.

Line 12

        std::priority_queue< double > priorities;

instantiates a **priority_queue** that stores **double** values and uses a **vector** as the underlying data structure. Lines 14 through 16 use function **push** to add elements to the **priority_queue**. The **while** structure at line 20 uses function **empty** (available in all containers) to determine if the **priority_queue** is empty. While there are more elements in the **priority_queue**, line 21 uses **priority_queue** function **top** to retrieve the highest priority element in the **priority_queue** for output. Line 22 physically removes the highest priority element in the **priority_queue** with function **pop** (available in all adapter classes).

20.5 Algorithms

Until STL, class libraries of containers and algorithms were essentially incompatible among vendors. Early container libraries generally used inheritance and polymorphism, with the associated overhead of **virtual** function calls. Early libraries had the algorithms built in to the container classes as class behaviors. STL separates the algorithms from the containers. This makes it much easier to add new algorithms. STL is implemented for efficiency. It avoids the overhead of **virtual** function calls. With STL, the elements of containers are accessed through iterators.

Software Engineering Observation 20.8

STL algorithms do not depend on the implementation details of the containers on which they operate. As long as the container's (or array's) iterators satisfy the requirements of the algorithm, STL algorithms can work on any C-style, pointer-based arrays as well as working on STL containers (and user-defined data structures).

Software Engineering Observation 20.9

Algorithms can be added easily to the STL without modifying the container classes.

20.5.1 `fill`, `fill_n`, `generate` and `generate_n`

Figure 20.26 demonstrates the **fill**, **fill_n**, **generate** and **generate_n** Standard Library functions. Functions **fill** and **fill_n** set every element in a range of container elements to a specific value. Functions **generate** and **generate_n** use a *generator function* to create values for every element in a range of container elements. The generator function takes no arguments and returns a value that can be placed in an element of the container.

```cpp
1   // Fig. 20.26: fig20_26.cpp
2   // Demonstrating fill, fill_n, generate, and generate_n
3   // Standard Library methods.
4   #include <iostream>
5
6   using std::cout;
7   using std::endl;
8
9   #include <algorithm>
10  #include <vector>
11
12  char nextLetter();
13
14  int main()
15  {
16     std::vector< char > chars( 10 );
17     std::ostream_iterator< char > output( cout, " " );
18
19     std::fill( chars.begin(), chars.end(), '5' );
20     cout << "Vector chars after filling with 5s:\n";
21     std::copy( chars.begin(), chars.end(), output );
22
23     std::fill_n( chars.begin(), 5, 'A' );
24     cout << "\nVector chars after filling five elements"
25          << " with As:\n";
26     std::copy( chars.begin(), chars.end(), output );
27
```

Fig. 20.26 Demonstrating Standard Library functions **fill**, **fill_n**, **generate** and **generate_n** (part 1 of 2).

```
28        std::generate( chars.begin(), chars.end(), nextLetter );
29        cout << "\nVector chars after generating letters A-J:\n";
30        std::copy( chars.begin(), chars.end(), output );
31
32        std::generate_n( chars.begin(), 5, nextLetter );
33        cout << "\nVector chars after generating K-O for the"
34              << " first five elements:\n";
35        std::copy( chars.begin(), chars.end(), output );
36
37        cout << endl;
38        return 0;
39   }
40
41   char nextLetter()
42   {
43        static char letter = 'A';
44        return letter++;
45   }
```

```
Vector chars after filling with 5s:
5 5 5 5 5 5 5 5 5

Vector chars after filling five elements with As:
A A A A A 5 5 5 5

Vector chars after generating letters A-J:
A B C D E F G H I J

Vector chars after generating K-O for the first five elements:
K L M N O F G H I J
```

Fig. 20.26 Demonstrating Standard Library functions **fill**, **fill_n**, **generate** and **generate_n** (part 2 of 2).

Line 19

```
std::fill( chars.begin(), chars.end(), '5' );
```

uses function **fill** to place the character **'5'** in every element of **vector chars** from **chars.begin()** up to, but not including, **chars.end()**. Note that the iterators supplied as the first and second argument must be at least forward iterators (i.e., they can be used for both input from a container and output to a container in the forward direction).

Line 23

```
std::fill_n( chars.begin(), 5, 'A' );
```

uses function **fill_n** to place the character **'A'** in the first five elements of **vector chars**. The iterator supplied as the first argument must be at least an output iterator (i.e., it can be used for output to a container in the forward direction). The second argument specifies the number of elements to fill. The third argument specifies the value to place in each element.

Line 28

```
std::generate( chars.begin(), chars.end(), nextLetter );
```

uses function **generate** to place the result of a call to generator function **nextLetter** in every element of **vector chars** from **chars.begin()** up to, but not including, **chars.end()**. The iterators supplied as the first and second arguments must be at least forward iterators. Function **nextLetter** (defined at line 41) begins with the character **'A'** maintained in a **static** local variable. The statement at line 44

```
return letter++;
```

increments the value of **letter** and returns the old value of **letter** each time **next-Letter** is called, then increments the value of **letter**.

Line 32

```
std::generate_n( chars.begin(), 5, nextLetter );
```

uses function **generate_n** to place the result of a call to generator function **nextLetter** in five elements of **vector chars** starting from **chars.begin()**. The iterator supplied as the first argument must be at least an output iterator.

20.5.2 equal, mismatch and lexicographical_compare

Figure 20.27 demonstrates comparing sequences of values for equality with Standard Library functions **equal**, **mismatch** and **lexicographical_compare**.

```
1    // Fig. 20.27: fig20_27.cpp
2    // Demonstrates standard library functions equal,
3    // mismatch, lexicographical_compare.
4    #include <iostream>
5
6    using std::cout;
7    using std::endl;
8
9    #include <algorithm>
10   #include <vector>
11
12   int main()
13   {
14      const int SIZE = 10;
15      int a1[ SIZE ] = { 1, 2, 3, 4, 5, 6, 7, 8, 9, 10 };
16      int a2[ SIZE ] = { 1, 2, 3, 4, 1000, 6, 7, 8, 9, 10 };
17      std::vector< int > v1( a1, a1 + SIZE ),
18                         v2( a1, a1 + SIZE ),
19                         v3( a2, a2 + SIZE );
20      std::ostream_iterator< int > output( cout, " " );
21
```

Fig. 20.27   Demonstrating Standard Library functions **equal**, **mismatch** and **lexicographical_compare** (part 1 of 2).

```
22        cout << "Vector v1 contains: ";
23        std::copy( v1.begin(), v1.end(), output );
24        cout << "\nVector v2 contains: ";
25        std::copy( v2.begin(), v2.end(), output );
26        cout << "\nVector v3 contains: ";
27        std::copy( v3.begin(), v3.end(), output );
28
29        bool result =
30           std::equal( v1.begin(), v1.end(), v2.begin() );
31        cout << "\n\nVector v1 " << ( result ? "is" : "is not" )
32           << " equal to vector v2.\n";
33
34        result = std::equal( v1.begin(), v1.end(), v3.begin() );
35        cout << "Vector v1 " << ( result ? "is" : "is not" )
36           << " equal to vector v3.\n";
37
38   `    std::pair< std::vector< int >::iterator,
39                   std::vector< int >::iterator > location;
40        location =
41           std::mismatch( v1.begin(), v1.end(), v3.begin() );
42        cout << "\nThere is a mismatch between v1 and v3 at "
43           << "location " << ( location.first - v1.begin() )
44           << "\nwhere v1 contains " << *location.first
45           << " and v3 contains " << *location.second
46           << "\n\n";
47
48        char c1[ SIZE ] = "HELLO", c2[ SIZE ] = "BYE BYE";
49
50        result = std::lexicographical_compare(
51                 c1, c1 + SIZE, c2, c2 + SIZE );
52        cout << c1
53           << ( result ? " is less than " :
54              " is greater than or equal to " )
55           << c2 << endl;
56
57        return 0;
58   }
```

```
Vector v1 contains: 1 2 3 4 5 6 7 8 9 10
Vector v2 contains: 1 2 3 4 5 6 7 8 9 10
Vector v3 contains: 1 2 3 4 1000 6 7 8 9 10

Vector v1 is equal to vector v2.
Vector v1 is not equal to vector v3.

There is a mismatch between v1 and v3 at location 4
where v1 contains 5 and v3 contains 1000

HELLO is greater than or equal to BYE BYE
```

Fig. 20.27 Demonstrating Standard Library functions **equal**, **mismatch** and **lexicographical_compare** (part 2 of 2).

Lines 29 and 30

```
bool result =
    std::equal( v1.begin(), v1.end(), v2.begin() );
```

uses function **equal** to compare two sequences of values for equality. Each sequence need not necessarily contain the same number of elements—**equal** returns **false** if the sequences are not the same length. Function **operator==** performs the comparison of the elements. In this example, the elements in **vector v1** from **v1.begin()** up to, but not including, **v1.end()** are compared to the elements in **vector v2** starting from **v2.begin()** (in this example, **v1** and **v2** are equal). The three iterator arguments must be at least input iterators (i.e., they can be used for input from a sequence in the forward direction). Line 34 uses function **equal** to compare **vector**s **v1** and **v3** which are not equal.

There is another version of function **equal** that takes a binary predicate function as a fourth parameter. The binary predicate function receives the two elements being compared and returns a **bool** value indicating whether or not the elements are equal. This can be useful in sequences that store objects or pointers to values rather than actual values, because you can define one or more comparisons. For example, you can compare **Employee** objects for age, social security number or location rather than comparing entire objects. You can compare what pointers refer to rather than comparing the pointer contents (i.e., the addresses stored in the pointers).

Lines 38 through 41

```
std::pair< std::vector< int >::iterator,
           std::vector< int >::iterator > location;
location =
    std::mismatch( v1.begin(), v1.end(), v3.begin() );
```

begin by instantiating a **pair** of iterators called **location** for a **vector** of integers. This object stores the result of the call to **mismatch**. Function **mismatch** compares two sequences of values and returns a **pair** of iterators indicating the location in each sequence of the mismatched elements. If all the elements match, the two iterators in the **pair** are equal to the last iterator for each sequence. The three iterator arguments must be at least input iterators. To determine the actual location of the mismatch in the **vector**s in this example, the expression at line 43 **location.first – v1.begin()** is used. The result of this calculation is the number of elements between the iterators (this is analogous to pointer arithmetic that we studied in Chapter 5). This corresponds to the element number in this example, because the comparison is performed from the beginning of each **vector**.

As with function **equal**, there is another version of function **mismatch** that takes a binary predicate function as a fourth parameter.

Lines 50 and 51

```
result = std::lexicographical_compare(
             c1, c1 + SIZE, c2, c2 + SIZE );
```

use function **lexicographical_compare** to compare the contents of two character arrays. This function's four iterator arguments must be at least input iterators. As you know, pointers into arrays are random-access iterators. The first two iterator arguments specify the range of locations in the first sequence. The last two iterator arguments specify the range of locations in the second sequence. While iterating through the sequences, if the element in the first sequence is less than the corresponding element in the second sequence, the function returns **true**. If the element in the first sequence is greater than or equal to the element in the second sequence, the function returns **false**. This function can be used to arrange sequences lexicographically. Typically such sequences contain strings.

20.5.3 `remove`, `remove_if`, `remove_copy` and `remove_copy_if`

Figure 20.28 demonstrates removing values from a sequence using the Standard Library functions **remove**, **remove_if**, **remove_copy** and **remove_copy_if**.

```cpp
1  // Fig. 20.28: fig20_28.cpp
2  // Demonstrates Standard Library functions remove, remove_if
3  // remove_copy and remove_copy_if
4  #include <iostream>
5
6  using std::cout;
7  using std::endl;
8
9  #include <algorithm>
10 #include <vector>
11
12 bool greater9( int );
13
14 int main()
15 {
16    const int SIZE = 10;
17    int a[ SIZE ] = { 10, 2, 10, 4, 16, 6, 14, 8, 12, 10 };
18    std::ostream_iterator< int > output( cout, " " );
19
20    // Remove 10 from v
21    std::vector< int > v( a, a + SIZE );
22    std::vector< int >::iterator newLastElement;
23    cout << "Vector v before removing all 10s:\n";
24    std::copy( v.begin(), v.end(), output );
25    newLastElement = std::remove( v.begin(), v.end(), 10 );
26    cout << "\nVector v after removing all 10s:\n";
27    std::copy( v.begin(), newLastElement, output );
28
29    // Copy from v2 to c, removing 10s
30    std::vector< int > v2( a, a + SIZE );
31    std::vector< int > c( SIZE, 0 );
32    cout << "\n\nVector v2 before removing all 10s "
33         << "and copying:\n";
34    std::copy( v2.begin(), v2.end(), output );
35    std::remove_copy( v2.begin(), v2.end(), c.begin(), 10 );
36    cout << "\nVector c after removing all 10s from v2:\n";
37    std::copy( c.begin(), c.end(), output );
38
```

Fig. 20.28 Demonstrating Standard Library functions **remove**, **remove_if**, **remove_copy** and **remove_copy_if** (part 1 of 3).

```
39        // Remove elements greater than 9 from v3
40        std::vector< int > v3( a, a + SIZE );
41        cout << "\n\nVector v3 before removing all elements"
42             << "\ngreater than 9:\n";
43        std::copy( v3.begin(), v3.end(), output );
44        newLastElement =
45           std::remove_if( v3.begin(), v3.end(), greater9 );
46        cout << "\nVector v3 after removing all elements"
47             << "\ngreater than 9:\n";
48        std::copy( v3.begin(), newLastElement, output );
49
50        // Copy elements from v4 to c2,
51        // removing elements greater than 9
52        std::vector< int > v4( a, a + SIZE );
53        std::vector< int > c2( SIZE, 0 );
54        cout << "\n\nVector v4 before removing all elements"
55             << "\ngreater than 9 and copying:\n";
56        std::copy( v4.begin(), v4.end(), output );
57        std::remove_copy_if( v4.begin(), v4.end(),
58                             c2.begin(), greater9 );
59        cout << "\nVector c2 after removing all elements"
60             << "\ngreater than 9 from v4:\n";
61        std::copy( c2.begin(), c2.end(), output );
62
63        cout << endl;
64        return 0;
65     }
66
67     bool greater9( int x )
68     {
69        return x > 9;
70     }
```

```
Vector v before removing all 10s:
10 2 10 4 16 6 14 8 12 10
Vector v after removing all 10s:
2 4 16 6 14 8 12

Vector v2 before removing all 10s and copying:
10 2 10 4 16 6 14 8 12 10
Vector c after removing all 10s from v2:
2 4 16 6 14 8 12 0 0 0

Vector v3 before removing all elements
greater than 9:
10 2 10 4 16 6 14 8 12 10
Vector v3 after removing all elements
greater than 9:
2 4 6 8
```

(continued at top of next page)

Fig. 20.28   Demonstrating Standard Library functions **remove**, **remove_if**, **remove_copy** and **remove_copy_if** (part 2 of 3).

(continued from bottom of previous page)

```
Vector v4 before removing all elements
greater than 9 and copying:
10 2 10 4 16 6 14 8 12 10
Vector c2 after removing all elements
greater than 9 from v4:
2 4 6 8 0 0 0 0 0 0
```

Fig. 20.28 Demonstrating Standard Library functions **remove**, **remove_if**, **remove_copy** and **remove_copy_if** (part 3 of 3).

Line 25

```
newLastElement = std::remove( v.begin(), v.end(), 10 );
```

uses function **remove** to eliminate all elements with the value **10** in the range **v.begin()** up to, but not including, **v.end()** from the **vector v**. The first two iterator arguments must be forward iterators so the algorithm can modify the elements in the sequence. This function does not modify the number of elements in the **vector** or destroy the eliminated elements, but it does move all elements that are not eliminated toward the beginning of the **vector**. The function returns an iterator positioned after the last **vector** element that was not deleted. Elements from the iterator position to the end of the **vector** have undefined values (in this example, each "undefined" position has value 0).

Line 35

```
std::remove_copy( v2.begin(), v2.end(), c.begin(), 10 );
```

uses function **remove_copy** to copy all elements that do not have the value **10** in the range **v2.begin()** up to, but not including, **v2.end()** from the **vector v2**. The elements are placed in **vector c** starting at position **c.begin()**. The iterators supplied as the first two arguments must be input iterators. The iterator supplied as the third argument must be an output iterator so the element being copied can be inserted into the copy location. This function returns an iterator positioned after the last element copied into **vector c**. Note on line 31 the use of the vector constructor that receives the number of elements in the **vector** and the initial values of those elements.

Lines 44 and 45

```
newLastElement =
    std::remove_if( v3.begin(), v3.end(), greater9 );
```

uses function **remove_if** to delete all elements in the range **v3.begin()** up to, but not including, **v3.end()** from the **vector v3** for which our user-defined unary predicate function **greater9** returns **true**. Function **greater9** is defined at line 67 to return **true** if the value passed to it is greater than 9, and to return **false** otherwise. The iterators supplied as the first two arguments must be forward iterators so the algorithm can modify the elements in the sequence. This function does not modify the number of elements in the **vector**, but it does move to the beginning of the **vector** all elements that are not eliminated. This function returns an iterator positioned after the last element in the **vector** that was not deleted. All elements from the iterator position to the end of the **vector** have undefined values.

Lines 57 and 58

```
std::remove_copy_if( v4.begin(), v4.end(),
                     c2.begin(), greater9 );
```

uses function **remove_copy_if** to copy all elements in the range **v4.begin()** up to, but not including, **v4.end()** from the **vector v4** for which the unary predicate function **greater9** returns **true**. The elements are placed in **vector c2** starting at position **c2.begin()**. The iterators supplied as the first two arguments must be input iterators. The iterator supplied as the third argument must be an output iterator so the element being copied can be inserted into the copy location. This function returns an iterator positioned after the last element copied into **vector c2**.

20.5.4 `replace`, `replace_if`, `replace_copy` and `replace_copy_if`

Figure 20.29 demonstrates replacing values from a sequence using the Standard Library functions **replace**, **replace_if**, **replace_copy** and **replace_copy_if**.

```cpp
1   // Fig. 20.29: fig20_29.cpp
2   // Demonstrates Standard Library functions replace, replace_if
3   // replace_copy and replace_copy_if
4   #include <iostream>
5
6   using std::cout;
7   using std::endl;
8
9   #include <algorithm>
10  #include <vector>
11
12  bool greater9( int );
13
14  int main()
15  {
16     const int SIZE = 10;
17     int a[ SIZE ] = { 10, 2, 10, 4, 16, 6, 14, 8, 12, 10 };
18     std::ostream_iterator< int > output( cout, " " );
19
20     // Replace 10s in v1 with 100
21     std::vector< int > v1( a, a + SIZE );
22     cout << "Vector v1 before replacing all 10s:\n";
23     std::copy( v1.begin(), v1.end(), output );
24     std::replace( v1.begin(), v1.end(), 10, 100 );
25     cout << "\nVector v1 after replacing all 10s with 100s:\n";
26     std::copy( v1.begin(), v1.end(), output );
27
```

Fig. 20.29 Demonstrating Standard Library functions **replace**, **replace_if**, **replace_copy** and **replace_copy_if** (part 1 of 3).

```
28      // copy from v2 to c1, replacing 10s with 100s
29      std::vector< int > v2( a, a + SIZE );
30      std::vector< int > c1( SIZE );
31      cout << "\n\nVector v2 before replacing all 10s "
32          << "and copying:\n";
33      std::copy( v2.begin(), v2.end(), output );
34      std::replace_copy( v2.begin(), v2.end(),
35                         c1.begin(), 10, 100 );
36      cout << "\nVector c1 after replacing all 10s in v2:\n";
37      std::copy( c1.begin(), c1.end(), output );
38
39      // Replace values greater than 9 in v3 with 100
40      std::vector< int > v3( a, a + SIZE );
41      cout << "\n\nVector v3 before replacing values greater"
42          << " than 9:\n";
43      std::copy( v3.begin(), v3.end(), output );
44      std::replace_if( v3.begin(), v3.end(), greater9, 100 );
45      cout << "\nVector v3 after replacing all values greater"
46          << "\nthan 9 with 100s:\n";
47      std::copy( v3.begin(), v3.end(), output );
48
49      // Copy v4 to c2, replacing elements greater than 9 with 100
50      std::vector< int > v4( a, a + SIZE );
51      std::vector< int > c2( SIZE );
52      cout << "\n\nVector v4 before replacing all values greater"
53          << "\nthan 9 and copying:\n";
54      std::copy( v4.begin(), v4.end(), output );
55      std::replace_copy_if( v4.begin(), v4.end(), c2.begin(),
56                            greater9, 100 );
57      cout << "\nVector c2 after replacing all values greater"
58          << "\nthan 9 in v4:\n";
59      std::copy( c2.begin(), c2.end(), output );
60
61      cout << endl;
62      return 0;
63   }
64
65   bool greater9( int x )
66   {
67      return x > 9;
68   }
```

```
Vector v1 before replacing all 10s:
10 2 10 4 16 6 14 8 12 10
Vector v1 after replacing all 10s with 100s:
100 2 100 4 16 6 14 8 12 100

Vector v2 before replacing all 10s and copying:
10 2 10 4 16 6 14 8 12 10
Vector c1 after replacing all 10s in v2:
100 2 100 4 16 6 14 8 12 100
```

(continued at top of next page)

Fig. 20.29 Demonstrating Standard Library functions **replace**, **replace_if**, **replace_copy** and **replace_copy_if** (part 2 of 3).

```
                                         (continued from bottom of previous page)
Vector v3 before replacing values greater than 9:
10 2 10 4 16 6 14 8 12 10
Vector v3 after replacing all values greater
than 9 with 100s:
100 2 100 4 100 6 100 8 100 100

Vector v4 before replacing all values greater
than 9 and copying:
10 2 10 4 16 6 14 8 12 10
Vector c2 after replacing all values greater
than 9 in v4:
100 2 100 4 100 6 100 8 100 100
```

Fig. 20.29   Demonstrating Standard Library functions `replace`, `replace_if`, `replace_copy` and `replace_copy_if` (part 3 of 3).

Line 24

```
std::replace( v1.begin(), v1.end(), 10, 100 );
```

uses function **replace** to replace all elements with the value **10** in the range **v1.begin()** up to, but not including, **v1.end()** from the **vector v1** with the new value **100**. The iterators supplied as the first two arguments must be forward iterators so the algorithm can modify the elements in the sequence.

Lines 34 and 35

```
std::replace_copy( v2.begin(), v2.end(),
                   c1.begin(), 10, 100 );
```

uses function **replace_copy** to copy all elements in the range **v2.begin()** up to, but not including, **v2.end()** from the **vector v2** replacing all elements with the value **10** with the new value **100**. The elements are copied into **vector c1** starting at position **c1.begin()**. The iterators supplied as the first two arguments must be input iterators. The iterator supplied as the third argument must be an output iterator so the element being copied can be inserted into the copy location. This function returns an iterator positioned after the last element copied into **vector c2**.

Line 44

```
std::replace_if( v3.begin(), v3.end(), greater9, 100 );
```

uses function **replace_if** to replace all elements in the range **v3.begin()** up to, but not including, **v3.end()** from the **vector v3** for which the unary predicate function **greater9** returns **true**. Function **greater9** is defined at line 65 to return **true** if the value passed to it is greater than 9 and **false** otherwise. The value **100** replaces each value greater than 9. The iterators supplied as the first two arguments must be forward iterators so the algorithm can modify the elements in the sequence.

Lines 55 and 56

```
std::replace_copy_if( v4.begin(), v4.end(), c2.begin(),
                      greater9, 100 );
```

uses function **replace_copy_if** to copy all elements in the range **v4.begin()** up to, but not including, **v4.end()** from the **vector v4**. Elements for which the unary predicate function **greater9** returns **true** are replaced with the value **100**. The elements are placed in **vector c2** starting at position **c2.begin()**. The iterators supplied as the first two arguments must be input iterators. The iterator supplied as the third argument must be an output iterator so the element being copied can be inserted into the copy location. This function returns an iterator positioned after the last element copied into **vector c2**.

20.5.5 Mathematical Algorithms

Figure 20.30 demonstrates some common mathematical algorithms from the STL, including **random_shuffle**, **count**, **count_if**, **min_element**, **max_element**, **accumulate**, **for_each** and **transform**.

```cpp
1   // Fig. 20.30: fig20_30.cpp
2   // Examples of mathematical algorithms in the Standard Library.
3   #include <iostream>
4
5   using std::cout;
6   using std::endl;
7
8   #include <algorithm>
9   #include <numeric>        // accumulate is defined here
10  #include <vector>
11
12  bool greater9( int );
13  void outputSquare( int );
14  int calculateCube( int );
15
16  int main()
17  {
18      const int SIZE = 10;
19      int a1[] = { 1, 2, 3, 4, 5, 6, 7, 8, 9, 10 };
20      std::vector< int > v( a1, a1 + SIZE );
21      std::ostream_iterator< int > output( cout, " " );
22
23      cout << "Vector v before random_shuffle: ";
24      std::copy( v.begin(), v.end(), output );
25      std::random_shuffle( v.begin(), v.end() );
26      cout << "\nVector v after random_shuffle: ";
27      std::copy( v.begin(), v.end(), output );
28
29      int a2[] = { 100, 2, 8, 1, 50, 3, 8, 8, 9, 10 };
30      std::vector< int > v2( a2, a2 + SIZE );
31      cout << "\n\nVector v2 contains: ";
32      std::copy( v2.begin(), v2.end(), output );
33      int result = std::count( v2.begin(), v2.end(), 8 );
34      std::cout << "\nNumber of elements matching 8: " << result;
```

Fig. 20.30 Demonstrating some mathematical algorithms of the Standard Library (part 1 of 2).

```
35
36        result = std::count_if( v2.begin(), v2.end(), greater9 );
37        cout << "\nNumber of elements greater than 9: " << result;
38
39        cout << "\n\nMinimum element in Vector v2 is: "
40             << *( std::min_element( v2.begin(), v2.end() ) );
41
42        cout << "\nMaximum element in Vector v2 is: "
43             << *( std::max_element( v2.begin(), v2.end() ) );
44
45        cout << "\n\nThe total of the elements in Vector v is: "
46             << std::accumulate( v.begin(), v.end(), 0 );
47
48        cout << "\n\nThe square of every integer in Vector v is:\n";
49        std::for_each( v.begin(), v.end(), outputSquare );
50
51        std::vector< int > cubes( SIZE );
52        std::transform( v.begin(), v.end(), cubes.begin(),
53                      calculateCube );
54        cout << "\n\nThe cube of every integer in Vector v is:\n";
55        std::copy( cubes.begin(), cubes.end(), output );
56
57        cout << endl;
58        return 0;
59    }
60
61    bool greater9( int value ) { return value > 9; }
62
63    void outputSquare( int value ) { cout << value * value << ' '; }
64
65    int calculateCube( int value ) { return value * value * value; }
```

```
Vector v before random_shuffle: 1 2 3 4 5 6 7 8 9 10
Vector v after random_shuffle: 5 4 1 3 7 8 9 10 6 2

Vector v2 contains: 100 2 8 1 50 3 8 8 9 10
Number of elements matching 8: 3
Number of elements greater than 9: 3

Minimum element in Vector v2 is: 1
Maximum element in Vector v2 is: 100

The total of the elements in Vector v is: 55

The square of every integer in Vector v is:
25 16 1 9 49 64 81 100 36 4

The cube of every integer in Vector v is:
125 64 1 27 343 512 729 1000 216 8
```

Fig. 20.30 Demonstrating some mathematical algorithms of the Standard Library (part 2 of 2).

Line 25

```
std::random_shuffle( v.begin(), v.end() );
```

uses function **random_shuffle** to randomly order the elements in the range **v.begin()** up to, but not including, **v.end()** in **vector v**. This function takes two random-access iterator arguments.

Line 33

```
int result = std::count( v2.begin(), v2.end(), 8 );
```

uses function **count** to count the elements with the value **8** in the range **v2.begin()** up to, but not including, **v2.end()** in **vector v2**. This function requires its two iterator arguments to be at least input iterators.

Line 36

```
result = std::count_if( v2.begin(), v2.end(), greater9 );
```

uses function **count_if** to count elements in the range **v2.begin()** up to, but not including, **v2.end()** in **vector v2** for which the predicate function **greater9** returns **true**. Function **count_if** requires its two iterator arguments to be at least input iterators.

Lines 39 and 40

```
cout << "\n\nMinimum element in Vector v2 is: "
     << *( std::min_element( v2.begin(), v2.end() ) );
```

uses function **min_element** to locate the smallest element in the range **v2.begin()** up to, but not including, **v2.end()** in **vector v2**. The function returns an input iterator located at the smallest element or, if the range is empty, returns the iterator itself. The function requires its two iterator arguments to be at least input iterators. A second version of this function takes as its third argument a binary function that compares the elements in the sequence. The binary function takes two arguments and returns a **bool** value.

Good Programming Practice 20.2

It is a good practice to check that the range specified in a call to **min_element** *is not empty and to check that the return value is not the "past the end" iterator.*

Lines 42 and 43

```
cout << "\nMaximum element in Vector v2 is: "
     << *( std::max_element( v2.begin(), v2.end() ) );
```

use function **max_element** to locate the largest element in the range **v2.begin()** up to, but not including, **v2.end()** in **vector v2**. The function returns an input iterator located at the largest element. The function requires its two iterator arguments to be at least input iterators. A second version of this function takes as its third argument a binary predicate function that compares the elements in the sequence. The binary function takes two arguments and returns a **bool** value.

Lines 45 and 46

```
cout << "\n\nThe total of the elements in Vector v is: "
     << std::accumulate( v.begin(), v.end(), 0 );
```

use function **accumulate** (the template of which is in header file **<numeric>**) to sum the values in the range **v.begin()** up to, but not including, **v.end()** in **vector v**. The function's two iterator arguments must be at least input iterators. A second version of this function takes as its third argument a general function that determines how elements are accumulated. The general function must take two arguments and return a result. The first argument to this function is the current value of the accumulation. The second argument is the value of the current element in the sequence being accumulated. For example, to accumulate the sum of the squares of every element, you could use the function

```
int sumOfSquares( int accumulator, int currentValue )
{
   return accumulator + currentValue * currentValue;
}
```

that receives the previous total as its first argument (**accumulator**) and the new value to square and add to the total as its second argument (**currentValue**). When the function is called, it squares **currentValue**, adds **currentValue** to **accumulator** and returns the new total.

Line 49

```
std::for_each( v.begin(), v.end(), outputSquare );
```

uses function **for_each** to apply a general function to every element in the range **v.begin()** up to, but not including, **v.end()** in **vector v**. The general function should take the current element as an argument and should not modify that element. Function **for_each** requires its two iterator arguments to be at least input iterators.

Lines 52 and 53

```
std::transform( v.begin(), v.end(), cubes.begin(),
               calculateCube );
```

use function **transform** to apply a general function to every element in the range **v.begin()** up to, but not including, **v.end()** in **vector v**. The general function (the fourth argument) should take the current element as an argument, should not modify the element and should return the **transform**ed value. Function **transform** requires its first two iterator arguments to be at least input iterators and its third argument to be at least an output iterator. The third argument specifies where the **transform**ed values should be placed. Note that the third argument can equal the first.

20.5.6 Basic Searching and Sorting Algorithms

Figure 20.31 demonstrates some basic searching and sorting capabilities of the Standard Library, including **find**, **find_if**, **sort** and **binary_search**.

Line 24

```
location = std::find( v.begin(), v.end(), 16 );
```

uses function **find** to locate the value **16** in the range **v.begin()** up to, but not including, **v.end()** in **vector v**. The function requires its two iterator arguments to be at least input iterators. The function returns an input iterator that either is positioned at the first element containing the value or indicates the end of the sequence.

```cpp
1   // Fig. 20.31: fig20_31.cpp
2   // Demonstrates search and sort capabilities.
3   #include <iostream>
4
5   using std::cout;
6   using std::endl;
7
8   #include <algorithm>
9   #include <vector>
10
11  bool greater10( int value );
12
13  int main()
14  {
15     const int SIZE = 10;
16     int a[ SIZE ] = { 10, 2, 17, 5, 16, 8, 13, 11, 20, 7 };
17     std::vector< int > v( a, a + SIZE );
18     std::ostream_iterator< int > output( cout, " " );
19
20     cout << "Vector v contains: ";
21     std::copy( v.begin(), v.end(), output );
22
23     std::vector< int >::iterator location;
24     location = std::find( v.begin(), v.end(), 16 );
25
26     if ( location != v.end() )
27        cout << "\n\nFound 16 at location "
28             << ( location - v.begin() );
29     else
30        cout << "\n\n16 not found";
31
32     location = std::find( v.begin(), v.end(), 100 );
33
34     if ( location != v.end() )
35        cout << "\nFound 100 at location "
36             << ( location - v.begin() );
37     else
38        cout << "\n100 not found";
39
40     location = std::find_if( v.begin(), v.end(), greater10 );
41
42     if ( location != v.end() )
43        cout << "\n\nThe first value greater than 10 is "
44             << *location << "\nfound at location "
45             << ( location - v.begin() );
46     else
47        cout << "\n\nNo values greater than 10 were found";
48
49     std::sort( v.begin(), v.end() );
50     cout << "\n\nVector v after sort: ";
51     std::copy( v.begin(), v.end(), output );
52
```

Fig. 20.31 Basic searching and sorting algorithms of the Standard Library (part 1 of 2).

```
53      if ( std::binary_search( v.begin(), v.end(), 13 ) )
54         cout << "\n\n13 was found in v";
55      else
56         cout << "\n\n13 was not found in v";
57
58      if ( std::binary_search( v.begin(), v.end(), 100 ) )
59         cout << "\n100 was found in v";
60      else
61         cout << "\n100 was not found in v";
62
63      cout << endl;
64      return 0;
65   }
66
67   bool greater10( int value ) { return value > 10; }
```

```
Vector v contains: 10 2 17 5 16 8 13 11 20 7

Found 16 at location 4
100 not found

The first value greater than 10 is 17
found at location 2

Vector v after sort: 2 5 7 8 10 11 13 16 17 20

13 was found in v
100 was not found in v
```

Fig. 20.31 Basic searching and sorting algorithms of the Standard Library (part 2 of 2).

Line 40

```
location = std::find_if( v.begin(), v.end(), greater10 );
```

uses function **find_if** to locate the first value in the range **v.begin()** up to, but not
including, **v.end()** in **vector v** for which the unary predicate function **greater10**
returns **true**. Function **greater10** is defined at line 67 to take an integer and return a
bool value indicating if the integer argument is greater than 10. Function **find_if** requires its two iterator arguments to be at least input iterators. The function returns an input
iterator that either is positioned at the first element containing a value for which the predicate function returns **true** or indicates the end of the sequence.

Line 49

```
std::sort( v.begin(), v.end() );
```

uses function **sort** to arrange the elements in the range **v.begin()** up to, but not including, **v.end()** in **vector v** in ascending order. The function requires its two iterator arguments to be random-access iterators. A second version of this function takes a third
argument that is a binary predicate function taking two arguments that are values in the sequence and returning a **bool** indicating the sorting order—if the return value is **true**, the
two elements being compared are in sorted order.

Common Programming Error 20.5

Attempting to **sort** *a container by using an iterator other than a random-access iterator is a syntax error. Function* **sort** *requires a random-access iterator.*

Line 53

```
if ( std::binary_search( v.begin(), v.end(), 13 ) )
```

uses function **binary_search** to determine if the value 13 is in the range **v.begin()** up to, but not including, **v.end()** in **vector v**. The sequence of values must be sorted in ascending order first. Function **binary_search** requires its two iterator arguments to be at least forward iterators. The function returns a **bool** indicating whether or not the value was found in the sequence. A second version of this function takes a fourth argument that is a binary predicate function taking two arguments that are values in the sequence and returning a **bool**. The predicate function returns **true** if the two elements being compared are in sorted order.

20.5.7 swap, iter_swap and swap_ranges

Figure 20.32 demonstrates functions **swap**, **iter_swap** and **swap_ranges** for swapping elements.

```cpp
1   // Fig. 20.32: fig20_32.cpp
2   // Demonstrates iter_swap, swap and swap_ranges.
3   #include <iostream>
4
5   using std::cout;
6   using std::endl;
7
8   #include <algorithm>
9
10  int main()
11  {
12     const int SIZE = 10;
13     int a[ SIZE ] = { 1, 2, 3, 4, 5, 6, 7, 8, 9, 10 };
14     std::ostream_iterator< int > output( cout, " " );
15
16     cout << "Array a contains:\n";
17     std::copy( a, a + SIZE, output );
18
19     std::swap( a[ 0 ], a[ 1 ] );
20     cout << "\nArray a after swapping a[0] and a[1] "
21        << "using swap:\n";
22     std::copy( a, a + SIZE, output );
23
24     std::iter_swap( &a[ 0 ], &a[ 1 ] );
25     cout << "\nArray a after swapping a[0] and a[1] "
26        << "using iter_swap:\n";
27     std::copy( a, a + SIZE, output );
28
```

Fig. 20.32 Demonstrating **swap**, **iter_swap** and **swap_ranges** (part 1 of 2).

```
29          std::swap_ranges( a, a + 5, a + 5 );
30          cout << "\nArray a after swapping the first five elements\n"
31              << "with the last five elements:\n";
32          std::copy( a, a + SIZE, output );
33
34          cout << endl;
35          return 0;
36      }
```

```
Array a contains:
1 2 3 4 5 6 7 8 9 10
Array a after swapping a[0] and a[1] using swap:
2 1 3 4 5 6 7 8 9 10
Array a after swapping a[0] and a[1] using iter_swap:
1 2 3 4 5 6 7 8 9 10
Array a after swapping the first five elements
with the last five elements:
6 7 8 9 10 1 2 3 4 5
```

Fig. 20.32 Demonstrating **swap**, **iter_swap** and **swap_ranges** (part 2 of 2).

Line 19

```
std::swap( a[ 0 ], a[ 1 ] );
```

uses function **swap** to exchange two values. In this example, the first and second elements of array **a** are exchanged. The function takes as arguments references to the two values being exchanged.

Line 24

```
std::iter_swap( &a[ 0 ], &a[ 1 ] );
```

uses function **iter_swap** to exchange the two elements. The function takes two forward iterator arguments (in this case, pointers to elements of an array) and exchanges the values in the elements to which the iterators refer.

Line 29

```
std::swap_ranges( a, a + 5, a + 5 );
```

uses function **swap_ranges** to exchange the elements in the range **a** up to, but not including, **a + 5** with the elements beginning at position **a + 5**. The function requires three forward iterator arguments. The first two arguments specify the range of elements in the first sequence that will be exchanged with the elements in the second sequence starting from the iterator in the third argument. In this example, the two sequences of values are in the same array, but the sequences can be from different arrays or containers.

20.5.8 **copy_backward**, **merge**, **unique** and **reverse**

Figure 20.33 demonstrates Standard Library functions **copy_backward**, **merge**, **unique** and **reverse**.

```cpp
1   // Fig. 20.33: fig20_33.cpp
2   // Demonstrates miscellaneous functions: copy_backward, merge,
3   // unique and reverse.
4   #include <iostream>
5
6   using std::cout;
7   using std::endl;
8
9   #include <algorithm>
10  #include <vector>
11
12  int main()
13  {
14     const int SIZE = 5;
15     int a1[ SIZE ] = { 1, 3, 5, 7, 9 };
16     int a2[ SIZE ] = { 2, 4, 5, 7, 9 };
17     std::vector< int > v1( a1, a1 + SIZE );
18     std::vector< int > v2( a2, a2 + SIZE );
19
20     std::ostream_iterator< int > output( cout, " " );
21
22     cout << "Vector v1 contains: ";
23     std::copy( v1.begin(), v1.end(), output );
24     cout << "\nVector v2 contains: ";
25     std::copy( v2.begin(), v2.end(), output );
26
27     std::vector< int > results( v1.size() );
28     std::copy_backward( v1.begin(), v1.end(), results.end() );
29     cout << "\n\nAfter copy_backward, results contains: ";
30     std::copy( results.begin(), results.end(), output );
31
32     std::vector< int > results2( v1.size() + v2.size() );
33     std::merge( v1.begin(), v1.end(), v2.begin(), v2.end(),
34                 results2.begin() );
35     cout << "\n\nAfter merge of v1 and v2 results2 contains:\n";
36     std::copy( results2.begin(), results2.end(), output );
37
38     std::vector< int >::iterator endLocation;
39     endLocation =
40        std::unique( results2.begin(), results2.end() );
41     cout << "\n\nAfter unique results2 contains:\n";
42     std::copy( results2.begin(), endLocation, output );
43
44     cout << "\n\nVector v1 after reverse: ";
45     std::reverse( v1.begin(), v1.end() );
46     std::copy( v1.begin(), v1.end(), output );
47
48     cout << endl;
49     return 0;
50  }
```

Fig. 20.33 Demonstrating **copy_backward**, **merge**, **unique** and **reverse** (part 1 of 2).

```
Vector v1 contains: 1 3 5 7 9
Vector v2 contains: 2 4 5 7 9

After copy_backward results contains: 1 3 5 7 9

After merge of v1 and v2 results2 contains:
1 2 3 4 5 5 7 7 9 9

After unique results2 contains:
1 2 3 4 5 7 9

Vector v1 after reverse: 9 7 5 3 1
```

Fig. 20.33 Demonstrating **copy_backward**, **merge**, **unique** and **reverse** (part 2 of 2).

Line 28

```
std::copy_backward( v1.begin(), v1.end(), results.end() );
```

uses function **copy_backward** to copy elements in the range **v1.begin()** up to, but not including, **v1.end()** in **vector v1** and place the elements in **vector results** starting from the element before **results.end()** and working toward the beginning of the **vector**. The function returns an iterator positioned at the last element copied into the **vector results** (i.e., the beginning of **results**, because we are going backwards). The elements are placed in **results** in the same order as **v1**. This function requires three bidirectional iterator arguments (iterators that can be incremented and decremented to iterate forwards and backwards through a sequence, respectively). The main difference between **copy** and **copy_backward** is that the iterator returned from **copy** is positioned *after* the last element copied and the iterator returned from **copy_backward** is positioned *at* the last element copied (which is really the first element in the sequence). Also, **copy** requires two input iterators and an output iterator as argument.

Lines 33 and 34

```
std::merge( v1.begin(), v1.end(), v2.begin(), v2.end(),
            results2.begin() );
```

use function **merge** to combine two sorted ascending sequences of values into a third sorted ascending sequence. The function requires five iterator arguments. The first four arguments must be at least input iterators and the last argument must be at least an output iterator. The first two arguments specify the range of elements in the first sorted sequence (**v1**), the second two arguments specify the range of elements in the second sorted sequence (**v2**) and the last argument specifies the starting location in the third sequence (**results2**) where the elements will be merged. A second version of this function takes as its fifth argument a binary predicate function that specifies the sorting order.

Note that line 32 creates vector **results** with the number of elements **v1.size() + v2.size()**. Using the **merge** function as shown here requires that the sequence where the results are stored be at least the size of the two sequences being merged. If you do not want to allocate the number of elements for the resulting sequence before the **merge** operation, you can use the following statements:

```
vector< int > results2();
merge ( v1.begin(), v1.end(), v2.begin(), v2.end(),
        back_inserter( results2 ) );
```

The argument **back_inserter(results2)** uses function template **back_inserter** (header file **<iterator>**) for the container **results2**. A **back_inserter** calls the container's default **push_back** function to insert an element at the end of the container. More importantly, if an element is inserted into a container that has no more elements available, the container grows in size. Thus, the number of elements in the container does not have to be known in advance. There are two other inserters—**front_inserter** (to insert an element at the beginning of a container specified as its argument) and **inserter** (to insert an element before the iterator supplied as its second argument in the container supplied as its first argument).

Lines 39 and 40

```
endLocation =
    std::unique( results2.begin(), results2.end() );
```

use function **unique** on the sorted sequence of elements in the range **results2.begin()** up to, but not including, **results2.end()** in **vector results2**. After this function is applied to a sorted sequence with duplicate values, only a single copy of each value remains in the sequence. The function takes two arguments that must be at least forward iterators. The function returns an iterator positioned after the last element in the sequence of unique values. The values of all elements in the container after the last unique value are undefined. A second version of this function takes as a third argument a binary predicate function specifying how to compare two elements for equality.

Line 45

```
std::reverse( v1.begin(), v1.end() );
```

uses function **reverse** to reverse all the elements in the range **v1.begin()** up to, but not including, **v1.end()** in **vector v1**. The function takes two arguments that must be at least bidirectional iterators.

20.5.9 inplace_merge, unique_copy and reverse_copy

The program of Fig. 20.34 demonstrates Standard Library functions **inplace_merge**, **unique_copy** and **reverse_copy**. [*Note:* The following program does not compile in Borland C++.]

```
1  // Fig. 20.34: fig20_34.cpp
2  // Demonstrates miscellaneous functions: inplace_merge,
3  // reverse_copy, and unique_copy.
4  #include <iostream>
5
6  using std::cout;
7  using std::endl;
8
```

Fig. 20.34 Demonstrating **inplace_merge, unique_copy** and **reverse_copy**.

```
 9    #include <algorithm>
10    #include <vector>
11    #include <iterator>
12
13    int main()
14    {
15       const int SIZE = 10;
16       int a1[ SIZE ] = { 1, 3, 5, 7, 9, 1, 3, 5, 7, 9 };
17       std::vector< int > v1( a1, a1 + SIZE );
18
19       std::ostream_iterator< int > output( cout, " " );
20
21       cout << "Vector v1 contains: ";
22       std::copy( v1.begin(), v1.end(), output );
23
24       std::inplace_merge( v1.begin(), v1.begin() + 5, v1.end() );
25       cout << "\nAfter inplace_merge, v1 contains: ";
26       std::copy( v1.begin(), v1.end(), output );
27
28       std::vector< int > results1;
29       std::unique_copy( v1.begin(), v1.end(),
30                            std::back_inserter( results1 ) );
31       cout << "\nAfter unique_copy results1 contains: ";
32       std::copy( results1.begin(), results1.end(), output );
33
34       std::vector< int > results2;
35       cout << "\nAfter reverse_copy, results2 contains: ";
36       std::reverse_copy( v1.begin(), v1.end(),
37                            std::back_inserter( results2 ) );
38       std::copy( results2.begin(), results2.end(), output );
39
40       cout << endl;
41       return 0;
42    }
```

```
Vector v1 contains: 1 3 5 7 9 1 3 5 7 9
After inplace_merge, v1 contains: 1 1 3 3 5 5 7 7 9 9
After unique_copy results1 contains: 1 3 5 7 9
After reverse_copy, results2 contains: 9 9 7 7 5 5 3 3 1 1
```

Fig. 20.34   Demonstrating **inplace_merge**, **unique_copy** and
reverse_copy.

Line 24

```
std::inplace_merge( v1.begin(), v1.begin() + 5, v1.end() );
```

uses function **inplace_merge** to merge two sorted sequences of elements in the same container. In this example, the elements from **v1.begin()** up to, but not including, **v1.begin() + 5** are merged with the elements from **v1.begin() + 5** up to, but not including, **v1.end()**. This function requires its three iterator arguments to be at least bi-directional iterators. A second version of this function takes as a fourth argument a binary predicate function for comparing elements in the two sequences.

Lines 29 and 30

```
std::unique_copy( v1.begin(), v1.end(),
                  back_inserter( results1 ) );
```

use function **unique_copy** to make a copy of all the unique elements in the sorted sequence of values from **v1.begin()** up to, but not including, **v1.end()**. The copied elements are placed into vector **results1**. The first two arguments must be at least input
iterators and the last argument must be at least an output iterator. In this example, we did
not preallocate enough elements in **results1** to store all the elements copied from **v1**.
Instead, we use function **back_inserter** (defined in header file **<iterator>**) to add
elements to the end of **vector v1**. The **back_inserter** uses class **vector**'s capability to insert elements at the end of the **vector**. Because the **back_inserter** inserts an
element rather than replacing an existing element's value, the **vector** is able to grow to
accommodate additional elements. A second version of the **unique_copy** function takes
as a fourth argument a binary predicate function for comparing elements for equality.

Lines 36 and 37

```
std::reverse_copy( v1.begin(), v1.end(),
                   back_inserter( results2 ) );
```

use function **reverse_copy** to make a reversed copy of the elements in the range
v1.begin() up to, but not including, **v1.end()**. The copied elements are inserted into
the **vector results2** using a **back_inserter** object to ensure that the **vector** can
grow to accommodate the appropriate number of elements copied. The **reverse_copy**
function requires its first two iterator arguments to be at least bidirectional iterators and its
third iterator argument to be at least an output iterator.

20.5.10 Set Operations

Figure 20.35 demonstrates Standard Library functions **includes**, **set_difference**,
set_intersection, **set_symmetric_difference** and **set_union** for manipulating sets of sorted values. To demonstrate that Standard Library functions can be applied to arrays and containers, this example uses only arrays (remember, a pointer into an
array is a random-access iterator).

Line 26

```
if ( std::includes( a1, a1 + SIZE1, a2, a2 + SIZE2 ) )
```

calls function **includes** as the condition in an **if** structure. Function **includes** compares two sets of sorted values to determine if every element of the second set is in the first
set. If so, **includes** returns **true**; otherwise, **includes** returns **false**. The first two
iterator arguments must be at least input iterators and describe the first set of values. In this
example, the first set consists of the elements from **a1** up to, but not including, **a1 +
SIZE1**. The last two iterator arguments must be at least input iterators and describe the second set of values. In this example, the second set consists of the elements from **a2** up to,
but not including, **a2 + SIZE2**. A second version of function **includes** takes a fifth argument that is a binary predicate function for comparing elements for equality.

```cpp
1    // Fig. 20.35: fig20_35.cpp
2    // Demonstrates includes, set_difference, set_intersection,
3    // set_symmetric_difference and set_union.
4    #include <iostream>
5
6    using std::cout;
7    using std::endl;
8
9    #include <algorithm>
10
11   int main()
12   {
13      const int SIZE1 = 10, SIZE2 = 5, SIZE3 = 20;
14      int a1[ SIZE1 ] = { 1, 2, 3, 4, 5, 6, 7, 8, 9, 10 };
15      int a2[ SIZE2 ] = { 4, 5, 6, 7, 8 };
16      int a3[ SIZE2 ] = { 4, 5, 6, 11, 15 };
17      std::ostream_iterator< int > output( cout, " " );
18
19      cout << "a1 contains: ";
20      std::copy( a1, a1 + SIZE1, output );
21      cout << "\na2 contains: ";
22      std::copy( a2, a2 + SIZE2, output );
23      cout << "\na3 contains: ";
24      std::copy( a3, a3 + SIZE2, output );
25
26      if ( std::includes( a1, a1 + SIZE1, a2, a2 + SIZE2 ) )
27         cout << "\na1 includes a2";
28      else
29         cout << "\na1 does not include a2";
30
31      if ( std::includes( a1, a1 + SIZE1, a3, a3 + SIZE2 ) )
32         cout << "\na1 includes a3";
33      else
34         cout << "\na1 does not include a3";
35
36      int difference[ SIZE1 ];
37      int *ptr = std::set_difference( a1, a1 + SIZE1,
38                    a2, a2 + SIZE2, difference );
39      cout << "\nset_difference of a1 and a2 is: ";
40      std::copy( difference, ptr, output );
41
42      int intersection[ SIZE1 ];
43      ptr = std::set_intersection( a1, a1 + SIZE1,
44            a2, a2 + SIZE2, intersection );
45      cout << "\nset_intersection of a1 and a2 is: ";
46      std::copy( intersection, ptr, output );
47
48      int symmetric_difference[ SIZE1 ];
49      ptr = std::set_symmetric_difference( a1, a1 + SIZE1,
50            a2, a2 + SIZE2, symmetric_difference );
51      cout << "\nset_symmetric_difference of a1 and a2 is: ";
52      std::copy( symmetric_difference, ptr, output );
53
```

Fig. 20.35 Demonstrating **set** operations of the Standard Library (part 1 of 2).

```
54        int unionSet[ SIZE3 ];
55        ptr = std::set_union( a1, a1 + SIZE1,
56                   a3, a3 + SIZE2, unionSet );
57        cout << "\nset_union of a1 and a3 is: ";
58        std::copy( unionSet, ptr, output );
59        cout << endl;
60        return 0;
61    }
```

```
a1 contains: 1 2 3 4 5 6 7 8 9 10
a2 contains: 4 5 6 7 8
a3 contains: 4 5 6 11 15
a1 includes a2
a1 does not include a3
set_difference of a1 and a2 is: 1 2 3 9 10
set_intersection of a1 and a2 is: 4 5 6 7 8
set_symmetric_difference of a1 and a2 is: 1 2 3 9 10
set_union of a1 and a3 is: 1 2 3 4 5 6 7 8 9 10 11 15
```

Fig. 20.35 Demonstrating **set** operations of the Standard Library (part 2 of 2).

Lines 37 and 38

```
int *ptr = std::set_difference( a1, a1 + SIZE1,
                   a2, a2 + SIZE2, difference );
```

use function **set_difference** to determine the elements from the first set of sorted values that are not in the second set of sorted values (both sets of values must be in ascending order). The elements that are different are copied into the fifth argument (in this case the array **difference**). The first two iterator arguments must be at least input iterators for the first set of values. The next two iterator arguments must be at least input iterators for the second set of values. The fifth argument must be at least an output iterator indicating where to store a copy of the values that are different. The function returns an output iterator positioned immediately after the last value copied into the set to which the fifth argument points. A second version of function **set_difference** takes a sixth argument that is a binary predicate function indicating the order in which the elements were originally sorted. The two sequences must be sorted using the same comparison function.

Line 43 and 44

```
ptr = std::set_intersection( a1, a1 + SIZE1,
               a2, a2 + SIZE2, intersection );
```

use function **set_intersection** to determine the elements from the first set of sorted values that are in the second set of sorted values (both sets of values must be in ascending order). The elements common to both sets are copied into the fifth argument (in this case array **intersection**). The first two iterator arguments must be at least input iterators for the first set of values. The next two iterator arguments must be at least input iterators for the second set of values. The fifth argument must be at least an output iterator indicating where to store a copy of the values that are different. The function returns an output iterator positioned immediately after the last value copied into the set to which the fifth argument points. A second version of function **set_intersection** takes a sixth argument that is a binary predicate function indicating the order in which the elements were originally sorted. The two sequences must be sorted using the same comparison function.

Lines 49 and 50

```
ptr = std::set_symmetric_difference( a1, a1 + SIZE1,
            a2, a2 + SIZE2, symmetric_difference );
```

use function **set_symmetric_difference** to determine the elements in the first set that are not in the second set and the elements in the second set that are not in the first set (both sets of values must be in ascending order). The elements that are different are copied from both sets into the fifth argument (in this case the array **symmetric_difference**). The first two iterator arguments must be at least input iterators for the first set of values. The next two iterator arguments must be at least input iterators for the second set of values. The fifth argument must be at least an output iterator indicating where to store a copy of the values that are different. The function returns an output iterator positioned immediately after the last value copied into the set to which the fifth argument points. A second version of function **set_symmetric_difference** takes a sixth argument that is a binary predicate function indicating the order in which the elements were originally sorted. The two sequences must be sorted using the same comparison function.

Lines 55 and 56

```
ptr = std::set_union( a1, a1 + SIZE1,
            a3, a3 + SIZE2, unionSet );
```

use function **set_union** to create a set of all the elements that are in either or both of the two sorted sets (both sets of values must be in ascending order). The elements are copied from both sets into the fifth argument (in this case the array **unionSet**). Elements that appear in both sets are only copied from the first set. The first two iterator arguments must be at least input iterators for the first set of values. The next two iterator arguments must be at least input iterators for the second set of values. The fifth argument must be at least an output iterator indicating where to store the copied elements. The function returns an output iterator positioned immediately after the last value copied into the set to which the fifth argument points. A second version of function **set_union** takes a sixth argument that is a binary predicate function indicating the order in which the elements were originally sorted. The two sequences must be sorted using the same comparison function.

20.5.11 **lower_bound**, **upper_bound** and **equal_range**

Figure 20.36 demonstrates the **lower_bound**, **upper_bound** and **equal_range** Standard Library functions.

Line 23

```
lower = std::lower_bound( v.begin(), v.end(), 6 );
```

uses function **lower_bound** to determine the first location in a sorted sequence of values at which the third argument could be inserted in the sequence and the sequence would still be sorted in ascending order. The first two iterator arguments must be at least forward iterators. The third argument is the value for which to determine the lower bound. The function returns a forward iterator pointing to the position at which the insert can occur. A second version of function **lower_bound** takes as a fourth argument a binary predicate function indicating the order in which the elements were originally sorted.

```cpp
1   // Fig. 20.36: fig20_36.cpp
2   // Demonstrates lower_bound, upper_bound and equal_range for
3   // a sorted sequence of values.
4   #include <iostream>
5
6   using std::cout;
7   using std::endl;
8
9   #include <algorithm>
10  #include <vector>
11
12  int main()
13  {
14     const int SIZE = 10;
15     int a1[] = { 2, 2, 4, 4, 4, 6, 6, 6, 6, 8 };
16     std::vector< int > v( a1, a1 + SIZE );
17     std::ostream_iterator< int > output( cout, " " );
18
19     cout << "Vector v contains:\n";
20     std::copy( v.begin(), v.end(), output );
21
22     std::vector< int >::iterator lower;
23     lower = std::lower_bound( v.begin(), v.end(), 6 );
24     cout << "\n\nLower bound of 6 is element "
25          << ( lower - v.begin() ) << " of vector v";
26
27     std::vector< int >::iterator upper;
28     upper = std::upper_bound( v.begin(), v.end(), 6 );
29     cout << "\nUpper bound of 6 is element "
30          << ( upper - v.begin() ) << " of vector v";
31
32     std::pair< std::vector< int >::iterator,
33                std::vector< int >::iterator > eq;
34     eq = std::equal_range( v.begin(), v.end(), 6 );
35     cout << "\nUsing equal_range:\n"
36          << "   Lower bound of 6 is element "
37          << ( eq.first - v.begin() ) << " of vector v";
38     cout << "\n   Upper bound of 6 is element "
39          << ( eq.second - v.begin() ) << " of vector v";
40
41     cout << "\n\nUse lower_bound to locate the first point\n"
42          << "at which 5 can be inserted in order";
43     lower = std::lower_bound( v.begin(), v.end(), 5 );
44     cout << "\n   Lower bound of 5 is element "
45          << ( lower - v.begin() ) << " of vector v";
46
```

Fig. 20.36 Demonstrating **lower_bound**, **upper_bound** and **equal_range** (part 1 of 2).

```
47        cout << "\n\nUse upper_bound to locate the last point\n"
48             << "at which 7 can be inserted in order";
49        upper = std::upper_bound( v.begin(), v.end(), 7 );
50        cout << "\n    Upper bound of 7 is element "
51             << ( upper - v.begin() ) << " of vector v";
52
53        cout << "\n\nUse equal_range to locate the first and\n"
54             << "last point at which 5 can be inserted in order";
55        eq = std::equal_range( v.begin(), v.end(), 5 );
56        cout << "\n    Lower bound of 5 is element "
57             << ( eq.first - v.begin() ) << " of vector v";
58        cout << "\n    Upper bound of 5 is element "
59             << ( eq.second - v.begin() ) << " of vector v"
60             << endl;
61        return 0;
62    }
```

```
Vector v contains:
2 2 4 4 4 6 6 6 6 8

Lower bound of 6 is element 5 of vector v
Upper bound of 6 is element 9 of vector v
Using equal_range:
   Lower bound of 6 is element 5 of vector v
   Upper bound of 6 is element 9 of vector v

Use lower_bound to locate the first point
at which 5 can be inserted in order
   Lower bound of 5 is element 5 of vector v

Use upper_bound to locate the last point
at which 7 can be inserted in order
   Upper bound of 7 is element 9 of vector v

Use equal_range to locate the first and
last point at which 5 can be inserted in order
   Lower bound of 5 is element 5 of vector v
   Upper bound of 5 is element 5 of vector v
```

Fig. 20.36   Demonstrating **lower_bound**, **upper_bound** and **equal_range**
(part 2 of 2).

Line 28

```
upper = std::upper_bound( v.begin(), v.end(), 6 );
```

uses function **upper_bound** to determine the last location in a sorted sequence of values at which the third argument could be inserted in the sequence and the sequence would still be sorted in ascending order. The first two iterator arguments must be at least forward iterators. The third argument is the value for which to determine the upper bound. The function returns a forward iterator pointing to the position at which the insert can occur. A second version of function **upper_bound** takes as a fourth argument a binary predicate function indicating the order in which the elements were originally sorted.

Line 34

```
eq = std::equal_range( v.begin(), v.end(), 6 );
```

uses function **equal_range** to return a **pair** of forward iterators containing the combined results of performing both a **lower_bound** and an **upper_bound** operation. The first two iterator arguments must be at least forward iterators. The third argument is the value for which to determine the equal range. The function returns a **pair** of forward iterators for the lower bound (**eq.first**) and upper bound (**eq.second**), respectively.

Functions **lower_bound**, **upper_bound** and **equal_range** are often used to locate insertion points in sorted sequences. Line 43 uses **lower_bound** to locate the first point at which **5** can be inserted in order in **v**. Line 49 uses **upper_bound** to locate the last point at which **7** can be inserted in order in **v**. Line 55 uses **equal_range** to locate the first and last points at which **5** can be inserted in order in **v**.

20.5.12 Heapsort

Figure 20.37 demonstrates the Standard Library functions for performing the heapsort sorting algorithm. Heapsort is a sorting algorithm in which an array of elements is arranged into a special binary tree called a *heap*. The key features of a heap are that the largest element is always at the top of the heap and the values of the children of any node in the binary tree are always less than or equal to that node's value. A heap arranged in this manner is often called a *maxheap*. Heapsort is generally discussed in computer science courses called "Data Structures" and "Algorithms."

Line 21

```
std::make_heap( v.begin(), v.end() );
```

uses function **make_heap** to take a sequence of values in the range **v.begin()** up to, but not including, **v.end()** and create a heap that can be used to produce a sorted sequence. The two iterator arguments must be random-access iterators, so this function will only work with arrays, **vector**s and **deque**s. A second version of this function takes as a third argument a binary predicate function for comparing values.

Line 24

```
std::sort_heap( v.begin(), v.end() );
```

uses function **sort_heap** to sort a sequence of values in the range **v.begin()** up to, but not including, **v.end()** that are already arranged in a heap. The two iterator arguments must be random-access iterators. A second version of this function takes as a third argument a binary predicate function for comparing values.

Line 34

```
std::push_heap( v2.begin(), v2.end() );
```

uses function **push_heap** to add a new value into a heap. We take one element of array **a** at a time, append that element to the end of **vector v2** and perform the **push_heap** operation. If the appended element is the only element in the **vector**, the **vector** is already a heap. Otherwise, function **push_heap** rearranges the elements of the **vector** into a heap. Each time **push_heap** is called, it assumes that the last element currently in the **vector** (i.e., the one that is appended before the **push_heap** function call) is the element being added to the heap and that all other elements in the **vector** are already arranged as a heap. The two iterator arguments to **push_heap** must be random-access iterators. A second version of this function takes as a third argument a binary predicate function for comparing values.

```cpp
1   // Fig. 20.37: fig20_37.cpp
2   // Demonstrating push_heap, pop_heap, make_heap and sort_heap.
3   #include <iostream>
4
5   using std::cout;
6   using std::endl;
7
8   #include <algorithm>
9   #include <vector>
10
11  int main()
12  {
13     const int SIZE = 10;
14     int a[ SIZE ] = { 3, 100, 52, 77, 22, 31, 1, 98, 13, 40 };
15     int i;
16     std::vector< int > v( a, a + SIZE ), v2;
17     std::ostream_iterator< int > output( cout, " " );
18
19     cout << "Vector v before make_heap:\n";
20     std::copy( v.begin(), v.end(), output );
21     std::make_heap( v.begin(), v.end() );
22     cout << "\nVector v after make_heap:\n";
23     std::copy( v.begin(), v.end(), output );
24     std::sort_heap( v.begin(), v.end() );
25     cout << "\nVector v after sort_heap:\n";
26     std::copy( v.begin(), v.end(), output );
27
28     // perform the heapsort with push_heap and pop_heap
29     cout << "\n\nArray a contains: ";
30     std::copy( a, a + SIZE, output );
31
32     for ( i = 0; i < SIZE; ++i ) {
33        v2.push_back( a[ i ] );
34        std::push_heap( v2.begin(), v2.end() );
35        cout << "\nv2 after push_heap(a[" << i << "]): ";
36        std::copy( v2.begin(), v2.end(), output );
37     }
38
39     for ( i = 0; i < v2.size(); ++i ) {
40        cout << "\nv2 after " << v2[ 0 ] << " popped from heap\n";
41        std::pop_heap( v2.begin(), v2.end() - i );
42        std::copy( v2.begin(), v2.end(), output );
43     }
44
45     cout << endl;
46     return 0;
47  }
```

Fig. 20.37 Using Standard Library functions to perform a heapsort (part 1 of 2).

```
Vector v before make_heap:
3 100 52 77 22 31 1 98 13 40
Vector v after make_heap:
100 98 52 77 40 31 1 3 13 22
Vector v after sort_heap:
1 3 13 22 31 40 52 77 98 100

Array a contains: 3 100 52 77 22 31 1 98 13 40
v2 after push_heap(a[0]): 3
v2 after push_heap(a[1]): 100 3
v2 after push_heap(a[2]): 100 3 52
v2 after push_heap(a[3]): 100 77 52 3
v2 after push_heap(a[4]): 100 77 52 3 22
v2 after push_heap(a[5]): 100 77 52 3 22 31
v2 after push_heap(a[6]): 100 77 52 3 22 31 1
v2 after push_heap(a[7]): 100 98 52 77 22 31 1 3
v2 after push_heap(a[8]): 100 98 52 77 22 31 1 3 13
v2 after push_heap(a[9]): 100 98 52 77 40 31 1 3 13 22
v2 after 100 popped from heap
98 77 52 22 40 31 1 3 13 100
v2 after 98 popped from heap
77 40 52 22 13 31 1 3 98 100
v2 after 77 popped from heap
52 40 31 22 13 3 1 77 98 100
v2 after 52 popped from heap
40 22 31 1 13 3 52 77 98 100
v2 after 40 popped from heap
31 22 3 1 13 40 52 77 98 100
v2 after 31 popped from heap
22 13 3 1 31 40 52 77 98 100
v2 after 22 popped from heap
13 1 3 22 31 40 52 77 98 100
v2 after 13 popped from heap
3 1 13 22 31 40 52 77 98 100
v2 after 3 popped from heap
1 3 13 22 31 40 52 77 98 100
v2 after 1 popped from heap
1 3 13 22 31 40 52 77 98 100
```

Fig. 20.37 Using Standard Library functions to perform a heapsort (part 2 of 2).

Line 41

```
std::pop_heap( v2.begin(), v2.end() - i );
```

uses **pop_heap** to remove the top heap element. This function assumes that the elements in the range specified by its two random-access iterator arguments are already a heap. Repeatedly removing the top heap element results in a sorted sequence of values. Function **pop_heap** swaps the first heap element (**v2.begin()** in this example) with the last heap element (the element before **v2.end() – i** in this example), then ensures that the elements up to, but not including, the last element still form a heap. Notice in the output that after the **pop_heap** operations, the **vector** is sorted in ascending order. A second version of this function takes as a third argument a binary predicate function for comparing values.

20.5.13 `min` and `max`

Algorithms **min** and **max** determine the minimum of two elements and the maximum of two elements, respectively. The program of Fig. 20.38 demonstrates **min** and **max** for **int** and **char** values. [*Note:* Microsoft's Visual C++ compiler does not support the STL **min** and **max** algorithms, because they conflict with functions by the same name in Microsoft Foundation Classes—Microsoft's reusable classes for creating Windows applications. The program of Fig. 20.38 was compiled with Borland C++.]

20.5.14 Algorithms Not Covered in This Chapter

Figure 20.39 discusses the algorithms that are not covered in this chapter.

```cpp
1   // Fig. 20.38: fig20_38.cpp
2   // Demonstrating min and max
3   #include <iostream>
4
5   using std::cout;
6   using std::endl;
7
8   #include <algorithm>
9
10  int main()
11  {
12     cout << "The minimum of 12 and 7 is: "
13          << std::min( 12, 7 );
14     cout << "\nThe maximum of 12 and 7 is: "
15          << std::max( 12, 7 );
16     cout << "\nThe minimum of 'G' and 'Z' is: "
17          << std::min( 'G', 'Z' );
18     cout << "\nThe maximum of 'G' and 'Z' is: "
19          << std::max( 'G', 'Z' ) << endl;
20     return 0;
21  }
```

```
The minimum of 12 and 7 is: 7
The maximum of 12 and 7 is: 12
The minimum of 'G' and 'Z' is: G
The maximum of 'G' and 'Z' is: Z
```

Fig. 20.38 Demonstrating algorithms **min** and **max**.

Algorithm	Description
`inner_product`	Calculate the sum of the products of two sequences by taking corresponding elements in each sequence, multiplying those elements and adding the result to a total.

Fig. 20.39 Algorithms not covered in this chapter (part 1 of 3).

Algorithm	Description
adjacent_difference	Beginning with the second element in a sequence, calculate the difference (using operator −) between the current and previous elements, and store the result. The first two input iterator arguments indicate the range of elements in the container and the third output iterator argument indicates where the results should be stored. A second version of this algorithm takes as a fourth argument a binary function to perform a calculation between the current element and the previous element.
partial_sum	Calculate a running total (using operator +) of the values in a sequence. The first two input iterator arguments indicate the range of elements in the container and the third output iterator argument indicates where the results should be stored. A second version of this algorithm takes as a fourth argument a binary function that performs a calculation between the current value in the sequence and the running total.
nth_element	Use three random-access iterators to partition a range of elements. The first and last arguments represent the range of elements. The second argument is the partitioning element's location. After this algorithm executes, all elements to the left of the partitioning element are less than that element and all elements to the right of the partitioning element are greater than or equal to that element. A second version of this algorithm takes as a fourth argument a binary comparison function.
partition	This algorithm is similar to **nth_element**, but it requires less powerful bidirectional iterators, making it more flexible than **nth_element**. Algorithm **partition** requires two bidirectional iterators indicating the range of elements to partition. The third element is a unary predicate function that helps partition the elements so that all elements in the sequence for which the predicate is **true** are to the left (toward the beginning of the sequence) of all elements for which the predicate is **false**. A bidirectional iterator is returned indicating the first element in the sequence for which the predicate returns **false**.
stable_partition	This algorithm is similar to **partition** except that elements for which the predicate function returns **true** are maintained in their original order and elements for which the predicate function returns **false** are maintained in their original order.
next_permutation	Next lexicographical permutation of a sequence.

Fig. 20.39 Algorithms not covered in this chapter (part 2 of 3).

Algorithm	Description
prev_permutation	Previous lexicographical permutation of a sequence.
rotate	Use three forward iterator arguments to rotate the sequence indicated by the first and last argument by the number of positions indicated by subtracting the first argument from the second argument. For example, the sequence 1, 2, 3, 4, 5 rotated by two positions would be 4, 5, 1, 2, 3.
rotate_copy	This algorithm is identical to **rotate** except that the results are stored in a separate sequence indicated by the fourth argument—an output iterator. The two sequences must have the same number of elements.
adjacent_find	This algorithm returns an input iterator indicating the first of two identical adjacent elements in a sequence. If there are no identical adjacent elements, the iterator is positioned at the **end** of the sequence.
partial_sort	Use three random-access iterators to sort part of a sequence. The first and last arguments indicate the sequence of elements. The second argument indicates the ending location for the sorted part of the sequence. By default, elements are ordered using operator **<** (a binary predicate function can also be supplied). The elements from the second argument iterator to the end of the sequence are in an undefined order.
partial_sort_copy	Use two input iterators and two random-access iterators to sort part of the sequence indicated by the two input iterator arguments. The results are stored in the sequence indicated by the two random-access iterator arguments. By default, elements are ordered using operator **<** (a binary predicate function can also be supplied). The number of elements sorted is the smaller of the number of elements in the result and the number of elements in the original sequence.
stable_sort	The algorithm is similar to **sort** except that all equal elements are maintained in their original order.

Fig. 20.39   Algorithms not covered in this chapter (part 3 of 3).

20.6 Class **bitset**

Class **bitset** makes it easy to create and manipulate *bit sets*. Bit sets are useful for representing a set of bit flags. **bitset**s are fixed in size at compile time. The declaration

```
bitset< size > b;
```

creates **bitset b** in which every bit is initially **0**. The statement

```
b.set( bitNumber );
```

sets bit **bitNumber** of **bitset b** "on." The expression **b.set()** sets all bits in **b** "on."

The statement

```
b.reset( bitNumber );
```

sets bit **bitNumber** of **bitset b** "off." The expression **b.reset()** sets all bits in **b** "off." The statement

```
b.flip( bitNumber );
```

"flips" bit **bitNumber** of **bitset b** (e.g., if the bit is on, **flip** sets it off). The expression **b.flip()** flips all bits in **b**. The statement

```
b[ bitNumber ];
```

returns a reference to the bit **bitNumber** of **bitset b**. Similarly,

```
b.at( bitNumber );
```

performs range checking on **bitNumber** first. Then, if **bitNumber** is in range, **at** returns a reference to the bit. Otherwise, **at** throws an **out_of_range** exception. The statement

```
b.test( bitNumber );
```

performs range checking on **bitNumber** first. Then, if **bitNumber** is in range, **test** returns **true** if the bit is on and **false** if the bit is off. Otherwise, **test** throws an **out_of_range** exception. The expression

```
b.size()
```

returns the number of bits in **bitset b**. The expression

```
b.count()
```

returns the number of bits that are set in **bitset b**. The expression

```
b.any()
```

returns **true** if any bit is set in **bitset b**. The expression

```
b.none()
```

returns **true** if none of the bits are set in **bitset b**. The expressions

```
b == b1
b != b1
```

compare the two **bitset**s for equality and inequality, respectively.

Each of the bitwise assignment operators **&=**, **|=** and **^=** can be used to combine **bit-set**s, For example,

```
b &= b1;
```

performs a bit-by-bit logical AND between **bitset**s **b** and **b1**. The result is stored in **b**. Bitwise logical OR and bitwise logical XOR are performed by

```
b |= b1;
b ^= b2;
```

The expression

```
b >>= n;
```

shifts the bits in **bitset b** right by **n** positions. The expression

```
b <<= n;
```

shifts the bits in **bitset b** left by **n** positions. The expressions

```
b.to_string()
b.to_ulong()
```

convert **bitset b** to a **string** and an **unsigned long**, respectively.

Figure 20.40 revisits the Sieve of Eratosthenes for finding prime numbers we discussed in Exercise 4.29. A **bitset** is used instead of an array to implement the algorithm. The program displays all the prime numbers from 2 to 1023, then allows the user to enter a number to determine if that number is prime.

```cpp
1   // Fig. 20.40: fig20_40.cpp
2   // Using a bitset to demonstrate the Sieve of Eratosthenes.
3   #include <iostream>
4
5   using std::cin;
6   using std::cout;
7   using std::endl;
8
9   #include <iomanip>
10
11  using std::setw;
12
13  #include <bitset>
14  #include <cmath>
15
16  int main()
17  {
18     const int size = 1024;
19     int i, value, counter;
20     std::bitset< size > sieve;
21
22     sieve.flip();
23
24     // perform Sieve of Eratosthenes
25     int finalBit = sqrt( sieve.size() ) + 1;
26
27     for ( i = 2; i < finalBit; ++i )
28        if ( sieve.test( i ) )
29           for ( int j = 2 * i; j < size; j += i )
30              sieve.reset( j );
31
32     cout << "The prime numbers in the range 2 to 1023 are:\n";
33
```

Fig. 20.40 Demonstrating class **bitset** and the Sieve of Eratosthenes (part 1 of 2).

```
34      for ( i = 2, counter = 0; i < size; ++i )
35         if ( sieve.test( i ) ) {
36            cout << setw( 5 ) << i;
37
38            if ( ++counter % 12 == 0 )
39               cout << '\n';
40         }
41
42      cout << endl;
43
44      // get a value from the user to determine if it is prime
45      cout << "\nEnter a value from 1 to 1023 (-1 to end): ";
46      cin >> value;
47
48      while ( value != -1 ) {
49         if ( sieve[ value ] )
50            cout << value << " is a prime number\n";
51         else
52            cout << value << " is not a prime number\n";
53
54         cout << "\nEnter a value from 2 to 1023 (-1 to end): ";
55         cin >> value;
56      }
57
58      return 0;
59   }
```

```
The prime numbers in the range 2 to 1023 are:
    2    3    5    7   11   13   17   19   23   29   31   37
   41   43   47   53   59   61   67   71   73   79   83   89
   97  101  103  107  109  113  127  131  137  139  149  151
  157  163  167  173  179  181  191  193  197  199  211  223
  227  229  233  239  241  251  257  263  269  271  277  281
  283  293  307  311  313  317  331  337  347  349  353  359
  367  373  379  383  389  397  401  409  419  421  431  433
  439  443  449  457  461  463  467  479  487  491  499  503
  509  521  523  541  547  557  563  569  571  577  587  593
  599  601  607  613  617  619  631  641  643  647  653  659
  661  673  677  683  691  701  709  719  727  733  739  743
  751  757  761  769  773  787  797  809  811  821  823  827
  829  839  853  857  859  863  877  881  883  887  907  911
  919  929  937  941  947  953  967  971  977  983  991  997
 1009 1013 1019 1021

Enter a value from 1 to 1023 (-1 to end): 389
389 is a prime number

Enter a value from 2 to 1023 (-1 to end): 88
88 is not a prime number

Enter a value from 2 to 1023 (-1 to end): -1
```

Fig. 20.40 Demonstrating class **bitset** and the Sieve of Eratosthenes (part 2 of 2).

Line 20

```
std::bitset< size > sieve;
```

creates a **bitset** of **size** bits (**size** is 1024 in this example). We ignore the bits at positions 0 and 1 in this program. By default, all the bits in the **bitset** are set "off." The code

```
// perform Sieve of Eratosthenes
int finalBit = sqrt( sieve.size() ) + 1;

for ( i = 2; i < finalBit; ++i )
   if ( sieve.test( i ) )
      for ( int j = 2 * i; j < size; j += i )
         sieve.reset( j );
```

determines all the prime numbers from 2 to 1023. The integer **finalBit** is used to determine when the algorithm is complete. The basic algorithm is that a number is prime if it has no divisors other than 1 and itself. Starting with the number 2, once we know a number is prime, we can eliminate all multiples of that number. The number 2 is only divisible by 1 and itself, so it is prime. Therefore, we can eliminate 4, 6, 8, and so on. The number 3 is only divisible by 1 and itself. Therefore, we can eliminate all multiples of 3 (keep in mind that all even numbers have already been eliminated).

20.7 Function Objects

Function objects and function adapters are provided to make STL more flexible. A *function object* contains a function that may be treated syntactically and semantically as a function using **operator()**. STL's function objects and adaptors are defined in header **<functional>**. A function object may also encapsulate data with the enclosed function. The standard function objects are **inline**d for performance. STL function objects are shown in Fig. 20.41.

STL function objects	Type
divides< T >	arithmetic
equal_to< T >	relational
greater< T >	relational
greater_equal< T >	relational
less< T >	relational
less_equal< T >	relational
logical_and< T >	logical
logical_not< T >	logical
logical_or< T >	logical
minus< T >	arithmetic

Fig. 20.41   Function objects in the Standard Library (part 1 of 2).

STL function objects	Type
modulus< T >	arithmetic
negate< T >	arithmetic
not_equal_to< T >	relational
plus< T >	arithmetic
multiplies< T >	arithmetic

Fig. 20.41 Function objects in the Standard Library (part 2 of 2).

The program of Fig. 20.42 demonstrates the **accumulate** numeric algorithm (discussed in Fig. 20.30) to calculate the sum of the squares of the elements in a **vector**. The fourth argument to **accumulate** is a binary function object or a function pointer to a binary function that takes two arguments and returns a result. Function **accumulate** is demonstrated twice—once with a function pointer to a binary function and once with a function object.

```cpp
1   // Fig. 20.42: fig20_42.cpp
2   // Demonstrating function objects.
3   #include <iostream>
4
5   using std::cout;
6   using std::endl;
7
8   #include <vector>
9   #include <algorithm>
10  #include <numeric>
11  #include <functional>
12
13  // binary function adds the square of its second argument and
14  // the running total in its first argument and
15  // returns the sum
16  int sumSquares( int total, int value )
17     { return total + value * value; }
18
19  // binary function class template which defines an overloaded
20  // operator() that adds the square of its second
21  // argument and the running total in its first argument and
22  // returns the sum
23  template< class T >
24  class SumSquaresClass : public std::binary_function< T, T, T >
25  {
26  public:
27     const T operator()( const T &total, const T &value )
28        { return total + value * value; }
29  };
30
```

Fig. 20.42 Demonstrating a binary function object (part 1 of 2).

```
31   int main()
32   {
33      const int SIZE = 10;
34      int a1[] = { 1, 2, 3, 4, 5, 6, 7, 8, 9, 10 };
35      std::vector< int > v( a1, a1 + SIZE );
36      std::ostream_iterator< int > output( cout, " " );
37      int result = 0;
38
39      cout << "vector v contains:\n";
40      std::copy( v.begin(), v.end(), output );
41      result =
42         std::accumulate( v.begin(), v.end(), 0, sumSquares );
43      cout << "\n\nSum of squares of elements in vector v using "
44         << "binary\nfunction sumSquares: " << result;
45
46      result = std::accumulate( v.begin(), v.end(), 0,
47                                SumSquaresClass< int >() );
48      cout << "\n\nSum of squares of elements in vector v using "
49         << "binary\nfunction object of type "
50         << "SumSquaresClass< int >: " << result << endl;
51      return 0;
52   }
```

```
vector v contains:
1 2 3 4 5 6 7 8 9 10

Sum of squares of elements in vector v using binary
function sumSquares: 385

Sum of squares of elements in vector v using binary
function object of type SumSquaresClass< int >: 385
```

Fig. 20.42 Demonstrating a binary function object (part 2 of 2).

Lines 16 and 17

```
int sumSquares( int total, int value )
   { return total + value * value; }
```

define function **sumSquares** that squares its second argument **value**, adds that square and its first argument **total**, and returns the sum. Function **accumulate** will pass each of the elements of the sequence over which it iterates as the second argument to **sumSquares** in the example. On the first call to **sumSquares**, the first argument will be the initial value of the **total** (which is supplied as the third argument to **accumulate**; **0** in this program). All subsequent calls to **sumSquares** receive as the first argument the running sum returned by the previous call to **sumSquares**. When **accumulate** completes, it returns the sum of the squares of all the elements in the sequence.

Lines 23 through 29

```
template< class T >
class SumSquaresClass : public std::binary_function< T, T, T >
{
public:
    const T &operator()( const T &total, const T &value )
        { return total + value * value; }
};
```

define class **SumSquaresClass** that inherits from class **binary_function** (in header file **<functional>**). Classes that inherit from **binary_function** define the overloaded **operator()** function with two arguments. Class **SumSquaresClass** is used to define function objects for which the overloaded **operator()** functions perform the same task as function **sumSquares**. The three type parameters (**T**) to the template **binary_function** are the type of the first argument to **operator()**, the type of the second argument to **operator()** and the return type of **operator()**, respectively. Function **accumulate** will pass the elements of the sequence over which it iterates as the second argument to function **operator()** of the object of class **SumSquaresClass** that is passed to the **accumulate** algorithm. On the first call to **operator()**, the first argument will be the initial value of the **total** (which is supplied as the third argument to **accumulate**: **0** in this program). All subsequent calls to **operator()** receive as the first argument the result returned by the previous call to **operator()**. When **accumulate** completes, it returns the sum of the squares of all the elements in the sequence.

Lines 41 and 42

```
result =
    std::accumulate( v.begin(), v.end(), 0, sumSquares );
```

call function **accumulate** with a pointer to function **sumSquares** as its last argument. The statement at lines 46 and 47

```
result = std::accumulate( v.begin(), v.end(), 0,
                          SumSquaresClass< int >() );
```

call function **accumulate** with an object of class **SumSquaresClass** as the last argument. The expression **SumSquaresClass< int >()** creates an instance of class **SumSquaresClass** that is passed to **accumulate** which sends the object the message (invokes the function) **operator()**. The preceding statement could be written as two separate statements as follows:

```
SumSquaresClass< int > sumSquaresObj;
result = accumulate( v.begin(), v.end(), 0, sumSquaresObj );
```

The first line defines an object of class **SumSquaresClass**. That object is then passed to function **accumulate** and is sent the message **operator()**.

Software Engineering Observation 20.10

Unlike function pointers, a function object can also encapsulate data.

SUMMARY

- Using STL can save considerable time and effort, and result in higher quality programs.
- The choice of what Standard Library container to use in a particular application is often based on performance considerations.
- STL containers are all templates so that you can tailor them to hold the type of data relevant to your particular applications.
- STL includes many popular data structures as containers and provides many algorithms that programs use to process data in these containers.
- STL containers are in three major categories—*sequence containers*, *associative containers* and *container adapters*. The sequence containers and associative containers are collectively referred to as the *first-class containers*.
- Four other types are considered "near-containers" because they exhibit similar capabilities to the first-class containers, but do not support all the capabilities of first-class containers—array, **string**, **bitset** and **valarray**.
- A **vector** provides rapid insertion and deletion at the back of the **vector** and direct access to any element. **vector**s support random-access iterators.
- A **deque** provides rapid insertion and deletion at the front or back of the **deque** and direct access to any element. **deque**s support random-access iterators.
- A **list** provides rapid insertion and deletion anywhere in the **list** and supports bidirectional iterators.
- A **set** provides rapid lookup of a key. No duplicate keys are allowed. **set**s support bidirectional iterators.
- A **multiset** provides rapid lookup of a key. Duplicate keys are allowed. **multiset**s support bidirectional iterators.
- A **map** provides rapid lookup of a key and its corresponding "mapped" value. No duplicate keys are allowed (i.e., a one-to-one mapping is specified). **map**s support bidirectional iterators.
- A **multimap** provides rapid lookup of a key and its corresponding "mapped" values. Duplicate keys are allowed (i.e., a one-to-many mapping). **multimap**s support bidirectional iterators.
- A **stack** provides a last-in-first-out (LIFO) data structure.
- A **queue** provides a first-in-first-out (FIFO) data structure.
- A **priority_queue** provides a first-in-first-out (FIFO) data structure with the highest priority item always at the front of the **priority_queue**.
- STL has been carefully designed so that the containers provide similar functionality. There are many generic operations that apply to all containers, and other operations that apply to subsets of similar containers. This contributes to the extensibility of the STL.
- STL avoids **virtual** functions in favor of using generic programming with templates to achieve better execution-time performance.
- It is important to ensure that the type of element being stored in an STL container supports a minimum set of functionalities (the constraints of the template), including a copy constructor, an assignment operator and—for associative containers—a less-than operator (**<**).
- Iterators are used with sequences that may be in containers, or may be input sequences or output sequences.
- Input iterators are used to read an element from a container. An input iterator can move only in the forward direction (i.e., from the beginning of the container to the end of the container) one element at a time. Input iterators support only one-pass algorithms.

- Output iterators are used to write an element to a container. An output iterator can move only in the forward direction one element at a time. Output iterators support only one-pass algorithms.

- Forward iterators combine the capabilities of input and output iterators. Forward iterators support multi-pass algorithms.

- Bidirectional iterators combine the capabilities of a forward iterator with the ability to move in the backward direction.

- Random-access iterators combine the capabilities of a bidirectional iterator with the ability to directly access any element of the container, i.e., to jump forward or backward by an arbitrary number of elements.

- The category of iterator supported by each container determines whether that container can be used with specific algorithms in the STL. Containers that support random-access iterators can be used with all algorithms in the STL.

- Pointers into arrays may be used in place of iterators in all STL algorithms.

- STL has approximately 70 standard algorithms. Mutating-sequence algorithms result in modifications to container elements. Nonmutating-sequence algorithms do not modify container elements.

- Functions **fill** and **fill_n** set every element in a range of container elements to a specific value.

- Functions **generate** and **generate_n** use a generator function to create values for every element in a range of container elements.

- Function **equal** compares two sequences of values for equality.

- Function **mismatch** compares two sequences of values and returns a **pair** of iterators indicating the location in each sequence of the mismatched elements. If all the elements match, the **pair** contains the result of function **end** for each sequence.

- Function **lexicographical_compare** compares the contents of two sequences to determine if one sequence is less than another sequence (similar to a string comparison).

- Functions **remove** and **remove_copy** delete all elements in a sequence that match a specified value. Functions **remove_if** and **remove_copy_if** delete all elements in a sequence for which the unary predicate function passed to the functions returns **true**.

- Functions **replace** and **replace_copy** replace all elements in a sequence that match a specified value. Functions **replace_if** and **replace_copy_if** replace with a new value all elements in a sequence for which the unary predicate function passed to the functions returns **true**.

- Function **random_shuffle** randomly orders the elements in a sequence.

- Function **count** counts the elements with the specified value in a sequence. Function **count_if** counts the elements in a sequence for which the supplied unary predicate function returns **true**.

- Function **min_element** locates the smallest element in a sequence. Function **max_element** locates the largest element in a sequence.

- Function **accumulate** sums the values in a sequence. A second version of this function receives a pointer to a general function that takes two arguments and returns a result. The general function determines how the elements in a sequence are accumulated.

- Function **for_each** applies a general function to every element in a sequence. The general function takes one argument (that it should not modify) and returns **void**.

- Function **transform** applies a general function to every element in a sequence. The general function takes one argument (that it can modify) and returns the **transform**ed result.

- Function **find** locates an element in a sequence and, if the element is found, returns an iterator to the element; otherwise, **find** returns an iterator indicating the end of the sequence. Function **find_if** locates the first element for which the supplied unary predicate function returns **true**.

- Function **sort** arranges the elements in a sequence in sorted order (ascending order by default, or in the order indicated by a supplied binary predicate function).
- Function **binary_search** determines if an element is in a sorted sequence.
- Function **swap** exchanges two values.
- Function **iter_swap** exchanges two values referred to by iterators.
- Function **swap_ranges** exchanges the elements in two sequences of elements.
- Function **copy_backward** copies elements in a sequence and places the elements in another sequence starting from the last element in the second sequence and working toward the beginning of the second sequence.
- Function **merge** combines two sorted ascending sequences into a third sorted sequence. Note that **merge** also works on unsorted sequences, but would not produce a sorted sequence.
- A **back_inserter** uses the container's default capability for inserting an element at the end of the container. When an element is inserted into a container that has no more elements available, the container grows in size. There are two other inserters—**front_inserter** and **inserter**. A **front_inserter** inserts an element at the beginning of a container (specified as its argument), and an **inserter** inserts an element before the iterator supplied as its second argument in the container supplied as its first argument.
- Function **unique** removes all duplicates from a sorted sequence.
- Function **reverse** reverses all the elements in a sequence.
- Function **inplace_merge** merges two sorted sequences of elements in the same container.
- Function **unique_copy** makes a copy of all the unique elements in a sorted sequence. Function **reverse_copy** makes a reversed copy of the elements in a sequence.
- Function **includes** compares two sorted sets of values to determine if every element of the second set is in the first set. If so, **includes** returns **true**; otherwise, **includes** returns **false**.
- Function **set_difference** determines the elements from the first set of sorted values that are not in the second set of sorted values (both sets of values must be in ascending order using the same comparison function).
- Function **set_intersection** determines the elements from the first set of sorted values that are in the second set of sorted values (both sets of values must be in ascending order using the same comparison function).
- Function **set_symmetric_difference** determines the elements in the first set that are not in the second set and the elements in the second set that are not in the first set (both sets of values must be in ascending order using the same comparison function).
- Function **set_union** creates a set of all the elements that are in either or both of the two sorted sets (both sets of values must be in ascending order using the same comparison function).
- Function **lower_bound** determines the first location in a sorted sequence at which the third argument can be inserted in the sequence and the sequence would still be sorted in ascending order.
- Function **upper_bound** determines the last location in a sorted sequence at which the third argument could be inserted in the sequence and the sequence would still be sorted in ascending order.
- Function **equal_range** returns a **pair** of forward iterators containing the combined results of performing both a **lower_bound** and an **upper_bound** operation.
- Heapsort is a sorting algorithm in which an array of elements is arranged into a special binary tree called a heap. The key features of a heap are that the largest element is always at the top of the heap and that the values of the children of any node in the binary tree are always less than or equal to that node's value. A heap arranged in this manner is often called a maxheap.

- Function **make_heap** takes a sequence of values and creates a heap that can be used to produce a sorted sequence.
- Function **sort_heap** sorts a sequence of values that are already arranged in a heap.
- Function **push_heap** adds a new value into a heap. **push_heap** assumes that the last element currently in the container is the element being added to the heap and that all other elements in the container are already arranged as a heap. Function **pop_heap** removes the top element of the heap. This function assumes that the elements are already arranged as a heap.
- Function **min** determines the minimum of two values. Function **max** determines the maximum of two values.
- Class **bitset** makes it easy to create and manipulate bit sets. Bit sets are useful for representing a set of boolean flags. **bitset**s are fixed in size at compile time.

TERMINOLOGY

accumulate()	**for_each()**
adapter	forward iterator
adjacent_difference()	**front()**
adjacent_find()	**<functional>**
<algorithm>	function object
assign()	**generate()**
assignment	**generate_n()**
associative array	generic programming
associative container	**inplace_merge()**
back()	input iterator
begin()	**insert()**
bidirectional iterator	**istream_iterator**
binary_search()	iterator
const_iterator	**<iterator>**
const_reverse_iterator	**iter_swap()**
container	last-in-first-out (LIFO)
container adapter classes	**lexicographical_compare()**
copy()	**<list>**
copy_backward()	**list** sequence container
count()	**lower_bound()**
count_if()	**make_heap()**
creating an association	**<map>**
<deque>	**map** associative container
deque sequence container	**max()**
deque<T>	**max_element()**
deque<T>::iterator	**max_size()**
empty()	**merge()**
end()	**min()**
equal()	**min_element()**
equal_range()	**mismatch()**
erase()	**multimap** associative container
fill()	**multiset** associative container
fill_n()	mutating-sequence algorithm
find()	**namespace std**
first-class containers	non-mutating-sequence algorithm
first-in-first-out (FIFO)	**nth_element**

COMMON PROGRAMMING ERRORS

20.1   Attempting to dereference an iterator positioned outside its container is a run-time logic error. In particular, the iterator returned by **end()** cannot be dereferenced or incremented.

20.2   Attempting to create a non-**const** iterator for a **const** container is a syntax error.

20.3   The **vector** must not be empty; otherwise, results of the **front** and **back** functions are undefined.

20.4   Erasing an element that contains a pointer to a dynamically allocated object does not **delete** the object.

20.5   Attempting to **sort** a container by using an iterator other than a random-access iterator is a syntax error. Function **sort** requires a random-access iterator.

GOOD PROGRAMMING PRACTICES

20.1   Use **typedef**s to make code with long type names (such as **multiset**s) easier to read.

20.2   It is a good practice to check that the range specified in a call to **min_element** is not empty and to check that the return value is not the "past the end" iterator.

PERFORMANCE TIPS

20.1   For any particular application, several different STL containers could be appropriate. Select the most appropriate container that achieves the best performance (i.e., balance of speed and size) for that application. Efficiency was a crucial consideration in STL's design.

20.2   Standard Library capabilities are implemented to operate efficiently across a wide variety of applications. For some applications with unique performance requirements, it may be necessary to write your own customized implementations.

20.3   STL generally avoids inheritance and **virtual** functions in favor of using generic programming with templates to achieve better execution-time performance.

20.4   Know your STL components. Choosing the most appropriate container for a given problem can maximize performance and minimize memory requirements.

20.5   Insertion at the back of a **vector** is efficient. The **vector** simply grows if necessary to accommodate the new item. It is expensive to insert (or delete) an element in the middle of a **vector**—the entire portion of the **vector** after the insertion (or deletion) point must be moved, because **vector** elements occupy contiguous cells in memory just like a C or C++ "raw" array.

20.6   Applications that require frequent insertions and deletions at both ends of a container normally use a **deque** rather than a **vector**. Although we can insert and delete elements at the front and back of both a **vector** and a **deque**, class **deque** is more efficient than **vector** for doing insertions and deletions at the front.

20.7   Applications with frequent insertions and deletions in the middle and/or at the extremes of a container normally use a **list**, due to its efficient implementation of insertion and deletion anywhere in the data structure.

20.8   Choose the **vector** container for the best random-access performance.

20.9   Objects of class **vector** provide rapid indexed access with the overloaded subscript operator **[ ]** because they are stored in contiguous storage like a C or C++ raw array.

20.10 It is faster to insert many elements at once than one at a time

20.11 It may be wasteful to double the size of a **vector** when more space is needed. For example, a full **vector** of 1,000,000 elements resizes to accommodate 2,000,000 elements when a new element is added. This leaves 999,999 elements unused. Programmers may use **resize()** to better control space usage.

20.12 Once a storage block is allocated for a **deque**, in several implementations the block is not deallocated until **deque** is destroyed. This makes the operation of a **deque** more efficient than if memory were repeatedly allocated, deallocated and reallocated. But this means that the **deque** is more likely to use memory inefficiently (than a **vector**, for example).

20.13 Insertions and deletions in the middle of a **deque** are optimized to minimize the number of elements copied to maintain the illusion that the elements of the **deque** are contiguous.

20.14 For performance reasons, **multiset**s and **set**s are typically implemented as so-called *red–black binary search trees*. With this internal representation, the binary search tree tends to be balanced, thus minimizing average search times.

20.15 A **multimap** is implemented to efficiently locate all values paired with a given key.

20.16   Each of the common operations of a **stack** is implemented as an **inline** function that calls the appropriate function of the underlying container. This avoids the overhead of a second function call.

20.17   For the best performance, use class **deque** or **vector** as the underlying container for a **stack**.

20.18   Each of the common operations of a **queue** is implemented as an **inline** function that calls the appropriate function of the underlying container. This avoids the overhead of a second function call.

20.19   For the best performance, use class **deque** as the underlying container for a **queue**.

20.20   Each of the common operations of a **priority_queue** is implemented as an **inline** function that calls the appropriate function of the underlying container. This avoids the overhead of a second function call.

20.21   For the best performance, use class **vector** as the underlying container for a **priority_queue**.

PORTABILITY TIPS

20.1   STL is certain to become the favored means of programming with containers. Programming with STL will enhance the portability of your code.

20.2   Because STL algorithms process containers only indirectly through iterators, one algorithm can often be used with many different containers.

SOFTWARE ENGINEERING OBSERVATIONS

20.1   The STL approach allows general programs to be written so that the code does not depend on the underlying container. Such a programming style is called *generic programming*.

20.2   Avoid reinventing the wheel; program with the reusable components of the C++ Standard Library. STL includes many of the most popular data structures as containers and provides various popular algorithms programs use to process data in these containers.

20.3   The equality and less than operators are technically not required for the elements stored in a container unless the elements need to be compared. However, when creating code from a template, some compilers require all parts of the template to be defined whereas other compilers require only the parts of the template that are actually used in the program.

20.4   Using the "weakest iterator" that yields acceptable performance helps produce maximally reusable components.

20.5   STL is implemented concisely. Until now, class designers would have associated the algorithms with the containers by making the algorithms member functions of the containers. STL takes a different approach. The algorithms are separated from the containers and operate on elements of the containers only indirectly through iterators. This separation makes it easier to write generic algorithms applicable to many other container classes.

20.6   STL is extensible. It is straightforward to add new algorithms and to do so without changes to STL containers.

20.7   STL algorithms can operate on STL containers and on pointer-based, C-like arrays.

20.8   STL algorithms do not depend on the implementation details of the containers on which they operate. As long as the container's (or array's) iterators satisfy the requirements of the algorithm, STL algorithms can work on any C-style, pointer-based arrays as well as working on STL containers (and user-defined data structures).

20.9   Algorithms can be added easily to the STL without modifying the container classes.

20.10   Unlike function pointers, a function object can also encapsulate data.

TESTING AND DEBUGGING TIPS

20.1   When programming pointer-based data structures and algorithms, we must do our own debugging and testing to be sure our data structures, classes and algorithms function properly. It is easy to make errors when manipulating pointers at this low a level. Memory leaks and memory-access violations are common in such custom code. For most programmers, and for most of the applications they will need to write, the prepackaged, templatized data structures of the STL are sufficient. Using the STL's code can avoid a great deal of testing and debugging time. One caution is that for large projects, template compile time can be significant.

20.2   The * (dereferencing) operator of any **const** iterator returns a **const** reference to the container element, thus disallowing the use of non-**const** member functions.

20.3   Operations performed on a **const_iterator** return **const** references to prevent modification to elements of the container being manipulated. Use **const_iterator**s in preference to **iterator**s where appropriate. This is another example of the principle of least privilege.

20.4   Only random-access iterators support **<**. It is better to use **!=** and **end()** to test for end of container.

SELF-REVIEW EXERCISES

20.1   (T/F) The STL makes abundant use of inheritance and **virtual** functions.

20.2   The two types of STL containers are sequence containers and _____ containers.

20.3   STL avoids using **new** and **delete** in favor of using _____ to enable a variety of means of controlling memory allocation and deallocation.

20.4   The five main iterator types are _____, _____, _____, _____ and _____.

20.5   (T/F) A pointer is a generalized form of iterator.

20.6   (T/F) STL algorithms can operate on C-like pointer-based arrays.

20.7   (T/F) STL algorithms are encapsulated as member functions within each container class.

20.8   (T/F) The **remove** algorithm does not decrease the size of the **vector** from which elements are being removed.

20.9   Memory allocation and deallocation are performed in the STL with _____ objects.

20.10 The three STL container adapters are_____, _____ and _____.

20.11 (T/F) Container member function **end()** yields the position of the last element of the container.

20.12 STL algorithms operate on container elements indirectly using _____.

20.13 The **sort** algorithm requires a _____ iterator.

ANSWERS TO SELF-REVIEW EXERCISES

20.1   False. These were avoided for performance reasons.

20.2   Associative.

20.3   Allocators.

20.4   Input, output, forward, bidirectional, random access.

20.5   False. It is actually vice versa.

20.6   True.

20.7   False. STL algorithms are not member functions. They operate indirectly on containers through iterators.

20.8   True.

20.9   Allocator.

20.10   **stack**, **queue**, **priority_queue**.

20.11   False. It actually yields the position just after the end of the container.

20.12   Iterators.

20.13   Random-access.

EXERCISES

20.14   Write a function template **palindrome** that takes as a parameter a **const vector** and returns **true** or **false** depending upon whether the **vector** does or does not read the same forwards as backwards (e.g., a **vector** containing 1, 2, 3, 2, 1 is a palindrome and a **vector** containing 1, 2, 3, 4 is not).

20.15   Modify the program of Fig. 20.29, the Sieve of Eratosthenes, so that if the number the user inputs into the program is not prime, the program displays the prime factors of the number. Remember that a prime number's factors are only 1 and the prime number itself. Every number that is not prime has a unique prime factorization. For example, consider the number 54. The factors of 54 are 2, 3, 3 and 3. When these values are multiplied together, the result is 54. For the number 54, the prime factors output should be 2 and 3.

20.16   Modify Exercise 20.15 so that if the number the user inputs into the program is not prime, the program displays the prime factors of the number and the number of times that prime factor appears in the unique prime factorization. For example, the output for the number 54 should be

      The unique prime factorization of 54 is: 2 * 3 * 3 * 3

STL RESOURCES ON THE INTERNET AND THE WORLD WIDE WEB

The following is a collection of Internet and World Wide Web STL resources. These sites include tutorials, references, FAQs, articles, books, interviews and software.

Tutorials

http://www.cs.brown.edu/people/jak/programming/stl-tutorial/tutorial.html
This STL tutorial is organized by examples, philosophy, components and extending STL. You will find code examples using the STL components, useful explanations and helpful diagrams.

http://web.ftech.net/~honeyg/articles/eff_stl.htm
This STL tutorial provides information on the STL components, containers, stream and iterator adaptors, transforming and selecting values, filtering and transforming values, and objects.

http://www.xraylith.wisc.edu/~khan/software/stl/os_examples/examples.html
This site is helpful for people just learning about the STL. You will find an introduction to the STL and ObjectSpace STL Tool Kit examples.

References

http://www.sgi.com/Technology/STL/other_resources.html
This site has a list of many STL-related Web sites and a list of suggested books on the STL.

http://www.cs.rpi.edu/projects/STL/stl/stl.html
This is the Standard Template Library Online Reference Home Page from Rensselaer Polytechnic Institute. You will find detailed explanations of the STL as well as links to other useful resources for information about the STL.

http://www.sgi.com/Technology/STL/
The Silicon Graphics Standard Template Library Programmer's Guide is a useful resource for STL information. You can download the STL from this site, and find the latest information, design documentation, and links to other STL resources.

http://www.dinkumware.com/refcpp.html
This site contains useful information about the ANSI/ISO Standard C++ Library and contains extensive information about the Standard Template Library.

http://www.roguewave.com/products/xplatform/stdlib/
Rogue Wave Software's Standard C++ Library web page. You can download whitepapers related to their version of the Standard C++ Library.

FAQs

ftp://butler.hpl.hp.com/stl/stl.faq
This FTP site is a FAQ sheet for the STL maintained by Marian Corcoran, a member of the ANSI committee and a C++ expert.

Articles, Books and Interviews

http://www.sgi.com/Technology/STL/other_resources.html
This site has a list of over 15 STL-related Web sites and a short list of suggested books on the STL.

http://www.byte.com/art/9510/sec12/art3.htm
The *Byte Magazine* site has a copy of an article on the STL written by Alexander Stepanov. Stepanov, one of the creators of the Standard Template Library, provides information on the use of the STL in generic programming.

http://www.sgi.com/Technology/STL/drdobbs-interview.html
An interview with Alexander Stepanov that has some interesting information about the creation of the Standard Template Library. Stepanov talks about how the STL was conceptualized, generic programming, the acronym "STL" and more.

ANSI/ISO C++ Standard

http://www.ansi.org/
You can purchase a copy of the C++ standard document from this site.

Software

http://www.cs.rpi.edu/~musser/stl.html
The RPI STL site includes information on how STL differs from other C++ libraries and on how to compile programs that use STL, list of main STL include files, example programs that use STL, STL Container Classes, and STL Iterator Categories. It also provides a STL-compatible compiler list, FTP sites for STL source code and related materials.

http://www.mathcs.sjsu.edu/faculty/horstman/safestl.html
Download SAFESTL.ZIP, a tool designed to find errors in programs using the STL.

http://www.objectspace.com/jgl/
Object Space provides information about porting C++ to Java. You can download their Standards<ToolKit> portable class libraries free. Key features of the toolkit include containers, iterators, algorithms, allocators, strings and exceptions.

http://www.cs.rpi.edu/~wiseb/stl-borland.html
"Using the Standard Template Library with Borland C++." This site is a useful reference for people using the Borland C++ compiler. The author has sections on warnings and incompatibilities.

http://msdn.microsoft.com/visualc/
This is the Microsoft Visual C++ home page. Here you can find the latest Visual C++ news, updates, technical resources, samples and downloads.

http://www.borland.com/bcppbuilder/
This is the Borland C++Builder home page. Here you can find a variety of C++ resources including several C++ newsgroups, information on the latest product enhancements, FAQs and many other resources for programmers using C++Builder.

STL BIBLIOGRAPHY

(Am97)   Ammeraal, L., *STL for C++ Programmers,* New York, NY: John Wiley, 1997.

(Gl95)   Glass, G., and B. Schuchert, *The STL <Primer>,* Upper Saddle River, NJ: Prentice Hall PTR, 1995.

(He97)   Henricson, M., and E. Nyquist, *Industrial Strength C++: Rules and Recommendations,* Upper Saddle River, NJ: Prentice Hall, 1997.

(Jo99)   Josuttis, N., *The C++ Standard Library: A Tutorial and Handbook*, Reading, MA: Addison-Wesley, 1999.

(Ko97)   Koenig, A., and B. Moo, *Ruminations on C++,* Reading, MA: Addison-Wesley, 1997.

(Mu94)   Musser, D. R., and A. A. Stepanov, "Algorithm-Oriented Generic Libraries," *Software Practice and Experience,* Vol. 24, No. 7, July 1994.

(Mu96)   Musser, D. R., and A. Saini, *STL Tutorial and Reference Guide: C++ Programming with the Standard Template Library,* Reading, MA: Addison-Wesley, 1996.

(Ne95)   Nelson, M., *C++ Programmer's Guide to the Standard Template Library,* Foster City, CA: Programmers Press, a Division of IDG Books Worldwide, Inc., 1995.

(Po97)   Pohl, I., *C++ Distilled: A Concise ANSI/ISO Reference and Style Guide,* Reading, MA: Addison-Wesley, 1997.

(Po97a) Pohl, I., *Object-Oriented Programming Using C++,* Second Edition, Reading, MA: Addison-Wesley, 1997.

(Ro00)   Robson, R., Using the STL: The C++ Standard Template Library, Springer Verlag, 2000.

(Sc99)   Schildt, H., STL Programming from the Ground Up, Osborne McGraw-Hill, 1999.

(Sr94)   Stroustrup, B., "Making a **vector** Fit for a Standard," *The C++ Report,* October 1994.

(Sr94a) Stroustrup, B., *The Design and Evolution of C++,* Reading, MA: Addison-Wesley, 1994.

(Sr97)   Stroustrup, B., *The C++ Programming Language,* Third Edition, Reading, MA: Addison-Wesley, 1997.

(St95)   Stepanov, A., and M. Lee, "The Standard Template Library," *Internet Distribution,* Published at **ftp://butler.hpl.hp.com/stl**, July 7, 1995.

(Vi94)   Vilot, M. J., "An Introduction to the Standard Template Library," *The C++ Report,* Vol. 6, No. 8, October 1994.

21

Standard C++ Language Additions

Objectives

- To understand and use data type **bool**.
- To be able to use cast operators: **static_cast**, **const_cast** and **reinterpret_cast**.
- To understand the concept of **namespace**s.
- To understand and use run-time type information (RTTI) and operators **typeid** and **dynamic_cast**.
- To understand operator keywords.
- To understand **explicit** constructors.
- To use **mutable** members in **const** objects.
- To understand and use class member pointer operators **.*** and **->***.
- To understand the role of **virtual** base classes in multiple inheritance.

What's in a name? that which we call a rose
By any other name would smell as sweet.
William Shakespeare, Romeo and Juliet

O Diamond! Diamond! thou little knowest the mischief done!
Sir Isaac Newton

...to thine own self be true,...
William Shakespeare, Hamlet

The die is cast.
Julius Caesar

Outline

Summary • Terminology • Common Programming Errors • Good Programming Practices • Performance Tip • Portability Tips • Software Engineering Observations • Testing and Debugging Tips • Self-Review Exercises • Answers to Self-Review Exercises • Exercises

21.1 Introduction

We now consider some standard C++ features including data type **bool**, cast operators, **namespace**s, run-time type information (RTTI) and operator keywords. We also discuss pointers-to-class-member operators and **virtual** base classes.

21.2 bool Data Type

The C++ standard provides data type **bool** whose values may be **false** or **true** as a preferred alternative to the old style of using **0** to indicate false and nonzero to indicate true. The program of Fig. 21.1 demonstrates data type **bool**.

```
1   // Fig. 21.1: fig21_01.cpp
2   // Demonstrating data type bool.
3   #include <iostream>
4
5   using std::cout;
6   using std::endl;
7   using std::cin;
8   using std::boolalpha;
9
```

Fig. 21.1   Demonstrating the fundamental data type **bool** (part 1 of 2).

```
10   int main()
11   {
12      bool boolean = false;
13      int x = 0;
14
15      cout << "boolean is " << boolean
16           << "\nEnter an integer: ";
17      cin >> x;
18
19      cout << "integer " << x << " is"
20           << ( x ? " nonzero " : " zero " )
21           << "and interpreted as ";
22
23      if ( x )
24         cout << "true\n";
25      else
26         cout << "false\n";
27
28      boolean = true;
29      cout << "boolean is " << boolean;
30      cout << "\nboolean output with boolalpha manipulator is "
31           << boolalpha << boolean << endl;
32
33      return 0;
34   }
```

```
boolean is 0
Enter an integer: 22
integer 22 is nonzero and interpreted as true
boolean is 1
boolean output with boolalpha manipulator is true
```

Fig. 21.1   Demonstrating the fundamental data type **bool** (part 2 of 2).

Line 12

        bool boolean = false;

declares variable **boolean** to be of type **bool** and initializes **boolean** to **false**. Variable **x** is declared and initialized to **0**. Line 15

        cout << "boolean is " << boolean

outputs **boolean**'s value. The value **0** is output rather than the keyword **false**. Numeric values are the default display for **bool**s.

The value of **x** (input on line 17) is used as an **if/else**'s condition in line 23. If **x** is **0**, the condition is **false**. Otherwise the condition is **true**. Note that negative values are nonzero and therefore **true**.

Line 28 assigns **true** to **boolean**. The value of **boolean** (**1**) is output on line 29. A **bool** variable outputs as **0** or **1** by default. The stream insertion operator **<<** has been overloaded to display **bool**s as integers.

Lines 30 and 31

```
cout << "\nboolean output with boolalpha manipulator is "
     << boolalpha << boolean << endl;
```

uses the stream manipulator **boolalpha** to set the output stream to display **bool** values as the strings "**true**" and "**false**." Manipulator **boolalpha** can also be used on input.

Pointers, **int**s, **double**s, etc. can be implicitly converted to **bool**s. Zero values convert to **false** and nonzero values convert to **true**. For example the expression

```
bool dc = false + x * 2 - b && true;
```

would assign **true** to **dc** assuming **x** is **3**, and **b** is **true**. Note that the right-hand portion of the assignment expression evaluates to **5**, but this value is implicitly converted to **true**.

Good Programming Practice 21.1

*When creating state variables to indicate truth or falsity, use **bool**s in preference to **int**s.*

Good Programming Practice 21.2

*Using **true** and **false** instead of zero and nonzero values makes programs clearer.*

21.3 `static_cast` Operator

The C++ standard contains four cast operators to use in preference to the "old-style" casting that has been used in C and C++. The new casts are less powerful and more specific than old-style casting, which gives the programmer more precise control. Casting is dangerous and can often be a source of errors so the new-style casts are also easier to spot and to search for using automated tools. Another advantage to the new-style casts is that the four casts have completely separate purposes, whereas with the old-style casting the philosophy was "one cast fits all."

C++ provides the **static_cast** operator for conversion between types. Type checking is performed at compile time. Operator **static_cast** performs standard conversions (e.g., **void *** to **char ***, **int** to **double**, etc.) and their inverses. Figure 21.2 demonstrates operator **static_cast**.

Common Programming Error 21.1

*Performing an illegal cast with operator **static_cast** is a syntax error. Illegal casts include casting from **const** types to non-**const** types, casting pointers and references between types that are not related by **public** inheritance and casting to a type for which there is not an appropriate constructor or conversion operator to perform the cast.*

The program declares classes **BaseClass** and **DerivedClass**. Each class defines a member function **f**. Lines 23 and 24

```
double d = 8.22;
int x = static_cast< int >( d );
```

declare and initialize both **d** and **x**. The **static_cast** operator converts **d** from **double** to **int**. The **static_cast** operator can be used for most conversions between fundamental data types such as **int**, **float**, **double**, etc.

```
1   // Fig. 21.2: fig21_02.cpp
2   // Demonstrating the static_cast operator.
3   #include <iostream>
4
5   using std::cout;
6   using std::endl;
7
8   class BaseClass {
9   public:
10     void f( void ) const { cout << "BASE\n"; }
11  };
12
13  class DerivedClass : public BaseClass {
14  public:
15     void f( void ) const { cout << "DERIVED\n"; }
16  };
17
18  void test( BaseClass * );
19
20  int main()
21  {
22     // use static_cast for a conversion
23     double d = 8.22;
24     int x = static_cast< int >( d );
25
26     cout << "d is " << d << "\nx is " << x << endl;
27
28     BaseClass * basePtr = new DerivedClass;
29     test( basePtr );    // call test
30     delete basePtr;
31
32     return 0;
33  }
34
35  void test( BaseClass * basePtr )
36  {
37     DerivedClass *derivedPtr;
38
39     // cast base class pointer into derived class pointer
40     derivedPtr = static_cast< DerivedClass * >( basePtr );
41     derivedPtr->f();    // invoke DerivedClass function f
42  }
```

```
d is 8.22
x is 8
DERIVED
```

Fig. 21.2   Demonstrating operator **static_cast**.

Software Engineering Observation 21.1

*With the additions to the C++ standard of the new cast operators (e.g., **static_cast**), old C-style casts are obsolete.*

Good Programming Practice 21.3

Use the safer and more reliable **static_cast** *operator in preference to the C-style cast operator.*

BaseClass pointer **basePtr** is assigned a **new DerivedClass** object on line 28 and passed to function **test** on line 29. The address passed into **test** is received in pointer **basePtr**. **DerivedClass** pointer **derivedPtr** is declared on line 37. Line 40

derivedPtr = static_cast< DerivedClass * >(basePtr);

uses **static_cast** to *downcast* from **BaseClass *** to **DerivedClass ***. Although (as we saw in Chapter 9) *downcasting* from a base class pointer to a derived class pointer is a potentially dangerous operation, **static_cast** permits the cast. Function **f** is invoked using **derivedPtr** (line 41).

21.4 const_cast Operator

C++ provides the **const_cast** operator for casting away **const** or **volatile**. The program of Fig. 21.3 demonstrates the use of **const_cast**.

```cpp
1   // Fig. 21.3: fig21_03.cpp
2   // Demonstrating the const_cast operator.
3   #include <iostream>
4
5   using std::cout;
6   using std::endl;
7
8   class ConstCastTest {
9   public:
10     void setNumber( int );
11     int getNumber() const;
12     void printNumber() const;
13  private:
14     int number;
15  };
16
17  void ConstCastTest::setNumber( int num ) { number = num; }
18
19  int ConstCastTest::getNumber() const { return number; }
20
21  void ConstCastTest::printNumber() const
22  {
23     cout << "\nNumber after modification: ";
24
25     // the expression number-- would generate compile error
26     // undo const-ness to allow modification
27     const_cast< ConstCastTest * >( this )->number--;
28
29     cout << number << endl;
30  }
31
```

Fig. 21.3   Demonstrating the **const_cast** operator (part 1 of 2).

```
32   int main()
33   {
34      ConstCastTest x;
35      x.setNumber( 8 );   // set private data number to 8
36
37      cout << "Initial value of number: " << x.getNumber();
38
39      x.printNumber();
40      return 0;
41   }
```

```
Initial value of number: 8
Number after modification: 7
```

Fig. 21.3   Demonstrating the **const_cast** operator (part 2 of 2).

Lines 8–15 declare class **ConstCastTest** that contains three member functions and **private** variable **number**. Two of the member functions are declared **const**. Function **setNumber** sets **number**'s value. Function **getNumber** returns **number**'s value.

The **const** member function **printNumber** modifies **number**'s value in line 27

```
const_cast< ConstCastTest * >( this )->number--;
```

In **const** member function **printNumber**, the data type of the **this** pointer is **const ConstCastTest ***. The preceding statement casts away the "**const**-ness" of the **this** pointer with operator **const_cast**. The type of the this pointer for the remainder of that statement is now **ConstCastTest ***. This allows **number** to be modified. Operator **const_cast** cannot be used to directly cast away a constant variable's "**const**-ness."

21.5 reinterpret_cast Operator

C++ provides the **reinterpret_cast** operator for *nonstandard casts* (e.g., casting from one pointer type to a different pointer type, etc.). Operator **reinterpret_cast** cannot be used for standard casts (i.e., **double** to **int**, etc.). Figure 21.4 demonstrates the use of the **reinterpret_cast** operator.

```
1    // Fig. 21.4: fig21_04.cpp
2    // Demonstrating the reinterpret_cast operator.
3    #include <iostream>
4
5    using std::cout;
6    using std::endl;
7
8    int main()
9    {
10      int x = 120, *ptr = &x;
11
12      cout << *reinterpret_cast<char *>( ptr ) << endl;
```

Fig. 21.4   Demonstrating operator **reinterpret_cast** (part 1 of 2).

```
13
14      return 0;
15  }
```

```
x
```

Fig. 21.4   Demonstrating operator `reinterpret_cast` (part 2 of 2).

The program declares an integer and a pointer. Pointer **ptr** is initialized to the address of **x**. Line 12

```
cout << *reinterpret_cast<char *>( ptr ) << endl;
```

uses operator `reinterpret_cast` to cast **ptr** (of type **int ***) to **char ***. The address returned is dereferenced.

Testing and Debugging Tip 21.1

It is easy to use **reinterpret_cast** *to perform dangerous manipulations that could lead to serious execution-time errors.*

Portability Tip 21.1

Using **reinterpret_cast** *can cause programs to behave differently on different platforms.*

21.6 namespaces

A program includes many identifiers defined in different scopes. Sometimes a variable of one scope will "overlap" (i.e., collide) with a variable of the same name in a different scope, potentially creating a problem. Such overlapping can occur at many levels. Identifier overlapping occurs frequently in third-party libraries that happen to use the same names for global identifiers (such as functions). When this occurs, compiler errors are usually generated.

Good Programming Practice 21.4

Avoid beginning identifiers with the underscore character, which can lead to linker errors.

The C++ standard attempts to solve this problem with **namespace**s. Each **namespace** defines a scope where identifiers and variables are placed. To use a **namespace** *member*, the member's name must be qualified with the **namespace** name and the binary scope resolution operator (**::**) as in

> *namespace_name***::***member*

or a **using** statement must occur before the name is used; typically **using** statements are placed at the beginning of the file in which members of the **namespace** are used. For example, the statement

> **using namespace** *namespace_name***;**

at the beginning of a source code file specifies that members of **namespace** *namespace_name* can be used in the file without preceding each member with the *namespace_name* and the scope resolution operator (**::**).

Good Programming Practice 21.5

*Precede a member with its **namespace** name and the scope resolution operator (::) if the possibility exists of a scoping conflict.*

Not all **namespaces** are guaranteed to be unique. Two third-party vendors may inadvertently use the same **namespace**. Figure 21.5 demonstrates the use of **namespaces**.

```cpp
1  // Fig. 21.5: fig21_05.cpp
2  // Demonstrating namespaces.
3  #include <iostream>
4  using namespace std;   // use std namespace
5
6  int myInt = 98;        // global variable
7
8  namespace Example {
9     const double PI = 3.14159;
10    const double E = 2.71828;
11    int myInt = 8;
12    void printValues();
13
14    namespace Inner {   // nested namespace
15       enum Years { FISCAL1 = 1990, FISCAL2, FISCAL3 };
16    }
17 }
18
19 namespace {             // unnamed namespace
20    double d = 88.22;
21 }
22
23 int main()
24 {
25    // output value d of unnamed namespace
26    cout << "d = " << d;
27
28    // output global variable
29    cout << "\n(global) myInt = " << myInt;
30
31    // output values of Example namespace
32    cout << "\nPI = " << Example::PI << "\nE = "
33       << Example::E << "\nmyInt = "
34       << Example::myInt << "\nFISCAL3 = "
35       << Example::Inner::FISCAL3 << endl;
36
37    Example::printValues();   // invoke printValues function
38
39    return 0;
40 }
41
42 void Example::printValues()
43 {
44    cout << "\nIn printValues:\n" << "myInt = "
45       << myInt << "\nPI = " << PI << "\nE = "
```

Fig. 21.5   Demonstrating the use of **namespaces** (part 1 of 2).

```
46              << E << "\nd = " << d << "\n(global) myInt = "
47              << ::myInt << "\nFISCAL3 = "
48              << Inner::FISCAL3 << endl;
49    }
```

```
d = 88.22
(global) myInt = 98
PI = 3.14159
E = 2.71828
myInt = 8
FISCAL3 = 1992

In printValues:
myInt = 8
PI = 3.14159
E = 2.71828
d = 88.22
(global) myInt = 98
FISCAL3 = 1992
```

Fig. 21.5   Demonstrating the use of **namespace**s (part 2 of 2).

Line 4

```
using namespace std;
```

informs the compiler that **namespace std** is being used. The contents of header file
<iostream> are all defined as part of **namespace std**. [*Note: Most C++ program-mers consider it poor practice to write a* **using** *statement such as line 4 because the entire contents of the* **namespace** *are included.*]

The **using namespace** statement specifies that members of a **namespace** will be used frequently throughout a program. This allows the programmer access to all the members of the **namespace** and to write more concise statements such as

```
cout << "d = " << d;
```

rather than

```
std::cout << "d = " << d;
```

Without line 4, every **cout** and **endl** in Fig. 21.5 would have to be qualified with **std::**. The **using namespace** statement can be used for predefined **namespace**s (e.g., **std**) or programmer-defined **namespace**s.

Lines 8 through 17

```
namespace Example {
    const double PI = 3.14159;
    const double E = 2.71828;
    int myInt = 8;
    void printValues();

    namespace Inner {    // nested namespace
        enum Years { FISCAL1 = 1990, FISCAL2, FISCAL3 };
    }
}
```

use the keyword **namespace** to define **namespace Example**. The body of a **namespace** is delimited by braces (**{}**). Unlike class bodies, **namespace** bodies do not end in semicolons. **Example**'s members consist of two constants (**PI** and **E**), an **int** (**myInt**), a function (**printValues**) and a *nested* **namespace** (**Inner**). Note that member **myInt** has the same name as global variable **myInt**. Variables that have the same name must have different scopes—otherwise syntax errors occur. A **namespace** can contain constants, data, classes, nested **namespace**s, functions, etc. Definitions of **namespace**s must occupy the global scope or be nested within other **namespace**s.

Lines 19 through 21

```
namespace {
    double d = 88.22;
}
```

create an *unnamed* **namespace** containing the member **d**. Unnamed **namespace** members occupy the *global* **namespace**, are directly accessible and do not have to be qualified with a **namespace** name. *Global variables* are also part of the global **namespace** and are accessible in all scopes following the declaration in the file.

Software Engineering Observation 21.2

Each separate compilation unit has its own unique unnamed **namespace**, *i.e., the unnamed* **namespace** *replaces the* **static** *linkage specifier.*

Line 26 outputs the value of **d**. Member **d** is directly accessible as part of the unnamed **namespace**. Line 29 outputs the value of global variable **myInt**. Lines 32 through 35

```
cout << "\nPI = " << Example::PI << p\nE = "
     << Example::E << "\nmyInt = "
     << Example::myInt << "\nFISCAL3 = "
     << Example::Inner::FISCAL3 << endl;
```

output the values of **PI**, **E**, **myInt** and **FISCAL3**. **PI**, **E** and **myInt** are **Example** members and are therefore qualified with **Example::**. Member **myInt** must be qualified because a global variable has the same name. Otherwise, the global variable's value is output. **FISCAL3** is a member of nested **namespace Inner** and is qualified with **Example::Inner::**.

Function **printValues** is a member of **Example** and can directly access other members of the same **namespace** without using a **namespace** qualifier. The **cout** on line 44 outputs **myInt**, **PI**, **E**, **d**, global variable **myInt** and **FISCAL3**. Notice that **PI** and **E** are not qualified with **Example**, **d** is still accessible, the global version of **myInt** has been qualified with the unary scope resolution operator (**::**) and **FISCAL3** has been qualified with **Inner::**. When accessing members of a nested **namespace**, the members must be qualified with the **namespace** name (unless you are inside the nested **namespace**).

Keyword **using** can also be used to allow an individual **namespace** member to be used. For example, the line

```
using Example::PI;
```

would allow **PI** to be used without **namespace** qualification. This is done typically when only one **namespace** member is frequently used. Namespaces can be aliased. For example the statement

```
namespace CPPHTP3E = CPlusPlusHowToProgram3E;
```

creates the alias **CPPHTP3E** for **CPlusPlusHowToProgram3E**.

Common Programming Error 21.2

Placing **main** *in a* **namespace** *is a syntax error.*

Software Engineering Observation 21.3

Ideally in large programs, every entity should be declared in a class, function, block or **namespace**. *This helps clarify every entity's role.*

21.7 Run-Time Type Information (RTTI)

Run-time type information (RTTI) provides a means of determining an object's type at run time. Two important RTTI operators are discussed in this section: **typeid** and **dynamic_cast**. The program of Fig. 21.6 demonstrates **typeid** and the program of Fig. 21.7 demonstrates **dynamic_cast**.

Testing and Debugging Tip 21.2

In order to use RTTI, some compilers require RTTI capabilities to be enabled. Check your compiler's documentation for RTTI use.

```cpp
1   // Fig. 21.6: fig21_06.cpp
2   // Demonstrating RTTI capability typeid.
3   #include <iostream>
4
5   using std::cout;
6   using std::endl;
7
8   #include <typeinfo>
9
10  template < typename T >
11  T maximum( T value1, T value2, T value3 )
12  {
13     T max = value1;
14
15     if ( value2 > max )
16        max = value2;
17
18     if ( value3 > max )
19        max = value3;
20
21     // get the name of the type (i.e., int or double)
22     const char *dataType = typeid( T ).name();
23
24     cout << dataType << "s were compared.\nLargest "
25        << dataType << " is ";
26
27     return max;
28  }
29
```

Fig. 21.6   Demonstrating **typeid** (part 1 of 2).

```
30   int main()
31   {
32      int a = 8, b = 88, c = 22;
33      double d = 95.96, e = 78.59, f = 83.89;
34
35      cout << maximum( a, b, c ) << "\n";
36      cout << maximum( d, e, f ) << endl;
37
38      return 0;
39   }
```

```
ints were compared.
Largest int is 88
doubles were compared.
Largest double is 95.96
```

Fig. 21.6   Demonstrating **typeid** (part 2 of 2).

Line 8 includes header file **<typeinfo>**. When using the result of **typeid**, **<typeinfo>** is required. The program defines a function template **maximum** that takes three arguments of the specified data type **T** and determines and returns the largest. Keyword **typename** is used in place of keyword **class**. In this situation, **typename** behaves identically to **class**.

Line 22

```
const char *dataType = typeid( T ).name();
```

uses function **name** to return an implementation defined, C-style string, representing **T**'s data type. Operator **typeid** returns a reference to a **type_info** object. A **type_info** object is a system-maintained object that represents a type. Note that the string returned by **name** is owned by the system and should not be **delete**d by the programmer.

 Good Programming Practice 21.6

Using **typeid** *in* **switch***-like tests is a misuse of RTTI. Use* **virtual** *functions instead.*

Operator **dynamic_cast** ensures that proper conversions take place at run time (i.e., the compiler cannot verify whether or not it is a proper conversion). Operator **dynamic_cast** is often used for *downcasting* from a base-class pointer to a derived-class pointer. The program of Fig. 21.7 demonstrates **dynamic_cast**.

```
1   // Fig. 21.7: fig21_07.cpp
2   // Demonstrating dynamic_cast.
3   #include <iostream>
4
5   using std::cout;
6   using std::endl;
7
8   const double PI = 3.14159;
```

Fig. 21.7   Demonstrating **dynamic_cast** (part 1 of 3).

```cpp
 9
10   class Shape {
11      public:
12         virtual double area() const { return 0.0; }
13   };
14
15   class Circle : public Shape {
16   public:
17      Circle( int r = 1 ) { radius = r; }
18
19      virtual double area() const
20      {
21         return PI * radius * radius;
22      };
23   protected:
24      int radius;
25   };
26
27   class Cylinder : public Circle {
28   public:
29      Cylinder( int h = 1 ) { height = h; }
30
31      virtual double area() const
32      {
33         return 2 * PI * radius * height +
34                2 * Circle::area();
35      }
36   private:
37      int height;
38   };
39
40   void outputShapeArea( const Shape * );        // prototype
41
42   int main()
43   {
44      Circle circle;
45      Cylinder cylinder;
46      Shape *ptr = 0;
47
48      outputShapeArea( &circle );     // output circle's area
49      outputShapeArea( &cylinder );   // output cylinder's area
50      outputShapeArea( ptr );         // attempt to output area
51      return 0;
52   }
53
54   void outputShapeArea( const Shape *shapePtr )
55   {
56      const Circle *circlePtr;
57      const Cylinder *cylinderPtr;
58
59      // cast Shape * to a Cylinder *
60      cylinderPtr = dynamic_cast< const Cylinder * >( shapePtr );
61
```

Fig. 21.7   Demonstrating **dynamic_cast** (part 2 of 3).

```
62      if ( cylinderPtr != 0 )   // if true, invoke area()
63         cout << "Cylinder's area: " << shapePtr->area();
64      else {   // shapePtr does not refer to a cylinder
65
66         // cast shapePtr to a Circle *
67         circlePtr = dynamic_cast< const Circle * >( shapePtr );
68
69         if ( circlePtr != 0 )   // if true, invoke area()
70            cout << "Circle's area: " << circlePtr->area();
71         else
72            cout << "Neither a Circle nor a Cylinder.";
73      }
74
75      cout << endl;
76   }
```

```
Circle's area: 3.14159
Cylinder's area: 12.5664
Neither a Circle nor a Cylinder.
```

Fig. 21.7   Demonstrating **dynamic_cast** (part 3 of 3).

The program defines a base class **Shape** (line 10) that contains **virtual** function **area**, a derived class **Circle** (line 15) that **public**ly inherits **Shape** and a derived class **Cylinder** (line 27) that **public**ly inherits **Circle**. Both **Circle** and **Cylinder** override function **area**.

In function **main** at lines 44 through 46, an object of class **Circle** called **circle** is instantiated, an object of class **Cylinder** called **cylinder** is instantiated and a pointer to a **Shape** called **ptr** is declared and initialized to zero. Lines 48 through 50 call function **outputShapeArea** (defined at line 54) three times. Each call to **output-ShapeArea** will display one of three results—the area of a **Circle**, the area of a **Cylinder** or an indication that the **Shape** is not a **Circle** or a **Cylinder**. Function **outputShapeArea** receives a pointer to a **Shape** as an argument—the first call receives the address of **circle**, the second call receives the address of **cylinder** and the third call receives a base-class **Shape** pointer called **ptr**.

Line 60

```
cylinderPtr = dynamic_cast< const Cylinder * >( shapePtr );
```

dynamically downcasts **shapePtr** (a **const Shape ***) to a **const Cylinder *** using the cast operator **dynamic_cast** As a result, **cylinderPtr** is assigned either the address of the **cylinder** object or **0** to indicate that the **Shape** is not a **Cylinder**. If the result of the cast is not **0**, the area of the **Cylinder** is output.

Line 67

```
circlePtr = dynamic_cast< const Circle * >( shapePtr );
```

dynamically downcasts **shapePtr** to a **const Circle *** using the cast operator **dynamic_cast**. As a result, **circlePtr** is assigned either the address of the **circle** object or **0** to indicate that the **Shape** is not a **Circle**. If the result of the cast is not **0**, the area of the **Circle** is output.

Common Programming Error 21.3

*Attempting to use **dynamic_cast** on a pointer of type **void** * is a syntax error.*

Software Engineering Observation 21.4

*RTTI is intended for use with polymorphic inheritance hierarchies (with **virtual** functions).*

21.8 Operator Keywords

The C++ standard provides *operator keywords* (Fig. 21.8) that can be used in place of several C++ operators. Operator keywords can be useful for programmer's keyboards that do not support certain characters such as !, &, ^, ~, |, etc.

The program of Fig. 21.9 demonstrates the use of the operator keywords. This program was compiled with Microsoft Visual C++ which requires the header file **<iso646.h>** to use the operator keywords. Other compilers may differ, so check documentation for your compiler to determine the header file to include (the compiler may not require any header file to use these keywords).

The program declares and initializes two integers **a** and **b**. Logical and bitwise operations are performed with **a** and **b** using the various operator keywords. The result of each operation is output.

Operator	Operator keyword	Description
Logical operator keywords		
&&	and	logical AND
||	or	logical OR
!	not	logical NOT
Inequality operator keyword		
!=	not_eq	inequality
Bitwise operator keywords		
&	bitand	bitwise AND
|	bitor	bitwise inclusive OR
^	xor	bitwise exclusive OR
~	compl	bitwise complement
Bitwise assignment operator keywords		
&=	and_eq	bitwise AND assignment
|=	or_eq	bitwise inclusive OR assignment
^=	xor_eq	bitwise exclusive OR assignment

Fig. 21.8   Operator keywords as alternatives to operator symbols.

```
1   // Fig. 21.9: fig21_09.cpp
2   // Demonstrating operator keywords.
3   #include <iostream>
4
5   using std::cout;
6   using std::endl;
7   using std::boolalpha;
8
9   #include <iso646.h>
10
11  int main()
12  {
13     int a = 8, b = 22;
14
15     cout << boolalpha
16            <<    "   a and b: " << ( a and b )
17            << "\n     a or b: " << ( a or b )
18            << "\n      not a: " << ( not a )
19            << "\na not_eq b: " << ( a not_eq b )
20            << "\na bitand b: " << ( a bitand b )
21            << "\na bit_or b: " << ( a bitor b )
22            << "\n    a xor b: " << ( a xor b )
23            << "\n    compl a: " << ( compl a )
24            << "\na and_eq b: " << ( a and_eq b )
25            << "\n a or_eq b: " << ( a or_eq b )
26            << "\na xor_eq b: " << ( a xor_eq b ) << endl;
27
28     return 0;
29  }
```

```
a and b: true
   a or b: true
    not a: false
a not_eq b: false
a bitand b: 22
a bit_or b: 22
   a xor b: 0
   compl a: -23
a and_eq b: 22
 a or_eq b: 30
a xor_eq b: 30
```

Fig. 21.9   Demonstrating the operator keywords .

21.9 `explicit` Constructors

In Chapter 8, "Operator Overloading," we discussed that any constructor that is called with one argument can be used by the compiler to perform an *implicit conversion* in which the type received by the constructor is converted to an object of the class in which the constructor is defined. The conversion is automatic and the programmer need not use a cast operator. In some situations implicit conversions are undesirable or error-prone. For example, our **Array** class in Fig. 8.4 defines a constructor that takes a single **int** argument. The intent of this constructor is to create an **Array** object containing the number of elements specified by the **int** argument. However, this constructor can be misused by the compiler to perform an implicit conversion. The program of Fig. 21.10 uses a simplified version of class **Array** from Chapter 8 to demonstrate an improper implicit conversion.

```
1   // Fig 21.10: array2.h
2   // Simple class Array (for integers)
3   #ifndef ARRAY2_H
4   #define ARRAY2_H
5
6   #include <iostream>
7
8   using std::ostream;
9
10  class Array {
11     friend ostream &operator<<( ostream &, const Array & );
12  public:
13     Array( int = 10 );   // default/conversion constructor
14     ~Array();            // destructor
15  private:
16     int size; // size of the array
17     int *ptr; // pointer to first element of array
18  };
19
20  #endif
```

Fig. 21.10   Single-argument constructors and implicit conversions—**array2.h**.

```
21  // Fig 21.10: array2.cpp
22  // Member function definitions for class Array
23  #include <iostream>
24
25  using std::cout;
26  using std::ostream;
27
28  #include <cassert>
29  #include "array2.h"
30
31  // Default constructor for class Array (default size 10)
32  Array::Array( int arraySize )
33  {
34     size = ( arraySize > 0 ? arraySize : 10 );
35     cout << "Array constructor called for "
36          << size << " elements\n";
37
38     ptr = new int[ size ]; // create space for array
39     assert( ptr != 0 );     // terminate if memory not allocated
40
41     for ( int i = 0; i < size; i++ )
42        ptr[ i ] = 0;          // initialize array
43  }
44
```

Fig. 21.10   Single-argument constructors and implicit conversions—**array2.cpp** (part 1 of 2).

```
45   // Destructor for class Array
46   Array::~Array() { delete [] ptr; }
47
48   // Overloaded output operator for class Array
49   ostream &operator<<( ostream &output, const Array &a )
50   {
51      int i;
52
53      for ( i = 0; i < a.size; i++ )
54         output << a.ptr[ i ] << ' ' ;
55
56      return output;      // enables cout << x << y;
57   }
```

Fig. 21.10 Single-argument constructors and implicit conversions—`array2.cpp` (part 2 of 2).

```
58   // Fig 21.10: fig21_10.cpp
59   // Driver for simple class Array
60   #include <iostream>
61
62   using std::cout;
63
64   #include "array2.h"
65
66   void outputArray( const Array & );
67
68   int main()
69   {
70      Array integers1( 7 );
71
72      outputArray( integers1 );    // output Array integers1
73
74      outputArray( 15 );   // convert 15 to an Array and output
75
76      return 0;
77   }
78
79   void outputArray( const Array &arrayToOutput )
80   {
81      cout << "The array received contains:\n"
82           << arrayToOutput << "\n\n";
83   }
```

```
Array constructor called for 7 elements
The array received contains:
0 0 0 0 0 0 0

Array constructor called for 15 elements
The array received contains:
0 0 0 0 0 0 0 0 0 0 0 0 0 0 0
```

Fig. 21.10 Single-argument constructors and implicit conversions—`fig21_10.cpp`.

Line 70 in **main**

```
Array integers1( 7 );
```

defines **Array** object **integers1** and calls the single argument constructor with the **int** value **7** to specify the number of elements in the **Array**. We modified the **Array** constructor so it outputs a line of text indicating that the **Array** constructor was called and the number of elements that were allocated in the **Array**. Line 72

```
outputArray( integers1 );    // output Array integers1
```

calls function **outputArray** (defined at line 79) to output the contents of the **Array**. Function **outputArray** receives as its argument a **const Array &** to the **Array**, then outputs the **Array** using the overloaded stream insertion operator **<<**. Line 74

```
outputArray( 15 );  // convert 15 to an Array and output
```

calls function **outputArray** with the **int** value **15** as an argument. There is no function **outputArray** that takes an **int** argument, so the compiler checks class **Array** to determine if there is a conversion constructor that can convert an **int** into an **Array**. Because class **Array** provides a conversion constructor, the compiler uses that constructor to create a temporary **Array** object containing **15** elements and passes the temporary **Array** object to function **outputArray** to output the **Array**. The output shows that the **Array** conversion constructor was called for a **15**-element **Array** and the contents of the **Array** were output.

C++ provides the keyword **explicit** to suppress implicit conversions via conversion constructors. A constructor that is declared **explicit** cannot be used in an implicit conversion. The program of Fig. 21.11 demonstrates an **explicit** constructor.

```
1   // Fig. 21.11: array3.h
2   // Simple class Array (for integers)
3   #ifndef ARRAY3_H
4   #define ARRAY3_H
5
6   #include <iostream>
7
8   using std::ostream;
9
10  class Array {
11     friend ostream &operator<<( ostream &, const Array & );
12  public:
13     explicit Array( int = 10 );  // default constructor
14     ~Array();                    // destructor
15  private:
16     int size; // size of the array
17     int *ptr; // pointer to first element of array
18  };
19
20  #endif
```

Fig. 21.11 Demonstrating an **explicit** constructor—**array3.h**.

```
21   // Fig. 21.11: array3.cpp
22   // Member function definitions for class Array
23   #include <iostream>
24
25   using std::cout;
26   using std::ostream;
27
28   #include <cassert>
29   #include "array3.h"
30
31   // Default constructor for class Array (default size 10)
32   Array::Array( int arraySize )
33   {
34      size = ( arraySize > 0 ? arraySize : 10 );
35      cout << "Array constructor called for "
36          << size << " elements\n";
37
38      ptr = new int[ size ]; // create space for array
39      assert( ptr != 0 );      // terminate if memory not allocated
40
41      for ( int i = 0; i < size; i++ )
42         ptr[ i ] = 0;            // initialize array
43   }
44
45   // Destructor for class Array
46   Array::~Array() { delete [] ptr; }
47
48   // Overloaded output operator for class Array
49   ostream &operator<<( ostream &output, const Array &a )
50   {
51      int i;
52
53      for ( i = 0; i < a.size; i++ )
54         output << a.ptr[ i ] << ' ' ;
55
56      return output;    // enables cout << x << y;
57   }
```

Fig. 21.11   Demonstrating an **explicit** constructor—**array2.cpp**.

```
58   // Fig. 21.11: fig21_11.cpp
59   // Driver for simple class Array
60   #include <iostream>
61
62   using std::cout;
63
64   #include "array3.h"
65
66   void outputArray( const Array & );
67
```

Fig. 21.11   Demonstrating an **explicit** constructor—**fig21_11.cpp** (part 1 of 2).

```
68   int main()
69   {
70      Array integers1( 7 );
71
72      outputArray( integers1 );    // output Array integers1
73
74      // ERROR: construction not allowed
75      outputArray( 15 );  // convert 15 to an Array and output
76
77      outputArray( Array( 15 ) ); // really want to do this!
78
79      return 0;
80   }
81
82   void outputArray( const Array &arrayToOutput )
83   {
84      cout << "The array received contains:\n"
85           << arrayToOutput << "\n\n";
86   }
```

Borland C++ command-line compiler error message

```
Fig21_11.cpp:
Error E2064 Fig21_11.cpp 18: Cannot initialize 'const Array &'
   with 'int' in function main()
Error E2340 Fig21_11.cpp 18: Type mismatch in parameter 1 (wanted
   'const Array &', got 'int') in function main()
*** 2 errors in Compile ***
```

Microsoft Visual C++ compiler error message

```
Compiling...
Fig21_11.cpp
Fig21_11.cpp(18) : error C2664: 'outputArray' : cannot convert
parameter 1 from 'const int' to 'const class Array &'
        Reason: cannot convert from 'const int' to 'const class Array'
        No constructor could take the source type, or constructor
        overload resolution was ambiguous
```

Fig. 21.11   Demonstrating an **explicit** constructor—**fig21_11.cpp** (part 2 of 2).

The only modification to the program of Fig. 21.10 was the addition of the keyword **explicit** to the declaration of the single-argument constructor at line 13. When the program is compiled, the compiler produces an error message indicating that the integer value passed to **outputArray** at line 75 cannot be converted to a **const Array &**. The compiler error message is shown in the output window. Line 77 illustrates how to create an **Array** of 15 elements and pass it to **outputArray** using the **explicit** constructor.

Common Programming Error 21.4

*Attempting to invoke an **explicit** constructor for an implicit conversion is a syntax error.*

Common Programming Error 21.5

Using the **explicit** *keyword on data members or member functions other than a single argument constructor is a syntax error.*

Software Engineering Observation 21.5

Use the **explicit** *keyword on single-argument constructors that should not be used by the compiler to perform implicit conversions.*

21.10 `mutable` Class Members

In Section 21.4, we introduced the **const_cast** operator which allowed "**const**-ness" to be cast away. C++ provides the storage class specifier **mutable** as an alternative to **const_cast**. A **mutable** data member is always modifiable even in a **const** member function or **const** object. This reduces the need to cast away "**const**-ness."

Portability Tip 21.2

The effect of attempting to modify an object that was defined as constant, regardless of whether that modification was made possible by a **const_cast** *or C-style cast, varies among compilers.*

Both **mutable** and **const_cast** allow a data member to be modified; each is used in different contexts. For a **const** object with no **mutable** data members, operator **const_cast** must be used every time a member is to be modified. This greatly reduces the chance of a member being accidently modified because the member is not permanently modifiable. Operations involving **const_cast** are typically hidden in a member function's implementation. The user of a class may not be aware that a member is being modified.

Software Engineering Observation 21.6

mutable *members are useful in classes that have "secret" implementation details that do not contribute to the logical value of an object.*

The program of Fig. 21.12 demonstrates using a **mutable** member. The program defines class **TestMutable** (line 8) that contains a constructor, two functions and **private mutable** data member **value**. Line 11

```
void modifyValue() const { value++; }
```

defines function **modifyValue** as a **const** function that increments **mutable** data member **value**. Normally, a **const** member function cannot modify data members unless the object on which the function operates—i.e., to one to which **this** points—is cast (using **const_cast**) to a non-**const** type. Because **value** is **mutable**, this **const** function is able to modify the data. Function **getValue** (line 12) is a **const** function that returns **value**. Note that **getValue** could change **value** because **value** is **mutable**.

Line 19 declares **const TestMutable** object **t** and initializes it to **99**. Line 21 outputs the contents of **value**. Line 23 calls the **const** member function **modifyValue** to add one to **value**. Note that both **t** and **modifyValue** are **const**. Line 24 outputs the contents of **value** (**100**) to prove that the **mutable** data member was indeed modified.

```
1    // Fig. 21.12: fig21_12.cpp
2    // Demonstrating storage class specifier mutable.
3    #include <iostream>
4
5    using std::cout;
6    using std::endl;
7
8    class TestMutable {
9    public:
10      TestMutable( int v = 0 ) { value = v; }
11      void modifyValue() const { value++; }
12      int getValue() const { return value; }
13   private:
14      mutable int value;
15   };
16
17   int main()
18   {
19      const TestMutable t( 99 );
20
21      cout << "Initial value: " << t.getValue();
22
23      t.modifyValue();    // modifies mutable member
24      cout << "\nModified value: " << t.getValue() << endl;
25
26      return 0;
27   }
```

```
Initial value: 99
Modified value: 100
```

Fig. 21.12 Demonstrating a **mutable** data member .

21.11 Pointers to Class Members (. * and –>*)

C++ provides the . * and –>* operators for accessing class members. Pointers to class members are not the same kind of pointers we have discussed previously. Attempting to use the –> or * operator with a pointer to member generates syntax errors. The program of Fig. 21.13 demonstrates the pointer-to-class member operators.

Common Programming Error 21.6

*Attempting to use the –> or * operator with a pointer to class member is a syntax error.*

The program declares class **Test** which provides **public** member function **function** and **public** data member **value**. Function **function** outputs "**function**". Lines 14 and 15 prototype functions **arrowStar** and **dotStar**. In lines 19 and 21, object **t** is instantiated and data member **value** of **t** is set to **8**. Lines 22 and 23 call functions **arrowStar** and **dotStar**; each call passes the address of **t**.

Line 29

```
void ( Test::*memPtr )() = &Test::function;
```

in function **arrowStar** declares and initializes **memPtr** as a pointer to a member of class **Test** that is a function with a **void** result and no parameters. We start by examining the left side of the assignment. First, **void** is the member function's return type. The empty parentheses indicate that this member function takes no arguments. The middle parentheses specify a pointer **memPtr** which points to a member of class **Test**. The parentheses around **Test::*memPtr** are required. Note that **memPtr** is a standard function pointer if **Test::** is not specified. Next we examine the right value of the assignment.

```cpp
1   // Fig. 21.13 fig21_13.cpp
2   // Demonstrating operators .* and ->*
3   #include <iostream>
4
5   using std::cout;
6   using std::endl;
7
8   class Test {
9   public:
10     void function() { cout << "function\n"; }
11     int value;
12  };
13
14  void arrowStar( Test * );
15  void dotStar( Test * );
16
17  int main()
18  {
19     Test t;
20
21     t.value = 8;
22     arrowStar( &t );
23     dotStar( &t );
24     return 0;
25  }
26
27  void arrowStar( Test *tPtr )
28  {
29     void ( Test::*memPtr )() = &Test::function;
30     ( tPtr->*memPtr )();   // invoke function indirectly
31  }
32
33  void dotStar( Test *tPtr )
34  {
35     int Test::*vPtr = &Test::value;
36     cout << ( *tPtr ).*vPtr << endl;   // access value
37  }
```

```
function
8
```

Fig. 21.13 Demonstrating the **.*** and **->*** operators .

Common Programming Error 21.7

Declaring a member function pointer without enclosing the pointer name in parentheses is a syntax error.

Common Programming Error 21.8

*Declaring a member function pointer without preceding the pointer name with a class name followed by the scope resolution operator (**::**) is a syntax error.*

The right side of the assignment uses the address operator (**&**) to get the name of the member function called **function** (which must return **void** and take no arguments). Pointer **memPtr** is initialized to this offset. Note that both the left side and right side of the assignment in line 29 do not refer to any specific object. Only the class name is used with the binary scope resolution operator (**::**). Without the **&Test::**, the right side of the assignment in line 29 is a standard function pointer. Line 30

```
( tPtr->*memPtr )();
```

invokes the member function name stored in **memPtr** (i.e., **function**) using the **->*** operator. Line 35

```
int Test::*vPtr = &Test::value;
```

declares and initializes **vPtr** as a pointer to an **int** data member of class **Test**. The right side of the assignment specifies the name of the data member **value**. Note that without the **Test::**, **vPtr** becomes an **int *** pointer to the address of **int value**.

The next line

```
cout << ( *tPtr ).*vPtr << endl;
```

uses the **.*** operator to access the member named in **vPtr**. Note that in client code we can only use pointer-to-member operators for accessible members. In this example, both **value** and **function** are **public**. In a member function of the class, all members of the class are accessible.

Common Programming Error 21.9

*Placing space(s) between the two characters of **.*** or **->*** is a syntax error.*

Common Programming Error 21.10

*Reversing the order of the symbols in **.*** or **->*** is a syntax error.*

21.12 Multiple Inheritance and **virtual** Base Classes

In Chapter 9, we discussed multiple inheritance, the process by which one class inherits from two or more classes. Multiple inheritance is used, for example, in the C++ standard library to form class **iostream** (Fig. 21.14).

Class **ios** is the base class for both **ostream** and **istream**, each of which is formed with single inheritance. Class **iostream** inherits from both **ostream** and **istream**. This enables objects of class **iostream** to provide the functionality of both **istream**s and **ostream**s. In multiple inheritance hierarchies, the situation described in Fig. 21.14 is referred to as *diamond* inheritance.

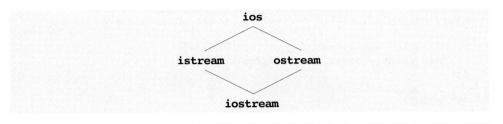

Fig. 21.14 Multiple inheritance to form class `iostream`.

Because classes **ostream** and **istream** each inherit from **ios**, a potential problem exists for **iostream**. Class **iostream** could contain duplicate *superclass objects* (e.g., **ios** is inherited into both **ostream** and **istream**). A problem could arise when an **iostream** pointer is upcast to an **ios** pointer. Two **ios** subobjects could exist. Which would then be used? Such a situation would be ambiguous and would result in a syntax error. Figure 21.15 demonstrates this kind of ambiguity but through implicit conversion rather than upcasting; of course, **iostream** does not really suffer from the problem we mentioned. In this section, we will explain how using **virtual** base classes solves the problem of duplicate subobjects.

Performance Tip 21.1

Duplicate subobjects consume memory.

```
1   // Fig. 21.15: fig21_15.cpp
2   // Attempting to polymorphically call a function
3   // multiply inherited from two base classes.
4   #include <iostream>
5
6   using std::cout;
7   using std::endl;
8
9   class Base {
10  public:
11     virtual void print() const = 0;   // pure virtual
12  };
13
14  class DerivedOne : public Base {
15  public:
16     // override print function
17     void print() const { cout << "DerivedOne\n"; }
18  };
19
20  class DerivedTwo : public Base {
21  public:
22     // override print function
23     void print() const { cout << "DerivedTwo\n"; }
24  };
25
```

Fig. 21.15 Attempting to call a multiply inherited function polymorphically (part 1 of 2).

```
26   class Multiple : public DerivedOne, public DerivedTwo {
27   public:
28      // qualify which version of function print
29      void print() const { DerivedTwo::print(); }
30   };
31
32   int main()
33   {
34      Multiple both;    // instantiate Multiple object
35      DerivedOne one;   // instantiate DerivedOne object
36      DerivedTwo two;   // instantiate DerivedTwo object
37
38      Base *array[ 3 ];
39      array[ 0 ] = &both;    // ERROR--ambiguous
40      array[ 1 ] = &one;
41      array[ 2 ] = &two;
42
43      // polymorphically invoke print
44      for ( int k = 0; k < 3; k++ )
45         array[ k ] -> print();
46
47      return 0;
48   }
```

Borland C++ command-line compiler error message

```
Borland C++ 5.5 for Win32 Copyright (c) 1993, 2000 Borland
Fig21_15.cpp:
Error E2034 Fig21_15.cpp 39: Cannot convert 'Multiple *' to 'Base *'
   in function main()
*** 1 errors in Compile ***
```

Microsoft Visual C++ compiler error message

```
Compiling...
Fig21_15.cpp
fig21_15.cpp(39) : error C2594: '=' : ambiguous conversions from
'class Multiple *' to 'class Base *'
```

Fig. 21.15 Attempting to call a multiply inherited function polymorphically (part 2 of 2).

The program defines class **Base** which contains pure **virtual** function **print**. Classes **DerivedOne** and **DerivedTwo** **public**ly inherit from **Base** and override **print**. Class **DerivedOne** and class **DerivedTwo** each contain a **Base** "subobject."

Class **Multiple** multiply inherits from **DerivedOne** and **DerivedTwo**. Function **print** is overridden to call **DerivedTwo**'s **print**. Note the qualification to specify which subobject version to call.

In **main**, an object of each class in the hierarchy is created. An array of **Base *** pointers is also declared. Each array element is initialized to the address of an object. An error occurs when the address of **both** (of multiply inherited type **Multiple**) is implicitly converted to **Base ***. Object **both** contains duplicate subobjects inherited from **Base** and this, of course, makes calls to function **print** ambiguous. A **for** loop is written to polymorphically call **print** for each of the objects pointed to by **array**.

The problem of duplicate subobjects is resolved with **virtual** inheritance. When a base class is inherited as **virtual**, only one subobject will appear in the derived class—a process called **virtual** *base class* inheritance. The program of Fig. 21.16 revises the program of Fig. 21.15 to use a **virtual** base class.

```
1   // Fig. 21.16: fig21_16.cpp
2   // Using virtual base classes.
3   #include <iostream>
4
5   using std::cout;
6   using std::endl;
7
8   class Base {
9   public:
10      // implicit default constructor
11
12      virtual void print() const = 0; // pure virtual
13   };
14
15   class DerivedOne : virtual public Base {
16   public:
17      // implicit default constructor calls
18      // Base default constructor
19
20      // override print function
21      void print() const { cout << "DerivedOne\n"; }
22   };
23
24   class DerivedTwo : virtual public Base {
25   public:
26      // implicit default constructor calls
27      // Base default constructor
28
29      // override print function
30      void print() const { cout << "DerivedTwo\n"; }
31   };
32
33   class Multiple : public DerivedOne, public DerivedTwo {
34   public:
35      // implicit default constructor calls
36      // DerivedOne and DerivedTwo default constructors
37
38      // qualify which version of function print
39      void print() const { DerivedTwo::print(); }
40   };
41
```

Fig. 21.16 Using **virtual** base classes (part 1 of 2).

```
42   int main()
43   {
44      Multiple both;    // instantiate Multiple object
45      DerivedOne one;   // instantiate DerivedOne object
46      DerivedTwo two;   // instantiate DerivedTwo object
47
48      Base *array[ 3 ];
49      array[ 0 ] = &both;
50      array[ 1 ] = &one;
51      array[ 2 ] = &two;
52
53      // polymorphically invoke print
54      for ( int k = 0; k < 3; k++ )
55         array[ k ] -> print();
56
57      return 0;
58   }
```

```
DerivedTwo
DerivedOne
DerivedTwo
```

Fig. 21.16 Using **virtual** base classes (part 2 of 2).

Class **Base** is defined and contains pure **virtual** function **print**. Class **DerivedOne** inherits from **Base** with the line

```
class DerivedOne : virtual public Base {
```

and class **DerivedTwo** inherits from **Base** with the line

```
class DerivedTwo : virtual public Base {
```

Both classes inherit from **Base**—each contains one subobject from **Base**. Class **Multiple** inherits from both **DerivedOne** and **DerivedTwo**. Only one subobject of **Base** is inherited into class **Multiple**. The compiler now allows conversion to occur (**Multiple *** to **Base ***). In **main**, an object is created for each class in the hierarchy. An array of **Base** pointers is also declared. Each **array** element is initialized to the address of an object. Note that the upcast from **both**'s address to **Base *** is now permitted. A **for** loop walks along **array** and polymorphically calls **print** for each object.

Designing hierarchies with **virtual** base classes is straightforward if default constructors are used for base classes. The previous two examples use compiler-generated default constructors. If a **virtual** base class provides a constructor, the design becomes more complicated because the *most derived class* must initialize the **virtual** base class.

In our two examples, **Base**, **DerivedOne**, **DerivedTwo** and **Multiple** are each the most derived class. If creating a **Base** object, **Base** is the most derived class. If creating a **DerivedOne** (or **DerivedTwo**) object, **DerivedOne** (or **DerivedTwo**) is the most derived class. If creating a **Multiple** object, **Multiple** is the most derived class. No matter how far down the hierarchy a class is, it is therefore the most derived class and responsible for initializing the **virtual** base class. In Exercise 21.17 we ask the reader to exercise the concept of most derived class.

Software Engineering Observation 21.7

Providing a default constructor for **virtual** *base classes simplifies hierarchy design.*

21.13 Closing Remarks

We sincerely hope you have enjoyed learning C++ and object-oriented programming in this course. The future seems clear. We wish you success in pursuing it!

We would greatly appreciate your comments, criticisms, corrections and suggestions for improving the text. Please address all correspondence to our email address:

    deitel@deitel.com

Good luck!

SUMMARY

- The C++ standard provides data type **bool** (with values of **false** or **true**) as a preferred alternative to the old style of using **0** to indicate false and nonzero to indicate true.
- The stream manipulator **boolalpha** sets the output stream to display **bool** values as the strings "**true**" and "**false**."
- The C++ standard introduces four new cast operators to use in preference to "old-style" casting used in C and C++.
- C++ provides the **static_cast** operator for conversion between types. Type checking is performed at compile time.
- The **const_cast** operator casts away the **const**-ness of objects.
- The **reinterpret_cast** operator is provided for nonstandard casts between unrelated types.
- Each **namespace** defines a scope where identifiers and variables are placed. To use a **namespace** member, the member's name must be qualified with the **namespace** name and the binary scope resolution operator (**::**) or a **using** statement must occur before the name is used.
- A **namespace** can contain constants, data, classes, nested **namespace**s, functions, etc. Definitions of **namespace**s must occupy the global scope or be nested within other **namespace**s.
- Unnamed **namespace** members occupy the global **namespace**.
- Run-time type information (RTTI) provides a means of determining an object's type at run time.
- The compile-time operator **typeid** returns a reference to a **type_info** object. A **type_info** object is a system-maintained object that represents a type.
- Operator **dynamic_cast** ensures that proper conversions take place at run time. The result of a **dynamic_cast** is **0** for invalid cast operations.
- The C++ standard provides operator keywords that can be used in place of several C++ operators.
- C++ provides the keyword **explicit** to suppress implicit conversions via conversion constructors. A constructor that is declared **explicit** cannot be used in an implicit conversion.
- A **mutable** data member is modifiable even in a **const** member function or **const** object.
- C++ provides the **.*** and **->*** operators to access class members via pointers to those members.
- Multiple inheritance can create duplicate subobjects which can be resolved with **virtual** inheritance. When a base class is inherited as **virtual**, only one subobject will appear in the derived class—a process called virtual base class inheritance.

TERMINOLOGY

->*	nested **namespace**
.*	**not**
and	**not_eq**
and_eq	operator keywords
anonymous **namespace**	**or**
bitand	**or_eq**
bitor	pointer to class member operator
bool	pointer to data member
boolalpha	pointer to member function
compl	**reinterpret_cast**
const_cast	RTTI (run-time type information)
diamond inheritance	static_cast
downcast	subobject
dynamic_cast	true
explicit	typeid
explicit conversion	typeinfo
false	typeinfo.h
global **namespace**	**type_info**
global variables	using
implicit conversion	virtual
most derived class	virtual base class
mutable	**xor**
name	**xor_eq**
namespace	

COMMON PROGRAMMING ERRORS

21.1 Performing an illegal cast with operator **static_cast** is a syntax error. Illegal casts include casting from **const** types to non-**const** types, casting pointers and references between types that are not related by **public** inheritance and casting to a type for which there is not an appropriate constructor or conversion operator to perform the cast.

21.2 Placing **main** in a **namespace** is a syntax error.

21.3 Attempting to use **dynamic_cast** on a pointer of type **void** * is a syntax error.

21.4 Attempting to invoke an **explicit** constructor for an implicit conversion is a syntax error.

21.5 Using the **explicit** keyword on data members or member functions other than a single argument constructor is a syntax error.

21.6 Attempting to use the **->** or * operator with a pointer to class member is a syntax error.

21.7 Declaring a member function pointer without enclosing the pointer name in parentheses is a syntax error.

21.8 Declaring a member function pointer without preceding the pointer name with a class name followed by the scope resolution operator (**::**) is a syntax error.

21.9 Placing space(s) between the two characters of **.*** or **->*** is a syntax error.

21.10 Reversing the order of the symbols in **.*** or **->*** is a syntax error.

GOOD PROGRAMMING PRACTICES

21.1 When creating state variables to indicate truth or falsity, use **bool**s in preference to **int**s.

21.2 Using **true** and **false** instead of zero and nonzero values makes programs clearer.

21.3   Use the safer and more reliable **static_cast** operator in preference to the C-style cast operator.

21.4   Avoid beginning identifiers with the underscore character, which can lead to linker errors.

21.5   Precede a member with its **namespace** name and the scope resolution operator (**::**) if the possibility exists of a scoping conflict.

21.6   Using **typeid** in **switch**-like tests is a misuse of RTTI. Use **virtual** functions instead.

PERFORMANCE TIP

21.1   Duplicate subobjects consume memory.

PORTABILITY TIPS

21.1   Using **reinterpret_cast** can cause programs to behave differently on different platforms.

21.2   The effect of attempting to modify an object that was defined as constant, regardless of whether that modification was made possible by a **const_cast** or C-style cast, varies among compilers.

SOFTWARE ENGINEERING OBSERVATIONS

21.1   With the additions to the C++ standard of the new cast operators (e.g., **static_cast**), old C-style casts are obsolete.

21.2   Each separate compilation unit has its own unique unnamed **namespace**, i.e., the unnamed **namespace** replaces the **static** linkage specifier.

21.3   Ideally in large programs, every entity should be declared in a class, function, block or **namespace**. This helps clarify every entity's role.

21.4   RTTI is intended for use with polymorphic inheritance hierarchies (with **virtual** functions).

21.5   Use the **explicit** keyword on single-argument constructors that should not be used by the compiler to perform implicit conversions.

21.6   **mutable** members are useful in classes that have "secret" implementation details that do not contribute to the logical value of an object.

21.7   Providing a default constructor for **virtual** base classes simplifies hierarchy design.

TESTING AND DEBUGGING TIPS

21.1   It is easy to use **reinterpret_cast** to perform dangerous manipulations that could lead to serious execution-time errors.

21.2   In order to use RTTI, some compilers require RTTI capabilities to be enabled. Check your compiler's documentation for RTTI use.

SELF-REVIEW EXERCISES

21.1   Fill in the blanks for each of the following:
   a) The _____ operator qualifies a member with its **namespace**.
   b) The _____ operator allows an object's "**const**-ness" to be cast away.
   c) The _____ operator allows conversions between types.

21.2   State which of the following are true and which are false. If a statement is false, explain why.
   a) **namespace**s are guaranteed to be unique.
   b) **namespace**s cannot have **namespace**s as members.
   c) Data type **bool** is a fundamental data type.

ANSWERS TO SELF-REVIEW EXERCISES

21.1   a) binary scope resolution (::).   b) **const_cast**.   c) C-style, **dynamic_cast**, **static_cast** or **reinterpret_cast**.

21.2   a) False. One programmer may inadvertently choose the same **namespace** as another.
   b) False. **namespace**s can be nested.
   c) True.

EXERCISES

21.3   Fill in the blanks for each of the following:
   a) Operator _____ is used to determine an object's type at run-time.
   b) Keyword _____ specifies that a **namespace** or **namespace** member is being used.
   c) Operator _____ is the operator keyword for logical OR.
   d) Storage specifier _____ allows a member of a **const** object to be modified.

21.4   State which of the following are true and which are false. If a statement is false, explain why.
   a) The validity of a **static_cast** operation is checked at compile-time.
   b) The validity of a **dynamic_cast** operation is checked at run-time.
   c) The name **typeid** is a keyword.
   d) Keyword **explicit** may be applied to constructors, member functions and data members.

21.5   What does each expression evaluate to? (*Note:* Some expressions may generate errors; if so, say what the cause of the error is.)
   a) `cout << false;`
   b) `cout << ( bool b = 8 );`
   c) `cout << ( a = true );    // a is of type int`
   d) `cout << ( *ptr + true && p );    // *ptr is 10 and p is 8.88`
   e) `// *ptr is 0 and m is false`
      `bool k = ( *ptr * 2 || ( true + 24 ) );`
   f) `bool s = true + false;`
   g) `cout << boolalpha << false << setw( 3 ) << true;`

21.6   Write a **namespace Currency** which defines constant members **ONE**, **TWO**, **FIVE**, **TEN**, **TWENTY**, **FIFTY** and **HUNDRED**. Write two short programs that use **Currency**. One program should make all constants available and the other program should only make **FIVE** available.

21.7   Write a program that uses the **reinterpret_cast** operator to cast different pointer types to **int**. Do any conversions result in syntax errors?

21.8   Write a program that uses the **static_cast** operator to cast some fundamental data types to **int**. Does the compiler allow the casts to **int**?

21.9   Write a program that demonstrates upcasting from a derived class to a base class. Use the **static_cast** operator to perform the upcast.

21.10   Write a program that creates an **explicit** constructor that takes two arguments. Does the compiler permit this? Remove **explicit** and attempt an implicit conversion. Does the compiler permit this?

21.11   What is the benefit of an **explicit** constructor?

21.12   Write a program that creates a class containing two constructors. One constructor should take a single **int** argument. The second constructor should take one **char *** argument. Write a driver program that constructs several different objects, each object having a different type passed into the constructor. Do not use **explicit**. What happens? Now use **explicit** only for the constructor that takes one **int**. What happens?

21.13   Given the following **namespace**s, answer whether or not each statement is *true* or *false*. Explain any *false* answers.

```
1   #include <string>
2   namespace Misc {
3      using namespace std;
4      enum Countries { POLAND, SWITZERLAND, GERMANY,
5                       AUSTRIA, CZECH_REPUBLIC };
6      int kilometers;
7      string s;
8
9      namespace Temp {
10        short y = 77;
11        Car car;    // assume definition exists
12     }
13  }
14
15  namespace ABC {
16     using namespace Misc::Temp;
17     void *function( void *, int );
18  }
```

    a)   Variable **y** is accessible within **namespace ABC**.
    b)   Object **s** is accessible within **namespace Temp**.
    c)   Constant **POLAND** is not accessible within **namespace Temp**.
    d)   Constant **GERMANY** is accessible within **namespace ABC**.
    e)   Function **function** is accessible to **namespace Temp**.
    f)   Namespace **ABC** is accessible to **Misc**.
    g)   Object **car** is accessible to **Misc**.

21.14   Compare and contrast **mutable** and **const_cast**. Give at least one example of when one might be preferred over the other. Note: This exercise does not require any code to be written.

21.15   Write a program that uses **const_cast** to modify a **const** variable. (*Hint:* Use a pointer in your solution to point to the **const** identifier.)

21.16   What problem does **virtual** base classes solve?

21.17   Write a program that uses **virtual** base classes. The class at the top of the hierarchy should provide a constructor that takes at least one argument (i.e., do not provide a default constructor). What challenges does this present for the inheritance hierarchy?

21.18   Find the error(s) in each of the following. When possible, explain how to correct each error.
    a)   ```namespace Name {
         int x, y;
         mutable int z;
      };```
    b)   `int integer = const_cast< int >( double );`
    c)   `namespace PCM( 111, "hello" );   // construct namespace`
    d)   `explicit int x = 99;`

Operator Precedence Chart

Operators are shown in decreasing order of precedence from top to bottom.

Operator	Type	Associativity
`::`	binary scope resolution	left to right
`::`	unary scope resolution	
`()`	parentheses	left to right
`[]`	array subscript	
`.`	member selection via object	
`->`	member selection via pointer	
`++`	unary postincrement	
`--`	unary postdecrement	
`typeid`	run-time type information	
`dynamic_cast< ` *type* ` >`	run-time type-checked cast	
`static_cast< ` *type* ` >`	compile-time type-checked cast	
`reinterpret_cast< ` *type* ` >`	cast for non-standard conversions	
`const_cast< ` *type* ` >`	cast away **const**-ness	
`++`	unary preincrement	right to left
`--`	unary predecrement	
`+`	unary plus	
`-`	unary minus	
`!`	unary logical negation	
`~`	unary bitwise complement	*(this level of*
`( ` *type* ` )`	C-style unary cast	*precedence*
`sizeof`	determine size in bytes	*continued on*
`&`	address	*next page)*

Fig. A.1   Operator precedence chart (part 1 of 2).

Operator	Type	Associativity
* **new** **new[]** **delete** **delete[]**	dereference dynamic memory allocation dynamic array allocation dynamic memory deallocation dynamic array deallocation	*(this level of precedence continued from previous page)*
.* **->***	pointer to member via object pointer to member via pointer	left to right
* **/** **%**	multiplication division modulus	left to right
+ **-**	addition subtraction	left to right
<< **>>**	bitwise left shift bitwise right shift	left to right
< **<=** **>** **>=**	relational less than relational less than or equal to relational greater than relational greater than or equal to	left to right
== **!=**	relational is equal to relational is not equal to	left to right
&	bitwise AND	left to right
^	bitwise exclusive OR	left to right
|	bitwise inclusive OR	left to right
&&	logical AND	left to right
||	logical OR	left to right
?:	ternary conditional	right to left
= **+=** **-=** ***=** **/=** **%=** **&=** **^=** **|=** **<<=** **>>=**	assignment addition assignment subtraction assignment multiplication assignment division assignment modulus assignment bitwise AND assignment bitwise exclusive OR assignment bitwise inclusive OR assignment bitwise left shift assignment bitwise right shift with sign	right to left
,	comma	left to right

Fig. A.1   Operator precedence chart (part 2 of 2).

ASCII Character Set

ASCII character set

	0	1	2	3	4	5	6	7	8	9
0	nul	soh	stx	etx	eot	enq	ack	bel	bs	ht
1	nl	vt	ff	cr	so	si	dle	dc1	dc2	dc3
2	dc4	nak	syn	etb	can	em	sub	esc	fs	gs
3	rs	us	sp	!	"	#	$	%	&	'
4	(	)	*	+	,	-	.	/	0	1
5	2	3	4	5	6	7	8	9	:	;
6	<	=	>	?	@	A	B	C	D	E
7	F	G	H	I	J	K	L	M	N	O
8	P	Q	R	S	T	U	V	W	X	Y
9	Z	[	\	]	^	_	'	a	b	c
10	d	e	f	g	h	i	j	k	l	m
11	n	o	p	q	r	s	t	u	v	w
12	x	y	z	{	|	}	~	del		

Fig. B.1 ASCII Character Set.

The digits at the left of the table are the left digits of the decimal equivalent (0-127) of the character code, and the digits at the top of the table are the right digits of the character code. For example, the character code for "**F**" is 70, and the character code for "**&**" is 38.

Number Systems

Objectives

- To understand basic number systems concepts such as base, positional value, and symbol value.
- To understand how to work with numbers represented in the binary, octal, and hexadecimal number systems
- To be able to abbreviate binary numbers as octal numbers or hexadecimal numbers.
- To be able to convert octal numbers and hexadecimal numbers to binary numbers.
- To be able to covert back and forth between decimal numbers and their binary, octal, and hexadecimal equivalents.
- To understand binary arithmetic, and how negative binary numbers are represented using two's complement notation.

Here are only numbers ratified.
William Shakespeare

Nature has some sort of arithmetic-geometrical coordinate system, because nature has all kinds of models. What we experience of nature is in models, and all of nature's models are so beautiful.
It struck me that nature's system must be a real beauty, because in chemistry we find that the associations are always in beautiful whole numbers—there are no fractions.
Richard Buckminster Fuller

C.1 Introduction

In this appendix, we introduce the key number systems that programmers use, especially when they are working on software projects that require close interaction with "machine-level" hardware. Projects like this include operating systems, computer networking software, compilers, database systems, and applications requiring high performance.

When we write an integer such as 227 or -63 in a program, the number is assumed to be in the *decimal (base 10) number system*. The *digits* in the decimal number system are 0, 1, 2, 3, 4, 5, 6, 7, 8, and 9. The lowest digit is 0 and the highest digit is 9—one less than the *base* of 10. Internally, computers use the *binary (base 2) number system*. The binary number system has only two digits, namely 0 and 1. Its lowest digit is 0 and its highest digit is 1—one less than the base of 2. Fig. C.1 summarizes the digits used in the binary, octal, decimal and hexadecimal number systems.

As we will see, binary numbers tend to be much longer than their decimal equivalents. Programmers who work in assembly languages and in high-level languages that enable programmers to reach down to the "machine level," find it cumbersome to work with binary numbers. So two other number systems the *octal number system (base 8)* and the *hexadecimal number system (base 16)*—are popular primarily because they make it convenient to abbreviate binary numbers.

In the octal number system, the digits range from 0 to 7. Because both the binary number system and the octal number system have fewer digits than the decimal number system, their digits are the same as the corresponding digits in decimal.

The hexadecimal number system poses a problem because it requires sixteen digits—a lowest digit of 0 and a highest digit with a value equivalent to decimal 15 (one less than the base of 16). By convention, we use the letters A through F to represent the hexadecimal digits corresponding to decimal values 10 through 15. Thus in hexadecimal we can have numbers like 876 consisting solely of decimal-like digits, numbers like 8A55F consisting of digits and letters, and numbers like FFE consisting solely of letters. Occasionally, a hexadecimal number spells a common word such as FACE or FEED—this can appear strange to programmers accustomed to working with numbers. Fig. C.2 summarizes each of the number systems.

Each of these number systems uses *positional notation*—each position in which a digit is written has a different *positional value*. For example, in the decimal number 937 (the 9, the 3, and the 7 are referred to as *symbol values*), we say that the 7 is written in the *ones position*, the 3 is written in the *tens position*, and the 9 is written in the *hundreds position*. Notice that each of these positions is a power of the base (base 10), and that these powers begin at 0 and increase by 1 as we move left in the number (Fig. C.3).

Binary digit	Octal digit	Decimal digit	Hexadecimal digit
0	0	0	0
1	1	1	1
	2	2	2
	3	3	3
	4	4	4
	5	5	5
	6	6	6
	7	7	7
		8	8
		9	9
			A (decimal value of 10)
			B (decimal value of 11)
			C (decimal value of 12)
			D (decimal value of 13)
			E (decimal value of 14)
			F (decimal value of 15)

Fig. C.1 Digits of the binary, octal, decimal and hexadecimal number systems.

Attribute	Binary	Octal	Decimal	Hexadecimal
Base	2	8	10	16
Lowest digit	0	0	0	0
Highest digit	1	7	9	F

Fig. C.2 Comparison of the binary, octal, decimal and hexadecimal number systems.

Positional values in the decimal number system			
Decimal digit	9	3	7
Position name	Hundreds	Tens	Ones
Positional value	100	10	1
Positional value as a power of the base (10)	10^2	10^1	10^0

Fig. C.3 Positional values in the decimal number system.

For longer decimal numbers, the next positions to the left would be the *thousands position* (10 to the 3rd power), the *ten-thousands position* (10 to the 4th power), the *hundred-thousands position* (10 to the 5th power), the *millions position* (10 to the 6th power), the *ten-millions position* (10 to the 7th power), and so on.

In the binary number 101, we say that the rightmost 1 is written in the *ones position*, the 0 is written in the *twos position*, and the leftmost 1 is written in the *fours position*. Notice that each of these positions is a power of the base (base 2), and that these powers begin at 0 and increase by 1 as we move left in the number (Fig. C.4).

For longer binary numbers, the next positions to the left would be the *eights position* (2 to the 3rd power), the *sixteens position* (2 to the 4th power), the *thirty-twos position* (2 to the 5th power), the *sixty-fours position* (2 to the 6th power), and so on.

In the octal number 425, we say that the 5 is written in the *ones position*, the 2 is written in the *eights position*, and the 4 is written in the *sixty-fours position*. Notice that each of these positions is a power of the base (base 8), and that these powers begin at 0 and increase by 1 as we move left in the number (Fig. C.5).

For longer octal numbers, the next positions to the left would be the *five-hundred-and-twelves position* (8 to the 3rd power), the *four-thousand-and-ninety-sixes position* (8 to the 4th power), the *thirty-two-thousand-seven-hundred-and-sixty eights position* (8 to the 5th power), and so on.

In the hexadecimal number 3DA, we say that the A is written in the *ones position*, the D is written in the *sixteens position*, and the 3 is written in the *two-hundred-and-fifty-sixes position*. Notice that each of these positions is a power of the base (base 16), and that these powers begin at 0 and increase by 1 as we move left in the number (Fig. C.6).

For longer hexadecimal numbers, the next positions to the left would be the *four-thousand-and-ninety-sixes position* (16 to the 3rd power), the *sixty-five-thousand-five-hundred-and-thirty-six position* (16 to the 4th power), and so on.

Positional values in the binary number system			
Binary digit	1	0	1
Position name	Fours	Twos	Ones
Positional value	4	2	1
Positional value as a power of the base (2)	2^2	2^1	2^0

Fig. C.4   Positional values in the binary number system.

Positional values in the octal number system			
Decimal digit	4	2	5
Position name	Sixty-fours	Eights	Ones
Positional value	64	8	1
Positional value as a power of the base (8)	8^2	8^1	8^0

Fig. C.5   Positional values in the octal number system.

Positional values in the hexadecimal number system			
Decimal digit	**3**	**D**	**A**
Position name	Two-hundred-and-fifty-sixes	Sixteens	Ones
Positional value	**256**	**16**	**1**
Positional value as a power of the base (16)	16^2	16^1	16^0

Fig. C.6   Positional values in the hexadecimal number system.

C.2 Abbreviating Binary Numbers as Octal Numbers and Hexadecimal Numbers

The main use for octal and hexadecimal numbers in computing is for abbreviating lengthy binary representations. Fig. C.7 highlights the fact that lengthy binary numbers can be expressed concisely in number systems with higher bases than the binary number system.

Decimal number	Binary representation	Octal representation	Hexadecimal representation
0	0	0	0
1	1	1	1
2	10	2	2
3	11	3	3
4	100	4	4
5	101	5	5
6	110	6	6
7	111	7	7
8	1000	10	8
9	1001	11	9
10	1010	12	A
11	1011	13	B
12	1100	14	C
13	1101	15	D
14	1110	16	E
15	1111	17	F
16	10000	20	10

Fig. C.7   Decimal, binary, octal, and hexadecimal equivalents.

A particularly important relationship that both the octal number system and the hexadecimal number system have to the binary system is that the bases of octal and hexadecimal (8 and 16 respectively) are powers of the base of the binary number system (base 2). Consider the following 12-digit binary number and its octal and hexadecimal equivalents. See if you can determine how this relationship makes it convenient to abbreviate binary numbers in octal or hexadecimal. The answer follows the numbers.

Binary Number	Octal equivalent	Hexadecimal equivalent
100011010001	**4321**	**8D1**

To see how the binary number converts easily to octal, simply break the 12-digit binary number into groups of three consecutive bits each, and write those groups over the corresponding digits of the octal number as follows

100	**011**	**010**	**001**
4	**3**	**2**	**1**

Notice that the octal digit you have written under each group of thee bits corresponds precisely to the octal equivalent of that 3-digit binary number as shown in Fig. C.7.

The same kind of relationship may be observed in converting numbers from binary to hexadecimal. In particular, break the 12-digit binary number into groups of four consecutive bits each and write those groups over the corresponding digits of the hexadecimal number as follows

1000	**1101**	**0001**
8	**D**	**1**

Notice that the hexadecimal digit you wrote under each group of four bits corresponds precisely to the hexadecimal equivalent of that 4-digit binary number as shown in Fig. C.7.

C.3 Converting Octal Numbers and Hexadecimal Numbers to Binary Numbers

In the previous section, we saw how to convert binary numbers to their octal and hexadecimal equivalents by forming groups of binary digits and simply rewriting these groups as their equivalent octal digit values or hexadecimal digit values. This process may be used in reverse to produce the binary equivalent of a given octal or hexadecimal number.

For example, the octal number 653 is converted to binary simply by writing the 6 as its 3-digit binary equivalent 110, the 5 as its 3-digit binary equivalent 101, and the 3 as its 3-digit binary equivalent 011 to form the 9-digit binary number 110101011.

The hexadecimal number FAD5 is converted to binary simply by writing the F as its 4-digit binary equivalent 1111, the A as its 4-digit binary equivalent 1010, the D as its 4-digit binary equivalent 1101, and the 5 as its 4-digit binary equivalent 0101 to form the 16-digit 1111101011010101.

C.4 Converting from Binary, Octal, or Hexadecimal to Decimal

Because we are accustomed to working in decimal, it is often convenient to convert a binary, octal, or hexadecimal number to decimal to get a sense of what the number is "really" worth. Our diagrams in Section D.1 express the positional values in decimal. To convert a number to decimal from another base, multiply the decimal equivalent of each digit by its positional value, and sum these products. For example, the binary number 110101 is converted to decimal 53 as shown in Fig. C.8.

To convert octal 7614 to decimal 3980, we use the same technique, this time using appropriate octal positional values as shown in Fig. C.9.

To convert hexadecimal AD3B to decimal 44347, we use the same technique, this time using appropriate hexadecimal positional values as shown in Fig. C.10.

Converting a binary number to decimal

Positional values:	32	16	8	4	2	1
Symbol values:	1	1	0	1	0	1
Products:	1*32=32	1*16=16	0*8=0	1*4=4	0*2=0	1*1=1
Sum:	= 32 + 16 + 0 + 4 + 0 + 1 = 53					

Fig. C.8   Converting a binary number to decimal.

Converting an octal number to decimal

Positional values:	512	64	8	1
Symbol values:	7	6	1	4
Products	7*512=3584	6*64=384	1*8=8	4*1=4
Sum:	= 3584 + 384 + 8 + 4 = 3980			

Fig. C.9   Converting an octal number to decimal.

Converting a hexadecimal number to decimal

Positional values:	4096	256	16	1
Symbol values:	A	D	3	B
Products	A*4096=40960	D*256=3328	3*16=48	B*1=11
Sum:	= 40960 + 3328 + 48 + 11 = 44347			

Fig. C.10   Converting a hexadecimal number to decimal.

C.5 Converting from Decimal to Binary, Octal, or Hexadecimal

The conversions of the previous section follow naturally from the positional notation conventions. Converting from decimal to binary, octal, or hexadecimal also follows these conventions.

Suppose we wish to convert decimal 57 to binary. We begin by writing the positional values of the columns right to left until we reach a column whose positional value is greater than the decimal number. We do not need that column, so we discard it. Thus, we first write:

Positional values: 64   32   16   8   4   2   1

Then we discard the column with positional value 64 leaving:

Positional values: 32   16   8   4   2   1

Next we work from the leftmost column to the right. We divide 32 into 57 and observe that there is one 32 in 57 with a remainder of 25, so we write 1 in the 32 column. We divide 16 into 25 and observe that there is one 16 in 25 with a remainder of 9 and write 1 in the 16 column. We divide 8 into 9 and observe that there is one 8 in 9 with a remainder of 1. The next two columns each produce quotients of zero when their positional values are divided into 1 so we write 0s in the 4 and 2 columns. Finally, 1 into 1 is 1 so we write 1 in the 1 column. This yields:

Positional values:	32	16	8	4	2	1
Symbol values:	1	1	1	0	0	1

and thus decimal 57 is equivalent to binary 111001.

To convert decimal 103 to octal, we begin by writing the positional values of the columns until we reach a column whose positional value is greater than the decimal number. We do not need that column, so we discard it. Thus, we first write:

Positional values:	512	64	8	1

Then we discard the column with positional value 512, yielding:

Positional values:	64	8	1

Next we work from the leftmost column to the right. We divide 64 into 103 and observe that there is one 64 in 103 with a remainder of 39, so we write 1 in the 64 column. We divide 8 into 39 and observe that there are four 8s in 39 with a remainder of 7 and write 4 in the 8 column. Finally, we divide 1 into 7 and observe that there are seven 1s in 7 with no remainder so we write 7 in the 1 column. This yields:

Positional values:	64	8	1
Symbol values:	1	4	7

and thus decimal 103 is equivalent to octal 147.

To convert decimal 375 to hexadecimal, we begin by writing the positional values of the columns until we reach a column whose positional value is greater than the decimal number. We do not need that column, so we discard it. Thus, we first write

Positional values:	4096	256	16	1

Then we discard the column with positional value 4096, yielding:

Positional values:	256	16	1

Next we work from the leftmost column to the right. We divide 256 into 375 and observe that there is one 256 in 375 with a remainder of 119, so we write 1 in the 256 column. We divide 16 into 119 and observe that there are seven 16s in 119 with a remainder of 7 and write 7 in the 16 column. Finally, we divide 1 into 7 and observe that there are seven 1s in 7 with no remainder so we write 7 in the 1 column. This yields:

Positional values:	256	16	1
Symbol values:	1	7	7

and thus decimal 375 is equivalent to hexadecimal 177.

C.6 Negative Binary Numbers: Two's Complement Notation

The discussion in this appendix has been focussed on positive numbers. In this section, we explain how computers represent negative numbers using *two's complement notation*. First we explain how the two's complement of a binary number is formed, and then we show why it represents the negative value of the given binary number.

Consider a machine with 32-bit integers. Suppose

```
int value = 13;
```

The 32-bit representation of **value** is

    00000000 00000000 00000000 00001101

To form the negative of **value** we first form its *one's complement* by applying C++'s bitwise complement operator (~), which is also called the *bitwise NOT operator*.

```
onesComplementOfValue = ~value;
```

Internally, **~value** is now **value** with each of its bits reversed—ones become zeros and zeros become ones as follows:

```
value:
00000000 00000000 00000000 00001101
```

```
~value  (i.e., value's ones complement):
11111111 11111111 11111111 11110010
```

To form the two's complement of **value** we simply add one to **value**'s one's complement. Thus

```
Two's complement of value:
11111111 11111111 11111111 11110011
```

Now if this is in fact equal to -13, we should be able to add it to binary 13 and obtain a result of 0. Let us try this:

```
 00000000 00000000 00000000 00001101
+11111111 11111111 11111111 11110011
-----------------------------------
 00000000 00000000 00000000 00000000
```

The carry bit coming out of the leftmost column is discarded and we indeed get zero as a result. If we add the one's complement of a number to the number, the result would be all 1s. The key to getting a result of all zeros is that the twos complement is 1 more than the one's complement. The addition of 1 causes each column to add to 0 with a carry of 1. The carry keeps moving leftward until it is discarded from the leftmost bit, and hence the resulting number is all zeros.

Computers actually perform a subtraction such as

```
x = a - value;
```

by adding the two's complement of **value** to **a** as follows:

```
x = a + ( ~value + 1 );
```

Suppose **a** is 27 and **value** is 13 as before. If the two's complement of **value** is actually the negative of **value**, then adding the two's complement of value to a should produce the result 14. Let us try this:

```
a  (i.e., 27)      00000000 00000000 00000000 00011011
+(~value + 1)     +11111111 11111111 11111111 11110011
                  -----------------------------------
                   00000000 00000000 00000000 00001110
```

which is indeed equal to 14.

SUMMARY

- When we write an integer such as 19 or 227 or -63 in a program, the number is automatically assumed to be in the decimal (base 10) number system. The digits in the decimal number system are 0, 1, 2, 3, 4, 5, 6, 7, 8, and 9. The lowest digit is 0 and the highest digit is 9—one less than the base of 10.

- Internally, computers use the binary (base 2) number system. The binary number system has only two digits, namely 0 and 1. Its lowest digit is 0 and its highest digit is 1—one less than the base of 2.

- The octal number system (base 8) and the hexadecimal number system (base 16) are popular primarily because they make it convenient to abbreviate binary numbers.

- The digits of the octal number system range from 0 to 7.

- The hexadecimal number system poses a problem because it requires sixteen digits—a lowest digit of 0 and a highest digit with a value equivalent to decimal 15 (one less than the base of 16). By convention, we use the letters A through F to represent the hexadecimal digits corresponding to decimal values 10 through 15.

- Each number system uses positional notation—each position in which a digit is written has a different positional value.

- A particularly important relationship that both the octal number system and the hexadecimal number system have to the binary system is that the bases of octal and hexadecimal (8 and 16 respectively) are powers of the base of the binary number system (base 2).

- To convert an octal number to a binary number, simply replace each octal digit with its three-digit binary equivalent.

- To convert a hexadecimal number to a binary number, simply replace each hexadecimal digit with its four-digit binary equivalent.

- Because we are accustomed to working in decimal, it is convenient to convert a binary, octal or hexadecimal number to decimal to get a sense of the number's "real" worth.

- To convert a number to decimal from another base, multiply the decimal equivalent of each digit by its positional value, and sum these products.

- Computers represent negative numbers using two's complement notation.

- To form the negative of a value in binary, first form its one's complement by applying C++'s bitwise complement operator (~). This reverses the bits of the value. To form the two's complement of a value, simply add one to the value's one's complement.

TERMINOLOGY

base	digit
base 2 number system	hexadecimal number system
base 8 number system	negative value
base 10 number system	octal number system
base 16 number system	one's complement notation
binary number system	positional notation
bitwise complement operator (~)	positional value
conversions	symbol value
decimal number system	two's complement notation

SELF-REVIEW EXERCISES

C.1   The bases of the decimal, binary, octal, and hexadecimal number systems are _____, _____, _____, and _____ respectively.

C.2   In general, the decimal, octal, and hexadecimal representations of a given binary number contain (more/fewer) digits than the binary number contains.

C.3   (True/False) A popular reason for using the decimal number system is that it forms a convenient notation for abbreviating binary numbers simply by substituting one decimal digit per group of four binary bits.

C.4   The (octal / hexadecimal / decimal) representation of a large binary value is the most concise (of the given alternatives).

C.5   (True/False) The highest digit in any base is one more than the base.

C.6   (True/False) The lowest digit in any base is one less than the base.

C.7   The positional value of the rightmost digit of any number in either binary, octal, decimal, or hexadecimal is always _____.

C.8   The positional value of the digit to the left of the rightmost digit of any number in binary, octal, decimal, or hexadecimal is always equal to _____.

C.9   Fill in the missing values in this chart of positional values for the rightmost four positions in each of the indicated number systems:

	1000	100	10	1
decimal	**1000**	**100**	**10**	**1**
hexadecimal	**. . .**	**256**	**. . .**	**. . .**
binary	**. . .**	**. . .**	**. . .**	**. . .**
octal	**512**	**64**	**8**	**1**

C.10   Convert binary **110101011000** to octal and to hexadecimal.

C.11   Convert hexadecimal **FACE** to binary.

C.12   Convert octal **7316** to binary.

C.13   Convert hexadecimal **4FEC** to octal. (Hint: First convert 4FEC to binary then convert that binary number to octal.)

C.14   Convert binary **1101110** to decimal.

C.15   Convert octal **317** to decimal.

C.16   Convert hexadecimal **EFD4** to decimal.

C.17   Convert decimal **177** to binary, to octal, and to hexadecimal.

C.18   Show the binary representation of decimal **417**. Then show the one's complement of **417**, and the two's complement of **417**.

C.19   What is the result when the one's complement of a number is added to itself?

SELF-REVIEW ANSWERS

C.1   **10, 2, 8, 16**.

C.2   Fewer.

C.3   False.

C.4   Hexadecimal.

C.5   False. The highest digit in any base is one less than the base.

C.6   False. The lowest digit in any base is zero.

C.7   **1** (the base raised to the zero power).

C.8   The base of the number system.

C.9   Fill in the missing values in this chart of positional values for the rightmost four positions in each of the indicated number systems:

decimal	1000	100	10	1
hexadecimal	4096	256	16	1
binary	8	4	2	1
octal	512	64	8	1

C.10   Octal **6530**; Hexadecimal **D58**.

C.11   Binary **1111 1010 1100 1110**.

C.12   Binary **111 011 001 110**.

C.13   Binary **0 100 111 111 101 100; Octal 47754**.

C.14   Decimal **2+4+8+32+64=110**.

C.15   Decimal **7+1*8+3*64=7+8+192=207**.

C.16   Decimal **4+13*16+15*256+14*4096=61396**.

C.17   Decimal **177**
to binary:

```
256 128 64 32 16 8 4 2 1
128 64 32 16 8 4 2 1
(1*128)+(0*64)+(1*32)+(1*16)+(0*8)+(0*4)+(0*2)+(1*1)
10110001
```

to octal:

```
512 64 8 1
64 8 1
(2*64)+(6*8)+(1*1)
261
```

to hexadecimal:

```
256 16 1
16 1
(11*16)+(1*1)
(B*16)+(1*1)
B1
```

C.18   Binary:

```
512 256 128 64 32 16 8 4 2 1
256 128 64 32 16 8 4 2 1
(1*256)+(1*128)+(0*64)+(1*32)+(0*16)+(0*8)+(0*4)+(0*2)+
(1*1)
110100001
```

One's complement: **001011110**
Two's complement: **001011111**
Check: Original binary number + its two's complement

```
110100001
001011111
---------
000000000
```

C.19   Zero.

EXERCISES

C.20   Some people argue that many of our calculations would be easier in the base **12** number system because **12** is divisible by so many more numbers than **10** (for base **10**). What is the lowest digit in base **12**? What might the highest symbol for the digit in base **12** be? What are the positional values of the rightmost four positions of any number in the base **12** number system?

C.21   How is the highest symbol value in the number systems we discussed related to the positional value of the first digit to the left of the rightmost digit of any number in these number systems?

C.22   Complete the following chart of positional values for the rightmost four positions in each of the indicated number systems:

	1000	100	10	1
decimal	**1000**	**100**	**10**	**1**
base 6	...	...	**6**	...
base 13	...	**169**	...	...
base 3	**27**	...	...	...

C.23   Convert binary **100101111010** to octal and to hexadecimal.

C.24   Convert hexadecimal **3A7D** to binary.

C.25   Convert hexadecimal **765F** to octal. (Hint: First convert **765F** to binary, then convert that binary number to octal.)

C.26   Convert binary **1011110** to decimal.

C.27   Convert octal **426** to decimal.

C.28   Convert hexadecimal **FFFF** to decimal.

C.29   Convert decimal **299** to binary, to octal, and to hexadecimal.

C.30   Show the binary representation of decimal **779**. Then show the one's complement of **779**, and the two's complement of **779**.

C.31   What is the result when the two's complement of a number is added to itself?

C.32   Show the two's complement of integer value **−1** on a machine with 32-bit integers.

C++ Internet and Web Resources

This appendix contains a list of valuable C++ resources on the Internet and the World Wide Web. These resources include FAQs (Frequently Asked Questions), tutorials, how to obtain the ANSI/ISO C++ standard, information about popular C++ compilers and how to obtain free compilers, demos, books, tutorials, software tools, articles, interviews, conferences, journals and magazines, on-line courses, newsgroups and career resources.

For more information about the American National Standards Institute (ANSI) or to purchase standards documents, visit ANSI at **http://www.ansi.org/**.

D.1 Resources

http://www.progsource.com/index.html
The Programmer's Source is a great resource for information on many programming languages, including C++. You will find lists of tools, compilers, software, books and other C++ resources.

http://www.intranet.ca/~sshah/booklist.html#C++
The Programmer's Book List has a section for C++ books with 30+ titles.

http://www.genitor.com/resources.htm
The Developer Resources site has links to C++ compilers, useful C++ tools, source code from the *C/C++ Users Journal* and publications.

http://www.possibility.com/Cpp/CppCodingStandard.html
The C++ Coding Standard site has an extensive amount of information about the C++ programming language as well as a great list of C++ resources on the Web.

http://help-site.com/cpp.html
Help-site.com provides links to C++ resources on the Web.

http://www.glenmccl.com/tutor.htm
This site is a good reference for users with C/C++ knowledge. Topics are accompanied by detailed explanations and example code.

http://www.programmersheaven.com/zone3/cat353/index.htm
This site offers an extensive collection of C++ libraries. These libraries are available for free download.

http://www.programmersheaven.com/zone3/cat155/index.htm
This site offers tools and libraries for C/C++.

http://www.programmersheaven.com/wwwboard/board3/wwwboard.asp
This message board allows users to post C/C++ programming questions and comments to the website **developer.com**. A list of frequently asked questions with answers is provided.

http://www.hal9k.com/cug/
This site provides C++ resources, journals, shareware, freeware, etc.

**http://developer.earthweb.com/directories/pages/
dir.c.developmenttools.html**
A popular Web site for programmers, *Developer.com* provides an extensive list of resources for programmers using C and C++.

http://www.devx.com
DevX is a comprehensive resources for programmers. The section provides the latest news, tools and techniques for various programming languages. The C++ zone section of the site is dedicated to C++.

D.2 Tutorials

http://info.desy.de/gna/html/cc/index.html
This *Introduction to Object-Oriented Programming Using C++* tutorial is available to download or you can register for a Web-based course. Check out the recommended books on object-oriented programming and the C++ programming language.

http://uu-gna.mit.edu:8001/uu-gna/text/cc/Tutorial/tutorial.html
This *Introduction to Object Oriented Programming Using C++* tutorial is broken down into 10 chapters, each with a set of exercises and solutions to the exercises.

http://www.icce.rug.nl/docs/cplusplus/cplusplus.html
This tutorial by a university professor is designed for C programmers who want to learn C++.

http://www.rdw.tec.mn.us/
Red Wing/Winona Technical College offers on-line C++ courses for credit.

http://www.zdu.com/zdu/catalog/programming.htm
ZD Net University offers a variety of on-line courses related to the C++ programming language.

http://library.advanced.org/3074/
This tutorial is designed for Pascal programmers who want to learn C++.

ftp://rtfm.mit.edu/pub/usenet/news.answers/C-faq/learn-c-cpp-today
This site has a list of C++ tutorials this site also contains information about various C++ compilers.

http://www.icce.rug.nl/docs/cplusplus/cplusplus.html
A site for users who already know C and want to learn C++.

http://www.cprogramming.com/tutorial.html
This site includes a step-by-step tutorial that includes sample code.

http://www.programmersheaven.com/zone3/cat34/index.htm
This site contains a list of tutorial topics. Tutorial levels range from beginner to expert.

D.3 FAQs

http://reality.sgi.com/austern/std-c++/faq.html
This is a FAQ site devoted to questions about the C++ ANSI/ISO standard, the design of the C++ programming language and the latest changes to the language.

http://www.trmphrst.demon.co.uk/cpplibs1.html
This is a C++ libraries FAQ. You will find an extensive list of answers to the questions frequently asked about the C++ standard libraries.

http://pneuma.phys.ualberta.ca/~burris/cpp.htm
The Internet Link Exchange is another great resource for C++ information. This site has links to FAQs related to **comp.lang.c++** and the C++ standard libraries.

http://www.math.uio.no/nett/faq/C-faq/faq.html
The **comp.lang.c** list of frequently asked questions (FAQs) and answers.

http://lglwww.epfl.ch/~wolf/c_std.html
A list of FAQs on the ANSI/ISO standard for the C programming language.

http://www.cerfnet.com/~mpcline/C++-FAQs-Lite/
This site has an abundance of FAQs broken down into 35 categories.

http://www.faqs.org/faqs/by-newsgroup/comp/comp.lang.c++.html
This site consists of a series of links to FAQs and tutorials gathered from the **Comp.Lang.C++** newsgroup.

http://www.cerfnet.com/~mpcline/C++-FAQs-Lite/
This is a FAQ site with an extensive array of topics. Each topic includes several questions with answers.

http://www.eskimo.com/~scs/C-faq/top.html
This FAQ list contains topics such as pointers, memory allocation and strings.

D.4 Visual C++

http://chesworth.com/pv/languages/c/visual_cpp_tutorial.htm
This is a good tutorial for a beginner learning Microsoft Visual C++. The tutorial gives the user a brief overview of C++.

D.5 comp.lang.c++

http://weblab.research.att.com/phoaks/comp/lang/c++/resources0.html
Wow! This site is a tremendous resource for information related to **comp.lang.c++**. The title of the page, *People Helping One Another Know Stuff*, summarizes what this site is all about. You will find links to over 40 additional resources for C++ information.

http://www.r2m.com/windev/cpp-compiler.html
This site contains links to many C++ related sites.

http://home.istar.ca/~stepanv/
This site has many links to sites with articles and information related to C++ programming. Topics listed on this site include object-oriented graphics, the ANSI C++ standard, the Standard Template Library, MFC resources, and tutorials.

http://kom.net/~dbrick/newspage/comp.lang.c++.html
Visit this site to connect to newsgroups related to the **comp.lang.c++** hierarchy.

http://www.austinlinks.com/CPlusPlus/
Quadralay Corporation's Web site has links to C++ resources including Visual C++/MFC Libraries, C++ programming information, C++ career resources, and a list of tutorials and other on line tools to help you learn C++.

http://db.csie.ncu.edu.tw/~kant_c/C/chapter2_21.html
This Web site has a list of ANSI C standard library functions

**http://wwwcn1.cern.ch/asd/geant/geant4_public/coding_standards/
coding/coding_2.html**
An excellent and extensive resource for C++ Standard information.

http://cuiwww.unige.ch/OSG/Vitek/Compilers/Year86/msg00046.html
"The C standard on segmented machines."

http://www.csci.csusb.edu/dick/c++std/
This site has links to the ANSI/ISO C++ Draft Standard and the Usenet group **comp.std.c++**
which provides new information about the standard.

http://ibd.ar.com/ger/comp.lang.c++.html
The Green Eggs Report lists over 100 URLs within **comp.lang.C++**.

http://www.ts.umu.se/~maxell/C++/
This is site provides code examples for some of the C++ classes.

http://www.quadralay.com/CPlusPlus/
This is a great resource for C++ programming information, learning C++, C++ career resources, and
other C++ related information.

http://www.research.att.com/~bs/homepage.html
This is the *home page for Bjarne Stroustrup*, designer of the C++ programming language. He provides
a list of C++ resources, FAQs and other useful C++ information.

http://www.cygnus.com/misc/wp/draft/index.html
This site has the "working draft" of the ANSI C++ Standard in HTML format (December 1996).

http://www.austinlinks.com/CPlusPlus/
This site has a list of C++ resources including suggested books, career resources, information about
the C++ programming language and links to sites with lists of C++ resources.

ftp://research.att.com/dist/c++std/WP/CD2/
This site has the current ANSI/ISO C++ draft standard.

http://ai.kaist.ac.kr/~ymkim/Program/c++.html
This Web site offers tutorials, libraries, popular compilers, FAQs and newsgroups.

http://www.cyberdiem.com/vin/learn.html
Learn C/C++ Today is the title of this site which provides a number of in depth tutorials on C/C++.

http://www.trumphurst.com/cpplibs1.html
The C++ Libraries FAQ is compiled by programming professionals for the use and benefit of other
C++ programmers. The Library is updated regularly and is a good source for current information.

http://www.experts-exchange.com/comp/lang/cplusplus/
The Experts Exchange is a free resource for high-tech professionals who wish to share information
with their colleagues. Members can post questions and answers.

http://www.execpc.com/~ht/vc.htm
This site is a compilation of C++ programming links that include general information sites, tutorials,
magazines and libraries.

http://cplus.about.com/compute/cplus/
This is the *About.com* site for C/C++ programming languages. You will find tutorials, freeware/share-
ware, dictionaries, jobs, magazines and many other related items.

**http://pent21.infosys.tuwien.ac.at/cetus/
oo_c_plus_plus.html#oo_c_plus_plus_general_newsgroups**
On this site you will find a general explanation of C++. This site contains news groups.

news:comp.lang.c++
This is a newsgroup dedicated to object-oriented C++ language issues.

`news:comp.lang.c++.moderated`
This is a more technically oriented newsgroup dedicated to the C++ language.

D.6 Compilers

`http://www.progsource.com/index.html`
The Programmer's Source is a great resource for information on many programming languages, including C++. You will find lists of tools, compilers, software, books and other C++ resources. The list of compilers is organized by platform.

`http://www.cygnus.com/misc/gnu-win32/`
The *GNU development environment* is available at no charge from the Cygnus Web site.

`http://www.remcomp.com/lcc-win32/`
The *LCC-Win32 compiler* for Windows 95/NT can be downloaded for free from this Web site.

`http://www.microsoft.com/visualc/`
The *Microsoft Visual C++ home page* provides product information, overviews, supplemental materials, and ordering information for the Visual C++ compiler.

`http://www.powersoft.com/products/languages/watccpl.html`
Powersoft product news and information for the *Watcom C/C++ version 11.0*. This compiler cannot be downloaded from the Web site. Purchasing information is provided.

`http://netserv.borland.com/borlandcpp/cppcomp/turbocpp.html`
The *Borland Turbo C++ Visual Edition* for Windows compiler Web site.

`http://www.symantec.com/scpp/fs_scpp72_95.html`
Symantec C++ 7.5 for Windows 95 and Windows NT.

`http://www.metrowerks.com/products/`
Metrowerks CodeWarrior for Macintosh or Windows.

`http://www.faqs.org/faqs/by-newsgroup/comp/comp.compilers.html`
This is a site that has created a list of FAQs generated within the **comp.compilers** newsgroup.

`http://www.ncf.carleton.ca/%7Ebg283/`
This is a DOS based C++ compiler called the *Miracle C compiler*. The compiler is free for download, but the source code is not available until you pay a registration fee.

`http://www.borland.com/bcppbuilder/`
This is a link to the *Borland C++ Builder 5.5* A free command-line version is available for download.

`http://www.compilers.net/`
Compilers.net is a site designed to help you find compilers.

`http://sunset.backbone.olemiss.edu/%7Ebobcook/eC/`
This C++ compiler is designed for beginning C++ users who wish to transition from Pascal to C++.

`http://developer.intel.com/vtune/compilers/cpp/`
The *Intel C++ compiler*. Platforms supported are Windows 98, NT and 2000.

`http://www.kai.com/C_plus_plus/index.html`
The *Kai C++ compiler* is available for a thirty-day free trial.

D.7 Development Tools

`http://www.quintessoft.com/`
Quintessoft Engineering, Inc. offers Code Navigator for C++, a C++ development tool for Windows 95/NT. You will find product information, customer comments, free trial edition downloads and pricing information for the product.

D.8 Standard Template Library

Tutorials

`http://www.cs.brown.edu/people/jak/programming/stl-tutorial/`
`tutorial.html`
This STL tutorial is organized by examples, philosophy, components and extending STL. You will find code examples using the STL components, useful explanations and helpful diagrams.

`http://web.ftech.net/~honeyg/articles/eff_stl.htm`
This STL tutorial provides information on the STL components, containers, stream and iterator adaptors, transforming and selecting values, filtering and transforming values, and objects.

`http://www.xraylith.wisc.edu/~khan/software/stl/os_examples/`
`examples.html`
This site is helpful for people just learning about the STL. You will find an introduction to the STL and ObjectSpace STL Tool Kit examples.

References

`http://www.sgi.com/Technology/STL/other_resources.html`
This site has a list of many STL-related Web sites and a list of suggested books on the STL.

`http://www.cs.rpi.edu/projects/STL/stl/stl.html`
This is the *Standard Template Library Online Reference Home Page* from Rensselaer Polytechnic Institute. You will find detailed explanations of the STL as well as links to other useful resources for information about the STL.

`http://www.sgi.com/Technology/STL/`
The *Silicon Graphics Standard Template Library Programmer's Guide* is a useful resource for STL information. You can download the STL from this site, and find the latest information, design documentation, and links to other STL resources.

`http://www.dinkumware.com/refcpp.html`
This site contains useful information about the ANSI/ISO Standard C++ Library and contains extensive information about the Standard Template Library.

`http://www.roguewave.com/products/xplatform/stdlib/`
Rogue Wave Software's Standard C++ Library web page. You can download whitepapers related to their version of the Standard C++ Library.

FAQs

`ftp://butler.hpl.hp.com/stl/stl.faq`
This FTP site is a FAQ sheet for the STL maintained by Marian Corcoran, a member of the ANSI committee and a C++ expert.

Articles, Books and Interviews

`http://www.sgi.com/Technology/STL/other_resources.html`
This site has many STL-related Web sites and a short list of suggested books on the STL.

`http://www.byte.com/art/9510/sec12/art3.htm`
The *Byte Magazine* site has a copy of an article on the STL written by Alexander Stepanov. Stepanov, one of the creators of the Standard Template Library, provides information on the use of the STL in generic programming.

`http://www.sgi.com/Technology/STL/drdobbs-interview.html`
An interview with Alexander Stepanov that has some interesting information about the creation of the Standard Template Library. Stepanov talks about how the STL was conceptualized, generic programming, the acronym "STL" and more.

ANSI/ISO C++ Standard

http://www.ansi.org/

You can purchase a copy of the C++ standard document from this site.

Software

http://www.cs.rpi.edu/~musser/stl.html

The RPI STL site includes information on how STL differs from other C++ libraries and on how to compile programs that use STL, list of main STL include files, example programs that use STL, STL Container Classes, and STL Iterator Categories. It also provides a STL-compatible compiler list, FTP sites for STL source code and related materials.

http://www.mathcs.sjsu.edu/faculty/horstman/safestl.html

Download SAFESTL.ZIP, a tool designed to find errors in programs using the STL.

http://www.objectspace.com/jgl/

Object Space provides information about porting C++ to Java. You can download their *Standards<ToolKit>* portable class libraries free. Key features of the toolkit include containers, iterators, algorithms, allocators, strings and exceptions.

http://www.cs.rpi.edu/~wiseb/stl-borland.html

"Using the Standard Template Library with Borland C++." This site is a useful reference for people using the Borland C++ compiler. The author has sections on warnings and incompatibilities.

http://msdn.microsoft.com/visualc/

This is the *Microsoft Visual C++ home page*. Here you can find the latest Visual C++ news, updates, technical resources, samples and downloads.

http://www.borland.com/bcppbuilder/

This is the *Borland C++ Builder home page*. Here you can find a variety of C++ resources including several C++ newsgroups, information on the latest product enhancements, FAQs and many other resources for programmers using C++Builder.

Bibliography

(Al92)   Allison, C., "Text Processing I," *The C Users Journal,* Vol. 10, No. 10, October 1992, pp. 23–28.

(Al92a)   Allison, C., "Text Processing II," *The C Users Journal,* Vol. 10, No. 12, December 1992, pp. 73-77.

(Al93)   Allison, C., "Code Capsules: A C++ Date Class, Part I," *The C Users Journal,* Vol. 11, No. 2, February 1993, pp. 123–131.

(Al94)   Allison, C., "Conversions and Casts," *The C/C++ Users Journal,* Vol. 12, No. 9, September 1994, pp. 67–85.

(Am95)   Almarode, J., "Object Security," *Smalltalk Report,* Vol. 5, No. 3 November-December 1995, pp. 15–17.

(An90)   ANSI, *American National Standard for Information Systems–Programming Language C (ANSI Document ANSI/ISO 9899: 1990),* New York, NY: American National Standards Institute, 1990.

(An94)   *American National Standard, Programming Language C++.* [Approval and technical development work is being conducted by Accredited Standards Committee X3, Information Technology and its Technical Committee X3J16, Programming Language C++, respectively. For further details, contact X3 Secretariat, 1250 Eye Street, NW, Washington, DC 20005.]

(An92)   Anderson, A. E., and W. J. Heinze, *C++ Programming and Fundamental Concepts,* Englewood Cliffs, NJ: Prentice Hall, 1992.

(Ba92)   Baker, L., *C Mathematical Function Handbook,* New York, NY: McGraw Hill, 1992.

(Ba93)   Bar-David, T., *Object-Oriented Design for C++,* Englewood Cliffs, NJ: Prentice Hall, 1993.

(Be94)   Beck, K., "Birds, Bees, and Browsers–Obvious Sources of Objects," *The Smalltalk Report,* Vol. 3, No. 8 June 1994, p. 13.

(Be93a)   Becker, P., "Conversion Confusion," *C++ Report,* October 1993, pp. 26-28.

(Be93)   Becker, P., "Shrinking the Big Switch Statement," *Windows Tech Journal,* Vol. 2, No. 5, May 1993, pp. 26–33.

(Bd93)   Berard, E. V., *Essays on Object Oriented Software Engineering: Volume I,* Englewood Cliffs, NJ: Prentice Hall, 1992.

(Bi95)   Binder, R. V., "State-Based Testing," *Object Magazine,* Vol. 5, No. 4, August 1995, pp. 75–78.

(Bi95a)   Binder, R. V., "State-Based Testing: Sneak Paths and Conditional Transitions," *Object Magazine,* Vol. 5, No. 6, October 1995, pp. 87–89.

(Bl92)   Blum, A., *Neural Networks in C++: An Object-Oriented Framework for Building Connectionist Systems,* New York, NY: John Wiley & Sons, 1992.

(Bo91)   Booch, G., *Object-Oriented Design with Applications,* Redwood City, CA: The Benjamin/Cummings Publishing Company, Inc., 1991.

(Bo94)   Booch, G., *Object-Oriented Analysis and Design,* Second Edition, Reading, MA: Addison-Wesley Publishing Company, 1994.

(Bo96)   Booch, G., *Object Solutions,* Reading, MA: Benjamin/Cummings, 1996.

(Ca92)   Cargill, T., *Programming Style,* Reading, MA: Addison-Wesley Publishing Company, 1992.

(Ca95)   Carroll, M. D., and M. A. Ellis, *Designing and Coding Reusable C++,* Reading, MA: Addison-Wesley Publishing Company, 1995.

(Co95)   Coplien, J. O., and D. C. Schmidt, *Pattern Languages of Program Design,* Reading, MA: Addison-Wesley Publishing Company, 1995.

(C++98)   ANSI/ISO/IEC: *International Standard: Programming Languages—C++.* ISO/IEC 14882:1998(E). Published by the American National Standards Institute, New York, NY: 1998.

(De90)   Deitel, H. M., *Operating Systems,* Second Edition, Reading, MA: Addison-Wesley, 1990.

(De00)   Deitel, H. M., and P. J. Deitel, *Java How to Program,* Third Edition, Upper Saddle River, NJ: Prentice Hall, 2000.

(De00a)   Deitel, H. M., and P. J. Deitel, *The Java Multimedia Cyber Classroom,* Third Edition, Upper Saddle River, NJ: Prentice Hall, 2000.

(De01)   Deitel, H. M., and P. J. Deitel, *C How to Program* (Third Edition), Upper Saddle River, NJ: Prentice Hall, 2000.

(Du91)   Duncan, R., "Inside C++: Friend and Virtual Functions, and Multiple Inheritance," *PC Magazine,* Vol. 10, No. 17, October 15, 1991, pp. 417–420.

(El90)   Ellis, M. A., and B. Stroustrup, *The Annotated C++ Reference Manual,* Reading, MA: Addison-Wesley, 1990.

(Em92)   Embley, D. W.; B. D. Kurtz; and S. N. Woodfield, *Object-Oriented Systems Analysis,* Englewood Cliffs, NJ: Yourdon Press, 1992.

(En90)   Entsminger, G., *The Tao of Objects: A Beginner's Guide to Object-Oriented Programming,* Redwood City, CA: M&T Books, 1990.

(Fl93)   Flamig, B., *Practical Data Structures in C++,* New York, NY: John Wiley & Sons, 1993.

(Ga95)   Gamma, E,; R. Helm; R. Johnson; and J. Vlissides, *Design Patterns: Elements of Reusable Object-Oriented Software,* Reading, MA: Addison-Wesley Publishing Company, 1995.

(Ge89)   Gehani, N., and W. D. Roome, *The Concurrent C Programming Language,* Summit, NJ: Silicon Press, 1989.

(Gi92)   Giancola, A., and L. Baker, "Bit Arrays with C++," *The C Users Journal,* Vol. 10, No. 7, July, 1992, pp. 21–26.

(Gl95)   Glass, G., and B. Schuchert, *The STL <Primer>,* Upper Saddle River, NJ: Prentice Hall PTR, 1995.

(Go95)   Gooch, T., "Obscure C++," *Inside Microsoft Visual C++,* Vol. 6, No. 11, November 1995, pp. 13–15.

(Ha90)   Hansen, T. L., *The C++ Answer Book,* Reading, MA: Addison-Wesley, 1990.

(He97)   Henricson, M., and E. Nyquist, *Industrial Strength C++: Rules and Recommendations,* Upper Saddle River, NJ: Prentice Hall, 1997.

(Ja93)   Jacobson, I., "Is Object Technology Software's Industrial Platform?" *IEEE Software Magazine,* Vol. 10, No. 1, January 1993, pp. 24–30.

(Ja89)   Jaeschke, R., *Portability and the C Language,* Indianapolis, IN: Hayden Books, 1989.

(Ke88)   Kernighan, B. W., and D. M. Ritchie, *The C Programming Language* (Second Edition), Englewood Cliffs, NJ: Prentice Hall, 1988.

(Kn92)   Knight, A., "Encapsulation and Information Hiding," *The Smalltalk Report,* Vol. 1, No. 8 June 1992, pp. 19-20.

(Ko90)   Koenig, A., and B. Stroustrup, "Exception Handling for C++ (revised)," *Proceedings of the USENIX C++ Conference,* San Francisco, CA, April 1990.

(Ko91)   Koenig, A., "What is C++ Anyway?" *Journal of Object-Oriented Programming,* April/May 1991, pp. 48–52.

(Ko94)   Koenig, A., Implicit Base Class Conversions," *C++ Report,* Vol. 6, No. 5, June 1994, pp. 18–19.

(Ko97)   Koenig, A., and B. Moo, *Ruminations on C++,* Reading, MA: Addison-Wesley, 1997.

(Kr91)   Kruse, R. L.; B. P. Leung; and C. L. Tondo, *Data Structures and Program Design in C,* Englewood Cliffs, NJ: Prentice Hall, 1991.

(Le92)   Lejter, M.; S. Meyers; and S. P. Reiss, "Support for Maintaining Object-Oriented Programs," *IEEE Transactions on Software Engineering,* Vol. 18, No. 12, December 1992, pp. 1045–1052.

((Li91)   Lippman, S. B., *C++ Primer* (Second Edition), Reading, MA: Addison-Wesley Publishing Company, 1991.

(Lo93)   Lorenz, M., *Object-Oriented Software Development: A Practical Guide,* Englewood Cliffs, NJ: Prentice Hall, 1993.

(Lo94)   Lorenz, M., "A Brief Look at Inheritance Metrics," *The Smalltalk Report,* Vol. 3, No. 8 June 1994, pp. 1, 4–5.

(Ma93)   Martin, J., *Principles of Object-Oriented Analysis and Design,* Englewood Cliffs, NJ: Prentice Hall, 1993.

(Ma95)   Martin, R. C., *Designing Object-Oriented C++ Applications Using the Booch Method,* Englewood Cliffs, NJ: Prentice Hall, 1995.

(Ma93a)   Matsche, J. J., "Object-Oriented Programming in Standard C," *Object Magazine,* Vol. 2, No. 5, January/February 1993, pp. 71–74.

(Mc94)   McCabe, T. J., and A. H. Watson, "Combining Comprehension and Testing in Object-Oriented Development," *Object Magazine,* Vol. 4, No. 1, March/April 1994, pp. 63–66.

(Me88)   Meyer, B., *Object-Oriented Software Construction,* C. A. R. Hoare Series Editor, Englewood Cliffs, NJ: Prentice Hall, 1988.

(Me92)   Meyer, B., *Advances in Object-Oriented Software Engineering,* Edited by D. Mandrioli and B. Meyer, Englewood Cliffs, NJ: Prentice Hall, 1992.

(Me92a)   Meyer, B., *Eiffel: The Language,* Englewood Cliffs, NJ: Prentice Hall, 1992.

(Me92b)   Meyers, S., *Effective C++: 50 Specific Ways to Improve Your Programs and Designs,* Reading, MA: Addison-Wesley Publishing Company, 1992.

(Me95)   Meyers, S., *More Effective C++: 35 New Ways to Improve Your Programs and Designs,* Reading, MA: Addison-Wesley Publishing Company, 1995.

(Me95a)   Meyers, S., "Mastering User-Defined Conversion Functions," *C/C++ Users Journal,* Vol. 13, No. 8, August 1995, pp. 57–63.

(Mu93)   Murray, R., *C++ Strategies and Tactics,* Reading, MA: Addison-Wesley Publishing Company, 1993.

(Mu94)   Musser, D. R., and A. A. Stepanov, "Algorithm-Oriented Generic Libraries," *Software Practice and Experience,* Vol. 24, No. 7, July 1994.

(Mu96)   Musser, D. R., and A. Saini, *STL Tutorial and Reference Guide: C++ Programming with the Standard Template Library,* Reading, MA: Addison-Wesley Publishing Company, 1996.

(Ne95)   Nelson, M., *C++ Programmer's Guide to the Standard Template Library,* Foster City, CA: Programmers Press, 1995.

(Ne920   Nerson, J. M., "Applying Object-Oriented Analysis and Design," *Communications of the ACM,* Vol. 35, No. 9, September 1992, pp. 63–74.

(Ni92)   Nierstrasz, O.; S. Gibbs; and D. Tsichritzis, "Component-Oriented Software Development," *Communications of the ACM,* Vol. 35, No. 9, September 1992, pp. 160–165.

(Pi90)   Pinson, L. J., and R. S. Wiener, *Applications of Object-Oriented Programming,* Reading, MA: Addison-Wesley, 1990.

(Pi93)   Pittman, M., "Lessons Learned in Managing Object-Oriented Development," *IEEE Software Magazine,* Vol. 10, No. 1, January 1993, pp. 43–53.

(Pl92)   Plauger, P. J., *The Standard C Library,* Englewood Cliffs, NJ: Prentice Hall, 1992.

(Pl93)   Plauger, D., "Making C++ Safe for Threads," *The C Users Journal,* Vol. 11, No. 2, February 1993, pp. 58–62.

(Po97)   Pohl, I., *C++ Distilled: A Concise ANSI/ISO Reference and Style Guide,* Reading, MA: Addison-Wesley, 1997.

(Po97a)   Pohl, I., *Object-Oriented Programming Using C++,* Second Edition, Reading, MA: Addison-Wesley Publishing Company, 1997.

(Pr92)   Press, W. H., et al, *Numerical Recipies in C,* Second Edition, Cambridge, MA: Cambridge University Press, 1992.

(Pr93)   Prieto-Diaz, R., "Status Report: Software Reusability," *IEEE Software,* Vol. 10, No. 3, May 1993, pp. 61–66.

(Pr92)   Prince, T., "Tuning Up Math Functions," *The C Users Journal,* Vol. 10, No. 12, December 1992.

(Pr95)   Prosise, J., "Wake Up and Smell the MFC: Using the Visual C++ Classes and Applications Framework," *Microsoft Systems Journal,* Vol. 10, No. 6, June 1995, pp. 17–34.

(Ra90)   Rabinowitz, H., and C. Schaap, *Portable C,* Englewood Cliffs, NJ: Prentice Hall, 1990.

(Re91)   Reed, D. R., "Moving from C to C++," *Object Magazine,* Vol. 1, No. 3, September/October 1991, pp. 46–60.

(Ri78)   Ritchie, D. M.; S. C. Johnson; M. E. Lesk; and B. W. Kernighan, "UNIX Time-Sharing System: The C Programming Language," *The Bell System Technical Journal,* Vol. 57, No. 6, Part 2, July–August 1978, pp. 1991–2019.

(Ri84)   Ritchie, D. M., "The UNIX System: The Evolution of the UNIX Time-Sharing System," *AT&T Bell Laboratories Technical Journal,* Vol. 63, No. 8, Part 2, October 1984, pp. 1577–1593.

(Ro84)   Rosler, L., "The UNIX System: The Evolution of C–Past and Future," *AT&T Laboratories Technical Journal,* Vol. 63, No. 8, Part 2, October 1984, pp. 1685–1699.

(Ro00)   Robson, R., Using the STL: The C++ Standard Template Library, Springer Verlag, 2000.

(Ru92)   Rubin, K. S., and A. Goldberg, "Object Behavior Analysis," *Communications of the ACM,* Vol. 35, No. 9, September 1992, pp. 48–62.

(Ru91)   Rumbaugh, J.; M. Blaha; W. Premerlani; F. Eddy; and W. Lorensen, *Object-Oriented Modeling and Design,* Englewood Cliffs, NJ: Prentice Hall, 1991.

(Sa93)   Saks, D., "Inheritance," *The C Users Journal,* May 1993, pp. 81–89.

(Sc99)   Schildt, H., STL Programming from the Ground Up, Osborne McGraw-Hill, 1999.

(Se92)   Sedgwick, R., *Algorithms in C++,* Reading, MA: Addison-Wesley, 1992.

(Se92a)   Sessions, R., *Class Construction in C and C++,* Englewood Cliffs, NJ: Prentice Hall, 1992.

(Sk93)   Skelly, C., "Pointer Power in C and C++," *The C Users Journal,* Vol. 11, No. 2, February 1993, pp. 93–98.

(Sm92)   Smaer, S., and S. J. Mellor, *Object Lifecycles: Modeling the World in States,* Englewood Cliffs, NJ: Yourdon Press, 1992.

(Sm90)   Smith, J. D., *Reusability & Software Construction in C & C++,* New York, NY: John Wiley & Sons, 1990.

(Sn93)   Snyder, A., "The Essence of Objects: Concepts and Terms," *IEEE Software Magazine,* Vol. 10, No. 1, January 1993, pp. 31–42.

(St95)   Stepanov, A., and M. Lee, "The Standard Template Library," Internet Distribution, Published at `ftp://butler.hpl.hp.com/stl`, July 7, 1995.

(St84)   Stroustrup, B., "The UNIX System: Data Abstraction in C," *AT&T Bell Laboratories Technical Journal,* Vol. 63, No. 8, Part 2, October 1984, pp. 1701–1732.

(St88)   Stroustrup, B., "What is Object-Oriented Programming?" *IEEE Software,* Vol. 5, No. 3, May 1988, pp. 10–20.

(St88a)   Stroustrup, B., "Parameterized Types for C++," *Proceedings of the USENIX C++ Conference,* Denver, CO, October 1988.

(St91)   Stroustrup, B., *The C++ Programming Language* (Second Edition), Reading, MA: Addison-Wesley Series in Computer Science, 1991.

(St93)   Stroustrup, B., "Why Consider Language Extensions?: Maintaining a Delicate Balance," *C++ Report,* September 1993, pp. 44–51.

(St94)   Stroustrup, B., "Making a **vector** Fit for a Standard," *The C++ Report,* October 1994.

(St94a)   Stroustrup, B., *The Design Evolution of C++,* Reading, MA: Addison-Wesley Publishing Company, 1994.

(St97)   Stroustrup, B., *The C++ Programming Language,* Third Edition, Reading, MA: Addison-Wesley Publishing Company, 1997.

(Ta94)   Taligent Inc., *Taligent's Guide to Designing Programs: Well-Mannered Object-Oriented Design in C++,* Reading, MA: Addison-Wesley Publishing Company, 1994.

(Ta92)   Taylor, D., *Object-Oriented Information Systems,* New York, NY: John Wiley & Sons, 1992.

(To89)   Tondo, C. L., and S. E. Gimpel, *The C Answer Book,* Englewood Cliffs, NJ: Prentice Hall, 1989.

(Ur92)   Urlocker, Z., "Polymorphism Unbounded," *Windows Tech Journal,* Vol. 1, No. 1, January 1992, pp. 11–16.

(Va95)   Van Camp, K. E., "Dynamic Inheritance Using Filter Classes," *C/C++ Users Journal,* Vol. 13, No. 6, June 1995, pp. 69–78.

(Vi94)   Vilot, M. J., "An Introduction to the Standard Template Library," *The C++ Report,* Vol. 6, No. 8, October 1994.

(Vo91)   Voss, G., *Object-Oriented Programming: An Introduction,* Berkeley, CA: Osbourne McGraw-Hill, 1991.

(Vo93)   Voss, G., "Objects and Messages," *Windows Tech Journal,* February 1993, pp. 15–16.

(Wa94)   Wang, B. L., and J. Wang, "Is a Deep Class Hierarchy Considered Harmful?" *Object Magazine,* Vol. 4, No. 7, November-December 1994, pp. 35–36.

(We94)   Weisfeld, M., "An Alternative to Large Switch Statements," *The C Users Journal,* Vol. 12, No. 4, April 1994, pp. 67–76.

(We92)   Weiskamp, K., and B. Flamig, *The Complete C++ Primer,* Second Edition, Orlando, FL: Academic Press, 1992.

(Wi93)   Wiebel, M., and S. Halladay, "Using OOP Techniques Instead of *switch* in C++," *The C Users Journal,* Vol. 10, No. 10, October 1993, pp. 105–112.

(Wi88)   Wiener, R. S., and L. J. Pinson, *An Introduction to Object-Oriented Programming and C++,* Reading, MA: Addison-Wesley, 1988.

(Wi92)   Wilde, N., and R. Huitt, "Maintenance Support for Object-Oriented Programs," *IEEE Transactions on Software Engineering,* Vol. 18, No. 12, December 1992, pp. 1038–1044.

(Wl93)   Wilde, N.; P. Matthews; and R. Huitt, "Maintaining Object-Oriented Software," *IEEE Software Magazine,* Vol. 10, No. 1, January 1993, pp. 75–80.

(Wi96)   Wilson, G. V., and P. Lu, *Parallel Programming Using C++,* Cambridge, MA: MIT Press, 1996.

(Wt93)   Wilt, N., "Templates in C++," *The C Users Journal,* May 1993, pp. 33–51.

(Wi90)   Wirfs-Brock, R.; B. Wilkerson; and L. Wiener, *Designing Object-Oriented Software,* Englewood Cliffs, NJ: Prentice Hall, 1990.

(Wy92)   Wyatt, B. B.; K. Kavi; and S. Hufnagel, "Parallelism in Object-Oriented Languages: A Survey," *IEEE Software,* Vol. 9, No. 7, November 1992, pp. 56–66.

(Ya93)   Yamazaki, S.; K. Kajihara; M. Ito; and R. Yasuhara, "Object-Oriented Design of Telecommunication Software," *IEEE Software Magazine,* Vol. 10, No. 1, January 1993, pp. 81–87.

Index

End-User License Agreement for Microsoft Software

IMPORTANT-READ CAREFULLY: This Microsoft End-User License Agreement ("EULA") is a legal agreement between you (either an individual or a single entity) and Microsoft Corporation for the Microsoft software products included in this package, which includes computer software and may include associated media, printed materials, and "online" or electronic documentation ("SOFTWARE PRODUCT"). The SOFTWARE PRODUCT also includes any updates and supplements to the original SOFTWARE PRODUCT provided to you by Microsoft. By installing, copying, downloading, accessing or otherwise using the SOFTWARE PRODUCT, you agree to be bound by the terms of this EULA. If you do not agree to the terms of this EULA, do not install, copy, or otherwise use the SOFTWARE PRODUCT.

SOFTWARE PRODUCT LICENSE

The SOFTWARE PRODUCT is protected by copyright laws and international copyright treaties, as well as other intellectual property laws and treaties. The SOFTWARE PRODUCT is licensed, not sold.

1.   GRANT OF LICENSE. This EULA grants you the following rights:

    1.1   License Grant. Microsoft grants to you as an individual, a personal nonexclusive license to make and use copies of the SOFTWARE PRODUCT for the sole purposes of evaluating and learning how to use the SOFTWARE PRODUCT, as may be instructed in accompanying publications or documentation. You may install the software on an unlimited number of computers provided that you are the only individual using the SOFTWARE PRODUCT.

    1.2   Academic Use. You must be a "Qualified Educational User" to use the SOFTWARE PRODUCT in the manner described in this section. To determine whether you are a Qualified Educational User, please contact the Microsoft Sales Information Center/One Microsoft Way/Redmond, WA 98052-6399 or the Microsoft subsidiary serving your country. If you are a Qualified Educational User, you may either:

(i)   exercise the rights granted in Section 1.1, OR

(ii)   if you intend to use the SOFTWARE PRODUCT solely for instructional purposes in connection with a class or other educational program, this EULA grants you the following alternative license models:

(A)   Per Computer Model. For every valid license you have acquired for the SOFTWARE PRODUCT, you may install a single copy of the SOFTWARE PRODUCT on a single computer for access and use by an unlimited number of student end users at your educational institution, provided that all such end users comply with all other terms of this EULA, OR

(B)   Per License Model. If you have multiple licenses for the SOFTWARE PRODUCT, then at any time you may have as many copies of the SOFTWARE PRODUCT in use as you have licenses, provided that such use is limited to student or faculty end users at your educational institution and provided that all such end users comply with all other terms of this EULA. For purposes of this subsection, the SOFTWARE PRODUCT is "in use" on a computer when it is loaded into the temporary memory (i.e., RAM) or installed into the permanent memory (e.g., hard disk, CD ROM, or other storage device) of that computer, except that a copy installed on a network server for the sole purpose of distribution to other computers is not "in use". If the anticipated number of users of the SOFTWARE PRODUCT will exceed the number of applicable licenses, then you must have a reasonable mechanism or process in place to ensure that the number of persons using the SOFTWARE PRODUCT concurrently does not exceed the number of licenses.

2.   DESCRIPTION OF OTHER RIGHTS AND LIMITATIONS.

- Limitations on Reverse Engineering, Decompilation, and Disassembly. You may not reverse engineer, decompile, or disassemble the SOFTWARE PRODUCT, except and only to the extent that such activity is expressly permitted by applicable law notwithstanding this limitation.

- Separation of Components. The SOFTWARE PRODUCT is licensed as a single product. Its component parts may not be separated for use on more than one computer.

- Rental. You may not rent, lease or lend the SOFTWARE PRODUCT.

- Trademarks. This EULA does not grant you any rights in connection with any trademarks or service marks of Microsoft.

- Software Transfer. The initial user of the SOFTWARE PRODUCT may make a one-time permanent transfer of this EULA and SOFTWARE PRODUCT only directly to an end user. This transfer must include all of the SOFTWARE PRODUCT (including all component parts, the media and printed materials, any upgrades, this EULA, and, if applicable, the Certificate of Authenticity). Such transfer may not be by way of consignment or any other indirect transfer. The transferee of such one-time transfer must agree to comply with the terms of this EULA, including the obligation not to further transfer this EULA and SOFTWARE PRODUCT.

- **No Support.** Microsoft shall have no obligation to provide any product support for the SOFTWARE PRODUCT.

- **Termination.** Without prejudice to any other rights, Microsoft may terminate this EULA if you fail to comply with the terms and conditions of this EULA. In such event, you must destroy all copies of the SOFTWARE PRODUCT and all of its component parts.

3. **COPYRIGHT.** All title and intellectual property rights in and to the SOFTWARE PRODUCT (including but not limited to any images, photographs, animations, video, audio, music, text, and "applets" incorporated into the SOFTWARE PRODUCT), the accompanying printed materials, and any copies of the SOFTWARE PRODUCT are owned by Microsoft or its suppliers. All title and intellectual property rights in and to the content which may be accessed through use of the SOFTWARE PRODUCT is the property of the respective content owner and may be protected by applicable copyright or other intellectual property laws and treaties. This EULA grants you no rights to use such content. All rights not expressly granted are reserved by Microsoft.

4. **BACKUP COPY.** After installation of one copy of the SOFTWARE PRODUCT pursuant to this EULA, you may keep the original media on which the SOFTWARE PRODUCT was provided by Microsoft solely for backup or archival purposes. If the original media is required to use the SOFTWARE PRODUCT on the COMPUTER, you may make one copy of the SOFTWARE PRODUCT solely for backup or archival purposes. Except as expressly provided in this EULA, you may not otherwise make copies of the SOFTWARE PRODUCT or the printed materials accompanying the SOFTWARE PRODUCT.

5. **U.S. GOVERNMENT RESTRICTED RIGHTS.** The SOFTWARE PRODUCT and documentation are provided with RESTRICTED RIGHTS. Use, duplication, or disclosure by the Government is subject to restrictions as set forth in subparagraph (c)(1)(ii) of the Rights in Technical Data and Computer Software clause at DFARS 252.227-7013 or subparagraphs (c)(1) and (2) of the Commercial Computer Software-Restricted Rights at 48 CFR 52.227-19, as applicable. Manufacturer is Microsoft Corporation/One Microsoft Way/ Redmond, WA 98052-6399.

6. **EXPORT RESTRICTIONS.** You agree that you will not export or re-export the SOFTWARE PRODUCT, any part thereof, or any process or service that is the direct product of the SOFTWARE PRODUCT (the foregoing collectively referred to as the "Restricted Components"), to any country, person, entity or end user subject to U.S. export restrictions. You specifically agree not to export or re-export any of the Restricted Components (i) to any country to which the U.S. has embargoed or restricted the export of goods or services, which currently include, but are not necessarily limited to Cuba, Iran, Iraq, Libya, North Korea, Sudan and Syria, or to any national of any such country, wherever located, who intends to transmit or transport the Restricted Components back to such country; (ii) to any end-user who you know or have reason to know will utilize the Restricted Components in the design, development or

production of nuclear, chemical or biological weapons; or (iii) to any end-user who has been prohibited from participating in U.S. export transactions by any federal agency of the U.S. government. You warrant and represent that neither the BXA nor any other U.S. federal agency has suspended, revoked, or denied your export privileges.

7. NOTE ON JAVA SUPPORT. THE SOFTWARE PRODUCT MAY CONTAIN SUPPORT FOR PROGRAMS WRITTEN IN JAVA. JAVA TECHNOLOGY IS NOT FAULT TOLERANT AND IS NOT DESIGNED, MANUFAC-TURED, OR INTENDED FOR USE OR RESALE AS ON-LINE CONTROL EQUIPMENT IN HAZARDOUS ENVIRONMENTS REQUIRING FAIL-SAFE PERFORMANCE, SUCH AS IN THE OPERATION OF NUCLEAR FACILITIES, AIRCRAFT NAVIGATION OR COMMUNICATION SYS-TEMS, AIR TRAFFIC CONTROL, DIRECT LIFE SUPPORT MACHINES, OR WEAPONS SYSTEMS, IN WHICH THE FAILURE OF JAVA TECH-NOLOGY COULD LEAD DIRECTLY TO DEATH, PERSONAL INJURY, OR SEVERE PHYSICAL OR ENVIRONMENTAL DAMAGE.

MISCELLANEOUS

If you acquired this product in the United States, this EULA is governed by the laws of the State of Washington.

If you acquired this product in Canada, this EULA is governed by the laws of the Prov-ince of Ontario, Canada. Each of the parties hereto irrevocably attorns to the jurisdiction of the courts of the Province of Ontario and further agrees to commence any litigation which may arise hereunder in the courts located in the Judicial District of York, Province of Ontario.

If this product was acquired outside the United States, then local law may apply.

Should you have any questions concerning this EULA, or if you desire to contact Microsoft for any reason, please contact

Microsoft, or write: Microsoft Sales Information Center/One Microsoft Way/Red-mond, WA 98052-6399.

LIMITED WARRANTY

LIMITED WARRANTY. Microsoft warrants that (a) the SOFTWARE PRODUCT will perform substantially in accordance with the accompanying written materials for a period of ninety (90) days from the date of receipt, and (b) any Support Services provided by Mi-crosoft shall be substantially as described in applicable written materials provided to you by Microsoft, and Microsoft support engineers will make commercially reasonable efforts to solve any problem. To the extent allowed by applicable law, implied warranties on the SOFTWARE PRODUCT, if any, are limited to ninety (90) days. Some states/jurisdictions do not allow limitations on duration of an implied warranty, so the above limitation may not apply to you.

CUSTOMER REMEDIES. Microsoft's and its suppliers' entire liability and your exclusive remedy shall be, at Microsoft's option, either (a) return of the price paid, if any, or (b) repair or replacement of the SOFTWARE PRODUCT that does not meet Microsoft's Limited Warranty and that is returned to Microsoft with a copy of your receipt. This Lim-ited Warranty is void if failure of the SOFTWARE PRODUCT has resulted from accident, abuse, or misapplication. Any replacement SOFTWARE PRODUCT will be warranted for the remainder of the original warranty period or thirty (30) days, whichever is longer. Outside the United States, neither these remedies nor any product support services offered by Microsoft are available without proof of purchase from an authorized international source.

NO OTHER WARRANTIES. TO THE MAXIMUM EXTENT PERMITTED BY APPLICABLE LAW, MICROSOFT AND ITS SUPPLIERS DISCLAIM ALL OTHER WARRANTIES AND CONDITIONS, EITHER EXPRESS OR IMPLIED, INCLUDING, BUT NOT LIMITED TO, IMPLIED WARRANTIES OR CONDITIONS OF MER-CHANTABILITY, FITNESS FOR A PARTICULAR PURPOSE, TITLE AND NON-INFRINGEMENT, WITH REGARD TO THE SOFTWARE PRODUCT, AND THE PROVISION OF OR FAILURE TO PROVIDE SUPPORT SERVICES. THIS LIMITED WARRANTY GIVES YOU SPECIFIC LEGAL RIGHTS. YOU MAY HAVE OTHERS, WHICH VARY FROM STATE/JURISDICTION TO STATE/JURISDICTION.

LIMITATION OF LIABILITY. TO THE MAXIMUM EXTENT PERMITTED BY APPLICABLE LAW, IN NO EVENT SHALL MICROSOFT OR ITS SUPPLIERS BE LIABLE FOR ANY SPECIAL, INCIDENTAL, INDIRECT, OR CONSEQUENTIAL DAMAGES WHATSOEVER (INCLUDING, WITHOUT LIMITATION, DAMAGES FOR LOSS OF BUSINESS PROFITS, BUSINESS INTERRUPTION, LOSS OF BUSI-NESS INFORMATION, OR ANY OTHER PECUNIARY LOSS) ARISING OUT OF THE USE OF OR INABILITY TO USE THE SOFTWARE PRODUCT OR THE FAILURE TO PROVIDE SUPPORT SERVICES, EVEN IF MICROSOFT HAS BEEN ADVISED OF THE POSSIBILITY OF SUCH DAMAGES. IN ANY CASE, MICROSOFT'S ENTIRE LIABILITY UNDER ANY PROVISION OF THIS EULA SHALL BE LIMITED TO THE GREATER OF THE AMOUNT ACTUALLY PAID BY YOU FOR THE SOFTWARE PRODUCT OR U.S.$5.00; PROVIDED, HOWEVER, IF YOU HAVE ENTERED INTO A MICROSOFT SUPPORT SERVICES AGREEMENT, MICROSOFT'S ENTIRE LIABILITY REGARDING SUPPORT SERVICES SHALL BE GOVERNED BY THE TERMS OF THAT AGREEMENT. BECAUSE SOME STATES/ JURISDICTIONS DO NOT ALLOW THE EXCLUSION OR LIMITATION OF LIA-BILITY, THE ABOVE LIMITATION MAY NOT APPLY TO YOU.

0495 Part No. 64358

The DEITEL & DEITEL Suite of Products...

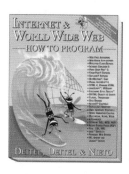

XML How to Program

BOOK / CD-ROM

© 2001, 1000 pp., paper
(0-13-028417-3)

This new book in the Deitels' *How to Program* series is a comprehensive guide to programming in XML. It explains how to use XML to create customized tags and includes several chapters that address standard custom markup languages for science and technology, multimedia, commerce and other fields. The authors include concise introductions to Java, VBScript, Active Server Pages and Perl/CGI, providing readers with the essentials of these programming languages and server-side development technologies to enable them to work effectively with XML. The book also includes cutting-edge topics such as XQL, SMIL and VoiceXML as well as a real-world e-commerce case study. A complete chapter on Web accessibility that addresses Voice XML is also included. It also includes tips such as valuable insights into Common Programming Errors, Software Engineering Observations, Portability Tips and Debugging Hints.

Perl How to Program

BOOK / CD-ROM

© 2001, 1000 pp., paper
(0-13-028418-1)

This comprehensive new guide to programming with Perl emphasizes the use of the Common Gateway Interface (CGI) with Perl to create powerful dynamic Web content for e-commerce applications. The book begins with a clear and careful introduction to the concepts of structured programming at a level suitable for beginners, and proceeds through advanced topics such as references and complex data structures. Key Perl topics such as regular expressions and string manipulation are covered in detail. The authors address important and topical issues such as object-oriented programming, the Perl database interface (DBI), graphics and security. Also included is a treatment of XML, a bonus chapter introducing the Python programming language, and a complete chapter on Web accessibility that addresses programming and technologies relevant to accessibility for people with disabilities. The text also includes tips such as valuable insights into Common Programming Errors, Software Engineering Observations, Portability Tips and Debugging Hints.

e-Business & e-Commerce for Managers

© 2001, 900 pp., paper
(0-13-032364-0)

This innovative new text is a comprehensive overview of building and managing an e-business. It explores topics such as the decision to bring a business online, choosing a business model, accepting payment, marketing strategies and security, as well as many other important issues. Features, Web resources and online demonstrations supplement the text and direct readers to additional materials. The book also includes an appendix that develops a complete Web-based shopping cart application using HTML, VBScript, Active Server Pages and an Access database. Plus, company-specific sections provide "real-world" examples of the concepts presented in the book.

Advanced Java How to Program

BOOK / CD-ROM

© 2001, 1100 pp., paper
(0-13-089560-1)

Expanding on the world's best-selling Java text, *Advanced Java How to Program* includes an in-depth discussion of advanced topics, aiding developers in producing significant, scalable Java applications and distributed systems. The book integrates such technologies as Swing, multithreading, RMI, JDBC, servlets, Java XML and Enterprise JavaBeans into a complete, rigorous, production-quality system, thus allowing developers to take better advantage of the leverage and platform-independence provided by the Java 2 platform.

Java How to Program
Third Edition
BOOK / CD-ROM

©2000, 1360 pp., paper bound w/CD-ROM (0-13-012507-5)

This edition of the world's best-selling Java textbook incorporates Sun Microsystems' latest version of Java, the Java 2 Software Development Kit (J2SDK). The introduction of new functionality in this upgrade has made Java a friendlier and more accessible programming language. Reviewers of the book were unanimous in praising the Deitels for making the best use of these enhancements and writing the introductory chapters in an engaging and accessible style. Designed for beginning through intermediate readers, it uses the Deitels' proven "live-code" approach with hundreds of complete working programs, valuable programming tips, more than 16,000 lines of code and over 1400 interesting and challenging exercises. The graphical user interface examples use Sun's new Swing GUI components. The authors have added significant coverage of JDBC, JavaBeans, RMI, Servlets, Java 2D, Java Media Framework, Collections, Serialization, Inner Classes and other topics. Includes several examples and projects on multi-tier, client/server systems development. The CD-ROM contains a complete Java Integrated Development Environment, source code for all examples in the text, and hyperlinks to valuable Java demos and resources on the Internet.

C++ How to Program
Third Edition
BOOK / CD-ROM

© 2001, 1168 pp., paper (0-13-089571-7)

The world's best-selling C++ text teaches programming by emphasizing structured and object-oriented programming, software reuse and component-oriented software construction. This comprehensive book uses the Deitels' signature "live-code" approach, presenting every concept in the context of a complete, working C++ program followed by a screen capture showing the program's output. It also includes a rich collection of exercises and valuable insights into Common Programming Errors, Software Engineering Observations, Portability Tips and Debugging Hints. The Third Edition includes a new case study that focuses on object-oriented design with the UML and illustrates the entire process of object-oriented design from conception to implementation. In addition, it adheres to the latest ANSI/ISO C++ standards. The accompanying CD-ROM contains Microsoft® Visual C++ 6.0 Introductory Edition software, source code for all examples in the text and hyperlinks to C++ demos and Internet resources.

C How to Program
Third Edition

BOOK / CD-ROM

©2001, 1253 pp., paper (0-13-089572-5)

Highly practical in approach, the Third Edition of the world's best-selling C text introduces the fundamentals of structured programming and software engineering and gets up to speed quickly. This comprehensive book not only covers the full C language, but also reviews library functions and introduces object-based and object-oriented programming in C++ and Java, as well as event-driven GUI programming in Java. The Third Edition includes a new 346-page introduction to Java 2 and the basics of GUIs, and the introduction to C++ has been condensed to 298 pages and updated to be consistent with the most current ANSI/ISO C++ standards. Plus, icons throughout the book point out valuable programming tips such as Common Programming Errors, Portability Tips and Testing and Debugging Tips.

Getting Started with Microsoft® Visual C++™ 6 with an Introduction to MFC

BOOK / CD-ROM

©2000, 163 pp., paper (0-13-016147-0)

This exciting book is intended to be a companion to the ANSI/ISO standard C++ best-selling book, *C++ How to Program, Second Edition*. Learn how to use Microsoft's Visual Studio 6 integrated development environment (IDE) and Visual C++ 6 to create Windows programs using the Microsoft Foundation Classes (MFC). The book includes 17 "live-code" Visual C++/MFC programs with screen captures, dozens of tips, recommended practices and cautions and exercises accompanying every chapter. It includes coverage of Win32 and console applications, online documentation and Web resources, GUI controls, dialog boxes, graphics, message handling, the resource definition language and the debugger.

Visual Basic® 6 How to Program

BOOK / CD-ROM

©1999, 1015 pp., paper bound w/CD-ROM (0-13-456955-5)

Visual Basic 6 is revolutionizing software development for conventional and Internet/Intranet-based applications. This text explains Visual Basic 6's extraordinary capabilities. Part of the Deitels' *Visual Studio* series, this book uses the Deitels' "live-code" approach to cover Internet/Intranet, World Wide Web, VBScript, ActiveX, ADO, multimedia, animation, audio, video, files, database, networking, graphics, strings, data structures, collections, GUI and control creation. The accompanying CD-ROM contains Microsoft's *Visual Basic 6 Working Model Edition* software, source code and hyperlinks to valuable Visual Basic resources.

BOOK/MULTIMEDIA PACKAGES

These complete packages include books and interactive multimedia CD-ROMs, and are perfect for anyone interested in learning Java, C++, Visual Basic, Internet/World Wide Web and e-commerce programming. They are exceptional and affordable resources for college students and professionals learning programming for the first time or reinforcing their knowledge.

The Complete Internet & World Wide Web Programming Training Course

BOXED SET

©2000, boxed book and software (0-13-085611-8)

Includes the book *Internet & World Wide Web How To Program* and the fully interactive browser-based *Internet & World Wide Web Programming Multimedia Cyber Classroom* CD-ROM that features:

- Fully searchable, electronic version of the textbook, complete with hyperlinks
- Hundreds of programs that can be run inside a browser
- Over 12 hours of audio explaining key Internet programming concepts
- Hundreds of exercises—many solved
- An integrated course completion and assessment summary feature to help you monitor your progress
- Practice exams with hundreds of short-answer test questions
- Hundreds of tips, terms and hints
- Master client- and server-side programming, including JavaScript, VBScript, ActiveX, ASP, SQL, XML, database and more!

Runs on Windows 95, 98, NT and Windows 2000

The Complete e-Business & e-Commerce Programming Training Course

BOXED SET

©2001, boxed book and software (0-13-089549-0)

Includes the book *e-Business & e-Commerce How To Program* and the fully interactive *e-Business & e-Commerce Programming Multimedia Cyber Classroom* CD-ROM that features:

- Fully searchable, electronic version of the textbook, complete with hyperlinks
- Over 13 hours of detailed audio descriptions of more than 15,000 lines of fully tested "live code"
- Hundreds of example programs that readers can run with the click of a mouse button
- Practice exams with hundreds of short-answer test questions
- Hundreds of self-review questions, all with answers
- Hundreds of programming exercises, half with answers
- Hundreds of tips, marked with icons, that show how to write code that is portable, reusable and optimized for performance
- An intuitive browser-based interface

Runs on Windows 95, 98, NT and Windows 2000

The Complete C++ Training Course Third Edition

BOXED SET

©2001, boxed book and software (0-13-089564-4)

Includes the complete, best-selling introductory book *C++ How to Program, Third Edition* and the fully interactive *C++ Multimedia Cyber Classroom* CD-ROM that features:

- Fully searchable, electronic version of the textbook, complete with hyperlinks
- 248 complete C++ programs that readers can edit and run with a click of the mouse in the Microsoft® Visual C++™ 6 Introductory Edition IDE included in the package
- Over 13 hours of detailed, expert audio descriptions of more than 13,000 lines of fully tested "live code"
- Hundreds of programming exercises, half with answers
- Practice exams with hundreds of short-answer test questions
- Hundreds of self-review questions, all with answers
- Hundreds of tips, marked with icons, that show how to write C++ code that is portable, reusable and optimized for performance
- An intuitive browser-based interface

Runs on Windows 95, 98, NT and Windows 2000

Coming Fall 2000, the award-winning Deitel & Deitel Cyber Classroom Series will be available from Prentice Hall over the World Wide Web. This is an ideal solution for students and programming professionals who prefer the convenience of Internet delivery to CD-ROM delivery, or who work on platforms not supported by the CD-ROM version of the Cyber Classrooms.

The Web-based Cyber Classrooms will run on any computer that supports version 4 of either Netscape Navigator or Internet Explorer and the free Real Networks RealPlayer version 7 or higher. The Web-based version will require a 56K modem or higher connection to the Internet.

The Web-based Cyber Classrooms will contain all of the features of the CD-ROM versions, including the Deitels' signature "live code" approach to teaching programming languages. All of the audio will be available through the Web, as will the sample program code, programming tips, exercises and so forth.

We are excited to announce enhanced Web-based versions of the Deitel & Deitel Cyber Classroom Series coming in 2001. The enhanced versions will attempt to recreate the experience of being in a live programming seminar. They will contain substantially more media than the current Cyber Classrooms, including extensive use of both audio and video. The enhanced versions will also include synchronous and asynchronous communications tools to support sophisticated instructor-to-student and student-to-student communication.

For more information, please visit **www.phptr.com/phptrinteractive**.

Turn back one page for details on the Cyber Classroom CD-ROMs and Complete Training Courses!

FORTHCOMING PUBLICATIONS FROM THE DEITELS

For those interested in
C++

Advanced C++ How to Program: This book builds on the pedagogy of *C++ How to Program, Third Edition*, and features more advanced discussions of templates, multiple inheritance, and other key topics. We are co-authoring this book with Don Kostuch, one of the world's most experienced C++ educators.

For those interested in
Microsoft® Visual C++

Visual C++ 7 How to Program: This book combines the pedagogy and extensive coverage of *C++ How to Program, Third Edition* with a more in-depth treatment of Windows programming in Visual Studio 7. We have carefully culled the best material from each of these areas to produce a solid, two-semester, introductory/intermediate level treatment.

Getting Started with Microsoft® Visual C++™ 7 with an Introduction to MFC, Second Edition: This book builds on the first edition introduced for Visual Studio 6. It features a much enhanced, yet still introductory, treatment of MFC.

For those interested in
C#

C# How to Program: This book discusses Microsoft's brand new C# language being introduced in Visual Studio 7.

For those interested in
Python

Python How to Program: This book introduces the increasingly popular Python language which makes many application development tasks much easier to accomplish than with traditional, recent object-oriented languages.

For those interested in
Flash

Flash 5 How to Program: Hundreds of millions of people browse Flash-enabled Web sites daily. This first book in our Multimedia series introduces the powerful features of Flash 5 and includes a detailed introduction to programming with the completely revamped Flash 5 scripting language.

For those interested in
Java

Java How to Program, Fourth Edition, Volume I and ***Java How to Program, Fourth Edition, Volume II:*** These books build on the pedagogy of *Java How to Program, Third Edition,* expanding our intermediate-level treatment of Java to two 1000-page volumes. The volumes include extensive treatments of XML and object-oriented design with UML.

For those interested in
Microsoft® Visual Basic

Visual Basic 7 How to Program, Second Edition: This book builds on the pedagogy of the first edition, which was developed for Visual Studio 6. It has a much enhanced treatment of developing Web-based e-business and e-commerce applications. The book includes an extensive treatment of XML.

New & Improved Deitel Web Site!
Deitel & Associates, Inc. is in the process of upgrading www.deitel.com. The new site will feature Macromedia Flash® enhancements and additional content to create a valuable resource for students, professors and professionals. Features will include FAQs, Web resources, e-publications and online chat sessions with the authors. We will include streaming audio clips where the authors discuss their publications. Web-based training demos will also be available at the site.

Turn the page to find out more about Deitel & Associates!

License Agreement and Limited Warranty

Using the CD-ROM

The contents of this CD are designed to be accessed through the interface provided in the file **AUTORUN.EXE**. If a startup screen does not pop up automatically when you insert the CD into your computer, double click on the icon for **AUTORUN.EXE** to launch the program or refer to the file **README.TXT** on the CD.

Contents of the CD-ROM

- Microsoft® Visual C++™ 6, Introductory Edition
- Live links to websites mentioned in the book *C++ How to Program, Third Edition*
- Live code examples from the book *C++ How to Program, Third Edition*

Software and Hardware System Requirements

- Intel Pentium 133 MHz or faster processor (200 MHz recommended)
- Microsoft Windows 95 or later, or
- Microsoft Windows NT 4.0 with Service Pack 3 (or later)
- Microsoft Internet Explorer 4.01 Service Pack 1 (included)
- 24 Mb RAM for Windows 95 or later (48 MB recommended)
- 32 Mb for Windows NT 4.0 or later (48 MB recommended)
- Hard disk space: 266 Mb typical install, 370 Mb maximum install
- CD-ROM drive
- Internet connection